WORDS AND PHRASES
legally defined

Volume 2: D–J

WORDS AND PHRASES
legally defined

THIRD EDITION

under the General Editorship of
John B Saunders
of Lincoln's Inn, Barrister

Volume 2: D–J

London
Butterworths
1989

United Kingdom   Butterworth & Co (Publishers) Ltd, 88 Kingsway, LONDON
                   WC2B 6AB and 4 Hill Street, EDINBURGH EH2 3JZ

Australia   Butterworths Pty Ltd, SYDNEY, MELBOURNE, BRISBANE, ADELAIDE,
                   PERTH, CANBERRA and HOBART

Canada   Butterworths Canada Ltd, TORONTO and VANCOUVER

Ireland   Butterworth (Ireland) Ltd, DUBLIN

New Zealand   Butterworths of New Zealand Ltd, WELLINGTON and AUCKLAND

Puerto Rico   Equity de Puerto Rico Inc, HATO REY

Singapore   Malayan Law Journal Pte Ltd, SINGAPORE

USA   Butterworth Legal Publishers, AUSTIN, Texas; BOSTON,
                   Massachusetts; CLEARWATER, Florida (D & S Publishers); ORFORD,
                   New Hampshire (Equity Publishing); ST PAUL, Minnesota; and
                   SEATTLE, Washington

First published 1989

British Library Cataloguing in Publication Data

Words and phrases legally defined.—3rd ed/edited by John B Saunders
    1. Commonwealth countries. Common law countries. Law—Encyclopaedias
I., Saunders, John B (John Beecroft), 1911—
342.009171'241

ISBN 0 406 08040 2 (set)
     0 406 08041 0 (vol 1)
     0 406 08042 9 (vol 2)
     0 406 08043 7 (vol 3)
     0 406 08044 5 (vol 4)

Typeset by Phoenix Photosetting, Chatham, Kent
Printed and bound in Great Britain by
Mackays of Chatham Ltd, Kent

OVERSEAS REVISING EDITORS

Australia
Arthur E Garcia   LLB(NSW), LLM(Syd)

Canada
Heather Probert   LLB
of the Ontario Bar

New Zealand
Hellen Papadopoulos   LLB
Barrister and Solicitor of the High Court of New Zealand

USA
Michael G Walsh
Assistant Professor in Business Law at the College of Commerce and Finance,
Villanova University, Villanova, Pennsylvania

EDITORIAL MANAGER

Margaret Cherry   LLB

The United Kingdom material in this volume states the law as at 28 February 1988. Material from jurisdictions outside the United Kingdom is up-to-date to 30 November 1988.

D

DAILY

'My personal opinion is that "daily labourer" means a man who, by the terms of his engagement or the course of his labour, is not only a labourer, but one who works every weekday and day by day. . . . In the English language the word "daily" has a well-known meaning, consecrated by long use in the sentence, "Give us each day our daily bread". That does not mean "once in every forty-eight hours", but every day. So, in my opinion, a daily labourer is one who goes out to his work every day.' *McDonald v Brown* (1918) 87 LJKB 1119 at 1121, DC, per Darling J

Australia '"Daily" is an adjective, the precise meaning of which is to be ascertained from the context in which it is used and particularly the substantive which it qualifies. The dictionaries show that "daily" may mean every week day and Sunday or every week day. . . . When a journal is spoken of as a "daily newspaper" the phrase is used to described a publication which is published day by day, rather than periodically, for example, at intervals of a week or a month.' *Foster v Howard* [1949] VLR 311 at 312, per Barry J

See, generally, 45 Halsbury's Laws (4th edn) para 1113.

DAIRY

In the following provisions [Part II] of this Act 'dairy'—
(i) includes any farm, cowshed, milking house, milk store, milk shop or other premises from which milk is supplied on or for sale, or in which milk is kept or used for purposes of sale or for the purposes of manufacture into butter, cheese, dried milk or condensed milk for sale, or in which vessels used for the sale of milk are kept, but
(ii) does not include a shop from which milk is supplied only in the properly closed and unopened vessels in which it is delivered to the shop, or a shop or other place in which milk is sold for consumption on the premises only.
(Food Act 1984, s 32(1)(a))

Dairy farm

'Dairy farm'—
(i) means any premises (being a dairy) on which milk is produced from cows, but
(ii) does not include any part of any such premises on which milk is manufactured into other products unless the milk produced on the premises forms a substantial part of the milk so manufactured.
(Food Act 1984, s 32(1)(b))

Dairy farmer

'Dairy farmer' means a dairyman who produces milk from cows. (Food Act 1984, s 32(1)(c))

Dairyman

'Dairyman' includes an occupier of a dairy, a cowkeeper, and a purveyor of milk. (Food Act 1984, s 32(1)(d))

DAM   *See also* BANK (Embankment); FISHING MILL DAM

The expression 'dam' includes any weir or other fixed obstruction used for the purpose of damming up water. (Salmon and Freshwater Fisheries Act 1975, s 41)

DAMAGE   *See also* INJURY

'Damage' includes destruction, and references to damaging shall be construed accordingly. (Army Act 1955, s 225(1); Air Force Act 1955, s 223(1))

'Damage' includes the death of, or injury to, any person (including any disease and any impairment of physical or mental condition). (Animals Act 1971, s 11)

'Neither in common parlance nor in legal phraseology is the word "damage" used as applicable to injuries done to the person, but solely as applicable to mischief done to property. Still less is this term applicable to loss of life, or injury resulting therefrom to a widow or surviving relative. We speak, indeed, of damages as compensation for injury done to the person; but the term "damage" is not employed interchangeably with the term "injury" with reference to mischief wrongfully occasioned to the person.' *Smith v Brown* (1871) LR 6 QB 729 at 731–733, per cur.

'Is the loss within the exception [in a bill of lading] as to insurance—"the shipowner is not to be liable for any damage to any goods which is capable of being covered by insurance"? I do not agree that "damage" is limited . . . to partial damage or injury, as distinguished from a total destruction of the thing; if goods were so much damaged as to be totally destroyed, that would be damage within the clause. But I think that it must be confined to cases where the goods receive damage from some peril which may be insured against; and that it does not extend to the case of a loss which is occasioned not by any damage or injury, but by the total bodily abstraction of the thing.' *Taylor v Liverpool & Great Western Steam Co* (1874) LR 9 QB 546 at 550, per Lush J

'The two clauses upon which the claimants have relied are the 6th and 16th clauses of the Railways Clauses Consolidation Act 1845. The first of those clauses provides for the payment to the class of claimants . . . "for all damage sustained by such owners, occupiers, and other parties, by reason of the exercise, as regards such lands, of the powers by this or the special Act, or any Act incorporated therewith vested in the company". In my opinion those words relate to damage sustained at or before the date of the claim, or at the latest, the date of the inquisition, and do not relate to future injury resulting in future damage. I substitute the word "injury" for "damage", because it appears to me that the word "damage" is used in the section of the statute which I have read for "injury"; and that although future injury cannot be claimed for . . . yet nevertheless future damage resulting from a past injury would be the subject of a claim for compensation.' *R v Poulter* (1887) 20 QBD 132 at 138, CA, per Fry LJ

[The Highways and Locomotives (Amendment) Act 1878, s 23 (repealed; see now the Highways Act 1980, s 59), enabled a highway authority to recover extraordinary expenses incurred by it in repairing a road by reason of the 'damage' caused by excessive weight or other extraordinary traffic.] 'I do not think "damage" means fair wear and tear. I think "damage" means that the road has been injured because I associate with the terms "excessive weight" and "extraordinary traffic"

the idea of something more than the road was intended normally to bear. . . . The more a road is used the more it justifies its position as a communally upkept road, and I do not think that in such a context you can say that the ordinary traffic of a road causes damage to it.' *Billericay Rural Council v Poplar Union & Keeling* [1911] 2 KB 801 at 813, CA, per Fletcher Moulton LJ

'The words "damages" and "damage" in law have more than one meaning, and great care has to be exercised in examining the context in which they severally appear. "Damage" may mean injury; "damage", and "damages" especially, may mean sums paid under the order of the Court for compensation for a breach of contract or a wrong.' *Swansea Corpn v Harpur* [1912] 3 KB 493 at 505, CA, per Fletcher Moulton LJ

'I shall try to distinguish between "damage" and "injury", following the stricter diction, derived from the civil law, which more especially prevails in Scottish jurisprudence. So used, "injury" is limited to actionable wrong, while "damage", in contrast with injury, means loss or harm occurring in fact, whether actionable as an injury or not.' *Crofter Hand Woven Harris Tweed Co Ltd v Veitch* [1942] AC 435 at 442, HL, per Lord Simon LC

Australia [In a contract for the carriage of goods a clause excluded the carrier from liability for 'any damage whatsoever to any goods'.] 'In the Oxford English Dictionary the word "damage" is defined as—"Injury, harm; esp. physical injury to a thing such as impairs its value or usefulness.". . . In my view, the phrase "damage to" when used in relation to goods, is a physical alteration or change, not necessarily permanent or irrepairable, which impairs the value of usefulness of the thing said to have been damaged. It follows that not every physical change to goods would amount to damage. What amounts to damage will depend upon the nature of the goods.' *Ranicar v Frigmobile Pty Ltd* (1983) Tas R 113 at 116, per Green CJ

Canada 'The words "damage" and "injury" are given as synonyms for each other. The first is generally used in respect to property and the second in relation to persons. . . . "Damage" has, I think, a more restricted meaning than "injury" as the latter word may mean a wrong which "damage" never does. The word "damage" includes "injury" when the latter word is used to denote physical harm to persons.' *Provincial Secretary-Treasurer v York*

(1957) 16 DLR (2d) 198 at 204, 205, NBCA, per Bridges J

Caused by ship

'The section [the Admiralty Court Act 1861, s 7 (repealed; see now Supreme Court Act 1981, s 20(2)(e)] indeed seems to me to intend by the words "jurisdiction over any claim", to give a jurisdiction over any claim in the nature of an action on the case for damage done by any ship, or in other words, over a case in which a ship was the active cause, the damage being physically caused by the ship. I do not say that damage need be confined to damage to property, it may be damage to person, as if a man were injured by the bowsprit of a ship. But the section does not apply to a case when physical injury is not done by a ship.' *The Vera Cruz (No 2)* (1884) 9 PD 96 at 99, CA, per Brett MR

'"Done by a ship" means done by those in charge of a ship with the ship as the noxious instrument.' Ibid, at 101, per Bowen LJ

'The question turns on the words in the Admiralty Court Act [1861 (repealed; see supra)] "damage done by any ship". I see no reason to doubt that the word "damage" is as applicable to damage done to a person as to damage done to property. It would be doing great violence to the ordinary meaning of the word to limit it to damage to property. . . . I must hold that the words "damage done by any ship" include damage to persons. Whilst, however, giving this meaning to the word "damage", I cannot think that the present case falls within the provisions of the Act of Parliament. Damage done by a ship is, I think, applicable only to those cases where, in the words of the Master of the Rolls in the *Vera Cruz* [supra], the ship is the "active cause" of the damage. . . . In this case, to put it at the highest, those in charge of the ship so placed a tarpaulin over the hatchway as to make a trap into which the plaintiff fell, whilst lawfully crossing the deck of the ship to reach his own vessel. The ship cannot be said to have been the active cause of the damage. The damage was done on board the ship, but was not, I think, within the meaning of the Act, done by the ship.' *The Theta* [1894] P 280 at 283, 284, per Bruce J

[The Supreme Court of Judicature (Consolidation) Act 1925, s 22(1)(a)(iv) (repealed; see now the Supreme Court Act 1981, s 20(2)(e)) gave the High Court jurisdiction in Admiralty matters to hear and determine any claim for 'damage' done by a ship.] 'It is clear that the plaintiffs' case is that the *New Perseverance* received damage to her deck and her elevator by the negligence of the defendants' servants in handling and using the gear of their ship *Minerva*. It also seems clear that the damage to the *New Perseverance* was done by the faulty gear of the *Minerva*, that is, by a part of the *Minerva* herself. The dropping of the elevator by the gear, and the dropping of the elevator and the gear together, did damage to the *New Perseverance*, her deck and her elevator. . . . I think the claim can be put under sub-s 4 as damage done by a ship. . . . I think the damage here may be said to be done by the derrick and its load falling on the *New Perseverance*. That is damage done by the defendants' ship. If part of the ship does the damage I think that is enough—e.g. if it were done by an anchor or by a propeller.' *The Minerva* [1933] P 224 at 228, 229, per Bateson J

See, generally, 43 Halsbury's Laws (4th edn) para 876.

'Loss or damage' in ticket condition

[A condition in a passenger ticket stated that the defendant steamship company would not be responsible for (inter alia) any 'loss or damage' arising from the perils of the sea, etc, or from any act, neglect, or default whatsoever of the pilot, master, or mariner. A passenger lost his life through the negligence of the defendants' servants.] 'Excluding the words which are not applicable to the present case, the stipulation would read thus—The company will not be responsible for any loss or damage arising from any act, neglect, or default whatsoever of the pilot, master or mariner. It was suggested that the word "damage" is not the correct word to apply to "personal injury". It is hardly usual to say that a man is damaged, but rather that he is hurt. "Personal injury" is not "loss", because a limb may be broken without being lost. The word "injury" would certainly have been more apt, but the word "damage" can certainly mean personal injury. Here the word occurs in a sentence which seems to be solely applicable to passengers personally. Therefore, upon consideration, we are unable to say that we think that injury to the person is not covered by the words of the stipulation.' *Hagh v Royal Mail Steam Packet Co Ltd* (1883) 52 LJQB 640 at 643, CA, per cur.

Pecuniary damage

'Pecuniary damage' or 'pecuniary loss' refers to any financial disadvantage, past or future, whether precisely calculable or not. Thus past loss of earnings and an assessment of loss of future earnings, loss due to damage to a chattel, loss on breach of a contract for the sale of goods, and loss of profits constitute pecuniary damage.

'Non-pecuniary damage' is exemplified by personal injuries, damage to reputation and interference with the enjoyment of property, although, of course, in each case pecuniary damage may have been sustained as well. (12 Halsbury's Laws (4th edn) para 1110)

DAMAGE FEASANT   *See* DISTRESS
DAMAGE FEASANT

DAMAGES   *See also* COMPENSATION

'Damages' are the pecuniary recompense given by process of law to a person for the actionable wrong that another has done him. (12 Halsbury's Laws (4th edn) para 1102)

Damages [are] given to a man by a jury, as a compensation and satisfaction for some injury sustained; as for a battery, for imprisonment, for slander, or for trespass. Here the plaintiff has no certain demand till after verdict; but, when the jury has assessed his damages, and judgement is given thereupon, whether they amount to twenty pounds or twenty shillings, he instantly acquires, and the defendant loses at the same time, a right to that specific sum. (2 Bl Com 438)

'Now, with respect to damages in general, they are of three kinds. First, nominal damages; which occur in cases where the judge is bound to tell the jury only to give such; as, for instance, where the seller brings an action for the non-acceptance of goods, the price of which has risen since the contract was made. The second kind is general damages, and their nature is clearly stated by Cresswell J in *Rolin v Steward* [(1854) 14 CB 595 at 605]. They are such as the jury may give when the judge cannot point out any measure by which they are to be assessed, except the opinion and judgment of a reasonable man. Thirdly, special damages are given in respect of any consequences reasonably or probably arising from the breach complained of.' *Prehn v Royal Bank of Liverpool* (1870) LR 5 Exch 92 at 99, 100, per Martin B

[The plaintiffs collected information as to transactions during the day on the Stock Exchange and supplied it on payment to their subscribers. The defendant surreptitiously invaded the plaintiffs' right of property in such information.] 'A man who does such a wrongful act as the defendant has done lays himself open to be told by the tribunal before whom he appears, "You have damaged the plaintiff. You have done a contemptible and fraudulent act against him, and have invaded his common law right, and therefore you must have damaged him." In such a case the jury may give any damages. It is not necessary to give proof of specific damages. The damages are damages at large.' *Exchange Telegraph Co Ltd v Gregory & Co* [1896] 1 QB 147 at 153, CA, per Lord Esher MR

'"Damages" to an English lawyer imports this idea, that the sums payable by way of damages are sums which fall to be paid by reason of some breach of duty or obligation, whether that duty or obligation is imposed by contract, by the general law, or legislation.' *Hall Brothers SS Co Ltd v Young* [1939] 1 KB 748 at 756, CA, per Greene MR

'Compensatory damages in a case in which they are at large may include several different kinds of compensation to the injured plaintiff. They may include not only actual pecuniary loss and anticipated pecuniary loss or any social disadvantages which result, or may be thought likely to result, from the wrong which has been done. They may also include natural injury to his feelings; the natural grief and distress which he may feel in being spoken of in defamatory terms; and, if there has been any kind of high-handed, oppressive, insulting or contumelious behaviour by the defendant which increases the mental pain and suffering which is caused by the defamation and which may constitute injury to the plaintiff's pride and self-confidence, those are proper elements to be taken into account in a case where the damages are at large.' *McCarey v Associated Newspapers Ltd* [1964] 3 All ER 947 at 957, CA, per Pearson LJ; also reported [1965] 2 QB 86

'It has been more than once pointed out the language of damages is more than usually confused. For instance, the term "special damage" is used in more than one sense to denominate actual past losses precisely calculated (as in a personal injuries action), or "material damage actually suffered" as in describing the factor necessary to give rise to the cause of action in cases, including cases of slander, actionable only on proof of "special damage". If it is not too deeply embedded in our legal language, I would like to see "special damage" dropped as a term of art in its latter sense and some phrase like "material loss" substituted. But a similar ambiguity occurs in actions of defamation, the expressions "at large", "punitive", "aggravated", "retributory", "vindictive" and "exemplary" having been used in, as I have pointed out, inextricable confusion. In my view it is desirable to drop the use of the phrase "vindictive" damages altogether, despite its use by the county court judge in *Williams v Settle* [[1960] 2 All ER 806]. Even when a purely punitive element is involved, vindictiveness is not a good motive for awarding punishment. In awarding "aggravated" damages the natural indignation of the court at the injury inflicted on the plaintiff is a perfectly legitimate motive in making a generous rather than a more moderate award to provide an adequate solatium. But that is because the injury to the plaintiff is actually greater and as the result of the conduct exciting the indignation demands a more generous solatium. Likewise the use of "retributory" is objectionable because it is ambiguous. It can be used to cover both aggravated damages to compensate the plaintiff and punitive or exemplary damages purely to punish the defendant or hold him up as an example. As between "punitive" or "exemplary", one should, I would suppose, choose one to the exclusion of the other, since it is never wise to use two quite interchangeable terms to denote the same thing. Speaking for myself, I prefer "exemplary", not because "punitive" is necessarily inaccurate, but "exemplary" better expresses the policy of the law as expressed in the cases. It is intended to teach the defendant and others that "tort does not pay" by demonstrating what consequences the law inflicts rather than simply to make the defendant suffer an extra penalty for what he has done, although that does, of course, precisely describe its effect. The expression "at large" should be used in general to cover all cases where awards of damages may include elements for loss of reputation, injured feelings, bad or good conduct by either party, or punishment, and where in consequence no precise limit can be set in extent. It would be convenient if, as the appellants' counsel did at the hearing, it could be extended to include damages for pain and suffering or loss of amenity. Lord Devlin uses the term in this sense in *Rookes v Barnard* [[1964] 1 All ER 367, HL], when he defines the phrase as meaning all cases where "the award is not limited to the pecuniary loss that can be specifically proved". But I suspect that he was there guilty of a neologism. If I am wrong, it is a

convenient use and should be repeated. Finally, it is worth pointing out, although I doubt if a change of terminology is desirable or necessary, that there is danger in hypostatising "compensatory", "punitive", "exemplary" or "aggravated" damages at all. The epithets are all elements or considerations which may, but with the exception of the first need not, be taken into account in assessing a single sum. They are not separate heads to be added mathematically to one another.' *Cassell & Co Ltd v Broome* [1972] 1 All ER 801 at 825, 826, HL, per Lord Hailsham LC

Australia 'Damages may be either compensatory or exemplary. Compensatory damages are awarded as compensation for and are measured by the material loss suffered by the plaintiffs. Exemplary damages are given only in cases of conscious wrongdoing in contumelious disregard of another's rights.' *Whitfield v De Lauret & Co Ltd* (1920) 29 CLR 71 at 77, per Knox CJ

Australia 'Damages are, in their fundamental character, compensatory. Whether the matter complained of be a breach of contract or a tort, the primary theoretical notion is to place the plaintiff in as good a position, so far as money can do it, as if the matter complained of had not occurred. . . . This primary notion is controlled and limited by various considerations, but the central idea is compensation, or, as Blackstone (Vol 2, p 438, see supra) says— "compensation and satisfaction".' Ibid at 80, per Isaacs J

Australia 'I think the word "damages" in that undertaking [an undertaking as to damages included in an order granting an interim injunction] is to be given a very general meaning, and is not necessarily to be given the same meaning as the word "damages" when used in connection with breaches of contracts. "Damages" in this case seems to me to mean real harm, rather than to have any strictly defined meaning.' *Victorian Onion & Potato Growers Assocn v Finnigan* [1922] VLR 819 at 822, per Cussen J

Aggravated damages

In certain circumstances the court may award more than the normal measure of damages, by taking into account the defendant's motives or conduct, and the damages may be 'aggravated damages', which are compensatory, or 'exemplary damages', which are punitive. (12 Halsbury's Laws (4th edn) para 1112)

New Zealand 'Aggravated damages are extra compensation to a plaintiff for injury to his feelings and dignity caused by the manner in which the defendant acted. Exemplary damages, on the other hand, are damages which, in certain instances only, are allowed to punish a defendant for his conduct in inflicting the harm complained of.' *Huljich v Hall* [1973] 2 NZLR 279 at 287, per McCarthy J

New Zealand 'The essential distinction in this context [a breach of promise case] between aggravated compensatory damages and exemplary or punitive damages is that the former represents a solatium to the plaintiff, the latter a punishment of the defendant.' *A v B* [1974] 1 NZLR 673 at 677, per Mahon J

Exemplary damages

[The award of exemplary damages was considered in *Rookes v Barnard* [1964] 1 All ER 367, HL, where, at 410, 411, Lord Devlin stated that in his view there are two categories of cases in which exemplary damages are awarded, viz (i) where there has been oppressive, arbitrary, or unconstitutional action by the servants of the government, and (ii) where the defendant's conduct has been calculated by him to make a profit which may well exceed the compensation payable to the plaintiff.

Rookes v Barnard was not followed in Australia: see headnote to *Australian Consolidated Press Ltd v Uren* [1967] 3 All ER 523, PC; but the principles formulated in *Rookes v Barnard* were upheld in *Cassell & Co Ltd v Broome* (supra), Lord Hailsham LC saying: 'I would hope very much that in the light of observations made on *Rookes v Barnard* in this case, Commonwealth courts might see fit to modify some of their criticisms of it.']

General damages   *See also* SPECIAL DAMAGES

'"General damages", as I understand the term, are such as the law will presume to be the direct natural or probable consequence of the act complained of.' *Ströms Bruks Akt v Hutchison* [1905] AC 515 at 525, HL, per Lord Macnaghten

Incidental damages

United States Incidental damages to an aggrieved seller include any commercially reasonable charges, expenses or commissions incurred in stopping delivery, in the transportation, care and custody of goods after the buyer's breach, in connection with return or resale of the goods or otherwise resulting from the breach. (Uniform Commercial Code 1978, s 2–710)

United States Incidental damages resulting from the seller's breach include expenses reasonably incurred in inspection, receipt, transportation and care and custody of goods rightfully rejected, any commercially reasonable charges, expenses or commissions in connection with effecting cover and any other reasonable expense incident to the delay or other breach. (Uniform Commercial Code 1978, s 2–715(1))

Liquidated damages

The parties may agree by contract that a particular sum is payable on the default of one of them, and, if the agreement is not obnoxious as a 'penalty', such a sum constitutes 'liquidated damages' and is payable by the party in default. The term is also applied to sums expressly made payable as liquidated damages under a statute.

In every other case, where the court has to quantify or assess the damages or loss, whether pecuniary or non-pecuniary, the damages are 'unliquidated'. (12 Halsbury's Laws (4th edn) para 1109)

Liquidated damages and penalty distinguished

The parties to a contract may agree at the time of entering into it that in the event of a breach the party in default shall pay a stipulated sum of money to the other. If this sum is a genuine pre-estimate of the loss which is likely to flow from the breach, then it represents the agreed damages, called 'liquidated damages', and it is recoverable without the necessity of proving the actual loss suffered. If, however, the stipulated sum is not a genuine pre-estimate of the loss but is in the nature of a penalty intended to secure performance of the contract, then it is not recoverable, and the plaintiff must prove what damages he can. (12 Halsbury's Laws (4th edn) para 1116)

'The hinge on which the decision in every particular case turns, is the intention of the parties, to be collected from the language they have used. The mere use of the term "penalty", or the term "liquidated damages", does not determine that intention, but, like any other question of construction, it is to be determined by the nature of the provisions and the language of the whole instrument. One circumstance, however, is of great importance towards the arriving at a conclusion; if the instrument contains many stipulations of varying importance, or relating to objects of small value calculable in money, there is the strongest ground for supposing that a stipulation, applying generally to a breach of all, or any of them, was intended to be a penalty, and not in the way of liquidated damages.' *Dimech v Corlett* (1858) 12 Moo PCC 199 at 229, 230, PC, per cur.

'Here there are a number of covenants . . . in respect of the breach of which it is said that £5,000 shall be liquidated damages. Now in what cases have the Courts said that in those circumstances you shall construe the words "liquidated damages", not as what they mean—as a sum assessed between the parties—but only as a penal sum, leaving the real damages to be ascertained? Undoubtedly the authorities do say this, that when a stipulation applies to a breach of a number of covenants, and one of those is a covenant for the payment of a sum of money where the damage for the breach of it is according to English law capable of being actually defined, then where a sum is said to be liquidated damages the stipulation applies not distributively to the different covenants but equally to all, and you must hold that the sum cannot be damages assessed by the parties as in the case of a particular covenant with respect to which damages are incapable of being ascertained and are by law fixed in a different way; but you must look upon it as a mere penalty, and ascertain when the breach occurs what is the damage sustained in respect of the particular breach.' *Wallis v Smith* (1882) 21 Ch D 243 at 268, CA, per Cotton LJ

'I shall content myself with stating succinctly the various propositions which I think are deducible from the decisions which rank as authoritative: 1. Though the parties to a contract who use the words "penalty" or "liquidated damages" may prima facie be supposed to mean what they say, yet the expression used is not conclusive. The Court must find out whether the payment stipulated is in truth a penalty or liquidated damages. This doctrine may be said to be found *passim* in nearly every case. 2. The essence of a penalty is a payment of money stipulated as *in terrorem* of the offending party; the essence of liquidated damages is a genuine covenanted pre-estimate of damage (*Clydebank Engineering & Shipbuilding Co v Don Jose Ramos Yzquierdo y Castaneda* [[1905] AC 6]). 3. The question whether a sum stipulated is penalty or liquidated damages is a question of construction to

be decided upon the terms and inherent circumstances of each particular contract, judged of as at the time of the making of the contract, not as at the time of the breach (*Public Works Comr v Hills* [[1906] AC 368, PC]).' *Dunlop Pneumatic Tyre Co Ltd v New Garage & Motor Co Ltd* [1915] AC 79 at 86, 87, per Lord Dunedin

Nominal damages

A plaintiff is entitled to 'nominal damages' where (1) his rights have been infringed, but he has not in fact sustained any actual damage from the infringement, or he fails to prove that he has; or (2) although he has sustained actual damage, the damage arises not from the defendant's wrongful act but from the conduct of the plaintiff himself; or (3) the plaintiff is not concerned to raise the question of actual loss, but brings his action simply with the view of establishing his right.

Nominal damages have been defined as a sum of money that may be spoken of but that has no existence in point of quantity, or a mere peg on which to hang costs. In practice, however, a small sum of money is awarded, usually £2. Nominal damages must be distinguished from small or contemptuous damages, which indicate the court's opinion that the action ought not to have been brought. (12 Halsbury's Laws (4th edn) para 1114)

'The question for consideration is, whether, where a sum of money is due upon simple contract, and the creditor is entitled to claim nominal damages for its detention, the debtor is discharged by the creditor's acceptance, before action brought, of the amount of the debt, or whether the former may afterwards sue for such nominal damages. I apprehend he cannot. Nominal damages are a mere peg on which to hang costs. . . . Nominal damages, in fact, mean a sum of money that may be spoken of, but that has no existence in point of quantity.' *Beaumont v Greathead* (1846) 2 CB 494 at 499, per Maule J

'"Nominal damages" is a technical phrase which means that you have negatived anything like real damage, but that you are affirming by your nominal damages that there is an infraction of a legal right which, though it gives you no right to any real damages at all, yet gives you a right to the verdict or judgment because your legal right has been infringed. But the term "nominal damages" does not mean small damages. The extent to which a person has a right to recover what is called by the compendious phrase damages, but may be also represented as compensation for the use of something that belongs to him, depends upon a variety of circumstances, and it certainly does not in the smallest degree suggest that because they are small they are necessarily nominal damages.' *Mediana (Owners) v Comet (Owners, etc), The Mediana* [1900] AC 113 at 116, per Lord Halsbury LC

Pecuniary damages

New Zealand [The Judicature Amendment Act 1936 (NZ), s 2(1) (repealed; see now the Judicature Amendment Act (No 2) 1955, s 2(1) (amended by Judicature Amendment Act 1977, s 9(1)) applied to actions in which the only relief claimed was payment of a debt or 'pecuniary damages' or the recovery of chattels. Section 3 provided for the trial of actions by a judge without a jury.] 'It is contended on behalf of the respondent that the sum of money claimed is not "pecuniary damages", because it is claimed by virtue of a statutory indemnity under s 50 of the Workers' Compensation Act 1922 [NZ]. I do not accept this view. I respectfully adopt the view expressed in the following language used by Ostler J, in *John Cobbe and Co Ltd v Viles (NIMU Insurance Co, Third Party* [[1939] NZLR 377, 379]: "In this case, although a statutory right to be indemnified is given by s 50 of the Workers' Compensation Act, if that section had never been enacted, in my opinion the plaintiff company would, in the circumstances of this case, have had a claim for damages against the defendant for the amount they had lost in paying compensation to their servant by reason of the defendant's negligence. This claim is in substance and in fact a claim for damages. It is a claim to be indemnified—i.e., to be put in the same position by a money payment as the plaintiff company would have been in if the defendant had not acted negligently. That is exactly what a claim for damages is." Ostler J's decision was the subject of an appeal reported as *NIMU Insurance Co Ltd (Third Party) v Viles* [[1939] NZLR 981]. All the members of the Court of Appeal were of opinion that the appeal should be dismissed. . . . This is not a proceeding for contribution, and, in my opinion, what is sought here is not an equitable remedy. An action by A against B alleging that B's negligence has compelled A to pay C a sum of money which A therefore seeks to recover from B is, in my opinion, an action for damages. Nor are there here any statutory provisions as to procedure which indicate that the Legislature intended such a claim to come before a judge alone. Indeed, the tasks facing a tribunal which has to adjudicate upon a claim for contribution differ substantially from the tasks which will confront the tribunal which tries this petition of right. Section 17 of the Law Reform Act 1936 [NZ], casts upon the Court the duty of determining what amount of contribution is just and equitable for a party to pay, having regard to his responsibility for the damage, and empowers the Court to exempt a party altogether, or to direct a party to make complete indemnity. On the hearing of this petition, there will be no such questions, nor will any assessment of unliquidated damages be necessary. The questions for determination will be what really happened on the wharf when this worker was killed; and who, if anyone, was to blame for what happened. It is not, I think, irrelevant to the interpretation of the words "pecuniary damages" in s 2 of the Judicature Amendment Act 1936 [NZ], to remark that these are questions of just such a kind as it appears to be the policy of the Legislature, as disclosed by that Act, to entrust to the determination of a jury. I conclude, therefore, that this is a claim for "pecuniary damages", and that the case comes within s 2 of the Judicature Amendment Act 1936.' *Richardson & Co Ltd v R* [1942] NZLR 211 at 212–214, per Callan J; also reported [1942] GLR 149 at 150

Prospective damages

The term 'prospective damages' is applied to the damages which are awarded to a plaintiff, not as compensation for the ascertained loss which he has sustained at the time of trial, but in respect of future damage or loss which is recoverable in law. In the case of pecuniary loss it is usual to quantify separately the past and prospective loss; in the case of general damages for pain and suffering and loss of amenity, one sum is given for past and future suffering. (12 Halsbury's Laws (4th edn) para 1111)

Special damages

In current usage, 'special damage' or 'special damages' relate to past pecuniary loss calculable at the date of trial, whilst 'general damage' or 'general damages' relates to all other items of damage whether pecuniary or non-pecuniary. The terms 'special damage' and 'general damages' are used in corresponding senses. Thus, in a personal injuries claim, 'special damage' refers to past expenses and loss of earnings, whilst 'general damages' will include anticipated future loss as well as damages for pain and suffering and loss of amenity.

Distinctions, other than those set out above, have been drawn between 'special damage' on the one hand and 'general damage' on the other, although it may now be better, except in the foregoing context, to avoid a term which (as has been said in relation to 'special damage') is intelligible enough in particular contexts, but tends when successively employed in more than one context and with regard to different subject matter to encourage confusion of thought. Thus 'general damage' has been used to describe the damage which the law 'implies' in wrongs actionable per se, whilst 'special damage' has been said to be the gist of wrongs derived from the action on the case. The term 'general damages' has also been applied to damages falling under the first rule in *Hadley v Baxendale* [(1854) 9 Exch 341], relating to damages arising in the usual course, damages under the second rule, relating to special circumstances, being 'special'. The term 'special damage' has also been used to distinguish the special disadvantage which a member of the public must prove to succeed in a private action based on a public nuisance. (12 Halsbury's Laws (4th edn) para 1113)

'The term "special damage", which is found for centuries in the books, is not always used with reference to similar subject-matter, nor in the same context. At times (both in the law of tort and of contract) it is employed to denote that damage arising out of the special circumstances of the case which, if properly pleaded, may be superadded to the general damage which the law implies in every breach of contract and every infringement of an absolute right: see *Ashby v White* [(1703) 2 Ld Raym 936]. In all such cases the law presumes that some damage will flow in the ordinary course of things from the mere invasion of the plaintiff's rights, and calls it general damage. Special damage in such a context means the particular damage (beyond the general damage) which results from the particular circumstances of the case, and of the plaintiff's claim to be compensated, for which he ought to give warning in his pleadings in order that there may be no surprise at the trial. But where no actual and positive right (apart from the damage done) has been disturbed, it is the damage done that is the wrong; and the expression "special damage" when used of this damage, denotes the actual and temporal loss which has, in fact, occurred. . . . The term "special damage" has also been used in actions on the case brought for a public nuisance, such as the obstruction of a river or highway, to

denote that actual and particular loss which the plaintiff must allege and prove beyond what is sustained by the general public.' *Ratcliffe v Evans* [1892] 2 QB 524 at 528, 529, CA, per cur.

'"Special damages". . . are such as the law will not infer from the nature of the act. They do not follow in ordinary course. They are exceptional in their character, and, therefore, they must be claimed specially and proved strictly. In cases of contract, special or exceptional damages cannot be claimed unless such damages were within the contemplation of both parties at the time of the contract.' *Ströms Bruks Akt Bolag v Hutchison* [1905] AC 515 at 525, 526, per Lord Macnaghten

Statutory damages

The phrase 'statutory damages' is inexact and inelegant. However, damages may be associated with statutes in various ways. Some statutes, for example the factories legislation, impose a duty the breach of which will give rise to civil action by an individual suffering damage. The right has its origin in the statute, but the remedy is provided by the common law. In some cases, on a proper construction of the statute, no individual rights are given. A statute may create a civil action for damages directly, and may define the criteria for the assessment of damages. By statute, common law remedies may be excluded or limited, or a limit put on the damages recoverable. (12 Halsbury's Laws (4th edn) para 1115)

Unliquidated damages   *See* LIQUIDATED DAMAGES

DAMNUM   *See* NUISANCE

DANGER   *See also* ENDANGER

'Danger' means danger of bodily harm or injury or danger to property. (Gas Act 1965, s 28)

New Zealand   [The Civil Aviation Act 1964, s 24 provides that where an aircraft is operated in such a manner as to be the cause of unnecessary 'danger' to any person or property, the pilot or the person in charge of the aircraft, and also the owner thereof, shall be liable on summary conviction.] 'The primary meaning of danger given in the Shorter Oxford English Dictionary is "Liability or exposure to harm or injury; risk, peril". Liability is there defined as, inter alia, "exposed or open to; prone to or liable to suffer from something damaging, deleterious or disadvantageous". These definitions make no distinction between potential and actual danger. We accept that there may be degrees of danger and that a danger may range from something that is no more than possible to something that is probable and that in some contexts danger will be so speculative or unreal as to be insufficient to be regarded as a danger in any real sense. In the end whether an allegedly dangerous situation is caught by a statutory provision which is aimed at its prevention must be considered in the light of the statutory context in which it is used.' *Fowler v Police* [1983] NZLR 701 at 702, 703, CA, per McMullin J

Danger building

. . . Every building in which any process of the manufacture [of gunpowder] is carried on or in which gunpowder or any ingredients thereof, either mixed or partially mixed, are kept, or in the course of manufacture are liable to be (in this Act referred to as a danger building) . . . (Explosives Act 1875, s 10(2))

In coal mine

[The Coal Mines Regulation Act 1908, s 1(2) (as amended by the Sex Discrimination Act 1975) provides that no contravention of the provisions of s 1(1) shall be deemed to take place in the case of a worker who is below ground for the purpose of rendering assistance in the event of accident, or for meeting any 'danger' or apprehended danger, or for dealing with any emergency or work uncompleted through unforeseen circumstances which requires to be dealt with without interruption in order to avoid serious interference with ordinary work in the mine.] 'There is, in the first place, the ordinary attention bestowed on the pit by repairers and brushers, whose business it is—always a more or less dangerous one —to keep the ways and works of the pit in a safe condition. Things are constantly occurring which, although slight at the moment, may, if not attended to, ultimately become dangerous, and it is the regular and ordinary work of the skilled repairer to detect and deal with these occurrences. In the second place, in such pits there are frequent occurrences which are more serious, and which obviously amount to danger or apprehended danger, distinguishable from these ordinary occurrences to which I have referred. Looking at the words of the clause of exceptions in s 1(2) of the Act and the context

in which they occur, I think they do not refer to the danger which will always be present in a pit if it is not looked after, but to some abnormal and exceptionally serious occurrence.' *Thorneycroft v Archibald* 1913 SC (J) 45 at 49, per the Lord Justice-Clerk (Sir John MacDonald)

Of seas or navigation

[A cargo of cheese was shipped under a bill of lading containing the ordinary exception clause—'The Act of God, the Queen's enemies, fire and all and every other danger and accident of the seas, rivers and navigation' etc. At the end of the voyage, the cheese was found to have been eaten and damaged by rats.] 'We agree . . . that the true question is, whether damage by rats falls within the exception, and we are clearly of opinion that it does not. The only part of the exception under which it possibly could be contended to fall is, as "a danger or accident of the sea and navigation"; but this we think includes only a danger or accident of the sea or navigation, properly so called, viz.: one caused by the violence of the wind and waves (a vis major) acting upon a seaworthy and substantial ship, and does not cover damage by rats, which is a kind of destruction not peculiar to the sea or navigation, or arising directly from it, but one to which such a commodity as cheese is equally liable in a warehouse on land as in a ship at sea.' *Laveroni v Drury* (1852) 8 Exch 166 at 170, 171, per cur.

'The words in the bills of lading—"dangers of the seas"—must, of course, be taken in the sense in which they are used in a policy of insurance. It is a settled rule of the law of insurance, not to go into distinct causes, but to look exclusively to the immediate and proximate cause of the loss. . . . Their Lordships . . . are of opinion, that the conclusion proper to be drawn from the evidence is this, that from the nature and collocation of this cargo of animal, vegetable, and (to some extent) putrescible matter, sea damage was done to a portion of the cargo; that by the packing and cramming of the ship so as to prevent any circulation of air, and the closing of the hatches, the atmosphere in the ship's hold became heated, damp and vitiated, without means of escape; and that this atmosphere was the proximate cause of the damage to the oil-cake which is the subject of this suit. This proximate cause cannot be brought within the legal import of the exception of dangers of the seas.' *The Freedom* (1871) LR 3 PC 594 at 601–603, per cur.

[A charterparty contained the following clause: 'The freight to be paid on unloading and right delivery of the cargo . . . (the Act of God, the Queen's enemies, restraint of princes and rulers, fire and all and every other dangers and accidents of the seas, rivers and navigation always excepted).'] 'The charter party here in question, like many others, contains in addition to the exception of perils of the sea the expression "all dangers or accidents of navigation". What is the true construction of that expression? Must it be construed as identical with "perils of the sea"; or must some further effect be given to those additional words? . . . The question which the Court has to determine, having regard to its knowledge of what happens at sea, is whether a loss of which the moving and direct cause is a collision caused by the negligence of another ship is not caused by a "danger or accident of navigation" within the meaning of those words in the charter, notwithstanding that such collision has been held not to be a peril of the sea. A peril of the sea is a peril caused by some action of the elements, but what is a peril of navigation? Navigation is the act of navigating ships. . . . One class of dangers which would most readily occur to the minds of persons accustomed to the sea would be the dangers caused by the negligent navigation of other ships. There are other dangers, but this is perhaps the principal and most obvious kind of danger which may happen at sea other than those included in the expression "perils of the sea". . . . Is such a danger then within the words "dangers of navigation"? I should say that it most certainly is. Though not a peril of the sea it is in my opinion clearly a danger of navigation. If the loss were occasioned by the negligent navigation of the ship carrying the cargo, I do not think that would be a danger of navigation within the words; that would be a loss brought about by the act or default of the shipowner's servants for which he would be liable. It would be a danger, not of navigation, but caused by his employing inefficient servants.' *Garston Sailing Ship Co Ltd v Hickie, Borman & Co* (1886) 18 QBD 17 at 21, 22, per Lord Esher MR

'It may be asked, why should the expression "danger of navigation" cover a loss occasioned by negligence of the other ship, when the expression "peril of the sea" does not? The answer appears to me to be that the one expression properly refers to dangers caused

by the elements and beyond human control; whereas navigation is a process subject to human control, and that dangers caused by the negligent navigation of other ships are therefore properly within the meaning of the term "dangers of navigation", but not within the term "perils of the sea".' Ibid, at 24, per Lopes LJ

'I think the idea of something fortuitous and unexpected is involved in both words, "peril" or "accident"; you could not speak of the danger of a ship's decay—you would know that it must decay; and the destruction of the ship's bottom by vermin is assumed to be one of the natural and certain effects of an unprotected wooden vessel sailing through certain seas.' *Hamilton, Fraser & Co v Pandorf & Co* (1887) 57 LJQB 24 at 26, 27, per Lord Halsbury LC

'It seems to me that the accident which caused the damage was one of the excepted perils or accidents. . . . It was an accidental and unforeseen incursion of the sea that could not have been guarded against by the exercise of reasonable care. I agree, therefore, with the judgment of Lopes LJ [in *Pandorf & Co v Hamilton, Fraser & Co* (1885) 16 QBD 629]. I do not think the case could be summed-up better than it was by him in the words . . . "Sea damage occurring at sea and nobody's fault".' Ibid, at 30, per Lord Macnaghten

DANGEROUS

'Anything, in a manner of speaking, is dangerous if, either owing to negligence, or owing to the fact that it is impossible for everybody on every occasion, however carefully they may conduct themselves, to avoid some mischance of hand or eye, injury may be caused. . . . Almost everything is dangerous from one point of view, but one has to see whether the danger should be reasonably anticipated from the use of things without protection.' *Kinder v Camberwell Borough Council* [1944] 2 All ER 315 at 316, 317, per Lord Caldecote CJ

Australia 'What chattels are dangerous in themselves? "The doctrine of dangerous things is one that I do not think I have ever fully grasped": *Beckett v Newalls Insulation Co Ltd* [1953] 1 All ER 250; [1953] 1 WLR 8, per Stable J at p 12. I humbly place myself beside the learned judge. Fullagar J, in extra-judicial statement expressed the view that the distinction between things dangerous in themselves and things not dangerous in themselves must surely now be regarded as abolished (25 ALJ 278, at p 287). Since the extension of the liability of a manufacturer in respect of defective manufacture since *Donoghue (or McAlister) v Stevenson* [1932] AC 562; [1932] All ER Rep 1, to a class of persons much wider than was previously thought to be the object of obligation, the necessity for the distinction has abated. The distinction originally served the purpose of extending the range of duty so as to include persons who would not otherwise be within the range. Nevertheless the distinction continues and, if in the case of goods dangerous in themselves no knowledge of the danger is necessary in the distributor but in the case of goods not dangerous in themselves knowledge, actual or imputed, is necessary before a distributor can be made liable in negligence, then the distinction would seem to be a lively one. However, one can reach no conclusion on the necessity or otherwise of the ingredient of knowledge of the danger until one has analysed what is meant by a thing dangerous in itself. An analysis of the cases on things dangerous in themselves with all the variety and variation which appear in those cases leads me to the conclusion that a thing is dangerous in itself when the danger of such a thing is of such public notoriety that a defendant will not be heard to say that he in particular did not know of the danger. The notorious danger may arise spontaneously or only when the thing is used in some way in which it may reasonably be foreseen that it may be used, but in any case the danger must be publicly notorious.' *Imperial Furniture Pty Ltd v Automatic Fire Sprinklers Pty Ltd* [1967] 1 NSWR 29 at 38, per Jacobs JA

DANGEROUS BUSINESS

'Dangerous business' means the business of the manufacture of matches or of other substances liable to sudden explosion, inflammation or ignition or of turpentine, naphtha, varnish, tar, resin or Brunswick black or any other manufacture dangerous on account of the liability of the substances employed therein to cause sudden fire or explosion. (London Building Act 1930 s 5)

DANGEROUS DOG

'In this case the magistrates dismissed the summons, without having heard all the evidence that was tendered on behalf of the complainant, on the ground that to justify an order under s 2 of the Dogs Act 1871 [which enables a court of summary jurisdiction to make an order directing a "dangerous" dog to be destroyed], there must be evidence that the dog is dangerous, not only to animals, but also to mankind. . . . I can see no reason why the word "dangerous" in s 2 of the Act of 1871 should be construed as meaning only "dangerous to mankind".' *Williams v·Richards* [1907] 2 KB 88 at 90, per Lord Alverstone CJ

'A dog with a disposition or propensity to bite small children or postmen, or any other class of persons, it seems to me, may well be dangerous though nobody could fairly describe the dog as ferocious; the disposition or propensity might spring from some uncertainty of temper, from some past unfortunate experience which it had suffered, or fear or nervousness, or something of that sort, and something quite different from actual savagery or ferocity or nature.' *Keddle v Payn* [1964] 1 All ER 189 at 191, 192, per Fenton Atkinson J

See, generally, 2 Halsbury's Laws (4th edn) paras 368–370.

DANGEROUS DRIVING   *See* DRIVE—DRIVER

DANGEROUS DRUGS   *See* DRUGS

DANGEROUS GOODS

For the purposes of this Part of this Act [Part V; Safety] the expression 'dangerous goods' means aquafortis, vitriol, naphtha, benzine, gunpowder, lucifer matches, nitroglycerine, petroleum, any explosives within the meaning of the Explosives Act 1875, and any other goods which are of a dangerous nature. (Merchant Shipping Act 1894, s 446(3))

[As to the meaning of 'Explosives' in the Explosives Act 1875, *see* EXPLOSIVES.]

DANGEROUS MACHINERY

A part of machinery is a dangerous part if it may be a reasonably foreseeable cause of injury to anybody acting in a way in which a human being may reasonably be expected to act in circumstances which may reasonably be expected to occur. (20 Halsbury's Laws (4th edn) para 568)

'It seems to me that machinery or parts of machinery is and are dangerous if in the ordinary course of human affairs danger may be reasonably anticipated from the use of them without protection. No doubt it would be impossible to say that because an accident had happened once therefore the machinery was dangerous. On the other hand, it is equally out of the question to say that machinery cannot be dangerous unless it is so in the course of careful working. In considering whether machinery is dangerous, the contingency of carelessness on the part of the workman in charge of it, and the frequency with which that contingency is likely to arise, are matters that must be taken into consideration. It is entirely a question of degree.' *Hindle v Birtwistle* [1897] 1 QB 192 at 195, 196, per Wills J

[A steam motor lorry was left on a highway. To start it, it was necessary to pull out a safety-pin, and manipulate three different levers. Two soldiers managed to send it in reverse into a shop-front. The question arose as to whether this was a case of a dangerous article being left about.] '"Dangerous" is not the word whereby to describe a machine which cannot move by mere accident, but only after a series of operations so complicated as to be beyond the power of a person unacquainted with the mechanism.' *Ruoff v Long & Co* [1916] 1 KB 148 at 153, DC, per Avory J

'It may be said that all moving parts of a machine—and indeed many parts which do not themselves move—are dangerous in the sense that they are capable of causing injury to workmen or other persons (careful or careless) who use the machine, or are brought into proximity to it; and in a literal sense the cutting or grinding parts of all machines designed to perform the operations of cutting or grinding may be said to be within the description of "dangerous".' *Lauder v Barr & Stroud* 1927 SC (J) 21 at 24, 25, per the Lord Justice-Clerk

'In considering whether machinery is dangerous you must not assume that everybody will always be careful . . . A part of machinery is dangerous if it is a possible cause of injury to anybody acting in a way in which a human being may be reasonably expected to act in circumstances which may be reasonably expected to occur.' *Walker v Bletchley Flettons Ltd* [1937] 1 All ER 170 at 175, per du Parcq J

'The first question is, I think, correctly stated in the appellant's case in these words: "Whether the words 'every dangerous part' referred to in s 14 of the Factories Act 1937 [repealed; see now s 14 of the Factories Act 1961] refer only to parts which are directly dangerous by reason

that the part itself is liable to cause injury so that such parts only are required to be fenced by the said section, or whether the said words 'every dangerous part' includes parts which are indirectly dangerous in that they are liable to throw out material with such force that the material is liable to cause injury to the worker so that such parts also are required to be fenced by the said section." My Lords, I have no doubt that this question should be answered by saying that the words "every dangerous part" in their context refer only to parts which are directly dangerous by reason that the part itself is liable to cause injury.' *Nicholls v Austin (F) (Leyton) Ltd* [1946] AC 493 at 504, HL, per Lord Simmonds

'One has to have regard to the purpose of the Factories Act 1937 [repealed; see supra] and that purpose is to protect operatives from danger. If danger does exist from the operation of the machine and if a part becomes dangerous from the operation of the machine, it seems to me that that is a "dangerous part" of the machinery, and the fact that it is not dangerous when no operation is taking place is quite irrelevant.' *Hoare v Grazebrook (M & W) Ltd* [1957] 1 All ER 470 at 474, per Lynskey J

'For my part, I am unable to see the distinction between parts of a machine which are dangerous because they eject pieces of material when the machine is in motion and parts of a machine which are dangerous because the operator may come in contact with them. If the section [s 14(1) of the Factories Act 1937 (repealed; see supra)] requires fencing against the one danger, it would be logical to suppose that fencing was required against the other.' *Close v Steel Co of Wales Ltd* [1961] 2 All ER 953 at 974, HL, per Lord Guest

'The construction of s 14 of the Factories Act 1937 [repealed; see supra] has been considered in a number of cases, and three propositions, derived from the general subject-matter of the section and its detailed provisions, have been established, which are relevant for the present case. (i) A distinction is drawn between dangerous parts of machinery and materials or articles which are dangerous in motion in the machine. The dangerous parts of machinery are dealt with by s 14(1) and are, subject to certain exemptions, required to be fenced. The dangerous materials or articles (which are sometimes . . . conveniently referred to as "components" because they are destined to become components of other machines) are not required by the section itself to be fenced, but there is a power under the concluding words of the section to make regulations requiring them to be fenced. No relevant regulations have been made, and one can see the difficulty of drafting general provisions for the fencing of things so variable as components. . . . (ii) The nature of the danger envisaged by s 14(1) is that a workman may suffer injury directly by coming into contact with a dangerous part of the machinery, and indirect causation is not envisaged. . . . (iii) As regards the degree of danger envisaged, a part of machinery is "dangerous" within the meaning of the section if it is a reasonably foreseeable cause of injury to anybody acting in a way in which a human being may be expected to act in circumstances which may reasonably be expected to occur.' *Eaves v Morris Motors Ltd* [1961] 3 All ER 233 at 241, CA, per Pearson LJ; also reported [1961] 2 QB 385 at 400, 401

[The Factories Act 1961, s 14(1) provides that every 'dangerous' part of any 'machinery', other than prime movers and transmission machinery, shall be securely fenced unless it is in such a position or of such construction as to be as safe to every person employed or working on the premises as it would be if securely fenced. A workman was injured by the revolving body of a mobile crane.] 'Sometimes one finds in the authorities references to dangerous machines; but that is not what the section says, and to ask the question—is this machine dangerous?—can easily lead to error. A vehicle is a dangerous machine in the sense that, if it is driven in a dangerous manner, it may run into someone and injure him. What, then, are the dangerous parts of the machine? It is not the parts of the machine which are dangerous but the machine as a whole; if one had to specify dangerous parts, presumably in the case of an ordinary motor car they would be the bumper, the mudguards and the grille or casing which in more modern cars is found in front of the radiator, but they are not parts of the machinery at all. Of course it would be impossible to fence against this kind of danger; but s 14 is not dealing with this kind of danger; it is dealing with parts of machinery where danger arises from their not being fenced and is obviated by fencing. So it appears to me that the fact that vehicles in motion create a kind of danger which does not exist with stationary or fixed machinery is no reason for not requiring the fencing of parts of the machinery in vehicles which are dangerous whether the vehicle is in motion or not.' *British Railways Board v Liptrot* [1967] 2 All ER 1072 at 1081, HL, per Lord Reid

Australia 'In the majority of cases it would be unnecessary to insist upon a definition of danger in relation to machinery as the existence of danger is a question of fact and generally the circumstances surrounding the particular accident are ample in themselves to furnish a completely satisfactory answer to any contentions, one way or the other, that may be offered. As a guide, however, it has been said that machinery is dangerous when it is in such a condition that possibly it may injure anybody acting in a way in which a human being may be reasonably expected to act in circumstances which may reasonably be expected to occur: per du Parc J, *Walker v Bletchley and Flettons Ltd* supra. Such a test should be adequate.' *Inglis v NSW Fresh Food & Ice Co Ltd* [1944] NSWSR 87 at 99, 100, per Davidson J

DANGEROUS PERFORMANCE

The expression 'performance of a dangerous nature' includes all acrobatic performances and all performances as a contortionist. (Children and Young Persons Act 1933, s 30)

DARK SMOKE   *See* SMOKE

DARKNESS   *See* HOURS OF DARKNESS

DATA

'Data' means information recorded in a form in which it can be processed by equipment operating automatically in response to instructions given for that purpose. (Data Protection Act 1984, s 1(2))

Data equipment

'Data equipment' means equipment for the automatic processing of data or for recording information so that it can be automatically processed. (Ibid, s 41)

DATE

'. . . it has been pointed out by the Court, that in fact "the date thereof" and "the day of the date thereof" are synonymous, and that when a certain time is to begin to run from a particular date, the term begins to run from the day following.' *Williams v Nash* (1859) 28 LJ Ch 886 at 887, per Romilly MR

[Under RSC 1965, Ord 6, r 8(1), a writ, for the purpose of service, is valid in the first instance for twelve months beginning with the 'date' of its issue.] 'It was suggested for the plaintiff that the word "date" should be construed as meaning "time", so that the twelve months ran from 3.5 pm on Sept 10, 1965, to 3.5 pm on Sept 10, 1966: and that the service was good as it was before that time. In support of this suggestion, reference was made to the Shorter Oxford Dictionary, which gives one of the meanings as "the precise time at which anything takes place". I cannot accept this suggestion. When we speak of the *date* on which anything is done, we mean the date by the calendar, such as: "The *date* today is May 2, 1967." We do not divide the *date* up into hours and minutes. We take no account of fractions of a *date*. If authority were needed for so obvious a proposition, it can be found in the judgment of Lord Mansfield CJ in *Pugh v Duke of Leeds* [(1777) 2 Cowp 714 at 720]. Speaking of the date of delivery of a deed, he said: "For what is 'the date'? The date is a memorandum of the day when the deed was delivered: in Latin it is 'datum': and 'datum tali die' is, delivered on such a day. Thus in point of law, there is no fraction of a day: it is an indivisible point . . . 'Date' does not mean the hour or the minute, but the day of delivery: and in law there is no fraction of a day." Applying these words, we must take no account of the time, 3.5 pm. We must regard the writ as issued on Sept 10, 1965, just as if that date were an indivisible point. The whole day of the date of issue must either be *included* or *excluded* in calculating the twelve months. If it is *included*, then, in point of fact, the period for service is less than twelve months by a few hours. If it is *excluded*, it is more than twelve months by a few hours. Which is it to be? I may add that a similar situation arises with the period of limitation. The "date" on which the cause of action accrues is either *included* or *excluded* in the three years.' *Trow v Ind Coope (West Midlands) Ltd* [1967] 2 All ER 900 at 904, CA, per Lord Denning MR

'The law does not as a rule take account of fractions of the day unless there is some necessity for it, as for instance in the dog licence case (*Campbell v Strangeways* [(1877) 3 CPD 105]), and there is no such necessity here. That case turned on the fact that the dog licence was taken out during the day in question. It was therefore clear that during so much of that day

as preceded the issue of the licence, the dog was not licensed. During the rest of the day the dog was licensed. It was therefore necessary to split the day into the period before and the period after the issue of the licence. To construe it otherwise would be to fly in the face of the facts because it was certainly true that during part of the day the dog was unlicensed and during the subsequent part of the day it was licensed. Accordingly, "date" in that case must mean "time", but in the absence of any such necessity, "date" and "time" are in contradistinction one from the other. "Date" is the whole period of twenty-four hours and "time" is the moment during that period which is critical.' Ibid at 908, per Harman LJ

[It was held that 'date' in Ord 6, r 8(1) meant 'day', and that the time of day when the writ was served was immaterial.]

DATE OF ACQUISITION   *See* ACQUISITION

DAUGHTER   *See also* SON

'The gift [in a will] is "to each of the sons and daughters of his late cousin Thomas Holyoake". There are sufficient persons alive to satisfy the word "sons", for Thomas Holyoake had two legitimate sons. It is therefore impossible to say, that illegitimate sons are let in by these words. But he had no legitimate daughter, and I do not see how it is possible to exclude the illegitimate daughter, and though the word is "daughters" in the plural, it does not alter the case. It is a gift to the legitimate sons and to the only daughter.' *Edmunds v Fessey* (1861) 29 Beav 233 at 234, 235, per Romilly MR

'It has been contended on behalf of the defendants that the term daughter means "female child". As, however, in this case the testator left no female children in the legal sense of the word, there are no persons to whom this term, in its literal construction, can apply. . . . I am of opinion that the testator by these words "my daughters" did mean those persons who were recognised by him as his daughters. The evidence shews that the testator treated these children as his daughters, that he called them "daughters", that they called him "father", and that he had introduced them to his acquaintances as his children. That evidence shews, in my opinion, that when the testator spoke of "my daughters" in his will, he meant those persons whom he had shewn to his friends as his daughters, and no others.' *Laker v Hordern* (1876) 45 LJ Ch 315 at 317, 318, per Bacon V-C

DAY *See also* DEMURRAGE; RUNNING DAYS; WORKING DAY

The term 'day' is, like the terms 'year' and 'month', used in more senses than one. A day is strictly the period of time which begins with one midnight and ends with the next. It may also denote any period of twenty-four hours, and again it may denote the period of time between sunrise and sunset. (45 Halsbury's Laws (4th edn) para 1113)

[A proviso in a will required the devisee to be personally present in the house devised for a certain number of days in each year.] 'If the owner be personally present at the house for any part of one day, that will be a sufficient residence for that day.' *Walcot v Botfield* (1854) Kay 534 at 550, per Page Wood V-C

[Under a charterparty, the charterers were to load and discharge as fast as the ship could work, but a minimum of seven days to be allowed merchants, and ten days on demurrage over and above the said lying days, at £25 per day. Lying days were exhausted when ship reached port. Discharge occupied one day and a fraction of the next.] 'There is no ground for saying that in the case of demurrage there can be any division of a day without express stipulation to that effect. The inconvenience of such a proceeding would be very great, and the justice of the case seems the other way. It might be that by the detention of a few hours the ship had lost the whole day, or a tide; and even if she could get out for another port for a fresh voyage, very possibly she might not be able to get to the other place in time for loading. Therefore convenience and the language of the charterparty point the same way. If not discharged within the lay days, the charterer must pay for every day and fraction of a day at the stipulated rate of demurrage.' *Commercial SS Co v Boulton* (1875) LR 10 QB 346 at 349, per Lush J

'"Days" and "lay days" are really the same in a charterparty. "Days" or "lay days" may be calculated in a different manner. They may be described, and sometimes they are described, in a charterparty as days of so many working hours. Then the number of days is fixed, but the length of each day is also fixed. The days may be described as "working days". . . . Working days in an English charterparty, if there is nothing to show a contrary intention, do not include Christmas Day and some other days, which are well known to be holidays. Therefore "working days" mean days on which, at the port, according to the custom of the port, work is done in loading and unloading ships, and the phrase does not include Sundays. . . . "Days" include every day. If the word "days" is put into the charterparty—so many days for loading and unloading—and nothing more, that includes Sundays and it includes holidays. "Working days" are distinguished from "days".' *Nielsen v Wait* (1885) 16 QBD 67 at 71, 72, CA, per Lord Esher MR

'The insurance is expressed by the policy to be "at and from Portland, Oregon, by any route to Algoa Bay and for 30 days in port after arrival". The "arrival" so mentioned in the earlier part of the policy is clearly defined in the subsequent part of it, which describes the risk as continuing "until the said ship with all her ordnance . . ., &c, shall be arrived . . ., until she hath there moored at anchor in good safety.". . . It appears to me that, in order to give effect to the intention of the parties, the expression "30 days" in the policy must be construed as meaning . . . thirty consecutive periods of twenty-four hours after the arrival of the ship.' *Cornfoot v Royal Exchange Assurance Corpn* [1904] 1 KB 40 at 54, CA, per Mathew LJ

[Two truckloads of goods, intended for the defendant, arrived at the plaintiffs' station on a Friday. An advice note was sent the same day stating that demurrage would be charged at a specified rate per wagon per day or part of a day if the wagons were not discharged within forty-eight hours. The goods were to be sent for not later than 6 pm, or on Saturday, not later than 1 pm. The defendant received the notice on Saturday and unloading was carried on up to 1 pm on that day and on Monday and was finished on Tuesday. The plaintiffs claimed demurrage for the detention of one of the trucks on the Tuesday.] 'The question is whether the plaintiffs are entitled to charge the defendant . . . demurrage for the detention of a wagon for one day. The notice was despatched on Friday . . . and it is admitted that, if Saturday is to count as a day, inasmuch as Saturday and Monday passed without the completion of the unloading of the trucks, there was a part of the goods which was not unloaded within two days, or forty-eight hours, within the meaning of the contract. But it is said that a day means a working day of twenty-four hours. I think that the language of the advice note shows that that is not a sound contention, for a part of a day is alluded to in the contract as a day, and on the true construction of the contract it is manifest that Saturday was to count as a day for the purpose of calculating the two days within which the delivery of the goods was to be taken.' *Lancashire & Yorkshire Rly Co v Swann* [1916] 1 KB 263 at 267, DC, per Lord Coleridge J

[Under the Companies Act 1929, s 117 (repealed; see now the Companies Act 1985, s 378(2)) a special resolution had to be passed at a general meeting, of which not less than 'twenty-one days' notice' had been given.] 'The first point to be decided is what is meant by the phrase "not less than twenty-one days' notice" contained in subsection 2 of s 117 of the Companies Act 1929. . . . I do not think there is any doubt about its meaning and I propose to found my decision on *R v Turner* [[1910] 1 KB 346, CCA] and *Chambers v Smith* [(1843) 12 M & W 2] and to decide that the phrase means twenty-one clear days exclusive of the day of service and exclusive of the day on which the meeting is to be held.' *Re Hector Whaling Ltd* [1936] Ch 208 at 210, per Bennett J

Australia [The Country Fire Authority Act 1958–1986 (Vic), s 40(1) prohibits the lighting of any fire in the open on any 'day' in respect of which a warning has been broadcast.] 'In my opinion, on a proper reading of s 40(1), the word "day" should be read as meaning a calendar day. The section contemplates a day being specified as a day of acute fire danger . . . and that specification would naturally be achieved by reference to a calendar day, a certain day in the week or the month. . . . It is true, of course, that in an appropriate setting the word "day" does denote the period between sunrise and sunset. "Day" is there used in contradistinction to "night". The "day" ends and the "night" begins. The Legislature in s 40 is not concerned with this distinction. It is concerned to prevent fires being lit or suffered to remain alight in the open air during a specified day. Whether it is day or night is of no consequence.' *Taig v Fawcett* [1962] VR 58 at 60, per Herring CJ

DAYS OF GRACE

Three days, called days of grace, are, in every case where the bill itself does not otherwise provide, added to the time of payment, as fixed by the bill, and the bill is due and payable on the last day of grace. (Bills of Exchange Act 1882, s 14)

DAYTIME

'It is plain from all the authorities that a distress for rent must be made in the daytime; and the only question is, whether "daytime" is to be considered as the time after sunrise and before sunset, or after daybreak and before dusk. We think that sunrise and sunset form the true limits. . . . It is sufficient to say that in Co Lit 142a, it is laid down: "For a rent service the landlord cannot distrain in the night, but in the daytime"; and the reference is to the Mirrour of Justices c 2, s 26, where it is expressly laid down that daytime is after sunrise and before sunset. So far as we can ascertain, there is not a single authority to the contrary.' *Tutton v Darke, Nixon v Freeman* (1860) 5 H & N 647 at 655, per cur.

DE BONIS NON

Where a sole or last surviving executor dies intestate without having fully administered the testator's estate, the deceased executor's administrator does not become the representative of the original testator, and it is accordingly necessary to appoint an administrator to administer the goods of the original testator left unadministered. This is a grant of administration cum testamento annexo de bonis non administratis (that is, 'with the will annexed for unadministered estate'). A grant for the administration of unadministered estate is also made where the deceased dies intestate and the original administrator did not complete the administration of the estate. Both types of grant are described as 'de bonis non'. (17 Halsbury's Laws (4th edn) para 984)

DE FACTO POSSESSION *See*
POSSESSION

DEAD FREIGHT *See* FREIGHT

DEAD RENT *See* RENT

DEAD STOCK *See* LIVESTOCK

DEAL—DEALER

The expression 'dealer' means a person who in the normal course of his business attends sales by auction for the purpose of purchasing goods with a view to reselling them. (Auctions (Bidding Agreements) Act 1927, s 1(2))

'Dealer' means a person engaged in the business of making, supplying, selling (including selling by auction) or exchanging articles of precious metal or in other dealing in such articles. (Hallmarking Act 1973, s 22(1))

'Dealer' means a person carrying on a business of selling goods, whether by wholesale or by retail. (Resale Prices Act 1976, s 14)

'I take it that the strict definition of "dealing" is "distributing". A dealer is one who distributes.' *Allen v Sharp* (1848) 17 LJ Ex 209 at 212, per Alderson B (arguendo)

Australia ['Dealing' is defined in the New South Wales Code in a similar way to its definition in s 4 of the Securities Industry Act, 1979–1980 (SA), namely: 'dealing', in relation to securities, means (whether as principal or agent) acquiring, disposing of, subscribing for or underwriting the securities or making or offering to make, or inducing or attempting to induce a person to make or to offer to make an agreement—(a) for or with respect to acquiring, disposing of, subscribing for or underwriting securities; or (b) for the purpose or purported purpose of which is to secure a profit or gain to a person who acquires, disposes of, subscribes for or underwrites the securities or to any of the parties to the agreement in relation to securities.'] '. . . The definition of "dealing" in the Companies Acquisition of Shares Code is in pari materia with that in s 4 of the Securities Industry Act except that, in the first mentioned Code, a reference is made to "sub underwriting" as well as to underwriting securities. It is notable, however, that throughout that Code, where appropriate, the word "acquisition" of shares is used and not the word "dealing" in shares. Notwithstanding the inclusion in the definition of "dealing" in securities of acquiring, disposing of, and subscribing for securities the mere acquisition, disposition or subscription cannot, in my view, properly be described as "dealing" in securities. The acquisition disposition or subscription may be part of a dealing.' *Von Doussa v Owens (No 1)* (1982) 30 SASR 367 at 376–377, per Mitchell J

United States The term 'dealer' means any person engaged in the business of buying and selling securities for his own account, through a broker or otherwise, but it does not include a bank, or any person insofar as he buys or sells securities for his own account, either individually or in some fiduciary capacity, but not as part of a regular business. (Securities Exchange Act of 1934, s 3(a)(5))

Motor dealer

'Motor dealer' means a person carrying on the business of selling or supplying mechanically propelled vehicles. (Vehicles (Excise) Act 1971, s 38(1))

DEALING COMPANY *See* COMPANY

DEAN AND CHAPTER *See* CATHEDRAL; CHAPTER

DEATH *See also* DIE

'The testator gives the houses to his daughter Emma Sarah and her children lawfully begotten; and it is properly argued that this alone would give her an absolute interest. He then proceeds: "And in default of such issue, and in case of her death," he gives them over. These are words of double contingency—default of issue, and death. Does it not evidently mean if she dies without issue? It is argued from authority that the words "in case of her death" must be taken to be descriptive of dying in the testator's life time. But the reason of the case alluded to does not apply here. If there is a gift to AB, and in case of his death to CD, words applying to contingency being used, with reference to an event as to which none exists, it is supposed that some contingency must be meant, and it is considered to apply to death in the life-time of the testator. That is because there is no other construction to be put upon it; but where there is an intelligible contingency it must be looked at. Here, by coupling together the words "in default of such issue", and "in case of her death", it means in case of her dying without issue; and there is a contingency, without resorting to the construction contended for.' *Gawler v Cadby* (1821) Jac 346 at 347, 348, per Plumer MR

'It is proper to notice a difference which occurs in the wording of the gift over of the two moieties of the residue, one is, "in case of the death of any or either of them before my said wife Elizabeth," and the other is, "in case of the death of any or either of them," without specifying any period within which the death was to take place, and which period therefore might have reference to the death of the testator, or to the death of the tenant for life. I am of opinion, however, that these words, in both cases, must be held to apply to the same event, viz, the contingency of death before the death of the tenant for life, and that no just argument can be deduced from the absence of these words, "before my said wife Elizabeth", in the disposition of the second moiety of the residue, but that the same principle and rule of construction applies to both.' *Ive v King* (1852) 16 Beav 46 at 54, 55, per Romilly MR

[A testatrix by her will disposed of the residue of her estate in the following terms—viz. '. . . and in case of the death of any of my daughters her share shall be equally divided between her children, and if any of my daughters die leaving no children her share shall be equally divided between my grandchildren.'] 'The death of a daughter spoken of in the first part of the clause means death in the lifetime of the testatrix, and therefore it also means the same in the second part of the clause, and accordingly in consequence of the daughters having survived their mother they become absolutely entitled to the residuary estate in equal shares.' *Re Reeves, Edwards v Reeves-Hughes* (1907) 51 Sol Jo 325 at 325, per Joyce J

'The vital provision [in a will] is "in the case of my wife's decease, the same is to go to my son". The rule is that such words are deemed in law to mean "decease in the testator's lifetime". This has been called "the first rule in *Edwards v Edwards* [(1852) 15 Beav 357]." The fourth rule in that case was set aside by the House of Lords in *O'Mahoney v Burdett* [(1874) LR 7 HL 388], but not the first rule. It has been established by an unbroken series of decisions. Its great strength was shown in *Trotter v Williams* [(1697) 2 Eq Ca Ab 344] where the words "then living" were used in a context which would have taxed the rule severely but for its strength. Words such as "in the case of an event" usually indicate that the event may or may not happen. They mean "if it happens". He who uses them normally provides for a contingency. If he uses them in relation to death he is deemed not to mean death at any time, for death at some time would be a certainty, not a contingency. Therefore it is supposed that he must mean "death within some definite period", and, if no such period is indicated by the will, the Courts seize upon the period of the testator's lifetime as the only period to which the contingency can be referred. As Fitzgibbon LJ said in *In re Neary's*

Estate [(1881) 7 LR Ir 311] "It is a corollary, *ex necessitate rei* forced upon the Court," and in *Montgomery v Montgomery* [(1845) 2 Ir Eq R 161] it was laid down that this rule of interpretation will never be applied except *ex necessitate rei*. If there is another period than the lifetime of the testator indicated by the will to which the contingency can be referred, that other period will be adopted.' *Re Hall, Hall v Hall* [1944] IR 54 at 57, per Black J

Resulting from injury

'If death in fact resulted from the injury, it is not relevant to say that death was not the natural or probable consequence thereof. The question whether death resulted from the injury resolves itself into an inquiry into the chain of causation. If the chain of causation is broken by a *novus actus interveniens*, so that the old cause goes and a new one is substituted for it, that is a new act which gives a fresh origin to the after-consequence.' *Dunham v Clare* [1902] 2 KB 292 at 296, CA, per Collins MR

'The claimant under the Workmen's Compensation Act [repealed; see now the Social Security Act 1975, s 50] must prove an accident arising out of and in the course of his employment and that injury or death resulted from it. The result need not be a direct or a natural or even a probable consequence of the accident if in fact it is a result of the accident. It is enough that the accident caused or contributed to or accelerated death and it appears from the authorities that an accident may contribute to the death if the accident has caused such a state of things in the man's body that he has become physically more susceptible to the cause which ultimately kills him.' *Comery v New Hucknall Colliery Co Ltd* (1919) 88 LJKB 462 at 465, CA, per Scrutton LJ

'What is laid down . . . in numerous . . . cases is this. If you can find that there is, as a result of an accident or of the shock resulting from an accident, a condition of nervous derangement which leads to the man committing suicide the applicant can get compensation under the Workmen's Compensation Act [repealed; see supra]. If you cannot find that the accident has caused any physical derangement, but can only find this, that, there being an accident with a physical result, the man when faced with it, thinking it over, brooding over it, loses his moral courage to face it and thinks that the only way out is to kill himself, that is not a consequence of the accident. The line runs very fine . . . but it is still a question of fact.'

Dixon v Sutton Heath & Lea Green Colliery Ltd (No 2) (1930) 23 BWCC 135 at 138, CA, per Scrutton LJ

DEBENTURE   *See also* DEBENTURE STOCK

No precise definition of 'debenture' can be found, but various forms of instruments are called debentures. A debenture is a document which either creates or acknowledges a debt. A document may be a debenture even though under its terms, the debt is only to be repaid out of a part of the profits. The term 'debenture' is usually associated with a company of some kind, and most debentures are securities given by companies, but they are often granted by clubs and occasionally by individuals. (7 Halsbury's Laws (4th edn) para 813)

'Debenture' includes debenture stock, bonds and any other securities of a company whether constituting a charge on the assets of the company or not. (Companies Act 1985, s 744)

'The term itself [debenture] imports a debt—an acknowledgment of a debt—and speaking of the numerous and various forms of instruments which have been called debentures without anyone being able to say the term is incorrectly used, I find that generally, if not always, the instrument imports an obligation or covenant to pay. This obligation or covenant is in most cases at the present day accompanied by some charge or security. So that there are debentures which are secured, and debentures which are not secured. . . . I am not bound to hold that an instrument is a debenture because it is called a debenture by the company issuing it, nor to hold it is not a debenture because it is not so called by the company. I must look at the substance of the instrument itself. . . . I have seen debentures of various kinds and classes, and it is a mistake to say that to be debentures the instruments must be issued and numbered *seriatim*. I have seen even a single debenture issued to one man.' *Edmonds v Blaina Furnaces Co, Beesley v Blaina Furnaces Co* (1887) 36 Ch D 215 at 219–221, per Chitty J

'Now what is a debenture? . . . A debenture means a document which either creates a debt or acknowledges it, and any document which fulfils either of these conditions is a "debenture".' *Levy v Abercorris Slate & Slab Co* (1887) 37 Ch D 260 at 263, 264, per Chitty J

'It has been said by a wiser man than myself that it is impossible to give an exhaustive defi-

nition of the word debenture. . . . But there are certain characteristics which, if found in a document, have usually in legal and commercial transactions been held to constitute that document a debenture. One of these is that the document is an acknowledgement of indebtedness.' *Lemon v Austin Friars Investment Trust Ltd* [1926] Ch 1 at 17, CA, per Warrington LJ

'Now, what the correct meaning of "debenture" is I do not know. I do not find anywhere any precise definition of it. . . . You may have mortgage debentures, which are charges of some kind on property. You may have debentures which are bonds. . . . You may have a debenture which is nothing more than an acknowledgement of indebtedness.' Ibid at 172, 173, per Lindley J; adopted in *R v Findlater* [1939] 1 KB 594 at 599, CCA

Australia 'The Oxford English Dictionary defines "debenture", inter alia, to mean: "An acknowledgement of indebtedness by a corporation, private person, etc." I am concerned with the meaning of the word in the Stamp Duties Act. Notwithstanding that it could be used to describe an acknowledgement of indebtedness by an individual, the fact is that that is a rare usage and, over a long period of time, the word has, both in the commercial world and in the courts, had a special relationship to documents given by companies. The definition in the Act could fairly be regarded as taken from the Companies Act, except that it uses the term "body corporate" instead of "company". This is explicable upon the footing that the definition is operating upon debentures of corporations whether incorporated in New South Wales or not, and the expression "body corporate" can be regarded as somewhat more specific than the word "company".' *Broad v Comr of Stamp Duties* [1980] 2 NSWLR 40 at 48–49, per Lee J

Canada 'A debenture is merely a specialty debt of a corporation. It may or may not be accompanied by security. In fact several series of debentures issued by large corporations in this Province, not having security behind them, come readily to my mind.' *Re Shipman Boxboards Ltd* [1942] OR 118 at 121, per Urquhart J

New Zealand 'Whatever may be the full definition of "a debenture", the term includes this much at least: that it is a written instrument containing an undertaking for the payment of a sum of money at a time fixed by, or ascertainable from the terms of, the instrument itself, with interest (if interest is payable) fixed or ascertainable in like manner.' *Union Bank of Australia Ltd v South Canterbury Building & Investment Co Ltd* (1894) 13 NZLR 489 at 512, CA, per cur.

DEBENTURE STOCK

Debenture stock is generally constituted and secured by a trust deed containing a charge upon the property of the company. A stock certificate is issued to each allottee or transferee of stock stating, inter alia, in the case of registered stock, that the person named in it is the registered proprietor or, in the case of bearer stock, that the bearer is the proprietor of the amount of stock mentioned in it, and having printed on it the conditions on which the stock is issued and held. (7(1) Halsbury's Laws (4th edn) para 1097)

DEBT

The legal acceptation of debt is, a sum of money due by certain and express agreement. (3 Bl Com 153)

[The Companies Act 1862, s 80 (repealed; see now Insolvency Act 1986, s 122), dealt with the winding up of companies because of inability to pay 'debts'.] 'With regard to the payment of debts, there are certain things given as *indicia* of inability to pay debts, followed by the general clause empowering the Court to make the order whenever it is proved to its satisfaction that the company is unable to pay its debts. . . . I think that the petitioners have not made out a case at all in any sense of inability to pay debts within the meaning of the Act of Parliament. I apprehend . . . that inability to pay debts must refer to debts absolutely due— that is to say, debts for which a creditor may go at once to the company's office and demand payment.' *Re European Life Assurance Society* (1869) LR 9 Eq 122 at 127, per James V-C

'I should say, apart from any authority, that a debt legal or equitable can be attached whether it be a debt owing or accruing; but it must be a debt, and a debt is a sum of money which is now payable or will become payable in the future by reason of a present obligation. . . . An accruing debt, therefore, is a debt not yet actually payable, but a debt which is represented by an existing obligation. . . . The result seems to me to be this; you may attach all debts, whether equitable or legal: but only debts can be attached; and moneys which may or may not become payable from a trustee to his *cestui que trust* are not debts.' *Webb v Stenton* (1883) 11 QBD 518 at 526–528, CA, per Lindley LJ

'It was urged that a call [in respect of shares] constitutes a debt from the time when the testator became a shareholder. I am of opinion that it does not, and that there is no debt till the call is made. We were referred to the Companies Act 1862, s 16 [repealed; see now Companies Act 1985, s 14(2)], which enacts that "all moneys payable by any member to the company . . . shall be deemed to be a debt due from such member to the company.". . . They are to be a debt; but when are they to be a debt? When they become payable according to the regulations of the company, and by the articles the shareholder is only to make the payment when he is called upon by the directors to do so. There is therefore no debt until a call is made.' *Whittaker v Kershaw* (1890) 45 Ch D 320 at 326, CA, per Cotton LJ

'The word "debts", no doubt, means something recoverable by an action for debt, and nothing can be recovered in an action for debt except what is ascertained or can be ascertained. A claim for an amount which is uncertain, and cannot be adjusted in an account, cannot, I think, be justly called a "debt".' *Ogdens Ltd v Weinberg* (1906) 95 LT 567 at 567, HL, per Lord Davey

'A purchaser is bound in law to pay the purchase money of goods he purchases. He may also be bound in certain circumstances to pay interest upon this sum while it remains unpaid. He may be sued for the recovery of it. His property may be taken in execution, seized and sold to satisfy a judgment recovered in respect of it. If the purchaser be an individual he may, in most cases, be made a bankrupt in the event of non-payment. If a company it may in certain circumstances be wound up, or equitable execution in the shape of the appointment of a receiver be obtained. It does not appear to me that an obligation for the breach of which or the non-performance of which no relief of any of these kinds can be obtained is an obligation . . . amounting to a debt within the meaning of that word in its ordinary natural sense and meaning as used by business men in their commercial or business dealings.' *Inland Revenue Comrs v Port of London Authority* [1923] AC 507 at 517, 518, per Lord Atkinson

Australia   'The debts referred to in s 94(1) [of the Life Insurance Act 1945–1986 (Cth)] as "his or her debts", that is, the debts of "the person whose life is insured", are, so far as concerns the situation after that person's death, those debts contracted by that person during his lifetime which devolve upon his personal representatives and are payable by them out of, and to the extent of, the assets in his estate. Death duty, whose characteristics as a debt are defined by provisions of the Stamp Duties Act . . . is not, and is not converted by those provisions into, a debt of the person whose life is insured, in that sense.' *Re Estate of Black, Thomas v Comr of Stamp Duties* (1965) 66 SR (NSW) 348 at 356, per Sugerman, Walsh and Moffitt JJ

Australia 'A debt accruing has been defined in *Webb v Stenton* [supra] where the Master of the Rolls, Sir Baliol Brett, . . . described it as "*debitum in praesenti, solvendum in futuro*", a present debt which is not yet payable, and as not including anything which may be a debt however probable and however soon it may be a debt. . . . Fry LJ, at p 258 said: "In my opinion the defendants' counsel is right in contending that the words 'is indebted' (in Order 45 Rule 2 which is in the same form as the present County Court rule)" and the words "debts owing or accruing" refer to the same subject matter. It appears to be plain that to satisfy either of these two expressions there must be an actual present debt. . . . In our opinion, these authorities establish that a debt "accruing due" must be a debt based upon a present obligation but which is payable at a definable approaching future date and not one which is payable only on the performance of a condition precedent.' *Re Australia and New Zealand Savings Bank* [1972] VR 690 at 692 per cur.

Canada 'The word "debt" has a well-defined judicial meaning as a sum payable in respect of a liquidated money demand. It does not include an unliquidated claim for damages.' *Pizzolati & Chittaro Manufacturing Co Ltd v May* [1971] 3 OR 768 at 770, Ont SC, per Houlden J revsd, without affecting definition, [1972] 2 OR 606, Ont CA

Bankruptcy

United States '[D]ebt' means liability on a claim. . . . (Bankruptcy Act 1978, s 101(11))

DEBT COLLECTOR

United States The term 'debt collector' means any person who uses any instrumentality of interstate commerce or the mails in any business the principal purpose of which is the collection of any debts, or who regularly collects or attempts to collect, directly or indirectly, debts owed or due or asserted to be owed or due another. . . . [T]he term includes any creditor who, in the process of collecting his own debt, uses any name other than his own which would indicate that a third person is collecting or attempting to collect such debts. For the purpose of section 1692f(6) of this title, such term also includes any person who uses any instrumentality of interstate commerce or the mails in any business the principal purpose of which is the enforcement of security interests. . . . (Fair Debt Collection Practices Act 1977, s 803(6))

DEBTOR   *See also* JUDGMENT DEBTOR

'The debtor', in relation to an attachment of earnings order, or to proceedings in which a court has power to make an attachment of earnings order, or to proceedings arising out of such an order, means the person by whom payment is required by the relevant adjudication to be made. (Attachment of Earnings Act 1971, s 2)

'The operative words of the Act [Deeds of Arrangement Act 1887 (repealed; see now Deeds of Arrangement Act 1914)] read shortly are "a deed made by a debtor for the benefit of his creditors shall be registered, and shall be void unless registered". Is there any legitimate way of reading these words so as not to include the deed of a foreigner? . . . It is, at least, as legitimate to read "debtor" as meaning "debtor subject to our jurisdiction" as it is to limit the word "void", and say it means "void as regards property within our jurisdiction.". . . On the whole it seems to me that . . . I am justified in . . . saying that "debtor" means "debtor subject to the Bankruptcy Acts".' *Dulaney v Merry & Sons* [1901] 1 KB 536 at 546, per Channell J

Secured transactions

United States 'Debtor' means the person who owes payment or other performance of the obligation secured, whether or not he owns or has rights in the collateral, and includes the seller of accounts or chattel paper. Where the debtor and the owner of the collateral are not the same person, the term 'debtor' means the owner of the collateral in any provision of the Article dealing with the collateral, the obligor in any provision dealing with the obligation, and may include both where the context so requires. . . . (Uniform Commercial Code 1978, s 9–105(1)(d))

DECEASE   *See* DEATH

DECEIVE

[The Trade Marks Act 1938, s 12 enacts that no trade mark shall be registered if it so nearly resembles an existing trade mark as to be likely to 'deceive' or cause confusion. (The phrase in the Trade Marks Act 1905, s 19 (repealed) was 'calculated to deceive.')] 'It seems to me that in registering trade-marks, the principle to which the enactment so plainly refers ought to be applied without any qualification whatever, and that the Comptroller . . . ought to reject words which involve a misleading allusion or a suggestion of that which is not strictly true, as well as words which contain a gross and palpable falsehood.' *Eno v Dunn* (1890) 15 App Cas 252 at 263, per Lord Macnaghten.

'To deceive is, I apprehend, to induce a man to believe that a thing is true which is false, and which the person practising the deceit knows or believes to be false. To defraud is to deprive by deceit: it is by deceit to induce a man to act to his injury. More tersely it may be put, that to deceive is by falsehood to induce a state of mind; to defraud is by deceit to induce a course of action.' *Re London & Globe Finance Corpn Ltd* [1903] 1 Ch 728 at 732, 733, per Buckley J

'The words "calculated to deceive" [in the Trade Marks Act 1905, s 19 (repealed; see now Trade Marks Act 1938, s 12, where the words are 'likely to deceive or cause confusion')] do not necessarily imply fraud, or anything of that kind; they are satisfied by the marks, if that is the case, being so nearly alike as to be calculated to cause confusion.' *Re Egg Products Ltd's Application* (1922) 39 RPC 155 at 163, per Sargant J

Australia [Any person who drives or uses upon a public street any unregistered motor vehicle or trailer, having upon it any number, number plate, or registration label of a description prescribed to be fixed to registered motor vehicles or trailers, and calculated to deceive, is guilty of an offence under s 13(d) of the Traffic Act 1925 (Tas).] 'The expression, "calculated to deceive" is a well-known expression under various trademark statutes, and does not necessarily imply fraud in the

person responsible. The words ordinarily mean, likely or apt to deceive. . . . In the trademark statutes, the expression ordinarily refers to trademarks of a kind which are likely or apt to deceive as to the true nature, quality, etc, of the goods. In the present context, the expression means, in my opinion, apt or likely to deceive in respect of whether the vehicle is registered, and whether it is registered under a particular registered number.' *Gunton v Jackman* [1981] Tas R 369 at 374, per Neasey J

DECEPTION

For the purposes of this section [obtaining property by deception] 'deception' means any deception (whether deliberate or reckless) by words or conduct as to fact or as to law, including a deception as to the present intentions of the person using the deception or any other person. (Theft Act 1968, s 15(4))

[The above definition is also applied to s 16 (obtaining pecuniary advantage by deception) and s 20 (suppression etc of documents) of the Act of 1968.]

[The Theft Act 1968, s 16(1) provides that a person who by any 'deception' dishonestly obtains for himself or another any pecuniary advantage shall on conviction be liable to imprisonment for a term not exceeding five years.] 'The deception, for the purposes of s 16(2)(a) [under which "pecuniary advantage" included a debt which was evaded or deferred], must at least normally be a deception which operates on the mind of the person deceived so as to influence him to do or to refrain from doing something whereby the debt is deferred or evaded.' *R v Aston, R v Hadley* [1970] 3 All ER 1045 at 1048, CA, per cur.

[Section 16(2)(a) of the Theft Act 1968 was repealed by s 5(5) of the Theft Act 1978, which creates additional offences, including those of obtaining services from another by deception and of evading liability by deception.]

'The physical acts of the accused that are an essential element of any offence under s 15 [of the Theft Act 1968] must amount to a "deception", i.e. the making to the person from whom the property is obtained of a representation of fact, law or intention that is false. The essential state of mind of the accused at the time of doing those physical acts is his knowledge of the falsity of the representation or his indifference as to whether it is true or false, and his intentions (1) that the false representation should be communicated to the person from whom the property is to be obtained; (2) that such person should believe the representation to be true; (3) that this belief should induce that person to part with ownership, possession or control of property to the accused himself or to some other person, and (4) that the accused himself or that other person should assume the rights of owner of the property so obtained.' *Director of Public Prosecutions v Stonehouse* [1977] 2 All ER 909 at 915, HL, per Lord Diplock

DECISION

South Africa 'To "decide" a matter means to take it into consideration and to settle it.' *Judes v Registrar of Mining Rights Krugerdorfs* 1907 TS 1049 per Innes CJ

DECK CARGO *See* CARGO

DECLARATORY JUDGMENT *See* JUDGMENT

DECLARE

'The terms of the deed are "it is declared", etc; and the question is, whether that amounts to a contract on the part of the trustee. . . . I am of opinion that when the parties to a deed frame it in the terms of *declaring* that such and such things shall be done, the term "declare" is sufficient to constitute a contract.' *Richardson v Jenkins* (1853) 1 Drew 477 at 482, 483, per Kindersley V-C

[An article of association of a company required a director to 'declare' his interest in any contract made by the company.] 'A man declares his opinion or his intentions when he states what his opinion is, or what his intentions are, not that he has an opinion or that he has intentions; and so, in my opinion, a man declares his interest, not when he states that he has an interest, but when he states what his interest is.' *Imperial Mercantile Credit Assocn (Liquidators) v Coleman* (1873) LR 6 HL 189 at 205, per Lord Cairns

DECLINE

'With regard to the question as to the contingency which would justify an appointment [of trustees under a power of appointment in a

will], one is the case of a trustee declining to act. A question has been raised, whether declining to act is not limited to a trustee declining to act without ever having accepted or acted; but I do not think that such a contention, which would have the effect of narrowing the utility of the power, can be allowed to prevail. I see no more reason for such a construction, than for holding that the case of a trustee dying or becoming incapable to act is not within the power, unless he had so died or become incapable before he ever acted. It appears to me that the contingency of a trustee who had acted, declining to act any longer, is one on which a new trustee might be appointed.' *Travis v Illingworth* (1865) 2 Drew & Sm 344 at 346, per Kindersley V-C

Canada [Upon applying for an insurance policy, an insurer answered 'No' to the question whether any underwriter or insurance company had 'declined' to insure her.] 'The Shorter Oxford English Dictionary, 3rd ed, vol 1, p 465, contains the following definition of the word "decline": "1. To turn aside. 2. To turn aside from. 3 (a) Not to consent to engage in, practice or do; (b) not to consent or agree to doing, or to do; hence practically = refuse, but a milder expression; (c) *not to accept (something offered)*; implying polite refusal. . . ." (The emphasis is mine.) In the absence of evidence proving an offer by or on behalf of Mrs Chenier to a particular insurer and the failure of that insurer to accept the specific risk offered, I cannot consider that the inability of a particular agent, or agents, to place the . . . coverage constitutes proof that an underwriter or insurance company had declined to insure Mrs Chenier. It has not been proved to my satisfaction that an application was made to an insurer to accept this risk, nor has it been proved that an insurer having been offered the specific risk did not accept it. Accordingly, I am of the view that it has not been proved that Mrs Chenier's answer to that question constituted misrepresentation, because I do not feel that the defendant has proved that the answer was untrue.' *Chenier v Madill* (1973) 2 OR (2d) 361 at 374, Ont SC, per Galligan J

DECORATION

'Decoration' includes medal, medal ribbon, clasp and good-conduct badge. (Army Act 1955, s 225(1); Air Force Act 1955, s 223(1); Naval Discipline Act 1957, s 135(1))

DEDICATION

A road or other way becomes a highway by reason of the dedication of the right of passage to the public by the owner of the soil and of an acceptance, that is user, of the right by the public. 'Dedication' means that the owner of the soil has either said in so many words, or so conducted himself as to lead the public to infer that he meant to say, that he was willing that the public should have this right of passage. From the moment that a dedicated way has been accepted by the public there is a right of passage by the public. (21 Halsbury's Laws (4th edn) para 62)

'It is necessary to shew in order that there may be a right of way established, that it has been used openly as of right, and for so long a time that it must have come to the knowledge of the owners of the fee that the public were so using it as of right, and from this apparent acquiescence of the owners, a jury might fairly draw the inference that they chose to consent, in which case there would be a dedication.' *Greenwich Board of Works v Maudslay* (1870) LR 5 QB 397 at 404, per Blackburn J

'A highway becomes such by being dedicated to the public, and proof of user by the public is in general sufficient evidence of dedication, unless it is shewn that during the period of user there was no person who could dedicate the land to the public. But dedication to the public may be proved in another way, by proof of acts and declarations of the owner.' *Spedding v Fitzpatrick* (1888) 38 Ch D 410 at 414, CA, per Cotton LJ

'It is clear law that a dedication must be made with intention to dedicate, and that the mere acting so as to lead persons into the supposition that a way is dedicated to the public does not of itself amount to dedication.' *Simpson v A-G* [1904] AC 476 at 493, 494, per Lord Macnaghten

'Dedication . . . as between the owner of the soil on the one hand, and the controlling authority on the other, involves something more than the mere occupation by the public of the surface. It involves the dedication of so much of the subjacent soil as is necessary for the proper maintenance of the surface as a road or street. How much of the subsoil is necessarily dedicated for this purpose is a matter of evidence in each case. It may be that the subsoil is of such a nature that only a very shallow stratum is required for the maintenance of the surface as a road; on the other hand it may be that the character of the subsoil renders a much thicker stratum necessary.' *Schweder v Worthing Gas Light & Coke Co (No 2)* [1913] 1 Ch 118 at 124, per Eve J

'The expression "dedicated to public use" is used in reference to land which itself remains the property of the owner in fee of the soil, but for some definite purposes is dedicated to public use.' *Porter v Ipswich Corpn* [1922] 2 KB 145 at 151, DC, per Greer J

DEED

A deed is an instrument which complies with the following requirements. First, it must be written on parchment or paper. Secondly, it must be executed in the manner specified below by some person or corporation named in the instrument. Thirdly, as to subject matter, it must express that the person or corporation so named makes, confirms, concurs in or consents to some assurance (otherwise than by way of testamentary disposition) of some interest in property or of some legal or equitable right, title, or claim, or undertakes or enters into some obligation, duty or agreement enforceable at law or in equity, or does or concurs in some other act affecting the legal relations or position of a party to the instrument or of some other person or corporation. (12 Halsbury's Laws (4th edn) para 1301)

A deed is a writing sealed and delivered by the parties. It is sometimes called a charter, *carta*, from its materials; but most usually, when applied to the transactions of private subjects, it is called a deed, in Latin *factum* . . . because it is the most solemn and authentic act that a man can possibly perform, with relation to the disposal of his property; and therefore a man shall always be estopped by his own deed, or not permitted to aver or prove any thing in contradiction to what he has once so solemnly and deliberately avowed. (2 Bl Com 293)

[An instrument under seal contained a covenant with trustees that the covenantor in his lifetime or his executors within twelve months after his decease would invest £60,000 in the names of trustees upon charitable trusts. It was executed by the covenantor but was not communicated to the trustees.] 'It appears to us that this instrument is a deed. . . . The instrument has all the requisites of a deed; it is in the form of an indenture, it is sealed and delivered by the covenantor in the presence of the attesting witness: and the collateral circumstance, that it had been kept in the possession of the covenantor, does not render it less a deed. No case has been cited showing that such an instrument is not a deed, whatever else it may also be.' *Alexander v Brame* (1855) 7 De GM & G 525 at 530, per cur.

'The term [deed] is clearly not confined to contracts. A charter of feoffment, for instance, is a deed; so is a gift or grant, power of attorney, a release, or a disclaimer. I would go further, and say that any instrument delivered as a deed, and which either itself passes an interest or property, or is in affirmance or confirmation of something whereby an interest or property passes is a deed.' *R v Morton* (1873) LR 2 CCR 22 at 27, per Bovill CJ

'In my judgment, in this day and age, we can, and we ought to, hold that a document purporting to be a deed is capable in law of being such although it has no more than an indication where the seal should be.' *First National Securities Ltd v Jones* [1978] 2 All ER 221 at 228, CA, per Goff LJ

Australia 'There is very little authority on the substantial requirements of a deed . . . In Spelman's Glossary, a deed is defined as *"Scriptum solemne quo firmatur donum, concessio, pactum, contractus, et hujusmodi"* which very freely translated means a solemn writing which confirms a gift, a concession, a pact, a contract and things of this mode. Other ancient law dictionaries give similar definitions. . . . In New South Wales, by the Conveyancing Act, s 38, the requirements were reduced to four, namely, signing, sealing, delivery and attestation though some modifications are made in what constitutes sealing.' *Manton v Parabolic Pty Ltd* [1985] 2 NSWLR 361 at 368–369, per Young J

New Zealand 'A deed is a writing on paper or parchment signed and attested in the manner required by s 4 of the Property Law Act 1952, whereby an interest, right or property passes or an obligation binding on some person is created, or which is in affirmance of some act whereby an interest, right or property has passed. The fact that a document describes itself otherwise than as a deed (e.g. as an agreement) does not mean that it is not a deed; nor is every instrument which is signed and attested in conformity with s 4 of the Property Law Act necessarily a deed.' *Re Wilson's Settlements* [1972] NZLR 13 at 22, per Quilliam J

DEED POLL   *See also* INDENTURE

A deed poll is a deed made by and expressing the active intention of one party only, or made by two or more persons joining together in expressing a common active intention of them all. A deed poll is so called because the parchment required for such deeds has usually been polled or shaven even at the top. (12 Halsbury's Laws (4th edn) para 1303)

DEEM

'Generally speaking, when you talk of a thing being deemed to be something, you do not mean to say that it is that which it is to be deemed to be. It is rather an admission that it is not what it is to be deemed to be, and that, notwithstanding it is not that particular thing, nevertheless . . . it is to be deemed to be that thing.' *R v Norfolk County Council* (1891) 60 LJQB 379 at 380, DC, per Cave J

'It is, of course, quite permissible to "deem" a thing to have happened when it is not known whether it happened or not. It is an unusual but not an impossible conception to "deem" that a thing happened when it is known positively that it did not happen. To deem, however, that a thing happened when not only is it known that it did not happen, but it is positively known that precisely the opposite of it happened, is a conception which to my mind . . . amounts to a complete absurdity.' *Batcheller (Robert) & Sons Ltd v Batcheller* [1945] Ch 169 at 176, per Romer J

'The word "deemed" is used a great deal in modern legislation. Sometimes it is used to impose for the purposes of a statute an artificial construction of a word or phrase that would not otherwise prevail. Sometimes it is used to put beyond doubt a particular construction that might otherwise be uncertain. Sometimes it is used to give a comprehensive description that includes what is obvious, what is uncertain and what is, in the ordinary sense, impossible.' *St Aubyn (LM) v A-G (No 2)* [1951] 2 All ER 473 at 498, HL, per Lord Radcliffe

'I bear in mind what Lord Radcliffe said in *St Aubyn's* case [supra] about the word "deem" but nevertheless regard its primary function as to bring in something which would otherwise be excluded.' *Barclays Bank Ltd v Inland Revenue Comrs* [1961] AC 509 at 523, HL, per Viscount Simonds

'The word "deems" normally means only "is of opinion" or "considers", or at most "decides", and there is no implication of steps to be taken before the opinion is formed or the decision is taken.' *R v Brixton Prison (Governor), ex p Soblen* [1962] 3 All ER 641 at 669, CA, per Pearson LJ; also reported in [1963] 2 QB 243 at 315

Australia 'The word "deemed" . . . is more commonly used for the purpose of creating . . . a "statutory fiction". . . . that is, for the purpose of extending the meaning of some term to a subject-matter which it does not properly designate. When used in that sense, it becomes very important to consider the purpose for which the statutory fiction is introduced.' *Muller v Dalgety & Co Ltd* (1909) 9 CLR 693 at 696, per Griffith CJ

Australia 'When the legislature uses the word "deemed" in legislation, it requires acceptance of a fictional state of affairs that would be otherwise if one were not so required by the legislation. In *Hunter Douglas Australia Pty Ltd y Perma Blinds* [(1970) 122 CLR 49] the High Court considered the word "deemed" in s 53(2) of the Trade Marks Act 1955–1986 (Cth). Windeyer J [at 65] said, "The words 'deem' or 'deemed' when used in a statute thus simply state the effect or meaning which some matter or thing has—the way in which it is to be adjudged. This need not import artificiality or fiction. It may be simply the statement of an indisputable conclusion".' *Wainer v Rippon* [1980] VR 129 at 135, per O'Bryan J

Australia 'In *Muller v Dalgety & Co Ltd* [supra], Griffith CJ said that "deemed" is commonly used "for the purpose of creating . . . a 'statutory fiction' . . . that is, for the purpose of extending the meaning of some term to a subject matter which it does not properly designate. When used in that sense it becomes very important to consider the purpose for which the statutory fiction is introduced". This passage has been often quoted in Australian courts. It is a recognition that the verb "deem", or derivatives of it, can be used in statutory definitions to extend the denotation of the defined term to things it would not in ordinary parlance denote. This is often a convenient device for reducing the verbiage of an enactment. But that the word can be used in that way and for that purpose does not mean that whenever it is used it has that effect. After all, to deem means simply to judge or reach a conclusion about something . . . The words "deem" and "deemed" when used in a statute thus simply state the effect of meaning which

some matter or thing has—the way in which it is to be adjudged. This need not import artificiality or fiction. It may be simply the statement of an indisputable conclusion, as if for example one were to say that on attaining the age of twenty-one years a man is deemed to be of full age and no longer an infant. . . . There is no presumption, still less any rule, that wherever the word "deemed" appears in a statute it demonstrates a "fiction" or some abnormality of terminology. Sometimes it does. Often it does not.' *Hunter Douglas Australia Pty Ltd v Perma Blinds* (1969) 122 CLR 49 at 65–67, per Windeyer J

Canada 'The word . . . "deemed" . . . is not inflexible. It may but does not always mean "adjudged and determined". Certainly, when the doing or abstaining from doing a particular thing is to be "deemed" to have a particular consequence, this is a very natural meaning, though the same result might be attained by attributing to it the meaning "shall be regarded as".' *Hickey v Stalker* (1924) 53 OLR 414 at 418, per Middleton J

Canada [The Insurance Act RSO 1950, s 134(1) (repealed; see now RSO 1970, c 224, s 148) provided that a contract was 'deemed' to be made in Ontario if the place of residence of the insured was stated to be Ontario or if the place of residence was not stated but the actual place was Ontario.] 'In the case at bar, and in many cases which can easily be imagined, to construe the word "deemed" in s 134(1) as "held conclusively" would be to impute to the Legislature the intention (i) of requiring the Court to hold to be the fact something directly contrary to the true fact, and (ii) of asserting the power to alter the terms of a contract made and to be wholly performed and in fact wholly performed in a foreign state. This result can, and in my opinion should, be avoided by construing the word to mean "deemed until the contrary is proved".' *Gray v Kerslake* (1957) 11 DLR (2d) 225 at 239, SCC, per Cartwright J

Canada 'The words "deem", "deemed" and "shall be deemed" when used in statutes usually imply an element of finality, but that meaning is not inflexible or invariable. In some cases these words, or words of identical import, are construed to establish a conclusive presumption. . . . In *Re Rogers and McFarland* [(1909) 19 OLR 622] the . . . court held that "deemed" . . . meant nothing less than "adjudged" . . . or "conclusively considered" for the purpose of the legislation.' *St Leon*

Village Consolidated School District No 1425 v Roncevay (1960) 31 WWR 385 at 391, 392, Man CA, per Schulz JA

Canada 'The word "deemed" is capable of meaning "rebuttably presumed", that is, presumed until the contrary is proved.' *Credit Foncier Franco-Canadien v Bennett and A-G (BC)* (1963) 43 WWR 545 at 547, per Sheppard JA

Canada [The City of Toronto Act 1967, s 6(6)(c) provided that municipal lien for costs of executing work orders should be 'deemed to be taxes'.] 'The primary function of the words "shall be deemed" is to bring in something that would otherwise be excluded. A lien on land is not in the nature of taxes and rates though a tax may be secured by a lien on land. To my mind the "deeming provision" ("shall be deemed to be taxes") in the later part of cl (c) of s 6(6) is expansive of the words "shall have a lien for any amount expended" used in the earlier part of the same clause. Putting the best construction I can on s 6(6)(c) it seems to me that the Legislature intended that the amount expended for repairs as ascertained and fixed by the Clerk of the municipality is to be considered as taxes on land with all the attendant consequences. A consequence of such a construction would be, in my judgment, to bring the amount due as ascertained and fixed by the Clerk of the municipality within the ambit of s 511 of the Municipal Act so that the municipality would have a special lien.' *Re Scarbim Realty Ltd and City of Toronto* (1978) 90 DLR (3d) 747 at 753, 754, Ont SC, per Pennell J

New Zealand 'While this term, which is popular with legal draftsmen, is commonly used to create a statutory fiction and to extend a meaning to a subject-matter which the latter does not literally embrace . . . this connotation cannot apply throughout s 224(1) [of the Companies Act 1955] which provides (inter alia) that "unless the court on proof of fraud or mistake, thinks fit otherwise to direct, all proceedings taken in the voluntary winding up shall be *deemed* to have been validly taken" in the event of a later petition for a winding up by the court. In that context, I think "deemed" must be given a significance which does not necessarily imply an artificial quality attributed to the commencement of winding up but should be read as the equivalent of "conclusively considered" for the purposes of the Act . . . or "to all intents and purposes . . ."'

Ross v P J Heeringa Ltd [1970] NZLR 170 at 173, per Haslam J

DEER

'Deer' means deer of.any species and includes the carcase of any deer or any part thereof. (Deer Act 1963, s 9; Deer Act 1980, s 8).

[Close times have been established for deer by the Deer Act 1963. As to the offence of taking or killing deer, see the Deer Act 1980, s 1.]

DEFACE

Australia 'The various dictionary definitions which were cited all shew that the word [deface] means "to mar the face of an object" and it is commonly used in that sense in relation to a monument, and, in particular, according to Webster's Dictionary, it means to mar the face or external appearance, or to mar by effacing an important feature or portion. To remove a plaque from a wall of a monument by undoing the bolts attaching it, so that either the bolts are left protruding from the wall or the bolt holes are left exposed, and so as to leave a distinct mark on the wall is, in my opinion, ample to amount to defacing the monument.' *Bolton v Dance* [1968] VR 631 at 643, per Gowans J

DEFALCATION

Australia 'The Oxford English Dictionary defines "defalcation" as "a fraudulent deficiency in money matters", and Webster as "misappropriation of money: embezzlement". Apart from these definitions I consider . . . that the ordinary meaning of the word essentially involves the presence of fraudulent or dishonest dealing.' *Daly v Sydney Stock Exchange* (1982) 2 NSWLR 421 at 428, per Samuels JA

DEFAMATION

A defamatory statement is a statement which tends to lower a person in the estimation of right thinking members of society generally or to cause him to be shunned or avoided or to expose him to hatred, contempt or ridicule, or to convey an imputation on him disparaging or injurious to him in his office, profession, calling, trade or business. (28 Halsbury's Laws (4th edn) para 10)

The essence of a defamatory statement is its tendency to injure the reputation of another person. There is no complete or comprehensive definition of what constitutes a defamatory statement, since the word 'defamatory' is nowhere precisely defined. Generally speaking, a statement is defamatory of the person of whom it is published if it tends to lower him in the estimation of right thinking members of society generally or if it exposes him to public hatred, contempt or ridicule or if it causes him to be shunned or avoided. A person's reputation is not confined to his general character and standing but extends to his trade, business or profession, and words will be defamatory if they impute lack of qualification, knowledge, skill, capacity, judgment or efficiency in the conduct of his trade, business or professional activity. (28 Halsbury's Laws (4th edn) para 42)

'Judges and textbook writers alike have found difficulty in defining with precision the word "defamatory". The conventional phrase exposing the plaintiff to hatred, ridicule and contempt is probably too narrow. The question is complicated by having to consider the person or class of persons whose reaction to the publication is the test of the wrongful character of the words used. I do not intend to ask your Lordships to lay down a formal definition, but after collating the opinions of many authorities I propose in the present case the test: Would the words tend to lower the plaintiff in the estimation of right-thinking members of society generally?' *Sim v Stretch* [1936] 2 All ER 1237 at 1240, per Lord Atkin

[*See*, generally, and particularly as to unintentional defamation, the Defamation Act 1952.]

DEFAULT   *See also* ACT OR DEFAULT; WILFUL; WRONGFUL ACT OR DEFAULT

'Default' means failure to pay, or want of sufficient distress to satisfy, any fine or other sum of money, or failure to do or abstain from doing any thing required to be done or left undone. (Criminal Justice Act 1961, s 39)

'I do not know a larger or looser word than "default". Abstracted from other words, what does it mean? In the expressions "judgment by default", and "a juror making default", we understand it differently. In its largest and

most general sense it seems to mean, failing.' *Doe* d *Dacre v Dacre (Lady)* (1798) 1 Bos & P 250 at 258, per Eyre CJ

'"Default" must mean a default where something is not done by the mere act of omission of the one party, and not an omission with the concurrence of the other party.' *Albert v Grosvenor Investment Co Ltd* (1867) LR 3 QB 123 at 128, per Cockburn CJ

'It [default] means nothing more, nothing less, than not doing what is reasonable under the circumstances—not doing something which you ought to do, having regard to the relations which you occupy towards the other persons interested in the transaction.' *Re Young and Haston's Contract* (1885) 31 Ch D 168 at 174, per Bowen LJ

'"Default" must, I think, involve either not doing what you ought or doing what you ought not, having regard to your relations with the other parties concerned in the transaction; in other words, it involves the breach of some duty you owe to another or others.' *Re Bayley-Worthington & Cohen's Contract* [1909] 1 Ch 648 at 656, per Parker J

[By an exception clause in a towage contract a tug owner was not responsible (inter alia) for any damage or loss that might arise to any vessel or craft being towed, or about to be towed, or having been towed, whether such damage arose from or was occasioned by 'default' of the steam tug owner.] 'I do not think it is necessary to say that in no case can the words "default of the owner" refer to a breach of contract, but I think that the whole clause points to the exceptions being confined to a time when the tug owner is doing something or omitting to do something in the actual performance of the contract, and do not apply during a period when, as in this case, he has ceased even for a time to do anything at all and has left the performance of his duties to some one else. In other words, I think the exception extends to cover a default during the actual performance of the duties of the contract, and not to an unjustified handing over of those obligations to some one else for performance.' *The Cap Palos* [1921] P 458 at 468, CA, per Lord Sterndale MR

'The act, default or sufferance referred to in s 94 of the Public Health Act 1875 [repealed; see now Public Health Act 1936, s 93] is an act, default or sufferance related to the nuisance which it is sought to abate, and default no less than sufferance within the meaning of that section can occur without the breach of an obligation arising from contractual agreement.' *Clayton v Sale Urban District Council* [1926] 1 KB 415 at 425, per Lord Hewart CJ

'For purposes of clearness and to avoid possible misunderstanding hereafter . . . I do not think that the ambit of "default" as an element disabling the plea of frustration to prevail has as yet been precisely and finally determined. "Self-induced" frustration . . . involves deliberate choice, and . . . a man cannot ask to be excused by reason of frustration if he has purposely so acted as to bring it about. "Default" is a much wider term and in many commercial cases dealing with frustration is treated as equivalent to negligence.' *Joseph Constantine SS Line Ltd v Imperial Smelting Corpn Ltd* [1942] AC 154 at 166, HL, per Lord Simon LC

'I cannot construe the word "default" here [in s 259 of the Public Health Act 1936] in the way in which we have been asked to do so by the appellants. I do not think "default" means in this case merely doing nothing, unless the obligation to do something is imposed by the Act. There was no act here which caused the obstruction [in a natural watercourse due to debris washed down by a stream] either to arise or to continue. I can well understand that there may be circumstances whereby a person failing to do something which he ought to do, as, for instance, preventing material going into a river from his own premises may be said to cause the obstruction by his default. In this case . . . there is nothing to show that the respondents did anything which caused this obstruction to arise or to continue, nor do I think that there is anything which can properly be called a default. There might have been facts which amounted to a sufferance, but sufferance is not mentioned in this section.' *Neath RDC v Williams* [1950] 2 All ER 625 at 632, per Lord Goddard CJ; [1951] KB 115 at 126

Australia 'In *Doe* d *Dacre v Dacre* [supra] Eyre CJ, said: "I do not know a larger or looser word than 'default' . . . In its largest and most general sense it seems to mean, failing. It is a relative term and takes its colour from the context. . . . 'Default' means not doing something which you ought to do having regard to the relations which you occupy towards the other persons interested in the transaction (*Re Bayley-Worthington and Cohen's Contract* [supra]). Similarly, in *Grein v Imperial Airways Ltd* [[1937] 1 KB at 88] Greene MR says: "The word 'default' is a word of wide

signification and in its ordinary use does, I think, include a breach of contract".' *Woolworths Ltd v Crotty* (1942) 66 CLR 603 at 620, per Rich J

'The words "default" and "wrongful default" are not in their ordinary meaning just equivalents for "tort" and the word "wrongdoer" for "tortfeasor". "Default" and "wrongful default" include a breach of contract, and "wrongdoer" a person guilty of a breach of contract.' Ibid at 623, per McTiernan J

Australia 'Section 379(8) of the Companies Ordinance (1962 (ACT)) states that "the phrase officer who is in default . . . includes an officer of the company or corporation who knowingly and wilfully authorizes or permits the commission of an offence". I agree with their Honours that this provision is intended to specify and define one way, which might otherwise have been in doubt, in which an officer may be in default. According to the Shorter Oxford Dictionary "default" as a noun means "1. Fault. 2. An imperfection, defect, blemish. 3. Failure to act; neglect; failure to perform some legal requirement or obligation. 4. Culpable neglect of some duty or obligation. 5. A failure in duty; a fault, misdeed, offence. 6. Failure: esp. to meet financial engagements" hence "remiss" . . . Section 379(8) is an inclusive definition and should not be read as covering all cases in which officers may be in default.' *Lillyman v Pinkerton (No 2)* (1981) 71 FLR 135 at 143, per Gallop J

Canada 'Default is in the legal sense at any rate synonymous with negligence, and is best defined by the synonym failure. . . . "Default" in common parlance assuredly calls to mind negative conduct, a failure in any given situation to take care, or to do an act required by law, and is foreign to the conception of intended and deliberate acts which owing to their consequence to others may prove actionable in law.' *Costello v Calgary* [1943] 2 WWR 327 at 331, per McLaurin J

DEFEASANCE

A provision for defeasance of the security, within the meaning of the statutory provision, is one which defeats or limits the operation of the bill or stipulates for its discharge in stated events. A stipulation is not a defeasance for the purpose of the Bills of Sale Acts unless it is a term which is part and parcel of the agreement under which the bill is given. A subsequent agreement varying or determining a bill of sale is not a defeasance within the Acts, though it may itself be registrable as a bill of sale. Similarly, a mortgage granted prior to the bill is not a defeasance of the bill. . . .

The essence of a defeasance is that it in some way defeats or limits the operation of the bill. A condition which does not defeat but fulfils the operation of the deed, such as a condition for sale on default, is not a defeasance; nor is a condition which does not come into operation until after enforcement of the bill, such as a condition that upon sale by the grantee the purchaser shall not be bound to inquire whether default has been made. (4 Halsbury's Laws (4th edn) para 704)

A defeasance is a collateral deed, made at the same time with a feoffment or other conveyance, containing certain conditions, upon the performance of which the estate then created may be *defeated* or totally undone. And in this manner mortgages were in former times usually made; the mortgagor enfeoffing the mortgagee, and he at the same time executing a deed of defeasance, whereby the feoffment was rendered void on re-payment of the money borrowed at a certain day. And this, when executed at the same time with the original feoffment, was considered as part of it by the antient law; and, therefore only indulged: no subsequent secret revocation of a solemn conveyance, executed by livery of seisin, being allowed in those days of simplicity and truth; though, when uses were afterwards introduced, a revocation of such uses was permitted by the courts of equity. But things that were merely executory, or to be completed by matter subsequent, (as rents, of which no seisin could be had till the time of payment; and so also annuities, conditions, warranties, and the like) were always liable to be recalled by defeasances made subsequent to the time of their creation. (2 Bl Com 327)

'As I have always understood, a "defeasance" is something which defeats the operation of a deed, but is contained in some other deed or document. If it is contained in the same deed it is called a condition. *Re Storey, ex p Popplewell* (1882) 21 Ch D 73 at 80, CA, per Jessel MR

'The words "defeasance or condition" as used in the sub-section [Bills of Sale Act 1878, s 10(3)] mean an agreement between the parties to the bill of sale affecting either the right of the grantor to redeem the goods or of the grantee to seize them.' *Stott v Shaw & Lee Ltd* [1928] 2 KB 26 at 37, CA, per Shearman J

DEFECT

'"Defect" means a lack or absence of something essential to completeness.' *Tate v Latham & Son* [1897] 1 QB 502 at 506, per Bruce J

'In all these cases between vendor and purchaser, the vendor knows what the property is, and what the rights with regard to it are. The purchaser is generally in the dark. I think, therefore, that, in considering what is a latent defect and what a patent defect, one ought to take the general view, that a patent defect, which can be thrust upon the purchaser, must be a defect which arises either to the eye, or by necessary implication from something which is visible to the eye. It would not be fair to hold that a purchaser is to be subjected to all the rights which he might have found out, if he had pursued an inquiry based upon that which was presented to his eye. I think he is only liable to take the property subject to those defects which are patent to the eye, including those defects which are a necessary consequence of something which is patent to the eye.' *Yandle & Sons v Sutton, Young v Sutton* [1922] 2 Ch 199 at 210, per Sargant J

[The relevant parts of an exception in a bill of lading were as follows: 'A. The act of God . . . and loss or damage resulting from any of the following causes or perils are excepted, viz. . . . loss or damage from rust, accidents to, or defects in, hull, tackle, or machinery . . . or navigation . . . of whatever nature or kind and howsoever caused.'] 'I think that this exception with regard to defects cannot displace the warranty of seaworthiness which is at the root of a bill of lading contract. . . . The word "defects" in this exception should be given a narrower interpretation, as referring to defects which might develop during the voyage in a ship which at the beginning of the voyage was seaworthy.' *Tudor Accumulator Co Ltd v Oceanic Steam Navigation Co Ltd* (1924) 41 TLR 81 at 83, per Rowlatt J

[The Mines and Quarries Act 1954, s 81(1) provides that all parts and working gear shall be of good construction, suitable material, adequate strength and free from 'patent defect'.] 'A patent defect is not latent when there is none to observe it. The natural meaning of the word "patent" is objective, not subjective. It means "observable", not "observed". A patent defect must be apparent on inspection, but it is not dependent on the eye of the observer; it can "blush unseen". In this case, although the defect was in darkness, it was patent. Had the plaintiff or his mate shone his lamp on it at the relevant moment, he would have seen it. The construction of the word "patent" for which the defendants contend involves the conclusion that a patent defect at the belt head becomes a latent defect immediately it has turned over the rollers and is making its hidden journey in the darkness, and that it is intermittently latent or patent according to its position. Such a construction is unreasonable and would severely limit the protection given by s 81(1) in a way that Parliament cannot have intended.' *Sanderson v National Coal Board* [1961] 2 All ER 796 at 799, CA, per Holroyd Pearce LJ; also reported [1961] 2 QB 244 at 251

In machinery or plant

'A defect in the machinery would be the absence of some part of the machinery, or a crack, or anything of that kind.' *McGiffin v Palmer's Shipbuilding & Iron Co Ltd* (1882) 10 QBD 5 at 9, per Stephen J

'I take defect to include anything which renders the plant etc. unfit for the use for which it is intended, when used in a reasonable way and with reasonable care: and, if a horse intended for drawing trolleys is from any cause unfit for such work, and a person is driving him with reasonable care, and is injured by reason of the unfitness of the horse for his work, such person may be properly said to be injured by reason of a defect in plant.' *Yarmouth v France* (1887) 19 QBD 647 at 658, DC, per Lindley LJ

'I am . . . quite unable to regard "latent defect in the machinery" as covering a weakness of design. It is not a natural interpretation of the words or a meaning which any man of business reading the expression in a commercial document would attach to it. The phrase "defect in machinery" in a business document means a defect of material, in respect either of its original composition or in respect of its original or its after-acquired condition. . . . The phrase . . . does not in my view cover the erroneous judgment of the designer as to the effect of the strain which his machinery would have to resist.' *Jackson v Mumford*

(1902) 51 WR 91 at 91, per Kennedy J; affd (1904) 52 WR 342, CA

DEFECT OF TITLE

Any fact calculated to prevent the purchaser obtaining such a title to the property as he was led to expect constitutes a defect of title. The following are examples of defects of title: where title is to be shown for less than the full statutory period, the fact that the deed forming the stipulated root of title is a voluntary one, upon which ordinarily there would not have been an investigation of the title; the existence or alleged existence of an easement over the property, or of covenants restricting its use and enjoyment; in the case of leasehold property, the onerous or unusual nature of the covenants in the lease under which the property is held; the existence of restrictions as to the use for certain trades of premises described as leasehold business premises; or of a covenant to expend a specified sum in building within a limited time on land described in general terms as freehold building land; or of a party structure notice under the London building legislation, and an award made under it imposing a pecuniary liability on the owner of the property sold. Similary it is a defect of title if the maxim cujus est solum ejus est usque ad coelum et ad inferos is not applicable to the property sold, owing to the vendor's title not extending to an underground cellar or to the subjacent minerals, or owing to a third party having a right to overhang part of the property. All such matters must be disclosed by the vendor. (42 Halsbury's Laws (4th edn) para 63)

DEFECTIVE   *See also* MENTAL
DISORDER

In this Act 'defective' means a person suffering from a state of arrested or incomplete development of mind which includes severe impairment of intelligence and social functioning. (Sexual Offences Act 1956, s 45(1), as amended by the Mental Health Amendment Act 1982, s 65(1), Sch 3, Part I, para 29)

DEFENCE

'When an indictment is preferred and process goes to bring in the defendants, and they say nothing until they come into Court, in obedience to process, and then plead guilty, that does not constitute a "defence". We must understand that word in its ordinary sense as meaning something which a man does in order to defend himself from the legal consequences of the proceedings instituted against him.' *R v Denton (Inhabitants)* (1864) 5 B & S 821 at 828, per Cockburn CJ

DEFERRED SHARES   *See* SHARES

DEFICIENCY OF MEN

[A charterparty provided (inter alia) that hire should not be paid in certain circumstances, including periods in which the vessel suffered from a 'deficiency of men'. The vessel was delayed for a week owing to the refusal of her officers and men to sail except in convoy.] 'Looking at the words as they stand, and endeavouring to give them a meaning which practical business men would give them, I think that "deficiency of men" means deficiency of men; it does not mean "deficiency of willingness in men to work". There is no doubt that the men on board this ship amounted to a full complement of officers and crew. That is what the owners agreed to provide—a full complement of officers and crew, and they did provide them. These men by a mere change of mind would have been competent at once to work this ship. It was not even as if they were sick. I am not sure that I agree with Sellers J, when he said that inability of officers and men to work through sickness or injury would amount to "deficiency of men"; but we have not to decide that point because these men were not sick. They were quite able and competent to do their work. Therefore, I think, giving the words "deficiency of men" their ordinary sense, the facts in this case do not come within those words.' *Royal Greek Government v Minister of Transport, The Ilissos* [1949] 1 KB 525 at 528, 529, CA, per Bucknill LJ

DEFRAUD   *See also* DECEIVE; FRAUD

'To defraud *is by* deceit to induce a course of action.' *Re London & Globe Finance Corpn Ltd* [1903] 1 Ch 728 at 733, per Buckley J

'I . . . express the opinion that the words "defraud" and "fraudulent purpose", where

they appear in the section in question [s 275 of the Companies Act 1929 (repealed; see now the Companies Act 1985, s 458)] are words which connote actual dishonesty involving, according to current notions of fair trading among commercial men, real moral blame. No judge, I think, has ever been willing to define "fraud", and I am attempting no definition. I am merely stating what, in my opinion, must be one of the elements of the word as used in this section.' *Re Patrick & Lyon Ltd* [1933] Ch 786 at 790, per Maugham J

[The appellant was convicted of uttering forged documents, knowing them to be forged with intent to 'defraud', contrary to the Forgery Act 1913, s 6 (repealed; see infra).] 'I think that there are one or two things that can be said with confidence about the meaning of this word "defraud". It requires a person as its object; that is, defrauding involves doing something to someone. Although in the nature of things it is almost invariably associated with the obtaining of an advantage for the person who commits the fraud, it is the effect on the person who is the object of the fraud that ultimately determines its meaning. This is none the less true because, since the middle of the last century, the law has not required an indictment to specify the person intended to be defrauded or to prove intent to defraud a particular person. Secondly, popular speech does not give, and I do not think ever has given, any sure guide as to the limits of what is meant by "to defraud". It may mean to cheat someone. It may mean to practise a fraud on someone. It may mean to deprive someone by deceit of something which is regarded as belonging to him or, though not belonging to him, as due to him or his right. It passes easily into metaphor, as does so much of the English natural speech. Murray's New English Dictionary instances such usages as defrauding a man of his due praise or his hopes. Rudyard Kipling in the First World War wrote of our "angry and defrauded young". There is nothing in any of this that suggests that to defraud is, in ordinary speech, confined to the idea of depriving a man by deceit of some economic advantage or inflicting on him some economic loss. Has the law ever so confined it? In my opinion, there is no warrant for saying that it has. What it has looked for in considering the effect of cheating on another person and so in defining the criminal intent is the prejudice of that person; what Blackstone's Commentaries, Vol 4, p 245, called "to the prejudice of another's right".' *Welham v Director of Public*

Prosecutions [1960] 1 All ER 805 at 808, HL, per Lord Radcliffe; also reported [1961] AC 103 at 123, 124

'I think it is fairly clear that the word "defraud" in this subsection [s 172(1) of the Law of Property Act 1925 (conveyance of property made with intent to defraud creditors)] is designed to reproduce the expression "hinder, delay or defraud" in the Statute of Elizabeth [1571], and is not intended to be confined to cases of fraud in the ordinary modern sense of that word, i.e. as involving actual deceit or dishonesty. It is quite inconceivable that if Parliament had meant to circumscribe the effect of the old provision it would not have done so in clear terms. The word "defraud" in the context of s 172, and having regard to the history of its statutory predecessor, must, I think, carry the meaning of depriving creditors of timely recourse to property which would otherwise be applicable for their benefit.' *Lloyd's Bank Ltd v Marcan* [1973] 2 All ER 359 at 367, per Pennycuick V-C

'I have not the temerity to attempt an exhaustive definition of the meaning of "defraud". . . . Words take colour from the context in which they are used, but the words "fraudulently" and "defraud" must ordinarily have a very similar meaning. If, as I think, and as the Criminal Law Revision Committee [(1966) Cmnd. 2977] appears to have thought, "fraudulently" means "dishonestly" then "to defraud" ordinarily means in my opinion to deprive a person dishonestly of something which is his or of something to which he is or would or might but for the perpetration of the fraud, be entitled.' *Scott v Metropolitan Police Comr* [1974] 2 All ER 1032 at 1038, HL, per Viscount Dilhorne

Australia 'Was there evidence of an intent to defraud the revenue—that is, to get out of the revenue something that was already in it, or to prevent something from getting into the revenue which the revenue was entitled to get? That, I think, would be defrauding the revenue.' *Stephens v Abrahams* (1902) 27 VLR 753 at 767, per Hodges J

Australia 'In the case of the common law offence of conspiracy to defraud it has been held that the expression "to defraud" means to deprive a person dishonestly of something which is his, or of something to which he is or would or might, but for the perpetration of the fraud, be entitled: *Scott v Metropolitan Police Comr* [supra]. That decision also established

that deceit is not an essential ingredient of the offence at common law. Under s 430 of the [Criminal] Code [Qld] "deceit or any fraudulent means" is expressly an element of the offence. In the case of the cognate offence of obtaining by false pretences, s 427 of the Code uses the expression "with intent to defraud". In *Balcombe v De Simoni* (1972) 126 CLR 576, 596, Gibbs J (as he then was) held that that expression in the corresponding section of the Western Australian Criminal Code made it necessary that "the accused person should have made the false pretence with the intention of inducing another person to part with property"; cf. also *R v Proctor & Perry* [1963] Qd R 335, 343.' *R v Finn and Niblock* [1985] 1 Qd R 212 at 213, per McPherson J

DEL CREDERE AGENT

A del credere agent is one who, usually for extra remuneration, undertakes to indemnify his employer against loss arising from the failure of persons with whom he contracts to carry out their contracts. (1 Halsbury's Laws (4th edn) para 713)

'I apprehend that a del credere agent, like any other agent, is to sell according to the instructions of his principal, and to make such contracts as he is authorised to make for his principal; and he is distinguished from other agents simply in this, that he guarantees that those persons to whom he sells shall perform the contracts which he makes with them.' *Re Nevill, ex p White* (1871) 6 Ch App 397 at 403, per Mellish LJ

'The proposition which the learned judge [in the court below] affirms . . . seems to me absolutely correct. After pointing out that it is not necessary for him to determine whether the obligation of a del credere agent extends beyond the case of insolvency to a case of inability, by reason of a debtor being beyond the seas or something of that kind, to obtain immediate payment, and that it is not necessary to decide what his obligations are as regards making payment in default of payment by the buyer, he goes on to say this: "I think it is quite clear that it" (that is, the obligation of the del credere agent) "does not extend to make him the person with whom the seller is entitled, if he wishes, to litigate any disputes that arise out of the contract and ascertain what is due upon it. . . ." The liability of the del credere agent is a contingent pecuniary liability, not a liability to perform the contract;

it is a pecuniary liability to make good in any event the default of the buyer in respect of a pecuniary liability. It does not extend to other obligations of the contract.' *Gabriel (Thomas) & Sons v Churchill & Sim* [1914] 3 KB 1272 at 1278, 1279, CA, per Buckley LJ

DELAY   *See also* LACHES

[The question was whether a settlement was one made to 'delay', hinder, or defraud creditors within the Stat (1571) 13 Eliz c 5 (repealed) making voidable voluntary conveyances with intent to defraud creditors; see now Law of Property Act 1925, s 172.] 'The solution of that question depends on this: will the settlement if it stands take anything out of the reach of the creditors, or, in other words, will they be in any worse position than if the settlement had never been executed?' *Ideal Bedding Co Ltd v Holland* [1907] 2 Ch 157 at 166, per Kekewich J

'A contract often provides that in the event of "delay" through specified causes, the contract is not to be dissolved, but merely suspended, yet such a provision has been held not to apply where the delay was so phenomenal, so pre-emptive, as to fall outside what the parties could possibly have contemplated in the suspension clause—in other words, "delay" though literally describing what has occurred, has been read as limited to normal, moderate delay, and as not extending to an interruption so differing in degree and magnitude from anything which could have been contemplated as to differ from it in kind.' *Parkinson & Co Ltd v Public Works Comrs* [1950] 1 All ER 208 at 228, CA, per Asquith LJ; [1949] 2 KB 632

[A building contract between an employer and a contractor provided that the contractor should pay liquidated damages for 'delay'.] 'Much argument was directed by the employer to the meaning of the word "delay" in condition 23(g). Counsel for the sub-contractor in the course of his argument, which lost nothing of its persuasiveness by its brevity, contended that there was delay if the sub-contractor failed to do anything it was required to do under the contract by the due date of performance. I have no doubt that counsel's contention is right. Looking at condition 23 by itself, that condition is concerned with delay in the completion of the main contract and in condition 23(g) and (h) it would be surprising if the word "delay" meant something other than a failure to perform by the due date whether it be

by nominated sub-contractors or nominated suppliers or artists, tradesmen or others engaged by the employer. Condition 27(a)(iv) . . . (which provides that a contract made with a nominated sub-contractor must include a provision for the payment of damages if the sub-contractor fails to complete the sub-contract works within the specified time), supports the conclusion that delay occurs when there is a failure to complete in due time.' *Westminster City Council v Jarvis (J) & Sons Ltd* [1970] 1 All ER 943 at 948, HL, per Viscount Dilhorne

New Zealand 'The dictionary meaning of the noun "delay" is "the putting off" or "the deferring". These latter words, in our opinion, in their ordinary meaning connote postponement of performance of some act or step beyond the point of time when the act or step should have been performed.' *Cable (William) Ltd v Trainor* [1957] NZLR 337 at 345, CA, per cur.

Inordinate delay

'Delay in the course of the proceedings which would have been acceptable if they had been begun promptly may become inordinate and inexcusable if it occurs after a late start. Similarly, whilst the defendant must show prejudice flowing from delay in the course of the proceedings, the degree of prejudice created by any given period of delay may be greatly heightened if proceedings were not begun promptly. Contrary to legend, it was not the last straw which broke the camel's back. It was the addition of that straw. The defendant must show that straws of the appropriate kinds were heaped on his back during the course of the proceedings, but the court must have regard to the load which he was already carrying when the proceedings began.' *Bremer Vulkan Schiffbau und Maschinenfabrik v South India Shipping Corpn* [1979] 3 All ER 195 at 197, per Donaldson J

DELEGATED LEGISLATION   *See* SUBORDINATE LEGISLATION

DELEGATION

Delegation by an agent, that is the entrusting to another person by an agent of the exercise of a power or duty entrusted to him by his principal, is in general prohibited, under the maxim *delegatus non potest delegare*, without the express authority of the principal, or authority derived from statute. Where there is personal confidence reposed in or skill required from the agent there normally may be no delegation, however general the nature of the duties, unless urgent necessity compels the handing over of the responsibility to another. (1 Halsbury's Laws (4th edn) para 747)

'Delegation, as the word is generally used, does not imply a parting with powers by the person who grants the delegation, but points rather to a conferring of an authority to do things which otherwise the person would have to do himself. The best illustration of the use of the word is afforded by the maxim, *Delegatus non potest delegare*, as to the meaning of which it is significant that it is dealt with in Broom's Legal Maxims under the law of contracts: it is never used by legal writers, so far as I am aware, as implying that the delegating person parts with his power in such a manner as to denude himself of his rights. If it is correct to use the word in the way in which it is used in the maxim, as generally understood, the word "delegate" means little more than an agent.' *Huth v Clarke* (1890) 25 QBD 391 at 395, per Wills J

'It appears that the man [a publican charged with selling intoxicating liquor to a child] had never given up the control of his business, but he was in the active conduct of his business. He was at times in the cellar and at times serving, although I think that he had not served upon this day until eleven o'clock. . . . It is impossible to say that they [the magistrates] were wrong in saying that, although absent from the bar, he had not delegated the control of the bar to the barmaid.' *McKenna v Harding* (1905) 69 JP 354 at 355, per Lord Alverstone CJ

'The word "delegation" when used in connection with the statutory duty of the employer does not mean the same thing as "employment". An employer does not, merely by employing his servant to work a crane, delegate to him the statutory duty of seeing that the crane is not overloaded. The theory of delegation of a statutory duty is intelligible where the duty is a positive duty such as to keep the guard of a power saw in adjustment. In the case of a negative duty such as not to overload a crane, the conception of delegation presents considerable difficulty.' *Gallagher v Dorman, Long & Co Ltd* [1947] 2 All ER 38 at 41, 42, CA, per Wrottesley LJ

'My own view is that for there to be a delegation of a statutory duty it must be made clear that it is a statutory duty that is being delegated, and that what is being said is not mere instruction common to all workmen as to how the workmen should carry out the work.' *Manwaring v Billington* [1952] 2 All ER 747 at 750, CA, per Birkett LJ

[The entrusting of an ocean-going ship to ship-repairers of high repute for the carrying out of necessary repairs was held not to be a 'delegation' of the duty, under art III, r 1 (a) of the Hague Rules, to exercise due diligence to make the ship seaworthy.] 'In my judgment, the fallacy in the argument on behalf of the cargo owners lies in the use of the word "delegation" to cover every occasion when the shipowner engages some other person to do some work on the ship. I see a distinction between employing someone else to carry on one's own business and engaging someone else to perform something which is his business. Any master delegates to his own servants the work of carrying on his own business. Equally I think he may be said to delegate when he employs some outside person to act as his representative.' *Riverstone Meat Co Pty Ltd v Lancashire Shipping Co Ltd* [1960] 1 All ER 193 at 220, CA, per Willmer J

DELETERIOUS DRUG   *See* DRUGS

DELIBERATE

Australia 'Deliberation . . . connotes not only collective discussion, but the collective acquisition and exchange of facts preliminary to the ultimate decision.' *Harris v Australian Broadcasting Corpn* (1983) 50 ALR 551 at 560, per Beaumont J

Canada [The distinction between capital and non-capital murder depends upon deliberation. Here Fauteux J was dissenting, but the Court's opinion did not disturb this point.] 'To dispose of the merits of this appeal, this Court . . . must unavoidably determine the meaning of the word "deliberate" under these provisions [s 202A (2)(a) (see now RSC 1970, c C-34, s 214, amended by 1973–74 (Can), c 38, s 11)] of the Criminal Code and their legal effect in the case. In the Shorter Oxford Dictionary, the word is thus defined: "Deliberate: well weighed or considered; carefully thought out; done of set purpose; studied; not hasty or rash. Of persons: Characterised by deliberation; considering carefully . . . Leisurely,

slow, not hurried.'' The first part of the definition is related to an action; the second part is
related to a person. Under the provisions of the
section the word ''deliberate'' qualifies not the
person charged but his action, i.e. the murder.
In the French version of these provisions, the
expression ''*de propos délibéré*'' stands for the
word ''deliberate'', and, according to the Lar-
ousse XXe siècle, means ''*à dessein—de parti
pris—de dessein formé, arrêté à l'avance*''. In
Harrap's Standard French and English Dictionary [Part Two], the expression ''of set purpose'' is translated ''*de propos délibéré, de parti
pris*''. In the same dictionary, the word ''pre-
determination'' is translated ''*détermination
prise d'avance; dessein arrêté*''. Thus it appears
from both the English and French versions,
which in the consideration of a Federal statute
must be read together, . . . that a time element
is the material feature common to both the
definition of the word ''planned'' and the definition of the word ''deliberate''. This feature
was not a constitutive element of murder under
the state of the law as it was prior to the
enactment of s 202A(2)(a). All of which
reasonably indicates that what Parliament
intended, by adding it as such, was to exclude
from the offence, henceforth categorised as
capital murder, a murder committed on the
spur of the moment.' *More v R* [1963] 3 CCC
289 at 297, 298, SCC, per Fauteux J

DELINEATE

'The 23rd section of the Act [a railway company's Act] . . . was in these words: "It shall
be lawful for the Company . . . to make and
maintain the railways hereinafter described . . . upon the lands 'delineated' on the
. . . plans.'' . . . I consider that ''delineated'' cannot in this Act be interpreted as
meaning surrounded in every part by
lines. . . . I think it means sketched or represented, or so shewn that landowners would
have notice that the land might be taken.'
*Dowling v Pontypool, Caerleon & Newport
Rly Co* (1874) LR 18 Eq 714 at 736, 740, per
Hall V-C

'We have to consider whether this land which it
is now proposed to take is delineated [on a
railway company's deposited plan]. . . . Is the
whole seventeen acres which consists of
nursery garden delineated? I cannot say that it
is. I have only got the sketches of paths ending
in nothing for a very small part of that land, and
to say that the whole of that nursery garden is
delineated in any sense you can put on the

word ''delineated'' seems to me to be out of the
question. It is not sketched; it is not represented; it is not shown in such a manner as that
the landowner would suppose that the whole
was going to be taken. . . . These paths are
indicated as unending, unlimited, obviously it
seems to me for the purpose of reproducing the
existing features of the ground . . . and not for
the purpose of delineating the land as land
which is to be taken. I think, therefore, that the
land proposed to be taken is in no sense
delineated.' *Protheroe v Tottenham & Forest
Gate Rly Co* [1891] 3 Ch 278 at 289, 290, CA,
per Fry LJ

Australia 'The core of the meaning of that
word is, to my mind, to trace the outline of
something as on a map or plan. To say that a
parcel of land has been delineated on a map or
plan signifies that its limits are shown thereon
by a line or lines; but it does not necessarily
imply that those limits are drawn with the
utmost degree of precision of which the professional surveyor is capable. The line or lines
may be drawn well or ill according to the circumstances. Sometimes the representation
under examination is executed so badly that it
cannot be called a delineation at all. Whether
it is a delineation is a question of fact: see
*Protheroe v Tottenham & Forest Gate Railway
Co* [supra], 3 Ch 278].' *Southern Centre of
Theosophy Incorporated v State of South Australia* (1979) 21 SASR 399 at 413, per Wells J

DELIVERABLE STATE

Goods are in a 'deliverable state' within the
meaning of this Act when they are in such a
state that the buyer would under the contract
be bound to take delivery of them. (Sale of
Goods Act 1979, s 61(5))

[The Sale of Goods Act 1893, s 18 (repealed;
see now the Sale of Goods Act 1979, s 18) laid
down rules for ascertaining the intention of the
parties as to the time at which the property in
the goods is to pass to the buyer, several of the
rules being dependent upon the goods being in
a 'deliverable state'.] 'A ''deliverable state''
does not depend upon the mere completeness
of the subject matter in all its parts. It depends
on the actual state of the goods at the date of
the contract and the state in which they are to
be delivered by the terms of the contract.'
*Underwood Ltd v Burgh Castle Brick &
Cement Syndicate* [1922] 1 KB 343 at 345, CA,
per Bankes LJ

DELIVERY   *See also* SPECIFIC DELIVERY

South Africa   'In order to constitute delivery there must be some overt act placing the purchaser in possession and giving him control of the property sold.' *Vorster v Vorster's Trustees* 1910 EDL 132 at 137 per Kotze JA

United States   'Deliver' includes [delivery by] mail. (Revised Model Business Corporation Act 1984, s 1.40(5))

Of chattels

'An act to constitute delivery must be one which in itself shows an intention of the donor to transfer the chattel to the donee. If the act in itself is equivocal—consistent equally with an intention of the husband to transfer the chattels to his wife or with an intention on his part to retain possession but give to her the use and enjoyment of the chattels as his wife—the act does not constitute delivery.' *Re Cole, ex p Trustee v Cole* [1963] 3 All ER 433 at 440, CA, per Pearson LJ

Of deed

'The law as to "delivery" of a deed is of ancient date. But it is reasonably clear. A deed is very different from a contract. On a contract for the sale of land, the contract is not binding on the parties until they have exchanged their parts. But with a deed it is different. A deed is binding on the maker of it, even though the parts have not been exchanged, as long as it has been signed, sealed and delivered. "Delivery" in this connection does not mean "handed over" to the other side. It means delivered in the old legal sense, namely, an act done so as to evince an intention to be bound. Even though the deed remains in the possession of the maker, or of his solicitor, he is bound by it if he has done some act evincing an intention to be bound, as by saying: "I deliver this my act and deed". He may, however, make the "delivery" conditional: in which case the deed is called an "escrow" which becomes binding when the condition is fulfilled.' *Vincent v Premo Enterprises (Voucher Sales) Ltd* [1969] 2 All ER 941 at 944, CA, per Lord Denning MR

Of goods

'Delivery' means voluntary transfer of possession from one person to another. It includes symbolic delivery and is not restricted to the physical transfer of the goods themselves, but covers also transfer of possession of documents of title to goods. Where the buyer takes possession pursuant to the leave of the seller, whether concurrent or antecedent, that is a voluntary transfer of possession. (41 Halsbury's Laws (4th edn) para 757)

'Delivery' means voluntary transfer of possession from one person to another. (Sale of Goods Act 1979, s 61(1))

'According to the ordinary understanding of the English language, as soon as an article is put into the hands of a party that is a delivery to him.' *Pettitt v Mitchell* (1842) 4 Man & G 819 at 841, per Maule J

'It is said that the delivery of a part is delivery of the whole [so as to effect the right of stoppage *in transitu*]. . . . If both parties intend it as a delivery of the whole, then it is a delivery of the whole; but if either of the parties does not intend it as a delivery of the whole, . . . then it is not a delivery of the whole. . . . I rather think that the onus is upon those who say that it was so intended.' *Kemp v Falk* (1882) 7 App Cas 573 at 586, HL, per Lord Blackburn

[The Factors Act 1889, s 9 deals with the effect of the 'delivery' of goods, under any agreement for sale, by a buyer in possession of the goods to a person receiving them in good faith and without notice of any right of the original seller.] 'It seems to me that it would be to restrict the natural meaning of the words "delivery under any agreement for sale" to hold that they apply only to cases where the goods are delivered to the person who receives them, pursuant to a sale of the goods by the person who delivers them to the person who receives them.' *Shenstone & Co v Hilton* [1894] 2 QB 452 at 456, 457, per Bruce J

'"Deliver as required" [in a contract for the sale of goods] means "within a reasonable time as required".' *Ross Brothers Ltd v Shaw & Co* [1917] 2 IR 367 at 379, per Wilson J

'Counsel for the defendants contended that in the phrase in s 35 [of the Sale of Goods Act 1893 (repealed; see now the Sale of Goods Act 1979, s 35)] ". . . when the goods have been delivered to him, and he does any act in relation to them which is inconsistent with the ownership of the seller . . ." the word "delivered" means physical delivery of the goods from the ship. If that were so, no dealing with the documents would be within the meaning of the section, because all such dealings would have been done before the goods had been delivered. I cannot take that view of it. I think that "delivery" means, as s 62(1) of the Act [now s 61(1) of the Act of 1979] defines it, a "voluntary transfer of possession", and, therefore, it means transfer of possession under the contract of sale.' *Chao v British Traders & Shippers Ltd* [1954] 1 All ER 779 at 795, per Devlin J

[Under RSC Ord 29, r 2A, the court may, on the application of any party to a cause or matter, make an order under s 4 of the Torts (Interference with Goods) Act 1977 for the 'delivery up' of goods.] 'The power to order the "delivery" or (as RSC Ord 29, r 2A(i) puts it) the "delivery up" of goods must be wide enough to cover an order requiring a defendant to allow the plaintiff to collect for himself goods which the defendant is unable or unwilling to deliver to him in the sense of collecting and transporting them, at all events, where as here, no objection to this course has been suggested. "Delivery" must, I think, include the process of merely transferring authority over something *in situ*, as with the delivery up of possession of land, or livery of seisin.' *Howard E Perry & Co Ltd v British Railways Board* [1980] 2 All ER 579 at 588, per Megarry V-C

New Zealand 'The appellant-plaintiffs sued the respondent-defendants for damages for the non-delivery of . . . carbide sold to the appellants under a contract in the following terms:— "Wellington, October 8th, 1917.—Particulars of sale: 15 tons carbide (Canadian) at £48 per ton net cife Wellington war risk included. Freight based on 31 dollars 20 cents, any difference to buyer's account. Delivery to arrive. Payment net cash against documents." . . . I think that this is the true meaning and purpose of the words "delivery to arrive". These words amount to a representation by the vendors that the goods are already *in transitu*, and an undertaking accordingly to perform the contract by delivery of the shipping documents within such time as is appropriate to such a state of things.' *Cardale & Scott v Clarke & Co* [1922] NZLR 83 at 87–89, per Salmond J; also reported [1921] GLR 693 at 696

See, generally, 41 Halsbury's Laws (4th edn) paras 757–789.

Of instruments

United States 'Delivery' with respect to instruments, documents of title, chattel paper, or certificated securities means voluntary transfer of possession. (Uniform Commercial Code 1978, s 1–201(14))

Of notice

New Zealand 'The provision in the condition [in a fire insurance policy] that "upon delivery" of the notice the policy shall cease infers that the notice is to be conveyed by something capable of delivery in a strict sense—that is, a document in writing or print. It is true that the word "delivery" is commonly used in connection with an oral message or a speech, and that where a notice is required to be given . . . and there is nothing more, an oral notice is sufficient; and, consequently, where a notice which is "given" is intended to be "in writing" it should be expressly so provided. This is illustrated by the present policy: in several instances in the conditions of the policy provision is made for "giving" notice; in only some of these the provision is expressly that the notice so to be given is to be "in writing". In the condition now in question there is a provision that the policy is to cease to be in force in case of the property insured passing from the assured otherwise than by will, "unless notice thereof be given to the company". No doubt, in that case a notice might be conveyed orally. The question may properly be asked, Why should there be a change of expression in the same condition if there was not intended to be a different meaning? . . . I think that a written notice is required by the condition.' *Elkington v Phœnix Assurance Co* (1895) 14 NZLR 237 at 241, 242, per Prendergast CJ

Of will

'Delivery of a will means the same as publication and consists in executing it in the presence of two witnesses and declaring it to be your will.' *Smith v Adkins* (1872) 41 LJ Ch 628 at 630, per Lord Romilly MR

Non-delivery

[A consignment note, framed with the object of relieving a railway company from liability as common carriers, provided that nothing therein should exempt the company from any liability they might otherwise incur in the case of 'non-delivery' of any package or consignment fully and properly addressed.] 'The respondent . . . undertakes for valuable consideration that his goods shall be carried at his own risk and not at the risk of the appellants, except in certain specified cases. I apprehend that such exception, to be effective, must be expressed with explicit accuracy. . . . It is for the respondent, who stipulates for an exception in his favour from his own clear obligation, to show clearly that the case falls within the terms of the exception, and in this, I think, he has failed. The particular exception upon which he relies is that last quoted—"Non-delivery of any package or consignment fully and properly addressed," and the question to be decided is simply what is meant by consignment. I am of opinion that, taking the words in their ordinary and grammatical meaning, it means the entire consignment, and not any part or parts of it. . . . Non-delivery of a consignment is one thing and short delivery of the same consignment is another and different thing . . . the non-delivery of a part does not prove the non-delivery of the whole.' *Great Western Rly Co v Wills* [1917] AC 148 at 157–159, per Lord Kinnear

'Was this then a case of "non-delivery"? That, of course, depends on what delivery means. I hold it to be free from doubt that delivery means the delivery of all and every part of the goods received. . . . Accordingly, if this be the case with regard to delivery, namely, that it means delivery of the whole and every part of the goods consigned, then the negation of that, namely, the case of non-delivery, arises when such delivery does not occur. When a part is not delivered I cannot see how it can be affirmed that the whole and every part has been delivered.' Ibid, at 161, 162, per Lord Shaw

To ship

[A charterparty provided that bills of lading should be conclusive evidence as to the quantity of goods 'delivered' to a ship.] 'Having regard to the other provisions of the charterparty, I think that the expression "delivered to ship" means delivered alongside in the sense that the goods have reached the ship and are under the control of the master.' *Crossfield & Co v Kyle Shipping Co Ltd* [1916] 2 KB 885 at 900, CA, per Bankes LJ

Writ of delivery

Where the judgment or order is for the delivery of goods or payment of their assessed value it may be enforced by one or more of the following means: (a) a writ of delivery to recover the goods or their assessed value: (b) with the leave of the court, a writ of specific delivery; and (c) where the defendant is required to do or abstain from doing any act, a writ of sequestration. The usual form of the writ of delivery orders the sheriff to deliver the specified goods to the plaintiff or to pay him the amount at which the value of the goods has been assessed

and the costs of the action. The defendant is thereby given the option either to return the goods or to pay the assessed value. (17 Halsbury's Laws (4th edn) para 503)

DELUSION *See also* MENTAL DISORDER

'In the well-known case of *Dew v Clark*, [1826] reported, 3 Addams, 97, but also reported, with the great advantage of the learned Judge's corrections, and published separately, by Dr Haggard, we find Sir John Nicholl stating, that mere eccentricity is not enough to constitute mental unsoundness, nor great caprice, nor violence of temper, but that there must be an aberration of reason; and he adopts a definition of delusion given by the learned Counsel in the cause, (now a member of this Court) deeming it well described by the expression, that "it is a belief of facts, which no rational person would have believed". Perhaps, in a strictly logical view, this definition is liable to one exception, or at least exposed to one criticism, namely, that it gives a consequence for a definition; and it may be more strictly accurate to term "delusion", the belief of things, as realities, which exist only in the imagination of the patient. The frame or state of mind which indicates his incapacity to struggle against such an erroneous belief, constitutes an unsound frame of mind. Sir John Nicholl justly adds, that such delusions are generally attended with eccentricities, often with violence, very often with exaggerated suspicions and jealousies.' *Waring v Waring* (1848) 6 Moo PCC 341 at 353, 354, per cur.

'Where the fact that the testator has been subject to any insane delusion is established, a will should be regarded with great distrust, and every presumption should in the first instance be made against it. Where insane delusion has once been shown to have existed, it may be difficult to say whether the mental disorder may not possibly have extended beyond the particular form or instance in which it has manifested itself. It may be equally difficult to say how far the delusion may not have influenced the testator in the particular disposal of his property. . . . But where in the result a jury are satisfied that the delusion has not affected the general faculties of the mind, and can have had no effect upon the will, we see no sufficient reason why the testator should be held to have lost his right to make a will, or why a will made under such circumstances should not be upheld.' *Banks v Goodfellow* (1870) LR 5 QB 549 at 570, per cur.

DEMAND   *See also* LIQUIDATED DEMAND

[By the Sheriffs Act 1887, s 29 a penalty is imposed upon any sheriff's officer who shall (inter alia) take or 'demand' any money or reward under any pretext whatever, other than the fees or sums allowed by or in pursuance of the Act.] 'In his judgment in this case Denman J adopted the view . . . that the demanding of money mentioned in clause (b) of sub-s 2 of s 29, refers only to a demand by the sheriff as a condition of doing the work. In that view I hesitate to concur. I can conceive that a demand of this sort might be made, after the work had been done, with either criminal negligence or a criminal mind. In such a case I think there would be an "offence" under s 29 although the demand might not be made as a condition precedent. The Master of the Rolls desires me to say that he entirely agrees with this view, and would state it even more strongly than I have done. He desires to express his opinion that a person who demands or takes money unlawfully—criminally, within the meaning of the language as we have already explained it—would be guilty of an "offence" although he did not make the demand as a condition of doing his work.' *Lee v Dangar, Grant & Co* [1892] 2 QB 377 at 351, CA, per Fry LJ

[The Theft Act 1968, s 21(1) provides that a person is guilty of blackmail if, with a view to gain for himself or another or with intent to cause loss to another, he makes any unwarranted 'demand' with menaces.] 'If a person went on to a remote and deserted shore and spoke words involving an unwarranted demand with menaces it would be fanciful to suggest that he had committed an offence under s 21. If a person put such a demand into writing in a letter which he then posted to an address in England and if after the letter was posted but before it was delivered the addressee of the letter died, I cannot think that it would be right to say that the demand was made. There would, I think, have been an attempt to make a demand. Making a demand or demanding involves effecting contact with a person so that effective communication is established with him. A demand is not made until it is communicated. If the demand is contained in a letter it is not made until the letter is received.' *Treacy v Director of Public Prosecutions* [1971] 1 All ER 110 at 116, 117, HL, per Lord Morris of Borth-y-Gest

Australia   'There must be a clear intimation that payment is required to constitute a demand; nothing more is necessary, and the word "demand" need not be used; neither is the validity of a demand lessened by its being clothed in the language of politeness; it must be of a peremptory character and unconditional, but the nature of the language is immaterial provided it has this effect.' *Re Colonial Finance, Mortgage, Investment & Guarantee Corpn Ltd* (1905) 6 SRNSW 6 at 9, per Walker J

DEMESNE   *See also* MANOR

'We think we are fully warranted in saying, that, though the word "demesne" may in some cases be applied to any fee-simple lands a man holds, yet it is more correct and usual to apply it to the lands of a manor, which the lord of that manor either actually has, or potentially may have, *in propriis manibus*.' *A-G v Parsons* (1832) 2 Cr & J 279 at 308, per cur.

DEMISE

The relationship of landlord and tenant is one of contract, but a lease also operates as a conveyance. The usual word for this purpose is 'demise', but neither this word nor any formal words of conveyance are necessary. Provided the instrument shows the parties' intent that the one is to divest himself of the possession and the other is to come into the possession for a determinate time, either immediately or in the future, it operates as a lease. This is so whether it is in the ordinary form of a demise, or in the form of a covenant or agreement, or in the form of an offer to let or take on certain terms and an acceptance appearing on correspondence. (27 Halsbury's Laws (4th edn) para 107)

'It is true that the word demise [in a lease] does imply a covenant for title, but only when there is no express covenant inconsistent with such a construction.' *Line v Stephenson* (1838) 5 Bing NC 183 at 186, per Lord Denman CJ

'The terms of the lease, in my opinion establish an exclusive occupation. The word "demise" *prima facie* alone would be sufficient to establish that. I do not go so far as to say that where the word "demise" is used in a lease or agreement no evidence would be admissible to displace the presumption arising from its use, but the word *prima facie* would establish an exclusive occupation.' *Young & Co v Liverpool Assessment Committee* [1911] 2 KB 195 at 215, DC, per Avory J

Of Sovereign

The Sovereign is regarded legally as immortal, the maxim of law being that 'the King never dies'. The death of the Sovereign in her natural body is therefore termed legally her demise, meaning the transfer of the kingdom to her successor. (8 Halsbury's Laws (4th edn) para 897)

DEMOCRATIC

Australia 'The "chief objects" of the Act [Conciliation and Arbitration Act 1904 (Cth)] are listed in s 2 and include:– "(f) to encourage the democratic control of organizations so registered and the full participation by members of such an organization in the affairs of the organization." . . . The word "democratic" is capable of a number of meanings ranging from total delegation of all power to elected representatives through to full participation by all members in every decision. Importantly, object 2(f) itself speaks of "the full participation by members of such an organization". In Lovell's case . . . Smithers and Evatt JJ emphasized the participatory aspect (35 FLR at 83): "It would seem that the democratic concept underlying the provisions of the Act is that of substantial participation by the whole of the membership, in the management of the organization. Democracy according to its ordinary current meaning may exist in various forms and in varying degrees. Government of the members, by the members, and for the members in some pure and undiluted form may be an ideal." Again, (at 84) their Honours stated that: "It is an object of Parliament to encourage full participation" (see also *Cook v Crawford* (1982) 43 ALR 83 at 147). In my opinion, one of the objects of the Act is to encourage participatory democracy—it seeks to achieve more than members merely voting for representatives and then not participating in union affairs.' *Wright v McLeod* (1983) 51 ALR 483 at 489 per Bowen CJ

DEMOLISH

'Demolition', in relation to a building which has been destroyed or damaged, includes non-restoration, and 'demolished' shall be construed accordingly. (Reorganisation Areas Measure 1944, s 53)

[Stat (1812) 52 Geo 3, c 130, s 2 (repealed; see now the Malicious Damage Act 1861, s 11), enacted that any person or persons who should unlawfully or with force 'demolish' or pull down any building therein mentioned, should be guilty of an offence.] 'I think burning is included in the general word "demolishing", etc. The Act meant to provide against destruction and spoliation; burning is only one of the means.' *Nesham v Armstrong* (1816) Holt NP 466 at 468, per Bayley J

'I think that, as the cottage was destroyed to such an extent as to be no longer a house, it is a sufficient demolition within this [repealed] statute. It can never be said that a house is not demolished because a few stones are left standing one upon another.' *R v Langford* (1842) Car & M 602 at 604, per Patteson J

'The stat [(1827)] 7 & 8 Geo 4, c 30, s 8 (repealed)], in the first place enacts, that if persons riotously and tumultuously assembled together to the disturbance of the public peace, demolish or pull down a house, or begin to demolish or pull down a house, etc, they shall be guilty of felony, and those words would rather point to a demolition of the house by separating from each other, by pulling down, the materials of which the house is composed.' *R v Harris* (1842) Car & M 661 at 667, per Tindal CJ

Australia 'The usual meaning of the word "demolish" is to destroy (particularly in relation to a building) by violent disintegration of its fabric; to pull or throw down; pull to pieces; reduce to ruins. "Demolition" is the act of demolishing (see New Oxford Dictionary—ed Murray). To extend "demolition" to cover the removal from the land upon which it stands of a house as an undamaged whole would be to give the word a new or at least a very unusual meaning.' *Nelson v Healy* [1948] VLR 415 at 417, per O'Bryan J

DEMOLITION ORDER

A demolition order is an order requiring that the premises—
(a) be vacated within a specified period (of at least 28 days) from the date on which the order becomes operative, and
(b) be demolished within six weeks after the end of that period or, if it is not vacated before the end of that period, after the date on which it is vacated or, in either case, within such longer period as in the

circumstances the local housing authority consider it reasonable to specify. (Housing Act 1985, s 267(1))

DEMONSTRATIVE LEGACY   *See*
LEGACY

DEMURRAGE

At the expiration of the lay days, the charterer may be allowed, in consideration of an additional payment called 'demurrage', a further number of days, known as 'demurrage days'. Sometimes no further time is expressly allowed, but it is simply stipulated that the charterer is to pay demurrage at the rate of so much a day for every day that the ship is detained beyond the lay days. (43 Halsbury's Laws (4th edn) para 469)

'The word "demurrage" no doubt properly signifies the agreed additional payment (generally per day) for an allowed detention beyond a period either specified in or to be collected from the instrument; but it has also a popular or more general meaning of compensation for undue detention, and from the whole of each charterparty containing the clause in question we must collect what is the proper meaning to be assigned to it.' *Lockhart v Falk* (1875) LR 10 Exch 132 at 135, per Cleasby B

'Now the days, which are given to the charterer in a charterparty, either to load or to unload without paying for the use of the ship, are "lay days". Other days are sometimes given also in favour of the charterer, which are called "demurrage days". Those are days beyond the lay days, but during which the amount that he has to pay for the use of the ship is a fixed sum, not necessarily what it costs the owner to keep his ship, but a fixed sum, which is usually about what it is supposed it costs the owner to keep the ship. This stipulation also is in favour of the charterer, because instead of being involved in a dispute as to what he would have to pay for the days during which the ship is kept idle, a sum is fixed, and he knows what he has to pay if he keeps the ship beyond the lay days. Those are the "demurrage days". If he keeps the ship beyond the lay days, when he pays nothing, and only the number of demurrage days, he pays a fixed sum for demurrage.' *Nielsen v Wait* (1885) 16 QBD 67 at 70, CA, per Lord Esher MR

'This is a contract by the freighter, by which he undertakes, under certain circumstances, to pay demurrage. It occurs in a document which is in constant use, and the stipulation is in an ordinary form, and has been construed frequently. It has been held that the demurrage contract, where a fixed number of lay-days is mentioned, is a contract by the freighter, that if the ship is detained over those days he will pay demurrage for so long as the ship is in such a condition that she cannot be handed back for the use of the shipper. This has been called an absolute and independent contract, and it is obvious that a contrast is intended to be drawn between such a contract and a conditional one, and that by an absolute contract is meant an unconditional one. The only condition attached to it is that the lay-days shall have commenced and run out, and, that condition being fulfilled, the obligation arises.' *Budgett & Co v Binnington & Co* [1891] 1 QB 35 at 37, 38, CA, per Lord Esher MR

'Demurrage is more applicable to a delay after a time expressly fixed, than to a delay after a time which is only implied as reasonable.' *Dunlop & Sons v Balfour, Williamson & Co* [1892] 1 QB 507 at 520, CA, per Fry LJ

'Demurrage is "agreed damages to be paid for delay of the ship in loading or unloading beyond an agreed period". In other words, the distinction between "demurrage" and damages for detention is that the one is liquidated damages and the other unliquidated. A claim under either head is a claim in respect of detention, and is in the nature of a claim of damages. Amongst mercantile men, indeed, "demurrage" is often used in a wider sense as including both demurrage strictly so called and damages for detention.' *Moor Line Ltd v Distillers Co Ltd* 1912 SC 514 at 520, per Lord Salvesen

DEMURRER

'The procedure of demurrer is of very considerable antiquity, but for practical purposes has long been regarded as obsolete. In Archbold's Pleading and Evidence (19th Edn) edited by Mr William Bruce in 1878, it is stated that special demurrers for merely formal defects, called demurrers in abatement, were rendered practically useless by 14 & 15 Vict c 100, in 1851, but that advantage might still be taken of general demurrers, founded on some substantial defect apparent on the indictment. Advantage was not often taken of them, however, because in cases of felony, judgment for the Crown was final. Demurrer was supplanted in practice by the safe and convenient procedures of motion to quash the indictment or motion in arrest of judgment. The information about demurrers available to students of Archbold become progressively less in successive editions. However the procedure could not be regarded as wholly extinct, because its existence is recognised in s 6 of the Criminal Law Act 1967, which may perhaps have inspired the enterprise in the present case. . . . Demurrer is an objection to the form or substance of the indictment, apparent on the face of the indictment, and is not to be decided by examination of the depositions.' *R v Deputy Chairman of Inner London Quarter Sessions, ex p Metropolitan Police Comr* [1969] 3 All ER 1537 at 1538, 1539, per Cantley J

'I hope that now demurrer in criminal cases will be allowed to die naturally.' Ibid, at 1541, per Lord Parker CJ

DENOMINATION

Canada 'The word "denomination" in the context in which it is used . . . in my view means a class, society or group of individuals called or identified by the same name. This meaning is to be found in a number of authoritative English language dictionaries. . . . With respect, I find no difficulty in accepting that the Sisters of St Joseph for the Diocese of Toronto in Upper Canada, recognised long ago by the Legislature to be "a religious order or association of women of the Roman Catholic faith" is properly described, notwithstanding the fact of incorporation, as a group of individuals called or identified by the same name. As already noted, the religious connotation is not questioned and I therefore hold that the applicant is a religious denomination.' *Re Sisters of St Joseph for the Diocese of Toronto in Upper Canada and City of Winnipeg* (1982) 135 DLR (3d) 177 at 178, 179, Man QB, per Dewar CJQB

DENTAL AUTHORITY

References in this Act to a dental authority are references to a medical authority who grant degrees, licences or other diplomas in dentistry. (Dentists Act 1984, s 3(4))

DENTAL DIPLOMA

'Diploma' means any diploma, degree fellowship, membership, licence, authority to practise, letters testimonial, certificate or other status or document granted by any university, corporation, college or other body or by any department of, or persons acting under the authority of, the government of any country or place whether within or without Her Majesty's dominions. (Dentists Act 1984, s 53(1))

DENTAL OPERATION

[The Dentists Act 1878, s 5 (repealed), provided that a person should not be entitled to recover any fee or charge in any court for the performance of any 'dental operation' or for any dental attendance or advice, unless he was registered under the Act, or was a legally qualified medical practitioner; cf now Dentists Act 1984, s 37(1).] 'In my opinion, *prima facie* certainly, the words in that section "dental operation" mean operation upon the person—on the mouth of the patient; "dental attendance" would mean advising in respect of the condition of the mouth, or as to what should be done, and "advice" would, of course, mean something of the same character.' *Hennan & Co Ltd v Duckworth* (1904) 90 LT 546 at 548, per Lord Alverstone CJ

DENTAL SURGEON

[The Dentists Act 1921, s 4(b) (repealed; see now the Dentists Act 1984, s 26(2)) enacted that a person registered under the Dentists Act 1878, shall not take or use any title or description reasonably calculated to suggest that he possesses any professional status or qualification other than a professional status or qualification which he in fact possesses and which is indicated by particulars entered in the register in respect of him.] 'The question whether the title "dental surgeon" falls within the prohibition in s 4(b) of the Dentists Act 1921, is a mixed question of fact and law. The questions of fact which arise are: What has been the user of the title in the past? And what meaning, owing to such user, has it acquired? The question of law is whether, regard being had to the evidence on the questions of fact, the title is . . . reasonably calculated to suggest that the user possesses a professional status or qualification other than the status or qualification which he in fact possesses, and which is indicated by the particulars entered on the register. First as to the questions of fact, evidence was adduced . . . that the title . . . had, for a period of upwards of fifty years . . . been used exclusively . . . by two classes of dental practitioners. The first class was composed of persons who had, by examination or otherwise, qualified themselves for and had obtained a diploma or degree in the art of dentistry. . . . The second class was composed of dental practitioners who had been bona fide in practice before July 22nd 1878 [when the Dentists Act was passed], but had not obtained a diploma or degree. . . . We then come to the further question whether . . . the title "dental surgeon" has . . . become indentified with persons who either had obtained a diploma or degree, or had practised dentistry prior to July 22nd 1878. . . . Weighing the evidence on both sides, it seems to me that . . . to the discerning and instructed person the title "dental surgeon" conveys the meaning that the practitioner using it has the status or qualification of either holding a diploma or degree or of having been in practice before July 22nd 1878.' *A-G v Weeks* [1932] 1 Ch 211 at 221–223, CA, per Lawrence LJ

See, generally, 30 Halsbury's Laws (4th edn) paras 199 et seq.

DENTISTRY

(1) For the purposes of this Act, the practice of dentistry shall be deemed to include the performance of any such operation and the giving of any such treatment, advice or attendance as is usually performed or given by dentists, and any person who performs any operation or gives any treatment, advice or attendance on or to any person as preparatory to or for the purpose of or in connection with the fitting, insertion or fixing of dentures, artificial teeth or other dental appliances shall be deemed to have practised dentistry within the meaning of this Act.
(2) Dental work shall not be treated for the purposes of this Act as amounting to the practice of dentistry if it is undertaken under the direct personal supervision of a registered dentist—
   (a) by a person recognised by a dental authority as a student of dentistry, or by a person recognised by a medical authority as a medical student, as part of a course of instruction approved by that authority for students of that kind, or as part of an examination so approved, or
   (b) by any person as part of a course of instruction which he is following in order to qualify for membership of a

class of dental auxiliaries or as part of examinations which must be passed in order to qualify for membership of a class of dental auxiliaries, but subject to that a person who undertakes dental work in the course of his studies (whether or not under the supervision of a registered dentist) shall be treated for the purposes of this Act as practising dentistry if he would have been treated for those purposes as practising dentistry if he had undertaken that work in the course of earning his livelihood.
(Dentists Act 1984, s 37(1), (2))

DEPART

[By a policy of insurance, a ship was warranted to 'depart' with convoy.] 'I take it, the meaning is, that he should go out with convoy, and so continue with him to the end of the voyage, without any default in him.' *Jefferyes v Legendra* (1691) 1 Show 320 at 326, per Eyres J

[On 9 September a ship weighed anchor at the port of Memel, but was beaten back by unfavourable weather and came to anchor within the harbour bar but nearer the sea. The question was, whether this constituted a departure from Memel before 15 September in compliance with a warranty in an insurance policy. The ship was unable to proceed further until 21 September.] 'To "depart", must be to depart from some particular place. It is said by the counsel for the plaintiff, that if the ship had got under way at Memel, and had been lost on her way to the sea mouth, that would have been a departure. I asked for his authority, but no case was cited. We must therefore construe it upon the reason of the case. It cannot mean a departure from the town of Memel. I see not then, what it can mean, except a departure from the port of Memel. I can see no other *terminus a quo*, and I think the ship had not departed from the port of Memel before the 15th of September.' *Moir v Royal Exchange Assurance Co* (1815) 6 Taunt 241 at 245, per Gibbs CJ

DEPARTMENT

Of school

'Department' means such part, if any, of a school as is organised under a separate head teacher. (Education Act 1946, s 16)

DEPARTMENTAL STORE

Canada 'I consider that a good test for determining whether a store is a "departmental store" is whether it deals in so many lines of goods that it has lost its identity as a store dealing in any particular line or lines of goods.' *City of London v Kingsmill's Ltd* [1956] OWN 715 at 717, Ont SC, per Aylen J

DEPENDANT

In this Act 'dependant' means—
(a) the wife or husband or former wife or husband of the deceased;
(b) any person who—
  (i) was living with the deceased in the same household immediately before the date of death; and
  (ii) had been living with the deceased in the same household for at least two years before that date; and
  (iii) was living during the whole of that period as the husband or wife of the deceased;
(c) any parent or other ascendant of the deceased;
(d) any person who was treated by the deceased as his parent;
(e) any child or other descendant of the deceased;
(f) any person (not being a child of the deceased) who, in the case of any marriage to which the deceased was at any time a party, was treated by the deceased as a child of the family in relation to that marriage;
(g) any person who is, or is the issue of, a brother, sister, uncle or aunt of the deceased.
(Fatal Accidents Act 1976, s 1(3), substituted by s 3(3) of the Administration of Justice Act 1982)

[The reference to the former wife or husband of the deceased in sub-s 3(a), supra, includes a reference to a person whose marriage to the deceased has been annulled or declared void as well as a person whose marriage to the deceased has been dissolved: ibid, sub-s (4).

See also sub-s (5) as to the deducing of relationships and the treatment of legitimate persons.]

'An illegitimate bachelor can have no dependant other than "parent or grandparent".' *McLean v Moss Bay Iron & Steel Co Ltd* [1909] 2 KB 521 at 523, CA, per Cozens-Hardy MR

'The wife does not necessarily cease to be dependent on the husband simply because the latter refuses to recognise or perform his obligation and succeeds in throwing the burden of her maintenance for the time being on the wife's parents or friend, or on the State. They may fulfil the husband's duty for him, but the wife's legal dependence is still on him and not on them and his death deprives her of the proper stay and support on which alone she is entitled to rely. The circumstances, however, are wholly different where the wife herself has for years clearly asserted and definitely maintained her complete independence of her husband.' *New Monckton Colleries Ltd v Keeling* [1911] AC 648 at 662, per Lord Robson

'I consider that the trustees, or if necessary the court, are quite capable of coming to a conclusion in any given case whether or not a particular candidate could properly be described as a dependant—a word that, as the learned judge [Brightman J in the court below] said, "conjures up a sufficiently distinct picture". I agree, too, that any one wholly or partly dependent on the means of another is a "dependant". There is thus no conceptual uncertainty inherent in that word.' *Re Baden's Deed Trusts (No 2), Baden v Smith* [1972] 2 All ER 1304 at 1311, per Sachs LJ

Australia 'It is established, I think, that the existence of an obligation to maintain has no part in the conception of dependency. Conversely, an obligation to maintain may exist, but, if it has not been performed and cannot be enforced, there is no dependency. These are the considerations which seem to me to show that the word "dependant" is, in a true sense, a technical term. If the evidence establishes that the alleged "dependant" relied or relies on another as the source, wholly or in part, of his or her means of subsistence, then dependency is established.' *Fenton v Batten* [1948] VLR 422 at 423, per Fullagar J

Australia 'The child concerned in the present action was a "dependant" [within s 3 of the Workers' Compensation Act 1927–1986 (Tas)] at the time of the death of the deceased notwithstanding that it was then unborn.' *Pegus v Associated Forest Holdings Pty Ltd* [1964] Tas SR 61 at 62, per Neasey J

Australia 'The question whether a person is a "dependant" within the meaning of the definition [in the Workers' Compensation Act 1912 (WA), s 5 (repealed; see now Workers'

Compensation and Assistance Act 1981–1986 (WA), s 5)] is a question of fact. If a person is acknowledged and treated as a dependant of a worker, although actual contributions or provision of sustenance are spasmodic or irregular, the provisions of the statute may be satisfied. In considering such a question, the fact that the person claiming dependency stands in a special relationship where the law will enforce payment of maintenance, e.g. wife, husband, child, is important (although not conclusive) in determining the issue. So is the fact that the person claiming has endeavoured to enforce the right to maintenance. If a worker has been furnishing regular support that is material as pointing to the fact of dependency. But dependency may exist notwithstanding that a worker ignores or successfully evades his responsibilities. Where, as already pointed out, a blood relationship exists which carries with it an enforceable obligation, the continued refusal or neglect to comply with the obligation may be more significant than where such an obligation is absent. If a wife throws in her lot with a man other than her husband and is kept by him and lives under his protection, these are circumstances pointing to the conclusion that she has ceased to be dependent upon her husband. A young child who is taken by his mother to a new family circle and supported in that circle by a *de facto* husband may also cease to be a dependant of his lawful father, although the inference is not so strong as in the case of his mother, because generally no act of conscious election comes from the child—it comes from the mother. Dependency may exist although actual contributions are suspended, as in *Borson v Hine & Co Pty Ltd* [[1965] WAR 19]. A wife who has been abandoned by her husband is not on that account to be denied her claim to be a dependant and the fact that he has managed to evade his responsibilities by going to some other State or place where she cannot locate him and cannot enforce her rights is not in itself sufficient to extinguish dependency. To hold otherwise would mean determining legal responsibility by the success of the worker in dodging his obligations.' *Re de Haan* [1969] WAR 161 at 164, 165, per Wolff CJ

DEPENDENCY   *See* COLONY; UNITED KINGDOM DEPENDENCY

DEPENDENT RELATIVE REVOCATION

'The revocation of a will may be relative to another disposition which has already been made or is intended to be made, and is so dependent on it that revocation is not intended unless that other disposition takes effect. Such a revocation is known as a 'dependent relative revocation', and, if from any cause the other disposition fails to take effect, the will remains operative as it was before the revocation. The doctrine also applies where the purported revocation is based on an assumption of fact which is false, the mistaken belief in that fact being the reason for the revocation.

The question may thus arise in the case of destruction of a will as part of the act of making a fresh will, which is not in fact made or is ineffectually made for want of due execution, or destruction in order to set up a prior will which needs revival. In order to involve the doctrine of dependent relative revocation, it is not necessary that there should be direct evidence of the physical destruction of the will which it is sought to set up. The question may also arise in the case of obliteration of the amount of a legacy, and the substitution, without proper formalities, of a different amount, or obliteration and substitution, in a similar manner, of a different donee or other person, or of a different event upon which the gift is to take effect. However, if a complete legacy has been obliterated and a new gift has been substituted which does not take effect (for example, for want of execution), the doctrine of dependent relative revocation does not apply and probate will be granted of the will with the parts obliterated blank. On the other hand, where some words in a legacy, as opposed to the whole legacy, have been obliterated and other words have been substituted for them, it may be possible to infer that the testator had no intention of revoking the original words unless the substituted words were effective, in which case the doctrine of dependent relative revocation applies and evidence outside the will itself will be admissible to show what the original words were. Thus, strips of paper covering the amounts of legacies may be removed to show what the original amounts were, but not strips obliterating whole legacies. Where it is not possible to infer that the testator only intended to revoke the original words if the words substituted were effective, the doctrine of dependent relevant revocation does not apply, and probate will be granted with the words obliterated blank.

In all these and other cases, however, the question is whether the disposition revoked is intended not to operate whatever happens, or is only to be destroyed if the provisions of the substituted instrument operate in its stead. The court must be satisfied that the testator did not intend to revoke the original will except conditionally, in so far as the other disposition could be set up. Thus, where a later will containing a revocatory clause is incomplete in material particulars, it and an earlier will may be admitted to probate, but without the revocatory clause in the later will. (50 Halsbury's Laws (4th edn) para 298)

DEPORTATION

'The word "deportation" has implicit in it the taking of the person in question from the country from which he is deported to some other place.' *R v Secretary of State for Foreign Affairs and Secretary of State for Colonies, ex p Greenberg* [1947] 2 All ER 550 at 555, per Jenkins J

DEPORTATION ORDER

Where a person is . . . liable to deportation, then . . . the Secretary of State may make a deportation order against him, that is to say an order requiring him to leave and prohibiting him from entering the United Kingdom; and a deportation order against a person shall invalidate any leave to enter or remain in the United Kingdom given him before the order is made or while it is in force. (Immigration Act 1971, s 5(1))

DEPOSIT

Certificate of deposit

'Certificate of deposit' means a document relating to money, in any currency, which has been deposited with the issuer or some other person, being a document which recognises an obligation to pay a stated amount to bearer or to order, with or without interest, and being a document by the delivery of which, with or without endorsement, the right to receive that stated amount, with or without interest, is transferable. (Finance Act 1968, s 55(3))

Of chattel

Bailment by deposit may be defined as a bailment of a chattel, to be kept by the bailor gratuitously, and returned upon demand. (2 Halsbury's Laws (4th edn) para 1506)

Of litter *See also* ACCUMULATION

[The Litter Act 1983, s 1(1), makes it an offence to throw down, drop, or otherwise 'deposit', and then leave, litter. In this case the matter deposited was a derelict motor car, which was held by a magistrates' court to constitute litter.] 'Observe that there are two ingredients there, the throwing down, dropping or otherwise depositing and the leaving. It is quite clear that not only the depositing but also the leaving is necessary, because it was not intended that an offence should be committed if somebody deposited litter and immediately cleared it up. Accordingly, although the act constituting the offence consists of throwing down, dropping or otherwise depositing, it is only an offence if it is not removed. The offence is not committed unless both of these things, the depositing and the leaving, occur. Depositing is an act fixed in point of time and not a continuing matter.' *Vaughan v Biggs* [1960] 2 All ER 473 at 474, per Lord Parker CJ

Of money

Subject to the provisions of this section, in this Act 'deposit' means a sum of money paid on terms—

(a) under which it will be repaid, with or without interest or a premium, and either on demand or at a time or in circumstances agreed by or on behalf of the person making the payment and the person receiving it; and

(b) which are not referable to the provision of property or services or the giving of security;

and references in this Act to money deposited and to the making of a deposit shall be construed accordingly. (Banking Act 1987, s 5(1))

Australia 'The underlying concept of a deposit in a simple case where completion is to take place within a short period is that it is to serve as it were as a guarantee that the purchaser means business, and any question of forfeiture will really only arise if the purchaser fails to come up with the balance of the price on the date fixed for completion; and in these circumstances there is no difficulty in treating a reasonable deposit as liquidated damages, and there can be no basis for treating it as a penalty against the forfeiture of which relief can be granted. But the position may be very different where the contract is to run for a long period before final completion, the purchaser meanwhile being bound by a variety of covenants of widely differing importance, so that one breach may produce substantial damage whereas another breach could produce only little damage or perhaps no actual damage at all. The wider the variety of contingencies on which forfeiture is to occur the more difficult it becomes to regard the deposit as liquidated ·damages.' *Coates v Sarich* [1964] WAR 2 at 15, per Hale J

DEPOSIT ACCOUNT

Secured transactions

United States 'Deposit account' means a demand, time, savings, passbook or like account maintained with a bank, savings and loan association, credit union or like organization, other than an account evidenced by a certificate of deposit. . . . (Uniform Commercial Code 1978, s 9–105(1)(e))

DEPOSIT SOCIETY   *See* FRIENDLY
SOCIETY

DEPOSITUM   *See* BAILMENT

DEPRAVE OR CORRUPT

Australia [The Objectionable Literature Act 1954–1986 (Qld), s 5 defines 'objectionable literature' as (inter alia) being of such a nature as to 'deprave or corrupt'.] 'We may take a modern meaning of each word, deprave, "to make morally bad" and corrupt "to render morally unsound". Moral badness or moral unsoundness is not confined to matters of sex alone. To convert a person from honesty is in my opinion to deprave that person and also to corrupt him. My view is that "to deprave or corrupt" is here used to describe any lowering of the moral level of persons so as to induce or incline them to conduct themselves in a manner, or to develop a moral outlook, which is disapproved by the ordinary respectable reasonable man.' *Literature Board of Review v Invincible Press, ex p Invincible Press & Truth and Sportsman Ltd* [1955] St R Qd 525 at 563, per Townley J

DEPRAVITY

Exceptional

Australia 'The most appropriate definition of "depravity" in the Oxford English Dictionary is, I think, "perversion of the moral qualities, corruption, viciousness, abandoned wickedness". In *Bowman v Bowman* [[1949] 2 All ER 127], Denning LJ (as he then was), said that cruelty, coupled with aggravated circumstances such as drunkenness and neglect, and with perverted lust would be exceptional depravity, and (as I understand his judgment) that adultery coupled with desertion or cruelty, or committed in aggravating circumstances, may constitute exceptional depravity. But he was not prepared to say (again as I understand him) that cruelty, coupled with drunkenness and neglect, or if it is exceptionally brutal or dangerous to health, constituted exceptional depravity. . . . But "exceptional depravity" does not mean depravity which is exceptional merely because the particular facts alleged are unusual, but conduct of an exceptional degree of depravity; see *Bowman v Bowman*, [supra], at p 356, per Denning LJ.' *Barratt v Barratt* [1964] ALR 720 at 722, 723, per Neasey J

Australia 'Depravity is defined in the Shorter Oxford Dictionary as "the quality or condition of being depraved or corrupt, moral perversion", and deprave means "to make bad, to pervert, to deteriorate, to corrupt". There are other meanings given besides these but these seem to me to be the ones in point here. The words "exceptional depravity" are used with respect to conduct in an Act dealing with matrimonial offences and I think that what the section is aiming at is some exceptional breach of the accepted standards of conduct. There must be a matrimonial offence, and not only a matrimonial offence, but there must be an exceptional as opposed to an ordinary departure from accepted standards of behaviour.' *Re Washington* [1967] QWN, No 10, per Hart J

DEPRECIATION

Canada [The appellant contended that in an assessment to income tax certain allowances for 'depreciation' and depletion were made in an arbitrary manner without regard to any principle and were inadequate.] 'The term "depreciation" apparently is here used in its commercial sense to apply only to wasting fixed assets, such as plant, machinery and equipment, which inevitably diminish in value while applied to the purpose of seeking profits, or advantage otherwise than by purchase and sale. In measuring annual depreciation in such cases the nearest approach to accuracy will ordinarily be obtained by estimating the whole-life period, in years, of each class of industrial plant, with due regard to all known facts, as well as to future probabilities, and distributing the cost, less the estimated remainder or scrap value, to future revenue accounts, in equal instalments over each year of the estimated whole-life period.' *National Petroleum Corpn Ltd v National Revenue Minister* [1942] Ex CR 102 at 102, Ex Ct, per Maclean J

Canada '"Depreciation" is an accounting term. It signifies, according to the evidence, the writing-off of the cost of an asset over its useful life. Mr P H Lyons, a chartered accountant, and an expert witness for the respondent, was asked: "Are we on common ground that the depreciation is an auditing word and not a tax word?" He replied: "Yes, it hasn't been a tax word since 1948." Capital cost allowance, on the other hand, is a tax term signifying the writing-off of the capital cost of an asset in an amount allowed by income tax regulations. There is no necessary connection between depreciation and capital cost allowance. It would appear from the evidence that it would be entirely fortuitous, or the result of a deliberate company policy, if the two were found to be identical.' *Canning v C F M Fuels (Ontario) Ltd* [1977] 2 SCR 207 at 214, 215 per Dickson J

DEPRIVATION

The censures to which a person found guilty of an offence under this Measure renders himself liable are the following, namely,—
(a) deprivation, that is to say, removal from any preferment which he then holds and disqualification from holding any other preferment except as hereinafter provided [e.g. on receiving a free pardon under s 53] and if he holds no preferment at the time the censure is pronounced, disqualification from holding any preferment in the future except as hereinafter provided. . . .
(Ecclesiastical Jurisdiction Measure 1963 (No 1), s 49(1))

DEPRIVE

(1) A person appropriating property belonging to another without meaning the other permanently to lose the thing itself is nevertheless to be regarded as having the intention of permanently depriving the other of it if his intention is to treat the thing as his own to dispose of regardless of the other's rights; and a borrowing or lending of it may amount to so treating it if, but only if, the borrowing or lending is for a period and in circumstances making it equivalent to an outright taking or disposal.
(2) Without prejudice to the generality of sub-s (1) above, where a person, having possession or control (lawfully or not) of property belonging to another, parts with the property under a condition as to its return which he may not be able to perform, this (if done for purposes of his own and without the other's authority) amounts to treating the property as his own to dispose of regardless of the other's rights.
(Theft Act 1968, s 6)

[The above section explains the word 'deprive' as it is used in s 1 of the Act of 1968. That section provides that a person is guilty of theft if he dishonestly appropriates property belonging to another with the intention of permanently 'depriving' the other of it.]

DERELICT *See also* ABANDONMENT OF SHIP; WRECK

'Derelict' is property, whether vessel or cargo, abandoned at sea by those in charge of it without hope on their part of recovering or intention of returning to it. A vessel is not derelict which is only left temporarily by her master and crew with the intention of returning to her, even though the management of the vessel may have passed into the hands of salvors. On the other hand, a vessel deserted by her master and crew with the intention of abandoning her does not cease to be derelict because they subsequently change their intention and try to recover her. Whenever the question arises whether a vessel is derelict or not, the test to be applied is the intention and expectation of the master and crew at the time of quitting her, and, in the absence of direct evidence, that is determined by consideration of all the circumstances of the case. (43 Halsbury's Laws (4th edn) para 1008)

'The term derelict applies where the vessel has been left *sine spe recuperandi* and *sine animo revertendi*.' *The Zeta* (1875) LR 4 A & E 460 at 462, per Phillimore J

'To constitute the ship a derelict, it must have been left (a) with that intention (*animo derelinquendi*): see *The John and Jane* [(1802) 4 Ch Rob 216]; (b) with no intention of returning to

her; and (c) with no hope of recovering her.'
Court Line Ltd v R, The Lavington Court
[1945] 2 All ER 357 at 362, CA, per Scott LJ

'A ship is derelict in the legal sense of the term
if the master and crew have abandoned her at
sea without any intention of returning to her
and without hope on their part of recovering
her. In *The Aquila* [(1798) 1 Ch Rob 37 at 41]
Sir William Scott said that to constitute
derelict—"It is sufficient if there has been an
abandonment at sea by the master and crew,
without hope of recovery: I say, without hope
of recovery; because a mere quitting of the ship
for the purpose of procuring assistance, from
shore, or with an intention of returning to her
again, is not an abandonment." . . . Once a
vessel has become derelict, I find it difficult to
think of any good reason why she should cease
to be derelict merely because she is not afloat
but is lying on the bed of the sea. To my mind it
is clear beyond doubt that a derelict which
sinks remains derelict. That view is supported
by authority.' *Pierce v Bernis, The Lusitania*
[1986] 1 All ER 1011 at 1014, 1015, per Sheen J

Canada '"Derelict" is a term legally applied
to a thing which is abandoned and deserted at
sea by those who were in charge of it, without
hope on their part of recovering it, and without
intention of returning to it.' *The Humboldt v
The Escort* (No 2) (1914) 21 Ex CR 179 at 181,
Ex Ct, per Martin LJA, quoting Kennedy on
Civil Salvage, 2nd edn, pp 61, 62

DERIVATIVE WORK

Copyrights

United States A 'derivative work' is a work
based upon one or more preexisting works,
such as a translation, musical arrangement,
dramatization, fictionalization, motion picture
version, sound recording, art reproduction,
abridgement, condensation, or any other form
in which the work may be recast, transformed,
or adapted. A work consisting of editorial
revisions, annotations, elaborations, or other
modifications which, as a whole, represent an
original work of authorship, is a 'derivative
work'. (Copyright Act of 1976, s 101)

DERIVE

'Their Lordships attach no special meaning to
the word "derived", which they treat as synonymous with arising or accruing.' *Taxation
Comrs v Kirk* [1900] AC 588 at 592, PC per cur.

Australia 'I see no difference between
income arising from a source and income
derived from a source.' *Harding v Federal
Comrs of Taxation* (1917) 23 CLR 119 at 131,
per Barton ACJ

Australia 'It is dependent on circumstances
whether anyone, other than the person beneficially entitled, "derives" income within the
meaning of the [Income Tax Assessment] Act
[see now Income Tax Assessment Act 1936,
s 136 AE(1)]. A person in fact carrying on and
controlling a business and appearing to the
outer world as the owner "derives" the income
produced by the business for the purpose of the
income tax. His accountability to another is
beside the point. "Derived" only means
"obtained" or "got" or "acquired". All
income is derived from something and by
someone.' *Federal Comr of Taxation v Clarke*
(1927) 40 CLR 246 at 260, per Isaacs ACJ

Australia 'The word "derived" does not connote that the profit must be a realised profit. It
is enough at least if it is an ascertained profit,
ascertained by a proper account.' *Evans v Federal Comr of Taxation (SA)* (1936) 55 CLR 80
at 101, per cur.

Canada 'In a taxing Act words must, generally speaking, be given their plain and ordinary meaning, and, according to such
meaning, the word "derived" covers a wider
field than the word "received", and when
applied to the word "income" it connotes the
source or origin of such income rather than its
immediate receipt.' *Kemp v Minister of
National Revenue* [1948] 1 DLR 65 at 71, Ex
Ct, per Thorson P

DEROGATION FROM GRANT

It is a well-established rule that a grantor
cannot be permitted to derogate from his
grant. Hence, on the grant by the owner of a
tenement of part of that tenement there will
pass to the grantee all those easements which
are necessary in order that the property may
be enjoyed reasonably for the purpose for
which it was granted. On the other hand, if
the grantor intends to reserve any right over
the tenement granted, he must do so
expressly, though to this rule there are certain
exceptions, notably in cases of what are
known as ways of necessity. (12 Halsbury's
Laws (4th edn) para 1354)

DESCENDANT

Whatever may have been its meaning in earlier times, 'descendants' now ordinarily refers to children, grandchildren and other issue of every degree of remoteness in descent. Although the word may be confined to mean children by a sufficiently strong context, the court does not restrict the word to that sense merely because the testator speaks of the descendants taking their parents' share. The class of descendants taking under a gift is ascertained according to the ordinary rules for ascertaining a class. When ascertained, the descendants prima facie take per capita and not per stirpes; but, in a gift to a group of persons or their descendants, the descendants prima facie take by way of substitution only, and not in competition with their parents, if living at the time of distribution. (50 Halsbury's Laws (4th edn) para 521)

[A testator, by his will, bequeathed to his wife the residue of his property, and then in the following terms: 'And after her decease to the brothers and sisters of myself and my said wife, and to their descendants, in such proportions as my said wife by her last will and testament may appoint'.] 'Where the word "descendants" is used as added to a gift to particular persons, the more obvious meaning is as describing persons to take by way of substitution. The authorities fail to justify me in holding anything contrary to the natural meaning of the testator's words. This construction is not only natural, but the most convenient. Therefore I must consider that I am bound to hold that the word "descendants" only applies to and describes the descendants of those brothers and sisters of this testator who are living at the death of the tenant for life.' *Tucker v Billing* (1856) 27 LTOS 132 at 132, per Stuart V-C

'In this case there appears to me to be a perfectly unambiguous word—"descendants"—a word which, I venture to say, no layman or lawyer would use to designate children only. Descendants means descendants, that is, children and their children, and their children to any degree, and it is difficult to conceive any context by which the word "descendants" could be limited to mean children only.' *Ralph v Carrick* (1879) 48 LJ Ch 801 at 808, CA, per James LJ

[A testatrix made a bequest to trustees upon trust for her brother, and after his death for his son, and from and after the decease of both of them upon trust to pay the dividends and annual proceeds to any immediate or direct 'descendants' of such brother or nephew.] 'This is a case in which the limitations were not intended to be confined to one particular taker, but were intended to include a series of persons taking as "descendants" in the ordinary sense of the word, that is to say, singly and separately and successively according to the ordinary mode of limitation or descent of a landed property.' *Re Roberts, Repington v Roberts-Gawen* (1881) 19 Ch D 520 at 524, CA, per Hall V-C

'The words of the gift [in a will] to be construed are "to the descendants of my Aunt Anna Stokes or their descendants living at my death". I think the words "living at my death" govern the whole sentence. . . . It has been said, and I think truly, that the meaning of the word "descendants" is less easy to control than the meaning of the word "issue". Laymen (in this respect more accurate, I think, in their use of language than lawyers) mean by "issue" children. With lawyers it has a technical and wider meaning and includes descendants of all degrees. It is not difficult to suppose that in using the word "issue" a testator may have intended the natural and not the technical meaning of the word. There is, on the other hand, no technical meaning attaching to the word "descendants" which embraces generation after generation. In the present case, however, if any meaning is given to the words "or their descendants", the meaning of "descendants" in the earlier part of the sentence must necessarily be limited. The gift is alternative. There cannot be a gift to A or A, and therefore, descendants in the later part of the sentence cannot mean the same class or persons as descendants in the first part. I think that a reasonable interpretation may be put upon the gift by reading "descendants" as descendants of a single generation whether immediate or more remote.' *Re Hickey, Beddoes v Hodgson* [1917] 1 Ch 601 at 604, 605, per Neville J

'Among the commonest forms of documents which are drafted and construed by professional lawyers are wills and settlements which create in favour of persons indicated by the document rights and liabilities in respect of property passing on the death of a deceased; and among the commonest classes of persons in favour of whom such rights are created are those who bore some family relationship to the deceased. "Descendant" is but one of a number of nouns which have been used in countless legal documents for a century or more to identify persons between whom and the deceased a particular family relationship existed. Like "son", "daughter", "children", "issue", "father" and "ancestor", it is one of those nouns denoting family relationship which have become terms of art. In the case of many of these other nouns, it has been laid down in well-known decisions of the courts that, unless there is something in the context of the document or in the surrounding circumstances to indicate the contrary, their meaning does not include persons whose only claim to the described relationship to or through a male is based on birth outside the bonds of wedlock. This rule of construction has been so uniformly applied to different nouns denoting family relationships that it has in my view become a general rule of construction applicable to all nouns within that class which have become terms of art.' *Sydall v Castings Ltd* [1966] 3 All ER 770 at 776, per Diplock LJ

Australia 'The word "issue" and the word "descendants" mean substantially the same thing, and prima facie at all events, are equivalent to "heirs of the body".' *Re Hickey* [1927] VLR 555 at 559, per McArthur J

DESCENT   *See also* HEIR

'All estates are taken either by *purchase* or by *descent*. Unquestionably the strict legal sense of the word "descent" means taking an estate by inheritance: that is, as heir of the former holder, but in common parlance the word is not properly, nor indeed commonly, confined to that meaning, but means succession merely.' *Bickley v Bickley* (1867) LR 4 Eq 216 at 220, per Lord Romilly MR

[As to the meaning of British citizen 'by descent' and British Dependent Territories citizen 'by descent' see the British Nationality Act 1981, ss 14, 25.]

DESCRIPTION   *See also* SALE; TRADE
     DESCRIPTION

'It is not necessary . . . to give a precise definition of the meaning of the word "description" as used in the Act [Bills of Sale Act (1878) Amendment Act 1882, Sch, which directs that the name, address and 'description' of the witness attesting a bill of sale must be given]; but in my opinion it includes a description of the profession, trade, or occupation of the witness, or, if he has no profession, trade, or occupation, his style.' *Sims v Trollope & Sons* [1897] 1 QB 24 at 27, CA, per Lopes LJ

'It seems at least clear that the words now appearing in s 14(1) [of the Sale of Goods Act 1893 (repealed; see now s 13 of the Sale of Goods Act 1979)] "and the goods are of a description which it is . . . the seller's business to supply" cannot mean more than "the goods are of a kind . . ." "Description" here cannot be used in the sense in which the word is used when the Act speaks of "sales by description", for s 14(1) is not dealing with sales by description at all. If this is so, I find no obstacle against reading "goods of that description" in a similar way in s 14(2). In both cases the word means "goods of that kind" and nothing more.' *Ashington Piggeries Ltd v Christopher Hill Ltd* [1971] 1 All ER 847 at 876, HL, per Lord Wilberforce

DESCRIPTIVE   *See* DISTINCTIVE

DESERT   *See* ABANDON OR DESERT

DESERTION

Matrimonial causes

In its essence desertion means the intentional permanent forsaking and abandonment of one spouse by the other without that other's consent, and without reasonable cause. It is a total repudiation of the obligations of marriage. In view of the large variety of circumstances and of modes of life involved, the court has discouraged attempts at defining desertion, there being no general principle applicable to all cases.

Desertion is not the withdrawal from a place but from a state of things, for what the law seeks to enforce is the recognition and discharge of the common obligations of the married state; the state of things may usually be termed, for short, 'the home'. There can be desertion without previous cohabitation by the parties, or without the marriage having been consummated. (13 Halsbury's Laws (4th edn) para 576)

'A wife is entitled to her husband's society, and the protection of his name and home, in cohabitation. The permanent denial of these rights may be aggravated by leaving her destitute, or mitigated by a liberal provision for her support; but if the cohabitation is put an end to against the consent of the wife, and without the intention of renewing it, the matrimonial offence of "desertion" is in my judgment complete.' *Yeatman v Yeatman* (1868) LR 1 P & D 489 at 491, per Wilde JO

'Desertion at any rate implies that the parties are living together at the time when the desertion takes place.' *Pape v Pape* (1887) 20 QBD 76 at 79, per Stephen J

'In order to constitute desertion there must be a cessation of cohabitation and an intention on the part of the accused party to desert the other. In most cases of desertion the guilty party actually leaves the other, but it is not always or necessarily the guilty party who leaves the matrimonial home. In my opinion, the party who intends bringing the cohabitation to an end, and whose conduct in reality causes its termination, commits the act of desertion. There is no substantial difference between the case of a husband who intends to put an end to a state of cohabitation, and does so by leaving his wife, and that of a husband who with the like intent obliges his wife to separate from him.' *Sickert v Sickert* [1889] P 278 at 282, per Gorell Barnes J

'Desertion means the cessation of cohabitation brought about by the fault or act of one of the parties. Therefore, the conduct of the parties must be considered. If there is good cause or reasonable excuse, it seems to me there is no desertion at all in law.' *Frowd v Frowd* [1904] P 177 at 179, per Jeune P

'Desertion does not necessarily involve that the wife desires her husband to remain with her. She may be thankful that he has gone, but he may nevertheless have deserted her.' *Harriman v Harriman* [1909] P 123 at 148, CA, per Buckley LJ

'In this case . . . the evidence of the wife, which I accept, I think entitles me to hold that she has been deserted. In March 1919, her husband forsook her bed, avoided her society, shut himself in a separate part of the house, refused her access to it, and told her that he was introducing another woman; and this condition continued until November 1921, when he found rooms elsewhere and left the house. Except that these two persons were sheltered by one and the same roof, there was desertion of this wife by her husband in every meaning of the word.' *Powell v Powell* [1922] P 278 at 279, 280, per Lord Buckmaster

'It is convenient, first, to observe that it is clear—and also agreed between counsel—that "desertion" postulates both (i) the *factum* of separation and (ii) a continuing *animus deserendi* on the part of the deserting spouse.' *Perry v Perry* [1952] 1 All ER 1076 at 1080, CA, per Evershed MR; also reported in [1952] P 203 at 212

'Desertion means in law separation without consent and without just cause.' *Pheasant v Pheasant* [1972] 1 All ER 587 at 590, per Ormrod J

Canada 'Desertion means absence without the intention of returning.' *R v Graves* (1918) 52 NSR 365 at 366, NSSC, per Drysdale J

Canada 'In its essence desertion means the abandonment of one spouse by the other, without the latter's consent, with the intention of forsaking the other, but in view of the variety of the circumstances and modes of life Courts have abstained from laying down a comprehensive definition.' *Re Mothers' Allowance Act, Re McDonald* [1943] 2 WWR 97 at 99, Alta CA, per Ford JA

Matrimonial causes—constructive desertion

'It is as necessary in cases of constructive desertion as it is in cases of actual desertion to prove both the *factum* and the *animus* on the part of the spouse charged with the offence of desertion. The practical difference between the two cases lies in the difference in the circumstances which will constitute such proof. In actual desertion the spouse charged must be shown to have abandoned the matrimonial *consortium* in fact and to have done so with the intention of deserting. In constructive desertion the spouse charged must be shown to have been guilty of conduct equivalent to "driving the other spouse away" [per Bucknill J in *Boyd v Boyd* [1938] 4 All ER 181 at 183] from the matrimonial home and to have done so with the intention of bringing the matrimonial *consortium* to an end. In each case the intention may, of course, be inferred if the circumstances are such as to justify the inference. In the case of actual desertion the mere act of one spouse in leaving the matrimonial home will in general make the inference an easy one. In the case of constructive desertion where there is no such significant act as a departure by the spouse who is alleged to be in desertion, the acts alleged to be equivalent to an expulsion of the complaining spouse must be of such gravity and so clearly established that they can fairly be so described. If they do not satisfy this test, not only is expulsion in fact not proved, but it is not legitimate to infer an intention to desert. A man may wish that his wife will leave him, but such a wish, unless accompanied by conduct which the court can properly regard as equivalent to expulsion in fact, can have no effect whatever. Conversely, where the conduct of the required nature is established, the necessary intention is readily inferred since no one can be heard to say that he did not intend the natural and probable consequences of his acts: *Sickert v Sickert* [[1899] P 278]. The crucial matter for consideration, therefore, is the nature of the conduct relied on as equivalent to an expulsion of the complaining spouse.' *Buchler v Buchler* [1947] 1 All ER 319 at 320, 321, CA, per Lord Greene MR

'On the findings of the commissioner the wife was a lazy and dirty woman who did not keep the house or the children in a clean and proper state, so much so that on that account the husband left the house. That is not sufficient to make the wife guilty of contructive desertion. The essential element of intention is wanting. The wife had no wish that the husband should leave. There is no evidence that the wife intended to bring the matrimonial consortium to an end, and there is no ground for inferring any such intention. Without such intention constructive desertion cannot be found.' *Bartholomew v Bartholomew* [1952] 2 All ER 1035 at 1037, CA, per Denning LJ

'For conduct to amount to constructive desertion, two elements are required, *factum* and *animus*. First, the conduct must be such that a reasonable spouse in the circumstances and environment of these spouses could not be expected to continue to endure. This, I apprehend, is what is meant by such expressions as "serious", "convincing", "grave and weighty", although I await with some philological excitement an example of conduct which is "grave" without being "weighty". The undue sensibility or eccentric phobias of the complaining spouse will not convert blameworthy behaviour which a reasonable spouse would endure, albeit unhappily, as part of the wear and tear of married life, into conduct capable of amounting to constructive desertion. . . . Secondly, there is the element of *animus*, namely, that *this* husband must have known that *this* wife would in all probability not continue to endure his conduct if he persisted in it.' *Hall v Hall* [1962] 3 All ER 518 at 526, 527, CA, per Diplock LJ

'The question which the court of re-hearing will have to ask itself is this: was the husband guilty of such grave and weighty misconduct that he must have known that his wife, if she acted like any reasonable woman in her position, would in all probability withdraw permanently from cohabitation? If they find that, then they should find that the husband was guilty of constructive desertion.' *Griffiths v Griffiths* [1964] 3 All ER 929 at 932, per Sir Jocelyn Simon P

Of ship

A person is guilty of desertion within the meaning of this Act if he—
(a) leaves or fails to attend at his unit, ship or place of duty with the intention of remaining permanently absent from duty without lawful authority, or, having left or failed to attend at his unit, ship or place of duty, thereafter forms the like intention, or
(b) absents himself without leave with intent to avoid serving at any place overseas, or to avoid service or any particular service when before the enemy.
(Naval Discipline Act 1957, s 15, as substituted by the Armed Forces Act 1971, s 11(3))

'There are reciprocal duties between masters and servants. From the servant, is due obedience and respect; from the master, protection and good treatment. Desertion is a forfeiture of wages; but if the captain conducts himself in such a way as puts the sailor into that situation, that he cannot without damage to his personal safety continue in his service, human nature speaks the language—a servant is justified in providing for that safety.' *Limland v Stephens* (1801) 3 Esp 269 at 270, per Lord Kenyon

[Three seamen, apprehending that by the tenor of the articles they were not bound to proceed to a certain country, went on shore to seek advice and whilst so occupied were arrested by the master and taken before a magistrate, by whom they were committed to prison on refusing to return on board their ship. The seamen's suit for wages was resisted by the owners, on the ground that the facts constituted desertion by the common maritime law.] 'I shall not . . . attempt any definition of desertion generally, but content myself with the observation that to constitute desertion in such a case as this, there must be a complete abandonment of duty, without justification on the part of the mariners; and such abandonment must, moreover, be by quitting the ship.' *The Westmorland* (1841) 1 Wm Rob 216 at 221, 222, per Dr Lushington

'The facts pleaded are, that the mariner quitted the ship, and remained absent for nine or ten consecutive days. These facts, if established, might, I think, constitute a legal desertion, provided an intention absolutely to quit can be inferred from the *res gestae* of the case. Without such an intention on the part of the mariner, there can be no absolute desertion. If there be an absence from the vessel, *animo revertendi*, whatever be its duration, it would not be a desertion forfeiting the whole of the wages . . . I hope that I have made myself clearly intelligible upon this point; that in order to establish a total desertion, there must be proved an intention absolutely to quit the ship; and this intention is to be inferred from the circumstances of the case.' *The Two Sisters* (1843) 2 Wm Rob 125 at 138, per Dr Lushington

'The plaintiff left the ship, contrary to his contract. The question is, whether the leaving amounted to desertion, which is a criminal act. If he left for a reasonable cause, he did not desert. It is said that this is a question of degree, and that, in order to justify the leaving, the violence apprehended must be such as would be dangerous to life or limb. For the plaintiff it is contended that great and unreasonable cruelty is sufficient. I think the argument for the plaintiff is right.' *Edward v Trevillick* (1854) 4 E & B 59 at 69, 70, per Erle J

'In my view, to constitute desertion by a seaman of his ship there must be complete abandonment of duty by him without jurisdiction. I take this definition from *The Westmorland* [supra]. H H Davies, the master, in his evidence gave what he regarded as the Merchant Navy's idea of desertion. He said: "I think a deserter is a man who leaves his ship and does not return to it with no other purpose than to break his agreement." This is not a legal definition, but it supports my view of the law that circumstances may exist which justify a man in leaving his ship and not returning to it, even though this may involve his abandoning his service agreement. If a man is brutally treated by the master it has been held that such treatment justifies him in refusing to carry out his agreement; equally, if the master fails to provide proper food for his crew a seaman is justified in leaving the ship and not returning to it.' *Moore v Canadian Pacific SS Co* [1945] 1 All ER 128 at 130, per Lynskey J

Under military law

For the purposes of this Act a person deserts who—
(a) leaves or fails to attend at his unit, ship or place of duty with the intention of

remaining permanently absent from duty without lawful authority, or, having left or failed to attend at his unit, ship or place of duty, thereafter forms the like intention, or
(b) absents himself without leave with intent to avoid serving at any place overseas, or to avoid service or any particular service when before the enemy, and references in this Act to desertion shall be construed accordingly.
(Army Act 1955, s 37(2), as substituted by the Armed Forces Act 1971, s 11(1); Air Force Act 1955, s 37(2), as so substituted)

DESERVING   *See* CHARITY—CHARITABLE

DESIGN

'By s 60 of the Patent and Designs Act of 1883 [Patents, Designs and Trade Marks Act 1883 (repealed; see now Registered Designs Act 1949, s 1(3))] "design" is defined as meaning any design applicable to any article of manufacture or to any substance "whether the design is applicable for the pattern, or for the shape or configuration, or for the ornament thereof." . . . Under the Designs part of the Act of 1883, I do not think the object which the designer has in view in adopting the particular shape, or the useful purpose that the shape is intended to serve, or does serve, ought to be regarded in considering what is the design protected. . . . When an infringement is alleged, the only question is, whether the shape of that which is impeached is the same, or whether the one is an obvious imitation of the other, without reference to whether it does or does not accomplish the same useful end.' *Hecla Foundry Co v Walker, Hunter & Co* (1889) 14 App Cas 550 at 554, 555, per Lord Herschell

'All that s 47 [of the Patents, Designs and Trade Marks Act 1883 (repealed; see now Registered Designs Act 1949, s 1), which enabled the Comptroller, on application, to register a design] and the following sections deal with is the question of "design"; that is the word used and the only word; but the word "design" is interpreted by the interpretation clause, s 60 [repealed; see *Hecla Foundry Co v Walker, Hunter & Co* (supra)]. In my opinion, the object of that interpretation clause was to make the word "design" as extensive as it reasonably ought to be. It was not intended to draw the distinction suggested as a sharp, hard and fast distinction between the design being "applicable for the pattern", or "for the shape or configuration", or "for the ornament". I do not think you can say that "pattern" as it is used in that section necessarily and always excluded the shape or configuration, and that nothing could be included in "shape" or "configuration" which might not fall to be considered under "pattern"; or again, that the "ornament thereof" might not be a part of the pattern, and included in certain cases within the word "pattern". The words have not a sharply defined meaning; but the intention is to include any design, because the word is repeated, "any design" applicable to any class of goods, and whether "applicable for a pattern", or "for the shape or configuration or ornament" or some or all of them. The object was to use words which would include everything which would ordinarily fall within the word "design" and to show that the word "design" was not intended to be used in any technical sense as excluding anything that would ordinarily fall within it.' *Heath & Sons v Rollason* [1898] AC 499 at 501, per Lord Herschell

[Section 93 of the Patents and Designs Act 1907 (repealed; see now s 1(3) of the Registered Designs Act 1949) defined 'design' as meaning only the features of shape, configuration, pattern or ornament applied to any article by any industrial process or means, whether manual, mechanical, or chemical, separate or combined, which in the finished article appealed to and were judged solely by the eye; but as not including any mode or principle of construction, or anything which was in substance a mere mechanical device.] 'From s 93 . . . I learn that a design means something which is applicable to an article by printing, painting, etc, or any other means whatever, manual, mechanical, or chemical. Design means, therefore, a conception or suggestion or idea of a shape or of a picture or of a device, or of some arrangement which can be applied to an article by some manual, mechanical, or chemical means. It is a conception, suggestion, or idea and not an article which is the thing capable of being registered. It may, according to the definition clause, be applicable to any article whether for the pattern or for the shape or configuration or for the ornament thereof (that is to say, of the article), or for any two or more of such purposes. The design, therefore, is not the article, but is the conception, suggestion, or idea of a shape, picture, device, or arrangement which is to be applied to the article by some one of the means mentioned in the definition clause. It is a suggestion of form or ornament to be applied to a physical body.' *Dover Ltd v Nürnberger Celluloidwaren Fabrik Gebrüder Wolff* [1910] 2 Ch 25 at 28, CA, per Buckley LJ

'The statutory definition of "design" now in force is found in s 19 of the Patents and Designs Act 1919 [repealed; see now s 1(3) of the Registered Designs Act 1949]. . . . The operative definition so far as here material is: "'design' means only the features of shape, configuration, pattern or ornament applied to any article by any industrial process or means, whether manual, mechanical, or chemical, separate or combined, which in the finished article appeal to and are judged solely by the eye." Thus, design involves certain elements. There must be features of shape, configuration, pattern, or ornament, and these must be applied (or intended to be applied in the words of s 22 of the Copyright Act [1911 (repealed; see now Copyright Act 1956, s 10)]) to any article by way of industrial means or process. Section 22 emphasises the same aspects. Designs to which the section is to apply are those used or intended to be used as models or patterns to be multiplied by any industrial process. Thus, a design may be the shape of a coal scuttle, a basin, a motor car, a locomotive engine or any material object. It may be the shape embodied in a sculptured or plastic figure, which is to serve as a model for commercial production, or it may be a drawing in the flat of a complex pattern intended to be used for the manufacture of linoleum or wallpaper. Design copyright is thus to be distinguished from artistic copyright. Indeed, though the design itself cannot acquire artistic copyright, a photograph or drawing of it may.' *King Features Syndicate Incorporated v Kleeman (O & M) Ltd* [1941] AC 417 at 438, 439, HL, per Lord Wright

'Design is defined in s 93 [of the Patents and Designs Act 1907 (repealed; see now s 1(3) of the Registered Designs Act 1949)] as meaning "only the features of shape, configuration, pattern or ornament applied to any article by any industrial . . . means . . . which in the finished article appeal to and are judged solely by the eye. . . ." In the appellants' submission, design means not the features of shape appearing in an article but a particular kind of article having a particular shape. The article referred to in a design when registered accordingly entered into and formed part of the registered design. In my view that is not the true construction of the definition. Its whole point is the isolation of the specified features. The use of the word "applied" in the definition is dictated by the reference to the means of application and is not directed to the inclusion in the design of the article featuring the design.' *Stenor Ltd v Whitesides (Clitheroe) Ltd* [1948] AC 107 at 138, per Lord Uthwatt

See, generally, 48 Halsbury's Laws (4th edn) paras 371 et seq.

Town planning

[Section 18(3) of the Town and Country Planning Act 1947 (repealed; see now the Town and Country Planning Act 1971, s 33), provided that where permission was granted for the erection of a building, the grant of permission might specify the purposes for which the building might be used; and if no purpose was so specified, the permission should be construed as including permission to use the building for the purpose for which it was 'designed'. Outline planning permission was given for the erection of an agricultural cottage.] 'If I am right in holding that the adjective "agricultural" describes the purpose for which the cottage is to be used, the grant of permission specifies the purpose for which the cottage may be used when erected. It thus falls within the first part of s 18(3) and includes planning permission to use the cottage for that purpose and that purpose only. But in any event it seems to me that it defines the purpose for which the cottage is designed, for "designed" in the context of an outline permission must mean "intended to be used". It cannot mean "of an architectural design suitable for a particular use", for at the time of the outline permission there may not be in existence, and there were not in this case any architectural designs for the cottage at all, and "designed" in the subsection cannot have a different meaning according to whether the permission is an outline permission granted before architectural designs are in existence or a final permission granted after architectural designs have been prepared. In the subsection in my view it bears the first meaning set out in the Concise Oxford Dictionary: "Set apart for, destined or intended".' *Wilson v West Sussex County Council* [1963] 1 All ER 751 at 760, CA, per Diplock LJ; also reported in [1963] 2 QB 764 at 783

DESIGNATED

'Now what is meant by the word "designated" [in a private Act in which "officer" was defined

as meaning every officer "designated" an officer in an established capacity]? . . . It is a peculiar word, which is not common in the statute book. What is its ordinary meaning? In my opinion it means "described as such", or "described as an officer", in other words, there must be some special description of him as an officer in an established capacity. It may be said that it means described *eo nomine*; I think it does mean in substance, that he is so designated. It does not mean merely "called". It is something more. "Designated" seems to me to involve the idea of being "specially described as".' *Newton v Marylebone Borough Council* (1914) 78 JP 169 at 171, per Channell J

DESIRABLE TENANT

'The vendors state that the property is let to a most desirable tenant, what does that mean? I agree that it is not a guarantee that the tenant will go on paying his rent, but it is to my mind a guarantee of a different sort, and amounts at least to an assertion that nothing has occurred in the relations between the landlords and the tenant which can be considered to make the tenant an unsatisfactory one. . . . In my opinion a tenant who had paid his last quarter's rent by driblets under pressure must be regarded as an undesirable tenant.' *Smith v Land & House Property Corpn* (1884) 28 Ch D 7 at 15, 16, CA, per Bowen LJ

DESPATCH   *See also* CARGO

[By a clause in a charterparty, the owners of a ship guaranteed (for a consideration) that the ship should be 'despatched' from a port of call within twenty-one days. The captain of the ship broke ground within twenty-one days with the *bona fide* intention of proceeding; but he was prevented from doing so by a mutiny of the crew, and was forced to put back.] 'It is clear that the ship was not despatched within twenty-one days within the meaning of this charterparty; *despatched* means really sailing on the voyage.' *Sharp v Gibbs* (1857) 1 H & N 801 at 806, per Martin B

DESPATCH MONEY

'In my opinion the words "despatch money" [in a charterparty] mean money earned by the use of greater promptitude than the contract provided for, and no other meaning can in a business sense be given to them.' *Maccoy v West* (1898) 15 TLR 84 at 84, per Kennedy J

DESPATCHES

'What are despatches? . . . They are all official communications of official persons, on the public affairs of the government.' *The Caroline* (1808) 6 Ch Rob 461 at 464, 465, per Sir W Scott

DESTINATION

'What is meant by sending goods "to their destination"? It seems to me that it means sending them to a particular place, to a particular person who is to receive them there, and not sending them to a particular place without saying to whom. . . . It can only be said that goods are sent to their "destination" when they are sent to the purchaser, or to the person to whom he directs them to be sent—to a particular person at a particular place. That is the meaning of "destination" in a business sense.' *Re Isaacs, ex p Miles* (1885) 15 QBD 39 at 43, 44, CA, per Brett MR

'For my own part as I understand it the verb "to destine" normally is a transitive verb meaning "to ordain or fix the fate or function or state of some person or object" and the noun "destination" is either the purpose, or the geographical context, the place to which the person or object is destined to go.' *Superheater Co Ltd v Customs & Excise Comrs* [1969] 2 All ER 469 at 477, per Blain J

Australia 'As to the word "destination". The ship's destination is never inserted in her official papers for the purpose of creating or authorising the voyage; but for the purpose of recording what the master asserts respecting his intended actual voyage, and then, assuming his representations to be true, of authorising the ship's departure from the port. Penalties are always provided for mis-statements as to that; but if the asserted and recorded voyage were to be conclusively deemed to be the real voyage, there never could be penalties, for there never could be mis-statements. "Port of destination" is a well known phrase, with a natural, not a technical, meaning, and always indicates the port where the voyage *qua* the subject matter is in reality intended to terminate.' *Merchant Service Guild of Australasia v Commonwealth SS Owners Assocn* (1913) 16 CLR 664 at 696, 697, per Isaacs J

DESTRUCTION

Of houses

'It was decided under that Act [Riot Act 1714 (repealed)] that there was no liability on the part of the hundred to make good damage done to houses unless the houses were feloniously demolished or destroyed, or commenced to be feloniously demolished under s 4: *Reid v Clarke* [(1798) 7 Term Rep 497)]. Then it was decided further that there was no destruction or demolition, which amounted to a felony within the Riot Act, unless there was a total destruction or the beginning of a total destruction, that is to say unless there was some intent or purpose to destroy the house, and the cases decided that if the mob attacked the house for the purpose of maliciously injuring it—not destroying it and with no purpose to destroy, but—breaking the windows and smashing the doors, that alone was not only no destruction and no commencement of destruction, but it was not an offence within the Act at all, unless there was something more to shew that they intended to destroy.' *Drake v Footitt, Drake v Hankin* (1881) 7 QBD 201 at 207, DC, per Lindley J

Of tree

[A tree preservation order under s 29(1) of the Town and Country Planning Act 1962 (repealed) prohibited the wilful 'destruction' of the trees specified.] 'We think it right as a matter of language not necessarily to treat destruction as a synonym for "obliteration"; a glass vase is destroyed when it falls to the ground and shatters, even though the fragments which once comprised it still remain. On the other hand "destruction" must have at least elements of finality and totality about it and must in our judgment go further than merely a material change in the life-span or stability of the tree. The difficulty in this case is to say precisely how much further one must go and how clearly to define in words the point at which one should stop. We think it right to start consideration of the problem with one of the dictionary definitions of destroy to which we have already referred, namely "to render useless". Before a tree can be said to be destroyed we feel that it must have been rendered useless—but rendered useless as what? This last enquiry raises immediately the question of the purpose for which the use of the tree may or may not continue to exist. Consequently in our judgment one must bear in mind in this case that the underlying purpose of the relevant legislation is the preservation of trees and woodlands as amenities, as living creatures providing pleasure, protection and shade; it is their use as such that is sought to be preserved and a tree the subject of a tree preservation order is destroyed in the present context when as a result of that which is done to it, it ceases to have any use as an amenity, as something worth preserving.' *Barnet London Borough Council v Eastern Electricity Board* [1973] 2 All ER 319 at 322, 323, per cur.

Of will   *See also* REVOCATION

A will may be revoked by being burnt, torn or otherwise destroyed by the testator or by some person in his presence and by his direction, with the intention of revoking it. For this purpose there must be both an act of destruction and an intention to revoke. A symbolical destruction is not sufficient so that mere abandonment will not suffice. Moreover, a will is not revoked by being destroyed by mistake, or in a fit of madness, as even the most complete form of destruction without intention does not revoke a will. (50 Halsbury's Laws (4th edn) para 291)

'I should think that if the names of the attesting witnesses were erased by the testator *animo revocandi*, it would be a sufficient revocation. It might be difficult to make it appear that the names of the witnesses were erased *animo revocandi*; but if it could appear, I should be of opinion that it would amount to a destruction of the will within the meaning of the Act of Parliament [Wills Act 1837, s 20]. I do not think that the words "otherwise destroying" mean that the material of the will must be destroyed, but that it must be something which would amount to a destruction of the will itself.' *Hobbs v Knight* (1838) 1 Curt 768 at 781, per Sir Herbert Jenner

'It is quite clear that a symbolical burning will not do, a symbolical tearing will not do, nor will a symbolical destruction. There must be the act as well as the intention. As it was put by Dr Deane in the Court below, "All the destroying in the world without intention will not revoke a will, nor all the intention in the world without destroying: there must be the two".' *Cheese v Lovejoy* (1877) 2 PD 251 at 253, CA, per James LJ

DETACHED   *See* STRUCTURALLY
DETACHED

DETAIN—DETENTION   *See also*
SEIZURE

Of goods

'The condition [in a railway consignment note] is that the company are not to be liable in respect of any loss or detention of, or injury to the said animals, or any of them, in the receiving, forwarding or delivery thereof, except upon proof that such loss, detention, or injury arose from the wilful misconduct of the company, or its servants. Does the word "detention" then apply—not merely to some stoppage in transit or mistake by which the cattle truck had been sent into a wrong siding or delivered in course of transit to the wrong person, or any such mistake causing delay, but—to the withholding of the cattle by the company under claim of a supposed right on which they insisted? I think that is not "detention" within the . . . condition. . . . It was not any "detention" which had delayed or prevented their arrival. The word "detention" alone may, no doubt, apply to an absolute refusal to deliver grounded on some cause which is supposed to give a right to refuse delivery. But I think that the word "detention" as used in this condition does not mean any detention by absolute refusal, but by something that prevents the company from delivering the cattle at the proper time.' *Gordon v Great Western Rly Co* (1881) 8 QBD 44 at 48, DC, per Grove J

'The clause of the charterparty relating to demurrage provides as follows: ". . . if longer detained consignees to pay steamer demurrage at the rate of. . . ." In this case the steamer was detained for a considerable number of days. Under those circumstances what was to be done? The answer is "If longer detained consignees to pay demurrage." There is no limitation upon those words in the document. Why then should I put any limitation upon them? . . . Apart from authority, I should have no hesitation in coming to the conclusion that "if longer detained" means if detained whether rightfully or wrongfully.' *Western Steamship Co v Amaral Sutherland & Co* [1913] 3 KB 366 at 370, per Bray J; judgment discharged on appeal on another ground, [1914] 3 KB 55, CA

'Now what is the meaning of the word "detain" [in the Army Act 1881, s 156(1)(a) (repealed), which enacts that in certain circumstances a person who "detains" any property therein mentioned commits an offence]? Mr Giveen . . . says that "detains" means withholding adversely. I agree with that definition.' *Pullen v Carlton* [1918] 2 KB 207 at 211, per Darling J

Of person

Canada [The right to counsel under s 10 of the Charter of Rights and Freedoms arises where there is a 'detention'.] 'In its use of the word "detention", s 10 of the Charter is directed to a restraint of liberty other than arrest in which a person may reasonably require the assistance of counsel but might be prevented or impeded from retaining and instructing counsel without delay but for the constitutional guarantee.

In addition to the case of deprivation of liberty by physical constraint, there is, in my opinion, a detention within s 10 of the Charter when a police officer or other agent of the State assumes control over the movement of a person by a demand or direction which may have significant legal consequence and which prevents or impedes access to counsel. . . . Most citizens are not aware of the precise legal limits of police authority. Rather than risk the application of physical force or prosecution for wilful obstruction, the reasonable person is likely to err on the side of caution, assume lawful authority and comply with the demand. The element of psychological compulsion, in the form of a reasonable perception of suspension of freedom of choice, is enough to make the restraint of liberty involuntary. Detention may be effected without the application or threat of application of physical restraint if the person concerned submits or acquiesces in the deprivation of liberty and reasonably believes that the choice to do otherwise does not exist.

For these reasons I am of the opinion that the s 235(1) demand to accompany the police officer to a police station and to submit to a breathalyzer test resulted in the detention of the respondent within the meaning of s 10 of the Charter.' *R v Therens* (1985) 18 DLR (4th) 655 at 678, 679, 680, SCC, per Le Dain J

Of suspect

'The first question that arises is whether this detention is something different from arrest or imprisonment. In law there can be no half-way house between the liberty of the subject, unfettered by restraint, and an arrest. If a person under suspicion voluntarily agrees to go to a police station to be questioned, his liberty is not interfered with, as he can change his mind at any time. If, having been examined, he is asked, and voluntarily agrees, to remain in the barracks until some investigation is made, he is still a free subject, and can leave at any time. But a practice has grown up of "detention", as distinct from arrest. It is, in effect, keeping a suspect in custody . . . without making any charge against him.' *Dunne v Clinton* [1930] IR 366 at 372, per Hanna J

DETAINMENT   *See* ARRESTS, RESTRAINTS AND DETAINMENTS

DETERMINATION   *See also* DETERMINE

'It is said that "termination" and "determination" do not mean the same thing; that "termination" means the thing coming to its natural end; "determination" means coming to what I may call a violent end, that is, an end which was not contemplated as the longest duration, such as coming to an end by an unexpected death. I do not think that this is either the popular or the legal distinction between the two terms. Supposing a term were created of fifty years, determinable at the death of A, would it be legally inappropriate to say, that such term is determinable either by effluxion of time or by the death of A? And as to the grammatical or popular use of the term, it is rather remarkable that, in Todd's edition of Johnson's Dictionary, the fourth sense given of the word "determination" is "expiration,"— "end". And the lexicographer adds, "Used only by lawyers; as, from and after the determination of the said lease." The word "determination" may properly, and according to legal as well as to ordinary use, signify the coming to an end in any way whatever. That appears to me to be the honest mode of construing the word.' *St Aubyn v St Aubyn* (1861) 1 Drew & Sm 611 at 618, 619, per Kindersley V-C

'The words of the condition [in a bond] are, "if the determination of the said action shall be in favour of the plaintiff," etc. We are of opinion that, as there was at the commencement of this action a judgment in favour of the plaintiff, and there was no stay of execution on the judgment, such a state of things amounts to "a determination" of the action in favour of the plaintiff within the meaning of the condition. . . . Where, as in this case, the plaintiff has obtained a judgment in his favour, and is in a condition to enforce it by execution, the action, as far as he is concerned, may be properly said to be determined in his favour.' *Burnaby v Earle* (1874) LR 9 QB 490 at 493, per Lush J

'There is a . . . context in Chapter 3 of the Income Tax Act 1952 [repealed], which relates to "Appeals and Relief for Mistake" and comprises s 50 to s 66. Thus, in s 50(2) there is the phrase "An appeal, once determined by the commissioners, shall be final, and neither the determination of the commissioners nor the assessment made thereon shall be altered, except . . ." It is plain that there the words "determined" and "determination" are equivalent to: decided and decision, and are quite incapable of being understood to mean an assessment or the amount stated in an assessment.' *Muir v Inland Revenue Comrs* [1966] 3 All ER 38 at 48, CA, per Winn LJ

[See now the Taxes Management Act 1970, s 33 (Part IV: error or mistake).]

Canada 'An appeal lies under s 762(1) [of the Criminal Code, RSC 1970, c c-34] against a "conviction, order, determination or other proceeding in a summary conviction court". The only ground on which the decision in the present case could be appealable is that the judge's decision was a "determination". In my opinion a "determination" as used in s 762 is a decision which is decisive of the issue raised in the information. "Determination" implies an ending or finality, the ending of a controversy. While a decision of the trial judge allowing the defendant's motion [for dismissal of a charge] would have ended the issue of the defendant's guilt or innocence of the offence charged, the decision to deny the motion did not have that effect and in my opinion was therefore not a "determination" against which an appeal by way of stated case was available.' *R v Appleby* (1974) 10 NBR (2d) 162 at 169, NBCA, per Hughes CJNB

New Zealand 'Article 19 [of a partnership agreement] . . . says: "Upon the determination of the partnership the assets of the firm shall be realised. . . ." The word "determination" appears to me to be used for "termination", and usage shows that they are now used interchangeably.' *Rushbrook v Bridgeman* (1910) 29 NZLR 1184 at 1189, per Stout CJ; also reported 13 GLR 178 at 180

DETERMINE

Australia [The Local Government Act 1958–1986 (Vic), s 588, makes certain provisions where any council 'determines' that the execution of any works for the construction of a private street is necessary.] 'Now it is quite clear that in this particular matter the council is not called upon to determine any matter inter partes, it is not making a decision between two people as to who is in the right or who is in the wrong or who has rights or powers against the other: it is doing no more than making up its mind whether certain works are necessary; it is acting in other words, in a governmental or executive capacity. I would have thought that when a council says, by resolution through its councillors, that "it is of opinion that so and so", it means quite clearly that it has made up its mind, or decided, or determined, whichever word you like to use, that these works are necessary. . . . The word "determines" in this context means no more than decides or forms the opinion.' *City of Heidelberg v McPherson* [1964] VR 783 at 785, per O'Bryan J

New Zealand 'Section 175 [of the Magistrates' Courts Act 1893 (repealed; see now the District Courts Act 1947, s 31(1)(a)] provides that, when the term and interest of the tenant of any tenement held by him at will, or for any term . . . has ended or been determined, either by the landlord or tenant, by a legal notice to quit or demand of possession, then, if such tenant refuses to go out, the landlord may enter a plaint in the Magistrate's Court, and the Magistrates can give him possession. . . . The word "ended" is contrasted with the word "determined". "Determined" means, put an end to by one of the parties; "ended" means, ended by effluxion of time, and not ended by the acts of the parties.' *Town v Stevens* (1899) 17 NZLR 828 at 829, 830, per Williams J

DEVASTAVIT

A personal representative in accepting the office accepts the duties of the office, and becomes a trustee in the sense that he is personally liable in equity for all breaches of the ordinary trusts which in courts of equity are considered to arise from his office. The violation of his duties of administration is termed a *devastavit*; this term is applicable not only to a misuse by the representative of the deceased's effects, as by spending or converting them to his own use, but also to acts of maladministration or negligence. (17 Halsbury's Laws (4th edn) para 1542)

DEVELOPMENT

Of disease

'It is clear that his [a workman's] disease was due to the nature of his employment: the only doubt is whether it was "developed" on or after the appointed day. I should regard this word as apt to cover equally an original outbreak of disease and a recrudescence of it after it had been inactive.' *Hales v Bolton Leathers Ltd* [1951] AC 531 at 540, 541, HL, per Lord Simmonds

Of property

(1) In this Act, except where the context otherwise requires, 'development', subject to the following provisions of this section, means the carrying out of building, engineering, mining or other operations in, on, over or under land, or the making of any material change in the use of buildings or other land.

(2) The following operations or uses of land shall not be taken for the purposes of this Act to involve development of the land, that is to say:

(a) the carrying out of works for the maintenance, improvement or other alteration of any building, being works which affect only the interior of the building or which do not materially affect the external appearance of the building and (in either case) are not works for making good war damage or works begun after 5th December 1968 for the alteration of a building by providing additional space therein below ground;

(b) the carrying out by a local highway authority of any works required for the maintenance or improvement of a road, being works carried out on land within the boundaries of the road;

(c) the carrying out by a local authority or statutory undertakers of any works for the purpose of inspecting, repairing or renewing any sewers, mains, pipes, cables or other apparatus, including the breaking open of any street or other land for that purpose;

(d) the use of any buildings or other land within the curtilage of a dwellinghouse for any purpose incidental to the enjoyment of the dwellinghouse as such;

(e) the use of any land for the purposes of agriculture or forestry (including afforestation) and the use for any of those purposes of any building occupied together with land so used;

(f) in the case of buildings or other land which are used for a purpose of any class specified in an order made by the Secretary of State under this section, [the use of the buildings or other land or, subject to the provisions of the order, of any part thereof] for any other purpose of the same class.

(3) For the avoidance of doubt it is hereby declared that for the purposes of this section—

(a) the use as two or more separate dwelling-houses of any building previously used as a single dwellinghouse involves a material change in the use of the building and of each part thereof which is so used;

(b) the deposit of refuse or waste materials on land involves a material change in the use thereof, notwithstanding that the land is comprised in a site already used for that purpose, if either the superficial area of the deposit is thereby extended, or the height of the deposit is thereby extended and exceeds the level of the land adjoining the site.

[(3A) For the purposes of this Act mining operations include—

(a) the removal of material of any description—

(i) from a mineral-working deposit;

(ii) from a deposit of pulverised fuel ash or other furnace ash or clinker; or

(iii) from a deposit of iron, steel or other metallic slags; and

(b) the extraction of minerals from a disused railway embankment.]

(4) Without prejudice to any regulations made under the provisions of this Act relating to the control of advertisements, the use for the display of advertisements of any external part of a building which is not normally used for that purpose shall be treated for the purposes of this section as involving a material change in the use of that part of the building.

(5) In this Act 'new development' means any development other than development of a class specified in Part I or Part II of Schedule 8 to this Act; and the provisions of Part III of that Schedule shall have effect for the purposes of Parts I and II thereof.

(Town and Country Planning Act 1971,

s 22, amended by the Housing and Planning Act 1986, s 49(1), Sch 11, para 1 and the Town and Country Planning (Minerals) Act 1981, s 1(1)).

[For Schedule 8 of the Act, referred to in sub-s (5) supra, see 46 Halsbury's Statutes (4th edn) pp 597–600.]

'The notion of a dwellinghouse on land involves the notion of vacant land round it essential to its effectiveness. And further, as houses are built to sell or let or live in, I think it involves so much land as would ordinarily be expected to go with a house of that size, if it is to be merchantable or livable. . . . I should express the referee's view "essential to its enjoyment" as "essential to its use as a dwelling-house by the class of persons who might, from the business point of view of a person dealing in houses, be expected to live in it"; and I regard the site of the house altogether with such an amount of adjoining land as complies with that definition as "developed" by the erection of such a house.' *Inland Revenue Comrs v Devonshire (Duke)* [1914] 2 KB 627 at 639, 640, per Scrutton LJ

'It was argued before us that this was only demolition, and that demolition is not "development" [within s 12(1) of the Town and Country Planning Act 1962 (repealed; see now the Town and Country Planning Act 1971, s 22 (supra))]. I can see that, if one entire building is demolished, it may not be "development"; but it is not necessary to pronounce on that today. Here we have the demolition of a part of a building which amounted to an alteration of it which affected its external appearance. That is, I think, development.' *Coleshill & District Investment Co Ltd v Minister of Housing and Local Government* [1968] 1 All ER 945 at 947, CA, per Lord Denning MR

[*Coleshill & District Investment Co Ltd v Minister of Housing and Local Government* was affirmed by the House of Lords. An extract from the speech of Lord Morris of Borth-y-Gest is given below.]
'My Lords, one question that was persistently raised in this appeal was formulated as being whether demolition constitutes development for the purposes of the Town and Country Planning Act 1962 [largely repealed; see now Town and Country Planning Act 1971]. Neat and arresting as the question so expressed may seem to be it is not in fact the direct question which calls for our decision. If someone propounded a question of comparable generality such as whether modernisation constitutes development someone else might ask for a ruling whether renovation constitutes development. No one of these enquiries has precision. If development needs permission, which in most cases it does, and if development is defined, as in the Act it is [see supra] the true path of enquiry first involves ascertaining exactly what it is that it is desired to do or exactly what it is that has been done and then to see whether that comes within the statutory definition of development. Once some completed or projected work or operation is fully and clearly described then the words of definition can be applied.' *Coleshill & District Investment Co Ltd v Minister of Housing and Local Government* [1969] 2 All ER 525 at 526, HL, per Lord Morris of Borth-y-Gest

Australia [Section 122 of the Income Tax Assessment Act (Cth) 1936–1986, provides that where a person carrying on mining operations (other than coal mining) in Australia, for the purpose of gaining or producing assessable income, incurs expenditure on necessary plant and 'development' of the mining property, an amount ascertained in accordance with the provisions of the section shall be an allowable deduction.] 'Perhaps the import of the section is best understood by regarding the use of the word "development" as intended to amplify the section and to cover capital works not covered by the word "plant". At all events I am satisfied that all other expenditure of a capital nature directly attributable to the establishment of the mine and to the working of it or to its expansion or extension from time to time should, for the purposes of the section, be regarded as expenditure on the development of the mining property.' *Mount Isa Mines Ltd v Federal Comr of Taxation* (1954) 92 CLR 483 at 490, per Taylor J

Canada '"Development" of a mine, in general terms, means to uncover the body or area which is to be the subject matter of the extraction process. Development is the preparation of the deposit or mining site for actual mining.' *Johnson's Asbestos Corpn v Minister of National Revenue* [1965] CTC 165 at 170, Ex Ct, per Jackett P

Canada 'Every building or structure is a development or redevelopment in one sense, but I do not believe that the Legislature intended to mean that the words "development" and "redevelopment" within s 35(a) [of the Planning Act, RSO, 1970, c 349; see now RSO 1980, c 379, s 39] were to be interpreted in such manner. It must have meant the definition to be read in a much broader sense than a building or structure, or else there would be no meaning to cl (c) of s-s (4) which prohibits the issuance of building permits until the plans had been filed and the agreements entered into. If it had meant it to cover all buildings and structures, it could more readily have said that on any application for a building permit for such building or structure, then agreements must be entered into and the plans must be approved in the manner set out in the section. There would have been no need to refer to development or redevelopment. I am of the opinion that the term "development" has a meaning analogous to "redevelopment" within s 35(a) of the Planning Act and that neither relate to minor construction such as a small portion of a building or structure.' *Re Slau Ltd and City of Ottawa* (1976) 74 DLR (3d) 181 at 185, 186, Ont Div Ct, per Steele J

DEVELOPMENT PLAN   *See also*
STRUCTURE PLAN

(1) For the purposes of this Act, any other enactment relating to town and country planning, the Land Compensation Act 1961 and the Highways Act 1980, the development plan for any district outside Greater London (whether the whole or part of the area of a local planning authority) shall be taken as consisting of—
   (a) the provisions of the structure plan for the time being in force for that area or the relevant part of that area, together with the Secretary of State's notice of approval of the plan;
   (b) any alterations to that plan, together with the Secretary of State's notices of approval thereof;
   (c) any provisions of a local plan for the time being applicable to the district, together with a copy of the authority's resolution of adoption or, as the case may be, the Secretary of State's approval of the local plan; and
   (d) any alterations to that local plan, together with a copy of the authority's resolutions of adoption or, as the case may be, the Secretary of State's notices of approval thereof.

(2) For the said purposes the development plan for any district in Greater London (whether the whole or part of the area of a London borough) shall be taken as consisting of—
   (a) the provisions of the Greater London development plan as in force for the time being, together with the notices given from time to time by the Secretary of State indicating his approval of any feature or element of the plan;
   (b) any alterations to that plan, together with the Secretary of State's notices of approval thereof;
   (c) any provisions of a local plan for the time being applicable to the district, together with a copy of the resolution of adoption of the relevant council or, as the case may be, the Secretary of State's notice of approval of the local plan; and
   (d) any alterations to that local plan, together with a copy of the resolution of adoption of the relevant council or, as the case may be, the Secretary of State's notices of approval thereof.
(Town and Country Planning Act 1971, s 20, as amended by the Town and Country Planning (Amendment) Act 1972, s 4(2) and the Highways Act 1980)

DEVIATION

Of line of works

'The respondents who are commissioners . . . obtained in . . . 1880 an Act enabling them to take water from the Dodder for the supply of the Rathmines and Rathgar township. . . . That clause [s 13 of the Act] provides that in the construction of the authorised works, the respondents may . . . deviate from the lines of such works to any extent not exceeding the limits of lateral deviation shown on the deposited plans and from the levels shown on the deposited sections. . . . Deviation, in its ordinary and natural sense, and also in the sense in which, so far as I am aware, it has invariably been used in Acts of Parliament, simply means shifting the work in its integrity from one site to another which may be deemed more suitable. It does not imply a right, not only to alter the situation of the work, but in doing so to dispense with a half or two thirds of it. . . . When the Legislature has specified, with much minuteness, the size and contour of basins like these, it appears to me that a subsequent power to deviate from their lines is simply a power to alter the shape and position of the works, without interfering with their capacity.' *Herron v Rathmines & Rathgar Improvement Comrs* [1892] AC 498 at 514, 515, 517, 518, HL, per Lord Watson

Of ship

There is a deviation from the voyage contemplated by the [marine insurance] policy (1) where the course of the voyage is specifically designated by the policy, and that course is departed from; or (2) where the course of the voyage is not specifically designated by the policy, but the usual and customary course is departed from. The intention to deviate is immaterial; there must be a deviation in fact to discharge the insurer from his liability under the contract. Where a ship, without lawful excuse, deviates from the voyage contemplated by the policy, the insurer is discharged from liability as from the time of deviation, and it is immaterial that the ship may have regained her route before any loss occurs. (25 Halsbury's Laws (4th edn) para 143)

Subject to any express term of a charterparty, the shipowner impliedly agrees to proceed from the loading port to the port of discharge by the usual route and without unreasonable delay. A voluntary departure from this route or an unreasonable delay, at any rate if wilful, constitutes a deviation. Unless it can be justified [as e.g. for the purpose of saving life, or owing to stress of weather] . . . a deviation precludes the shipowner from relying on any exception or other stipulation in his favour contained in the charterparty and renders him liable for any loss of or damage to the cargo, unless he can show that this loss or damage must have occurred even if there had been no deviation. (43 Halsbury's Laws (4th edn) para 431)

(1) Where a ship, without lawful excuse, deviates from the voyage contemplated by the policy, the insurer is discharged from liability as from the time of deviation, and it is immaterial that the ship may have regained her route before any loss occurs.

(2) There is a deviation from the voyage contemplated by the policy—
   (a) Where the course of the voyage is specifically designated by the policy, and that course is departed from; or
   (b) Where the course of the voyage is not specifically designated by the policy, but the usual and customary course is departed from.
(3) The intention to deviate is immaterial; there must be a deviation in fact to discharge the insurer from his liability under the contract. (Marine Insurance Act 1906, s 46)

'It is often a nice question on the facts whether an interruption of the voyage amounts to a deviation only or is a change of voyage [these terms appearing in a policy of marine insurance]. The usual test is whether the ultimate *terminus ad quem* remains the same.' *Thames & Mersey Marine Insurance Co Ltd v Van Laun & Co* (1905) HL, reported [1917] 2 KB 48 n at 53, per Davey LJ

'I think it is clear that a deviation would not be reasonable merely because it was convenient to the shipowner. Its reasonableness must depend upon what would be contemplated reasonably by both parties having regard to the exigencies of the route, known, or assumed to be known, to both parties. . . . In addition to that, account would have to be taken I think, of the various terms in the deviation clause.' *Foreman and Ellams Ltd v Federal Steam Navigation Co Ltd* [1928] 2 KB 424 at 431, per Wright J

'Such a word [reasonable] must be construed in relation to all the circumstances, for it is obvious that what may be reasonable under certain conditions may be wholly unreasonable when the conditions are changed. Every condition and every circumstance must be regarded, and it must be reasonable, too, in relation to both parties to the contract and not merely to one.' *Stag Line Ltd v Foscolo, Mango & Co* [1932] AC 328 at 335, per Lord Buckmaster

'The true test seems to be what departure from the contract voyage might a prudent person controlling the voyage at the time make and maintain, having in mind all the relevant circumstances existing at the time, including the terms of the contract and the interests of all parties concerned, but without obligation to consider the interests of any one as conclusive.' Ibid at 343, per Lord Atkin

New Zealand 'The distinction between a deviation and a change of voyage is thus dealt with in Joyce's Treatise on Insurance [Vol 2, p 1547]: "In the case of an intention to deviate only the usual course of the voyage is intended to be voluntarily departed from without necessity, and the intention of going ultimately to the *terminus ad quem* of the voyage insured is never absolutely lost sight of and given up. And herein lies the distinction between a deviation and a change or abandonment of the voyage insured. In the latter case the *terminus ad quem* of the voyage insured is absolutely lost sight of and given up."' *Union SS Co of New Zealand Ltd v Jakins & Bower* (1901) 19 NZLR 780 at 792, per Stout CJ; also reported 3 GLR 338 at 343

New Zealand 'An unjustifiable delay in the commencement or completion of the voyage is a deviation. So, also, is a deviation of necessity which would be otherwise justifiable, if the immediate cause of such necessity is the negligence or want of caution of the owners. . . . An unreasonable delay at any port at which the ship is authorised to touch and stay is a deviation.' Ibid at 799, 800, per Williams J

DEVICE

'The 15th section of 36 & 37 Vict c 71 [(1873) (repealed)] enacts that between certain days no person shall place in any inland water any device whatsoever to catch or obstruct fish descending the stream. . . . The words are "any device whatsoever". There is no doubt that when the floodgate is raised the structure in question is a most effective device for catching the fish, and it is quite immaterial whether it is of a permanent or a temporary nature.' *Briggs v Swanwick* (1883) 10 QBD 510 at 512, DC, per Field J

'It seems to me that by "placing a device" is intended what in more popular language would be called setting a trap.' Ibid at 513, per Mathew J

[See now the Salmon and Freshwater Fisheries Act 1975, s 12, where the word used is now 'contrivance'; but cf s 5 (use of 'electrical device').]

DEVISE   *See also* BEQUEATH

'The word "devise" is properly applicable to a disposition of real estate, which is prima facie its meaning. If a testator says, "I give, devise and bequeath," the words "give and bequeath" apply to the personal estate, and "devise" to the real estate. Here he "devises" "everything he may die possessed of", which is sufficient to cover real estate.' *Phillips v Beal* (1858) 25 Beav 25 at 27, per Romilly MR

'The word "devise" in this Act [Wills Act 1837] . . . does include, unless a contrary intention appears by the will, a devise by way of appointment under a special or a general power conferred on the testator as to property not his own: consequently, it is so to be read in s 25.' *Freme v Clement* (1881) 18 Ch D 499 at 515, per Jessel MR

'The words "devise" or "bequest", when used in the Wills Act [1837] without any indication of an intention that they should apply to appointments under powers, ought, prima facie, to be understood in their ordinary sense, viz., as referring to a gift by will of the testator's own property, and nothing else.' *Holyland v Lewin* (1884) 26 Ch D 266 at 272, CA, per Lord Selbourne LC

DEVOLVE—DEVOLUTION

'Devolution' is the passing of property from a person dying to a person living. (17 Halsbury's Laws (4th edn) para 1073)

'To devolve means to pass from a person dying to a person living.' *Parr v Parr* (1833) 1 My & K 647 at 648, per Leach MR

'Where the succession is by "disposition" the settlor is the "predecessor", and where by "devolution" the last possessor is the "predecessor". . . . If the appellant were to die leaving a son, the son would take by "devolution", the appellant being considered his "predecessor", and so it would go on by devolution from generation to generation.' *Saltoun (Lord) v Advocate-General* (1860) 3 Macq 659 at 673, 678, per Lord Campbell LC

'Devolution by law takes place whenever the title is such that an heir takes under it by descent from an "ancestor", according to the rules of law applicable to the descent of heritable estates; and in all cases of descent the estate of the successor is immediately "derived" from the "ancestor" from whom the estate descends.' *Zetland (Earl) v Lord Advocate* (1878) 3 App Cas 505 at 520, per Lord Selborne

See, generally, 17 Halsbury's Laws (4th edn) paras 1071–1115.

DEVOTED

Canada [Measure of expropriation compensation varied where land was 'devoted' to particular purpose so that there was no general market.] 'The expression "devoted to a purpose" relates specifically to the land and entails some restriction upon the adaptability of the land which would impair its ability to command a normal price in the open market. . . . Improved land is devoted to a purpose not by the use which is made of it but where improvements incorporated into it (a) fit it for use for that purpose and (b) unfit it for most if not all other purposes. From this it follows that the purpose to which land is devoted may be a broad general purpose or a narrower specific purpose depending upon the degree of restriction on use imposed upon the land by the improvements made to or incorporated into it. Land upon which is erected a building which is readily adaptable to a wide variety of light manufacturing processes would be devoted to the purpose of light manufacturing even though the use actually made was limited to the assembly of electronic recording devices, while land occupied by a brewery building, not adaptable to any other use, would be devoted to the purposes of brewing.' *Re Gray Coach Lines Ltd and City of Hamilton* (1971) 19 DLR (3d) 13 at 18, 19, Ont Ca, per Kelly JA; on appeal (1972) 30 DLR (3d) 1, SCC

DICTIONARY

'One of the main objects of every dictionary of the English language is to give an adequate and comprehensive definition of every word contained in it, which involves setting forth all the different meanings which can properly be given to the particular word.' *Mills v Cannon Brewery Co* [1920] 2 Ch 38 at 44, per Lawrence J

DICTUM

Statements which are not necessary to the decision, which go beyond the occasion and lay down a rule that it is unnecessary for the purpose in hand are generally termed 'dicta'. They have no binding authority on another court, although they may have some persuasive efficacy. Mere passing remarks of a judge are known as 'obiter dicta', whilst considered enunciations of the judge's opinion on a point not arising for decision, and so not part of the ratio decidendi, have been termed 'judicial dicta'. A third type of dictum may consist in a statement by a judge as to what has been done in other cases which have not been reported. (26 Halsbury's Laws (4th edn) para 574)

'Dicta are of different kinds and of varying degrees of weight. Sometimes they may be called almost casual expressions of opinion upon a point which has not been raised in the case, and is not really present to the judge's mind. Such dicta, though entitled to the respect due to the speaker, may fairly be disregarded by judges before whom the point has been raised and argued in a way to bring it under much fuller consideration. Some dicta, however, are of a different kind; they are, although not necessary for the decision of the case, deliberate expressions of opinion given after consideration upon a point clearly brought and argued before the court. It is open no doubt to other judges to give decisions contrary to such dicta, but much greater weight attaches to them than to the former class.' *Slack v Leeds Industrial Co-operative Society Ltd* [1923] 1 Ch 431 at 451, per Lord Sterndale MR

'Some authorities distinguish between obiter dicta and judicial dicta. The former are mere passing remarks of the judge, whereas the latter consist of considered enunciations of the judge's opinion of the law on some point which does not arise for decision on the facts of the case before him, and so is not part of the ratio decidendi. But there is, I think, a third type of dictum, so far innominate. If instead of merely stating his own view of the point in question the judge supports it by stating what has been done in other cases, not reported, then his statement is one which rests not only on his own unsupported view of the law but also on the decisions of those other judges whose authority he has invoked. He is, as it were, a reporter *pro tanto*. Such a statement of the settled law or accustomed practice carries with it the authority not merely of the judge who makes it but also of an unseen cloud of his judicial brethren. A dictum of this type offers, as it seems to me, the highest authority that any dictum can bear; and I think that a judge would have to be very sure of himself before he refused to follow.' *West (Richard) & Partners (Inverness) Ltd v Dick* [1969] 1 All ER 289 at 292, per Megarry J

DIE

'There can be no question that a bequest to any person, and in case of his death to another, is an absolute gift to the first legatee if he survives the testator; and this, whatever be the form of expression, as "if he die", "should he happen to die", "in case death should happen to him", and so forth. The event here contemplated being so inevitable that it cannot be deemed a contingency, the courts have held that something else must be intended than merely to provide for the case of the legatee dying at some time or other; and have said, that they will rather suppose the testator to have contemplated and provided for the case of the legatee dying in his own lifetime; and so have read those words as if they had been "in case of his death during the testator's lifetime", in which event alone they have allowed the bequest over to take effect.' *Home v Pillans* (1833) 2 My & K 15 at 20, 21, per Lord Brougham LC

[A testator by his will gave certain property to three persons in specified shares, and directed that if any of the three should die, the others should have his share. One of the three legatees was drowned with the testator in a vessel, and there was nothing to show who was the survivor.] 'The only question for me to determine in this case is what words am I to import into the will to explain the expression "in case one of the legatees dies". The unusual event has happened that the testator and one of the legatees have died in such a manner that there is nothing to show which died first. If I ask myself what the testator meant by the word "die", I answer that he meant "die in my lifetime". The contingency of his dying at the same moment as the legatee never occurred to him. Lord Hatherley says, in *O'Mahoney v Burdett* [(1874) LR 7 HL 388 at 401], that the only mode of construing such a gift is to understand the testator as saying, "This contingency referred to the case of A's death during my (the testator's) lifetime, in which case the legacy would remain undisposed of, and I therefore provide that in that event it shall go over to another." It appears to me that by a long series of cases it has been decided that where there is a gift to A, and if A dies to B, that means a gift to B, if A dies before the testator. I must apply that rule to this case, and the consequence is that as the deceased legatee is not shown to have died before the testator, the legacy falls into the residue.' *Elliott v Smith* (1882) 22 Ch D 236 at 237, 238, per Fry J

[The law as to commorientes dying after 31 December 1925, is now contained in s 184 of the Law of Property Act 1925, which provides that where two or more persons die in circumstances rendering it uncertain which survived the other or others, subject to any order of the court, for all purposes affecting the title to property the deaths shall be presumed to have occurred in order of seniority and the younger deemed to have survived the elder. The meaning of 'dying' given above is, however, unaffected.]

New Zealand 'In *Gorringe v Mahlstedt* [[1907] AC 225] Lord Halsbury says, "The proposition I propose to adopt is this: that unless the ordinary and usual meaning of the words leads to some absurdity or something which is, to use the language of Kindersley V-C, 'manifestly contrary to the testator's obvious intention,' I will simply construe the language of the will itself and give effect to the meaning of those words according to the ordinary and proper meaning of them." I venture to adopt this proposition in the present case. The ordinary and usual meaning of the words "shall die" refer to death in the future, and there is nothing in the will or in the surrounding circumstances to suggest that they have any wider meaning.' *Re Nicolson* (1913) 33 NZLR 203 at 211, 212, per Williams J; also reported 16 GLR 317 at 319

Without issue

'The Vice-Chancellor has . . . laid down accurately the rule that where there is a gift over in the event of death without issue, that direction must be held to mean death without issue at any time, unless a contrary intention appears in the will, and that the introduction of a previous life estate does not alter that principle of construction. . . . The will says "if any of my children should die without issue, then that child or children's share shall be divided, . . . among the children then living". . . . There is throughout this will only one period of division contemplated. . . . There is to be a division at the death of the tenant for life.' *Olivant v Wright* (1875) 1 Ch D 346 at 348, 349, CA, per James LJ

Australia 'I am not going to decide now whether "childless" means without leaving children or without leaving issue. . . . At present I only decide that the words "die childless" mean die without leaving a child or children surviving at her death, leaving open the question whether the gift over will take effect if the daughter should die leaving issue her surviving, but not a child or children.' *Re Raphael, Permanent Trustee Co of NSW Ltd v Lee* (1903) 3 SRNSW 196 at 200, per Simpson CJ in Eq

Australia 'As to the effect of the words "dying without lawful issue", I think that on the authorities cited, these words are equivalent to "dying without leaving lawful issue", and I so decide. . . . On the construction of the will there seems to me to be no reason for restricting the meaning of the words to death in the lifetime of the testator.' *Re Galligan* (1913) 13 SRNSW 291 at 294, per Harvey J

Australia 'The ordinary and primary sense of the words "die without leaving issue" is "die at any time without leaving issue"; and this is supported by the modern rule of interpreting wills according to their ordinary and natural meaning, unless some rule of law, or canon of construction, intervenes so as to compel the court to place some special meaning upon them.' *Flanagan v National Trustees, Executors & Agency Co of Australia Ltd* (1923) 32 CLR 468 at 484, per cur.

Australia 'In the present case the words "dying without issue" are in my opinion, not free from ambiguity. In their natural meaning they rather point to dying without *leaving* issue. . . . I think I am justified in holding— and I do hold—that "dying without issue" should be given a referential construction and should be construed as meaning "dying without having or having had children, who attain or have attained the age of 25 years".' *Re Benjamin, Mason v Benjamin* [1926] VLR 378 at 396, per McArthur J

DIE (plate)

'Die' means the whole or part of any plate, tool or instrument by means whereof any mark of the nature of a sponsor's mark or a hallmark is struck on any metal. (Hallmarking Act 1973, s 6(2))

The expression 'die' includes any plate, type, tool, or implement whatever used under the direction of the Commissioners for expressing or denoting any duty, or rate of duty, or the fact that any duty or rate of duty or penalty has been paid, or that an instrument is duly stamped, or is not chargeable with any duty or for denoting any fee, and also any part of any such plate, type, tool, or implement. (Stamp Duties Management Act 1891, s 27)

'Die' means the whole or part of any plate, tool or instrument by means whereof any mark of the nature of a sponsor's mark or a hallmark is struck on any metal. (Hallmarking Act 1973, s 6(2))

DIFFERENCE

[A private Act empowered the company to charge for services to traders and provided that any 'difference' should be determined by an arbitrator.] 'I propose to give no opinion upon the true construction of the statute, except this: that a condition precedent to the invocation of the arbitrator on whatever grounds is that a difference between the parties should have arisen; and I think that must mean a difference of opinion before the action is launched either by formal plaint in the county court or by writ in the superior courts.' *London & North Western & Great Western Joint Rly Cos v Billington (J H) Ltd* [1899] AC 79 at 81, per Lord Halsbury LC

New Zealand 'The word "difference" in an arbitration includes "a failure to agree".' *A-G v Barker Bros* [1976] 2 NZLR 495 at 502, CA, per Richmond P

DIFFERENCES

Stock Exchange

No proof is allowed on a contract for differences, that is, where the parties are gaming under the guise of contracts for the purchase and sale of shares or commodities, neither party intending that delivery shall take place, even when by the form of the contract delivery might be insisted on. Similarly no proof is allowed for stocks agreed to be given by the bankrupt to meet a balance admitted by him to be due on such a contract, though proof may be made in respect of cover not required which the creditor has deposited with the bankrupt as security. (3 Halsbury's Laws (4th edn) para 722)

DIG

Canada [Power of mining company to drill oil wells was alleged to be included in its power to 'dig' for minerals.] 'The words "to dig for" may not in the popular sense appear very apt to describe the process of boring an oil well of some thousands of feet deep, but the words as used must clearly receive a wide and special interpretation as they would be understood by those concerned with mining. Obviously you cannot obtain the mineral oil by digging with a spade, as the literal meaning might perhaps suggest, but the same is also true as regards all other minerals for mining in which modern machinery is employed. It could hardly be suggested that under this power the company is not entitled to bore for oil on its own property. The words, I think, cover any process by which the earth is broken into for the extraction of the minerals.' *Dome Oil Co v Alberta Drilling Co* (1915) 52 SCR 561 at 562, SCC, per Fitzpatrick CJ

DILAPIDATIONS

Dilapidations . . . are a kind of ecclesiastical waste, either voluntary, by pulling down; or permissive, by suffering the chancel, parsonage-house, and other buildings thereunto belonging, to decay; an action . . . lies, either in the spiritual court by the canon law, or in the courts of common law: and it may be brought by the successor against the predecessor, if living, or, if dead, then against his executors. (3 Bl Com 91)

DILIGENCE   *See also* DUE DILIGENCE

Australia 'I think that a sensible commercial construction of the phrase [reasonable diligence] is that the actual extent of work completed is of some significance. "Diligence" in this contract means, it seems to me, not only the personal industriousness of the defendant himself, but his efficiency and that of all those who worked for him. A similar provision in a shipping contract was so construed in *Dobell & Co v Steamship Rossmore Co Ltd* [[1895] 2 QB 408]. Moreover, it would be wrong to insist that "reasonable diligence" refers only to the personal characteristics of individuals, and that evidence of the actual conduct or misconduct of the defendant and his servants, is alone relevant, to the exclusion of evidence of the actual state of the work at a given time. I am of opinion that, construing this subcontract as a reasonable commercial document, I am entitled to accept, as evidence, that reasonable diligence had not been displayed by the defendant, evidence that the work was, at the material time, seriously incomplete, together with evidence that there were no circumstances preventing the defendant from overcoming this situation.' *Hooker Constructions Pty Ltd v Chris's Engineering Contracting Co* [1970] ALR 821 at 822, 823, per Blackburn J

DILUTION

'The question turns mainly on s 8 of the [Customs and Inland Revenue] Act [1885 (repealed; see now Alcoholic Liquor Duties Act 1979, ss 52(2), 72(1), (2))], and it is to be noted that there is a marked difference between its two subsections. The first subsection applies to the brewer, who is not to adulterate beer . . . while the second subsection, which is applicable to the retailer, prohibits him from adulterating or diluting it. . . . There is an obvious reason why in the one subsection, dilution should be specified, while it is not mentioned in the other; for brewers, who brew beer of different strengths, must in a sense dilute it, either with water or by blending it with other beer. . . . But the retailer is supposed to buy his beer ready brewed. . . . The policy of the Act is therefore that, after he has purchased the beer for retailing . . . it shall not be diluted. . . . Here the defendant undoubtedly did dilute beer, for he put a weaker and inferior beer into the stronger so as to reduce its specific gravity from 10 to 8; if that is not dilution, I am quite unable to say what is; what he did was to make Barclay's beer weaker or thinner, and that is the fair ordinary meaning of dilution.' *Crofts v Taylor* (1887) 19 QBD 524 at 527, per Grove J

DIMINISHED RESPONSIBILITY   *See also* ABNORMALITY OF MIND

DIOCESAN BOARD OF FINANCE

'Diocesan Board of Finance' means the body constituted as such for any diocese under the provisions of any Measure, and, pending the passing of such a Measure, the body recognised by the Bishop as the board of finance of the diocese. (Interpretation Measure 1925, s 3)

DIOCESAN CHANCELLOR   *See also* CHANCELLOR

DIOCESAN CONFERENCE

. . . 'Diocesan Conference' means an assembly of Clergy and Laity constituted as a

Diocesan Conference in accordance with the regulations of the Church Assembly for the time being in operation and containing lay representatives elected in accordance with the constitution. (Interpretation Measure 1925, s 3)

DIOCESAN PURPOSES

Australia 'I am not prepared to hold that the expression "diocesan purposes", whatever objects are comprised therein, is not plain language, and if so it follows that the trust cannot be limited by the ecclesiastical position of the bishop trustee. . . . In my view, a diocesan purpose is not necessarily what the bishop may regard as a diocesan purpose, still less what he may consider to be conducive to the proper administration of his diocese. . . . It is sufficient for the present to say that, in my view, every diocesan purpose proper is a religious purpose and charitable in the legal sense.' *Re MacGregor, Thompson v Ashton* (1932) 32 SRNSW 483 at 491, 498, per Long Innes J

DIOCESAN TRUST

'Diocesan trust' means in relation to any diocese any body holding property upon trust for diocesan or parochial purposes and recognised by the Bishop as a Diocesan Trust but not as an existing Board of Finance. (Diocesan Boards of Finance Measure 1925, s 5)

DIOCESE

A diocese is a legal division of a province and the circuit of a bishop's jurisdiction: it is divided into archdeaconries, each archdeaconry into deaneries, and each deanery into parishes. (14 Halsbury's Laws (4th edn) para 454)

'The words "see" and "diocese" seem to be employed as equivalent expressions, although probably the word "see" has strictly a more confined meaning than the word "diocese". The primary reason why a diocese, or, in other words a limited territorial space, was originally assigned to a bishop, was not, as I apprehend, because his functions or duties were confined to that space, but because, as the superintendence of the bishop was to be more effectual when exercised principally over a limited extent, a territorial district, termed a diocese, was assigned to him as the limits within which

he should principally exercise his authority.' *Natal (Bp) v Gladstone* (1866) LR 3 Eq 1 at 29, 30, per Lord Romilly MR

DIPLOMA

'Diploma' means any diploma, degree, fellowship, membership, licence, authority to practise, letters testimonial, certificate or other status or document granted by any university, corporation, college or other body or by any department of, or persons acting under the authority of, the government of any country or place (whether within or without Her Majesty's dominions). (Dentists Act 1984, s 53(1))

DIPLOMATIC AGENT

A 'diplomatic agent' is the head of the mission or a member of the diplomatic staff of the mission. (Diplomatic Privileges Act 1964, Sch 1)

DIPLOMATIC IMMUNITY   *See*
IMMUNITY

DIRECT (Adjective)

Direct cause

[A policy of insurance provided that if the insured sustained any personal injury caused by external and accidental violence, and the injury was the 'direct' and sole cause of the insured's death within a specified period, the insurance company would pay the sum stated in the policy. The insured accidentally inflicted a wound with his thumb-nail on the side of his leg, which became septic, and the insured died from septic pneumonia consequent upon such wound.] 'Once it is agreed that the same instrument inflicted the wound and introduced the poison, it seems to me to follow that the morbid condition of the lungs which ultimately proved fatal was directly and solely caused by the wound. Take the case of a man being bitten by a mad dog and eventually dying of hydrophobia; surely it would be accurate to say that the death was directly and solely caused by the bite, although what immediately preceded the death was the disease resulting from the introduction of the poison into the system.' *Mardorf v Accident Insurance Co* [1903] 1 KB 584 at 588, per Wright J

'When the disease or other cause is dependent

on the accident, I think it is right to say that the term "direct or proximate cause" [in a policy of insurance] covers in such a case not only the immediate result of the accident, but also all those things which may fairly be considered as results usually attendant upon the particular accident in question.' *Re Etherington & Lancashire & Yorkshire Accident Insurance Co* [1909] 1 KB 591 at 598, CA, per Vaughan Williams LJ

Direct sale

In this section 'direct sale' means a sale where negotiations on behalf of the vendor are not conducted by any agent other than a person employed by him under a contract of service. (Agriculture and Horticulture Act 1964, s 12)

Direct tax   *See* TAX

DIRECT (Adverb)

'Relief was to be given [by the Local Government Act 1929, s 136 (repealed)] on certain traffics which passed on the railways. Amongst those traffics were Agricultural Selected Traffics, and it is with one item . . . that we are concerned today namely, "Treacle delivered direct to Farmers". . . . The words, in their plain and natural sense, seem to me to have nothing to do, as regards the word "direct", with the purity of the thing delivered, but with the process of delivery, that is to say, it must go from one point direct to the other point, which is the farmer.' *United Molasses Co Ltd v Amalgamated Rly Cos* (1932) 21 Ry & Can Tr Cas 26 at 28, per cur.

DIRECT (Verb)

[Stat (1772) 12 Geo 3 c 69, s 36 (repealed), authorised commissioners to 'direct' and regulate the stands of hackney coaches and chairs.] 'Looking at the whole of this clause I think that "direct" means "appoint". And if the commissioners may appoint the stands of hackney-coachmen, that necessarily includes a power of saying that they shall not take their stand in a particular place, as well as that they may do so.' *R v Rawlinson* (1826) 6 B & C 23 at 26, per Abbott CJ

'The corporation may make orders [under the Town Police Clauses Act 1847, s 21] for the regulation of the traffic . . . and as part of the machinery for carrying out the orders, the corporation may give directions to the constables

to regulate the traffic. That is not merely an order to the constables that they shall direct the traffic; it is an order from the corporation to the constables that they shall direct the traffic. "Direct" implies "obey", and therefore disobedience of the direction which is a part of the order is disobedience of the order; and therefore under those circumstances a person disobeying the direction of the constable is infringing the order.' *Dudderidge v Rawlings* (1912) 108 LT 802 at 804, DC, per Coleridge J

DIRECTION

'Mr Hollins [counsel] has directed my attention to Murray's Oxford Dictionary, from which it is quite clear, as I should myself have supposed, that in certain contexts "order" and "direction" are interchangeable terms. A "direction" is said to be "an order to be carried out", and "order", for example, so far as the Supreme Court is concerned, is said to be "a direction other than final judgment".' *Benson v Benson* [1941] P 90 at 97, per Lord Merriman P

DIRECTLY

'The order given by the defendant was a conditional order, to send him five tons of cake, provided it could be shipped directly. That clearly means something different from a contract to be performed within a reasonable time.' *Duncan v Topham* (1849) 8 CB 225 at 230, per Coltman J

'"Directly" does not mean "instanter".' Ibid at 231, per Cresswell J

'The words [in an insurance policy which was subject to the condition that it did not insure against death "directly or indirectly" caused by, arising from, or traceable to war] which I find it impossible to escape from are "directly or indirectly". There does not appear to be any authority in which those words have been considered, and I find it impossible to reconcile them with the maxim *causa proxima non remota spectatur*. . . . In my judgment the only possible effect which can be given to those words is that the maxim . . . is excluded and that a more remote link in the chain of causation is contemplated than the proximate and immediate cause.' *Coxe v Employers' Liability Assurance Corpn Ltd* [1916] 2 KB 629 at 634, per Scrutton J

[The Agriculture Act 1920, s 10(6) (repealed; see now the Agricultural Holdings Act 1986, s 60(5)), provided that compensation for disturbance should be a sum representing loss or expense 'directly' attributable to the quitting of the holding.] 'I apprehend that we ought to construe the words "directly attributable" in a popular rather than a metaphysical sense. . . . One is remitted by these words to the task of discovering the effective or immediate cause of the loss sustained.' *McGregor v Board of Agriculture for Scotland* 1925 SC 613 at 620, per the Lord Justice-Clerk

DIRECTOR   *See also* CONTROLLING
DIRECTOR

In this section 'director', in relation to any body corporate established by or under any enactment for the purpose of carrying on under national ownership any industry or part of an industry or undertaking, being a body corporate whose affairs are managed by the members thereof, means a member of that body corporate. (Trade Descriptions Act 1968, s 20(2))

(1) In this Act, 'director' includes any person occupying the position of director, by whatever name called.
(2) In relation to a company, 'shadow director' means a person in accordance with whose directions or instructions the directors of the company are accustomed to act.
However, a person is not deemed a shadow director by reason only that the directors act on advice given by him in a professional capacity. (Companies Act 1985, s 741(1), (2))

[Subsection (3) of the section exempts corporate bodies from being treated as shadow directors of subsidiary companies.]

For the purposes of this Part [XI: Close Companies] 'director' includes any person occupying the position of director by whatever name called, any person in accordance with whose directions or instructions the directors are accustomed to act, and any person who—
(a) is a manager of the company or otherwise concerned in the management of the company's trade or business, and
(b) is, either on his own or with one or more associates, the beneficial owner of, or able, directly or through the medium of other companies or by any other indirect means, to control 20 per cent or over of the ordinary share capital of the company.
(Income and Corporation Taxes Act 1988, s 417(5))

For the purposes of this Chapter [Part V, Chap I (supplementary charging provisions) relating to the Schedule E charge] . . . 'director' means—
(a) in relation to a company whose affairs are managed by a board of directors or similar body, a member of that board or similar body;
(b) in relation to a company whose affairs are managed by a single director or similar person, that director or person; and
(c) in relation to a company whose affairs are managed by the members themselves, a member of the company,
and includes any person in accordance with whose directions or instructions the directors of the company (as defined above) are accustomed to act. (Income and Corporation Taxes Act 1988, s 168(8))

'It appears to me, that a director is simply a person appointed to act as one of a board, with power to bind the company when acting as a board, but having otherwise no power to bind them.' *Re Marseilles Extension Rly Co, ex p Credit Foncier & Mobilier of England* (1871) 7 Ch App 161 at 168, per Mellish LJ

Full-time working director

'Full-time working director' means a director who is required to devote substantially the whole of his time to the service of the company in a managerial or technical capacity. (Income and Corporation Taxes Act 1988, s 168(10))

Of corporation

United States 'Director' [for purposes of indemnification] means an individual who is or was a director of a corporation or an individual who, while a director of a corporation, is or was serving at the corporation's request as a director, officer, partner, trustee, employee, or agent of another foreign or domestic corporation, partnership, joint venture, trust, employee benefit plan, or other enterprise. A director is considered to be serving an employee benefit plan at the corporation's request if his duties to the corporation also impose duties on, or otherwise involve services by, him to the plan or to participants in or beneficiaries of the plan. 'Director' includes, unless the context requires otherwise, the estate or personal representative of a director. (Revised Model Business Corporation Act 1984, s 8.50(2))

Of nationalised industry

In this Part [Part I] of this Act . . . 'director', in relation to a body corporate which is established by or under any enactment for the purpose of carrying on under national ownership any industry or part of an industry or undertaking and whose affairs are managed by the members thereof, means a member of that body. (Criminal Justice Act 1967, s 36(1))

In this section [offences by bodies corporate under the Land Commission Act 1967] 'director', in relation to a body corporate established by or under any enactment for the purpose of carrying on under national ownership any industry or part of an industry or undertaking, being a body corporate whose affairs are managed by its members, means a member of that body corporate. (Land Commission Act 1967, s 97(2))

DISABILITY

'Disability' includes mental as well as physical disability. (National Assistance Act 1948, s 64)

For the purposes of this Act a person shall be treated as under a disability while he is an infant, or of unsound mind. (Limitation Act 1980, s 38(2))

[A testator by his will gave a moiety of his residuary estate to his son, with a gift over in case of his being under any 'legal disability' whereof he would be hindered in or prevented from taking the same for his own personal and exclusive benefit.] 'What did the testator mean by "legal disability"? I think he meant a disability by act of law; not a disability created by Carew [the son] himself, but a personal disability imposed on him by the law, not voluntarily created, but imposed *in invitum*, such, for instance, as bankruptcy, or conviction for felony, or attainder for treason, and, in my judgment, also lunacy. I cannot think, having regard to the words used in the will, that the testator ever intended that those words should include a mortgage or a charge, or that he ever thought of those being such a disability as he was dealing with.' *Re Carew, Carew v Carew* [1896] 2 Ch 311 at 316, per Lopes LJ

'The wife's own doctor, Dr Hodgson, said that he had been her medical attendant for some eight years and he considered her throughout that time to be unable to look after the house or family by reason of her mental illness, and incapable of managing her own affairs. A distinguished physician, a Dr Leigh, who had been through all the hospital records, said that from March, 1962, that is when the petition was served, to February, 1963, "she was suffering

from a mental illness and that, as a result, it was highly unlikely that she was able to appreciate the nature of a petition for divorce or the need to enter an appearance to any such suit in the protection of her own interests". So there is strong medical evidence to show that she was in fact a person under disability.' *Balloqui v Balloqui* [1963] 3 All ER 989 at 991, per Lord Denning MR

DISABLED PERSON

'Disabled person' means a person who, on account of injury, disease, or congenital deformity, is substantially handicapped in obtaining or keeping employment, or in undertaking work on his own account, of a kind which apart from that injury, disease or deformity would be suited to his age, experience and qualifications; and the expression 'disablement', in relation to any person, shall be construed accordingly. (Disabled Persons (Employment) Act 1944, s 1(1))

'Disabled person' means a person who is substantially and permanently handicapped by illness, injury or congenital infirmity. . . . (Land Compensation Act 1973, s 87(1))

'Disabled persons' means persons who are blind, deaf or dumb or who suffer from mental disorders of any description and other persons who are substantially and permanently handicapped by illness, injury or congenital deformity or such other disability as may be prescribed. (National Health Service Act 1977, s 128(1), as inserted by the Health and Social Services and Social Security Adjudications Act 1983, s 29, Sch 9)

New Zealand 'It seems to me that "disablement" as used in s 34 [of the Workers' Compensation Act 1956] should be interpreted as "incapacity", that is to say as "loss of or diminution in ability or capacity to earn wages".' *Wati v A-G* [1963] NZLR 139 at 143, per Dalglish J

DISABLEMENT

'Disablement', in relation to persons, means that they are blind, deaf or dumb or substantially and permanently handicapped by illness, injury or congenital deformity or any other disability prescribed by the Secretary of State. (Registered Homes Act 1984, s 20)

Australia [The Workers' Compensation Act

1927–1986 (Tas) by s 5(1) provides that if a worker is 'disabled' or dies as a result of a disease arising out of and in the course of the employment, his employer shall be liable to pay compensation.] 'Counsel for the plaintiff submitted that a worker is disabled when there is any physical interference with bodily function. But I do not think that the word "disabled" refers to some vague general disability of that kind but, instead, should be taken to refer to the loss or reduction of the ability to perform a particular function and, in my opinion, in the light of the history and of the purposes of the Act, that means a loss or reduction of the ability to work. The plaintiff's claim should fail because he has not shown that his working capacity has been lost or diminished because of industrial deafness.' *Boucher v Motors Pty Ltd* [1976] Tas SR 130

DISAFFECTION

South Africa '[Disaffection] means political alienation or discontent; a spirit of disloyalty to the government or existing authority, with the understanding that the words "government" and "existing authority" do not refer to the political party in power but to the system of government and authority which is in being.' *R v Malianga* 1963 (4) SA 229 (FS)

DISBURSEMENTS

By solicitor

As regards disbursements, a distinction must be drawn between professional disbursements, that is to say payments made by the solicitor in his professional capacity, which must be included in his bill of costs, and payments made by him merely as agent on behalf of his client, which must be inserted in a separate cash account, and not in the bill of costs.

Professional disbursements include payments which are necessarily made by the solicitor in pursuance of his professional duty, such as court fees or counsel's fees, or which are sanctioned as professional disbursements by the general and established custom of the profession. Payments which are made by the solicitor merely as a matter of convenience and not in pursuance of his professional duty, and which are therefore to be regarded as advances to the client, such as payments of money into court, as security for costs, payments of stamp duty, capital transfer tax or other duties, and payments due from the client, whether under a judgment or a contract, are not professional disbursements. (44 Halsbury's Laws (4th edn) para 164)

'Those payments only, which are made in pursuance of the professional duty undertaken by the solicitor, and which he is bound to perform, or which are sanctioned as professional payments, by the general and established custom and practice of the profession, ought to be entered or allowed as professional disbursements in the bill of costs.' *Re Remnant* (1849) 11 Beav 603 at 613, per Lord Langdale MR

'There are many things which must be paid by the solicitor for his client, and which are obviously disbursements made by him in his character of solicitor. There are frequently large amounts, such as court fees and counsel's fees, which it is the duty of the solicitor, and not of the client, to pay, and which are also disbursements of the solicitor in his professional character; and there are also items such as stamps, fees on the registration of deeds, etc, which are properly called disbursements. And the question whether a particular payment is properly a disbursement cannot depend on its mere amount. On the other side it is clear that where the payment is made by the solicitor purely as an agent, it is in no sense a disbursement by the solicitor in his professional character.' *Re Lamb* (1889) 23 QBD 5 at 6, per Pollock B; overruled on another point by *Sadd v Griffin* (infra).

'The Act [Solicitors Act 1843 (repealed; see now Solicitors Act 1974, s 67)] requires the bill [of costs] to include "disbursements", that is (I quote the Oxford English Dictionary edited by Murray, Vol 3, p 409), "That which has been disbursed: money paid out: expenditure." . . . The money must have been paid in order to support an action on the bill. . . . All disbursements should be made before the bill is paid. . . . For the purpose of taxation under the Solicitors Act "disbursements" means actual payments before the delivery of the bill.' *Sadd v Griffin* [1908] 2 KB 510 at 512, 513, CA, per cur.

[An action was settled on the terms that the defendants should pay (1) a certain sum to cover the plaintiff's costs as between solicitor and client, and (2) all items of the plaintiff's disbursements.] 'I feel great difficulty as to the latter part of the agreement as to disbursements, but I have come to the conclusion that every item to be allowed or paid must be of the character of a proper disbursement to qualify for inclusion. It must be an item which would be properly described as a disbursement in a solicitor's bill of costs.' *Barnato v Joel* (1928) 45 TLR 167 at 167, per Eve J

'A "disbursement" charged by a solicitor against his client for counsel's fees must always have meant a disbursement actually made—money paid out of the pocket of the solicitor—since *ex hypothesi* counsel's fees, being in law mere gratuities, and not constituting a debt from the solicitor to the barrister, cannot be "due" from the client to the solicitor until the latter has actually paid counsel.' *Re Taxation of Costs, Re Solicitor* [1936] 1 KB 523 at 530, CA, per cur.

In Admiralty practice

'The real meaning of the word "disbursement" in Admiralty practice is disbursements by the master, which he makes himself liable for in respect of necessary things for the ship, for the purposes of navigation, which he, as master of the ship, is there to carry out—necessary in the sense that they must be had immediately—and when the owner is not there, able to give the order, and he is not so near to the master that the master can ask for his authority, and the master is therefore obliged, necessarily, to render himself liable in order to carry out his duty as master.' *The Orienta* [1895] P 49 at 55, CA, per Lord Esher MR

In marine insurance policy

'It [the word "disbursements" in a policy of marine insurance] is well understood at Lloyds' to be a compendious term used to describe any interest which is outside the ordinary and well-known interests of "hull", "machinery", "cargo", and "freight".' *Buchanan & Co v Faber* (1899) 15 TLR 383 at 384, per Bigham J

DISCHARGE

[The respondent advertised for sale a hand-held electrical device designed to stun and temporarily incapacitate a victim by passing through his body, by means of electrodes placed on his skin, an electrical current. He was convicted of being in possession of a 'weapon . . . designed for the discharge of any noxious liquid, gas or other thing', contrary to the Firearms Act 1968, s 5(1)(b). He successfully appealed on the grounds that 'discharge' was to be given its wide general meaning of emission of a physical object or substance, and that there had been no discharge when the

electricity was released. The prosecution appealed for a ruling on the meaning of the word 'discharge' as used in s 5(1)(b).] 'If the so-called general, and non-technical, meaning of the word "discharge" is applied, to my mind it is quite clear that when the device is placed up against a human body or against the clothing of a human body and operated electricity is then transferred from the device and passes through the human body. Electricity has thus been emitted from the device and it is this emission which has caused the victim to be stunned. In common parlance, as the terms of the advertisement so clearly confirms, the victim has received an electrical discharge, which discharge has resulted in his temporary immobilisation.' *Flack v Baldry* [1988] 1 All ER 673 at 675, HL, per Lord Ackner

Australia [Criminal Code (Tas) s 345 provides: . . . '(3) If any such person as aforesaid is not indicted during the sessions next after such sessions as aforesaid, he shall, be discharged'.] 'Counsel for the accused submits that the order . . . had the effect of acquitting the accused of the crime. . . . In other areas of the law the word "discharge" is used in different senses—for examples see Jowitt's Dictionary of English Law, 2nd edn, pp 619, 620. Two of the senses in which the word is commonly used are to deprive an obligation of its binding force, for example when a debt is discharged, and setting a person at liberty by an order discharging him from imprisonment. . . . an order for discharge made under s 345(3) is not to acquit an accused person or to debar further proceedings against him, but to discharge him from the incidents of a committal order so that his obligation to appear on remand is discharged and he is released from custody or from his obligation to observe the conditions of his release upon bail.' *R v Hill* (1982) Tas R 1 at 3–5, per Green CJ

Canada [Accused alleged that as she had not been 'discharged' by customs officers, she was detained and thus her right to counsel under the Canadian Charter of Rights and Freedoms was violated by subsequent strip search.] 'One of the meanings given to the word "discharge" in the Shorter Oxford English Dictionary is: "The act of freeing from obligation, liability, or restraint; exoneration; exculpation; dismissal; liberation." The discharging of a person under s 144 [of the Customs Act, RSC 1970, c C-40] simply means that he or she is freed from any obligation to submit to a personal search. Furthermore the right to be taken before one of the officials in s 144 was a right which could only be exercised by the person to be searched. In this case the respondent never exercised that right so that the matter of her being discharged never arose for consideration.' *R v Simmons* (1984) 7 DLR (4th) 719 at 740, Ont CA, per Howland CJ

Marine pollution

New Zealand [The Marine Pollution Act 1974, s 3(1) creates an offence if any oil is 'discharged' into New Zealand waters from any ship. An information charged that oil or a mixture containing it was discharged into New Zealand waters from a specified ship on a specific day. It was common ground that the cause of spillage was a fractured pipe.] 'Section 2(3) of the Marine Pollution Act 1974 provides that any reference in the Act "to the discharge or escape of oil or any pollutant, or to any oil or pollutant being discharged, from any ship . . . includes, but is not limited to, spilling, leaking, pumping, pouring, emitting, or emptying of that oil or pollutant as the case may be, howsoever it is caused, and howsoever it occurs" . . . It follows that when on an information brought under s 3(1), charging that oil was discharged, it is proved that the oil escaped from the ship, the extended definition provided by s 2(3) is effective to include spilling, leaking, pumping, pouring, emitting or emptying. Therefore an information which alleges that oil was discharged is sufficient to cover any spillage, leaking, pumping, pouring, emitting, or emptying. In my view the two words "discharge" and "escape" are used interchangeably in order to achieve the broadest basis of reliability.' *Union Steamship Company of New Zealand Ltd v Northland Harbour Board* [1980] 1 NZLR 273 at 276, per McMullin J

Of cargo *See* CARGO

Of effluent

'The first point that arises is whether what took place constituted a discharge of effluent [within s 2(5) of the Public Health (Drainage of Trade Premises) Act 1937] from the new premises into the sewer? It has been suggested on behalf of the appellants that "discharge" must mean direct discharge. Having regard to the wording of the Act and the results which would follow if one narrowed the meaning of the word "discharge" to direct discharge, I take the view that "discharge" here means discharge directly or indirectly into the sewer.' *Yorkshire Dyeing and Proofing Co Ltd v Middleton Borough Council* [1953] 1 All ER 540 at 543, per Lynskey J

New Zealand 'In its dictionary meaning relevant to the context the word "discharge" means to disburden, to get rid of, or to send forth. Here the word is used in conjunction with the word "into". When one speaks of discharging something into something else there is an implication that what is discharged goes directly or immediately into whatever receives it. In my opinion, the expression "discharge . . . into" as used [in the Water and Soil Conservation Act 1967] carries this implication of directness or immediacy . . . On the facts found by the appeal board the company proposes to dispose of its mill effluent by irrigation over land. In so far as the company can be said thereby to discharge natural water or waste it is, in my view, discharging it onto ground. It is not discharging it into natural water, even though there be natural water under the ground.' *Watson v Nelson Regional Water Board* [1976] 2 NZLR 333 at 335, SC, per Wild CJ

Of order

Canada 'Here [in s 24 of the Wives and Children's Maintenance Act, RSM 1954, c 294 (repealed; see now RSM 1970, c W 170, s 24)] is an express power given to the court to "alter, vary, or discharge any order". Counsel for the wife would have us give a narrow interpretation to the word "discharge"—as meaning something less than the power to rescind or to revoke, but as meaning simply "put an end to", and hence effective so far only as *future* operation is concerned. By so narrowing the term he would deprive the court of any power to deal with arrears. But in my view, the term "discharge" has, and should here be given, a broader meaning. It connotes nothing less than a power to revoke or to rescind.' *Lamontagne v Lamontagne* (1964) 47 WWR 321 at 331, Man CA, per Freedman JA

DISCIPLINE

Australia [A police officer was charged with a breach of reg 41 of the Police Regulations 1958 (Tas), reg 41 (repealed; see now Police Regulations 1974–1986, s 47) which prohibits misconduct against the 'discipline' of the police force.] '"Discipline" in this sense involves more than mere obedience to lawful orders. It is a wide concept and I have no doubt extends to conduct of a police officer when off duty so far as that conduct may affect his fitness to discharge his duties as a police officer. Many of the powers of a police officer are exercised by him by virtue of the independent public office he holds and cannot be exercised on the responsibility of any person but himself. His duties are of a public nature and over a wide range of matters affecting the public he exercises original and not delegated authority. Discreditable conduct in his private life may therefore clearly affect his status and authority as a police officer in the discharge of his public duties and his relations with the public.' *Henry v Ryan* [1963] Tas SR 90 at 91, per Burbury CJ

DISCLAIMER

By trustee

'The use throughout s 54 [of the Bankruptcy Act 1914 (repealed; see now the Insolvency Act 1986, ss 315–321), relating to the 'disclaimer' by a trustee in bankruptcy of onerous property] of the words "disclaim" and "disclaimer" is in itself a strong indication of the scope of the section. The words, in my view, connote a renunciation of, or refusal to claim, rights or property which would automatically devolve on or accrue to the person making the disclaimer. . . . "Disclaime, disclamare . . . signifieth utterly to renounce . . .". Co Litt 102*a*. . . . And the word is habitually used in this sense at the present day with reference to the non-acceptance or renunciation of the office and estate of a trustee under a deed or of an executor and trustee under a will.' *Re Lister, ex p Bradford Overseers & Bradford Corpn* [1926] Ch 149 at 165, 166, CA, per Sargant LJ

'While the office of a trustee may be disclaimed before acceptance, once it has been accepted, it cannot be disclaimed. . . . [Counsel's] argument that the office of trustee can only be disclaimed where it has not been accepted is sound.' *Re Sharman's Will Trusts, Public Trustee v Sharman* [1942] Ch 311 at 314, per Bennett J

By trustee in bankruptcy

'. . . The effect of disclaimer . . . is to put an end to both the rights and the liabilities of the bankrupt and his trustee in respect of the disclaimed property. That is the primary object. By the disclaimer the trustee elects to have nothing to do with the property which is onerous and from which nothing can be got for the benefit of the creditors. He is at liberty to disclaim it and the effect of the disclaimer is to extinguish all the rights and liabilities both of the bankrupt and of the trustee himself.' *Re Finley, ex p Clothworkers' Co* (1888) 21 QBD 475 at 482, per Lindley LJ

See, generally, 3 Halsbury's Laws (4th edn) paras 701–708.

In patent law

[The Patents Act 1949, s 31(1) provides that after the acceptance of a complete specification, no amendment thereof shall be effected except by way of 'disclaimer', correction or explanation, etc.] 'Since, if not before, the decision of this House in *Ralston v Smith* [(1865) 11 HL Cas 223], the expressions "disclaimer" and "by way of disclaimer" have been understood in this branch of the law to connote, in the words used by Lord Chelmsford in *Ralston's* case, "the renunciation of some previous claim actually or apparently made, or supposed to be made". A disclaimer in this sense may arise by express words or by necessary implication, and it must, at the least, operate to curtail the ambit of the monopoly as originally claimed. If the amendments proposed have this effect and are, in their substance, amendments of the original claims, they will, at any rate in the absence of special circumstances, be "by way of disclaimer", since their main and unequivocal effect will be to renounce something of what has been claimed.' *Amp Incorporated v Hellerman Ltd* [1962] 1 All ER 673 at 682, HL, per Lord MacDermott

[Section 31 of the Patents Act 1949 is among those restricted to patents and applications existing on a day appointed for the purposes of the Patents Act 1977. Amendments, thereafter, will be dealt with under ss 27, 75, 76 of the Act of 1977.]

DISCLOSE

[Section 27 of the Common Law Procedure Act 1852 (repealed), enabled a judgment in default of appearance to be set aside upon an application supported by an affidavit 'disclosing' a defence upon the merits.] 'It may be that the legislature, by the adoption of the language in question in the proviso of s 27 intended that something more than the ordinary affidavit of merits should be required; but the word "disclose" is a very vague and general expression, and may mean no more than that the party shall state his defence. . . . The word "disclosing", if the proper sources are sought to obtain its true definition, apparently points to something more than "adverting to", or "stating" or simply "telling", which are some of its definitions. It was probably intended that something more was meant, but of that I am by no means certain. The legislature has made use of a word which does not necessarily convey more than the sense of "telling".' *Warrington v Leake* (1855) 11 Exch 304 at 307, per Pollock CB

'I wish to make the single observation that I myself, and my brethren who have agreed with me, are of opinion that the word "disclose" may admit of two interpretations, the discovery of what was not before known, and a statement of that which was before known; and we are only to look in each Act of Parliament to see in which sense it is used by the Legislature, knowing that in one set of statutes it is used in one sense and in another sense in other statutes.' *R v Skeen* (1859) Bell CC 97 at 133, 134, CCR, per Lord Campbell CJ

Australia 'Where the word "disclose" is used with reference to information to be provided it should in my opinion be understood as requiring a statement of the relevant information which is in the possession of the person who is required to make the disclosure for a particular purpose or to bring himself within some particular statutory or other provision. In other words, a person cannot be said to fail to disclose something which he never knew.' *Federal Comr of Taxation v Westgarth* (1950) 81 CLR 396 at 407, per Latham CJ

Australia 'In my opinion, it is not possible, according to the ordinary use of language, to "disclose" to a person a fact of which he is, to the knowledge of the person making a statement as to the fact, already aware. There is a difference between "disclosing" a fact and stating a fact. Disclosure consists in the statement of a fact by way of disclosure so as to reveal or make apparent that which (so far as the "discloser" knows) was previously unknown to the person to whom the statement was made.' *Foster v Federal Comr of Taxation* (1951) 82 CLR 606 at 614, 615, per Latham CJ

DISCONTINUE *See also* DISUSE

'The word "discontinued" does not necessarily mean permanently discontinued. One

discontinues many things that may be discontinued only for a time, and when one resumes what one has discontinued it does not mean there has never been any discontinuance. There has been a discontinuance followed by a revival or resumption.' *Postill v East Riding County Council* [1956] 2 All ER 685 at 688, per Donovan J

DISCOUNT

General meaning

'The word "discount" is in the Oxford English Dictionary defined, in its primary meaning, as an abatement or deduction from the amount, or from the gross reckoning or value of anything, and, as used in commerce (1) is defined to mean a deduction (usually at a certain rate per cent.) made for payment before it is due of a bill or account; or any deduction or abatement from the nominal value or price; (2) "the deduction made from the amount of a bill of exchange or promissory note by one who gives value for it before it is due". The profits made by the respondents by buying these bills from the Treasury at something less than their true face value, and selling them during their currency at an advanced price, or by keeping them till maturity when their face value was paid by the Treasury, are, in my opinion, profits "on discount" within the meaning of Case 3, r 2 of Sch D [see now the Income and Corporation Taxes Act 1988, s 18].' *Brown (Surveyor of Taxes) v National Provident Institution* [1921] 2 AC 222 at 251, HL, per Lord Atkinson

Australia '"Discount" is primarily a rebate, and, as such, an allowance in reduction of the total sum payable. It is subtracted from the amount owed, or price asked, for some commodity or right in consideration of prepayment before the due date. . . . It is in the nature of a reward for early settlement. . . . The amount refunded retains its character as a rebate, whether it be repaid, or allowed, at the time of settlement, or deferred to a later date or dates. As between the person paying and the payee it remains a rebate in either contingency.' *Maddaford v De Vantee* [1951] SASR 259 at 263, per Mayo J

In commercial document

'This document embodying the scheme [of arrangement and compromise with the creditors of a company] . . . is essentially a commercial document; and the question is what, in a commercial document of this kind, is the meaning of "under discount at the rate of 4 per cent. per annum"? The scheme provides for the payment of £25 per share by instalments, which are to be paid every three months, and to extend over four years altogether. Then it provides that any shareholder may, if he likes, pay the amount due on his shares in advance "under discount at the rate of 4 per cent. per annum". . . . I come to the conclusion, without a doubt, that the ordinary commercial meaning of these words is this: "If you pay me that which is due from you in advance you shall have a rebate at the rate of 4 per cent. per annum for that payment in advance." . . . I think the real meaning is . . . a rebate of interest.' *Re Land Securities Co, ex p Farquhar* [1896] 2 Ch 320 at 326, 328, CA, per Kay LJ

In negotiable instruments

'In the discounting of bills of exchange, Exchequer bills, etc, the discount is the reward and in the normal case (since such bills do not as a rule carry interest) the only reward which the person discounting the bill obtains for his money.' *Lomax v Peter Dixon & Co* [1943] 2 All ER 255 at 262, CA, per Lord Greene MR

In underwriting of shares

'A . . . question arises as to the meaning of the expression underwriting "at 15 per cent. discount". It appears from the evidence that the expression "discount" is an unusual term in connection with the underwriting of shares, and that it is not a term to which any meaning of art can be given; and it further appears that under an underwriting agreement a commission is paid on all the shares to which the agreement applies, whether taken by the public or by the underwriter himself. But the court must put a construction on the word. And I think that upon a fair construction of the words used, they mean not "discount" in the proper sense of the term, but merely "commission", the amount to be paid to the underwriter in respect of the shares which he underwrote. It is not really a sum to be deducted from the nominal amount of the shares when they are applied for and allotted, but a sum to be paid on all the shares underwritten.' *Re Licensed Victuallers' Mutual Trading Assocn, ex p Audain* (1889) 42 Ch D 1 at 6, 7, CA, per Cotton LJ

DISCOVER

To 'discover' means simply to find out, and applies to the discovery of an error in law and an error in fact. It does not mean 'ascertains by legal evidence' but 'comes to the conclusion from the examination he (the inspector of taxes) makes, and from any information he may choose to receive' or 'has reason to believe', or 'finds or satisfies himself', or 'honestly comes to the conclusion on the information before him'. (23 Halsbury's Laws (4th edn) para 1577)

[By s 52 of the Taxes Management Act 1880 (repealed; see now the Taxes Management Act 1970, s 29), if a surveyor (now inspector) of taxes 'discovered' that any properties or profits chargeable to income tax had been omitted from a first assessment, or that a person so chargeable had not made a proper return, then as regarded the duties chargeable under Sch D the additional Commissioners should make an additional first assessment.] 'The question which we have to consider is what is the meaning of the word "discovers". That word obviously has more than one meaning, and the question which we have to consider is what meaning it has in this section. . . . First of all, has the surveyor any right given to him to obtain legal evidence? I cannot find that he has any such right. He has no right whatever to examine the taxpayer on oath, or to require him to give the particulars of his profits and gains and to verify the same, or to call upon any one in his service to answer questions. It would therefore seem most unlikely that the Legislature should have intended by the word "discovers" that the surveyor was to ascertain by legal evidence. The Act provides for a later trial, if I may call it so, of the question if and when there is an appeal. The stage preceding an appeal is not that at which legal evidence is required, and it seems to me to be clear that the word "discovers" cannot mean ascertains by legal evidence. In my opinion it means comes to the conclusion from the examination he makes and from any information he may choose to receive. There is nothing to prevent him from getting such information as he can.' *R v Kensington Income Tax Comrs* [1913] 3 KB 870 at 889, 890, per Bray J

'In my opinion the word means "has reason to believe". If it is construed in that sense it is consistent, and only in that way is it consistent with the whole scheme of this legislation.' Ibid at 897, per Avory J

'If that section imposes as a condition precedent to the operation of that section an obligation on the part of the surveyor to obtain legal evidence that the return is defective, it is certainly remarkable that the statute which imposes that obligation contains no machinery for enabling the surveyor to obtain the evidence which it is said he must obtain before the jurisdiction under the section arises. . . . If we take "discovers" as I think it was intended to be taken, as equivalent to "finds" or "satisfies himself", the difficulty disappears.' Ibid at 898, per Lush J

[The Income Tax Act 1918 (repealed; see now the Taxes Management Act 1970, s 29), provided for an additional first assessment where the inspector 'discovered' that a person chargeable had been allowed, or had obtained from and in the first assessments, any unauthorised allowance, deduction, exemption, abatement, or relief.] 'The real question is whether, within the meaning of s 125 the inspector has "discovered" an undercharge in the first assessment. The word "discover" does not, in my view, include a mere change of opinion on the same facts and figures upon the same question of accountancy, being a question of opinion. . . . It is to be remembered that income tax is an annual tax for the service of the year, and when one finds a provision for an additional assessment within a period of six years one is led to expect machinery, not for a mere revision, but for the bringing in of something which had been overlooked.' *Anderton & Halstead Ltd v Birrell* [1932] 1 KB 271 at 281, per Rowlatt J

'The question . . . is whether a discovery that a mistake, essentially a mistake of law, has been made is a discovery within the meaning of s 125 [of the Income Tax Act 1918 (repealed; see supra)]. I think the word "discover" in itself, according to the ordinary use of language, may be taken simply to mean "find out". What has to be found or found out is that any properties or profits chargeable to tax have been omitted from the first assessment. . . . If there were any reason in the context for restricting the word "discover" to the discovery of an error in fact, that restriction would necessarily receive effect, but, in my opinion, the context points, not to any such restriction, but on the contrary to so wide a meaning that the word ought to be held to cover just the kind of discovery which was made here, when the Special Commissioners found out that, by reason of a misapprehension of the legal position, certain of the profits chargeable to tax had been omitted from the first assessment.' *Inland Revenue v Mackinlay's Trustees* 1938 SC 765 at 771, 772, per the Lord President (Lord Normand)

'It was said by Rowlatt J in the case of *Anderton & Halstead Ltd v Birrell* [supra], that a mere change of opinion by an inspector who, with full knowledge of the facts, had honestly held the opinion that tax was not payable, was not a discovery within the meaning of the section [Income Tax Act 1918, s 125 (repealed; see supra)]. Again, it is clear that in the case of *British Sugar Manufacturers v Harris* [[1938] 2 KB 220], as far as the arguments are concerned, the Court of Appeal were prepared to hold that what took place in that case was not discovery within the meaning of the section. On the other hand, there is the case of *Mackinlay's Trustees* [*Inland Revenue v Mackinlay's Trustees* (supra)] to the effect that a discovery of a mistake in law in a former assessment of a discovery within the section. . . . This is not . . . the case of a new inspector taking a different view of the law from that taken by the inspector whose place he had taken. But it was a question of refunding to the taxpayer income tax claimed to have been paid during the last assessment period. There were special obligations to scrutinise figures which had passed muster, and at their face value, in former returns, in view of the answers given by the company's accountants. Vouchers were called for by the company from their brokers. These could not be produced. Then, for the first time, did the inspector discover that the dividends, treated hitherto as having been received after the tax was deducted, were in fact entries in the "contango" accounts of the company's brokers and no more. Therefore . . . there was a discovery by the inspector entitling him to raise an additional assessment on the appellants under the provisions of the Income Tax Act 1918, s 125(1) [repealed; see supra].' *Multipar Syndicate Ltd v Devitt* [1945] 1 All ER 298 at 303, 304, per Wrottesley J

'If some other meaning is to be given to "discover" [within s 125(1) of the Income Tax Act 1918 (repealed; see supra)] than the natural meaning "to find out", I should like to learn what it is.' *Commercial Structures Ltd v Briggs (Inspector of Taxes)* [1948] 2 All ER 1041 at 1049, CA, per Cohen LJ

'I have expressed my reluctance to add to the many pronouncements on the subject of what "discovery" [as required by s 125 of the Income Tax Act 1918 (repealed; see supra)] is. To say that it means to "find out" does not seem to me to help very much. Is there perhaps, a distinction to be drawn between "finding" and "finding out"? Does a man discover a diamond by finding it in the ground believing it to be a piece of glass, that is, not finding out that what he has found is a diamond? . . . It seems to me that this is a true analogy:—A man finds or discovers in his land a diamond. He thinks it is only a piece of glass, but, though he did not at first find out it was a diamond, he had in the true sense discovered it on the day that he found it. . . . I think that the discovery need not be a complete and detailed or accurate discovery and that when the commissioners find out, or think that they have found out, the existence of an omission or other error it is not necessary for them to have probed the matter to its depths or to define precisely the ground on which they have made the assessments. Here the relevant facts were all known to them. What was lacking was a comprehension of those facts. The facts were there, the commissioners, to revert for a moment to my analogy, thought that the diamond which they had found was only a piece of glass, but it was none the less a discovery.' *Beatty (Earl) v Inland Revenue Comrs* [1953] 2 All ER 758 at 761, 762, per Vaisey J

Australia [Section 128 of the Stamp Duties Act 1920–1986 (NSW), provides that it shall be lawful for the Commissioner, if it is 'discovered' that any duty payable has not been fully assessed and paid, to make a further assessment of the duty so unpaid.] 'To "discover" means to obtain knowledge or become aware of some fact or circumstances for the first time, or in other words, as has been said in the English decisions, "to find out". If, to take another example, a motor car intended to be sold, was valued by an expert valuer within a day or two prior to the sale at a certain figure, and if when sold immediately after that valuation it realised a figure more than double the valuer's estimate, then in ordinary English language such a valuer could properly be said to have discovered after the sale that his valuation was incorrect.' *Francis v Comr of Stamp Duties* (1953) 53 SR (NSW) 257 at 263, per Street CJ

DISCOVERY

The term 'discovery' . . . is used to describe the process by which the parties to a civil cause or matter are enabled to obtain, within certain defined limits, full information of the existence and the contents of all relevant documents relating to the matters in question between them. The process of the discovery of documents operates generally in three successive stages, namely (1) the disclosure in writing by one party to the other of all the documents which he has or has had in his possession, custody or power relating to matters in question in the proceedings; (2) the inspection of the documents disclosed, other than those for which privilege from or other objection to production is properly claimed or raised; and (3) the production of the documents disclosed either for inspection by the opposite party or to the court. (13 Halsbury's Laws (4th edn) para 1)

'The course of practice is, that as between plaintiff and defendant, either party may require an affidavit for the discovery of documents and for the production of those which relate to the matters in the cause. The practice of the courts is against the proposition that the question of production and the question of discovery are the same. They are not the same thing, but entirely different. The defendants are bound to state by affidavit what documents they have in their possession, and when they have done so, then will arise the question of production. It may turn out that the plaintiff . . . is not entitled to production. The order will be that the defendants make the common affidavit, stating whether they have any, and if any what, documents in their possession or power relating to the matters in question, following the order in *Rumbold v Forteath* [(1857) 3 K & J 748].' *Quin v Ratcliff* (1860) 3 LT 363 at 366, per Stuart V-C

DISCRETION

'"Discretion" means when it is said that something is to be done within the discretion of the authorities that that something is to be done according to the rules of reason and justice, not according to private opinion: *Rooke's Case* [(1598) 5 Co Rep 99b]; according to law, and not humour. It is to be, not arbitrary, vague, and fanciful, but legal and regular. And it must be exercised within the limit to which an honest man competent to the discharge of his office ought to confine himself: *Wilson v Rastall* [(1792) 4 Term Rep at 757].' *Sharp v Wakefield* [1891] AC 173 at 179, HL, per Lord Halsbury LC

Australia 'It has been held in this court, in a series of cases, that a discretion or power to grant a licence, though conferred in very general terms, does not entitle the authority to which the discretion is granted, or upon which the power is conferred, to take into account what have been described as extraneous conditions. The discretion must be used and the power exercised bona fide and with the view of achieving ends or objects not outside the purpose for which the direction or power is conferred.' *Shrimpton v Commonwealth* (1945) 69 CLR 613 at 620, per Latham CJ

Canada [The premier of a province, in his capacity as attorney-general, wishing to hamper the activities of a religious sect of which he disapproved, procured the removal of a liquor licence from a member of the sect and thus destroyed his business. He argued that he was merely exercising his 'discretion'.] 'In public regulation of this sort there is no such thing as absolute and untrammelled "discretion", that is that action can be taken on any ground or for any reason that can be suggested to the mind of the administrator; no legislative Act can, without express language, be taken to contemplate an unlimited arbitrary power exercisable for any purpose, however capricious or irrelevant, regardless of the nature or purpose of the statute. Fraud and corruption in the Commission may not be mentioned in such statutes but they are always implied as exceptions. "Discretion" necessarily implies good faith in discharging public duty; there is always a perspective within which a statute is intended to operate; and any clear departure from its lines or objects is just as objectionable as fraud or corruption. Could an applicant be refused a permit because he had been born in another province, or because of the colour of his hair? The ordinary language of the legislature cannot be so distorted.' *Roncarelli v Duplessis* [1959] SCR 121 at 140, SCC, per Rand J

DISCRETIONARY TRUST   *See* TRUST

DISCRIMINATION

A person discriminates against another in any circumstances relevant for the purposes of any provision of this Act if—
(a) on racial grounds he treats that other less favourably than he treats or would treat other persons; or
(b) he applies to that other a requirement or condition which he applies equally or would apply equally to persons not of the same racial group as the other but—
  (i) which is such that the proportion of persons of the same racial group as that other who can comply with it is considerably smaller than the proportion of persons not of that racial group who can comply with it; and

  (ii) which he cannot show to be justifiable irrespective of colour, race, nationality or ethnic or national origins of the person to whom it is applied; and
  (iii) which is to the detriment of that other because he cannot comply with it.
(Race Relations Act 1976, s 1(1))

A person discriminates against a woman in any circumstances relevant for that purpose of any provision of this Act if—
(a) on the ground of her sex he treats her less favourably than he treats or would treat a man, or
(b) he applies to her a requirement or condition which applies or would apply equally to a man but—
  (i) which is such that the proportion of women who can comply with it is considerably smaller than the proportion of men who can comply with it, and
  (ii) which he cannot show to be justifiable irrespective of the sex of the person to whom it is applied, and
  (iii) which is to her detriment because she cannot comply with it.
(Sex Discrimination Act 1975, s 1)
[Sections 2, 3 and 4 respectively of the Act of 1975 relate to sex discrimination against men; discrimination against married persons in the employment field; and discrimination by way of victimisation.]

'It is not discrimination for mankind to treat womankind with the courtesy and chivalry which we have been taught to believe is right conduct in our society.' *Peake v Automotive Products Ltd* [1978] 1 All ER 106 at 108, CA, per Lord Denning MR

'A general policy concerning dismissal involving the dismissal of a woman solely because she has attained the qualifying age for a state pension, which age is different under national legislation for men and for women, constitutes discrimination on grounds of sex.' Case 152/84: *Marshall v Southampton and South West Hampshire Area Health Authority (Teaching)* [1986] 2 All ER 584 at 599, ECJ, per cur.

'A contractual provision which lays down a single age for the dismissal of men and women under a mass redundancy involving the grant of an early retirement pension, whereas the normal retirement age is different for men and women, does not constitute discrimination on grounds of sex.' Case 151/84: *Roberts v Tate &*

Lyle Industries Ltd [1986] 2 All ER 602 at 612, ECJ, per cur.

Australia 'I have some difficulty in understanding how "discrimination" in a precise sense can be shown in a law applying only to one person or class of persons in respect of a particular subject matter. Discrimination appears to me to involve differences in the treatment of two or more persons or subjects. Legislation with respect only to one or more persons or with respect only to one or more subjects is not, I suggest with respect, properly described as discriminating against other persons or other subjects simply because it leaves them alone.' *Lord Mayor, Councillors and Citizens of the City of Melbourne v Commonwealth* (1947) 74 CLR 31 at 60, per Latham CJ

Australia 'The word "Discrimination" is defined in the Oxford English Dictionary as "The action of discriminating or distinguishing; a distinction (made with the mind or in action); the condition of being discriminated or distinguished" . . . in my opinion the ordinary usage of the word in the community generally, in the 1970s and 1980s, implies not merely difference or distinction, but "unequal treatment" and it carries a very strong pejorative flavour against the person practising it; discrimination, in this sense, is generally thought to be a wrongful activity.' *Comalco Ltd v Australian Broadcasting Corpn* [1985] 64 ACTR 1 at 30–31, per Blackburn CJ

Canada 'The Act [Human Rights Act, CCSM, c H 175] does not define discrimination but I did not understand from the arguments of counsel that any difference of opinion existed as to its meaning for the purposes of the human rights legislation. . . . However, I will indicate for the record that a definition associated with the United States human rights legislation, where the wording is very similar to the Manitoba law, seems more consistent with the terminology used in our law. That definition is simply: "To discriminate is to make a distinction, to make a difference in treatment or favour".' *Re Canada Safeway Ltd and Steel* (1984) 9 DLR (4th) 330 at 336, Man QB, per Wright J; affd 13 DLR (4th) 314, Man CA. (Leave to appeal to SCC dismissed, 11 February 1985)

DISEASE

'Disease' shall be construed as including a physical or mental condition arising from imperfect development of any organ. (Disabled Persons (Employment) Act 1944, s 1(2))

'Disease' includes any injury, ailment, or adverse condition, whether of body or mind. (Medicines Act 1968, s 132(1))

Notifiable disease

In this Act 'notifiable disease' means any of the following diseases: (a) cholrea; (b) plague; (c) relapsing fever; (d) smallpox; and (e) typhus. (Public Health (Control of Disease) Act 1984, s 10)

Of the mind

'In its broadest aspects these appeals raise the question what is meant by the phrase "a defect of reason from disease of the mind" within the meaning of the M'Naghten Rules [*M'Naghten's Case* (1843) 10 Cl & Fin 200] . . . In our judgment no help can be obtained by speculating (because that is what we would have to do) as to what the judges who answered the House of Lords' questions in 1843 meant by disease of the mind, still less what Sir Matthew Hale meant in the second half of the 17th century [Pleas of the Crown (1682)]. A quick backward look at the state of medicine in 1843 will suffice to show how unreal it would be to apply the concepts of that age to the present time. Dr Simpson had not yet started his experiments with chloroform, the future Lord Lister was only 16 and laudanum was used and prescribed like aspirins are today. Our task has been to decide what the law means now by the words "disease of the mind". In our judgment the fundamental concept is of a malfunctioning of the mind caused by disease. A malfunctioning of the mind of transitory effect caused by the application to the body of some external factor such as violence, drugs, including anaesthetics, alcohol and hypnotic influences cannot fairly be said to be due to disease. Such malfunctioning, unlike that caused by a defect of reason from disease of the mind, will not always relieve an accused from criminal responsibility. A self-induced incapacity will not excuse, nor will one which could have been reasonably foreseen as a result of either doing, or omitting to do something, as, for example, taking alcohol against medical advice after using certain prescribed drugs, or failing to have regular meals whilst taking insulin.' *R v Quick* [1973] 3 All ER 347 at 349, 356, CA, per cur.

Australia [The relevant parts of s 103(1) Lunacy 1898 (NSW) provided: 'Where . . . any person is, through mental infirmity, arising from disease . . . incapable of managing his affairs, the court may . . . appoint any person . . . to undertake the . . . management of his property . . .'] 'The word "disease" is not defined in the Act of 1898; nor in any subsequent relevant Ordinance of the Australian Capital Territory; nor in any other comparable Act of a State in Australia or of the United Kingdom. . . . A guide to the relevant meaning of disease in the context of the case before me is provided by the Shorter Oxford English Dictionary, which defines, so far as relevant, the word "disease" as "a condition of the body or of some part of organ of the body in which its functions are disturbed or deranged".' *Re M, Application for Appointment of Managers* (1982) 59 FLR 102 at 107–108, per Lockhart J

Canada [Insanity defence included requirement of existence of 'disease of the mind'.] 'Although the term "disease of the mind" is not capable of precise definition, certain propositions may, I think, be asserted with respect to it. "Disease of the mind" is a legal term, not a medical term of art; although a legal concept, it contains a substantial medical component as well as a legal or policy component.

The legal or policy component relates to (a) the scope of the exemption from criminal responsibility to be afforded by mental disorder or disturbance, and (b) the protection of the public by the control and treatment of persons who have caused serious harms while in a mentally disordered or disturbed state. The medical component of the term, generally, is medical opinion as to how the mental condition in question is viewed or characterised medically. Since the medical component of the term reflects or should reflect the state of medical knowledge at a given time, the concept of "disease of the mind" is capable of evolving with increased medical knowledge with respect to mental disorder or disturbance.' *R v Rabey* (1977) 79 DLR (3d) 414 at 425, Ont CA, per Martin JA; affd 114 DLR (3d) 193, SCC

Canada 'In summary, one might say that in a legal sense "disease of the mind" embraces any illness, disorder or abnormal condition which impairs the human mind and its functioning, excluding however, self-induced states caused by alcohol or drugs, as well as transitory mental states such as hysteria or concussion. In order to support a defence of insanity the disease must, of course, be of such intensity as to render the accused incapable of appreciating the nature and quality of the violent act or of knowing that it is wrong.' *Cooper v R* [1980] 1 SCR 1149 at 1159, SCC, per Dickson J

DISFRANCHISEMENT

Disfranchisement is the expulsion of a corporator from membership and involves the total deprivation of all privileges, rights, interests, profits, and advantages which the individual member enjoyed whilst a corporator. The power to disfranchise is incident to a corporation at large, but not to a select body within the corporation, even though the latter may have a right to elect corporators unless by virtue of the charter or by prescription such a power is expressly and clearly given.

At the present day the vacation of office by members of a statutory corporation is usually governed by the statute, or by an instrument made under the statute, or, if the corporation is created by royal charter, by the charter. (9 Halsbury's Laws (4th edn) para 1253)

'The word "disfranchisement" signifies taking a franchise from a man for some reasonable cause.' *Symmers v R* (1776) 2 Cowp 489 at 502, per Lord Mansfield CJ

DISGRACEFUL

'The Architects (Registration) Act 1931, s 7, gives the council power to strike the name of an architect from the register if he has been "guilty of conduct disgraceful to him in his capacity as an architect". I cannot accept the argument that the term "disgraceful" is in any sense a term of art. In accordance with the usual rule it is to be given its natural and popular meaning; but it is qualified by the phrase "in his capacity as an architect". The effect of that qualification is twofold. First, the conduct must not only be what would ordinarily be considered disgraceful, but it must also be a disgrace which affects him professionally: to that extent the qualification diminishes the term. Secondly, conduct which is not disgraceful for an ordinary man may be disgraceful for a professional man: to that extent the qualification amplifies the term. The amplification does not, however, require that "disgraceful" is to be given any technical meaning: it requires only that the ordinary meaning of the word should be applied in relation to the special obligations and duties of a professional man. It must not be forgotten that if the finding of the committee stands, anyone may hereafter say of the appellant with impunity that he was struck off the register for disgraceful conduct and may add that that means what it says.' *Hughes v Architects' Registration Council of the United Kingdom* [1957] 2 All ER 436 at 442, per Devlin J; also reported in [1957] 2 QB 550 at 560, 561

DISHONEST

(1) A person's appropriation of property belonging to another is not to be regarded as dishonest—
  (a) if he appropriates the property in the belief that he has in law the right to deprive the other of it, on behalf of himself or of a third person; or
  (b) if he appropriates the property in the belief that he would have the other's consent if the other knew of the appropriation and the circumstances of it; or
  (c) (except where the property came to him as trustee of personal representative) if he appropriates the property in the belief that the person to whom the property belongs cannot be discovered by taking reasonable steps.
(2) A person's appropriation of property belonging to another may be dishonest notwithstanding that he is willing to pay for the property.
(Theft Act 1968, s 2)
[The above section immediately follows the definition of 'theft' in s 1 of the Act of 1968. A person is guilty of theft if he 'dishonestly' appropriates property belonging to another with the intention of permanently depriving the other of it.]

'In determining whether the prosecution has proved that the defendant was acting dishonestly, a jury must first of all decide whether according to the ordinary standards of reasonable and honest people what was done was dishonest. If it was not dishonest by those standards, that is the end of the matter and the prosecution fails. If it was dishonest by those standards, then the jury must consider whether the defendant himself must have realised that what he was doing was by those standards dishonest. In most cases, where the actions are obviously dishonest by ordinary standards, there will be no doubt about it. It will be obvious that the defendant himself knew that he was acting dishonestly. It is dishonest for a defendant to act in a way which he knows ordinary people consider to be dishonest, even if he asserts or genuinely believes that he is morally justified in acting as he did.' *R v Ghosh* [1982] 2 All ER 689 at 696, CA, per cur.

Australia 'In its ordinary meaning the primary meaning of the word "dishonestly" (despite the Latin origin of the word "honest") is not, I consider, "dishonourably". The latter word is, I consider, directed more to the community's assessment of a man's lack of or failure in respect of moral integrity or probity and in other cases to the individual's assessment of that lack or failure. The judgment of the individual in this sense may often be astray or at variance with that of the community's assessment of honesty and dishonesty, as is plainly exemplified by the case of *R v Gilks* [1972] 1 WLR 1341. The words "honesty" and "dishonesty" as used in ordinary parlance connote respectively compliance with or disregard of the dictates of the moral virtue of justice which acknowledges and gives effect to the rights of others to or in respect of material things, or of the relationship of one person to another, e.g. husband and wife, parent and child, master and pupil, vendor and purchaser, employer and employee, etc. The terms may in certain contexts connote respect for or disregard of the moral virtue of truth. The word "dishonestly" implies reference to a standard of morality underlying the law. The law sets standards of legality and illegality but cannot set and never has purported to set standards of morality. Standards of morality underlie the law: they derive not from the law but from the standard of ethics accepted by the community.' *R v Salvo* [1980] VR 401 at 407, per cur.

Canada [A fidelity bond referred to loss through any 'dishonest', fraudulent or criminal act of any of the employees.] '"Dishonest" is a word of such common use that I should not have thought that it could give rise to any serious difficulty, but in construing even plain words regard must be had to the context and circumstances in which they are used: *Canadian Indemnity Co v Andrews & George Co Ltd* [[1953] 1 SCR 19 at 24]. However, to try to put a gloss on an old and familiar English word which is in everyday use is often likely to complicate rather than to clarify. "Dishonest" is normally used to describe an act where there has been some intent to deceive or cheat. To use it to describe acts which are merely reckless, disobedient or foolish is not in accordance with popular usage or the dictionary meaning. It is such a familiar word that there should be no difficulty in understanding it. In the present case there is nothing in either circumstances or the context requiring the court to give it a meaning other than its popular sense.' *Lynch & Co v United States Fidelity & Guaranty Co* [1971] 1 OR 28 at 37, 38, Ont SC, per Fraser J

DISHONOUR

Commercial paper

United States   An instrument is dishonored when
(a) a necessary or optional presentment is duly made and due acceptance or payment is refused or cannot be obtained within the prescribed time or in case of bank collections the instrument is seasonably returned by the midnight deadline (Section 4–301); or
(b) presentment is excused and the instrument is not duly accepted or paid.
(Uniform Commercial Code 1978, 3–507(1))

DISINTERESTED PERSON

Bankruptcy

United States   '[D]isinterested person' means a person that—
(A) is not a creditor, an equity security holder, or an insider;
(B) is not and was not an investment banker for any outstanding security of the debtor;
(C) has not been, within three years before the date of the filing of the [bankruptcy] petition, an investment banker for a security of the debtor, or an attorney for such an investment banker in connection with the offer, sale, or issuance of a security of the debtor;
(D) is not and was not, within two years before the date of the filing of the petition, a director, officer, or employee of the debtor or of an investment banker specified in subparagraph (B) and (C) of this paragraph; and
(E) does not have an interest materially adverse to the interest of the estate or of any class of creditors or equity security holders, by reason of any direct or indirect relationship to, connection with, or interest in, the debtor or an investment banker specified in subparagraph (B) or (C) of this paragraph, or for any other reason. . . .
(Bankruptcy Act 1978, s 101(13))

DISMISS—DISMISSAL

(1) In this Part [Part V: Unfair dismissal], except as respects a case to which section 56 applies, 'dismissal' and 'dismiss' shall be construed in accordance with the following provisions of this section.

(2) Subject to sub-section (3), an employee shall be treated as dismissed by his employer if, but only if,—
(a) the contract under which he is employed by the employer is terminated by the employer, whether it is so terminated by notice or without notice, or
(b) where under that contract he is employed for a fixed term, that term expires without being renewed under the same contract, or
(c) the employee terminates that contract, with or without notice, in circumstances such that he is entitled to terminate it without notice by reason of the employer's conduct.
(3) Where an employer gives notice to an employee to terminate his contract of employment and, at a time within the period of that notice, the employee gives notice to the employer to terminate the contract of employment on a date earlier than the date on which the employer's notice is due to expire, the employee shall for the purposes of this Part be taken to be dismissed by his employer, and the reasons for the dismissal shall be taken to be the reasons for which the employer's notice is given.
(Employment Protection (Consolidation) Act 1978, s 55)
[Section 56 of the Act provides that failure to permit a woman to return to work after confinement is to be treated as dismissal.

For general provisions for determining whether any dismissal was fair or unfair, see ibid, s 57. See also ss 6, 8, 9 of the Employment Act 1980, and ss 2–9 of the Employment Act 1982.]

'"Dismissal" is a word of very ambiguous meaning. You can dismiss a servant, but I am unable to hold that you cannot dismiss a contractor. "Dismissal" is merely a convenient expression for the determination of an employment whatever its nature may be, and does not necessarily import the relationship of master and servant.' *Graham v Minister for Industry & Commerce & Molloy* [1933] IR 156 at 164, per Fitzgibbon J

New Zealand   [Section 6 of the Tramways Amendment Act 1910, makes provision (inter alia) for the hearing and determination of appeals by tramways employees against 'dismissals', etc.] 'The word "dismissal" may be used in the sense of either a peremptory or arbitrary dismissal or a dismissal after due notice or payment under the terms of the contract of employment.' *Auckland Transport Board v Nunes* [1952] NZLR 412 at 415, per Fair J; also reported [1952] GLR 259 at 260, *sub nom. Auckland Transport Board v Sinclair*

New Zealand 'Section 117 of the Industrial Relations Act uses several times the expressions "unjustifiable dismissal" or "unjustifiably dismissed". The concept is not a simple one. It is not in everyday use in the English language. Its permissible scope in the context of the Act is a question of interpretation and so of law. . . . Very broadly a dismissal may be said to be unjustifiable if it is unreasonable or procedurally unfair. . . . Obviously there is a dismissal when an employer in fact "dismisses" a worker in the ordinary meaning of the word. But the Arbitration Court has held in a line of cases that the concept is wider and includes constructive dismissal. In our opinion that is the correct approach. In the context of an Act aimed at good industrial relations it is right to assume that Parliament would have meant "dismissal" to cover cases where in substance the employer has dismissed a worker although technically there has been a resignation.' *Auckland Employees Union v Woolworths (NZ) Ltd* [1985] 2 NZLR 372 at 374, CA, per Cooke J

See, generally, 16 Halsbury's Laws (4th edn) para 616.

DISORDER   *See* MENTAL DISORDER; PSYCHOPATHIC DISORDER

DISORDERLY CONDUCT   *See also* IDLE AND DISORDERLY

'I agree that a person may be guilty of disorderly conduct which does not reach the stage that it is calculated to provoke a breach of the peace, but I am of opinion that not only must the behaviour seriously offend against those values of orderly conduct which are recognised by right-thinking members of the public but it must at least be of a character which is likely to cause annoyance to others who are present. I think that Henry J meant to be so understood.' *Melser v Police* [1967] NZLR 437 at 443, CA, per North P

'Disorderly conduct is conduct which is disorderly; it is conduct which, while sufficiently ill-mannered, or in bad taste, to meet with the disapproval of well-conducted and reasonable

men and women, is also something more—it must, in my opinion, tend to annoy or insult such persons as are faced with it—and sufficiently deeply or seriously to warrant the interference of the criminal law.' Ibid at 444, per Turner J

'I agree that an offence against good manners, a failure of good taste, a breach of morality, even though these may be contrary to the general order of public opinion, is not enough to establish this offence. There must be conduct which not only can fairly be characterised as disorderly, but also is likely to cause a disturbance or to annoy others considerably.' Ibid at 446, per McCarthy J

DISORDERLY HOUSE   *See also* BROTHEL

A person commits an indictable offence at common law who keeps a common, ill-governed and disorderly house. A house found to be kept open to, and frequented by, persons who conduct themselves in such a manner as to violate law and good order is a disorderly house. Where, however, the essence of the charge is the taking place of indecent performances or exhibitions, the fact that persons resorting to the premises are merely spectators does not prevent the premises constituting a disorderly house; nor need disorderly conduct be visible from the exterior of the house. A disorderly house may amount to a common nuisance, but this is not an essential ingredient of the offence. Where indecent performances or exhibitions are alleged as rendering premises a disorderly house, it must be shown that the matters performed or exhibited there are of such a character that their performance or exhibition in a place of common resort would (1) amount to an outrage of public decency, or (2) tend to corrupt or deprave, or (3) be otherwise calculated to injure the public interest so as to call for condemnation and punishment. (11 Halsbury's Laws (4th edn) para 1057)

'The prisoner, being the owner of a house, let it in different apartments to young women of immoral habits; but he did not live in the house, and had no control over the inmates. There was no doubt that the persons to whom the apartments were severally let, used them for the purposes of prostitution. The prisoner was indicted for keeping a disorderly house. We are of opinion that the house was not kept by him. He had no power to admit or refuse admission to anybody.' *R v Stannard* (1863) 33 LJMC 61 at 63, CCR, per Pollock CB

'It is admitted that the applicant is a man of good character, and the objection taken (inter alia) to the renewal of his licence is that the house in respect of which the licence is sought is of a disorderly character. Evidence was given of three convictions . . . against previous occupiers . . . which shew that in the judgment of the justices the house had the character of being a disorderly house. . . . A house of a disorderly character is a parliamentary phrase; the disorderly character of the house is distinguished from the disorderly character of the applicant. . . . It is plain to me that the house, apart from the person, may be of a disorderly character, and therefore this was a perfectly legal objection to take.' *R v Miskin Higher JJ* [1893] 1 QB 275 at 278, DC, per Lord Coleridge CJ

'In reliance partly on the decision in *Shaw v Director of Public Prosecutions* [[1961] 2 All ER 466] counsel for the Crown submitted a proposition which deserves to be recorded, particularly as both counsel for Quinn and counsel for Bloom were content to accept it as a correct statement of principle: "A disorderly house is a house conducted contrary to law and good order in that matters are performed or exhibited of such a character that their performance or exhibition in a place of common resort (a) amounts to an outrage of public decency or (b) tends to corrupt or deprave or (c) is otherwise calculated to injure the public interest so as to call for condemnation and punishment." Subject to two comments, we are of opinion that this statement of principle is correct in law. In the first place in the two appeals now before us the whole essence of the charge against the appellants was that indecent performances had taken place, and it was in relation to such a disorderly house that counsel for the Crown's statement of principle was put forward. A charge of keeping a disorderly house may be preferred on some ground other than indecent performances and, in our opinion, the statement of principle must be regarded as limited to cases in which indecent performances or exhibitions are alleged. Secondly, the statement contains three phrases expressed as alternatives which, for convenience, we have lettered (a), (b) and (c). In our view, these phrases should not be regarded as mutually exclusive; on the contrary, a case may well fall within all three.' *R v Quinn, R v Bloom* [1961] 3 All ER 88 at 91, 92, CCA, per cur.

'Many forms of conduct may fall within the scope of the offence [of keeping a disorderly house], and to attempt to establish a universal definition with precision is both undesirable and impossible. It is, however, both desirable and possible to indicate how a jury should be directed, where the ground on which the charge is based is that the premises are being used for the provision of sexual services. In such cases, the direction, adapting the definition in *R v Quinn, R v Bloom* [supra], would in our judgment be that, in order to convict, the jury must be satisfied that the services provided are open to those members of the public who wish to partake of them and are of such a character and are conducted in such a manner (whether by advertisement or otherwise) that their provision amounts to an outrage of public decency or is otherwise calculated to injure the public interest to such an extent as to call for condemnation and punishment. They should further be directed that the fact, if it be a fact, that the services are provided by a single prostitute to one client at a time and without spectators does not prevent the house being a disorderly house.' *R v Tan* [1983] 2 All ER 12 at 18, CA, per cur.

Canada 'The term "disorderly house" has acquired in criminal jurisprudence a definite legal meaning and it includes any house to which persons resort for criminal or immoral purposes and it is immaterial that the house is conducted quietly so as not to disturb the neighbours.' *R v Four Chinamen* (1907) 13 BCR 216 at 217, per Hunter CJ

DISORDERLY PERSON *See also* IDLE AND DISORDERLY; VAGRANT

Australia [Section 73(1) of the Police Offences Act 1953 (SA) (repealed; see now Summary Offences Act (SA) 1953–1986, s 73(1)) provides that any member of the police force may, whenever he thinks proper, enter into any place of public entertainment and order any common prostitute or reputed thief or 'disorderly person' who is in that place of public entertainment to leave it.] 'It is s 73(1)(b) in which the words "disorderly person" appear and it is to be noted that they appear in juxtaposition to the words "common prostitute" and "reputed thief". A member of either of those two categories of persons is quite clearly a person who bears a character or disposition which pre-dates her or his presence in the place of public entertainment. Thus a police officer may enter a place of public entertainment and if he sees a person there who bears the known character of being a "common prostitute" or "reputed thief" that person may be ordered to leave the premises irrespective of how she or he may be behaving at the particular time. That is to say that such a person need not be engaged in either soliciting for the purposes of prostitution or stealing, before the powers given to that police officer by s 73 may be invoked. It is enough if they bear the required character. Indeed, unless a person found soliciting for the purposes of prostitution or stealing in a place of public entertainment already bears the character of a "common prostitute" or "reputed thief" s 73 would not give a police officer the power to order them to leave. In either case there are adequate powers to enable the police to deal with such persons by arrest. Thus s 73 can be seen as clothing a police officer with power to prevent undesirable persons from frequenting places of public entertainment before they are actually detected in their undesirable activities. In my opinion, a similar interpretation should be given to the words "disorderly person". An analogy can be drawn between "disorderly person" in the Police Offences Act and "idle and disorderly person" in the Vagrant Act of 1824 in England. Speaking of the latter Act Cave J in *Pointin v Hill* [(1884) 12 QBD 306] said: "The statute was directed against a particular habit and mode of life." That is to say that unless the person is known to have the character of behaving in a disorderly manner either generally or in a given set of circumstances then s 73 cannot be used to order his removal. There may thus be a person who is known to interrupt, in a disorderly fashion, public entertainment of a particular sort, and being so known he could be ordered to leave such an entertainment, but not another.' *Brander v Lovegrove* (1981) 28 SASR 591 at 593, per Mohr J

DISPLAY

Copyrights

United States To 'display' a work means to show a copy of it, either directly or by means of a film, slide, television image, or any other device or process or, in the case of a motion picture or other audiovisual work, to show individual images nonsequentially. (Copyright Act of 1976, s 101)

DISPOSE—DISPOSAL

'Disposal', in relation to a dead body, means disposal by burial, cremation or any other means, and cognate expressions shall be construed accordingly. (Births and Deaths Registration Act 1953, s 41)

The expression 'dispose' means sell, give in exchange, pledge or otherwise hand over (whether apart from this section the handing over is lawful or not). (Army Act 1955, s 195(5); Air Force Act 1955, s 195(5); Naval Discipline Act 1957, s 98(3))

'Disposal', in relation to waste, includes the removal, deposit or destruction thereof, the discharge thereof, whether into water or into the air or into a sewer or drain or otherwise, or the burial thereof, whether underground or otherwise, and 'dispose of' shall be construed accordingly. (Radioactive Substances Act 1960, s 19(1))

'Disposal' means disposal by way of sale, exchange or lease, or by way of the creation of any easement, right or privilege, or in any other manner, except by way of appropriation, gift or mortgage, and 'dispose of' shall be construed accordingly. (Town and Country Planning Act 1971, s 290(1))

Australia [Section 59 of the Income Tax Assessment Act 1936–1986 (Cth), provides (inter alia) that where any property of a taxpayer, in respect of which depreciation has been allowed or is allowable under the Act, is 'disposed' of, lost or destroyed at any time in the year of income, the depreciated value of the property at that time, less the amount of any consideration receivable in respect of the disposal, loss or destruction, shall be an allowable deduction.] 'No doubt the notion primarily conveyed by the words "disposed of" is the notion of a disposition by the taxpayer; but it is not necessarily so confined, and the use of the passive voice, without specific words of restriction referring to the person by whose act the disposal takes place, leaves ample room for a construction in keeping with the general tenour of the section, and with its place in the scheme which ss 54 and 62 provide. The entire expression "disposed of, lost or destroyed" is apt to embrace every event by which property ceases to be available to the taxpayer for use for the purpose of producing assessable income, either because it ceases to be his, or because it ceases to be physically accessible to him, or because it ceases to exist. . . . The words "is disposed of" are wide enough to cover all forms of alienation, . . . and they should be understood as meaning no less than "becomes alienated from the taxpayer", whether it is by him or by another that the act of alienation is done.' *Henty House Pty Ltd (in voluntary liquidation) v Federal Comr of Taxation* (1953) 88 CLR 141 at 151, 152, per cur.

Australia [Section 7(1)(j) of the Probate Duty Act 1962–1986 (Vic) provides that any property of which, immediately prior to death, a deceased person was competent to 'dispose', otherwise than in a purely fiduciary capacity, shall be deemed to form part of that deceased's estate.] 'Many authorities have recognised that the word "dispose" has a very wide meaning and in its context in s 7(1)(j) of the Probate Duty Act 1962 (Vic), as amended, it includes any mode by which the property could, as a result of an act of the deceased, pass immediately before her death.' *Equity Trustees v Probate Comr* (1976) 10 ALR 131 at 133, per Gibbs J

Canada [A requirement in s 15(2), para 17, of the Business Corporations Act RSO 1970, applies where directors propose to sell, lease, exchange or otherwise 'dispose' of all or substantially all of the property of a corporation.] 'The word "dispose" has been defined by Logie J in *MacPherson v London Loan Assets Ltd & Royal Bank of Canada* [[1931] OR 109 at 115] where the learned judge said: "'Dispose' in the sense in which it is used, is defined in the Century Dictionary as follows: 'To make over, or part with as by gift, sale or other means of alienation, alienate or bestow'." Applying this definition to s 15(2), para 17, I conclude that the word dispose in that paragraph refers to an alienation of the property of the corporation. I would conclude that a pledge is not an alienation in that a pledge is delivery of property to a creditor as security for a debt. The pledgee is entitled to hold the property until payment or performance and may sell it upon failure of payment or performance, but until that time it may be redeemed by the pledgor. The pledgee has a special property in the goods pledged until the debt is paid off, but his right to the property vests only in so far as it is necessary to secure the debt.' *North Rock Explorations Ltd v Zahavy Mines Ltd* [1974] 3 OR (2d) 163 at 166, Ont SC, per Holland J

Canada [Section 2(1) of the Dependants' Relief Act, RSS 1978, c D-25, defines 'estate' as all the property of which a testator or an intestate has power to 'dispose' by will, otherwise than by virtue of a special power of appointment, less the amount of the usual debts, duties, etc.] 'In my opinion, the word "dispose" was intended to be given a strict or limited interpretation because it was followed by the exception "otherwise than by virtue of a special power of appointment". The right to change the designation of a beneficiary of life insurance (with statutory limitations) was not unlike such a power of appointment. When therefore the definition speaks of "dispose" that word should not be enlarged in meaning to include property already fully disposed of and in which was retained only a certain statutory power to retract that disposition and appoint another.' *Re Farrar, Farrar v Scammell* (1982) 11 ETR 316 at 319, Sask QB, per Rutherford J

DISPOSITION

'Disposition' and 'conveyance' include a mortgage, charge by way of legal mortgage, lease, assent, vesting declaration, vesting instrument, disclaimer, release and every other assurance except a will, and 'dispose of' or 'convey' has a corresponding meaning. (Universities and Colleges Estates Act 1925, s 43)

'Disposition' includes the grant of a tenancy, the renewal, extension or any other variation of a tenancy, and any other conveyance, assignment, transfer, grant, variation or extinguishment of an interest in or right over land, whether made by an instrument or otherwise. (Land Commission Act 1967, s 99)

'If the word "disposition" [in s 53 of the Law of Property Act 1925] is given its natural meaning, it cannot, I think, be denied that a direction given by Mr Hunter [a settlor] whereby the beneficial interest in the shares theretofore vested in him became vested in another or others is a disposition. But it is contended by the appellants that the word "disposition" is to be given a narrower meaning and (so far as relates to inter vivos transactions) is to be read as if it were synonymous with "grants and assignments" and that, given this meaning, it does not cover such a direction as was given in this case. . . . I am clearly of the opinion . . . that there is no justification for giving the word "disposition" a narrower meaning than it ordinarily bears.' *Grey v Inland Revenue Comrs* [1949] 3 All ER 603 at 605, HL, per Viscount Simonds

[Though the Law of Property Act 1925 was a consolidating Act, the consolidation included property legislation of 1922 and 1924 by which the law of real and personal property was profoundly changed, and accordingly the principle of construction that a consolidating Act is not intended to alter the law does not apply as between the Law of Property Act 1925 and enactments amended by the legislation of 1922 or 1924; in the particular instance of s 53 of the Law of Property Act 1925 (which reproduced provisions of the Statute of Frauds as incorporated with alterations by para 15 of Part 2 of Sch 3 to the Law of Property (Amendment) Act 1924) the word 'disposition' in sub-s (1)(c) of s 53 bears its natural meaning and is not limited to the same meaning as may have been attributed to the words 'grant' or 'assignment' in s 9 of the Statute of Frauds.]

'The word "disposition", taken by itself, and using it in its most extended meaning, is no doubt wide enough to include the act of extinguishment. To talk of disposing of one's enemy, no doubt, indicates his extinguishment; but the primary meaning of the word, at any rate in relation to property, is to deal with the property in one of a number of ways, the property remaining in existence.' *Re Leven (Earl) (decd), Inland Revenue Comrs v Williams Deacon's Bank Ltd* [1954] 3 All ER 81 at 85, per Wynn-Parry J

'Section 21(9)(b) of the Finance Act 1936 [repealed; see now the Income and Corporation Taxes Act 1988, s 670] provided that the expression "settlement" included any "disposition, trust, covenant, agreement, arrangement or transfer of assets", and counsel for the taxpayer has argued strenuously that a surrender is not a disposition. I should have great difficulty in holding that; I think that a surrender clearly is a disposition. A person can dispose of his interest in a fund or in a chattel or in anything else in a variety of ways, but, if, having an interest in a fund, although the interest may not then be in possession, he surrenders that interest, it seems to me that he disposes of it.' *Inland Revenue Comrs v Buchanan* [1957] 2 All ER 400 at 402, CA, per Lord Goddard CJ; also reported in [1958] Ch 289 at 296

Australia 'There is no doubt that when a loan of money is made by one person to another the property in the money lent passes, upon the loan being made, from the lender to the borrower. There is, upon payment to the borrower, a disposition of the money lent notwithstanding the fact that the borrower may have undertaken to *repay* the amount of the loan and I can see no reason why the wide words of the

definition of "disposition of property" [In s 4 of Gift Duty Assessment Act 1941–1986 (Cth); see now s 4(1)]—"any conveyance, transfer, assignment, settlement, delivery, payment, or other alienation of property"—does not fairly comprehend a payment by a lender to a borrower of a sum of money agreed to be lent by the former to the latter.' *McGain v Commissioner of Taxation* (1965) 112 CLR 523 at 528, per Taylor J

Australia 'A delivery to an auctioneer for the purpose of sale, on behalf of the person delivering, is not a disposition within the ordinary meaning of that word. In a legal context, disposition means the act of disponing or disposing of (see Shorter Oxford English Dictionary). Disposing of, in this sense, means dealing with definitely or a getting rid of or a getting done with a particular item (ibid). It usually refers in this particular meaning to a making over of an item by way of sale or bargain because then there is a definite dealing with the item and a getting rid of it, a finishing with it (ibid).' *Roache v Australian Mercantile Land & Finance Co Ltd (No 2)* [1966] 1 NSWR 384 at 386, per Jacobs JA

New Zealand 'Section 10 [of the Unclassified Societies Registration Act 1895 (repealed; see now s 6(i), (k) of the Incorporated Societies Act 1908)] provides that any society incorporated under the Act may make rules providing for, inter alia, "the control, investment, and disposition of the funds and property of the society." . . . The word "disposition", in my opinion, includes a mortgage. A sale is a larger power of disposition than a mortgage, and I cannot see why, if a sale is permitted, what is sometimes called a conditional sale—that is, a mortgage—see *Ball v Harris* [(1839) 4 My & Cr 264 at 267, 268]—should be prohibited.' *Forsythe v Wellington Central Mission* (1904) 24 NZLR 780 at 780, 781, per Stout CJ; also reported 7 GLR 251

New Zealand '"Disposition" is a very comprehensive term and in my opinion is wide enough to cover the withdrawal of moneys from a savings account.' *Thompson v Thompson* [1968] NZLR 504 at 508, per Wilson J

Of body   *See* SECRET DISPOSITION

Specific disposition

'Specific disposition' [in Part XVI of the Act (administration of estates)] means a specific devise or bequest made by a testator, and includes the disposition of personal chattels made by s 46 of the Administration of Estates Act 1925, and any disposition having, whether by virtue of any enactment or otherwise, under the law of another country an effect similar to that of a specific devise or bequest under the law of England and Wales.

Real estate included (either by a specific or general description) in a residuary gift made by the will of a testator shall be deemed to be a part of the residue of his estate and not to be the subject of a specific disposition. (Income and Corporation Taxes Act 1988, s 701(5))

DISPUTE   *See also* TRADE DISPUTE

[A berth note provided that in case of any 'dispute' arising at loading ports it should be submitted to a local arbitration court.] 'The question is, what is the meaning of clause 10 in this berth note or berth contract? On one side it is said that . . . "dispute" means "contention", and that therefore it arises where the contention is made. On the other hand it is said that "dispute" means the matter or question in dispute. If the latter be the right meaning, then the matter in dispute arose at the port of loading. Now I put to myself two questions, and the answers, in my view, determine the construction to be placed on clause 10. The first is, what is in dispute? It is this—and therefore the dispute is this—"what are the proper charges for stevedoring at Marioupol?" If that be the dispute, where does it arise? It arises, in my opinion, where the stevedoring work is done and where the charges which are in dispute are made. If that be so, clause 10 applies in this case, and there must be arbitration. Putting it in one word, in my view "dispute" in clause 10 means, not disputation, but matter in dispute.' *The Dawlish* [1910] P 339 at 342 per Evans P

DISQUALIFIED

'Section 34 [of the Licensing (Consolidation) Act 1910 (repealed; see now Licensing Act 1964, ss 3, 9)] provides that "a justices' licence shall not be granted, whether as a new licence or by way of renewal or transfer, to any person who is a disqualified person . . . and a justices' licence shall not be granted in respect of or removed to any premises which by virtue of this Act are disqualified premises during the continuance of the disqualification, and a justices' licence held by a person so disqualified or attached to premises so disqualified shall be

void". . . . Premises which fail to fulfil the requirement of the Act as to value are just as much "disqualified premises" as premises in respect of which there has been a conviction or order of a court rendering them disqualified from receiving a licence. Both are disqualified premises within the meaning of the Act.' *R v Kingston-upon-Hull Licensing JJ* [1913] 2 KB 425 at 430, 431, DC, per Ridley J

See, generally, 26 Halsbury's Laws (4th edn) paras 104 et seq.

[A certificate of motor insurance contained a proviso that the driver must hold a licence to drive and not be 'disqualified' for holding or obtaining such a licence.] 'The justices held that the words in the certificate of insurance "not disqualified for holding or obtaining such a licence" meant a disqualification by order of the court under s 4(6) [of the Road Traffic Act 1930 (repealed; see now the Road Traffic Act 1972, s 177, Sch 4 (as amended) and the Road Traffic Regulation Act 1984, s 98, Sch 7)]. In my opinion, they were right.' *Edwards v Griffiths* [1953] 2 All ER 874 at 876, per Lord Goddard CJ

See, generally, 40 Halsbury's Laws (4th edn) paras 515 et seq.

DISSOLUTION

'In my view the word "dissolution" relates to the marriage bond itself, whereas the word "divorce" relates to the parties to the marriage bond; and it is apt to refer to "divorce" when speaking of parties and "dissolution" when speaking of the bond.' *Deacock v Deacock*, [1958] 2 All ER 633 at 635, CA, per Hodson LJ; also reported [1958] P 230 at 233

Australia 'The "dissolution" of an unincorporated body appears to me to present no legal difficulty whatever. It is merely a legislative direction that the body shall not be allowed to continue to exist. The body is not a legal *persona*, and the "dissolution" can be made effective only by some other provisions dealing with the conduct of the natural persons who constitute the association.' *Adelaide Company of Jehovah's Witnesses Inc v Commonwealth* (1943) 67 CLR 116 at 138, per Latham CJ

Canada 'Does a decree nisi dissolve a marriage? I think not. A reading of ss 13, 16 and 17 of the Divorce Act, RSC 1970, c D–8, makes it clear that the marriage relationship is not finally determined until a decree absolute is granted. The words "dissolution of marriage" [in a limitation section] imply the termination of the existence of the relationship. How can the marriage relationship be said to have been terminated by the decree nisi when that order may be set aside on appeal, or may be rescinded or varied by reason of its having been obtained by collusion, by reason of the reconciliation of the parties or by reason of other material facts? The parties may marry again once the decree has been made absolute (s 16), and the Court of Appeal has no power to extend the time for appeal once the decree has been made absolute. The effect of these provisions is to dissolve the marriage tie upon the granting of a decree absolute.' *Re Pearce* [1974] 52 DLR (3d) 544 at 547, BCSC, per Macfarlane J

Partnership

United States The dissolution of a partnership is the change in the relation of the partners caused by any partner ceasing to be associated in the carrying on as distinguished from the winding up of the business. (Uniform Partnership Act 1914, s 29)

DISTANCE

Measurement of *See* MILE

In the measurement of any distance for the purposes of any Act, that distance shall, unless the contrary intention appears, be measured in a straight line on a horizontal plane. (Interpretation Act 1978, s 8)

DISTILLER—DISTILLERY

[Statute (1825) 6 Geo 4, c 80 (repealed), s 6 declared it unlawful for any person to have or keep any still whatever for the purpose of distilling . . . spirits without having first obtained a licence.] 'A chemist is a distiller if he chooses to manufacture his own spirits of wine, instead of buying them. If a man keeps a still for the purpose of manufacturing spirits, whether he afterwards uses them to drink, or to make other mixtures or preparations, he uses the still for making and distilling spirits, and comes within the penalties of the Act.' *A-G v Bailey* (1846) 16 M & W 74 at 76, per Parke B (arguendo)

'Distillery' means premises where spirits are manufactured, whether by distillation of a fermented liquor or by any other process. (Alcoholic Liquor Duties Act 1979, s 4(1))

DISTINCTIVE

'Distinctive' means adapted, in relation to the goods in respect of which a trade mark is registered or proposed to be registered, to distinguish goods with which the proprietor of the trade mark is or may be connected in the course of trade from goods in the case of which no such connection subsists, either generally or, where the trade mark is registered or proposed to be registered subject to limitations, in relation to use within the extent of the registration. Further, in determining whether a mark is adapted to distinguish, the tribunal may have regard to the extent to which (1) the mark is inherently adapted to distinguish, and (2) by reason of the use of the trade mark or of any other circumstances, the trade mark is in fact adapted to distinguish. Frequently, the exercise of judgment as to whether a mark is 'distinctive' within the meaning of these provisions is referred to as an exercise of discretion. (48 Halsbury's Laws (4th edn) para 34)

For the purposes of this section 'distinctive' means adapted, in relation to the goods in respect of which a trade mark is registered or proposed to be registered, to distinguish goods with which the proprietor of the trade mark is or may be connected in the course of trade from goods in the case of which no such connection subsists, either generally or, where the trade mark is registered or proposed to be registered subject to limitations, in relation to use within the extent of the registration. (Trade Marks Act 1938, s 9(2))

'The only question which I desire to discuss is whether this device is a distinctive device or label within 38 & 39 Vict c 91 [Trade Marks Registration Act 1875 (repealed), which enacted that a trade mark should consist of (inter alia) a 'distinctive device or label'; see now Trade Marks Act 1938, s 9 (supra)]; and it appears to me that this device cannot be registered under that Act as it is but the simple description of an article which every one in the trade may sell. A description may be in words or by a picture . . . and as this device is merely the description of a common article which everybody may sell I am of opinion that the objection is valid and that this appeal must fail.' *Re Anderson's Trade Mark* (1885) 54 LJ Ch 1084 at 1085, CA, per Bowen LJ

[The Trade Marks Registration Act 1875, s 10 (repealed), enacted that a trade mark should consist of (inter alia) a 'distinctive' mark; see now Trade Marks Act 1938, s 9 (supra).] 'The meaning of the word "distinctive" I understand to be this, that it must be a mark or device of such a kind that in case of infringement it shall be clear what it is that is being infringed, and that the mark is something different from all other marks used in the same class of goods.' *Re James's Trade Mark, James v Soulby* (1886) 33 Ch D 392 at 396, CA, per Lopes LJ

'By "distinctive device" it is meant that the device must be something which shall be capable of distinguishing the particular goods in relation to which it is to be used from other goods of a like character belonging to other people. In that view it is difficult to conceive that anything could well be more distinctive than the portrait of the man who professes to manufacture the particular article.' *Rowland v Mitchell, Re Rowland's Trade Mark* [1897] 1 Ch 71 at 74, CA, per Lord Russell of Killowen CJ

'Much of the argument before us . . . was based on an assumption that there is a natural and innate antagonism between distinctive and descriptive as applied to words, and that if you can show that a word is descriptive you have proved that it cannot be distinctive. To my mind this is a fallacy. Descriptive names may be distinctive and vice versa.' *Re Crosfield (Joseph) & Sons Ltd, Re California Fig Syrup Co, Re Brock (HN) & Co Ltd* [1910] 1 Ch 130 at 145–147, CA, per Fletcher Moulton LJ

'"Distinctive" [in the Trade Marks Act 1905 (repealed; see now s 9 of the Trade Marks Act 1938 (supra))] is defined as meaning "adapted to distinguish the goods of the applicant for registration from the goods of other persons". The definition is found for the first time in the Act of 1905, but the word "distinctive" was, I think, used in all the earlier Acts in the sense of "adapted to distinguish". . . . In my opinion, in order to determine whether a mark is distinctive it must be considered quite apart from the effects of registration. The question, therefore, is whether the mark itself, if used as a trade mark, is likely to become actually distinctive of the goods of the person so using it. The applicant for registration in effect says, "I intend to use this mark as a trade mark, i.e., for the purpose of distinguishing my goods from the goods of other persons" and the Registrar . . . has to determine . . . whether it is of such a kind that the applicant quite apart from the effects of registration is likely or unlikely to attain the object he has in view.' *Registrar of Trade Marks v Du Cros (W & G)*

Ltd [1913] AC 624 at 634, per Lord Parker of Waddington

[The Trade Marks Act 1905, s 9 (repealed), enabled a trade mark to be registered if it was a 'distinctive' mark; see now Trade Marks Act 1938, s 9 (supra).] 'I have . . . to ascertain whether this name ['Cadbury', under which the chocolate, cocoa and confectionery of Cadbury Brothers Ltd was sold] . . . is distinctive in the sense of being "adapted to distinguish the goods of the proprietor of a trade mark from those of other persons". In determining that question I am entitled to "take into consideration the extent to which . . . user has rendered such trade mark in fact distinctive of the goods in respect of which it is registered or proposed to be registered", and I have at all events the dicta of the Judges of the Court of Appeal to show that that means user as a trade mark. . . . What is meant by "distinctive" except that when you see the name your mind immediately refers to the person or firm or company who sold or manufactured the article, and to that one person or firm or company alone.' *Re Cadbury Brothers Ltd's Application* [1915] 1 Ch 331 at 339, per Neville J

DISTRESS *See also* ABANDONMENT; LEVY

The term 'distress' primarily connotes a summary remedy by which a person is entitled without legal process to take into his possession the personal chattels of another person, to be held as a pledge to compel the performance of a duty, or the satisfaction of a debt or demand. By almost universal sanction the term 'distress' is now used to designate both the process of taking, and the chattels taken, though originally it applied only to the taking. (13 Halsbury's Laws (4th edn) para 201)

'It is very rarely that we have a case about distress for rent. It is an archaic remedy which has largely fallen into disuse.' *Abingdon Rural District Council v O'Gorman* [1968] 3 All ER 79 at 82, CA, per Lord Denning MR

DISTRESSED

Distressed circumstances

'As regards both widows and children, the intended provision [in the rules of a friendly society] is strictly for those who are in what is called "distressed circumstances". . . . The words "distressed circumstances", although capable of many interpretations, grammatically, no doubt, mean, not only that a member is so sick that he cannot follow his ordinary employment, but that his position in life is such that he cannot live independently of that employment—that he is distressed in that sense.' *Re Buck, Bruty v Mackey* [1896] 2 Ch 727 at 734, per Kekewich J

Distressed seamen

[The Merchant Shipping Act 1894, s 191 (repealed), enabled provision to be made for the maintenance and sending home of 'distressed seamen'; see now Merchant Shipping Act 1970, s 62.] 'The question whether seamen are in distress or not seems to me to be a question of fact in each case. It is quite possible that a seaman who may have a family to support in England may be said to be in distress abroad, though he is paid his wages in a foreign place; but, on the other hand, on my reading of the Act, the fact that a seaman is shipwrecked is not conclusive evidence that he is a distressed seaman within the meaning of that term as used in the Act. A shipwrecked seaman might be a millionaire with plenty of money at his disposal, and in such a case he could hardly be called a distressed seaman who was entitled to maintenance and a passage home.' *Board of Trade v Sailing Ship Glenpark Ltd* [1904] 1 KB 682 at 687, CA, per Collins MR

DISTRIBUTABLE INCOME *See*
INCOME

DISTRIBUTE—DISTRIBUTION *See*
also PUBLISH

In this Part [VIII: Distribution of profits and assets] 'distribution' means every description of distribution of a company's assets to its members, whether in cash or otherwise, except distribution by way of—
(a) an issue of shares as fully or partly paid bonus shares,
(b) the redemption or purchase of any of the company's own shares out of capital (including the proceeds of any fresh issue of shares) or out of unrealised profits in accordance with Chapter VII of Part V [purchase by a company of its own shares],
(c) the reduction of share capital by extinguishing or reducing the liability of any of the members on any of the company's shares in respect of share capital not paid up, or by paying off paid up share capital, and

(d) a distribution of assets to members of the company on its winding up.
(Companies Act 1985, s 264(2))

'The will . . . is in the terms:—"I do hereby will and bequeath any money I shall die possessed of to the Rev W O'Brien to be distributed as he thinks right.". . . As the will does not designate any executor, the point to consider is . . . Did Father O'Brien take on the face of the will a beneficial interest, or does he take merely as trustee by virtue of the word "distribute"? . . . There is no decision that there is any necessary meaning of the word "distribute" standing alone; but there is nothing in the word itself to imply an absence of beneficial interest in property. . . . In this case the word "distribute" does not, in my opinion, show that it was intended that Father O'Brien should be merely a conduit pipe or donee of a power to appoint any beneficiaries. "Distribute" does not imply an absence of beneficial interest in the property, nor can I see any solid distinction in law or fact between "distribute" and "dispose of".' *O'Brien v Condon* [1905] 1 IR 51 at 54, 55, per Porter MR

'To distribute means to pay over.' *Re Mackinlay, Scrimgeour v Mackinlay* (1911) 56 Sol Jo 142 at 142, per Swinfen Eady J

[The appellant was convicted of committing a breach of the peace by distributing leaflets which incited violence. The evidence against him was that he offered the leaflets to passersby, some of whom looked at them. The leaflets never left the appellant's possession.] 'The findings make it absolutely plain that the leaflets never left the appellant's possession. At most he was offering them to passers-by but he all along retained possession of them, therefore he could not be held to have distributed them.' *Kelly v Tudhope* 1987 SCCR 445 at 447, per the Lord Justice-Clerk (Ross)

Canada 'In my opinion the question devolves on the meaning of the word "distribute". The general rule is that statutes are presumed to use words in their popular sense. This is especially so when the word is capable of one meaning only. It is difficult for me to imagine how things could be distributed to one person only. According to Murray's Oxford Dictionary the verb distribute comes from the Latin word *distribuere*. *Dis* means in various directions, and *tribuere* means to assign, grant, deliver. In this case the delivery of the handbill was made to one person only. The word distribute connotes the delivery of something to several persons.' *R v McNiven* [1944] 1 WWR 127 at 128, per Doiron J

Canada '"Distribution" is obviously a word of wider connotation than "sale" as sale is only one of a number of means by which distribution can be accomplished. There may, however, be cases where a sale would not be a distribution as in the case where all that evidence showed was that a single book had been sold to an individual. The word "distribution" seems to indicate the handing out of more than one article to more than one individual.' *R v Fraser, Harris & Fraser Book Bin Ltd* (1965) 52 WWR 712 at 717, BCCA, per Maclean J

United States 'Distribution' means a direct or indirect transfer of money or other property (except its own shares) or incurrence of indebtedness by a corporation to or for the benefit of its shareholders in respect of any of its shares. A distribution may be in the form of a declaration or payment of a dividend; a purchase, redemption, or other acquisition of shares; a distribution of indebtedness; or otherwise. (Revised Model Business Corporation Act 1984, s 1.40(6))

DISTRIBUTOR

United States The term 'distributor' means a person to whom a consumer product is delivered or sold for purposes of distribution in commerce, except that such term does not include a manufacturer or retailer of such product. (Consumer Product Safety Act 1972, s 3(a)(5))

Petroleum marketing

United States The term 'distributor' means any person, including any affiliate of such person, who—
(A) purchases motor fuel for sale, consignment, or distribution to another; or
(B) receives motor fuel on consignment for consignment or distribution to his own motor fuel accounts or to accounts of his supplier, but shall not include a person who is an employee of, or merely serves as a common carrier providing transportation service for, such supplier.
(Petroleum Marketing Practices Act 1978, s 101(6))

United States The term 'distributor' means any person who receives gasoline and distributes such gasoline to another person other than the ultimate purchaser. (Petroleum Marketing Practices Act 1978, s 201(16))

DISTRICT

'Mr Johnston Edwards' argument . . . is that the custom [of recreation and playing games on land situated in three parishes] is good if confined to inhabitants of a particular district, and that "district" may be construed as meaning two or three contiguous or adjoining parishes, in addition to the parish in which the land is situate. I cannot find any justification for that contention. . . . I do not . . . find in any of the cases anything that would justify me in saying that the use of the word "district" means more than the particular division known to the law in which the particular property is situate. It may be situate in a parish, or in a manor, or there might be some other division. I take it that the judges have used the word "district" as meaning some division of the county defined by and known to the law, as a parish is.' *Edwards v Jenkins* [1896] 1 Ch 308 at 312, 313, per Kekewich J

[Under the Workmen's Compensation Act 1897 (repealed), the jurisdiction of the county court depended on the 'district' in which the parties resided, or, if the parties resided in different districts, in which the accident occurred.] 'The word "district" is not a very technical word, but is of general application and is, I think, common to both England and Scotland. It is not so technical that a definition is necessary, and there seems to me to be no real difficulty in holding that "district" means the area over which the judge, whether county court judge or sheriff, has jurisdiction. If that is so, the difficulty arising from the use of that word is removed, and the word "district" can be treated as a word of general meaning, to be applied according as the context requires.' *R v Owen* [1902] 2 KB 436 at 443, per Channell J

[The Land Drainage Act 1930, s 24(7) (repealed; see now the Land Drainage Act 1976, s 68(4)) empowered a drainage board to determine that no rates should be levied by them in any portion of the 'district' which, in their opinion, either by reason of its height above sea level or for any other reason, ought to be exempted wholly from rating. The underground workings, of a National Coal Board colliery extended into a drainage district though they were five hundred feet below ground and derived no direct benefit from the drainage board's operations. The Coal Board claimed exemption from rates.] 'Land drainage is primarily concerned with the drainage of the surface although, in the course of doing so, it may be necessary to lay pipes and construct works underground. The district of a drainage board is defined by reference to the surface area of the land in the same way as the districts of a rural district and an urban district [were formerly] defined for the purposes of local government. In my opinion, the word "district" in the sub-section refers solely to the surface area within which they can exercise their functions. I do not therefore think that it is within the power of the appellants to exempt any land below the surface without at the same time exempting part of the surface. In other words, a "portion of their district" must include a part of the surface area.' *Trent River Authority v National Coal Board* [1970] 1 All ER 558 at 562, HL, per Viscount Dilhorne

DISTRICT NOTARY   *See* NOTARY

DISTURBANCE   *See also* ROUT

'Disturbance implies that something is taking place against the will of the person disturbed. If an owner is expelled from his house, the expense he is put to in removal is in no way connected with the value of his house. It is a loss which he has suffered, as it seems to me, by being expelled, whatever the value of the house may be.' *Horn v Sunderland Corpn* [1941] 1 All ER 480 at 499, CA, per Goddard LJ (dissenting)

Australia 'Shouting loudly in a public place or addressing a crowd in loud tones cannot possibly of itself amount to conduct creating a disturbance of the public peace. There must be some other element—use of insulting, abusive or threatening words or words inciting a breach of the peace. To hold otherwise would endanger free speech. It would bring within the ambit of the criminal law the street corner preachers, the Domain orators and the politicians on the hustings. Even shouting in a loud voice in a public place accompanied by the discordant tones of a cornet has been held not to constitute the offence of disturbing the public peace [*Beaty v Glenister* (1884) 51 LT 304]. Noise in public places may be an annoyance to citizens and may contravene city by-laws but it does not constitute a disturbance of the public peace in the legal sense. The "public peace" is not

"peace and quiet"—it is "public order".' *Neave v Ryan* [1958] Tas SR 58 at 59, 60, per Burbury CJ

Canada 'To support a conviction for the offence of causing a disturbance something more must be established than that the person charged fought, screamed, shouted, swore, sang or used insulting and obscene language. These acts constitute an offence only if a disturbance results . . . While it is difficult, if not impossible, to define with any degree of precision what is meant by a "disturbance" as used in s 171(a)(i) [of the Criminal Code] it is obvious it involves activities constituting a distraction to persons in or near public places who are pursuing their ordinary peaceable pursuits and includes a breach of the peace, a tumult, an uproar, a commotion and any other disorder. Where the acts specified in the section produce only annoyance or emotional upset not accompanied by activities in the nature of a disorder there is not in my opinion a disturbance of the kind contemplated by the section.' *R v CD* (1973) 13 CCC (2d) 206 at 208, 209, NBPB, per Hughes CJNB

Canada [Accused were charged under s 172(3) of the Criminal Code RSC 1970, c C–34, with disturbance of religious worship by kneeling to receive communion after directive requiring standing.] 'Not all conduct capable of being described as disturbing or creating a disturbance will fall within s 172(3). To found criminal liability under this sub-section, the actions must meet a definition of the term "disturbs" suitable in law to the context of the section and the offence thereby enacted. It is necessary for the conduct to be disorderly in itself or productive of disorder to be rendered criminal. Conduct which falls below this threshold will not be caught by the subsection. Parliament could not have intended that s 172(3) of the Criminal Code could be triggered by conduct which is not disorderly in itself or productive of disorder. The use of the all-encompassing term "anything" to describe the type of acts that can be the cause of the disturbance is an indication of the need to restrict the meaning of the word "disturb". If "disturb" in the context of s 172(3) is taken to encompass annoyance, anxiety or emotional upset, then "anything", no matter how trivial, which would lead to such annoyance, anxiety or emotional upset would be caught by the provision: a man might be convicted under the section for failing to take his hat off in church, or failing to keep it on in synagogue.' *Skoke-Graham v R* (1985) 16 DLR (4th) 321 at 331, SCC, per Dickson J

Of franchise

Disturbance of franchises happens, when a man has the franchise of holding a court-leet, of keeping a fair or market, of free-warren, of taking toll, of seizing waifs or strays, or (in short) any other species of franchise whatsoever; and he is disturbed or incommoded in the lawful exercise thereof. As if another by distress, menaces or persuasions, prevails upon the suitors not to appear at my court; or obstructs the passage to my fair or market; or hunts in my free-warren; or refuses to pay me the accustomed toll; or hinders me from seizing the waif or stray, whereby it escapes or is carried out of my liberty: in every case of this kind, which it is impossible here to recite or suggest, there is an injury done to the legal owner; his property is damnified, and the profits arising from such his franchise are diminished. (3 Bl Com 236)

DISUSE

'Each of us has a surname and it seems to me altogether fanciful to suggest that there is any real ambiguity in a requirement that I should adopt and use a surname in place of that which I at present have: for the requirement does no more nor less than postulate that I should thereafter use the new surname just as I at present use my existing name. Equally, as it seems to me, there is no real ambiguity in a divesting provision expressed to take effect if I should at any time "disuse" or "discontinue to use" the surname which I have adopted, though I do not say that there might not be circumstances in which a disuse from accident or in some other special circumstances will seriously raise the question of its application. Its general sense and meaning seem to me, I confess, no less clear than the general sense and meaning of the obligation to assume the name. As was observed by Diplock LJ, during the argument, when Dean Swift said that he had "disused family prayers for about five years", he must surely have meant that he had ceased at some date about five years before to have family prayers and had not since resumed them. In my judgment, therefore, and with all respect to the learned judges who since 1945 have thought otherwise, name and arms clauses substantially following the forms I have indicated ought not to be regarded as void

for uncertainty on the grounds which . . . appealed to those learned judges.' *Re Neeld (decd), Carpenter v Inigo-Jones* [1962] 2 All ER 335 at 346, CA, per Lord Evershed MR; also reported in [1962] Ch 643 at 667

DITCH

'Ditch' includes a culverted and a piped ditch but does not include a watercourse vested in or under the control of a drainage body. (Land Drainage Act 1976, s 40(4))

In this section [power to fill in roadside ditches] 'ditch' includes a watercourse and any part of a ditch or watercourse, and 'pipes' includes culverts, tunnels and other works. (Highway Act 1980, s 101(6))

DIVERT

'The expression "divert" [in s 85 of the Highway Act 1835 (repealed; see now the Highways Act 1980, s 116) which deals with proceedings for diverting highways] applied to a road suggests the giving of another road instead of the existing one, as a substitute for and to put an end to it.' *R v Surrey JJ* [1892] 1 QB 867 at 869, CA, per Lord Esher MR

See, generally, 21 Halsbury's Laws (4th edn) paras 143 et seq.

DIVIDE BETWEEN

[A testator by his will bequeathed property to be 'divided between' the Local Preachers' Mutual Aid Society and the heirs of his brother and sisters.] 'The . . . question is, how must the division between the charity, the testator's sisters and the deceased brother's heir be made? On that point there has been some difference of opinion, apart from slight differences in the language of testators. I think that Joyce J in *Re Walbran* [[1906] 1 Ch 64] did take the view that with regard to a gift "to be equally divided between the children of A and B", the prima facie meaning implied a division into two parts rather than into a greater number. I agree that he had some ground, which he mentioned, for thinking that that was what the testatrix in that case meant. But for my part I doubt whether that is the true natural popular meaning of a gift of personal estate "to be divided between the children of A and B". An ordinary man directing a sum to be divided between the children of his sister and, say, his nephew Jack, would in my opinion, be intending a division per capita. The history of the word "between" goes back, as does the history of many words in common use, to remote antiquity. Reference to the Oxford Dictionary, vol 1, p 834, shows that if you go as far back as Anglo-Saxon times, the word "between" was etymologically a reference to "two". But there is also in the Oxford Dictionary, vol 1, p 835, para v, 19, the statement that "in all senses, 'between' has been, from its earliest appearance, extended to more than two. In Old English and Middle English it was so extended in sense 1" (i.e. the sense of simple position) "in which 'among' is now considered better. It is still the only word available to express the relation of a thing to many surrounding things severally and individually, 'among' expressing a relation to them collectively and vaguely. . . ." The illustrations given show that in the opinion of the editor it is not, in strictness, right to direct a sum to be divided "among A, B and C", but that the correct phrase is, and for many years has been, "between A, B and C". Agreeing as I do with that view, I am disposed to follow the decision of Sargant J (as he then was) in *Re Harper* [[1914] 1 Ch 70]. In that case there was a gift of a fund "to be divided equally between the unmarried daughters of my brother-in-law Dr H and Dr G equally. Dr H had five daughters, of whom three were unmarried, and Dr G one daughter only, who was four years old, and Sargant J held that the gift was a gift to Dr G personally and not to his "unmarried daughter", and that the fund in question was divisible in equal fourth parts.

On the whole, I am of opinion that the gift in the present case ". . . to be divided between the Local Preachers' Mutual Aid Society and the heirs of my brother and sisters" is, according to the natural meaning of the words—which I have construed as meaning a gift to be divided between (for in this case I decline to use the word "among") the charity, the sisters, who were alive at the date of the testator's death, and the daughter of his deceased brother—a gift in equal fourth parts.' *Re Cossentine, Philp v Wesleyan Methodist Local Preachers' Mutual Aid Assocn Trustees* [1933] 1 Ch 119 at 123–125, per Maugham J

DIVIDEND

The ordinary meaning of 'dividend' is a share of profits, whether at a fixed rate or otherwise, allocated to the holders of shares in a company.

The term is generally used with reference to trading or other companies, and to payments made to members of a company as such and not by way of remuneration for services. Although it usually implies a share of profits periodically payable, it may also refer to such shares of profits as are divided only occasionally and are usually called 'bonuses' or 'bonus dividends'. The terms 'preference dividend', 'preferential dividend', and 'cumulative preferential dividend' refer to shares having preferential rights. An 'interim dividend' is a dividend payable at some date between the ordinary general meetings. A voucher or written authority for payment to a shareholder of the amount of a dividend on his shares is usually described as a dividend warrant. (7 Halsbury's Laws (4th edn) para 596)

The word 'dividends' includes (besides dividends strictly so called) all payments made by the name of dividend, bonus, or otherwise out of the revenue of trading or other public companies, divisible between all or any of the members of such respective companies, whether such payments shall be usually made or declared, at any fixed times or otherwise; and all such divisible revenue shall, for the purposes of this Act, be deemed to have accrued by equal daily increment during and within the period for or in respect of which the payment of the same revenue shall be declared or expressed to be made, but the said word 'dividend' does not include payments in the nature of a return or reimbursement of capital. (Apportionment Act 1870, s 5)

In this Part [Part III: Schedule C] 'dividends' means any interest, public annuities, dividends or shares of annuities. (Income and Corporation Taxes Act 1988, s 45)

'The [defendant] company were about to issue a set of shares. They experienced great difficulty in getting them into the market, except on giving favourable terms; and the terms they offer are these: that, for seven years certain, the persons taking these shares are to have a preference dividend of £7 per cent. per annum, with a liberty to the company, on account of this burden, of buying them up at any time. . . . I do not think the word "dividend" has in itself, *ex vi termini*, any such meaning as to give the company the power of saying it shall be merely a sum payable out of periodical divisions of the capital of the company. . . . These shareholders are to be paid out of the profits of the company. That is the only fund they are to look to.' *Crawford v North Eastern*

Rly Co (1856) 3 K & J 723 at 743, 744, per Page-Wood V-C

'The word "dividend", if we look to its derivation, means obviously the fund to be divided, not the share of any particular partner or person in that fund, and strict language would require us to speak, not of the dividend which each shareholder is entitled to receive, but of his *aliquot portion of the dividend.*' *Henry v Great Northern Rly Co* (1857) 27 LJ Ch 1 at 15, 16, CA, per Lord Cranworth LC

'The word as used in the places in which we have now to deal with it, means, I apprehend, share of profits.' Ibid at 18, per Knight Bruce LJ

'I suppose it [the word 'dividend'] is taken from *dividendum*, the thing to be divided; but it is used in ordinary commercial language as the share of the thing to be divided—that share which is coming to each person who is entitled to share in that division.' *Staples v Eastman Photographic Materials Co* [1896] 2 Ch 303 at 307, 308, CA, per Kay LJ

'By clause 5 of the memorandum and clause 6 of the articles the holders of the preference shares were entitled to a cumulative preferential dividend of 5 per cent. A dividend means prima facie a payment made to the shareholders while the company is a going concern; after the commencement of a winding-up dividend is no longer payable.' *Re Crichton's Oil Co* [1902] 2 Ch 86 at 95, CA, per Stirling LJ

'The prima facie meaning of dividend was thus stated by Stirling LJ in *Re Crichton's Oil Co* [supra]: "A dividend means prima facie a payment made to the shareholders while the company is a going concern." But, in the present case, finding, as I do, this word in a passage which refers to a winding up, it seems to me that one must give the meaning of "arrears of dividend" to it.' *Re de Jong (F) & Co Ltd* [1946] Ch 211 at 215, CA, per Morton LJ

Australia 'The expression "dividends on shares" imports a payment by a company to a person who holds shares in the company at the date when the dividend is, or ought in the ordinary course to be, declared.' *Taylor v Reid* (1929) 42 CLR 371 at 380, per cur.

Canada 'The word "dividend" is not a word of technical import. Primarily it appears to mean part of anything which is subject to be divided and it is, of course, also sometimes used to describe a share which one person

receives along with others equally entitled. It is commonly used in reference to the profits of a joint stock company distributed among the shareholders, but in no way . . . is it limited to this last meaning.' *Re McEwen* (1963) 40 DLR (2d) 273 at 277, Ont SC, per Wells J

Discriminatory dividend

Australia 'I would understand a discriminatory dividend to be one in the declaration of which a decision is involved to prefer some members or class of members over others, all of them being members whose shares carry such rights as would entitle those declaring the dividend, if they so chose, to provide equality of treatment.' *Duggan v Federal Taxation Comr* (1973) 47 ALJR 44 at 46, per Stephen J

Preference dividend

'Preference dividend' means a dividend payable on a preferred share or preferred stock at a fixed rate per cent. or, where a dividend is payable on a preferred share or preferred stock partly at a fixed rate per cent. and partly at a variable rate, such part of that dividend as is payable at a fixed rate per cent. (Income and Corporation Taxes Act 1988, s 832(1))

'The first part [of one of a company's articles of association] is this: "The said preferential shares shall carry a right to a fixed cumulative preferential dividend at the rate of six per cent. per annum on the capital for the time being paid up thereon respectively." That part of the sentence is clear. It is dealing with dividends payable out of the profits of the company, that is, dividends in the true and ordinary sense while the company is a going concern. It is to be noted that the word "preferential" clearly shows that the dividend on those preference shares is to have priority over the dividend on the ordinary shares.' *Re F de Jong & Co Ltd* [1946] Ch 211 at 214, CA, per Morton LJ

DIVIDING SOCIETY *See* FRIENDLY SOCIETY

DIVINE SERVICE

[The Ecclesiastical Courts Jurisdiction Act 1860, s 2 punishes any person guilty of riotous, etc. behaviour in any cathedral, church or chapel, whether during the celebration of 'divine service' or at any other time or of molesting or disturbing etc. any clergyman in holy orders celebrating any divine service, rite or office in any cathedral, church or chapel.]

'The words "divine service" are used in the earlier part of s 2 in their widest sense; and we think that the words in the latter part of the section "any divine service, rite, or office in any cathedral, church, or chapel" were used to cover all the services in the Church of England, including the celebration of the sacraments.' *Matthews v King* [1934] 1 KB 505 at 515, DC, per cur.

See, generally, 14 Halsbury's Laws (4th edn) paras 933 et seq.

DIVORCE

[The sole ground upon which a petition for divorce may be presented to the court by either party to a marriage is that the marriage has broken down irretrievably: see the Matrimonial Causes Act 1973, s 1.

Formerly, under s 3 of the Act of 1973, no petition for divorce could be presented to the court before the expiration of three years from the date of the marriage. A new s 3 has been substituted by s 1 of the Matrimonial and Family Proceedings Act 1984, which reduces the period within which the presentation of petitions is barred from three years to one year.]

'In my view the word "dissolution" relates to the marriage bond itself, whereas the word "divorce" relates to the parties to the marriage bond; and it is apt to refer to "divorce" when speaking of parties and "dissolution" when speaking of the bond.' *Deacock v Deacock* [1958] 2 All ER 633 at 635, CA, per Hodson LJ; also reported in [1958] P 230 at 233

See, generally, 13 Halsbury's Laws (4th edn) paras 501 et seq.

DO OR SUFFER   *See* SUFFER

DOCK

A dock is an artificial inclosure, connected with a harbour or a river, provided for the reception of vessels, and is generally shut off from the harbour or river by gates for regulating the inflow and outflow of water. It may be a dry or graving dock, used for the inspection and repair of vessels, or a wet dock, used for their loading and discharge. A dock may include a lock leading from it to a river. (36 Halsbury's Laws (4th edn) para 401)

For the purpose of this section [limiting the liability of harbour authorities and others] the term 'dock' shall include wet docks and basins, tidal docks and basins, locks, cuts, entrances, dry docks, graving docks, gridirons, slips, quays, wharves, piers, stages, landing-places, and jetties. (Merchant Shipping (Liability of Shipowners and others) Act 1900, s 2)

'Dock' means a dock used by sea-going ships. (Harbours Act 1964, s 57)

'Dock' includes any harbour, wharf, pier or jetty or other works in or at which vessels can ship or unship merchandise or passengers, not being a pier or jetty primarily used for recreation, and 'dock undertaking' shall be construed accordingly. (Capital Allowances Act 1968, s 7(5))

DOCK DUES   *See* DUES

DOCK WORKER

'Dock worker' means a person employed or to be employed in, or in the vicinity of, any port on work in connection with the loading, unloading, movement or storage of cargoes, or work in connection with the preparation of ships or other vessels for the receipt or discharge of cargoes or for leaving port. (Dock Workers (Regulation of Employment) Act 1946, s 6)

DOCKING

'Docking' means the deliberate removal of any bone or any part of a bone from the tail of a horse, and the expression 'docked' shall be construed accordingly. (Docking and Nicking of Horses Act 1949, s 3)

DOCKMASTER

'Dockmaster' means, in relation to a dock, a person appointed by the Port Authority to be a dockmaster and, in relation to a canal, a person appointed by the Port Authority to be a canal master or canal ranger and includes the deputies and assistants of persons so appointed. (Port of London Act 1968, s 2(1))

DOCKYARD PORT   *See* PORT

DOCTOR   *See also* MEDICAL
PRACTITIONER

'The term "doctor" is now commonly used to mean any medical practitioner, but when that word is used in conjunction with some particular branch of learning it means one who in any faculty has attained to the highest degree conferred by a university. We take this from the Oxford Dictionary. So a person who describes himself as a doctor of medicine represents that he has had this degree conferred on him by a university as the result of competent examination.' *Younghusband v Luftig* [1949] 2 KB 354 at 360, per cur.

DOCUMENT

The expression 'document' includes part of a document. (Official Secrets Act 1911, s 12)

'Documents' includes plans, sections, records of survey and similar things. (Coal Industry Nationalisation Act 1946, s 63)

In this Part [Part I: hearsay evidence] of this Act . . . 'document' includes, in addition to a document in writing—
(a) any map, plan, graph or drawing;
(b) any photograph;
(c) any disc, tape, sound track or other device in which sound or other data (not being visual images) are embodied so as to be capable (with or without the aid of some other equipment) of being reproduced therefrom; and
(d) any film, negative, tape or other device in which one or more visual images are embodied so as to be capable (as aforesaid) of being reproduced therefrom.
(Civil Evidence Act 1968, s 10(1))

[See also s 198B(4) of the Army Act 1955 and of the Air Force Act 1955, as substituted by s 9 of the Armed Forces Act 1981 (evidence derived from computer records).]

'It has been contended that the sealed envelope and what is inside it does not come within the term "document". I think that it is perfectly plain that the sealed envelope itself might be a document. . . . I should . . . say that any written thing capable of being evidence is properly described as a document. On behalf of the bank it has been contended that the sealed envelope and what is inside it does not come within the term "document". I think that it is perfectly plain that the sealed envelope itself might be a document. Nothing but the sealed envelope might be required. But I should myself say that any written thing capable of being evidence is properly described as a document and that it is immaterial on what the writing may be inscribed. It might be inscribed on paper, as is the common case now; but the common case once was that it was not on paper, but on parchment; and long before that it was on stone, marble, or clay, and it might be, and often was, on metal. So I should desire to guard myself against being supposed to assent to the argument that a thing is not a document unless it be a paper writing. I should say it is a document no matter upon what material it be, provided it is writing or printing and capable of being evidence.' *R v Daye* [1908] 2 KB 333 at 340, per Darling J

'Although the construction of an Act of Parliament must always be a question of law, I agree . . . that where the construction involves the right meaning to be given to a word in such common use in business as the word "document"—a word of which everyone thinks he knows the meaning—the court should endeavour to give to it a meaning with which the ordinary educated business man would agree. Whether I regard the derivation of the word "document" from Latin, or the decisions of the courts on the meaning of the word. I find that a document must be something which teaches you and from which you can learn something, i.e., it must be something which affords information. In the dictionaries the word is repeatedly defined as something which is "evidence", not in the sense that it is something admissible in a court of law, but as being something which makes evident that which otherwise would not be evident. To constitute a document, the form which it takes seems to me to be immaterial; it may be anything on which the information is written or inscribed—paper, parchment, stone or metal.' *Hill v R* [1945] KB 329 at 332, 333, per Humphreys J

'It is unnecessary for me to dwell at length on the width of the significance of the word "document". Etymologically, it means something which shows or teaches and is evidential or informative in its character. . . . Although there is a good deal to be said for the contentions which have been put forward by the plaintiffs, I think the safer course is to say that "documents" means, according to its ordinary significance, written documents. One may say that "documents" includes tombstones, but "documents", in the ordinary sense in which the ordinary business man uses it means written documents, documents which either record something or contain directions for the making of something or are used for reference in the course of business.' *Tucker (J H) & Co Ltd v Board of Trade* [1955] 2 All ER 522 at 522, 524, per Vaisey J

'It appears to me that written or printed words are, after all, only encapsulated sound—and in a sense badly encapsulated sound, in that they often do not, when they purport to be a record of direct speech, embody the tone of voice, the inflexions, the subtleties of phrasing and pauses, which form the warp and woof of real-life conversation. If two parties to litigation have a record of a vital conversation, one in the form of a shorthand note, and the other in the form of a tape recording, I think that both would be justified, under normal English usage, in saying that they held "documentary proof" of the conversation. If there was in existence a tape recording of Queen Elizabeth I's speech to her troops at Tilbury would not all the world say that that was a priceless historical document? It is, I think, noteworthy that instructional films have for many years now been called "documentary films". This strengthens my belief that in ordinary current English usage a document is primarily something that instructs and is by no means to be confined to "books, clothed in black and red, of Aristotle and his philosophie" which the Clerk of Oxenford had in days gone by, or things ejusdem generis therewith. A film is a documentary film, notwithstanding that the sound is, of course, incorporated in the print. I do not think that popular speech makes any distinction between the visual and oral parts of what is all one subject-matter. . . . In the upshot I conclude that a tape recording, provided of course that what is recorded is indeed information—relevant sounds of some description—is a document.' *Grant v Southwestern & County Properties Ltd* [1974] 2 All ER 465 at 475, per Walton J

Australia   'The word "document" is, etymologically, derived from the latin word *documentum*, that which teaches, a lesson, an example for instruction or warning. The common feature of documents, as the term is popularly understood, I think, is that the writing or printing or inscription is of something capable of being discerned by the eye, with or without the aid of optical instruments. The communication of the information onto the document is usually achieved through the organ of touch, and the apprehension of the information contained in the document is achieved usually by the organ of sight, or, sometimes, as in the case of a document in Braille, by the organ of touch.' *Beneficial Finance Corpn Co Ltd v Conway* [1970] VR 321 at 322, per McInerney J

[In the above case, McInerney J went on to hold that tape-recordings were not documents. The case was considered, but not followed, in *Grant v Southwestern & County Properties*, supra.]

New Zealand   'When such a point as this came before Hoare J in *Cassidy v Engwirda Construction Co* [[1967] QWN 16], he pointed out that much depends upon the text in which the word "document" is used, and that just as an engraving upon stone could be regarded as a document because of its permanence and its capacity to provide or furnish information, there can be no reason in principle why the recording in some other permanent or semi-permanent manner of a human voice or other sound should not be so regarded for the purpose of the relevant rule concerning discovery. He remarked that "nothing is more likely to destroy the effectiveness of the law and our legal system than a timid, restrictive interpretation of procedural provisions. I have no hesitation in concluding that the term 'document' as used in O 35 includes the repository of evidence or information preserved in the manner indicated." With respect, I agree entirely with the approach of the learned judge.' *Snow v Hawthorn* [1969] NZLR 776 at 777, per Woodhouse J

New Zealand   [The question was whether pages of three books displayed in a shop window were to be treated as 'documents' for the purposes of the Indecent Publications Act 1963, or as parts of 'books'.] 'I am satisfied on the facts of this case that each of the pictures exhibited must be viewed as "a document" and it will be for the learned magistrate to decide whether, in all the circumstances, such exhibition was indecent.' *Police v Brien* [1971] NZLR 119 at 121, per Roper J

False document   *See* FORGERY

Manorial document   *See* MANOR

Public document

'Baron Parke said in delivering the opinion of the Judges in the case of *The Irish Society v The Bishop of Derry* [(1846) 12 Cl & Fin 641]: ". . . In public documents made for the information of the Crown, or all the King's subjects who may require the information they contain, the entry by a public officer is presumed to be true when it is made, and is for that reason receivable in all cases, whether the officer or his successor may be concerned in such cases or not." . . . Now . . . taking that decision, the principle on which it goes is, that it should be a public inquiry, a public document, and made by a public officer. . . . I understand a public document there to mean a document that is made for the purpose of the public making use of it, and being able to refer to it.' *Sturla v Freccia* (1880) 5 App Cas 623 at 642, 643, per Lord Blackburn

DOCUMENT OF TITLE

'Document of title' shall include any bill of lading, dock warrant, warehouse-keeper's certificate, and warrant or order for the delivery of goods, and any other document used in the ordinary course of business as proof of the possession or control of goods, or authorising or purporting to authorise, either by endorsement or by delivery, the possessor of the document to transfer or receive goods thereby represented. (Factors Act 1889, s 1)

'A delivery order is not the less a document of title because it is created by the owner of the goods. It would be a curious result if the document by which the owner gets a title can, if passed on by him, give a title to some one else, but that a document created by himself cannot give a title when passed on because it is not a "transfer" but is only a delivery or issue.' *Ant Jurgens Margarinefabrieken v Dreyfus (Louis) & Co* [1914] 3 KB 40 at 44, per Pickford J

'In their Lordships' opinion the only possible conclusion is that, whenever any doubt arises as to whether a particular document is a "document showing title" or a "document of title" to goods . . . the test is whether the document in question is used in the ordinary course of business as proof of the possession or control of goods, or authorising or purporting to authorise, either by indorsement or by delivery, the possessor of the document to transfer or receive goods thereby represented.' *Ramdas Vithaldas Durbar v Amerchand (S) & Co, Ramdas Vithaldas Durbar v Chhaganlal Pitamber* (1916) 85 LJPC 214 at 215, per cur.

'The registration book of a car, or the "log-book" [now registration document] as it is called, may not itself be a document of title, but it is the best evidence of title. The transfer of the log-book does not itself transfer the property in the car'. *Bishopsgate Motor Finance Corporation Ltd v Transport Brakes Ltd* [1949] 1 All ER 37 at 46, per Denning LJ

United States 'Document of title' includes bill of lading, dock warrant, dock receipt, warehouse receipt or order for the delivery of goods, and also any other document which in the regular course of business or financing is treated as adequately evidencing that the person in possession of it is entitled to receive, hold and dispose of the document and the goods it covers. To be a document of title a document must purport to be issued by or addressed to a bailee and purport to cover goods in the bailee's possession which are either identified or are fungible portions of an identified mass. (Uniform Commercial Code 1978, s 1–201(15))

DOCUMENTARY DEMAND FOR PAYMENT   *See* DOCUMENTARY DRAFT

DOCUMENTARY DRAFT

Bank deposits and collections

United States 'Documentary draft' means any negotiable or non-negotiable draft with accompanying documents, securities or other papers to be delivered against honor of the draft. . . . (Uniform Commercial Code 1978, s 4–104(1)(f))

Letters of credit

United States A 'documentary draft' or 'documentary demand for payment' is one honor of which is conditioned upon the presentation of a document or documents. 'Document' means any paper including a document of title, security, invoice, certificate, notice of default and the like. (Uniform Commercial Code 1978, s 5–105(1)(b))

DOG

'Dog' includes any bitch, sapling, or puppy. (Protection of Animals Act 1911, s 15)

'There seems to be no foundation at all for any distinction between dogs. The nature of a dog is perfectly well known. For myself, I see no ground at all for saying that because a dog is a lurcher or, indeed, belongs to any other breed, therefore it is to be taken out of the ordinary category of dogs. It is a dog with the habits of a dog.' *Tallents v Bell & Goddard* [1944] 2 All ER 474 at 476, CA, per Finlay LJ

Guard dog

'Guard dog' means a dog which is being used to protect—
(a) premises; or
(b) property kept on the premises; or
(c) a person guarding the premises or such property.
(Guard Dogs Act 1975, s 8)

DOG RACE

'Dog race' means a race in which an object propelled by mechanical means is pursued by dogs, and 'dog racecourse' shall be construed accordingly. (Betting, Gaming and Lotteries Act 1963, s 55)

DOMESTIC ANIMAL   *See* ANIMAL

DOMESTIC BUILDING

For the purposes of this Part [Part V] of this Act the expression 'domestic building' does not include any buildings used or constructed or adapted to be used wholly or principally as offices or counting-houses. (London Building Act 1930, s 42)

'I should think a domestic building means something which is in the nature of a house, and which is in some way inhabited, though not necessarily slept in, and is used by human beings.' *Collins v Greenwood* (1910) 103 LT 36 at 38, DC, per Channell J

'The first question is whether or not this hospital can be brought within the description of a domestic establishment or *domus*. Such a description would no doubt apply to a boarding-school. It could . . . be applied also to a residential college and a university, and I have no doubt that it applies to a hospital. Indeed some hospitals are now commonly referred to as homes. A "nursing-home" is the expression used to describe a hospital run as a paying concern. There is also the expression "mental home". The term "domestic" may be applied to establishments of that kind. Those who live there regularly, as members of the staff, and temporarily as patients, may be regarded as a family in a wide sense, and certainly the establishment is of a domestic character as a whole.' *Cameron v Royal London Ophthalmic Hospital* [1941] 1 KB 350 at 358, per du Parcq LJ

DOMESTIC PREMISES

'Domestic premises' means premises occupied as a private dwelling (including any garden, yard, garage, outhouse or other appurtenance of such premises which is not used in common by the occupants of more than one such dwelling) and 'non-domestic' premises shall be construed accordingly. (Health and Safety at Work etc. Act 1974, s 53(1))

DOMESTIC PURPOSES

'A supply of water for domestic purposes' means a sufficient supply for drinking, washing, cooking and sanitary purposes, but not for any bath having a capacity (measured to the centre line of the overflow pipe, or in such other manner as the Minister may by regulations prescribe) in excess of fifty gallons; and includes—
(a) a supply for the purposes of a profession carried on in any premises the greater part whereof is used as a house; and
(b) where the water is drawn from a tap inside a house and no hosepipe or similar apparatus is used, a supply for watering a garden, for horses kept for private use and for washing vehicles so kept:
Provided that it does not include a supply of water for the business of a laundry or a business of preparing food or beverages for consumption otherwise than on the premises. (Water Act 1945, Sch 3, s 1)

'I agree that a householder might allow his dog or his cat to drink the water supplied for domestic purposes and might use the water for washing them. So again, as has been decided, he might use the water for washing his horse and carriage, and for watering the horse. There must, however, be some limitation. Suppose a wealthy proprietor chose to keep other tame animals—for instance, a tame elephant—would it be reasonable for him to call upon a water company to supply him with water to fill a special bath for the elephant? In my opinion that would not be a supply for domestic purposes.' *Barnard Castle Urban Council v Wilson* [1902] 2 Ch 746 at 755–757, CA, per Romer LJ

[The question was whether water supplied to a railway company on the platforms of its stations for sanitary and other purposes was supplied for 'domestic purposes' within a private water board Act.] 'It should not be assumed that domestic means civilised or domesticated or something appertaining to man, either the natural or the civilised man. It means, I think, something to do with man as occupying or using a house or dwelling. It may be that the occupation need not be through the night as well as the day. . . . It does not follow, because a man generally cooks, eats, and reads in his house, that the cooking of roasted chestnuts on a stall, or the eating of chocolate out of an automatic machine at a station, or the reading of a book . . . while walking along the street, is domestic. In the same way it does not seem to me to follow that the use of sanitary conveniences in some public place or some place of temporary resort during a journey is domestic.' *Metropolitan Water Board v London, Brighton & South Coast Rly Co* [1910] 1 KB 804 at 810, per Phillimore J

'Having thought the matter over again I retain my opinion [formed in *Metropolitan Water Board v London, Brighton & South Coast Rly Co*, supra] that "domestic" does not mean civilised or domesticated or something appertaining to man, but means something to do with man as occupying or using a house or dwelling. Such occupation need not be for day and night. In the previous case I gave certain examples of an occupation of premises without pernoctation which might yet make the use of water in connection with that occupation domestic. So, if a man has a bedroom and uses his club all day, his use of water in his club may well be a use for domestic purposes.' *Metropolitan Water Board v Colley's Patents Ltd* [1911] 2 KB 38 at 40, CA, per Phillimore J; affd [1911] 2 KB 44, CA

'According to the ordinary meaning of language, I take it that water supplied for domestic purposes would mean water supplied to satisfy or help to satisfy the needs, or perform or help in performing the services, which, according to the ordinary habits of civilised life, are commonly satisfied and performed in people's homes, as distinguished from those needs and services which are satisfied or performed outside those homes, and are not connected with, nor incident to, the occupation of them.' *Metropolitan Water Board v Avery* [1914] AC 118 at 126, 127, per Lord Atkinson

'I can imagine no more domestic purpose to which water can be applied than that of internal administration.' *Kingston-upon-Hull Corpn v Yuille* [1939] 2 KB 769 at 779, 780, CA, per Scott LJ

'A great variety of articles go to make a home, not because they are necessary, but because they are calculated to contribute to the comfort and well-being of people in the home. Such

articles may be said to be of a kind used for domestic purposes.' *A-G v Milliwatt Ltd* [1948] 1 All ER 331 at 332, per Cassels J

DOMESTIC SERVANT   *See also*
MENIAL SERVANT; SERVANT

Domestic servants are those employees who, forming part of the employer's residential establishment, are engaged upon work of such a character that it brings them into the close personal proximity of the employer and is mainly concerned with the household. Thus the following have been said to be domestic servants: a groom, a head gardener, a huntsman, a potman, a male nurse, a stoker at a hospital and persons employed in performing various duties at a club. The following have been held not to be domestic servants: a governess, the housekeeper of a hotel, a steward, a laundress, a caddy at a golf club and a hotel boy principally employed as a messenger. (16 Halsbury's Laws (4th edn) para 508)

[A testator by his will gave one year's wages to each 'servant in his domestic establishment' at the time of his death. The plaintiff, a gardener, was held not to be entitled.] 'For the purpose of ascertaining in what sense the testator used the expression "domestic establishment", it appears to me to be important to distinguish between a servant in the establishment and one out of the establishment, between what is called an indoor and an outdoor servant; and I cannot but think that the testator had this very distinction in view. The mere fact of splitting up the plaintiff's salary into weekly payments would not, in my opinion, have excluded him, but the construction which would include the plaintiff would also include a gamekeeper, or cowboy, which would clearly be not maintainable. . . . The word "domestic" . . . was introduced for the purpose of drawing a distinction between servants who were in the house not receiving board wages and servants not boarding in the house and receiving proportionately higher wages.' *Ogle v Morgan* (1852) 1 De GM & G 359 at 360, 361, per Lord Truro LC

'When one speaks of articles of domestic use and ornament, one means articles of household use and ornament, and in like manner a "domestic servant" is, in my opinion, a household servant as distinguished from an outdoor servant.' *Re Lawson, Wardley v Bringloe* [1914] 1 Ch 682 at 686, per Eve J

'I shall not endeavour to formulate a definition

of what is a "domestic servant". . . . But if I had, in my own words, to describe what are the characteristics of such a servant I should express it, . . . that domestic servants are servants, whose main or general function it is to be about their employers' persons, or establishments, residential or quasi-residential, for the purpose of ministering to their employers' needs or wants, or to the needs or wants of those who are members of such establishments, or of those resorting to such establishments, including guests,' *Re Junior Carlton Club* [1922] 1 KB 166 at 169, 170, per Roche J

'As a general rule, . . . without laying down anything intended to apply to every case, where there is what can properly be termed a domestic establishment, and some of the work in that establishment is done by a particular person for the purposes of the upkeep of the home, and for the convenience of the members of the family, that person is a domestic servant. Sometimes he is a highly skilled person. There are great houses where a chef is employed who would not hesitate to admit that he was a domestic servant, but who at the same time regards himself as an exponent of a great art. There may be a chauffeur who not only drives but also attends to the mechanism of his employer's car. He is a domestic servant. . . .' *Cameron v Royal London Ophthalmic Hospital*, [1941] 1 KB 350 at 358, 360, per du Parcq LJ

DOMICILE   *See also* ABODE; RESIDENCE

Domicile is the legal relationship between an individual and a territory with a distinctive legal system which invokes that system as his personal law. A person is domiciled in that country in which he either has or is deemed by law to have his permanent home. Every individual is regarded as belonging, at every stage in his life, to some community consisting of all persons domiciled in a particular country; the rules as to domicile are such that this legal idea may not correspond to the social realities of the situation. A person may have no permanent home, but the law requires him to have a domicile. He may have more than one home, but he may have only one domicile for any one purpose. He may have his home in one country, but be deemed to be domiciled in another.

The relationship of domicile is between a person and a country, and never arises from membership of a group as distinguished from the country in which the group is domiciled; but the municipal law of the country of domicile may itself distinguish between classes of its

subjects, and apply different rules according to the race, caste, creed or other characteristics of a particular person, so that after the domicile has been ascertained it may be further necessary to inquire into the other characteristics of the individual before the particular rule applicable to his case can be known. (8 Halsbury's Laws (4th edn) para 421)

'By domicil we mean home, the permanent home; and if you do not understand your permanent home, I am afraid that no illustration drawn from foreign writers or foreign languages will very much help you to it. I think the best I have ever heard is one which describes the home as the place (I believe there is one definition in which the *"lares"* [household gods] are alluded to) *"unde non sit discessurus sie nihil avocet; unde cum profectus est, peregrinari videtur"* [from which you cannot be separated if nothing removes you; when you depart from them you are seen as a stranger]. I think that is the best *illustration*, and I use that word rather than *definition*, to describe what I mean.' *Whicker v Hume* (1858) 7 HL Cas 124 at 160, per Lord Cranworth

'There are several definitions of domicil which appear to me pretty nearly to approach correctness. One very good definition is this: Habitation in a place with the intention of remaining there for ever, unless some circumstance should occur to alter his intention.' Ibid at 164, per Lord Wensleydale

'I would venture to suggest that the definition of an acquired domicil might stand thus: "That place is properly the domicil of a person in which he has voluntarily fixed the habitation of himself and his family, not for a mere special and temporary purpose, but with a present intention of making it his permanent home, unless and until something (which is unexpected or the happening of which is uncertain) shall occur to induce him to adopt some other permanent home".' *Lord v Colvin* (1859) 4 Drew 366 at 376, per Kindersley V-C

'Nothing is better settled with reference to the law of domicil than that the domicil can be changed only *animo et facto*, and although residence may be decisive as to the *factum*, it cannot, when looked at with reference to the *animus*, be regarded otherwise than as an equivocal act. The mere fact of a man residing in a place different from that in which he has been before domiciled, even although his residence there may be long and continuous, does not of necessity shew that he has elected that place as his permanent and abiding home.

He may have taken up and continued his residence there for some special purpose, or he may have elected to make the place his temporary home. But domicil, although in some of the cases spoken of as "home", imports an abiding and permanent home, and not a mere temporary one.' *Jopp v Wood* (1865) 4 De GJ & Sm 616 at 621, 622, per Turner LJ

'"Domiciled in England" means in England as distinguished from Scotland and Ireland as well as from foreign countries, because Scotland and Ireland have their own separate legal tribunals.' *Re Mitchell, ex p Cunningham* (1884) 13 QBD 418 at 423, per Cotton LJ

'The question whether a person is or is not domiciled in a foreign country is to be determined in accordance with the requirements of English law as to domicil, irrespective of the question whether the person in question has or has not acquired a domicil in the foreign country in the eyes of the law of that country.' *Re Annesley, Davidson v Annesley* [1926] Ch 692 at 705, per Russell J

'The general rule of jurisdiction in divorce in England is that English domicil only is the test and that has to be the domicil of the husband. Pausing there, the English conception of domicil is the most rigid in the world. It must be residence with the intention of permanent settlement in that place.' *Arnold v Arnold* [1957] 1 All ER 570 at 572, per cur; also reported in [1957] P 237 at 247

'Acquisition and abandonment are correlatives; in Lord Westbury's words [in *Udny v Udny* (1869) LR 1 Sc & Div at p 458], "Domicile of choice, as it is gained *animo et facto*, so it may be put an end to in the same manner". When *animus* and *factum* are each no more, domicile perishes also; for there is nothing to sustain it. If a man has already departed from the country, his domicile of choice there will continue so long as he has the necessary *animus*. When he no longer has this, in my judgment his domicile of choice is at an end, for it has been abandoned; and this is so even if his intention of returning has merely withered away and he has not formed any positive intention never to return to live in the country. In short, the death of the old intention suffices, without the birth of any new intention. In this way abandonment dovetails in with acquisition.' *Re Flynn, Flynn v Flynn* [1968] 1 All ER 49 at 58, per Megarry J

New Zealand   [Rule 517 of the Code of Civil Procedure (NZ) (now r 643 of the High Court

Rules) provided that every notice of motion for probate of the will or for letters of administration of the estate and effects of a deceased person, together with all affidavits, documents, and papers, shall be filed in the registry nearest to which the deceased person resided or was 'domiciled' at the time of his death. If the deceased person was not resident or 'domiciled in New Zealand', such notice of motion, etc, are to be filed in the principal registry of the judicial district where the property is.] 'The observations made by Denniston J in *Re Cleary* [(1893) 12 NZLR 151] and by Conolly J in *Re Taylor* [(1902) 22 NZLR 388] show that they took the view that the word "domiciled" in the first paragraph of what is now r 517 was used not in its proper sense as a legal conception whose area is a country subject to one system of law, but in the lax sense, meaning no more than "residence". . . . . This view appears to me to be consistent with the other language used in the rule, and I agree with it. In my opinion, however, the word "domiciled" is used in its proper sense in the expression "domiciled in New Zealand" in the second paragraph of the rule: cf. *Whitley v Stumbles* [[1930] AC 544, 547]. Moreover, I do not think a case falls within the second paragraph unless the deceased was at the time of his death both resident out of New Zealand and domiciled out of New Zealand.' *Re Raitt (Deceased)* [1955] NZLR 179 at 179, per Cooke J

Of choice

'Domicil of choice is a conclusion or inference which the law derives from the fact of a man fixing voluntarily his sole or chief residence in a particular place, with an intention of continuing to reside there for an unlimited time.' *Udny v Udny* (1869) LR 1 Sc & Div 441 at 458, HL, per Lord Westbury LC

'The domicil flows from the combination of fact and intention, the fact of residence and the intention of remaining for an unlimited time. The intention required is not an intention specifically directed to a change of domicil, but an intention of residing in a country for an unlimited time.' *Re Annesley, Davidson v Annesley* [1926] Ch 692 at 701, per Russell J

Australia   'The expression "domicil of choice" imports the notion that residence in that country must be the free and deliberate choice of the person concerned. . . .   If residence in the country is not the result of free and deliberate choice of the person concerned, but is something over which he has no control, can he by merely forming the intention that when he is free to choose he will continue permanently to reside there, acquire a domicil of choice in that country? I think not.' *Fitzgibbon-Lloyd v Fitzgibbon-Lloyd* [1944] VLR 29 at 30, per O'Bryan J

South Africa 'The onus of proving a "domicil" of choice is discharged once physical presence is proved and it is further proved that the de cujus had at the relevant time a fixed and deliberate intention to abandon his previous domicil, and to settle permanently in the country of choice. A contemplation of any certain or foreseeable future event on the occurrence of which residence in that country would cease, excludes such an intention. If he entertains any doubt as to whether he will remain or not, intention to settle permanently is likewise excluded.' *Eilon v Eilon* 1965 (1) SA 703 (A) per Potgieter AJA

Of origin

'The original domicil, or, as it is called, the *forum originis*, or the domicil of origin, is to prevail, until the party has not only acquired another, but has manifested and carried into execution an intention of abandoning his former domicil and taking another as his sole domicil. I speak of the domicil of origin rather than that of birth; for the mere accident of birth at any particular place cannot in any degree affect the domicil. . . . If the son of an Englishman is born upon a journey in foreign parts, his domicil would follow that of his father. The domicil of origin is that arising from a man's birth and connections.' *Somerville v Somerville (Lord)* (1801) 5 Ves 750 at 787, per Arden MR

'It was argued for the defendants, as a proposition of law, that domicil of origin, rightly understood, does not mean domicil at birth; but the last domicil imposed by the choice of the father, or other the guardian of an infant, who has authority to change the domicil of an infant by changing his own. . . . It was urged that great inconvenience and hardship would arise by holding that domicil of origin meant simply domicil at birth. . . . I pass by these questions of fact and law without expressing any opinion upon them, except by saying, as to the defendant's proposition of law, that I am not persuaded that it is well-founded, or that it can be supported upon a due examination of the authorities bearing on the subject.' *Re*

Craignish, Craignish v Hewitt [1892] 3 Ch 180 at 184, 185, per Chitty J

'Domicil of origin, or as it is sometimes called perhaps less accurately, "domicil of birth", differs from domicil of choice mainly in this— that its character is more enduring, its hold stronger, and less easily shaken off.' *Winans v A-G* [1904] AC 287 at 290, per Lord Macnaghten

Of origin and of choice distinguished

The law attributes to everyone at birth a domicile which is called a domicile of origin. This domicile may be changed, and a new domicile, which is called a domicile of choice, acquired; but the two kinds of domicile differ in the following respects:—

(1) The domicile of origin is received by operation of law at birth; the domicile of choice is acquired later by the actual removal of an individual to another country accompanied by his *animus manendi*;

(2) The domicile of origin is retained until the acquisition of a domicile of choice; it cannot be divested, although it remains in abeyance during the continuance of a domicile of choice; the domicile of choice is lost by abandonment whereupon the domicile of origin will revive unless some other domicile is acquired; the domicile of choice is destroyed when it is once lost, but may be acquired anew by fulfilling the same conditions as are required in the first instance.

(3) The domicile of origin is more durable than that of choice, in the sense that it is more difficult to establish a change of domicile when the domicile alleged to have been displaced is one of origin.

(8 Halsbury's Laws (4th edn) para 425)

DOMINANT TENEMENT   *See* EASEMENT

DONATIO INTER VIVOS   *See* GIFT

DONATIO MORTIS CAUSA

A donatio mortis causa is a gift inter vivos by which the donee is to have the absolute title to the subject of the gift, not at once, but if the donor dies. The donee's title becomes absolute at the moment of the donor's death so that the property given never vests in the donor's personal representative who is obliged if necessary to lend his name or give his indorsement to assist the donee in completing his title. (17 Halsbury's Laws (4th edn) para 1076)

A gift mortis causa is neither entirely inter vivos nor testamentary. It must be made in contemplation, though not necessarily in expectation, of the death of the donor, in circumstances which show that it is to take effect only in that event, and so as to be recoverable by the donor if that event does not occur, and void if the donee dies before it occurs. A gift mortis causa has in effect the nature of a legacy, and is only a gift on survivorship. It is not unusual for the evidence of this kind of gift to be that of the donee alone.

There must be delivery to the donee or his agent of the subject of the gift, or a transfer of the means or part of the means of getting at the property, although the actual delivery need not be by the donor himself, but may be by a person directed by him to make it; but the delivery must be to the donee or some one for the donee, for mere delivery to an agent in the character of agent for the donor amounts to nothing. It must clearly appear that the delivery was by way of gift, and not merely to take care of the object for the donor. The delivery to the donee may be as trustee for any other person or persons or for a special purpose. The expression of the trust or condition must form part of the donation, and be either contemporaneous with it or be so coupled with it by contemporaneous words of reference as, in effect, to be incorporated with it.

The donee's title can never be complete until the donor is dead. A gift mortis causa does not vest in the donor's personal representatives, and if on the donor's death the subject of the gift is not already completely vested in the donee the question arises whether he can call on the donor's personal representatives to make good his title. A good gift mortis causa, where the subject of the gift is not completely vested in the donee, raises by operation of law a trust, which was not within the Statute of Frauds, and the court, by the application of equitable principles, assists the donee to perfect his title. The donee is accordingly entitled to call upon the donor's representatives to lend him their name, or to give him their indorsement, in order that he may complete his title. The title remains in the donor until the event happens which is to divest him, that is his death, so that, if it appears that the donor intended to divest his interest at once, the

transaction will be treated as a gift inter vivos, complete or incomplete as the case may be, and not as a gift mortis causa.

There is an implied condition that the gift is to be retained only in the event of death, even though the donor does not expressly say so. The death may take place some time afterwards, or the donor may actually die from some other illness, but if the donor recovers from the illness during which the gift is made the donee has no title, and can only hold what was delivered to him in trust for the donor. (20 Halsbury's Laws (4th edn) paras 66, 67)

'For an effectual *donatio mortis causa* three things must combine; first, the gift or donation must have been made in contemplation, though not necessarily in expectation, of death; secondly, there must have been delivery to the donee of the subject matter of the gift; and, thirdly, the gift must be made under such circumstances as shew that the thing is to revert to the donor in case he should recover. This last requirement is sometimes put somewhat differently, and it is said that the gift must be made under circumstances shewing that it is to take effect only if the death of the donor follows; it is not necessary to say which way of putting it is the better.' *Cain v Moon* [1896] 2 QB 283 at 286, DC, per Lord Russell CJ

'A *donatio mortis causa* is a singular form of gift. It may be said to be of an amphibious nature, being a gift which is neither entirely *inter vivos* nor testamentary. It is an act *inter vivos* by which the donee is to have the absolute title to the subject of the gift not at once, but if the donor dies. If the donor dies, the title becomes absolute not under but as against his executor. In order to make the gift valid, it must be made so as to take complete effect on the donor's death.' *Re Beaumont, Beaumont v Ewbank* [1902] 1 Ch 889 at 892, 897, per Buckley J

'A *donatio mortis causa* is a well-recognised form of gift. It is one made in contemplation of the death of the donor, and is to take effect only in that event, being recoverable by the donor if that event does not occur. Such a gift is, in effect, I think, in the nature of a legacy, being subject to a condition, express or implied, that it is to take effect only in the event of the survivorship of the donee. There are . . . three essentials to constitute such a gift—namely:

(i) the gift must be made in contemplation of the death of the donor, although not necessarily in expectation of death;

(ii) there must be a delivery of the subject-matter of the gift to the donee, or, I think, a transfer of the means of, or part of the means of, getting at the property; and

(iii) the circumstances must be such as to establish that the gift is to take effect only on the death of the donor.

It follows that the title of the donee is not complete until the donor is dead.' *Delgoffe v Fader* [1939] 3 All ER 682 at 685, per Luxmoore LJ

'It has been decided in *Re Weston* [*Bartholomew v Menzies* [1902] 1 Ch 680] that the delivery of a Post Office Savings Bank book coupled with words of gift is capable of constituting a valid *donatio mortis causa* of money standing to the credit of the deceased in the Post Office Savings Bank. In this case there is no doubt that the book was in fact handed to the donee and the only question is as to the nature of the words of the gift. There is no doubt that the words of the gift must be words of present intention to give and not words of future gift.' *Re Ward, Ward v Warwick* [1946] 2 All ER 206 at 206, 207, per Roxburgh J

South Africa 'A gift made in contemplation of death. There are three modes in which such a gift may be effected: (1) the donor gives something in mere general contemplation of death, but without any fear of an early death or imminent danger, and with the understanding that it is not to become the property of the donee until the donor's death; (2) when the gift is made in imminent peril of death, but with the understanding that the property shall only pass upon the donor's death; (3) under circumstances similar to those of the last case, but with the understanding that the ownership of the property shall pass immediately, though if the donor survives the peril the property shall be returned to him.' *Ex p Steyl* 1951 (1) SA 277 (O)

DONATION *See* ENDOWMENT

DOUBLE INSURANCE *See* INSURANCE

DOUBLE PORTION *See* PORTION

DOUBT *See* REASONABLE DOUBT

DOWNPAYMENT

United States 'Downpayment' means an amount, including the value of any property used as a trade-in, paid to a seller to reduce the cash price of goods or services purchased in a credit sale transaction. A deferred portion of a downpayment may be treated as part of the downpayment if it is payable not later than the due date of the second otherwise regularly scheduled payment and is not subject to a finance charge. (Truth in Lending Regulations 1982, 12 CFR, s 266.2(a)(18))

DRAFT

'Now, the word "draft", no doubt, includes a bill of exchange as well as a cheque. It is a *nomen generale*, which embraces every request by the drawer upon the drawee to pay money.' *Hunter v Bowyer* (1850) 15 LTOS 281 at 281, per Pollock CB

DRAIN *See also* SEWER

'Drain' means a drain used for the drainage of one building or of any buildings or yards appurtenant to buildings within the same curtilage. (Public Health Act 1936, s 343)

'Drain' means a drain used for the drainage of one building or of buildings or yards appurtenant to buildings within the same curtilage, and includes any manholes, ventilating shafts, pumps or other accessories belonging to the drain. (Building Act 1984, s 126)

'I think "a drain or watercourse" [in the Highway Act 1835, s 67 (repealed; cf now the Highways Act 1980, s 100(9))] is applied to that sort of conveyance by which you direct the course of the water, and where you can follow the course of the water, and where you can correct any mischief which arises from an impediment to a flow of the water where you can do the repairs.' *Croft v Rickmansworth Highway Board* (1888) 39 Ch D 272 at 286, CA, per Fry LJ

'Looking at the character of the place, we find that the road that passes the spot rises on either side, and that the land on the side away from the defendant's land slopes to the road. Under these circumstances, water would run down to this spot and would be impounded on the surface of the road unless it is carried away by some means or other. There are catch-pits on either side of the road with a connection between them by which the water from the other side flows into the catch-pit on the east side, and the whole escapes by a pipe six feet long, which carries it through the hedge and discharges it on the defendant's land. . . . It is compatible with certain evidence that was given in the case that there had at one time been a ditch on the defendant's land which carried away the water from the point at which it entered the land. Upon this state of facts it seems to me that this convenience for carrying away the water was a drain within the meaning of the section [s 67 of the Highway Act 1835 (repealed; see supra)].' *A-G v Copeland* [1902] 1 KB 690 at 693, CA, per Collins MR

DRAINAGE

'Drainage' includes defence against water (including sea water), irrigation, other than spray irrigation, and warping. (Land Drainage Act 1976, s 116(1))

DRAMATIC WORK

'Dramatic work' includes a choreographic work or entertainment in dumb show if reduced to writing in the form in which the work or entertainment is to be presented, but does not include a cinematograph film, as distinct from a scenario or script for a cinematograph film. (Copyright Act 1956, s 48(1))

DRAW

'Although the word "drawing" is used [in a debenture trust deed] it is . . . obviously an inappropriate term to use concerning a debenture issued singly which is to be redeemed in order of its date. . . . A "drawing" properly so called can only take place among several debentures of even date.' *Finlay v Mexican Investment Corpn* [1897] 1 QB 517 at 523, per Charles J

DRAW OR PREPARE

[Section 20(1) of the Solicitors Act 1957 (repealed; see now the Solicitors Act 1974) made it an offence for any unqualified person to 'draw or prepare' any instrument of transfer.] 'The meaning of "draw or prepare" in this context is compose, to use the mind to select the words.' *Green v Hoyle* [1976] 2 All ER 633 at 638, per Lord Widgery CJ

DRAWBACK

Drawback is a repayment of, or in respect of the duties previously paid on imported goods, and is allowed on the exportation or shipment as stores of the goods, of articles incorporating them, or of goods produced or manufactured from them in the United Kingdom. (12 Halsbury's Laws (4th edn) para 553)

DRAWING

'Drawing' includes any diagram, map, chart or plan. (Copyright Act 1956, s 48(1))

'I think that these things [dies] which were registered [under the Fine Arts Copyright Act 1862, ss 1, 4 (repealed; see now Copyright Act 1956, s 3)] were drawings. It is quite true that their value consisted, not in the use of the original drawings for exhibition, but for the multiplication of copies of the originals by a particular process, but I do not think that prevents the original drawings from being "drawings", which are capable of registration under the Act; and I think that the copyright may well extend to the right of reproducing and multiplying copies by one or more methods.' *Millar & Lang Ltd v Polak* [1908] 1 Ch 433 at 440, per Neville J

DREDGING

In this section 'dredging' does not include things done otherwise than in the interests of navigation, but (subject to that) includes the removal of anything forming part of or projecting from the bed of the sea or of any inland water, by whatever means it is removed and whether or not at the time of removal it is wholly or partly above water; and this section shall apply to the widening of an inland waterway in the interests of navigation as it applies to dredging. (Capital Allowances Act 1968, s 67(10))

DRIFTWAY   *See also* HIGHWAY

'The grant of a right of way is the grant of a right of way having regard to the nature of the road over which it is granted and the purpose for which it is intended to be used; and both these circumstances may be legitimately called in aid in determining whether it is a general right of way, or a right of way restricted to foot-passengers, or restricted to foot-passengers and horsemen or cattle, which is generally called a drift way.' *Cannon v Villars* (1878) 8 Ch D 415 at 421, per Jessel MR

DRINK

'I do not think that it is necessary to consider the ingenious point counsel for the respondent took whether a non-alcoholic beverage is drink within the meaning of the Act [Road Traffic Act 1930, s 15(1) (repealed; see now the Road Traffic Act 1972, s 5, as amended)]. If it were necessary to do so, I should be inclined to apply the dictum of Martin B, which is on record, where the bailiff was sworn to keep the jury without meat or drink, or any light but candlelight, and a juryman asked if he might have a glass of water. Martin B, said: "Well, it is certainly not meat and I should not call it drink. He can have it." I think that drink means alcoholic drink.' *Armstrong v Clark* [1957] 1 All ER 433 at 435, per Lord Goddard CJ

DRIVE—DRIVER

Except for the purposes of section 1 [causing death by reckless or dangerous driving], 'driver', where a separate person acts as a steersman of a motor vehicle, includes that person as well as any other person engaged in the driving of the vehicle, and 'drive' shall be construed accordingly. (Road Traffic Act 1972, s 196(1))

'Driver'—
(a) in relation to a motor vehicle, includes any person who is in charge of the vehicle and, if a separate person acts as steersman, includes that person as well as any other person in charge of the vehicle or engaged in the driving of it, and
(b) in relation to a trailer, means any person who (in accordance with the preceding paragraph) is the driver of the motor vehicle by which the trailer is drawn.
(Road Traffic (Foreign Vehicles) Act 1972, s 7(1); International Carriage of Perishable Foodstuffs Act 1976, s 19(1))

'Driver', where a separate person acts as steersman of a motor vehicle, includes that person as well as any other person engaged in the driving of the vehicle, and 'drive' and 'driving' shall be construed accordingly (Road Traffic Regulation Act 1984, s 142(1))

[Section 78 of the Highway Act 1835 makes it an offence (inter alia) for a person to ride a horse or beast or drive a carriage so furiously as to endanger the life and limb of any passenger.] 'In this section the word "driver" is plainly used in an extended sense, for it includes drivers of "horses, mules or other beasts of draught or burthen"; and therefore it may have been intended by the legislature that the word "driver" shall include "rider" because a person riding must "drive" that is, guide or conduct the horse. The word "drive" is sometimes popularly used in this sense; and it is applied to a rider at the beginning of this very section, where it provides that, "if the driver of any waggon, cart, or other carriage of any kind shall ride . . . upon any horse or horses drawing the same" without the means of proper control, he shall commit an offence against the Act; it is also applied to the person who ought to be in charge of the vehicle, but who quits it and goes to the other side of the hedge. I therefore think it would not be an extravagant construction to hold that in the latter part of the penal clause "driver" means a person guiding or conducting, and therefore a "rider".' *Williams v Evans* (1876) 1 Ex D 277 at 282, 283, CA, per Grove J

'The question raised in this case is whether the respondent was driving the lorry at the time in question. The lorry, which he owned, was standing at the head of an incline. There was no petrol in the tank, and the respondent, having released the brake, set the lorry in motion by pushing it, got into the driving seat, and let the lorry go down the hill so as to get it into his garage. I dare say he thought he was not committing an offence, but it seems impossible to say that in those circumstances he was not "driving" the vehicle. He controlled it by operating the brakes and the steering wheel, and one cannot say that he was not the "driver" for the purposes of the Road Traffic Act.' *Saycell v Bool* [1948] 2 All ER 83 at 84, per Lord Goddard CJ

'"Driving away" in s 28(1) [of the Road Traffic Act 1930 (repealed; see now the Theft Act 1968, s 12] must be construed as causing the vehicle to move, and so a motor vehicle can be said to be driven if somebody pushes and somebody steers and thus it is made to move from the place where it has been standing.' *Shimmell v Fisher* [1951] 2 All ER 672 at 673, per Lord Goddard CJ

'I do not think it is impossible either in law or in fact to say that there can be two drivers at the same time, two people controlling the car. One may be controlling the starting and one may be controlling the stopping, and they may both be controlling the steering, though that may be rather a perilous thing to do.' *Langman v Valentine* [1952] 2 All ER 803 at 805, per Lord Goddard CJ

[See Road Traffic Regulation Act 1984, s 142(1), supra.]

'In the present case it is argued that if a man has stopped for something more than a mere moment the engine of a car which he has been driving he may be in charge of the vehicle, but in law he is not the driver. To give any such narrow meaning as that to the word "driver" would nullify the whole of s 22 [of the Road Traffic Act 1930 (repealed; see now the Road Traffic Act 1972, s 25)]. For the purposes of that section the "driver" is the person who takes out the vehicle, and he remains the driver until he finishes his journey.' *Jones v Prothero* [1952] 1 All ER 434 at 435, per Lord Goddard CJ

'In any ordinary case, when once it has been proved that the accused was in the driving seat of a moving car, there is prima facie an obvious and irresistible inference that he was driving it. No dispute or doubt will arise on that point unless and until there is evidence tending to show that by some extraordinary mischance he was rendered unconscious or otherwise incapacitated from controlling the car. Take the following cases. (1) The man in the driving seat is having an epileptic fit, so that he is unconscious and there are merely spasmodic movements of his arms and legs. (2) By the onset of some disease he has been reduced to a state of coma and is completely unconscious. (3) He is stunned by a blow on the head from a stone which passing traffic has thrown up from the roadway. (4) He is attacked by a swarm of bees so that he is for that time being disabled and prevented from exercising any directional control over the vehicle, and any movements of his arms and legs are solely caused by the action of the bees. In each of these cases it can be said that at the material time he is not driving and therefore not driving dangerously.' *Hill v Baxter* (1957) 42 Cr App Rep 51 at 60, 61, per Pearson J

'It seems to this court that the phrase "any person driving" [in s 2(1) of the Road Safety Act 1967 (repealed: see now s 8(1) of the Road Traffic Act 1972 as substituted by the Transport Act 1981, s 25(3), Sch 8)]—once one realises that it clearly cannot refer to the time when the vehicle is in motion—applies to what one might call generally "the driver", somebody who is not only at the steering wheel while the vehicle is in motion but somebody who is in the driving seat while the vehicle is stationary; and what is more, somebody who has got out of the driving seat albeit temporarily and can still be termed, in general terms, "the driver".' *R v Price* [1968] 3 All ER 814 at 816, AC, per cur.

'In determining the meaning of any word or phrase in a statute the first question to ask always is what is the natural or ordinary meaning of that word or phrase in its context in the statute? It is only when that meaning leads to some result which cannot reasonably be supposed to have been the intention of the legislature, that it is proper to look for some other possible meaning of the word or phrase. We have been warned again and again that it is wrong and dangerous to proceed by substituting some other words for the words of the statute. The second point of law certified by the Divisional Court in this case is "Whether the requirement [of a breath test] can only be made of a person who, though no longer actually driving can in general terms be described as the driver." I decline to answer that question. It asks me to choose between two phrases "actually driving" and "the driver", neither of which is to be found in the Act. It is in effect substituting "the driver" for the statutory words "person driving or attempting to drive". The two are not the same. A person can often be properly called the driver although for quite a long time he has neither been driving nor attempting to drive. Suppose several people go off for the day in a car to the seaside and only one is to do the driving; throughout their sojourn by the sea it would in ordinary parlance be proper to call that one person the driver, but it could not be said that throughout that period he was either driving or attempting to drive the car. I must therefore consider in what circumstances a person can, by the ordinary usage of the English language, properly be said to be driving a car. Clearly the term cannot be limited to periods during which the car is in motion. Suppose the car is held up in a traffic jam and is stationary for five or ten minutes. No one would say that the driver is not driving the car during that period. He may have switched off the engine and be reading a book or a map; or he may have got out to clean his windscreen; and I do not think that it would make any difference if he got out to buy a paper from a newsvendor on the pavement. But, on the other hand, suppose the driver pulls up at the kerb and leaves his car to go shopping. I do not think that it could be said that he is driving the car while he is buying groceries. And I do not think that it would make any difference if he remained in the car while his passenger was doing the shopping; he would then not be driving but waiting for his passenger. Can it, then, be said that to give this ordinary meaning to these words would defeat the manifest intention of Parliament? I do not think so. If a man stopped in a traffic jam is still driving so also he is still driving if stopped by a policeman, and it must then be a question of degree and of circumstances for how long thereafter he can properly be said to be still driving. The mere fact that he has got out of the car would not be enough.' *Pinner v Everett* [1969] 3 All ER 257 at 258, 259, HL, per Lord Reid

'A person in the driving seat preparing to drive by switching on is, in my view, driving. It is not necessary that the vehicle should be in motion. A person is obviously driving although he may be in an almost interminable traffic block or waiting at a level crossing or at traffic lights or if he merely fills up with petrol; nor can it make any difference if in a traffic block he switches the engine off to prevent it overheating or to save petrol. But if the driver leaves his driver's seat it is more difficult. If the driver leaves his seat, removes the ignition key and locks up the car for the night, he is quite clearly, in the words of Ashworth J in *Campbell v Tormey* [[1969] 1 All ER 961] "no longer driving or intending to drive the vehicle within the plain meaning of that expression".' Ibid at 266, per Lord Upjohn

'When spotted by the police and given a breath test, the appellant and another youth were guiding the car backwards down the Mound in Edinburgh. They had motored in to Edinburgh from Perth, and the car ran out of petrol while ascending the Mound. The appellant had his hand on the steering wheel of the car as it was going backwards down the slope. He and the other youth were walking on the road, pushing or rolling the car backwards. A third member of the party was in apparent safety inside it. As the police approached the car, it veered out towards the centre of the roadway and then stopped. The issue as to whether the appellant was driving within the meaning of the section [s 1(1) of the Road Safety Act 1967 (repealed; see now Road Traffic Act 1972, s 6 as substituted by the Transport Act 1981, s 25(3), Sch 8)] depends, in my view, upon whether he was in a substantial sense controlling the movement and direction of the car. It is not essential for the purpose of establishing that he was driving it that the engine was running at the time, and it is in my view not essential to constitute driving that the appellant should be sitting in the driving seat. In *Wallace v Major* [see note, supra] Lord Chief Justice Goddard put the matter in this way: "It is quite obvious that a person who is merely steering a towed vehicle cannot have proper control; he certainly cannot have full control; and though he might have as much control as could fairly be

attributed to a person on a towed vehicle, it is obvious he cannot retain a full view of the road and traffic ahead." The court therefore held that there was in that case no driving of the car. In *Saycell v Bool* [[1948] 2 All ER 83] the test again applied was whether the accused had complete control of the vehicle at the time when the offence was alleged to have been committed, and the same test was applied in *Shimmell v Fisher* [[1951] 2 All ER 672]. The circumstances in these cases were clearly distinguishable from the present. In my view, on the facts of the present case, the extent of the appellant's powers of intervention with the movement and direction of this vehicle was sufficient to establish that within the meaning of the section he was driving, and in these circumstances the question put to us, in my view, should be answered in the affirmative.' *Ames v MacLeod* 1969 SC(J) 1 at 2, per the Lord Justice-General (Clyde)

[Section 1(1) of the Road Safety Act 1967 (repealed; see now Road Traffic Act 1972, s 6, as substituted by the Transport Act 1981, s 25(3), Sch 8) provided that if a person drove or attempted to drive with a blood-alcohol concentration above a prescribed limit, he committed an offence. Section 2(1) (repealed; see now Road Traffic Act 1972, s 8) provided for the requirement, in certain circumstances, of a breath test from any such person 'driving or attempting to drive'. (See Transport Act 1981, Sch 8.)]

'In my view, the words "driving or attempting to drive", where they occur in s 2(1), do not refer to what the defendant is doing necessarily at the precise moment of the suspicion or of the requirement but describe in effect who he is or to what class of person he belongs, and relate back to the words "drives or attempts to drive" in s 1(1), namely, the only relevant factor for the purpose of establishing an offence under s 1(1) and the present participle is used as the "continuing present" known to some grammarians, because one transaction or a single sequence of events of precisely the kind which took place here was envisaged by Parliament when it enacted the section and the driving or attempting to drive is a continuous fact within it either for the whole, or, as the case may be, at least a significant part, of the time. This seems to me to emerge decisively from the following considerations, namely: (1) The words cannot be interpreted absolutely literally. This is universally conceded. (2) The fact that the breath test can be taken "there or nearby" clearly indicates that, at least for the purpose of the actual test, the defendant at least may be off the road. (3) The proviso in s 2(1)(b) shows quite clearly that the requirement at least in that case, may be "as soon as practicable" after the relevant suspicion of a moving traffic offence arose, and it is not sensible to suggest that a new decisive condition is intended whereby it must not only be as soon as practicable after the suspected commission of the moving traffic offence, but whilst the defendant continues to be "driving or attempting to drive", when the requirement is made. If that were the true construction, the motorist must not merely be driving (a) when the alleged offence under s 1 is committed and (b) when the suspected moving traffic offence is committed but also (c) still when, as soon as practicable thereafter, the requirement is made. (4) The results of rejecting this construction are really too bizarre to be borne unless one is absolutely constrained to do so. As it was accepted in argument, to suggest that the test whether the requirement is lawfully made fails if the driving has actually come to an end leads to the following ridiculous conclusion. A motorist as drunk as may be, having committed a series of moving traffic offences, is chased by a police car over five miles, and is then at last overtaken and stopped. He is approached by the constable when, abandoning all thought of driving any further, he runs out of his car across country, flinging his ignition keys into a nearby lake as he flees, and is ultimately caught by the constable and stopped at a distance from the road in a nearby copse where a breath test is required. His one motive, as he candidly admits, is to save his licence and to escape from the police. His motor car and his journey are abandoned, so that he cannot be said at the moment of capture to be "driving or attempting to drive". Does he thereby escape the test? The answer is Yes if some of the passages in *Pinner v Everett* [supra] are assumed to be literally correct. But, if the true construction of the section be that the phrase is describing, and relates back to, the moment when the offence is committed (admittedly in most cases a continuing one) throughout the single transaction or sequence of events, no such difficulty can arise and no strained or bizarre interpretation of the phrase "driving or attempting to drive" is really involved. In my view, this is the correct construction of the section.' *Sakhuja v Allen* [1972] 2 All ER 311 at 320, 321, HL, per Lord Hailsham of St Marylebone LC

'We do not think that any ordinary meaning of the word "drive" could extend to a man who is not in the motor car, who has both feet on the road, and who is making no use of the controls apart from an occasional adjustment of the steering wheel.' *R v MacDonagh* [1974] 2 All ER 257 at 260, CA, per cur.

Australia 'It is clear from the entry relating to the word "drive" in the Shorter Oxford Dictionary . . . that the word came into the English language from the old Germanic/Teutonic tongue. It is in no way cognate with words from Latin such as "direct" or "direction". Moreover, in the entries in the same dictionary relating to the words "direct" and "steer", the word "drive" is not given as a synonym. On reading through the full entry, I have become completely satisfied that, in whatever one of the multitude of situations in which the word "drive" can be used in the English language, it always conveys, as a part of its meaning, the application of motive force by the person doing the "driving". Even where it is used as a noun it carries with it the conception of the initiation or application of force. For instance to say of a man that he has "drive" is to say more than that he has a sense of direction. It is to say that he is impelling himself purposefully in a chosen direction. I am clearly of the view that a person cannot "drive" a motor vehicle unless, in addition to having control over the steering and braking systems of the vehicle, he also has control over its means of propulsion. This is something which the steersman of a towed vehicle simply does not have. In coming to this conclusion I rely simply on what I regard as the clear meaning of the term as a word in the English language. I do not regard it as necessary to call in aid the principle of construction of a penal section. However, that principle of construction clearly, in my view, would add weight to the construction I have arrived at. I realise that I am differing from the construction given to the word by English courts of high authority. However, with respect, I feel that that construction is not consonant with the proper meaning of the word as part of the English language. I am not bound by those decisions and I decline to follow them.' *Hampson v Martin* (1981) 2 NSWLR 782 at 796, per Foster J

Australia 'In my view the absence of a definition of "driving" in the legislation [Traffic Act 1949 Qld] (a situation which appears to be common to comparable legislation throughout Australia) is deliberate. The legislature intended that the term should bear its ordinary everyday meaning, and that it would be for the courts in each particular case to say whether the conduct in question constituted "driving". The Shorter Oxford English Dictionary provided the operative definition for the verb "drive": "to urge onward and direct the course of a vehicle . . .". As Nelson J said in delivering the judgment of the Victorian Full Court in *Rowe v Hughes* [1974] VR 60 at 62: "In its ordinary sense the word 'driving' would appear to involve the actual physical control over the operation and movement of the motor car . . ."' *Allan v Quinlan, ex p Allan* (1986) 3 MVR 343 at 347, per G N Williams J

Canada 'There is a shade in meaning and one may in some circumstances be "operating" a motor vehicle without necessarily carrying out all of the mechanical functions usually associated with driving. But when, though the means of propulsion is under the control of the driver of a towing vehicle, there is a person in charge of the towed vehicle who is manipulating the steering wheel and brakes and exercising a significant measure of control over the direction and movement of that vehicle, I consider that such person can be said to be operating or driving the motor vehicle.' *R v Morton* (1970) 75 WWR 335 at 342, BC Prov Ct, per Ostler Prov J

New Zealand 'The terms [of an agreement between two bus-proprietors] are "running, driving, or plying a bus". If the words had been "running or plying" it might probably have been argued with effect that driving a bus as an employee was not within the agreement, but the term "driving" is wide enough to include, and was, in my opinion, meant to include, the employment of the defendant by another bus-proprietor.' *Woodville v McConvill* (1907) 26 NZLR 1032 at 1033, per Cooper J

New Zealand 'The word "drive" is not defined in the [Transport Act 1962] but the appellant relied on a decision of a Divisional Court in England for the proposition that a man who was "the steersman" of a disabled car under tow could not be regarded as its driver because "the vehicle was in fact not being driven; it was being drawn". The case is *Wallace v Major* [see note, supra] and the passage relied on is contained in the judgment of Lord Goddard CJ. He said: ". . . giving the ordinary meaning to words in the English language, it is difficult to see how a person who is merely at the steering wheel of a car and having nothing to do with the propulsion of the car,

having nothing to do with making the car go, is driving the vehicle. The vehicle, in fact, was not being driven; it was being drawn." In *Caughey v Spacek* [[1968] VR 600] those words of Lord Goddard are referred to with approval as expressing "robust common sense". But with all respect I think the pithy attraction of the last sentence of the passage is misleading and has the effect of diverting attention from the real issue. It is not to the point that the energy which propelled the vehicle along the road caused it to be driven or drawn; but whether under tow it was subject to a measure of control by the person steering it and able to use its braking devices. The meaning of the verb "to drive" is not limited to activities which initiate or maintain the movement of something. It can also mean the act of guiding its progress. In the present case the towing operation clearly required the active co-operation of two persons if there was to be effective control and guidance of the two vehicles which formed the towing unit. And the appellant had an important part to play as one of those two persons. It certainly was not a passive function. It required a deliberate exercise of judgment and it took him beyond any concept of being merely in charge of the towed vehicle. He was its driver. It is for reasons of this sort that I think the emphasis put by Lord Goddard upon the car and its propulsion and the contrast drawn by him between a driven and a drawn vehicle results in a use of the word "drive" which is not apposite to the conduct of the driver.' *Hawkins v Transport Dept* [1972] NZLR 1013 at 1014, per Woodhouse J

New Zealand 'I conclude . . . that each case must depend largely upon its own facts and that where in particular the driver has left his vehicle it will be a question of degree as to whether he can still be said to be driving. Speaking generally, it will depend upon whether there has been a logical sequence of events connected with the act of driving or whether that sequence has been interrupted by some act which is inconsistent with the continued act of driving.' *Transport Ministry v Wilson* [1973] 1 NZLR 200 at 205, per Quilliam J

New Zealand [On two occasions the appellant, a disqualified driver, was seen sitting beside his wife, who was in the driving seat, and he had one or both of his hands on the steering wheel and at least at times he was in fact steering the vehicle. He was in a position to operate the clutch and the footbrake, but denied having done so.] 'The proper test in a case such as this is whether the accused played an active part in the operation of the vehicle. In each case, of course, whether the part a person plays in the operation of a moving vehicle is so active and material as to fairly entitle it to be said that he is driving, is a question of fact for the jury. Provided this test is satisfied, it seems to us . . . that it is no answer that some other person is also concerned in the operation of the vehicle.' *R v Clayton* [1973] 2 NZLR 211 at 215, CA, per cur.

New Zealand 'For present purposes I am concerned only with the suggestion that a motor vehicle may be said to be in the course of "being driven" within the terms of general exception 1(d) of this policy at a time when the driver has parked the vehicle and is away somewhere else. In my view, it is under such circumstances a misuse of language to say that the vehicle is "being driven".' *Mason v Century Insurance Co Ltd* [1973] 2 NZLR 216 at 221, per Mahon J

Careless driving

'The words of the section [s 12 of the Road Traffic Act 1930 (repealed; see now Road Traffic Act 1960, s 3)] are that it is an offence when a person drives a motor vehicle without due care and attention or without reasonable consideration for other persons using the road. . . . It is wrong to assume that the word "skill" is synonymous with the word "care". . . . The question is not a question dependent upon inexperience or lack of skill. . . . "Due care and attention" is something not related to the proficiency of the driver, but governed by the essential needs of the public on the highway.' *McCrone v Riding* [1938] 1 All ER 157 at 158, 159, per Lord Hewart CJ

Dangerous driving

Australia 'The section speaks of a speed or manner which is dangerous to the public. This imports a quality in the speed or manner of driving which either intrinsically in all circumstances, or because of the particular circumstances surrounding the driving, is in a real sense potentially dangerous to a human being or human beings who as a member or as members of the public may be upon or in the vicinity of the roadway on which the driving is taking place. It may be, of course, that potential danger to property on or in the vicinity to that roadway would suffice to make the speed or manner of driving dangerous to the public, but the need for death or injury to a person to result from impact with a vehicle so driven may make that question unlikely to arise, though the possibility of its doing so must be acknowledged. This quality of being dangerous to the public in the speed or manner of driving does not depend upon resultant damage, though to complete the offence under the section, impact causing damage must occur during that driving. Whilst the immediate result of the driving may afford evidence from which the quality of the driving may be inferred, it is not that result which gives it that quality. A person may drive at a speed or in a manner dangerous to the public without causing any actual injury: it is the potentiality in fact of danger to the public in the manner of driving, whether realised by the accused or not, which makes it dangerous to the public within the meaning of the section.' *McBride v R* [1966] ALR 753 at 757, per Barwick CJ

Canada 'As was held in *Mann v The Queen* [[1966] SCR 238] dangerous driving entails more than momentary inattention. It is conduct which is criminal and deserving of punishment by the state. Mens rea is required but the manner of the driving may itself be sufficient to prove the necessary state of mind.' *R v Beaudoin* [1973] 3 OR 1 at 4, 5, Ont CA, per Kelly JA

DRIVING-BELT

'Driving-belt' includes any driving strap or rope. (Factories Act 1961, s 176)

DRUGS

'Drug' includes medicine for internal or external use. (Food Act 1984, s 132(1))

'The only question which the justices ask this court is whether the taking of insulin by the respondent was, in the circumstances which occurred, to be regarded as taking a drug which would make him liable to be found guilty of an offence under s 15(1) [of the Road Traffic Act 1930 (repealed; see now the Road Traffic Act 1972, s 5]. In my opinion, for the purposes of this Act, it is a drug. Many things which are not drugs can be taken by a person, but a drug means what I might for convenience call a medicant or medicine, something given to cure or alleviate or assist an ailing body. That is one definition. The definitions which are given in the Oxford Dictionary are very comprehensive, but I do not think that the ordinary person would have any doubt that a person taking insulin is taking what, in ordinary parlance, would be called a drug in the sense of a medicine.' *Armstrong v Clark* [1957] 1 All ER 433 at 435, per Lord Goddard CJ

'The Shorter Oxford Dictionary defines, so far as need be mentioned, "drug" as "an original, simple medicinal substance, organic or inorganic"; "medicinal" as "(i) having healing properties or attributes; adapted to medical uses . . . (ii) of or relating to the science or the practice of medicine"; and "medical" as: "pertaining to the healing art". It similarly defines "medicine" as "a medicament", which it in turn defines as "a substance used in curative treatment". It further defines "medicine" in a sense other than a substance, namely "the science and art concerned with the cure, alleviation, and prevention of disease, and with the restoration and preservation of health". Both words "drug" and "medicine" thus refer to a substance used or adapted to heal and cure, and also to the prevention of disease and preservation of health—all, so it seems to me, with regard to their relation to the science or art of curing and preventing disease.' *Beecham Foods Ltd v Customs & Excise Comrs* [1969] 3 All ER 135 at 141, per Ungoed-Thomas J; affd 1972 1 All ER 498, HL

Australia 'I see no reason why "drug" should not be construed in its ordinary sense, which includes at least any organic or inorganic substance which is a narcotic or a poison. . . . A deleterious drug . . . in my opinion, means a drug which, unless used with care and a special knowledge of its propensity to do harm, may cause substantial injury to the life or health of the user. In considering whether a person is in possession of a deleterious drug, regard may be had to the quantity of the drug in his possession. A person may be in possession of such a small quantity of a drug that, however used, it could cause no real harm. In such a case I should think he could not be said to be in possession of a deleterious drug.' *McAvoy v Gray* [1946] ALR 459 at 461, per O'Bryan J

Dangerous drugs

[The Dangerous Drugs Acts 1965 and 1967 were repealed by the Misuse of Drugs Act 1971. 'Cannabis', 'cannabis resin' and 'prepared opium' are defined by s 37 of the new Act (the definition of 'cannabis' having been substituted by s 52 of the Criminal Law Act 1977); other definitions, including those of 'coca leaf', 'medicinal opium', 'opium poppy', 'poppy straw' and 'raw opium' are to be found in Sch 2, Part IV thereof.]

DRUNK *See also* HABITUAL DRUNKARD; INTOXICATION

For the purposes of this section a person is guilty of drunkenness if owing to the influence of alcohol or any drug, whether alone or in combination with any other circumstances, he is unfit to be entrusted with his duty or with any duty which [he might reasonably expect to be called upon to perform], or behaves in a disorderly manner or in any manner likely to bring discredit on Her Majesty's service. (Army Act 1955, s 43(2) and Air Force Act 1955, s 43(2), as amended by the Armed Forces Act 1971, s 15)

[See also the Naval Discipline Act 1957, s 28(1), as so amended.]

'The Divisional Court in *Isaacs v Keech* [[1925] 2 KB 354, DC] regarded themselves as bound by the decision of the Court of Appeal in *Trebeck v Croudace* [[1918] 1 KB 158, CA]. That, however, was a different case. There was there no overriding condition that the person arrested should answer to a general description. The power to arrest depended on the particular acts done or conduct exhibited. It was a power (inter alia) to arrest without a warrant every person found drunk while in charge of any carriage on a highway. While I do not wish to express any final opinion on a case not now before me, I am not prepared to dissent from the actual decision of the Court of Appeal that the arrest was justified if the constable reasonably believed that the man was drunk, even though eventually the magistrates dismissed the charge. As at present advised, I think that "drunk" in that context means "apparently drunk". The constable must act on what he sees at the moment, and should be held to be justified if the man's appearance and behaviour are those of a drunken man. Instant action is demanded by the needs of public safety which would be endangered if an intoxicated person were left in charge of a vehicle on the road. Swinfen Eady LJ [in *Trebeck v Croudace*, supra, at p 165], said that the nature of the offences specified required the construction that the authority to apprehend applied where the circumstances were such as to enable an honest belief on reasonable grounds to exist that the offence was being committed by the person being apprehended. In the particular classes of offences there considered, I may add that the constable must act on external appearances, and a reasonable inference from these appearances, and a word like "drunk" may well be construed in that context as contrasted with its meaning in a statute imposing penalties for being drunk while in charge of a vehicle, such as a motor car, to refer merely to external appearances, even though the appearances may be afterwards held to have been misleading. Bankes LJ said [in *Trebeck v Croudace*, supra, at p 167] that action must of necessity be founded on the circumstances of the moment and mainly probably on such information as the senses of a police constable, his sight and hearing, convey to him.' *Barnard v Gorman* [1941] AC 378 at 394, 395, HL, per Lord Wright

DUAL-PURPOSE VEHICLE   *See*
VEHICLE

DUCK   *See* WILD DUCK

DUE   *See also* BECOME DUE

[A testator left a property 'upon trust for all and every of my first cousins german, to be divided equally among them share and share alike . . . and in case any of my said cousins shall depart this life before their respective shares . . . shall become due or payable, leaving any lawful issue . . . such issue shall be entitled to the same share or shares.'] 'I think that the words "due or payable" are referable to the time of the testator's death, and that the share of the cousin german dying in the testator's lifetime who left issue belongs to his issue.' *Cort v Winder* (1844) 1 Coll 320 at 321, 322, per Knight Bruce V-C

[One of the articles of association of a company gave the company a lien on shares for all moneys due to it by the holder.] 'On the 7th article the argument addressed to me was this. It was said "moneys due" included moneys owing, but not at present payable. To that I answer . . . that the word "due" may mean either owing or payable, and what it means is determined by the context. . . . It is absurd to suppose that the company may sell the shares of a man, and apply the proceeds in payment of a bill of exchange which he has given, but which is not yet due, that is not yet payable; for that must be the meaning of the word "due" in that article. In the 7th article, then, the

word "due" means payable.' *Re Stockton Malleable Iron Co* (1875) 2 Ch D 101 at 103, per Jessel MR

[Under the Merchant Shipping Act 1894, s 552, where salvage is 'due' to any person under the Act the receiver must detain the vessel.] 'The question is peculiarly short in itself, and is. What is the true rendering of the words in s 552 of the Merchant Shipping Act 1894, "where salvage is due to any person under this Act?" . . . It is clear to me that the true rendering of the words . . . is not that the money should be actually due. . . . In my judgment the word "due" in this section means recoverable under the Act.' *The Fulham* [1899] P 251 at 259, 262, 263, CA, per A L Smith LJ

'A premium becomes due on the day specified in the body of the policy as the day on or before which it is to be paid as a condition of the company's liability to pay the sum insured. . . . The condition allowing days of grace means that if the premium is paid during those days of grace it shall be treated as if it had been paid on the due date.' *McKenna v City Life Assurance Co* [1919] 2 KB 491 at 496, per Scrutton LJ

'I think the words "due and payable" in s 264 of the Companies Act [1929] [repealed; see now the Companies Act 1985, Sch 19, para 7] are meant to refer to a liability in respect of which there had to be a payment, and the particular debt for additional rates must be deemed to have become due and payable within the period of the twelve months next before the relevant date. . . . Where one finds that the debt has been appropriated to a particular period one must deal with it as such, and see whether in that character it falls within the limitations of s 264(1).' *Re Airedale Garage Co Ltd, Anglo-South American Bank Ltd v Airedale Garage Co* [1933] 1 Ch 64 at 78, 79, CA, per Lord Hanworth MR

Australia   [Section 218 of the Income Tax Assessment Act 1936–1986 (Cth) enables the Deputy Commissioner of Taxation by notice to a third party to require that third party to pay amounts 'due' to the taxpayer direct to the Deputy Commissioner in satisfaction of unpaid tax.] 'The word "due" does not mean due and payable but refers to a presently existing liability to tax even though payment is not to be made until a later date.' *Deputy Federal Comr of Taxation (NSW) v Peacock* (1980) 11 ATR 103 (headnote)

New Zealand 'The order [an authority to receive moneys] does not, in terms, cover money subsequently to become due. Its terms are "any moneys due to me by your association". "Any moneys" means "any sums of money" and the word "due" means "presently owing or payable", and does not describe moneys which might thereafter become due.' *Re Beatty* [1932] NZLR 1092 at 1095, per Kennedy J

New Zealand 'In summary . . . while fully accepting that the debts owing by a debtor continue to exist after the date of the debtor's adjudication as a bankrupt, Bigham J and Darling J held, in *Re Moss* [[1905] 2 KB 307], that such debts no longer continued, after the date of adjudication, to be "due". Edwards J in *Saunders v Baker* [[1916] NZLR 1137; [1916] GLR 709] followed this decision where one of the vital words was "due". Edwards J in *Sole v Ward* [[1919] NZLR 212; [1919] GLR 124] again followed *Re Moss* in a case where the more appropriate word to apply might seem to be "owing", saying that he would follow his earlier decision until it was reversed by the Court of Appeal. It may be that the Court of Appeal, in *Bank of New Zealand v Baker* [[1926] NZLR 462; [1926] GLR 210], while perhaps raising some doubts as to the correctness of the decisions in *Re Moss* and *Saunders v Baker*, did not expressly disapprove of them in any way in respect of a case where the word "due" is of crucial importance. For these reasons I hold that, after the bankrupt's adjudication in the present case, there was no income tax or social security charge "due" by the bankrupt to the Commissioner in respect of the years prior to the adjudication.' *Re Gunson (A Bankrupt, ex p Official Assignee* [1966] NZLR 187 at 194, per Moller J

South Africa 'It seems to me that for a debt to be due there must be a liquidated money obligation presently claimable by the debtor, for which an action could presently be brought against the garnishee. If such an obligation exists, then, to my mind, a debt is due. And such an obligation need not necessarily arise from contract; it may, I think, be created by statute.' *Whatmore v Murray* 1908 TS 970 per Innes CJ

DUE CARE AND ATTENTION *See* CARE

DUE CAUSE *See* CAUSE

DUE DILIGENCE

'An obligation to exercise due diligence is to my mind indistinguishable from an obligation to exercise reasonable care.' *Riverstone Meat Co Pty Ltd v Lancashire Shipping Co Ltd* [1960] 1 All ER 193 at 219, CA, per Willmer LJ

DUE INQUIRY

To identify vehicle

Australia 'The expression "due inquiry and search" [in the Motor Traffic Ordinance 1936–1986, s 41A (see now s 85(3)) (ACT)] is . . . the expression of a compound idea. In my opinion, it ought not to have each of the integers segregated so as to require them each to be satisfied in every case. The concept, I think, is that there should be inquiry and that inquiries when they yield leads should be followed up. Asking questions without pursuing answers may very well be found insufficient. However, the controlling word for relevant purposes, it seems to me, is the word "due". This word, as has been pointed out in decisions of this Court, accommodates to the circumstances of the case the nature and extent of the inquiry and search which is required. It is, therefore, essential that close regard be had to the nature of the situation in which the need to establish the identity of a vehicle arises.' *Slinn v Nominal Defendant* [1965] ALR 667 at 669, per Barwick CJ

DUE NOTICE

[The court was considering a clause in a policy of marine insurance stating that any deviation by the vessel should be held covered at a premium to be arranged, provided 'due notice' be given by the assured on receipt of advice of such deviation.] 'I agree that it is impossible to construe the clause as giving an option to the assured to be covered or not as he chooses, but I think that in the event of the ship arriving safely the assured would be bound to give the notice and the underwriter would be entitled to his premium. On the other hand I do not think that the words "due notice" can be read as meaning that no notice is to be considered as "due" unless it is given at a time when the underwriter can protect himself by reinsurance. I think the clause must be read as an agreement to hold the assured covered subject to a proviso which is satisfied by the giving of such a notice as the assured could give after advice of the deviation.' *Mentz, Decker & Co v Maritime Insurance Co* [1910] 1 KB 132 at 135, per Hamilton J

DUE PROCESS OF LAW

Canada [Expropriation was challenged as not being by 'due process of law' within Canadian Bill of Rights, s 1(a).] 'The expression "due process of law", or in French "application régulière de la loi", in the present case at least, means the existing law governing the rights of any owner of expropriated property, but should also include the holding of a hearing in which the principles of fundamental justice recognized by our legal system would be applied. The word "law" here means not only the law to be found in the statutes, but is also used in its abstract or general sense, and includes what are known as the principles of natural justice.' *National Capital Commission v Lapointe* [1972] FCR 568 at 571, FCTD, per Noel ACJ

DUES   *See also* ECCLESIASTICAL DUES

'In my judgment the words "dock dues" as used in this charterparty are equivalent to the words "dock charges". . . . "Dock dues" in the ordinary meaning of the English language means charges made for the use of the dock; and what is intended by this commercial document is that all proper charges which can be and are imposed by the dock authority in respect of entrance into and the use of this dock by this vessel carrying this cargo are included in the words "dock dues".' *The Katherine* (1913) 30 TLR 52 at 53, DC, per Evans P

DUKE   *See* PEERAGE

DULY

[By a tenancy agreement, the plaintiff was given an option to purchase provided she should in the meantime have 'duly' paid the rent reserved.] 'I am of opinion that on the true construction of the clause creating the condition precedent in the present case "duly" does not mean punctually, and I think that, within the meaning of the clause, the plaintiff could truly say [on the date of exercise of the

option] . . . that she had since the commencement of her tenancy duly paid the rent reserved [although on one occasion when she paid it was seventeen days overdue].' *Starkey v Barton* [1909] 1 Ch 284 at 290, per Parker J

DUMB BARGE

'The barges used were what are called "dumb barges"—that is to say, barges which with the exception of two small cabins at the ends of the barge, one for stowing the tackle of the barge and the other for the use of the bargemen, are altogether undecked and open for the reception of the cargo.' *Akt Helios v Ekman & Co* [1897] 2 QB 83 at 87, CA, per Lord Esher MR

DUMPING

Subject to subsections (3) to (5) below, substances and articles are dumped in the sea for the purposes of this Act if they are permanently deposited in the sea from a vehicle, ship, aircraft, hovercraft or marine structure, or from a structure on land constructed or adapted wholly or mainly for the purpose of depositing solids in the sea. (Dumping at Sea Act 1974, s 1(2))

[Subsection (3) of the above section excludes discharges incidental to the normal operation of ships, aircraft, etc; sub-s (4) excludes certain deposits made by harbour or lighthouse authorities; while sub-s (5) excludes deposits made in the execution of works of maintenance in a harbour.]

DUPLEX

Canada 'The current understanding of a duplex at the time of passing of the byelaw [a building byelaw] here in question is well exemplified in the above decisions [a series of Ontario cases], namely, a building of two floors in separate occupation, with separate entrances. Thus a duplex normally accommodates two families in space which would otherwise be occupied by one family in one "private residence". In the case of the "quadruplex" here in question, there would appear to be four apartments. In my view, such a building cannot be said to be a duplex within the meaning of the byelaw.' *Toronto and Gillies v Unser (Wm) Ltd* [1954] 3 DLR 641 at 649, SCC, per Kellock J

DUPLEX QUERELA

If the bishop refuses institution or admission [of a clergyman to a living] on the grounds of doctrine or ritual or, refusing on some other ground sufficient in law, fails to signify his refusal to the patron and the presentee in writing or, apparently, refuses on some ground insufficient in law to justify the refusal the presentee may bring a suit of duplex querela against the bishop before the Court of Ecclesiastical Causes Reserved. Appeal lies to a Commission of Review. If another clergyman has also been presented he is made a co-defendant. The suit, however, cannot be brought after another clergyman has been inducted to the benefice, since a temporal right has been then acquired which can only be questioned in a temporal court. (14 Halsbury's Laws (4th edn) para 823)

'The promoter in this proceeding of *"duplex querela"* complains in his libel that having been duly presented to the rectory of Drayton-Parslow, within the diocese of Oxford, and having applied to the Bishop to be instituted thereto, the bishop has refused to institute him. The answer of the bishop put forward in his responsive plea is this: That he deputed the Venerable Archdeacon Pott, one of his chaplains, to examine the promoter "in order to ascertain whether he was worthy of the office and ministry", and that "the result of the said examination satisfied him (the defendant) that the promoter was *non idoneus et minus sufficiens in literatura*". It is objected against this as an answer, that the bishop is bound to go much further, and state distinctly in what respect the clerk is *"non idoneus"* and in what respect he fell short of that standard in education or acquirements which is described as *"sufficiens in literatura"*. On the part of the bishop it is broadly claimed that his judgment on these subjects is by law final, and not subject to review by this Court. . . . In Gibson's Codex, I find the following: Double quarrel.—This is, when a clerk who is presented to a benefice, offers himself to the bishop, or other person having power, for institution, and is refused or unreasonably and illegally delayed: In which case he may appeal to the immediate superior (to the archbishop, when the ordinary refuses; or to the Court of Delegates where the archbishop refuses), and thereupon obtain an instrument directed to the ordinary, and called *duplex querela*; containing a monition to institute within a certain day; or if he refuse, then to appear and shew cause why he doth not.' *Willis v Oxford (Bp)* (1877) 2 PD 192 at 198, 200, per Lord Penzance

DUPLICATE

'The term "duplicate" means a document which is essentially the same as some other instrument. It is a very different thing from an examined copy; although an examined copy may, in effect, be a duplicate under certain circumstances.' *Toms v Cuming* (1845) 7 Man & G 88 at 94, per Maule J

DUPLICATING PROCESS

'Duplicating process' means any process involving the use of an appliance for producing multiple copies. (Copyright Act 1956, s 41(7)).

DURATION

'Clause 2 of the main agreement [made by the War Office with a school of aviation] says that the contract is to be "for the duration of the war". It is agreed that there is no decision which throws light on the meaning of these words in such a contract as this. . . . Whilst fully aware of all the difficulties from any point of view, I shall hold that the parties here were contemplating as the "duration of the war" the substantial continuance of active hostilities.' *Ruffy-Arnell & Baumann Aviation Co v R* [1922] 1 KB 599 at 611, 613, per McCardie J

DURESS   *See also* UNDUE INFLUENCE

By duress is meant the compulsion under which a person acts through fear of personal suffering, as from injury to the body or from confinement, actual or threatened. (9 Halsbury's Laws (4th edn) para 297)

Undue influence . . . should be distinguished from duress, which is part of the common law and means the compulsion under which a person acts through fear of personal suffering as from physical injury or confinement actual or threatened, although the distinction is not always clear. (18 Halsbury's Laws (4th edn) para 332)

'Duress must be a question of degree, and may begin from a gentle form of pressure, to physical violence, accompanied by threats of death.' *Griffiths v Griffiths* [1944] IR 35 at 42, per Haugh J; see also *H (otherwise D) v H* [1953] 2 All ER 1229 at 1233, per Karminski J

'Duress is a matter of defence where a prisoner is forced by fear of violence or imprisonment to do an act which in itself is criminal. If the act is a criminal act, the prisoner may be able to show that he was forced into doing it by violence, actual or threatened, and to save himself from the consequences of that violence. There is very little learning to be found in any of the books or cases on the subject of duress and it is by no means certain how far the doctrine extends, though we have the authority both of Hale and of Fitzjames Stephen, that, while it does not apply to treason, murder and some other felonies, it does apply to misdemeanours, and offences against these regulations are misdemeanours. But here again, before any question of duress arises, a jury must be satisfied that the prisoner had the intention which is laid in the indictment.' *R v Steane* [1947] 1 All ER 813 at 816, CCA, per Lord Goddard CJ

'The first question that arises is whether duress is a defence to a charge of murder as a principal in the second degree. The law has never recognised such a defence; and there is considerable authority that duress, and closely cognate judicial concepts (such as "necessity" and "coercion"), do not extend to being defences to a charge of murder as a principal—if, indeed, to murder in any degree of participation. But it is argued on behalf of the appellant, first, that the law has already recognised duress as a defence to some crimes, and that there is no logical reason for its limitation; and, secondly, that a criminal law which exacts sanctions against persons who are terrorised into performing prohibited acts is both making excessive demands on human nature, and is also imposing penalties in circumstances where they are unjustified as retribution and irrelevant as deterrent. Before turning to examine these considerations, it is convenient to have a working definition of duress—even though it is actually an extremely vague and elusive juristic concept. I take it for present purposes to denote such [well-grounded] fear, produced by threats, of death or grievous bodily harm [or unjustified imprisonment] if a certain act is not done, as overbears the actor's wish not to perform the act, and is effective, at the time of the act, in constraining him to perform it. I am quite uncertain whether the words which I have put in square brackets should be included in any such definition. It is arguable that the test should be purely subjective, and that it is contrary to principle to require the fear to be a reasonable one. Moreover, I have assumed, on the basis of *R v Hudson* [[1971] 2 All ER 44], that threat of future injury may suffice, although Stephen [Digest of the Criminal Law

(1877)] is to the contrary. Then the law leaves it also quite uncertain whether the fear induced by threats must be of death or grievous bodily harm, or whether threatened loss of liberty suffices: cases of duress in the law of contract suggest that duress may extend to fear of unjustified imprisonment; but the criminal law returns no clear answer.' *Lynch v Director of Public Prosecutions for Northern Ireland* [1975] 1 All ER 913 at 931, HL, per Lord Simon of Glaisdale

[See also *Abbot v R* [1976] 3 All ER 140.]

'Duress, whatever form it takes, is a coercion of the will so as to vitiate consent. . . . In determining whether there was a coercion of will such that there was no true consent, it is material to enquire whether the person alleged to have been coerced did or did not protest; whether, at the time he was allegedly coerced into making the contract, he did or did not have an alternative course open to him such as an adequate legal remedy; whether he was independently advised; and whether after entering the contract he took steps to avoid it. All these matters are . . . relevant in determining whether he acted voluntarily or not.' *Pao On v Lau Yiu* [1979] 3 All ER 65 at 78, PC, per Lord Scarman

'As a matter of public policy, it seems to us essential to limit the defence of duress by means of an objective criterion formulated in terms of reasonableness. Consistency of approach in defences to criminal liability is obviously desirable. Provocation and duress are analogous. In provocation the words or action of one person break the self-control of another. In duress the words or actions of one person break the will of another. The law requires a defendant to have the self-control reasonably to be expected of the ordinary citizen in this situation. It should likewise require him to have the steadfastness reasonably to be expected of the ordinary citizen in his situation. So too with self-defence, in which the law permits the use of no more force than is reasonable in the circumstances. And, in general, if a mistake is to excuse what would otherwise be criminal, the mistake must be a reasonable one.' *R v Graham* [1982] 1 All ER 801 at 806, CA, per cur.

'It is, I think, already established law that economic pressure can in law amount to duress; and that duress, if proved, not only renders voidable a transaction into which a person has entered under its compulsion but is actionable as a tort, if it causes damage or loss: see *Barton v Armstrong* [[1975] 2 All ER 465] and *Pao On v Lau Yiu* [supra]. The authorities on which these two cases were based reveal two elements in the wrong of duress: (1) pressure amounting to compulsion of the will of the victim; and (2) the illegitimacy of the pressure exerted. There must be pressure, the practical effect of which is compulsion or the absence of choice. Compulsion is variously described in the authorities as coercion or the vitiation of consent. The classical case of duress is, however, not the lack of will to submit but the victim's intentional submission arising from the realisation that there is no other practical choice open to him. This is the thread of principle which links the early law of duress (threat to life or limb) with later developments when the law came also to recognise as duress first the threat to property and now the threat to a man's business or trade.' *Universe Tankships Inc of Monrovia v International Transport Workers' Federation* [1982] 2 All ER 67 at 88, HL, per Lord Scarman

DURING

'With respect to the words [in a statement contained in a ground of appeal] "during which years", it appears to me that in their strict and proper legal sense they mean for the whole of those years; and that the other meaning, namely, "at some time in those years", is colloquial and incorrect.' *R v Inhabitants of Anderson* (1846) 9 Ad & El 663 at 668, per Lord Denman CJ

'I think that the natural meaning of the word "during" in such passages as this [i.e. used of a hired servant serving for a whole year from May Day during which service he resided in the parish of C] is "during the whole".' *R v Clixby (Inhabitants)* (1847) 11 JP 568 at 568, per Patteson J

[A father by a bond gratuitously undertook to pay his son an annuity 'during' his (the father's) life. His son predeceased him.] 'In the present instance, if the appellant instead of binding himself to pay the annuity "during his lifetime" had bound himself to pay it for twenty years, I do not doubt that he would have been bound, if his son had died within the twenty years, to go on paying it to his son's representatives until the expiry of the twenty years. I cannot see any ground for reaching a different conclusion where the obligant binds himself to pay the annuity yearly during his lifetime.' *Reid v Coggans (or Reid)* [1944] AC 91 at 101, 102, HL, per Lord Macmillan

'I readily accept that, according to the ordinary

use of language, the word "during", when used as a preposition governing a stated period of time, is well capable of bearing the meaning "in the course of" in a proper context. Indeed, in many instances the context will show clearly that it bears that sense, because the activity or condition referred to by the relevant verb by its very nature cannot have continued throughout the whole of the designated period. For example, if someone were to tell me that during the afternoon X jumped into the lake, he would manifestly be using the word "during" in the sense of "in the course of". In my judgment, however, according to the ordinary use of English, the word "during" tends to point more naturally to the meaning "throughout the whole continuance of" than the meaning "in the course of" in any context where, having regard to the verb to which it is linked, it is capable of bearing the former sense. For example, if someone were to tell me that during the period 1880 to 1890 Rudolph was King of Ruritania, I would regard such statement as meaning prima facie that Rudolph reigned throughout the period 1880 to 1890 unless there were additional factors in the particular context which showed that the informant merely meant that Rudolph's reign fell within that period.' *Davenport (Inspector of Taxes) v Hasslacher* [1977] 3 All ER 396 at 400, per Slade J

DURING PLEASURE   *See* PLEASURE

DUSTBIN

'Dustbin' means a movable receptacle for the deposit of ashes or refuse. (Public Health Act 1936, s 343)

DUTY

New Zealand [Section 16 of the National Roads Act 1953 empowers delegation of 'all or any part or parts of the Board's duties in respect of the design, supervision, construction, or maintenance or the administration of any . . . State highway'.] 'I would read the word "duties" as being used in its popular sense as the equivalent of "functions", and in that sense as having a very wide meaning sufficient to include powers incidental to the exercise of functions. An illustration of the word "duties" being interpreted in this wide popular sense can be found in *Canadian Pacific*

Tobacco Co Ltd v Stapleton [(1952) 86 CLR 1].' *A-G v Cooper* [1974] 2 NZLR 713 at 720, CA, per Richmond J

DWELLING
DWELLING-HOUSE   *See also*
PRIVATE DWELLING

'Dwelling-house' means a building used or constructed or adapted to be used wholly or principally for human habitation. (London Building Act 1930, s 5)

'Dwelling-house' includes any part of a house where that part is occupied separately as a dwelling-house. (Representation of the People Act 1983, s 202(1))

'Dwelling-house' includes any building or part thereof which is occupied as a dwelling, and any yard, garden, garage or outhouse belonging to the dwelling-house and occupied therewith. (Matrimonial Homes Act 1983, s 10(1); Matrimonial and Family Proceedings Act 1984, s 27)

'Dwelling' means a building or part of a building occupied or intended to be occupied as a separate dwelling, together with any yard, garden, outhouses and appurtenances belonging to it or usually enjoyed with it. (Housing Act 1985, ss 237, 525; Housing Associations Act 1985, s 106(1))

A dwelling-house is a house if, and only if, it . . . is a structure reasonably so called;' so that—
(a) where a building is divided horizontally, the flats or other units into which it is divided are not houses;
(b) where a building is divided vertically, the units into which it is divided may be houses;
(c) where a building is not structurally detached, it is not a house if a material part of it lies above or below the remainder of the structure.
A dwelling-house which is not a house is a flat. (Housing Act 1985, s 183(2), (3))

'A house, as soon as built and fitted for residence, does not become a dwelling-house until some person dwells in it.' *R v Allison* (1843) 2 LTOS 288 at 289, per Maule J

'It is quite clear that part of a house, even a single room, may properly and legally be considered and described as a house or dwelling-

house. For instance, Lord Coke, in treating of burglary, in 3 Inst. 64–65, says: "A chamber or room, be it upper or lower, wherein any person doth inhabit or dwell, is *domus mansionalis* in law." . . . The following may also be mentioned as familiar instances of parts of houses being considered houses, viz., chambers in the Albany, chambers in the Inns of Court, rooms in the colleges at the universities . . . apartments in Hampton Court Palace.' *Thompson v Ward, Ellis v Burch* (1871) LR 6 CP 327 at 358, 359, per Bovill CJ

'A "dwelling-house" need not, in my opinion, be a separate building; it may be bounded by a horizontal plane just as well as by a vertical plane.' *Re Hecquard, ex p Hecquard* (1889) 24 QBD 71 at 75, CA, per Lindley LJ

'By a "dwelling-house" I understand a house in which people live or which is physically capable of being used for human habitation.' *Lewin v End* [1906] AC 299 at 304, per Lord Atkinson

'I am of opinion that the expression "dwelling-house" may include a whole tenement even although that tenement comprises four dwelling-houses. The whole question is one simply of identification.' *Kirkpatrick v Maxwelltown Town Council* 1912 SC 288 at 297, per the Lord President

'I am bound to say that in my view a dwelling-house does not cease to be a dwelling-house because the people who dwell in it are of such a character and live under such conditions as to make it a common lodging-house.' *Re Ross & Leicester Corpn* (1932) 96 JP 459 at 461, per Swift J

'It is, no doubt, true that the acts of sleeping upon premises at night and having meals upon them by day are acts which may be described as "residential" in character. But the use of premises as a dwelling-house is by no means necessarily confined to their use by the tenant for sleeping and eating. The experience of great numbers of Englishmen during the last six years provides many instances of sleeping and eating upon premises which could by no fair use of language on that account be described as dwelling-houses. In other words, to sleep on particular premises at night, or to have one's meals upon them by day, or both, ought not *ipso facto* to have the effect in law of making those premises a dwelling-house.' *Macmillan & Co Ltd v Rees* [1946] 1 All ER 675 at 677, CA, per cur.

'It is not difficult to see that the word dwelling-house may be used in different senses in different connections. Thus we may speak of a garden attached to or surrounding a dwelling-house. In this sense by "dwelling-house" we mean only the dwelling-house itself, the actual bricks and mortar. On the other hand, a conveyance or a devise of a dwelling-house would normally be construed as including all the land within the curtilage of the house.' *Belfast Corpn v Kelso* [1953] NI 160 at 163, per Black LJ

'Section 32(5) of the Housing Act 1961 [repealed; see now the Landlord and Tenant Act 1985, s 16] contains the following definition: "'lease of a dwelling-house' means a lease whereby a building or part of a building is let wholly or mainly as a private dwelling, and 'the dwelling-house' means that building or part of a building." For my part I have no doubt but that, as counsel for the plaintiff has correctly conceded, the definition given to "the dwelling-house" was intended to and does exclude from the ambit of the landlord's liability those parts of the demise that are not part of the building itself. In particular, to my mind, there would normally be excluded from the ambit of those liabilities a garden or a pond, and likewise the fences round or a gate leading to such a garden or pond. Similarly, there would normally be excluded the steps leading into a garden from a road. Equally, however, on the other hand, it would appear clear that in London where there are many buildings with areas and area steps leading down into them, those areas, and the steps into them, are not meant to be excluded from the ambit of liabilities.' *Brown v Liverpool Corpn* [1969] 3 All ER 1345 at 1347, per Sachs LJ

'I do not . . . take the view that the word "dwelling house" as it is found in a conveyance can be construed in a special sense to connote only that part of a building in which you dwell. It must in a conveyance, unless you find something to the contrary, be used in a physical sense and, in a conveyance which is not construed as a conveyance of all that is below the surface, so as to include at least the foundations and the surface of the earth on which the house stands. And where, as here, you find a cellar immediately under the sitting room floor with no separate ceiling and containing supports for that floor, it can, I think, be properly said to be part of the "dwelling house".' *Grigsby v Melville* [1973] 3 All ER 455 at 462, CA, per Stamp LJ

'Generally speaking "a dwelling-house let as a separate dwelling" envisages that at least someone, that someone being in most cases the tenant in occupation, will have the right to go to any part of the premises he chooses. It may well be that a tenant who takes a separate dwelling-house will sublet so as to preclude himself, vis-à-vis the sub-lessee, from entering another part of the premises for the period of the subletting; but that is something which occurs after the lease has been entered into and in one way detracts from the right of the tenant vis-à-vis the landlord to go to another room. The existence of someone able to go of his own right to all the rooms of the premises is one of the hallmarks of a dwelling house.' *St Catherine's College v Dorling* [1979] 3 All ER 250 at 255, CA, per Eveleigh LJ

Australia '"Dwelling" ordinarily signifies a place of abode or residence, a tenement, habitation, or house, which premises a person or persons are using as a place for sleeping, and usually for the provision of some or all of their meals. The word is not used as a term of art, and has to be interpreted in accordance with its ordinary, proper, and grammatical sense in the context in which it appears. . . . "Dwelling" is perhaps more comprehensive than "dwelling-house"; "house" may imply some additional requirement not necessitated by "dwelling".' *Campbell v O'Sullivan* (1947) SASR 195 at 201, per Mayo J

Australia 'Whether particular premises are a dwelling-house is a question to be decided on the facts of each case. . . . In deciding that question the test is whether at the material time the premises possessed the characteristics ordinarily found in buildings used or let for human habitation as homes.' *Bakes v Huckle* [1948] VLR 159 at 160, per Barry J

Canada [Insurer denied liability on ground inter alia that house was not a 'dwelling-house' by reason of the presence of lodgers.] 'With regard to the alleged misdescription of the premises as a dwelling-house, I am not able to concur in the holding that the presence of "lodgers", one or more, on the premises proves that the designation of dwelling-house was such a misdescription as vitiated the policy. A dwelling-house does not cease to be such simply because one or more lodgers are taken in by the occupants.' *Mahomed v Anchor Fire and Marine Insurance Co* (1913) 48 SCR 546 at 551, SCC, per Davies J

New Zealand [A house was insured as a dwelling-house, but was used to accommodate a small number of boarders.] 'In my opinion, there has been no alteration of the nature of the occupation of the insured premises. It was insured as a "dwelling-house". It continued to be a "dwelling-house" notwithstanding some boarders were taken in. . . . In *Rafferty v New Brunswick Insurance Co* [an American case] it was held that it is not a violation of a policy of insurance "that a house insured as a dwelling-house is afterwards occupied as a boarding-house, if keeping a boarding-house is not in the enumeration of things forbidden". It was said in that case by White J, "The defendants say the house was kept as a boarding-house, but . . . when so used it is still a 'dwelling-house', and a private house, as distinguished from a public house or tavern".' *Brown v Ocean Accident & Guarantee Corpn Ltd* [1916] NZLR 377 at 381, 384, per Cooper J; also reported [1916] GLR 276 at 278

New Zealand 'The fact is, or so it seems to me, that at the very time when the lease was granted, the premises, though a dwelling-house in the general sense, actually comprised a congeries of dwelling-houses inasmuch as each room in the house was then sublet as a separate dwelling. Secondly, the defendant at no time since the lease was granted, or indeed prior thereto, occupied the premises, or any portion thereof. It was at no time *his* dwelling-house. It is true that, so far as the defendant is concerned, the premises were let to him at one rental of five guineas per week, but I do not think that that is material if in fact at the time of the granting of the lease the premises were actually not a separate dwelling-house but a congeries of separate dwellings. If that is right, then the Act does not apply to the premises because, though a dwelling-house, that dwelling-house was not let as a separate dwelling.' *Meek v Horlock* [1946] NZLR 502 at 504, per Myers CJ; also reported [1946] GLR 317

New Zealand 'It may well be that, as a dwelling-place is a place where one lives, it cannot be said that a person really lives where he does nothing but sleep. On the other hand, does a man live where he cooks and eats, reads, and entertains his friends, but does not sleep? In this case, I think this tenant really dwells partly in one place and partly in the other. In that case, neither can correctly be described as his dwelling-house, but either can be described as only part of his dwelling-house.' *McCarthy v Preston* [1951] NZLR 1091 at 1092, 1093, per Northcroft J; also reported [1952] GLR 73 at 74

New Zealand 'The usual definition of "dwelling-house" accepted in all the legal dictionaries is wide enough to cover a block of flats.' *Carmichael v Ripley Finance Co Ltd* [1974] 1 NZLR 557 at 559, per Perry J

United States 'Dwelling' means a residential structure that contains 1 to 4 units, whether or not that structure is attached to real property. The term includes an individual condominium unit, cooperative unit, mobile home and trailer, if it is used as a residence. (Truth in Lending Regulations 1982, 12 CFR s 226.2(a)(19))

United States The term 'dwelling' means a residential structure or mobile home which contains one to four family housing units, or individual units of condominiums or cooperatives. (Truth in Lending Act 1968, s 103(v))

DYING DECLARATION

South Africa 'In order that a "dying declaration" may be admitted as evidence, the rule is that three things must have occurred: the person must have been in danger of impending death; he must have realised the extent of his danger so as to have given up all hope of life; and death must have ensued.' *R v Abdul* 1905 TS 122, per Innes CJ

E

E & OE

Australia 'The letters are, of course, the initials of "Errors and Omissions Excepted".

According to Jowitt's Dictionary of English Law, they are "appended to an account stated in order to excuse slight mistakes or oversights". . . . But although, in the ordinary case, it saves the creditor from being precluded from making an alteration which may be unwarranted by the facts, it is not notice that the creditor reserves the right to amend the account in any respect and to any extent at any time. At least I find that it would be not so understood by reasonable men. Specifically, I do not think a reasonable man would understand the initials on these statements of account as conveying that the plaintiff was thereby reserving the right to increase the amount stated in the account five or ten fold and perhaps a year or more after it was rendered.' *NW County District Council v J I Case (Australia) Pty Ltd* [1974] 2 NSWLR 511 at 520, per Jeffrey J

EARL   *See* PEERAGE

EARL MARSHAL   *See* ARMS

EARLY CLOSING DAY

'Early closing day' means as respects a shop, the day on which the shop is required to be closed for the serving of customers not later than one o'clock in the afternoon in pursuance of section 1 of this Act and the Shops (Early Closing Days) Act 1965. (Shops Act 1950, s 74(1), as substituted by the Shops (Early Closing Days) Act 1965, s 3)

EARNED INCOME   *See* INCOME

EARNEST

'It is somewhat difficult to give a precise definition of the word "earnest". Certain characteristics, however, seem to be clear. An earnest must be a tangible thing. . . . That thing must be given at the moment at which the contract is concluded, because it is something given to bind the contract, and, therefore, it must come into existence at the making or conclusion of the contract. The thing given in that way must be given by the contracting party who gives it, as an earnest or token of good faith, and as a guarantee that he will fulfil his contract, and subject to the terms that if, owing to his default, the contract goes off, it will be forfeited. If, on the other hand, the contract is fulfilled, an earnest may still serve a further purpose and operate by way of part payment. . . . In Benjamin on Sale (6th Edn),

p 255, . . . the author says: "The giving of earnest . . . has fallen so much into disuse, that the two expressions . . . 'give something in earnest' or 'in part payment' are often treated as meaning the same thing, although the language clearly intimates that the earnest is 'something to bind the bargain', or 'the contract', whereas it is manifest that there can be no part payment till after the bargain has been bound, or closed. Earnest may be money, or some gift or token . . . given by the buyer to the seller and accepted by the latter to mark the final conclusive assent of both sides to the bargain. . . . An earnest did not lose its character because the same thing might also avail as a part payment."' *Farr, Smith & Co v Messers Ltd* [1928] 1 KB 397 at 408, 409, per Wright J

EARNING CAPACITY

Australia   [Paragraph (k) of s 75(2) of the Family Law Act 1975 (Cth) which provides that the court shall take into account in exercising jurisdiction under s 74, 'the duration of the marriage and the extent to which it has affected the earning capacity of the party whose maintenance is under consideration'.] 'The words "earning capacity" in that paragraph refer to skills in earning money, whether by way of wages or by way of business acumen. Paragraph (k) cannot be read as if it referred to any loss of income as a result of a marriage. "Earning capacity" does not have the same meaning as income. It relates to the ability to earn income which may or may not be commensurate with the income actually received: *J v J* [1955] P 215.' *In the Marriage of J Hirst and E Rosen* (1982) 8 Fam LR 251 at 252, per Nygh J

Australia   '"Earning capacity" in our view, as expressed in the Family Law Act [1975 (Cth) s 75(2)(k)] must, as there is no provision in the Act to the contrary, be interpreted as having the same meaning as it has had since the first Maintenance Acts in Australia, namely, as a capacity to obtain income which could be used to provide maintenance for a wife or children and not merely as current income from personal exertion or from the use of personal skills. A spouse who has assets which are not income producing but which could be used for that purpose has a capacity to earn the amount which those assets reasonably invested or utilized would produce. See generally *Wearne v Wearne (No 3)* [1964] ALR 207. Ability to pay has a similar meaning and must be judged in the light of all the circumstances, mental and physical resources, money at his disposal, capital position and current necessary expenditure.' *In the Marriage of Beck* (1983) 48 ALR 470 at 472–473, per cur.

EARNINGS *See also* ANTICIPATED EARNINGS

(1) For the purposes of this Act, but subject to the following subsection, 'earnings' are any sums payable to a person—
   (a) by way of wages or salary (including any fees, bonus, commission, overtime pay or other emoluments payable in addition to wages or salary or payable under a contract of service);
   (b) by way of pension (including an annuity in respect of past services, whether or not rendered to the person paying the annuity, and including periodical payments by way of compensation for the loss, abolition or relinquishment, or diminution in the emoluments, of any office or employment);
   (c) by way of statutory sick pay.
(2) The following shall not be treated as earnings:—
   (a) sums payable by any public department of the Government of Northern Ireland or of a territory outside the United Kingdom;
   (b) pay or allowances payable to the debtor as a member of Her Majesty's forces;
   (c) pension, allowances or benefit payable under any of the enactments specified in Schedule 4 to this Act (being enactments relating to social security);
   (d) pension or allowances payable in respect of disablement or disability;
   (e) [except in relation to a maintenance order] wages payable to a person as a seaman, other than wages payable to him as a seaman of a fishing boat;
   (f) guaranteed minimum pension within the meaning of the Social Security Pensions Act 1975.
(Attachment of Earnings Act 1971, s 24, as amended)

In this Act 'earnings' includes any remuneration or profit derived from an employment; and 'earner' shall be construed accordingly. (Social Security Act 1975, s 3(1))

[Regulations may provide that certain sums are to be earnings for social security purposes: see s 18 of the Social Security (Miscellaneous Provisions) Act 1977.]

'Where the employment is of such nature that the habitual giving and receiving of "tips" is open and notorious and sanctioned by the employer, so that he could not complain of the retention by the servant of the money thus received, we think the money thus received with his knowledge and approval ought to be brought into account in estimating the average weekly earnings [under the Workmen's Compensation Act 1906, Sch I (repealed)].' *Penn v Spiers & Pond Ltd* [1908] 1 KB 766 at 770, CA, per cur.

'The question is whether the family allowance which is given to a married soldier whose wife is living separate from him by reason of the exigencies of the service is "earnings". . . . To my mind the answer is obvious. He is entitled to it and he does earn it, and none the less so because he is compelled to assent to the condition on which he earns it, namely, that it shall be paid direct to his wife.' *Doncaster Amalgamated Collieries Ltd v Leech* [1941] 1 KB 649 at 653, CA, per Scott LJ

New Zealand 'In my view, the phrase "is earning" in s 5(6) of the Workers' Compensation Act 1922 [repealed; see now s 14(4) of the Workers' Compensation Act 1956] means "is entitled to receive under subsisting contract of employment"; and "the weekly amount which the worker is earning after the accident" means the amount the worker would receive for a week's work if he worked a full week, and provided, of course, that time lost by reason of his original injury must be disregarded.' *Davis v Attorney-General* [1959] NZLR 454 at 455, Comp CT, per Archer J

United States 'Earnings' means compensation paid or payable to an individual for his account for personal services rendered or to be rendered by him, whether denominated as wages, salary, commission, bonus, or otherwise, and includes periodic payments pursuant to a pension, retirement, or disability program. (Uniform Consumer Credit Code 1969, s 1.301(8))

EARTHCLOSET

'Earthcloset' means a closet having a moveable receptacle for the reception of fæcal matter and its deodorisation by the use of earth, ashes or chemicals, or by other methods. (Building Act 1984, s 126)

EASEMENT

An easement is a right annexed to land to utilise other land of different ownership in a particular manner (not involving the taking of any part of the natural produce of that land or of any part of its soil) or to prevent the owner of the other land from utilising his land in a particular manner.

The piece of land in respect of which an easement is enjoyed is called 'the dominant tenement', and that over which the right is exercised is called 'the servient tenement', and the expressions 'dominant owner' and 'servient owner' bear corresponding meanings.

Since 1926 the only easements capable of subsisting at law are easements for an interest equivalent to an estate in fee simple absolute in possession or a term of years absolute. A legal easement is an easement capable of subsisting at law which has been validly created at law, namely by statute, deed or prescription. An easement which does not take effect as a legal easement takes effect as an equitable interest and is called an equitable easement. In the strict statutory meaning of the term an equitable easement is a proprietary interest in land such as would before 1926 have been recognised as capable of being conveyed or created at law, but which since 1926 takes effect only as an equitable interest. The class of equitable easements certainly includes those easements which, if created in the same manner before 1926, would have taken effect as legal easements, but which by virtue of the Law of Property Act 1925 are no longer capable of subsisting at law and thus take effect (if at all) as equitable interests. It is far from certain whether the class of equitable easements extends beyond this limited category. The term 'equitable easement' is also loosely but incorrectly applied to various other equitable rights over land which are not easements within the strict statutory meaning of the term.

The essential characteristics of an easement are (1) there must be a dominant and a servient tenement; (2) the easement must accommodate the dominant tenement; (3) the dominant and servient owners must be different persons; and (4) the easement must be capable of forming the subject matter of a grant. It is an essential characteristic of every easement that there is both a servient and a dominant tenement. The easement must be appurtenant to the dominant tenement.

A person possesses an easement in respect of his enjoyment of some estate or interest in a particular piece of land, and the easement is said to be appurtenant to that land. No one can possess an easement irrespective of his enjoyment of some estate or interest in a particular piece of land, for there is no such thing as an easement in gross. When validly annexed to the land constituting the dominant tenement an easement remains inseparably attached to that tenement so long as the easement continues to exist; the easement cannot be severed from the dominant tenement, nor can estates be created in it apart from the dominant tenement, nor can it be made a right in gross.

An easement which is created for a legal estate is to enure for the benefit of the land to which it is intended to be annexed, and nothing in the Law of Property Act 1925 affects the right of a person to acquire, hold or exercise an easement over or in relation to land for a legal estate in common with any other person or the power of creating or conveying that easement. (14 Halsbury's Laws (4th edn) paras 1, 2, 5, 6, 7, 8, 9)

In this Act 'similar right', where the reference is to an easement or similar right in relation to any land, means any of the following rights, that is to say, any right to take game or fish or other sporting right exercisable in respect of that land, any right to fell and remove trees standing thereon, any right to take timber or other wood, water, turf or other materials therefrom, any right to work minerals thereon (otherwise than by virtue of a mining lease or of an order conferring working rights), and any right to depasture cattle or other animals thereon, except any such sporting or other right which—

(a) subsists only as a right incidental to the ownership of the land in question, or to some other interest therein, or to a right to occupy that land, or

(b) is exercisable by virtue of a licence granted otherwise than for valuable consideration;

and any right over land which constitutes an easement or similar right in relation thereto, if apart from this subsection it would not constitute an interest in that land, shall be treated for the purposes of this Act as constituting an interest therein. (Opencast Coal Act 1958, s 51(3))

'There is a great difference between interests and profits, as rents, commons, etc and bare easements, such as are lights, ayre, gutters, stillicidia, and the like; for though while they are in one hand, they may be stopped, or fore-done, because a man cannot be said to wrong himself, yet if they be divided, things of that nature (still in being) do revive because they are of no less use of themselves in one hand than in divers, being equally (*rebus stantibus* in the same use and occupation) necessary for the several houses to which they belong but clearly, if even such things be foredone or altered, while they are in one hand, and so being the houses be again divided, they cannot be restored by law but must be taken as they were at the time of the conveyance.' *Robins v Barnes* (1615) Hob 131 at 131, per Hobart CJ

'The water of a spring, when it first issues from the ground . . . is no part of the soil, like sand, or clay, or stones; nor the produce of the soil, like grass, or turves, or trees. A right to take these by custom, claimed by all the inhabitants of a district, would clearly be bad; for they all come under the category of profit à prendre, being part of the soil or the produce of the soil. . . . As to customary rights claimed by reason of inhabitancy, the distinction has always been between a mere easement and profit à prendre. A custom for all the inhab-itants of a vill to dance on a particular close at all times of the year, at free will, for their recreation, has been held good, this being a mere easement . . . and we held [in *Bland v Lipscombe* (1854) 4 E & B 713 n.] . . . that, to a declaration for breaking and entering the plaintiff's close and taking his fish, a custom pleaded for all the inhabitants of the parish to angle and catch in the *locus in quo* was bad, as this was a profit à prendre, and might lead to the destruction of the subject-matter to which the alleged custom applied.' *Race v Ward* (1855) 4 E & B 702 at 709, 713, per cur.

'One of the earliest definitions of an easement with which we are acquainted is in the "Termes de la Ley", and it is "a privilege that one neigh-bour hath of another by writing or prescrip-tion, without profit, as a way or a sink through his land." In this definition custom is not men-tioned, prescription is, and it therefore seems to point to a privilege belonging to an indi-vidual, not a custom which appertains to many as a class.' *Mounsey v Ismay* (1865) 3 H & C 486 at 497, per cur.

'If a building is divided into floors or "flats", separately owned (an illustration which occurs in many of the authorities), the owner of each upper floor or "flat" is entitled . . . to vertical support from the lower part of the building, and to the benefit of such lateral support as

may be of right enjoyed by the building itself. . . . Any such right of support to a building, or part of a building, is an easement.' *Dalton v Angus* (1881) 6 App Cas 740 at 792, 793, per Lord Selborne LC

'An easement is some right which a person has over land which is not his own; but, if the land is his own, if he has an interest in it, then his right is not an easement. You cannot have an easement over your own land; and if your right is an interest in land it is a hereditament.' *Metropolitan Rly Co v Fowler* [1892] 1 QB 165 at 171, CA, per Lord Esher MR

'The term "easement" has, somewhat loosely and inaccurately perhaps, but still with suffi-cient accuracy for some purposes, been said to define the case of a public right of way, in which case there exists no dominant and servient tenement; but in strictness, and according to the proper use of legal language, the term "easement" does imply a dominant tenement in respect of which the easement is claimed, and a servient tenement upon which the right claimed is exercised.' *Hawkins v Rutter* [1892] 1 QB 668 at 671, DC, per Lord Coleridge CJ

'An easement . . . is a mere burden upon the proprietary right of the owner in fee. It may consist, either in restraining, for the benefit of the dominant tenement, certain uses which its owner might otherwise make of the servient land, or, in compelling him to submit to uses of that land by others, which are not incompatible with his retaining the right of property.' Ibid, on appeal [1893] AC 416 at 426, per Lord Watson

'An easement of necessity . . . means an easement without which the property retained cannot be used at all, and not one merely necessary to the reasonable enjoyment of that property.' *Union Lighterage Co v London Graving Dock Co* [1902] 2 Ch 557 at 573, CA, per Stirling LJ

'The right of a person who is owner or occupier of a building with windows, privileged as ancient lights, in regard to the protection of the light coming to those windows, is a purely legal right. It is an easement belonging to the class known as negative easements. It is nothing more or less than the right to prevent the owner or occupier of an adjoining tenement from building or placing on his own land anything which has the effect of illegally obstructing or obscuring the light of the dominant tenement.' *Colls v Home & Colonial Stores Ltd* [1904] AC 179 at 185, 186, per Lord Macnaghten

'There are two kinds of easement known to the law: positive easements, such as a right of way, which give the owner of land *a right himself to do something* on or to his neighbour's land: and negative easements, such as a right of light, which gives him *a right to stop his neighbour doing something* on his (the neighbour's) own land.' *Phipps v Pears* [1964] 2 All ER 35 at 37, CA, per Lord Denning MR; also reported [1965] 1 QB 76

EASTER BREAK

'Easter break' means the period beginning with the Thursday before and ending with the Tuesday after Easter Day. (Local Government Act 1972, s 270(1); Representation of the People Act 1983, s 40(1)

ECCLESIASTICAL BUILDING

[Building preservation orders could not be made in respect of 'ecclesiastical buildings' under s 30(2)(a) of the Town and Country Planning Act 1962 (repealed; see now the Town and Country Planning Act 1971, s 58.] 'It seems to me that a building, in order to be an ecclesiastical building, must be owned by the ecclesiastical authorities. It must be owned by them as freehold or as leasehold. In addition, it must, I think, have some further ecclesiastical attribute. Let me take some illustrations. Any church which is open for public religious worship is obviously an ecclesiastical building. So, also, is a vestry or a chapter house; equally, I should have thought a theological college; so, also, a bishop's palace. In such cases, in addition to ownership by the ecclesiastical authorities, there is also a further attribute showing that it has an ecclesiastical quality. What about a rectory? A rectory of the Church of England has for centuries been recognised to have special attributes connected with the church. It is vested in the incumbent for the time being as a corporation sole. It is a house set apart, not merely as his residence, but so as to be used by him for his spiritual, pastoral and parochial duties. He cannot leave it except with the consent of the bishop; and, if he fails to reside in it, the bishop can order him to go back, and any occupier can be expelled to make room for him. In *Bishop of Gloucester v Cunnington* [[1943] KB 101], this court held that, by reason of the special attributes attaching to a rectory or a parsonage, such houses did not come within the Rent Restriction Acts. Furthermore, within the last forty years, the ecclesiastical authorities of the Church of England,

under the Dilapidations Measure, which dates back to 1923 [see now the Repair of Benefice Buildings Measure 1972], do exercise control over any repairs, alterations or demolition of parsonage houses. In these circumstances, it is quite plain to my mind that a rectory or a parsonage house of the Church of England has special attributes, more than mere ownership, which show it to be an "ecclesiastical building".' *Phillips v Minister of Housing and Local Government* [1964] 2 All ER 824 at 825, CA, per Lord Denning MR; also reported [1965] 1 QB 156

'The first question is whether the Howard Church is an "ecclesiastical building". . . . To satisfy those words the building must be owned by the ecclesiastical authorities—as freehold or leasehold—and it must have some other ecclesiastical attribute marking it out as ecclesiastical. I think this building has such an attribute. It was designed as a church, built as a church, looks like a church and was used as a church for nearly 200 years. That stamps it with the mark "ecclesiastical" as much as anything could do. Even though it should fall into disuse, it would still remain an "ecclesiastical building". But, if it was put to some secular purpose, such as storing records or as a museum, it would then cease to be an "ecclesiastical building".' *A-G (on the relation of Bedfordshire County Council) v Trustees of the Howard United Reformed Church, Bedford* [1974] 3 All ER 273 at 276, CA, per Lord Denning MR; revsd. on other grounds [1975] 2 All ER 337, HL

'A church is a place for the worship of God, usually in public but in its broadest meaning not always so. I do not find it necessary to decide whether the word "ecclesiastical" is bound up with the practice of the Christian faith, and I would leave for decision hereafter whether the word "ecclesiastical" can accurately be applied to synagogues, mosques, or Hindu and Buddhist temples. It suffices for me that the words "ecclesiastical building" imply some connection with the worship of God.' Ibid, at 280, per Lawton J

ECCLESIASTICAL CHARITY   *See*
CHARITY

ECCLESIASTICAL CORPORATION

A corporation sole which is recognised by the law as having perpetual succession in right of an office or function of a spiritual character is an ecclesiastical corporation. A corporation aggregate which is constituted for a spiritual purpose is an ecclesiastical corporation. Archbishops, bishops, some deans, prebendaries, vicars choral, canons, all archdeacons and incumbents, including rectors and vicars and perpetual curates (now vicars), are corporations sole. They are all ecclesiastical corporations excepting a rector while the rectory is in lay hands. (14 Halsbury's Laws (4th edn) paras 1253, 1254)

Ecclesiastical corporations are where the members that compose it are entirely spiritual persons; such as bishops; certain deans, and prebendaries; all archdeacons, parsons, and vicars; which are sole corporations: deans and chapters at present, and formerly prior and convent, abbot and monks, and the like, bodies aggregate. These are erected for the furtherance of religion, and the perpetuating the rights of the church. (1 Bl Com 458)

'Ecclesiastical corporation' means a corporation in the Church of England, whether sole or aggregate, which is established for spiritual purposes. (Land Commission Act 1967, s 90)

ECCLESIASTICAL DUES

The expression 'ecclesiastical dues' includes offerings and oblations. (New Parishes Measure 1943, s 29)

ECCLESIASTICAL LAW

The term 'ecclesiastical law' may be used both in a general and in a technical sense. In its general sense it means the law relating to any matter concerning the Church of England administered and enforced in any court; in its technical sense it means the law administered by ecclesiastical courts and persons. This distinction is important, as different sanctions apply. Thus an order of certiorari does not lie to bring up to be quashed an order of a consistory court, but where it is alleged that an ecclesiastical court has exceeded its jurisdiction the prerogative remedy of prohibition is available. (14 Halsbury's Laws (4th edn) para 301)

'The ecclesiastical law of England is not a foreign law. It is a part of the general law of England—of the common law—in that wider sense which embraces all the ancient and approving customs of England which form law,

including not only that law . . . to which the term Common Law is sometimes in a narrower sense confined, but also that law administered in Chancery and commonly called Equity, and also that law administered in the Courts Ecclesiastical, that last law consisting of such canons and constitutions ecclesiastical as have been allowed by general consent and custom within the realm—and form, as is laid down in *Caudre's Case* [(1591) 5 Co Rep 1a] the King's ecclesiastical law.' *Mackonochie v Penzance (Lord)* (1881) 6 App Cas 424 at 446, per Lord Blackburn

ECCLESIASTICAL OFFICE

'Ecclesiastical office' means any bishopric, ecclesiastical dignity, or preferment within the meaning of the Church Discipline Act 1840 and includes any lay office in connection therewith, or in connection with any cathedral corporation. (Welsh Church Act 1914, s 38(1))

ECCLESIASTICAL PROPERTY

Property which is owned by any person in the capacity of a representative of the Church of England is ecclesiastical property. Where a person owns property and the relation between the person and the thing owned arises out of and can be defined by reference to spiritual functions to be performed on behalf of the Church of England, the property is owned by the person in the capacity of a representative of the Church of England, and is ecclesiastical property.

Thus ecclesiastical property includes every legal right and every description of property which is vested in any person for the purpose of furthering the spiritual work of the Church, such as the right to levy a church rate, the right to demand pew rents (where that right still subsists), and buildings or other property conveyed upon trust to be used for furthering the spiritual work of a parish or of the Church at large. (14 Halsbury's Laws (4th edn) para 1224)

In this section the expression 'ecclesiastical property' means land belonging to an ecclesiastical benefice of the Church of England, or being or forming part of a church subject to the jurisdiction of the bishop of any diocese of the Church of England or the site of a church so subject, or being or forming part of a burial ground so subject. (Harbours Act 1964, s 49; Land Commission Act 1971, s 90; Ancient

Monuments and Archaeological Areas Act 1979, s 51(5))

ECCLESIASTICAL PURPOSES

'Ecclesiastical purposes' shall mean the building, rebuilding, enlargement and repair of any church or chapel and any purpose to which by common or ecclesiastical law a church rate is applicable or any of such purposes. (Parochial Church Councils (Powers) Measure 1921, s 4(3))

ECCLESIASTICAL RESIDENCE

'Ecclesiastical residence' means any parsonage house and any house of residence provided for an assistant curate and any house of residence of any bishop or member or officer of a cathedral corporation and any offices belonging thereto. (Welsh Church Act 1914, s 38(1))

EDITION

Literary works are usually issued to the public in editions. Any fresh issue or publication of a work is an edition. It does not seem necessary that the type should be set up anew, or even that fresh copies should be printed, the essential factor being that there is a determination to reissue the work to the public.

Where under an agreement between an author and his publisher a licence is conferred on the publisher without limitation to any definite period, and where payment to the author is by royalties or by a share of the profits, the licence, although exclusive so long as it exists, is revocable; and the author can restrain the publication of any edition subsequent to the notice of revocation. (37 Halsbury's Laws (4th edn) para 1002)

'Now I apprehend, that, not merely in point of etymology, but having regard to what actually takes place in the publication of any work, an "edition" of a work is the putting of it forth before the public, and if this be done in batches at successive periods, each successive batch is a new edition; and the question whether the individual copies have been printed by means of moveable type or by stereotype, does not seem to me to be material. If moveable type is used, the type having been broken up, the new edition is prepared by setting up the type afresh, printing afresh, advertising afresh, and repeating all the other necessary steps to obtain a new circulation of the work. In that case the contemplated break between the two editions is more complete, because, until the type is again set up, nothing further can be done. But I apprehend it makes no substantial difference, as regards the meaning of the term "edition", whether the new "thousand" have been printed by a re-setting of moveable type, or by stereotype, or whether they have been printed at the same time with the former thousand, or subsequently. A new "edition" is published whenever, having in his storehouse a certain number of copies, the publisher issues a fresh batch of them to the public. This, according to the practice of the trade, is done, as is well known, periodically. And if, after printing 20,000 copies, a publisher should think it expedient, for the purpose of keeping up the price of the work, to issue them in batches of a thousand at a time, keeping the rest under lock and key, each successive issue would be a new "edition" in every sense of the word.' *Reade v Bentley* (1858) 4 K & J 656 at 667, per Page Wood V-C

EDITOR

Generally speaking, an editor is a person who superintends the publication of any literary work.

In the case of newspapers and periodicals, such a person is usually appointed by the proprietor to be responsible for the literary part of the journal, but no general statement can be made as to his duties or authority, because these must depend upon the contract entered into in each individual case. The mere fact that a person is appointed editor of a newspaper does not give him control of the conduct of the paper or of the material to be included, and, in the absence of special stipulations in the contract giving him control, he is subject to the directions of the proprietor. On the other hand, any undue interference with a person who holds a general appointment as editor in the performance of his duties may amount to a breach of contract.

The question whether a person is discharging editorial duties or is merely a contributor is a question of fact depending upon the terms of the contract of engagement, the nature of the work done and the mode of payment. (37 Halsbury's Laws (4th edn) para 1058)

EDUCATION   *See also* ADVANCEMENT

General meaning

In this Act . . . 'education' includes training. (Matrimonial Causes Act 1973, s 52(1))

[A document declaring the trusts of a fund which had been subscribed for the 'education' of the children of a deceased clergyman stated that the money was to be used as deemed necessary to defray the expenses of all the children, and that solely in the matter of education.] 'I deem myself entitled to construe "education" in the broadest possible sense, and not to consider the purpose exhausted because the children have attained such ages that education in the vulgar sense is no longer necessary. Even if it be construed in the narrower sense it is, in Wood V-C's language, merely the motive of the gift, and the intention must be taken to have been to provide for the children in the manner (they all being then infants) most useful.' *Re Andrew's Trust, Carter v Andrew* [1905] 2 Ch 48 at 52, 53, per Kekewich J

[The Royal Choral Society claimed exemption from income tax as a society established for charitable purposes only.] 'Dealing with the educational aspect from the point of view of the public who hear music, the Solicitor-General argued that nothing could be educational which did not involve teaching—as I understood him, teaching in the sense of a master teaching a class. He said that in the domain of art the only thing that could be educational in a charitable sense would be the education of the executants: the teaching of the painter, the training of the musician, and so forth. I protest against that narrow conception of education when one is dealing with aesthetic education. Very few people can become executants, or at any rate executants who can give pleasure either to themselves or to others; but a very large number of people can become instructed listeners with a trained and cultivated taste. In my opinion, a body of persons established for the purpose of raising the artistic taste of the country and established by an appropriate document which confines them to that purpose, is established for educational purposes, because the education of artistic taste is one of the most important things in the development of a civilised human being.' *Royal Choral Society v Inland Revenue Comrs* [1943] 2 All ER 101 at 104, 105, CA, per Lord Greene MR

'In one sense the word "education" may be used to describe any form of training, any manner by which physical or mental aptitude, which a man may desire to have for the purpose of his work, may be acquired.' *Chartered Insurance Institute v London Corpn* [1957] 2 All ER 638 at 643, per Devlin J

[Section 10(2) (repealed) of the Income and Corporation Taxes Act 1970 provided for child relief while the child was receiving full-time instruction at any university, college, school, or other educational establishment.] 'Looking at the matter apart from any findings on the facts of this particular case, an educational establishment must, I think, be an establishment whose primary function is that of education. In this context . . . I think it is clear that "education" denotes training of the mind, in contradistinction to training in manual skills.' *Barry v Hughes (Inspector of Taxes)* [1973] 1 All ER 537 at 543, per Pennycuick V-C

Australia 'Such public legislative recognitions of the words "educational" and "public education" as I have mentioned are only confirmatory of the general understanding of these words as connoting the sense of imparting knowledge or assisting and guiding the development of body or mind.' *Chesterman v Federal Taxation Comr* (1922) 32 CLR 362 at 386, per Isaacs J; reversed on another point (1925) 37 CLR 317, PC

Primary education

It shall be the duty of every local education authority to secure that there shall be available for their area sufficient schools . . . for providing primary education, that is to say, full-time education suitable to the requirements of junior pupils who have not attained the age of ten years and six months, and full-time education suitable to the requirements of junior pupils who have attained that age and whom it is expedient to educate together with junior pupils who have not attained that age. (Education Act 1944, s 8(1), as amended by the Education (Miscellaneous Provisions) Act 1948, s 3)

Secondary education

It shall be the duty of every local education authority to secure that there shall be available for their area sufficient schools . . . for providing secondary education, that is to say, full-time education suitable to the requirements of senior pupils, other than such full-time education as may be provided for senior pupils in pursuance of a scheme made under the provisions of this Act relating to further education, and full-time education for junior pupils who have attained the age of ten years and six months and whom it is expedient to educate together with senior pupils. (Education Act 1944, s 8(1), as amended by the Education (Miscellaneous Provisions) Act 1948, s 3)

Further education

(1) It shall be the duty of every local education authority to secure the provision for their area of adequate facilities for further education.
(2) Subject to the following provisions of this section, in this Act 'further education' means –
   (a) full-time and part-time education for persons over compulsory school age (including vocational, social, physical and recreational training); and
   (b) organised leisure-time occupation provided in connection with the provision of such education.
(3) In this Act 'further education' does not include higher education.
(Education Act 1944, s 41, as substituted by Education Reform Act 1988, s 120(2))
[For local authority functions and for higher and further education generally see Part II of the 1988 Act.]

Local education authority

'Local education authority' means, in relation to any area for which a joint education board is constituted as the local education authority . . . the board so constituted, and, save as aforesaid, means, in relation to a non-metropolitan county, the council of the county, and, in relation to a metropolitan district, the council of the district. (Education Act 1944, s 114(1), as amended by the Local Authorities (Miscellaneous Provisions) Order 1977, SI 1977/293)

EDUCATIONAL ENDOWMENT *See* ENDOWMENT

EDUCATIONAL PURPOSES *See* CHARITY—CHARITABLE

EELS

In this Act . . . 'eels' includes elvers and the fry of eels. (Salmon and Freshwater Fisheries Act 1975, s 41)

EFFECT

'It is important to notice that the words of the policy draw a distinction between "cause" and "effects". The company agree to pay the sum assured "if the assured shall sustain any injury caused by accident—that is to say, immediately caused by accident—and also if the assured shall die from the effects of such injury". The facts in this case seem to me to shew that death was caused by the natural consequences of the accident. The case finds that death was, in fact, caused by pneumonia, resulting from cold; the cold, and the fatal effects of the cold, being due to the condition of health to which the deceased had been reduced by the accident. It is also found as a fact that the deceased would not have died as and when he did if it had not been for the accident, and the case goes on to set out the condition to which the assured had been reduced by the accident. I am of opinion that the words "effects of such injury" do not mean the proximate cause of the result, but that we are entitled in deciding this case to see whether there was a series of natural consequences leading legitimately and directly by steps to the death. The consequences of the accident were weakness and inability to bear clothing, and a consequent liability to catch cold, which the man in his ordinary state would not have experienced. From that state results pneumonia and death. Therefore, if the question for us is whether these facts may be looked at to explain the policy, I think that the death was the effect of the natural results of the accident, and that the company is liable.' *Re an Arbitration between Isitt & Railway Passengers' Assurance Co* (1889) 58 LJQB 191 at 195, per Huddleston B

'The meaning of the expression "effect" in relation to an agreement may vary with the context in which it appears. Prima facie, it means those acts which the parties to the agreement thereby agree that one or more of them shall do or refrain from doing, but it is capable in the appropriate context of a wider meaning and of embracing the remoter consequences, including the economic consequences, of doing or refraining from doing those acts.' *Re Black Bolt and Nut Association of Great Britain's Agreement (No 2)* [1961] 3

All ER 316 at 319, 320, RPC, per cur; affd [1962] 1 All ER 139, CA

Canada 'The grammatical meaning of the words "on any sale effected" [in an agreement to pay commission] is perfectly plain to me. The word "effect" means "to bring about an event or result". The sense and usage of it in commercial transactions is illustrated in the phrases "to effect a sale": Murray's New English Dictionary, s.v. "effect", 1(d). The word effected does not require any modification of its ordinary meaning and sense to give proper effect and meaning to the agreement between the parties. A "sale effected" is a sale made by a vendor to a purchaser. I do not say that the purchase price has to be paid, the transfer of title must be completed, or that all obligations under such a contract have to be fulfilled, to bring a transaction within the meaning of the words "sale effected". There must, however, be a valid contract between the vendor and the purchaser.' *Gladstone v Catena* [1948] OR 182 at 187, Ont CA, per Laidlaw JA

New Zealand [A land agent was employed to sell or exchange the property of his client, and commission to be paid to him when he had 'effected' a sale or exchange of such property.] 'In my opinion the word "effected" means if a valid contract is made. It does not mean that the transfers, etc., have to be executed and the price or consideration paid. . . . A sale is "effected" when made, a title in equity being created.' *Nigro v Wilson* [1924] NZLR 834 at 839, per Stout CJ; also reported [1924] GLR 537 at 540

EFFECTIVE

'In dismissing the action, the judge considered the various grounds which were put forward, and we must consider those grounds, and consider whether the judge was right or wrong. The first ground was based on s 5(1) of the Factories Act 1961, and also on common law negligence. It is obvious that on this point the two run rather closely together, and I will first consider the provisions of s 5(1). The terms of that subsection are: "Effective provision shall be made for securing and maintaining sufficient and suitable lighting, whether natural or artificial, in every part of a factory in which persons are working or passing." . . . The point which really arises is that, assuming that there was sufficient and suitable lighting provided by the lamps to which I have referred,

was it effective within the meaning of s 5 of the Act? I have come to the conclusion that it was not. It seems to me, on the construction of this subsection, that "effective" means lighting which is functioning effectively, and lighting which may be admirable in construction and in the provision of proper bulbs and so on, is not effective when it is not turned on.' *Thornton v Fisher & Ludlow Ltd* [1968] 2 All ER 241 at 242, 243, CA, per Danckwerts LJ

EFFECTIVE DATE OF NOTICE

United States Written notice by a domestic or foreign corporation to its shareholder, if in a comprehensible form, is effective when mailed, if mailed postpaid and correctly addressed to the shareholder's address shown in the corporation's current record of shareholders. (Revised Model Business Corporation Act 1984, s 1.41(c))

EFFECTS   *See also* BELONGINGS; FURNITURE

Farming effects

[A farmer assigned 'the whole and every of my effects, stock, books and book debts' to a trustee for and on behalf of his creditors.] 'The assignment, if made bona fide, extends to all the property. "Effects" is a very comprehensive word. The general intent of the instrument, also, shews that the whole of the property [including cattle upon the farm] was intended to pass.' *Lewis v Rogers* (1834) 1 Cr M & R 48 at 54, per Alderson B

New Zealand 'The authorities cited . . . show clearly that the words "household effects" are sufficient to include a motor-car, and I think also that, as motor-cars are commonly used by farmers in connection with their business, the words "farming effects" would include a motor-car.' *Re Sim* [1917] NZLR 169 at 172, per Sim J

In will: generally

A gift of the testator's 'effects' without a context sufficient to control it, may include the whole of the testator's personal estate where that property is not otherwise disposed of by the will, and is prima facie confined to personal estate unless an inference to the contrary arises from the context, in which case even real estate may be comprised in the term. The term may also by the context be restricted to particular kinds of personal estate. Thus, in a gift of a house with its furniture and a class of articles which tend to the beneficial occupation and enjoyment of the house, ending with 'all other effects', the term may, by the ejusdem generis rule, be restricted to other articles of that nature; and 'effects' is frequently used in a restricted sense, meaning goods and movables, a sense especially applicable where other parts of the personal estate are separately disposed of, or where there is a subsequent residuary gift of personal estate. 'Personal effects' generally means physical chattels having some personal connection with the testator, such as articles of personal or domestic use or ornament, clothing and furniture, and so forth, but not money or securities for money. The expressions 'personal estate', 'personal estate and effects' and 'personal property' are prima facie confined to personal estate in the legal sense, but may, in the context of circumstances, include realty. (50 Halsbury's Laws (4th edn) para 473)

'The natural and true meaning of real effects in common language and speech is real property; and real and personal effects are synonymous to substance, which includes everything that can be turned into money.' *Hogan v Jackson* (1775) 1 Cowp 299 at 307, 308, per Lord Mansfield CJ; affd sub nom *Jackson v Hogan* (1776) 3 Bro Parl Cas 388

'The word "effects" may be taken to mean real estate, if, from other expressions coupled with it, it appear that such was the intention of the testator. . . . But here nothing appears from the words of the residuary clause to shew that the word "effects" was intended to carry the real estate. In general, the word "effects" is used to denote personalty, and "wheresoever" means in whatsoever place they were to be found: the other words "whatsoever, and of what nature, kind, or quality soever", do not carry the description beyond the notion of personal estate, which may well enough be described in that manner by amplification; they do not shew that the testatrix must have meant to include "real" estate.' *Camfield v Gilbert* (1803) 3 East 516 at 523, 524, per Lawrence J

'The question arises on the word "effects", as used in the residuary clause, from whence we are to collect what was the intention of the testatrix. "Effects" standing alone must certainly be taken to mean personalty; but it may be extended beyond that, and include real estate by other words used showing such an intent.' Ibid at 524, per Le Blanc J

'The word "effects" is capable of embracing the realty, if such appear to have been the meaning of a testator.' *Den d Franklin v Trout* (1812) 15 East 394 at 398, per Lord Ellenborough CJ

'The word "effects" used *simpliciter,* will carry the whole personal estate, as a gift "of all my effects", without more. But it is frequently used in a restricted sense, meaning "Goods and moveables", as in the common expression of "Furniture and Effects". In every case the court has to collect from the context the particular sense in which the testator has intended to use it. In *Campbell v Prescott* [(1808) 15 Ves 500], there were added to the word "effects", "of what nature and kind soever"; and this addition excluded its restricted sense. And it appears to me, that the words which follow "effects", in the present case, "that he shall die possessed of", lead to the same conclusion. It is further to be observed, that the words here are not "household goods, furniture and effects", but "household goods and furniture, and effects", which imports a distinct sense in the word "effects", particularly with the addition of the words "that he shall die possessed of"; and further, unless this testator intended to describe his general personal estate by the word "effects", he has omitted all notice of it in his will. I think, therefore, the best construction here is, that this testator meant to give to his daughters all the effects which he should die possessed of, or in other words, all his personal estate.' *Michell v Michell* (1820) 5 Madd 69 at 71, 72, per Leach V-C

'The words are "all my furniture, plate, linen and other effects that may be in my possession at the time of my death". It is alleged that the words "other effects" are to be cut down so as to mean that which is something like "furniture", "plate", "linen". But the answer is that the words of a will ought to have their natural meaning given to them unless there is some contrary intention appearing in the will. The mere fact that the testatrix enumerates some items before the words "other effects" does not alter the proper meaning of those words.' *Hodgson v Jex* (1876) 2 Ch D 122 at 123, per Jessel MR

'By these words, "I give all the rest, residue, moneys, chattels, and all other my effects", I am of opinion that the testator meant to include everything he had in the world, whether real property or personal property, and to pass all the residue of every kind soever not otherwise disposed of; and I also think that the testator did not intend to die intestate as to any of his property, but to pass everything under his will.' *Smyth v Smyth* (1878) 8 Ch D 561 at 567, 568, per Malins V-C

'The testator . . . makes a disposition to his wife and children and in language which is on the face of it very comprehensive: he gives and bequeaths "all my household property and effects of every kind whatsoever". Then he refers to the situation of his property "whatsoever and wheresoever". He includes the whole of his property in this disposition and the real estate passes. But the real estate would not pass under the words "effects" alone without taking the context into consideration. The tendency of modern decisions is to give effect to very slight indications of a testator's intentions. . . . In the present case all the testator's property was intended to be included in the words "all my household property and effects whatsoever and wheresoever".' *Re Fisher, Allan v Fisher* (1902) 46 Sol Jo 297 at 297, per Swinfen Eady J

'The principle of construction to be gathered from the cases is that prima facie the word "effects" is sufficient to carry the entire personal estate not otherwise disposed of by the will, unless the testator, by the terms of the will, shows that a different and narrower construction was intended.' *In the Goods of Curling* [1928] IR 521 at 523, per O'Byrne J

Australia 'I feel no difficulty about the word "effects" being sufficient to cover a motor car, even apart from authorities.' *Re Tormey, Tormey v Tormey* [1935] VLR 300 at 301, per Mann J

New Zealand 'The testator . . . made the following will: . . . "I give and bequeath . . . the house I now live in, the furniture, library, and all effects including the electrical appliances complete." . . . The only question now to be decided is whether the cash in the house and the cash on deposit passed . . . under the words "all effects". . . . I think that the words used amount to a general bequest of the testator's personal property.' *Moodie v Commins* (1903) 22 NZLR 510 at 511, 512, 513, per Williams J; also reported 5 GLR 198 at 199

In will: household effects

'It is clear that this testator, by adding to "household furniture" "other household effects", meant to carry his bequest further than merely to household furniture. The only

question is, how far the word "effects" is controlled by the word "household"; and though some doubt may be entertained with respect to the wines and liquors, the books, and the turning machinery, I do not see any sufficient reason for excluding any of them from the bequest.' *Cole v Fitzgerald* (1827) 3 Russ 301 at 303, per Lord Lyndhurst LC

'I cannot hold that the animals in question [a horse, cows and sheep] were included in the gift of household effects in and about the dwelling-house of the testator.' *Re Labron, Johnson v Johnson* (1885) 1 TLR 248 at 248, per Kay J

'The testator gives and devises his property known as Heathfield, with the offices, gardens, fields, and appurtenances belonging thereto, to the use of his wife, Sarah Harriet, during her life, and bequeathed all his furniture, pictures, plate, jewellery, horses and carriages, and other household effects, to his said wife absolutely. . . . He means her to have the house and contents, and he gives her £1,000 a year to enable her to live there, and he means her to have the house in the same way that he had it himself. After enumerating all these things it would be giving it a very narrow construction to say that the bequest does not include the wine which was put there for the use of the household. . . . I . . . hold that the wine did pass.' *Re Bourne, Bourne v Brandreth* (1888) 58 LT 537 at 538, per Kay J

[A testator by his will gave his nephew all the 'household furniture and effects' in his country residence.] '"Effects" . . . does not pass jewellery. . . . The proper grammatical construction is, "all the household furniture, and all the household effects"; "household" . . . governs the two. . . . Jewellery has never been held, as far as I am aware, to be household effects any more than it is household furniture, and certainly I am not disposed so to hold it.' *Northey v Paxton* (1888) 60 LT 30 at 31, per Kekewich J

'Household effects do not include all effects on the premises which would have passed under a gift of the house, and accordingly the outdoor effects do not pass. . . . The wearing apparel, etc, do not pass.' *Re Tweed, Buckmaster v Moss* (1902) 46 Sol Jo 634 at 634, per Farwell J

'The word "effects" may also be, and often is, qualified or localised by its context. In the present bequest it is both qualified by the word "household", and localised by the words "in my residence, Abbey-street". . . . In my opinion the word "household" in this bequest governs both "furniture" and "effects". All "effects" in his residence answering to the description "household", e.g. all effects contributing to the use or ornament of the house, or the use of the household would pass under it.' *McPhail v Phillips* [1904] 1 IR 155 at 160, per Barton J

'It is a question of intention that I have to determine whether the words "my household furniture and effects in Thornleigh (just as it now stands)" are sufficiently wide—qualified as they are by the word "household"—to include the motor cars in question. I think that it is clear on the will that the testator wanted the plaintiff to have the house just as they were living in it at that time, and having regard to the evidence, I cannot say that the motor cars did not form a very important part of the house as they were living in it down to and at the time of the testator's death. I am bound to hold on the authorities that "household effects" would include carriages and horses, and as a matter of construction of this will and following the authorities on the word "household effects" I have no doubt that the testator meant the motor cars to pass to the plaintiff, and I must so determine.' *Re Howe, Ferniehough v Wilkinson* [1908] WN 223 at 223, per Eve J

'These proceedings have been instituted to determine the true construction of clause 14 of the testator's will. It is in these terms: "I bequeath to my said adopted daughter Rosemary such of the furniture and household effects which . . . shall be in or about either of my residences . . . as she may select for the purpose of furnishing a residence for my said adopted daughter.". . . Does the bequest include motor-cars, consumable stores, garden implements and tools and movable plants? . . . I think that the . . . phrase "in or about" includes the motor-cars and the other three items enumerated in this question.' *Re Wavertree of Delamere (Baron), Rutherford v Hall-Walker* [1933] Ch 837 at 841, 842, per Eve J

Canada 'Here [in a bequest of 'all my household goods, furniture, effects . . .'] the word "effects" should be construed as a word of wide meaning, limited only by the general type of article obviously included by the testator in the paragraph in which it is found. In my view it is limited to effects used in or about or in the normal operation of the household. Under present conditions of life a motor car used in this fashion as apparently the testator used his

motor car in his lifetime, should be included under the word "effects".' *Re Pridham* [1953] 1 DLR 782 at 784, Ont SC, per Wells J

New Zealand [A testator, by his will, bequeathed to his wife all his 'household and personal furniture and effects'. The question was whether the testator's Austin A40 motor-car passed under the bequest.] 'The phrase "household and personal effects" can comprehend a motor-car, and will, I think, ordinarily do so unless its user for business purposes has been so considerable as to exclude it from inclusion in that category.' *Re Liverton, Liverton v Liverton* [1954] NZLR 612 at 613, 614, per Gresson J

Maritime law

'Effects' includes clothes and documents. (Merchant Shipping Act 1894, s 742)

'This action has been brought on a policy of marine insurance on goods on board the ship *Lion*, for a voyage from Catania, in Sicily, to any port in the United Kingdom. The goods insured were described in the policy as "master's effects". . . . The articles which constitute the "master's effects" have no natural or artificial connection with each other, but, of necessity, must be essentially different in their nature and kind, in their value, in the use to be made of them, and the mode in which they would be disposed on board. The word "effects" is obviously employed to save the task of enumerating the nautical instruments, the chronometer, the clothes, books, furniture, etc, at [sic] which they happened to consist.' *Duff v Mackenzie* (1857) 3 CBNS 16 at 28, 29, per cur.

EFFICIENT

'I agree . . . that we should not give any peculiar importance to the word "efficient". I shall use it as if the word "fit" were used. The clause [in this charterparty] in question is, "That in the event of loss of time from deficiency of men or stores, breakdown of machinery, want of repairs, or damage, whereby the working of the vessel is stopped for more than forty-eight consecutive working hours, the payment of hire shall cease until she be again in an efficient state to resume her service." I read, as I have said, "fit" for "efficient", "until she shall be in a fit state to resume her service".' *Hogarth v Miller, Brother & Co* [1891] AC 48 at 67, 68, HL, per Lord Morris

'In my judgment "an efficient guard" [on a

machine] is a guard that properly or effectively guards.' *Vickers v E Gomme Ltd* [1957] 2 All ER 60 at 65, per Jenkins LJ

EFFLUENT   *See* SEWAGE EFFLUENT; TRADE EFFLUENT

EGRESS   *See* INGRESS

EITHER

'The expression [in a will] is "if either of my said sisters shall be then dead". . . . I do not think it is according to the ordinary use of language to say that the expression "if either of my said sisters shall be then dead" means if both of them shall be then dead. "Either" is taken in the ordinary sense as one of the two and as not, in any sense, meaning both. . . . I do not think that the expression "if either of my said sisters shall be then dead" can be taken as expressing in ordinary English the contingency of both being dead.' *Re Pickworth, Snaith v Parkinson* [1899] 1 Ch 642 at 648, 649, CA, per Lindley MR.

Australia   ' "Either" is not a technical word, it is a distributive word, and may mean one of two, or each of two—depending upon the subject matter and the context. A common grammatical illustration will suffice: "You can take either side", that is one side or the other; "The river overflowed on either side", that is, on each side.' *Currie v Glen* (1936) 54 CLR 445 at 453, per Starke J

EJUSDEM GENERIS

Where the particular things named [in a document] have some common characteristic which constitutes them a genus, and the general words [following an enumeration of specific things or classes of things] can be properly regarded as in the nature of a sweeping clause designed to guard against accidental omissions, then the rule of ejusdem generis will apply, and the general words will be restricted to things of the same nature as those which have been already mentioned; but the absence of a common genus between the enumerated words will not necessarily prevent a restricted construction of the general words if justified by the context. The ejusdem generis construction will be assisted if the general scope or language of the deed, or the particular clause, indicates that the general words should receive a limited construction, or if an unlimited construction will produce some unforeseen loss to the grantor.

A common application of the ejusdem generis rule occurs in the construction of policies of insurance, where special enumerated risks are insured against, followed by a general clause insuring against all risks whatsoever, the last clause being construed as limited to risks of the same nature as those previously mentioned. (12 Halsbury's Laws (4th edn) para 1526)

South Africa   'The instrument of interpretation denoted by ejusdem generis or nascitur a sociis must always be borne in mind where the meaning of the general words in association with specific words has to be ascertained; but what is often a useful means of finding out what was meant by a provision in a contract or statute must not be allowed to substitute an artificial intention for what was clearly the real one.' *Grobbelaar v De Vyver* 1954 (1) SA 255 (A), per Schreiner JA

ELDEST

The description 'first son' or 'eldest son' of a certain person in the strict sense means the first-born son; and similarly for other sons. The circumstances of the case and the context of the will may, however, show that the testator intended the eldest son of the person at the date of the will (which is prima facie the sense of the words where the strict sense is inapplicable), or his eldest son for the time being at some future time, or the son taking a family estate. This last sense is normally the sense where the provision made by the will is for portions for younger children, and the eldest son is excluded, 'younger children' in such a case prima facie being taken to mean children other than a child taking the estate. It is possible that an eldest son may take under a limitation to, for example, 'second and other sons', but not where by the context of the will he is excluded. Where a first or second son is dead at the date of the will, the will is construed as meaning first or second son at the testator's death. (50 Halsbury's Laws (4th edn) para 517)

'The words "male lineal descendant" have already received one judicial construction by this House, by which we are unquestionably bound; they mean a male descendant claiming entirely through males. The sole question, therefore, is to the meaning of the word "eld-est" applied to such male lineal descendants with the context in this will. The word "eldest" is certainly capable of more meanings than one, as the term "elder" is. In Dr Johnson's Dictionary this word is said to be the compara-tive of old, changed to eld, and two of its meanings (the only meanings necessary to be considered in this case) are "surpassing in years" and "having the privileges of primo-geniture". In which of these two senses is it to be read in this place? I think it can hardly be disputed that in its primary, that is, as I con-ceive, its original or prima facie sense, or its strict sense . . . or perhaps in its ordinary and grammatical sense . . . is "surpassing in years", or is that person or thing which has existed the longest time, and when the word "elder" or "eldest" is used alone, or with reference simply to an individual person, the "eldest" man, for instance, it means eldest in years. But if applied to an individual having a particular character, it has a different meaning. The "eldest" or "senior magistrate", or "officer" does not mean that magistrate or officer who has lived the greatest number of years, nor indeed always him who has filled the office for the longest time, for it may indicate rank only. So by the term "the eldest Earl of England" is not generally intended the Earl the most advanced in years, but the eldest in point of family origin—the premier Earl. . . . I am inclined to think, that being used with reference to a line of male lineal descendants, it ought to be understood to mean, not the eldest *man*, or the eldest *in age* amongst the male lineal descendants, but the eldest *qua* male lineal descendant—the eldest in heritable blood in the male line.' *Thellusson v Rendlesham (Lord), Thellusson v Thellusson, Hare v Roberts* (1859) 7 HL Cas 429 at 520, 521, per Lord Wensleydale

'The property then is given, after the death of the survivor of the widow and unmarried daughters, equally amongst his two eldest children born in legitimate wedlock to each of his sons and daughters. Now of course it is possible that the testator by the words "the eldest children born" might have meant either the two eldest who were prior in date of birth, or the two eldest living at the particular period when the property was to be divided among them. Either of those suppositions is possible, and the whole question is, which did he mean? That does not depend on the vesting of the property; but the vesting in reality depends on the ascertaining of what it was that the testator

meant. If he meant the one class, those prior in date of birth, it might be conceded that the interest would be a vested one in those; but if he meant the other class, those who were to be the two eldest at the time of the distribution among the parties, then the interest could not be vested. It could not be vested because you could not tell until the period arrived, who might be those persons answering the descrip-tion. . . . I have come to the conclusion that in the case of the eldest son there is an exclusion of the one who died, . . . but an admission of the third who has become one of the two eldest living at the time of the distribution. In the other case it was the second who died. The original eldest is still living and there is a third. It will, therefore, be the original eldest and the third who will take, in other words it will be the two eldest living at the period of distribution who must be held to have been intended by the testator.' *Madden v Ikin* (1862) 2 Drew & Sm 207 at 210, 211, 215, per Kindersley V-C

[An estate was limited in a marriage settlement to A and his heirs in tail male, 'save and except an eldest son'. The only son of the marriage claimed to be entitled.] 'It is by no means an uncommon use of language, even with regard to the term "eldest son", where there is only one, to speak of the first-born as the "eldest", and that for this reason. In speaking of those who may become a class as to whom there is an expectation that there naturally will be more than one . . . it is not only not an uncommon use, but the natural and ordinary use, of language to speak of the one (of that which is expected to be a class) who first comes into the world as being the first-born or the eldest, even at a time when no others have been added to the class.' *Tuite v Bermingham* (1875) LR 7 HL 634 at 644, per Lord Cairns LC

'I do not think the words "shall become the eldest son" of a person living at the date of the will are words which, unless controlled and explained by a context, extend in their opera-tion beyond the life-time of that person. . . . I do not think that without an explanatory con-text explaining and forcing the construction, a man is, by the death of his elder brother, said to become the eldest son of his father after his father's death. I think the words "become the eldest son" in their natural and ordinary mean-ing, point to the attaining a status perfectly well known and well understood, and con-nected with heirship of, and right of succession to a living man.' *Bathurst v Errington* (1877) 2 App Cas 698 at 711, 712, per Lord Cairns LC

'After certain limitations which have failed or

determined, he [the testator] disposed of a property . . . by giving it in these words: "To the eldest son of my sister Frances McKeand Gibney and his heirs for ever". It appears that at the time when the testator made his will Mrs Gibney had two sons. It was contended that the word "eldest" was not properly applicable to the elder of two persons, and that, if the testator had really meant Mrs Gibney's first-born son, he would have said "elder", not "eldest". In their Lordships' opinion that objection savours of hyper-criticism. If a man has two sons, and only two, the ordinary way of speaking of the first-born, if not designated by name, is to call him the eldest son of so-and-so. There being then a person in existence at the time answering the description in the will, their Lordships are of opinion that the person, though he died afterwards in the testator's lifetime, was the object of the testator's bounty. There is nothing in the context to warrant any departure from the proper and ordinary meaning of the words employed.' *Amyot v Dwarris* [1904] AC 268 at 271, PC, per cur.

'It seems to me . . . that, the testator having by the last clause of this devise clearly shown a general intention that the estate should not go over unless there was a default of male issue of George, I am at liberty . . . to construe the words "lawful eldest male issue" not as a *descriptio personæ*, but as *nomen collectivum*, embracing the whole line of male descendants, the word "eldest" merely indicating the order of succession.' *Re Finlay's Estate* [1913] 1 IR 143 at 152, 153, per Wylie J

ELECTION

Doctrine of election   *See also* APPROBATE AND REPROBATE; ESTOPPEL

Where a testator by his will purports to give property to A which in fact belongs to B and at the same time out of his own property confers benefits on B, the literal construction and application of the will would allow B to keep his own property to the disappointment of A, and also to take the benefits given to him by the will. Equity, however, in such circumstances, introduces the principle that a man shall not accept and reject the same instrument, and B is not allowed to take the full benefit given him by the will unless he is prepared to carry into effect the whole of the testator's dispositions. He is accordingly put to his election to take either under the instrument or against it. If he elects to take under the will he is bound, and

may be ordered, to convey his own property to A; if he elects to take against the will and to keep his own property, and so disappoints A, then he cannot take any benefits under the will without compensating A out of such benefits to the extent of the value of the property of which A is disappointed. It follows that if B's property is such that it cannot be assigned, as where it consists of heirlooms, he is not put to his election. (16 Halsbury's Laws (4th edn) para 1392)

'By the well settled doctrine which is known in Scotch law as the doctrine of "approbation and reprobation", and which in our own courts is known as the doctrine of "election", where a deed or a will professes to make a general disposition for the benefit of a person named in it, such person cannot accept that benefit without at the same time conforming to all the provisions of the instrument, and renouncing every right inconsistent with them.' *Codrington v Codrington* (1876) 45 LJR 660 at 664, per Lord Cairns LC

'The decree in this case is no extension of the doctrine of election, as suggested by the learned counsel for the appellant, but strictly within the principle on which that doctrine is founded. The principle is, that there is an implied condition that he who accepts a benefit under an instrument must adopt the whole of it, conforming to all its provisions, and renouncing every right inconsistent with it. It seemed to be considered in argument that the rule of the Scotch law that a person cannot approbate and reprobate under the same instrument was not altogether the same as the English doctrine of election, but Lord Redesdale, in *Birmingham v Kirwan* [(1805) 2 Sch & Lef 444], puts them exactly on the same footing. He there says, "The general rule is that a person cannot accept and reject the same instrument, and this is the foundation of the law or election".' Ibid at 666, per Lord Chelmsford

'The doctrine of election is this, that if a person whose property a testator effects to give away takes other benefits under the same will, and at the same time elects to keep his own property, he must make compensation to the person affected by his election to an extent not exceeding the benefits he receives.' *Rogers v Jones* (1876) 3 Ch D 688 at 689, per Jessel MR

'Where a party in his own mind has thought that he would choose one of two remedies, even though he has written it down on a memorandum or has indicated it in some other way, that alone will not bind him; but so soon as he had not only determined to follow one of his remedies but has communicated it to the other side in such a way as to lead the opposite party to believe that he has made that choice, he has completed his election and can go no further; and whether he intended it or not, if he has done an unequivocal act—I mean an act which would be justifiable if he had elected one way and would not be justifiable if he had elected the other way—the fact of his having done that unequivocal act to the knowledge of the persons concerned is an election.' *Scarf v Jardine* (1882) 7 App Cas 361, per Lord Blackburn

'The doctrine of election . . . is a principle which the courts apply in the exercise of an equitable jurisdiction enabling them to secure a just distribution in substantial accordance with the general scheme of the instrument. It is not merely the language used to which the court looks. A testator may, for instance, have obviously failed to realize that any question could arise. But the court will none the less hold that a beneficiary who is given a share under the will in assets, the total amount of which depends on the inclusion of property belonging to the beneficiary himself which the testator has ineffectively sought to include, ought not to be allowed to have a share in the assets effectively disposed of, excepting on terms. He must co-operate to the extent requisite to provide the amount necessary for the division prescribed by the will, either by bringing in his own property, erroneously contemplated by the testator as forming part of the assets, or by submitting to a diminution of the share to which he is prima facie entitled, to an extent equivalent to the value of his own property if withheld by him from the common stock.' *Brown v Gregson* [1920] AC 860 at 868, HL, per Viscount Haldane

'The equitable doctrine of election can, I think, be formulated in this way. If A by a disposition effected by an instrument such as a will confers a beneficial interest in property of which he is competent to dispose on B, and by the same instrument purports to confer a beneficial interest on C in property of which A is not competent to dispose, being the property of B, B may elect to adopt one of two courses. He may elect to accept the entire benefit under the will, in which case he will be equitably bound so far as he is able, to give effect to A's purported gift to C; or he may elect not to give effect to that purported gift. In the latter case, he will not forfeit his interest under the will,

but will be equitably bound to submit to C being compensated out of that interest, so far as practicable, for being deprived of the beneficial interest which A intended to give him.' *Re Gordon's Will Trusts, National Westminster Bank Ltd v Gordon* [1978] 2 All ER 969 at 973, CA, per Buckley LJ

Parliamentary election

'Parliamentary Election' means the election of a Member to serve in Parliament for a constituency. (Interpretation Act 1978, Sch 1)

ELECTION ADDRESS   *See* ADDRESS

ELECTION COURT

'Election court' means—
(a) in relation to a parliamentary election petition, the judges presiding at the trial;
(b) in relation to a petition questioning an election under the local government Act, the court constituted under this Act for the trial of that petition.
(Representation of the People Act 1983, s 202(1))

ELECTION EXPENSES

'Election expenses' in relation to an election means expenses incurred, whether before, during or after the election, on account of or in respect of the conduct or management of the election. (Representation of the People Act 1983, s 118)

'If another person pays an expense, and that expense is one of the ordinary expenses of the candidate, so that the doing of that by the third person relieves the candidate from part of his election expenses, then the candidate must treat that assistance as given to him in respect of his election expenses, and must treat the expenses as part of his expenses . . . and if a person instead of giving money gives a particular portion of the election expenses by providing the expenses of a meeting or doing something or other of that sort, then he does something in reference to "the conduct and management of the election".' *Cumberland, Cockermouth Division Case* (1901) 5 O'M & H 155 at 158, per Channell J

Personal expenses

'Personal expenses' as used with respect to the expenditure of any candidate in relation to any election includes the reasonable travelling expenses of the candidate, and the reasonable expenses of his living at hotels or elsewhere for the purposes of and in relation to the election. (Representation of the People Act 1983, s 118)

ELECTOR

'Elector', in relation to an election, means any person whose name is for the time being on the register to be used at that election, but does not include those shown in the register as below voting age on the day fixed for the poll. (Representation of the People Act 1983, s 202(1))

In this rule [subscription of nomination paper] 'elector' means a person (a) who is registered as a parliamentary elector in the constituency in the register to be used at the election or (b) who, pending the publication of that register, appears from the electors lists for that register as corrected by the registration officer to be entitled to be so registered, and accordingly includes a person shown in the register or electors lists as below voting age if it appears from it that he will be of voting age on the day fixed for the poll, but not otherwise. (Representation of the People Act 1983, Sch 1; Parliamentary Elections Rules r 7(6)). [Cf also s 91 of the 1983 Act.]

Local government elector

A person entitled to vote as an elector at a local government election in any electoral area is one who—
(a) is resident there on the qualifying date; and
(b) on that date and on the date of the poll—
(i) is not subject to any legal incapacity to vote (age apart); and
(ii) is either a Commonwealth citizen or a citizen of the Republic of Ireland; and
(c) is of voting age (that is, 18 years or over) on the date of the poll.
(Representation of the People Act 1983, s 2(1))

Parliamentary elector

A person entitled to vote as an elector at a parliamentary election in any constituency is one who—
(a) is resident there on the qualifying date (subject to subsection (2) below in relation to Northern Ireland); and
(b) on that date and on the date of the poll—
(i) is not subject to any legal incapacity to vote (age apart); and
(ii) is either a Commonwealth citizen or a citizen of the Republic of Ireland; and
(c) is of voting age (that is, 18 years or over) on the date of the poll.
(Representation of the People Act 1983, s 1(1))
[Entitlement to vote in Northern Ireland is dependent on three months' prior residence.]

ELECTRIC LINE

The expression 'electric line' means a wire or wires, conductor, or other means used for the purpose of conveying, transmitting, or distributing electricity with any casing, coating, covering, tube, pipe, or insulator enclosing, surrounding, or supporting the same, or any part thereof, or any apparatus connected therewith for the purpose of conveying, transmitting, or distributing electricity or electric currents. (Electric Lighting Act 1882, s 32)

ELECTRICAL FITTINGS   *See* FITTINGS

ELECTRICAL PLANT   *See* PLANT

ELECTRICITY

The expression 'electricity' means electricity, electric current, or any like agency. (Electric Lighting Act 1882, s 32)

ELEEMOSYNARY

[Section 268(3) of the Local Government Act 1933 (repealed; cf. now s 139 of the Local Government Act 1972) debarred a local authority from accepting any gift of property which, when accepted, would be held in trust for an 'eleemosynary' charity.] 'I have heard a great deal of able argument on the word "eleemosynary". As counsel have shown, that adjective has been used with a variety of meanings in different legal contexts. The particular term "eleemosynary charity" is not a term of art with a judicially established definition. . . . How then am I to ascertain the proper and natural meaning of the adjective in its place? I must have regard to the etymological origin of the word. It is an adjective derived from the Greek word which, through Latin, has come into our language as "alms". . . . I come to the conclusion that the term "eleemosynary charity" covers all charities directed to the relief of individual distress, whether due to poverty, age, sickness or other similar individual afflictions. Whether the term extends further it is not necessary for me to decide, and I express no opinion on the point.' *Re Armitage's Will Trusts, Ellam v City & County of Norwich* [1972] 1 All ER 708 at 711, per Goulding J

ELIGIBLE

'The Master of the Rolls was of opinion "that persons dissenting from the doctrines of the Church of England are eligible to be appointed, and to act as trustees of the charity", and he therefore confirmed the appointment which had been made. The word "eligible", as here used by the Master of the Rolls, is ambiguous. It may mean either "legally qualified", or "fit to be chosen".' *Baker v Lee* (1860) 8 HL Cas 495 at 522, 523, per Lord Chelmsford

[By the rules of a trade union, no person was 'eligible' for membership who had been convicted in a court of law of a criminal offence.] 'It is no doubt true . . . that the word "eligible" according to the dictionary may, in certain contexts, mean "suitable for election" as distinct from "qualified for election". As I have said, however, in the context of the phrase in the present rule I cannot for my part entertain any doubt but that, as a matter of English, the word "eligible" must mean and can only mean "legally qualified".' *Faramus v Film Artistes' Assocn* [1964] 1 All ER 25 at 28, HL, per Lord Evershed

'"Eligible" means the same as "qualified". The question whether a person is presently qualified in one respect or another will, more often than not, depend on whether certain conditions were satisfied in his case in the past. For instance a barrister is presently qualified if he was called to the Bar in the past, and a doctor is presently qualified if he acquired the necessary medical qualifications in the past.' *Jackson v Hall* [1979] 1 All ER 449 at 455, CA, per Brandon LJ

New Zealand [The Judicature Amendment Act 1972, s 3, defines 'statutory power of decision' as meaning a power or right conferred by or under any Act to make a decision deciding or prescribing (inter alia) the 'eligibility' of any person to receive, or to continue to receive, a benefit or licence, whether he is legally entitled to it or not.] 'It was held by Perry J that the expression "eligibility" as it appears in clause

(b) of the definition of "statutory power of decision" should be construed as if it meant "legally qualified" but in our respectful opinion the correct construction is the alternative meaning of suitability or fitness, including any question of legal qualification.' *Thames Jockey Club v New Zealand Racing Authority* [1975] 2 NZLR 768, CA, per Mahon J

ELSEWHERE

[A testator by his will devised to trustees all his lands, tenements and hereditaments 'in the three towns of Littleton, Marston and Milbrooke, or elsewhere'.] 'The question here is, are these words doubtful? I think not; I think that the word "elsewhere" is the same as if the testator has said "he devised all his land in the three towns particularly mentioned, or in any other place whatsoever"; and there is no reason to reject so plain, proper, and intelligible a word in a will as this, which probably was inserted to avoid the prolixity of naming the several other towns in which the premises lay, it being a great estate, and difficult, at the time of making the will, . . . to particularise all the towns. . . . The word elsewhere is therefore the most significant sensible and comprehensive word that could be used for that purpose, equivalent to the naming of them; and it would be of the most dangerous consequence, under pretence of construing this will, and assisting the testator's intentions, to reject a word so material to be made use of, both for the sake of brevity and security.' *Chester v Chester* (1730) 3 P Wms 56 at 61, per Lord King LC

'The word "elsewhere" [in a mariner's contract to serve on a voyage from London to New South Wales and India or elsewhere and to return to Europe] must, in its construction, vary much, according to the situation of the primary port of destination;—if it is applied to a country remote from all neighbouring settlements, it is entitled to a larger construction—if to one which is surrounded by many adjacent ports, the limitation would be much narrowed; and I cannot help observing here, that the captain has deprived himself of an extensive latitude, by describing his primary port to be in the neighbourhood of many adjacent ports which could supply cargoes.' *The Minerva* (1825) 1 Hag Adm 347 at 362, per Lord Stowell

[A company was formed to acquire mines in West Australia 'or elsewhere'.] 'I should think that the putting in of the words "West Australia" meant to point specially to West Australia;

and that it did not mean West Australia, California, Mexico, or any place you like to mention, or elsewhere. It did not mean anywhere in the world. It is not a reasonable thing to say that "West Australia or elsewhere" means anywhere in the world, especially where you have the other words, "to conduct all such businesses as are contemplated by, or permitted under, the Goldfields Regulations of the Colony of West Australia". What sense is there in such words as I have last read, if they are to be applied to mines in Mexico, or in California, or in Wales, or any place where minerals—or gold if you like—may be found? . . . I am not at all inclined to say that that clause means West Australia and any other part of the world. And I do not see how we can get as far as Victoria without letting in all the rest of the world. I should say that probably, or possibly, this meaning may be given to that word "elsewhere"—"elsewhere in reasonable business connection with something being done in West Australia".' *Re Coolgardie Consolidated Gold Mines Ltd* (1897) 76 LT 269 at 272, CA, per Rigby LJ

EMANCIPATION

'What is meant by "emancipation" has never been defined in any of the reported decisions. It was contended . . . that as soon as a daughter is married and leaves the parental home that in itself amounts to emancipation, which puts an end to any presumption of undue influence by a parent. I do not agree with this view. I think emancipation from the relationship which gives rise to the exceptional influence possessed by a parent over a child is a question of fact to be determined on the evidence given in each case.' *Lancashire Loans Ltd v Black* [1934] 1 KB 380 at 421, CA, per Greer LJ

EMBLEMENTS

At common law a tenant holding for an uncertain interest, whose interest determines otherwise than by or in consequence of his own act, has the right, under the name of emblements, to enter upon the land after determination to cut and carry away those crops that normally repay within the year the labour by which they are produced. (14 Halsbury's Laws (4th edn) para 1077)

EMBRACERY

Embracery is an indictable offence at common law and is committed by any person who attempts to corrupt, influence, or instruct a jury or to incline a jury to favour one side more than the other, whether by money, promises, letters, threats, or persuasion, or by any means other than by evidence and arguments in open court at the trial. To give jurors money after their verdict constitutes embracery, even though there was no previous promise to pay. (11 Halsbury's Laws (4th edn) para 953)

EMERGENCY

References in this Act to a case of emergency are references to a case in which a person lawfully requiring entry to the premises in question, in the exercise of a right of entry to which this Act applies, has reasonable cause to believe that circumstances exist which are likely to endanger life or property, and that immediate entry to the premises is necessary to verify the existence of those circumstances or to ascertain their cause or to effect a remedy. (Rights of Entry (Gas and Electricity Boards) Act 1954, s 3) [A similar definition is to be found in the Radioactive Substances Act 1960, s 12(9).]

[The Motorways Traffic Regulations 1959, reg 7(2), provided that no vehicle should remain at rest on any motorway verge except (inter alia) by reason of any accident, illness, or other 'emergency'.] 'There is no previous authority, we are told, on the meaning of the word "emergency" in this context. One comes to the dictionary and the first meaning given in the Shorter Oxford Dictionary is: "The sudden or unexpected occurrence of a state of things"; the alternative is "a sudden occurrence". Too much stress, however, in my judgment, must not be attached to the word "sudden" because in a somewhat different context, although a context which I find valuable, the meaning of an emergency has been considered by the House of Lords. The case is *Larchbank v British Petrol* [[1943] AC 299] and I take the extract from the speech of Lord Atkin. He said: "'Emergency' can be used to describe a state of things which is not the result of a sudden occurrence. A condition of things causing a reasonable apprehension of the near approach of danger would, I think, constitute an emergency. The gradual approach of a hostile invader might well at some time or other constitute an emergency. So might the position arising from the presence of a large hostile force encamped near the frontier and only awaiting favourable conditions for an advance." I am indebted to Lord Atkin for that guidance, and perhaps for preventing me from falling into the error of thinking that an element of suddenness is essential for the existence of an emergency in the present legislation.' *Higgins v Bernard* [1972] 1 All ER 1037 at 1040, per Lord Widgery CJ

EMERGENCY WORKS

'Emergency works' means works whose execution at the time when they are executed is requisite in order to put an end to, or to prevent the arising of, circumstances then existing or imminent which are calculated to cause danger to persons or property, interruption of a supply or service afforded by undertakers or by a transport authority, or substantial loss to undertakers or to such an authority, or in order to enable undertakers to satisfy an obligation created by an enactment to afford a supply or service within a time fixed by or under the enactment; and, in relation to works comprising items whereof some fall within the preceding definition and others do not, includes only such of them as fall within it and such others of them as cannot reasonably be severed therefrom. (Public Utilities Street Works Act 1950, s 39) [Extended by the Drought Act 1976, s 2(9).]

'Emergency works' means works whose execution at the time when they are executed is requisite in order to put an end to, or to prevent the arising of, circumstances then existing or imminent which are calculated to cause danger to persons or property, interruption of the conveyance by a pipe-line of any thing or a service afforded by undertakers (within the meaning of the Public Utilities Street Works Act 1950), or substantial loss to the owner of a pipe-line or to such undertakers. (Pipe-lines Act 1962, s 68)
[For the meaning of undertakers, see s 39 of the Public Utilities Street Works Act 1950.]

EMOLUMENTS

'Emoluments' includes any allowances, privileges or benefits, whether obtaining legally or by customary practice. (Electricity Act 1947, s 67(1))

'The question turns upon the meaning of the expression "annual emolument", and I find on looking at Johnson's Dictionary, that "emolument" is defined to be "profit or advantage",

and therefore it means the annual profit or advantage which the prosecutor has derived from the office. . . . In ascertaining what is the annual profit and advantage that he derived from his office, you must take into consideration the sum paid him for travelling expenses, and taking the whole of that into consideration, does he derive any annual profit or advantage from it? If he does, that is what he is entitled to, and that must be taken into consideration in calculating the amount of compensation. It appears to me to turn on that word, which has a wider meaning than the word "remuneration".' *R v Postmaster-General* (1876) 1 QBD 658 at 665, per Quain J

[Section 742 of the Merchant Shipping Act 1894, provides that the expression 'wages' includes emoluments.] 'It is not necessary to define "emoluments", which is a term not usually applicable to wages payable to a sailor, but it was meant to include something paid to him for his work over and above the wages actually agreed to be paid.' *Shelford v Mosey* [1917] 1 KB 154 at 159, per Lord Reading CJ

[Section 4 of the Superannuation (Metropolis) Act 1866 (repealed) provided that the allowance to be granted to an officer, who should have served for a certain period, should be an allowance of ten sixtieths of the salary and 'emoluments' of his office.] 'There is nothing very artificial in the meaning of the word "emolument". It simply means here the advantage or benefit which the plaintiff is entitled to in virtue of his office or employment in addition to his salary.' *Kiddie v Port of London Authority* (1929) 93 JP 203 at 205, per Maugham J

'It is perfectly plain that the council would never have got a whole-time officer to do the local fuel overseer's work for £150 a year. If they had tried to get somebody outside to hold such an office it would have cost them far more. Because the borough treasurer was getting a salary and was ready to do these extra duties, he did them. To my mind, it is quite plain that the £150 was an emolument which he was entitled to have brought into account [in the calculation of his superannuation allowance].' *Re Wickham & Paddington Corpn's Arbitration,* [1946] 2 All ER 68 at 79, per Atkinson J

Canada 'What . . . is the meaning of "emolument" in its usual and ordinary acceptation. It comes from the participle (*emolumentum*) of the latin verb *emolo, molo* to grind, originally meaning toll taken for grinding. It is now, according to the Imperial Dictionary and other reliable authorities, understood: "1. The profit arising from office or employment—that which is received as a compensation for services, or which is annexed to the possession of office, as salary, fees and perquisites. 2. Profit, advantage, gains in general;" and according to the same dictionary, "emolumental" means "producing profit, useful, profitable, advantageous".' *Lawless v Sullivan* (1879) 3 SCR 117 at 146, SCC, per Henry J, revd, without affecting definition, (1881) 6 App Cas 373

EMPLOY

A person who works about the business of a shop for the occupier thereof shall be deemed to be employed notwithstanding that he receives no reward for his labour. (Shops Act 1950, s 22)

'The word "employ" does not necessarily mean employed in actual work; but . . . may be fulfilled by keeping [a person] in . . . service.' *Emmens v Elderton* (1852) 4 HL Cas 624 at 654, per Wightman J

'The words "employ" and "employment" are capable of two meanings which are apt to cause confusion. They may relate to the general nature of a workman's employment, or they may be confined to the particular work or job, which he is doing under his contract of service at any particular moment of time. One must judge their true meaning in any particular case by the context.' *Meadows v Ellerman Lines Ltd* [1920] 3 KB 544 at 549, CA, per cur.

[The respondent had for a number of years carried on a quarry business with a partner. In 1935 they sold the business to the appellants, entering into a covenant not to compete. In 1938 the respondent's sons decided to start a quarry business on land adjacent to the appellant's quarry. The respondent provided capital and took part in the business negotiations.] 'I think that the words "employed in the business" cover the acts of the father in connection with those negotiations. It seems to me that the part that he took in those negotiations, representing his sons during their necessary absence on other work, was the part of an agent perhaps, or a clerk employed in the business. The acquisition of machinery and its installation was part of the business activities of these three sons, and on behalf of the sons and as representing the sons he negotiated in that matter and quite clearly also gave advice. In my opinion, the word "employed" is sufficient to cover what he did.' *Batts Combe Quarry Ltd v Ford* [1942] 2 All ER 639 at 640–642, CA, per Lord Greene MR

'It certainly cannot be said that the word "employed" in a statute automatically connotes an exclusion of periods when acts are done which are not within the scope of employment. Nor is there anything in the words of the section [Factories Act 1961, s 14(1)] to suggest such a connotation. Moreover, it would be difficult to conceive an apparently continuous employment as leading to an intermittent existence which temporarily ceased whenever the servant did things (or perhaps merely set out to do things) which were not within the scope of it. Nor is it easy to see at what exact point in the servant's acts one would say that employment temporarily ceased. On the narrow point of the construction of the section itself there is, therefore, nothing to justify the gloss that an employed person is to be protected only so long as he is acting within the scope of his employment.' *Uddin v Associated Portland Cement Manufacturers Ltd* [1965] 2 All ER 213 at 216, CA, per Lord Pearce; also reported [1965] 2 QB 582

Australia [The Workers' Compensation Act 1926–1986 (NSW) s 7(1)(a) deals with the case of an employer who has a place of employment in New South Wales, or is for the time being in New South Wales, and there 'employs' a worker.] 'The question is what does the word "employs" mean in the context being considered. . . . In my view the words "for the time being present in New South Wales" are strong to indicate the sense in which the Legislature used the word "employs". . . . The word "employs" is used to denote a particular act, that is, the engagement of a worker by an employer visiting the State, not the carrying out by the worker of a contract of employment in the State.' *Helmers v Coppins* (1961) 106 CLR 156 at 158–160, per McTiernan J

EMPLOYEE

For the purposes of this Act the term 'employee' means an individual who has entered into or works under a contract of service or apprenticeship with an employer whether by way of manual labour, clerical work or otherwise, whether such contract is expressed or implied, oral or in writing. (Employers' Liability (Compulsory Insurance) Act 1969, s 2(1))

'Employee' . . . means an individual who has entered into or works under (or, where the employment has ceased, worked under) a contract of employment, otherwise than in police service. (Trade Union and Labour Relations Act 1974, s 30(1))

'Employee' includes an articled clerk. (Solicitors Act 1974, s 87(1))

'Employee' means an individual who has entered into or works under (or, where the employment has ceased, worked under) a contract of employment. (Employment Protection (Consolidation) Act 1978, s 153(1))

Canada [The question in issue was whether a solicitor acting for a company was an 'employee' for the purpose of examination for discovery.] 'It may be true in a broad sense to say that one who is employed is an employee and it would certainly sound funny to refer to a bank president as an employee of his bank. While, however, it is strictly correct to say that everyone who is an employee is employed by another I do not think it is equally true to say that everyone who is employed by another is his employee. For instance, a solicitor who is engaged by a client to do certain work for him is employed by him for that purpose, as is a doctor who gives his professional skill to a patient, but no one would think of referring to either of these professional men as an employee of his client or his patient.' *Carter v Great West Lumber Co* [1919] 3 WWR 901 at 902, Alta SC, per Walsh J

Canada 'What . . . is the ordinary import of the word "employee" and its correlative, "employer"? "Employee" may designate someone who at the time in question is actually performing services for the employer. But its natural meaning goes beyond that. Black's Law Dictionary, revised 4th ed (1968), p 617, defines "employee" in terms of "position", "place", or "office": ". . . it is understood to mean some permanent employment or position. The word may be more extensive than 'clerk' or 'officer', and may signify any one in place, or having charge or using a function, as well as one in office." I therefore conclude that in its ordinary import, "employee" may designate someone who has a position or status relative to the employer. Provided that he continues to have that position or status . . . he does not cease to be an employee merely because he is not actually performing work at a given time.' *United Brotherhood of Carpenters and Joiners of America Local 1928 v Citation Industries Ltd, Employment Standards Board*

and A-G of British Columbia (1983) 46 BCLR 129 at 133–135, BCSC, per McLachlin J; affd (1984) 54 BCLR 283, BCCA

United States The term 'employee' shall include any employee, and shall not be limited to the employees of a particular employer, unless this subchapter explicitly states otherwise, and shall include any individual whose work has ceased as a consequence of, or in connection with, any current labor dispute or because of any unfair labor practice, and who has not obtained any other regular and substantially equivalent employment, but shall not include any individual employed as an agricultural laborer, or in the domestic service of any family or person at his home, or any individual employed by his parent or spouse, or any individual having the status of an independent contractor, or any individual employed as a supervisor, or any individual employed by an employer subject to the Railway Labor Act, as amended from time to time, or by any other person who is not an employer as herein defined. (Labor Management Relations Act of 1947, s 2(3))

United States 'Employee' means any individual employed by an employer, and includes any individual whose work has ceased as a consequence of, or in connection with, any current labor dispute or because of any unfair labor practice or because of exclusion or expulsion from a labor organization in any manner or for any reason inconsistent with the requirements of this chapter. (Labor-Management Reporting and Disclosure Act of 1959, s 3(f))

Corporations

United States 'Employee' includes an officer but not a director. A director may accept duties that make him also an employee. (Revised Model Business Corporation Act 1984, s 1.40(8))

EMPLOYER

'Employer', in relation to an employee, means the person by whom the employee is (or, in a case where the employment has ceased, was) employed. (Employment Protection (Consolidation) Act 1978, s 153(1); Wages Act 1986, s 8(1))

United States The term 'employer' includes any person acting as agent of an employer, directly or indirectly, but shall not include the United States or any wholly owned

Government corporation, or any Federal Reserve Bank, or any State or political sub-division thereof, or any person subject to the Railway Labor Act, as amended from time to time, or any labor organization (other than when acting as an employer), or anyone acting in the capacity of officer or agent of such labor organization. (Labor Management Relations Act of 1947, s 2(12), as amended 1974)

United States 'Employer' means any employer or any group or association of employers engaged in an industry affecting commerce (1) which is, with respect to employees engaged in an industry affecting commerce, an employer within the meaning of any law of the United States relating to the employment of any employees or (2) which may deal with any labor organization concerning grievances, labor disputes, wages, rates of pay, hours of employment, or conditions of work, and includes any person acting directly or indirectly as an employer or as an agent of an employer in relation to an employee but does not include the United States or any corporation wholly owned by the Government of the United States or any State or political sub-division thereof. (Labor-Management Reporting and Disclosure Act of 1959, s 3(e))

EMPLOYERS' ASSOCIATION

In this Act, except so far as the context otherwise requires, 'employers' association' means an organisation (whether permanent or temporary) which either—
(a) consists wholly or mainly of employers or individual proprietors of one or more descriptions and is an organisation whose principal purposes include the regulation of relations between employers of that description or those descriptions and workers or trade unions; or
(b) consists wholly or mainly of—
  (i) constituent or affiliated organisations which fulfil the conditions specified in paragraph (a) above (or themselves consist wholly or mainly of constituent or affiliated organisations which fulfil those conditions), or
  (ii) representatives of such constituent or affiliated organisations;
and in either case is an organisation whose principal purposes include the regulation of relations between employers and workers or between employers and trade unions, or include the regulation of relations between its constituent or affiliated organisations.

(Trade Union and Labour Relations Act 1974, s 28(2); Employment Protection (Consolidation) Act 1978, s 153(1)

'Employers' association' means any organisation representing employers and any association of such organisations or of employers and such organisations. (Wages Councils Act 1979, s 28)

EMPLOYMENT

'Employment' includes any trade, business, profession, office or vocation and 'employed' shall be construed accordingly except in the expression 'employed earner'. (Social Security Act 1973, s 99(1))

'Employment' includes (a) employment by way of a professional engagement or otherwise under a contract for services; (b) the reception in a private household of a person under an arrangement whereby that person is to assist in the domestic work of the household in consideration of receiving hospitality and pocket money or hospitality only. (Employment Agencies Act 1973, s 13(1))

In this section [s 29: meaning of 'trade dispute'] 'employment' includes any relationship whereby one person personally does work or performs services for another. (Trade Union and Labour Relations Act 1974, s 29(6))

'I do not think that employment means only where one man is set to work by others to earn money; a man may employ himself so as to earn profits in many ways.' *Partridge v Mallandaine* (1886) 18 QBD 276 at 277, 278, DC, per Denman J

[A clause of a time charterparty (form T.99A) provided that the master of a ship should be under the orders and directions of the charterers as regards 'employment', agency or other arrangements. The question on this clause was whether the employment referred to meant employment of persons or employment of the ship.] 'In my opinion, the "employment" referred to is "employment of the ship". . . . I think the word "employment" in cl. 9 . . . means the services which the ship is ordered to perform, such as the voyages to or from particular ports, with particular cargoes or in ballast.' *Larrinaga SS Co Ltd v R* [1945] AC 246 at 255, HL, per Lord Wright

'The word "employment" is one of very wide significance. But the words "employer" and "employee" are much more restricted in their meanings. Thus, I may be said to "employ" my time or my talents without being in any proper sense an employer, and I may also be said to be employed in some pursuit or activity without being an employee.' *Westall Richardson Ltd v Roulson* [1954] 2 All ER 448 at 451, per Vaisey J

South Africa 'It seems to me that to constitute employment there must be control by the employer over the employee—the right to give the employee instructions as to what he is to do.' *Martheze v The Rescue Works Committee of the Dutch Reformed Church* 1925 CPD 382, per Gardiner AJP

Casual employment

'Suppose that a host, when from time to time he entertains his friends at dinner or his wife gives a reception or a dance, has been in the habit for many years of employing the same men to come in and wait at his table or assist at the reception, it may be said that their employment is regular. But the employment is of a casual nature. It depends upon the whim or the hospitable instincts or the social obligations of the host whether he gives any, and how many, dinner parties or receptions, and the number of men he will want will vary with the number of his guests. In such a case the waiters may not incorrectly be said to be regularly employed in an employment of a casual nature.' *Hill v Begg* [1908] 2 KB 802 at 805, 806, CA, per Buckley LJ

Course of   *See* COURSE OF EMPLOYMENT

Place of employment

'Place of employment' in relation to any person, means the factory, workshop, farm or other premises or place at which he was employed, so however that, where separate branches of work which are commonly carried on as separate businesses in separate premises or at separate places are in any case carried on in separate departments on the same premises or at the same place, each of those departments shall for the purposes of this paragraph be deemed to be a separate factory or workshop or farm or separate premises or a separate place, as the case may be. (Social Security Act 1973, s 14(6))

EMPLOYMENT AGENCY

For the purposes of this Act 'employment agency' means the business (whether or not carried on with a view to profit and whether or not carried on in conjunction with any other business) of providing services (whether by the provision of information or otherwise) for the purpose of finding workers employment with employers or of supplying employers with workers for employment by them. (Employment Agencies Act 1973, s 13(2))

[Certain arrangements, services, functions or businesses are excluded by s 13(7) of the Act.]

EN VENTRE SA MÈRE   *See also* LIVING (ALIVE)

'I have no doubt on any view of this case. It is plain on the words of the will, that the testator meant that all the children whom his brother should leave behind him should be benefited; but independent of this intention, I hold that an infant en ventre sa mère, who by the course and order of nature is then living, comes clearly within the description of "children living at the time of his decease".' *Doe* d *Clarke v Clarke* (1795) 2 Hy Bl 399 at 400, per Eyre LCJ

'The child was en ventre sa mère at the time of the death of its grandmother, and was plainly then living, so as to bring it within the words of the will "in case she has issue living".' *Re Burrows, Cleghorn v Burrows* [1895] 2 Ch 497 at 498, per Chitty J

ENABLE

South Africa 'The word "enable" in Order 11, Rule 2 of the Magistrates Court (Civil) Rules, is not to be interpreted as imposing a duty to give particulars only when without them it would be impossible to plead, any more than ability to prepare for trial means that, without the particulars requested, it would be impossible to prepare for trial. In the context, ability to plead or prepare for trial means the ability properly to plead or prepare for trial.' *Timsecurity (Pvt) Ltd v Castle Hotel (Pvt) Ltd* 1972 (3) SA (RA) 114, per MacDonald ACJ

ENACTMENT   *See also* STATUTE

Whilst all statutes are properly referred to as enactments, 'enactment' may equally well be used to describe a particular provision in a statute. It is also used at times to include [General Synod] Measures, or particular provisions of them, and subordinate legislation. (44 Halsbury's Laws (4th edn) para 803)

'Enactment' includes any byelaw, regulation or other provision having effect under an enactment. (Education (Work Experience) Act 1973, s 1(4))

'The word "enactment" does not mean the same thing as "Act". "Act" means the whole Act, whereas a section or part of a section in an Act may be an enactment.' *Wakefield & District Light Rlys Co v Wakefield Corpn* [1906] 2 KB 140 at 145, 146, per Ridley J

South Africa 'Enactment is not a term of art and means any measure ordained and promulgated by any person or body possessing legislative authority.' *R v Conway* 1943 EDL 215, per Gutsche J

ENCLOSED *See* INCLOSED

ENCLOSED LAND

[A game licence is not necessary under the Game Licences Act 1960 where deer are killed on 'enclosed land' by the owner or occupier of such land or with his permission.] 'I think in this context the contrast is between enclosed lands, such as lands used for farming and enclosed by normal agricultural hedges, and moorland where there are no enclosures and where the deer can run free.' *Jemmison v Priddle* [1972] 1 All ER 539 at 543, per Lord Widgery CJ

ENCOURAGE

[By s 17(1) of the Children Act 1908 (repealed; see now s 28(1) of the Sexual Offences Act 1956), any person having custody of a girl under the age of sixteen, who causes or 'encourages' the seduction, etc, of her shall be guilty of a misdemeanour.] 'The Legislature . . . enacted that a person should be deemed to have caused or encouraged the seduction . . . of the girl, "if he has knowingly allowed the girl to consort with . . . any prostitute or person of known immoral character". . . . If it was proved that a father, knowing that his daughter was consorting with persons of known immoral character, stood by and allowed such intimacies to continue when it was in his power to prevent them, that might furnish evidence of causing or encouraging her unlawful carnal knowledge. But there is a wide difference between allowing and "knowingly allowing" within the meaning of this enactment.' *R v Chainey* [1914] 1 KB 137 at 141, 142, CCA, per Isaacs CJ

[Rule 4 of Sch 4 to the Betting, Gaming and Lotteries Act 1963 provides that neither the licensee of a betting office, nor any servant or agent of his, shall 'encourage' persons to bet.] 'In my judgment, "encourage" there merely means incite. It does not mean cause to be encouraged, but inciting someone to bet. There can be no incitement of anyone unless the incitement, whether by words or written matter, reaches the man whom it is said is being incited.' *Wilson v Danny Quastel (Rotherhithe) Ltd* [1965] 2 All ER 541 at 543, per Lord Parker CJ

ENCUMBRANCE *See also* INCUMBRANCE

Australia 'The word "encumbrances", in its ordinary connotation, means that a person or estate is burdened with debts, obligations or responsibilities. True, the word is in law especially used to indicate a burden on property, a claim, lien or liability attached to property. . . . But when we remember that the whole estate of the testator is liable in the hands of his executor for payment of debts and the expense of administering his estate, it is not an extravagant use of language to say that his "whole estate is not free from encumbrances" until those debts and expenses are paid. The estate would, in fact, be burdened with those debts, and no technical use of the word "encumbrances" can alter that result.' *Wallace v Love* (1922) 31 CLR 156 at 164, per cur.

Australia '"Mortgagor" is defined so as to mean a borrower and "mortgagee" a lender on the security of an estate or interest in land. "Encumbrancer" means any person not being a mortgagor who shall have charged any estate or interest in land with any annuity or sum of money other than a loan. "Encumbrancee" has a corresponding meaning, that is, a person "not being a mortgagee". There is not an exact correspondence between the definitions. If attention is confined to the distinction between a mortgage and an encumbrance it might be thought that an encumbrance included any security except one which merely secured a loan and that it therefore included a security given for both a loan and some other liability. However, when "encumbrancer" and "encumbrancee" are contrasted with "mortgagor" and "mortgagee", they indicate that an encumbrance is a security given for a debt other than a loan and that it therefore excludes any security given for both a loan and a debt.' *Cambridge Credit Corporation Ltd v Lombard Australia Ltd* (1977) 136 CLR 608 at 615–616, per cur.

Secured transactions

United States 'Encumbrance' includes real estate mortgages and other liens on real estate and all other rights in real estate that are not ownership interests. . . . (Uniform Commercial Code 1978, s 9–105(1)(g))

END   *See also* DETERMINE

Of engagement

'Section 4 of 43 & 44 Vict c 16 [Merchant Seamen (Payment of Wages and Rating) Act 1880 (repealed; see now Merchant Shipping Act 1970, ss 7, 8)] enacts that "in the case of foreign-going ships the owner or master of the ship shall pay to each seaman on account, at the time when he lawfully leaves the ship at the end of his engagement, two pounds", and so on. . . . It appears to me that "the end of his engagement" means that time at which his actual service terminates; that is to say, the language is sufficiently elastic to include the natural effluxion of the agreement, and the discharge of the seaman in breach of the contract. I think these words are used advisedly to include both cases. The words "at the end of his engagement" would, according to my view, include such a case as this, namely, the discharge by the captain of the seaman before the time at which, according to the agreement, and without breach of the agreement, he could discharge them, which is the present case.' *Re Great Eastern SS Co, Williams' Claim* (1885) 53 LT 594 at 596, per Chitty J

See, generally, 43 Halsbury's Laws (4th edn) paras 229 et seq.

Of voyage

[By the Merchant Shipping Act 1894, s 218 (repealed; see now the Merchant Shipping Act 1970, s 78) an unauthorised person who went on board a ship about to arrive, arriving, or having arrived 'at the end of her voyage', before the seamen lawfully left the ship or were discharged, was made liable to a fine. Section 219 provided for the application of s 218 to ships of a foreign country, where the government of that foreign country so desired.] 'Section 219 . . . provides: "Her Majesty in Council may order that those provisions [of s 218] shall apply to the ships of that foreign country, and have effect as if the ships of that country arriving, about to arrive, or having arrived at the end of their voyage, were British ships." . . . Of course it is quite possible . . . to read the word "voyage" as indicating a voyage or transit to British territory, notwithstanding the fact that when the foreign vessel goes out again she will go under the same contractual relation in regard to its seamen as before.' *R v Abrahams* [1904] 2 KB 859 at 864, DC, per Lord Alverstone CJ

'The end of the voyage means, in my opinion, for this purpose the end of the voyage into British territorial waters.' Ibid at 865, per Phillimore J

[A seaman signed articles of agreement for a voyage 'commencing at Cardiff, proceeding thence to Malta, thereafter trading to ports in any rotation, and to end at such port in the United Kingdom or continent of Europe, within home trading limits, as may be required by the master.'] 'The Merchant Shipping Acts from 1729 downwards do not in terms define the "end of a voyage", but there are three expressions which afford a fairly sure guide to what may be taken to be the place where a voyage is to end. "The place of unlivery of the cargo", "the final port of discharge", and "the final port of destination" are terms which will be found fairly frequently in the various Merchant Shipping Acts, and so far as I can judge are intended to be correlative terms, each pointing to what must be taken to be the end of a voyage: and reading them in this light it seems clear that the end of a voyage is the place where the final or home passage of the whole voyage terminates by reason that it is the place at which the cargo brought home is to be discharged finally.' *The Scarsdale* [1906] P 103 at 115, 116, CA, per Vaughan Williams LJ

See, generally, 43 Halsbury's Laws (4th edn) para 652 et seq.

Of will   *See* FOOT OR END

ENDANGER

New Zealand [Section 166(1) of the Crimes Act 1908 (NZ) (repealed; see now s 151(1) of the Crimes Act 1961) provided that any one who had charge of any other person unable to provide himself with the necessities of life was criminally responsible for omitting without lawful excuse to perform such duty if the death of such person was caused or if his life was 'endangered'.] 'Where death results from the gradual development of a disease, it must frequently be the case that the disease progresses through a series of stages until the stage is reached after which death immediately occurs. Can it be said, then, that the life is endangered only during the ultimate stage and that it is not endangered during the penultimate or any of the preceding stages? To answer that question in the affirmative would be, we think, to take an unrealistic view. In many diseases there may be a real danger to life long before the final stage is reached. We think that there is evidence to go to the jury, in a case such as this, that the life is endangered within the meaning of that expression in s 166 of the Crimes Act 1908, as soon as the disease has reached the stage at which it can be said that there exists a reasonable possibility that death will ensue if medical attention is not obtained.' *R v Moore* [1954] NZLR 893 at 899, 900, CA, per cur.

ENDEAVOUR TO PERSUADE *See* PERSUADE

ENDOW

Australia 'The person who endows does not keep up a perpetual series of payments, but he provides property or makes over some income or fruits of some property which he—the person who endows—owns or buys or causes to be bought. This is the meaning of the word "endow".... Pope has the line "Die, and endow a college or a cat".' *Fielding v Houison* (1908) 7 CLR 393 at 457, 458, per Higgins J

ENDOWED SCHOOL *See* SCHOOL

ENDOWMENT

'Endowments' includes any commutation or other payment charged on the common fund of the Commissioners and any money in their hands which represents the proceeds of a sale of land, or of a house of residence, or a fund for repair of a house of residence. (Episcopal Endowments and Stipends Measure 1943 (No 2), s 8(1))

'By the endowment of a school, an hospital or a chapel, is commonly understood, not the building or purchasing a site for a school, an hospital or a chapel, but the providing of a fixed revenue for the support of those institutions.' *Edwards v Hall* (1855) 6 De G M & G 74 at 87, per Lord Cranworth LC

[A testatrix gave her net residuary estate on trusts which included a provision that, in the events which had happened, one half of the residuary estate should be applied in 'endowing' beds for paying patients in a hospital.] 'In my opinion the words "endowing" or "endowment" are not limited to the provision out of capital expenditure for the actual amenity bed. I think that by "endowment" or "endow" may also be meant providing a capital sum out of which income will be produced that will pay for the services which it is desired will be provided in respect of the endowment in question. It seems to me in the present case, therefore, that it may be perfectly proper, if the opportunity arises and there is need for it, to apply the capital of the fund in question towards the cost of erection of new buildings, or the provision of actual beds, and so on; but "endowment" also includes the meaning of provision of a fund which, by the income thereby derived, pays for the purpose which is the object of the gift. A very simple illustration of that is gifts, for instance, to the National Trust. In that case there is a gift of land, and in addition the National Trust desires to have an endowment of the land given, that is to say, a fund which will provide means for the maintenance and upkeep of the land and buildings, the subject of the gift. In the same way the gift of an endowment of a hospital bed in my view includes the income of a fund which will provide some support for the patients who occupy the bed.' *Re Adams, Gee v Barnet Group Hospital Management Committee* [1967] 3 All ER 285 at 290, CA, per Danckwerts LJ

ENEMY *See also* ALIEN

Subject to the provisions of this section, the expression 'enemy' for the purposes of this Act means—
(a) any State, or Sovereign of a State, at war with [Her] Majesty,
(b) any individual resident in enemy territory,
(c) any body of persons (whether corporate or unincorporate) carrying on business in any place, if and so long as the body is controlled by a person who, under this section, is an enemy . . .
(d) any body of persons constituted or incorporated in, or under the laws of, a State at war with [Her] Majesty; and
(e) as respects any business carried on in enemy territory, any individual or body of persons (whether corporate or unincorporate) carrying on that business

but does not include any individual by reason only that he is an enemy subject. (Trading with the Enemy Act 1939, s 2(1))

[See also the similar definition in the Import, Export and Customs Powers (Defence) Act 1939, s 8.]

'Enemy' includes all persons engaged in armed operations against any of Her Majesty's forces, or any forces co-operating therewith, and also includes all armed mutineers, armed rebels, armed rioters and pirates. (Air Force Act 1955, s 223(1), as amended by the Armed Forces Act 1966, s 28; Army Act 1955, s 225(1), as so amended; Naval Discipline Act 1957, s 135(1), as amended by the Armed Forces Act 1966, s 36)

[Section 1 of the Official Secrets Act 1911 makes it an offence to make, or communicate to another person, any sketch, etc, which is calculated to be, or might be or is intended to be, useful to an 'enemy'.] 'When the statute uses the word "enemy" it does not mean necessarily some one with whom this country is at war, but a potential enemy with whom we might some day be at war.' *R v Parrott* (1913) 8 Cr App Rep 186 at 192, per Phillimore J

'A soldier in His Majesty's army who has been taken prisoner during war and is detained in enemy territory, is not an enemy in any sense of the word.' *Vandyke v Adams* [1942] Ch 155 at 157, per Farwell J

'The tribunal [Pensions Appeal Tribunal] held that the Minister had discharged the onus of proving that the injury was not a "war injury" as defined [in s 10 of the Pensions (Navy, Army, Air Force and Merchant Marine) Act 1939, and in the First Schedule to the War Pensions (Mercantile Marine) Scheme 1944]. They held that "enemy" in the section cited referred to "the normal armed forces in uniform" and not to persons or agents hostile to the British who might be in the pay of, or in sympathy with, the enemy. . : . In our opinion the tribunal's conclusion was justified. The collocation in which the word "enemy" occurs in the Act indicates that the reference is to war-like operations by the organised forces of the enemy. To give the word the wider meaning claimed by the appellant would impose on the Minister the impossible onus of accounting for almost any kind of unexplained mishap which might befall a British seaman in any part of the world. We derive no aid from the special extension given to the term "enemy" in the Army Acts and the Naval

Discipline Acts, in which the background and context are entirely different. . . . The appellant's only hope of success is to show that any person, irrespective of nationality or allegiance, who is a sympathiser with the enemy is an "enemy" for the purposes of the Act and relative Pension Scheme. Being unable to accept this view, we hold that the appeal fails.' *Laird v Minister of Pensions* 1946 SLT 363 at 364, 365, per the Lord Justice-Clerk (Cooper)

Canada 'With reference to civil rights "enemy" means . . . a person, of whatever nationality, who resides or carries on business in enemy territory.' *Lampel v Berger* (1917) 40 OLR 165 at 167, per Mulock C of Ex

See, generally, 49 Halsbury's Laws (4th edn) paras 148 et seq.

ENEMY ALIEN   *See* ALIEN

ENEMY SUBJECT

The expression 'enemy subject' means—
(i) an individual who, not being either a British subject or a British protected person, possesses the nationality of a State at war with [Her] Majesty, or
(ii) a body of persons constituted or incorporated in, or under the laws of, any such State.
(Import, Export and Customs Powers (Defence) Act 1939, s 8)

ENEMY TERRITORY

The expression 'enemy territory' means any area which is under the sovereignty of, or in the occupation of, a Power with whom [Her] Majesty is at war, not being an area in the occupation of [Her] Majesty or of a Power allied with [Her] Majesty. (Import, Export and Customs Powers (Defence) Act 1939, s 8)

ENFORCE

Australia 'I would harbour considerable doubt, as matter of grammar or syntax, whether the word "enforced" extends to cover the institution of proceedings for breach of a provision of a statute. The relevant meaning assigned in the Shorter Oxford English Dictionary is that to enforce means "to compel observance of". That is, I think, its ordinary meaning.' *R v*

Bates [1982] 2 NSWLR 894 at 895, per Samuels JA

ENFRANCHISEMENT

'Enfranchisement of leaseholds in the eye of the tenant is the acquisition of the fee or the getting rid of the rent. Having got rid of that he is master of his property; it belongs to him.' *Re Bruce, Halsey v Bruce* [1905] 2 Ch 372 at 378, per Kekewich J

ENGAGED

[A private Act enacted that a lighter should be exempt from the payment of rates so long as such lighter should be bona fide 'engaged' in discharging or receiving ballast or goods.] 'A lighter is engaged in discharging not merely while the goods are being removed, but also during her entrance to the dock, her departure from it, and any other operations reasonably required in order that she may discharge. It is one single piece of business in several stages.' *London & India Docks Co v McDougall & Bonthron Ltd, London & India Docks Co v Page, Son & East Ltd* [1909] AC 25 at 26, 27, per Lord Loreburn LC

'An employer "engages" a servant when he makes an agreement with him for his services. A workman is "engaged" on work when he is actually carrying it out.' *Benninga (Mitcham) Ltd v Bijstra* [1946] KB 58 at 62, CA, per MacKinnon LJ

[A restrictive covenant provided that an outgoing partner should not carry on or be 'engaged' in a similar business for a period of five years.] 'In my opinion, the words "carry on or be engaged or interested in any business similar to or competing with the business of the partnership" are apt, particularly in view of the word "engaged", to include a case where the party subject to the restriction takes employment in a business of either of the kinds mentioned at a salary or wages, as well as a case in which he embarks on such a business on his own account or partnership.' *Ronbar Enterprises Ltd v Green* [1954] 2 All ER 266 at 268, 269, CA, per Jenkins LJ

Australia 'In some contexts you may speak about a person being engaged in an occupation for however short a period he may be occupied therein. In another context, however, the word "engaged" conveys a different meaning, i.e. it excludes mere casual or intermittent employment and rather connotes such a degree of employment as occupies the whole or at least a substantial part of the person's time.' *Buntine v Hume* [1943] VLR 123 at 128, per O'Bryan J

ENGAGED IN

Australia [The plaintiff was riding a motor cycle on a road as a means of transport. At the relevant time he was insured under a policy of insurance, which was subject to an exception from liability with respect to any event which might happen to the plaintiff whilst 'engaging in' motor cycling.] 'A person who is driving or riding a motor cycle as a means of transport is not engaging in motor cycling. The word "engaging" refers to motor cycling of a recreation, sporting or competitive nature.' *Dufty v City General Mutual Insurance Ltd* [1977] Qd R 94, per Kneipp J

ENGAGEMENT   *See* ATTACK

ENGINE   *See also* FIXED ENGINE

[Section 3 of the Game Act 1831 makes it an offence for any person to use a dog, gun, net, or other 'engine' or instrument for the purpose of killing or taking game on a Sunday.] 'The word engine, derived from *ingenium*, includes a snare which is a device or contrivance—an engine— for killing game.' *Allen v Thompson* (1870) LR 5 QB 336 at 339, per Blackburn J

[Section 31 of the Offences Against the Person Act 1861, makes it a misdemeanour to set or place any spring gun, man trap or other 'engine' calculated to destroy human life or inflict grievous bodily harm upon a trespasser or other person. The appellant hung a live electric wire by a window so that any person entering through the window would be liable to receive a severe shock.] 'There are quite clearly two distinct meanings, amongst others, of the word "engine". One is the perfectly general one derived from the Latin "ingenium", of any instance or product of ingenuity, a contrivance, a device, and this wide meaning would no doubt cover this electrical contrivance. On the other hand, another well recognised meaning of "engine" is a mechanical contrivance,—a machine. What is said in the present case is that this is a penal statute and if there be any ambiguity this narrower meaning ought to be given to the words. The court has come to the conclusion that, particularly as this is a penal statute, the meaning to be given to the word "engine" in s 31 of the Offences Against the Person Act 1861, is the more limited meaning of "engine" as meaning a mechanical contrivance.' *R v Munks* [1963] 3 All ER 757 at 758, 759, CCA, per cur; also reported in [1964] 1 QB 304 at 306

ENGINEERING OPERATIONS

'Engineering operations' includes the formation or laying out of means of access to highways. (Town and Country Planning Act 1971, s 290(1))

ENGLAND

'England' shall include the town of Berwick-on-Tweed, but shall not include any part of England or Wales to which the Welsh Church Act 1914, applies. (Interpretation Measure 1925, s 2)

'England' means, subject to any alteration of boundaries under Part IV of the Local Government Act 1972, the area consisting of the counties established by section 1 of that Act, Greater London and the Isles of Scilly. (Interpretation Act 1978, Sch 1)

'The judgment of the Court in *R v Keyn* [(1876) 46 LJMC 17], is binding on all the Courts in Westminster Hall, and as I understand the *ratio decidendi* in that case it is that, except where the jurisdiction has been extended by an Act of Parliament, England and the sovereignty of the Queen stop at low water mark.' *Harris v Franconia (Owners)* (1877) 46 LJQB 363 at 364, per Lord Coleridge CJ

ENGRAVING

'Engraving' includes any etching, lithograph, woodcut, print or similar work, not being a photograph. (Copyright Act 1956, s 48(1))

ENJOY

'The claim of the plaintiff is vested on s 3 of 2 & 3 Will 4, c 71 [Prescription Act 1832], which enacts that "when the access and use of light to and for any dwelling-house . . . shall have been actually enjoyed therewith for the full period of twenty years without interruption, the right thereto shall be deemed absolute and indefeasible". . . . I take "enjoyed" to mean "having had the amenity or advantage of using" the access of light; that is nearly equivalent to "having had the use".' *Cooper v Straker* (1888) 40 Ch D 21 at 26, 27, per Kay J

'The question in dispute between the parties is whether the roadway is, as the plaintiffs contend, a private roadway or is, as the defendants contend, a public highway. . . . In the first place, it is necessary to decide how the words "actually enjoyed by the public as of right" are to be construed. . . . I think it is right . . . to interpret those words as involving that he who asserts the right must establish as a matter of fact on the one hand the actual enjoyment of the right by the public as of right, and on the other hand the actual suffering of the exercise of that right by the landowner for the full period of twenty years. I take the word "enjoyed" to mean, as Stirling J said in *Smith v Baxter*, [[1900] 2 Ch 138] "having had the amenity or advantage of using".' *Merstham Manor Ltd v Coulsdon & Purley Urban District Council* [1936] 2 All ER 422 at 423, 426, per Hilbery J

'The grant is this: the right as now enjoyed in common with others having the like right to the water supply to the hereditaments hereinbefore described through pipes from a spring . . . it seems to me clear beyond the possibility of doubt that the right conferred by the words which I have read is . . . to receive . . . all the water required at their farm, subject to this, that they could get only what was left after the persons entitled to draw down the existing branch pipes had taken what they wanted.' *Beauchamp v Frome Rural District Council* [1938] 1 All ER 595 at 597, CA, per Greene MR

ENJOYMENT   *See* BENEFICIAL ENJOYMENT; QUIET ENJOYMENT

ENLARGEMENT   *See also* EXTENSION

'Enlargement', in relation to any school premises, includes any modification of the existing premises which has the effect of increasing the number of pupils for whom accommodation can be provided, and 'enlarge' shall be construed accordingly. (Education Act 1944, s 114(1), inserted by s 1, Sch 1 to the Education Act 1968)

'The power [conferred by a private Act] is to enlarge and improve the market place, the market place being, as I understand it, the place where the market is held. Then what is the meaning of the word "enlarge"? We have had a great deal of criticism on the subject, but it appears to me that it is sufficient to say that it will bear this meaning "to increase the space in which the market is held".' *A-G v Cambridge Corpn* (1873) LR 6 HL 303 at 310, per Lord Chelmsford

'Churches are consecrated or dedicated to Almighty God and are intended primarily for His worship. The purpose of an enlargement must, therefore, be closely connected with worship. But that, by itself, is not enough. There must also be a reasonable degree of contiguity with the original building before a new one can fairly be described as an enlargement of the existing church.' *Re St Ann's Church, Kew* [1976] 1 All ER 461 at 464, Southwark Consistory Court, per the Chancellor

Australia 'As applied to a building, "enlarge" means to make bigger and more commodious by additions.' *Re Church of St Jude* [1956] SASR 46 at 53, per Hannan AJ

ENTAILED INTEREST

Estates tail, now sometimes called entailed interests, arose from the operation of the Statute of Westminster the Second [1285] on conditional fees at common law.

At common law a limitation to a man and a special class of heirs, such as the heirs male of his body by a specified wife, was a conditional fee simple. The condition was performed by the birth of issue of the prescribed class, and thereafter the grantee had a fee simple absolute for the purpose of alienation; but, if he died without having alienated the land, the form of the gift was observed, and it followed the prescribed course of descent. The statute enacted that the will of the grantor according to the form of the grant should thenceforth be observed, so that the grantee of the land under such a condition should have no power to alienate the land, but that it should remain to the issue after the death of the grantee, or should revert to the grantor or his heirs on failure of the prescribed issue of the grantee, whether because there was no such issue, or because, after issue born, the line of issue failed. Therefore, the statute prevented the estate from ever becoming a fee simple absolute, and converted it into an estate of inheritance of a restricted nature, whence the estate was called feodum talliatum, or an estate tail.

An estate in tail in its widest form is where lands or tenements are limited to a man and the heirs of his body without restriction as to the wife of whom the heirs are to be born or of the sex of the heirs; and similarly where the limitation is to a woman and the heirs of her body. Such an estate is called an 'estate in tail general'. However often the donee in tail is married, his or her issue of every such marriage, whether male or female, are, in successive order, capable of inheriting under the entail; so that elder sons and their issue will inherit in order before younger sons; sons and their issue will inherit before daughters and their issue; and daughters will inherit equally inter se, the issue of each daughter taking her share.

An estate in tail general may be restricted to heirs male or heirs female, and is called, accordingly, an 'estate in tail male general', or an 'estate in tail female general'. Under a limitation in tail male general only male issue claiming continuously through male issue can inherit; and under a limitation in tail female general only female issue claiming continuously through female issue can inherit. However, the second limitation does not occur in practice, since a limitation in tail male followed by a remainder in tail female does not exhaust the possible issue; the appropriate remainder after a limitation in tail male is a limitation in tail without restriction of sex.

An estate in tail may be restricted to the heirs of the body of two specified persons, and then it is known as an 'estate in tail special'. This may be, first, where the limitation is to a single donee and the heirs of his or her body by a specified wife or husband; and, secondly, where the limitation is to a man and woman who are either married or are capable of lawful marriage. In the first case, the donee has an estate in tail special; in the second case, the donees have a joint estate in tail special. An estate in tail special may be further restricted in the same way as an estate in tail general to male heirs of the body or female heirs of the body. (39 Halsbury's Laws (4th edn) paras 418, 419, 420, 421)

ENTER   *See also* FORCIBLE ENTRY

'Stat 1 & 2 Will 4, c 32 [Game Act 1831], s 30, enacts that, if any person "shall commit any trespass by entering or being, in the day time, upon any land, in search or pursuit of game", he may be convicted. . . . I think that the Legislature contemplated that the offender must personally be or enter on the land. Had the words been only "commit any trespass on land in pursuit of game", I should have said that sending a dog upon the land was within the meaning of the words: but, when I find the words are "commit any trespass by entering or being" "upon any land", I think that the construction of the section is that there must be a personal entering and being on the land.' *R v Pratt* (1855) 4 E & B 860 at 864, 865, CCR, per Lord Campbell CJ

ENTERTAINMENT

In this Act 'exempt entertainment' [exemption of small lotteries] means a bazaar, sale of work, fete, dinner, dance, sporting or athletic event or other entertainment of a similar character, whether limited to one day or extending over two or more days. (Lotteries and Amusements Act 1976, s 3(1))

'The question turns upon whether this house was a place for "public refreshment, resort and entertainment", within the meaning of the 23 & 24 Vict c 27 [Refreshment Houses Act 1860 (repealed; see now the Late Night Refreshment Houses Act 1969, s 1)]. . . . If I found in some other Acts of parliament that word [entertainment] coupled with the word "refreshment", I should be strongly disposed to think it meant amusement and gratification rather than food or drink. But I agree with my brother Martin that the word "entertainment", as here used, is only another expression for "refreshment", and probably means something more substantial than simple refreshment. The word "entertainment" has unquestionably an ambiguous meaning, and being found in connection with the word "refreshment", I should have thought that if the legislature meant it to signify something not ejusdem generis, but quite different, they would have said, "All houses kept open for public refreshment, resort, and entertainment such as music, dancing and other similar entertainment." But, finding the word where it is, I think it means refreshment ejusdem generis.' *Taylor v Oram* (1862) 1 H & C 370 at 376, per Pollock CB

'The real question is as to the meaning of the word "entertainment" in s 6 of the Act [Refreshment Houses Act 1860 (repealed; see supra)]. . . . This house was kept open for public resort. . . . The main objection is, that there was no public entertainment, for that means a musical or other public performance. I think that is wrong. . . . Entertainment is something connected with the enjoyment of refreshment-rooms, tables, and the like. It is something beyond refreshment; it is the accommodation provided, whether that

includes a musical or other amusement or not.' *Muir v Keay* (1875) LR 10 QB 594 at 598, per Lush J

'An entertainment is the gathering together of a number of people to carry out some activity or to be present at some activity presumably with a view to enjoying themselves.' *Bow v Heatly* 1960 SLT 311 at 313, per the Lord Justice-Clerk (Thomson)

'Parliament . . . left the term "entertainment" to receive its meaning in ordinary language, and that meaning in this connection is "amusement".' Ibid at 313, per Lord Patrick

New Zealand   'I am of the opinion that the playing of music in the lounge bar by the two performers was the provision of entertainment for the licensee's customers within the common or popular sense of the word "entertainment". It was a public performance by the two musicians and in ordinary parlance that would be described as the giving of entertainment by them. I do not think it matters that the music was being played softly or that it was . . . merely "background music": the music may well have been all the more agreeable for that reason.' *Mackenzie v Police* [1964] NZLR 1021 at 1023, per Macarthur J

Place of public entertainment

[A local Act enacted that no theatre or other 'place of public entertainment' should be used without a licence.] 'Apart from authority, the respondents argued that "public entertainment" involves the existence of entertainers and persons entertained, and that, where persons resort to premises where there are no entertainers, and entertain themselves . . . the place is not one of public entertainment. The case under this head was persuasively put by asking whether persons who hire a tennis court in a public park and possibly racquets and balls take part in a public entertainment. The answer to this is, we think, no. . . . We think a satisfactory working definition of "public entertainment" was one suggested by counsel for the appellant in argument: ". . . a place open to members of the public without discrimination who desire to be entertained and where means of entertainment are provided." Judged by this test, or indeed, by the ordinary use of language, these funfairs were, in our view, places of "public entertainment", and none the less so because no fee was charged for admission to the premises.' *Allen v Emmerson* [1944] 1 All ER 344 at 347, 348, DC, per cur.

ENTIRE CONTRACT

An entire contract is one where the complete performance of one party is a condition precedent to his right to call for the performance of the other party's obligation. Where the contractor undertakes to complete the works and the contract on its true construction is entire, the employer is entitled to insist on completion before his obligation to pay arises. If the building contractor leaves the work unfinished to a substantial degree he cannot claim a corresponding percentage of the contract sum or recover on a quantum meruit basis for that part of the work he has completed; moreover, he will be liable in damages to the employer for breach of contract. Nevertheless, if he can show that he has substantially completed the works (even though some minor items might remain unfinished) he will be entitled to claim payment. (4 Halsbury's Laws (4th edn) para 1145)

ENTITLED

'The word "entitled" has no defined legal meaning—that is, as between the sense of being entitled in possession and entitled in interest; and as Lord Cranworth says in *Jupp v Wood* [(1865) 2 De GJ & Sm 323 at 329)], "The whole case depends on our putting a proper interpretation on the word entitled. That word may, without any violence to language, mean entitled in interest, or entitled in possession"; and in that particular case the Lord Chancellor held that it meant entitled in possession.' *Re Maunder, Maunder v Maunder* [1902] 2 Ch 875 at 878, per Joyce J; affd. [1903] 1 Ch 451, CA

'Clause 6 . . . [of an Order made by the former Board of Education] . . . goes on to provide that . . . "no nominated or co-optative manager" shall be entitled to act as a foundation manager until he has signed a declaration that he is a member of the Church of England. . . . I think the words "be entitled to" do qualify the nature of the prohibition . . . and that they are used as equivalent to the words "be qualified to".' *Meyers v Hennell* [1912] 2 Ch 256 at 267, per Eve J

Australia 'In my opinion "entitled" usually means "entitled in possession", "entitled to have the thing", not merely that you will be entitled or may be entitled to get something at some future time.' *In the Will of Borger* [1912] VLR 310 at 313, per Hodges J

In possession

'Section 5(2) [of the Settled Land Act 1882 (repealed; see now Settled Land Act 1925, s 19(1))] says that "the person who is for the time being, under a settlement, beneficially entitled to possession of settled land, for his life, is for purposes of·this Act the tenant for life of that land, and the tenant for life under that settlement". I take it that the words "entitled to possession" in that sub-section mean entitled in possession as contradistinguished from reversion, and that it is immaterial whether there are or are not any surplus rents which the person entitled can in fact receive.' *Re Atkinson, Atkinson v Bruce* (1885) 30 Ch D 605 at 612, per Pearson J

New Zealand 'An infant, who cannot demand the receipt of his income or sue for it, but who must submit to the accumulation of any balance unexpended by the trustee on his behalf, cannot be said to be "entitled in possession" to the receipt of that income under the trust during the income year.' *Doody v Commissioner of Taxes* [1941] NZLR 452 at 458, per Smith J; also reported [1941] GLR 218 at 220

See, generally, 35 Halsbury's Laws (4th edn) paras 1111 et seq.

ENTITY

United States 'Entity' includes corporation and foreign corporation; not-for-profit corporation; profit and not-for-profit unincorporated association; business trust, estate, partnership, trust, and two or more persons having a joint or common economic interest; and state, United States, and foreign government. (Revised Model Business Corporation Act 1984, s 1.40(9))

ENTRUST

'Intrusting with the document is essentially different from enabling a person to become possessed of it—from giving him the means of obtaining it. An instance of the difference was well put in the argument, when it was said . . . that one who gives another the key of his bureau to get out one paper, may enable him to procure any other that he pleases to take, but does not intrust him with it. . . . Principals can never be deemed to have intrusted the agents with a document which the agents obtained in breach of their trust, against the intention of their principals, in violation of their duty towards them, and which document never would have existed at all, if it had not been for the fraud of the agents against their employers.' *Phillips v Huth* (1840) 6 M & W 572 at 598, 599, per cur.

'There must, I think, be a personal entrusting of the security [under the Stat (1827) 7 & 8 Geo 4, c 29, s 49 (repealed)]. . . . The prisoner is directed to buy exchequer bills; he goes out, and upon his return admits that he has them; they are then left in his possession to keep safely. This is I think an entrusting within the Act.' *R v Nairne* (1850) 14 JP 305 at 306, per Patteson J

'A person may be entrusted with property, or may receive it for or on account of another person, within the meaning of this section [Larceny Act 1901, s 1 (repealed; cf. now ss 1–6 of the Theft Act 1968)] notwithstanding that the property is not delivered to him directly by the owner and that in fact the owner does not know of his existence and has no intention of entrusting the property to him. . . . For the purpose of determining whether the offence has been committed, the words "being entrusted" should not be read as being limited to the moment of the sending or delivering of the property by the owner, but may cover any subsequent period during which a person becomes entrusted with the property.' *R v Grubb* [1915] 2 KB 683 at 689, CCA, per cur.

[Section 43 of the Matrimonial Causes Act 1973 empowers the court to make a care order where it appears that it is impracticable or undesirable for a child to be 'entrusted' to either of the parties to a marriage or to any other individual.] 'The condition of the operation of that section is that the court is satisfied that there are exceptional circumstances making it impracticable or undesirable to entrust the child to either of the parents or any other individual. By that verb I understand the section to be describing a state of affairs in which the parent or other individual is clothed with the totality of the responsibility for the upbringing of the child. Nothing short of that, in my judgment, amounts to entrusting the child to that parent or individual. Not only is that in my view the natural meaning of the words but in the context in which it finds itself, in a context which contrasts that entrusting with the committing of the child to the local authority, it seems to me inevitable that the largest interpretation must be given to the

word "entrust".' *R v G (Surrey County Council intervening)* [1984] 3 All ER 460 at 467, CA, per Sir John Arnold P

Australia 'Although . . . the exact meaning to be attributed to the word "entrusted" (or its variant "intrusted") is to be determined by the context in which it is used, nonetheless [various] . . . authorities seem to proceed on the basis that at the very core of the concept of the words "entrust" and "intrust" is the situation of a person obtaining or assuming the control of property under circumstances in which the control is to be exercised for the benefit of, or for and at the direction of, another person. That this should be so is, in the light of the derivation of the word "entrust", hardly surprising.' *Daly v Sydney Stock Exchange* [1981] 2 NSWLR 179 at 196, per Powell J

[See also *Francis v Law Society of New South Wales* [1982] 2 NSWLR 191.]

Australia [Section 5(1) of the Factors (Mercantile Agents) Act 1923 (NSW) deals with cases where a mercantile agent is 'entrusted' with goods.] '"Entrustment" involves the obtaining of possession of the goods by the agent from or, at least, with the consent of the true owner.' *Associated Midland Corpn v Sanderson Motors Pty Ltd* [1983] 3 NSWLR 395 at 400, per Clarke J

United States 'Entrusting' includes any delivery and any acquiescence in retention of possession [of goods] regardless of any condition expressed between the parties to the delivery or acquiescence and regardless of whether the procurement of the entrusting or the possessor's disposition of the goods have been such as to be larcenous under the criminal law. (Uniform Commercial Code 1978, s 2–403(3))

ENTRY   *see* FORCIBLE ENTRY

EQUAL

'It comes really to this, whether or not the deed [of composition] provides equally for the benefit of all the creditors, as well assenting as dissenting. By "equal benefit", is meant not only equal benefit upon the face of the deed, but equal remedy, so that one man is placed in a position as good and as favourable to him as another. It is quite idle to say that to give to one man a clear and plain remedy which he can enforce at any moment, whilst you give to another merely a doubtful suit in equity, is giving an equal benefit to both.' *Re Senders, ex p Senders* (1864) 11 LT 574 at 575, per cur.

'If clause 20 of the charter-party [which provided that all derelicts and salvage should be for owners' and charterers' 'equal benefit'] stood alone there could, I take it, be no doubt as to its meaning. "Equal benefit" cannot be accorded to shipowner and charterer without taking into account what each has contributed towards securing the benefit.' *Booker & Co v Pocklington SS Co* [1899] 2 QB 690 at 694, per Bigham J

Australia 'A gift to persons "equally", if there is nothing else in the will to show a contrary intention, will constitute a gift to them as tenants in common. In other words, "equally" is itself an indication of intention that the beneficiaries are to take as tenants in common.' *Rentoul v Rentoul* [1944] VLR 205 at 206, per Gavan Duffy J

New Zealand [In a contract for the supply of ammunition to the Crown it was provided that the Government should pay to the company for service ammunition delivered under the contract a price 'equal to' the current price for the time being paid by the War Office in England to contractors for similar ammunition.] 'I regard the words "equal to" as meaning "equal in value to" or "equivalent to".' *Colonial Ammunition Co Ltd v R* [1938] NZLR 354 at 365, CA, per Myers CJ; also reported [1938] GLR 205 at 210.

EQUAL REGULATION

United States A class of persons or markets is subject to 'equal regulation' if no member of the class has a competitive advantage over any other member thereof resulting from a disparity in their regulation under this chapter which the [Securities and Exchange] Commission determines is unfair and not necessary or appropriate in furtherance of the purposes of this chapter. (Securities Exchange Act of 1934, s 3(a)(36))

EQUALITY

'The maxim *Qui prior est tempore, potior est jure* is in the plaintiffs' favour, and it seems strange that they should, without any default of their own, lose a security which they once possessed. But the above maxim is, in our law, subject to an important qualification, that, where equities are equal, the legal title prevails. Equality, here, does not mean or refer to priority in point of time, as is shewn by the cases on tacking. Equality means the non-existence of any circumstances which affects the conduct of one of the rival claimants, and makes it less meritorious than that of the other.' *Bailey v Barnes* [1894] 1 Ch 25 at 36, CA, per cur.

Canada [Under s 1(b) of the Canadian Bill of Rights 1960, every individual is entitled to 'equality before the law'.] 'We were referred to decisions of American courts . . . but it does not appear to me that any of such decisions directly touch upon the meaning of "equality before the law", although opinions are expressed in some as to what is meant by "equal protection of the laws" and "equality of the laws". I think these are different matters to "equality before the law". . . . The meaning of the word "equality" is well known. In my opinion, the word "before" in the expression "equality before the law", in the sense in which that expression is used in s 1(b) means "in the presence of". It seems to me this is the key to the correct interpretation of the expression and makes it clear that "equality before the law" has nothing to do with the application of the law equally to everyone and equal laws for everyone in the sense for which appellant's counsel contends, namely, the same laws for all persons, but to the position occupied by persons to whom a law relates or extends. They shall be entitled to have the law as it exists applied equally and without fear or favour to all persons to whom it relates or extends.' *R v Gonzales* (1962) 37 WWR 257 at 263, 264, BCCA, per Tysoe JA

EQUIP

'Equipping' in relation to a ship shall include the furnishing a ship with any tackle, apparel, furniture, provisions, arms, munitions, or stores, or any other thing which is used in or about a ship for the purpose of fitting or adapting her for the sea or for naval service, and all words relating to equipment shall be construed accordingly. (Foreign Enlistment Act 1870, s 30)

EQUIPMENT

'Equipment' (without prejudice to the generality of that expression) includes weapons, vehicles, aircraft and animals. (Land Powers (Defence) Act 1958, s 6(6))

In this Part [Part III: credits and grants for construction of ships and offshore installations] of this Act 'equipment', in relation to a ship or installation, means the installation on or in it, or the provision for it, of fixed or movable equipment, or apparatus or furnishings of any kind. (Industry Act 1972, s 12(1))

'Equipment' includes any machinery, apparatus or appliance, whether fixed or not, and any vehicle. (National Health Service Act 1977, s 128(1))

'"Equipment" [in a gift by will for the rebuilding and 'equipment' of a hospital] scarcely needs definition, but it may be useful to add that in my opinion it covers anything and everything which is required to convert an empty building, or part of an empty building, into a hospital, or part of a hospital, with all modern appliances.' *Re Unite, Edwards v Smith* (1906) 75 LJ Ch 163 at 165, per Kekewich J

[The Roads Act 1920, s 7(6) (repealed; see now Road Traffic Act 1972, s 194), provided that the weight unladen of a vehicle should be taken to be the weight of the vehicle exclusive of (inter alia) loose 'equipment'.] 'Boxes, baskets, trays of one kind or another, and cans are familiarly used in tradesmen's delivery vans; but it would hardly occur to anyone to regard them as parts of the unladen vehicle. . . . What then are they in the phraseology of the section? I see no difficulty in regarding them as included under the statutory term "loose equipment", and loose equipment is not to be included in the unladen weight.' *Darling v Burton* 1928 SC(J) 11 at 14, per the Lord Justice-General (Lord Clyde)

Fixed equipment

'Fixed equipment' includes any building or structure affixed to land and any works on, in, over or under land, and also includes anything grown on land for a purpose other than use after severance from the land, consumption of the thing grown or of produce thereof, or amenity, and references to fixed equipment on land shall be construed accordingly (Agriculture Act 1947, s 109; Agricultural Holdings Act 1986, s 96(1))

In this Part of this Act [Part II: financial assistance for hotel development] . . . 'fixed equipment' means equipment, including furniture, which in the opinion of the Tourist Board concerned is fixed to, or incorporated in, a building in such a manner as not to be easily detachable therefrom. (Development of Tourism Act 1969, s 16(1))

Secured transactions

United States Goods are . . . 'equipment' if they are used or bought for use primarily in business (including farming or a profession) or by a debtor who is a non-profit organization or a governmental subdivision or agency or if the goods are not included in the definitions of inventory, farm products or consumer goods. . . . (Uniform Commercial Code 1978, s 9–109(2))

Weighing or measuring equipment

'Weighing or measuring equipment' means equipment for measuring in terms of length, area, volume, capacity, weight or number, whether or not the equipment is constructed to give an indication of the measurement made or other information determined by reference to that measurement. (Weights and Measures Act 1985, s 94(1))

EQUITY—EQUITABLE

Early authorities refer to 'conscience', 'reason', and 'good faith' as the principles which guided the Court of Chancery, and the term 'equity' implies a system of law which is more consonant than the ordinary law with opinions current for the time being as to a just regulation of the mutual rights and duties of men living in a civilised society. Yet there was never a time in the history of the court when the Chancellor was at liberty to follow generally either his own, or professional, or common opinions as to what was right and convenient. Law and the administration of law are, in all systems, intended as a means of attaining justice, but the means are imperfect. The special imperfections of mediæval common law were, as to the law itself, that its rules were too strict, and that it did not cover the whole field of obligations; as to its administration, that it had no effectual means of extracting truth from the parties, that its judgments were not capable of being adapted to meet special circumstances, and that they were often unenforceable through the opposition of the defendant, or were turned into a means of oppression.

In so far as it remedied these defects, the Court of Chancery afforded an improved system of attaining justice, but this was the extent of the difference between law and equity. Each had the same object; each attained it only imperfectly—equity somewhat less imperfectly than law. Both, moreover, were developed in the same way, by decisions given in accordance with precedents and subject to professional criticism. From the beginning, the Court of Chancery acted on the maxim that 'equity follows the law', and in cases where the legal analogy clearly applied, the rule of law was adopted, however harsh it might be.

As to matters not ordinarily dealt with at common law, such as trusts and legacies, equity was free to go to new sources of law, and the Roman law and the canon law were laid under contribution; and for a time, in laying the foundations of a new system of jurisprudence, the Chancellors acted, when necessary, on their own initiative, and made precedents. They made as few innovations on the common law as possible, and the usual course was to disclaim the free following of any such notion as natural justice and to adhere to precedents. By the time that Lord Eldon's chancellorship closed, equity was a system of rules as well settled as ever the common law had been, and it had become incapable of judicial alteration except by the application of old rules to new subjects or to fresh circumstances, a process that is continually going on both at law and in equity. (16 Halsbury's Laws (4th edn) para 1204, 1205)

'Now equity is no part of the law, but a moral virtue, which qualifies, moderates, and reforms the rigour, hardness, and edge of the law, and is an universal truth; it does also assist the law where it is defective and weak in the constitution (which is the life of the law) and defends the law from crafty evasions, delusions, and new subtilties, invented and contrived to evade and delude the common law, whereby such as have undoubted right are made remediless; and this is the office of equity, to support and protect the common law from shifts and crafty contrivances against the justice of the law. Equity therefore does not destroy the law, nor create it, but assist it.' *Dudley (Lord) v Dudley (Lady)* (1705) Prec Ch 241 at 244, per Lord Cowper LC

Equitable assignment *See* ASSIGNMENT

Equitable charge

An equitable charge on land is a security which does not create a legal estate, but only confers an equitable interest in the land upon the creditor. It entitles the holder to have the property comprised in it sold by an order of the court to raise the money charged on it, but, in the absence of any express provision to that effect, or unless it is a mortgage by deposit of title deeds, it does not amount to an agreement to give a legal mortgage, although it may, if duly registered, take priority over a legal estate. Even if the security provides for a legal mortgage to be granted, it is still an equitable charge as distinguished from a mortgage.

Unlike an equitable charge of land, an equitable charge of a chose in action usually takes the form of an assignment of the property, but trust receipts, by which the borrowers agree that goods purchased with advances should be held by them as agents for and in trust for the bank, may create an equitable charge on the goods, and a letter may amount to an equitable assignment by way of security and therefore a charge on book debts. (32 Halsbury's Laws (4th edn) para 406)

'Every valid equitable charge is now also legal in the sense that it is recognised and enforceable at law as well as in equity; and a legal mortgage is, as always, enforceable in equity, and in that sense an equitable charge. . . . The only way . . . in which the charge now under consideration [a statutory charge for estate duty] differs from any other equitable charge is that it is created by statute, not by contract between parties. It is none the less an "equitable charge".' *Re Bowerman, Porter v Bowerman* [1908] 2 Ch 340 at 342–344, per Joyce J

Equitable execution

'Confusion of ideas has arisen from the use of the term "equitable execution". The expression tends to error. It has often been used by judges, and occurs in some orders, as a short expression indicating that the person who obtains the order gets the same benefit as he would have got from legal execution. But what he gets by the appointment of a receiver is not execution, but equitable relief, which is granted on the ground that there is no remedy by execution at law; it is a taking out of the way a hindrance which prevents execution at common law.' *Re Shephard, Atkins v Shephard* (1889) 43 Ch D 131 at 135, 136, CA, per Cotton LJ

See, generally, 17 Halsbury's Laws (4th edn) paras 574 et seq.

Equitable interest   *See also* ESTATE

All estates, interests and charges in or over land (other than those which can subsist at law) such as estates tail, life interests and remainders, take effect as equitable interests. To ensure that no beneficial forms of property are lost by this rearrangement of estates and interests, all interests in land validly created or arising after the commencement of the Law of Property Act 1925 which are not capable of subsisting as legal estates must take effect as equitable interests; and, save as otherwise expressly provided by statute, interests in land which, under the Statute of Uses or otherwise, could before such commencement have been created as legal interests are capable of being created as equitable interests. (39 Halsbury's Laws (4th edn) para 347)

Equitable lien   *See* LIEN

Equitable mortgage   *See* MORTGAGE

Equitable power   *See* POWER

Equitable waste   *See* WASTE

Equity of exoneration   *See also* EXONERATION

'If a married woman charges her property with money for the purpose of paying her husband's debts and the money raised by her is so applied, she is prima facie regarded in equity, and as between herself and him, as lending him and not giving him the money raised on her property, and as entitled to have her property exonerated by him from the charge she has created. This doctrine is purely equitable, and . . . is based on an inference to be drawn from the circumstances of each particular case.' *Paget v Paget* [1898] 1 Ch 470 at 474, CA, per cur.

Equity of redemption

Incident to every mortgage is the right of the mortgagor to redeem, a right which is called his equity of redemption, and which continues notwithstanding that he fails to pay the debt in accordance with the proviso for his redemption. This right arises from the transaction being considered as a mere loan of money secured by a pledge of the estate. Any provision inserted in the mortgage to prevent redemption on payment of the debt or performance of the obligation for which the

security was given is termed a clog or fetter on the equity of redemption, and is void. The right to redeem is so inseparable an incident of a mortgage that it cannot be taken away by an express agreement of the parties that the mortgage is not to be redeemable or that the right is to be confined to a particular time or to a particular description of persons. This is especially illustrated in the case of mortgages by building societies where, although redemption is not contemplated for periods usually varying between fifteen and twenty-five years, nevertheless the mortgage may expressly allow redemption at any time. The right continues unless and until, by judgment for foreclosure or, in the case of a mortgage of land where the mortgagee is in possession, by the running of time, the mortgagor's title is extinguished or his interest is destroyed by sale either under the process of the court or of a power in the mortgage incident to the security. (32 Halsbury's Laws (4th edn) para 407)

Equity security

'Equity security' in relation to a company means a relevant share in the company (other than a share shown in the memorandum to have been taken by a subscriber to the memorandum or a bonus share), or a right to subscribe for, or to convert securities into, relevant shares in the company. (Companies Act 1985, s 94(2))

United States   The term 'equity security' means any stock or similar security; or any security convertible, with or without consideration, into such a security, or carrying any warrant or right to subscribe to or purchase such a security; or any such warrant or right; or any other security which the [Securities and Exchange] Commission shall deem to be of similar nature and consider necessary or appropriate, by such rules and regulations as it may prescribe in the public interest or for the protection of investors, to treat as an equity security. (Securities Exchange Act of 1934, s 3(a)(11))

United States   '[E]quity security' means—
(A) share in a corporation, whether or not transferable or denominated "stock", or similar security;
(B) interest of a limited partner in a limited partnership; or
(C) warrant or right, other than a right to convert, to purchase, sell, or subscribe to a share, security, or interest of a kind

specified in subparagraph (A) or (B) of this paragraph. . . .
(Bankruptcy Act 1978, s 101(15))

Equity share capital

'Equity share capital' means, in relation to a company, its issued share capital excluding any part of that share capital which, neither as respects dividends nor as respects capital, carries any right to participate beyond a specified amount in a distribution. (Companies Act 1985, s 744)

ERECT

'Erect' includes extend, alter and re-erect, and 'erection' shall be construed accordingly. (Local Authorities (Land) Act 1963, s 14)

[A testator devised the residue of his estate to his trustees to 'erect' a hospital for the support and maintenance of poor old men.] 'There is no direction in this will, that any part of this money should be laid out in building a hospital; for erect as well imports foundation as building; and so is *erigimus* construed in charters of the crown and private foundations.' *Vaughan v Farrer* (1751) 2 Ves Sen 182 at 187, 188, per Lord Hardwicke LC

'Directions in a will to erect a school-house in general, imports an intention to purchase.' *A-G v Hyde* (1775) Amb 751 at 752, 753, per Lord Aspley LC

Australia 'The word "erect" would seem to cover an act of setting up above the surface of the ground in a permanent or quasi-permanent position, and, therefore, to denote something which is not necessarily built on a foundation let into the ground, and which also may differ from placing in a temporary position for a passing purpose. Direct fixation into the soil is in my view not a requisite to "erecting". Such structures as barricades, scaffolds and hoardings might properly be said to be erected, although they have no foundations below the surface.' *Subiaco Municipal Council v Walmsley* (1930) 32 WALR 49 at 56, 57, per Dwyer J

Australia 'One can envisage cases where alterations and even renovations to an existing building might be sufficient to come within the meaning of "erecting a house" as those words are used in the instant [restrictive] covenant; if the result of alterations or renovations is to convert a building into a house then this would

be sufficient; the true meaning of the word "erect" is to be found more in the notion of setting up rather than putting up. One can imagine cases where what was already a house might be so altered, enlarged, or perhaps renovated, that the acts of construction could be said to bring into being a house and as such to amount to a breach of a covenant such as the present not to erect a house; but in order to constitute such a breach it would be necessary in my view still to be able to say that by the acts of construction a house has been brought into being—if what results is in substance the same house although in an enlarged or improved condition then the erection of a house has not occurred.' *Lawton v SHEV Pty Ltd* [1969] 2 NSWR 238 at 242, per Helsham J

ERECTION

'Erection' in relation to buildings . . . includes extension, alteration and re-erection. (Town and Country Planning Act 1971, s 290(1))

[Land was leased to an oil-refiner together with the 'erections' and buildings then already erected and built or to be erected and built thereon.] 'The word "erection" must mean other things than mere brick or stone houses. Here there are large cisterns bricked up to the brim, and I think it is impossible to say that they are not "erections".' *Bidder v Trinidad Petroleum Co* (1868) 17 WR 153 at 154, per Romilly MR

'The erection [of a building] . . . is commenced as soon as the foundation has been excavated, and a building is erected upon the site upon which it is built none the less because no part of it is raised above the ground level as existing at the date of its erection.' *St Nicholas Acons (Rector & Churchwardens) v London County Council* [1928] AC 469 at 474, per cur.

[The vendor sold a market garden. At the time of the sale two greenhouses stood on concrete supports but they were not bolted down or fixed in any other way. They were not specifically mentioned in the conveyance. The question was whether the greenhouses passed with the land as 'erections' under s 62(1) of the Law of Property Act 1925.] 'These greenhouses were not even bolted down to the concrete dollies on which they rested; they simply remained there by their own weight and were clearly not part or parcel of the land. But it is said, and the learned county court judge so held, that they were erections. So in a sense they were. But are they "erections" within the meaning of the general words of s 62(1)? In my opinion, clearly not. Nothing is an "erection" within the meaning of that section which is not something which is part and parcel of the land conveyed.' *Dibble (H E) Ltd v Moore* [1966] 3 All ER 1465 at 1470, CA, per Harman LJ

ERROR

[An inventory stated that a vessel and her stores were to be taken with all faults, as they then lay, without allowance for any defect or 'error' whatever.] 'We find the word "error", which has been introduced for further protection; and I cannot put any construction upon that word, except that of "unintentional misdescription". According to the contract, it must be a "barque" that is sold; but if there is any involuntary misdescription of such a vessel, that is covered by the word "error". The term "error", when used with reference to the purchase of real estate, has been construed to mean a misstatement or misdescription erroneously and not wilfully introduced: *The Duke of Norfolk v Worthy* [(1808) 1 Camp 337], *Wright v Wilson* [(1832) 1 Mood & R 207]. So, in this case, I construe the word "error" to mean any "unintentional misdescription".' *Taylor v Bullen* (1850) 5 Exch 779 at 786, per Parke B

New Zealand 'There was . . . a mistake common to both parties as to an essential attribute of the thing agreed to be sold, and this affected the substance of the whole consideration. Such a mistake amounts to what Sir Frederick Pollock calls "fundamental error". It excludes any real consent, and this prevents the formation of any contract. The general rule is that in such a case the agreement is void.' *Mackley v Brighton* (1914) 34 NZLR 314 at 316, per Sim J; 17 GLR 323 at 324

Of judgment

'Error in judgment [included as one of the exceptions in a bill of lading], whether in navigating a ship or otherwise, on the largest interpretation that one could possibly give to the word "otherwise"—and I think it is a large word there—could not, in my opinion, cover such a thing as a misreading of the document under which the captain was acting. It is something totally different altogether, and a thing which one would not at all expect to be provided for by this kind of exception.' *SS Knutsford Ltd v Tillmanns (E) & Co* (1908) 99 LT 399 at 401, HL, per Channell J

'The expression "error of judgment" is not a term of art. It is, in fact, one of the vaguest possible description. It can, colloquially, be used to describe either a negligent act or one which, though mistaken, is not negligent.' *Simpson v Peat* [1952] 1 All ER 447 at 448, 449, per Lord Goddard CJ; [1952] 2 QB 24 at 27

On face of award

'An error in law on the face of the award means, in their Lordships' view, that you can find in the award or a document actually incorporated thereto, as for instance a note appended by the arbitrator stating the reasons for his judgment, some legal proposition which is the basis of the award and which you can then say is erroneous.' *Champsey Bhara & Co v Jivraj Balloo Spinning & Weaving Co* [1923] AC 480 at 487, PC, per cur.

ESCAPE

From prison

Escape is an indictable offence at common law, punishable by imprisonment and fine at the discretion of the court, and is committed by a person (1) who, without the use of force, escapes from prison either when serving a sentence or when awaiting trial, or (2) who, having a person in his lawful custody, whether before or after conviction, voluntarily or negligently permits him to escape. It is also an indictable offence at common law, similarly punishable, for a person to escape from lawful custody on a criminal charge, without using force but by artifice or similar means. It is an indictable offence at common law, punishable by imprisonment and fine at the discretion of the court, to aid a person to escape from lawful custody on civil process. (11 Halsbury's Laws (4th edn) para 967)

Rule in *Rylands v Fletcher*

The rule in *Rylands v Fletcher* applies only to things likely to do mischief if they escape. A wide variety of things have been held to come within the rule, for example water, sewage, fires deliberately made or brought on to the land or arising accidentally in a dangerous object which is likely to catch fire easily or to do damage if it escapes, gas, electricity, gas oil, acid smuts, fumes, explosives, decayed wire rope, colliery spoil, trees, vibrations, a flagpole, a chair-o-plane, and even caravan dwellers who committed nuisances. . . . The rule in *Rylands v Fletcher* only applies where the thing which does the damage has escaped. For the purposes of the rule, escape means escape from a place where the defendant has occupation or control over land to a place which is outside his occupation or control. (32 Halsbury's Laws (4th edn) paras 341, 342)

[The appellant was employed by the Ministry of Supply at an ordnance factory filling shells with high explosives. Whilst lawfully in the shell-filling shop in discharge of her duties the appellant was injured by the explosion of a shell.] '"Escape", for the purpose of applying the proposition in *Rylands v Fletcher* [supra] means escape from a place which the defendant has occupation of, or control over, to a place which is outside his occupation or control. Blackburn J, several times refers to the defendant's duty as being the duty of "keeping a thing in" at the defendant's peril and by "keeping in" he means, not preventing an explosive substance from exploding, but preventing a thing which may inflict mischief from escaping from the area which the defendant occupies or controls.' *Read v Lyons & Co Ltd* [1946] 2 All ER 471 at 474, HL, per Lord Simon

ESCHEAT

Escheat is a term of art and derived from the French word *escheate* that is *cadere, excidere* or *accidere* and signifyeth properly when by accident the lands fall to the lord of whom they are holden. (Co Litt 13 a)

The last consequence of tenure in chivalry was escheat; which is the determination of the tenure, or dissolution of the mutual bond between the lord and tenant, from the extinction of the blood of the latter by either natural or civil means: if he died without heirs of his blood, or if his blood was corrupted and stained by commission of treason or felony; whereby every inheritable quality was intirely blotted out and abolished. In such cases the land escheated, or fell back, to the lord of the fee; that is, the tenure was determined by breach of the original condition, expressed or implied in the feodal donation. In the one case, there were no heirs subsisting of the blood of the first feudatory or purchaser, to which heirs alone the grant of the feud extended: in the other, the tenant, by perpetrating an atrocious crime, shewed that he was no longer to be trusted as a vasal, having forgotten his duty as a subject; and therefore forfeited his feud, which he held under the implied condition that he should not be a traitor or felon. The consequence of which in both cases was, that the gift, being determined, resulted back to the lord who gave it. (2 Bl Com 72, 73)

Formerly, when a tenancy in fee simple came to an end for any reason, the land went back to the lord of whom the tenant held, and he was said to take by escheat. The commonest instances were escheat for want of heirs (propter defectum sanguinis), which occurred when a tenant in fee simple died intestate without leaving an heir-at-law, and escheat on conviction of felony (propter delictum tenentis), but both these have been abolished. Escheat in other cases is still possible but rare. (39 Halsbury's Laws (4th edn) para 597)

'The legal right of escheat arises under the law of enfeoffment, by which, with us, the lord gave the land to the tenant and his heirs, under a tacit condition to revert, if the tenant died seised without heirs. . . . It is said the writ of escheat lieth where the tenant, who hath an estate in fee-simple of any lands or tenements, and holdeth them of another, dieth seised without heir general or special, the lord shall have the writ of escheat against him who is tenant after the death of his tenant; and by this writ he shall recover his land, because he shall have the same in lieu of his services. Now the books are uniform, that in this event alone (except in the case of tortfaisors), the escheat took place. As long as the tenant in fee stood by himself, or his real representatives as tenant, or by his own act, or implied assent, to the seisin of another, supplied the lord with a tenant, the lands could never escheat.' *Burgess v Wheate A-G v Wheate* (1759) 1 Eden 177 at 241–243, per Lord Henley, Lord Keeper

'From the use of the word "revert", in the writ of escheat is manifestly derived the language of some authorities which speak of escheat as a species of reversion.' *A-G for Ontario v Mercer* (1883) 8 App Cas 767 at 772, PC, per cur.

ESCROW

An intended deed may, after sealing and any signature required for execution as a deed, be delivered as an escrow (or scroll), that is as a simple writing which is not to become the deed of the party expressed to be bound by it until some condition has been performed. Thus, a conveyance on sale or a mortgage or a surrender discharging a mortgage may be delivered in escrow so as to be binding on the grantor only if the grantee pays the consideration money or only if the grantee executes a counterpart or some other deed or document as agreed with the grantor.

Like delivery as a deed, delivery as an escrow may be made in words or by conduct although it need not be made in any special form or accompanied with any particular words, the essential thing in the case of delivery as an escrow being that the party should expressly or impliedly declare his intention to be bound by the provisions inscribed, not immediately, but only in the case of and upon performance of some condition then stated or ascertained. In the absence of direct evidence whether or not a deed of conveyance was delivered as an escrow, the fact that only part of the purchase price has been paid at the time of delivery justifies the inference that the deed was delivered as an escrow pending payment of the balance. (12 Halsbury's Laws (4th edn) para 1332)

'A deed may be delivered on a condition that it is not to be operative until some event happens or some condition is performed. In such a case it is until then an escrow only.' *Macedo v Stroud* [1922] 2 AC 330 at 337, PC, per cur.

'A document which is intended to take effect as a deed when certain conditions have been fulfilled may be executed as an escrow; that is to say, with all the formalities of a deed save that the vital unconditional delivery, which is essential for the proper execution of a true deed, is missing, it is replaced by a conditional delivery, usually express, but capable of being assumed. At this stage, the document is not a deed; and although of course it contains within itself the possibility of becoming an effective deed, a deed rising phoenix-like from the ashes of the escrow, at the stage before the condition is fulfilled it is of no effect whatsoever.' *Terrapin International Ltd v Inland Revenue Comrs* [1976] 2 All ER 461 at 465, 466, per Walton J

'The doctrine of "escrow" is a relic of medieval times. It dates from the time when conveyances were made by feoffment and livery of seisin. It has survived to the present day and often operates in regard to conveyances of land or the creation or disposition of estates and interests in land such as a term of years. It has changed its features much since the days of Sheppard's Touchstone (1st Edn, 1641; 7th Edn, 1820) and Preston's Abstracts of Title (1st Edn, 1818–19; 2nd Edn, 1823–24). We no

longer speak of a first delivery or a second delivery. But it does predicate a document which is executed and delivered. The accustomed formula is "signed, sealed and delivered". When that formula is used in the document and it is signed by the party (or in the case of a company its seal is affixed) and attested by a witness with intent by the maker that it should be binding on him, it is conclusively presumed to be "signed, sealed and delivered". If it is handed over to another unconditionally, it is delivered as a deed. If it is handed over to another conditionally, it is delivered as an escrow. It only becomes a deed when the conditions are fulfilled.' *Alan Estates Ltd v WG Stores Ltd* [1981] 3 All ER 481 at 486, CA, per Lord Denning MR

Canada 'In early times escrow may have been used exclusively when delivering deeds. Today however "escrow", like many other words has acquired a much wider application. It may apply to money, company stock, securities and other items of property. The modern day application of the word is provided in Black's Law Dictionary, 5th ed, p 489: "Escrow. A writing, deed, money, stock, or other property delivered by the grantor, promisor or obligor into the hands of a third party, to be held by the latter until the happening of a contingency or performance of a condition, and then by him delivered to the grantee, promisee or obligee. A system of document transfer in which a deed, bond, or funds is delivered to a third person to hold until all the conditions in a contract are fulfilled; e.g., delivery of deed to escrow agent under instalment land sale contract until full payment for land is made." The Concise Oxford Dictionary states as follows: "Escrow. Written legal engagement to do something, kept in third person's custody until some condition has been fulfilled; money or goods so kept".' *Tooton v Atkinson* (1985) 52 Nfld 8 PEIR 167 at 174, Nfld District Ct, per Riche DCJ

ESQUIRE   *See also* GENTLEMAN

Esquires and gentlemen are confounded together by Sir Edward Coke, who observes, that every esquire is a gentleman, and a gentleman is defined to be one *qui arma gerit*, who bears coat armour, the grant of which adds gentility to a man's family: in like manner as civil nobility, among the Romans, was founded in the *jus imaginum*, or having the image of one ancestor at least, who had borne some curule office. It is indeed a matter somewhat unsettled, what constitutes the distinction, or who is a real *esquire*: for it is not an estate, however large, that confers this rank upon it's owner. Camden, who was himself a herald, distinguishes them the most accurately; and he reckons up four sorts of them: 1. The eldest sons of knights, and their eldest sons, in perpetual succession. 2. The younger sons of peers, and their eldest sons, in like perpetual succession: both which species of esquires Sir H. Spelman entitles *armigeri natalitii*. 3. Esquires created by the king's letters patent, or other investiture; and their eldest sons. 4. Esquires by virtue of their offices; as justices of the peace, and others who bear any office of trust under the crown. To these may be added the esquires of knights of the bath, each of whom constitutes three at his installation; and all foreign, nay, Irish peers; and the eldest sons of peers of Great Britain, who, though generally titular lords, are only esquires in the law, and must so be named in all legal proceedings. As for *gentlemen*, says Sir Thomas Smith, they be made good cheap in this kingdom: for whosoever studieth the laws of the realm, who studieth in the universities, who professeth liberal sciences, and (to be short) who can live idly, and without manual labour, and will bear the port, charge, and countenance of a gentleman, he shall be called master, and shall be taken for a gentleman. A *yeoman* is he that hath free land of forty shillings by the year; who is thereby qualified to serve on juries, vote for knights of the shire, and do any other act, where the law requires one that is *probus et legalis homo*. (1 Bl Com 393, 394)

ESTABLISH

Canada 'The main argument before this court turned on the meaning to be attached to the word "establishes" as it occurs in s 224A(1)(a) of the Code [Criminal Code, 1953–54 (Can) c 51 (now RSC 1970, c C–34, s 237)]. It will be seen that the Court of Appeal treated this word as being equivalent to "raises a reasonable doubt", but with the greatest respect, I am unable to distinguish between the word "establishes" as used in s 224A(1)(a) and the word "proves" as used in other sections of the Code.' *R v Appleby* (1971) 16 CRNS 35 at 38, SCC, per Ritchie J

Canada [Gift by will to municipality was expressed to be given provided it 'established' a general public hospital within specified time.] 'All the authorities as to the meaning of the word establish have a common thread running through each of the meanings attributable to the word establish; that is, the word has a notion of stability and permanence as an integral part of its meaning. The word means more when applied to an institution than simply setting it up. It must be set up with a degree of permanence and stability.' *Re O'Brien* (1977) 77 DLR (3d) 397 at 403, NSSC, per Hallett J; affd (sub nom *Re O'Brien; Dalhousie University v Dartmouth* (1978) 85 DLR (3d) 532, NSCA

New Zealand [Under the Local Authorities Loans Act 1956, s 34(5) proviso the council had to 'establish' the names of all ratepayers eligible for a poll.] 'The word "establish" as used in the proviso to s 34(5) simply means "to verify, substantiate or prove".' *Blincoe v Wellington City Council* (1985) 5 NZAR 375 at 384, per Davison CJ

ESTABLISHMENT

Of business

[Section 274 of the Companies (Consolidation) Act 1908 (repealed; see now the Companies Act 1985, s 691), required every company incorporated outside the United Kingdom which established a place of business within the United Kingdom to do certain things within one month from such establishment.] 'When the legislature selected the phrase "establishes a place of business", it meant something other than "carrying on business". . . . That expression seems to me clearly to point to this, that the company must have what I may call a local habitation of its own.' *Lord Advocate v Huron & Erie Loan & Savings Co* 1911 SC 612 at 616, per the Lord President

'The establishment of a new trade or industry is, in my opinion, a different thing altogether from the entry of a particular person into an existing trade or industry.' *Re Robin Electric Lamp Co's Petition* [1915] 1 Ch 780 at 791, per Warrington J

[A testator gave trustees power to make advancement to his son for the purpose of 'establishing' him in business or enabling him to become a partner in any business whether established or not.] 'By the word "establish" the testator meant both "start in a new business" and "strengthen or confirm in business", so that the trustee could, under the power of advancement, advance money to William Henry Mead for the purpose both of starting him in the new business and of establishing him in the business in which he was already engaged.' *Re Mead, Public Trustee v Mead* (1918) 88 LJ Ch 86 at 86, 87, CA, per Swinfen Eady MR

'"Established or conducted for profit" in s 8(1) of the Act [Rating and Valuation (Miscellaneous Provisions) Act 1955 (repealed; see now s 40(5) of the General Rate Act 1967)] means established for the purpose of making profit or conducted for the purpose of making profit, and does not extend to every organisation which in any circumstances or at any stage in its activities receives something which might be considered in itself to constitute a profit.' *Guinness Trust (London Fund) Founded 1890 Registered 1902 v West Ham Corpn* [1959] 1 All ER 482 at 488, CA, per Jenkins LJ

Of identity of vehicle

Australia [Where a person injured by an unidentified motor vehicle sues a nominal defendant under s 47(1) of the Motor Car Act 1951 (Vic) (see now Motor Car Act 1958–1986, s 49), the burden of proof lies on him to show that he has complied with the proviso to that section, which stipulates that he must, as soon as possible after he knew that the identity of the vehicle could not be 'established', give notice of his intention to make a claim.] 'What is meant by the expression "the identity of the car cannot be established"? The word "established" does not seem to mean "proved by admissible evidence to the satisfaction of a court"; although doubtless it is capable of that meaning. Cases may be imagined where the identity of the car is known but there is a lack of admissible evidence to prove it. Rather the word seems to mean "ascertained definitely or with reasonable certainty".' *Vines v Djordjevitch* [1955] ALR 431 at 434, per cur.

Of school

'Upon the true construction of the will, the school was to be established by a school-house

being built. Many senses might, no doubt, be given to the word "establishing". It might mean, by directing a payment to be made to a school-master for giving instruction; and if this meaning could properly be ascribed to the testator, then within the distinction taken in the *Attorney-General v Williams* [(1794) 2 Cox 387] the bequest might be good. The first part of the language of the will, the direction to apply the legacy towards the establishing a school near the Angel Inn, Edmonton, pointed to a particular locality, and rather indicated an intention to occupy a site in the neighbourhood referred to; but upon these words alone there might perhaps be a doubt, whether they would not admit of another meaning being attributed to the word "establish". The latter part of the bequest, however, removed all doubt, "provided a further sum can be raised in aid thereof, if found necessary". It was clear that the testator contemplated the establishment of the school, not by a succession of small payments, but by an immediate expenditure of a sum of money, which might be greater than the amount of the legacy. . . . The intention was, that land should be purchased, and a building erected for the purpose of the proposed school.' *A-G v Hull* (1852) 9 Hare 647 at 648, 649, per Turner V-C

[The testator bequeathed a sum of money to be applied for the 'establishment' of a charity school.] 'The testator directs the school to be "established". He therefore points to a permanent establishment, and how can this be effected without a school, which must stand on land to be procured for the purpose?' *Re Clancy* (1852) 16 Beav 295 at 296, per Romilly MR

[A testator left £2,000 to pay a master and mistress of a school which he wished to have 'established' after his death.] 'I consider that a school may be established without necessarily purchasing a schoolhouse, or land whereon to erect a schoolhouse. The money may be expended in the hire of a house for the purposes of holding the school; and if that be so the bequest is good.' *Hill v Jones* (1854) 23 LTOS 253 at 253, per Wood V-C

ESTATE   *See also* PERSONAL ESTATE; REAL ESTATE

'Estate' has two meanings. In its narrower meaning it denotes the fee simple of land and any of the various interests into which it could formerly be divided at law, whether for life, or for a term of years or otherwise; and, where there was an estate at law, there could be a corresponding estate in equity. In its wider meaning it denotes any property whatever and is divided into real and personal estate. 'Real estate' is a technical term and is, generally, to be construed in its technical sense. It comprises all freehold (and formerly copyhold) lands, tenements and hereditaments, but not leasehold interests, although for the purposes of devolution on death under the Administration of Estates Act 1925, it includes chattels real. Before 1926, freehold estates were either estates of mere freehold, that is estates for life or lives, or estates of inheritance. Real estate includes, also, any rights in land, such as a rentcharge, which admit of being limited in the same manner as freehold estates or interests. (39 Halsbury's Laws (4th edn) para 302)

The word 'estate' shall extend to an estate in equity as well as at law, and shall also extend to any interest, charge, lien, or incumbrance in, upon, or affecting lands, either at law or in equity, and shall also extend to any interest, charge, lien, or incumbrance in, upon, or affecting money subject to be invested in the purchase of lands. (Fines and Recoveries Act 1833, s 1)

For the purposes of this Act, a person's estate is the aggregate of all the property to which he is beneficially entitled, except that the estate of a person immediately before his death does not include excluded property. (Inheritance Tax Act 1984, s 5(1))

['Excluded property' includes property situated outside the United Kingdom and certain reversionary interests; see ss 6 and 48 of the Act.]

'If a man be seised in fee, and devise "his estate", the inheritance shall pass without any other circumstance to manifest his intent; merely by devising his estate. Without this construction the words of the will cannot stand; for the word "estate" implies a fee simple, for that is the general estate that every man is supposed to be seised of. "Estate" comes from "stando", because it is fixed and permanent, and imports the most absolute property that a man can have.' *Bridgewater (Countess) v Bolton (Duke)* (1704) 6 Mod Rep 106 at 107, 109, per cur.

'The word "estate" primarily imports the interest a person has in anything, but secondarily the thing itself, because it is impossible to have the interest without the thing.' *Barry v*

Edgworth (1729) Mos 172 at 175, per Jekyll MR

'The general rule is, that the word estate includes not only the lands, or thing which is the subject of the devise, but also the estate or interest therein.' *Goodwyn v Goodwyn* (1748–9) 1 Ves Sen 226 at 228, per Lord Hardwicke LC

'Wherever the word "estate" or "estates" is restrained to personalty, it is done upon the ground of the testator's shewing his intention by joining it with words which relate to personalty only; but on the other hand, where such other words are in themselves sufficient to pass all the personal estate, then in order to give some effect to the word "estate", it is holden to pass realty.' *Jongsma v Jongsma* (1787) 1 Cox Eq Cas 362 at 362, per Kenyon MR

[A testator made a bequest of 'money, goods, chattels, estates, and effects'.] 'Unless the realty be included under the words "estate" and "estates", those words are mere superfluities, for the words "goods, chattels, and effects" would of themselves carry the personalty. This is the will of an unlearned man, and I think that I should act against the soundest rules of construction, if I were to hold the general words "estates" and "estate" to be limited by the other words. I must, therefore, hold, that the real estate passes by the will.' *Midland Counties Rly Co v Oswin* (1844) 1 Coll 74 at 79, per Knight Bruce V-C

[A testator made a bequest of 'all the rest and residue of my estate and effects'.] 'One rule is, that the word "estate", simply, is sufficient to pass real "estate"; but in most cases the word "estate" is not used simply; and another rule is, that, supposing there is nothing in other parts of the will to control the meaning of the gift, the effect of the word "estate", coupled with other words, is this: if the other words would without the word "estate" not be sufficient to pass the whole personal estate the word "estate" will be considered as used to effect a complete passing of the "personal estate"; but if the other words are sufficient to pass *all* the personal estate then the word "estate" must be read as intended to apply to *real* estate. It is equally clear that, consistently with the general principles, there may be words in the will which show that the language used may have an interpretation different from their ordinary and proper interpretation; but the rule being that the word "estate" is sufficient to pass real estate, and the other words used in this case being "effects", which is sufficient to pass *all* the personal estate, so far as the language is considered, prima facie the word "estate" here would comprise the "real estate".' *D'Almaine v Moseley* (1853) 1 Drew 629 at 632, per Kindersley V-C

'There can be no question that the first words, taken alone, are sufficient to include the real estate: they are "All estate, effects and property, etc." . . . No words can be larger than these, and I have not the slightest doubt that these words are sufficient to include real estate.' *Coard v Holderness* (1855) 20 Beav 147 at 152, per Romilly MR

'As far as I know, independently of authority, no one would treat the word "property" or the word "estate" which is used here [by a company who issued debentures whereby they bound "themselves and their successors and their real and personal estate" for payment of the sums advanced], when applied to a partnership, as including the liability of the individual partners to make good a deficiency of that very estate to pay the creditors in full. . . . When we speak of the property of a partnership or the estate and effects of a partnership we speak of that which belongs to the firm.' *Re Colonial Trusts Corpn, ex p Bradshaw* (1879) 15 Ch D 465 at 470, per Jessel MR

'I have to determine the effect of a few words in a decree made by the . . . President of the Probate Division in a probate action. After pronouncing against the validity of the will, the decree goes on to order the costs of the plaintiffs . . . to come "out of the estate". What does that mean? . . . "Estate" now by virtue of the Act [Land Transfer Act 1897 (repealed; see now s 1(1) of the Administration of Estates Act 1925)] means real and personal estate. . . . The order in this probate action says that the costs are to come out of "the estate", and, the personal estate being insufficient, the real estate is not only charged with the payment of the costs in question, but must bear them.' *Re Vickerstaff, Vickerstaff v Chadwick* [1906] 1 Ch 762 at 765–767, per Kekewich J

Australia 'At common law the Crown is the supreme owner or lord paramount of every parcel of land in the realm and all land is holden of some lord or other and immediately or mediately of the King. The word "estate" is therefore especially used to denote the extent of the interest that the subject has in his land, and an estate in fee simple, which is the greatest interest in and which a subject may

have, is wellnigh equivalent to absolute property.' *Minister of State for the Army v Dalziel* (1944) 68 CLR 261 at 298, per Williams J

Australia [A divorced husband, in settlement of a claim for alimony, executed an indenture charging his 'estate' with payment. His assets at the time of his death included certain policies of insurance on his own life.] 'Mr Sholl [counsel for the defendant] . . . said what the testator charged in the indenture was his "estate", and, since the policy moneys were not liable for payment of debts, the word "estate" should not be construed so as to cover them. I cannot accept this contention. The policies are part of the property he owns when he dies, they pass to his executor and they are liable for administration expenses, estate duty and any other tax levied on the estate. They are in my opinion clearly comprised within the word "estate".' *Re Lesser, National Trustees Executors & Agency Co of Australasia Ltd v Lesser* [1944] VLR 210 at 213, per Gavan Duffy J

Australia 'The word "estate" is of general import and prima facie covers all the disposable property of the testatrix.' *Re Seccombe (decd), Queensland Trustees Ltd v Seccombe* [1948] St R Qd 11 at 17, per Douglas J

Australia 'The Act [Testator's Family Maintenance and Guardianship of Infants Act (NSW) 1916–1986] contains no definition of the "estate" out of which the court is empowered by s 3(1) to make provision for members of the family. It is, however, clear that it cannot mean the gross estate passing to the executor but must be confined to the net estate available to answer the dispositions made by the will.' *Schaefer v Schuhmann* [1972] AC 572 at 585; [1972] 1 All ER 621

Canada 'To us, whether lawyer or layman, in this Island [Newfoundland], it [estate] means only one of two things: (a) If the deceased is long since dead, the totality of his real property, if that, as often happens, has been kept together identifiably. We speak, geographically, of a house being "on Smith's Estate" in St John's, he having been dead a hundred years, perhaps; and (b) If the deceased is recently dead, the totality of what he leaves behind him; his real and personal possessions, his choses in action, indeed all his substance.' *Re Harvey, Assessor of Taxes v*

Walsh (1950) 24 MPR 360 at 392, Nfld SC, per Dunfield J

Estate and interest

'Unless there are indications of a contrary intention, the words "all my estate and interest" cover everything which the testator had to dispose of in the lands, and . . . the phrase is equivalent to "all and every my estate", or "all my estate and every interest which I have in the lands".' *Mackesy v Mackesy* [1896] 1 IR 511 at 518, per Porter MR

'The question is whether the words "all my estate and interest" passed all that the testatrix had in the lands, as well the "landed estate", which was realty, as charges on the land, legal or equitable, which were personalty. . . . In my opinion, the words she used were enough to pass, and did pass, all that she had in the lands, either as estate, or as charge.' *Kilkelly v Powell* [1897] 1 IR 457 at 461, 462, CA, per FitzGibbon LJ

Estate for life   *See* LIFE INTEREST

Estate in possession   *See* POSSESSION

Estate owner

'Estate owner' means the owner of a legal estate, but an infant is not capable of being an estate owner. (Law of Property Act 1925, s 205)

Estate tail   *See* ENTAILED INTEREST

Legal estate

'Legal estates' mean the estates, interests and charges, in or over land (subsisting or created at law) which are by this Act authorised to subsist or to be created as legal estates; 'equitable interests' mean all the other interests and charges in or over land or in the proceeds of sale thereof; an equitable interest 'capable of subsisting as a legal estate' means such as could validly subsist or be created as a legal estate under this Act. (Law of Property Act 1925, s 205)

'Legal estates' mean the estates charges and interests in or over land (subsisting or created at law) which are by statute authorised to subsist or to be created at law; and 'equitable interests' means all other interests and charges in or over land or in the proceeds of sale thereof. (Administration of Estates Act 1925, s 55(1))

'Legal estate' means an estate interest or charge in or over land (subsisting or created at law) which is by statute authorised to subsist or to be created at law. (Settled Land Act 1925, s 117)

Unadministered estate

'Unadministered estate' means all the property for the time being held by the personal representatives of a testator or intestate as such, excluding property devolving on the personal representatives otherwise than as assets for payment of his debts and property that is the subject of a specific disposition. (Finance Act 1938, s 47(5))

ESTATE AGENT

'Estate agent' means a person who, by way of profession or trade, provides services for the purpose of finding premises for persons seeking to acquire them or assisting in the disposal of premises. (Sex Discrimination Act 1975, s 82(1))

New Zealand   'An agent who specialises in finding suitable properties for purchaser clients is prima facie within the Act [Real Estate Agents Act 1976] although he may well not negotiate contracts or handle money.' *Previews Inc v UEB Industries* [1985] 1 NZLR 468 at 477, CA, per Cooke J

ESTIMATE

Australia   'So far from being a promissory expression, "estimated speed 15 mph" indicated, in our opinion, an expression of opinion as the result of approximate calculation based on probability.' *J J Savage & Sons v Blakney* (1970) 119 CLR 435 at 442, per cur.

ESTOPPEL   *See also* RES JUDICATA

There is said to be an estoppel where a party is not allowed to say that a certain statement of fact is untrue, whether in reality it is true or not. Estoppel, or 'conclusion' as it is frequently called by the older authorities, may therefore be defined as a disability whereby a party is precluded from alleging or proving in legal proceedings that a fact is otherwise than it has been made to appear by the matter giving rise to that disability. Estoppel is often described as a rule of evidence, but the whole concept is more correctly viewed as a substantive rule of law. (16 Halsbury's Laws (4th edn) para 1501)

An 'estoppel' is . . . a special plea in bar: which happens where a man hath done some act, or executed some deed, which estops or precludes him from averring any thing to the contrary. (3 Bl Com 308)

'A man shall not be allowed to blow hot and cold—to affirm at one time and deny at another—making a claim on those whom he has deluded to their disadvantage, and founding that claim on the very matters of the delusion. Such a principle has its basis in common sense and common justice, and whether it is called "estoppel", or by any other name, it is one which Courts of law have in modern times most usefully adopted.' *Cave v Mills* (1862) 7 H & N 913 at 927, 928, per Wilde B

'The word "estoppel" only means stopped. You will find it explained by Coke in his Commentaries on Littleton (at 352a). It was brought over by the Normans. They used the old French "estoupail". That meant a bung or cork by which you stopped something from coming out. It was in common use in our courts when they carried on all their proceedings in Norman-French. Littleton writes in the law-French of his day (fifteenth century) using the words "pur ceo que le baron est estoppe dire ceo", meaning simply that the husband is *stopped* from saying something. From that simple origin there has been built up over the centuries in our law a big house with many rooms. It is the house called Estoppel. In Coke's time it was a small house with only three rooms, namely, estoppel by matter of record, by matter in writing, and by matter "in pais". But by our time we have so many rooms that we are apt to get confused between them. Estoppel *per rem judicatam*, issue estoppel, estoppel by deed, estoppel by representation, estoppel by conduct, estoppel by acquiescence, estoppel by election or waiver, estoppel by negligence, promissory estoppel, proprietary estoppel, and goodness knows what else. These several rooms have this much in common: they are all under one roof. Someone is stopped from saying something or other, or doing something or other, or contesting something or other.' *McIlkenny v West Midlands Police Force* [1980] 2 All ER 227 at 235, CA, per Lord Denning MR

'The doctrine of estoppel is one of the most flexible and useful in the armoury of the law. . . . It has evolved during the last 150 years in a sequence of separate developments: proprietary estoppel, estoppel by representation of fact, estoppel by acquiescence and promissory estoppel. At the same time it has

been sought to be limited by a series of maxims: estoppel is only a rule of evidence; estoppel cannot give rise to a cause of action; estoppel cannot do away with the need for consideration, and so forth. All these can now be seen to merge into one general principle shorn of limitations. When the parties to a transaction proceed on the basis of an underlying assumption (either of fact or of law, and whether due to misrepresentation or mistake, makes no difference), on which they have conducted the dealings between them, neither of them will be allowed to go back on that assumption when it would be unfair or unjust to allow him to do so. If one of them does seek to go back on it, the courts will give the other such remedy as the equity of the case demands.' *Amalgamated Investment & Property Co Ltd v Texas Commerce International Bank Ltd* [1981] 3 All ER 577 at 584, CA, per Lord Denning MR

'Mere silence or inaction cannot amount to a representation unless there be a duty to disclose or act: see *Greenwood's* case [[1933] AC 51]. And their Lordships would reiterate that unless conduct can be interpreted as amounting to an implied representation, it cannot constitute an estoppel: for the essence of estoppel is a representation (express or implied) intended to induce the person to whom it is made to adopt a course of conduct which results in detriment or loss.' *Tai Hing Cotton Mill Ltd v Liu Chong Hing Bank* [1985] 2 All ER 947 at 959, PC, per Lord Scarman

Canada 'Estoppel is a complex legal notion, involving a combination of several essential elements—statement to be acted upon, action on the faith of it, resulting detriment to the actor. Estoppel is often described as a rule of evidence, as indeed it may be so described. But the whole concept is more correctly viewed as a substantive rule of law. The purchaser or other transferee must have acted upon it to his detriment. . . . It is also true that he cannot be said to rely on the statement if he knew that it was false; he must reasonably believe it to be true and therefore act upon it. Estoppel is different from contract both in its nature and consequences. But the relationship between the parties must also be such that the imputed truth of the statement is a necessary step in the constitution of the cause of action. But the whole case of estoppel fails if the statement is not sufficiently clear and unqualified.' *Canada & Dominion Sugar Co Ltd v Canadian National (West Indies) Steamships Ltd* [1946] 3 WWR 759 at 774, PC, per Lord Wright

Agency by

Agency by estoppel arises where one person has so acted as to lead another to believe that he has authorised a third person to act on his behalf, and that other in such belief enters into transactions with the third person within the scope of such ostensible authority. (1 Halsbury's Laws (4th edn) para 725)

Approbation and reprobation

On the principle that a person may not approbate and reprobate, a species of estoppel has arisen which seems to be intermediate between estoppel by record and estoppel in pais. The principle that a person may not approbate and reprobate expresses two propositions, (1) that the person in question, having a choice between two courses of conduct, is to be treated as having made an election from which he cannot resile, and, (2) that he will not be regarded, in general at any rate, as having so elected unless he has taken a benefit under or arising out of the course of conduct which he has first pursued and with which his subsequent conduct is inconsistent.

Thus a plaintiff, having two inconsistent claims, who elects to abandon one and pursue the other, may not, in general, afterwards choose to return to the former claim and sue on it; but this rule of election does not apply where the two claims are not inconsistent and the circumstances do not show an intention to abandon one of them.

The common law principle which puts a man to his election between alternative inconsistent courses of conduct has no connection with the equitable doctrine of election and relates mainly, though not exclusively, to alternative remedies in a court of justice. (16 Halsbury's Laws (4th edn) para 1507)

By conduct

'Seeing that here we are considering the doctrine of estoppel by conduct, I would like to state the basis of it. It is this: starting with an innocent person who has been led to believe in a state of affairs which he takes to be correct . . . and has acted on it, the first question is how has this innocent person been led into this belief? If it has been brought about by the conduct of another . . . who, though not solely responsible, nevertheless has contributed so large a part to it that it would be unfair or unjust to allow him to depart from it, then he is not allowed to go back on it so as to prejudice the innocent person who has acted on it. In so stating the basis of estoppel by conduct, I am relying on the well-considered analysis by Dixon J in *Thompson v Palmer* [(1933) 49 CLR 547], and *Grundt v Great Boulders* [(1937) 59 CLR 675]. His formulation of the principle is the most satisfactory that I know. As he points out, the basis of estoppel is that it would be unfair or unjust to allow a party to depart from a particular state of affairs which another has taken to be correct; but the law does not leave the question of fairness or justice at large. It has defined with more or less completeness the kinds of participation by a party which will suffice to work an estoppel against him. They are to be found in the decided cases.' *Central Newbury Car Auctions Ltd v Unity Finance Ltd* [1956] 3 All ER 904 at 909, CA, per Denning LJ (dissenting)

By deed

Where there is a statement of fact in a deed made between parties and verified by their seals, an estoppel results, and is called 'estoppel by deed'. If upon the true construction of the deed the statement is that of both or all the parties, the estoppel is binding on each party; if otherwise, it is only binding on the party making it. It seems that an estoppel also arises upon a deed poll, the mode of its execution being equally solemn with that of a deed made inter partes. (16 Halsbury's Laws (4th edn) para 1504)

By judgment

'Once the final appellate court has pronounced its judgment, the parties and those who claim through them are concluded; and, if the judgment is as to the status of a person, it is called a judgment *in rem* and everyone must accept it. A line can thus be drawn closing the account between the contestants. Important though the issues may be, how extensive soever the evidence, whatever the eagerness for further fray, society says: "We have provided courts in which your rival contentions have been heard. We have provided a code of law by which they have been adjudged. Since judges and juries are fallible human beings, we have provided appellate courts which do their own fallible best to correct error. But in the end you must accept what has been decided. Enough is enough." And the law echoes: "*res judicata*, the matter is adjudged." The judgment creates an estoppel—which merely means that what has been decided must be taken to be established as a fact, that the decided issue cannot be reopened by those who are bound by the judgment, that the clamouring voices must be stilled, that the bitter waters of civil contention (even though channelled into litigation) must be allowed to subside.' *Ampthill Peerage Case* [1976] 2 All ER 411 at 423, 424, HL (Committee for Privileges), per Lord Simon of Glaisdale

By representation

'For the purpose of this case, I think that the elements of estoppel by representation can be stated as follows. A person seeking to rely on an estoppel by representation must prove: (1) that a representation was made to him by or on behalf of the person against whom he seeks to rely on the estoppel; (2) that it was the intention of the person making the representation that the person to whom the representation was made should act on it as correct; (3) that the person to whom it was made did act on it; (4) that the representation was not correct and that as a result of acting on it he suffered detriment.' *Moorgate Mercantile Co Ltd v Twitchings* [1975] 3 All ER 314 at 326, CA, per Browne LJ

Feeding the estoppel

Canada   'Perhaps a brief word should be said about the implications flowing from the expression "feeding the estoppel". An interest in land is created by estoppel when the grantor has no legal estate or interest therein at the time of the grant, and although a title by estoppel is not good as against all the world but only against the grantor, who is estopped by his own deed as against him, it has all the elements of a real title. Where the grantor subsequently acquires a legal title to the premises which he has purported to grant that legal estate or interest is said to feed the estoppel, and the original grant then takes effect in interest and not by estoppel, but the grantor is estopped from saying that he had no interest at the time of the grant. Thus through the instrumentality of what is a pure legal fiction, i.e. by operation of law, the grantee's erstwhile estate by estoppel valid only as against his grantor became an estate in interest valid as against the rest of the world without the necessity of the grantee obtaining a further or supplementary grant from the grantor, or without any other or further documentation.' *Reference re Certain Titles to Land in Ontario* [1973] 2 OR 613 at 629, CA, per cur.

In pais

Where a person has by words or conduct made to another a representation of fact, either with knowledge of its falsehood or with the intention that it should be acted upon, or has so conducted himself that another would, as a reasonable man, understand that a certain representation of fact was intended to be acted on, and that the other has acted on the representation and thereby altered his position to his prejudice, an estoppel arises against the party who made the representation and, he is not allowed to aver that the fact is otherwise than he represented it to be. (16 Halsbury's Laws (4th edn) para 1505)

Issue estoppel

[Although a comparatively new phrase, issue estoppel has for long been recognised as a form of estoppel *per rem judicatam.* As opposed to action estoppel, issue estoppel arises where some issue between the same parties was incidental to a decision in a former action.] 'The requirements of issue estoppel still remain (i) that the same question has been decided; (ii) that the judicial decision which is said to create the estoppel was final; and (iii) that the parties to the judicial decision or their privies were the same persons as the parties to the proceedings in which the estoppel is raised or their privies.' *Carl-Zeiss-Stiftung v Rayner & Keeler Ltd (No 2)* [1966] 2 All ER 536 at 565, HL, per Lord Guest

'Issue estoppel is a particular application of the general rule of public policy that there should be finality in litigation. That general rule applies also to criminal proceedings, but in a form modified by the distinctive character of criminal as compared with civil litigation. Here it takes the form of the rule against double jeopardy . . . I think with great respect that the use of that expression [issue estoppel] in criminal and civil proceedings alike may lead to confusion, for there are obvious differences—lack of mutuality is but one—between the application of the rule against double jeopardy in criminal cases, and the rule that there should be finality in civil litigation.' *Mills v Cooper* [1967] 2 All ER 100 at 105, per Diplock LJ

'Issue estoppel can be said to exist when there is a judicial establishment of a proposition of law or fact between parties to earlier litigation and when the same question arises in later litigation between the same parties. In the later litigation the established proposition is treated as conclusive between those same parties.'

R v Hogan [1974] 2 All ER 142 at 145, per Lawson J

[The above case, which had purported to apply the doctrine of issue estoppel to criminal proceedings, was held to be wrong, and was accordingly overruled by the House of Lords, in *Director of Public Prosecutions v Humphrys* [1976] 2 All ER 497, [1977] AC 1, HL.]

'It is my own view, which I understand is shared by all your Lordships, that it would be best, in order to avoid confusion, if the use of the description "issue estoppel" *in English law, at any rate* (it does not appear to have been adopted in the United States), were restricted to that species of estoppel *per rem judicatam* that may arise in civil actions between the same parties or their privies, of which the characteristics are stated in a judgment of my own in *Mills v Cooper* [supra] that was adopted and approved by this House in *Director of Public Prosecutions v Humphrys* [supra], the case in which it was also held that "issue estoppel" had no place in English criminal law.' *Hunter v Chief Constable of West Midlands* [1981] 3 All ER 727 at 733, HL, per cur.

'In English law, when a plaintiff, who, basing his claim on a particular set of facts, has already sued the defendant to final judgment in a foreign court of competent jurisdiction and lost, then seeks to enforce a cause of action in an English court against the same defendant based on the same set of facts, the defendant's remedy against such double jeopardy is provided by the doctrine of issue estoppel. It is far too late, at this stage of the development of the doctrine, to question that issue estoppel can be created by the judgment of a foreign court if that court is recognised in English private international law as being a court of competent jurisdiction. Issue estoppel operates regardless of whether or not an English court would regard the reasoning of the foreign judgment as open to criticism. . . . To make available an issue estoppel to a defendant to an action brought against him in an English court on a cause of action to which the plaintiff alleges a particular set of facts give rise, the defendant must be able to show (1) that the same set of facts has previously been relied on as constituting a cause of action in proceedings brought by that plaintiff against that defendant in a foreign court of competent jurisdiction and (2) that a final judgment has been given by that foreign court in those proceedings.' *D S v Silo-und Verwaltungsgesellschaft mbH v Sennan*

(Owners), The Sennan [1985] 2 All ER 104 at 106, HL, per Lord Diplock

Of record

Estoppel of record or quasi of record, also known as estoppel per rem judicatam, arises (1) where an issue of fact has been judicially determined in a final manner between the parties by a tribunal having jurisdiction, concurrent or exclusive, in the matter, and the same issue comes directly in question in subsequent proceedings between the same parties (this is sometimes known as cause of action estoppel); (2) where the first determination was by a court having exclusive jurisdiction, and the same issue comes incidentally in question in subsequent proceedings between the same parties (this is sometimes known as issue estoppel); (3) in some cases where an issue of fact affecting the status of a person or thing has been necessarily determined in a final manner as a substantive part of a judgment in rem of a tribunal having jurisdiction to determine that status, and the same issue comes directly in question in subsequent civil or criminal proceedings between any parties whatever. Where the earlier decision is that of a court of record, the resulting estoppel is said to be 'of record'; where it is that of any other tribunal, whether constituted by agreement of the parties or otherwise, the estoppel is said to be 'quasi of record'. (16 Halsbury's Laws (4th edn) para 1503)

Per rem judicatam

'The estoppel relied on . . . is estoppel *per rem judicatam*. However, . . . that is a generic term which in modern law includes two distinct species. One, cause of action estoppel, is that which prevents a party to an action from asserting or denying against the other party the existence of a particular cause of action, the existence or non-existence of which has already been determined by a court of competent jurisdiction in previous litigation between the same parties. The cause of action is merged in the judgment on the previous determination and its place is taken by the rights created by the judgment, so that no second action may be brought on that cause of action. The other species, issue estoppel, is that which prevents a party to an action from raising against the other party any issue whether of fact or law which has already been determined by a court of competent jurisdiction in previous litigation between the same parties. Issue estoppel, therefore, prevents contradiction of a previous determination, whereas cause of action estoppel prevents reassertion of the cause of action the subject of the previous determination.' *Lawlor v Gray* [1984] 3 All ER 345 at 349, 350, per Peter Gibson J

Promissory estoppel

When one party has, by his words or conduct, made to the other a promise or assurance which was intended to affect the legal relations between them and to be acted on accordingly, then, once the other party has taken him at his word and acted on it, the one who gave the promise or assurance cannot afterwards be allowed to revert to their previous legal relations as if no such promise or assurance had been made by him, but he must accept their legal relations subject to the qualification which he himself has so introduced. (16 Halsbury's Laws (4th edn) para 1514)

ESTOVERS

Common of estovers is the profit which a man has in the soil of another to cut or prune from his forest or other wastes wood for his building, enclosing and firing or other necessary purposes. (16 Halsbury's Laws (4th edn) para 579)

ESTRAYS

Estrays are valuable animals of a tame or reclaimable nature which are found wandering in any manor or lordship, and whose owner is unknown. They belong to the Sovereign as general owner and lord paramount by way of recompense for the damage done, and to preserve the animal alive, unless, as is more generally the case today, they belong to the lord of the manor by grant or prescription. (8 Halsbury's Laws (4th edn) para 1517)

ESTUARY

'The word "estuary" . . . means the tidal part of a river.' *Birrel v Dryer* (1884) 9 App Cas 345 at 347, HL, per Lord Selborne LC

ET CETERA

'It [a gift by will] goes on with the words, if properly speaking they can be called words, "etc, etc," the proper interpretation of which is "and all other things".' *Gover v Davis* (1860) 29 Beav 222 at 225, per Romilly MR

[In a contract for the sale of two plots of land, 'and buildings, material &c,' no mention was made of a right of way thereto. The purchaser claimed that the words 'et cetera' carried the right of way.] 'I think the contention of the vendor is right. . . . On the land sold lay the bricks and other debris of two cottages which had fallen to pieces, and on the true construction of the contract I think the words "et cetera" are limited to the word "material" which immediately precedes them and refer to something of the same character as "material". . . . The expression "et cetera" cannot be held to include the right of way now in dispute.' *Re Walmsley & Shaw's Contract* [1917] 1 Ch 93 at 97, per Eve J

'When you find in a will a list of things . . . and the list concludes with the general words like "et cetera" the meaning of the general words is restricted to things of the same class as those which are contained in the list.' *Milne's Trustees v Davidson* 1956 SLT 34 at 35, per the Lord Justice-Clerk (Thomson)

ETHNIC

[The Race Relations Act 1976, s 3(1) defines 'racial group' as a group of persons defined by reference to colour, race, nationality or 'ethnic' or national origins.] 'For a group to constitute an ethnic group in the sense of the 1976 Act, it must, in my opinion, regard itself, and be regarded by others, as a distinct community by virtue of certain characteristics. Some of these characteristics are essential; others are not essential but one or more of them will commonly be found and will help to distinguish the group from the surrounding community. The conditions which appear to me to be essential are these: (1) a long shared history, of which the group is conscious as distinguishing it from other groups, and the memory of which it keeps alive; (2) a cultural tradition of its own, including family and social customs and manners, often but not necessarily associated with religious observance. In addition to those two essential characteristics the following characteristics are, in my opinion, relevant: (3) either a common geographical origin, or descent from a small number of common ancestors; (4) a common language, not necessarily peculiar to the group; (5) a common literature peculiar to the group; (6) a common religion different from that of neighbouring groups or from the general community surrounding it; (7) being a minority or being an oppressed or a dominant group within a larger community, for example a conquered people (say, the inhabitants of England shortly after the Norman conquest) and their conquerers might both be ethnic groups.' *Mandla v Dowell Lee* [1983] 1 All ER 1052 at 1066, 1067, HL, per Lord Fraser of Tullybelton

EUROPEAN

Australia 'The expression "an European language" means a standard form of speech recognised as the received and ordinary means of communication among the inhabitants in an European community for all the purposes of the social body. Scottish Gaelic is not such a language.' *R v Wilson, ex p Kisch* (1934) 52 CLR 234 at 241, per Rich J

EVADE

'It does not appear to their Lordships that an examination of the decisions in which the word "evade" has been the subject of comment leads to any tangible result. Everybody agrees that the word is capable of being used in two senses; one which suggests underhand dealing, and another which means nothing more than the intentional avoidance of something disagreeable.' *Simms v Registrar of Probates* [1900] AC 323 at 334, PC, per cur.

'There are two ways of construing the word "evade": one is that a person may go to a solicitor and ask him how to keep out of an Act of Parliament—how to do something which does not bring him within the scope of it. That is evading in one sense, but there is nothing illegal in it. The other is, when he goes to his solicitor, and says "Tell me how to escape from the consequences of the Act of Parliament, although I am brought within it." That is an act of quite a different character.' *Bullivant v A-G for Victoria* [1901] AC 196 at 207, HL, per Lord Lindley

Australia 'The distinction in meaning between the words "evade" and "avoid" is well established, and a charge of evading payment is not made out by evidence which proves no more than that the person charged failed or omitted to pay an amount payable by him.' *Wilson v Chambers & Co Pty Ltd* (1926) 38 CLR 131 at 136, per Knox CJ

Australia [Section 120 of the Excise Act 1901 (Cth) is in the following terms: 'A person shall not . . . (iv) evade payment of any duty

which is payable'.] 'In the context of considering the meaning of the word "evasion" in the Income Tax (Management) Act 1936 (NSW), Dixon J said in *Denver Chemical Manufacturing Co v Commissioner of Taxation (NSW)* (1949) 79 CLR 296 at 313, that it was unwise to attempt to define the word. He then went on to say that some blameworthy act or omission on the part of the taxpayer is contemplated. He said an intention to withhold information lest the Commissioner should consider the taxpayer liable to a greater extent than the taxpayer is prepared to concede is conduct which, if the result is to avoid tax, would justify finding evasion. This meaning was adopted by Fullagar J in *Australasian Jam Co Pty Ltd v FC of T* (1953) 88 CLR 23 at 38–9. It is appropriate, in my view, to apply the meaning enunciated by Dixon J in the penal provisions now under consideration, namely, that the word "evade" means more than the intentional withholding of information or the mere furnishing of misleading information, but requires some blameworthy act or omission on the part of the appellants.' *Ludwigs Canberra Bond Cellar Pty Ltd v Sheen* (1982) 46 ACTR 13 at 20, per Gallop J

EVASION

'An obligation is evaded if by some contrivance the debtor avoids or gets out of fulfilling or performing his obligation. In the days when such things happened, a welshing bookmaker not only evaded his pursuers, he also evaded his obligations. Evasion does not necessarily mean permanent escape. If the bookmaker evaded his pursuers on Monday, the fact that he is caught and made to pay up on Tuesday does not alter the fact that he evaded his obligations on Monday. Unlike reducing and deferring an obligation, evading an obligation is a unilateral operation. It leaves the obligation untouched and does not connote any activity on the part of the creditor. When the evasion ceases he can seek to recover the debt in any way open to him.' *Director of Public Prosecutions v Turner* [1973] 3 All ER 124 at 127, HL, per Lord Reid

EVENING

'I am of opinion that the tender [which was made five minutes after a bank closed for the day] was made "before the evening of the 10th", as in terms provided by the notice. What other meaning can be placed on the words "before the evening of the 10th" except that any time before sunset would be in time? There is nothing to shew that the evening ceased at the time the banks chose to close on the 10th.' *Re Quebrada Co Ltd, Clarke's Case* (1873) 42 LJ Ch 277 at 279, per Romilly MR

EVENT

Costs following event

[Order 65 of RSC 1883 formerly contained a proviso to the effect that in cases of trial by jury the costs should follow the 'event'. This proviso was annulled in 1929. See now however RSC 1965, Ord 62 r 3, as to when costs shall 'follow the event'.]

'I wish to guard myself against being taken to hold that, where distinct, separate, substantive matters in difference are referred to arbitration, with a provision that the costs shall abide the event of the award, and some of those matters are decided in favour of one party and some in favour of the other, the word "event" must there be taken to be applicable only to one general event, so as to prevent either party from obtaining costs. . . . Where the matters referred are clearly distinct and separate, it seems to me that it would be fraught with very great inconvenience and injustice to hold that the word "event" may not be construed in the larger sense of "events", so that the costs may be distributed according to the decision of the arbitrator upon the different matters brought under his notice.' *Re Marsack & Webber* (1860) 2 E & E 637 at 650, 651, per Cockburn CJ

'The word "event" [in Ord 55, r 1 of RSC 1875, replaced by Ord 65 of RSC 1883 (see note, supra)] is to be construed distributively, and if in the same action the plaintiff obtains a verdict and judgment as to one distinct cause of action and the defendant obtains a verdict and judgment as to another cause of action, these are two events.' *Myers v Defries* (1879) 41 LT 659 at 660, per cur.

'It is . . . argued on behalf of the plaintiff that the word "event" ought to be read distributively, as if the term "events" had been employed. . . . It cannot be denied that this is the general interpretation of the term, and I see nothing in this particular case to make another interpretation the correct one. I am of opinion that . . . the reason of the thing is to treat "event" distributively.' *Ellis v Desilva* (1881) 6 QBD 521 at 524, per Bramwell LJ

'I think the term "event" in the order of reference [to an arbitrator] must be construed distributively, and that the costs of the action must abide the event of the action, and the costs of the matters in difference must abide the event of the matters in difference.' *Hawke v Brear* (1885) 14 QBD 841 at 843, per Mathew J

'What is the meaning of the word "event" in Order 65, r 1 [see note, supra] . . . An "event" within the meaning of the rule is an outcome of the presentation to the tribunal of some claim made by the plaintiff against the defendant which results in a finding that the plaintiff is or is not entitled to relief against the defendant.' *Howell v Dering* [1915] 1 KB 54 at 62, 63, CA, per Buckley LJ

EVERY

[A testator gave by his will £100 to 'every' of the sons and daughters of his late cousin JD.] 'In order to admit this claim, the words must be construed as extending generally to all sons and daughters, whether legitimate or not. Then it would be impossible to exclude any other bastards of JD who may possibly hereafter claim. This construction would be monstrous, where there exists one that answers the legal description of the persons to take.' *Hart v Durand* (1796) 3 Anst 684 at 685, per Thompson B

[The custom of a borough corporation was that 'every' freeman's son should be admitted a freeman.] 'The expression "every freeman's son" must be understood, with reference to the usage, to mean, that one son of a freeman shall be admitted in right of his father; and the expression cannot be construed to mean *every son* of a freeman.' *R v Rye Corpn* (1828) 7 LJOSKB 107 at 108, per Lord Tenterden CJ

EVERYONE

Canada 'I would hold that "everyone" as used in s 8 [of the Charter of Rights and Freedoms] should include all human beings and all entities that are capable of enjoying the benefit of security against unreasonable search. This then would include corporations. That interpretation would not be inconsistent in the other sections where the word "everyone" is used where only human beings can enjoy the rights given.' *Southam Inc v Hunter* (1982) 68 CCC (2d) 356; sub nom *Southam Inc v Director* *of Investigation & Research of Combines Investigations Branch* (Alta QB) at 364, CCC, per Cavanagh J; revd (1982) 65 CPR (2d) 116, Alta CA; affd [1984] 2 SCR 145; approved in *Crain (RL) Inc v Couture* (1983) 6 DLR (4th) 478, Sask QB

EVERYTHING

Everything else

[A testator provided in his will that 'all my goods, furniture, plate, books, pictures, and every thing else which at my decease shall be at my house at Lea, shall remain there, and be enjoyed by the person who for the time being shall be in possession of the said house.'] '"Every thing else, which at my decease shall be at my house", must be construed things *ejusdem generis*, such as are proper to go with the house as heir-looms.' *Boon v Cornforth* (1751) 2 Ves Sen 277 at 280, per Lord Hardwicke LC

'Everything I possess'

'The testatrix goes on: "Everything I am possessed of I leave to my sister, Sophia Plumptre, for her life." In my opinion, having regard to the Wills Act, and having regard to the expressions used, Sophia Plumptre does take this property [real property] for life. I wish to say that distinctly. I do not wish to be misunderstood, but she takes it because she takes everything. There is nothing I can find to cut down the meaning of the word "everything"—"everything I am possessed of". Why should it not mean everything? But although everything is left to a person for life, it does not follow that everything is to be left after her decease.' *Re Methuen & Blore's Contract* (1881) 29 WR 656 at 658, per Jessel MR

'I am clearly of opinion that that gift to Elsie Tranter of "everything that I die possessed of" is a general residuary gift, which covers everything which the testator could, according to law, dispose of by his will, including property over which he had any general power of disposition. This last observation is justified by s 27 of the Wills Act [1837].' *Re Hayter, Hayter v Tranter* [1937] 2 All ER 110 at 112, per Clauson J

EVICTION

The tenant is not liable for rent accruing due after he has been evicted from the premises either by the landlord, or by a person lawfully claiming by title paramount, so long as the

eviction continues. To constitute an eviction for this purpose, it is not necessary that there should be an actual physical expulsion from any part of the premises. Any wrongful act of a permanent character done by the landlord or his agent with the intention of depriving the tenant of the enjoyment of the demised premises, or any part thereof, will operate as an eviction. (27 Halsbury's Laws (4th edn) para 236)

'It is extremely difficult at the present day to define with technical accuracy what is an eviction. Latterly, the word has been used to denote that which formerly it was not intended to express. In the language of pleading, the party evicted was said to be expelled, amoved, and put out. The word eviction, from *evincere*, to evict, to dispossess by a judicial course,— was formerly used to denote an expulsion by the assertion of a title paramount, and by process of law. But that sort of eviction is not necessary to constitute a suspension of the rent, because it is now well settled, that, if the tenant loses the benefit of the enjoyment of any portion of the demised premises, by the act of the landlord, the rent is thereby suspended. The term "eviction" is now popularly applied to every class of expulsion or amotion. Getting rid thus of the old notion of eviction, I think it may now be taken to mean this,—not a mere trespass and nothing more, but something of a grave and permanent character done by the landlord with the intention of depriving the tenant of the enjoyment of the demised premises.' *Upton v Townend, Upton v Greenless* (1855) 17 CB 30 at 64, 65, per Jervis CJ

'It seems to me that the act of the landlord (or his agent) in order to constitute an eviction at law must at least have certain characteristics which, though they have not been (and may not indeed be capable of being) precisely defined, will be regarded as satisfied or not satisfied according to the standards of common sense and ordinary understanding in the light of the facts of each particular case. I leave aside at this stage the question of the "wrongfulness" of the landlord's act. But apart from any requisite of wrongfulness, the landlord's act must (i) be of a "permanent character", and (ii) be done with a particular "intention", viz, that of disabling the tenant from continuing to "hold" the subject of his demise, or of depriving him of the "enjoyment" of the thing demised, or some part thereof.' *Comrs of Crown Lands v Page* [1960] 2 All ER 726 at 729, CA, per Lord Evershed MR; also reported in [1960] 2 QB 274 at 281, 282

EVIDENCE

Evidence is the usual means of proving or disproving a fact or matter in issue. The law of evidence indicates what may properly be introduced by a party (that is, what is admissible), and also what standard of proof is necessary (that is, the quality or quantity of evidence necessary in any particular case). In short, the law of evidence governs the means and manner in which a party may substantiate his own case, or refute that of his opponent.

Modern evidential principles still reflect the now obsolete assumption that all cases are tried by judge and jury, the former deciding on matters of admissibility, the latter on the value of the evidence admitted. While this is untrue in civil cases, . . . the distinction between admissibility and value (or weight) is fundamental to a proper understanding of the English law of evidence for, although evidence has recently been the subject of significant statutory revision, its principles are largely those of nineteenth and twentieth century case law.

Two further principles are important. First, cases are tried solely on the evidence adduced by the parties, which may be limited as a matter of agreement or tactics; the judge does not pursue any independent inquiry. Secondly, in a minority of cases evidence may not be necessary to enable a party to establish a particular fact; there may be formal admissions, what is contended for may be a matter of which judicial notice may be taken, or a presumption of sufficient strength may operate. (17 Halsbury's Laws (4th edn) para 1)

'I think, of the essence of "evidence", according to English ideas, when used with reference to judicial or quasi-judicial matters, that it should consist of oral statements or documents in writing which are made in the presence of or communicated to both parties before the tribunal reaches its decision. This is not in my view confined to judicial tribunals bound by legal rules of evidence, but is equally applicable to a quasi-judicial tribunal such as a pensions appeal tribunal, which is expressly required to have regard to the onus of proof in its adjudications.' *Moxon v Minister of Pensions* [1945] KB 490 at 501, per Tucker J

Australia 'I think the word "evidence" is not to be limited to evidence which can be used against the person who gives it or in favour of the person who requires it. To give evidence in my opinion means to make statements on oath before a person duly authorised to administer an oath.' *Re Williams Brothers Ltd* (1928) 29 SRNSW 248 at 248, per Harvey CJ in Eq

Australia 'In this case, the law places on the liquidator, in a voluntary winding-up, the responsibility of working out the affairs of the company. It affords him the means of obtaining information, that is, evidentiary facts, enabling him to come to a conclusion as to ultimate facts. The information obtained as prescribed through the instrumentality of the Court and on oath is properly described as "evidence". It is "evidence" for the purpose intended by the law.' *Cheney v Spooner* (1929) 41 CLR 532 at 537, per cur.

Canada 'The association of the word "evidence" with the words "and the exhibits" in [Criminal] Code, s 512(a) [see now RSC 1970, c C-34, ss 531] is a strong indication that "evidence" was not intended to embrace statements taken from prospective witnesses. . . . The word "evidence" must mean testimony given at a judicial hearing relating to the subject-matter of the charge against the accused, such as a preliminary hearing or a hearing under Code, s 613 [see now RSC 1970, c C-34, s 634], and the expression "his own statement" must mean the accused's statement made at the preliminary hearing under Code, s 454(1) and (2) [see now RSC 1970, c C-34, s 469]. I would add that, in my opinion, the making of a statement by a person does not constitute the giving of evidence by him, even though that statement be put into writing and signed by him. At most it is an expression of what he will say if and when he is put in the witness-box to give evidence.' *R v Lantos* (1963) 45 WWR 409 at 410, BCCA, per Tysoe J

New Zealand 'If . . . there is any difference in meaning between the two words, "testimony" is somewhat narrower than "evidence"; for "evidence" includes not only the testimony of persons who attest, but also what is called real evidence—that is, the evidence of things and events, from which we draw conclusions for ourselves. For instance, a footprint in the sand is evidence that someone has been walking there; it can hardly be said to be testimony.' *Harvey v Church* (1898) 17 NZLR 19 at 20, 21, per Pennefather J; also reported 1 GLR 20

Best evidence

That evidence should be the best that the nature of the case will allow is, besides being a matter of obvious prudence, a principle with a considerable pedigree. However, any strict interpretation of this principle has long been obsolete, and the rule is now only of importance in regard to the primary evidence of private documents. The logic of requiring the production of an original document where it is available rather than relying on possibly unsatisfactory copies, or the recollections of witnesses, is clear, although modern techniques make objections to the first alternative less strong. When a deed has superseded a written agreement it must be produced, and evidence embodied in depositions can only be given in the absence of the deponent in certain circumstances. The best evidence rule does not apply to cases in which the issue concerns the state of a chattel, such as the correspondence of the bulk of goods to a sample, and the chattel need not be produced. (17 Halsbury's Laws (4th edn) para 8)

'What the best evidence is must depend upon circumstances. Generally speaking, the original document is the best evidence; but circumstances may arise in which secondary evidence of the contents may be given.' *Macdonnell v Evans* (1852) 11 CB 930 at 941, per Jervis CJ

Conclusive evidence   *See* CONCLUSIVE

Fresh evidence

'I need not go at large into the meaning of the words "upon fresh evidence". Suffice it to say that the passage in the judgment of Hill J in *Timmins v Timmins* [(1919) P 75, 80], in which, relying on the decision in *Johnson v Johnson* [(1900) P 19], he says, "fresh evidence . . . means evidence of something which has happened since the former hearing or has come to the knowledge of the party applying since the hearing, and could not by reasonable means have come to his knowledge before that time", has received favourable notice in the Court of Appeal.' *Underwood v Underwood* [1946] P 84 at 86, 87, per Lord Merriman P

[A decision of a medical board might be reviewed, under s 40(1) of the National Insurance (Industrial Injuries) Act 1946 (repealed), in the light of 'fresh evidence'.] 'If an appellant had knowledge of some material fact at the time when he was appearing before a medical appeal tribunal, but if for some reason he decided not to disclose the material fact, and if a decision were given, I cannot think that he could then seek to review the decision by bringing the material fact before the medical

board and asserting that he had "fresh evidence". In my judgment, he would not have "fresh evidence". "Fresh evidence", it seems to me, must have the quality of newness, or the feature of having become newly available and obtainable.' *R v Medical Appeal Tribunal (North Midland Region), ex p Hubble* [1959] 3 All ER 40 at 47, CA, per Morris LJ; also reported [1959] 2 QB 408

Further evidence

'The first question to be decided is, what is the meaning of the words "further evidence" [in RSC Ord 58, r 5; see now RSC 1965 Ord 59, r 10(2)]? In my opinion they mean evidence not used at the trial or hearing in the Court below. . . . All appeals are by way of rehearing, that is by trial over again, on the evidence used in the Court below; but there is special power to receive further evidence.' *Re Chennell, Jones v Chennell* (1878) 8 Ch D 492 at 504, 505, CA, per Jessel MR

Hearsay evidence

Hearsay evidence in its legal sense is evidence given by a testifying witness of a statement made on some other occasion, when it is intended as evidence of the truth of what was asserted. It is essential to appreciate that evidence is only hearsay when tendered to prove the truth of the facts asserted, not when tendered simply to show that the statement was made. Hearsay may be first hand, when a witness says what he heard someone else say, or second hand (or even more distant) when he relates what he was told that someone else said. It may be oral or documentary, of fact or of opinion. With certain very significant exceptions, hearsay evidence was not admissible at common law. Now, in civil proceedings, first-hand hearsay is admissible to the extent provided by statute, or by agreement of the parties, but not otherwise. Its admissibility is in general dependent upon compliance with procedural requirements of notice, although the court has a discretion to admit it without compliance. (17 Halsbury's Laws (4th edn) para 53)
[In any civil proceedings a statement other than one made by a person while giving oral evidence in those proceedings shall be admissible only by virtue of the Civil Evidence Act 1968, or other statutory provision or by agreement. See generally Part I of the Civil Evidence Act 1968.]

'A statement made otherwise than by a

witness in giving evidence is called "hearsay" when the object of such evidence is to establish the truth of what is contained in the statement and is generally deemed to be irrelevant and inadmissible.' *R v Harz, R v Power* [1966] 3 All ER 433 at 449, CCA, per Thesiger J

'Evidence of a statement made to a witness by a person who is not himself called as a witness may or may not be hearsay. It is hearsay and inadmissible when the object of the evidence is to establish the truth of what is contained in the statement. It is not hearsay and is admissible when it is proposed to establish by the evidence, not the truth of the statement but the fact that it was made.' *Subraminean v Public Prosecutor* [1956] 1 WLR 965 at 970, PC, per cur.

'The authorities relating to the application of the hearsay rule contrast two distinct situations. In the first situation evidence is sought to be adduced of a statement made to a witness in order to prove the truth of the facts stated. This is hearsay evidence and must be excluded, unless it can be brought within one of the recognised exceptions to the hearsay rule. In the second situation evidence is sought to be adduced of a statement made to a witness in order to prove, not the truth of any facts stated, but the state of mind either of the person who made the statement or of the person to whom it was made. This evidence is not within the hearsay rule at all; it is direct and primary evidence of the state of mind of the maker or recipient of the statement. . . . Hearsay evidence is not excluded because it has no logically probative value. Given that the subject matter of the hearsay is relevant to some issue in the trial, it may clearly be potentially probative. The rationale of excluding it as inadmissible, rooted as it is in the system of trial by jury, is a recognition of the great difficulty, even more acute for a juror than for a trained judicial mind, of assessing what, if any, weight can properly be given to a statement by a person whom the jury have not seen or heard and which has not been subject to any test of reliability by cross-examination. As Lord Normand put it, delivering the judgment of the Privy Council in *Teper v R* [[1952] 2 All ER 447 at 449, [1952] AC 480 at 486]: "The rule against admission of hearsay evidence is fundamental. It is not the best evidence and it is not delivered on oath. The truthfulness and accuracy of the person whose words are spoken to by another witness cannot be tested by cross-examination, and the light which his demeanour would throw on his testimony is lost". The danger

against which this fundamental rule provides a safeguard is that untested hearsay evidence will be treated as having a probative force which it does not deserve.' *R v Blastland* [1985] 2 All ER 1095 at 1098, 1099, HL, per Lord Bridge of Harwich

In support of alibi   *See* ALIBI

Personal

Australia 'I think "personal evidence" means evidence personally deposed to by any means admissible before the particular tribunal in which the question of proof arises, and, on a habeas corpus application, evidence by affidavit is commonly received.' *R v Governor of Metropolitan Gaol, ex p Di Nardo* [1963] VR 61 at 63, per Sholl J

'Present testimony'

New Zealand 'The only question really involved in the present case is as to the meaning of the words "present testimony" in s 10 of the Evidence Act 1908. That section was passed for the purpose of enabling a witness to be discredited in a manner in which if it had not been passed he could not have been discredited. Counsel for the accused has sought to confine the words "present testimony" to testimony given by the witness in his examination-in-chief. It is difficult to see why the words should be so narrowed. If testimony is given by a witness at any stage of the proceedings which is relevant to the issue, that testimony would properly be called "present testimony". There is no reason why it should not be so denominated. If a witness on cross-examination makes statements which are relevant to the issue, but in respect of which he has on some previous occasion made inconsistent statements, there is no reason on the grounds of public policy or convenience why the section should not be applied to them, and why evidence that he has made such inconsistent statements should not be admitted.' *R v Rolton* (1909) 29 NZLR 272 at 275, 276, CA, per Williams ACJ; also reported 12 GLR 261

New Zealand   'I am of the same opinion. I have never felt any doubt that the statements in question were relative to the subject-matter of the proceedings. The only possible doubt was as to whether the evidence of a witness given in cross-examination came within the meaning of the words "present testimony" in the section. The witness, however, is sworn to speak the truth, the whole truth, and nothing but the truth. I think his testimony given at the trial includes every answer which he is liable to give to questions put to him while in the witness-box; but he can only be contradicted as to statements which he has previously made relative to the subject-matter of the proceedings and inconsistent with his present testimony.' Ibid at 277, per Edwards J

Secondary evidence

In the unavoidable absence of the best or primary evidence of documents, the court will accept secondary evidence. This is evidence which suggests, on the face of it, that other and better evidence exists. A party tendering it ought therefore to show that he is unable to obtain the best evidence. Public and judicial documents are usually proved by copies, without accounting for the absence of the originals. (17 Halsbury's Laws (4th edn) para 9)

Tape recordings *See* DOCUMENT

EVIDENCE TO THE CONTRARY

Canada 'Evidence that an accused broke and entered a place is proof that he broke and entered with intent to commit an indictable offence therein, in the absence of any evidence to the contrary.' *R v Proudlock* [1979] 1 SCR 525 at 536, SCC, per Estey J

Canada '"Evidence to the contrary", as regards an analyst's conclusions set out in a certificate, as those words are meant in s 9 [of the Narcotic Control Act, RSC 1970, c N-1], is any evidence upon which a trier of fact could as a matter of law rest a reasonable doubt as to that analyst's conclusions had he testified as an expert witness in court.' *Oliver v R* [1981] 2 SCR 240 at 249, 250, SCC, per Lamer J

EVIDENTIAL UNCERTAINTY *See* UNCERTAINTY

EX GRATIA

'It is, I think, common experience amongst practitioners of the law that litigation or threatened litigation is frequently compromised on the terms that one party shall make to the other a payment described in express terms as "ex gratia" or "without admission of liability". The two phrases are, I think, synonymous. No one would imagine that a settlement, so made, is unenforceable at law. The words "ex gratia" or

"without admission of liability" are used simply to indicate—it may be as a matter of *amour propre* or it may be to avoid a precedent in subsequent cases—that the party agreeing to pay does not admit any pre-existing liability on his part; but he is certainly not seeking to preclude the legal enforceability of the settlement itself by describing the contemplated payments as "ex gratia".' *Edwards v Skyways Ltd* [1964] 1 All ER 494 at 500, per Megaw J

EX SHIP

'These goods were [by a contract for their carriage] to be put on rail ex ship. . . . The expression "ex ship" does not exclude taking the goods into warehouse for the purpose of despatching them by cart to the railway.' *Essex Counties Farmers' Co-operative Assocn Ltd v Newhouse & Co Ltd* (1916) 86 LJKB 172 at 174, per Rowlatt J

'In the case of a sale "ex ship", the seller has to cause delivery to be made to the buyer from a ship which has arrived at the port of delivery and has reached a place therein, which is usual for the delivery of goods of the kind in question. The seller has therefore to pay the freight, or otherwise to release the shipowner's lien and to furnish the buyer with an effectual direction to the ship to deliver. Till this is done the buyer is not bound to pay for the goods. Till this is done he may have an insurable interest in profits, but none that can correctly be described as an interest "upon goods", nor any interest which the seller, as seller, is bound to insure for him. If the seller insures, he does so for his own purposes and of his own motion.' *Yangtsze Insurance Assocn v Lukmanjee* [1918] AC 585 at 589, PC, per Lord Sumner

United States (1) Unless otherwise agreed a term for delivery of goods 'ex-ship' (which means from the carrying vessel) or in equivalent language is not restricted to a particular ship and requires delivery from a ship which has reached a place at the named port of destination where goods of the kind are usually discharged.
(2) Under such a term unless otherwise agreed
    (a) the seller must discharge all liens arising out of the carriage and furnish the buyer with a direction which puts the carrier under a duty to deliver the goods; and
    (b) the risk of loss does not pass to the buyer until the goods leave the ship's

tackle or are otherwise properly unloaded.
(Uniform Commercial Code 1978, s 2–322)

EXAMINATION

'As the canon [canon 48 of the canon of 1603 which relates to the licensing of curates] lays down no method of examination it appears to me that "examination and admission" means "investigate and see" whether a licence should be granted.' *R v Liverpool (Bp)* (1904) 20 TLR 485 at 486, per Lord Alverstone CJ

'Prima facie one would expect that when two different words, although practically synonymous in ordinary use, are employed in different parts of the same regulation dealing with the same kind of topic, they are intended to have some different meaning. It seems to me, when I look at the pattern of reg 18, reg 19 and reg 21 [of the Docks Regulations 1934], that "examination" in those regulations is a more thorough and scientific process than "inspection" under those regulations. Indeed, "examination", like "testing" and "annealing", may require technical qualifications, as reg 21 recognises. Although something less than "examination", "inspection" is something more than a mere casual glance; I think that it involves looking carefully and critically at the gear with the naked eye, but no more than that.' *Gibson v Skibs A/S Marina* [1966] 2 All ER 476 at 478, per Cantley J

New Zealand [Section 17 of the Coroners Act 1951 (NZ), requires the coroner at an inquest to 'examine' on oath all persons who tender their evidence respecting the facts in issue, and all other persons whom he thinks it expedient to examine. Section 17(2) gives a right to persons who have a sufficient interest in the subject or the result of the inquest, to cross-examine witnesses.] 'The word "examine" which is used in s 17(1), particularly when it appears in a section which later provides that other persons may cross-examine, can, in my view, mean only one thing—namely, the process of obtaining from a witness evidence upon some matter by asking the witness the appropriate questions necessary to elicit his evidence in the form of his answers. . . . I have no doubt that it is irregular . . . for the coroner to accept as the evidence of a witness called before him a previously-prepared written statement, upon the witness after having been sworn stating that the statement contains the truth.' *Re Ford's Inquest* [1956] NZLR 805 at 809, per Shorland J

EXCAVATION   *See also* PIT

[Regulation 77 of the Building (Safety, Health and Welfare) Regulations 1948 (revoked; see now the Construction (Working Places) Regulations 1966), required that every accessible part of an 'excavation', pit or opening into the ground which an employee was liable to fall more than a specified depth should be protected.] 'It is plain that some limit must be put on those words, "excavation, pit or opening in the ground". Counsel for the plaintiff submits that any hole (again to use a neutral term) comes within the ambit of these regulations when it is a hole into which some one engaged on the work is liable to fall; he says that this man did fall; and that, accordingly, it is a hole within the ambit of that regulation. Such a hole might be anywhere on the land on which the workmen are engaged. Some limitation must be put on those words, and I think that, in the context in which they appear, they are limited to excavations, pits or openings made by the contractor in the course of his work on the site.' *Knight v Lambrick Contractors Ltd* [1956] 3 All ER 746 at 747, CA, per Parker LJ; [1957] 1 QB 562 at 565

EXCEPTION

'The rent, heriots, suit of mill, and suit of court, are the only things which, according to the legal sense and meaning of the word, are reservations. For we are of opinion, that what relates to the privilege of hawking, hunting, fishing, and fowling, is not either a reservation or an exception in point of law; and it is only a privilege or right granted to the lessor, though words of reservation and exception are used. And we think, that what relates to the wood and the underground produce is not a reservation but an exception. Lord Coke, in his commentary on Littleton, 47*a*, says, "Note a diversity between an exception (which is ever of part of the thing granted, and of a thing *in esse*), for which, *exceptis, salvo, praeter*, and the like, be apt words; and a reservation which is always of a thing not *in esse*, but newly created or reserved out of the land or tenement demised".' *Doe* d *Douglas v Lock* (1835) 2 Ad & El 705 at 743, 744, per Lord Denman CJ

'It is to be observed that a right of way cannot, in strictness, be made the subject either of exception or reservation. It is neither parcel of the thing granted, nor is it issuing out of the thing granted, the former being essential to an exception, and the latter to a reservation.'

Durham & Sunderland Rly. Co v Walker (1842) 2 QB 940 at 967, per Tindal CJ

EXCEPTIONAL

Hardship or depravity

[The Matrimonial Causes Act 1965 was repealed, and s 3 of the Matrimonial Causes Act 1973, which barred petitions for divorce within three years of marriage, provided that, by leave of a judge, a petition might be presented within the specified period in a case of exceptional hardship suffered by the petitioner or of exceptional depravity on the part of the respondent.

Now, by s 1 of the Matrimonial and Family Proceedings Act 1984, a new s 3 has been substituted in the Act of 1973, which reduces the period within which the presentation of petitions is barred to one year, and no longer makes provision for exceptional hardship or depravity cases.

Two cases below illustrate the position as it was under the original s 3.]

'Hardship is a concept with which judges are familiar in various contexts though it is often difficult to decide whether it can properly be called exceptional. A considerable degree of hardship is inevitable when a marriage breaks down in the first three years. Exceptional depravity, on the other hand, is much more difficult. The word "depravity" has fallen out of general use (it is not included in Fowler's Modern English Usage) so that it now conveys only a vague idea of very unpleasant conduct. In 1937 [date of the Matrimonial Causes Act 1937 (repealed)] it may have carried to contemporary minds a much more specific meaning, but norms of behaviour, particularly in the sexual sense, have changed greatly in the last 40 years. It is unlikely that the meaning of "depravity" and "exceptional depravity" suggested by Denning LJ in *Bowman v Bowman* [[1949] 2 All ER 127] would find much support today. In contrast, the change in the basis of divorce from the matrimonial offence to irretrievable breakdown with the expectation of relatively easy divorce may have increased the hardship involved in waiting for the specified period to elapse. . . . It is now accepted that in dealing with these applications the judge may properly take into account hardship arising from the conduct of the other spouse, present hardship, and hardship arising from having to wait until the specified period

has elapsed. In these circumstances it seems to be unnecessary in the great majority of these cases to rely on exceptional depravity with all its unpleasant overtones and difficulties.' *C v C* [1979] 1 All ER 556 at 559, 560, CA, per Ormrod LJ

'It is not possible to define with any precision what is meant by "exceptional" hardship or depravity. The imprecision of these concepts with the resultant impossibility of definition must have been deliberately accepted as appropriate by the legislature and is itself an indication that the determination of what is exceptional is essentially a matter for the judge. All that can be said with certainty is . . . that the hardship suffered by the applicant (or the respondent's depravity) must be shown to be something out of the ordinary. There must, therefore, be evidence in a hardship case of the extent of the applicant's suffering, e.g. evidence of ill-health, of nervous sensitivity or tension resulting in severe emotional or mental stress or breakdown. In particular, evidence should be given of the circumstances relied on as constituting the exceptional character of the hardship suffered.' *Fay v Fay* [1982] All ER 922 at 926, HL, per Lord Scarman

Australia 'Depravity is defined in the Shorter Oxford Dictionary as "the quality or condition of being depraved or corrupt, moral perversion", and deprave means "to make bad, to pervert, to deteriorate, to corrupt". There are other meanings given besides these but these seem to me to be the ones in point here. The words "exceptional depravity" are used with respect to conduct in an Act dealing with matrimonial offences and I think that what the section is aiming at is some exceptional breach of the accepted standards of conduct. There must be a matrimonial offence, and not only a matrimonial offence, but there must be an exceptional as opposed to an ordinary departure from accepted standards of behaviour.' *Re Washington* [1967] QWN, No 10, per Hart J

EXCESSIVE WEIGHT

[Section 23 of the Highways and Locomotives (Amendment) Act 1878 (repealed; see now the Highways Act 1980, s 59), contained provisions as to 'excessive weight' and other extraordinary traffic.] 'We have first to ascertain what is meant by "excessive weight" and "extraordinary traffic". It appears to me that those words must mean excessive and extraordinary with reference to the ordinary use and traffic upon and over the road. If anything is done of an unusual and extraordinary kind, the person doing it must pay for the damage thereby occasioned. It is the ordinary nature of the traffic over the road which is to be the standard.' *Aveland (Lord) v Lucas* (1879) 5 CPD 211 at 223, per Lindley J

EXCHANGE *See also* SALE

Australia 'The expression "exchange" when used in a will may denote one of two things, either (a) the difference in value between the currencies of the place of the testator's domicile and of the place of payment, or (b) the costs of transmission, which may be either foreign or inland exchange.' *Thompson v Wylie* (1938) 38 SRNSW 328 at 334, per Long Innes CJ in Eq

United States The term 'exchange' means any organization, association, or group of persons, whether incorporated or unincorporated, which constitutes, maintains, or provides a market place or facilities for bringing together purchasers and sellers of securities or for otherwise performing with respect to securities the functions commonly performed by a stock exchange as that term is generally understood, and includes the market place and the market facilities maintained by such exchange. (Securities Exchange Act of 1934, s 3(a)(1))

EXCISE

Australia 'In Australia a duty of excise is a tax on goods imposed at any point from and including their manufacture or production to the point of their consumption. It will be such a tax if it taxes a step in a process of bringing goods into existence or to a consumable state, or of passing them down the line which reaches from the earliest stage in production to the point of receipt by the consumer. . . . I have no doubt that to tax the receipt of the purchase price or any part of the purchase price of the sale of goods is to tax a step in the movement of goods into consumption. It is . . . a tax upon the transaction of sale itself and, to my mind, is clearly of the essential nature of a duty of excise.' *State of Western Australia v Chamberlain Industries Ltd* [1970] ALR 483 at 486, 488, per Barwick J

EXCISE DUTIES

Excise duties fall under three main headings: (1) those charged on articles or commodities produced or manufactured in the United Kingdom; (2) those charged on certain betting and gaming activities; and (3) those charged on excise licences, which are called excise licence duties. This last category includes licences for mechanically propelled vehicles, licences relating to the manufacture or production of articles or commodities, and licences relating to the carrying on of a trade, business or other activity. (12 Halsbury's Laws (4th edn) para 775)

'"Excise" is a word of vague and somewhat ambiguous meaning. . . . The word is usually (though by no means always) employed to indicate a duty imposed on home-manufactured articles in the course of manufacture before they reach the consumer. So regarded, an excise duty is plainly indirect. A further difficulty in the way of the precise application of the word is that many miscellaneous taxes, at any rate in this country, are classed as "excise" merely because they are for convenience collected through the machinery of the Board of Excise—the tax on owning a dog, for example.' *Atlantic Smoke Shops Ltd v Conlon & A-G for Canada* [1943] AC 550 at 564, 565, PC, per cur.

Australia 'The term "duties of excise" is used in several sections of the Constitution. . . . It will be noticed that whenever in the Constitution the expression "duties of excise" is used, it is used in close juxtaposition with the expression "duties of customs", as being a term relating to things of the same nature, and governed by the same rules. They are indeed in every respect analogous. . . . The conclusion is almost inevitable that . . . it is intended to mean a duty analogous to a customs duty imposed upon goods either in relation to quantity or value when produced or manufactured, and not in the sense of a direct tax or personal tax.' *Peterswald v Bartley* (1904) 1 CLR 497 at 505, 506, 509, per Griffith CJ

Australia [Section 90 of the Commonwealth Constitution [Commonwealth of Australia Constitution Act 1901–1986] provides, inter alia, that on the imposition of uniform duties of customs the power of the Parliament to impose 'duties of customs and excise', and to grant bounties on the production or export of goods, shall become exclusive.] 'If an exaction is to be classed as a duty of excise, it must, of course, be a tax. Its essential distinguishing feature is that it is a tax imposed "upon" or "in respect of" or "in relation to" goods: *Matthews v Chicory Marketing Board* [(1938) 60 CLR 263].

It would perhaps be going too far to say that it is an essential element of a duty of excise that it should be an 'indirect' tax. But a duty of excise will generally be an indirect tax, and, if a tax appears on its face to possess that character, it will generally be because it is a tax upon goods rather than a tax upon persons.' *Downs Transport Pty Ltd v Kropp* [1959] ALR 1 at 14, per cur

EXCLUSIVE LICENCE

'Exclusive licence' means a licence from a patentee which confers on the licensee, or on the licensee and persons authorised by him, to the exclusion of all other persons (including the patentee), any right in respect of the patented invention, and 'exclusive licensee' shall be construed accordingly. (Patents Act 1949, s 101)

EXCLUSIVE OCCUPATION

'I agree . . . that exclusive occupation does not mean the power of excluding everyone else from the land, but does mean the exclusive power of using the rights given him in the soil.' *Back v Daniels* [1925] 1 KB 526 at 543, CA, per Scrutton LJ

[The question was whether a contract was one to which s 2(1) of the Furnished Houses (Rent Control) Act 1946 (repealed; see now the Rent Act 1977, s 19(6)), applied because the tenant had 'exclusive occupation'.] 'Exclusive occupation means exclusive occupation as a residence, and the fact that there is reserved to the landlord a right of access from time to time does not of itself destroy that right to exclusive occupation as a residence, when the furniture and keys have been handed over by the landlord. It amounts to no more than the right of a landlord to have access for the purposes of repair, and so on.' *R v Battersea Rent Tribunal, ex p Parikh* [1957] 1 All ER 352 at 356, per Lynskey J

EXCLUSIVE USE

'In the deed of 1839 certain parcels are conveyed to Wimbush which beyond all question he takes absolutely, and then follow these important words: "Together with the exclusive use of the said gateway into Oxford Street, being 10 ft 11 in in the clear on the north side, 11 ft 7 in on the south side, in depth 41 ft 6 in and in height 15 ft, be the said several dimensions, little more or less." Now what passed in respect of this gateway? . . . I think ownership passed. The exclusive use of the said gateway was given. The exclusive or unrestricted use of a piece of land, I take it, beyond all question passes the property or ownership in that land, and there is no easement known to law which gives exclusive and unrestricted use of a piece of land. It is not an easement in such a case, it is property that passes.' *Reilly v Booth* (1890) 44 Ch D 12 at 26, 27, per Lopes LJ

EXCLUSIVELY

'The plaintiffs are an insurance company . . . and they appointed Mr Harvey what they called their supervisor. . . . Mr Harvey agrees to "act exclusively for" the plaintiffs in so far as to tender to them all risks obtained by him or under his control. . . . Now the whole difficulty arises from the introduction of the word "exclusively" into the clause which I have read, namely that the supervisor agrees to "act exclusively for" the association in so far as to tender to them all risks obtained by him or under his control. Bearing in mind that Mr Harvey is bound to do the best he can under that clause for the plaintiffs, what does it mean? Does it mean that he is to do more than send to the plaintiffs such life assurance risks as he can procure for them? Supposing that a person goes to him and asks him to send on a risk to a totally different company, and Mr Harvey, acting bona fide, says, "I am the agent for the Mutual Reserve Association, give me a risk for them". . . . I should say on the true construction of this contract, that he is bound to do that. Supposing, however, a person says "No, I will not have anything to do with that company", there is nothing whatever in the contract, under those circumstances, to prevent Mr Harvey from sending the risk on to somebody else, for this simple reason that in the case I put the risk would not be risk "obtained by him, or under his control", such as is contemplated by the contract.' *Mutual Reserve Fund Life Assocn v New York Life Insurance Co & Harvey* (1896) 75 LT 528 at 530, CA, per Lindley LJ

[Sections 7 and 74 of the Elementary Education Act 1870 (repealed; see now s 39(2)(b) of the Education Act 1944), provided in effect that a child should not be required to attend school on any day 'exclusively set apart for religious observance' by the religious body to which his parent belonged.] 'The words "exclusively set apart for religious observance" do not mean that all other things than religious practice should be excluded on the days indicated as holy days, but only that such things should be excluded as the rules of the particular religious body require to be excluded, and for as long a time as those rules require. The words "set apart" would in my opinion suffice, and the phrase "exclusively set apart" is merely an instance of emphasis in the not uncommon guise of repetition.' *Marshall v Graham, Bell v Graham* [1907] 2 KB 112 at 124, per Darling J

EXCOMMUNICATION

'Excommunication, in the meaning of the law of the English Church, is not merely an expulsion from the Church of England, but from the Christian Church generally. The ecclesiastical law excommunicates papists. The ecclesiastical law excommunicates Presbyterians. Dissenters of all descriptions from the Church of England are liable to excommunication. But what is meant by the Church of England by the term of excommunication can be best explained by the articles of that church. By the 33rd article it is expressly stated, "That person which by open denunciation of the church is rightly cut off from the unity of the church and excommunicated ought to be taken of the whole multitude of the faithful as an heathen and publican until he be openly reconciled by penance, and received into the church by a judge that hath authority thereunto": that is, he is no longer to be considered as a Christian, no longer to be considered as a member of the Christian Church universal, but he is to be considered "as an heathen and a publican", for those are the words of the article.' *Kemp v Wickes* (1809) 3 Phillim 264 at 271, 272, per Sir John Nicholl

EXCURSION   *See* SHIP

EXECUTE

'Executed' and 'execution', with reference to instruments not under seal, mean signed and signature. (Stamp Act 1891, s 122(1))

Australia [Section 12(2) of the Wills Act 1936–1986 (SA) provides that a document purporting to embody the testamentary intentions of a deceased person shall, notwithstanding that it has not been executed with the formalities required by this Act, be deemed to be a will of the deceased person if the Supreme Court . . . is satisfied that there can be no reasonable doubt that the deceased intended the document to constitute his will.] 'I am unable to agree with the contention that the words "has not been executed with the formalities required by this Act" imply that there must be a signature to the document. I think that the relevant meaning of the word "execute" is the third meaning given in the English Oxford Dictionary (1961), namely "to go through the formalities necessary to the validity of (a legal act, e.g. a bequest, agreement, mortgage etc). Hence to complete and give validity to (the instrument by which such act is effected) by performing what the law requires to be done, as by signing sealing etc." To execute a document is to do what the law requires to be done to give validity to the document. Section 8 sets out the legal requirements or formalities for execution of a will. If those formalities are not complied with, there is no execution. Execution and signature are, of course, not synonymous. Execution is the validation of a document by going through the formalities required by law for that purpose. Signature is simply one of the formalities required by the Act for valid execution.' *In the Estate of Williams, Deceased* (1984) 36 SASR 423 at 425, per King CJ

EXECUTED CONTRACT   *See* CONTRACT

EXECUTED OR EXECUTORY TRUST   *See* TRUST

EXECUTION

The word 'execution' in its widest sense signifies the enforcement of or giving effect to the judgments or orders of courts of justice. In a narrower sense, it means the enforcement of those judgments or orders by a public officer under the writs of fieri facias, elegit, capias, sequestration, attachment, possession, delivery, fieri facias de bonis ecclesiasticis, etc. (17 Halsbury's Laws (4th edn) para 401)

'The first point raised is as to the meaning of the words "taken in execution", and it seems to me that the obvious meaning of the words is that when a sheriff goes into possession on a writ of *fi. fa.* the goods that he seizes are taken in execution.' *Marylebone Vestry v London (Sheriff)* [1900] 2 QB 591 at 594, CA, per Smith LJ

'To my mind, "to proceed to execution on", or "to proceed to the enforcement of", a judgment is only a way of saying "to execute" or "to enforce", that is, to go to the length of executing, or to go to the length of enforcement, and I do not think that normally anyone, whether a lawyer or a layman, would say that a party who applies for an order for the examination of the judgment debtor as to means is executing or enforcing the judgment.' *Fagot v Gaches* [1943] 1 KB 10 at 12, CA, per du Parcq LJ

'The word "execution" is not defined in the Act [Administration of Justice Act 1956]. It is, of course, a word familiar to lawyers. "Execution" means, quite simply, the process for enforcing or giving effect to the judgment of the court: and it is "completed" when the judgment creditor gets the money or other thing awarded to him by the judgment. That this is the meaning is seen by reference to that valuable old book Termes de la Ley, where it is said: "*Execution* is, where judgment is given in any action, that the plaintiff shall recover the land, debt, or damages, as the case is; and when any writ is awarded to put him in possession, *or to do any other thing whereby the plaintiff should the better be satisfied his debt or damages*, that is called a writ of *execution*; and when he hath the possession of the land or is paid the debtor damages, or hath the body of the defendant awarded to prison, then he hath *execution*". The same meaning is to be found in *Blackman v Fysh* [[1892] 3 Ch 209], when Kekewich J said that execution means the "process of law for the enforcement of a judgment creditor's right and in order to give effect to that right". In cases when execution was had by means of a common law writ, such as *fieri facias* or elegit, it was *legal* execution: when it was had by means of an equitable remedy, such as the appointment of a receiver, then it was *equitable* execution. In either case it was "execution" because it was the process for enforcing or giving effect to the judgment of the court.' *Re Overseas Aviation Engineering (GB) Ltd* [1962] 3 All ER 12 at 16, CA, per Lord Denning MR; also reported in [1963] Ch 24 at 39

Canada 'Execution is the enforcement of a judgment. In Coke Upon Littleton, 17th edn, vol 1, p 154a, it is said: "Execution signifieth in law the obtaining of actuall possession of anything required by judgment of law, or by a fine executory levied, whether it be by the sherife or by the entry of the party". . . . Execution is aptly described as "putting the sentence of the law into force". The means of putting the

sentence in force must necessarily vary with the nature of the subject-matter.' *Thakar Singh v Pram Singh* [1942] 1 WWR 737 at 750, 751, BCCA, per O'Halloran JA

Irregular or wrongful

An execution is wrongful when it is neither authorised nor justified by the writ of execution or by the judgment under which it is issued; or where the writ is issued maliciously and without reasonable or probable cause; or when unfair means, such as the procuring of a search warrant, are used to enable the bailiff to enter into the premises of the execution debtor. (17 Halsbury's Laws (4th edn) para 457)

An execution is irregular where any of the requirements of the rules of court have not been complied with, and the proceedings may be set aside or amended or otherwise dealt with in such manner and upon such terms as the Court thinks fit. (17 Halsbury's Laws (4th edn) para 459)

Of deed or will

'The deed [of settlement of a joint stock company] itself requires that the persons who should become such shareholders should not only seal and deliver, but subscribe the deed. The words are, "whose names and seals should be thereunto subscribed, and who had sealed and delivered, or who might from time to time seal and deliver the same". . . . It is contended that the allegation in the latter part of the declaration [which recited the deed of settlement] "that whilst the defendant was such shareholder and proprietor of 200 shares in the capital of the said company, and after the execution by the defendant of the said indenture or deed of settlement as aforesaid", does not imply either that the defendant sealed or subscribed his name to that instrument. . . . Now "executed" is a very general word. "Executed as aforesaid" must mean executed with all the formalities necessary to the completion of the deed.' *Sutherland v Wills, Murray v Wills* (1850) 5 Exch 715 at 717, 718, per Patteson J

'Counsel for the Crown is perfectly correct in his submission that execution of a deed is a process rather than a single matter at a single instant of time. It consists of signature, sealing and delivery unconditionally. Obviously, a live grantor must sign and seal; but he may entrust the resultant document to others (including his personal representatives) to deliver unconditionally. And if he has himself first delivered it conditionally, then he may not himself withhold, nor can his personal representatives on his behalf withhold, the unconditional delivery to the grantee if the condition is fulfilled. It matters not by whose hand that unconditional delivery may take place.' *Terrapin International Ltd v Inland Revenue Comrs* [1976] 2 All ER 461 at 466, per Walton J

Australia 'In the Shorter Oxford Dictionary "execution" is defined as "the due performance of all formalities, as signing, sealing, etc, necessary to give validity to a legal transaction"; while the word "execute" is defined in a precisely corresponding way as "to go through the formalities necessary to the validity of. Hence to complete and give validity to, as by signing, sealing, etc." I think that the words "executed" and "execution" where used in s 12 of the [Money Lenders] Ordinance [1936] (ACT); repealed, see now Credit Ordinance 1985] are to be taken generally as relating to documents which lack nothing, whether, for example, signing, sealing, dating or filling up of blanks left, to make them physically complete.' *J & S Holdings Pty Ltd v NRMA Insurance Ltd* (1981) 57 FLR 385 at 401, per Kelly J

EXECUTOR

An executor is the person appointed, ordinarily by the testator by his will or codicil, to administer the testator's property and to carry into effect the provisions of the will. A special executor may be appointed or is deemed to be appointed in regard to settled land.

An executor de son tort is one who takes upon himself the office of an executor, or intermeddles with the goods of a deceased person, without having been appointed an executor by the testator's last valid will or by a codicil to that will, or without having obtained a grant of administration from a competent court; and the term is thus equally applicable in the case of an intestacy as in the case of testacy for there is no such term known to the law as an administrator de son tort. (17 Halsbury's Laws (4th edn) para 702)

Executor de son tort

Canada 'An executor *de son tort* is one who takes upon himself the office of executor by intrusion, not being so constituted by the deceased and in the absence of that constitution not being substituted by competent authority to act as administrator. . . . An act of intermeddling with a deceased's assets makes a person an executor *de son tort*.' *Blinkoff (J N) v Minister of National Revenue* [1973] CTC 636 at 673, Fed Ct, per Cattanach J; affd (sub nom *Henderson v Minister of National Revenue* [1975] CTC 485, Fed CA

Executorship expenses

'I cannot distinguish between "executorship expenses" and "testamentary expenses". It seems to me the words "executorship expenses" amount to this: they are expenses incident to the proper performance of the duty of the executor in the same way as testamentary expenses are, neither more or less. Now what is the proper performance of that duty? It is to ascertain the debts and liabilities due from the testator's estate, to pay such debts and liabilities, and to attend to the legal and proper distribution between the persons entitled. It has been decided that if the executor is unable to decide these questions for himself, he may obtain the assistance of a Court of Equity to decide them for him, and the costs occasioned by a suit instituted by him for that purpose will be allowed him, that is, not only his own costs, but the costs of the other parties to the suit. Again it has been held that it makes no difference as regards the costs, that instead of the executor coming as plaintiff to ask for the direction of the Court, one of the beneficiaries comes and asks for the same direction in a proper case. In that case also the administration costs, that is, the costs of the suit, are borne in the same way as if the executor himself had paid them. That being so, where a testator directs "executorship expenses" to be paid out of a given fund, he does, in my opinion, include the expenses of the distribution of the fund whether incurred in an administration suit, or simply by taking the advice of a solicitor and a counsel outside the administration suit.' *Sharp v Lush* (1879) 48 LJ Ch 231 at 232, per Jessel MR

EXECUTORY CONTRACT   *See* CONTRACT

EXEMPLARY DAMAGES   *See* DAMAGES

EXEMPT

[By a private Act, the defendant company was enabled to make a canal from Leeds to Liverpool, and to charge tolls which should be 'exempt' from the payment of any taxes, rates, assessments, or impositions whatsoever.] 'The word *exempt* may be taken to mean precluded from being chargeable. The meaning of the clause of exemption was, that the land or space occupied by the canal should be liable to be taxed, as it was before, that is as the land was before: but the tolls were not rated before, for they had no existence; and therefore are exempted.' *R v Leeds & Liverpool Canal Co* (1804) 5 East 325 at 331, per Lord Ellenborough CJ

New Zealand 'In my opinion, the Solicitor-General is right in his submission that income cannot be said to be "exempt from taxation" within the meaning of that expression in sub-s (2) of s 149 [of the Land and Income Tax Act 1954 (NZ)] unless that income would, but for an exemption, be subject to taxation in New Zealand.' *Australian Mutual Provident Society v Comr of Internal Revenue* [1961] NZLR 497 at 500, 501, per Barrowclough CJ; affd, [1962] NZLR 449, PC

EXEMPTION

Australia '"Non-liability" and "exemption" are different concepts: the first connotes that the subject was never in the tax net, while the latter connotes that it was, but has been permitted to escape.' *Re Sharpe, Queensland Trustees Ltd v Comr of Stamp Duties* [1944] St R Qd 26 at 33, per Philp J

EXERCISE

Of invention

'It is said . . . that he [the defendant in an action for infringement of patent] has "exercised" the invention within the jurisdiction. It is remarkable that this word, which has been found in letters patent at least since 1621, so far as I am aware, has never been construed. I think, however, that it can only mean "put in practice".' *Saccharin Corpn v Reitmeyer & Co* (1900) 69 LJ Ch 761 at 763, per Cozens-Hardy J

Of trade

'The question whether a trade is exercised in the United Kingdom [within the Income Tax Acts] is a question of fact, and it is undesirable to attempt to lay down any exhaustive test of what constitutes such an exercise of trade; but I think it must now be taken as established that in the case of a merchant's business, the primary object of which is to sell goods at a profit, the trade is (speaking generally) exercised or carried on (I do not myself see much difference between the two expressions) at the place where the contracts are made. No doubt reference has sometimes been made to the place where payment is made for the goods sold or to the place where the goods are delivered, and it may be that in certain circumstances these are material considerations; but the most important, and indeed the crucial, question is, where are the contracts of sale made?' *Maclaine & Co v Eccott* [1926] AC 424 at 432, per Lord Cave LC

EXHIBIT—EXHIBITION

[Section 1 of the Cinematograph Act 1909 (repealed; see now the Cinemas Act 1985, s 1), makes provision against the 'exhibition' of pictures by a cinematograph apparatus except in licensed premises.] 'There must be some limitation put upon the word "exhibition". . . . It cannot possibly be held to include every occasion on which a film is run through a cinematograph machine. I think that I ought to construe the Act as referring to places of public entertainment where an exhibition of a cinematograph picture takes place, and that I ought not to construe it as including a case where a dealer . . . bona fide, in the exercise of his trade of selling and renting, for this purpose only, runs his films through his machine, in the presence of one or more customers.' *A-G v Vitagraph Co Ltd* [1915] 1 Ch 206 at 213, per Astbury J

'By reg. 5 of the Shops Regulations 1934, the notice had to "be kept constantly exhibited". I see no escape from the conclusion that, when the statute and that regulation said that the form was to be exhibited, they were using "exhibited" in the ordinary sense of that word. I think it impossible to hold that a form was exhibited which was included with a number of other forms in a folder and hung up behind a door in circumstances in which it could not be seen or read without opening the folder, and when the form had to be found amongst other forms in order that it might be read.' *Tinn v Cunningham* (1938) 82 Sol Jo 435 at 435, 436, DC, per Branson J

[The appellants operated an amusement arcade where coin-operated video games were played. The licensing authority took the view that the premises required to be licensed under the Cinematograph Act 1909, s 1(1) (repealed; see supra) on the grounds that video games constituted a cinematograph exhibition.] 'The section, as amended, now includes cinematograph exhibitions however they are produced with the exception of simultaneous reproduction of television programmes. But I can attach no different meaning to "cinematograph exhibition" to that which, in my view, it clearly bears in the earlier Acts, namely a film show. Video games were not within the purview of the 1909 and 1952 Acts for the simple reason that they had not been invented. If it had been the intention to bring these games within the 1982 Act, which involve an activity on the part of the player so utterly different in kind to the passive participation of a cinema audience, I should have expected a clearer indication than the alteration of the definition of a "cinematograph exhibition" necessitated by the need to keep the Acts abreast of modern technology.

The crucial words are: "In this Act 'cinematograph exhibition' means any exhibition of moving pictures . . ." The judge and the majority of the Court of Appeal accepted the argument that because the screen of a video game displays moving objects there was therefore an exhibition of moving pictures within the meaning of the Act. . . . This approach fails in my opinion to take into account the different shades of meaning attached in the English language to the use of the word "exhibition" according to the context in which it is used and, in particular, fails to give sufficient weight to the primary dictionary meaning of "exhibit": "*esp.* to show publicly for the purpose of amusement or instruction . . ." It is true that the 1982 Act now covers exhibitions for private gain (in order to catch the pornographic cinema clubs) but reading the Act as a whole and the regulations made thereunder, I have no doubt that exhibition is used in the sense of a show to an audience and not in the sense of a display of moving objects on the screen of a video game.' *BACTA v Westminster City Council* [1988] 1 All ER 740 at 744–745, HL, per Lord Griffiths

[The term used in the Cinemas Act 1985 is 'film exhibition', but the definition (s 21) is in substantially the same terms as that for 'cinematograph exhibition'.]

New Zealand 'In my opinion, "exhibits" in s 21(1)(f) [of the Indecent Publications Act 1963] is used in its ordinary meaning and, as such, does not include "plays" [in relation to an indecent tape recording].' *Harris v Police* [1966] NZLR 153 at 154, per Wilson J

Indecent publications

New Zealand [Once the Indecent Publications Tribunal has classified a book as indecent in the hands of persons under a certain age, s 21(1)(f) then makes it an offence to sell, deliver, 'exhibit' or offer the book to persons within that category.] 'In this context, the meaning of "exhibit" is directed at the positive act of bringing the work in question to the attention of others. It is not limited to cases where one person physically presents the work to another for the latter's perusal. It covers the common situation where the action taken has a continuing effect; where it brings the work to the attention of anyone who at any time comes to the place where it is displayed. The very purpose of a bookseller in putting books face up on a table in his shop is to draw them to the attention of persons coming into that part of the premises. The bookseller's action is designed to encourage people to examine the books and, having done that, to buy them. Whether or not individual customers pick up the books to examine them, the effect of displaying the books in that manner is to bring them to the notice of customers. Any book exposed to view in that way is exhibited to all members of the public, including those within the restricted age group, who come in the ordinary course to that point in the shop. When a bookseller places books upon a display table in a shop for the public to see he exhibits those books to those who come there just as a painter, who hangs his canvas upon a wall in a gallery to which the public are invited, exhibits his painting.' *London Bookshop in Kirkcaldies Ltd v Police* [1980] 1 NZLR 292 at 296, per McMullin J

EXONERATION

If the property of a married woman is mortgaged or charged in order to raise money for the payment of her husband's debts, or otherwise for his benefit, it is presumed, in the absence of evidence showing an intention to the contrary, that she meant to charge her property merely by way of security, and in such case she is in the position of surety, and is entitled to be indemnified by her husband, and to throw the debt primarily on his estate to the exoneration of her own.

The right to exoneration is, however, a presumptive right only; it depends on the intention of the parties to be ascertained from all the circumstances of each particular case. It may be rebutted by evidence showing that the wife intended to make a gift of the property to her husband, and it has been held to be rebutted where the money was raised to pay debts which, though legally the husband's, had been contracted by reason of the extravagant mode of living of both parties.

No presumption of a right to exoneration arises where the money is raised to discharge the wife's debts or obligations, or otherwise for her benefit; and where the mortgage of the wife's estate is contemporaneous with a settlement of it, the whole will be presumed to be one transaction, so as to exclude her claim to indemnity, especially if the money is raised for the purpose of discharging any of the wife's debts or charges on the estate, even though more money has been raised than is necessary for that purpose. A wife's equity of exoneration is waived and barred if she disclaims her right, and her husband's executors pay legacies on the faith of the disclaimer. (22 Halsbury's Laws (4th edn) para 1071)

EXPECT

'The question is simply, what do the words "expected ready to load" by a certain date, mean? Counsel for the respondents has suggested three possible meanings: (1) That the vessel was, in fact at the time, in such a position that any ordinary man who knew her position would expect her to be ready to load at the date given; in other words, it meant "so situated that she will be ready to load by that date". (2) "Expected" means expected by the seller, and does not mean expected by the shipping world generally. (3) That the sellers honestly, though without grounds, expect that the vessel will be in the River Plate at the time indicated. It is difficult to see how the third meaning differs much from the second, for an honest expectation could hardly be formed without some grounds upon which it could be based, and an ordinary man would read "expected" as meaning expected by the person putting that clause in. In my view, the second suggested meaning is the correct one, namely, that in view of the facts known to the sellers at the time, the expectation was one which they ought to have held honestly and on reasonable grounds.' *Sandy & Co v Keighley Maxted & Co* (1922) 91 LJKB 624 at 624, 625, CA, per Sterndale MR

[The Solicitors Act 1932, s 47(1) (repealed; see now the Solicitors Act 1974, s 22(1)) provided that any person other than a barrister or solicitor who prepared a legal instrument was liable to a fine unless he proved that it was not done for or in the 'expectation' of a fee, etc.]

'We think . . . that the section provides that the act must not be done for or in expectation of any fee, gain or reward, and that the word "expectation" clearly indicates that there need be no legal right to recover, but merely an expectation or hope that some reward will be forthcoming as a result of the action taken.' *Pacey v Atkinson* [1950] 1 KB 539 at 543, per Lord Goddard CJ

Canada 'The meaning of the words "expected ready to load" [in a charterparty] by a given date has been explained by the Courts on several occasions. . . . The words mean, as has been said by the learned editors of Scrutton on Charter-parties (14th edn) at p 95, that in view of the facts known to the promisor when making his contract he honestly expects that the vessel will be ready as stated, and that his expectation is based on reasonable grounds. The promise is broken if either he does not honestly expect it, or he has not reasonable grounds for his expectations. The words are not a mere representation but a contractual statement, part of the contract between the parties. The statement amounts to a condition precedent to obligations under the charter: *Corkling v Massey* (1873) [LR 8 CP 395, 42 LJCP 153]. The fact that failure to comply with such a condition precedent results from perils excepted in the charter will not prevent its being a breach of such condition precedent so as to entitle the charterers to cancel, though the exception may protect the owner from a claim for damages.' *Re Empire Shipping Co Ltd & Hall Bryan Ltd* [1940] 1 WWR 97 at 102, BCSC, per Manson J

EXPECTANCY   *See also* INTEREST IN   EXPECTANCY

'The title of the Act [Infant Settlements Act 1855] is "An Act to enable infants, with the approbation of the Court of Chancery, to make binding settlements of their real and personal estate on marriage." Then this object is worked out by s 1 thus: "It shall be lawful for every infant upon or in contemplation of his or her marriage, with the sanction of the Court of Chancery, to make a binding settlement . . . of all or any part of his or her property, or property over which he or she has any power of appointment, whether real or personal, and whether in possession . . . or expectancy". . . . These words are very large. . . . The Act is not addressed only to property of the infant. It applies also to property over which the infant "has any power of appointment", and those words expressly cover that which is not the infant's own property. . . . In the passage which Mr Justice Kay in *Re Parsons* [(1890) 45 Ch D 51 at 57] quoted from Watkins on Conveyancing [8th edn, p 219] the word "expectancy" is expressly applied to such an interest as that which is now in question— *viz*, "the hope of inheritance entertained by the heir".' *Re Johnson, Moore v Johnson* [1891] 3 Ch 43 at 51–53, per North J

EXPECTATION OF LIFE

Loss of *See* LOSS

EXPEDIENT

'Section 57 of the Trustee Act [1925] . . . is undoubtedly framed in very wide terms. . . . It is: "Where in the management or administration of any property vested in trustees, any sale, lease, mortgage, surrender, release, or other disposition, or any purchase, investment, acquisition, expenditure, or other transaction". Pausing there for a moment, to come within the section the matter must be one which arises in the management or administration of property vested in trustees; but so long as the matter does so arise, there is nothing in those words which limits the power of the Court under the section. Then the section goes on: "is in the opinion of the Court expedient, but the same cannot be effected by reason of the absence of any power for that purpose", etc., the Court may authorise it to be done. The word "expedient" there quite clearly must mean expedient for the trust as a whole. It cannot mean that however expedient it may be for one beneficiary if it is inexpedient from the point of view of the other beneficiaries concerned the Court ought to sanction the transaction. In order that the matter may be one which is in the opinion of the Court expedient, it must be expedient for the trust as a whole.' *Re Craven's Estate, Lloyds Bank Ltd v Cockburn (No 2)* [1937] Ch 431 at 436, per. Farwell J

Australia [Under s 81 of the Trustee Act 1925–1986 (NSW), the Court may, if satisfied that it is 'expedient' in the interest of the trust property as a whole so to do, confer certain powers upon the trustees where neither the trust instrument nor the Act confers the power.] 'If a literal construction yields a literal result, you must interpret literally. So all you have to do is to see whether a proposed course is "expedient", that is, likely to be for the financial advantage of the trust fund, and, if you find it is "expedient" in that sense, give authority for the proposed course.' *Riddle v Riddle* (1952) 85 CLR 202 at 227, per Fullagar J

EXPEDITE

Australia 'The adjective "expeditious" and the corresponding verb "expedite" have received, in common parlance and in realms of power where jungle English (I acknowledge A P Herbert as the originator of that expression) is preferred to the Queen's English, a meaning that implies a hastening, or a speeding of the progress, of something. Its true and primary meaning, however, still derives from its Latin origin *expedire* (which itself is compounded of the ingredients *ex* and *pes (pedis)*). The primary meaning of that verb is to free one caught by a foot (as in a snare). It is easy to see how the secondary meaning came to be attributed to it. "Expedite", therefore, truly and primarily means in English to clear something of difficulties, thus helping forward or hastening the progress of it; and the word "expeditious" ought to be given a corresponding meaning.' *Director of Planning v Uren* (1976) 40 LGRA 70 at 76, per Wells J

EXPENDITURE

[A house owner having improved his property by his own labour claimed an allowance for 'expenditure' wholly and exclusively incurred by him on the property within the Finance Act 1965, Sch 6, para 4(1)(6).] 'It seems to me that, although one does in general terms talk about expenditure of time and expenditure of effort, having regard particularly to the opening words of para 4(1), where the expenditure is to be "a deduction", the primary matter which is thought of by the legislature in para 4(1)(b) is something which is passing out from the person who is making the expenditure. That will most normally and naturally be money, accordingly presenting no problems in calculation; but that will not necessarily be the case. I instance the case . . . of the taxpayer employing a bricklayer to do some casual bricklaying about the premises, the remuneration for the bricklayer being three bottles of whisky at the end of the week. It seems to me that that would be expenditure by the taxpayer, because out of his stock he would have to give something away to the person who was laying the bricks, and I do not think that that would present any real problems of valuation or other difficulty. But when one comes on to his own labour, it does not seem to me that that is really capable of being quantified in this sort of way. It is not something which diminishes his stock of anything by any precisely ascertainable amount; it is something which would have to be estimated. It has been estimated here by taking the very modest sum of £1 an hour, but the fact that the taxpayer has been modest in his demands does not enable one to escape from the crucial crunch, which is how, in a case which was contested and where the amount claimed was something which was larger than was obviously right, one would test it. It seems to me that there would undoubtedly have to be found in the end some machinery for translating into money terms the work put in by the owner of the asset himself, if that was to be allowable. But it seems to me that does not fall into the ordinary meaning of "the amount of any expenditure wholly and exclusively incurred on the asset by him or on his behalf". The wording, to my mind, just does not fit that sort of situation. It is perhaps a matter of first impression that the word "expenditure" makes on one, but I think that the whole group of words, "expenditure", "expended", "expenses" and so on and so forth, in a revenue context, mean primarily money expenditure and, secondly, expenditure, in money's worth, something which diminishes the total assets of the person making the expenditure, and I do not think that one can bring one's own work, however skilful it may be and however much sweat one may expend on it, within the scope of para 4(1)(b).' *Oram (Inspector of Taxes) v Johnson* [1980] 2 All ER 1 at 5, 6, per Walton J

EXPENSES

'What do you "expend"? You "expend" that which you have. A man cannot spend what he has not got—he can mortgage or pledge, but he cannot actually spend.' *Re Bristol's (Marquis) Settled Estates* [1893] 3 Ch 161 at 166, per Kekewich J

'In England "expenses" is not a term of art; it is a vague and general term. . . . This difficulty would have been avoided if the referee . . . had used the word "costs" instead of "expenses" because an award of an arbitrator

awarding costs is not bad merely because he does not fix the amount. . . . I have before me an order of a referee ordering payment of expenses of unascertained amount. I cannot make the amount certain through the taxing officers of this Court. Therefore the decision of the referee is bad on this point because it does not assess the amount of the expenses, and the amount of expenses cannot be assessed by a taxing master taxing costs.' *Simpson v Inland Revenue Comrs* [1914] 2 KB 842 at 845, 846, per Scrutton J

'In the case of a debt owing to the deceased it is plain that its extinguishment would not involve the deceased in any "expense" in the sense of paying out money. Nevertheless such extinguishment would rightly be described as having been effected at his expense, in that by extinguishing the debt he deprived himself of his right to recover it.' *Re Stratton's Deed of Disclaimer, Stratton v Inland Revenue Comrs* [1957] 2 All ER 594 at 600, CA, per Jenkins LJ; also reported in [1958] Ch 42

[A testatrix left the residue of her estate to certain persons after all her debts, and funeral, and 'expenses' were paid.] 'I have to deal with the words which I find, and as "expenses" (in the context) are something other than funeral expenses, then I cannot see why I should limit them more than would be the natural course in any ordinary will. It seems to me that "expenses" must include not only testamentary expenses (which by reason of the rules which have been adopted in regard to wills, would include estate duty payable out of the general estate), but also would include the expenses of administration of the testatrix' estate.' *Re Berrey's Will Trusts, Greening v Warner* [1959] 1 All ER 15 at 17, per Danckwerts J

Capital expenditure   *See* CAPITAL

Election, of   *See* ELECTION EXPENSES

Executorship   *See* EXECUTOR

Indemnification of director of corporation

United States   'Expenses' include counsel fees (Revised Model Business Corporation Act 1984, s 8.50(3))

Personal expenses

'Personal expenses' as used with respect to the expenditure of any candidate in relation to any election includes the reasonable travelling expenses of the candidate, and the reasonable expenses of his living at hotels or elsewhere for the purposes of and in relation to the election. (Representation of the People Act 1983, s 118)

EXPERT

The expression 'expert' . . . includes engineer, valuer, accountant and any other person whose profession gives authority to a statement made by him. (Companies Act 1985, s 62)

EXPERT WITNESS   *See* WITNESS

EXPIRE

'The primary meaning of "expiry" of a right prestable for a tract of time is the passing of that term. It is only in a secondary sense that the word could be used to denote the extinction of a right through the voluntary action of the person entitled to the right. Few people would say "my tenancy of the cottage expired" if what really happened was that the tenancy was given up.' *Middleton's Trustees v Middleton* 1955 SLT 68 at 72, 73, per Lord Patrick

Australia 'Probably all that one can say is that the time of the expiry of a lease may mean the date on which the term granted will come to an end, or it may mean the date when the relationship of landlord and tenant under the lease is otherwise determined. It depends upon the context.' *A'Beckett v Federal Comr of Taxation* (1959) 104 CLR 508 at 515, per Windeyer J

EXPIRY

At the expiration

New Zealand   [A lease for ten years provided that the rental payable under the terms thereof should be subject to review 'at the expiration' of five years from the commencement of the term.] 'In my view, the sensible interpretation of the words "at the expiration" is to say that they do not mean "contemporaneous with the expiration" but "within a reasonable time of the expiration of the period fixed".' *Aetna Life of Australia & New Zealand Ltd v Grace Bros Ltd* [1975] 2 NZLR 577 at 579, per McMullin J

EXPLANATION

Australia   [An amendment to a specification must be, inter alia, in the nature of an explanation.] 'I think that the term "explanation" includes any information as to any matters which the persons to whom the specification is deemed to be addressed already know, but which may not be possessed by other persons not so familiar with the subject . . . it certainly enlarges the number of persons who can understand it when it is presented to them, and I think that is a very reasonable meaning of the word "explanation".' *Minerals Separation Ltd v Potter's Sulphide Ore Treatment Ltd* (1909) 8 CLR 779 at 793, per Griffith CJ

EXPLOIT

Canada   [A definition of offence of obscenity included undue 'exploitation' of sex.] 'I consider the significance of the word "exploit" to be that sex is used for a purpose other than that for which it may be said to be primarily intended, namely, procreation or mutual solace and comfort between the sexes, those for which it is by nature designed. There is no doubt that in our society today sex is used for many additional purposes, from the selling of consumer goods to the entertainment of the public, and I believe it is in this sense that the word "exploit" is to be understood.' *R v O'Reilly* (1970) 13 DLR (3d) 257 at 269, Ont Co Ct, per Lyon Co Ct J

EXPLORATION

Canada   '"Exploration", in general terms, is the operation of testing for the existence and the extent of an ore body and includes prospecting. In relation to asbestos, I take it that, for the purpose of this definition, "ore body" means an area of rock containing veins of asbestos in such quantity and of such quality as to make the removal of the rock containing the asbestos a commercially feasible proposition.' *Johnson's Asbestos Corpn v Minister of National Revenue* [1965] CTC 165 at 169, 170, Ex Ct, per Jackett P

EXPLOSION

Insurance policy

New Zealand   [The plaintiff sought to recover from the defendant insurance company for loss arising from damage to a cement silo. As a result of air being pumped into the unventilated silo the roof had lifted causing distortion. The issue was whether the pumping of air in this manner could amount to an 'explosion'.] 'A consistent synonym for explode is burst, accompanied by noise. The bursting can and usually does result from development of internal pressure. I think it is fair to acknowledge that in the natural and ordinary meaning of explosion one would expect it to be accompanied by noise. I think the noise sufficient to satisfy this element must be clearly audible within a reasonable range for a listener. The tonal quality of the noise I do not think important.' *Golden Bay Cement Co Ltd v South British Insurance Co Ltd* [1980] 1 NZLR 348 at 352, 353, per Jeffries J

EXPLOSIVE

'Explosive' in this Act—
(1) Means gunpowder, nitro-glycerine, dynamite, gun-cotton, blasting powders, fulminate of mercury or of other metals, coloured fires, and every other substance, whether similar to those above mentioned or not, used or manufactured with a view to produce a practical effect by explosion or a pyrotechnic effect; and
(2) Includes fog-signals, fireworks, fuzes, rockets, percussion caps, detonators, cartridges, ammunition of all descriptions, and every adaptation or preparation of an explosive as above defined.
(Explosives Act 1875, s 3)

[The above general definition of 'explosives' must be read in conjunction with Orders in Council classifying and defining explosives and the list of authorised explosives periodically issued by HM Stationery Office.]

The expression 'explosive substance' shall be deemed to include any materials for making any explosive substance; also any apparatus, machine, implement, or materials used, or intended to be used, or adapted for causing, or aiding in causing, any explosion in or with any explosive substance; also any part of any such apparatus, machine, or implement. (Explosive Substances Act 1883, s 9)

'Explosive' means any article manufactured for the purpose of producing a practical effect by explosion, or intended by the person having it with him for that purpose. (Theft Act 1968, s 10(1)(c))
[Under s 10, a person is guilty of aggravated burglary if he commits any burglary and at the same time has with him any firearm or imitation firearm, any weapon of offence, or any explosive.]

'Explosive' means any article manufactured for the purpose of producing a practical effect, by explosion, or intended for that purpose by a person having the article with him. (Aviation Security Act 1982, s 38(1))

EXPORT

'The question is, whether the goods laden on board this ship, having broken ground in the Thames, and not having left the port of London, may be said to have been exported. I am of opinion that the goods shipped could not be considered as exported until the ship had cleared the limits of the ports.' *A-G v Pougett* (1816) 2 Price 381 at 393, 394, per Wood B

'There is nothing in the language of the Act [Tyne Coal Dues Act 1872] to shew that the word "exported" was used in any other than its ordinary sense, namely, "carried out of the port". . . . We feel bound to hold that coals carried away from the port, not on a temporary excursion, as in a tug or pleasure boat, which intends to return with more or less of the coals on board, and which may be regarded as always constructively within the port, but taken away for the purpose of being wholly consumed beyond the limits of the port, are coals "exported" within the meaning of the Act.' *Muller v Baldwin* (1874) LR 9 QB 457 at 461, per cur.

EXPORTER

'Exporter', in relation to goods for exportation or for use as stores, includes the shipper of the goods and any person performing in relation to an aircraft functions corresponding to those of a shipper. (Customs and Excise Management Act 1979, s 1(1))

EXPOSE

'There is no magic about the word "exposed" [in the Coal Mines Act 1911, s 55 (repealed; see now s 82(1) of the Mines and Quarries Act 1954)] and I am not going to define it. The word speaks for itself. . . . "Exposed" is not limited in its effect; "exposed" means "at all exposed".' *Carey v Ocean Coal Co Ltd, Carey v Richards, Carey v Rees* [1938] 1 KB 365 at 373, per Lord Hewart CJ

EXPOSE FOR SALE

'I think the words "exposed for sale" mean exposed to view in the shop in the sight of the purchaser. If . . . margarine is put in the shop for sale, and put in a place where it is visible to customers, then it is exposed for sale within the meaning of the Act [Margarine Act 1887 (repealed)].' *Crane v Lawrence* (1890) 25 QBD 152 at 155, per A L Smith J

'The decision in *Crane v Lawrence* [supra] . . . is simply that margarine which cannot in any sense be seen by the purchaser is not exposed for sale. . . . The expression "exposed for sale" is a well-understood term, and cannot be limited so as to mean only "exposed to view".' *Wheat v Brown* [1892] 1 QB 418 at 421, per Wright J

'Milk . . . was in a pan on the counter of the respondent's shop; it was not intended to be sold alone, but only for the purpose of mixing it with cups of tea, etc. On these facts the magistrate held that the milk was not exposed to sale. . . . I do not agree with that view. In my opinion, although the milk was going to be mixed with something else it was none the less exposed to sale.' *McNair v Terroni* [1915] 1 KB 516 at 519, 520, per Ridley J

'It seems to me that the primary meaning of "exposed for sale" [in s 16(5) of the Food and Drugs (Adulteration) Act 1928 (repealed; see now the Food Act 1984, s 91(2)] means exposed for the purpose of sale—that is to say, exposed in order to attract offers to purchase from the public.' *Clark v Strachan* 1940 SC(J) 29 at 31, per the Lord Justice-General (Lord Normand)

EXPOSURE

Of child

'We have considered this case, and we are of opinion that the conviction was right, and ought to be affirmed. The prisoner was indicted, under 24 & 25 Vict c 100 [Offences against the Person Act 1861], s 27, for unlawfully abandoning and exposing a child, under the age of two years, whereby its life was endangered. On the facts stated in the case the objection was taken that there was no evidence of abandonment or exposure. Now, the prisoner was the father of the child, and as such was entitled to the custody and control of it, and was not only morally but legally bound to provide for it. Then it appears that when the child was lying at the door he saw it, stepped over it, and left it there. Afterwards, when the child was in the road, he knew it was there. I am clearly of opinion that there was evidence here upon which the jury might and ought to convict the prisoner. Instead of protecting and providing for the child, as it was his duty to do, he allowed it to remain lying, first at his door, and afterwards in the road, insufficiently clothed, and at a time of year when the result was likely to be the child's death. I think, therefore, he was guilty both of abandonment and exposure.' *R v White* (1871) LR 1 CCR 311 at 313, per Bovill CJ

'The appellant has been indicted under s 12 of the Children's Act 1908 [repealed; see now s 1 of the Children and Young Persons Act 1933] for neglecting and exposing his children [he tramped on with his children through the night, when he might have got accommodation for them]. . . . The court will not decide whether he has neglected the children, for the word "exposed" in the indictment is sufficient. Mr Ward wishes us to say that exposure must consist of a physical placing somewhere with intent to injure, but the statute does not say that. The object is to prevent the causing of unnecessary suffering to children, and the appellant has certainly exposed his children in a manner to cause them unnecessary suffering.' *R v Williams* (1910) 26 TLR 290 at 290, per cur.

EXPRESS

[Regulation 21 of the Building (Safety, Health and Welfare) Regulations 1948 (revoked; see now the Construction (Working Places) Regulations 1966), provides that an employer must take 'express' steps to see that a scaffold, once erected, is stable.] 'The use of the adjective "express" is somewhat ungrammatical and peculiar. Nobody suggests that it means "quick". I assume that the intention was that the steps must be such as were directed, and directed specifically, to the question . . . whether the scaffold was stable.' *Clarke v Wright (ER) & Son* [1957] 3 All ER 486 at 490, 491, per Lord Evershed MR

Canada [Section 287 of the Corporations Act, RSO 1960, c 71 (see now RSO 1980, c 95, s 274), applies unless otherwise 'expressly' provided in an Act or instrument.] 'The definition of "express" contained in Murray's English Dictionary, when the word is applied to a law, stipulation or grant, etc, is that it is used in the sense of "expressed and not merely implied; definitely formulated; definite, explicit". In my opinion the word "expressly" is used in s 287 in this sense—meaning that a provision of the Act or instrument creating the corporation does not have the effect sought to be attributed to it unless it is stated in express and positive terms, directly, and not merely by implication from the language used.' *Walton v Bank of Nova Scotia* [1964] 1 OR 673 at 682, Ont CA, per Schroeder JA; affd (sub nom *Eisenberg v Bank of Nova Scotia*) [1965] SCR 681

EXPRESS MALICE   *See* MALICE

EXPRESS TRUST   *See* TRUST

EXPRESSLY

'The statute 13 & 14 Vict c 21 [Lord Brougham's Act 1850 (repealed; see now Interpretation Act 1978, s 6)] . . . enacts, in s 4, that, in all Acts of Parliament, words importing the masculine gender shall be deemed to include females, unless the contrary be expressly provided. . . . That word [expressly] does not necessarily mean "expressly excluded by words". . . . The word "expressly" often means no more than plainly, clearly, or the like.' *Chorlton v Lings* (1868) LR 4 CP 374 at 393, 394, per Byles J

[Section 1 of the Innkeepers' Liability Act 1863 (repealed; see now the Hotel Proprietors Act 1956, s 2(3)(6)), limited the liability of an innkeeper to make good a loss of his guest's goods to £30 (now £100), unless the goods had been deposited 'expressly' for safe custody with the innkeeper.] 'The word "expressly" is not used without a purpose. It means that an intention by the bailor is not enough. That intention must be brought to the mind of the bailee or his agent in some reasonable and intelligible manner, so that he may, if so minded, insist on the precautions specified in the Act. The pursuer's traveller caused to be placed in the office, without a word spoken, a bag of undeclared contents, which was laid in a corner of the room. . . . The Act meant to secure for the innkeeper, by warning, an opportunity of safeguarding himself when a heavy risk is placed on him. There is no ground for saying he had such a warning here.' *Whitehouse v Pickett* [1908] AC 357 at 361, per Lord Loreburn LC

'I do not think that any form of words was needed, but something should be said or done by the guest that would clearly convey to the innkeeper that goods were being deposited with him for safe keeping.' Ibid at 362, per Lord Ashbourne

Provided by law

Canada   'When the expression "unless some penalty or punishment of other mode of proceeding is expressly provided by law" [in the Criminal Code] is read as an entity or unit as though included in parentheses, the natural meaning to be attributed to the words "by law" contained therein is "by statute law". For one thing, such law is clearly "expressly provided" beyond argument. Any other law, however it may originate, cannot be so readily described as "expressly provided".' *R v Clement* (1981) 127 DLR (3d) 419 at 426, SCC, per Estey J

EXPROPRIATION

South Africa   'The effect of expropriation is to vest the ownership of the land in the Government notwithstanding that the land still stands registered in the plaintiff's name and has not been transferred to the Government. No doubt dominium in land does not as a rule pass without delivery. But the principle that such dominium may pass without such delivery or transfer by mere operation of law is well known to the common law, though it applies in certain definite cases only, e.g. marriage in community. And it is quite in the power of the legislature to effect such a passing over of the dominium by operation of law, without delivery or transfer. Such a passing over is involved in the very nature of expropriation, where the legislature empowers the Government to take the land of a private owner for certain purposes, against his will. If the property expropriated be a movable, can it be doubted that on its expropriation no further delivery on the part of the former owner is necessary to pass the dominium. The principle is the same in regard to land.' *Mathiba v Mosckhe* 1920 AD 364, per Juta AJA

EXTEND

Beyond limits of State

Australia   'The facts disclose . . . a dispute in the shipping industry which includes a great number of shipowners and their employés in various States of Australia, so that the dispute as a whole is one which, in the ordinary sense, extends beyond the bounds of any one State within the meaning both of the Constitution [Commonwealth of Australia Constitution Act 1901] and the Act [Commonwealth Conciliation and Arbitration Act 1904; see now Conciliation and Arbitration Act 1904–1986, s 71(1)]. . . . If the dispute be a composite dispute, that is, if it be concerned with conditions partly in Australia and partly in America or India or partly in Australia and partly on the high seas, then, if it be separable, the Court can deal with the Australian part, and ignore the foreign part; but if the parties claiming the demands insist that they are not making separable but inseparable claims, then, in my opinion, they are insisting upon something that stretches beyond the ambit of jurisdiction contained in sub-s 35 so far as it is unaided by any further provision in the Constitution Act.' *Merchant Service Guild of Australasia v Commonwealth SS Owners Assocn* (1913) 16 CLR 664 at 686–691, per Isaacs J

Australia 'The words "extending beyond the limits of any one State" as applied to a dispute mean that the dispute is one "existing in two or more States", or, in other words, "covering Australian territory comprised within two or more States".' *Holyman's Case* (1914) 18 CLR 273 at 285, 286, per Isaacs J

EXTENSION

'The word extension imports the continuance of an existing thing, and must have its full effect given to it where it occurs.' *Brooke v Clarke* (1818) 1 B & Ald 396 at 403, per Lord Ellenborough CJ

Australia [The proviso to s 197(5)(b) of the Local Government Act 1928 (Vic.) (see now the Local Government Act 1958–1986, s 197(7)) enacts that no by-law shall preclude the continuance of the use of any building for any purpose for which it was used immediately before the coming into operation of the by-law or the enlargement, rebuilding or 'extension' of any building used for any such purpose.] 'The question is: What is the meaning of the word "extension" in this connection? That it is not used in the sense of "enlargement" is clear from the context, for if so read it would add nothing to the words that go before. "Enlargement" involves an increase in the size of an existing building, and no doubt when it involves an increase in the area covered by the

building there may be said to be an "extension" of it. But it would not cover the case where an additional wing or annex is added to an existing building. In such a case there is a spreading out or "extension", and it seems to me that the word "extension" in the proviso covers the building of additional or supplementary buildings. No doubt on many occasions such additions will be built on to an existing building, as a new wing may be built on to an existing factory. But it would, I think, be taking far too narrow a view to hold that such a wing would cease to be an "extension" of the factory just because it was detached. I think a new detached wing could just as properly be regarded as an extension of the factory as one that was built on to it. And, *a fortiori*, where there are a number of detached buildings, as for example, in an explosive factory or a poultry farm, it would be proper to describe additional detached buildings as an "extension" of the existing building.' *R v Shire of Ferntree Gully, ex p Hamley* [1946] ALR 558 at 564, 565, per Herring CJ

Of credit

Canada [The accused was charged, pursuant to s 320(1)(c)(iv) of the Criminal Code of Canada, with committing the offence of making a false statement in writing in order to obtain from the bank an 'extension of credit', or in the French version of the Code, 'ouverture d'un crédit'.] 'The words "extend" (verb) and "extension" (noun) have, like many other words in English, several connotations, which certainly include the notions of prolongation or continuation in space or in time, e.g., the extension of delay, of a railway. But they have another quite different connotation which does not conflict with the clearer meaning of the French wording; that sense is "grant" or "accord", and I am satisfied that the word "extension" is used in that sense in the subsection here involved. Particularly, but not only in commercial circles, that meaning is common, e.g., "I wouldn't extend five cents worth of credit to that man"; one extends, i.e., grants or accords, hospitality, greetings or assistance.' *R v Cohen* (1984) 15 CCC (3d) 231 at 236–237, Quebec CA, per Tyndale JA

EXTENUATING CIRCUMSTANCES

Australia 'In the Shorter Oxford English Dictionary, . . . "extenuating circumstances" means circumstances that "seem [ed] to lessen the seeming magnitude of guilt . . . by partial excuses". I would add a reference to Murray's New English Dictionary which gives a similar meaning, namely, "circumstances that tend to diminish culpability" . . . [A] person who had committed an offence which caused financial loss to another person. If such an offender subsequently made restitution, . . . the fact of restitution would be an extenuating circumstance within the meaning of s 4(2a) [Offenders Probation Act 1913 (SA)], whereas it would not be an extenuating circumstance under which the offence was committed . . . that a very substantial show of remorse by the offender in an endeavour to undo the harm would be an extenuating circumstance.' *Beavan v Rankine* (1983) 36 SASR 120 at 125, per Matheson J

[See also *Lanham v Brake* (1983) 74 FLR 284]

South Africa 'In our view an extenuating circumstance in this connection [belief in witchcraft] is a fact associated with the crime which serves in the minds of reasonable men to diminish, morally albeit not legally, the degree of the prisoner's guilt. The mentality of the accused may furnish such a fact.' *R v Biyana* 1938 EDL 310, per Lansdown JP

EXTERNAL

[A lease contained a covenant that the lessee should not make any 'external' alteration whatsoever in the premises.] 'I think the alterations here were external within the meaning of the covenant. At first I was inclined to think that this part of the covenant was intended to apply to that portion of the premises which had an outside and an inside. But I have come to the conclusion that the word "external" was meant to apply to everything external to the house, or, as it is popularly called, "out of doors".' *Perry v Davis* (1858) 3 CBNS 769 at 776, 777, per Williams J

Canada 'In the policy under consideration, looking, as I am bound to, to the whole of the policy and also to the things that are excepted from it, as applied to a hoist with a structural mast, the word "external" means "situate outside"; "situate outside the object under consideration" or "arising or acting from without". It must be taken to mean the opposite to "internal". The word "cause" has a number of meanings but, in my opinion, the best definition is "that which produces an effect".' *Capital City Oil Well Servicing Co Ltd*

v Non Marine Underwriters Member of Lloyd's (1959) 27 WWR 241 at 254, Alta SC, per Greschuk J

External debt *See* NATIONAL DEBT

External injury

[A policy of insurance covered injury caused by violent, accidental, 'external', and visible means.] 'The word "external" is that which has caused me most doubt; but I feel sure that in this policy, looking, as we are bound to, at the rest of the policy, and the things that are excepted from it, the expression must be taken to mean the antithesis of "internal". If the injury had happened by reason of something internal, it would not be within the policy; but that is not the case, and I think we must say that because the cause of the injury was not internal it must have been "external", and in that case it was also "visible" within the meaning of the policy.' *Hamlyn v Crown Accidental Insurance Co* [1893] 1 QB 750 at 753, CA, per Lord Esher

External waters

'External waters' means the whole of the sea adjacent to the United Kingdom which is within the seaward limits of the territorial waters adjacent thereto. (Marine, &c, Broadcasting (Offences) Act 1967, s 9)

EXTORTION

'Extortion, whether by a sheriff or any other officer, was a misdemeanour at common law; see Comyn's Digest, title "Extortion", and *Smythe's Case* [(1622), Palm. 318]. . . . Extortion is defined to be "in a large sense any oppression under colour of right". In a strict sense the taking of money by any officer by colour of his office, either where none at all is due, or not so much is due, or where it is not yet due (Hawkins, PC, bk 1, c 66).' *Shoppee v Nathan & Co* [1892] 1 QB 245 at 250, per Collins J

[A debtor, appealing from a receiving order, contended that the petitioning creditor had been guilty of attempted 'extortion'.] 'The following conclusions . . . may in our judgment be drawn. (i) There is no such hard and fast rule as counsel for the debtor suggested, namely, that any arrangement or agreement made by a petitioning creditor with his debtor, after the institution or under the shadow of bankruptcy proceedings, whereby the creditor is able to get more than that "to which he was legally entitled" (that is, more than he could have recovered at law at the time of the bankruptcy proceedings being started or threatened) amounts to extortion in bankruptcy law, notwithstanding the absence of any *mala fides* or anything amounting to oppression in fact. In our judgment, the decision in *Re Bebro* [[1900] 2 QB 316] involves, necessarily, the rejection of such a proposition. (ii) There is equally no rule that extortion has, in bankruptcy law, a special and artificial significance divorced altogether from the ordinary implication of the word. (iii) The so-called "rule" in bankruptcy is, in truth, no more than an application of a more general rule that court proceedings may not be used or threatened for the purpose of obtaining for the person so using or threatening them some collateral advantage to himself, and not for the purpose for which such proceedings are properly designed and exist; and a party so using or threatening proceedings will be liable to be held guilty of abusing the process of the court, and, therefore, disqualified from invoking the powers of the court by proceedings which he has abused. (iv) On the other hand, having regard to what Jenkins LJ [in *Re A Judgment Summons (No 25 of 1952), ex p Henlys Ltd* [1953] 1 All ER 424], called the "potent instrument of oppression" which bankruptcy proceedings (with their potential consequences on property and status) provide, the court will always look strictly at the conduct of a creditor using or threatening such proceedings; and, if it concludes that the creditor has used or threatened the proceedings at all oppressively (for example in order to obtain some payment or promise from the debtor or some other collateral advantage to himself properly attributable to the use of the threat) the court will not hesitate to declare the creditor's conduct extortionate and will not allow him to make use of the process which he has abused. (v) In every case it is a question of fact in all the circumstances of the case whether there has been, in truth, extortion.' *Re A Debtor (No 757 of 1954), ex p Debtor v Dumont (FA) Ltd* [1955] 2 All ER 65 at 78, CA, per Evershed MR

South Africa 'The crime of extortion (*concussio*) may be committed either by a public official or by a private individual under colour of authority but illegitimate pressure in some shape is a necessary element to constitute the offence.' *Notaris v R* 1903 TS 484, per Innes CJ

South Africa 'It is inherent in the description and presentation of the crime (*concussio*) . . .

that the advantage sought to be obtained by illegitimate pressure must be something which is not due. It is distinguished from robbery in that the extorter takes property, not by violence, but by inspiring fear.' *R v Jansen* 1959 (1) SA 779 (C), per Rosenow J

EXTRADITION

Extradition is the formal surrender by one country to another, based on reciprocal arrangements partly judicial and partly administrative, of an individual accused or convicted of a serious criminal offence committed outside the territory of the extraditing country and within the jurisdiction of the requesting country which, being competent by its own law to try and punish him, demands the fugitive's surrender. (18 Halsbury's Laws (4th edn) para 201)

'The conditions of extradition, the fulfilment of which we have in this case to consider, are the following: (1) the imputed crime must be within the treaty [extradition treaty with another country]; (2) it must be a crime against the law of the country demanding extradition; (3) it must be a crime within the English Extradition Acts 1870 and 1873; and (4) there must be such evidence before the committing magistrate as would warrant him in sending the case for trial, if it were an ordinary case in this country.' *Re Arton (No 2)* [1896] 1 QB 509 at 513, per cur.

EXTRAORDINARY TRAFFIC

'We have first to ascertain what is meant by "excessive weight" and "extraordinary traffic". It appears to me that those words must mean excessive and extraordinary with reference to the ordinary use and traffic upon and over the road. If anything is done of an unusual and extraordinary kind, the person doing it must pay for the damage thereby occasioned. It is the ordinary nature of the traffic over the road which is to be the standard. Now, the case shews that the appellant about four or five times a week passed along the road in question with a traction-engine and waggon, the concentrated weight of which when loaded exceeded twenty-four tons. That appears to me excessive weight and extraordinary traffic to impose upon an ordinary highway, utterly regardless of whether or not a locomotive was used, and must cause extraordinary expense.' *Aveland (Lord) v Lucas* (1879) 5 CPD 211 at 223, 224, per Lindley J

'The only question . . . is, whether this was extraordinary traffic within the meaning of the section [s 23 of the Highways and Locomotives Amendment Act 1878 (repealed; see now the Highways Act 1980, s 59)]. . . . The facts before us are that the road is in a large agricultural district near a railway station. There are no doubt broad main roads . . . repaired so as to bear the traffic in question. But there is also a particular road communicating with one of these main roads and principally used by farmers whose premises adjoin it. Over this road locomotives have gone very rarely and then in dry weather, but on the particular occasion a traction engine with loaded trucks made during several days two journeys a day upon it with the result of practically squeezing the road into the ditch and seriously damaging it. . . . Having regard to the character of this road and to the mode in which it was generally used, it is impossible to hold that the use of such engines was an ordinary incident of the traffic upon it.' *R v Ellis (Jesse) & Co* (1882) 8 QBD 466 at 469, 470, per Field J

'Extraordinary traffic [in s 23 of the Highways and Locomotives (Amendment) Act 1878 (repealed; see supra)] is really a carriage of articles over the road, at either one or more times, which is so exceptional in the quality or quantity of articles carried, or in the mode or time of user of the road, as substantially to alter and increase the burden imposed by ordinary traffic on the road, and to cause damage and expense thereby beyond what is common.' *Hill v Thomas* [1893] 2 QB 333 at 340, 341, CA, per cur.

'The question in this case is as to the proper construction of the 23rd section of the Highways and Locomotives (Amendment) Act 1878 [repealed; see supra], which is headed "Extraordinary Traffic". . . . The phraseology of the section is somewhat obscure. In the first place, the words "extraordinary traffic", appear to be used in two distinct senses. In the heading to the section the phrase is apparently used as equivalent both to excessive weight and to the narrower sense in which it is used in the body of the section, where it appears to be used as meaning something other than excessive weight. It is a condition precedent to the jurisdiction of the justices that it must be shown that extraordinary expenses have been incurred in repairing a highway by reason of the damage caused by excessive weight passing along the same, or extraordinary traffic, both of which

are contemplated as causes of damage. . . . It is obvious that extraordinary traffic means, primarily, traffic which is beyond that which is ordinary in point of quantity, since it is in that way alone that damage can be caused to a highway. No matter how extraordinary in kind the traffic may be, I do not see how it can cause damage to the road unless the vehicles used are of an unusual weight, or the traffic is unusual in amount. It may be that the Legislature intended that the traffic should be extraordinary in kind as well; but it must obviously be extraordinary in quantity, or it will not produce the damage at which this part of the section is aimed. . . . With the exception . . . of the dictum of Lopes J [in *Pickering Lythe East Highway Board v Barry* (1881) 45 LT 655] . . . there seems to be a clear concurrence of authority that "extraordinary traffic" in the section in question is something distinct from "excessive weight", that it must be extraordinary in kind as well as in quantity, and that the comparison must be made not between the use complained of and the ordinary use of other roads in the neighbourhood, but between the use complained of and the ordinary use of the same road.' *Etherley Grange Coal Co v Auckland District Highway Board* (1893) 69 LT 286 at 289, 291, 292, per cur.

'I think that the words of s 23 [of the Highways and Locomotives (Amendment) Act 1878 (repealed; see supra)] are so selected as to show the intention of the Legislature to bring such traffic as that of the appellants within the principle of the section as soon as it is shown that it has caused extraordinary expense for repair to the road in question to fall on the road authority by reason of the excess of weight of such traffic over the average of that for roads in the neighbourhood similar to the road in question, or, analogously, of an extraordinary kind of traffic compared with that on such neighbouring roads.' *Butt (Henry) & Co v Weston-super-Mare Urban District Council* [1922] 1 AC 340 at 353–354, per Lord Haldane

[As to the recovery by highway authorities, etc., of expenses incurred in maintaining highways, see now the Highways Act 1980, s 59, which deals specifically with the recovery of expenses due to 'extraordinary traffic', including damage caused by excessive weight passing along the highway; such sums are recoverable in the High Court or (where not exceeding £500) in the county court. *See also* 21 Halsbury's Laws (4th edn) para 241 et seq.]

F

FC & S CLAUSE *See* FREE OF CAPTURE
OR SEIZURE

FOB *See* FREE ON BOARD

FABRICATE

'The word "fabricate" occurs [in the Local
Government Act 1858, s 13 (repealed)] along
with the words "alters, defaces, abstracts, or
purloins any voting paper, or personates any
person", all of which import a criminal
intention—a *mens rea*; and the legislature must
mean such an act as the person doing it must
know is wrong, and not such as he believes to
be right.' *Aberdare Local Board v Hammett*
(1875) LR 10 QB 162 at 165, per Mellor J

'"Fabricate" implies fraud or falsehood, a
false or fraudulent concoction, knowing it to be
wrong and contrary to the Act.' Ibid at 166, per
Quain J

FACILITIES

New Zealand [Section 165(4) of the Sale of
Liquor Act 1962 requires the Licensing Control Commission, when considering the grant
or renewal of a club charter, to have regard to
the 'facilities' then existing in the locality in
which the club is situated for social amenities,
recreation or refreshment.] 'The facilities to
which the Commission is required to have
regard in considering an application for the
grant of a club charter are not confined to such
facilities in other clubs (not necessarily
chartered clubs); the Commission is required
to have regard also to such facilities provided in
hotels or institutions other than clubs.' *Hodgson v Buller Workingmen's Club (No 2)* [1967]
NZLR 636 at 638, per Wild CJ

FACT

Australia [The Evidence Act 1958–1986,
(Vic), s 55 makes admissible certain documents which contain statements by deceased

persons tending to establish any 'fact'.] 'It may
be that the phrase "a fact" must be given an
expanded meaning equivalent to some matter
in issue to be established in the proceedings.
Indeed, Wigmore, in his work on Evidence,
3rd edn, vol 1, p 1, para 1, points out that, in
one sense, "everything in the cosmos is a fact
or a phenomenon". In my view, it would be
contrary to the policy of the legislation to give a
restricted meaning to the word "fact" so as to
exclude a statement of opinion by an expert. In
this context, I agree with the view recently
expressed by Hart J, *Lenehan v Queensland
Trustees Ltd* [1965] Qd R 559 at 565, 566, that
the word "statement" is wide enough to
include a statement of opinion.' *Morley v
National Insurance Co* [1967] VR 566 at 567,
per McInerney J

FACTOR *See also* BROKER; MERCANTILE
AGENT

A factor is a mercantile agent who in the ordinary course of business is entrusted with possession of goods or of the documents of title
thereto. (1 Halsbury's Laws (4th edn) para
712)

'A factor, who has the possession of goods,
differs materially from a broker. The former is
a person to whom goods are sent or consigned,
and he has not only the possession, but in consequence of its being usual to advance money
upon them, has also a special property in them,
and a general lien upon them. When, therefore, he sells in his own name, it is within the
scope of his authority: and it may be right
therefore, that the principal should be bound
by the consequences of such sale; amongst
which, the right of setting-off a debt due from
the factor is one.' *Baring v Corrie* (1818) 2 B &
Ald 137 at 148, per Holroyd J

'The word "factor" is not a term of the Civil
Law; it is not to be found in the language in
which that system of laws is written. I believe it
has a French origin in the word "facteur", and,
in common parlance, it continues in a sense of
great latitude to signify any agent whatever. In
the northern district of this island, it is very

generally applied to land-stewards, bailiffs, and managers of estates. . . . In seaport towns, where there are great manufactories, besides the great manufacturers themselves, there may be factors to export upon commission: a very great part of the commerce of this great town is conducted on foreign goods imported, and our own manufactures to be exported. But I take the real and established distinction in our statutes to be, that a merchant buys and sells for his own direct mercantile profit, and the factor only buys or sells upon commission. . . . To be a factor, he must be empowered to sell by commission; and if not so empowered, he is not a factor, whatever else he may do.' *The Matchless* (1822) 1 Hag Adm 97 at 100, 101, per Lord Stowell

'The definition of a factor I thought always was that which is laid down in Smith's Mercantile Law, where it is said: "There are two extensive classes of mercantile agents, namely, factors who are entrusted with the possession as well as the disposition of property, and brokers, who are employed without being put into possession of the goods." As for limiting that definition by restricting it to persons entrusted with goods from abroad, I never before heard of such a limitation, and I think it must be rejected.' *Re Henley, ex p Dixon* (1876) 4 Ch D 133 at 137, CA, per Brett JA

'A factor is an agent, but an agent of a particular kind. He is an agent entrusted with the possession of goods for the purpose of sale. That is the true definition of a factor.' *Stevens v Biller* (1883) 25 Ch D 31 at 37, CA, per Cotton LJ

'I think the word "factor" is used in that section [the Income Tax Act 1842, s 41 (repealed)] in its proper legal sense, viz, as meaning an agent who has possession of the goods of his principal.' *Grainger & Son v Gough* [1895] 1 QB 71 at 80, CA, per Lord Esher MR

FACTORY *See also* MANUFACTORY; MILL

(1) Subject to the provisions of this section, the expression 'factory' means any premises in which, or within the close or curtilage or precincts of which, persons are employed in manual labour in any process for or incidental to any of the following purposes, namely:—
   (a) the making of any article or of part of any article; or
   (b) the altering, repairing, ornamenting,

finishing, cleaning, or washing or the breaking up or demolition of any article; or
   (c) the adapting for sale of any article;
   (d) the slaughtering of cattle, sheep, swine, goats, horses, asses, or mules; or
   (e) the confinement of such animals as aforesaid while awaiting slaughter at other premises, in a case where the place of confinement is available in connection with those other premises, is not maintained primarily for agricultural purposes within the meaning of the Agriculture Act 1947, or, as the case may be, the Agriculture (Scotland) Act 1948, and does not form part of premises used for the holding of a market in respect of such animals;
being premises in which, or within the close or curtilage or precincts of which, the work is carried on by way of trade or for purposes of gain and to or over which the employer of the persons employed therein has the right of access or control.
(2) The expression 'factory' also includes the following premises in which persons are employed in manual labour (whether or not they are factories by virtue of subsection (1) of this section), that is to say,
   (a) any yard or dry dock (including the precincts thereof) in which ships or vessels are constructed, reconstructed, repaired, refitted, finished or broken up;
   (b) any premises in which the business of sorting any articles is carried on as a preliminary to the work carried on in any factory or incidentally to the purposes of any factory;
   (c) any premises in which the business of washing or filling bottles or containers or packing articles is carried on incidentally to the purposes of any factory;
   (d) any premises in which the business of hooking, plaiting, lapping, making-up or packing of yarn or cloth is carried on;
   (e) any laundry carried on as ancillary to another business, or incidentally to the purposes of any public institution;
   (f) except as provided in subsection (10) of this section, any premises in which the construction, reconstruction or repair of locomotives,

vehicles or other plant for use for transport purposes is carried on as ancillary to a transport undertaking or other industrial or commercial undertaking;

(g) any premises in which printing by letterpress, lithography, photogravure, or other similar process, or bookbinding is carried on by way of trade or for purposes of gain or incidentally to another business so carried on;

(h) any premises in which the making, adaptation or repair of dresses, scenery or properties is carried on incidentally to the production, exhibition or presentation by way of trade or for purposes of gain of cinematograph films or theatrical performances, not being a stage or dressing-room of a theatre in which only occasional adaptations or repairs are made;

(j) any premises in which the business of making or mending nets is carried on incidentally to the fishing industry;

(k) any premises in which mechanical power is used in connection with the making or repair of articles of metal or wood incidentally to any business carried on by way of trade or for purposes of gain;

(l) any premises in which the production of cinematograph films is carried on by way of trade or for purposes of gain, so, however, that the employment at any such premises of theatrical performers within the meaning of the Theatrical Employers Registration Act 1925, and of attendants on such theatrical performers shall not be deemed to be employment in a factory;

(m) any premises in which articles are made or prepared incidentally to the carrying on of building operations or works of engineering construction, not being premises in which such operations or works are being carried on;

(n) any premises used for the storage of gas in a gasholder having a storage capacity of not less than 140 cubic metres.

(3) Any line or siding (not being part of a railway or tramway) which is used in connection with and for the purposes of a factory, shall be deemed to be part of the factory; and if any such line or siding is used in connection with more than one factory belonging to different occupiers, the line or siding shall be deemed to be a separate factory.

(4) A part of a factory may, with the approval in writing of the chief inspector, be taken to be a separate factory and two or more factories may, with the like approval, be taken to be a single factory.

(5) Any workplace in which, with the permission of or under agreement with the owner or occupier, two or more persons carry on any work which would constitute the workplace a factory if the persons working therein were in the employment of the owner or occupier, shall be deemed to be a factory for the purposes of this Act, and, in the case of any such workplace not being a tenement factory or part of a tenement factory, the provisions of this Act shall apply as if the owner or occupier of the workplace were the occupier of the factory and the persons working therein were persons employed in the factory.

(6) Where a place situate within the close, curtilage, or precincts forming a factory is solely used for some purpose other than the processes carried on in the factory, that place shall not be deemed to form part of the factory for the purposes of this Act, but shall, if otherwise it would be a factory, be deemed to be a separate factory.

(7) Premises shall not be excluded from the definition of a factory by reason only that they are open air premises.

(8) Where the Minister by regulations so directs as respects all or any purposes of this Act, different branches or departments of work carried on in the same factory shall be deemed to be different factories.

(9) Any premises belonging to or in the occupation of the Crown or any municipal or other public authority shall not be deemed to be a factory, and building operations or works of engineering construction undertaken by or on behalf of the Crown or any such authority shall not be excluded from the operation of this Act, by reason only that the work carried on thereat is not carried on by way of trade or for purposes of gain.

(10) Premises used for the purpose of housing locomotives or vehicles where only cleaning, washing, running repairs or

minor adjustments are carried out shall not be deemed to be a factory by reason only of paragraph (f) of subsection (2) of this section, unless they are premises used for the purposes of a railway undertaking where running repairs to locomotives are carried out. (Factories Act 1961, s 175 as amended by SI 1983/978, reg 3(1))

'In order that premises may be a factory within the meaning of the Factories Act 1937, s 151(1) [repealed; see now the Factories Act 1961, s 175 (supra)], all that, in my opinion, is required is that within these premises persons be employed in manual labour in some activity directed towards or incidental to the processing of articles by way of trade or for purposes of gain. I thus read the words "in any process" as used in the section as equivalent to "in any activity". I do not think these words mean "process" in a technical sense, seeing that "processing" in such a sense is covered by the later words of the definition which deal with the "making, altering or repairing of articles". It is further, in my opinion, unnecessary that the person making the claim in respect of an accident within a factory should himself be employed by the person who occupies the factory. . . . I am clearly of opinion that, in addition to the employees of the occupier of the factory, all persons who are legitimately present within the premises are equally entitled to invoke the safeguards which are introduced by the Act. I think further that it is quite consistent with the statutory definitions that the same area should be at once a notional factory in terms of s 107 [see now s 127 of the Act of 1961] and an actual factory in terms of s 151.' *Ward v Coltness Iron Co Ltd* 1944 SC 318 at 324, per Lord Moncrieff

Australia [The Lottery and Gaming Act 1936–1986 (SA), s 4 defines 'public place' as meaning (inter alia) any 'factory', and the appurtenances of any factory.] 'In its modern use the word "factory" is a shortened form of "manufactory", and the primary meaning is "a building or place in which goods are manufactured or made". This is the opinion expressed by the late Sir Samuel Way in *Ross v Smith, Timms & Co* [[1909] SASR 128 at 133, 134]. . . . It is true that goods are usually manufactured in a building or under cover, and that there is, therefore, a tendency to think and speak of a "factory" as "a building or range of buildings with plant for the manufacture of goods". This is a possible meaning. . . . I have no hesitation in inferring that the statute law of this State uses the word "factory" with the meaning of a building or place in which goods are manufactured or made and—with Way, CJ—"I cannot doubt that 'works' in the open may be as much a factory or manufactory as if carried on within a building or range of buildings".' *O'Sullivan v Arriola* [1951] SASR 108 at 110, 111, per Napier CJ

Factory or workshop

'Factory or workshop' means any premises on which any manual labour is exercised by way of trade, or for purposes of gain, in or incidental to the following purposes or any of them; that is to say,
(a) In or incidental to the making any article or part of an article; or
(b) In or incidental to the altering repairing ornamenting finishing of any article; or
(c) In or incidental to the adapting for sale any article.
(Bills of Sale Act 1878, s 5)

Tenement factory

'Tenement factory' means any premises where mechanical power from any prime mover within the close or curtilage of the premises is distributed for use in manufacturing processes to different parts of the same premises occupied by different persons in such manner that those parts constitute in law separate factories. (Factories Act 1961, s 176)

'I am of opinion that this group of buildings is not a tenement factory within the meaning of s 14 of the Factory and Workshop Act 1901 [repealed; see now Factories Act 1961]. That section provides that all factories in which more than forty persons are employed shall be furnished with reasonable means of escape in case of fire for the persons employed therein. And by sub-s 7 for the purposes of that section "the whole of a tenement factory . . . shall be deemed to be one factory". Then s 149 [see now Factories Act 1961, s 176 (supra)] defines what a tenement factory is: "The expression 'tenement factory' means a factory where mechanical power is supplied to different parts of the same building occupied by different persons for the purpose of any manufacturing process or handicraft, in such manner that those parts constitute in law separate factories; and for the purposes of the provisions of this Act with respect to tenement factories all buildings situate within the same close or curtilage shall be treated as one building." . . . I understand that expression "supplied to" to mean supplied from one and the same source.' *Brass v*

London County Council [1904] 2 KB 336 at 339, 340, DC, per Lord Alverstone CJ

Textile factory

In this section 'textile factory' means any factory in which mechanical power is used in the spinning, weaving or knitting of cotton, wool, hair, silk (including artificial silk), flax, hemp, jute, tow, china-grass, cocoanut fibre, asbestos, or other like material, either separately or mixed together, or mixed with any other material, or any fabric made thereof or in any process preparatory or incidental thereto, whether or not carried on in the same premises. (Factories Act 1961, s 135)

FAIL

'Fail' [to provide a specimen for a laboratory blood-alcohol test] includes refuse. (Road Traffic Act 1972, s 12(2) as substituted by the Transport Act 1981, s 25, Sch 8)

'The first question is whether Mr Martineau [the arbitrator named in an arbitration clause which added that "failing him" another should be named] failed on August 1 within the meaning of the contract. What happened afterwards may clearly be looked at to see if there was at that date a "failure" in fact. But, apart from what happened subsequently, the facts on August 1 are clear. . . . Mr Martineau was not within reach; he was in America on business, and he would not be likely to give up his business there in order to return to England and hold this arbitration. It was idle to assume that he would come back at once, and even if he had it might have been too late. Therefore Mr Martineau was not available, and had "failed" within the meaning of the contract.' *Re Wilson & Son & Eastern Counties Navigation & Transport Co Ltd* (1892) 8 TLR 264 at 265, per Lord Esher MR

[The defendant, by agreement, was to have the first claim on the services of the plaintiff as a jockey, and in case the plaintiff should die or should 'fail' to procure a licence during the said term the agreement was to be at an end.] 'It seems to me that the word "fail" must have some meaning given to it, and fairly construed it points to something in the nature of a failure by reason either of misconduct on his part or a want of due diligence in trying to obtain a licence.' *Loates v Maple* (1903) 88 LT 288 at 290, per Wright J

[The Road Traffic Act 1930, s 49 (repealed; see now Road Traffic Act 1972, s 22(1)(b)) provided that where a police constable was for the time being engaged in the regulation of traffic in a road, any person driving or propelling a vehicle who neglected to stop the vehicle, or to make it proceed in or keep to a particular line of traffic when directed so to do by the police constable in the execution of his duty, should be guilty of an offence.] 'As I understand Mr Lyne's argument, "failing" to make a vehicle proceed in accordance with police instructions is not the same thing as "neglecting" to do so. He says that neglecting imports negligence, and therefore that the justices might have applied minds to the question of failure only, and not to the question whether the failure was accompanied by negligence. But the words of the information are "did unlawfully fail" and that, to my mind, includes failure through negligence.' *Pontin v Price* (1933) 150 LT 177 at 178, per Lawrence J

'According to the primary and natural meaning of the words a testamentary provision "fails" when (either because of the death of the chosen beneficiary or for some other reason) it (a) is incapable of receiving effect, or (b) becomes incapable of ever receiving further effect. . . . I am unable to adopt the alternative suggestion that a provision "fails" only if it never becomes operative at all.' *Thomson's Trustees v Thomson* 1946 SLT 339 at 342, per the Lord Justice-Clerk (Cooper)

Australia [The Excise Act 1901–1986 (Cth), s 60(1), deals with circumstances where a person who has or has been entrusted with the possession, custody or control of excisable goods which are subject to the control of the Customs 'fails' to keep those goods safely.] '"Safely" seems to mean safe from loss or destruction: for the subject is excise duty, not the condition of the goods. The provision is pointed at the loss of goods involving the loss of excise duty. . . . The hypothesis is that by the loss of the goods duty has been escaped. There must be some doubt whether the destruction of the goods was also contemplated but upon the words of the section destruction is certainly covered. It is said, however, for the defendant that "fail" involves some want of care, some neglect or default. Considering the object of the provision and the place it takes, this ground must "fail". It means to place on the person having possession, custody or control, an absolute duty . . . to keep the goods safe from loss or destruction. . . .' *Marcusson v Southern Shipping Co Ltd* [1962] ALR 758 at 760, per Dixon CJ

'The word "fails" in my opinion, is not strong enough to impose upon the person concerned so onerous a duty as that of avoiding the unavoidable. . . . *Lex non cogit ad impossibilia*.' Ibid at 763, per McTiernan J

'In one context the word "fails" may import the notion of fault. In another it may mean no more than "omits" or "does not" [*Ingram v Ingram* (1938) 38 SR (NSW) 407 at 410, per Jordan CJ]. In the context in which the word is found here, I think the latter meaning should be given to it.' Ibid at 773, per Owen J

Australia 'The meaning of words is notoriously the subject of controversy, particularly in the English language with its rich etymological history. It is rare that a word will have one meaning only. Certainly, the word "fails" is not such a word. In *Ingram v Ingram* (1938) SR (NSW) 407 at 410, Jordan CJ pointed out that the word "fail" may have at least three possible meanings: (1) simply the omission to do a thing in question, irrespective of any reasons; (2) an omission by reason of some carelessness or delinquency; but not an omission caused by impossibility; (3) an omission to do the thing including by impossibility arising from some clause being included and others being excluded. There are doubtless several other combinations of circumstances which do or do not attract the verb to fail.' *CBS Productions Pty Ltd v O'Neill* (1985) 1 NSWLR 601 at 608, 609, per Kirby P (dissenting)

Australia 'The problem which the words pose is a simple one: it depends, in the end, upon the meaning to be given to "fails". "Fail" may denote mere non-fulfilment. . . . If it has that meaning, then there is a failure whatever be the cause of non-fulfilment. Alternatively, "fail" may denote, not every non-fulfilment of the commitment, but only those cases where non-fulfilment arises from certain kinds of causes.' Ibid at 615, per Mahoney JA

New Zealand 'I am unable to agree that the word "fail" in its ordinarily accepted meaning bears the connotation of wrongfulness. There can, of course, be no failure to maintain at common law unless there is a breach of a legal duty to maintain, but in my view it is sufficient under the Act for a wife to prove that there has, in fact, been such a failure, without being obliged to prove, in addition, "the element of wrongful intention", on the husband's part.' *Wilson v Wilson* [1965] NZLR 625 at 627, per Wilson J

New Zealand [The defendant was required by a traffic officer to provide a specimen of his breath but due to a lung condition he could not inflate the bag fully. The question was whether he had 'failed' to supply a specimen of his breath within the meaning of that term as used in the Transport Act 1962, s 59C(1) as amended by the Transport Amendment Act 1970.] 'The word "fail" in this context means fail *simpliciter*: it means the omission, from whatever cause, to provide a specimen of breath.' *Transport Dept v Taylor* [1971] NZLR 622 at 629, per Macarthur J

New Zealand [The defendant, after failing a breath test, was required by a traffic officer to allow a medical practitioner to take a sample of his blood for analysis. He signed a form consenting to the taking of such sample but at the doctor's surgery he refused to allow a sample to be taken from his arm but offered to permit one to be taken from his thumb, toe or leg. No reason was advanced for his refusal to allow the sample to be taken from his arm, and it was held that he had failed or refused to permit a sample to be taken and was thus guilty of an offence against the Transport Act 1962, s 58C]. 'The continuing duty of the person concerned to facilitate the successive procedures by accepting directions from the prescribed authority is emphasised by the use of the words "fails or refuses" at various stages in the sections, e.g., s 58A(2)(b); s 58A(3); s 58B(1)(a). In each of those instances the failure or refusal is one of the pre-requisites to a further step in law enforcement on the part of a constable or traffic officer. In my opinion, it becomes a question of fact whether the person concerned has failed or refused·to permit a specimen of blood to be taken in terms of s 58C(1). In my opinion, the present appellant was clearly "required" by the traffic officer in terms of para (a) of the last subsection, and cannot be assisted by a transient compliance in signing the form, for he repudiated that consent in the doctor's surgery. There was no reason on the face of the evidence why he should not have submitted to the extraction of venous blood from his arm and his rejection of the request of both the traffic officer and the medical practitioner made him guilty of an offence under both paras (a) and (b) thereof.' *Fleetwood v Ministry of Transport* [1972] NZLR 798 at 800, per Haslam J

Fail or determine

'The precise meaning of the words "fail or determine" is rather difficult to define, but I think that the words "or determine" are added to this quite common conveyancing phrase so as to meet the case of what may in a sense be termed a partial failure. Quite commonly clauses of this kind with regard to the ultimate trusts are introduced simply by the words "if the trusts hereinbefore declared shall fail", and that I should have thought would in all ordinary circumstances be quite enough; but it might possibly be argued in certain circumstances that, although the trusts of the fund or of the particular share had come to an end, they could not be said to have failed. A simple reference to failure, it might be argued, is appropriate only to total failure, so that where income has been applied, or powers have been exercised, in favour of a beneficiary entitled to a limited interest or contingently entitled and then the trusts fail, it might be said that the words "shall fail" *simpliciter* would not be appropriate to such a case, because the trusts have come into operation and have been in operation up to a point and to a certain extent, and then have come to an end. All doubts of that sort would be resolved by adding the words "or determined". That makes it quite clear that such partial failure as I have endeavoured to describe would suffice to bring the accruer or the ultimate trust, whatever it may be, into operation.' *Re Huntington's Settlement Trusts, Struthers v Mayne* [1949] Ch 414 at 422, per Jenkins J

To make payment

Canada   [For the purpose of committal proceedings], 'It should I think be readily admitted that "fails to make any payment so ordered" is equivalent, or may be taken to have a similar meaning, to such terms as (1) refuses to pay; (2) wilfully abstains from paying; or (3) knowingly omits to pay.' *Prette v Smith* (No 3) [1942] 3 WWR 689 at 689, 690, Man KB, per Donovan J; revd on other grounds, [1943] 1 WWR 9, Man CA

FAILURE

Petroleum marketing

United States   The term 'failure' does not include—
(A) any failure which is only technical or unimportant to the franchise relationship; or
(B) any failure for a cause beyond the reasonable control of the franchisee.
(Petroleum Marketing Practices Act 1978, s 101(13))

FAIR (Noun)   *See also* MARKET

At common law a fair is a franchise conferring a right to hold a concourse of buyers and sellers. Fair is applied also to the like right when conferred by Act of Parliament.

As regards legal incidents, there seems to be no distinction, at common law, between a market and a fair. It has been laid down that every fair is a market, but every market is not a fair; and a fair has accordingly been defined as a great sort of market, which is usually kept once or twice in the year, and a market to be less than a fair, being usually kept once or twice in the week. It seems that the legal incidents of a fair do not include the amusements which often accompany the holding of fairs, although their presence has been recognised by statute. Therefore, the difference seems to lie merely in the size or frequency of the gathering; and whether a particular gathering should be called a market or a fair must depend usually upon the term chosen for it in the instrument by which it is authorised. The two franchises are of equal dignity. (29 Halsbury's Laws (4th edn) paras 602, 603)

[Section 126 of the Walsall Corporation Act 1890 imposed a penalty on any occupier of land within the borough who held or permitted to be held any market or 'fair' thereon without the corporation's licence.] 'It is not only as a law term that the word fair is well defined; it is well recognised in ordinary language as a meeting of people for buying and selling. Allusion was made during the argument to Vanity Fair as described by Bunyan. He was a great master of English, and he describes the fair as "a fair wherein should be sold all sorts of vanity". Therefore at this fair are all such merchandise sold as houses, lands, trades, honours, preferments. No doubt, in connection with the great annual or quarterly fairs, amusements and sports were provided for the people; but these were merely incident to the business of the fair. In modern times the commercial importance of fairs has greatly diminished, and the amusements which accompany the holding of fairs often excite much more attention than the buying and selling. But it seems to me that this circumstance does not alter the meaning of the word fair. No doubt words may, and often do, undergo a change of meaning, and a word that was originally used to signify one thing may by usage come to be properly applied to something different. But I cannot find any authority for the use of the word fair as applied to a wake, or a show, or an exhibition. A cattle fair still means a fair where cattle are sold, a fancy fair where fancy articles are sold. There are many occasions where shows and exhibitions are gathered together—for instance, at horse race meetings, at boat races, at great football matches, and other outdoor meetings; yet I think such gatherings cannot properly be spoken of as fairs. It is said that there are such things as pleasure fairs. I am not sure that there is any such phrase in common use [see now the Public Health Act 1961, s 75 (infra)]. But if there is it can, I think, only mean a fair at which toys, trinkets, and such like articles are sold. The fair mentioned in the old song to which the young man went to buy blue ribbon for his sweetheart may have been a pleasure fair, but it was a fair at which blue ribbon was sold, and I suppose other like commodities. From what I have said I should think, if the word fair stood alone in the section of the Act of Parliament, that it would not apply to a mere collection of contrivances for amusement. But the words used are "any market or fair", and although the word "or" is disjunctive, still I think it is interpretative or expository, and that the proximity of the word market emphasises the sense in which the word fair is used.' *Collins v Cooper* (1893) 68 LT 450 at 452, 453, DC, per Bruce J

'I quite agree that the chief idea in the word "fair" is that of buying and selling, but amusements have always been a consequence of people coming together for buying and selling.' Ibid at 453, 454, per Lawrence J

[Section 7 of the Town Moor Act 1774, preserved to a corporation the right to use a certain parcel of land on which 'the fairs commonly called the Cowhill Fairs' had been held.] 'The festival [a temperance gathering with roundabouts and shows] for which the corporation gave possession of some seventy-eight acres of the Town Moor to the defendants was not a horse race nor the fair "commonly called the Cowhill Fair". I cannot think that, in the sense in which "fair" ought to be understood where it occurs in this statutory provision, it was a "fair" at all.' *Walker v Murphy* [1915] 1 Ch 71 at 83, CA, per Kennedy J

'The word "fair" is a term of art and connotes a concourse of buyers and sellers for the purchase and sale of commodities pursuant to a franchise (i.e., a privilege granted under the Crown prerogative) with an optional addition of provision for amusement.' *Wyld v Silver* [1961] 3 All ER 1014 at 1019, per Lloyd-Jacob J

Pleasure fair

(1) A local authority may make byelaws—
  (a) for regulating the hours during which pleasure fairs and roller skating rinks may be open to the public;
  (b) for securing safe and adequate means of ingress to, and egress from, any pleasure fair or roller skating rink;
  (c) for the prevention and suppression of nuisances, and the preservation of sanitary conditions, cleanliness, order and public safety, at any pleasure fair or roller skating rink;
  (d) without prejudice to the generality of the preceding paragraph, for preventing outbreaks of fire which might endanger—
    (i) stands, stalls or other structures used or intended for use in connection with any pleasure fair, or
    (ii) caravans used or intended for use as sleeping accommodation in connection with any pleasure fair, and for reducing the risk of, and the spread of fire from, such outbreaks
and it shall be the duty of the local authority to enforce byelaws made by them under this section.
(2) In this section—
  (a) 'pleasure fair' means any place—
    (i) which is for the time being used wholly or mainly for providing, whether or not in combination with any other entertainment, any entertainment to which this section applies, and
    (ii) for admission to which, or for the use of the contrivances in which, a charge is made;
  (b) 'roller skating rink' means any place which is for the time being used wholly or mainly for roller skating and for admission to which a charge is made.
(3) Subject to the provisions of the next following subsection, the entertainments to which this section applies are the following:—
  (a) circuses;
  (b) exhibitions of human beings or of performing animals;
  (c) merry-go-rounds, roundabouts, swings, switchback railways;
  (d) coco-nut shies, hoop-las, shooting galleries, bowling alleys;
  (e) dodgems or other mechanical riding or driving contrivances;
  (f) automatic or other machines intended for entertainment or amusement;

(g) anything similar to any of the foregoing.
(Public Health Act 1961, s 75, as amended by the Local Government (Miscellaneous Provisions) Act 1976, s 22)

'If the phrase "pleasure fair" [in the Betting, Gaming and Lotteries Act 1963] is not to be regarded as a term of art but as a noun qualified by an adjective, each word being understood in its ordinary sense, it can only mean a fair principally devoted to providing entertainment and amusement in contradistinction to a trade or market fair which has the promotion of commerce as its object. How is the definition of a pleasure fair in this sense to be attempted? All fairs are places of public resort, and it is a simple step to decide that pleasure fairs are places of public resort for entertainment and amusement of a traditional character. What then is the common denominator of such diversions as coconut shies, hoop-la, exhibitions of freaks, dodgem cars and so on? The attribute shared by these and other forms of the fun of the fair is that the entertainment afforded is of a rudimentary and sometimes a crude kind. It demands neither intellectual judgment nor aesthetic appreciation; and if it involves any skill at all, it is at a minimal level and of a simple sort. The game of prize bingo . . . conforms in all respects to these common characteristics of the fun of the fair. What particular form the entertainment or amusement provided takes must depend on the mood of the time. Traditional forms become outmoded or cease to entertain and fresh ones take their place. Roll-a-penny gives way to bingo and so on. Variety cannot be an essential so long as a popular form of amusement is provided. If a particular amusement has for the time being caught the imagination or interest of a substantial part of the public, why should it not be purveyed by itself for general enjoyment at a fair? Bearing in mind the considerations earlier adverted to, which demand a liberal construction of an exemption from a statutory provision which may operate harshly, I would hold on first principles that the expression "pleasure fair" is apt to include premises where facilities are provided for playing prize bingo whether or not any form of amusement or entertainment is available.' *R v Herrod, ex p Leeds City District Council* [1976] 1 All ER 273 at 291, CA, per Shaw LJ; affd sub nom *Walker v Leeds City Council* [1976] 3 All ER 709, HL

Travelling showmen's pleasure fair

'Travelling showmen's pleasure fair' means a pleasure fair consisting wholly or mainly of amusements provided by travelling showmen which is held on any day of a year on premises not previously used in that year on more than twenty-seven days for the holding of such a pleasure fair. (Gaming Act 1968, s 52(1))

FAIR (Adjective)

Fair and reasonable

'By s 9 [of the Attorneys and Solicitors Act 1870 (repealed; see now the Solicitors Act 1974, s 61(2)] the court may enforce an agreement [with a solicitor] if it appears that it is in all respects fair and reasonable. With regard to the fairness of such an agreement, it appears to me that this refers to the mode of obtaining the agreement, and that if a solicitor makes an agreement with a client who fully understands and appreciates that agreement that satisfies the requirement as to fairness. But the agreement must also be reasonable and in determining whether it is so the matters covered by the expression "fair" cannot be re-introduced. As to this part of the requirements of the statute, I am of opinion that the meaning is that when an agreement is challenged the solicitor must not only satisfy the court that the agreement was absolutely fair with regard to the way in which it was obtained, but must also satisfy the court that the terms of that agreement are reasonable.' *Re Stuart, ex p Cathcart* [1893] 2 QB 201 at 204, 205, CA, per Lord Esher, MR

Fair, large and liberal

New Zealand [Section 5(j) of the Acts Interpretation Act 1924 requires every Act to receive such 'fair, large and liberal' construction and interpretation as will best ensure the attainment of the object of the Act and of such provision or enactment according to its true intent, meaning and spirit.] 'As it is obvious that (just as beauty is said to lie in the eye of the beholder) the effect to be given to s 5(j) of the Acts Interpretation Act must depend upon the viewpoint of the reader, it is important to decide at this stage what that viewpoint should be. From the viewpoint of those concerned with the administration of a statute it is desirable that its provisions should receive as "large and liberal" a construction as possible; whereas from the viewpoint of those whose affairs are affected by the statute the emphasis desired is on the word "fair". Neither of these is the correct approach for a court of construction, which, in accordance with s 5(j) must give a statutory provision not merely a "fair", or a "large" or a "liberal" construction, but one which combines all three elements in such a way as will best ensure the attainment of the object of the statute as a whole and the provision under consideration in particular, according to its true "intent, meaning and spirit". The word "fair", of course, refers to the construction of the relevant provision, not to the result of that construction, so that, if the words fairly mean something which may operate unfairly, nevertheless that meaning is to be adopted provided it accords with the "true intent, meaning, and spirit" of the provision.' *Union Motors Ltd v Motor Spirits Licensing Authority* [1964] NZLR 146 at 150, per Wilson J

FAIR COMMENT

The defence of fair comment is in the nature of a general right, and enables any member of the public to comment on matters of public interest. Like the defence of justification it must be based on facts proved to be true, but, it differs from justification in that it is available only in relation to statements which are expressions of opinion and not defamatory statements of fact. Where the defendant seeks to justify his comment, he must prove that the facts and inferences from both fact and comment are true.

The comment must be (1) on a matter of public interest; (2) based on a fact or facts that are truly stated; and (3) a fair comment on such fact or facts, within the wide limits which the law allows. It is for the trial judge to decide whether the matter is one of public interest, and for the jury to decide whether the fact or facts on which the comment is based have been sufficiently proved and whether the comment on such fact or facts is fair. (28 Halsbury's Laws (4th edn) paras 131, 132)

'Every person has a right to comment on the acts of a public man, which concern him as a subject of the realm, if he do not make his comments the vehicle of malice or slander.' *Turnbull v Bird* (1861) 2 F & F 508 at 524, per Erle CJ

'The jury were told that they must be satisfied that the article was an honest and fair comment on the facts,—in other words, that, in the first place, they must be satisfied that the comments had been made with an honest belief in their justice; but that this was not enough, inasmuch as such belief might originate in the blindness of party zeal, or in personal or political

aversion; that a person taking upon himself publicly to criticise and to condemn the conduct or motives of another, must bring to the task, not only an honest sense of justice, but also a reasonable degree of judgment and moderation, so that the result may be what a jury shall deem, under the circumstances of the case, a fair and legitimate criticism on the conduct and motives of the party who is the object of censure. Considering the direction thus given to have been perfectly correct, we are of opinion that . . . this rule must be discharged.' *Wason v Walter* (1868) LR 4 QB 73 at 96, per cur.

'There are many cases where a man might speak ill of his neighbour and not be liable in such an action as the present one, as the occasion would be privileged. Of course, nobody can take advantage of the privilege of the occasion to exercise private malice, nor will the privilege shield him if he makes charges against another recklessly or inconsiderately. One of the cases in which privilege can be claimed is the present one, as it is that of a public writer writing for the public on matters of public interest, but the privilege would not avail the defendant if the matter complained of by the plaintiff had been anything more than a comment at once fair and *bona fide*.' *Williams v Beresford-Hope* (1886) 3 TLR 20 at 21, per Lord Coleridge CJ

'What is the meaning of a "fair comment"? I think the meaning is this: is the article in the opinion of the jury beyond that which any fair man, however prejudiced or however strong his opinion may be, would say of the work in question? Every latitude must be given to opinion and to prejudice, and then an ordinary set of men with ordinary judgment must say whether any fair man would have made such a comment on the work.' *Merivale v Carson* (1887) 20 QBD 275 at 280, CA, per Lord Esher MR

'It is only when the writer goes beyond the limits of fair criticism that his criticism passes into the region of libel at all. . . . The criticism is to be "fair", that is, the expression of it is to be fair. The only limitation is upon the mode of expression. In this country a man has a right to hold any opinion he pleases, and to express his opinion, provided that he does not go beyond the limits which the law calls "fair", and, although we cannot find in any decided case an exact and rigid definition of the word "fair", this is because the judges have always preferred to leave the question what is "fair" to the jury. The nearest approach, I think, to an exact definition of the word "fair" is contained in the judgment of Lord Tenterden CJ, in *Macleod v Wakley* [(1828) 3 C & P 311 at 313], where he said, "whatever is fair, and can be reasonably said of the works of authors or of themselves, as connected with their works, is not actionable, unless it appears that, under the pretext of criticising the works, the defendant takes an opportunity of attacking the character of the author; then it will be a libel".' Ibid at 283, per Bowen LJ

'With regard to the question whether the comment was fair, how can it be said to depend upon the names of the persons who gave the information, or upon whether they were acting maliciously? . . . How can the names of the informants be important or in any way effective upon the question whether the defendant's statements are fair? I cannot see how the knowledge of those names would aid in solving that question.' *Hennessy v Wright* (No 2) (1888) 24 QBD 445 at 447 n, CA, per Lord Esher, MR

'Comment, in order to be fair, must be based upon facts, and if a defendant cannot show that his comments contain no misstatements of fact, he cannot prove a defence of fair comment.' *Digby v Financial News Ltd* [1907] 1 KB 502 at 507, per Lord Collins MR

'The defence of fair comment assumes that the matter to which it relates would be defamatory if it were not protected by the defence of fair comment. . . . Comment which tends to prejudice may still be fair; it may convey imputations of bad motive as far as the facts truly stated justify such an imputation. It is for the jury to say whether the facts justify the imputation or not.' *Hunt v Star Newspaper Co Ltd* [1908] 2 KB 309 at 323, CA, per Buckley LJ

'I have been referring . . . to fair comment, because that is the technical name which is given to this defence, or, as I should prefer to say, which is given to the right of every citizen to comment on matters of public interest. The expression "fair comment" is a little misleading. It may give the impression that you, the jury, have to decide whether you agree with the comment, whether you think that it is fair. If that were the question which you had to decide, you realise that the limits of freedom which the law allows would be greatly curtailed. People are entitled to hold and to express freely on matters of public interest strong views, views which some of you, or indeed all of you, may think are exaggerated,

obstinate, or prejudiced, provided—and this is the important thing—that they are views which they honestly hold. The basis of our public life is that the crank, the enthusiast, may say what he honestly thinks just as much as the reasonable man or woman who sits on a jury, and it would be a sad day for freedom of speech in this country if a jury were to apply the test of whether it agrees with the comment instead of applying the true test: was this an opinion, however exaggerated, obstinate or prejudiced, which was honestly held by the writer?' *Silkin v Beaverbrook Newspapers Ltd* [1958] 2 All ER 516 at 518, per Diplock J

Australia 'The test whether comment is capable of being regarded as unfair is not whether reasonable men might disagree with it, but whether they might reasonably regard the opinion as one that no fair-minded man could have formed or expressed. The opinion must, of course, be germane to the subject matter criticised. Thus if a critic denounced a book for its indecency it would not be beyond the bounds of fair comment if he also denounced the author for publishing such a book. But dislike of an artist's style would not justify an attack upon his morals or his manners. Whistler obtained his verdict, not because Ruskin had accused him of "flinging a pot of paint in the public's face", but because he was in judicious enough to call him a coxcomb into the bargain, and to suggest that he was guilty of wilful imposture.' *Gardiner v John Fairfax & Sons Pty Ltd* [1942] NSWSR 171 at 174, per Jordan CJ

Rolled-up plea

The defendant may plead that, insofar as the words complained of consist of statements of fact they are true in substance and in fact, and insofar as they are expressions of opinion they are fair comment. This is known as 'the rolled-up plea', and is a plea of fair comment, not justification. Particulars must be given stating which of the words complained of are alleged to be statements of fact, and of the facts or matters relied on in support of the allegation that the words are true. In consequence of this requirement, the plea is no longer in general use. (28 Halsbury's Laws (4th edn) para 188)

FAIR DEALING

'It could not be contended that the mere republication of a copyright work was a "fair dealing" [within s 2(1) of the Copyright Act

1911 (repealed; see now Copyright Act 1956, ss 6, 9)] because it was intended for purposes of private study, nor, if an author produced a book of questions for the use of students, could another person with impunity republish the book with the answers to the questions. Neither case would, in my judgment, come within the description of "fair dealing".' *University of London Press Ltd v University Tutorial Press Ltd* [1916] 2 Ch 601 at 613, 614, per Peterson J

'The defendants . . . contended that the acts which they have done, and threatened to do, are acts that, having regard to the proviso in s 2, sub-s 1 of the Copyright Act 1911 [repealed; see supra], do not constitute an infringement of the plaintiffs' copyright. That proviso, so far as material for the present purpose, is in these terms: "Provided that the following acts shall not constitute an infringement of copyright: (1) any fair dealing with any work for the purposes of private study, research, criticism, review or newspaper summary." . . . Dealing with an unpublished literary work would not . . . in my opinion, be a "fair dealing" with the work.' *British Oxygen Co v Liquid Air Ltd* [1925] 1 Ch 383 at 392, 393, per Romer J

'It is said by the defendants that they are protected by the first proviso to s 2, sub-s 1 of the Act [Copyright Act 1911 (repealed; see *supra*)] which enacts that amongst the acts which shall not constitute an infringement of copyright are "Any fair dealing with any work for the purposes of . . . newspaper summary". Mr Macgillivray has asked us to hold that a cinematograph screen when displaying items of news is a newspaper within the meaning of that proviso. I see obvious difficulties in so holding. But let me assume it is a newspaper. Even then, what the defendants have done cannot be described as a "fair dealing with any work for the purposes either of criticism, review, or newspaper summary". . . . The item of news with which we are dealing is the item of news that . . . the Prince of Wales reviewed the boys of the Naval School . . . and that they marched past him to the tune of "Colonel Bogey". Of course, any newspaper is entitled to say that, and that would be a summary of an item of news. . . . But what they would not be entitled to do would be to say "For the benefit of those who were not able to be present, we publish the principal 28 bars of the 'Colonel Bogey march'." That is just what the defendants have done.' *Hawkes & Son (London) Ltd v Paramount Film Service*

Ltd [1934] Ch 593 at 609, CA, per Romer LJ

'The substantiality of the part reproduced is . . . an element which the court will take into consideration in arriving at a conclusion whether what has been done is a fair dealing or not.' *Johnstone v Bernard Jones Publications Ltd* [1938] Ch 599 at 603, per Morton J

FAIR PRICE   *See* MARKET PRICE; PRICE

FAIR REPORT

'The action is one of libel against Lloyds for publishing a report of the trial of one Guerra for conspiracy to commit fraud, he having been alleged to have conspired with the plaintiff who was not however tried with him. At the trial of this action the question of privilege was reserved, the Lord Chief Justice of the Common Pleas expressing a doubt whether Lloyds had the same privilege as an ordinary newspaper, and, inasmuch as no evidence was given in the report but only the speeches of the prosecuting counsel and the summing up of the judge, whether the report could possibly be considered fair. It appears to me upon the authorities that there is no foundation for the doubts thus expressed. I cannot think that there is any difference between the privilege of a newspaper and a pamphlet, unless some question be raised of malice. . . . I also think that the fact that the report only published the summing up and the speech of the prosecuting counsel and omitted the evidence, does not shew that the report was unfair; it would clearly be impossible to report trials if that were so. It is sufficient to publish a fair abstract. I do not see that the reporter is to be blamed if he takes the judge's abstract instead of one of his own, though I do not lay it down as law that the summing up is necessarily fair.' *Milissich v Lloyds* (1877) 46 LJQB 404 at 406, CA, per Mellish LJ

'The judge may have given a fair analysis of the speeches of both counsel, then if you have published the Judge's speech you have really given a fair report.' Ibid at 407, per Brett JA

FAIR TRIAL

'The right to prosecute and the right to lead admissible evidence in support of its [the prosecution's] case are not subject to judicial control. Of course when the prosecutor reaches court he becomes subject to the directions as to the conduct of the trial by the judge, whose duty it then is to see that the accused has a fair trial according to law. What does "fair" mean in this context? It relates to the process of trial. No man is to be compelled to incriminate himself: *nemo tenetur se ipsum prodere*. No man is to be convicted save on the probative effect of legally admissible evidence. No admission or confession is to be received in evidence unless voluntary. If legally admissible evidence be tendered which endangers these principles the judge may exercise his discretion to exclude it, thus ensuring that the accused has the benefit of principles which exist in the law to secure him a fair trial; but he has no power to exclude admissible evidence of the commission of a crime, unless in his judgment these principles are endangered.' *R v Sang* [1979] 2 All ER 1222 at 1246, HL, per Lord Scarman

FAIR VALUE

Australia 'In finding the fair or real value of shares at the time of purchase or allotment, the fact that it is then possible to sell the shares at a price that will go far to cover the outlay may be disregarded, if that price is delusive or fictitious, is the result of a fraudulent prospectus, manipulation of the market or some other improper practice on the part of the defendant or those associated with him: see *Twycross v Grant* [(1877) 2 CPD 469 at 489]; *Broome v Speak* [[1903] 1 Ch 586 at 606].' *Potts v Miller* (1940) 64 CLR 282 at 299, per Dixon J

Australia 'The use of the phrase "fair market value" does not, in my view, connote anything different from "value to the owner"; the mere introduction of the word "fair" as a qualification of the measure provided by market value appears to me to require the same approach to the assessment of compensation as is generally applied under statutes which expressly or impliedly provide for payment of "value" *simpliciter*, or "value to the owner".' *Cattanach v Water Conservation and Irrigation Commission* [1963] NSWR 304 at 308, 309, per Else-Mitchell J

New Zealand [The articles of a private company contained restrictions as to transfers of shares to persons who were not shareholders, and gave the governing director of the company an absolute right to purchase from any shareholder the whole or any portion of the shares held by him, at such price as might be agreed upon by the governing director and the shareholder, and, in default of agreement, at the 'fair value', as fixed by the auditor for the time being of the company. On a special case stated by the auditor, as arbitrator:] 'In my view, what is a "fair value" is not in the circumstances what a man desiring to buy the shares would have had to pay for them to a vendor willing to sell at a fair price but not desiring to sell. Having regard to the constitution of the company, and the circumstances of this case, I think it would be unreal to try to imagine hypothetical buyers and sellers of shares of this company for the purpose of ascertaining the price at which they would deal. The arbitrator has to arrive at a "*fair* value"—that is to say, a value fairly attributable to these shares having regard to all the factors proper to be considered. . . . The basis upon which the arbitrator is to proceed in the valuation of the 4,000 shares in question is that he will decide what he considers to be the fair value of the shares having regard to—(a) The assets of the company including goodwill. (b) The past earnings of the company and the present prospects of future earnings. (c) The possibility that all future profits may not be distributed as dividends but may be retained and become additional assets. (d) The fact that in this case the purchaser is the governing director who has special privileges in relation to dividends. The arbitrator will ignore all the special provisions of the articles relating to transfer, and will value the shares as if they were not subject to any such provision.' *Re an Arbitration, Fletcher, Humphreys & Co Ltd v Middleton* [1944] NZLR 502 at 507, 508 per Northcroft J; also reported [1944] GLR 262 at 265

United States 'Fair value', with respect to a dissenter's shares, means the value of the shares immediately before the effectuation of the corporate action to which the dissenter objects, excluding any appreciation or depreciation in anticipation of the corporate action unless exclusion would be inequitable. (Revised Model Business Corporation Act 1984, s 13.01(3))

FAIR WEAR AND TEAR *See* WEAR AND TEAR

FAIRLY

[The defendant agreed to take a colliery at a certain sleeping rent, and to continue to work it so long as it was 'fairly' workable.] 'The defendants were not obliged, under this agreement, to go on working so long as there was any coal to be found; for, I am of opinion, that, under the words "fairly workable", they were not obliged to work at a dead loss.' *Jones v Shears* (1836) 7 C & P 346 at 347, per Coleridge J

'The learned judge [in the court of first instance] . . . goes on to say that the duty of the shipowner is to put the timber into the lighters "in such a way and to such an extent as that the lighters may fairly be deemed to be loaded"; . . . I think what the judge meant by "fairly loaded" was this. The shipowner has to discharge into the lighter the timber which has been brought by the ship. His obligation would not be satisfied by putting two or three pieces of timber on board the barge. His obligation is to put a fair cargo on the barge.' *Akt Helios v Ekman & Co* [1897] 2 QB 83 at 91, 92, CA, per Chitty LJ

FAIRWAY

'Taking it upon the finding of the jury, that the steamer at the time of the collision, was out of the fairway or mid-channel of the river, it becomes necessary to look at the 17 & 18 Vict c 104 [Merchant Shipping Act 1854 (repealed; see now Collision Regulations and Distress Signals Order 1977] and see what rule it lays down. The 297th section, says that "Every steam ship, when navigating any narrow channel shall, whenever it is safe and practicable, keep to that side of the fairway or mid-channel which lies on the starboard side of such ship." . . . The jury have found that there is a fairway or mid-channel as distinct from the channel itself, and in my opinion they are wrong in that finding, because the terms "fairway or mid-channel" mean every navigable part of the river. If a vessel is excluded from navigating a particular part of the river by tiers of shipping, that part would not be the fairway or mid-channel within the meaning of the Act. I think that the jury ought to have found that the fairway or mid-channel extends as close to the shore as there is depth of water on ordinary occasions. If the term "fairway or mid-channel" is taken to mean some arbitrary stream of which there is no indication, it would be difficult, if not impossible for persons navigating the river to know how to regulate their course so as to comply with the Act of Parliament. In my opinion the fairway or mid-channel extends to so much of the river as is commonly navigable.' *Smith v*

Voss (1857) 2 H & N 97 at 101–103, per Bramwell B

'The word "fairway" means, we think, a clear passage-way by water. Wherever there is an open navigable passage used by vessels proceeding up and down a river or channel, that may be said to be a fairway.' *The Blue Bell* [1895] P 242 at 246, PC, per cur

FALSA DEMONSTRATIO NON NOCET

'The rule is, that where any property in a will is sufficiently ascertained by the description, it passes by the devise, although all the particulars stated in the will with reference to it may not be true. The question here is, does this testator mean to devise any particular estate which can be ascertained from the will? If he does, then the describing it to be freehold instead of leasehold would not affect the devise; for the maxim is—*Falsa demonstratio non nocet.'* *Doe* d *Dunning v Cranstoun* (1840) 7 M & W 1 at 10, 11 per Parke B

'That maxim to which I refer is applicable to a case where some subject-matter is devised as a whole under a denomination which is applicable to the entire land, and then the words of description that include and denote the entire subject-matter are followed by words which are added on the principle of enumeration, but do not completely enumerate and exhaust all the particulars which are comprehended and included within the antecedent, universal, or generic denomination. Then the ordinary principle and rule of law, which is perfectly consistent with common sense and reason, is this: that the entirety which has been expressly and definitely given shall not be prejudiced by an imperfect and inaccurate enumeration of the particulars of the specific gift.' *West v Lawday* (1865) 11 HL Cas 375 at 383, 384, per Lord Westbury LC

FALSE

'If by a number of statements you intentionally give a false impression and induce a person to act upon it, it is not the less false although if one takes each statement by itself there may be a difficulty in showing that any specific statement is untrue.' *Aaron's Reefs v Twiss* [1896] AC 273 at 281, HL, per Lord Halsbury LC

[Section 25 of the Weights and Measures Act 1878 (repealed; see now Weights and Measures

Act 1985, s 17), made it an offence to use for trade any weighing machine which was 'false or unjust'.] 'If, with the most honest purpose and at the request of the purchaser, you try to obtain an adjustment by an alteration of the machine itself, which affects its accuracy as an instrument, you are then using a machine for trade which is false or unjust. . . . If the machine itself is altered, so that as it stands the weight of the contents of the scale or scoop which holds the goods is not truly represented on the index, I think that s 25 has been contravened, and that there has been a user of an instrument which is false or unjust within the meaning of the section.' *London County Council v Payne & Co* [1904] 1 KB 194 at 202–204, per Kennedy J

'In the opinion of this court there was ample evidence on which the jury could come to the conclusion that this prospectus was false in a material particular in that it conveyed a false impression. The falsehood . . . consisted in putting before intending investors, as material on which they could exercise their judgment as to the position of the company, figures which apparently disclosed the existing position, but in fact hid it.' *R v Kylsant (Lord)* [1932] 1 KB 442 at 448, CCA, per cur.

Australia 'It would be extravagant to apply the epithet "false" to a story merely because it contains some inaccuracies in detail or because it is somewhat exaggerated.' *Mountford v Crofter* [1942] SASR 244 at 249, per Richards J

Australia [Income Tax Assessment Act 1936 provides in s 227(1) any person who makes or delivers a return which is false in any particular . . . shall be guilty of an offence.] 'As a matter of ordinary English usage the word "false" is capable, depending upon its context, of meaning either erroneous or deceitful and for this reason I turn to the context in which the word appears in the statute. A comparison of s 227 [see now s 8K Taxation Administration Act 1953] with ss 229 and 230 suggests that when Parliament has intended to proscribe deceitful conduct it has used the words "knowingly" and "wilfully" which tends to suggest that in s 227 "false" should be given some other meaning, namely its more common meaning of erroneous or incorrect.' *Federal Commissioner of Taxation v Turner* (1984) 73 FLR 24 at 26, per Olney J

Australia [Section 234 of the Customs Act 1901 (Cth) provides that it is an offence to evade payment of any duty which is payable, . . . or make or give any entry which is false in any particular. . . .] 'There is, . . . authority which compels me to conclude that the words "false in any particular" in s 234(1)(d) means "contrary to fact", guilty knowledge or belief forming no ingredient in the offence—*Davidson v Watson* (1953) 28 ALJ 63; *Sternberg v R* (1953) 88 CLR 646 at 653. . . . It is plain that the word "false" has two accepted meanings—"untrue in fact" and "intentionally untrue". Its use in s 229(1)(i) in conjunction with "or wilfully misleading" gives force to the view, at which I have arrived, that in the context in which it is found, it does not mean merely "untrue in fact" but involves proof that the entry, answers, statements etc were intentionally or deliberately false.' *Farmer v Murphy* (1986) 67 ALR 114 at 119, 122, per Yeldham J

Canada [Section 19(1)(c)(viii) of the Immigration Act, RSC 1952, c 325 (now RSC 1970, c I-2, s 18(1)(e)(viii)), refers to a person who comes into Canada or remains therein with a 'false' or improperly issued passport, visa, medical certificate or other document pertaining to his admission or by reason of any 'false' or misleading information, force, stealth or other fraudulent or improper means, whether exercised or given by himself or by any other person.] 'The juxtaposition of "false document" and "false or misleading information" in the one paragraph conveys to me different senses in which the word "false" is used. "False document" is not defined in the Immigration Act. In context, it appears to me that a document does not become false merely because it contains false information. A person may be in possession of a passport or visa or other document which is an authorized one from an authorized source being what it purports to be, and yet it may contain false or misleading information so as to bring him within the second part of s 19(1)(c)(viii).' *Minister of Manpower and Immigration v Brooks* (1973) 36 DLR (3d) 522 at 530, SCC, per Laskin J

FALSE ACCOUNTING

(1) Where a person dishonestly, with a view to gain for himself or another or with intent to cause loss to another,—
   (a) destroys, defaces, conceals or falsifies any account or any record or document made or required for any accounting purpose; or

(b) in furnishing information for any purpose produces or makes use of any account, or any such record or document as aforesaid, which to his knowledge is or may be misleading, false or deceptive in a material particular;

he shall, on conviction on indictment, be liable to imprisonment for a term not exceeding seven years.

(2) For purposes of this section a person who makes or concurs in making in an account or other document an entry which is or may be misleading, false or deceptive in a material particular, or who omits or concurs in omitting a material particular from an account or other document, is to be treated as falsifying the account or document.

(Theft Act 1968, s 17)

[The Falsification of Accounts Act 1875 (repealed; see now the Theft Act 1968 s 17 [supra]) made it an offence for a servant wilfully and with intent to defraud to 'falsify' any account belonging to his employer.] 'It is not disputed that the figures on these sheets were incorrect . . . because the prisoner had driven [a] cab with the flag up, and so the taximeter from which the figures are taken gave no record of the miles actually run. . . . The prisoner . . . has certified that the amount recorded is the correct amount received. He has therefore clearly concurred in making a false entry in the taximeter sheet, which is an account. . . . Further than this . . . an offence under this statute was committed when the prisoner falsified the mechanical record from which the calculation of the amount received was made up. . . . It would be a serious thing to say that to falsify the mechanical means whereby an account is brought into existence is not to falsify an account within the meaning of this Act.' *R v Solomons* [1909] 2 KB 980 at 986, CCA, per cur.

FALSE IMPRISONMENT

The gist of the action of false imprisonment is the mere imprisonment. The plaintiff need not prove that the imprisonment was unlawful or malicious, but establishes a prima facie case if he proves that he was imprisoned by the defendant; the onus then lies on the defendant of proving a justification. (45 Halsbury's Laws (4th edn) para 1325)

FALSE PRETENCES

[Under the former Larceny Act 1916, any person who by any false pretence, with intent to defraud, obtained from any other person any chattel, money or valuable security, etc was guilty of a misdemeanour—

The crime of obtaining by false pretences has now been replaced by that of obtaining property by deception under the Theft Act 1968, s 15. The Larceny Act 1916 was repealed by the Act of 1968, s 33(3), Sch 3.]

FALSE TRADE DESCRIPTION

(1) A false trade description is a trade description which is false to a material degree.

(2) A trade description which, though not false, is misleading, that is to say, likely to be taken for such an indication of any of the matters specified in s 2 of this Act [which defines 'trade description'] as would be false to a material degree, shall be deemed to be a false trade description.

(3) Anything which, though not a trade description, is likely to be taken for an indication of any of those matters and, as such an indication, would be false to a material degree, shall be deemed to be a false trade description.

(4) A false indication, or anything likely to be taken as an indication which would be false, that any goods comply with a standard specified or recognised by any person or implied by the approval of any person shall be deemed to be a false trade description, if there is no such person or no standard so specified, recognised or implied.

(Trade Descriptions Act 1968, s 3).

[Notwithstanding sub-s (1) above, a trade description which indicates the fineness (whether in parts per thousand or otherwise) of any precious metal shall be a false trade description if that indication is false to any extent or degree (except by understating the fineness). See Hallmarking Act 1973, s 1(4).]

'The section [the Merchandise Marks Act 1887, s 3 (repealed; see supra)] goes on to define a "false trade description" as "a trade description which is false in a material respect as regards the goods to which it is applied". It is said that the present case does not come within that definition, because the purchaser got an article which was as good as that which he asked for, but if once what I may call the doctrine of equivalents is to be admitted, I can see no answer to the illustration which I put in the course of the argument, which was that of a man selling American hams as Yorkshire hams, who, according to the respondents' contention, would be entitled to an acquittal, if he were able to show that, as a matter of fact, American hams were as good as, or better than, Yorkshire hams. . . . I cannot think that the legislature can have contemplated that to prove the goods supplied to be of a quality equal to those ordered, should afford an answer to such a charge as that made in the present case.' *Kirshenboim v Salmon & Gluckstein* [1898] 2 QB 19 at 26, DC, per Lord Russell of Killowen CJ

'It strikes me that the materiality of the trade description cannot be made dependent on a comparison of the quality of the goods supplied to the purchaser with that of other goods.' Ibid at 27, per Hawkins J

Australia [The defendant company was charged with a breach of the Trade Practices Act 1974 (Cth) that in contravention of s 53(a) of the Act it did 'falsely represent' that the goods were of a particular quality.] 'The next matter is to consider whether the words "falsely represent" in s 53(a) of the Act are satisfied if the representation is not correct or whether it must be known to be false by the person making the representation. It was also argued for the defendant that, since it was a corporation, the representation must be one false to the knowledge of a person of sufficient seniority in the company to be able to bind the company. . . . I am satisfied that if a representation is in fact not correct, it comes within the words of the section, even if it is not false to the knowledge of the person making the representation, and even if the person making the representation is a servant of the company or of insufficient seniority in the company for his knowledge, according to the ordinary principles of the common law, to be deemed to be the knowledge of the company. There is nothing novel in equating "false" with "contrary to fact".' *Given v C V Holland (Holdings) Pty Ltd* (1977) 15 ALR 439 at 443, per Franki J

FAMILY   *See also* CHILD

For the purposes of this Act a family shall consist of the following members of a household—

(a) a man or woman engaged, and normally engaged, in remunerative full-time work; and

(b) if the person mentioned in the preceding paragraph is one of a married or unmarried couple, the other member of the couple; and

(c) the child or children whose requirements are provided for, in whole or in part, by the person or either of the persons mentioned in the preceding paragraphs

except that persons who include a married or unmarried couple shall not be a family for the purposes of this Act if one of the couple is engaged and normally engaged as aforesaid and the other member of the couple is receiving such payments as may be specified by regulations. (Family Income Supplements Act 1970, s 1(1), as amended by the Social Security Act 1980, s 7).

In this section . . . 'family' means, in relation to an individual, the husband or wife of the individual, and a relative of the individual or the individual's husband or wife, and 'relative' means brother, sister, ancestor or lineal descendant. (Capital Gains Tax Act 1979, s 124(8))

'Now what is . . . [the] *family*, except those persons who reside with him, of whom he is the *pater-familias*, or head. The son is one of them so long as he remains under his father's protection; . . . but when he becomes the head of a family himself, he is emancipated.' *R v Darlington (Inhabitants)* (1792) Nolan 124 at 128, 129, per Lord Kenyon CJ

'It is evident that the word "family" is capable of so many applications that if any one particular construction were attributed to it in wills, the intention of testators would be more frequently defeated than carried into effect. Under different circumstances it may mean a man's household, consisting of himself, his wife, children, and servants; it may mean his wife and children, or his children excluding the wife. . . . In the case of a will we must endeavour to ascertain the meaning in which the testator employed the word, by considering the circumstances and situation in which he was placed, the object he had in view, and the context of the will.' *Blackwell v Bull* (1836) 1 Keen 176 at 181, per Lord Langdale MR

'I have looked into the authorities, which have confirmed the opinion which I entertained during the argument, that the primary meaning of the word "family" is "children", and that there must be some peculiar circumstance, arising either on the will itself or from the situation of the parties, to prevent that construction being given to it. In ordinary parlance, the word "family" means children.' *Re Terry's Will* (1854) 19 Beav 580 at 581, per Romilly MR

'I have in this case to consider the will of a shopkeeper, who at the date of his will had a wife and seven children living; some of the children were twenty-one, others under that age; and he had at least one child married who had children. . . . The question is, who are meant by the word "family". . . . The word "family" has various meanings. In one sense it means the whole household, including servants, and, perhaps, lodgers. In another sense it means everybody descended from a common stock, that is to say, all blood relations; and it may, perhaps, include the husbands and wives of such persons. In the sense I have just mentioned, the family of A includes A himself; A must be a member of his own family. In a third sense, the word includes children only; thus when a man speaks of his wife and family, he means his wife and children. Now, every word which has more than one meaning has a primary meaning. . . . What, then, is the primary meaning of "family"? It is "children". . . . I hold, therefore, that the children of the testator can alone take under the words "my said family".' *Pigg v Clarke* (1876) 3 Ch D 672 at 674, per Jessel MR

'Although the word "family" may ordinarily mean children and nothing else, it is, I think, not unreasonable that a natural child who has been treated and recognised as a child by the parent should be so included.' *Humble v Bowman* (1877) 47 LJ Ch 62 at 65, per Hall V-C

'On the main point [counsel] relied strongly on the fact that, on marrying, a son becomes the head of a new family. It does not follow that on marrying he ceases to be a member of the original family. . . . This seems to me no more to follow from [counsel's] premiss than it follows . . . from the fact that a man on marrying becomes his wife's husband that he ceases to be his mother's son. One can be a member of two families simultaneously.' *Standingford v Probert* [1950] 1 KB 377 at 386, CA, per Asquith LJ

'Family', when looked at as an object of a power, means anybody with blood relationship and is not confined to those nearest of kin or the statutory next of kin of the testator.' *Re Perowne, Perowne v Moss* [1951] Ch 785 at 788, per Harman J

'I begin with the word "family". Certain authorities have been put before me on the use of this word adjectivally, as in "family mansion"; but I think that by common consent these authorities are to be regarded as standing some distance away from what I have to decide. The word appears in many combinations, from "family jewels" and "family home" to "family tree", "family history" and even "family way". I think it is a Janus-like word, often looking backwards ancestrally, but sometimes looking forward to posterity. In relation to "arms", I can see no real reason why the word should be used merely ancestrally especially when it is also said to exclude the maternal line and apply only to the paternal line. It seems to me that the function of the word is far more general than that. Counsel for the first, second and third defendants contended that its function was to indicate arms that were descendible. Arms could be said to be "family arms" if they were arms that had been lawfully granted so as to descend to the grantee's family. The term thus excluded arms unlawfully assumed, which were not descendible, and also arms granted to the grantee alone without any limitation to his descendants. . . . This explanation appears to me to satisfy requirements both of technical accuracy and of ordinary usage, and I accept it.' *Re Neeld, Inigo-Jones v Inigo-Jones* [1969] 2 All ER 1025 at 1028, per Megarry J

[A woman who had been mistress of W for a great many years continued to live in rented premises after his death. She claimed the protection of the Rent Acts as a member of the original tenant's 'family'.] 'Between 1950 and 1975 there have been many changes in the law effected by statute and decisions of the courts. Many changes have their foundation in the changed needs and views of society. Such changes have occurred in the field of family law and equitable interests in property. The popular meaning given to the word "family" is not fixed once and for all time. I have no doubt that with the passage of years it has changed. The cases reveal that it is not restricted to blood relationships and those created by the marriage ceremony. It can include *de facto* as well as *de jure* relationships. The popular meaning of "family" in 1975 would, according to the answer of the ordinary man, include the appellant as a member of Mr W's family. This is not to say that every mistress should be so regarded. Relationships of a casual or intermittent character and those bearing indications of impermanence would not come within the popular concept of a family unit.' *Dyson Holdings Ltd v Fox* [1975] 3 All ER 1030 at 1035, CA, per James LJ

'The meaning to be given to the words "a member of the original tenant's family" [now in para 3 of Sch 1 to the Rent Act 1977] is in my view a question of law. "Family" is a word the content of which varies with the context in which it is used. When used in a statute, it has not in my opinion the same meaning as the word "household". While a household may consist only of members of a family, it can include persons not capable of being so regarded. I accordingly cannot accept the argument that "family" in the Act can be read as meaning "household".' *Carega Properties SA v Sharratt* [1979] 2 All ER 1084 at 1087, HL, per Viscount Dilhorne

'The House [in *Carega Properties SA v Sharratt* (supra)] decided that "family" was not a term of art but was used in its ordinary popular meaning and that in that meaning it requires at least a broadly recognisable *de facto* familial nexus.' *Kavanagh v Lyroudias* [1985] 1 All ER 560 at 563, CA, per cur.

Australia 'The primary meaning of the word "family" is children. If it be intended by the testator to give the word "family" some meaning other than its primary meaning, there must be some indication of such intention shewn in the will itself.' *Re McGrath's Will* (1899) 20 NSWLR (B & P) 55 at 57, 58, per Walker J

Australia [A testator devised certain property on trust for his nephew for life subject to certain conditions. One of these conditions was that he should not marry a member of a certain 'family'.] 'The word "family" is a word of most uncertain import. It can mean many things according to its context, and in some contexts it is impossible to say in what particular sense it is used. In this condition I do not know what the testator intended to cover. I would think he meant to cover more than its own daughters—but how far lineally or laterally he wanted the word to extend it is impossible to know. He apparently had a very fixed determination that the beneficiary should not marry into that family, and determinations of that character are usually as indeterminate of ambit as they are relentless of purpose. I have no hesitation in holding that this condition is void for uncertainty.' *Re Brewis, Brewis v Brewis* [1946] VLR 199 at 202, per O'Bryan J

Australia 'The term "the family" is nowhere defined in the Act [Family Law Act 1975 (Cth)]. The juxtaposition of the phrase "the family constituted by the parties to the marriage" with what follows in the subsection suggests that this expression is intended to embrace a wider concept than that of children. It is clear, in my view, that the ordinary grammatical meaning of the word "family" is "children". As one would expect many of the authorities dealing with the construction of that word are concerned with wills.

In the subsection under consideration [s 79(4)(c)], it is the addition of the words "constituted by the parties to the marriage" which in my opinion widens the class of persons ordinarily comprehended in the expression "family" to include other relatives and members of the household. Two extended definitions of "family" appear in the Concise Oxford Dictionary, namely: (i) "members of a household, parents, children, servants, etc"; and (ii) "set of parents and children, or of relations, living together or not". I am of the opinion that the word "family" is used in the subsection in one or both of these senses.' *In the Marriage of H M and F Mehmet* (1986) 10 Fam LR 1035 at 1042, 1043, per Rourke J

Canada 'As to the construction of the word "family", it appearing from the evidence that Mrs Burgess has a husband and four infant children, I hold that "family" should be taken as referring only to children.' *Re McKeown* [1942] 3 DLR 796 at 797, Man KB, per Donovan J

Canada 'The word "family" is an elastic term, having various meanings in varying circumstances and must be considered in relation to the particular subject-matter. In *Dodge v Boston & Providence Railroad Corp* (1891) 154 Mass 299 at 301 the court said: The word "family" has several meanings. Its primary meaning is the collective body of persons who live in one house under one head or management. Its secondary meaning is those who are of the same lineage or descend from one common progenitor. Unless the context manifests a different intention, the word "family" is usually construed in its primary sense.' *Charlottetown v Charlottetown Association for Residential Services* (1979) 100 DLR (3d) 614 at 621, 622, PE I, SC, per McQuaid J

New Zealand 'That the word "family", used by a married man in his will, means "children" has been established by the cases of *Pigg v Clarke* [supra], *Re Hutchinson and Tenant* [(1878) 8 Ch D 540], and other cases, and does not seem to be contested.' *Re Cundy* (1899) NZLR 53 at 58, per Edwards J; also reported 1 GLR 246 at 248

FAMILY ARRANGEMENT

A family arrangement is an agreement between members of the same family, intended to be generally and reasonably for the benefit of the family either by compromising doubtful or disputed rights or by preserving the family property or the peace and security of the family by avoiding litigation or by saving its honour.

The agreement may be implied from a long course of dealing, but it is more usual to embody or to effectuate the agreement in a deed to which the term 'family arrangement' is applied. . . .

Family arrangements are governed by principles which are not applicable to dealings between strangers. When deciding the rights of parties under family arrangements or a claim to upset such an arrangement, the court considers what in the broadest view of the matter is most for the interest of the family, and has regard to considerations which, in dealing with transactions between persons not members of the same family, would not be taken into account. Matters which would be fatal to the validity of similar transactions between strangers are not objections to the binding effect of family arrangements. Conversely, an intention to create a legally enforceable contract may be negatived more readily where the parties to an arrangement are members of the same family than where they are not.

Although usually and necessarily present where a family arrangement is made, parental influence will not by itself render the transaction voidable, but where, at a time when he is not fully emancipated from his parent's influence, a child enters into a family arrangement under which the parent benefits to the total exclusion of the child or benefits to an extent out of all proportion to the benefit accruing to the child, there is a presumption of undue influence. The presumption will be rebutted if it appears that, when the arrangement was entered into, the child was able to form a free and unfettered judgment independent of any sort of control. (18 Halsbury's Laws (4th edn) para 304)

FAMILY COMPANY *See* COMPANY

FARE

The expression 'fare' includes any payment to be made for the carriage of luggage on a cab. (London Cab and Stage Carriage Act 1907, s 6)

'Fares' includes sums payable in respect of a contract ticket or season ticket. (Transport Charges &c (Miscellaneous Provisions) Act 1954, s 13; Road Traffic Act 1960, s 257(1))

FARM

Farm, or *feorme*, is an old Saxon word signifying provisions: and it came to be used instead of rent or render, because antiently the greater part of rents were reserved in provisions; in corn, in poultry, and the like; till the use of money became more frequent. So that a farmer, *firmarius*, was one who held his lands upon payment of a rent or *feorme*: though at present, by a gradual departure from the original sense, the word farm is brought to signify the very estate or lands so held upon farm or rent. (2 Bl Com 318)

'The emphatic meaning of the word "farm" is this. That it means lands which have not been held in hand by the owner, but granted out and occupied by another person. Where that is the case, where that description applies to lands, the interest of the lessor or the lessee may pass with the description of "farm", but where it is contained in a devise of real estate upon limitations which import the fee, I have no hesitation in saying it carries the fee simple farms, and fee simple farms only.' *Holmes v Milward* (1878) 47 LJ Ch 522 at 525, per Fry J

Dairy farm *See* DAIRY

Farm buildings

'"Farming buildings" [in a will] include farmhouses.' *Cooke v Cholmondeley* (1858) 4 Drew 326 at 328, per Kindersley V-C

Farm labourer

Canada 'A "farm labourer" is not simply one who works on a farm—as that might include carpenters, electricians and others engaged in carrying on their trade temporarily on farm lands. It seems to me that "a farm labourer" must be considered as one who works in or at a farming activity. His time and attention might be solely devoted to cultivation of the soil, or in caring for livestock, or in hauling produce to market—but his primary or basic function must be related to farming.

It would seem to me that "farm labourer" indicates a type of occupation. It does not depend on whether the person works on one small farm or on a large farm of many acres, nor whether he works for a corporation or an individual farmer, nor whether he works for one farmer or several, nor whether he does one class of farm work only or a number of classes of farm work. It would not matter whether he lived on a farm or commuted to work from a town. To give the words their natural meaning "a farm labourer" would be one engaged in work that is considered, in the society in which he lives and works, as part of the business of farming. His work must be primarily for farm purposes—that is, devoted to the growing of crops and the primary production of food in all its many forms such as cattle and livestock operations, dairying, bee-keeping, growing seed, fodder, or any combination or variety of these things and others ordinarily considered as part of or a type of "farming".' *R v Alberta Board of Industrial Relations, ex parte Eastern Irrigation District* (1970) 13 DLR (3d) 709 at 715, 716, Alta SC, per MacDonald J

Farm land

'Farm land' means land in the United Kingdom wholly or mainly occupied for the purposes of husbandry, but excluding any dwelling or domestic offices, and excluding market garden land, and 'farming' shall be construed accordingly. (Income and Corporation Taxes Act 1988, s 832(1))

Canada [Issue arose as to the meaning of the word 'farmland' as found in s 2(d) of the Farm Land Security Act, SS 1984–85, c F-8.01.] 'There is a definition of farmland contained in s 2 of the Act and that definition is as follows: (d) "farmland" means land in Saskatchewan that is used for the purposes of farming and is subject to a mortgage. The affidavit filed by the defendant discloses that the parcel of land contains the family farm house, four grain bins and a machine shed—workshop. The affidavit also states that the parcel of land is the headquarters and operative base of a farm operation and enterprise. In my opinion, the land itself does not have to be farmed to come within the provisions of the Act, as long as it is used in the operation of a farm. Relying upon the defendant's affidavit, which is not contradicted by any material filed on behalf of the plaintiff, I am satisfied that the parcel of land is used for the purposes of farming within the meaning and the intent of the Act.' *Bank of Montreal v Ducheminsky Farms Ltd* (1985) 38 Sask R 293 at 293, 294 Sask QB, per McLellan J

FARM PRODUCTS

Secured transactions

United States Goods are . . . 'farm products' if they are crops or livestock or supplies used or produced in farming operations or if they are products of crops or livestock in their unmanufactured states (such as ginned cotton, wool-clip, maple syrup, milk and eggs), and if they are in possession of a debtor engaged in raising, fattening, grazing or other farming operations. If goods are farm products they are neither equipment nor inventory. . . . (Uniform Commercial Code 1978, s 9–109)

FARMER

'Farmer' means any person (not being an incorporated company or society) who, as tenant or owner of an agricultural holding, cultivates the holding for profit. (Agricultural Credits Act 1928, s 5)

Canada 'I feel that the word "farmer" as used in the Act [Farmers' Creditors Arrangement Act 1934 (see now RSC 1970, c F–5)] refers to one who runs the land "for his own profit" and does not refer to a hired man who tills the land only and does not receive the profit from the operation or suffer the loss in the event of crop failure. Nor does it include someone who does a few odd chores on the farm, when the person who runs the farm for his own profit is away or otherwise busy. A person may be a farmer all his life, and have no other occupation. When he becomes aged he may retire from farming, let his sons have the whole operation of the farm and take the profits, in which case he is in my opinion not a farmer and efficient producer within the meaning of the Act but a "retired farmer".' *Re Beck* [1940] 1 WWR 609 at 619, Sask KB, per Bryant LM

Canada [Section 2(1)(f) of the Farmers' Creditors Arrangement Act 1934 (see supra) defined a 'farmer' as a person whose principal occupation consisted in farming or the tillage of the soil.] 'It is not necessary for a woman to do any manual labour, such as driving a tractor or binder, to be a farmer. In fact it is not the custom generally among Canadian women to do heavy manual labour in the fields. She may hire it all done or she may get help from her husband or children or neighbours. A corporation may be a farmer within the above subsection: *Re Barickman Hutterian Mutual Corpn; Barickman Hutterian Mutual Corpn v Nault* [1939] SCR 223, 20 CBR 314.' *Prudential Insurance Co v Liboiron* [1940] 2 WWR 623 at 627, Sask KB, per Anderson J; revd on other grounds, [1940] 3 WWR 556, Sask CA

Canada 'By s 2(1)(f) [of the Farmers' Creditors Arrangement Act 1934 (see supra)] it is provided that unless the context otherwise requires or implies the expression "farmer" means a person whose principal occupation consists in farming or tillage of the soil. It is clear that having or carrying on another occupation than that of farming does not exclude a person from the benefit of the Act. It seems clear also that residence on a farm is not essential.' *Northern Trusts Co v Eckert* [1942] 2 WWR 382 at 385, Alta CA, per Ford JA

Actively engaged in farming

New Zealand 'In my opinion the words "actively engaged in farming" mean a person who derives his livelihood substantially from "farming". That is farming in the sense of active participation in the cultivation of land or the raising of stock. He is one who is effectively committed to farm work as a means of livelihood to the extent that, if asked his occupation, he could fairly reply "farmer".' *Re Cowley (decd)* [1971] NZLR 468 at 470, per Roper J, in an unreported judgment but quoted with approval by Richmond J, delivering the judgment of the Court of Appeal

FARMING   *See also* HUSBANDRY

'The Act [Income Tax Act 1952] is somewhat less than explicit on the meaning of the word "farming". By s 526(1) [repealed; see now the Income and Corporation Taxes Act 1988, s 832(1)], except so far as is otherwise provided or the context otherwise requires, "farm land" means: "land in the United Kingdom wholly or mainly occupied for the purposes of husbandry, not being market garden land, and includes the farmhouse and farm buildings, if any, and "farming" shall be construed accordingly." In relation to what I am concerned with in this case, the meaning of "farming" thus principally depends on the meaning of "husbandry"; and as one of the ordinary meanings of "husbandry" is "farming", here again there is some degree of circularity. "Market garden land", which is excluded from "farm land" and so from the meaning of "farming", is defined

by s 526(1) [repealed; see supra] as meaning: "land in the United Kingdom occupied as a nursery or garden for the sale of the produce (other than land used for the growth of hops) and 'market gardening' shall be construed accordingly". Thus neither by inclusion nor by exclusion is much assistance provided. I therefore propose to assume that the word "farming" means "farming" in the sense of the carrying on of activities appropriate to land recognisable as farm land. It must at least include the raising of beasts, the cultivation of land and the growing of crops; and the words "wholly or mainly" seem to me to be of some importance. I do not think that a farmer ceases to farm merely because he arranges for others to reap instead of himself.' *Lowe (Inspector of Taxes) v Ashmore (J W) Ltd* [1971] 1 All ER 1057 at 1065, per Megarry J

New Zealand 'It seems to me, beyond question, that the development of land for the purpose of farming is a use that falls naturally within the general category of "farming". If a farmer who is in the process of bringing in unimproved land is confronted with some inconvenient irregularity in the surface of the land, then he obviously can get rid of this, either by bulldozing adjoining land, if that is a suitable procedure, or by filling it in with suitable material. This, I think, would clearly still be a use that falls naturally within the general class of farming use. Once this point is reached then I cannot see that it matters whether he carts filling material from some other part of his own farm or imports it from some external source.' *Onehunga Timber Holdings Ltd v Rotorua City* [1972] NZLR 349 at 352, per Richmond J

FARMING OPERATION

Bankruptcy

United States '[F]arming operation' includes farming, tillage of the soil, dairy farming, ranching, production or raising of crops, poultry, or livestock, and production of poultry or livestock products in an unmanufactured state. . . . (Bankruptcy Act 1978, s 101(18))

FARMING STOCK

'Farming stock' means crops or horticultural produce, whether growing or severed from the land, and after severance whether subjected to any treatment or process of manufacture or not; live stock, including poultry or bees, and the produce and progeny thereof; and any agricultural or horticultural produce whether subjected to any treatment or process of manufacture or not; seeds and manures; agricultural vehicles, machinery, and other plant; agricultural tenants' fixtures and other agricultural fixtures which a tenant is by law authorised to remove. (Agricultural Credits Act 1928, s 5)

In will

'"All my farming stock", in common and popular language, does not include crops on the ground.' *Vaisey v Reynolds* (1828) 5 Russ 12 at 19, per Leach MR [But see *Evans v Williamson*, infra]

'Is it possible to say these words "farming stock and effects upon the farm" do not carry the corn, wool and sheep ready for sale to the trustees? The clear intention of the testator was, that they should pass to his executors, and if proper be sold by them. . . . It is possible that the wool would not be included in the words "live or dead farming stock", but I have no doubt it comes under the word "effects".' *Harvey v Harvey* (1863) 32 Beav 441 at 444, 445, per Romilly MR

'I feel no doubt whatever that when the testator made this bequest of "all the live and dead farming stock belonging to him in and about his farm", he intended to give everything which in the ordinary sense of the words is comprised under the term "farming stock". I understand those words to include all the undisposed of produce of the farm. The "livestock" must include all the animals, and the term "dead stock" will apply to the wheat, wool, cheese, ricks of hay and other articles enumerated in the schedule. In my opinion, they all pass under this bequest.' *Burbridge v Burbridge* (1867) 37 LJ Ch 47 at 48, per Malins V-C

'The gift is of "all the household furniture, farming stock, goods, chattels and effects which shall be in or about Frondeg". Now, I do not see how it is possible to hold, after Lord Ellenborough's decision [in *West v Moore* (1807) 8 East, 339], that the words "farming stock" are not an indication of an intention to give the crops. Lord Ellenborough said, "The case of *Cox v Godsalve* [(1699) 6 East 604 n.] . . . must conclude it, though, but for that case, I should have been more inclined to think that stock on the farm meant movable stock." By that he evidently means that that decision included stock not movable.' *Evans v Williamson* (1880) 50 LJ Ch 197 at 198, per Jessel MR

FARRIERY

'Farriery' means any work in connection with the preparation or treatment of the foot of a horse for the immediate reception of a shoe thereon, the fitting by nailing or otherwise of a shoe to the foot or the finishing off of such work to the foot. (Farriers (Registration) Act 1975, s 18)

FAST

[A steamer was to be discharged as 'fast' as she could deliver. Certain customs as to the method of discharge operated at her port of arrival.] 'It appears to me that shipowners, when they enter a dock of this character, and place themselves, as they have done in this case, in the hands of the dock company to carry out the discharge in accordance with what appears to be, upon the evidence, the invariable practice of the port, must in so doing leave these agents to deal with the matter of the discharge in the customary way; and that when the shipowners assert that the vessel has not been discharged as fast as she can deliver, it rests upon them to show, having regard to the way in which the discharge must be done, that she has not been discharged as fast as she could deliver—in effect, that she could have delivered, under the circumstances in which she was placed, at a greater rate than in fact was the case.' *The Jaederen* [1892] P 351 at 359, per Gorell Barnes J

'"To be discharged as fast as steamer can deliver, as customary", means that the discharge and delivery is to be as fast as the custom of the port would allow, and that the shipowner took the risk of a delay in that discharge and delivery owing to the custom of the port.' *Good & Co v Isaacs* [1892] 2 QB 555 at 564, CA, per Kay LJ

[The cargo of a ship was to be loaded 'as fast as steamer can receive' in accordance with a clause in her charterparty. On the ship's arrival at the named port the only suitable berth was occupied, and on account of this delay the ship did not complete loading until after the time fixed by the charterparty. The owners of the chartered ship claimed demurrage.] 'When the ship was an arrived ship, what was the obligation of the defendant? It was to load as fast as she could receive; that, in a business document drawn by business men and to be interpreted according to a business meaning, does not mean that she was to be loaded either all night or by unusual or by impracticable methods, but that she was to be loaded in the usual and customary manner—i.e. the obligation of the charterer was to use with reasonable diligence the usual and available means for loading . . . the obligation of the charterer to load did not commence . . . until it was possible to load.' *Temple, Thomson & Clarke v Runnalls* (1901) 18 TLR 18 at 19, per Bigham J; affd (1902) 18 TLR 822, CA

'Although . . . the words . . . are unambiguous, I have no doubt they must be construed reasonably, and that the extent of the consignee's obligation may depend a good deal upon the circumstances existing in the particular case. For example, if the shipowner devised some means by which the cargo could be discharged much faster than the consignee had any reason to anticipate or be prepared for, I do not think that his failure to take delivery as fast as it was tendered would be a breach of his obligation.' *Crown SS Co Ltd v Leitch* 1908 SC 506 at 512, per Lord Low

'The initial words of the clause [in a bill of lading] "cargo to be received at destination as fast as vessel can deliver", do not, in my opinion, mean that the consignee is bound to take delivery in the shortest time the ship could, in the circumstances affecting her, put the goods out. Consideration must also be paid to the circumstances so far as they affect the receivers of the goods. If they take the cargo as fast as was possible in the circumstances with the exercise of reasonable skill and diligence then they fulfil their part of the contract.' *Rickinson Sons & Co v Scottish Co-operative Wholesale Society, SS Arachne* 1918 SC 440 at 461, per Lord Mackenzie

FAST AND LOOSE

In the Greenland whale fishery, for example, the rule of 'fast and loose' applies. A whale is said to be a 'fast fish' at any time while a harpoon remains in it and the line continues attached to it and remains in the striker's power or management, or where the harpoon does not remain in the body of the whale but the whale is attached to the boat of the first striker by any means, such as the entanglement of the line round it. If, while the whale is a fast fish, it is struck by a harpoon from another ship, the second harpoon is called a 'friendly harpoon' and the whale remains the property of the first striker, even though it subsequently frees itself from the first harpoon and remains fast to the second. Similarly, if, while the whale

remains fast to the harpoon of the first striker, another, unsolicited, so disturbs the whale that it breaks from the first harpoon, the property remains in the first striker even though the second striker afterwards secures it. But if the first harpoon or line breaks, or the line attached to the first harpoon is not in the striker's power, the whale is a 'loose fish' and will become the property of any other person who strikes and obtains it. A whale is not in the striker's power if his line runs out and he attaches the end of the line to a 'drog' or buoy which he throws overboard; but in the Southern whale fishery among the Galapagos Islands, this part of the 'fast and loose' rule is subject to a modification whereby the person who first struck the whale with a harpoon and drog is entitled to one-half of the proceeds from the person who kills it.' (18 Halsbury's Laws (4th edn) para 919)

'There has prevailed in the Northern Whale Fishery for a very considerable period of time—probably ever since the time when these fisheries came into the possession of this country—a rule with regard to the property in whales that are harpooned and captured, which rule has received the technical denomination of "fast and loose", and has been known by that designation among the parties engaged in the fishery, and has become the subject of various decisions in English courts of justice. The object of the rule was to prevent disputes and quarrels among persons engaged in the capture of whales. The rule is intended to denote that the person who first harpoons a fish, and retains his hold of that fish until it is finally captured, is to be regarded as the proprietor of the fish, although the actual capture and killing of the whale may be accomplished by the assistance of other persons. But the rule also involves this consideration—that if the fish, after it has been harpooned, breaks away from the person who first harpoons it, or if the fish is subsequently abandoned; then the fish, though dying in consequence of the wound originally inflicted by the harpoon, is regarded as a loose fish, and becomes the property of the person who first finds it, and takes possession of it.' *Aberdeen Arctic Co v Sutter* (1862) 6 LT 229 at 230, per Lord Westbury LC; also reported (1862) 4 Macq 355.

FATHER

'I take it that, *prima facie*, the titles of "father" and "mother" belong only to those who have become so in the manner known to and approved by the law.' *Re C T (an infant)* [1956] 3 All ER 500 at 504, per Roxburgh J; also reported in [1957] Ch 48 at 56

FATSTOCK

'Fatstock' means fat cattle, fat sheep and fat pigs and the carcases of those animals. (Agriculture Act 1967, s 25)

FAULT

'Fault' means wrongful act or default. (Sale of Goods Act 1979, s 61(1))

'Fault' means negligence, breach of statutory duty or other act or omission which gives rise to a liability in tort or would, apart from this Act, give rise to the defence of contributory negligence. (Law Reform (Contributory Negligence) Act 1945, s 4)

[Rule D of the York-Antwerp Rules 1950 provides that rights to contribution in general average shall not be affected though the event that gave rise to the sacrifice or expenditure may have been due to the 'fault' of one of the parties to the adventure.] 'It appears . . . that for the relevant purpose a "fault" is a legal wrong which is actionable as between the parties at the time when the general average sacrifice or expenditure is made.' *Goulandris Bros Ltd v Goldman (B) & Sons Ltd* [1957] 3 All ER 100 at 114, per Pearson J; also reported in [1958] 1 QB 74 at 104]

'We would state briefly what in our judgment the law was and is on this question of fault in the offence of driving in a dangerous manner. It is not an absolute offence. In order to justify a conviction there must be, not only a situation which, viewed objectively, was dangerous, but there must also have been some fault on the part of the driver, causing that situation. "Fault" certainly does not necessarily involve deliberate misconduct or recklessness or intention to drive in a manner inconsistent with proper standards of driving. Nor does fault necessarily involve moral blame. Thus there is fault if an inexperienced or a naturally poor driver, while straining every nerve to do the right thing, falls below the standard of a competent and careful driver. Fault involves a failure; a falling below the care or skill of a competent and experienced driver, in relation to the manner of the driving and to the relevant circumstances of the case.' *R v Gosney* [1971] 3 All ER 220 at 224, CA, per cur.

United States 'Fault' means wrongful act, omission or breach. (Uniform Commercial Code 1978, s 1–201(16))

With all faults

'The meaning of the advertisement [describing a ship as "a copper-fastened vessel to be taken wth all her faults"] must be, that the seller will not be responsible for any faults which a copper-fastened ship may have. Suppose a silver service sold "with all faults", and it turns out to be plated; can there be any doubt that the vendor would be liable? "With all faults" must mean with all faults which it may have consistently with its being the thing described.' *Shepherd v Kain* (1821) 5 B & Ald 240 at 241, per cur.

[A contract for the sale of goods provided that the goods were to be taken 'with all faults' and defects, damaged or inferior, if any, at valuation to be arranged mutually or by arbitration.] 'That clause in my opinion only applies to goods which answer the trade description, and does not shut out the overriding warranty or condition implied by law under the Sale of Goods Act [1893 s 13 (repealed; see now the Sale of Goods Act 1979, s 13(1))] which says that where there is a contract for the sale of goods by description there is an implied condition that the goods shall correspond with the description.' *Robert A Munro & Co Ltd v Meyer* [1930] 2 KB 312 at 327, per Wright J

FAULTY

Design

Australia 'To design something that won't work simply because at the time of its designing insufficient is known about the problems involved and their solution to achieve a successful outcome is a common enough instance of faulty design. The distinction which is relevant is that between "faulty", i.e., defective, design and design free from defect. We have not found sufficient ground for reading the exclusion in this policy as not covering loss from faulty design when, as here, the piers fell because their design was defective although, according to the finding, not negligently so. The exclusion is not against loss from "negligent designing"; it is against loss from "faulty design", and the latter is more comprehensive than the former.' *Manufacturers' Mutual Insurance Ltd v Queensland Government Railways* (1968) 118 CLR 314 at 321, per cur.

FAVOUR   *See* IN FAVOUR OF

FEE FARM RENT

Fee farm rent is rent reserved upon a grant in fee. It is included in the definition of 'rentcharge' in the Law of Property Act 1925, and is for practical purposes indistinguishable. Chief rent and quit rent were manorial incidents, which have been extinguished by statute. In certain parts of England it was a common practice to sell building land in consideration of a perpetual rentcharge. These rentcharges were sometimes incorrectly called chief rents. (39 Halsbury's Laws (4th edn) para 1206)

FEE SIMPLE

A fee . . ., in general, signifies an estate of inheritance; being the highest and most extensive interest that a man can have in a feud: and, when the term is used simply, without any other adjunct, or has the adjunct of simple annexed to it (as, a fee, or, a fee-simple), it is used in contradistinction to a fee conditional at the common law, or a fee-tail by the statute; importing an absolute inheritance, clear of any condition, limitation, or restrictions to particular heirs, but descendible to the heirs general, whether male or female, lineal or collateral. And in no other sense than this is the king said to be seised in fee, he being the feudatory of no man. (2 Bl Com 106)

The statutory expression *fee simple absolute in possession* . . . is the only *freehold* interest capable of existing as a legal estate. The word *fee* had by Littleton's day come to denote that the estate was inheritable, that is to say, that it would endure until the person entitled to it *for the time being*—whether the original donee or some subsequent alienee—died intestate and left no heir. The word *simple* showed that the fee was one which was capable of passing to the heirs *general* and was not restricted to passing to a particular class of heirs. This last fact therefore distinguishes a fee simple from another kind of fee which used to be called a fee tail and is now called an entailed interest, for this is a freehold that passes, on the intestacy of its owner, only to the particular class of lineal descendants specified in the instrument of creation. Thus if a tenant in fee simple died intestate before 1926, his estate passed to his nearest heir, who according to the circumstances might be a descendant or an ascendant, a lineal or a collateral relative.

An entailed interest, on the other hand (and this is still the law), was capable of passing only to lineal descendants, and these might, according to the terms of the instrument of gift, be either lineal descendants in general or a restricted class of descendants, such as male heirs or the issue of the tenant by a specified wife. The characteristic of general inheritability is still the attribute of a fee simple, but the significance of this is now modified . . . by the abolition of the doctrine of heirship except in the case of the entailed interest. The land itself no longer passes to the nearest heir but upon the death of the owner intestate is held by the administrators on trust for sale, the proceeds of the sale being distributed among the nearest relatives according to a scheme introduced by the Administration of Estates Act 1925, as amended by the Intestates' Estates Act 1952 and the Inheritance (Provision for Family and Dependants) Act 1975. The relatives specified by the Act, however, comprise descendants and ascendants, both lineal and collateral, and it is therefore still true to say that a fee simple is an estate which, though in the converted form of money, is the subject of general inheritability.

But it is not every fee simple that is a legal estate, for the Law of Property Act [1925] confines that attribute to a fee simple absolute in possession. Postponing for the moment the consideration of the last two words, we must inquire what is meant by the word 'absolute'. This is not defined in the Act, but it clearly excludes an estate that is defeasible either by the breach of a condition or by the possibility that it may pass to some new owner upon the happening of a specified event. More than a hundred years ago Preston [Elementary Treatise on Estates 125, 126] explained the purport of *absolute* in the following words: 'The epithet *absolute* is used to distinguish an estate extended to any given time, without any condition to defeat or collateral limitation to determine the estate in the mean time, from an estate subject to a condition or collateral limitation. The term absolute is of the same signification with the word pure or simple, a word which expresses that the estate is not determinable by any event besides the event marked by the clause of limitation.'

Thus a fee simple absolute is distinguished from a *determinable* fee simple, i.e. one which according to the express terms of its limitation may determine by some event before the completion of the full period for which it may possibly continue. . . .

Finally, to have the character of a legal

estate, a fee simple absolute must be *in posses-sion*. 'Possession' is not here confined to its popular meaning, for it includes receipt of rents and profits or the right to receive the same. Therefore a tenant in fee simple who has leased the land to a tenant for years is the owner of a legal estate even though he is not in physical possession of the land. If, however, he is entitled to the fee simple only at some time in the future, as for instance in the case of a limitation 'to A for life and then to B in fee simple', he has a mere equitable interest.

FEE TAIL   *See* ENTAILED INTEREST

FELL

'Felling' [of trees] includes wilfully destroying by any means. (Forestry Act 1967, s 35)

FELO DE SE   *See* SUICIDE

FELONY

[The distinction between felonies and mis-demeanours has been abolished; see the Criminal Law Act 1967, s 1(1). On all matters on which a distinction was previously made, including mode of trial, the law and practice in relation to all offences cognisable under English law (including piracy) is that applic-able at the commencement of the Act (1 January 1968) in relation to misdemeanours.]

FEME SOLE

'The defendant is a spinster. She is described in all the documents in the title as otherwise—as a "feme sole". That is quite a wrong way in which to describe a female party who is a spinster. It is appropriate to one who has been married, is no longer married, but is not a widow.' *Ross v Collins* [1964] 1 All ER 861 at 866, CA, per Russell LJ

FEN

'Now the word "fen" would in my opinion include a piece of water like this broad, which was a shallow expanse of water covering many acres—its deepest part in the centre being only about five feet—very shallow as to the greater part of it, and in many places covered by reeds. The definitions of the word in the numerous

dictionaries to which I was referred show this. I will take one as an example—Cunningham's Law Dictionary of 1771, where the word is defined as "low marshy grounds or lakes for water for draining whereof in this country several Acts have been passed"—references being made to instances, and in particular to Whittlesea fen or mere.' *Micklethwait v Vincent* (1892) 67 LT 225 at 229, per Romer J

FENCE   *See also* BOUNDARY; SECURELY FENCED

Although fences are frequently used to mark the situation of boundaries, none the less they are primarily guards against intrusion, or barriers to prevent persons or animals straying out, and therefore in this sense the term includes not only hedges, banks, and walls, but also ditches. (4 Halsbury's Laws (4th edn) para 877)

For the purposes of this section [matters to be dealt with by byelaws] the word 'fence' includes a wall. (London Building Acts (Amendment) Act 1939, s 97(2))

'Fencing' includes the construction of any obstacle designed to prevent animals from straying. (Animals Act 1971, s 11)

'Whatever provisions the general inclosure act [Inclosure Consolidation Act 1801 (repealed)] may have very wisely introduced, yet we cannot say that a ditch may not be in legal construction a fence; and if it may be, then the jury in this case have found that this ditch was a sufficient fence.' *Ellis v Arnison* (1822) 1 B & C 70 at 74, per cur.

Canada   [The extended coverage for an insurance policy included 'fences'. During a fire water flowed down a hill and through a dry stone retaining wall, where it froze and damaged the wall.] 'A fence as used in this insurance policy refers to a structure which encloses wholly or partially some piece of property so as to impede ingress and egress. It may be composed of anything so long as it creates a line of obstacle serving this purpose. . . . A reasonable underwriter and a reasonable insurer would not consider this dry stone retaining wall as used on these premises a fence.' *Lahey v Hartford Fire Insurance Co* [1968] 1 OR 727 at 728, 729, Ont SC, per Haines J; affd [1969] 2 OR 883, CA

FERAE NATURAE   *See* ANIMAL

FERRY

A public ferry is a public highway of a special description and its termini must be in places where the public have rights, as, towns or vills, or highways leading to towns or vills. The right of the grantee is, in the one case, an exclusive right of carrying from town to town, in the other of carrying from one point to the other, all who are going to use the highway to the nearest town or vill to which the highway leads on the other side.' *Huzzey v Field* (1835) 2 Cr M & R 432 at 442, per Lord Abinger CB

'A ferry is a highway for all the Queen's subjects paying the toll; and whether it is described in the declaration, as it is in most cases, as a ferry for *all* persons having occasion to use it, or, as it is in some, *for persons* having occasion to use it, the right is the same.' *North & South Shields Ferry Co v Barker* (1848) 2 Exch 136 at 149, per cur.

'A ferry exists in respect of persons using a right of way, where the line of way is across water. There must be a line of way on land, coming to a landing-place on the water's edge (as, in this case, to Potter's Ferry Stairs), or, where the ferry is from or to a vill, from or to one or more landing-places in the vill. The franchise is established to secure convenient passage; and the exclusive right is given because in an unpopulous place there might not be profit sufficient to maintain the boat, if there was no monopoly. The ferry is unconnected with the occupation of land, and exists only in respect of persons using the right of way. The questions, whence they come, and whither they go, are irrelevant to the exercise of that right: and the ferryman has no inchoate right in respect of any of them, unless they come to his passage.' *Newton v Cubitt* (1862) 12 CBNS 32 at 58, per cur.

'A ferry has been said to be the continuation of a public highway across a river or other water for the purpose of public traffic from the termination of the highway on the one side to its recommencement on the other side; and as such the existence of a ferry is obviously for the benefit of the public. The advantage to the public is so great that the Crown has from time to time granted rights of ferry, and all common ferries have their origin in royal grant, or in prescription, which presumes such grant. Such a right of ferry is an exclusive right or monopoly, and, as such, it is in itself an evil, being in derogation of common right, for by common right any person may carry passengers across a

river. But as a compensation for that derogation of common right, there is this great advantage to the public, that they have at all times at hand, by reason of the ferry, the means of travelling on the King's highway, of which the ferry forms a part; for the owner of the ferry is under the obligation of always providing proper boats, with competent boatmen, and all other things necessary for the maintenance of the ferry in an efficient state and condition for the use of the public; and this he is bound to do under pain of indictment; and if he be found in default, he would, as it is expressed, be liable to be grievously amerced.' *Letton v Goodden* (1866) LR 2 Eq 123 at 130, 131, per Kindersley V-C

'All ancient ferries have their origin in Royal grant or in prescription, which presumes a Royal grant. A right of ferry is in derogation of common right, for by common right any person entitled to cross a river in a boat is entitled to carry passengers too. Within the limits of an ancient ferry no one is permitted to convey passengers across but the owner of the ferry. No one may disturb the ferry. The ferry carries with it an exclusive right or monopoly. In consideration of that monopoly the owner of the ferry is bound to have his ferry always ready.' *Simpson v A-G* [1904] AC 476 at 490, HL, per Lord Macnaghten

Road-ferry

'Road-ferry' means a ferry connecting the termination of a highway which is, or is to become, a highway maintainable at the public expense with the termination of another highway which is, or is to become, such a highway. (Highways Act 1980, s 329(1))

FETTER   *See also* CLOG; MORTGAGE

'Whenever a transaction is in reality one of mortgage, equity regards the mortgaged property as security only for money, and will permit of no attempt to clog, fetter, or impede the borrower's right to redeem and to rescue what was, and still remains in equity his own.' *Northampton (Marquess) v Pollock* (1890) 45 Ch D 190 at 215, CA, per Bowen LJ; affd [1892] AC 1

FETTLE

'A man of average education knows of the noun "fettle". A horse may be in "high fettle", or a man may be in "good fettle". But the verb created out of that word is not, I think, generally so well known. "To fettle", I suppose, must mean to put into good fettle and, therefore, might be a very general expression. It is of no significance, however, to look in the dictionary and, divorcing the word from its context, arrive at its etymological or other definition. Words must be construed according to the context in which they appear, and this word appears in the schedule to the Protection of Eyes Regulations 1938. It refers to a process of "fettling of metal castings". From the evidence that was given in this case, and indeed from the reports of the cases at nisi prius, it seems that that is a well-known activity. Fettlers are people who do a well demarcated job, not a highly skilled one. It is a kind of trimming up of the castings as they come from the foundry.' *Prophet v Platt Bros & Co Ltd* [1961] 2 All ER 644 at 647, 648, CA, per Harman LJ

FICTITIOUS

[Section 7 (3) of the Bills of Exchange Act 1882 enacts that when the payee is a 'fictitious person' the bill may be treated as payable to bearer.] 'Turning to the interpretation of the word "fictitious" in Dr Johnson's Dictionary, I find amongst the meanings given are "counterfeit", "feigned". It seems to me, then, that where the name inserted [in a bill of exchange] as that of the payee is so inserted by way of pretence only, it may, without impropriety, be said that the payee is a feigned or pretended, or, in other words, a fictitious person.' *Bank of England v Vagliano Brothers* [1891] AC 107 at 153, per Lord Herschell

'It was said that the proper meaning of fictitious is "imaginary". I do not think so, I think the proper meaning of the word is "feigned" or "counterfeit".' Ibid at 161, per Lord Macnaghten

'The question I have to decide . . . is, what is the true construction of s 7, sub-s 3, of the Bills of Exchange Act 1882 . . . that is to say, in other words, I have to decide whether in the case before me the payees of certain cheques were fictitious or non-existing persons within the meaning of that 3rd sub-section. . . . Independently of authority, what am I to say is meant by "fictitious"? It seems to me this at all events must be true. It cannot be fictitious in the abstract. You must look at the circumstances of the particular case, and say whether the name of the person inserted in the bill is the name of a fictitious person having regard to all

those circumstances.' *Vinden v Hughes* [1905] 1 KB 795 at 799, 800, 802, 803, per Warrington J

'The . . . cases seem to establish this, that in order to have a fictitious payee within the meaning of the section [s 7 of the Bills of Exchange Act 1882], you must always find that the drawer knew and intended that the payee was to be an unreality, but that if his intention was to have a real payee and a real transaction, there cannot be a fictitious payee so far as the drawer is concerned.' *Town & Country Advance Co Ltd v Provincial Bank of Ireland Ltd* [1917] 2 IR 421 at 427, per Campbell CJ

FIDUCIARY

'The fiduciary relation [Lat, *fiducia*, trust] as it is called, does not depend upon any particular circumstances. It exists in almost every shape. It exists, of course, notoriously in the case of trustee and *cestui que trust*; it exists in the case of guardian and ward, of parent and child, of solicitor and client.' *Plowright v Lambert* (1885) 52 LT 646 at 652, per Field J

FIERI FACIAS

The most usual method of enforcement of a money judgment is by writ of fieri facias (commonly called fi fa). The writ lies to enforce a judgment or order for the payment to any person of a sum of money or costs. It must be in the prescribed form appropriate in the particular case, and is expressed in the form of a royal command directing the sheriff of the county in which the judgment debtor's goods are situate to seize in execution such of the judgment debtor's goods, chattels and other property as are authorised to be seized by law, and thereout to 'cause to be made' (namely to sell) so much of the same as may be sufficient to satisfy the amount of the judgment debt and the costs of execution, and also interest on the amount of the judgment from its date until payment. The writ must correspond with the judgment as to the names of the parties and the subject matter of the judgment, and must bear the date of the day of its issue. (17 Halsbury's Laws (4th edn) para 462)

De bonis ecclesiasticis

Where it appears upon the return of any writ of fieri facias that the person against whom it was issued is the incumbent of a benefice named in the return but has no goods or chattels in the county of the sheriff to whom the writ was directed, then, after the return has been made, the party by whom the writ of fieri facias was issued may apply for leave to issue a writ of fieri facias de bonis ecclesiasticis or a writ of sequestrari de bonis ecclesiasticis directed to the bishop of the diocese within which that benefice is.

When sealed, the writ must be delivered to the bishop to be executed by him, and when returned by him must be delivered to the parties or solicitors by whom it was sued out and filed in the Central Office. The bishop or his officers may not take or be allowed any fees for execution other than such as are allowed by lawful authority. In executing the writ the bishop is said to be in the nature of an ecclesiastical sheriff. (17 Halsbury's Laws (4th edn) para 520)

FILE

'The word "filing", in reference to matters of practice, is very commonly used to express the duty of bringing to the proper office, as the case may be, writs, pleadings, affidavits and other such matters for safe custody, or enrolment. The duty of filing in this sense may be properly considered as included under the word "returning".' *Hunter v Caldwell* (1847) 10 QB 60 at 81, per cur.

'The Act [s 14 of the Companies Act 1900 (repealed; cf now Companies Act 1985, s 395, where the word 'file' is no longer used)] says . . . "(d) a floating charge on the undertaking or property of the company, shall . . . be void against the liquidator and any creditor of the company, unless filed with the registrar for registration . . . within twenty-one days after the date of its creation. . . ." . . . "Filed with the registrar" really means "supplied to the registrar for registration" or "furnished to the registrar for registration".' *Re Yolland, Husson & Birkett Ltd, Leicester v Yolland, Husson & Birkett Ltd* [1908] 1 Ch 152 at 157, CA, per Cozens-Hardy MR

New Zealand 'What is the meaning of the word "filed"? Filing, it has been said, is the means adopted of keeping Court documents. . . . In its primitive meaning "filing" means putting the documents on a file; but now documents are kept together by other methods. "Filing" now really means depositing in a Court office. It has, in my opinion, acquired this secondary meaning; and in Wharton's Law Lexicon it is said that "to file"

means to deposit at an office.' *Re Commercial Union Assurance Co Ltd* (1899) 18 NZLR 585 at 588, per Stout CJ

FILM *See also* CINEMATOGRAPH FILM

'Film' includes any form of video-recording. (Protection of Children Act 1978, s 7(5))

In this section [films to which Act applies] 'film' includes any record, however made, of a sequence of visual images, which is a record capable of being used as a means of showing that sequence as a moving picture. (National Film Finance Corporation Act 1981, s 2(8))

Film exhibition

'Film exhibition' means any exhibition of moving pictures which is produced otherwise than by the simultaneous reception and exhibition of—
(a) television programmes broadcast by the British Broadcasting Corporation or the Independent Broadcasting Authority, or
(b) programmes included in a cable programme service which is, or does not require to be, licensed under section 4 of the Cable and Broadcasting Act 1984.
(Cinemas Act 1985, s 21(1))

FINAL

'The second point is the effect of s 36(3) of the National Insurance (Industrial Injuries) Act 1946 [repealed; see now the Social Security Act 1975, s 117] which provides that "any decision of a claim or question . . . shall be final". Do those words preclude the Court of Queen's Bench from issuing a *certiorari* to bring up the decision? This is a question which we did not discuss in *R v Northumberland Compensation Appeal Tribunal, ex p Shaw* [[1952] 1 All ER 122], because it did not there arise. It does arise here, and on looking again into the old books I find it very well settled that the remedy by *certiorari* is never to be taken away by any statute except by the most clear and explicit words. The word "final" is not enough. That only means "without appeal". It does not mean "without recourse to *certiorari*". It makes the decision final on the facts, but not final on the law. Notwithstanding that the decision is by a statute made "final", *certiorari* can still issue for excess of jurisdiction or for error of law on the face of the record.' *Re Gilmore's Application* [1957] 1 All ER 796 at 801, CA, per Denning LJ

'When Parliament says that a decision of an inferior tribunal is to be "final", it does so on the assumption that the tribunal will observe the law. Parliament only gives the impress of "finality" to the decision on the condition that it is reached in accordance with law: and the Queen's courts will see to it that this condition is fulfilled. Accordingly if a tribunal goes wrong in law and the error apears on the face of the record, the High Court will interfere by *certiorari* to quash the decision. It is not to be deterred by the enactment that the decision is "final". The decision may be final on the facts, but it is not final on the law.' *Tehrani v Rostron* [1971] 3 All ER 790 at 793, CA, per Lord Denning MR

Canada 'In my opinion, the question whether an order or decision is interlocutory or final should be determined by looking at the order or decision itself, and its character is not affected by the nature of the order or decision which could have been made had a different result been reached. If the nature of the order or decision as made finally disposes of, or substantially decides the rights of the parties, it ought to be treated as a final order or decision. If it does not, and the merits of the case remain to be determined, it is an interlocutory order or decision.' *Bourque v New Brunswick Province, Leger and Leger* (1982) 41 NBR (2d) 129 at 133, NBCA, per Stratton JA

New Zealand 'Subsection (5) of this section [s 144 of the Summary Proceedings Act 1957] provides in terms that: "The decision of the Court of Appeal on any appeal under this section shall be final." I have no doubt that the word "final" where used in this section means "unappealable"—see *Re Ell, ex p Austin and Hoskins* [(1886) 4 NZLR 114 at 126]; *Re Bruce's Patent Oatmeal and Milling Co Ltd* [(1890) 8 NZLR 598 at 608; *Ewing v Scandinavian Water-Race Co* [(1904) 24 NZLR 271 at 291]; *Kydd v Liverpool Watch Committee* [[1908] AC 327]; *R v Medical Appeal Tribunal, ex p Gilmore* [[1957] 1 QB 574 at 583, 587]. The words of sub-s (5) amount therefore to a declaration by the Legislature that the decision of this court in this case may not be the subject of appeal.' *Nunns v Licensing Control Commission* [1968] NZLR 7 at 62, per Turner J

Final and binding

New Zealand [Section 175(3) of the Land Act 1948 (NZ), provided that the determination of the Board on any matter arising under the section should be 'final and binding' on all persons interested therein.] 'Decisions made without jurisdiction, e.g. where the basis necessary for the exercise of jurisdiction purported to have been exercised are not, of course, within the words of prohibition. The words here are "final and binding", but I am unable to perceive any material difference between those words and the words "final and conclusive". In my view the important word for present purposes is "final", and I think it is intended to mean, and should be construed as meaning, final in the sense of admitting of no further disputation. I am of opinion, accordingly, that s 175(3) is to be construed as a prohibition of any appeal from a decision of the Board made pursuant to the jurisdiction conferred by s 175.' *Re McCosh's Application* [1958] NZLR 731 at 734, per Shorland J

Final award

'The only way in which it is possible to ascertain what was the real effect of this award is to construe its language. Unless it can be found that, according to its terms, the powers of the arbitrator were so exercised that, in any event, his duties under the arbitration were ended, and that he reserved to himself no further power in any event, then the award cannot be regarded as final.' *Cogstead (C T) & Co v Newsum (H) Sons & Co* [1921] 2 AC 528 at 532, 533, per Lord Buckmaster

Final destination

[A policy of marine insurance covering a cargo of timber included the Timber Trade Federation Insurance Clauses, by clause 2 of which the cover was extended to include risks of non-delivery until discharged at port of destination and whilst in transit by land and/or water to 'final destination' there or in the interior.] 'For the purposes of this case, and this particular parcel of goods, I think the final destination was reached when the goods were discharged, and the mere fact that they had been moved to a shed or another part of it and there piled according to their marks seems to me to make no difference at all. It is quite conceivable that the goods might have been put under their marks and sizes as they were delivered from the ship, but according to the usage of the port the goods are bulked without regard to marks or sizes, and the fact that they were moved to another place does not, in my view, prevent the place on to which they had been discharged from being the place where they reached their final destination.' *Renton (GH) & Co Ltd v Black Sea & Baltic General Insurance Co Ltd* [1941] 1 KB 206 at 210, 211, per Lord Caldecote CJ

Final distribution

Australia 'I am prepared to accept the view that there has been a final distribution of an estate, when the executors have got in all the estate and have completed their executorial duties and have assented to the dispositions of the will taking effect, so that thereafter they hold the estate as trustee for the person entitled.' *Brown v Holt* [1961] VR 435 at 441, per Pape J

Final judgment   *See* JUDGMENT

Final order   *See* ORDER

Final port

[A ship was insured at and from St Vincent, Barbadoes, and all or any of the West India Islands to her port or ports of discharge and loading in the United Kingdom, during her stay there, and thence back to Barbadoes, and all or any of the West India colonies, until the ship should have arrived at her final port as aforesaid.] 'I think the words, "final port as aforesaid", must be construed with reference to the voyage insured. That voyage was to the ship's port or ports of discharge and loading in the United Kingdom, and thence back to Barbadoes, and all or any of the West India colonies. The voyage must be concluded on the discharge of the cargo in Barbadoes, or any of the West India colonies.' *Moore v Taylor* (1834) 1 Ad & El 25 at 30, per Patteson J

'The policy [of insurance on a ship] consists of a printed form with blanks which are filled up in writing. The filled-up parts in this case so far as material are as follows: "Doth make assurance and cause themselves . . . to be insured, lost or not lost, at and from . . . any port or ports, place or places on the River Plate and/or tributaries to any port or ports, place or places in France and/or the United Kingdom (Final Port) excluding Mediterranean via any ports in any order." . . . I hold that the expression "final port" in this policy was equivalent to "final port of discharge". . . . I agree that the final port might have been in the United Kingdom, but once dissociate "final port" from "final port of discharge" then there seems to me no *termini habiles* to fix what is the final port.' *Marten v Vestey Brothers Ltd* [1920] AC 307 at 318, 319, per Lord Dunedin

FINANCE

New Zealand   'The use of the phrase "subject to finance" implies that the purchaser at the time of signing the contract has insufficient cash available to complete the purchase. In the context, therefore, the word "finance" must, I think, be used in a somewhat narrower sense than that of "pecuniary resources". I think that it simply means "the raising of money or credit".' *Eastmond v Bowis* [1962] NZLR 954 at 958, per Richmond J

FINANCIAL CORPORATION

Australia   'In my opinion a financial corporation [for the purposes of s 51 (xx) of the Constitution [Commonwealth of Australia Constitution Act 1901] and s 4(1) of the Trade Practices Act 1974] is one which borrows and lends or otherwise deals in finance as its principal or characteristic activity or, depending on which approach one takes, it is a corporation formed for the purpose of borrowing and lending or otherwise dealing in finance. If it does so in the way of trade it may also be a trading corporation, but that is not a necessary feature of a financial corporation.' *Re Ku-ring-gai Co-operative Building Society (No 12) Ltd* (1978) 36 FLR 134 at 138, per Bowen CJ

FINANCIAL INTERMEDIARY

Investment securities

United States   A 'financial intermediary' [in the context of the transfer of a security] is a bank, broker, clearing corporation, or other person (or the nominee of any of them) which in the ordinary course of its business maintains security accounts for its customers and is acting in that capacity. A financial intermediary may have a security interest in securities held in account for its customer. (Uniform Commercial Code 1978, s 8–313(4))

FINANCIAL NEEDS

Australia   'The use of the phrase "financial needs" suggests that the long term situation should be looked at. Indeed, in the context of s 75(2)(g) [Family Law Act 1975 (Cth)] . . ., the phrase "financial needs" in s 75(2)(d) means in my opinion, "those requirements reasonably necessary to maintain a standard of living which is in all the circumstances reasonable".' *In the Marriage of L and V Lawrie* (1981) 7 Fam LR 560 at 570, per Gee J

FINANCIAL RESOURCE

Australia 'Under s 73 of the [Family Law Act 1975 (Cth)] the parties to the marriage are liable according to the respective financial resources to maintain the children of the marriage, who have not attained the age of 18. In *Crapp and Crapp* (1979) 5 Fam LR 47; Fogarty J defined the words "financial resource" to include "a means of applying some want or deficiency, a stock or reserve upon which one can draw when necessary". In *Kelly and Kelly (No 2)* (1981) 7 Fam LR 762; the Full Court in a unanimous judgment, approved the definition of "financial resource" adopted by the trial judge in the following terms (at 76,802): "A financial stock or reserve over which a party has sufficient control as a matter of fact to draw upon when necessary towards supplying some financial want or deficiency of the party."' *In the Marriage of S and A Vartikian* (1984) 10 Fam LR 165 at 175, per Gee J

FINANCIAL YEAR

'Financial year' means, in relation to matters relating to the Consolidated Fund, the National Loans Fund, or to the Exchequer or to central taxes or finance, the twelve months ending with 31 March. (Interpretation Act 1978, Sch 1)

[The year of assessment and charge to income tax is 6 April to 5 April; see Income and Corporation Taxes Act 1988, s 2. See also the Companies Act 1985, s 742(1)(d).]

'Financial year' means each period of twelve months at the end of which the balance of the accounts of the insurance company is struck, or, if no such balance is struck, means the calendar year. (Insurance Companies Act 1982, s 96(1))

FINANCING AGENCY

United States 'Financing agency' means a bank, finance company or other person who in the ordinary course of business makes advances against goods or documents of title or who by arrangement with either the seller or the buyer intervenes in ordinary course to make or collect payment due or claimed under the contract for sale, as by purchasing or paying the seller's draft or making advances against it or by merely taking it for collection whether or not documents of title accompany

the draft. 'Financing agency' includes also a bank or other person who similarly intervenes between persons who are in the position of seller and buyer in respect to the goods. (Section 2–707) (Uniform Commercial Code 1978, s 2–104(2))

FIND

'The rule of law on this subject [appropriation of objects by a finder] seems to be, that if a man find goods that have been actually lost, or are reasonably supposed by him to have been lost, and appropriates them, with intent to take the entire dominion over them, really believing when he takes them, that the owner cannot be found, it is not larceny. But if he takes them with the like intent, though lost, or reasonably supposed to be lost, but reasonably believing that the owner can be found, it is larceny.' *Thurborn's Case* (1849) 1 Den 387 at 396, per Parke B

[This case was decided some years before the passing of the Larceny Act 1861. Both that Act and the Larceny Act 1916 have been repealed, but the substance of the common law rule relating to finding is preserved by the Theft Act 1968, s 2(1)(c).]

'The first meaning attributed to the verb "find" in the New English Dictionary is not that of discovering the whereabouts of something but that of coming across, falling in with or lighting on something. If I say that a certain place is the best in which to find purchasers for a certain commodity, I mean that it is the best place in which to meet them with a hope of doing business.' *Re R* [1966] 3 All ER 613 at 616, per Buckley J

Australia 'In its ordinary sense . . . "found" implies something more than merely "seen", proof of presence. . . . The word can convey the sense of discovering, the exposing or unmasking of someone in a situation that has elements of secrecy or hiding, or of dissimulation by the alleged offender to conceal or screen presence, identity, conduct, purpose, or other circumstance. Or, possibly, the word suggests some aspect of surprise, or of the unexpected.' *Abbott v Pulbrook* [1947] SASR 57 at 62, per Mayo J   .

Found committing offence

Australia 'When the section [the Local Government Act 1919, s 644 (as amended)] speaks of a council servant or member of the police force "who finds a person committing an offence under this Act" it refers to and deals with the discovery "*in flagrante delicto*" which may be translated somewhat topically as catching the offender "red handed". There is a world of difference between catching such a person in the actual commission of an offence on the one hand and finding on the other hand someone who had not committed the particular offence, does not know who has, but for reasons best known to himself is willing to accept the blame for it and take all the legal consequences.' *Hazell v Parramatta City Council* [1968] 1 NSWR 165 at 177, per Isaacs J

Found drunk

Australia 'I think the phrase "found drunk in a public place" means no more than that the appellant was in a public place and was drunk and that he was seen in that condition in that place by the constable who arrested him contemporaneously.' *Sheehan v Piddington, ex p Piddington* [1955] St R Qd 574 at 581, per Macrossan CJ

Found in public place

New Zealand [The accused was charged under the Summary Offences Act 1981, s 28(1) of being 'found in a public place' behaving in a manner from which it could reasonably be inferred that he was preparing to commit a crime.] 'If there is a finding of a person in a public place but no concurrent behaviour from which an inference of preparation can be drawn, there is no finding for the purposes of s 28(1). I say that with the qualification that whether behaviour is too remote in time from the moment the alleged offence is first seen must always be a matter of fact and degree. And I see no reason why, if there is a contemporaneity of observation and proscribed behaviour, subsequent behaviour should not be taken into account in accordance with the ordinary rules of evidence as similar fact evidence to rebut any defence that the "found" conduct, from which the inference of preparation can itself be drawn, was accidental or involuntary. But subsequent conduct cannot be used to put a complexion on earlier conduct, innocent in itself, which does not give rise to that inference.' *Palmer-Brown v Police* [1985] 1 NZLR 365 at 369, CA, per McMullin J

'A person is "found" when he is seen or discovered or perceived to be present.' Ibid at 369, per Somers J

Found on premises

[Section 25 of the Licensing Act 1872 (repealed), made it an offence to be 'found on premises' in closing hours.] 'This case turns on the meaning to be given to the words in the 25th section of the Licensing Act "found on premises". The appellant was seen to go into the licensed house, and in three minutes after to come out with a bottle. The question is, whether he could be said to be "found on the premises"? In my opinion, it is enough to satisfy these words if the person has been detected or seen, or clearly ascertained to have been, on the premises at the time alleged.' *Thomas v Powell* (1893) 57 JP 329 at 329, per Bruce J

'I agree. I cannot see any other intelligent meaning to put on these words except to hold that the fact of seeing the appellant going in, and then coming out, was equivalent to his being found on the premises in question.' Ibid at 329, per Kennedy J

'What is the true construction to be put upon the words of the section [Vagrancy Act 1824, s 4] . . . which defines the offence as "being found in or upon any dwelling-house . . . for any unlawful purpose". In order to be found upon premises a person must be upon those premises, and the offence, therefore, consists in being upon premises for an unlawful purpose and being found there. . . . What constitutes a finding within the meaning of the section? The simplest case would be a case of apprehension upon the premises. Actual apprehension upon the premises is, however, in my opinion, not necessary to constitute the offence. . . . There may be many cases in which a person is found upon the premises within the meaning of the section although he is not apprehended until after he has quitted the premises. To constitute the offence a person must . . . be discovered upon the premises doing the acts or things which of themselves constitute the unlawful purpose. It may be that evidence is admissible of what a person did before he entered the premises or after he left them to explain the nature of the acts or things which he was discovered doing upon the premises themselves; such evidence must, however, . . . be strictly confined to this purpose.' *Moran v Jones* (1911) 104 LT 921 at 922, 923, DC, per Bray J

'The . . . contention is that for the appellant to be brought within the terms of s 7 [of the Prevention of Crimes Act 1871 (repealed by the Criminal Law Act 1967, s 10 Sch 3)] he must have been arrested then and there at the place where he is alleged to have been "found" about to commit an offence. We are not inclined to agree that there is any necessity for this court to hold that "found" is equivalent to "arrested". Certainly that is not so in the ordinary use of the English language. It would have been easy for the legislature to have provided, had they wished to do so, that a person who is arrested in the circumstances detailed in the section might be found guilty of an offence, but that is not what is provided by the section and here charged. The court is indebted to Mr Blundell for bringing to their attention the unanimous decision of a Divisional Court in *Moran v Jones* [supra]. . . . That decision has the full approval of this court, and we see no reason why the word "found" should not be given the same meaning in s 7 of the Act of 1871 and the view of the court is that it means no more than "discovered" or "seen".' *R v Goodwin* [1944] KB 518 at 522, 523, CCA, per cur

[The appellant was convicted of being 'found' by night in a building with intent to steal, contrary to the Larceny Act 1916, s 28(4) (repealed by the Theft Act 1968).] ' "Found in" does not necessarily mean that he must be caught or apprehended in the building, or that the finder should be in the building as well as the person who is charged with the offence, but the subsection must mean that, if a person is to be convicted of an offence under it, there must be clear and unmistakable evidence that he has been, as the subsection says, found in the building.' *R v Lumsden* [1951] 1 All ER 1101 at 1102, CCA, per Cassels J; also reported in [1951] 2 KB 513 at 515

Found trespassing

Australia [The Impounding Act 1930, s 18 (repealed; see now the Local Government Act 1962–1985, (Tas) s 578(1)) provides, inter alia, for the impounding of an animal 'found trespassing'.] 'It is plain that, in this section, "found trespassing" must mean "first found trespassing" otherwise the period would be capable of repetitive renewal and the owner could detain the animal indefinitely. There is no reason for finding any distinction in the meaning of the phrase wherever it appears in the Act, and I hold that "found trespassing" means "first found trespassing".' *Ryan v Vince* [1962] Tas SR 222 at 225, per Crawford J

FINE

In this section 'fine' includes—

(a) any pecuniary penalty, pecuniary forfeiture or pecuniary compensation payable under a conviction, and

(b) any non-pecuniary forfeiture on conviction by, or under an order of, a magistrates' court so far as the forfeiture is converted into or consists of money. (Justices of the Peace Act 1979, s 61(7))

'Fine', except for the purposes of any enactment imposing a limit on the amount of any fine, includes any pecuniary penalty or pecuniary forfeiture or pecuniary compensation payable under a conviction. (Magistrates' Courts Act 1980, s 150(1))

FINE (Premium)

'Fine' includes premium or fore-gift, and any payment, consideration, or benefit in the nature of a fine, premium, or fore-gift. (Law of Property Act 1925, s 205(1)(xxiii))

'Section 2, sub-s 9 of the Conveyancing Act 1881 . . . contains a definition of a "fine" which makes that expression include "premium or foregift, and any payment, consideration or benefit in the nature of a fine, premium or foregift". . . . I am of opinion that it is expressly intended thereby to make the word "fine" when used in these Acts include any valuable consideration given or required under such circumstances that, if it were money, it would be what is commonly known as a "fine". The phrase "in the nature of a fine", when applied to the case of obtaining consent to assign, means nothing more than "paid as the price for" such consent.' *Waite v Jennings* [1906] 2 KB 11 at 17, 18, CA, per Fletcher Moulton LJ

FINE ARTS

[Under the Scientific Societies Act 1843 (repealed by the Rating and Valuation Act 1961), rating relief was given to societies instituted for the purposes of science, literature, or the 'fine arts'. The Act of 1961 is now largely repealed by the General Rate Act 1967, under s 40(5) of which rating authorities may again reduce or remit the payment of rates in the case of organisations concerned with (inter alia) the 'fine arts'.]

'We were referred to various definitions of the terms "art", "fine art" and "the fine arts" in the Oxford English Dictionary and in the seventh and eighth editions of the Encyclopaedia Britannica, covering the period from

1830 to 1860 and thus spanning the date of the Scientific Societies Act 1843. The Oxford English Dictionary has under "Art": "10. A pursuit or occupation in which skill is directed towards the gratification of taste or production of what is beautiful. Hence *The Arts*: (specifically) = 'The Fine Arts' . . . 11. . . . (a) . . . *Industrial, mechanical, useful arts*: those in which the hands and body are more concerned than the mind. *Fine Arts*: those in which the mind and imagination are chiefly concerned." The Oxford English Dictionary has, under "Fine". "Fine art . . . In plural, the arts which are concerned with 'the beautiful', or which appeal to the faculty of taste; in the widest use including poetry, eloquence, music, etc, but often applied in a more restricted sense to the arts of design, as painting, sculpture, and architecture." The seventh and eighth editions of the Encyclopaedia Britannica have under "The Fine Arts" the following introductory passage: "Fine Arts. The term Fine Arts may be viewed as embracing all those arts in which the powers of imitation or invention are exerted, chiefly with a view to the production of pleasure by the immediate impression which they make on the mind. But the phrase has of late, we think, been restricted to a narrower and more technical signification; namely, to painting, sculpture, engraving and architecture, which appeal to the eye as the medium of pleasure; and, by way of eminence, to the two first of these arts." I am prepared to accept the wider meaning assigned to "the fine arts" in the above definitions and to treat them as including, for example, poetry, eloquence, and music as well as such "arts of design" as painting, sculpture, and architecture. We are, indeed, bound for the present purpose to include music amongst them: see *Royal College of Music v Westminster Vestry* [[1898] 1 QB 809], a decision of this court. It is possible that dramatic art should also be included: see the *Nonentities Society*'s case [*Nonentities Society v Linley (Valuation Officer)* (1954) 47 R & I T 426]. . . . If music and drama rank as fine arts, I see no justification for holding, as a general proposition, that dancing, which in some of its forms is closely allied to music and the drama, can never do so. I observe that the Oxford English Dictionary under the word "Ballet" says that it is "now for the most part regarded as an artistic exhibition of skill in dancing", and this perhaps affords an example of a form of dancing fit to be recognised as one of the fine arts. It by no means follows, however, that all dancing is in itself fine art, or that everybody who dances any form of dance on any occasion is practising

the fine art of dancing. An artistic exhibition of skill in dancing may be a fine art, but I cannot bring myself to hold that dancing of the sort in which the assembled company take part for their own amusement at a ball or similar function can properly or reasonably be so described. Dancing of that sort is, to my mind, no more than a recreation or pastime—dancing as a social amusement as distinct from dancing as a fine art.' *O'Sullivan (Valuation Officer) v English Folk Dance & Song Society* [1955] 2 All ER 845 at 857, 858, CA, per Jenkins LJ

FINENESS   *See also* CARAT

'Fineness' in relation to any precious metal means the number of parts by weight of that fine metal in one thousand parts by weight of alloy. (Hallmarking Act 1973, s 22(1))

FIRE

There is no fire within the meaning of a fire insurance policy unless there is ignition, either of the property insured or of the premises where it is situated; heating or fermentation unaccompanied by ignition is not sufficient. That which is ignited must be something which was not intended to be ignited. Therefore, if property in proximity to a source of heat in ordinary use is damaged by the excessive heat thrown out, but is not actually ignited, the damage is not within the policy, since there is no ignition except such ignition as was intended and nothing has been burned except what ought to have been burned. (25 Halsbury's Laws (4th edn) para 618)

Loss by fire: marine insurance

Loss by fire covers fire caused by lightning, or by an enemy, or by the ship being burnt in order to prevent capture, or to prevent the spread of a contagious disease or the like; and, where a loss of freight is due to steps taken in order to prevent a fire which, but for such steps, would have broken out and destroyed the cargo, the underwriter is liable for that loss of freight. Mere heating, which has not arrived at the stage of incandescence or ignition, is not within the specific word 'fire', although it may be within the general words of the policy as ejusdem generis. (25 Halsbury's Laws (4th edn) para 155)

[In order to prevent her from falling into the hands of the enemy, a ship was set on fire by her captain. The ship was insured against 'loss by fire'.] 'If the ship is destroyed by fire, it is of no consequence whether this is occasioned by a common accident, or by lightning, or by an act done in duty to the state. Nor can it make any difference whether the ship is thus destroyed by third persons, subjects of the king, or by the captain and crew acting with loyalty and good faith. Fire is still the *causa causans*, and the loss is covered by the policy.' *Gordon v Rimmington* (1807) 1 Camp 123 at 123, 124, per Lord Ellenborough

'Fire did not actually break out, but it is reasonably certain that it would have broken out and the condition of things was such that there was an actual existing state of peril of fire, and not merely a fear of fire. The case is peculiar, and not exactly analogous to that of any other peril. The danger was present, and, if nothing were done, spontaneous combustion and fire would follow in natural course. In effect the concession of the defendants admits this, because they do not dispute their liability for the share of the loss in general average. But in order to give rise to general average there must have been imminent danger to ship and cargo—that is to say, real substantial danger. I have found that such danger existed in this case. Then does it may any difference that the fire had not actually broken out? I think not in the circumstances. There was imminent danger of fire, and an existing condition of things producing this danger, and if this cannot, strictly speaking, be termed a loss by fire, it is, in my opinion, a loss ejusdem generis, and covered by the general words "all other losses and misfortunes, etc".' *The Knight of St Michael* [1898] P 30 at 34, 35, per Gorell Barnes J

'Undoubtedly this cargo was damaged partly by fire, partly by the smoke resulting from the fire, and partly by the water used to put out the fire, and I hold that the water and smoke were matters which occurred by reason of the fire. That is the only reasonable interpretation of the statute [Merchant Shipping Act 1894, s 502 (prospectively repealed by the Merchant Shipping Act 1979, s 50(4))].' *The Diamond* [1906] P 282 at 287, per Bargrave Dean J

[Section 66(6) of the Marine Insurance Act 1906 enacts that in the absence of express stipulation, the insurer is not liable for any general average loss or contribution where the loss was not incurred for the purpose of avoiding, or in connection with the avoidance of, a peril insured against.] 'The underwriters insured against fire in fact, and if there had been a fire they would have had to pay. But why are they

to pay if in fact there was no fire? They did not insure against an error of judgment on the part of the captain in deciding whether there was a peril or not. It has been contended that this was a loss incurred "for the purpose of avoiding, or in connection with the avoidance of, a peril insured against" within the meaning of s 66, sub-s 6 of the Act. . . . I am of opinion that the effect of the subsection is to bring in losses collateral to the main process of avoiding a peril insured against, and that it does not touch losses incurred in a mistaken attempt to avoid a peril in fact non-existent.' *Watson (Joseph) & Son Ltd v Firemen's Fund Insurance Co of San Francisco* [1922] 2 KB 355 at 359, per Rowlatt J

[A fire broke out on a jetty some distance from goods insured against fire, and in order to prevent the fire spreading the authorities jettisoned a portion of the insured goods, and other portions were damaged by water.] 'In my judgment, it is right to say that the cause of the loss was the fire. It is quite true that fire never touched the goods; they were touched by the enemy of fire, that is to say, by water, and they were damaged by water. But it has long been decided, and for a long time been acted upon in relation to fire insurance on land, that damage by water done to save the consequence of fire and damage by the destruction of property to prevent the spreading of the fire, can be held to be the consequence of the fire and within a policy of fire insurance.' *Symington & Co v Union Insurance Society of Canton* (1928) 97 LJKB 646 at 652, CA, per Greer LJ

Loss by fire: non-marine insurance

'The expression in the policy which we have to construe is, "loss or damage occasioned by fire". Those words are to be construed as ordinary people would construe them. They mean loss or damage either by ignition of the article consumed, or by ignition of part of the premises where the article is: in the one case there is a loss, in the other a damage, occasioned by fire.' *Everett v London Assurance* (1865) 19 CBNS 126 at 133, per Byles J

'The action is upon a policy of insurance on plate-glass. . . . The insurance is against "loss or damage originating from any cause whatsoever, except fire, breakage during removal, alteration, or repair of premises". The defendants contend that this loss originated from fire or from breakage during removal, and so is within the exception. The circumstances were these:—The glass insured was plate-glass in the plaintiff's shop-front. A fire occurring in some premises adjoining the plaintiff's, and communicating with a distant part of the plaintiff's house, the plaintiff got some of his neighbours to assist him in removing his furniture and stock-in-trade; and, whilst they were thus engaged, the assembled mob feloniously broke in the windows for the purpose of plunder. Hence, no doubt, the remote cause of the damage was fire, but the proximate cause was the lawless violence of the mob. I think the general rule of insurance law, that the proximate and not the remote cause of the loss is to be regarded, is the rule which must govern our decision in this case.' *Marsden v City & County Assurance Co* (1865) LR 1 CP 232 at 238, 239, per Erle CJ

[A policy of fire insurance covered premises against 'loss by fire', with various exceptions.] 'Any loss resulting from an apparently necessary and bona fide effort to put out a fire, whether it be by spoiling the goods by water, or throwing the articles of furniture out of window, or even the destroying of a neighbouring house by an explosion for the purposes of checking the progress of the flames, in a word, every loss that clearly and proximately results, whether directly or indirectly, from the fire, is within the policy.' *Stanley v Western Insurance Co* (1868) LR 3 Exch 71 at 74, per Kelly CB

'Is a fire insurance a contract of indemnity? It appears to me it is quite as much a contract of indemnity as a marine insurance is: the differences between the two are caused by the diversity of the subject matters. . . . What is it that is insured in a fire policy? Not the bricks and the materials used in building the house, but the interest of the assured in the subject matter of insurance, not the legal interest only, but the beneficial interest.' *Castellain v Preston* (1883) 11 QBD 380 at 397, CA, per Bowen LJ

'A red hot cinder jumps from the fire and sets some paper of value on fire—admittedly there is liability. A draught from the window blows the same paper into the same fire. Is that any less an accidental loss by fire? Are the words in the policy any less applicable to the latter than the former? A draught blows the flame of a candle against a curtain—admittedly there is liability. But what if the curtain is blown against the flame of the candle? Surely the result must be the same? If it is not the same the result is an absurdity. If it is the same, why should the result be different if one substitutes a fire in a grate for the lighted candle in a candle-

stick? . . . There is loss or damage caused by fire when there has been ignition of insured property which was not intended to be ignited, or when insured property has been damaged otherwise than by ignition as a direct consequence of the ignition of other property not intended to be ignited.' *Harris v Poland* [1941] 1 KB 462 at 464, 465, 468, 473, per Atkinson J

FIREARM

In this Act, the expression 'firearm' means a lethal barrelled weapon of any description from which any shot, bullet or other missile can be discharged and includes—
(a) any prohibited weapon, whether it is such a lethal weapon as aforesaid or not; and
(b) any component part of such a lethal or prohibited weapon; and
(c) any accessory to any such weapon designed or adapted to diminish the noise or flash caused by firing the weapon; and so much of section 1 of this Act as excludes any description of firearm from the category of firearms to which that section applies shall be construed as also excluding component parts of, and accessories to, firearms of that description. (Firearms Act 1968, s 57(1))

['Prohibited weapons' under s 5 of the Act of 1968 are (a) any firearm which is so designed or adapted that, if pressure is applied to the trigger, missiles continue to be discharged until pressure is removed from the trigger or the magazine containing the missiles is empty; or (b) any weapon of whatever description designed or adapted for the discharge of any noxious liquid, gas or other thing; or (c) any ammunition containing, or designed or adapted to contain, any such noxious thing. Firearms excluded by s 1 of the Act are (a) a shotgun (that is to say a smooth-bore gun with a barrel not less than 24 inches in length, not being an air gun) and (b) an air weapon (that is to say, an air rifle, air gun or air pistol not of a type declared by rules made by the Secretary of State to be specially dangerous).]

See also the Firearms Act 1982 (imitation firearms.)

'Firearm' includes an air gun or air pistol, an "imitation firearm" means anything which has the appearance of being a firearm, whether capable of being discharged or not. (Theft Act 1968, s 10(1)(a))

[Under s 10, a person is guilty of aggravated burglary if he commits any burglary and at the same time has with him any firearm or imitation firearm, any weapon of offence, or any explosive.]

'Firearm' includes an air gun or air pistol (Aviation Security Act 1982, s 38(1))

'If one compares the air gun, which was the weapon carried by the respondents in this case, with a modern rifle, one can say with confidence that the two weapons are substantially identical, save only for the nature of the propellant, i.e. save only for the fact that the propellant in one case is compressed air and in the other case is cordite. One puts oneself in the position when an air gun has become part of the modern armoury of sport, and one tries to envisage the discussions which would take place when this new-fangled weapon had been taken into use and Parliament had been accustomed to it. For my part, I think that the attitude at that time would have been for people to compare the similarity of the two weapons, to observe, as I have observed, that it is only the nature of the propellant which distinguishes them, and I do not think that the use of the phrase "firearm" should be regarded as unsuitable for an air gun merely because of that difference in the propellant. In my judgment, the ordinary meaning of the word requires us to say that the expression "firearm" does include an air gun.' *Seamark v Prouse* [1980] 3 All ER 26 at 27, 28, per Lord Widgery CJ

Canada 'The word "firearm" as used . . . in its popular sense means any portable smallarm from which a missile may be propelled by an explosive. It is, in common parlance, a "shooting weapon". A rifle is simply a firearm having rifling on the surface of its bore.' *Re R v Desjarlais* (1961) 38 WWR 125 at 126, Sask KB, per Disbery J

Canada 'When reading the definition of firearm [in the Criminal Code] it first appears that what is being principally considered is a barrelled weapon that is actually "capable of causing serious bodily injury or death", because it can be loaded and fired. This to me includes unloaded guns.' *R v Covin* [1983] 1 SCR 725 at 728, SCC, per Lamer J

Imitation firearm

'Imitation firearm' means any thing which has the appearance of being a firearm (other than such a weapon as is mentioned in s 5(1)(b) of this Act (see supra)) whether or not it is capable of discharging any shot, bullet or other missile (Firearms Act 1968, s 57(4); cf s 10(1)(a) of the Theft Act, supra and the Firearms Act 1982, s 1)

Meaning of 'lethal'

'The definition of "firearm" in s 32, sub-s 1, of the Act [Firearms Act 1937 (repealed; see now s 57(1) of the Firearms Act 1968, supra)] is "any lethal barrelled weapon of any description from which any shot, bullet, or other missile can be discharged". If a weapon is a lethal weapon, which means a weapon capable of causing injury, and if such a weapon is barrelled and a shot, bullet, or other missile can be discharged from it, it is a firearm.' *Read v Donovan* [1947] KB 326 at 327, per Lord Goddard CJ

[Section 32(1) of the Firearms Act 1937 (repealed; see supra) defines 'firearm' as any 'lethal' barrelled weapon of any description from which any shot, bullet or other missile can be discharged.] 'The sole question was whether this "Diana" airgun was a firearm within the statute and within s 19(1) [which deals with the sale of firearms to persons under seventeen years of age]. The justices held that it was not, and they came to that conclusion really on these grounds: that, having regard to the definition in s 32(1) and, in particular the word "lethal", the weapon in question must be one likely to cause injury of the sort which might result in death. They rejected a contention that a lethal weapon was one which was merely capable of causing injury though not injury of the sort likely to cause death. In saying that, I understand that they were giving effect to the word "lethal" in this sense: that the weapon must be a sort which causes injury of a type from which death would in the ordinary way result. For my part, I think that they were fully entitled to give effect to the word "lethal" in the sense that the injury must be of a kind which may cause death. That is the ordinary meaning of the word, but it is to be observed that in this connexion one is not considering whether a firearm is designed or intended to cause injury from which death results, but rather whether it is a weapon which, however misused, may cause injury from which death may result.' *Moore v Gooderham* [1960] 3 All ER 575 at 576, per Lord Parker CJ

Shot gun

A smooth-bore gun with a barrel not less than 24 inches in length, not being an air gun. (Firearms Act 1968, s 1(3)(a))

'Shot gun' has the meaning assigned to it by

s 1(3)(a) of this Act [supra] and in the definition of 'firearms dealer' [infra] includes any component part of a shot gun and any accessory to a shot gun designed or adapted to diminish the noise or flash caused by firing the gun. (Firearms Act 1968, s 57(4))

FIREARMS DEALER

'Firearms dealer' means a person who, by way of trade or business, manufactures, sells, transfers, repairs, tests or proves firearms or ammunition to which s 1 of this Act applies, or shot guns. (Firearms Act 1968, s 57(4))

FIREPLACE

'Fireplace' includes any furnace, grate or stove, whether open or closed. (Clean Air Act 1956, s 34(1))

FIRM   See also FOREIGN FIRM

Persons who have entered into partnership with one another are for the purposes of this Act called collectively a firm, and the name under which their business is carried on is called the firm-name. (Partnership Act 1890, s 4(1))
[A person, e.g. a solicitor, in sole practice is therefore not a 'firm': see *Oswald Hickson Collier & Co (a firm) v Carter-Ruck* [1984] 2 All ER 15, CA]

'The word "firm", I believe, like many mercantile terms, is derived from an Italian word, which means simply "signature", and it is as much the name of the house of business, as John Nokes or Thomas Stiles is the name of an individual. The name of a firm is a very important part of the goodwill.' *Churton v Douglas* (1859) 28 LJ Ch 841 at 845, per Wood V-C

Australia 'It is undoubtedly true that a firm is not any entity known to the law. It is an unincorporated body, comprised of certain members who carry on business in partnership. It, as distinct from its members, is incapable of committing an offence against the criminal law or an offence of a quasi-criminal nature, unless a statute otherwise provides.' *McLeod v Trethowan* [1965] VR 672 at 672, per O'Bryan J

FIRM OFFER

United States An offer by a merchant to buy or sell goods in a signed writing which by its terms gives assurance that it will be held open is not revocable, for lack of consideration, during the time stated or if no time is stated for a reasonable time, but in no event may such period of irrevocability exceed three months; but any such term of assurance on a form supplied by the offeree must be separately signed by the offeror. (Uniform Commercial Code 1978, s 2–205)

FIRST   See IN THE FIRST PLACE

FIRST-CLASS

[By a deed it was agreed that a certain piece of land should be sold for use as a 'first-class' station or place for the purposes of taking up and setting down passengers travelling on the railway.] 'First-class must mean something, and must mean that the station shall be in a position at least equal to any other station.' *Hood v North Eastern Rly Co* (1870) 5 Ch App 525 at 528, per Lord Hatherley LC

FIRST COUSIN   See COUSIN

FIRST REFUSAL

[By an agreement between a racecourse company and a canal company, if the racecourse were at any time proposed for use for dock purposes, the racecourse company were to give the canal company the 'first refusal' thereof.] 'There appear to be two possible meanings of the words "first refusal"; one is that they mean the opportunity of refusing a "fair and reasonable offer" by the racecourse company to sell the lands *en bloc* to the canal company; the other is that they mean the opportunity of refusing the land at a price acceptable to the racecourse company offered by some person other than the canal company, which is what we understand by the term "right of preemption".' *Manchester Ship Canal Co v Manchester Racecourse Co* [1901] 2 Ch 37 at 46, 47, CA, per cur.

Australia [The owner of land covenanted that upon the death of the survivor of himself and his wife his executors would give to the tenant of the land the right of 'first refusal' to purchase the land for £13,000.] 'The term "first refusal" is not a technical term. It is a colloquial term, and indeed a somewhat inept term, because what the potential offeree wants is an opportunity of accepting an offer rather than an opportunity of refusing an offer. . . . It seems clear that a mere promise to give the first refusal should be taken prima facie as conferring no more than a pre-emptive right.' *Woodroffe v Box* [1954] ALR 474 at 479, per Fullagar and Kitto J

New Zealand [A clause in a lease provided that three months before the expiration of the lease the lessor would grant the lessee 'first refusal' of a further five years' lease. At the expiration of the term, the lessor stated he did not propose again to lease the premises for a further period, and he had made no offer to the tenant. In holding that the clause could not be treated as a covenant for renewal:] 'The covenant on the part of the lessor is, however, to grant a first refusal of a further five years' lease, and the lessor's obligation must be limited to that. There is no evidence that the lessor
• intends to lease the property again. If he had proposed to lease and wanted a tenant, the applicant was entitled, if he had performed the conditions of the lease, to first refusal on the terms mentioned. A refusal connotes an offer. If the lessor does not propose to lease the hotel for a further period and he makes no offer to the tenant, then there can be no refusal.' *Scott v Skinner* [1947] NZLR 528 at 531, per Johnson J; also reported [1947] GLR 137 at 138

FIRST SON

'I cannot quite agree, that "first son" is to be always taken strictly in the sense of *primogenitus*; but in the sense of an elder son, *senior* or *maximus natu*.' *Lomax v Holmden* (1749) 1 Ves Sen 290 at 294, per Lord Hardwicke LC

[By a strict settlement of real estate made in 1876 the property was limited to the use of the settlor's eldest son for life with remainder to his 'first and other sons' successively according to seniority in tail male.] 'The important words in the limitation I am considering are the words "first and other sons", and I think that . . . there is a general principle of construction not confined to wills which binds me to hold that these words connote successive interests. That principle is, in my opinion, established by *Lewis v Waters* [(1805) 6 East 336]. In that case . . . Grose J said: "The limitation to the 'first and other sons' imports that they were to take successively according to priority of birth;

it is the abridged language of conveyancers." . . . It appears clear from this judgment that, in the view of Grose J, the words "first and other sons" in conveyances, and not merely in wills, do import the idea of successive interests. That being so, I think I am bound to place the same meaning on those words in the limitations in the deed before me.' *Re Gosset's Settlement, Gribble v Lloyds Bank Ltd* [1943] Ch 351 at 354, 355, per Cohen J

FISCAL PERIOD

Canada 'Under s 2(s) of the Act [Income War Tax Act, RSC 1927, c 97 (repealed; see now the Income Tax Act, RSC 1970, C I–5, s 203)] there is such a thing as a "fiscal period", and this means the period for which the accounts of the business of the taxpayer have been, or are ordinarily made up and accepted for purposes of assessment under the Act, and in the absence of such an established practice the fiscal period shall be that which the taxpayer adopts, but it must not exceed a period of twelve months.' *Malkin v National Revenue Minister* [1942] Ex CR 113 at 123, Ex Ct, per Maclean J

FISH

'Fish' includes molluscs and crustaceans. (Harbours Act 1964, s 57)

[As to the offence of unlawfully taking or destroying fish, see the Theft Act 1968, Sch 1.]

'Fish' includes crustaceans and molluscs of any kind. (Agricultural Marketing Act 1983, s 8)

Fish farming

'Business of fish farming' means business of keeping live fish (whether or not for profit) with a view to their sale or to their transfer to other waters. (Diseases of Fish Act 1937, as inserted by s 4(2) of the Diseases of Fish Act 1983)

Freshwater fish

'Freshwater fish' means any fish living in fresh water exclusive of salmon and trout and of any kinds of fish which migrate to and from tidal waters and of eels. (Salmon and Freshwater Fisheries Act 1975, s 41(1))

'Freshwater fish' means any fish living in fresh

water including eels and the fry of eels, but excluding salmon. (Import of Live Fish (England and Wales) Act 1980, s 4)

Migratory trout *See* TROUT

Right of fishing

'What passed to the grantees by the words "exclusive right of fishing"? Mr Bramwell Davis [counsel for the appellant] contended that they only gave the right of catching fish, and did not include the right of taking away the fish caught; that it was a licence to hook the fish and leave the fish, when hooked, in the water or somewhere else. . . . If a person chooses to pay for the amusement of catching fish and leaving them in the water, of course he can do so; but that is not what is understood by lawyers or men of sense as a right of fishing. The right of fishing includes the right to take away fish unless the contrary is expressly stipulated.' *Fitzgerald v Firbank* [1897] 2 Ch 96 at 100, 101, CA, per Lindley LJ

Salmon *See* SALMON

Sea fish

'Sea fish' means fish of any description found in the sea, including shellfish and salmon and migratory trout. (Sea Fish Industry Act 1962, s 33)

'Sea fish' means fish of any description found in the sea including shellfish but does not include—
(a) fish of the salmon species, or
(b) trout which migrate to and from the sea.
(Sea Fisheries Regulation Act 1966, s 20)

[See also s 8 of the Fishery Limits Act 1976.]

'Sea fish' means fish, whether fresh or cured, of any kind found in the sea, including shellfish, and any parts of any such fish but (except in ss 4, 4A, 5, 6, 7 and 9) does not include salmon or migratory trout. (Sea Fish (Conservation) Act 1967, s 22(1), as amended by the Fisheries Act 1981, s 21(2)(c))

[Section 4 of the Act deals with the licensing of British fishing boats; s 4A prohibits unauthorised trans-shipment of fish; s 5 gives powers to restrict fishing for sea fish; ss 6, 7 regulate the landing of sea fish; s 9 exempts operations for scientific or certain other purposes.]

'Sea fish' means fish of any description found in the sea, other than fish of the salmon species, and includes shellfish. (Sea Fisheries (Shellfish) Act 1967, s 22)

Shellfish

'Shellfish' includes crustaceans and molluscs of any kind, and includes any part of a shellfish and any (or any part of any) brood, ware, half-ware or spat of shellfish, and any spawn of shellfish, and the shell, or any part of the shell, of a shellfish, and references in this Act to shellfish of any particular description shall be construed accordingly. (Sea Fish Industry Act 1962, s 33; Sea Fisheries (Shellfish) Act 1967, s 22(2))

'Shellfish' includes crustaceans and molluscs of any kind and any spat or spawn of shellfish. (Sea Fish (Conservation) Act 1967, s 22(1))

'The habit of taking and removing [oyster] spawn is extremely ancient. . . . Shell-fish is the proper description of this species of fish.' *Bridger v Richardson* (1814) 2 M & S 568 at 572, per Lord Ellenborough CJ

Trout *See* TROUT

FISHERY

The general principle is that fisheries are in their nature mere profits of the soil over which the water flows, and that the title to a fishery arises from the right to the soil. A fishery may be severed from the soil and it then becomes a profit à prendre *in alieno solo* and an incorporeal hereditament. The term corporeal fishery is, accordingly, used to describe a corporeal hereditament; that is, in tidal waters, a several fishery coupled with the soil under it and, in non-tidal waters, the soil coupled with a right of fishing thereover. A corporeal fishery may be owned by one who owns no land adjacent to it. The term 'incorporeal fishery' is used to describe an incorporeal hereditament, that is, a mere right to take fish or a specified class of fish in a defined stretch of water without interference with the soil. An incorporeal fishery cannot be exercised by means of engines fixed in the soil unless there is a special provision in the grant, for the mere grant of such a fishery does not confer the right to occupy the soil, but the temporary driving in of stakes for holding a net in position may be regarded as ancillary to the grant.

A fishery may be vested in the public at large, in which case it is described as a public fishery, or it may be vested in one or more individuals, in which case it is called a private fishery. A private fishery may be either a several fishery or a common of fishery. (18 Halsbury's Laws (4th edn) paras 601, 602)

'The general principle is that fisheries are in their nature mere profits of the soil over which the water flows, and that the title to a fishery arises from the right to the *solum*. A fishery may of course be severed from the *solum*, and it then becomes a profit à prendre *in alieno solo* and an incorporeal hereditament. The severance may be effected by grant or by prescription, but it cannot be brought about by custom, for the origin of such a custom would be an unlawful act. But apart from the existence of such severance by grant or prescription the fishing rights go with the property in the *solum*.' *A-G for British Columbia v A-G for Canada* [1914] AC 153 at 167, 168, PC, per cur.

Common of fishery

Common of fishery is a liberty of fishing in another man's waters in common with certain other persons. It may be held as either appurtenant to a house or land (but not to a pasture), or in gross, but if appurtenant may not be without stint. When not held in gross it may be claimed under the Prescription Act 1832. (18 Halsbury's Laws (4th edn) para 618)

Franchise fishery

There is one special right of fishery which is a franchise, that is to say a royal privilege in the hands of a subject. This is the right to take whales and sturgeon, which are royal fish, within the waters of the realm. Unless he is a grantee of the Crown the captor has no property in such fish, even though he is the owner of a several fishery at the spot where the fish is caught. Subject to this exception, it is doubtful whether any fishery can be a franchise. (18 Halsbury's Laws (4th edn) para 619)

Oyster fishery

'The words oyster-layings would not pass the privilege of getting oysters; because those words only import a privilege of laying oysters there, and it might be doubtful whether it would give a right to take them.' *Scratton v Brown* (1825) 4 B & C 485 at 503, 504, per Littledale J

'For a long series of years the plaintiff and his predecessors have been the occupiers of certain oyster beds, which are constructions of the nature of artificial ponds, high up on the foreshore of the locality, into which beds or ponds oysters that have been dredged elsewhere are brought to be laid down in order to fatten, and to be taken from those beds to the market. . . . I have come to the conclusion that an oyster bed of this kind, which I prefer to call by the older and unambiguous term of an "oyster laying", has nothing whatever to do with a several oyster fishery, and can exist quite independently of the existence of such a fishery. If we consider what is the purpose of such a bed, one sees that it has nothing in common with rights of fishing. Rights of fishing signify the right to catch that species of creatures known as *feræ naturæ* which exist in the sea, and there is no doubt that when, as in a several oyster fishery, or in a public oyster fishery, you dredge oysters from their natural beds, you are fishing, you are taking things in respect of which, in the case of a public fishery, nothing in the nature of a proprietary right exists in anyone, and are appropriating them and making them your own property. But an "oyster laying" does not come into operation until the act of appropriation is finished. It exists only for the purpose of being used in connection with chattels the property of which is in some individual. The oysters are first caught or purchased by the owner, they are then laid down in the "oyster laying" for the purpose of improving, and, unless the owner by so laying them down has committed an act of abandonment, the property still remains in him. . . . The position where these "oyster layings" are usually placed is high up on the foreshore, where they are formed in the shape of shallow ponds, covered by the flux and reflux of the tide, but by no means in places where natural beds of oysters exist. It cannot be said that their existence de facto limits any rights of taking oysters from their natural beds; they are usually put in places on ground belonging to some individual, that is to say, on parts of the waste of the manor, quite away from those places in which the fishing for what I may call wild oysters would take place. In my mind, oysters in an "oyster laying" do not differ substantially, as regards legal status, from lobsters that are in a lobster pot. Everyone has a right to take lobsters in the sea, unless he is thereby interfering with the rights of a several fishery; but, if a lobster is in a lobster pot, and a stranger takes it out, that is not fishing, but taking something the property in which has passed to some individual. If we go a little further, and consider the practice which exists in some parts of the coast, I believe, of placing lobsters that have been captured in larger wicker cages where a considerable number of them can be kept till it is convenient to send them to market, we see a still closer analogy to these "oyster layings". It is quite true that in such cages the lobsters are wholly enclosed, but that is because it is impossible in the case of such fish to keep them safely unless they are so enclosed. The fact that the mature oyster has practically no means of locomotion makes it quite unnecessary that you should place oysters in a wholly enclosed space in order to confine them, but the oysters in an "oyster laying" are just as much kept in captivity as would be the lobsters in a wicker construction of the character that I have described. It therefore seems to me that, in the absence of authority that these "oyster layings" are not capable of legal existence except as part of a several fishery, there is no ground in good sense why we should suppose that they must necessarily be parcel of or appurtenant to such a fishery.' *Foster v Warblington Urban Council* [1906] 1 KB 648 at 678, 680–682, CA, per Fletcher Moulton LJ

Several fishery

A private right of fishing, whether in tidal or non-tidal waters, is either a right of several fishery or of common of fishery. A several fishery is an exclusive right of fishing in a given place, either with or without the property in the soil. By exclusive is meant that no other person has a co-extensive right with the owner. The fact that some other person (1) has a right to a particular class of fish in the fishery, (2) has a right to fish in common with the owner of the several fishery, or (3) is entitled to fish at a certain time of the year under a presumed trust in his favour or otherwise, does not destroy the severalty of the fishery. (18 Halsbury's Laws (4th edn) para 617)

'In order to constitute a several fishery, it is requisite that the party claiming it should so far have the right of fishing, independent of all others, as that no person should have a co-extensive right with him in the subject claimed: (for, where any person has such co-extensive right, there is only a free fishery). But we think that a partial independent right in another, or a limited liberty, does not derogate from the right of the general owner.' *Seymour v Courtenay* (1771) 5 Burr 2814 at 2817, per Lord Mansfield

'The fishery in this case is sufficiently described as a "several" fishery, which means an exclusive right to fish in a given place, either with or without the property in the soil.' *Malcomson v O'Dea* (1863) 10 HL Cas 593 at 619, per Willes J

'A several fishery means an exclusive right to fish in a given place for which I may refer to *Malcomson v O'Dea* [supra] and *Holford v Bailey* [(1849) 13 QB 426]. A several fishery may exist either apart from or as incident to the ownership of the soil over which the river flows; but since *Attorney-General v Emerson* [[1891] AC 649] it must be taken as settled that where a several fishery is proved to exist, the owner of the fishery is to be presumed to be the owner of the soil, unless there is evidence to the contrary.' *Hanbury v Jenkins* [1901] 2 Ch 401 at 411, per Buckley J

FISHING BOAT

The expression 'fishing boat' means a vessel of whatever size, and in whatever way propelled, which is for the time being employed in sea fishing or in the sea-fishing service, but save as otherwise expressly provided, that expression shall not include a vessel used for catching fish otherwise than for profit. (Merchant Shipping Act 1894, s 370)

'Fishing boat' has the same meaning as in Part IV of the principal Act [Merchant Shipping Act 1894 (supra)] except that it includes a vessel which is being constructed for the purpose of being employed in sea fishing or in the sea-fishing service. (Merchant Shipping Act 1950, s 7(1))

'Fishing boat' means any vessel for the time being employed in fishing operations or any operations ancillary thereto. (Fishery Limits Act 1976, s 8)

FISHING INTERROGATORIES *See* INTERROGATORIES

FISHING MILL DAM

'Fishing mill dam' means a dam used or intended to be used partly for the purpose of taking or facilitating the taking of fish, and partly for the purpose of supplying water for milling or other purposes. (Salmon and Freshwater Fisheries Act 1975, s 41(1))

FISHING VESSEL

'Fishing vessel' means a vessel which is for the time being used for or in connection with sea fishing but does not include a vessel used for fishing otherwise than for profit. (Fishing Vessels (Safety Provisions) Act 1970, s 9(1))

'The . . . question is, whether these vessels [which only carried fish from one port to another] come within the description of "coasting vessels" or "fishermen". They certainly do not come within the description of "fishermen". A fishing vessel is a vessel from which persons fish either with a line or net, and not a vessel merely used for carrying fish.' *Shepherd v Hills* (1855) 11 Exch 55 at 67, per Parke B

FISHING WEIR

'Fishing weir' means any erection, structure, or obstruction fixed to the soil either temporarily or permanently across, or partly across, a river or branch of a river, and used for the exclusive purpose of taking or facilitating the taking of fish. (Salmon and Freshwater Fisheries Act 1975, s 41(1))

FIT

Fit for human habitation

[Section 1(1) of the Housing Act 1925 (repealed; see now the Landlord and Tenant Act 1985, s 8, provided that in any contract for letting a dwelling house at a rent not exceeding certain sums, there should be implied a condition that the house was, at the commencement of the tenancy, 'in all respects reasonably fit for human habitation'.] 'The Housing Act 1925 . . . imposes a liability on the landlord to keep the house in all respects reasonably fit for human habitation. . . . The standard which was suggested . . . is one which commends itself to me, which is that if the state of repair of a house is such that by ordinary user damage may naturally be caused to the occupier, either in respect of personal injury to life or limb or injury to health, then the house is not in all respects reasonably fit for human habitation.' *Morgan v Liverpool Corpn* [1927] 2 KB 131 at 144, 145, CA, per Atkin LJ

'The claim is based on s 2, sub-s 1 of the Housing Act 1936 [repealed; see now the Landlord and Tenant Act 1985, s 8], which is the latest embodiment of a legislative measure going back to 1857. The subsection provides that in any contract for letting for human habitation a house at a rent not exceeding £26 a year (I take the figure which applies in Salford) there shall, notwithstanding any stipulation to the contrary, be implied a condition that the house is at the commencement of the tenancy, and an

undertaking that the house shall be kept by the landlord during the tenancy, in all respects reasonably fit for human habitation. . . . The section only applies to low-rented tenements. In these small houses it may be assumed that every room is in full use, and I think that the statutory condition is intended to ensure that every room is fit for use. It was contended that it is the house, and not every room in the house, which is required to fulfil the condition, but, in my opinion, that contention is inconsistent both with the language and the object of the section. "In all respects" must mean in all respects material to the enjoyment of the tenement, and the unfitness of one room may be a most material detraction from that enjoyment. "Human habitation" is in contrast with habitation by pigs, horses or other animals, or with use as warehouses and the like, but I think it also imports some reference to what we call humanity or humaneness. MacKinnon LJ observed [in the court below] that the words used are not words of art taken from the usual provisions of covenants in leases, and described them as "words almost of journalistic generality". But that is natural enough. The measure is a new departure. The construction of usual covenants in leases has often been justified, whether rightly or wrongly, on the ground that the words have acquired a recognised and conventional meaning, but here the condition is not derived from the agreement of the parties. It is imposed compulsorily by Parliament. Older cases, however, have used similar words. Thus in *Smith v Marrable* [(1843) 11 M & W 5], the well-known case of a furnished house, the side note describes the implied condition to be that it is "reasonably fit for habitation". The phrase used by Parke B was "fit for decent and comfortable habitation". The words of the Act are meant to be wide and elastic, because they are to be applied to the needs and circumstances of poor people living in confined quarters. The court has to condescend to realise what these are.' *Summers v Salford Corpn* [1943] AC 283 at 292–294, per Lord Wright

Fit person

[By s 23(2) of the Licensing (Consolidation) Act 1910 (repealed; see now ss 3(1), 12(7) of the Licensing Act 1964), an application for the transfer of a justices' licence might be allowed or refused by the licensing justices in the exercise of their discretion provided that the transferee was a 'fit' and proper person in the opinion of the justices to be the holder of the licence.] 'Lord Alverstone CJ, in giving his judgment [in *R v Hyde JJ* (1912) 106 LT 152] said: "The prima facie meaning of the words 'fit and proper person' in s 23(2), cl(b), of the Licensing (Consolidation) Act 1910 . . . is that the applicant must be a fit and proper person to hold a licence and carry on the business of the licence-holder." . . . One of the grounds which it is natural and proper to take into consideration upon the question whether the proposed transferee is a fit and proper person, is the kind or degree of his interest in the licensed premises and the good conduct of the licensed premises. . . . The question remains in every case whether the person put forward as manager has such a real and effective interest in the licensed premises as to be a fit and proper person to hold the licence.' *R v Holborn Licensing JJ, ex p Stratford Catering Co Ltd* (1926) 136 LT 278 at 279, 280, DC, per Lord Hewart CJ

Fitted or provided with

Canada 'That section [Criminal Code, 1953–54 (Can) c 51, s 169(b); see now RSC 1970, c C–34, s 180] provides that "if any house, room, or place is found fitted or provided with any such machine [a slot-machine] there shall be an irrebuttable presumption that such house, room or place is a common gaming house". . . . If the machine was in storage on the premises then one would not in ordinary speech refer to the room or place where it was as "fitted and provided with" the machine. But the mere fact that, for the moment while cleaning-up was in progress, the machine was pulled out from the wall, would not mean very much. It could be very quickly put back in position just as could the chairs and tables with which, no doubt, the same room was fitted or provided.' *R v Carusetta* [1942] 2 DLR 644 at 645, Ont CA, per Robertson CJO

FITNESS *See* QUALITY

FITTINGS *See also* FIXTURES

Electrical fittings

'Electrical fittings' means electric lines, fittings, apparatus and appliances designed for use by consumers of electricity for lighting, heating, motive power and other purposes for which electricity can be used. (Electricity Act 1947, s 67(1))

Gas fittings

'Gas fittings' means gas pipes and meters, and fittings, apparatus and appliances designed for use by consumers of gas for heating, lighting, motive power and other purposes for which gas can be used. (Gas Act 1986, s 48(1))

Water fittings

'Water fittings' includes pipes (other than mains), taps, cocks, valves, ferrules, meters, cisterns, baths, water-closets, soil-pans and other similar apparatus used in connection with the supply and use of water. (Water Act 1945, s 59; ibid, Sch III(1))

FIXED

Copyrights

United States A work is 'fixed' in a tangible medium of expression when its embodiment in a copy or phonorecord, by or under the authority of the author, is sufficiently permanent or stable to permit it to be perceived, reproduced, or otherwise communicated for a period of more than transitory duration. A work consisting of sounds, images, or both, that are being transmitted, is 'fixed' for purposes of this title if a fixation of the work is being made simultaneously with its transmission. (Copyright Act of 1976, s 101)

FIXED ASSETS *See* ASSETS

FIXED CAPITAL

Part of the capital of a company may consist of fixed capital and part of circulating capital. Fixed capital means that capital which a company retains in the shape of assets upon which the subscribed capital has been expended and which assets either themselves produce income independently of any further action by the company, or, being retained by the company, are made use of to produce income or gain profits. (7 Halsbury's Laws (4th edn) para 600)

'What is fixed capital? That which a company retains, in the shape of assets upon which the subscribed capital has been expended, and which assets either themselves produce income, independent of any further action by the company, or being retained by the company are made use of to produce income or gain profits.' *Ammonia Soda Co v Chamberlain* [1918] 1 Ch 266 at 286, CA, per Swinfen Eady LJ

FIXED ENGINE

'Fixed engine' includes—
(a) stake net, bag net, putt, or putcher; and
(b) any fixed implement or engine for taking or facilitating the taking of fish; and
(c) any net secured by anchors and any net or other implement for taking fish fixed to the soil, or made stationary in any other way; and
(d) any net placed or suspended in any inland or tidal waters unattended by the owner or a person duly authorised by the owner to use it for taking salmon or trout, and any engine, device, machine, or contrivance, whether floating or otherwise, for placing or suspending such a net or maintaining it in working order or making it stationary.
(Salmon and Freshwater Fisheries Act 1975, s 41(1))

'The definition in s 92(1) of the Act [Salmon and Freshwater Fisheries Act] of 1923 [repealed; see now the Salmon and Freshwater Fisheries Act 1975, s 41(1), supra] . . . is: "The expression 'fixed engine' includes . . . (c) any net secured by anchors and any net or other implement for taking fish fixed to the soil, or made stationary in any other way, not being a fishing weir or fishing mill dam. . . ." That definition is not an absolute definition, as it states what a "'fixed engine' includes", but the first thing I should say with regard to a "fixed engine" is that it must be fixed. I do not see how, whatever the definition clause says that the expression is to include, it could remove the necessity for a "fixed engine" to be fixed, and, if a thing is fixed, it seems to me, it must be stationary.' *Percival v Stanton* [1954] 1 All ER 392 at 394, per Lord Goddard CJ

FIXED EQUIPMENT   *See* EQUIPMENT

FIXED ODDS

A bet is a bet at fixed odds within the meaning of this section only if each of the persons making it knows or can know, at the time he makes it, the amount he will win, except in so far as that amount is to depend on the result of the event or events betted on, or on any such event taking place or producing a result, or on the numbers taking part in any such event, or on the starting prices or totalisator odds for any such event, or on there being totalisator odds on any such event, or on the time when his bet is received by any person with or through whom it is made.

In this subsection—
'starting prices' means, in relation to any event, the odds ruling at the scene of the event immediately before the start, and
'totalisator odds' means—
(a) in relation to a race which is a recognised horse race within the meaning of section 55(1) of the Betting, Gaming and Lotteries Act 1963, the odds paid on bets on that race made by way of sponsored pool betting, and
(b) in relation to any other event, the odds paid on bets made by means of a totalisator at the scene of the event.
(Betting and Gaming Duties Act 1981, s 10(2))

FIXED PRICE

Australia 'It may be conceded, and, indeed, it appears to have been decided, that a bare power to "fix" a price cannot be validly exercised without naming a money sum, or prescribing a certain standard by the application of which it can be calculated or ascertained definitely. Otherwise the price is not "fixed".' *Fraser Henleins Pty Ltd v Cody* (1945) 70 CLR 100 at 128, per Dixon J

FIXED TERM

'In my opinion a "fixed term" is one which cannot be unfixed by notice. To be a "fixed term", the parties must be bound for the term stated in the agreement; and unable to determine it by notice on either side. If it were only determinable for misconduct, it would, I think, be a "fixed term"—because that is imported by the common law anyway. But determination by notice is destructive of any "fixed term".' *British Broadcasting Corpn v Ioannou* [1975] 2 All ER 999 at 1005, CA, per Lord Denning MR

FIXTURES   *See also* CHATTELS

In accordance with the general rule of law that anything fixed to the freehold becomes part of the freehold, chattels affixed to premises at the date of a lease by a landlord, or some prior owner or tenant, will pass under the demise unless expressly or impliedly excluded. Chattels so affixed, and chattels affixed subsequent to the commencement of the lease, must be delivered up to the landlord on the determination of the tenancy, unless the tenant is entitled to remove them by virtue of some special rule of law, statute, or agreement, in accordance with the rule of law that whatever has once become part of the inheritance cannot be severed by a limited owner, whether he is owner for life or for years, without the commission of waste. Two questions usually arise for consideration with regard to articles attached to premises, first, whether the attachment is such that they are to be regarded as forming part of the premises, that is to say, as fixtures; and, secondly, if they are fixtures, whether they can be removed by some person other than the owner of the freehold by virtue of some special rule of law, statute, or agreement. For the purposes of distinction, fixtures which the tenant may not remove are usually referred to as 'landlord's fixtures'. This term includes fixtures attached to the premises at the date of the demise, those fixed by the landlord during the term, and also those fixed by the tenant which he is not entitled to remove. Those removable by the tenant are usually referred to as 'tenant's fixtures', and while attached to the premises they form part of the realty. If the fixtures are not removed by the tenant, they pass to the landlord, and a subsequent tenant takes no interest in them. In practice, the theoretical distinction between articles which are removable by the tenant because they have never become fixtures, and articles which have become fixtures and are so removable as 'tenant's fixtures' has often become blurred. (27 Halsbury's Laws (4th edn) para 142)

'Fixtures, when they belong to the owner of the inheritance, are, in contemplation of law, a component part of the entire estate, to all intents and purposes. They may be, however, and often are, the property of different owners; but they are still deemed part and parcel of the realty, whether the owner have a right to remove them, or not. Whether they belong to the landlord, or tenant—to the mortgagor, or the mortgagee,—the heir, or the executor,—they are still fixtures, in the eye of the law, as long as they continue locally stationed in the places to which they are affixed and adapted. The right to unfix and carry them away, does not alter their nature or condition; and the very assertion of that right involves an admission of their character of fixtures.' *Re Walsh, ex p King* (1840) 1 Mont D & De G 119 at 123, 124, per Sir John Cross

'Here the question is as to fixtures, trade fixtures, and what I may call domestic fixtures, and I wish to state that by "fixtures" we, . . . understand such things as are ordinarily affixed to the freehold for the convenience of the occupier, and which may be removed without material injury to the freehold, such will be machinery, using a generic term, and, in houses, grates, cupboards and other like things.' *Re Gawan, ex p Barclay* (1855) 5 De GM & G 403 at 410, per Lord Cranworth LC

'This is an action on a covenant in a lease. The lessees covenanted to "keep the inside of the demised premises, including all landlord's fixtures" in good repair. . . . The expression "landlord's fixtures", as I understand it, covers all those chattels which have been so affixed by way of addition to the original structure, and were so affixed either by the landlord, or, if by the tenant, under circumstances in which they were not removable by him.' *Boswell v Crucible Steel Co* [1925] 1 KB 119 at 123, CA, per Atkin LJ

'From the examination of many cases it would seem that the definition cited from Adkin and Bowen in Fixtures and adopted by counsel for the defendants conveys the essential matters: "A fixture is an article which by its annexation to the land has lost its chattel nature and has become, in the eye of the law, part and parcel of the realty." To make these printing machines in this case fixtures, therefore, they must be annexed to the realty; and in deciding whether annexation has taken place physical attachment is only one of the considerations to be kept in mind. An article, not physically attached to the land, in certain circumstances may yet have become part and parcel of the land and have lost its chattel character. The question of annexation depends on a number of circumstances, and the cases show that each case must be considered and decided on its own circumstances, applying the principles of law which have been laid down.' *Hulme v Brigham* [1943] 1 All ER 204 at 207, per Birkett J

'What is a fixture? First, the commonest fixture is a house. A house is built into the land, so the house, in law, is regarded as part of the land; the house and the land are one thing. Anything which is an integral part of the house, such as, for instance, lead pipes, will also be a fixture and will be attached to or form part of the land. A thing which, in its nature, is a chattel may or may not be a fixture. If it is affixed in some way, the true test, it seems to me is: was it meant to be a temporary fixture, and not part of the house or the land? In a house it may be for decoration. Many questions have arisen as regards such things as tapestries, fireplaces, and ornamental chimney-pieces. I think the matter is summed up admirably in Halsbury's

Laws of England [see now 4th edn, Vol 27, para 143] . . .: "Whether a chattel has been so affixed to the land or buildings as to become a fixture depends on the object and purpose of the annexation, and if the chattel can be removed without doing irreparable damage to the premises, neither the method nor the degree of annexation, nor the quantum of damage that would be done to the chattel or to the premises by the removal, affect the question save in so far as they throw a light upon the object and purpose of the annexation. If the object and purpose was for the permanent and substantial improvement of the land or building, the article will be deemed to be a fixture, but if it was attached to the premises merely for a temporary purpose or for the more complete enjoyment and use of it as a chattel, then it will not lose its chattel character and it does not become part of the realty." That is a useful exposition of the law, and if one wants authority to support it, a very good instance is *Holland v Hodgson* [(1872) LR 7 CP 328], where Blackburn J, than whom there was no higher authority on these matters, giving his judgment also emphasised that one has to consider the circumstances.' *Billing v Pill* [1953] 2 All ER 1061 at 1063, per Lord Goddard CJ; also reported in [1954] 1 QB 70 at 75

Australia 'If an article is embedded in the soil or is attached to any building or permanent erection thereon by cement, mortar, solder, bolts, screws, nails, spikes or other permanent fastening, it is prima facie a fixture.' *Re May Bros Ltd* [1929] SASR 508 at 512, per Murray CJ

Australia '"The meaning of the word [fixtures] is anything annexed to the freehold, that is, fastened to or connected with it, not in mere juxtaposition with the soil. Whatever is so annexed becomes part of the realty, and the person who was the owner of it when it was a chattel loses his property in it, which immediately vests in the owner of the soil. . . . But an exception has long been established in favour of a tenant erecting fixtures for the purposes of trade, allowing him the privilege of removing them during the continuance of the term (*Bain v Brand* [[1876] 1 App Cas 762 at 772])." And in determining whether or not a chattel becomes a fixture, the intention of the person affixing it to the soil is material only so far as it can be presumed from the degree and object of the annexation.' *Geita Sebea v Territory of Papua* (1941) 67 CLR 544 at 553, per Starke J

Australia 'On the whole, though unwillingly, I have come to the conclusion that the bulk of English authority is in favour of treating the maxim *quicquid solo plantatur solo cedit* as having full force and resulting in things fixed sufficiently and for a sufficient purpose changing their nature and becoming part of the freehold and so remaining while fixed, whatever rights any person may have in or in regard to them by custom, by contract or otherwise.' *Neon Electric Signs Ltd v Caldwell* [1943] VLR 1 at 28, per Gavan Duffy J

FLAGGED

'Kerbed does not mean flagged. Kerbed might answer paved, but not flagged. Flagged means with flagged stones.' *A-G v Bidder* (1881) 47 JP 263 at 264, per Jessel MR

FLAGRANT

New Zealand [The Copyright Act 1962, s 24(3) refers to the 'flagrancy' of an infringement.] 'What can rightly be described as "flagrant" . . . covers wilful or deliberate copyright infringements of varying kinds.' *International Credit Control Ltd v Axelsen* [1974] 1 NZLR 695 at 705, per Mahon J

FLARE-UP LIGHT

'The third officer of the *Tovarisch* burned a green pyrotechnic light, holding it out from the starboard side of the bridge. . . . The defendants say this was a light authorised by the regulations. If authorised it must be by art 12 [of the Regulations for Preventing Collisions at Sea 1910 (revoked; see now the Collision Regulations and Distress Signals Order 1977)], "Every vessel may, if necessary in order to attract attention, in addition to the lights which she is by these rules required to carry, show a flare-up light. . . ." . . . I am concerned with the meaning of "a flare-up light". The defendants say it may be of any colour, shown from any part of the ship. I cannot agree. In my opinion, in the language of the sea, it means a light, which is not in a lamp, and is produced by setting fire to something which burns with an ordinary flame, and does not include specially coloured flames. . . . Flare-up lights are not screened, and show all round the horizon.' *The Tovarisch* [1929] P 293 at 296, 297, 300, per Hill J

FLAT

'Flat' means a separate set of premises, whether or not on the same floor, which—
(a) forms part of a building,
(b) is divided horizontally from some other part of the building, and
(c) is constructed or adapted for use for the purposes of a dwelling and is occupied wholly or mainly as a private dwelling.
(Landlord and Tenant Act 1985, s 30)

'A flat is, in ordinary language, as defined in the Oxford Dictionary, "a suite of rooms on one floor, forming a complete residence". The term is itself derived from an old English word, meaning "floor".' *Boyle v Fitzsimons* [1926] IR 378 at 383, per Hanna J

Australia 'It does not appear to me that in order to be a flat premises must be self-contained in the sense that they must possess for their own exclusive use all the facilities which are commonly found in a complete single dwelling house, such as a bathroom, a toilet and a laundry. It is common knowledge that many premises described in ordinary usage as flats do not possess all these facilities. The expression "self-contained flat" is itself in common usage by way of referring to a flat which has its own kitchen, bathroom and toilet and of distinguishing it from flats which are lacking in some of these facilities. . . . The distinguishing characteristic of a "flat", in addition to that already mentioned, is that it is reasonably recognisable as a separate private dwelling even though it may not possess all the facilities which such a dwelling could possess.' *Slazengers (Aust) Pty Ltd v Emerson* (1967) 69 SR (NSW) 144 at 148, per Sugarman JA

FLESH   *See* HORSEFLESH

FLIGHT

'Flight' means a journey by air beginning when the aircraft takes off and ending when the aircraft next alights thereafter. (Civil Aviation (Licensing) Act 1960, s 10)

'Flight' means a journey by air beginning when the aircraft in question takes off and ending when it next lands. (Civil Aviation Act 1982, s 105(1))

For the purposes of this Act the period during which an aircraft is in flight shall be deemed to include any period from the moment when all its external doors are closed following embarkation until the moment when any such door is opened for disembarkation, and, in the case of a forced landing, any period until the competent authorities take over responsibility for the aircraft and for persons and property on board. (Aviation Security Act 1982, s 38(3)(a))

Aerial flight

Canada [An insurer appealed from a judgment allowing a beneficiary's action for proceeds under a life insurance policy. The insured died accidentally as a result of a fall whilst using a hang glider kite which was tethered to the ground. The policy excluded liability for loss resulting from 'aerial flight'. The appeal was allowed and judgment set aside.] 'The word "aerial" is defined in the Oxford English Dictionary, as "existing or moving in the atmosphere, above the earth, flying or floating in the air". The word "flight" is defined in the same dictionary, as "the action or manner of flying or moving through the air with or as with wings". In *Holmes v Sun Life Assurance Company of Canada* [[1977] ILR 765 at 770] Moore J said: "The words contained in the aviation exclusion provisions should in my view be given their simple meaning. The word 'travel' simply means to go from one place to another. 'Flight' in the context of the provision surely includes the movement of an aircraft on the ground or in the air from the moment its motion commences until its motion comes to a stop. A 'pilot' is a person who operates the controls of an aircraft in motion. A 'member of a crew' within the meaning of the provision surely means any person who assists in any way with the conduct of an aircraft in flight whether as a co-pilot, navigator, radio communicator, or any other person whose actions assist the movement of the aircraft on the ground or in the air." . . . It is, I think, clear that the Muller hang kite or glider which the late Mr Gowan was operating at the time of his death was a device designed to carry one person in flight through the air by the dynamic action of the air against the kite's surfaces and that it was a form of aircraft. It is, I think, also clear that the usual, ordinary and commonly accepted meaning of the words "aerial flight" is moving or flying in or through the air. Even if one were to accept the submission . . . that because the Muller hang kite or glider being operated by Mr Gowan was tied to the ground and was incapable of free flight, and that what he was doing was more akin to flying a kite from the ground, it is my opinion that from the moment such a kite or glider leaves the ground, it is in "aerial flight" of a kind and the person on it is making an "aerial flight".' *Gowan v North American Life Assurance Co* (1981) 34 NBR (2d) 187 at 194, 195, 200, New Brunswick CA, per Stratton JA

FLOATABLE

Canada 'There is a distinction between "floatable" and "navigable" [when applied to a river]. The former means floatable for loose logs; the latter navigable for boats of any character or even for rafts of logs.' *Flewelling v Johnston* (1921) 16 Alta LR 409 at 412, Alta CA, per Beck J

FLOATING CHARGE   *See also*
FLOATING SECURITY

The terms 'floating charge' and 'floating security' mean a charge or security which is not to be put into immediate operation, but is to float so that the company is to be allowed to carry on its business. It contemplates, for instance, that book debts may be extinguished by payment, and other book debts may come in and take the place of those that have disappeared. While a specific charge is one that, without more, fastens on ascertained and definite property or property capable of being ascertained or defined, a floating charge moves with the property which it is intended to affect, until some event occurs or some act is done which causes it to settle and fasten on the subject of the charge within its reach and grasp. It is of the essence of a floating charge that it remains dormant until the undertaking charged ceases to be a going concern, or until the person in whose favour the charge is created intervenes. (7 Halsbury's Laws (4th edn) para 824)

'A floating security is an equitable charge on the assets for the time being of a going concern. It attaches to the subject charged in the varying condition in which it happens to be from time to time. It is of the essence of such a charge that it remains dormant until the undertaking charged ceases to be a going concern, or until the person in whose favour the charge is created intervenes. His right to intervene may of course be suspended by agreement. But if there is no agreement for suspension, he may exercise his right whenever he pleases after

default.' *Governments Stock & Other Securities Investment Co Ltd v Manila Rly Co Ltd* [1897] AC 81 at 86, per Lord Macnaghten

'I certainly do not intend to attempt to give an exact definition of the term "floating charge" . . . but I certainly think that if a charge has the three characteristics that I am about to mention it is a floating charge. (1) If it is a charge on a class of assets of a company present and future; (2) if that class is one which, in the ordinary course of the business of the company, would be changing from time to time; and (3) if you find that by the charge it is contemplated that, until some future step is taken by or on behalf of those interested in the charge, the company may carry on its business in the ordinary way as far as concerns the particular class of assets I am dealing with.' *Re Yorkshire Woolcombers Assocn Ltd, Houldsworth v Yorkshire Woolcombers Assocn Ltd* [1903] 2 Ch 284 at 295, CA, per Romer LJ

'I should have thought there was not much difficulty in defining what a floating charge is in contrast to what is called a specific charge. A specific charge, I think, is one that without more fastens on ascertained and definite property or property capable of being ascertained and defined; a floating charge, on the other hand, is ambulatory and shifting in its nature, hovering over and so to speak floating with the property which it is intended to affect until some event occurs or some act is done which causes it to settle and fasten on the subject of the charge within its reach and grasp.' *Illingworth v Houldsworth* [1904] AC 355 at 358, HL, per Lord Macnaghten

'A floating charge is ambulatory and hovers over the property until some event occurs which causes it to settle and crystallise into a specific charge.' *Barker (George) v Eynon* [1974] 1 All ER 900 at 905, CA, per Edmund Davies LJ

Canada 'A floating charge cannot be said to be a legal mortgage for it requires as an essential ingredient that there be a present conveyance of the legal estate to the mortgagee subject to defeasance or reconveyance on non-payment. A floating charge, however, can be termed an equitable mortgage because it is a charge by which property is made a security for a debt owing which entitles the holder to payment out of the property. A chattel mortgage on specified property differs in this respect as the legal title vests in the mortgagee immediately upon the giving of the mortgage.' *JR Auto Brokers Ltd v Hillcrest Autolease Ltd* [1968] 2 OR 532 at 537, 538, Ont SC, per Lieff J

FLOATING POLICY

(1) A floating policy is a policy which describes the insurance in general terms, and leaves the name of the ship or ships and other particulars to be defined by subsequent declaration.

(2) The subsequent declaration or declarations may be made by indorsement on the policy, or in other customary manner.

(Marine Insurance Act 1906, s 29)

FLOATING SECURITY *See also*
CRYSTALLISE

'It was urged that this [debenture] was a "floating security". That term only expresses what is more fully expressed in the conditions indorsed on the debentures, viz that the company shall, notwithstanding the debentures, be at liberty to carry on its business, and in the ordinary course of such business to dispose of the property, as if the debentures did not exist. That is the ordinary meaning of the term "floating security".' *Driver v Broad* [1893] 1 QB 744 at 748, 749, per Kay LJ

'What is the precise effect of a "floating security" of this nature? Does it create a present charge, or is there no effective charge until the debenture-holders apply for a receiver? I think the true view is this. A floating security gives an immediate equitable charge on the assets, subject to a right to the company in the ordinary course and for the purposes of the business of the company, but not otherwise, to dispose of the assets as though the charge had not existed.' *Wallace v Evershed* [1899] 1 Ch 891 at 894, per Cozens-Hardy J

FLOOD

[A policy of insurance covered a householder against damage by 'storm, tempest or flood'. The insured claimed for damage caused, over a period of many months, by seepage of rainwater.] 'It seems apparent that what the policy was intending to cover, whatever may be the colloquial use of the word "flood" in common parlance, were three forms of natural phenomena which were related not only by the fact that they were natural, but also that they were unusual manifestations of those phenomena: that is to say, "storm" meant rain accompanied by strong wind; "tempest" denoted an even more violent storm; and "flood" was not something which came about by seepage or by trickling or dripping from some natural source, but involved "a large movement, an erruption of water", as one of the definitions in the Oxford Dictionary puts it. The slow movement of water, which can often be detected so that the damage threatened can be limited, is very different from the sudden onset of water where nothing effective can be done to prevent the damage, for it happens too quickly. It is because the word "flood" occurs in the context it does, that I have come to the conclusion that one must go back to first impressions, namely that it is used there in the limited rather than the wider sense; that it means something which is a natural phenomenon which has some element of violence, suddenness or largeness about it.' *Young v Sun Alliance and London Insurance Ltd* [1976] 3 All ER 561 at 563, CA, per Shaw LJ

FLOOD WARNING SYSTEM

'Flood warning system' means any system whereby, for the purpose of providing warning of any danger of flooding, information with respect to—
(a) rainfall, as measured at a particular place within a particular period, or
(b) the level or flow of any inland water, or part of an inland water, at a particular time, or
(c) other matters appearing to the authority providing the system to be relevant for that purpose
is obtained and transmitted whether automatically or otherwise, with or without provision for carrying out calculations based on such information and for transmitting the results of those calculations. (Land Drainage Act 1976, s 32(5))

FLOOR

'In my view, there is no sufficient reason for holding that the so-called sand floor of the foundry in this case was not a floor within the meaning of s 25(3) of the Factories Act 1937 [repealed; see now the Factories Act 1961, s 28(4)]. It is true that it was a floor made of sand as distinct from materials such as timber or cement, but, nevertheless, it seems to me that it was a floor, and a floor of such a kind that pits or openings could be made in it and re-filled at will as the exigencies of the work demanded. I think, therefore, that the hole into which the plaintiff fell was an opening in a floor within the meaning of s 25(3) of the Act.' *Harrison v Metropolitan-Vickers Electrical Co Ltd* [1954] 1 All ER 404 at 406, CA, per Jenkins LJ

[Planks were laid across the steel framework of a gantry carrying cranes, with gaps in various places. The question was whether the planks constituted a 'floor' required to be securely fenced under s 25(3) of the Factories Act 1937 (repealed; see supra.).] 'The question is: what is a floor? There is no definition in the Act to help the court. The ordinary and natural meaning of a floor is something within walls, indoors, on which people walk or stand. A plank-run such as this on a gantry—or on a staging or on a scaffolding—does not seem to me to be within the ordinary meaning of a "floor". There would be great difficulty in applying the word "floor" to this plank-run. If it is a floor, what is the edge of the floor, as distinct from an opening in it? Does the floor go round the stanchions or is there a gap in it, and so forth? That all goes to show that this is not properly described as a floor at all. It can be described as a plank-run or a gangway or a plat-form, but it is not a floor.' *Tate v Swan Hunter & Wigham Richardson Ltd* [1958] 1 All ER 150 at 152, CA, per Lord Denning

[Section 28(1) of the Factories Act 1961, pro-vides that all 'floors' shall be kept free from any obstruction.] 'The expression "floors" in this context and in the light of the word "obstruction", which means "blocking or being blocked, making or becoming more or less impassable", is, in my view, limited to those parts of the factory on which workmen are intended or likely to pass and repass. Where a part of the factory floor is used for storing, as in this case, and properly used for storing, it seems to me that the articles which are stored there, whether stored on racks or whether stored on the floor, are not obstructions on the floor within the meaning of s 28(1) of the Act of 1961.' *Pengelley v Bell Punch Co Ltd* [1964] 2 All ER 945 at 947, CA, per Diplock LJ

'I think that the normal and ordinary meaning of a floor is the lower surface of an enclosed space, such as a room or similar place. It can, in ordinary use of language, also be used to des-cribe certain surfaces on which people walk or stand or on which objects are placed and which are designed or constructed or adapted for people to walk or stand on or to hold objects. A natural cave may have a floor, although no work of construction or adaptation has been done to its lower surface. A floor can be con-strued in the open air, but it will depend upon the whole circumstances whether floor is an apt word to describe a constructed surface in the open air. I do not think that, in its ordinary meaning, the unmade earthen surface of an open yard can be a floor.' *Sullivan v Hall Russell & Co Ltd* 1964 SLT 192 at 193, per Lord Kissen

Australia [A planning scheme ordinance defined 'storey' as 'a floor other than a floor (a) used principally for storage; or (b) used wholly or partly for parking'. The term 'floor' was not defined. Clause 51 of the draft ordinance pro-hibited, within the relevant zone, the erection of a building either containing more than four floors or more than three storeys.] 'In the con-text of cl 51 "floor" in its ordinary sense, means level, layer or stratum, rather than "the under surface of the interior of a room" (Shorter Oxford English Dictionary) or "the lower surface of a closed space" (*Sullivan v Hall Russell & Co Ltd* (1964) SLT 192 at 193). Although cl 3(1) of the ordinance defines "storey" in terms of "floor", and not the other way about, I think that "floor" in cl 51 bears the meaning attributed to "storey" by the Shorter Oxford English Dictionary, namely, "each of the stages or portions one above the other of which a building consists". I would add "levels" as a current and relevant synonym for "stages" or "portions". But the phrase "one above the other" does not mean "one directly above the other", because "above" does not ordinarily mean "directly above" i.e. in precisely the same vertical plane, but only "higher than". Usually, it is true, the floors, storeys or levels of a building are found directly one above the other or others; but this circum-stance cannot determine the meaning ordin-arily given to those words. The idea of multiple or comparative levels involves difference in the horizontal plane. Hence a difference in level is established whenever one object, assuming a common datum point, is higher or lower than another. In that event there are two levels, even though the higher level is not superim-posed directly above the lower. Assume a building, stepped back into a rising slope with ten "steps" incorporated in its structure, none of which is directly above the "step" below, in the fashion of the treads and risers of an ordinary staircase. . . . In my opinion, "floor" in cl 51 means an interior level forming part of the structure of the building. In order to ascertain whether this building contains more than three floors it is necessary only to start at the bottom and count the different interior levels as they ascend.' *Leichhardt Municipal Council v Daniel Callaghan Pty Ltd* (1983) 46 LGRA 29 at 37, per Samuels JA (S Ct of NSW)

FLOTSAM   *See also* WRECK

It is to be observed, that in order to constitute a legal *wreck*, the goods must come to land. If they continue at sea, the law distinguishes them by the barbarous and uncouth appellations of *jetsam, flotsam*, and *ligan*. Jetsam is where goods are cast into the sea, and there sink and remain under water: flotsam is where they continue swimming on the surface of the waves: ligan is where they are sunk in the sea, but tied to a cork or buoy, in order to be found again. These are also the king's, if no owner appears to claim them; but, if any owner appears, he is entitled to recover the possession. For even if they be cast overboard, without any mark or buoy, in order to lighten the ship, the owner is not by this act of necessity construed to have renounced his property: much less can things ligan be supposed to be abandoned, since the owner has done all in his power, to assert and retain his property. These three are therefore accounted so far a distinct thing from the former, that by the king's grant to a man of wrecks, things jetsam, flotsam, and ligan will not pass. (1 Bl Com 282)

Flotsam is where a ship is wrecked and the goods float on the sea *Sir Henry Constable's Case* (1601) 5 Co Rep 106*a*; (8 Halsbury's Laws (4th edn) para 1506n)

'According to the well-known meaning of flotsam, as stated in the Termes de la Ley, it refers to goods having been at sea in a ship and separated from it by some peril.' *Palmer v Rouse* (1858) 3 H & N 505 at 510, per Martin B

FODDER

'Fodder' means hay or other substance commonly used for food of animals. (Animal Health Act 1981, s 89(1))

[A local Act provided that no tolls should be demanded for any horse emplyed in carrying 'fodder' for cattle grown on land in the occupation of the owner of such fodder.] 'No doubt there is some difficulty, at first sight, in saying that barley in the course of transit to a mill for the purpose of being ground into meal, to be afterwards eaten by cattle, is already fodder for cattle; but giving a fair and liberal construction to the words of the statute, I think that everything which is ultimately destined to be used as food for cattle is fodder for them, although it may not have gone through the final process which will make it such.' *Clements v Smith* (1860) 3 E & E 238 at 242, 243, per Cockburn CJ

FOLDCOURSE

Foldcourse is a right of feeding sheep on another's land, also known as a sheepwalk, which grew out of the ancient right of foldage, and could not exist except in cases where the lord of the manor or other paramount lord claimed the right of foldage. The right of foldcourse was not originally a right of common, but something reserved out of the original grant by the lord; but in modern times it means nothing more than a right of common for so many sheep appurtenant to certain lands where a sheepwalk formerly stood. (6 Halsbury's Laws (4th edn) para 575)

[*Note.*—'Foldage' was the right (now extinguished) of the lord or other person to whom it had been granted to have the sheep of his tenants folded on his land at night for the purpose of manuring it.]

FOOD

In this section [registration of hawkers of food and premises] 'food' means food and ingredients of food for human consumption, including—
(a) drink (other than water);
(b) chewing gum and like products,
    but does not include—
    (i)   milk and cream;
    (ii) live animals and birds;
    (iii) articles or substances used only as drugs.
(Local Government (Miscellaneous Provisions) Act 1982, s 19(12))

'Food' includes any food or drink produced or processed for human or animal consumption (including game of any kind) and any ingredient of such food or drink. (Agriculture Marketing Act 1983, s 8)

'Food' includes drink, chewing gum and other products of a like nature and use, and articles

and substances used as ingredients in the preparation of food or drink or of such products, but does not include—
(a) water, live animals or birds,
(b) fodder or feeding stuffs for animals, birds or fish, or
(c) articles or substances used only as drugs.
(Food Act 1984, s 131(1))

[Section 2 of the Sale of Food and Drugs Act 1875 (repealed; see now Food Act 1984, s 131(1), supra), enacted that the term 'food' should include every article used for food or drink by man other than drugs or water.] 'It could be truly said that pure ground rice is an article of food for man; but it would cease to be so if it were mixed with an equal quantity of alum and 20 per cent of bicarbonate of soda, and sold in little penny packets of an ounce each. Who would venture to describe such a mixture as food for man? With equal truth, might not powder composed of poison, mixed with flour, be called food for man because pure flour is used? Possibly it may be said that the injurious ingredient when mixed with the other materials of which an article of food is composed becomes a part and parcel of such article; but that is no argument against the vendor of such injurious ingredient unless such ingredient can be treated as an article of food at the time of the sale. That is the moment when the test of its character is to be applied, and if it is not then an article of food no offence is committed by the vendor of it, though the purchaser or any other person who afterwards mixes it with an article of food intended for sale would be guilty of an offence. We are clearly of opinion that the baking powder in question is not an article of food, and that neither the sale of it, nor the admixture of it with an article of food, unless such article is intended for sale, is prohibited by the statute. For his own use anybody may use it if he thinks fit, and it would certainly seem strange if for selling such a mixture, to a person who had a right to mix it with the ingredients forming his own bread or pastry, the vendor could be convicted of a criminal offence. We do not, however, in anything we have said intend to convey it as our opinion that nothing can be deemed to be an article of food unless it be made up into an eatable or drinkable form and fit for immediate use, for we have no doubt that the substantial and requisite materials for making, and which are to form part of the unadulterated article when made—e.g. flour, butter, salt, mustard, pepper, etc—are articles of food; for though nobody would ordinarily dream of eating them alone, yet they are articles intended to form substantial components of articles of food, or to be eaten as adjuncts thereto.' *James v Jones* [1894] 1 QB 304 at 308, 309, DC, per Hawkins J

'I desire to repeat it, that tea is not in itself a food in the sense that it is not nutritious, that you cannot live on it, that it will not increase the amount of tissue in a person as the drinking of milk would— food may be solid food or liquid food—it is not simply because it is a drink that tea is not a food; that is an entire mistake—supposing tea were capable of adding to the tissues as milk will do, then it would be quite right to call it simply a food. Tea appears to be nothing in the world but a stimulant.' *Sainsbury v Saunders* (1918) 88 LJKB 441 at 445, DC, per Darling J

'I am not . . . prepared to assent to the proposition that in order that any article should be food [within a wartime regulation against hoarding] . . . it must be something which is eaten, as distinguished from something which people drink. I am not prepared to hold that things consumed by drinking may not be food. I do not confine the word "food" to things that are consumed by eating. The word "food" must be interpreted in its primary sense—namely, as something taken into the system as nourishment, and not merely as a stimulant.' *Hinde v Allmond* (1918) 87 LJKB 893 at 894, per Avory J

FOOT OR END

Australia 'When the testator makes plain what he intends to be the order in which his dispositions are to be read, it does not matter where he signs the document so long as his signature is intended to authenticate the whole document. . . . In such a case "the foot or end" is where he signs.' *Re Brown* [1944] VLR 24 at 25, per Lowe J

Australia 'It must now be taken to be established that the "foot or end" of a will for this purpose is not necessarily the foot or end physically; that is, the execution need not physically follow the whole of the dispositive provisions.' *Will of Ellen Rose Witts* [1962] NSWR 1045 at 1045, per Myers J

See, generally, 50 Halsbury's Laws (4th edn) para 256.

FOOTPATH

'Footpath' means a highway over which the public have a right of way on foot only, other than such a highway at the side of a public road.

(National Parks and Access to the Countryside Act 1949, s 27)

'Footpath' means a highway over which the public have a right of way on foot only, not being a footway. (Highways Act 1980, s 329(1))

'Footpath' means a way over which the public have a right of way on foot only. (Road Traffic Act 1972, s 196(1))

'The question turns upon the construction to be put on the first part of s 72 of 5 & 6 Wm 4, c 50 [Highway Act 1835, which imposes a penalty on any person, 'who shall wilfully ride upon any footpath or causeway by the side of any road made or set apart for the use or accommodation of foot-passengers'], and it appears to me very clear that the construction to be put upon it is, that it only extends to a footpath set apart for the use of foot-passengers by the side of a road. . . . It was intended to prevent persons who drive or ride along a road from riding or driving over the footpaths by the side of the road, and so damaging the path and endangering the safety of the foot-passengers; and this part of s 72 is a most useful enactment, giving a summary mode of punishment for such wanton misconduct; and as footpaths may be, and often are, level with the road, it was necessary to insert "footpath" as well as "causeway".' *R v Pratt* (1867) LR 3 QB 64 at 65, 66, per Cockburn CJ

FOOTWAY

'Footway' means any part of a street made or set apart for the use or accommodation of foot-passengers or any way so made or set apart at the side of a street or any street which does not contain a carriageway. (London County Council (General Powers) Act 1958, s 35(2))

'Footway' means a way comprised in a highway which also comprises a carriageway, being a way over which the public have a right of way on foot only. (Highways Act 1980, s 329(1))

'Construing the word "footway" from the company in which it is found—"the soil and pavement of", "streets", "lanes", "passages",—the legislature [in a water company's private Act] appears to have meant those paved footways in large towns which are too narrow to admit of carriages and horses.' *Scales v Pickering* (1829) 4 Bing 448 at 452, per Best CJ

'Looking at the general purview of the Act, and the context, it is clear that the word footway means one of those paved ways running by

adjacent buildings, and not a path over a private ground.' Ibid at 453, per Burrough J

FOR

'"During" and "for" are words which are very awkward in their application to "payments" and "periods of payments". If you are describing something that is continuous and occupies a certain length of time, like a tenure, or like the presence in a particular place, or the existence of any state of affairs, then "during" and "for" are admirable words to use; but when you are speaking of a series of payments, on particular days of limited number, and if you say they are to be during a period embracing those days, or for a period embracing those days, it seems to me, as far as I can see at present, that "during" and "for" must mean really "in respect of the succession of those number of years".' *Inland Revenue Comrs v St Luke's Hostel Trustees (Registered)* (1930) 144 LT 50 at 51, per Rowlatt J; rvsd on other grounds, 144 LT 52, CA

FOR THE BENEFIT OF

Australia 'Such expressions as acting "for the benefit of" . . . the trust estate or in the discharge of his duty as a trustee are used indiscriminately in the judgments, but they all mean the same thing, namely, that the question is whether the costs, charges and expenses are properly incurred by the trustee as an incident of his administration of the estate.' *National Trustees Executors & Agency Co of Australasia Ltd v Barnes* (1941) 64 CLR 268 at 279, per Williams J

FOR THE PURPOSE OF

[Section 8 of the Rating and Valuation (Miscellaneous Provisions) Act 1955 (repealed; see now the General Rate Act 1967, s 40(5)), which provided for the limitation of rates, applied, inter alia, to any hereditament occupied 'for the purposes of' a club, society, etc, which was not established or conducted for profit.] 'I think that the words "for the purposes of" in this paragraph must in their context refer to the mode of use of the hereditament and may be paraphrased as "in carrying on the activities of". For example, a hereditament is occupied for the purposes of a shop, factory or school, if its use has been the carrying on of the activities of a shop, factory or school.' *Parker v Borough of Ealing* [1961] 1 All ER 147 at 149, per Pennycuick J

FOR THE TIME BEING

'The words "for the time being" are capable of different interpretations, according to the context; for example, they might be used with a context shewing clearly that they were intended to point one single period of time; and a case was put of a person intending to give a promissory note to a company, and giving it to the secretary "for the time being", meaning clearly the person who appeared to be the secretary at the particular time when the note became payable. It might be, according to the context, that the same words would apply to a succession of periods. Take the common case of a petition for payment of dividends to the rector of a certain parish "for the time being", which, of course, would point, not to a single period but a succession of periods.' *Ellison v Thomas* (1862) 31 LJ Ch 867 at 869, per Kindersley V-C

FORAGE

'Forage' includes all feeding stuffs for animals, whether natural, artificial, dried, or undried. (Essential Commodities Reserves Act 1938, s 6)

FORCE

'The first question . . . is to ascertain exactly what is meant by force in this context, the context being the use of force to prevent the true owner from recovering possession of his property, and I turn to *Russell on Crime* [12th edn, p 286], where this passage appears: "Forcible detainer is where a man, who enters peaceably, afterwards detains his possession by force; and the same circumstances of violence or terror which will make an entry forcible will also make a detainer forcible. It seems to follow that whoever keeps in his house an unusual number of people, or unusual weapons, or threatens to do some bodily hurt to the former possessor, if he dare return, is guilty of a forcible detainer, though no attempt is made to re-enter. . . ." With the assistance of counsel we have checked the authorities from which that passage is derived, and it clearly contains a correct statement of the law as it stands, and that means that accumulating an unusual number of people or unusual

weapons, or making other preparations of such a kind which indicate in themselves that any attempt to enter will be opposed by force may amount to the use of force in detaining the premises even though the owner is deterred and never makes the attempt at all.' *R v Robinson* [1970] 3 All ER 369 at 372, CA, per cur.

[But see FORCIBLE ENTRY.]

[By the Criminal Law Act 1967, s 2(6) a constable may enter any place, if need be by 'force', for the purpose of making an arrest.] 'First of all, let me define what I think is meant by "force". In the contest of outside premises of course there is no problem about force unless there is a gate or something of that sort. The constable simply enters the place and is authorised to do so by sub-s (6). But if he meets an obstacle, then he uses force if he applies any energy to the obstacle with a view to removing it. It would follow that, if my view is correct, where there is a door which is ajar but it is insufficiently ajar for someone to go through the opening without moving the door and energy is applied to that door to make it open further, force is being used. *A fortiori* force is used when the door is latched and you turn the handle from the outside and then ease the door open. Similarly, if someone opens any window or increases the opening in any window, or indeed dislodges the window by the application of any energy, he is using force to enter, and in all those cases a constable will have to justify the use of force.' *Swales v Cox* [1981] 1 All ER 115 at 119, per Donaldson LJ

FORCE MAJEURE

[A live-stock shipping contract contained the words 'The vessel . . . not to call at any port or ports before landing her live-stock except in case of *force majeure*.'] 'The words in question appear to me to amount to an absolute undertaking by the shipowners that the vessel should not before landing her live-stock call at any port, whether in or out of the ordinary course of the voyage, except in case of *force majeure*. I think that this undertaking is made subject to one exception and one exception only, which is, the case of *force majeure*. What, then, is the meaning of *force majeure*? The vessel might be seized and carried into some port by her captors. This would be a plain, though unusual, case of *force majeure*. A more ordinary case would be where, in consequence of some casualty occurring in the course of the voyage, the master is compelled to put into a port for the safety of the ship or cargo, or of both. . . . I think that if the steamer ran short of coals, not in consequence of any casualty, but simply because by some mistake she had not when she left Buenos Ayres sufficient coals for the voyage to St Vincent, there was no case of *force majeure*.' *Yrazu v Astral Shipping Co* (1904) 20 TLR 153 at 154, 155, per Walton J

'The words "*force majeure*" are not words which we generally find in an English contract. They are taken from the *Code Napoléon*, ... In my construction of the words "*force majeure*" I am influenced to some extent by the fact that they were inserted by this foreign gentleman. . . . At the same time I cannot accept the argument that the words are interchangeable with "*vis major*" or "*act of God*". I am not going to attempt to give any definition of the words "*force majeure*", but I am satisfied that I ought to give them a more extensive meaning than "act of God" or "*vis major*". The difficulty is to say how much more extensive. . . . I think that the complete dislocation of business . . . as a consequence of the universal coal strike . . . did come within the reasonable meaning of the words "*force majeure*". . . . So far as the shipwrights' strike is concerned it comes within the very words of the exceptions clause. As to delay due to breakdown of machinery it comes within the words "*force majeure*", which certainly cover accidents to machinery. The term "*force majeure*" cannot, however, in any view, be extended to cover bad weather, football matches, or a funeral.' *Matsoukis v Priestman & Co* [1915] 1 KB 681 at 685–687, per Bailhache J

'It was argued that the inability of the master to procure the necessary funds for his voyage brought the *Concadoro* under art 2 [of the Hague Convention No VI of 1907], and that she was unable to leave the enemy port within the days of grace "*par suite de circonstances de force majeure*". In their Lordships' opinion, this contention cannot be maintained. The "*force majeure*" contemplated in the article is one which renders the vessel unable to leave the port, and cannot be construed to include the circumstance that the master has not been provided by the owners with sufficient financial resources to continue his voyage.' *The Concadoro* [1916] 2 AC 199 at 202, PC, per cur.

[By a local Order, a borough council were bound to supply energy to premises in their district when requested, and they were liable to a penalty on default unless the court should be of opinion that such default was caused by inevitable accident or '*force majeure*'.] 'I regret the introduction of foreign words into English Statutes and Orders without any definition of them being given. In my view *force majeure* in this case means some physical or material restraint, and does not include a reasonable fear or apprehension of such a restraint.' *Hackney Borough Council v Doré* [1922] 1 KB 431 at 437, DC, per Sankey J

FORCE OF LAW   *See* LAW

FORCES   *See* ROYAL FORCES

FORCIBLE ENTRY

[The offences of forcible entry and forcible detainer were abolished, and the Forcible Entry Acts were repealed, by the Criminal Law Act 1977, s 13. New offences were created in their place by ss 6–10 of the latter Act, e.g. the use of violence for securing entry, adverse occupation of residential premises, etc.]

FORECAST

Australia   'Section 37(2) [Companies (Acquisition of Shares) Act 1980 (Cth)] so far as it is material, provides that a target company . . . or a person associated therewith, shall not make or issue or cause to be made or issued, any statement to the public or to all or any members of the target company . . . "that contains a forecast in respect of the profits or profitability of the target company, or, if the person . . . is a corporation a forecast in respect of their profits or profitability of that corporation". The most relevant meaning ascribed to the word "forecast" in the Oxford English Dictionary is: "A conjectural estimate or account, based on present indications, of the course of events or state of things in the future, especially with regard to the weather." Some guidance is to be obtained in a general way from the way in which those responsible for the London Rule and the Commission's [National Companies and Securities Commission] policy statement appear to have understood the word. I have taken these indications into account, but I consider that in the context in which it appears the dictionary definition I have quoted provides the best guide as to the meaning of the word.' *Bond Corpn Holding*

Ltd v Grace Bros Holding Ltd (1983) 48 ACTR 3 at 33, per Sheppard J

FOREIGN

'Foreign', in relation to any postal packet means either posted in the British postal area [United Kingdom, Channel Islands and Isle of Man] and sent to a place outside that area, or posted in a place outside that area and sent to a place within that area, or in transit through the British postal area to a place outside that area. (Post Office Act 1953, s 87)

FOREIGN AGENT

The expression 'foreign agent' includes any person who is or has been or is reasonably suspected of being or having been employed by a foreign power either directly or indirectly for the purpose of committing an act, either within or without the United Kingdom, prejudicial to the safety or interests of the State, or who has or is reasonably suspected of having, either within or without the United Kingdom, committed, or attempted to commit, such an act in the interests of a foreign power. (Official Secrets Act 1920, s 2)

FOREIGN COUNTRY

'Foreign country' means a country other than the United Kingdom, a dependent territory, a country mentioned in Sch 3 and the Republic of Ireland. (British Nationality Act 1981, s 50(1))

[For s 1(3) of the Act *see* BRITISH SUBJECT.]

FOREIGN CURRENCY

'Foreign currency' means any currency other than sterling. (Air Corporations Act 1967, s 33; Gas and Electricity Act 1968, s 7(1))

FOREIGN PROCEEDING

Bankruptcy

United States '[F]oreign proceeding' means proceeding, whether judicial or administrative and whether or not under bankruptcy law, in a foreign country in which the debtor's domicile, residence, principal place of business, or principal assets were located at the commencement of such proceeding, for the purpose of liquidating an estate, adjusting debts by composition, extension, or discharge, or effecting a reorganization. . . . (Bankruptcy Act 1978, s 101(19))

FOREIGN REPRESENTATIVE

Bankruptcy

United States '[F]oreign representative' means duly selected trustee, administrator, or other representative of an estate in a foreign proceeding. . . . (Bankruptcy Act 1978, s 101(20))

FORESEEABLE

'What is "foreseeable" depends on the knowledge of the foreseer: what is "reasonably foreseeable" depends on the knowledge which a reasonable person entering into the contract in question might reasonably be expected to possess as well as any additional information communicated to him by the other party to the contract.' *The Heron II, Czarnikow Ltd v Koufos* [1966] 2 All ER 593 at 604, CA, per Diplock LJ

FORESHORE   *See also* SEASHORE

'Foreshore' includes the shore and bed of the sea and of every channel, creek, bay, estuary and navigable river as far up it as the tide flows. (Salmon and Freshwater Fisheries Act 1975, s 41)

'Foreshore' means the shore and bed of the sea and of any tidal water, below the line of the medium high tide between the spring tides and the neap tides. (Limitation Act 1980, Sch 1, para 11(3))

FOREST

A certaine territorie of woody grounds and fruitful pastures, privileged for wilde beasts and foules of forest, chase and warren, to rest and abide in, in the safe protection of the King, for his princely delight and pleasure, which territorie of ground, so privileged, is meered and bounded with unremovable markes, meeres, and boundaries, either known by matter of record, or else by prescription, and also replenished with wilde beasts of venerie or chase, and with great coverts of vert [i.e. green-leaved trees, bushes, etc] for the succour of the said wilde beasts, to have their abode in: for the preservation and continuance of which said place, together with the vert and venison, there are certaine particular lawes, priviledges, and officers belonging to the same, meete for that purpose, that are only proper unto a forest, and not to any other place. (Manwood's Forest Laws (1598 Edn) 1)

[Most of the ancient forest laws, the earliest still on the statute book being a charter of 1297, were repealed by the Wild Creatures and Forest Laws Act 1971. The statute abolished any franchises of forest, free chase, park or free warren, and abrogated the forest law except in so far as it relates to the appointment and functions of verderers.]

FORESTRY

In this Act . . . 'forestry' includes—
(i) the use of land for nursery grounds for trees, and
(ii) the use of land for woodlands where that use is ancillary to the use of land for other agricultural purposes.
(Rent (Agriculture) Act 1976, s 1(1))

FORESTRY LAND

'Forestry land' means woodlands in the United Kingdom in respect of which an election is in force for assessment and charge to tax under Schedule D by virtue of section 54 of the principal Act [Income and Corporation Taxes Act 1988], and any houses or other buildings in the United Kingdom which are occupied together with, and wholly or mainly for the purposes of, such woodlands. (Capital Allowances Act 1968, s 69)

FORFEITURE *See also* DEFEASANCE

Forfeiture is a punishment annexed by law to some illegal act, or negligence, in the owner of lands, tenements, or hereditaments; whereby he loses all his interest therein, and they go to the party injured, as a recompense for the wrong which either he alone, or the public together with himself, hath sustained. (2 Bl Com 267)

[In a settlement of real estate the trustees were to pay the rents and profits to L for life or until he should commit an act of bankruptcy, or commit any act, etc, whereby the rents should be 'forfeited' to or become vested in any other person, in which case there was a gift over.]

'The word "forfeit", the noun substantive, is defined in Dr Johnson's Dictionary to be "something lost by the commission of a crime;—something paid for the expiation of the crime, a fine, a mulct". By the same authority the verb "to forfeit" is defined to mean "to lose by some breach of condition, to lose by some offence", and he gives certain illustrations, as usual, in his dictionary, and this is one: "A father cannot alien the power he has over his child; he may perhaps to some degree forfeit it, but cannot transfer it.—Locke." There "forfeit" is contrasted with "alien or transfer". "Forfeit", the participial adjective, is defined to be "liable to penal seizure; alienated by a crime, lost either as to right or possession by breach of conditions". Then he gives these lines from Shakespeare: "All the souls that were, were forfeit once; And He that might the vantage best have took, Found out the remedy" (Measure for Measure). And, again: "Beg that thou may'st have leave to hang thyself; And yet, thy wealth being forfeit to the state, Thou hast not left the value of a cord". Clearly the word "forfeit" means not merely that which is actually taken from a man by reason of some breach of condition, but includes also that which becomes liable to be so taken. In this very sentence the word "forfeited" is contrasted with the words "vested in any other person". Therefore "forfeited" means something less than become "vested in any other person", and that shews that forfeited is used quite accurately as meaning liable to be taken from him.' *Re Levy's Trusts* (1885) 30 Ch D 119 at 124, 125, per Kay J

'I think that the word [forfeiture] is here used with the meaning assigned to it in the Imperial Dictionary, where it is said "in regard to property 'forfeiture' is a loss of the right to possess"; and that it includes cesser, or determination on bankruptcy, alienation, remarriage, or any other event.' *Re Sumner's Settled Estates* [1911] 1 Ch 315 at 319, per Eve J

FORFEITURE RULE

In this Act, the 'forfeiture rule' means the rule of public policy which in certain circumstances precludes a person who has unlawfully killed another from acquiring a benefit in consequence of the killing. (Forfeiture Act 1982, s 1(1))

[Unlawful killing includes aiding and abetting, counselling or procuring the death of another: ibid, sub-s (2).]

FORGERY

A person is guilty of forgery if he makes a false instrument, with the intention that he or another shall use it to induce somebody to accept it as genuine, and by reason of so accepting it to do or not to do some act to his own or any other person's prejudice. (Forgery and Counterfeiting Act 1981, s 1)

[For the fuller interpretation of this section, see ibid, ss 8–10.]

'I agree in the definition of forgery at common law, that it is the forging of a false document to represent a genuine document.' *R v Smith* (1858) Dears & B 566 at 574, CCR, per Willes J

'Forgery supposes the possibility of a genuine document, and that the false document is not so good as the genuine document, and that the one is not so efficacious for all purposes as the other.' Ibid at 575, per Bramwell B

'Forgery is the false making of an instrument purporting to be that which it is not, it is not the making of an instrument which purports to be what it really is, but which contains false statements.' *R v Windsor* [1865] Cox CC 118 at 123, per Blackburn J

'By 24 & 25 Vict c 98 [Forgery Act 1861 (repealed; see now Forgery and Counterfeiting Act 1981, s 1 (supra))], s 20, it is felony to "forge" any deed with intent to defraud. The material word in this section is "forge". There is no definition of "forge" in the statute, and we must therefore inquire what is the meaning of the word. The definition in Comyns (Dig, tit Forgery, A I) is "forgery is where a man fraudulently writes or publishes a false deed or writing to the prejudice of the right of another"—not making an instrument containing that which is false, which . . . would not be forgery, but making an instrument which purports to be that which it is not. Bacon's Abr (tit Forgery, A), which, it is well known, was compiled from the MS of Chief Baron Gilbert, explains forgery thus, "The notion of forgery doth not so much consist in the counterfeiting of a man's hand and seal . . . but in the endeavouring to give an appearance of truth to a mere deceit and falsity, and either to impose that upon the world as the solemn act of another which he is in no way privy to, or at least to make a man's own act appear to have been done at a time when it was not done, and by force of such a falsity to give it an operation which in truth and justice it ought not to have". The material words, as applicable to the facts of the present case, are, "to make a man's own

act appear to have been done at a time when it was not done". When an instrument professes to be executed at a date different from that at which it really was executed, and the false date is material to the operation of the deed, if the false date is inserted knowingly and with a fraudulent intent, it is a forgery at common law.' *R v Ritson* (1869) LR 1 CCR 200 at 203, 204, per Blackburn J

'In 1796 all the judges of England laid down the definition of forgery as "the false making a note or other instrument *with intent to defraud*": see *R v Parkes & Brown* [(1797) 2 Leach 775 at 785], and ever since that time it has been held that the very essence of forgery is an *intent to defraud* and it must be laid in the indictment.' *Welham v Director of Public Prosecutions* [1960] 1 All ER 805 at 814, HL, per Lord Denning; also reported [1961] AC 103 at 131

FORGIVE

Australia 'The word "forgive" has at least two meanings, which, though related, are different. It may mean an abandonment of resentment over a wrong done, as in the common expression "forgive and forget". Or it may mean the giving up of any claim to restitution or remedy for a wrong done as in the expression "to forgive a debt". So the noun "forgiveness" has two corresponding meanings.' *Hemsworth v Hemsworth* [1947] VLR 292 at 303, per cur.

FORGO

New Zealand [On 3 March 1933, a meeting of the majority of the debenture-holders of a company decided that they were willing to 'forgo' their 25,000 vendors' shares and accept £50,000 for their debentures in order to facilitate a sale of substantially all the timberlands of the company at a price of not less than £80,000. At the annual general meeting of the company held on 13 October 1933, a motion confirming the action of the directors in disposing of the property referred to the resolution passed by vendor shareholders 'with reference to the surrender by the vendor shareholders of their claims in respect of vendors' shares'.] 'The proposals of the holders of debenture stock and vendors' shares made to the company and accepted by it on March 3 or 4, 1933, express the willingness of the vendor shareholders to "forgo" their shares. This word is, in the circumstances, equivalent to "surrender". This meaning is confirmed by the minutes of the meeting of March 3. As at no time during the negotiations was the questions of a dividend considered as remotely possible, the shareholders' resolution of October 6 also confirms this meaning. The shareholders, at the annual general meeting of October 13, in their resolution, expressly referred to it as a "surrender" of the shares.' *Re Matahina Rimu Co Ltd (In Liquidation)* [1941] NZLR 490 at 496, per Fair J; [1941] GLR 304, 306

FORM

New Zealand [Section 5(i) of the Acts Interpretation Act 1924 provides that wherever 'forms' are prescribed, slight deviations therefrom, but to the same effect and not calculated to mislead, shall not vitiate them. It was sought to apply this provision to a traffic notice which did not comply with the provision of the appropriate regulations, the Heavy Motor Vehicle Regulations 1969 (SR 1969/231).] 'In my opinion s 5(i) should not be invoked to make the word "form" become a general term appropriate for application to a wooden structure.' *Transport Ministry v Picton Carriers Ltd* [1973] 1 NZLR 353 at 356, per Beattie J

FORSWEAR

[Action upon the case was brought for these words: 'Thou art forsworn, and I will make thee flower the pillory, or else it shall cost me a hundred pounds.'] 'An action lies not; for Anderson said, there is a great difference betwixt the words "forsworn" and "perjured". For "forsworn" is where he swears against the truth in ordinary discourse; but *perjurium est quando jus alterius pervertitur*. . . . But to say, "he was forsworn in such a court", or betwixt such parties an action lies.' *Anon.* (1595) Cro Eliz 395 at 395, per cur.

FORTHWITH   *See also* IMMEDIATELY

[It was agreed to hire a vessel to be made ready to take on board 'forthwith'.] 'The terms of the contract are, that the vessel shall be ready "forthwith". . . . The word "forthwith" indeed, in strictness, means immediately; but it is plain that this cannot be the construction to be affixed to it here. It was known that she required some repairs; at least to be coppered, and some time must be allowed for that.'

Simpson v Henderson (1829) Mood & M 300 at 301, 302, per Lord Tenterden CJ

'I agree that the word "forthwith" is not to receive a strict construction like the word "immediately", so that whatever follows, must be done immediately after that which has been done before. By referring to s 50 [of a private Act] it seems that whatever is to be done under it, ought to be done without any unreasonable delay. I think the word "forthwith" there used, must be considered as having that meaning.' *R v Worcestershire JJ* (1839) 7 Dowl 789 at 790, per Coleridge J

'With regard to the term "forthwith" [in an award], I think it is the same as if the arbitrator had fixed a certain day and place for the execution of the deeds respectively by each of the parties, or as if he had said that the two acts should be done at the same time, or contemporaneously. It would be impossible for any person to misunderstand that.' *Boyes v Bluck, Bluck v Boyes, Clossman v Bluck, Bluck v Clossman* (1853), 13 CB 652 at 673, per Cresswell J

'It was . . . contended on behalf of the defendants that the vessel having been delayed by perils of the seas upon her outward voyage, she did not "forthwith proceed" to Barbados within the meaning of the charterparty. If this contention were to be upheld, it would strike the clause as to perils of the seas out of the charterparty. "Forthwith" means without unreasonable delay. The difference between undertaking to do something "forthwith" and within a specified time is familiar to everyone conversant with law. To do a thing "forthwith" is to do it as soon as is reasonably convenient.' *Hudson v Hill* (1874) 43 LJCP 273 at 280, per Grove J

'To act "forthwith", . . . seems to mean "reasonably soon in the circumstances".' *Brown v Bonnyrig Magistrates* 1936 SC 258 at 262, per Lord Carmont (Lord Ordinary)

'In my opinion, the statutory injunction [in the Housing (Scotland) Act 1930, s 16] to proceed "forthwith" was inserted in the statute for the purpose of spurring on a local authority to a zealous and active prosecution of its duty to close houses which are unfit for human habitation.' Ibid at 265, per the Lord President (Lord Normand)

[On 5 May 1961 a local authority served on the owner of a house which was unfit for human habitation a notice under s 16 of the Housing Act 1957, giving a return date on 31st May

1961, and proposing to make a demolition order on 27th June 1961. The owner attended to be heard on 31st May, and did not oppose the making of a demolition order, which was made on 27th June, and served on the owner. A dispute arose whether the demolition order served was properly signed, but this order disappeared. On 26th January 1962 the local authority made and served a further demolition order, relying on the 5th May notice under s 16. The owner contended that the 1962 demolition order was invalid because it had not been made 'forthwith' as required by s 17(1) of the Act of 1957. The owner suffered no detriment from, and in fact benefited by, the delay between 27th June 1961 and 26th January 1962.] 'Under s 16 there are various alternatives under which the person on whom the original notice is served may submit counter-offers and so on; but nothing of that sort happened in this case. Therefore, under s 17(1), no undertaking to restore or repair having been given ". . . then, subject to the provisions of this section, the local authority shall forthwith make a demolition order for the demolition of the premises to which the notice given under the last foregoing section relates". Such demolition orders were made in this case. It is said that they were void because they were not made "forthwith". It is said that "forthwith" means on the next convenient opportunity, and that that would have been the moment in 1961 at which originally the demolition order—the so-called ineffective demolition order—was made, namely, 27th June 1961, and that waiting a half year after that makes it not "forthwith". The first reason why I think that that is a bad point is that I cannot see that if the local authority fail to observe the spur given to it by the statute and do not do it forthwith that makes the whole of their notice bad in the absence of some detriment suffered by the person on whom the notice is served. It is not said that there was such detriment here. Indeed there was an advantage, because the owner continued to collect rents from these horrible places for a year after he should not have been entitled to do so. Therefore I do not think that, even if the notices were not "forthwith", that is good enough to defeat them. Apart from that, however, "forthwith" is not a precise time and, provided that no harm is done, "forthwith" means any reasonable time thereafter.' *London Borough of Hillingdon v Cutler* [1967] 2 All ER 361 at 363, 364, CA, per Harman LJ

Australia 'A promise to do an act forthwith

does not mean that it is to be done instanter. Sometimes . . . the word may be treated as practically synonymous for some purposes . . . with "within a reasonable time".' *Measures v McFadyen* (1910) 11 CLR 723 at 729, per Griffith CJ

Australia [The Police Offences Act 1953 (SA) s 78 (see now the Summary Offences Act 1953–1986 (SA) s 78(1)) requires that a person apprehended without warrant should be delivered 'forthwith' into the custody of the member of the police force who is in charge of the nearest police station in order that that person may be brought before a justice or released on bail.] 'The word "forthwith" must of course be reasonably understood and applied. But it clearly prohibits an arrest for the purpose of interrogating the person arrested as a preliminary to bringing him before the justice.' *Drymalik v Feldman* [1966] SASR 227 at 234, per cur.

Australia 'It [a determination of an industrial court] alleges that the defendant was under an obligation to pay a specified amount of holiday pay to the worker "forthwith" at the end of a period of employment. The use of the word "forthwith" creates some difficulty of meaning. In ordinary English usage it means "immediately" or "without delay". In the context in which the word is used in the determination it means as soon as reasonably possible or practicable. . . . It may also mean within a reasonable time, or without unreasonable delay. . . . Quite clearly, in the context in which the word "forthwith" is used [in the determination] it cannot be intended to stipulate a definite time or date for payment after which time or date the obligation to pay is spent. Different situations relating to the employment may require different meanings to be given to the obligation to pay holiday pay. . . . But, in every case, it is the obligation to pay the amount due that is the essential element involved. Where an offence is charged and it is alleged that the obligation has not been met by the employer the use of the word "forthwith" in the information does not introduce any essential element into the offence. The offence is the failure to pay the amount due under the determination and the obligation to pay continues until payment is made.' *R v Industrial Appeals Court, ex p Circle Realty Pty Ltd* [1980] VR 459 at 463, per O'Bryan J

Canada 'Where the word "forthwith" occurs in a statute it has usually been construed as meaning "within a reasonable time in view of the circumstances of the case and of the subject matter".' *R v Cuthbertson* [1950] Ex CR 83 at 87, Ex Ct, per O'Connor J

Canada [Section 193(1) of the Vehicles Act, RSS 1965, c 377 (see now RSS), requires a person involved in a motor accident to report it 'forthwith'.] 'A careful consideration of [the] authorities satisfies me that the meaning that should be ascribed to "forthwith" in the section in question is "as promptly as is reasonably possible or practicable under all the circumstances".' *R v Bell* [1969] 2 Can CC 9 at 18, Sask QB, per Tucker J

Canada [Sections 465(d) and 457(1) of the Criminal Code, RSC 1970, c C-34 permit a justice to adjourn the proceedings and remand the accused 'forthwith' to custody in prison by warrant.] 'The warrant of remand provided for by the Code requires the peace officers to whom it is addressed to forthwith convey the prisoner to the prison specified in the warrant. In my view "forthwith" in the context means as soon as possible in the circumstances [see 45 Halsbury's Laws (4th edn) para 1148; cf *John Lewis & Co Ltd v Tims* [1952] AC 676, where 'forthwith' was contrasted with 'within a reasonable time']. I do not wish to be taken as holding that in every case the prisoner must be taken to prison immediately. It is possible to imagine circumstances in which delay in conveying the accused to a prison may be justifiable, for example, where the accused's assistance is sought to find a missing child or to locate a concealed bomb. . . . The practice, of course, of detaining a prisoner in holding cells connected with the court until other prisoners have been dealt with does not infringe the provisions of the Code.' *R v Precourt* (1976) 39 CCC 311 at 322, Ont CA, per Martin JA

Canada 'The inclusion of the words "payable forthwith after taxation" [in a court order] are, in my view, nothing but an exercise in judicial prolixity. Even so, I suppose they do have a certain ominous or encouraging ring to them, depending on whether one is required to pay or entitled to receive the costs. I do not think the inclusion of these words relating to payment can have any effect on when the costs should be taxed.' *Anchor Shoring Ltd v Halton Conservation Authority* (1979) 12 CPC 220 at 221, 222, Ont SC, per Taxing Officer McBride

New Zealand 'I think that the obvious meaning of "forthwith" in this subsection

[s 59B(1) of the Transport Act 1962] is "as soon as reasonably practicable".' *Chesham v Wright* [1970] NZLR 247 at 251, per Beattie J

New Zealand 'For the purpose of the several sections [in the Transport Act 1962] dealing with breath and blood tests the word "forthwith" means "as soon as reasonably practicable". This was the opinion of McGregor J in *Fraser v Police* [[1967] NZLR 447] and Beattie J in *Chesham v Wright* [supra] whose opinions have been followed in several unreported judgments of this court. In *Transport Ministry v Walker* McMullin J said: "The word 'forthwith' connotes urgency. Where an act is required to be done 'forthwith' it may require to be construed 'as soon as possible'. 'Forthwith' has been judicially interpreted to have that meaning. When so interpreted it will mean something more urgent than 'as soon as practicable' and even more urgent than 'as soon as convenient'. But it is important to consider the word in the statute in which it is used and a review of any standard judicial dictionary will show that the meaning will vary according to the statutory setting in which it appears." And he went on to refer to *Sameen v Abeyewickrema* [[1963] AC 597] and *Re Southam, ex p Lamb* [see Main Vol] as demonstrating that the word is also used circumstantially, that is, that what is practicable must depend upon the *circumstances of the case*.' *Police v Maugham* [1975] 2 NZLR 385 at 391, per Chilwell J

New Zealand 'Throughout the various stages of this case it has not been disputed that the prosecution based on the evidential breath test could not succeed unless the defendant had failed or refused to undergo a breath-screening test "forthwith". . . . "Forthwith" is recognised not to be synonymous with "instantly". Certainly it imports that there must be no significant delay, but it does allow a little elasticity. . . . In our view "forthwith" in s 58A [of the Transport Act 1962] as elsewhere in these sections, should be accepted to mean as soon as reasonably practicable.' *Scott v Ministry of Transport* [1983] NZLR 234 at 236, CA, per Cooke J

FORTUITOUS

'Mr Miller [counsel for the defendant] has argued that before a claim can attach on a policy of insurance there must be a loss of an accidental or fortuitous character, there must be in some form or another a casualty. There is no doubt that that is a general statement of the law. The difficulty at times is to find out in these cases what interpretation one has to put upon the words so often used "accident or fortuitous casualty". It is quite clear that the words have a wider meaning than something in the nature of an accidental fire or a destruction of the goods by the forces of nature, such as a flood or a hurricane; because it cannot be denied that theft of goods would be a loss coming within the policy, and that theft is a conscious and wilful act of another person. There is nothing fortuitous and nothing accidental about that. It is accidental and fortuitous in the sense that the assured is deprived by some unexpected acts of his property in the goods or of his possession of the goods.' *London & Provincial Leather Processes Ltd v Hudson* [1939] 2 KB 724 at 730, per Goddard LJ

New Zealand 'The expression, "external fortuity" [in an insurance policy] like "fortuitous accidents" or "casualties of the seas" means that there must be some casualty, something which could not be foreseen as one of the necessary incidents of the adventure.' *Techni-Chemicals Products Co Ltd v South British Insurance Co Ltd* [1977] 1 NZLR 311 at 318, SC, per Beattie J

FORTUNE

'The question I have to consider is as to the meaning of the words "the residue of my fortune. . .". The will, although an English will, executed according to the ceremonies required by the law of England, is expressed in the French language; and the translation which I have before me appears to be a reasonably good translation of the French original. The term "fortune" appears there. The word "fortune" in the English language is a word of wide import with regard to personal property. It is a term used in settlement, when it is said that a lady's fortune is so and so, and a gentleman's fortune is so and so. If it occurred in an English will it would be equivalent to saying "all my real and personal property": at any rate that is the largest meaning which could be given to it.' *Baring v Ashburton* (1886) 54 LT 463 at 464, per Chitty J

FORWARD CONTRACT

'Forward contract' means a contract of sale under which the date on which the cereals to which the contract relates are required to be delivered cannot fall within the month in which the contract is made or within the month immediately following that month. (Cereals Marketing Act 1965, s 24)

FOSSILS   *See* MINERALS

FOSTER CHILD

1. Subject to section 2 below, a child is a foster child for the purposes of this Act if he is below the upper limit of the compulsory school age and his care and maintenance are undertaken by a person who is not a relative, guardian or custodian of his.
2.(1) A child is not a foster child while he is in the care of a local authority or a voluntary organisation or is boarded out by a local authority or a local education authority.
    (2) A child is not a foster child while he is in the care of any person—
        (a) in premises in which any parent, adult relative or guardian of his is for the time being residing;
        (b) in any voluntary home within the meaning of Part VI of the Child Care Act 1980;
        (c) in any school within the meaning of the Education Act 1944 in which he is receiving full-time education;
        (d) in any hospital, or in any nursing home registered or exempted from registration under the Registered Homes Act 1984; or
        (e) in any home or institution not specified in this subsection or subsection (5) below but maintained by a public or local authority.
    (3) A child is not a foster child at any time while his care and maintenance are undertaken by any person—
        (a) who is not a regular foster parent and at that time does not intend to, and does not in fact, undertake his care and maintenance for a continuous period of more than 27 days; or
        (b) who is a regular foster parent but at that time does not intend to, and does not in fact, undertake his care and maintenance for a continuous period of more than six days.
    In this subsection 'regular foster parent' means a person who—
        (i) during the period of 12 months immediately preceding the date on which he begins to undertake the care

and maintenance of the child in question, and

(ii) otherwise than as a relative or guardian,

had the care and maintenance of one or more children either for a period of, or periods amounting in the aggregate to, not less than three months or for at least three continuous periods each of which was of more than six days.

(4) A child is not a foster child while he is in the care of any person in compliance with a supervision order within the meaning of the Children and Young Persons Act 1969 or a supervision requirement within the meaning of the Social Work (Scotland) Act 1968.

(5) A child is not a foster child while he is liable to be detained or subject to guardianship under the Mental Health Act 1983, or is resident in a residential care home within the meaning of Part I of the Registered Homes Act 1984.

(6) A child is not a foster child—

(a) while he is placed in the care and possession of a person who proposes to adopt him under arrangements made by an adoption agency within the meaning of section 1 of the Adoption Act 1976 or section 1 of the Adoption (Scotland) Act 1978; or

(b) while he is a protected child within the meaning of Part III of the Adoption Act 1976.

(Foster Children Act 1980, ss 1, 2, as amended)

Canada [A testator who left the residue of his estate to his children, defined children as including 'foster-children'.] 'There are apparently no cases in this jurisdiction or indeed in any of the Commonwealth countries that counsel have been able to find dealing with this term. I have, however, been referred to one case from the United States which is *Re Norman's Estate* [(1940) 295 NW 63], which is a decision of the Supreme Court of Minnesota. That case accepts the dictionary definition of foster-mother or father as a woman or man who has performed the duties of a parent to a child of another by rearing the child as an own child. Foster-child is defined as one who has been cared for by a foster-parent. This definition, which commended itself to the Minnesota Court, also commends itself to me.' *Re Page* [1973] 3 OR 903 at 904, Ont SC, per Zuber J

FOUND (Discovered)   *See* FIND

FOUND (Establish)

'Dealing with the language of the will, "To the Belgrave Hospital for Children to found a bed . . ." it is quite obvious that the intention of the testator was to establish something. He says "to found a bed", which involves the idea of establishing it; and it is established by providing a capital sum, the revenue from which may maintain it or be applied to its maintenance.' *A-G v Belgrave Hospital* [1910] 1 Ch 73 at 75, 76, per Swinfen Eady LJ

FOUNDATION

'Foundation' in relation to a wall means the solid ground or artificially formed support resting on solid ground on which the wall rests. (London Building Acts (Amendments) Act 1939, s 44)

FOUNDATION GOVERNOR   *See* GOVERNOR

FOUNDED ON

'The fair meaning of the words "action founded on tort" in s 116(2) [of the County Courts Act 1888 (repealed; see now County Courts Act 1984, s 19(1))] is that a tort should be the gist of the action, and . . . the section is not applicable to an action which, though nominally to recover damages for a tort, includes, as the main relief sought, a claim for an injunction.' *Keates v Woodward* [1902] 1 KB 532 at 537, CA, per Collins MR

'The words "founded on any breach or alleged breach of the contract" . . . mean this: an action in which you cannot get any relief unless you proceed upon and are dependent upon a contract.' *Hughes v Oxenham* [1913] 1 Ch 254 at 257, CA, per Cozens-Hardy MR

FOUNDERS SHARES   *See* SHARES

FOWL

'Fowl' includes any cock, hen, chicken, capon, turkey, goose, gander, duck, drake, guinea-fowl, peacock, peahen, swan, or pigeon. (Protection of Animals Act 1911, s 15)

'Here is not the nature of the wildfowl stated; for wildfowl are of several sorts; ducks, teal, mallard, and indeed all birds that are wild are wildfowl. . . . It is true in the large signification of the word they are so; and also the word fowl comprehends all birds and poultry: but wildfowl are taken in a more restrained sense; pheasants and partridges are not thereby understood, for they are fowl of warren.' *Keeble v Hickeringill* (1809) 11 East 574 n at 575 n, per Holt CJ

FRAME

Australia 'The phrase "to frame" a person is a slang expression which, as ordinarily used, means to fabricate false evidence in order to make it appear that he has committed an offence of which he is innocent.' *Grigg v Consolidated Press Ltd* (1945) 45 SR (NSW) 247 at 251, per Jordan CJ

FRANCHISE

Franchise and liberty are used as synonymous terms: and their definition is, a royal privilege, or branch of the king's prerogative, subsisting in the hands of a subject. Being therefore derived from the crown, they must arise from the king's grant; or, in some cases, may be held by prescription, which, as has been frequently said, presupposes a grant. The kinds of them are various, and almost infinite: I will here briefly touch upon some of the principal; premising only, that they may be vested in either natural persons or bodies politic; in one man, or in many: but the same identical fanchise, that has before been granted to one, cannot be bestowed on another; for that would prejudice the former grant.

To be a county palatine is a franchise, vested in a number of persons. It is likewise a franchise for a number of persons to be incorporated, and subsist as a body politic, with a power to maintain perpetual succession and do other corporate acts: and each individual member of such corporation is also said to have a franchise or freedom. Other franchises are, to hold a court leet: to have a manor or lordship; or, at least, to have a lordship paramount: to have waifs, wrecks, estrays, treasure-trove, royal fish, forfeitures, and deodands: to have a court of one's own, or liberty of holding pleas, and trying causes: to have the cognisance of pleas; which is a still greater liberty, being an exclusive right, so that no other court shall try causes arising within that jurisdiction: to have a bailiwick, or liberty exempt from the sheriff of the county, wherein the grantee only, and his

officers, are to execute all process: to have a fair or market; with the right of taking toll, either there or at any other public places, as at bridges, wharfs, and the like; which tolls must have a reasonable cause of commencement, (as in consideration of repairs, or the like) else the franchise is illegal and void: or, lastly, to have a forest, chase, park, warren, or fishery, endowed with privileges of royalty. (2 Bl Com 37, 38)

'I am prepared to say that the term "franchise" in the County Court Act 1888 [s 56 (repealed in part; see now County Courts Act 1984, s 15(2)(b))], includes a privilege granted by the Crown in respect of its prerogative, and that so a grant of a patent comes within the exception, and the power of the County Court to try a case involving the title to a patent is ousted by it.' *R v Halifax County Court Judge* [1891] 2 QB 263 at 266, per Lord Esher MR

'A franchise is a Royal privilege or branch of the King's prerogative subsisting in a subject by a grant from the King: Chitty on Prerogatives, p 119.' So long as it is attached to the Crown it is called prerogative, but when granted to a subject it is called franchise: Chitty on Prerogatives, p 118.' *A-G v British Museum Trustees* [1903] 2 Ch 598 at 612, per Farwell J

Australia 'What . . . the respondent bought was in substance the sole selling rights throughout Australia of Ford products and parts and the right to be supplied with such products and parts. Such rights as these are known in the motor trade as a "franchise".' *Comr of Taxes v Ford Motor Co of Australia Pty Ltd* [1941] St R Qd 233 at 245, per Philp J

Canada 'The words "franchise" and "concession" [in the context of capital cost allowances for income tax purposes] must be given the meaning or sense in which they are employed by businessmen on this continent and . . . in this sense, they extend, not only to certain kinds of rights, privileges or monopolies conferred by or pursuant to legislation or by governmental authority, but also to analogous rights, privileges or authorities created by contract between private parties. I do not propose, however, to attempt to formulate a definition of the kinds of rights, privileges or monopolies that can fall within those words. It is sufficient for the purposes of this appeal to say that, in my view, those words are used to refer to some right, privilege or monopoly that enables the concessionaire or franchise holder to carry on his business, or that facilitates the carrying on of his business, and that they are not used to refer to a contract under which a person is entitled to remuneration for the performance of specified services.' *Investors Group v Minister of National Revenue* [1965] CTC 192 at 194, 195, Ex Ct, per Jackett P

United States The term 'franchise' means any contract—
(i) between a refiner and a distributor,
(ii) between a refiner and a retailer,
(iii) between a distributor and another distributor, or
(iv) between a distributor and a retailer,
under which a refiner or distributor (as the case may be) authorizes or permits a retailer or distributor to use, in connection with the sale, consignment, or distribution of motor fuel, a trademark which is owned or controlled by such refiner or by a refiner which supplies motor fuel to the distributor which authorises or permits such use. (Petroleum Marketing Practices Act 1978, s 101(1)(A))

Franchise relationship

United States The term 'franchise relationship' means the respective motor fuel marketing or distribution obligations and responsibilities of a franchisor and a franchisee which result from the marketing of motor fuel under a franchise. (Petroleum Marketing Practices Act 1978, s 101(2))

Franchisee

United States The term 'franchisee' means a retailer or distributor (as the case may be) who authorizes or permits, under a franchise, a retailer or distributor to use a trademark in connection with the sale, consignment, or distribution of motor fuel. (Petroleum Marketing Practices Act 1978, s 101(4))

Franchisor

United States The term 'franchisor' means a refiner or distributor (as the case may be) who authorizes or permits, under a franchise, a retailer or distributor to use a trademark in connection with the sale, consignment, or distribution of motor fuel. (Petroleum Marketing Practices Act 1978, s 101(3))

FRANCHISE CORONER *See* CORONER

FRANCHISE FISHERY *See* FISHERY

FRATERNITY *See also* CORPORATION

'A fraternity is some people of a place united together, in respect of a mystery and business, into a company.' *Cuddon v Eastwick* (1704) 1 Salk 192 at 193, per cur.

FRAUD *See also* CONCEALMENT; DEFRAUD; FRAUDULENT; UNDUE INFLUENCE

The court has never ventured to lay down as a general proposition, what constitutes fraud. Actual fraud arises from acts and circumstances of imposition. It usually takes the form of a statement of what is false or a suppression of what is true. The withholding of information (suppressio veri) is not in general fraudulent unless there is a special duty to disclose it. Thus upon a contract of sale the maxim caveat emptor applies both at law and in equity, and a party who has special knowledge of the property is not bound to disclose it unless there is some obligation of disclosure arising otherwise than out of the relation of vendor and purchaser. The obligation of disclosure may arise from the relation of the parties as where they are agent and principal; or from the nature of the contract, as where it is uberrimae fidei, such as a contract of partnership or of marine insurance; or in ordinary contracts from circumstances occurring during the negotiation, as where a statement made with honest belief is subsequently discovered to be false. The partial statement of fact, and the withholding of essential qualifications may make that which is stated absolutely false and bring it under the head of suggestio falsi. (16 Halsbury's Laws (4th edn) para 1219)

'Ever since 1845 [i.e. since the decision in *Ormrod v Huth* (1845) 14 M & W 651] it has been clear and established law that, in considering the principles governing this class of cases [actions of deceit], the term "fraud" must be used and understood in the common meaning of the word, as it is ordinarily used in the English language, and as implying some base conduct and moral turpitude.' *Joliffe v Baker* (1883) 11 QBD 255 at 270, per Watkin Williams J

'"Fraud", in my opinion, is a term that should be reserved for something dishonest and morally wrong, and much mischief is, I think, done, as well as much unnecessary pain inflicted by its use where "illegality" and "illegal" are the really appropriate expressions.' *Re*

Companies Acts, ex p Watson (1888) 21 QBD 301 at 309, DC, per Wills J

'I think the authorities establish the following propositions: First, in order to sustain an action of deceit, there must be proof of fraud, and nothing short of that will suffice. Secondly, fraud is proved when it is shewn that a false representation has been made (1) knowingly, or (2) without belief in its truth, or (3) recklessly, careless whether it be true or false. . . . Thirdly, if fraud be proved, the motive of the person guilty of it is immaterial. It matters not that there was no intention to cheat or injure the person to whom the statement was made.' *Derry v Peek* (1889) 14 App Cas 337 at 374, per Lord Herschell

[Section 17 of the Gaming Act 1845 makes guilty of fraudulent conduct any person who wins any sum of money from others by 'any fraud or unlawful device or ill practice in playing at cards'.] 'What is known as the three card trick is a game in which one player backs his ability to indicate the position of a particular card, and the other player by sleight of hand and quickness of movement in manipulating the cards in such a way as to deceive the eye induces the former to indicate the wrong card. That in my opinion does not amount to fraud or unlawful device or ill practice; it is sleight of hand and nothing more.' *R v Brixton Prison (Governor), ex p Sjoland & Metzler* [1912] 3 KB 568 at 570, per Lord Alverstone CJ

See, generally, 18 Halsbury's Laws (3rd edn) 189.

'Counsel says that a charge of robbery is a charge of fraud. Robbery includes stealing, he says, and stealing includes fraud. I cannot accept this argument. "Fraud" in ordinary speech means the using of false representations to obtain an unjust advantage: see the definition in the Shorter Oxford English Dictionary. Likewise in law "fraud" is proved when it is shown that a false representation has been made knowingly, or without belief in its truth, or recklessly, careless whether it be true or false: see *Derry v Peek* [supra] per Lord Herschell. In any case "fraud" involves a false representation. Robbery does not. It involves violence, not fraud. Nor is he on a charge of robbery.' *Barclays Bank Ltd v Cole* [1966] 3 All ER 948 at 950, CA, per Lord Denning MR

'The general direction as to fraud in the summing-up [of the judge in the court below] commences by stating that to amount to fraud the conduct must be deliberately dishonest.

That is plainly right.' *R v Sinclair* [1968] 3 All ER 241 at 246, CA, per cur.

[Section 6(1)(a) of the Administration of Justice Act 1933 (repealed; see now s 169(1)(a) of the Supreme Court Act 1981) provided for the trial of an action by jury in certain cases of charges of 'fraud'.] 'The word "fraud" is used not in any general sense of dishonesty, but as meaning an intentional misrepresentation (or in some cases concealment) of fact made by one party with the intention of inducing another party to act on it, and thereby inducing the other party to act on it to his detriment.' *Stafford Winfield Cook & Partners Ltd v Winfield* [1980] 3 All ER 759 at 766, per Megarry V-C

Australia 'Fraud is conduct which vitiates every transaction known to the law. It even vitiates a judgment of the Court. It is an insidious disease, and if clearly proved spreads to and infects the whole transaction (*Jonesco v Beard* [1930] AC 298 at 301, 302). A registration of a trade mark procured by fraud, whether another trader or the Registrar was defrauded, would be equally open to attack. In most cases a registration obtained in fraud of the rights of another trade would also involve a fraud on the Registrar.' *Farley (Aust) Pty Ltd v Alexander (J R) & Sons (Queensland) Pty Ltd* (1947) 75 CLR 487 at 493, per Williams J

Australia 'The essence of the fraud . . . charged is that advantage was taken of weakness, ignorance and other disabilities on the side of the respondent and the contract was derived from such behaviour and it is an unfair bargain. Lord Hardwicke said in *Earl of Chesterfield v Janssen* [(1751) 2 Ves Sen 125]: "This Court has an undoubted jurisdiction to relieve against every species of fraud." It appears by his judgment in that case that one species is getting bargains by taking surreptitious advantage of persons unable to judge for themselves by reason of weakness, necessity or ignorance. The word surreptitious would imply that the bargain was snatched.' *Blomley v Ryan* (1956) 99 CLR 362 at 385, 386, per McTiernan J

New Zealand 'By fraud in these Acts [New Zealand Land Transfer Acts of 1870 and 1885 (repealed; see supra)] is meant actual fraud, i.e. dishonesty of some sort, not what is called constructive or equitable fraud—an unfortunate expression and one very apt to mislead, but often used, for want of a better term, to denote transactions having consequences in equity similar to those which flow from fraud. . . . Fraud by persons from whom he [a person who presents a document for registration] claims does not affect him unless knowledge of it is brought home to him or his agents. The mere fact that he might have found out fraud if he had been more vigilant, and had made further inquiries which he omitted to make, does not of itself prove fraud on his part. But if it be shown that his suspicions were aroused and that he abstained from making inquiries for fear of learning the truth, the case is very different, and fraud may be properly ascribed to him.' *Assets Co Ltd v Mere Roihi* [1905] AC 176 at 210, PC, per cur.

New Zealand 'With respect I adopt the view that in the section of our own Companies Act under which this summons was issued [s 216 of the Companies Act 1933 (NZ) (repealed; see now s 263 of the Companies Act 1955 (NZ))], as in the English section which Lord Macnaghten was discussing [in *Re Patrick and Lyon Ltd* [1933] Ch 786], fraud is that "which connotes actual dishonesty involving, according to current notions of fair trading among commercial men, real moral blame".' *Re Brighton Coalmines Ltd (In Liquidation)* [1944] NZLR 275 at 280, per Northcroft J; also reported [1944] GLR 97 at 102

Constructive fraud

A court of equity will set aside a transaction entered into as the result of conduct which, though not amounting to actual fraud or deceit, is contrary to good conscience. Such conduct, which is described as 'constructive fraud', includes the procurement of a gift or other benefit by the exertion of undue influence and the making of an unconscionable bargain. Whilst not seeking to put too precise a definition on the meaning of constructive fraud, the courts have acted on the principle of saving persons not from the consequences of their own folly but from being victimised by other people, and of preventing an unfair advantage being taken as a result of an inequality of bargaining power between the parties. (18 Halsbury's Laws (4th edn) para 329)

Fraud on power

'The term fraud in connection with frauds on a power does not necessarily denote any conduct on the part of the appointor amounting to fraud in the common law meaning of the term

or any conduct which could be properly termed dishonest or immoral. It merely means that the power has been exercised for a purpose, or with an intention, beyond the scope of or not justified by the instrument creating the power. Perhaps the most common instance of this is where the exercise is due to some bargain between the appointor and appointee, whereby the appointor, or some other person not an object of the power, is to derive a benefit. But such a bargain is not essential. It is enough that the appointor's purpose and intention is to secure a benefit for himself, or some other person not an object of the power.' *Vatcher v Paull* [1951] AC 372 at 378, PC, per Lord Parker of Waddington; applied, *Re Merbon's Settlement, Public Trustee v Wilson* [1953] 2 All ER 707

Intent to defraud

[Section 275(1) of the Companies Act 1929 (repealed; see now the Companies Act 1985, s 458), provided that if, in the course of the winding-up of a company, it appeared that any business of the company had been carried on with 'intent to defraud creditors', the court might declare the directors personally responsible for the liabilities of the company.] 'I must hold with regard to the meaning of the phrase carrying on business "with intent to defraud creditors" that, if a company continues to carry on business and to incur debts at a time when there is to be the knowledge of the directors no reasonable prospect of the creditors ever receiving payment of those debts, it is, in general, a proper inference that the company is carrying on business with intent to defraud.' *Re Leitch (Wm C) Brothers Ltd* [1932] 2 Ch 71 at 77, per Maugham J

'Put shortly, "with intent to defraud" means "with intent to practise a fraud" on someone or other. It need not be anyone in particular. Someone in general will suffice. If anyone may be prejudiced in any way by the fraud, that is enough.' *Welham v Director of Public Prosecutions* [1960] 1 All ER 805 at 815, HL, per Lord Denning; also reported [1961] AC 103 at 133

Australia [Section 87 of the Trade Marks Act 1905 (repealed; see now Trade Marks Act 1955–1986 (Cth) s 99), provided that whoever sold or exposed for sale any goods to which any forgery of a registered trade-mark was applied should be guilty of an offence unless he proved (inter alia) that he acted without 'intent to defraud'.] 'In this case the only question that arises is whether upon the particular evidence the magistrate was entitled to find that the defendant had no intent to defraud. . . . The expression "intent to defraud" in the section means intent to induce purchasers to believe that the goods which they are purchasing, and which are manufactured by the defendant, have been manufactured by somebody else.' *Jones v Gedje* (1909) 9 CLR 263 at 264, per Griffith CJ

New Zealand   'In s 222 of the Crimes Act 1961 no express mention is made of colour of right and the word "fraudulently" is used on its own. We think that in order to act fraudulently an accused person must certainly . . . act deliberately and with knowledge that he is acting in breach of his legal obligation. But we are of opinion that if an accused person sets up a claim that in all the circumstances he honestly believed that he was justified in departing from his strict obligation, albeit for some purpose of his own, then his defence should be left to the jury for consideration provided at least that there is evidence on which it would be open to a jury to conclude that in all the circumstances his conduct, although legally wrong, might nevertheless be regarded as honest. In other words the jury should be told that the accused cannot be convicted unless he has been shown to have acted dishonestly.' *R v Coombridge* [1976] 2 NZLR 381 at 387, CA, per Richmond P

Patent in fraud of another's rights

'The question still remains, was it [a patent], in the language of the statute, "obtained in fraud of the rights" of the petitioner? The first point to be determined in answering that question is the sense in which the word "fraud" is used in the statute. I have not to deal with a statute nearly 300 years old, like the Statute of Monopolies of James I, nor with one in which there is any context to fix the sense in which the word is used. It would be wrong, in my judgment, to construe such a word in an Act passed little more than three years ago [Patents, Designs and Trade Marks Act 1883 (repealed; see now Patents Act 1949)], and, in the absence of a context imperatively demanding such a construction, otherwise than in accordance with the ordinary meaning of the English language, and, consequently, as involving dishonesty or grave moral culpability on the part of the person obtaining the patent.' *Re Avery's Patent* (1887) 36 Ch D 307 at 319, per Stirling J

FRAUD (Slang)

'The agent is said to have called the pursuer "the greatest liar and fraud that ever came into Greenock". Now, it is perfectly true that to accuse a man of committing a fraud is a slander; but if slang is used it must be taken according to its ordinary meaning. Here it is nothing else than slang; and calling a man a fraud does not mean that he has committed a fraud. All that is meant, is that he is not nearly so good as he pretends to be; and it may be that in a great many walks of life, or in what can scarcely be called walks of life, a man may be called a fraud, e.g. with reference to his pretensions even to play a game well, or to be an authority on a certain branch of knowledge. . . . Therefore, to call a man a liar and a fraud is not slanderous.' *Agnew v British Legal Life Assurance Co Ltd* (1906) 8 F (Ct of Sess) 422 at 428, per the Lord President (Lord Dunedin)

FRAUDULENT

'The word "fraudulent" in connection with conversion, however important it may be in a criminal matter, is, in the civil action of conversion, so far as regards the cause of action, nothing more than an abusive epithet.' *Beaman v ARTS Ltd* [1949] 1 All ER 465 at 467, CA, per Lord Greene MR; [1949] 1 KB 550

[Section 1(1) of the Larceny Act 1916 (repealed; cf now ss 1, 15 of the Theft Act 1968) provided that a person stole who, without the consent of the owner, 'fraudulently' and without a claim of right made in good faith, took and carried away anything capable of being stolen with intent, at the time of such taking, permanently to deprive the owner thereof.] 'If a person honestly believes that he has a right to the property, and the taking is in vindication of, or in exercise of, a bona fide claim of right, he is not acting feloniously. But sub-s (1) says "fraudulently and without a claim of right", and counsel for the appellants rightly says that it is the duty of the court to give a meaning to every word in the section. He submitted that the word "fraudulently" means intending to act to the detriment of any person against the person's wishes. The court thinks that the word "fraudulently" does add, and is intended to add, something to the words "without a claim of right", and it means (though I am not saying that the words I am about to use will fit every case, but they certainly will fit this particular case) that the taking must be intentional and deliberate, that is to say, without mistake. You must know, when you take the property, that it is the property of another person and that you are taking it deliberately, not by mistake, and with an intention to deprive the person of the property in it.' *R v Williams* [1953] 1 All ER 1068 at 1070, CCA, per cur; also reported in [1953] 1 QB 660 at 666

FRAUDULENT MISREPRE-
SENTATION *See* MISREPRESENTATION

FRAUDULENT PREFERENCE

'When we speak of fraudulent preference, we do not mean by it anything involving or meriting blame; the term only signifies that the act is contrary to the declared and recognised policy of the bankrupt law.' *Exley v Inglis* (1868) LR 3 Exch 247 at 256, per Channell B

'The question is, was the payment made with intent to prefer the particular creditor to whom it was made? It is not within the section [s 48 of the Bankruptcy Act 1883 (repealed; see now s 44 of the Bankruptcy Act 1914)] if the debtor pays one creditor in order to benefit another. Still less is it within the section if he pays a creditor with intent to benefit someone else who is not a creditor. In the present case, the debtor made a payment to Whittaker. The County Court judge has found that, in making that payment, he did not intend to benefit Whittaker, but intended to benefit Greenwood. To hold that that was a fraudulent preference would be to come to a decision in direct conflict with that in *ex p Taylor* [(1886) 18 QBD 295], and to do what the court says in that case cannot be done, namely, to strike out from the section the words, "with a view of giving such creditor a preference over the other creditors".' *Re Mills, ex p Official Receiver* (1888) 58 LT 871 at 872, CA, per Lord Esher MR

'I have always understood that to ascertain whether there has been a fraudulent preference, it is necessary to consider what the dominant or real motive of the person making the preference was, whether it was to defraud some creditors by preferring others, or for some other motive.' *New, Prance & Gerrard's Trustees v Hunting* [1897] 2 QB 19 at 29, per Smith LJ

'The Legislature has thought fit to state that certain acts are to be deemed a fraudulent preference and to be invalid accordingly. A

fraudulent preference within the meaning of the Companies Act 1929 [repealed; see now Companies Act 1985], or the Bankruptcy Act 1914 [repealed; see now Insolvency Act 1986], whether in the case of a company or of an individual, possibly may not involve moral blame at all. For example, there may be a discrimination between creditors, irrespective of pressure, on grounds with which most people would sympathise.' *Re Patrick & Lyon Ltd* [1933] Ch 786 at 790, per Maugham J

'In my opinion, in these cases the onus is on those who claim to avoid the transaction to establish what the debtor really intended, and that the real intention was to prefer. The onus is only discharged when the court upon a review of all the circumstances is satisfied that the dominant intent to prefer was present. That may be a matter of direct evidence or of inference, but where there is not direct evidence and there is room for more than one explanation it is not enough to say, there being no direct evidence, the intent to prefer must be inferred.' *Peat v Gresham Trust Ltd* [1934] AC 252 at 262, per Lord Tomlin

'A fraudulent preference, as has often been pointed out, is a misleading term. A preference can be "fraudulent" within the statute [Bills of Exchange Act 1882] without there being any element of common law fraud involved. When one looks at the language of s 44(1) of the Bankruptcy Act 1914, it provides (and I leave out the immaterial words): "Every conveyance or transfer of property, or charge thereon made . . . by any person unable to pay his debts as they become due from his own money in favour of any creditor, or of any person in trust for any creditor. With a view of giving such creditor, or any surety or guarantor for the debt due to such creditor, a preference over the other creditors, shall, if the person making, taking, paying or suffering the same is adjudged bankrupt on a bankruptcy petition presented within [six] months after the date of making, taking, paying or suffering the same, be deemed fraudulent and void as against the trustee in bankruptcy.' It has often been pointed out that the phrase is an inept one and that a better phrase than "fraudulent preference" is "voidable preference". Of course a so-called fraudulent preference is void as against the relevant parties. But I take the view that in the relevant sections of the 1882 Act, "fraud" means common law fraud.' *Osterreichische Länderbank v S'Elite Ltd* [1980] 2 All ER 651 at 654, CA, per Roskill LJ

FRAUDULENTLY

Australia [The Crimes Act 1900 (NSW), s 173 penalises a director, officer, or member, of any body corporate, or public company, who fraudulently takes, or applies, company property for his own use or benefit.] 'We are satisfied that the course of judicial decision in the hundred years or so since these new statutory offences were created has assigned to the term "fraudulently" a meaning interchangeable with "dishonestly".' *R v Glenister* [1980] 2 NSWLR 597 at 604, per cur.

New Zealand 'In cases under s 222 and s 224 of the Crimes Act 1961 where it is alleged that an accused acted fraudulently, it must be shown that he acted deliberately and with knowledge that he was acting in breach of his legal obligation. But if, that being established, the accused sets up a claim of honest belief that he was justified in departing from his strict obligations, even for some purpose of his own, then his defence must be left to the jury if there is some evidence from which the jury might conclude that his conduct, though legally wrong, might nevertheless be regarded as honest.' *R v Williams* [1985] 1 NZLR 294 at 308, per Greig J

FREE

Australia 'The word "free" in s 92 [of the Constitution [Commonwealth of Australia Constitution Act 1901], which declares that trade, commerce and intercourse among the States shall be absolutely free] means free from any restriction conditioned upon the circumstance of passing from one State into another, but in all other respects subject to the laws of the Commonwealth or the States, as the case may be, regulating the conduct of persons and their rights with respect to property within the jurisdiction of the Legislature which makes the law.' *Duncan v State of Queensland* (1916) 22 CLR 556 at 574, per Griffith CJ

Australia 'The word "free" is used in many senses, and the meaning of the word varies almost indefinitely with the context. A man is said to be free when he is not a slave, but he is also said to be free when he is not imprisoned, and is not subject to any other form of physical restraint. In another sense a man is only truly free when he has freedom of thought and expression, as well as of physical movement. But in all these cases an obligation to obey the laws which apply generally to the community is not regarded as inconsistent with freedom. . . . In *James v The Commonwealth* [[1936] AC 578] the Privy Council dealt with the meaning of the words "absolutely free" in s 92 of the Constitution. It was there said: "Free", in itself is vague and indeterminate. It must take its colour from the context. Compare, for instance, its use in free speech, free love, free dinner and free trade. Free speech does not mean free speech; it means speech hedged in by all the laws against defamation, blasphemy, sedition and so forth. . . . Free love, on the contrary, means licence or libertinage, though even so, there are limitations based on public decency and so forth. Free dinner generally means free of expense. . . . Free trade means, in ordinary parlance, freedom from tariffs". Thus there is no dictionary meaning of the word "free" which can be applied in all cases.' *Adelaide Company of Jehovah's Witnesses v Commonwealth* (1943) 67 CLR 116 at 126, 127, per Latham CJ

Australia 'It is difficult . . . to hold that the word "free" in s 92 [of the Commonwealth of Australia Constitution Act 1901] relates to freedom from all legislative control and regulation. If s 92 were interpreted in this sense, it would be impossible for any Parliament in Australia to make any law which applied to such trade and commerce. It cannot be supposed that any such impossible result was intended. Accordingly, the problem was that of reconciling some degree of legislative control with what was described as absolute freedom. The solution was discovered in drawing a distinction between laws of such a character that they did not interfere with the freedom which was guaranteed by s 92 and other laws which did interfere with such freedom. Thus a distinction was drawn between a law directed against interstate transport, or merely prohibiting interstate transport on the one hand, and, on the other hand, a law which, though it incidentally affected interstate transport, was not directed against it, but introduced a system of regulation which included interstate transport and which did not amount to a mere prohibition thereof.' *Gratwick v Johnson* (1945) 70 CLR 1 at 13, per Latham CJ

Australia 'It is . . . trade, commerce and intercourse that s 92 [of the Commonwealth of Australia Constitution Act 1901] requires shall be "absolutely free". . . . That means "freedom as at the frontier" or in other words across state boundaries.' *Bank of New South Wales v Commonwealth* (1948) 76 CLR 1 at 309, per Starke J

Canada [The Motor-Vehicle Act 1957, s 171(2) (repealed; see now RSC 1979, c 288, s 188(2)) provided that no person should park a vehicle so as to obstruct the 'free' passage of traffic on the highway.] 'Since every act of parking on the roadway must constitute an obstruction of some sort, and thus cut down in part the completely free passage of traffic, the phrase "free passage" must be interpreted in a relative rather than an absolute sense. I find a fair interpretation is to read "free" to mean "reasonable".' *White v Derban* (1960) 33 WWR 542 at 545, BCSC, per Ruttan J

Free and voluntary

Australia 'It is a long established principle of the common law that to be admissible a confession or admission must be "free and voluntary". . . . But it seems that in the common law principle the expression "free and voluntary" has a different and more restricted meaning than that which the expression bears in common parlance. It excludes cases where there has been a threat, a promise or any inducement by a person in authority, but stops there. . . . It seems that there must be something improper or unlawful in the behaviour of a person in authority which induces the admission before such admission is to be excluded.' *Hyde v Kenyon* (1957) 2 LGRA 1 at 4, 5, per Stephen DCJ

Free from average   *See* AVERAGE

FREE GRANT

Canada 'The term "free grants" mentioned in the statute [53 Vict c 4(D)] meant free so far as the Crown granting the lands was concerned. It meant free from any of the customary charges made by the Government in selling its vacant lands to settlers or others, and from any charges of any kind by or on behalf of the Crown excepting those expressly mentioned for survey fees. It could not, in my opinion, be intended to exempt the beneficial interest of the railway company in the lands from liability to local taxation which it otherwise would be subject to after it came into existence, and before the patent issued. The term "free grant" meant free as far as the

Crown granting the lands was concerned, not free from liens or charges which might attach to the lands by law by virtue or in consequence of the acquisition by the railway company of a beneficial interest therein. Such a construction as that claimed involves, I think, an unwarrantable extension of the language of the statute, the meaning of which seems reasonably clear to me.' *Calgary and Edmonton Land Co v Attorney General of Alberta* (1911) 45 SCR 170 at 176, 177, SCC, per Davies J

Free of conditions

New Zealand [A contract for the sale of land required the vendor, on settlement, to give the purchaser a registrable transfer of the land 'free of all conditions except any now registered against the title of the said property'. The local authority had a declared policy that the building on the property must be reconstructed with the outer walls in permanent material and the question for the court was whether this policy was a breach of the vendor's obligation to transfer 'free of all conditions'.] 'On my reading of cl(1), the concluding passage is directed to the transfer of title. The operative phrase defining what shall happen on settlement is "we shall receive a registrable transfer. . . ." and, in my opinion, the adjective "free" describes the noun "transfer". The succeeding words "of the property" are, in my view, redundant. I read the phrase "free of all conditions except any now registered against the title of the said property" as going no further than guaranteeing the purchaser against unregistered limitations on the title itself.' *Savage v New Zealand Properties Ltd* [1964] NZLR 319 at 322, 324, per Haslam J; affd [1965] NZLR 341

Free of deductions

[A testator by his will gave an annuity to his wife 'free of deductions and abatements'.] 'It is possible to give a meaning to the word "abatements" because . . . the income might not be enough to pay the annuity, and in that case the word "abatements" might mean that it should come out of capital. But it seems difficult to give a meaning to the word "deductions" when coupled with "abatements", in the case of an annuity to a wife. . . . Without speculating on what the testator might have meant, I must adhere to the rule of construction laid down in the decisions, and consequently I am not at liberty to treat income tax as being a deduction.' *Gleadow v Leetham* (1882) 22 Ch D 269 at 274, per Kay J

'I think the covenant [that he, the said H H, will at such time or times during his life as he shall think fit, or within twelve calendar months after his death, pay to "the trustees . . . the sum of £10,000 sterling free from all deductions whatsoever"] only means "I or my executors will pay to the trustees £10,000 from which neither I nor they shall be entitled to make any deductions".' *Re Higgins, Day v Turnell* (1885) 31 Ch D 142 at 147, CA, per Lindley LJ

'I approach this will, and ask myself whether there is in it anything which shows that the testator intended the expression "deductions" to include income tax. In my judgment there is. The annuity is given free of all duties, and, unless the direction that it is "to be paid free of all deductions whatsoever" is meaningless and entirely ineffective, the expression "deductions" must include income tax. I cannot hold the direction to be wholly meaningless and ineffective, and therefore decide that the expression "deductions" in this will includes income tax, and that the annuity is payable to the widow free of income tax.' *Re Cowlishaw, Cowlishaw v Cowlishaw* [1939] 1 Ch 654 at 655, per Bennett J

'If a testator directs payment of an annuity out of the income of his estate, the annuity is not payable free of income tax unless there is a direction in the will to that effect. . . . It is not a sufficient direction to give an annuity "free of all deductions".' *Re Skinner, Milbourne v Skinner* [1942] Ch 82 at 83, per Morton J

Free of duty

'I cannot myself see any reason for saying that "free from duty" means free from one kind of duty payable by the executors more than from another kind of duty so payable.' *Re Turnbull, Skipper v Wade* [1905] 1 Ch 726 at 733, per Farwell J

'The words "free of all duties" when used with regard to a fund, and not expressed to be with regard to successive interests in the fund, or with regard to the interests of beneficiaries in the fund, would be satisfied by applying them to the duties which would be paid at the time when the fund was handed over, and need not be extended so as to include the duties which will be payable on a subsequent devolution; because it is the fund that is being dealt with

and considered.' *Re Fenwick* [1922] 2 Ch 775 at 799, per Sargant J

'In the absence of authority, I hold that, where an English testator by an English will gives a pecuniary legacy "free of duty", the only duties payable out of his estate in respect of the legacy are duties imposed by English law, unless there are words in the will which make it clear that duties imposed by the law of a foreign country are to be paid thereout.' *Re Norbury, Norbury v Fahland* [1939] 1 Ch 528 at 530, per Bennett J

'It is well . . . that I should shortly state my opinion on the question whether a gift of a legacy "free of death duties" or even "free of all death duties" suffices, without more, to exonerate the bequest not only from United Kingdom duties, but also from those imposed in respect of the gift under the laws of a foreign state. In my judgment, an exonerating provision in either of the above terms, if found in a will, executed in Great Britain and in accordance with the testamentary formalities required by our law, of a domiciled British subject is prima facie confined in its operation to death duties exigible by the laws of this country, but if, in any given case, there are attendant circumstances of a quality and degree sufficient to show beyond reasonable doubt that the testator must have intended to include freedom from foreign duties also, then effect will be given to the intention so disclosed.' *Re Goetze, National Provincial Bank Ltd v Mond* [1953] 1 All ER 76 at 85, CA, per Romer LJ (also reported in [1953] Ch 96 at 113, 114)

New Zealand [A clause in a will was as follows: 'I direct my trustees . . . to pay all my just debts and testamentary expenses in New Zealand and succession and death duties in New Zealand or South Australia so that every legacy gift and bequest in this my will contained . . . shall be paid free of succession and death duty and expense of every kind'.] 'The testator may not have had in his mind the assessment of duty upon his personal estate, which was physically in New Zealand, but constructively in England, by the English revenue authorities; but what he intended is quite clear—i.e. that those to whom he had given specific legacies by his New Zealand will should receive them without deduction. . . . The rule is that if the Court can find any language in the will by which it can reasonably gather an intention that specific legacies are to be paid without deduction, it must give effect

to it.' *Fitzherbert v Waterhouse* (1908) 27
NZLR 600 at 602, 603, per Cooper J

Free of tax

'I think that when the testator gave the lady an
income and directed that the amount of it
should be calculated free of payment of all
taxes including income tax and duties, he was
only contemplating such taxes and duties as
were properly payable from time to time under
the laws of this country and that he did not
contemplate or intend to include a tax to which
the lady has become liable solely by reason of
her change of residence after his death.' *Re
Frazer, Frazer v Hughes* [1941] Ch 326 at 330,
per Farwell J

[By his will a testator provided that his trustees
should pay, out of the residue of his estate, a
life annuity of £100 'free of income tax'. The
sum required to yield £100 per annum after
deduction of tax at the standard rate was £160,
and the trustees accounted to the Revenue
Commissioners for £60 per annum and paid
£100 to the annuitant. The annuitant, having
no other income, recovered from the Revenue
Commissioners £52 10s. per annum in respect
of the £60 per annum deducted by the trustees.
The point at issue was whether the annuitant
must account to the trust estate for such
refunds.] 'The first outstanding difficulty, as I
see the matter, is that the annuitant's supposed
liability to hand over to the trustee her annual
recoupment of £52 10s. can be extracted from
this particular will only by making the words
"free of income tax" bear a dual meaning,
where they must first mean "free of tax at the
standard rate" for the purposes of the
quarterly payments in advance; having done
that duty, the words cannot be read as then
meaning something else—"free of the tax for
which the annuitant is actually liable", for the
purpose of depriving her of the beneficial
interest in her recoupments; I cannot impose
that double duty on the single and solitary
phrase "free of income tax" in its collocation
here, because the first operation exhausts the
language. I do not see how I can import into the
will a right in the trustee to future tax
recoveries, solely dependent on the
slenderness of the particular annuitant's
resources, when the testator himself, far from
recovering so mean a spirit towards his poor
housekeeper, confined himself to directing the
trustee to withhold tax at the standard rate and
made no further provision whatever from
which I can infer an intention that his vast
possessions are to profit by her penury. . . . In

my opinion, the trust has no concern whatever
with the lady's claim to a recoupment of £52
10s. per annum, nor with her actual recovery of
£52 10s. per annum or any other sum that may
from time to time be repaid to her by the
Revenue authorities.' *Re Swan, Hibernian
Bank Ltd v Munro* [1945] IR 216 at 221–223,
per Gavan Duffy J

'Trustees directed to pay an annuity free of
income tax do not deduct tax but they pay the
full sum to the beneficiary. But that is not the
end of the matter. When the beneficiary has to
make a return of his total income he does not
merely return the net sum paid to him by the
trustees. He must "gross it up"; he must return
as his income such sum as after deduction of tax
leaves the sum which he received free of tax.
The trustees, who normally pay out of money
which has borne tax, are notionally regarded as
having set aside that gross sum and then
deducted the tax from it before paying to the
annuitant the net sum which is the sum they
have been directed to pay free of tax. And the
difference between the gross and net sums, the
tax which they have retained, is regarded as tax
borne by the beneficiary. If the trustees were
paying out of capital they would in fact have to
set aside the gross sum, deduct tax from it, and
account to the revenue for that tax. If the
beneficiary is entitled to recover tax for any
reason e.g. because his total income is small,
he can recover it from the revenue out of the
tax notionally retained by the trustees in the
first case, or out of the tax actually retained and
paid by the trustees to the revenue in the
second case. So when under a will a beneficiary
receives an annual payment free of income tax
he receives a greater benefit than he would if
there had been no provision that the payment
was to be free of income tax.' *Ferguson v
Inland Revenue Comrs* [1969] 1 All ER 1025 at
1029, HL, per Lord Reid

New Zealand 'The testator knew, as appears
from the will and codicils, that the appellant,
Mrs Rennick, who was his daughter, was living
in England and that other annuitants resided
abroad, one of them in San Francisco; and, as
already pointed out, in 1933, when there was a
depreciation in New Zealand currency, the
testator made a third codicil in which he
expressly declared and directed these
annuitants, so long as they continued to reside
in England or America, or as the case was,
should have their annuities paid in English
currency. All the annuities were to be paid

"free of duty and income tax". Some of them were in continuation of similar sums which the testator had been paying in his lifetime, and it is plain, in my opinion, from the language of the will and codicils that the testator intended that the annuitants should benefit under his will to precisely the same extent as they had benefited by his bounty in his lifetime, and no less. In his lifetime the payments he made to these persons to whom by his will and codicils he has given annuities were gifts which did not attract income tax in the hands of the recipients. Upon his death, however, a different position arose, and foreign income tax is payable upon the annuities in the hands of the annuitants, so that if the income tax has to be borne by the annuitants themselves the benefits that they receive will be to that extent less than the benefits which they received from the testator during his lifetime. In my opinion, upon the true construction of the will and codicils, the expression "free of duty and income tax" must be read as including not only New Zealand income tax but also foreign income tax. That is so, however, only where the annuitants who are living abroad continue to reside in the countries in which they are described in the will and codicils as resident: it does not apply to tax payable in some other country, if, as in *Re Frazer, Frazer v Hughes* [supra], the annuitant chooses to change her residence to such other foreign country.' *Re Paterson, Rennick v Guardian, Trust & Executors Co of New Zealand Ltd* [1944] NZLR 104 at 127, 128, CA, per Myers CJ; [1944] GLR 72, 77

FREE ALONGSIDE

United States Unless otherwise agreed the term F.A.S. vessel (which means 'free alongside') at a named port, even though used only in connection with the stated price, is a delivery term under which the seller must
(a) at his own expense and risk deliver the goods alongside the vessel in the manner usual in that port or on a dock designated and provided by the buyer; and
(b) obtain and tender a receipt for the goods in exchange for which the carrier is under a duty to issue a bill of lading.
(Uniform Commercial Code 1978, s 2–319(2))

FREE FROM AVERAGE *See* AVERAGE

FREE OF CAPTURE AND SEIZURE
See also PORT

The ordinary form of the Lloyd's policy includes, among the perils insured against 'men of war, enemies and surprisals, takings at sea, arrests, restraints, and detainments of all princes and peoples'. Since the time of the Napoleonic wars, however, it has been customary to exclude some of these risks by a 'warranty', commonly known as the f c and s clause, the scope of which has been widened from time to time. The form in use during the early part of the 1939–45 war was as follows: 'Warranted free of capture, seizure, arrest, restraint, or detainment and the consequences thereof or of any attempt thereat, also from the consequences of hostilities or warlike operations, whether there be a declaration of war or not. Further warranted free from the consequences of civil war, revolution, rebellion, insurrection, or civil strife arising therefrom, or piracy'.

This f c and s clause was later modified by the inclusion of a proviso, in the following terms: 'but this warranty shall not exclude collision, contact with any fixed or floating object (other than a mine or torpedo), stranding, heavy weather or fire unless caused directly (and independently of the nature of the voyage or service which the vessel concerned or, in the case of a collision, any other vessel involved therein, is performing) by a hostile act by or against a belligerent power; and for the purposes of that warranty "power" includes any authority maintaining naval, military or air forces in association with a power'. (25 Halsbury's Laws (4th edn) para 156)

FREE ON BOARD

F o b (free on board) contracts [are contracts] where the seller's duty is to deliver the goods on board ship at his own expense, upon which prima facie the property and the risk pass to the buyer, who is liable for subsequent charges and payment for the goods becomes due; however, commonly the fob contract contains special terms as to payment, for example by providing for 'cash against documents' in a similar manner to the c i f contract. (41 Halsbury's Laws (4th edn) para 612)

'Delivery "free on board" only means "The price shall be that which we stipulate for, and you shall not have to pay for the waggons or carts necessary to carry the clay from the place where it is dug; we will bear all those charges and put it free on board the ship, the name of which you are to furnish." *Re Cock, ex p Rosevear China Clay Co* (1879) 11 Ch D 560 at 564, CA, per Bacon CJ

'A contract in writing is made for the purchase of a certain quantity of sugar upon the terms "free on board", and the question is, what is the true construction of that contract made between two persons who both knew the course of business . . . in that trade? . . . if the goods dealt with by the contract were specific goods, it is not denied but that the words "free on board", according to the general understanding of merchants, would mean more than merely that the shipper was to put them on board at his expense; they would mean that he was to put them on board at his expense on account of the person for whom they were shipped; and . . . the goods so put on board . . . would be at the risk of the buyer. . . . Can there be a contract with the terms "free on board" which can be fulfilled without the delivery of specific goods at the time of shipment? Is there any mercantile or legal reason why a person should not agree to sell so much out of a bulk cargo on board or ex such a ship upon the terms that if the cargo be lost the loss shall fall upon the purchaser, and not upon the seller? I can see no reason why he should not; and if such a contract can be made, and in a contract to buy and sell a certain quantity ex ship or ex bulk there is put in the terms "free on board", one must . . . give some meaning to those words. . . . What meaning can be given to them with regard to . . . the goods which is the subject-matter of the contract, but the same meaning as is given to those words with regard to goods attributed to the contract?' *Stock v Inglis* (1884) 12 QBD 564 at 572, 573, per Brett MR; affirmed on appeal *Inglis v Stock* (1885) 10 App Cas 263, HL

'It is well settled that, on an ordinary f o b contract, when "free on board" does not merely condition the constituent elements in the price but expresses the seller's obligations additional to the bare bargain of purchase and sale, the seller does not "in pursuance of the contract of sale" or as seller send forward or start the goods to the buyer at all except in the sense that he puts the goods safely on board, pays the charge of doing so, and for the buyer's protection but not under a mandate to send, gives up possession of them to the ship only upon the terms of a reasonable and ordinary bill of lading or other contract of carriage. There his contractual liability as seller ceases,

and delivery to the buyer is complete as far as he is concerned. In such a case the goods are not "sent by the seller to the buyer", though they then begin a journey which will end in the buyer's hands. In law, as between buyer and seller, they are then and there delivered by the seller to the buyer, and thereafter it is by the buyer and his agent, the carrier, and not by the seller, that the goods are "sent" to their destination.' *Wimble Sons & Co v Rosenberg & Sons* [1913] 3 KB 743 at 756, 757, CA, per Hamilton LJ

United States   Unless otherwise agreed the term f o b (which means 'free on board') at a named place, even though used only in connection with the stated price, is a delivery term under which
(a) when the term is f o b the place of shipment, the seller must at that place ship the goods in the manner provided in this Article (s 2–504) and bear the expense and risk of putting them into the possession of the carrier; or
(b) when the term is f o b the place of destination, the seller must at his own expense and risk transport the goods to that place and there tender delivery of them in the manner provided in this Article (s 2–503);
(c) when under either (a) or (b) the term is also f o b vessel, car or other vehicle, the seller must in addition at his own expense and risk load the goods on board. If the term is fob vessel the buyer must name the vessel and in an appropriate case the seller must comply with the provisions of this Article on the form of bill of lading (s 2–323).
(Uniform Commercial Code 1978, s 2–319(1))

FREEBOARD

Ship

The 'freeboard' assigned is the distance measured vertically downwards at the side of the ship amidships from the upper edge of the deck line to the upper edge of the load line mark. (Merchant Shipping (Safety and Load Line Conventions) Act 1932, Sch 2, Annex 1, r 1)

FREEDOM OF THE PRESS

That degree of freedom from restraint which is essential to enable proprietors, editors and journalists to advance the public interest by publishing the facts and opinions without which a democratic electorate cannot make responsible judgments. (Report of Royal Commission on the Press, Cmnd 6810, 1977)

FREEHOLD

Australia [An option was given, for valuable consideration, to purchase the defendant's conditionally purchased and conditionally leased lands at a given price 'calculated on a freehold basis'.] 'The words "calculated on a freehold basis" are, in my opinion, plain and unambiguous. They are not words of art, but ordinary English words to be interpreted as applied to the subject-matter. In a contract for the sale of land at so much per acre it is implied, if no more appears, that the title to the land is freehold and that the vendor will make a clear title. If the title to a great part of the land is, as in the present case, not freehold, but capable of being converted into freehold at the option of the purchaser, such an implication might or might not arise. But the words in question . . . can only mean that the price is to be fixed on the assumption that the land for which it is given is to be made freehold before or after transfer, so that the purchaser will acquire a freehold title, and so that if the vendor does not make them freehold a deduction must be made from the named sum equivalent to what the purchaser will have to pay to acquire the freehold. In any other sense they would at best, be merely surplusage.' *Goldsborough, Mort & Co Ltd v Quinn* (1910) 10 CLR 674 at 680, 681, per Griffith CJ

In will

'Though in a grant of all one's freehold houses, leasehold houses cannot pass; and, in the case of a will, had there been any freehold houses to satisfy the will, the leasehold houses should not have passed; yet the plain intention of the testator in the principal case being to pass some houses, and he having no freehold houses there the word [freehold] should rather be rejected, than the will be wholly void; and the leasehold should pass.' *Day v Trig* (1715) 1 P Wms 286 at 287, per Tracy J

'The word "freehold", as used in this will, seems to me a necessary part of the description, which cannot be rejected. If it had been omitted, the probability is, that the leasehold in question would have been held to pass. Again, if the whole of the farm had been leasehold, the insertion of the word "freehold"

would probably not have been material. But there is a subject here which properly answers the description given in the will. There is a freehold farm called Wick, which contains 200 acres, or thereabouts (incorrectness, if there be any incorrectness in that respect, is immaterial), and which is occupied by Eeley [the farm tenant]. Being of opinion that the freehold part of the farm is properly described by those words in the will, although the leasehold should be abstracted from it, I am obliged to say that not any leasehold land, although used and treated as freehold, can pass under this devise.' *Hall v Fisher* (1844) 1 Coll 47 at 53, per Knight Bruce V-C

'The fields in dispute are not strictly freeholds, but they are usually known as freeholds or customary freeholds in the locality, and in devising her "freehold land and hereditaments at Morland" the testatrix was not, I think, using the word "freehold" in the strict technical sense of tenure. I am of opinion that both the freeholds and the customary freeholds passed to the defendant.' *Re Steel, Wappett v Robinson* [1903] 1 Ch 135 at 137, per Swinfen Eady J

FREEHOLD   *See also* ANTICIPATED FREIGHT; CARGO

'Freight' includes the profit derivable by a shipowner from the employment of his ship to carry his own goods or moveables, as well as freight payable by a third party, but does not include passage money. (Marine Insurance Act 1906, s 90)

'Freight' is the profit earned by the shipowner in the carriage of goods on board his ship; and an insurance upon freight is an insurance made in order to secure that profit to the shipowner, in case he is prevented by any of the perils insured against from actually earning such profit.' *Forbes v Aspinall* (1811) 13 East 323 at 325, per Lord Ellenborough CJ

'Money paid in advance by a charterer, or shipper of goods, is not in strictness freight; it has been called more properly "the price of the privilege of putting the goods on board the ship to be conveyed to their place of destination": but great latitude is allowed in describing the interest in a policy of insurance, provided that the nature of it is intelligibly disclosed: and there seems no reason why the money advanced may not be insured a freight as well as the money to grow due on the charter, which is undoubtedly insurable as freight, although not properly freight, and rather the price of the hire of the ship.' *Hall v Janson* (1855) 4 E & B 500 at 509, per cur.

'Freight is the reward payable to the carrier for the safe carriage and delivery of goods; it is payable only on the safe carriage and delivery; if the goods are lost on the voyage, nothing is payable. On the other hand, if the goods are safely carried the master of the ship has a lien on the goods for the amount of the freight due for such carriage, and cannot be compelled to part with the goods till such freight be paid. These incidents to freight exist by rule of law, without reference to any bill of lading, or other written contract between the parties.' *Kirchner v Venus* (1859) 12 Moo PCC 361 at 390, per cur.

'According to the law of England, as a rule, freight is earned by the carriage and arrival of the goods ready to be delivered to the merchant, though they may be in a damaged state when they arrive. If the shipowner fails to carry the goods for the merchant to the destined port, the freight is not earned. If he carry part, but not the whole, no freight is payable in respect of the part not carried, and freight is payable in respect of the part carried unless the charterparty make the carriage of the whole a condition precedent to the earning of any freight,—a case which has not within our experience arisen in practice.' *Dakin v Oxley* (1864) 15 CBNS 646 at 665, per cur.

'"Freight" has a definite meaning. It is described . . . as signifying "the earnings or profit derived by the shipowner or hirer of the ship from the use of it himself or by letting it to others to be used, or for carrying goods for others"; and by Lord Tenterden in *Flint v Flemyng* [(1830) 1 B & Ad 45] as importing "the benefit derived from the employment of the ship".' *Allison v Bristol Marine Insurance Co* (1876) 1 App Cas 209 at 250, per Lord O'Hagan

'"Freight" as distinguished from "contingency freight" means the freight which the assured has had to pay or had already at the date of the loss become liable to pay, and that is the only freight which can be taken into account in arriving at the value of the goods under the clause "Invoice cost plus freight and insurance plus 10 per cent".' *King v Methuen* (1906) 23 TLR 69 at 71, per Channell J

'It has often been said that freight involves the possession of goods implying a contract to carry or a legal right to have goods for carriage with a view to earning freight. But I cannot find

that the words freight, or chartered freight, or freight as if chartered have ever been applied to the expectation, however well founded, that a ship's agents will procure a cargo for her where there is no actual binding engagement to that effect.' *Scottish Shire Line Ltd v London & Provincial Marine & General Insurance Co Ltd* [1912] 3 KB 51 at 65, per Hamilton J

See, generally, 43 Halsbury's Laws (4th edn) paras 443 et seq.

Chartered freight

'The term chartered freight is free from ambiguity, and means the freight, if any, made payable by the terms of the charterparty, i.e. in this case the lump sum of £3,000. The phrase "chartered or as if chartered" is alternative in form; if there is a chartered freight for certain goods, or for a certain space in the ship, that is the freight insured. . . . The alternative "or as if chartered" applies to freight, or what in business is treated as freight. . . . The phrase "as if chartered" would also cover freight payable under a charterparty entered into after the date of the policy, if the policy without those words would not extend to such freight.' *Williams & Co v Canton Insurance Office Ltd* [1901] AC 462 at 475, CA, per Lindley LJ

Contract of affreightment

A contract for the carriage of goods in a ship is called in law a contract of affreightment. In practice these contracts are usually written and most frequently are expressed in one or other of two types of document called respectively a charterparty and a bill of lading. (43 Halsbury's Laws (4th edn) para 401)

Dead freight

If without lawful excuse the charterer ships a less quantity of goods than that required by the charterparty, or if the goods shipped are not in accordance with the charterparty, the measure of damages is the difference between the freight actually earned, including any profit earned by carrying the goods of third persons, and the freight that would have been earned if the charterer had fulfilled his obligation. Such damages are usually known as 'deadfreight'. (43 Halsbury's Laws (4th edn) para 591)

'It must be admitted that the term "dead freight" is an inaccurate expression of the thing signified by it. "It is", as Lord Ellenborough said in *Phillips v Rodie* [(1812), 15 East, 547, at 554] "not freight, but an unliquidated

compensation for the loss of freight recoverable in the absence and place of freight." . . .
In construing the charterparty it must be assumed that the parties understood the meaning of the terms they employed, and that, amongst others, the term "dead freight" meant (according to Lord Ellenborough's definition) "an unliquidated compensation for the loss of freight".' *McLean & Hope v Fleming* (1871) LR 2 Sc & Div 128 at 131, 133, HL, per Lord Chelmsford

'Dead freight is not freight at all properly so called, but is in reality damages for breach of contract for convenience nicknamed dead freight.' *Kish v Taylor* [1912] AC 604 at 621, 622, HL, per Lord Atkinson

'I have come to the conclusion that the plaintiffs are entitled to succeed in their claim for what is called dead freight, which in legal terminology is damages for failure to load a full and complete cargo.' *Akt Reidar v Arcos Ltd* [1926] 2 KB 83 at 85, per Greer J; affirmed on appeal [1927] 1 KB 352, CA

See, generally, 43 Halsbury's Laws (4th edn) para 591.

FREQUENT (Verb)

'It is plain that "frequenting" means being at a place long enough for the purpose aimed at. We decided in the unreported case of *Jones v Scott* that a man being in a street for a quarter of an hour, walking up and down in a space of some fifteen to twenty yards, and taking money and slips from eleven different men, on a certain day, that being long enough to carry out his betting operations, was frequenting the place.' *Airton v Scott* (1909) 100 LT 393 at 394, per Lord Alverstone CJ

FRESH

'Fish which has been preserved from decay by artificial means for months or years is not fresh in any ordinary sense of the term. It may be as good as when it came out of the water, but, however this may be, it is not fresh. It owes its good condition to the process to which it has been subjected.' *Warner's (William) Sons & Co v Midland Rly Co* [1918] AC 616 at 618, per Lord Finlay, LC

FRESH (Noun)

New Zealand 'The "freshes" referred to in the evidence are not, in our opinion,
equivalent to what are called floods in the English cases. A "fresh" in a New Zealand river, when the water is confined within the banks of the river, is nothing more than what may be termed the ordinary condition of the river during the rainy season.' *Kingdon v Hutt River Board* (1905) 25 NZLR 145 at 157, per cur; 7 GLR 634 at 636

FRESH EVIDENCE   *See* EVIDENCE

FRESHET

Canada 'The dictionary meaning of the word "freshet" is the same as the statutory and popular meaning, and that is, a flood or inundation by means of rains or (and) melted snow.' *Hunt v Beck* (1915) 34 OLR 609 at 612, Ont SC, per Boyd C; affd 36 OLR 333, Ont CA

FRIEND

In deed

'The defendants are a limited company, formed for the purpose of providing for ladies engaged in professional or other avocations in London a home in which are to be provided sleeping apartments and a suite of reception rooms—in few words, a home with as little trouble as possible to the inmates. There are at the present time residing in this home a number of ladies as to whom the question arises whether they are entitled to use the garden. The plaintiffs . . . want . . . to have the true construction of the deed of 1852 determined. The question turns upon the language of the deed [by which the use of the garden was granted to the purchaser of the fee his heirs administrators and assigns and for his and their "friends"]. . . . What is the meaning of the word "friends"? Are these ladies the "friends" of the defendant company? . . . I do not intend to lay down exactly and exhaustively what the expression "friends"means; but can these ladies be, in any proper sense, called the friends of the company? I think not. If I am to give them a name they are not friends, but customers. These ladies come to the defendants' club, not from motives of friendship, but for the purposes of commercial relations and because it answers their purpose to come. It may be exceedingly difficult to draw the line between who is a friend and who is not. . . . All I have to decide in this case is whether or not these ladies, members of the club, are within the words of the deed. I hold that they are not." *Keith v Twentieth Century Club Ltd* (1904) 73 LJ Ch 545 at 548, 549, per Buckley J

In will

[A testator instructed his trustees to give the residue of his estate among his 'friends' and relations.] 'Where trustees have power to distribute generally according to their discretion without any object pointed out or rule laid down, the court interposes not, unless in case of charity, which is different, the court exercising a discretion as having the general government and regulation of charity. But here is a rule laid down; and the *friends* is synonymous to *relations*; otherwise it is absurd.' *Gower v Mainwaring* (1750) 2 Ves Sen 87 at 89, per Lord Hardwicke LC

'I think the court must necessarily put some limit upon the term "friends", and that the only limit to be put upon it is to give it the same construction as the word "relations", as was done in that case before Lord Hardwicke of *Gower v Mainwaring* [supra]. In that case the words were "friends *and* relations" in the conjunctive, and in the present case they are "relations or friends" in the disjunctive; but that difference does not in my opinion afford a sufficient reason why they should not receive the same construction. I must therefore consider the word "friends" as being in effect synonymous with "relations", and that the wife's power was a special power to appoint by will to her relations.' *Re Caplin's Will* (1865) 2 Drew & Sm 527 at 531, per Kindersley V-C

'Friendship, of course, is a phrase particularly blurred in outline, but its context, and the circumstances of the case, may well fill in what would otherwise be vague. A circumstance to which I have particular regard is the power of appointment vested in the testator's widow. In my judgment, it is quite plain that this gift contemplates a degree of intimacy sufficiently close to make its detection quite easy. It is to be observed that the opening words (which may not have any imperative force, but which, none the less, are not to be ignored in construing the gift) are: "If my wife feels that I have forgotten any friend". Therefore, it must be somebody who was realised by the wife to be a friend at the moment of the testator's death. That is emphasised by the fact that in the margin of the will the testator, as it were, picks up his own words: "I have forgotten Richard Hurton and

C G Chapple Mark Francis and Miss Jennings but my wife will put that right". I am sure that the emphasis in the "I have forgotten" is on the word "have", and in the words which follow the testator gives again to his wife a plain clue as to the sort of friends whom he had in mind. Then he directs that his wife may nominate such friends. It is to be noted that it is not any friends, but is the friends that his wife feels that he has forgotten. What may she nominate them? Not a fortune but "a sum not exceeding £25 per friend". That in itself indicates that the purpose here is sentimental, not financial. Again, to show that his purpose is sentimental, he provides that there shall be "a maximum aggregate payment of £250". That is the limit of the widow's power of appointment. Then, to close any possible gap, he says "so that such friends may buy a small memento of our friendship". Quite obviously that indicates to my mind that the testator was thinking of friends whom he would wish to remember him and who, he thinks, would wish him to remember them. In those circumstances it appears to me that friends of a considerable degree of intimacy are only to be included in this gift.' *Re Coates (decd)* [1955] 1 All ER 26 at 28, 29, per Roxburgh J

FRIENDLY SOCIETY

Friendly societies are unincorporated mutual insurance associations in which members subscribe for provident benefits for themselves and their families. They form part of a main group of voluntary benefit thrift and provident societies. There is a close affinity in the early history and legislation relating to societies in this group. The expression 'friendly societies' is sometimes used to refer to all the societies registered under the Friendly Societies Act 1974, but friendly societies are only one of the six classes of societies which can be registered under that Act. (19 Halsbury's Laws (4th edn) para 10)

FRINGE BENEFIT

Australia 'The expression "fringe benefit" is . . . defined by s 136(1) of the [Fringe Benefits Tax Act 1986], in terms of a benefit provided, or deemed to be provided, to the employee or an associate of the employee in respect of the employment of the employee, whether the benefit be provided by the employer, an associate of the employer or another person under an arrangement with the employer or an associate of the employer. The definition of "fringe benefit" excludes a long list of benefits too numerous to mention. Wages, salary and superannuation benefits are among the benefits thereby excluded.' *State of Queensland v Commonwealth of Australia* (1987) 18 ATR 158 at 169, per Mason, Brennan and Dean JJ

FRIVOLOUS ACTION

'There is an inherent power in every Court to stay and dismiss actions or applications which are frivolous and vexatious and abusive of the process of the Court. . . . In order to bring a case within the description it is not sufficient merely to say that the plaintiff has no cause of action. It must appear that his alleged cause of action is one which on the face of it is clearly one which no reasonable person could properly treat as bona fide, and contend that he had a grievance which he was entitled to bring before the Court.' *Norman v Mathews* (1916) 85 LJKB 857 at 859, per Lush J

FROM   *See also* AT

'"From" [a particular date] may in the vulgar use, and even in the strict propriety of language, mean either inclusive or exclusive [of that date]; . . . the parties necessarily understood and used it in that sense which made their deed effectual; . . . courts of justice are to construe the words of parties so as to effectuate their deeds, and not to destroy them; more especially where the words themselves abstractedly may admit of either meaning.' *Pugh v Leeds (Duke)* (1777) 2 Cowp 714 at 725, per cur.

'The point principally relied upon is that the word "from" is exclusive. In *Rex v Stevens* [(1804) 5 East 244] the word "until" was the subject of discussion: and it was considered to admit a different interpretation according to the subject-matter and context. Supposing that the word prima facie has an exclusive meaning, there is no rule that prevents us from interpreting it so as to be inclusive, if the use of the word in the transaction leads us to do so. Now here, if we advert to the whole of the count, we find an averment that the plaintiff entered into the service, on the terms of the contract, on the day itself. The contract, if so, must have included that day. To say that the word is necessarily exclusive would, I think, be

erroneous.' *Wilkinson v Gaston* (1846) 9 QB 137 at 146, per Williams J

'The sailing of a ship insured "from London" is "a sailing from the docks, from the place where she was, where she first broke ground and commenced the voyage".' *The Samuel Hicks, Anderson v Thornton* (1852) 8 LT 93 at 93, per Pollock CB

'I feel no doubt on this question. The words are perfectly plain. If any one spoke of the kings of England "from William the Conqueror downwards", he would certainly mean to include William the Conqueror. The testatrix gives "from Sophia downwards"—that is, from Sophia the second child down to the youngest inclusive.' *Lett v Osborne* (1882) 51 LJ Ch 910 at 911, per Bacon V-C

'The first question raised is whether or not November 24, 1888, the day on which this event occurred, is included in the period covered by the policy. The insurance being "for twelve calendar months from November 24, 1887", obviously either November 24, 1887 or November 24, 1888 must be excluded, for otherwise the period covered would exceed twelve calendar months by one day. I decide . . . that the former date is excluded and the latter included. . . . I cannot but think that, as regards time, "from" is akin to "after", and excludes the date fixed for the commencement of the computation.' *South Staffordshire Tramways Co v Sickness & Accident Assurance Assocn* [1891] 1 QB 402 at 404, 405, per Day J

Australia 'There is no general rule as to the consequences of the use of the preposition "from", whether it be in the computation of the period of time, or in any other connexion. In general, in computing a period of time from a date, the period will commence at the end of the day of that date, but there is no universally operating rule to that effect, see, for example, the illustration given in the note at p 1068 of the report of *R v Stevens and Agnew* [(1804) 102 ER 1063] and *Wilkinson v Gaston* [supra]. When as here, a change is to take place from a stated time, the general "rule" as to the computation of a period of time is not of direct significance, though it is illustrative of the separating effect of the preposition "from". In my opinion, it does not usually have an inclusive but rather an exclusive or separatist quality. But unquestionably it may have either. Thus, the preposition derives its relevant quality from the context in which it is found, which includes the purpose which the document in which it is found is evidently designed to effect.' *Associated Beauty Aids Pty Ltd v Federal Comr of Taxation* [1966] ALR 104 at 113, per Barwick CJ

Canada 'I think it may . . . be taken as settled that where a term is expressed to commence from a given date without the addition of other words which make it clear that the word "from" is to be inclusive or exclusive of the date then the context or subject-matter must be looked at to determine in which sense the words are used, since as Lord Mansfield said in the *Pugh* case [*Pugh v Leeds (Duke)* (supra)], at p 725, "'from' may in the vulgar use, and even in strict propriety of language, mean either inclusive or exclusive". Here the lease provides for an annual tenancy with rent payable in equal monthly instalments commencing September 1, 1943, and on the first day of each month thereafter during the said term. I am of opinion that the word "from" in that context must be read as inclusive of September 1, 1943.' *West v Barr* [1945] 1 WWR 337 at 344, BCCA, per Bird JA

From loading

'Looking as we are obliged to do to the policy, and to the policy alone, in order to collect the intention of the parties as to the commencement and duration of the adventure thereby protected, we cannot feel ourselves at liberty to disjoin in point of effect and construction the words, "at all or any port or place on the coast of Brazil" from the words, "from the loading thereof aboard the said ship", by which they are immediately preceded and with which by immediate context they appear to us to be necessarily united. . . . Feeling, therefore, the impossibility of assigning to these words any other place in or with reference to this contract than what the parties themselves have done; and feeling the impossibility of assigning to them in that place, and with the context which attends them, any other meaning than what they obviously and in their plain grammatical sense import, we are obliged to say, that the adventure could only attach on goods and ship after a loading of goods had taken place on the coast of Brazil: and as that circumstance or event never took place in the present instance, that the policy of course never attached at all.' *Robertson v French* (1803) 4 East 130 at 140–142, per cur.

[A policy of insurance on goods from Gottenburgh to any port in the Baltic contained the printed words 'beginning the adventure upon the said goods, from the loading thereof on board the said ship'. At the foot of the policy were added the words: 'In continuation of five policies . . .' and the policies were enumerated.] 'A very strict, and certainly a construction not to be favoured, and still less to be extended, was adopted in the case of *Spitta v Woodman* [(1810) 2 Taunt 416] where it was holden that the words beginning the adventure from the loading on board were to be confined to the place from whence the risk commenced. But if there be any thing to indicate that a prior loading was contemplated by the parties, it will release the case from that strict construction. Then can there be any thing more indicative of such an understanding between the parties than the statement made at the foot of this policy, that it was in continuation of former policies, which were distinctly upon a voyage from Virginia. This was taking up the voyage from a period in the former policies. The conclusion, therefore, which was drawn in *Spitta v Woodman*, is completely rebutted by the reference in this policy to an antecedent loading.' *Bell v Hobson* (1812) 16 East 240 at 243, per Lord Ellenborough CJ

[A cargo of goods was insured at and from Gottenburgh to the ship's port of discharge, beginning the adventure on the said goods from the loading thereof aboard the ship.] 'To construe the . . . words "from the loading, etc." to mean only the same thing as "being loaded", would be giving them no effect. . . . If the word loading is to be understood in a grammatical sense as descriptive of an act to be done, and not of the goods being in a loaded state, it can only be applied to one specific place, viz. where the cargo is to be taken on board; whereas if it is to be understood as "being loaded" it will be descriptive of a loading at every place. The former is the more obvious and strictly grammatical construction. We are of opinion after much consideration that we shall not violate any rule of construction by construing this policy according to the construction of *Spitta v Woodman* [supra], which is the only case precisely in point with the present.' *Mellish v Allnutt* (1813) 2 M&S 106 at 110, 111, per cur.

'One of the usual printed parts of a policy . . . is that the "insurance shall commence on the freight and goods and merchandise from the loading of the said goods and merchandise on board the said ship or vessel at as above". . . . That means that the underwriters are not responsible for the goods until they are put on board the ship for the voyage that is insured against, unless there is something stated to the contrary; and so it has been decided. But then in *Bell v Hobson* [supra], which rather derogates from that rule, Lord Ellenborough says it had been held that the words "beginning the adventure from the loading on board" were to be confined to the place from whence the risk commenced. "But", he says, "if there be anything to indicate that a prior loading was contemplated by the parties, it will release the case from that strict construction". That I understand to mean, that if there be anything on the face of the written instrument (we cannot construe it as importing other matters) to shew that the loading was to commence at a prior time, or that the word loading was used in a sense different from the mere putting on board, then it shall prevail.' *Joyce v Realm Marine Insurance Co* (1872) LR 7 QB 580 at 583, 584, per Blackburn J

[A policy of insurance upon freight provided that the adventure upon 'the said goods or freight' should begin 'from the loading thereof'.] 'The words "from the loading thereof" exclude the goods not actually loaded, and also the freight for them.' *Hopper v Wear Marine Insurance Co* (1882) 46 LT 107 at 108, per Mathew J

FROM TIME TO TIME

[By s 3 of Sir H Meux's Settled Estate Act 1863: 'The Lord Chancellor may from time to time . . . order or direct to be done . . . all and whatsoever Sir Henry Meux, if of sound mind, might do'.] 'The words "from time to time" are words which are constantly introduced where it is intended to protect a person who is empowered to act from the risk of having completely discharged his duty when he has once acted, and therefore not being able to act again in the same direction. The meaning of the words "from time to time" is that after he [in this case, the Lord Chancellor] has made one order he may make a fresh order to add something to it, or take something from it, or reverse it altogether; and as that meaning gives sufficient force to the words and explains the use of them here it seems to me that your Lordships ought not to go further and to narrow these words by any construction which would throw impediments in the way of carrying on the business, whereas the object of the Act was to facilitate it.' *Lawrie v Lees*

(1881) 7 App Cas 19 at 29, 30, HL, per Lord Penzance

'Section 25 [of the Waterworks Clauses Act 1847 (repealed; see now Water Act 1945, Sch III (16))] . . . is to this effect: "Except where otherwise provided for by agreement, the undertakers shall, from time to time, pay to the owner, lessee, or occupier of any mines of coal . . . for any mines or minerals, not purchased by the undertakers, which cannot be obtained by reason of making and maintaining the said works". . . . I have no doubt that what was meant was this, that "from time to time" meant as the occasion should arise. . . .' *Holliday v Wakefield Corpn* (1887) 57 LT 559 at 562, 563, per Mathew J

Australia ' "From time to time" is a well-known phrase which occurs in various statutes and documents. The words have been held to mean "as occasion may arise"—per Williams J in *Bryan v Arthur* [(1839) 11 Ad & El 108 at 117]. The words "from time to time" are words which are constantly introduced where it is intended to protect a person who is empowered to act from the risk of having completely discharged his duty when he has once acted, and, therefore, not being able to act again in the same direction. The meaning of the words "from time to time" is that after once acting the donee of the power may act again (per Lord Penzance in *Lawrie v Lees* [supra])." *Boettcher v Boettcher* [1948] St R Qd 73 at 77, per Stanley AJ

FRONT *See also* ADJOIN

[The taking down of the 'front' of a building for the purpose of rebuilding entitled the local authority to prescribe a new building line under s 155 of the Public Health Act 1875 (repealed; see now s 74 of the Highways Act 1980).] 'It would certainly seem to me an abuse of language to call the exterior wall and shop window of the ground floor of Nos 104 and 106 High Street north the "front" of those two houses to the exclusion of the exterior walls and windows of the first and second floors, and I therefore, quite apart from authority, come to the conclusion that the "front" of the houses . . . so far as s 155 of the Public Health Act 1875 is concerned includes the exterior walls and windows of the first and second floors of those houses as well as the exterior wall and windows of the ground floor.' *A-G v Prices' Tailors (1928) Ltd* [1930] 2 Ch 316 at 322, 323, per Luxmoore J

Australia 'A piece of land may front, and does front, any street the alignment of which constitutes a boundary of the land in question.' *Kingsford v Phillips & Jutsum* [1931] St R Qd 122 at 132, per Macrossan SPJ

FRONTAGE

New Zealand 'I think that by the word "frontage" [as applied to a building] is meant a side towards the street, such side having no other erection between it or any part of it and the street; and a "frontage" in that sense means the whole of the side which is towards the street.' *Doyle v Bishop* (1898) 17 NZLR 574 at 575, per Prendergast CJ

FRUIT

'The question in this case is, whether looking to the subject-matter of the demise, and the several clauses of the lease, fruit trees where clearly intended to be excepted, or whether there be any reasonable degree of doubt whether that were intended or not. Now a grant of "timber trees and other trees" will not pass fruit trees. Here the exception is, "of all timber trees, and other trees, but not the annual fruit thereof". Some meaning must, undoubtedly, be given to the latter words, for if the fruit saved was the fruit of orchard trees, it would follow that the bodies of those trees would be within the exception. But the term fruit in legal acception is not confined to the produce of those trees which in popular language are called fruit trees, but applies also to the produce of oak, elm, and walnut trees.' *Bullen v Denning* (1826) 5 B & C 842 at 847, per Bayley J

FRUSTRATION

The doctrine of frustration operates to excuse from further performance [of a contract] where (1) it appears from the nature of the contract and the surrounding circumstances that the parties have contracted on the basis that some fundamental thing or state of things will continue to exist, or that some particular person will continue to be available, or that some future event which forms the basis of the contract will take place, and (2) before breach, an event in relation to the matter stipulated in (1) renders performance impossible or only possible in a very different way from that contemplated, but without default of either party. (9 Halsbury's Laws (4th edn) para 950)

'I must briefly explain my conception of what is meant in this context by impossibility of performance, which is the phrase used by Blackburn J [in *Taylor v Caldwell* (1863) 3 B & S 826 at 839]. In more recent days the phrase more commonly used is "frustration of the contract" or more shortly "frustration". But "frustration of the contract" is an elliptical expression. The fuller and more accurate phrase is "frustration of the adventure or of the commercial or practical purpose of the contract". This change in language corresponds to a wider conception of impossibility, which has extended the rule beyond contracts which depend on the existence, at the relevant time, of a specific object, as in the instances given by Blackburn J to cases where the essential object does indeed exist, but its condition has by some casualty been so changed as to be not available for the purposes of the contract either at the contract date, or, if no date is fixed, within any time consistent with the commercial or practical adventure. For the purposes of the contract the object is as good as lost. Another case, often described as frustration, is where by State interference or similar overriding intervention the performance of the contract has been interrupted for so long a time as to make it unreasonable for the parties to be required to go on with it. Yet another illustration is where the actual object still exists and is available, but the object of the contract as contemplated by both parties was its employment for a particular purpose, which has become impossible, as in the Coronation cases [e.g. *Krell v Henry* [1903] 2 KB 740]. In these and similar cases, where there is not in the strict sense impossibility by some casual happening, there has been so vital a change in the circumstances as to defeat the contract. What Willes J described as substantial performance is no longer possible. The common object of the parties is frustrated.' *Joseph Constantine SS Line Ltd v Imperial Smelting Corpn Ltd* [1942] AC 154 at 182, 183, HL, per Lord Wright

'Frustration of a contract, which, though as an expression criticised in the past, has now received legislative sanction in a recent Act—the Law Reform (Frustrated Contracts) Act 1943—has been described by Professor Winfield, at 235, in the 11th edition of Pollock on Contracts which he has edited in the following terms: "After the formation of a contract, certain sets of circumstances arise which, owing to the fault of neither party, render fulfilment of the contract by one or both of the parties impossible in any sense or mode contemplated by them. These sets of circumstances have been more or less defined by the courts and are held by them to release both parties from any further obligation to fulfil the contract". The rule has sometimes been described as an exception to the general principle that parties must perform their obligations or pay damages for breach of contract. I should prefer to describe it as a substantive and particular rule which the common law has evolved. Where it applies there is no breach of contract. What happens is that the contract is held on its true construction not to apply at all from the time when the frustrating circumstances supervene.' *Denny, Mott & Dickson Ltd v Fraser (James B) & Co Ltd* [1944] AC 265 at 273, 274, per Lord Wright

'Frustration may be defined as the premature determination of an agreement between parties, lawfully entered into and in course of operation at the time of its premature determination, owing to the occurrence of an intervening event or change of circumstances so fundamental as to be regarded by the law both as striking at the root of the agreement, and as entirely beyond what was contemplated by the parties when they entered into the agreement. If, therefore, the intervening circumstance is one which the law would not regard as so fundamental as to destroy the basis of the agreement, there is no frustration. Equally, if the terms of the agreement shew that the parties contemplated the possibility of such an intervening circumstance arising, frustration does not occur. Neither, of course, does it arise where one of the parties has deliberately brought about the supervening event by his own choice. (See the cases collected in *Joseph Constantine Steamship Line Ltd v Imperial Smelting Corporation Ltd* [supra].) But where it does arise frustration operates to bring the agreement to an end as regards both parties forthwith and quite apart from their volition.' *Cricklewood Property & Investment Trust Ltd v Leighton's Investment Trust Ltd* [1945] AC 221 at 228, HL, per Lord Simon LC

'If there is an event or change of circumstances which is so fundamental as to be regarded by the law as striking at the root of the contract as a whole, and as going beyond what was contemplated by the parties and such that to hold the parties to the contract would be to bind them to terms which they would not have made had they contemplated that event or those circumstances, then the contract is frustrated by that event immediately and irrespective of the volition or the intention of the parties, or their knowledge as to that particular event, and this even although they have continued for a time to treat the contract as still subsisting.' *Morgan v Manser* [1948] 1 KB 184 at 191, per Streatfield J

'If the decisions in "frustration" cases are regarded as illustrations of the power and duty of a court to put the proper construction on the agreement made between the parties, having regard to the terms in which that agreement is expressed and to the surrounding circumstances in which it was made, including any necessary implication, such decisions are seen to be examples of the general judicial function of interpreting a contract when there is disagreement as to its effect. What distinguishes "frustration" cases is that the interpretation involves the consequence that, in view of what has happened, further performance is automatically ended. This is because the frustrating event (such, for example, as war or prolonged delay) must be regarded as introducing a new situation to which no limit can be put.' *British Movietonews Ltd v London and District Cinemas Ltd* [1951] 2 All ER 617 at 625, per Viscount Simon

'The doctrine of frustration is not an easy one, and there are rival theories as to the foundation on which it rests. Some high judicial authorities have supposed that it rests on an implied contract or on a term which must be deemed to be implicit in the contract as applied to some unforeseen, unpredictable, and unknown state of circumstances which has, in fact, arisen. The other view is that frustration depends on some such consideration as that the event which has happened has so completely destroyed the subject-matter and altered the circumstances that the contract can no longer be carried out or recognised in any shape or form and on that ground must be deemed (in equity, I suppose for this, of course, is an executory contract) to be no longer enforceable, and, indeed, no longer in existence, so that it can be neither specifically performed by either party nor can any damages be recovered for any alleged breach of it.' *Hillingdon Estate Co v Stonefield Estates Ltd* [1952] 1 All ER 853 at 855, per Vaisey J (also reported in [1952] Ch 627 at 630, 631).

'Before I refer to the facts, I must say briefly

what I understand to be the legal principle of frustration. It is not always expressed in the same way, but I think that the points which are relevant to the decision of this case are really beyond dispute. The theory of frustration belongs to the law of contract and it is represented by a rule which the courts will apply in certain limited circumstances for the purpose of deciding that contractual obligations, ex facie binding, are no longer enforceable against the parties. The description of the circumstances that justify the application of the rule and, consequently, the decision whether, in a particular case, those circumstances exist are, I think, necessarily questions of law. Frustration occurs whenever the law recognises that, without default of either party, a contractual obligation has become incapable of being performed because the circumstances in which performance is called for would render it a thing radically different from that which was undertaken by the contract. *Non haec in foedera veni*. It was not this that I promised to do.' *Davis Contractors Ltd v Fareham Urban District Council* [1956] 2 All ER 145 at 160, HL, per Lord Radcliffe

'Frustration is a doctrine only too often invoked by a party to a contract who finds performance difficult or unprofitable, but it is very rarely relied on with success. It is in fact a kind of last ditch, and, as Lord Radcliffe says in effect in his speech in the most recent case [*Davis Contractors Ltd v Fareham UDC* (supra)], it is a conclusion which should be reached rarely and with reluctance. The doctrine used to be spoken of as that of "frustration of the adventure", which seems to me to be more accurate than the modern expression "frustration of the contract". . . . I have always favoured the view that this doctrine when analysed proves to depend on the true construction of the contract. A man may only be released under this doctrine if he can truly say . . . "This was not the bargain that I made; the contract properly construed does not provide for the event which has happened and is therefore not binding because it has no application." Hardship or unexpected expense falling on one of the parties to a commercial adventure can never excuse him from it so long as the adventure remains recognisably that on which the parties embarked.' *Tsakiroglou & Co Ltd v Noblee & Thorl* [1960] 2 All ER 160 at 171, CA, per Harman LJ; affd [1961] 2 All ER 179, [1962] AC 93, HL

'Frustration of a contract takes place when there supervenes an event (without default of either party and for which the contract makes no sufficient provision) which so significantly changes the nature (not merely the expense or onerousness) of the outstanding contractual rights and/or obligations from what the parties could reasonably have contemplated at the time of its execution that it would be unjust to hold them to the literal sense of its stipulations in the new circumstances; in such case the law declares both parties to be discharged from further performance.' *National Carriers Ltd v Panalpina (Northern) Ltd* [1981] 1 All ER 161 at 175, HL, per Lord Simon of Glaisdale

'There can be no doubt that an agreement to refer a dispute to arbitration can in theory, like any other contract, be discharged by frustration. Lord Diplock expressly recognised this in his speech in *Bremer Vulkan* [[1981] 1 All ER 289 at 297]. Before this can happen, however, the usual requirements necessary to give rise to frustration of a contract must be present. What those requirements are appear clearly from the various pronouncements of high authority on the doctrine of frustration on contract conveniently gathered together by Griffiths LJ in his dissenting judgment in this case [see [1982] 3 All ER 394 at 406, 407]. Those pronouncements, which I do not consider that it is necessary for me to quote again myself, show that there are two essential factors which must be present in order to frustrate a contract. The first essential factor is that there must be some outside event or extraneous change of situation, not foreseen or provided for by the parties at the time of contracting, which either makes it impossible for the contract to be performed at all, or at least renders its performance something radically different from what the parties contemplated when they entered into it. The second essential factor is that the outside event or extraneous change of situation concerned, and the consequences of either in relation to the performance of the contract, must have occurred without either the fault or the default of either party to the contract.' *Paal Wilson & Co A/S v Partenreederei Hannah Blumenthal, The Hannah Blumenthal* [1983] 1 All ER 34 at 44, HL, per Lord Brandon of Oakbrook

Australia 'The world is more full of the frustration of hopes and endeavours than ever before and perhaps from this cause frustration has given its name to a fashionable legal doctrine and has a mint of phrases in its train. . . . In my opinion it is of especial importance in "frustration" cases to remember the golden rule that judgments are to be read in relation to the particular facts of each case. No rule or principle of law can be discovered by examining the differing words and phrases in which learned Judges have described or commented upon the facts or the consequences of them. The fashion of the moment is to seize upon every new judicial phrase or illustration as the foundation for a new so-called principle by which law may be brought into conformity with, or replaced by somebody's conception of reason and justice. . . . I venture the following summary of the effect of the decisions upon what is called the doctrine of frustration. Frustration is an excuse for default in fulfilling a contract—using default as meaning non-performance. In so far as "frustration" has become a term of art at all, its first requirement is proof of frustration in fact, that is impossibility arising from external forces. So much being shown, the question then and only then arises, whether the defendant is to be relieved of the usual consequences of default.' *Neon Electric Signs Ltd v Caldwell* [1943] VLR 1 at 8, 14, per Mann CJ

FUEL OR FIELD GARDEN ALLOTMENT   *See* ALLOTMENT

FUGITIVE

'The Act [Fugitive Offenders Act 1881 (repealed; see now Fugitive Offenders Act 1967)] was passed to deal with the return of "fugitives", and s 2 provides: "Where a person accused of having committed an offence . . . in one part of Her Majesty's dominions has left that part, such person (in this Act referred to as a fugitive from that part) if found in another part of Her Majesty's dominions, shall be liable to be apprehended and returned in manner provided by this Act to the part from which he is a fugitive. A fugitive may be so apprehended under an indorsed warrant or a provisional warrant". Thus, although the word "fugitive" is used, it applies, not merely to a person who has left one part of His Majesty's dominions for the express purpose of avoiding trial, but to any person who is accused of having committed an offence in one part and is found in another part of His Majesty's dominions.' *Re Henderson, Henderson v Secretary of State for Home Affairs* [1950] 1 All ER 283 at 286, CA, per Tucker LJ

FUGITIVE CRIMINAL

'Fugitive criminal' means any person accused or convicted of an extradition crime committed within the jurisdiction of any foreign state who is in or is suspected of being in some part of Her Majesty's dominions; and the term 'fugitive criminal of a foreign state' means a fugitive criminal accused or convicted of an extradition crime committed within the jurisdiction of that state. (Extradition Act 1870, s 26)

'In this case the applicant [for a writ of habeas corpus] has been convicted of the crime of robbery with violence, a crime mentioned in the treaty [of extradition], and he broke out of prison and came to this country. In those circumstances, I think the applicant is a "fugitive criminal"; he is a fugitive criminal who has been convicted of an extradition crime, and it seems to me therefore that the committal order is right.' *Ex p Moser* [1915] 2 KB 698 at 701, per Atkin J

'Section 10 of the Extradition Act 1870, speaks of "a fugitive criminal alleged to have been convicted of an extradition crime", and provides that the magistrate may commit him for extradition. That obviously means a criminal who has been convicted and has not served his sentence.' Ibid at 702, per Lord Reading CJ

'The question turns on the meaning of "fugitive criminal", and whatever might be the meaning of those words if no definition of them existed, as far as English law is concerned they have been defined by s 26 of the Extradition Act 1870 [supra]. As Smith J pointed out in *Reg v Nillins* [(1884) 53 LJMC 157 at 159], the words in s 26 are "who is in" this country, not "who has fled to this country". Avory J has pointed out that the term fugitive criminal does not mean any fugitive person accused who is in any part of His Majesty's dominions. The word "fugitive" is not inserted before "person" but is inserted before "criminal" in the latter part of the definition. In the first part therefore it means any person accused.' *R v Godfrey* [1923] 1 KB 24 at 30, DC, per Sankey J

See, generally, 18 Halsbury's Laws (4th edn) para 210 et seq

FULL

Canada [A treaty with Indians reserved to them the 'full and free privilege' to hunt over ceded lands.] 'First, I do not think that, properly understood, the words used convey the broad and unlimited meaning that would otherwise be necessary. I agree that the word "full", in the context, is difficult to define; but if it seems to connote a plenary quality, a completeness of the right, it is, in my view, strictly as regards the right of the owner or possessor of the land. As to the word "free", to me it simply means that no consideration is to be exacted from those entitled to hunt and fish in exercise of the right.' *Pawis v R* (1979) 102 DLR (3d) 602 at 609, FCTD, per Marceau J

FULL AGE

[By the Family Law Reform Act 1969, s 1 the age of majority was reduced from twenty-one years to eighteen years and all statutory references to minority and infancy are to be construed accordingly. Section 9 of the Act of 1969 further provides that the time at which a person attains a particular age expressed in years shall be the commencement of the relevant anniversary of the date of his birth. The old common law rule that a person was deemed to attain a particular age at the first moment of the day immediately preceding the relevant anniversary of this birth was thus abolished]

The heir apparent or heir presumptive to the Throne shall be deemed for all the purposes of the Regency Act 1937, to be of full age if he or she has attained the age of eighteen years. (Regency Act 1953, s 2)

'The words "of full age" are not, so far as I know, technical words or words of art at all. I think it is obvious that throughout this Act [Settled Land Act 1925] as indeed throughout the Law of Property Act [1925] the words "of full age" are used in relation to a person in contrast with the word "infant", and that I ought to treat the words "of full age" as meaning no more than this, "not being an infant".' *Re Carnarvon's (Earl) Chesterfield Settled Estates, Re Carnarvon's (Earl) Highclere Settled Estates* [1927] 1 Ch 138 at 143–145, per Romer J

Australia 'A day is not in law divisible and a person is deemed in law for the purpose of computing his age to have lived through the whole of the first day of his life. He would thus have been deemed to have attained full age with the expiration of the day preceding the 21st anniversary of his birth were it not for an ancient though artificial rule treating him as of full age throughout the whole of the day

preceding that anniversary. As I understand the rule of law applicable to the matter a person is deemed to have become of full age coincidentally with the passing of midnight.' *Prowse v McIntyre* [1963] ALR 243 at 246, per McTiernan J

'In calculating a person's age the law says that the day of his birth is to be included. At whatever time of the day he is born, that day is counted; and, a day not being divisible, it is as if he were born at the first instant of that day. When on this basis does he come to full age? . . . He is to be regarded as having become of age at the beginning of that day— that is at the first instant of the day before his birthday. . . . During the whole of the day before the anniversary of his birth a man is of full age and capacity in law. He is not during that day coming of age. He had come of age when the day began. The days of his non-age had at that instant passed. . . . It follows that in computing a period after a man's coming to full age the day before his 21st birthday must in law be counted as the first day of that period.' Ibid at 252, 253, per Windeyer J

FULL AMOUNT

[The Income Tax Act 1918, Sch D, Case V, r 1 (repealed; see now the Income and Corporation Taxes Act 1988, ss 64, 65), provided that the tax in respect of income arising from stocks, shares or rent in any place out of the United Kingdom was to be computed on the 'full amount' thereof on an average of the three preceding years.] 'If the taxpayer in the year of assessment receives anything falling within the description of income arising from stocks, shares or rents in any place out of the United Kingdom he is assessable upon the basis of the average of the three preceding years of all receipts falling within the same description. . . . The phrase "the full amount thereof" in r 1 of Case V, in my opinion means the full amount of the "income arising from stocks, shares or rents in any place, out of the United Kingdom, i.e. the full amount of all the income having any of the origins mentioned.' *Diggines v Forestal Land, Timber & Rlys Co* [1931] AC 380 at 394, per Lord Tomlin

FULL SALARY

'The next question is, what "full salary" means? The legacy [to the office and warehouse employees of the testator] is to be "six months' full salary"; and it is said that "full salary" means that it is to be free from duty. I do not take that view. I see no reason for saying that that is the meaning of the language used. . . . I think the expresson "full salary" refers to this: it is to be the full salary for six months—that is to say, it is to be calculated without any incidental deductions that might be made, either by the custom of trade, or owing to illness, or anything of that sort. It means that it is to be the salary for six months without deduction, but does not mean in any way to relieve the person who receives the legacy from the incidental charges that the law casts upon it—namely the payment of duty.' *Re Marcus, Marcus v Marcus* (1887) 56 LJ Ch 830 at 838, per North J

FUMES

'Fume' includes gas or vapour. (Factories Act 1961, s 176)

'Fumes' means any airborne solid matter smaller than dust. (Clean Air Act 1968, s 13(1))

FUNCTUS OFFICIO

Canada [Issue arose as to whether after making a provisional tax assessment for 1975 a Minister was *functus officio* and thus unable subsequently to reassess the taxpayer for the same year.] 'I . . . wish to comment on the use of the term *functus officio* in the following portion of the judgment of Macfarlane J in *Herman Sawmill* [*Re Herman Sawmill Ltd and Minister of Finance* (1972) 24 DLR (3d) 476] (see 483): "It was further contended by the appellant that the Minister, having exercised his discretion when the original assessments were made, *and there being no new relevant facts brought to his attention with respect to the matter* that he was *functus officio* and could not re-exercise his discretion: see *Clarke v MNR* (1952) 7 Tax ABC 137 at 152. In my opinion *there were no grounds upon which the Minister could properly re-exercise his discretion* in regard to the granting of capital cost allowance in this case." [The italics are mine.] I think it is inappropriate to use the term *functus officio* in that context. To me the term means that the person who decides something is precluded from again considering the matter even if new evidence or arguments are presented to him. An example would be a judge who reaches

retirement age and cannot thereafter consider a decision made before retirement.' *MacMillan Bloedel Ltd v Minister of Finance* (1985), 60 BCLR 145 at 162–163 (British Columbia Court of Appeal) per Taggart JA

FUND   *See also* FUNDED DEBT

'I think the words "the Funds" must be taken to mean the same as the "Government Funds" or "Public Funds". There is no other interpretation which can be put upon the term that would not let in every species of property that the imagination might suggest. . . . Originally we know, as matter of history, that particular funds were appropriated to particular debts, but afterwards they were all consolidated together, and made one fund; and the term "the Funds" has ever since, for a century at least, been taken to mean that portion of the public debt which is payable out of the Consolidated Fund.' *Slingsby v Grainger* (1859) 7 HL Cas 273 at 280, per Lord Cranworth

'The word "fund" may mean actual cash resources of a particular kind (e.g. money in a drawer or a bank), or it may be a mere accountancy expression used to describe a particular category which a person uses in making up his accounts.' *Allchin v Coulthard* [1942] 2 KB 228 at 234, CA, per Lord Greene MR; affd [1943] AC 607, HL

FUNDAMENTAL

'There was much discussion during the argument on the phrases "fundamental breach" and "breach of a fundamental term", and I think that it is true that in some of the cases these terms have been used interchangeably; but in fact they are quite different. I believe that all of your lordships are agreed and, indeed, it has not seriously been disputed before us that there is no magic in the words "fundamental breach"; this expression is no more than a convenient shorthand expression for saying that a particular breach or breaches of contract by one party is or are such as to go to the root of the contract which entitles the other party to treat such breach or breaches as a repudiation of the whole contract. Whether such breach or breaches do constitute a fundamental breach depends on the construction of the contract and on all the facts and circumstances of the case. The innocent party may accept that breach or those breaches as a repudiation and treat the whole contract at an end and sue for damages generally, or he may at his option prefer to affirm the contract and treat it as continuing on foot, in which case he can sue only for damages for breach or breaches of the particular stipulation or stipulations in the contract which has or have been broken. But the expression "fundamental term" has a different meaning. A fundamental term of a contract is a stipulation which the parties have agreed either expressly or by necessary implication or which the general law regards as a condition which goes to the root of the contract so that *any* breach of that term may at once and without further reference to the facts and circumstances be regarded by the innocent party as a fundamental breach and thus is conferred on him the alternative remedies at his option that I have just mentioned.' *Suisse Atlantique Société d'Armement Maritime SA v NV Rotterdamsche Kolen Centrale* [1966] 2 All ER 61 at 85, 86, HL, per Lord Upjohn

[As to 'fundamental breach' of contract, see *Photo Production Ltd v Securicor Transport Ltd* [1980] 1 All ER 556, and *George Mitchell (Chesterhall) Ltd v Finney Lock Seeds Ltd* [1983] 2 All ER 737 at 741, HL, per Lord Bridge

FUNDED DEBT   *See also* NATIONAL DEBT

'It has been rightly said that there is no definition in law of "funded debt", and I do not intend to attempt to give one which is in any way exhaustive; I merely intend to deal with the expression "funded debt" so far as is necessary for the purpose of this case. I did take the trouble to see what definitions were given for the general public in the best dictionaries and I found this definition of "fund" as a verb: "to provide a fund, hence to convert a floating debt into a more or less permanent debt at a fixed rate of interest". I also found the following definition of "funded": "That which has been made part of the permanent debt of the State with provision for regular payment of interest at a fixed rate". Of course, this definition overlooks the fact that it need not be a debt of the State at all; it may be a debt of a company as well as that of the State.' *A-G v South Wales Electrical Power Distribution Co* [1920] 1 KB 552 at 555, 556, CA, per Lord Sterndale MR

FUNGIBLE

United States 'Fungible' with respect to goods or securities means goods or securities of which any unit is, by nature or usage of trade, the equivalent of any other like unit. Goods which are not fungible shall be deemed fungible for the purposes of this Act to the extent that under a particular agreement or document unlike units are treated as equivalents. (Uniform Commercial Code 1978, s 1–201(17))

FURNISHED

Canada '"Furnished" means provided for use . . . and in such a position as will reasonably enable one to make use of what is furnished.' *Kime v Hamilton Radial Electric Rly Co* (1921) 50 OLR 113 at 116, Ont CA, per Riddell J

FURNITURE   *See also* EFFECTS

'Both MacKinnon and du Parcq LJJ [*Gray v Fidler* [1943] 2 All ER 289], took the view that the word "furniture" in the section there under review was to be construed as a common English word, and neither accepted the view that fixtures cannot be furniture. I borrow the language of MacKinnon LJ, in that case and found my judgment in this part of the case on it. What he said was this: "It is not denied, of course, that beds and wardrobes are pieces of 'furniture'; but it is said that, to be 'furniture' within the section, a bed or a wardrobe must be a movable article, whereas these beds and wardrobes, and most of the articles specified in Sch 2, are affixed by screws or other connections to the walls or floors of the building. And being so fixed, and not movable in their normal user (sic), they cannot be 'furniture' within the section. It was first said that 'furniture' must be 'movable', and the definition of the New Oxford English Dictionary was invoked. This is as follows: Movable articles in a dwellinghouse, place of business, or a public building (now the prevailing sense) dating from 1573. I cannot agree that to constitute furniture the articles notoriously within that description must be movable. It seems to me that it would be absurd to say that members of the Bar have the use of no furniture in this court, and that my brethren and I have the use of no furniture except the chairs on which we are now sitting. Of course, articles of furniture are usually movable, and the definition of the New Oxford English Dictionary is amply justified; but if a pedant had said to the late Dr Murray: 'Barristers in the law courts sit on very uncomfortable wooden seats with very inconvenient desks in front of them. Those seats and desks are fixed to the floor. Do you say those seats and desks are not furniture?' I feel sure he would have replied that he did not.

I, personally, have no doubt that it is no part of the proper definition of 'furniture', in its ordinary meaning, that it must consist of movable articles. The briefest mental survey of my own house recalls many things that are fixed to the wall—mirrors, a bracket-clock, corner cupboards, many book-shelves, a medicine cupboard—which everyone would describe as articles of furniture. In houses I knew in my earlier days there were many articles of Victorian mahogany which were certainly not movable (except by a powerful crane), and to screw them to floor or wall would have been a superfluity. But they were certainly 'furniture' though not movable by unaided human effort. A billiard table is only movable after it has been taken to pieces. . . . Then it was said that, because these articles are fixed to the walls or floor they pass to the tenant under the demise of the flat, and the tenant does not enjoy their use under a contract for the use of chattels. Most of us have had experience of taking furnished houses for a term. But I have never known such an agreement to specify separately payment for the demised house, and payment for the use of the furniture. Indeed, the section now under consideration obviously contemplates a single amount payable to the landlord, and the judge has to inquire how much, if any, of that single payment by way of 'rent' is for the use of 'furniture'. I think the word 'furniture' in this section is to be construed as a common English word, or, as Bankes LJ said in *Wilkes v Goodwin* [[1923] 2 KB 86], 'the popular meaning of the word'. For articles to be 'furniture' within that meaning I do not think it is essential that they shall be movable, and though, of course, articles of furniture are commonly movable, I do not think they pass out of the popular meaning of furniture because they are fixed by a nail or a screw to wall or floor, I think that the judge was right in treating these beds and wardrobes as articles which come within the ordinary and popular meaning of furniture. In strictness, perhaps, one should add 'the ordinary or popular meaning of furniture at the present day'. For no doubt the ambit of the word has changed. The closetstool of our ancestors is as obsolete as the triclinium: the round bath and its accompanying can of my undergraduate days is gone. No one would speak of their substitutes, the apparatus of the water closet, or the bath in the bathroom as furniture. But, that would not be because they are fixed to the floor or wall, but merely because they are not within the common or popular meaning of the word. A contrasted change may be that, whereas no one would include a fireplace within furniture, the electric fire which can stand anywhere, with a wire to a wall plug, probably would be called a piece of furniture. But there again that is not because it is movable, but because it is within the common or popular meaning." Du Parcq LJ gave a judgment which was to the same effect. Viscount Simon in *Palser v Grinling* [[1948] 1 All ER 1] in a speech with which the other lords of appeal agreed, did not accept the view expressed by the majority of the court in *Gray v Fidler* [supra] that for the purposes of the Rent Acts furniture must be given its ordinary, popular meaning, but I do not understand him to have disagreed with the judgments of MacKinnon and du Parcq LJJ as to that popular meaning; on the contrary he, I think, recognised (although not for the purpose of the section which he was considering) that fixtures might be furniture in the popular sense. In my judgment, ordinary English words such as "furniture", where found in the Purchase Tax Act 1963 [repealed]—which affects millions of Her Majesty's subjects and I know not how many tens of thousands of traders unfamiliar with legal language—ought to be given their popular meaning.' *F Austin (Leyton) Ltd v Comrs of Customs & Excise* [1968] 2 All ER 13 at 17, 18, per Stamp J

'In our opinion a clock, whether long case or bracket is an article of furniture in the ordinary sense of the word, and it matters not whether it is keeping good or bad time or no time at all, whether it is standing in the room in the testator's house which is in everyday use or stored in a locked room therein, or stored at a repository, or on loan to a museum.' *Re Crispin's Will Trusts, Arkwright v Thurley*, [1974] 3 All ER 772 at 775, CA, per cur.

See, generally, 27 Halsbury's Laws (4th edn) paras 622, 623.

In bequest

'By the word furniture, the defendant is not entitled to the marble slabs, or chimney-pieces, or any thing fixed to the freehold, in the house in the country, on the testator's own estate; and glasses in pannels are to be considered as part of the freehold, but not if they are screwed in; and there is a great difference between the heir and the devisee, or the executor and devisee, and a landlord and tenant. Books are not furniture; and the watch and gold-headed cane will not pass either as jewels or plate.' *Allen v Allen* (1729) Mos 112 at 113, per Lord King LC

'I am clearly of the opinion, that a library of books will not pass as furniture.' *Bridgman v*

Dove (1744) 3 Atk 201 at 202, per Lord Hardwicke LC

'The word household-furniture [in a bequest in a will] has as general a meaning as possible. It is incapable of a definition. It is capable only of a description. It comprises every thing that contributes to the use or convenience of the householder, or ornament of the house.' *Kelly v Powlet* (1763) Amb 605 at 610, 611 per Clarke MR

'The words are "I give and bequeath my household furniture . . . and all and singular . . . my household furniture and effects." . . . I think it is clear, that, by that description, nothing that was merely a personal ornament would pass, but only those articles which . . . were adapted for the use and ornament of the house.' *Tempest v Tempest* (1856) 2 K & J 635 at 644, per Page Wood V-C

'I dissent most emphatically from the proposition that where the owner of a leasehold house containing tenant's fixtures bequeaths the house to A and the furniture to B, that entitles B to remove the mantel-pieces, stoves, kitchen dressers and shelves, and articles of that kind. In my opinion, it is clear that whether you regard the ordinary use of language or the technicalities of the law relating to fixtures, such articles do not pass under the word "furniture". . . . It may be stated as a general rule that the word "furniture" will not pass tenant's fixtures.' *Finney v Grice* (1878) 10 Ch D 13 at 14, 15, per Jessel MR

'The testator says this "I desire that the furniture, goods and chattels be not sold during my wife's lifetime, but at her decease be divided among the executors". . . . I cannot entertain any doubt that the rule *ejusdem generis* applies to this particular case, and that nothing passes . . . beneficially to the executors, but the things which were actually in the house and were necessary for the use and comfort of the testator's wife in the enjoyment of the life interest which he gave her; . . . that it is literally confined to those things which, if the house had been put up to be let to a tenant as a furnished house, would have been passed over to that tenant in order that he might occupy the house.' *Manton v Tabois* (1885) 30 Ch D 92 at 97, 98, per Bacon V-C

'The first question I have to decide is, whether the library as a whole passes under the bequest to her of furniture. In my opinion it does not. There may be cases in which the word "furniture" ought to be held to include books, but in this case I find nothing in the surrounding circumstances, nor in the will itself, which leads me to come to that conclusion. It is admitted that prima facie the word "furniture" does not denote or include books, . . . and, in the absence of anything to enlarge the prima facie meaning of the word, I hold that the library does not pass to the legatee of the furniture.' *Re Zouche (Baroness) Dugdale v Zouche (Baroness)* [1919] 2 Ch 178 at 184, per Lawrence J

In Rent Acts

In this Part [Part IX] of this Act unless the context otherwise requires, 'furniture' includes fittings and other articles. (Rent Act 1977, s 128(1))

[The Increase of Rent and Mortgage Interest (Restrictions) Act 1920, s 12(2) (repealed), provided that the Act did not apply to a dwelling-house bona fide let at a rent which included payments in respect of the use of 'furniture'.] 'The subsection does not say "at a rent that includes 'the use of a piece of linoleum'", but "use of furniture"; and before it can be said that rent includes use of furniture there must be in the house something substantial in the way of furniture. Otherwise the Act would be reduced to an absurdity, and a frying-pan might be held to be furniture. There must be furniture—not a single piece of furniture, but a series of things which would justify the use of the word "furniture". A single chair or table or a piece of linoleum does not seem to me to satisfy the word "furniture" in the Act.' *Crane v Cox* (1923) 92 LJKB 544 at 545, DC, per Bailhache J

'In seeking where to draw the line between the fabric of the building and its furniture for the purposes of the section [the Rent and Mortgage Interest Restrictions Act 1923; s 10(1) (repealed)] it is difficult to suppose that the legislature intended to marshal as furniture objects—such as built-in wardrobes and cupboards—which, though performing the functions of conventional furniture, could only be detached at the cost of altering the design or arrangement of the building or of appreciable damage to it or themselves. Nor is it easy to think that "furniture" can include a fixture which on detachment becomes so altered as to lose the utility it previously possessed, as, for example, a table affixed to the wall and depending for support on a wall-bracket. On the other hand, however, it is no less difficult, having regard to the obvious intendment of the section, to suppose that the legislature in speaking of the "use of furniture" meant to recognise the law of real property to the extent of excluding from "furniture" each and every fixture whatever the nature and degree of its attachment. In my opinion the true view is that articles belonging to the landlord otherwise entitled to rank as "furniture" for the purposes of s 10 should, if affixed to the fabric, be regarded as part thereof if they cannot be detached without appreciable damage to or alteration of the fabric or themselves; otherwise they should be regarded as furniture.' *Palser v Grinling Property Holding Co Ltd v Mischeff* [1948] AC 291 at 313, 314, per Viscount Simon

FURTHER EDUCATION   *See*
EDUCATION

FURTHER EVIDENCE   *See* EVIDENCE

FURTHERANCE   *See* CONTEMPLATION OR
FURTHERANCE

FUTURE GOODS

'Future goods' means goods to be manufactured or acquired by the seller after the making of the contract of sale. (Sale of Goods Act 1979, s 6(1))

G

GAIN   *See also* ANNUAL PROFITS OR GAINS;
PROFIT

'Gain' is not limited to pecuniary gain or confined to commercial profits only, and a company is formed for the acquisition of gain which is formed to acquire something, as distinguished from a company formed for spending something. (7 Halsbury's Laws (4th edn) para 20)

For purposes of this Act 'gain' and 'loss' are to be construed as extending only to gain or loss in money or other property, but as extending to any such gain or loss whether temporary or permanent; and—
(i) 'gain' includes a gain by keeping what one has, as well as a gain by getting what one has not; and
(ii) 'loss' includes a loss by not getting what one might get, as well as a loss by parting with what one has.
(Theft Act 1968, s 34(2)(a))

'The 4th section [of the Companies Act 1862 (repealed; see now Companies Act 1985, s 716(1))] applies to companies or associations having for their object the acquisition of gain either by the company or association or the individual members thereof. Now, if you come to the meaning of the word "gain" it means acquisition. It has no other meaning that I am aware of. Gain is something obtained or acquired. It is not limited to pecuniary gain. We should have to add the word "pecuniary" so to limit it. . . . The word used, it must be observed,

is not "gains" but "gain" in the singular. Commercial profits, no doubt, are gain, but I cannot find anything limiting gain simply to a commercial profit.' *Re Arthur Average Assocn for British, Foreign & Colonial Ships, ex p Hargrove & Co* (1875) LR 10 Ch App 545 n at 546, 547 n per Jessel MR

Australia '"Gain" is not restricted to pecuniary or commercial profits, it includes other considerations of value obtained.' *Re Commonwealth Homes & Investment Co Ltd* [1943] SASR 211 at 228, per Mayo J

Australia '"Gain" was said by Simonds J to be a word that was "not susceptible of precise or scientific definition". He thought the test . . . was "whether that which is being done is what ordinary persons would describe as the carrying on of a business for gain" [*Armour v Liverpool Corporation* [1939] Ch 422 at 437]. The most appropriate definition to be found in a dictionary may be "increase in resources or business advantages resulting from business transactions or dealings".' *Re Riverton Sheep Dip* [1943] SASR 344 at 347, per Mayo J

Canada '"Gain" is "that which is acquired or comes as a benefit, profit, or advantage", and it may be derived indirectly as well as directly.' *R v James* (1903) 6 OLR 35 at 38, Ont CA, per Osler JA

New Zealand [The Law Reform Act 1936 (NZ), s 7 (repealed; see now the Deaths by Accident Compensation Act 1952, s 7(2)) provided that in assessing damages in any action under the principal Act (the Deaths by Accidents Compensation Act 1908) there should not be taken into account any 'gain', whether to the estate of the deceased or to any person for whose benefit the action was brought, that was consequent on the death of the deceased person.] 'I agree that the word "gain" must be given the same meaning as applied to both species of gain referred to in the section. But what is the meaning of the word? The section is speaking of damages and must therefore refer to financial gain. The words "any gain" mean no more than "any increase in financial resources". Giving the words that meaning it is clear that the section has specified two species of gain which are not to be taken into account in diminution of damages: (i) any gain or increase in financial resources to the estate of the deceased consequent on his death; and (ii) any gain or increase in financial resources to the person for whose benefit the action is brought—i.e. a dependant—consequent on the death. The word "gain" has the same meaning in each species of gain referred to, but the second species of gain is defined widely enough to include every kind of property which a dependant receives from the estate of the deceased person either under a will or upon his intestacy. . . . In assessing the damages no profit to the dependant in consequence of the death can be taken into account. That being so, all evidence as to such gain or profit is irrelevant to the inquiry, and therefore inadmissible, for only relevant evidence is admissible. . . . For the reasons given, the questions of law asked in the summons will be answered as follows: (i) Any capital or income received by the widow or children of the deceased is a gain consequent upon the deceased's death within the meaning of s 7 of the Law Reform Act 1936; and (ii) no evidence can be given at the trial of the acquisition of property under the will by the widow and children of the deceased in order to reduce the damages.' *Alley v Alfred Buckland & Sons Ltd* [1941] NZLR 575 at 584, 585, per Ostler J; also reported [1941] GLR 333 at 336

In law of distress

'He [the plaintiff] relies on 51 Hen 3 stat 4. I refer to it as 51 Hen 3, stat 4, although the date of the statute is uncertain [see *Chitty's Statutes*, vol 7, p 428]. . . . Although it relates primarily to the King's debts it contains words of apparently broader operation. As given into English by Chitty they are these: "Yet it is provided that no man of religion, nor other shall be distrained by his beasts, that gain his land". . . . I presume that the word "gain" is derived from the French "gagner" and that it may be applicable to beasts which either pull the plough, or, for example, draw a cart which is used for carrying corn from the harvestfield.' *McCreagh v Cox & Ford* (1923) 92 LJKB 855 at 856, 857, per McCardie J

'It is said that the five milking cows are within the rule of the ancient document, the alleged statute, as being animals "ke gaignent sa terre" or, in the translation in Ruffhead's edition of the Statutes of the Realm "beasts that gain his land". . . . As regards that I can express my view quite shortly. I think that, whatever originally may have been the meaning of animals "ke gaignent sa terre" the uniform decision of the Courts for a good many centuries has treated that as meaning "beasts of the plough". In the old days they were very likely bullocks as well as horses, but that, I think, is the real meaning of the phrase.' *Swaffer v Mulcahy, Hooker v Mulcahy, Smith v Mulcahy* [1934] 1 KB 608 at 633, 634, per MacKinnon J

Private gain

[Promoters of a lottery were convicted for applying the proceeds for 'private gain', contrary to s 4(1)(c) of the Small Lotteries and Gaming Act 1956 (repealed; see now s 41(5) of the Gaming Act 1968).] 'I am quite satisfied that . . . the repeated reference . . . to private gain in connexion with the promotion of lotteries is clearly a reference to private gain to the organisers of the lottery or those to whom they represent.' *Payne v Bradley* [1961] 2 All ER 36 at 40, per Lord Parker CJ; affd [1961] 2 All ER 882, HL

GAINS   *See* ANNUAL PROFITS OR GAINS

GALE

A free miner of coal or iron has the right to require a grant to himself of specified veins of coal or iron in a specified situation. The grant, as also the subject matter of the grant, is known as a 'gale'. No gale may be made of any enclosed land belonging to the Crown. (31 Halsbury's Laws (4th edn) para 848)

'The word "gale" is used in many senses, sometimes as the grant itself of a right to mine, sometimes as the licence conferred by the grant, and more frequently as the corporeal property affected by the grant, having a site and capable of being defined by metes and bounds. It is in this latter sense that I find it used in the two documents which I have to construe, in one of which . . . it is expressly made equivalent to "colliery".' *Great Western Forest of Dean Collieries Co Ltd v Trafalgar Colliery Co Ltd* (1887) 3 TLR 724 at 725, per Kekewich J

GAMBLING

New Zealand 'A man is not, it is true, ordinarily designated a "gambler" if he occasionally, or perhaps even habitually, plays during his hours of recreation at a game of chance for moderate or nominal stakes, but the fact that the stakes are moderate or nominal does not alter the nature of the game. In my opinion, where one of the elements of a particular game is the element of chance, and where that game is played for money or money's worth, playing at that game is "gambling" within the meaning of s 44 [of the Licensing Acts Amendment Act 1904 (repealed; see now s 248(1)(b) of the Sale of Liquor Act 1962)]. . . . It may be . . . that the use in the Act of 1904 of the word "gambling" excludes from the operation of the section the playing for money at a game which is purely a game of skill, . . . but it is, in my opinion, impossible to hold that the Legislature intended to limit the operation of s 44 to games of chance with stakes for a large amount, and to exclude games of chance where stakes for a small or nominal amount were played for.' *Fuller v Fouhy* (1905) 24 NZLR 753 at 756, 757, per Cooper J

GAME (Animals or birds) *See also* BIRD; POULTRY

There is no comprehensive statutory definition of the term game, but it has been variously defined for the purposes of particular Acts. Thus in the Game Act 1831, game is deemed to include hares, pheasants, partridges, grouse, heath or moor game and black game. This definition appears also in the Night Poaching Act 1828, but with the addition of bustards. The Poaching Prevention Act 1862, however, omits bustards and heath game and adds rabbits, woodcock, snipe, and the eggs of pheasants, partridges, grouse and black or moor game. In the Game Licences Act 1860, deer, as well as rabbits, woodcock and snipe, are added to the game in respect of which a licence to take or kill is required. . . . The term ground game was introduced by the Ground Game Act 1880, and

means hares and rabbits. (2 Halsbury's Laws (4th edn) para 211)

For the purposes of this section the word 'game' shall be deemed to include hares, pheasants, partridges, grouse, heath or moor game, black game, bustards, woodcocks and snipes. (Game Laws (Amendment) Act 1960, s 4(5))

'Game is of a character intermediate between that of animals which are domesticated and thus the subject of property, and that of animals which are wild and thus not the subject of property.' *Cattell v Ireson* (1858) EB & E 91 at 99, per Erle J

'I am of opinion that these pheasants, as long as they are under the care and protection of the hen which hatched them, are to be considered the "property" of the owner of the hen. Being his property they are not "game" within the meaning of this statute [Night Poaching Act 1828], for that term necessarily implies something which is not the subject of property.' *R v Garnham* (1861) 2 F & F 347 at 348, per Pollock CB

'There is a qualified or special right of property in game, that is in animals *ferae naturae* which are fit for the food of man.' *Blades v Higgs* (1865) 11 HL Cas 621 at 631, per Lord Westbury LC

'As to the authority I referred to—*Graham v Ewart* [(1855) 11 Exch 326],—I have had an opportunity of speaking to my Brother Martin about it; and I find, as I had supposed, that the expression "game" commonly so called, was not intended to limit it to what had in acts of parliament been from time to time called game; but to such things as are usually sported after,—excluding small birds and vermin which are beneath the notice of a sportsman.' *Jeffryes v Evans* (1865) 19 CBNS 246 at 266, per Willes J

'Partridges' eggs . . . are game within the meaning of the Poaching Prevention Act 1862.' *Stowe v Benstead* [1909] 2 KB 415 at 419, per Darling J

Trespass in pursuit of

'The respondent, standing in his own land, fires over the land of another person and kills a grouse sitting there. He does not do anything more at that moment and the act was not followed up immediately; but some little time after he does go on the land where he had killed the grouse. If he had gone under an impulse not connected with what he had previously done, that would have been one state of facts; but here he went under such circumstances as satisfied the magistrates that he went in search of what he had killed. That is sufficient to connect the two things together. It seems to me that, in so going upon the land in search of what he had killed, he was committing the offence in s 30 of the Game Act 1831; that is that he was "committing a trespass by entering or being upon the land in search or pursuit of game".' *Horn v Raine* (1898) 19 Cox CC 119 at 121, 122, DC, per Lord Russell CJ

GAME (Pastime)

'I think that an ordinary man, when talking of playing a game, is talking of something which involves entertainment, he is talking of something which involves excitement and fun in the common pursuit by a number of competitors of a similar and known object, and it seems to me exceedingly difficult to produce those elements which the common man would ascribe to a game if the participants are in separate places with no communication between them whilst the activity is going on, and thus no sort of opportunity of seeing how their competitors are progressing and, I would have thought, none of the excitement and entertainment which any true game can provide.' *Adcock v Wilson* [1967] 1 All ER 1028 at 1037, per Widgery J

GAME OF CHANCE

(1) In this Act . . . 'game of chance' does not include any athletic game or sport, but, with that exception, and subject to subsection (6) of this section, includes a game of chance and skill combined and a pretended game of chance or of chance and skill combined; . . .

(6) In determining for the purposes of this Act whether a game, which is played otherwise than against one or more other players, is a game of chance and skill combined, the possibility of superlative skill eliminating the element of chance shall be disregarded.
(Gaming Act 1968, s 52)

[Section 3 of the Vagrant Act Amendment Act 1873 (repealed; see now the Gaming Act 1968 s 52), extended the provisions of the Vagrancy Act 1824, by imposing a penalty on every person playing or betting, etc, with any table or instrument of gaming, or any coin, card, token or other article etc., at any 'game or pretended game of chance'.] 'I think that in order to commit an offence under this section a person must be found to have been playing or betting by way of wagering at some game or pretended game which is in itself a game of chance. I do not think it can be said that dog-racing, any more than

horse-racing, is a game of chance.' *Everett v Shand* [1931] 2 KB 522 at 534, per Humphreys J

GAMING   *See also* BET

It may be deduced from the early cases that gaming is playing a game, whether of chance or skill, for stakes hazarded by the players, but for the purposes of the Gaming Act 1968, it is defined as 'the playing of a game for winnings in money or money's worth, whether any person playing the game is at risk of losing any money or money's worth or not'. Gaming may take place by means of a machine, but a machine is not to be treated as being used for gaming when it is so used that a player, or a person claiming to be a player, cannot receive or be entitled to receive any article, benefit or advantage other than either (1) the opportunity afforded by the automatic action of the machine to play one or more further games without the insertion of any cash or token, or (2) the delivery by means of the machine of one or more coins or tokens where one or more coins or tokens of an equal or greater value or aggregate value were inserted in order to play that game. It would seem that there must be some form of active participation by a player for gaming to take place. (4 Halsbury's Laws (4th edn) para 2)

(1) In this Act . . . 'gaming' (subject to subsections (3) to (5) of this section) means the playing of a game of chance for winnings in money or money's worth, whether any person playing the game is at risk of losing any money or money's worth or not; . . .
(3) where apart from this subsection the playing of a game of chance would constitute gaming and also constitutes a lottery, then if—
  (a) in so far as it is a lottery, it is a lottery promoted as mentioned in section 3 (small lotteries incidental to certain entertainment, 4 (private lotteries), 5 (societies' lotteries) or 6 (local lotteries) of the Lotteries and Amusements Act 1976, and
  (b) each winner of a prize is ascertained by reference to not more than three determining factors, each of those factors being either the result of a draw or other determination or the outcome of an event,
  the playing of the game shall not constitute gaming for the purposes of this Act.
(4) In this Act 'gaming' does not include the making of bets by way of pool betting.
(5) For the purposes of this Act a machine shall be taken not to be used for gaming if it is

used in such a way that no game played by means of the machine can result in a player, or a person claiming under a player, receiving or being entitled to receive any article, benefit or advantage other than one (but not both) of the following, that is to say—

(a) an opportunity afforded by the automatic action of the machine to play one or more further games without the insertion of any cash or token;

(b) the delivery by means of the machine of one or more coins or tokens as a prize in respect of a game where one or more coins or tokens of an equal or greater value or aggregate value were inserted into the machine by or on behalf of the player in order to play that game.

(Gaming Act 1968, s 52 as amended by the Lotteries and Amusements Act 1976, s 25(2), Sch 4, para 6(2)).

Without prejudice to the following provisions of this section [requirement for gaming licenses], the games to which this section applies are baccarat, punto banco, big six, blackjack, boule, chemin de fer, chuck-a-luck, craps, crown and anchor, faro, faro bank, hazard, poker dice, pontoon, French roulette, American roulette, trente et quarante, vingt-et-un, and wheel of fortune. (Betting and Gaming Duties Act 1981, s 13(3)).

[The following provisions of the section enable other games to be added by order; games essentially similar to those mentioned above are included even if described by another name.]

'There were four men playing at ten-pins for a pint of beer each game, and the games went on till twenty or thirty had been played and twenty or thirty pints of beer had been lost and won. Each of the players had his share of the beer, but instead of each paying his portion of the price, they agreed by playing these games to determine who as losers should pay for those who won. This is simply gaming.' *Danford v Taylor* (1869) 20 LT 483 at 484, per Cockburn CJ

'The essence of gaming and wagering is that one party is to win and the other to lose upon a future event, which at the time of the contract is of an uncertain nature—that is to say, if the event turns out one way A will lose, but if it turns out the other way he will win.' *Thacker v Hardy* (1878) 4 QBD 685 at 695, CA, per Cotton LJ

'The question turns upon the construction of s 18 of the Gaming Act 1845, which says that "all contracts or agreements, whether by parole or in writing by way of gaming or wagering, shall be null and void". Now is this a contract "by way of gaming or wagering" within that section? Of course, it is an agreement simply to buy and sell stock . . . the statute has no application. But . . . if the real effect of this contract is to stipulate for the payment of differences, it is plainly a gambling transaction. . . . If you have an agreement which is a wagering agreement for differences, and superadded to that the purchaser has the option of purchasing the stock, that is none the less an agreement for gaming or wagering. It is a gaming transaction plus something else.' *Re Gieve* [1899] 1 QB 794 at 798–800, per Lord Lindley MR

'If the parties meant that no legal bargain should be effected between them, and that there should be no right to demand a payment of differences except a moral right, the contract is a gaming contract. But if the parties intended to enter into a legal contract, which gave legal rights and imposed legal obligations, then the contract though it deals with speculative transactions is enforceable.' *Barnett v Sanker* (1925) 41 TLR 660 at 661, 662, per McCardie J

[A competition, consisting of a series of puzzle pictures, was advertised in a newspaper. A money prize was offered to the reader sending in the best solution on the form provided, together with an entrance fee. The action was brought to test the legality of the competition.] 'The nature of the competition appears from studying the notice in the paper, which describes the way in which it is conducted, and in which the result is arrived at. . . . The way I approach the subject is this. I ask myself whether this is a competition success in which depends on the exercise of skill. The words are few, but very often a few words are pregnant with suggestion of what the interpretation of them is. . . . I am limiting myself to the question whether, if this competition were put forward as a competition initiated and conducted as has been detailed, the Court would not put to itself the question, and the only question which is material: Is this a competition which involves the exercise of skill on the part of those who attempt to solve it? In my view it is. . . . the solution does depend on the exercise of considerable skill, and in those circumstances I do not feel justified in saying that it is within the mischief of s 26, sub-s 1(a) and (b) of the Betting and Lotteries Act 1934 [repealed; see now s 14(1)(b) of the Lotteries and Amusements Act 1976, which makes it unlawful to conduct any competition success in which does not depend substantially upon the exercise of skill]. I have already said that, in my opinion, it is not a game within s 1 of the Betting Act 1853 [repealed], and it is a competition. Throughout, there has been a distinction made between game and competition, and I should therefore not be prepared to hold the word "game" as covering such a competition as this, in the absence of any authority to that effect.' *Witty v World Service Ltd* [1936] 1 Ch 303 at 307, 308, per Eve J

[The Betting and Gaming Act 1960, s 17(2)(b) (repealed; see now the Gaming Act 1968, s 34(2)), made it a condition that the stake hazarded in order to play a 'game' once on a gaming machine should not exceed sixpence (now 10p).] '"Game" is not defined in the Act of 1960 but "gaming" is defined in s 28 as meaning "the playing of a game of chance. . . ." I think that in ordinary language "gaming" is often used to denote gambling activities where there is no game in the ordinary sense. I do not read this definition as intended to restrict the ordinary meaning of gaming and I think that there are clear indications in the Act of 1960 that "game" is used in an unusually wide sense. For example, s 25 applies to "a game played by means of a machine" in accordance with conditions and the first condition begins "(a) the game is made playable by the insertion of a coin. . . ." So inserting the coin is not part of the game. One assumes that words are used in the same sense throughout an Act unless there is some indication of a contrary intention. So I assume that inserting coins is not part of the game referred to in s 17(2)(b). The game in this case must then consist solely in pulling the lever, and playing the game once must mean pulling the lever once.' *Rosenbaum v Burgoyne* [1964] 2 All ER 988 at 989, HL, per Lord Reid; also reported [1965] AC 430

'I am in entire agreement . . . that the introduction of the word "winnings" first in the Act of 1960 [Betting and Gaming Act 1960 (repealed)] and then in the Act of 1963 [Betting, Gaming and Lotteries Act 1963] has done nothing directly or by inference to alter the law as it previously existed, namely that "gaming" only takes place where there is the chance not only of winning but also of losing, in other words where some stake has been hazarded.' *McCollom v Wrightson* [1968] 1 All ER 514 at 516, 517, per Lord Hodson

Australia 'The transactions, no doubt, were speculative transactions. But were the contracts in question "by way of" gaming or wagering, which "means contracts 'for' gaming and wagering, and relates only to contracts which are of themselves contracts by way of gaming and wagering" (*Ellesmere (Earl) v Wallace* [[1929] 2

Ch 1 at 33 (and see 48, where the distinction is said to be subtle)]? In *Thacker v Hardy* [supra] Cotton LJ says: "The essence of gaming and wagering is that one party is to win and the other to lose upon a future event, which at the time of the contract is of an uncertain nature—that is to say, if the event turns out one way A will lose, but if it turns out the other way he will win". This definition was approved by Lord Herschell in *Forget v Ostigny* [[1895] AC 318 at 326]. . . . In considering questions of this kind one must ascertain the real nature of the transaction as to whether the contracts are genuine or are merely camouflaged contracts by way of gaming or wagering.' *Morley v Richardson* (1942) 65 CLR 512 at 517, per Rich J

New Zealand '"Gaming", in my opinion, in its ordinary grammatical sense can mean nothing but the playing of a game upon the result of which a stake depends, and it is just as much gaming if the game is a game of skill as if it is a game of chance. Not only so, but games of skill, such as the game of billiards undoubtedly is, are frequently made the means of determining gambling bets, just as much as if they were games of chance.' *Marshall v Creen* (1906) 26 NZLR 161 at 165, per Edwards J; also reported 9 GLR 95 at 96

GAMING AND WAGERING POLICY

'The . . . question arises whether these policies are insurances on some event wherein the assured has no interest, or insurances by way of gaming or wagering within the meaning of the Act of 1774 [Life Assurance Act 1774] and consequently illegal and void. In my opinion the fact that the policies contain the p p i ["policy proof of interest"] clause does not of itself prove that the assured has no insurable interest in the subject matter of the insurance, or that the policies are gaming or wagering policies. . . . In my judgment, however, the facts disclosed by the evidence here are such that it is impossible to hold that the assured had any insurable interest. In my opinion the description of the subject matter of the insurance, the existence of the p p i and f i a clause ["full interest admitted"] on all the policies, and the absence of any attempt on the part of the claimants to prove that the original assured had any insurable interest, lead to the irresistible inference that these policies were insurances by way of gaming or wagering, and I should require the clearest possible evidence to convince me to the contrary.' *Re London County Commercial Reinsurance Office* [1922] 2 Ch 67 at 79, 80, per Lawrence J

GAMING-HOUSE

Australia 'The statute [Gaming and Betting Act 1912–1986 (NSW)] must be taken, as it and similar legislation have always been taken, as importing the common law definition of a common gaming house. This may be best stated in the words which Street J, as he then was, used in *Eggins v Wilcox* [(1943) 60 WN (NSW) 215], 'At common law in order to constitute a common gaming house the premises must be kept for gaming in such a manner and under such circumstances as to constitute a public mischief, or a nuisance injurious to public morals, or in other words there must be some pernicious tendency in the keeping of those particular premises".' *Grigg v Bell* [1966] 2 NSWR 170, per Sugerman J

GAMING MACHINE

(1) This Part [Part III: gaming by means of machines] applies to any machine which—
   (a) is constructed or adapted for playing a game of chance by means of the machine, and
   (b) has a slot or other aperture for the insertion of money or money's worth in the form of cash or tokens.
(2) In the preceding subsection the reference to playing a game of chance by means of a machine includes playing a game of chance partly by means of a machine and partly by other means if (but only if) the element of chance in the game is provided by means of the machine.
(Gaming Act 1968, s 26).

[A] machine is a gaming machine for the purposes of this Act if it is of the following description—
(a) it is constructed or adapted for playing a game of chance by means of it;
(b) a player pays to play the machine (except where he has an opportunity to play without payment as the result of having previously played successfully), either by inserting a coin or token into the machine or in some other way; and
(c) the outcome of the game is determined by the chances inherent in the action of the machine, whether or not provision is made for manipulation of the machine by a player.
(Betting and Gaming Duties Act 1981, s 25(1))

[Subsection (2) of the above section defines (for the purposes of sub-s (1)) 'game of chance' (*q.v.*); sub-s (3) exempts certain types of machine; sub-s (4) (amended by the Finance Act 1982 ss 8, 157, Sch 6, Pt V, para 13, Sch 22, Pt III makes provisions regarding machines which two or more persons can play simultaneously.]

'Gaming machine' means a machine in respect of which the following conditions are satisfied, namely—
(a) it is constructed or adapted for playing a game of chance by means of it; and
(b) a player pays to play the machine (except where he has an opportunity to play payment-free as a result of having previously played successfully), either by inserting a coin or token into the machine or in some other way; and
(c) the element of chance in the game is provided by the machine.
(Value Added Tax Act 1983, s 13(4)).

GANGWAY

'There is no definition of "gangway" in the Factories Act 1937 [repealed; see now the Factories Act 1961], and I know not whether the first syllable of the word is of German or Scottish origin, but it seems to me that "gangway" must mean a way over which one goes, and I think that a plank placed across a duct for the purpose of people crossing it is a "gangway" within the meaning of s 25(1) of the Act [see now s 28(1) of the Act of 1961].' *Hosking v De Havilland Aircraft Co Ltd* [1949] 1 All ER 540 at 541, 542, per Lewis J

'The regulations [Building (Safety, Health and Welfare) Regulations 1948 (revoked; see now the Construction (Working Places) Regulations 1966, SI 1966/94 (as amended by SI 1984/1593)] contain no separate definition of "working platform" or "gangway". In the absence of any definition, I think that the question whether part of a building constitutes a working platform or a gangway must be decided as a matter of common sense. It seems to me that there is more to be said for this gutter amounting to a gangway than a working platform. The word "gangway" suggests a place where men may pass and re-pass in the course of their work, whereas a working platform suggests something more static.' *Curran v William Neill & Son (St Helens) Ltd* [1961] 3 All ER 108 at 116, CA, per Willmer LJ

GARAGE

'Now what is a garage? No evidence was given to suggest or prove that the word "garage" in the trade had got any special meaning, and it was agreed to take the four dictionary definitions set out in the agreed statement of facts. The four definitions were these. From the Shorter Oxford Dictionary: "A building for the storage or refitting of motor vehicles". From the New Century Dictionary: "A building for sheltering, cleaning or repairing motor vehicles. To put or keep in a garage". From the New Standard Dictionary: "A building for stabling or storing of motor vehicles of all kinds". From Nuttal's Standard Dictionary: "A storehouse for motor vehicles". Those are four definitions from leading dictionaries all containing at any rate one word in common, and that is "building". As there is no evidence as to how the general public understand the word "garage" I suppose one is entitled to use one's own knowledge. I am inclined to think that the ordinary man in the street does not regard a garage as connoting some sort of a building; how far he would go I do not know. I do not know whether he would think that there should be a wall all round it, or whether it would be sufficient if there were three sides walled in and a roof. I have one in mind where there is a row of sheds without any protection in front, which are commonly spoken of as "garages", but I am going to apply here the test suggested by counsel for the insured. He said "A garage is a place where one can get reasonable protection and shelter for a car". Can I say that you are getting reasonable protection and shelter for a car, if there is nothing to protect the car from above—if there is no roof of any sort? I think the ordinary man, as counsel for the insurers suggested, who took a house with a garage, if he came and found merely an open shed without any roof, would think he had been swindled, however high the walls might be. I cannot think that one is entitled to say that it is adequate or reasonable protection or shelter if there is no roof; but this is worse than that, though I agree that the walls are very good here. Wherever you put a car in this yard, in addition to there being no shelter from above, there will be no shelter on two sides. That seems to me to be really conclusive.' *Barnett & Block v National Parcels Insurance Co Ltd* [1942] 1 All ER 221 at 223, CA, per Atkinson J

GARDEN *See also* ALLOTMENT (GARDEN); MARKET GARDEN

'I am not of opinion that the word "gardens" [in an endowment] would of itself carry garden-stuff, or things originally grown in gardens, if grown elsewhere.' *Williams v Price* (1817) 4 Price 156 at 159, per Richards CB

[The Telegraph Act 1863, s 21 (repealed) permitted the placing of a telegraph across any land not being a 'garden'.] 'The gardens are raised or roof-gardens made on buildings already erected. Are these "gardens" within the meaning of s 21? The original company are empowered to place and maintain their telegraphs over any building or land, not being a garden or pleasure-ground. The exception is only made in respect of *land* when it is a garden or pleasure-ground. It is not made in respect of buildings. Therefore, a garden existing on the roof of a building is not, I think, within the section.' *Stevens v National Telephone Co Ltd, Lee (Edward) & Co Ltd v National Telephone Co Ltd* [1914] 1 IR 9 at 15, per Ross J

'My Lords, in my opinion, far the most distinctive quality which differentiates a garden within the rule [r 8 of the Income Tax Act 1918, Sch B (repealed; see now s 53(1) of the Income and Corporation Taxes Act 1988] from a farm taxable under r 1 [of Sch B] is the mode of cultivation employed. It is the character and nature of the operations on the land which mainly determine whether or not it is a garden for the sale of produce. I agree with Scott LJ, that the distinction between farm and "garden" may be expressed in general words as the difference between lands cultivated by agricultural methods and lands on which horticultural methods are employed. Produce which requires the attention of skilled men would generally be found grown in a garden. The use of the plough in such a place would be something of a rarity. The soil in the garden would usually be prepared by the employment of the homely spade and the tiresome operation of trenching and digging in manure. At any rate, I am confident that that was the case when the words "gardens for the sale of the produce" were employed in the early Acts relating to income tax. Certainly, hand-labour would usually be employed, and it would be very unusual to find (as in this case) that the land was for the most part both machine-planted and machine-hoed. It is not altogether irrelevant to note that in the census returns gardeners and nurserymen and "gardeners' labourers" are enumerated separately from "agricultural labourers". The greater care employed in raising vegetables in a market-garden generally results in better shape and quality in the produce. Peas and beans, as I have pointed out, may be grown both on farms and gardens, but they will not usually have quite the same taste and quality.' *Bomford v Osborne* [1941] 2 All ER 426 at 437, 438, per Lord Maugham

'It does not follow that, because certain produce is grown in gardens, any land on which it is grown is necessarily a garden. The word "garden" is not used in r 8 in a technical sense. It is an ordinary word, to be understood as in ordinary popular usage. However, whatever else may be included in the word "gardens" in the rule, I think that it cannot be wholly divorced from its root idea of a substantially homogeneous area, substantially devoted to the growth of fruits, flowers and vegetables. The dictionary definitions of "garden" include the idea of its being an enclosed space. Thus. for instance, in the Oxford Dictionary, "garden" is defined as: "An enclosed piece of ground devoted to the cultivation of flowers, fruit, or vegetables; often preceded by some defining word, as flower, fruit kitchen, market, strawberry garden, etc." I do not say that in modern times gardening operations falling within r 8 may not be carried on in open fields, but the essential characteristic of the statutory "garden" and the idea material to this case is that it should be, within reasonable limits, a defined unit of cultivation in relation to space. That is not inconsistent with the inclusion in the unit of some lands used at some particular time for other purposes. This is necessary for rotation of crops, but it must be possible to predicate a substantial and relatively permanent unity of character and purpose.' Ibid at 442, 443, per Lord Wright

'Counsel for the tenant says that you can have a formal cultivated garden and a wild garden, and no doubt it is true that some people do have such a corner, or part, in their pleasure garden. But when you have, as here, a cultivated garden and a piece of rough pasture ground separated from one another, and apparently marked as separate in the lease plan, I do not think it is possible to regard that rough pasture (the paddock) as being garden.' *Methuen-Campbell v Walters* [1979] 1 All ER 606 at 616, CA, per Goff LJ

New Zealand 'The word "garden" was defined by Collins J in *Cooper v Pearse* [[1896] 1 QB 562] as "a plot of ground on which fruit, vegetables, and flowers are grown for food or pleasure". In that case, a piece of land in the occupation of a seedsman for the purposes of his business and chiefly planted with trade bulbs was held not to be a garden. . . . So, too, in *R v Hodges* [(1829) Moo & M 341], upon a direction by Parke J a piece of ground chiefly used for growing grafted seedling pear trees for sale was held by a jury, as a question of fact, not a "garden". It would appear that the ordinary meaning of "garden" would not include an enclosure or paddock used

as a horse-paddock, or a cow-paddock, nor an area used as a pig-run or a fowl-run. These instances are adverted to for the purpose of illustrating that the use of the word "garden" would, probably, not of itself include all land which might ordinarily be found used in conjunction with an ordinary dwelling, not producing anything for sale or business purposes.' *Dalzell v Smith* [1946] NZLR 421 at 427, 428, 429, per Fair J; also reported [1946] GLR 187 at 189

GARDENING

'Gardening' includes destroying weeds in drives, paths and courtyards. (Farm and Garden Chemicals Act 1967, s 5)

GARNISHEE PROCEEDINGS *See also* ATTACHMENT

Garnishee proceedings are a process of enforcing a money judgment by the seizure or attachment of the debts due or accruing due to the judgment debtor which form part of his property available in execution. It is thus a species of execution upon debts, for which the ordinary methods of execution are inapplicable. By this process the court has power to order a third person to pay direct to the judgment creditor the debt due or accruing due from him to the judgment debtor, or as much of it as may be sufficient to satisfy the amount of the judgment and the costs of the garnishee proceedings. For this purpose the third person who is indebted to the judgment debtor is called the garnishee, the requisite proceedings are known as garnishee proceedings, and the order to attach the debt due or accruing due from the garnishee is called a garnishee order. Garnishee proceedings are taken in the action in which the judgment or order for the payment of money is given or made, and may be regarded as part of the proceedings in that action or as being themselves independent proceedings. (17 Halsbury's Laws (4th edn) para 525)

[By Order 26, r 1, of the County Court Rules 1903 (now Ord 30, rr 1, 4 of the County Court Rules 1981), 'Any person who has obtained a judgment or order for the recovery or payment of money may, . . . upon lodging with the registrar of the Court . . . an affidavit by himself or his solicitor stating that judgment has been recovered or an order made, and that it is still unsatisfied, and to what amount, and that any other person (hereinafter called the garnishee) is indebted to such debtor, . . . enter a plaint to obtain payment to him of the amount of the debt due to the said debtor from the garnishee'.] 'We have to construe the terms of Order 26, r 1, of the County Court Rules. . . . I think that garnishee proceedings are a species of execution, and that a judgment creditor ought not to be allowed to take out a garnishee summons, or get an order thereon, under Order 26, r 1, if the state of things is such that he cannot issue execution against the judgment debtor's chattels.' *White, Son & Pill v Stennings* [1911] 2 KB 418 at 426, 427, CA, per Vaughan Williams LJ

'The word "garnishee" is derived from the Norman-French. It denotes one who is required to "garnish", that is, to furnish, a creditor with the money to pay off a debt. A simple instance will suffice. A creditor is owed £100 by a debtor. The debtor does not pay. The creditor gets judgment against him for the £100. Still the debtor does not pay. The creditor then discovers that the debtor is a customer of a bank and has £150, at his bank. The creditor can get a "garnishee" order against the bank by which the bank is required to pay into court or direct to the creditor, out of its customer's £150, the £100 which he owes to the creditor. These are two steps in the process. The first is a garnishee order *nisi. Nisi* is Norman-French. It means "unless". It is an order on the bank to pay the £100 to the judgment creditor or into court within a stated time *unless* there is some sufficient reason why the bank should not do so. Such reason may exist if the bank disputes its indebtedness to the customer for one reason or other. Or if payment to this creditor might be unfair by preferring him to other creditors. . . . If no sufficient reason appears, the garnishee order is made *absolute*, to pay to the judgment creditor, or into court, whichever is the more appropriate. On making the payment, the bank gets a good discharge from its indebtedness to its own customer, just as if he himself directed the bank to pay it. If it is a deposit on seven days' notice, the order *nisi* operates as the notice. As soon as the garnishee order *nisi* is served on the bank, it operates as an injunction. It prevents the bank from paying the money to its customer until the garnishee order is made absolute, or is discharged, as the case may be. It binds the debt in the hands of the garnishee, that is, creates a charge in favour of the judgment creditor. . . . The money at the bank is then said to be "attached", again derived from Norman-French. But the attachment is not an order to pay. It only freezes the sum in the hands of the bank until the order is made absolute or is discharged. It is only when the order is made absolute that the bank is liable to pay.' *Choice Investments Ltd v Jeromnimon (Midland Bank Ltd garnishee)* [1981] 1 All ER 225 at 328, 329, CA, per Lord Denning MR

GAS

'Gas' includes fume or vapour. (Mines and Quarries Act 1954, s 182)

[A fire insurance policy contained the exception 'neither will the Company be responsible for loss or damage by explosion except for such loss or damage as shall arise from explosion by gas'. The premises of the plaintiff caught fire through the explosion of a vapour evolved in the course of his business of extracting oil from shoddy.] 'The words of the policy are to be construed not according to their strictly philosophical or scientific meaning, but in their ordinary and popular sense. Now in the ordinary language, not only of men of business and the owners of property (the subject of insurance) but even of scientific men themselves, the explosion in the present case would not be said to have been caused by gas. It was not, therefore, within the saving to the exception, which, indeed, was obviously intended by the parties only to refer to gas in the more limited sense of ordinary illuminating gas.' *Stanley v Western Insurance Co* (1868) LR 3 Exch 71 at 73, per Kelly CB

Australia [The issue was whether the word 'gas' in s 418 of the Local Government Act 1919–1986 (NSW) included liquefied petroleum gas or was confined to coal gas.] 'The Act here speaks of "gas", not of coal gas. In my opinion, it thus selects the genus, and not any particular species of gas. I can see no reason why, whilst the connotation of the word "gas" will be fixed, its denotation cannot change with changing technologies.' *Lake Macquarie Shire Council v Aberdare Shire Council* [1971] ALR 362 at 364, per Barwick CJ

GAS FITTINGS *See* FITTINGS

GASOLINE RETAILER

United States The term 'gasoline retailer' means any person who markets automotive gasoline to the general public for ultimate consumption. (Petroleum Marketing Practices Act 1978, s 201(4))

GASWORKS

'Gasworks' means works for the manufacture of gas and gas holders, and any works used in connection with such works or holders. (Gas Act 1972, s 48(1))

GAVELKIND

'Gavelkind' was not, properly speaking, the name of a tenure, but it denoted certain special customs which affected lands of socage tenure in Kent and elsewhere. The chief of these customs related to descent. On the death of the owner intestate, primogeniture was excluded, and there was equal division of descendible estates among all the sons or other male heirs. Other customs existing up to 1st January 1926 were: (1) tenancy by the curtesy was in one-half the land, did not depend on birth of heritable issue, and ceased on remarriage; (2) dower was in one-half the land and continued while the widow remained chaste and unmarried; and (3) an infant could alienate his land by feoffment after attaining fifteen years, but it was necessary to show that he received full consideration, and he had to make the foeffment in person. (139 Halsbury's Laws (4th edn) para 322)

GAZETTE

'Gazette' shall include the London Gazette, the Edinburgh Gazette, and the Dublin Gazette, or any of such Gazettes. (Documentary Evidence Act 1868, s 5)

GENDER AND NUMBER

In any Act, unless the contrary intention appears—
(a) words importing the masculine gender include the feminine;
(b) words importing the feminine gender include the masculine;
(c) words in the singular include the plural and words in the plural include the singular.
(Interpretation Act 1978, s 6)

GENERAL AVERAGE   *See* AVERAGE

GENERAL DAMAGES   *See* DAMAGES

GENERAL INTANGIBLES

Secured transactions

United States 'General intangibles' means any personal property (including things in action) other than goods, accounts, chattel paper documents, instruments, and money. (Uniform Commercial Code 1978, s 9–106)

GENERAL MEDICAL COUNCIL

(1) There shall continue to be a body corporate known as the General Medical Council . . . having the functions assigned to them by this Act.
(2) The General Council shall be constituted as provided by Her Majesty by Order in Council under this section subject to the provisions of Part I of Schedule I to this Act.
(Medical Act 1983, s 1(1), (2))

[Part I of Schedule I to the Act provides for elected members, appointed members (to be chosen by universities and certain other bodies) and nominated members (to be nominated by the Queen with the advice of her Privy Council)]

GENERAL MEDICAL PRACTITIONER   *See* MEDICAL PRACTITIONER

GENERAL STRIKE   *See* STRIKE

GENERATE

[The respondents were under contract to establish an electric light station in Bulawayo and to provide street and other lighting. In consideration thereof the appellants were, by the same contract, bound to pay at such rates as would yield to the contractors a return equal to 10 per cent over the actual cost of 'generating' the light.] 'What is the meaning of the expression "generating the light"? . . . Their Lordships agree with the Chief Justice in thinking that "the term 'generating the light' was intended to include not only the generation of the current, but also the transmission of the current to the points where the light is finally evolved". The language is certainly not altogether accurate, but their Lordships are satisfied that this compendious expression was intended to cover the whole process—the whole series of operations—leading up to the production of the light in the street lamps.' *Bulawayo Municipality v Bulawayo Waterworks Co Ltd* [1908] AC 241 at 246, per cur.

GENERATING STATION

The expression 'generating station' means any station for generating electricity, including any buildings and plant used for the purpose, and the site thereof, and a site intended to be used for a generating station, but does not include any station for transforming, converting, or distributing electricity:

The expression 'railway generating station' means a station for generating electricity for use solely or mainly by a railway company for the purposes of their undertaking. (Electricity (Supply) Act 1919, s 36)

GENOCIDE

In the present Convention, genocide means any of the following acts committed with intent to destroy, in whole or in part, a national, ethnical, racial or religious group, as such:
(a) Killing members of the group;
(b) Causing serious bodily or mental harm to members of the group;
(c) Deliberately inflicting on the group conditions of life calculated to bring about its physical destruction in whole or in part;
(d) Imposing measures intended to prevent births within the group;
(e) Forcibly transferring children of the group to another group.
(Genocide Act 1969, Sch).

[The Convention referred to, Article II of which is set out in the above Schedule, is the Convention on the Prevention and Punishment of the Crime of Genocide approved by the General Assembly of the United Nations on 9 December 1948]

GENTLEMAN   *See also* ESQUIRE

'It appears that, by the will of Mr Hunstone, he directed his charity to be for the benefit of such decayed gentlemen as can make it appear unto his trustees that they are of his name and family, and of the age of forty years; or else so impotent as not to be otherwise able to get a living. . . . The word "gentlemen" . . . is a word of somewhat vague meaning; and it will be well therefore, to give some more accurate description of it; at all events enumerating some classes, so as to make the objects of the charity more definite, and the duties of the trustees

more easy in future. . . . The Master . . . will . . . consider how to define the word "gentleman" more clearly—as, for instance, by stating that magistrates, esquires, members of the three learned professions, graduates of the universities, attornies, surgeons, apothecaries, and the like shall be considered, if otherwise eligible, objects of this charity.' *A-G v Holland* (1837) 2 Y & C Ex 683 at 704–707, per Alderson B

'I am not disposed to extend the use of the term "gentleman", which is a vague one, and gives no information; but I cannot suggest . . . any better description of the attesting witness in this case. It has been suggested that he should have been described as of no occupation, but that would not assist any person in identifying him any more than the term "gentleman". . . . He had no definite occupation; he had drawn bills of sales, written letters, and collected debts, but only on rare occasions. He was living on an allowance from his mother, and ready to do any job to eke it out. I do not see how any other description than "gentleman" would have assisted more to identify him.' *Smith v Cheese* (1875) 1 CPD 60 at 61, 62, per Grove J

'He was, and I suppose is, a grocer, spirit dealer, and draper; and without at all saying or thinking that a person so occupied may not be in the fullest sense of the word a gentleman, I am unable to hold that the latter designation is a correct statement of his title, trade, or profession, within the meaning of the Act [an Irish Act]. I should draw no distinction between "gentleman" and "esquire" for this purpose. I should simply hold that where a man has no title (of honour or otherwise), but has a trade or profession, it is not sufficient, under the statute, to call him merely a gentleman. It is quite different where he has no trade or profession. There it is hard to see how he can be described otherwise than as a gentleman or esquire—no one has suggested that "human being" would be a proper description. For the purposes of the Act, I should put upon the words "gentleman" or "esquire" the very loosest and most popular meaning, and entirely decline to go to Selden or Coke for their definition.' *Spaddacini v Treacy* (1889) LR 21 Ir 553 at 559, per Porter MR

GENUINE

United States   'Genuine' means free of forgery or counterfeiting. (Uniform Commercial Code 1978, s 1–201(18))

GEOGRAPHICAL NAME

[By the Patents, Designs and Trade Marks Act 1883, s 64(1)(e) (repealed; see now Trade Marks Act 1938, s 9(1)(d)) a word, to be registered as a trade mark, must inter alia not be a 'geographical name'.] 'Mr Neville [counsel] . . . says geography means in the first instance and properly a description of the divisions of the earth. That is so accepted. Then he says that means continents, countries, towns, villages, and so forth, and not a spring such as this, with the establishment for the supply of water which may be changed at the will of the owner to-morrow and be named something quite different. If it were changed, there might be something to be said; but when for forty years a place has had a particular name, though at the will of the owners, and has found its way into common parlance, and I doubt not, though it has not been proved, into the maps and guide-books, and other places where one looks for distinctive names, it is part of the geography of the country, and it has passed for the moment into that geography . . .' *Re Apollinaris Co's Trade Marks* [1891] 2 Ch 186 at 203, 204, CA, per Kekewich J

'The object of the legislature was to prevent a trader from acquiring a monopoly in the name of a place, and from thereby suggesting that the goods had a local origin or a local connection.' *Re Sir Titus Salt Sons & Co's Application* [1894] 3 Ch 166 at 169, per Chitty J

'A word does not become a geographical name simply because some place upon the earth's surface has been called by it.' *Re Magnolia Metal Co's Trade Marks* [1897] 2 Ch 371 at 392, 393, CA, per cur.

GIFT   *See also* CHARITY—CHARITABLE
PURPOSES; DONATIO MORTIS CAUSA

In this Part of this Act the expression 'gift' includes devise, bequest, appointment, conveyance, assignment, transfer and any other assurance of property. (Historic Buildings and Ancient Monuments Act 1953, s 9)

In this Chapter [Chapter III of Part II: exempt transfers] 'gift', in relation to any transfer of value, means the benefit of any disposition or rule of law by which, on the making of the transfer, any property becomes (or would but for any abatement become) the property of any person or applicable for any purpose; 'given' shall be construed accordingly; 'specific gift' means any gift other than a gift of residue or of a share in residue. (Inheritance Tax Act 1984, s 42(1))

'A gift at law, or in equity, supposes some act to pass the property: in donations inter vivos . . . if the subject is capable of delivery, delivery; if a chose in action, a release, or equivalent instrument; in either case, a transfer of the property, is required.—An intention to give, is not a gift.' *Hooper v Goodwin* (1818) 1 Swan 485 at 491, per Plumer MR

'By the law of England, in order to transfer property by gift there must either be a deed or instrument of gift, or there must be an actual delivery of the thing to the donee.' *Irons v Smallpiece* (1819) 2 B & Ald 551 at 552, per Abbott CJ

'In order to make a valid gift, there must be perfect knowledge in the mind of the person making the gift of the extent of the beneficial interest intended to be conferred, and of which it is intended to divest oneself in making it.' *Howard v Fingall* (1853) 22 LTOS 12 at 13, per Stuart V-C

'In order to perfect a gift to a volunteer the thing purported to be given must be so completely disposed of as to be no longer within the control of the donor.' *Roberts v Roberts* (1865) 13 LT 492 at 493, per Stuart V-C

'I have come to the conclusion that in ordinary English language, and in legal effect, there cannot be a "gift" without a giving and taking. The giving and taking are the two contemporaneous reciprocal acts which constitute a "gift". They are a necessary part of the proposition that there has been a "gift". They are not evidence to prove that there has been a gift, but facts to be proved to constitute the proposition that there has been a gift.' *Cochrane v Moore* (1890) 25 QBD 57 at 76, CA, per Lord Esher MR

'The difference between a gift to named individuals, and a gift to a class, in reference to lapse, is firmly established. A gift by will to a class is taken, in law and in equity, to be a gift, where it is immediate, to those only who survive the testator; and, where it is not immediate but postponed, to be a gift to those only who survive the testator, or come into being before the period of distribution.' *Re Harvey's Estate, Harvey v Gillow* [1893] 1 Ch 567 at 570, per Chitty J

'My understanding of the matter is . . . that a gift made in consideration of marriage is a transfer made on the occasion of marriage, contingently on the marriage taking place, and containing such limitations, if made by way of settlement, as amount to the customary provision for the spouses and the issue of the marriage. No doubt a settlement that contained ultimate trusts for other persons to take effect subject to the interests of the family, if they failed, would be within the category: so, I should suppose, would be one in which a man bringing property into settlement reserves a limited power to withdraw a proportion of it to provide for issue of a later marriage. But I do not think that the words are satisfied unless the terms of the settlement are such that they unequivocally secure provision for the spouses and their issue and by so doing declare that the marriage is the consideration on which the transfer is to be rested.' *Inland Revenue Comrs v Rennell (Lord)* [1963] 1 All ER 803 at 809, HL, per Viscount Radcliffe; also reported in [1964] AC 173 at 196

Australia [Section 78(1)(a) of the Income Tax Assessment Act 1936–1986 provides that certain 'gifts' made by the taxpayer to a public benevolent institution shall be allowable deductions] 'The ordinary notion of gift and "gift" in its technical meaning have common features: a transfer of a beneficial interest in property by way of benefaction, and an absence of a pecuniary or proprietary benefit passing to the transferor by way of return. But the relevant circumstances in which these indicia may be found are more narrowly confined when the enquiry is as to a gift in the technical sense than when the enquiry is as to a gift according to ordinary notions. The former enquiry is narrower in scope, for it is more confined in its purpose. Its purpose is to ascertain whether a beneficial interest in property has been transferred by a mode which falls within the classification of gift. The intention of the transferor and transferee as to the ownership of the beneficial interest and the form of its transfer exhaust the matters for investigation as to the divesting and investing of the interest, and the absence of consideration passing from the transferee to the transferor serves to distinguish a gift from other modes of transferring property. But an enquiry into the making of a gift according to ordinary notions requires reference to wider circumstances. In the first place, it is relevant to enquire as to the return (if any) which a disponor seeks and receives by disposing of the relevant property. The ordinary notions of a gift do not pay much regard to the difference between a return to a disponor which he receives as consideration under a contract and a return which is furnished under some other

arrangement or understanding; nor is it of great importance that the return does not come directly from a disponee, but indirectly. It will always be of significance that a disponor has received from a disponee, either directly or indirectly, the return sought for making the disposition. Secondly, it is relevant to enquire whether the disponee is, to the knowledge of the disponor, free to enjoy without burden the property disposed of; or whether, to the knowledge of the disponor, the taking of that property under the disposition is the occasion and reason for incurring a liability. . . . Thirdly, and most importantly, if the disponor is moved to dispose of his property, not to confer a benefaction on the disponee, but to acquire a pecuniary or proprietary benefit for himself, his disposition of that property with the object of effecting the result denies an essential characteristic of a gift according to ordinary notions.' *Leary v Federal Comr of Taxation* (1980) 11 ATR 145 at 159, per Brennan J

New Zealand 'The term "gift" is not defined in the Matrimonial Property Act. At common law it refers to a transaction whereby the owner of property conveys the ownership of that property to another without consideration. The distinction is between gifts which are always gratuitous dispositions of property and grants which are dispositions for consideration (2 Blackstone's Commentaries (14 ed) 440; 20 Halsbury's Laws of England (4 ed, para 1). Unless the context of s 10 otherwise requires, "gift" in s 10 must be read in that settled general sense.' *Mills v Dowdall* [1983] 2 NZFLR 210 at 214, per Richardson J

New Zealand 'In general a gift is something truly gratuitous, although it is possible that nominal or very small considerations may not prevent trasactions from being classed as gifts for some purposes'. Ibid, at 212, per Cooke J

Class gift

Prima facie a class gift is a gift to a class of persons included and comprehended under some general description and bearing a certain relation to the testator or another person or united by some common tie. Thus, where a testator divides his residue into as many equal shares as he shall have children surviving him, or predeceasing him leaving issue, and gives a share to or in trust for each such child, the gift is to a class. There may also be a class compounded of persons answering one or other of alternative descriptions, as, for example, 'the children of A and the children of B', or 'the children of A who attain twenty-one and the issue of such as die under that age'. A gift may be none the less a gift to a class because some of the members are referred to by name, or because a person who would otherwise fall within the class is excluded by name. On the other hand, a gift to one person and the children of another is not regarded as a class gift, unless there is something in the context to show that the testator intended to form a class or group; and gifts to several persons designated by name or number or by reference are not class gifts, and are liable to lapse unless a joint tenancy is created, or words are added implying a contingency. (50 Halsbury's Laws (4th edn) para 362)

Inter vivos

A gift inter vivos may be defined shortly as the transfer of any property from one person to another gratuitously while the donor is alive and not in expectation of death. It is an act whereby something is voluntarily transferred from the true possessor to another person, with the full intention that the thing shall not return to the donor, and with the full intention on the part of the receiver to retain the thing entirely as his own without restoring it to the giver. (20 Halsbury's Laws (4th edn) para 1)

Mortis causa   See DONATIO MORTIS CAUSA

Personal gift

'Tips received by a man as a reward for services rendered, voluntary gifts made by people other than the employers, are assessable to tax as part of the profits arising out of the employment if given in the ordinary way; but, on the other hand . . . personal gifts, which means gifts to a man on personal grounds, irrespective of and without regard to the question whether services have been rendered or not, are not assessable. The commissioners have obviously misunderstood what is meant by a personal gift. They have not found that the tips were personal gifts; they have found that they were gifts given to the respondent personally, which is a totally different thing. Every tip is given to a man personally, but that merely means that it is given to him for his own benefit, and not for that of the employers. Having listened to the cases, the commissioners thought the words "personal gift" meant given to him personally, whereas it is quite clear from the cases that what is meant by "personal gift" is a condensation of the full sentence, "personal gifts given on personal grounds other than for services rendered".'

Calvert (Inspector of Taxes) v Wainwright [1947] KB 526 at 527, per Atkinson J

GIPSY

'Gipsies' means persons of nomadic habit of life, whatever their race or origin, but does not include members of an organised group of travelling showmen, or of persons engaged in travelling circuses, travelling together as such. (Caravan Sites Act 1968, s 6)

[The Highways Act 1959, s 127 (repealed; cf now the Highways Act 1980, s 148 where the word 'gipsy' no longer occurs) make it an offence for a hawker or other itinerant trader, or a 'gipsy', to pitch a booth, stall or stand, or to encamp, on the highway.] 'That a man is of the Romany race is, as it seems to me, something which is really too vague of ascertainment, and impossible to prove; moreover, it is, I think, difficult to think that Parliament intended to subject a man to a penalty in the context of causing litter and obstruction on the highway merely by reason of his race. I think that, in this context, "gipsy" means no more than a person leading a nomadic life with no, or no fixed, employment and with no fixed abode. In saying that, I am hoping that those words will not be considered as the words of a statute, but merely as conveying the general colloquial idea of a gipsy.' *Mills v Cooper* [1967] 2 All ER 100 at 103, per Lord Parker CJ

'As members of this race first appeared in England not later than the beginning of the sixteenth century, and have not in the intervening centuries been notorious for the abundance of their written records, it would be impossible to prove Romany origin even as far back as the sixteenth century, let alone through the earlier centuries of their peripatetic history from India to the shores of this island. The section so far as it referred to "gipsy", would be incapable in practice of having any application at all. Confronted by these difficulties, counsel for the respondent only faintly argued that the word "gipsy" in the context of the section does not bear its popular meaning, which I would define as a person without fixed abode who leads a nomadic life, dwelling in tents or other shelters, or in caravans or other vehicles. If this meaning is adopted, it follows that being a gipsy is not an unalterable status. It cannot be said "once a gipsy always a gipsy". By changing his way of life a modern Borrow may be a gipsy at one time and not a gipsy at another.' Ibid at 104, per Diplock LJ

GIVE

[The plaintiff was induced by fraud to give a cheque for £3,000 for the alleged purposes of a good investment. The money was in fact used to pay betting debts owed to the defendant who took the cheque in good faith.] 'The cheque was not "given" for an illegal consideration within the meaning of 9 Anne c 14, s 1; or 5 and 6 Will 4 c 41, s 1 [Gaming Acts 1710 and 1835]—the word applies only to the original giving of the cheque and not to its subsequent negotiations.' *Barkworth v Gant* (1909) 25 TLR 722 at 723, per Ridley J

Canada 'The primary meaning of the word ["give"] appears to have been the placing of a material object in the hands of another person; the usual sense now however is that of freely and gratuitously conferring on a person the ownership of something as an act of bounty.' *Zdrok (Shukin Estate) v Shukin (No 2)* [1948] 1 WWR 724 at 727, Sask CA, per Martin CJS

Canada [The words 'give', 'deliver' and 'distribute' are used in the Narcotic Control Act, RSC 1970, c N–1). 'In each case the word contemplates a physical act involving two or more persons and it is important to note that these verbs can operate independently of and without reference to the ownership or change of ownership of the object given, delivered or distributed. In other words, one can "give", "deliver" or "distribute" an object to another or others regardless of whether that object is owned by the one, another or others or all or none of them' *R v Taylor* (1974) 17 CCC (2d) 36 at 40, per Carrothers JA

GIVE WAY

'The expression "giving way", means not crossing a vessel's bows, but going under her stern.' *The Rose* (1843) 2 Wm Rob 1 at 5, per cur.

GLEBE

The glebe of a benefice includes all land of any kind, houses or other buildings forming part of its endowments but does not include the parsonage house and grounds occupied with it. A parsonage house is a house which belongs to or is parcel of the parsonage, namely, of the endowments of the benefice. The house and glebe are both comprehended under the word 'manse'. The parsonage house and glebe are owned by the incumbent as a corporation sole for the benefit of himself and his successors in the incumbency, and he is entitled to use them for his own enjoyment or profit so far as such use is consistent with the due preservation of them for the use of his successors. (14 Halsbury's Laws (4th edn) para 1139)

Glebe building

'Glebe building' means any building, wall, fence or work which the incumbent of a benefice is bound by virtue of his office to maintain in repair, not being a parsonage house or comprised in a parsonage house. (Repair of Benefice Buildings Measure 1972, s 31(1))

GOAT

'Goat' includes a kid. (Protection of Animals Act 1911, s 15)

GOING CONCERN

Australia [In an advertisement for tenders for a business it was described as a 'going concern'.] 'The words "as a going concern" are merely intended to mean that the shop is being kept open, instead of having been closed up, and that the customers are being kept together, so that if the purchaser wishes to keep on the business he can do so; that . . . the vendors only propose to sell the stock and fixtures, and they leave it to the person who buys to decide whether he will carry on the business or not, and that meanwhile, lest the purchaser should care to carry on the business, they keep it open for his advantage till he takes his choice. In some cases they shut up the shop prior to the sale; in other cases they keep it "going" so that the trade may not be broken and dispersed.' *Ferne v Wilson* (1900) 26 VLR 422 at 437, per Madden CJ

Australia 'To describe an undertaking as a "going concern" imports no more than that, at the point of time to which the description applies, its doors are open for business; that it is then active and operating, and perhaps also that it has all the plant, etc which is necessary to keep it in operation, as distinct from its being only an inert aggregation of plant.' *Reference under Electricity Commission (Balmain Electric Light Co Purchase) Act 1950* [1957] SR (NSW) 100 at 131, per Sugerman J

GOLD   *See also* HALLMARK

Where English law is the proper law of the contract under which a debt is payable, any reference in the contract to gold or gold coin will prima facie be construed as an indication of the means by which the amount of the debt is to be measured, and not as a requirement to make actual payment in gold; but in some cases a reference to gold in connection with a particular currency may be no more than part of the description of that currency. (32 Halsbury's Laws (4th edn) para 103)

GOLD PLATE   *See* PLATE

GOOD CHARACTER   *See* CHARACTER

GOOD CONSTRUCTION

[The Factories Act 1937, s 23(1)(a) (repealed; see now the Factories Act 1961, s 26(1)) provided that no chain, rope or lifting tackle should be used unless it was of 'good construction', sound material, adequate strength and free from patent defect.] 'The question is . . . raised as to the meaning of the phrase "good construction". Does the phrase import or denote suitability for some particular purpose? The decision in *Beadsley v United Steel Companies Ltd* [[1950] 2 All ER 872] shows that it does not. The case dealt with the words "good construction". Singleton LJ in his judgment said Ibid at 874]: "If the legislation had intended to make the occupiers of a factory responsible because a chain or lifting tackle which was not suitable was used, it would have been quite easy to say: 'No chain, rope or lifting tackle shall be used unless it is of good construction, sound material, adequate strength, free from patent defect and suitable for the purposes for which it is used.' Those last words do not appear in the subsection." Birkett LJ in his judgment ibid at 875], said that the words "good construction" meant "well made".' *Gledhill v Liverpool Abbattoir Utility Co Ltd* [1957] 3 All ER 117 at 120, 121, CA, per cur.

GOOD DEFENCE

Canada [Registration of judgment for reciprocal enforcement was to be refused where debtor would have had a 'good defence' to an action on the judgment.] 'I find no reason to believe that the word "good" . . . has any special significance other than its ordinary meaning of adequate, effectual, thorough or valid (Oxford English Dictionary). In that sense a "good defence" is one which would be effective or successful and not just "any defence" which a resourceful pleader might frame (short of purposes of embarrassment or delay) however unlikely to induce a judge or jury to decide in the defendant's favour.' *Re Aero Trades Western Ltd and Ben Hocum & Son Ltd* (1974) 51 DLR (3d) 617 at 621, 622, Man Co Ct, per Molloy Co Ct J

GOOD FAITH   *See also* BONA FIDES; UBERRIMA FIDES

A thing is deemed to be done in good faith within the meaning of this Act when it is in fact done honestly, whether it is done negligently or not. (Bills of Exchange Act 1882, s 90; Sale of Goods Act 1979, s 61(3))

In this section 'a purchaser in good faith' means a person dealing with an appointee of the age of not less than twenty-five years for valuable consideration in money or money's worth, and without notice of the fraud, or of any circumstances from which, if reasonable inquiries had been made, the fraud might have been discovered. (Law of Property Act 1925, s 157)

'What does "good faith" mean? What is meant by those two English words which are the exact equivalent in every sense of the expression which is perhaps more commonly used, though not more correctly or properly, bona fides? I think that the best way of defining the expression, so far as it is necessary or safe to define it, is by saying that it is the absence of bad faith—of mala fides.' *Mogridge v Clapp* [1892] 3 Ch 382 at 391, CA, per Kekewich J

[The Leasehold Reform Act 1967, Sch 3, para 4(1), provides that where a tenant makes a claim to acquire the freehold or an extended lease of any property, then during the currency of the claim no proceedings to enforce any right of re-entry or forfeiture terminating the tenancy shall be brought in any court without the leave of that court, and leave shall not be granted unless the court is satisfied that the claim was not made in 'good faith'. 'The words "in good faith" are often used in statutes but rarely defined. . . . To my mind under this Act a claim is made "in good faith" when it is made honestly and with no ulterior motive.' *Central Estates (Belgravia) Ltd v Woolgar* [1971] 3 All ER 647 at 649, CA, per Lord Denning MR

'The words "in good faith", in my opinion, mean "honestly". A claim is not made honestly if it is made with the intention of committing a criminal offence, or of facilitating the commission of a future offence. It does not make it any the less a dishonest claim because the intended criminal offence is itself not what is called an offence involving dishonesty.' Ibid at 651, per Phillimore LJ

[The word 'purchaser' was defined by r 2(2) of the Land Registration (Official Searches) Rules, 1969 (revoked; see now SI 1988 No 629), as any person who in 'good faith' and for valuable consideration acquires or intends to acquire a legal estate in land.] 'The question of good faith . . . is partly one of law and partly one of fact. So far as law is concerned, in my judgment if a purchaser acts honestly he is acting "in good faith" within the meaning of r 2 of the 1969 rules, and I so hold.' *Smith v Morrison, Smith v Chief Land Registrar* [1974] 1 All ER 957 at 973, per Plowman J

United States 'Good faith' means honesty in fact in the conduct of transaction concerned. (Uniform Commercial Code 1978, s 1–201(19))

GOOD HEALTH

'According to the ordinary and only intelligible sense of the term in the circumstances in which it was used [a proposal for life insurance], she was in "good health", if she neither was conscious of nor exhibited the slightest symptoms of disease.' *Hutchinson v National Loan Fund Life Assurance Co* (1845) 7 D 467 at 480, per Lord Fullerton

Australia 'If a person is not in conscious enjoyment of all his faculties and functions, and is conscious that he is not free from any ailment, affecting them, or of symptoms of ailment, he is not in good health. . . . In my opinion, a sufficient definition of the term "good health" . . . is that it means that the person in question is free from any apparent sensible disease or symptom of disease, and is unconscious of any derangement of the bodily functions by which health can be tested.' *National Mutual Life Assocn of Australasia Ltd v Kidman* (1905) 3 CLR 160 at 167, 168, per Griffith CJ

GOOD HUSBANDRY *See* FARMING; HUSBANDRY

GOOD REPAIR *See* REPAIR

GOOD SHIP *See* SHIP

GOOD TITLE *See* TITLE

GOODS

The words 'goods' shall include wares and merchandise of every description, and all articles in respect of which rates or duties are payable under the special Act. (Harbours, Docks, and Piers Clauses Act 1847, s 3)

The expression 'goods' includes every description of wares and merchandise. (Merchant Shipping Act 1894, s 492)

The term 'goods' means goods in the nature of merchandise, and does not include personal effects or provisions and stores for use on board.

In the absence of any usage to the contrary, deck cargo and living animals must be insured specifically, and not under the general denomination of goods. (Marine Insurance Act 1906, Sch 1, para 17)

'Goods' includes vehicles, vessels, aircraft and animals, and generally includes articles and property of any description. (Trading Stamps Act 1964, s 10)

'Goods' includes fish, livestock and animals of all descriptions. (Harbours Act 1964, s 57)

'Goods' includes ships and aircraft, things attached to land and growing crops. (Trade Descriptions Act 1968, s 39(1))

'Goods', except in so far as the context otherwise requires, includes money and every other description of property except land, and includes things severed from the land by stealing. (Theft Act 1968, s 34(2)(b))

'Goods' includes goods, wares, merchandises, and articles of every kind whatsoever, except live animals and cargo which by the contract of carriage is stated as being carried on deck and is so carried. (Carriage of Goods by Sea Act 1971, Sch (Hague Rules, Article 1(c))

'Goods' includes goods or burden of any description. (Road Traffic Act 1972, s 196(1))

'Goods' includes buildings and other structures, and also includes ships, aircraft and hovercraft, but does not include electricity. (Fair Trading Act 1973, s 137(2); see also Competition Act 1980, s 33)

'Goods' includes ships and aircraft, minerals, substances and animals (including fish), and references to the production of goods include references to the getting of minerals and the taking of such animals. (Restrictive Trade Practices Act 1976, s 43(1))

'Goods' includes stores and baggage. (Customs and Excise Management Act 1979, s 1(1))

'Goods' includes all chattels personal other than things in action and money. (Torts (Interference with Goods) Act 1977, s 14(1))

'Goods' includes all personal chattels other than things in action and money, and in Scotland all corporeal moveables except money; and in particular 'goods' includes emblements, industrial growing crops, and things attached to or forming part of the land which are agreed to be severed before sale or under the contract of sale. (Sale of Goods Act 1979, s 61(1)). [See also s 1(1) of the Customs and Excise Management Act 1979]

'Goods' includes animals, parcels and mails. (London Regional Transport Act 1984, s 68)

'Goods' includes baggage. (County Courts Act 1984, s 175)

In this Part of this Act [Part I: Packaged goods] . . . 'goods', in relation to a package, excludes the container included in the package. (Weights and Measures Act 1985, s 68(1))

'Personal actions are as well included within this word "goods", in an Act of Parliament, as goods in possession.' *Ford & Sheldon's Case* (1606) 12 Co Rep 1 at 2, per cur.

'I think that the words "other goods" in the section [s 23 of the Merchant Shipping Act 1876 (repealed; see now Merchant Shipping Act 1894, s 85(1))] must have their natural meaning in regard to the subject-matter with which the section was dealing, namely, deck cargo, and must be treated as comprising all goods that may be carried on deck as part of the cargo. Bales of cotton carried in the hold would be goods forming part of the cargo; and why, if carried on deck, should they not be regarded . . . as goods carried as deck cargo? In this case the question arises with regard to horses and cattle. They also are according to the ordinary use of language "goods" carried as part of the cargo. I think that we ought to construe the word "goods" as including them and anything else that may be carried as cargo on deck.' *Richmond Hill SS Co v Trinity House Corpn* [1896] 2 QB 134 at 137, 138, CA, per Lord Esher MR

'At first sight the word "goods" might seem to be

an . . . inappropriate description [of securities]. It must, however, be observed that the word is of very general and quite indefinite import, and primarily derives its meaning from the context in which it is used. . . . The content of the word "goods" differs greatly according to the context in which it is found and the instrument in which it occurs. . . . "Goods" are not limited to things which are of considerable bulk or weight. . . . The documents . . . were things of price, the subjects of sale and delivery, irreplaceable and unalterable. No doubt can be entertained that they are within the descriptive word "goods". . . .' *The Noordam (No 2)* [1920] AC 904 at 908–910, PC, per cur.

'The Customs Consolidation Act 1876, s 43 . . . is in these terms: "The importation of arms, ammunition, gunpowder, or any other goods may be prohibited by proclamation or Order in Council". . . . I am of opinion that the ejusdem generis rule must be applied to the construction of s 43, and that the meaning of the general words must be restricted to that of the particular words which precede them, and that "any other goods" means goods of the class of arms, ammunition, and gunpowder.' *A-G v Brown* [1920] 1 KB 773 at 795, 799, per Sankey J; on appeal, [1921] 3 KB 29, CA, these words were not considered

'The seventeenth of the Rules for Construction [of Policies, in the 1st Schedule to the Marine Insurance Act 1906] is as follows: "17. The term 'goods' means goods in the nature of merchandise, and does not include personal effects or provisions and stores for use on board. In the absence of any usage to the contrary, deck cargo and living animals must be insured specifically, and not under the general denomination of goods." The construction of this rule has given rise to a great deal of controversy, and it is now necessary that we should endeavour to settle this vexed question of construction. Rule 17 is very oddly worded, but it appears to me that on its true reading it leaves the law as to insurance of deck cargo very much as it was before the Marine Insurance Act passed. The rule prescribes that deck cargo and living animals must be insured specifically in the absence of any usage to the contrary. What is the meaning of the provision that deck cargo and living animals 'must be insured specifically"? I think "specifically" in this connection means "as such". In the case of deck cargo there must, in addition to the ordinary description of the goods, be an intimation in the policy that the goods are to be carried on deck, by inserting "for carriage on deck", or other similar words.' *British &*

Foreign Marine Insurance Co v Gaunt [1921] 2 AC 41 at 53, per Lord Finlay

'There can be no question, it appears to me, but that apart from some special use in a special Act of Parliament the word "goods" is wide enough to cover what are known as industrial growing crops. The word "goods", as defined in the Sale of Goods Act [see now the Act of 1979, supra], which it is to be remembered is a codifying Act, in terms includes, in the definition of "goods", industrial growing crops, and that definition is nothing new.' *Stephenson v Thompson* [1924] 2 KB 240 at 247, 248, per Atkin LJ

[The owner of a car left it with a dealer to put in his showroom, but not to sell without first referring inquiries to the owner. The owner took away the ignition key but accidentally left the registration book. The car was sold without the owner's authority.] 'I agree . . . that the car, with or without the car key and the registration book, must be "goods" within the meaning of the Factors Act [1889, s 2]. In my view, the word "goods" must include all chattels of which physical possession is possible, notwithstanding that they are not easily movable without wheels or an ignition key, or are subject to difficulties in satisfying a purchaser in the absence of the registration book.' *Stadium Finance Ltd v Robbins* [1962] 2 All ER 633 at 639, CA, per Danckwerts LJ; also reported in [1962] 2 QB 664 at 676

United States 'Goods' includes goods not in existence at the time the transaction is entered into and merchandise certificates, but excludes money, chattel paper, documents of title, and instruments. (Uniform Consumer Credit Code 1969, s 2.105(1))

United States 'Goods' means all things (including specially manufactured goods) which are movable at the time of identification to the contract for sale other than the money in which the price is to be paid, investment securities (Article 8 [of the Uniform Commercial Code]) and things in action. 'Goods' also includes the unborn young of animals and growing crops and other identified things attached to realty as described in the section on goods to be severed from realty (Section 2–107). (Uniform Commercial Code 1978, s 2–105(1))

Carriage of goods *See* CARRIAGE OF GOODS

Consumer goods

United States Goods [in the context of secured

transactions are 'consumer goods' if they are used or bought for use primarily for personal, family or household purposes . . . . (Uniform Commercial Code 1978, s 9–109.)

Conveyance of goods *See* CONVEY

Future goods

United States Goods must be both existing and identified before any interest in them can pass. Goods which are not both existing and identified are 'future' goods. A purported present sale of future goods or of any interest therein operates as a contract to sell. (Uniform Commercial Code 1978, s 2–105(2))

Household goods

'A man deviseth his household goods and stuff to his wife, and died, having made his daughter executrix. The question was, whether or no by his devise the wife should have the plate that was commonly used about the house, viz. a silver tankard, twelve silver spoons. . . . The tankard and spoons, commonly used about the house, will pass by the devise of household goods.' *Flay v Flay* (1680) Freem Ch 64 at 64, per the Lord Chancellor

'By a devise of all rings and household goods, plate used in the house does not pass.' *Jesson v Essington* (1702) Prec Ch 207 at 207, per the Lord Keeper

'The words of the bequest here are "household goods . . . which shall belong to me at the time of my decease". . . . A clock is, in its very nature, within the term "household goods", and using, as he has done, these large words, the best conclusion I can form is, that he [the testator] intended to sweep over everything that could be called household furniture, and the clock must go over to Mrs Pellew [the testator's widow].' *Pellew v Horsford* (1856) 25 LJ Ch 352 at 353, 354, per Wood V-C

In marine insurance policy

[T]he term 'goods' means goods in the nature of merchandise, and does not include personal effects, or food or stores for use on board, and in the absence of any usage to the contrary deck cargo and living animals must be insured specifically and not under the general denomination of goods. The term includes money, bullion or jewels if put on board as merchandise, but does not comprise jewels, ornaments, cash, etc., not intended for trade and carried about or belonging to persons on board;

and it probably does not include banknotes or bills of exchange. (25 Halsbury's Laws (4th edn) para 113)

Secured transactions

United States 'Goods' includes all things which are movable at the time the security interest attaches or which are fixtures (Section 9–313), but does not include money, documents, instruments, accounts, chattel paper, general intangibles, or minerals or the like (including oil and gas) before extraction. 'Goods' also includes standing timber which is to be cut and removed under a conveyance or contract for sale, the unborn young of animals, and growing crops . . . (Uniform Commercial Code 1978, s 9–105(1)(h))

GOODS AND CHATTELS

'The words "goods and chattels" are words of most extensive import. Unless controlled by the context, they comprise all the personal estate of whatsoever nature or description.' *Bartlett v Bartlett* (1857) 1 De G & J 127 at 139, per Turner LJ

'These words "goods and chattels" are words of very extensive signification, and undoubtedly comprise both tangible property and property which is not tangible.' *Re Baldwin, Ex p Foss, Ex p Baldwin* (1858) 2 De G & J 230 at 238, 239, per Turner LJ

GOODS VEHICLE

'Goods vehicle' means a motor vehicle constructed or adapted for use for the carriage of goods, or a trailer so constructed or adapted. (Road Traffic Act 1972, s 196(1) and cf the Road Traffic (Foreign Vehicles) Act 1972, s 7(1))

'Goods vehicle' means a motor vehicle constructed or adapted for the carriage of goods or burden of any description, on a trailer as constructed or adapted. (Road Traffic Regulation Act 1984, s 138(1))

'Goods vehicles are ones "constructed or adapted for use for the conveyance of goods or burden of any description". Accordingly, a vehicle may become a goods vehicle by construction or adaptation, whereas it is only by construction that a vehicle can become a passenger vehicle.' *Fry v Bevan* (1937) 81 Sol Jo 60 at 60, DC, per Lord Hewart CJ

Articulated goods vehicle

'Articulated goods vehicle' means a motor vehicle which is so constructed that a trailer designed to carry goods may by partial superimposition be attached thereto in such a manner as to cause a substantial part of the weight of the trailer to be borne by the motor vehicle, and 'articulated goods vehicle combination' means an articulated goods vehicle with a trailer so attached. (Road Traffic Act 1972, s 110, as inserted by the Road Traffic (Drivers' Ages and Hours of Work) Act 1976, s 1, Sch 1)

Foreign goods vehicle

'Foreign goods vehicle' (except in s 4 of this Act [examiner's right to production of documents]) means a goods vehicle which has been brought into Great Britain and which, if a motor vehicle, is not registered in the United Kingdom or, if a trailer, is drawn by a motor vehicle not registered in the United Kingdom which has been brought into Great Britain. (Road Traffic (Foreign Vehicles) Act 1972, s 7(1))

Heavy goods vehicle

'Heavy goods vehicle' means any of the following vehicles—
(a) an articulated goods vehicle;
(b) a large vehicle, that is to say, a motor vehicle (not being an articulated goods vehicle) which is constructed or adapted to carry or to haul goods and the permissible maximum weight of which exceeds 7.5 tonnes.
(Road Traffic Act 1972, s 124, as substituted by the Road Traffic (Drivers' Ages and Hours of Work) Act 1976, s 1 Sch 1)

Small goods vehicle

'Small goods vehicle' means a motor vehicle (other than a motor cycle or invalid carriage) which is constructed or adapted to carry or to haul goods and is not adapted to carry more than 9 persons inclusive of the driver and the permissible maximum weight of which does not exceed 3.5 tonnes. (Road Traffic Act 1972, s 110, as inserted by the Road Traffic (Drivers' Ages and Hours of Work) Act 1976, Sch 1)

GOODWILL

The goodwill of a business is the whole advantage of the reputation and connection formed with customers together with the circumstances, whether of habit or otherwise, which tend to make that connection permanent. It represents in connection with any business or business product the value of the attraction to customers which the name and reputation possesses. . . . A distinction has been drawn between personal goodwill, which is merely the advantage of the recommendation of the owner of a business and of the use of his name, and local goodwill, which is attached to premises, and must be taken into account in calculating the value of such premises. There may be a goodwill attached to a business which depends upon personal relations between the man who carries it on and his clients or customers, such as the business of a stockbroker, or a solicitor, or a notary, or a surgeon or doctor, or a dentist; and even though a successor may not use the old name, it may be an advantage of appreciable value merely to be a successor, though in some cases such goodwill may be so worthless as to be unsaleable. (35 Halsbury's Laws (4th edn) paras 1106, 1109)

'The goodwill, which has been the subject of sale, is nothing more than the probability, that the old customers will resort to the old place.' *Cruttwell v Lye* (1810) 17 Ves 335 at 346, per Lord Eldon LC

'There is considerable difficulty in defining, accurately, what is included under this term goodwill; it seems to be that species of connection in trade which induces customers to deal with a particular firm.' *Wedderburn v Wedderburn (No 4)* (1856) 22 Beav 84 at 104, per Romilly MR

'Where a trade is established in a particular place, the goodwill of that trade means nothing more than the sum of money which any person would be willing to give for the chance of being able to keep the trade connected with the place where it has been carried on. It was truly said in argument that "goodwill" is something distinct from the profits of a business, although in determining its value the profits are necessarily taken into account; and it is usually estimated at so many years' purchase upon the amount of these profits.' *Austen v Boys* (1858) 2 De G & J 626 at 635, 636, per Lord Chelmsford LC

'"Goodwill", I apprehend, must mean every advantage—every positive advantage, if I may so express it, as contrasted with the negative advantage of the late partner not carrying on the business himself—that has been acquired by the old firm in carrying on its business, whether connected with the premises in which the business was previously carried on, or with the name of the late firm, or with any other matter

carrying with it the benefit of the business.' *Churton v Douglas* (1859) John 174 at 188, per Page Wood V-C

'It is quite plain that the goodwill of a public-house passes with the public-house. In such a case the goodwill is the mere habit of the customers resorting to the house. It is not what is called a personal goodwill.' *Re Kitchin, Ex p Punnett* (1880) 16 Ch D 226 at 233, CA, per Jessel MR

'It [goodwill] is the connection thus formed, together with the circumstances, whether of habit or otherwise, which tend to make it permanent, that constitutes the goodwill of a business. It is this which constitutes the difference between a business just started, which has no goodwill attached to it, and one which has acquired a goodwill. The former trader has to seek out his customers. . . . The latter has a custom ready made. He knows what members of the community are purchasers of the articles in which he deals, and are not attached by custom to any other establishment.' *Trego v Hunt* [1896] AC 7 at 17, 18, per Lord Herschell

'What is goodwill? It is a thing very easy to describe, very difficult to define. It is the benefit and advantage of the good name, reputation, and connection of a business. It is the attractive force which brings in custom. It is the one thing which distinguishes an old-established business from a new business at its first start. . . . If there is one attribute common to all cases of goodwill it is the attribute of locality. For goodwill has no independent existence. It cannot subsist by itself. It must be attached to a business. Destroy the business, and the goodwill perishes with it, though elements remain which may perhaps be gathered up and be revived again.' *Inland Revenue Comrs v Muller & Co's Margarine Ltd* [1901] AC 217 at 223, 224, HL, per Lord Macnaghten

'The dispute in this case . . . resolves itself into a question whether amongst the assets of the partnership for the purpose of winding up is to be included the goodwill. For the purpose of answering that question one must necessarily consider . . . what is meant by the expression "goodwill". . . . In *Trego v Hunt* [supra] . . . Lord Macnaghten . . . says, "Generally speaking, it means much more than what Lord Eldon took it to mean in the particular case actually before him in *Cruttwell v Lye* [supra] where he says: 'The goodwill which has been the subject of sale is nothing more than the probability that the old customers will resort to the old place'. Often it happens that the goodwill is the very sap and life of the business, without which the business would yield little or no fruit. It is the whole advantage, whatever it may be, of the reputation and connection of the firm, which may have been built up by years of honest work or gained by lavish expenditure of money". Lord Herschell expresses the same thing in rather different words. He says this: "It is the connection thus formed, together with the circumstances, whether of habit or otherwise, which tend to make it permanent, that constitutes the goodwill of a business". I summarise that by saying, the goodwill of a business is the advantage, whatever it may be, which a person gets by continuing to carry on and being entitled to represent to the outside world that he is carrying on a business which has been carried on for some time previously. That seems to me to be the meaning of "goodwill".' *Hill v Fearis* [1905] 1 Ch 466 at 471, per Warrington J

Australia 'My opinion is that while it [the goodwill] cannot be said to be absolutely and necessarily inseparable from the premises or to have no separate value, prima facie at any rate it may be treated as attached to the premises and whatever its value may be should be treated as an enhancement of the value of the premises.' *Daniell v Federal Comr of Taxation* (1928) 42 CLR 296 at 302, 303, per Knox CJ

Australia 'Goodwill has been said to be "the attractive force which brings in custom" (*Inland Revenue Comrs v Muller & Co's Margarine Ltd* [supra]). Hence to determine the nature of the goodwill in any given case, it is necessary to consider the type of business and the type of customer which such a business is inherently likely to attract as well as all the surrounding circumstances. . . . The goodwill of a business is a composite thing referable in part to its locality, in part to the way in which it is conducted and the personality of those who conduct it, and in part to the likelihood of competition, many customers being no doubt actuated by mixed motives in conferring their custom.' *Federal Comr of Taxation v Williamson* (1943) 67 CLR 561 at 564, per Rich J

Australia 'The goodwill of a business is the advantage, whatever it may be, which a person gets by continuing to carry on and being entitled to represent to the outside world that he is carrying on a business which has been carried on for some time previously.' *Re Jacobson* [1970] VR 180 at 182, 183, per Gowans J

Australia 'The meaning of the word "goodwill" is discussed by Warrington J in *Hill v Fearis* [1905] 1 Ch 466 at 471, I summarise by saying, the goodwill of business is the advantage, whatever it may be, which a person gets by continuing to carry on and being entitled to represent to the outside world that he is carrying on a business which has been carried on for some time previously. That seems to me to be the meaning of "goodwill". The latter part of this passage was cited by Isaacs J in *Bacchus Marsh Concentrated Mild Co Ltd (in liq) v Joseph Nathan & Co Ltd* (1919) 26 CLR 410 at 438, accompanying it with this observation: "Goodwill is property, but, as such, is inseparable from a particular "business", in the sense of a particular going concern. It is an asset of that business, and enhances its value."' *Re Jacobson, deceased* [1970] VR 180 at 182–183, per Gowans J

GOVERN

[A clause in a bill of lading provided that the contract should be 'governed' by the law of England.] 'It is to my mind impossible to say that English law "governs" the contract in any practical or real sense when the only function of the English law is to direct that the relevant Australian law must prevail.' *Ocean SS Co Ltd v Queensland State Wheat Board* [1941] 1 KB 402 at 416, CA, per Du Parcq LJ

GOVERNMENT

From the legal point of view, government may be described as the exercise of certain powers and the performance of certain duties by public authorities or officers, together with certain private persons or corporations exercising public functions. The structure of the machinery of government, and the regulation of the powers and duties which belong to the different parts of this structure, are defined by the law, which also prescribes, to some extent, the mode in which these powers are to be exercised or these duties are to be performed. (8 Halsbury's Laws (4th edn) para 804)

'For the purposes of our judgment the two policies of insurance on the construction of which the question arises for our decision are substantially identical. The learned judge below, in construing the material clauses, dealt with two contentions raised by the assured. The first contention was that the expression "the Government of the country in which the property is situated" means the Government of that country in power at the date of the policy. In my opinion, the learned judge was right in refusing to accept that view of the construction of the policy. It seems to me that the material date to be considered is the date of the loss happening as the result of the acts of Government therein mentioned; such acts of Government being the acts of the executive body occupying the position of Government at the time the acts in question were committed.' *White, Child & Beney Ltd v Simmons, White Child & Beney Ltd v Eagle Star & British Dominions Insurance Co* (1922) 127 LT 571 at 583, CA, per Warrington LJ

'The words "government regulations and restrictions" [used in a charter-party containing the words "Subject to Indian Government Licence . . . and in all respects to customs and other Government regulations, restrictions or otherwise affecting the normal shipment of the cargo and clearances and sailing of the vessel"] do not include local regulations made by the port authorities and affecting the time or manner of leading in the port.' *Hogarth v Cory Brothers & Co* (1926) 95 LJPC 204 at 207, per cur.

[By a war risks clause in a charter-party a vessel had liberty to comply with directions given by the 'government' of the nation under whose flag it was sailing, or any other 'government'.] 'I would read the words "by the government of the nation under whose flag the vessel sails . . . or by any other government" as referring to the same type of government, not to contrasting or different types. The clause refers to national governments, not to a subservient authority such as a municipal or provincial government. The qualities of character required by the body giving the order or on whose behalf it was given or purported to be given must, therefore, include essentially the exercise of full executive and legislative power over an established territory.' *Luigi Monta of Genoa v Cechofracht Co Ltd* [1956] 2 All ER 760 at 773, per Sellers J (also reported in [1956] 2 QB 552 at 564)

GOVERNOR

Foundation governor of school

'Foundation governors' means, in relation to any voluntary school governors appointed otherwise than by a local education authority or a minor authority for the purpose of securing, so far as is practicable, that the character of a school as a voluntary school is preserved and developed, and, in particular, that the school is conducted in accordance with the provisions of any trust deed relating thereto . . . (Education Act 1944, s 114(1), as amended by Education Act 1980, s 1(3), Sch 1, para 13)

Of dependent territory

The term 'Governor' usually means any officer appointed by the Crown to administer the government of a dependent territory, though in protectorates and other dependencies outside Her Majesty's dominions the Crown's representative will normally be styled 'High Commissioner'. In constituting his office, provision is always made for the administration of the government in case of a vacancy or the absence or incapacity of the Governor. Usually there is also an authorisation for the Governor to appoint a deputy with such powers as the Governor thinks fit whenever he is about to be absent from the capital, or visit a dependency (or, sometimes, an adjacent territory), or when temporarily incapacitated through illness; but the Governor retains all his own powers. (6 Halsbury's Laws (4th edn) para 1033)

'Governor', in relation to a dependent territory, includes the officer for the time being administering the government of that territory. (British Nationality Act 1981, s 50(1))

GOVERNMENT BILL

'Government bill' means any bill, note or other obligation of a Government in any part of the world, being a document by the delivery of which, with or without endorsement, title is transferable, and not being an obligation which is or has been legal tender in any part of the world, and 'Government bill' includes in particular a Treasury bill. (Finance Act 1968, s 55(3))

GRANDCHILDREN

'As to great-grandchildren, I incline to think that the word grandchildren would, without further explanation, comprehend them; for in common parlance, which is the true way of interpreting words in a will, the word grandchildren is used rather in opposition to, and exclusive of, children, than as confined to the next descent, the children of children, and must, I think, have the effect of comprehending both, unless the intention appear to the contrary; but in the present case there is no necessity to give any opinion upon that point, as here the testatrix has, in so many words, declared, that she meant to comprehend great grandchildren under the word grandchildren; for she has given the specific legacy of china to her grand-daughter, Miss Hussey, who is, in fact, her great grand-daughter, the daughter of her grand-daughter, Mrs Hussey; that, I think, is decisive of the question.' *Hussey v Berkeley* (1763) 2 Eden 194 at 196, per Lord Henley LC

[Construction of a will and settlement as not comprehending great-grandchildren under the description of children and 'grandchildren' and when there are persons who answer to the description of children or grandchildren.] 'How stands the present case in these respects? There is a limitation over to Harriet Churchill, but in the event of the tenant for life dying, not without issue, but without children or grandchildren living at his death; and here is a grandchild of the tenant for life living at his death. There is no room therefore for the argument, that, where there is a total want of persons, who properly answer the description, other persons, who do not so completely answer it, may be let in to take in their stead. I never knew an instance, where there were children, to answer the proper description, that grandchildren were permitted to share along with them; although, where there is a total want of children, grandchildren have been let in under a liberal construction of the word "children". I am therefore clearly of opinion, that the great grandchild of Charles Churchill, the tenant for life, is not entitled to any share of the £30,000.' *Orford (Earl) v Churchill* (1814) 3 Ves & B 59 at 69, per Grant MR

[A testator gave his property to trustees to divide the same between his 'grandchildren then living . . . or the issue of such as may have died (such issue taking a parent's share only)'.] 'The only gift to grandchildren in the present case being to those then living, and therefore wholly contingent until the death of the last survivor of the children, and no interest of any sort or kind being made to vest in any grandchild before the period when the distribution was to take place, the gift to great-grandchildren by virtue of the words "or the issue of such as may have died (such issue taking a parent's share only)" appears to me to be in no sense substitutional, but a distinct independent substantive, or, as it is sometimes called, an original gift.' *Re Woolley, Wormald v Woolley* [1903] 2 Ch 206 at 208, 209, per Joyce J

'The first of the two cases is *Hussey v Dillon* [(1763) 2 Amb 603], in which the then Lord Chancellor, Lord Henley, said, in his judgment: "Grandchildren is a word of large extent, and, in

common parlance, takes in everybody descended from the testator, and will have that effect, unless the intention appears to the contrary". I do not rely on that statement as a binding decision that the word "grandchildren" takes in everybody descended from the testator unless anything appears to the contrary; but at least it tends to show that at the date of the report, the year 1763, the then Lord Chancellor was of the opinion that "grandchildren" was a word of large extent and, in common parlance, took in everybody descended from the testator. The second decision dealing with the point is *Earl of Orford v Churchill* [supra]. That was a case arising out of the construction of a will and a settlement, and it was unsuccessfully argued, inter alia, that the word "grandchildren" would comprehend great-grandchildren. In my opinion, however, the judgment is no authority for the view that in a will the word "grandchildren" with a suitable context may not properly be construed to include great-grandchildren and other descendants; and although it is now well settled that prima facie the word "grandchildren" means descendants of the second degree, it is not impossible to find cases in which it is used in a wider sense. The derivation of the word, as I have pointed out, does not in any way indicate that it may not be be so used.' *Re Hall, Hall v Hall* [1932] 1 Ch 262 at 266, 267, per Maugham J

Australia 'The word "grandchildren" in its ordinary acceptation cannot include the children of a stepdaughter.' *Re Moyle's Will, Howie v Moyle* [1920] VLR 147 at 150, per Schutt J

GRANT

Canada [Reduction of capital cost allowance claim was required in respect of 'grant, subsidy'.] 'In the Shorter Oxford English Dictionary (3rd edn) "grant" is defined as "An authoritative bestowal or conferring of a right, etc; a gift or assignment of money etc out of a fund". In addition it also has the legal meaning of a conveyance by deed. In Jowitt, The Dictionary of English Law, "grant" is defined as "the term commonly applied to rights created or transferred by the Crown, e.g., grants of pensions, patents, charters, franchises. It is also used in reference to public money devoted to special purposes". Again referring to the dictionary meanings of the words "grant" and "subsidy" there is one common thread throughout, that is a gift or assignment of money by government or public authority out of public funds to a private or individual or commercial enterprise deemed to be beneficial to the public interest. Subject to minor refinements the words "grant" and "subsidy" appear from their dictionary meanings to be almost synonymous.' *GTE Sylvania Canada Ltd v R* [1974] 1 FCR 726 at 735, 736, FCTD, per Cattanach J; affd [1974] 2 FCR 212, FCA

From Crown

'The proper meaning of the expression "grant from the Crown" in the case of a land grant is a conveyance by letters patent under the Great Seal. And although, of course, Crown lands may be transferred to a subject by Act of Parliament, such a transfer would not ordinarily or properly be described as a "grant from the Crown".' *R v Canadian Pacific Rly Co* [1911] AC 328 at 334, PC, per cur.

Of licence

'Grant' in relation to a justices' licence includes a grant by way of renewal, transfer or removal and 'application' shall be construed accordingly. (Licensing Act 1964, s 201)

Of watercourse

The grant of a watercourse does not . . . mean the grant of the water itself. It may mean any one of three things, namely, a grant of the easement or the right to the running of water, or a grant of the channel-pipe or drain which contains the water, or a grant of the land over which the water flows. The meaning in the case of each particular grant is to be drawn from the context, and if there is no context from which the meaning can be gathered the word 'watercourse' prima facie means an easement. (14 Halsbury's Laws (4th edn) para 186)

GRANTOR

'What is the prima facie meaning of the words "the grantor of the lease"? I think they mean quite plainly the man who puts his hand and seal to the document in question—the man who grants the land for the term for which it is to be vested in the lessee.' *Bodega Co Ltd v Read* [1914] 2 Ch 283 at 290, per Warrington J

GRASSUM

'What is "grassum"? Grassum [in Scots law] is taking, beforehand, that which otherwise would be taken half-yearly, or annually, according to

the terms of a lease: It appears to me that "grassum", "rental", "rent", or whatever word may be used, are, in reality, one and the same thing.' *Queensberry Leases Case* (1819) 1 Bli 339 at 523, 524, per Lord Redesdale

GRATUITOUS

'The subject-matter of the action is a well in a . . . village. It has been used by the inhabitants of the village from time immemorial, and is of considerable advantage to them. . . . Under s 64 of the Public Health Act 1875 [repealed; see now Public Health Act 1936, s 124], in order that the well should vest in them [the local authority] it is essential for them to show, not only that it is a public well, but that it is used for the gratuitous supply of water and that it is used for the supply of water to the inhabitants of their district. The word "gratuitous" does not prevent voluntary contributions from being made by persons using the well, but it means that there must be no charge.' *A-G v Tonkin* (1901) 18 TLR 29 at 29, per Kekewich J

GRATUITY

'I . . . read "gratuity" [in a local Act] as wide enough to cover any money gratuitously granted or paid, whether it is paid in one sum or in instalments.' *Holloway v Poplar Corpn* [1940] 1 KB 173 at 178, per Asquith J

Canada 'One of the meanings ascribed to the word "gratuity" in the Oxford English Dictionary is: A gift or present (usually of money) often in return for favours or services, the amount depending upon the inclination of the giver. . . . Now applied exclusively to such a gift made to a servant or inferior official; a "tip".

The Oxford English Dictionary also says that another meaning, viz, "payment; wages" is obsolete. Webster's Third New International Dictionary gives as one of the meanings of "gratuity": "something given voluntarily or over and above what is due, usually in return for or in anticipation of some service".' *Re Vladicka and Board of School Trustees of Calgary School District No 19* (1974) 45 DLR (3d) 442 at 448, Alta SC, per McDonald J

GRAVE

'I think we must come to the conclusion that when Parliament introduced the word "grave" before the word "misconduct" [in a repealed superannuation Act] it meant that the misconduct must be not only of a character which could properly be described as misconduct, but also that the misconduct must be such as would amount to misconduct of a grave—that is serious and even very serious—character.' *Poad v Scarborough Union* [1914] 3 KB 959 at 968, CA, per Lord Reading CJ

GRAVE CRIME

'Grave crime' shall be construed as meaning any offence punishable (on a first conviction) with imprisonment for a term that may extend to five years or with a more severe sentence. (Consular Relations Act 1968, s 1(2))

GRAVITY

(a) 'gravity' in relation to any liquid, means the ratio of the weight of a volume of the liquid to the weight of an equal volume of distilled water, the volume of each liquid being computed as at [20°C];
(b) where the gravity of any liquid is expressed as a number of degrees that number shall be the said ratio multiplied by 1,000; and
(c) 'original gravity' in relation to any liquid in which fermentation has taken place means its gravity before fermentation.
(Alcoholic Liquor Duties Act 1979, s 3(1), as amended by the Alcoholic Liquors (Amendment of Enactments Relating to Strength and to Units of Measurement) Order 1979, SI 1979/241)

GRAZIER

Australia 'A grazier is commonly understood to be a person who carries on the occupation of sheep farming or cattle farming, mostly (in this country) [Australia] on a large scale, though in the more settled districts it is not uncommon to combine that occupation with a certain amount of agricultural farming.' *Terry v McGirr* (1922) 22 SRNSW 453 at 458, per Cullen CJ

GRAZING LAND   See ROUGH GRAZING
LAND

GREEN

[A town green or a village green] may or may not be subject to rights of common, but the essential characteristic of a town or village green is that by immemorial custom the inhabitants of the town, village, or parish should have acquired the right of playing lawful games thereon and of enjoying it for purposes of recreation. (6 Halsbury's Laws (4th edn) para 525)

Until the passing of the Commons Registration Act 1965 [see infra] a 'village green', or, as it is sometimes called, a town green, had not been defined by statute. The essential characteristic was that the inhabitants of the particular locality had an immemorial customary right to use it for exercise and recreation, including the playing of lawful games. The custom had to be reasonably exercised by those entitled to it. (34 Halsbury's Laws (4th edn) para 507)

'Town or village green' means land which has been allotted by or under any Act for the exercise or recreation of the inhabitants of any locality or on which the inhabitants of any locality have a customary right to indulge in lawful sports and pastimes or on which the inhabitants of any locality have indulged in such sports and pastimes as of right for not less than twenty years. (Commons Registration Act 1965, s 22)

GRIEVOUS BODILY HARM

'You must be satisfied that the prisoner had an intent to do grievous bodily harm. It is not necessary that such harm should have been actually done, or that it should be either permanent or dangerous, if it be such as seriously to interfere with comfort or health, it is sufficient.' *R v Ashman* (1858) 1 F & F 88 at 88, 89, per Willes J

'My lords, I confess that, whether one is considering the crime of murder or the statutory offence [under s 11 (repealed) of the Offences against the Person Act 1861], I can find no warrant for giving the words "grievous bodily harm" [see s 18 of the Act of 1861] a meaning other than that which the words convey in their ordinary and natural meaning. "Bodily harm" needs no explanation and "grievous" means no more and no less than "really serious".' *Director of Public Prosecutions v Smith* [1960] 3 All ER 161 at 171, HL, per Viscount Kilmuir LC

[The question which arose in *Director of Public Prosecutions v Smith* (supra) was whether the intent required had to be subjective or objective, and it was held that the objective test (viz. the test of what a reasonable man would contemplate as the probable result of his acts and, therefore, would intend) was the right test. Following considerable criticism of this decision the Law Commission considered the matter and came to the conclusion that the test of intent in murder should be subjective and that the same subjective test should be applied in regard to all other offences where it was necessary to ascertain the existence of intent or foresight. As a result of the Law Commission's report, s 11 of the Offences against the Person Act 1861 (which contained a definition of "grievous bodily harm" closely following *R v Ashman* (supra)) was repealed by the Criminal Law Act 1967, s 10(2), Sch 3 (III). Proof of criminal intent is now governed by s 8 of the Criminal Justice Act 1967. See the comments of Lord Hailsham of St Marylebone in *Hyam v Director of Public Prosecutions* [1974] 2 All ER 41 at 46, 47, HL.]

'For over a century judges have almost daily directed juries as to the essential elements required to constitute the offence of wounding with intent to do grievous bodily harm, contrary to s 18 of the Offences against the Person Act 1861. The adjective "grievous" is out moded. Therefore the words "really serious" have been properly and sensibly used to describe the nature of the bodily harm that must be intended.' *R v Belfon* [1976] 3 All ER 46 at 47, CA, per cur.

Australia 'Grievous bodily harm consists of any injury which materially and seriously interferes with the health or comfort of the person injured.' *R v Newman* [1948] VLR 61 at 64, per Barry J

Australia 'In many cases, "grievous bodily harm" is explained to the jury as meaning "really serious bodily injury" (*Cunningham* [1981] 3 WLR 223 at 226) or in other words which make clear that the intention must be to cause some life threatening harm. An assault with intention of breaking a toe or a finger may cause "serious bodily harm" but is not the kind of assault or intention relevant to the crime of murder (ibid). Where the words "serious bodily harm" are used without further explanation, there will often be no misdirection because the assault in the particular case is with a gun or a knife or a club and aimed at a vital part of the body so that grievous bodily harm could ordinarily be expected in the circumstances. However, where the particular assault is of a less obviously dangerous nature, for example performed with the hands in the form of blows to the face or temporary pressure to the neck, the distinction between an intention to do "grievous bodily harm" and to do "serious bodily harm" can

become significant and less of a semantic difference.' *R v Perks* (1986) 20 A Crim R 201 at 210, per White J

GROSS

'In the first part of the clause [in the articles of a company], what is contemplated is a sum which will remain after deduction of income tax from a larger sum. Such a sum would naturally be described as a "clear sum". In the latter part of the clause, what is contemplated is a sum from which income tax at a certain rate is to be deducted, and it is not inappropriate to describe such a sum as a "gross" sum.' *Friends etc Life Office v Investment Trust Corpn Ltd* [1951] 2 All ER 632 at 636, HL, per Lord Morton of Henryton

GROSS INCOME   *See* INCOME

GROSS NEGLIGENCE   *See* NEGLIGENCE

GROSS PRICE

New Zealand [Authority was given to a firm of licensed land agents to sell or exchange the respondent's farm as follows: 'You are hereby authorised to sell or exchange the property described hereunder on commission of 2½ per cent on the gross price'.] 'I think . . . that the term "gross price" means the price per acre at which the agent is authorised to dispose of the property. If it had been intended to limit the commission to 2½ per cent of the amount remaining after deducting the amount of the incumbrances the term used would have been "net price".' *Hamill & Co v Loughlin* [1917] NZLR 784 at 787, 788, per Cooper J; [1917] GLR 453, 454

GROSS VALUE

'Gross value' means the wholesale price, or, if there be no such price, the estimated value, with, in either case, freight, landing charges, and duty paid beforehand; provided that, in the case of goods or merchandise customarily sold in bond, the bonded price is deemed to be the gross value. 'Gross proceeds' means the actual price obtained at a sale where all charges on sale are paid by the sellers. (Marine Insurance Act 1906, s 71(4))

'Gross value', in relation to a hereditament,

means the rent at which the hereditament might reasonably be expected to let from year to year if the tenant undertook to pay all usual tenant's rates and taxes and the landlord undertook to bear the cost of the repairs and insurance and the other expenses, if any, necessary to maintain the hereditament in a state to command that rent. (General Rate Act 1967, s 19)

GROUND

[Section 17 of the Larceny Act 1861 (repealed by the Theft Act 1968) dealt with the taking at night of hares or rabbits in a warren or 'ground'.] 'The word "ground" must mean something ejusdem generis with "warrens", as for instance, places where hares are preserved.' *Bevan v Hopkinson* (1876) 34 LT 142 at 143, DC, per Cleasby B

GROUND GAME   *See* GAME

GROUND LEASE   *See* LEASE

GROUND STOREY

'Ground storey' means that storey of a building to which there is an entrance from the outside on or near the level of the ground and where there are two such storeys then the lower of the two but does not include any storey of which the upper surface of the floor is more than four feet below the level of the adjoining pavement. (London Building Act 1930, s 5)

GUARANTEE

A guarantee is an accessory contract by which the promisor undertakes to be answerable to the promisee for the debt, default or miscarriage of another person, whose primary liability to the promisee must exist or be contemplated. As in the case of any other contract its validity depends upon the mutual assent of the parties to it, their capacity to contract; and consideration, actual or implied. An additional statutory requirement is that the contract must either be in writing or be evidenced by a written note or memorandum signed by or on behalf of the party to be charged. A guarantee is often termed a 'collateral' or 'conditional' contract, in order to distinguish it from one that is 'original' or 'absolute'. But the word 'collateral' does not occur in the provision relating to guarantees contained in the Statute of Frauds, and cannot, therefore, safely be

accepted as affording a certain criterion whether a promise is or is not within that enactment. Moreover the use of this word, without any proper definition, is apt to cause a misapprehension of its meaning. A guarantee, being merely an accessory contract, does not, even when under seal, cause a merger with it of the principal debtor's simple contract debt to which it relates and, generally, when the principal contract or liability is determined, the guarantee itself is also determined. A continuing guarantee is one which extends to a series of transactions and is not exhausted by nor confined to a single credit or transaction. (20 Halsbury's Laws (4th edn) para 101)

Anything in writing is a guarantee if it contains or purports to contain some promise or assurance (however worded or presented) that defects will be made good by complete or partial replacement, or by repair, monetary compensation or otherwise. (Unfair Contract Terms Act 1977, s 5(2)(b))

'Guarantee' includes any contract to indemnify, whether wholly or in part, against loss of any description and shall be construed in accordance with section 10(a)(i) above. (Export Guarantees and Overseas Investment Act 1978, s 15(1))

[Section 10(a)(i) of the Act provides that where a company is controlled by any person then any contract entered into by the Secretary of State with that person shall, in so far as it provides for the Secretary of State to make payments to that person in respect of any loss of that company or in respect of any deficit on an account relating both to activities of that company and to activities of that person be deemed a contract to indemnify that person against loss and a guarantee within the meaning of the Act.]

'In general, contracts of guarantee are between persons who occupy, or ultimately assume, the positions of creditor, debtor and surety, and thereby the surety becomes bound to pay the debt or make good the default of the debtor.' *Seaton v Heath, Seaton v Burnand* [1899] 1 QB 782 at 793, CA, per Romer LJ

[It was argued for the defendants that the word 'guarantee' in a contract implied an understanding by a third party.] 'The word "guarantee" is often used in other than its legal sense. An example of the word meaning simply an undertaking by the contracting party can be found in *Barker v M'Andrew* [(1865) 18 CBNS 759]. The learned judge says this: "Again I think one has to bear in mind that commercial men do not look at these things quite from a lawyer's point of view. To a lawyer to say: 'I guarantee that I will perform my contract' is quite worthless, but a commercial man would regard the guarantee, perhaps furnished in a proper form of letter, as having some value as underlining, as it were, the promise that had been undertaken. He does not think in terms of damages, liquidated damages, penalty clauses and the rest of it; he says to himself 'I have got it in writing and if for any reason these goods do not come forward I will get ten per cent of their price', and he may well think that is a valuable thing".' *Heisler v Anglo-Dal Ltd* [1954] 2 All ER 770 at 772, CA, per Somervell LJ

Australia [A prospectus issued by a company stated that the company gave a 'guaranteed accumulated revisionary bonus'.] 'The word "guaranteed" is not used in its strict legal signification, which is concerned with the solvency or fidelity of persons, but in a sense not uncommon in mercantile circles (e.g. *Wilson v Wiles* [[1921] NZLR 798]). It is capable of meaning an obligation amounting to a warranty.' *Re Commonwealth Homes & Investment Co Ltd* [1943] SASR 211 at 219, per Mayo J

Australia 'A person cannot guarantee the payment of money by himself. He may undertake an additional obligation to pay money which he is already bound to pay, but that added obligation cannot be described as a guarantee. A guarantee is essentially a promise to answer for the debt, default or miscarriage of another, and it does not include as such the case of a person incurring an additional liability in respect of a sum of money for which he is already liable.' *Bank of New South Wales v Permanent Trustee Co of New South Wales Ltd* (1943) 68 CLR 1 at 11, per Latham CJ

Continuing   *See* CONTINUE (Continuing guarantee)

In charterparty

[A charterparty stipulated that the vessel should with all convenient speed proceed to the usual loading place 'guaranteed' for cargo.] 'It appears to me . . . that the owner has made a stipulation that he is not to be responsible for delay caused by a peril of the seas, rivers, or navigation whilst the vessel is proceeding to the place of loading, subject to the construction to be put upon the word "guaranteed". I am not aware that that word has any technical meaning, except in the case of a guarantee for the debt or default of another. As used in this charterparty, it means no more than a contract or engagement on the part of the owner that the vessel shall be ready at the loading place to receive her cargo within the stipulated time unless prevented by an accident happening from a peril of the sea without any default on his part; and that, if the vessel is not so ready, the other party may treat it as a warranty, and throw up the charterparty. I entirely adopt the argument . . . that "guaranteed" is to be taken with the exception,—that it means guaranteed, subject to the defendant not being prevented by the excepted perils.' *Barker v M'Andrew* (1865) 18 CBNS 759 at 773, per Willes J

In will

'This testator gives a great many legacies, and adds, that the payment of these legacies shall be guaranteed by certain leaseholds and freehold estates mentioned in the will; and he afterwards gives a great many other legacies. The estates, which are referred to as the guarantee, are not sufficient for the payment of the legacies for which they were made a guarantee, and those legacies cannot be paid in full without a participation in the general personal estate. . . . The Vice-Chancellor was of opinion, that the testator's intention was, that the general personal estate should contribute to the payment of all the legacies; though, as the general personal estate might be insufficient for the payment of all the legacies in full, the produce of certain particular estates was to be applied exclusively in paying a particular class of legacies, for which the testator had thought fit to provide what he calls a guarantee. . . . I never before met the word "guarantee" used as it is by this testator; and I have not been able to find any authority as to the construction, which, under such circumstances, ought to be put upon it. But my opinion is, that the decree of the Vice-Chancellor is right.' *Willox v Rhodes* (1826) 2 Russ 452 at 454, 455, per Lord Eldon LC

GUARD

[Regulation 27(2) of the Building (Safety, Health & Welfare) Regulations 1948 (revoked; see now reg 29(2) of the Construction (Working Places) Regulations 1966, SI 1966/94, as amended by SI 1984/1593), makes it necessary for all gangways, runs and stairs from which a person is liable to fall more than a certain distance to be provided with suitable 'guard-rails'.] 'I think that in this context guard-rails must be construed as rails of such a character as will provide a physical barrier against the possibility of falling over the side.' *Carn v Weir's*

Glass (Hanley) Ltd [1960] 2 All ER 300 at 303, CA, per Willmer LJ

[Regulation H5 of the Building Regulations 1965 provided that the side of any landing or similar space forming part of a stairway or directly overlooking a stairwell should be 'guarded' by a wall, balustrade, etc.] 'It is pointed out that the regulation in question does not define what the spaces between the rails or balustrade or the like shall be, although the erection contemplated is one which is not solid, but will contain apertures in it. These are nowhere defined. Accordingly it is said that providing even a guard rail and nothing more was put, the regulation has been complied with. For my part I am quite unable to accept that contention. True the words used are not "securely guarded". True there is no definition of what will be treated as a proper guard, but it seems to me that once one asks the question "Guarded against what?" it is clearly contemplating a guard which will afford reasonable safety to any person, and by "person" I include children as well as adults, who may from time to time occupy the house. It is not without interest that in the next reg H6, which deals with external balconies, platforms and roofs, the word "guard" is not specifically referred to, but it is provided that they are to be constructed so as to afford reasonable safety for any person using such balcony, platform, roof or other external area. I would define "guard" in the same way; on the facts here it is quite clear, as the justices found, that the stairwell was not "guarded" applying that test, and accordingly I would dismiss the appeal on those informations.' *Sunley Homes Ltd v Borg* [1969] 3 All ER 332 at 336, per Lord Parker CJ

GUARD DOG   *See* DOG

GUARDIAN

Minors, both naturally and at law, are subject to incapacities which make it necessary for their interests to be safeguarded by persons of full age. In its widest sense, the relationship of guardian and ward may arise by nature, for nurture or by parental right. It may be created by appointment, whether by a court of competent jurisdiction or out of court, in which case the appointment may be by a parent or by the minor himself. Guardianship may be either of the minor's person or of his estate or both. A guardian of the person has no authority over the minor's property, and a guardian of his estate has no authority over his person. Guardianship is an office of trust and the relationship between guardian and ward is that of trustee and beneficiary. The court's inherent guardianship jurisdiction is grounded in the role of the Crown as parens patriae and in the general power and authority which it has over all trusts, and its powers in respect of the appointment or removal of a guardian have probably never been dependent upon the minor holding property. (24 Halsbury's Laws (4th edn) para 527)

'Guardian' means—
(a) a person apointed by deed or will in accordance with the provisions of the Guardianship of Infant Acts 1886 and 1925 or the Guardianship of Minors Act 1971 or by a court of competent jurisdiction to be the guardian of the child, and
(b) in the case of an illegitimate child, includes the father where he has custody of the child by virtue of an order under section 9 of the Guardianship of Minors Act 1971, or under section 2 of the Illegitimate Children (Scotland) Act 1930.
(Adoption Act 1976, s 72(1))

'The relation of guardian and ward is strictly that of trustee and cestui que trust. I look on it as a peculiar relation to trusteeship, and this appears from the case of *Beaufort (Duke) v Berty* [(1721) 1 P Wms 703]. A guardian is not only a trustee of the property, as in an ordinary case of trustee, but he is also the guardian of the person of the infant, with many duties to perform, such as to see to his education, and maintenance. Lord Macclesfield [in *Beaufort (Duke) v Berty,* supra] said, "that guardians were but trustees, and that the jurisdiction of the Court was grounded upon the general power and jurisdiction which it had over all trusts, and a guardianship is most plainly a trust". This shews that the important and principal part of the relation is not confined to the property, but extends beyond it. I consider that it is not confined to that relation, and that of all the property which he gets into his possession in the character of guardian, he is a trustee for the benefit of the infant ward.' *Mathew v Brise* (1851) 14 Beav 341 at 345, per Romilly MR

'It is not to be disputed that if a person is appointed guardian, in that character possesses himself of any of his ward's property, of that property he becomes a trustee, although he is only a trustee by construction, and not appointed by name.' *Sleeman v Wilson* (1871) LR 13 Eq 36 at 42, per Bacon V-C

'What does the word "guardian", standing alone, generally mean? I suppose guardian of the person. An infant may have several guardians; he may have a guardian of the person, or a guardian in socage, or in gavelkind or, if he has a copyhold estate [which tenure has been abolished], a guardian according to the custom of the manor. But I suppose "guardian" of an infant means guardian of the person.' *Rimington v Hartley* (1880) 14 Ch D 630 at 632, per Jessel MR

GUARDIAN AD LITEM

An appointment of a guardian ad litem where the interests of the child or young person may conflict with those of the parent or guardian must be made by order, and the person to be appointed is to be selected from the panel established by regulations or, if this is not practicable, is to be some other suitable person. In either case, the person selected must not be a member, officer or servant of a local authority or authorised person which is a party to the proceedings. The appointment may be revoked and new guardian ad litem appointed where it appears to the court to be desirable.

With a view to safeguarding the interests of the relevant infant before the court the guardian ad litem must: (1) so far as it is reasonably practicable, investigate all circumstances relevant to the proceedings and for that purpose interview such persons and inspect such records as he thinks appropriate; (2) in the light of that investigation, consider whether it is in the infant's best interests that the application to which the proceedings relate should succeed; (3) in the light of that consideration, decide how the case should be conducted on behalf of the infant and, where appropriate, instruct a solicitor to represent the infant; (4) where the infant is not legally represented, conduct the case on his behalf, unless the infant otherwise requests; (5) where the guardian ad litem thinks that it would assist the court, make a report in writing to the court; (6) perform such other duties as the court directs.

When the court has finally disposed of the case the guardian ad litem must consider whether it would be in the infant's best interests to appeal to the Crown Court and, if he considers that it would be, he must give notice of appeal on the infant's behalf. (24 Halsbury's Laws (4th edn) para 765)

'A minor, whose father is alive, neither has nor can have any guardian except his father. . . . If . . . an action is brought against a minor, or a minor has to be made a party to any proceedings in a court of justice, a guardian ad litem may be appointed, but such person does not thereby become the guardian of the minor generally.' *Re Salisbury (Marquis) & Ecclesiastical Comrs* (1876) 2 Ch D 29 at 36, CA, per Mellish LJ

GUEST

'If one come to an inn, and make a previous contract for lodging for a set time, and do not eat or drink there, he is no guest, but a lodger, and as such is not under the innkeeper's protection; but if he eat and drink there it is otherwise.' *Parker v Flint* (1698) 12 Mod Rep 254 at 255, per Holt CJ

'The real question is whether there was any evidence to justify the county court judge in finding that the plaintiff was a guest at the defendant's inn. . . . The room he went into was the dining-room of the hotel. It is said that to make him a guest he must be a wayfarer and traveller. The facts are that he was on his way home; he was on his way to the station from which he travelled home by railway. Why was he not a wayfarer? . . . But I do not take the more restricted view of what constitutes a guest at an inn. I think a guest is a person who uses the inn, either for a temporary or a more permanent stay, in order to take what the inn can give. He need not stay the night. I confess I do not understand why he should not be a guest if he uses the inn as an inn for the purpose merely of getting a meal there.' *Orchard v Bush & Co* [1898] 2 QB 284 at 287, DC, per Wills J

Australia 'Various dictionary meanings of the word "guest" could be referred to, e.g. one who is entertained at the house or table of another, a visitor entertained without payment or a person to whom hospitality is extended; very often, of course, the word is used to indicate persons to whom hospitality is extended without such persons actually contributing to the cost but I do not think that, even in relation to social gatherings in a private home, it could always be postulated that it would be a misuse of language to describe people as guests in the home even though they might, in particular circumstances, be contributing to the cost of the refreshments which the householder makes available to them.' *Ex p Fry, Re Maher* [1965] NSWR 1590 at 1595, per Maguire J

Canada 'It would appear that for the person being transported by a motor vehicle to be a guest, the person transporting him must be extending something to him in the nature of hospitality as to the facilities afforded by the motor vehicle, and that the person to whom this hospitality is extended must voluntarily accept it (unless perhaps, he is in the custody of someone else, as, for example, where he is an infant in arms, when possibly the person in charge of him may accept it). For example, a person forcibly put into a motor vehicle by the driver and carried off would not, in my view, be a guest, nor would a person entering it under any form of duress on the part of the driver.' *Keddy v Campbell* (1959) 19 DLR (2d) 735 at 738, NSSC, per Ilsley CJNs

GUILD CHURCH   *See* CHURCH

GUILTY BUT INSANE

[Section 2 of the Trial of Lunatics Act 1883, as amended by the Criminal Procedure (Insanity) Act 1964, empowers a jury to return the special verdict of 'not guilty by reason of insanity'. The former special verdict was 'guilty but insane'.] 'The jury came to the conclusion that the appellant committed the act complained of, but was insane at the time. . . . It is now quite clear that that special verdict amounts to an acquittal of the person tried; and that being so he is not a person who has been convicted.' *R v Taylor* [1915] 2 KB 709 at 712, 713, CAA, per cur.

H

HABEAS CORPUS

The writ of habeas corpus, the most celebrated writ in the English law. Of this there are various kinds made use of by the courts at Westminster, for removing prisoners from one court into another for the more easy administration of justice. Such is the *habeas corpus ad respondendum*, when a man hath a cause of action against one who is confined by the process of some inferior court; in order to remove the prisoner, and charge him with this new action in the courts above. Such is that *ad satisfaciendum*, when a prisoner hath had judgment against him in an action, and the plaintiff is desirous to bring him up to some superior court to charge him with process of execution. Such also are those *ad prosequendum, testificandum, deliberandum, &c*; which issue when it is necessary to remove a prisoner, in order to prosecute or bear testimony in any court, or to be tried in the proper jurisdiction wherein the fact was committed. Such is, lastly the common writ *ad faciendum et recipiendum*, which issues out of any of the courts of Westminsterhall, when a person is sued in some inferior jurisdiction, and is desirous to remove the action into the superior court; commanding the inferior judges to produce the body of the defendant, together with the day and cause of his caption and detainer (whence the writ is frequently denominated an *habeas corpus cum causa*) to *do and receive* whatsoever the king's court shall consider in that behalf. This is a writ grantable of common right, without any

motion in court; and it instantly supersedes all proceedings in the court below. (3 Bl Com 129, 130)

Ad deliberandum and recipiendum

The object of the writ of habeas corpus ad deliberandum et recipiendum is to enable the removal of prisoners from one custody to another for the purpose of their trial. This writ is obsolete, modern legislation having facilitated the removal of prisoners from one custody to another for various purposes. (11 Halsbury's Laws (4th edn) para 1511)

Ad respondendum

The object of the writ of habeas corpus ad respondendum is to bring up prisoners who are detained in custody under civil or criminal process before magistrates or courts of record for trial or examination on any other charge. However, persons, who are in custody and under recognisances to come up for trial for any criminal offence can now be brought up on an indictment by order without a writ of habeas corpus ad respondendum. (11 Halsbury's Laws (4th edn) para 1510)

Ad subjiciendum

The writ of *habeas corpus ad subjiciendum*, which is commonly known as the writ of habeas corpus, is a prerogative process for securing the liberty of the subject by affording an effective means of immediate release from unlawful or unjustifiable detention, whether in prison or in private custody. It is a prerogative writ by which the Queen has a right to inquire into the causes for which any of her subjects are deprived of their liberty. By it the High Court and the judges of that Court, at the instance of a subject aggrieved, command the production of that subject, and inquire into the cause of his imprisonment. If there is no legal justification for the detention, the party is ordered to be released. Release on habeas corpus is not, however, an acquittal, nor may the writ be used as a means of appeal. (11 Halsbury's Laws (4th edn) para 1452)

In this Act 'application for habeas corpus' means an application for a writ of habeas corpus ad subjiciendum and references to a criminal application or civil application shall be construed according as the application does or does not constitute a criminal cause or matter. (Administration of Justice Act 1960, s 17(2))

Ad testificandum

The object of the writ of habeas corpus ad testificandum is to enable a person who is in legal custody in prison to be brought up before the court for the purpose of giving evidence as a witness. The judges of the High Court may award writs of habeas corpus for the purpose of bringing up prisoners before any court of record in England to be examined as witnesses in any cause or matter, civil or criminal, or before any arbitrator or umpire, or before courts-martial or commissioners acting under commission or warrant from the Crown. . . . Applications for writs of habeas corpus ad testificandum must be made on affidavit to a judge in chambers, and the writ may be awarded whether the person whose evidence is required is detained in custody under civil or criminal process. It is, however, now rarely necessary to resort to the writ in the case of a person in prison, for the secretary of state may order the attendance of any prisoner at any place, if it is proved to his satisfaction that such attendance is desirable in the interests of justice or for the purpose of any public inquiry. Judges of the High Court and of county courts have power to order a prisoner to be brought up to give evidence, except when the prisoner is confined under civil process. (11 Halsbury's Laws (4th edn) para 1509)

HABITUAL

Australia [The Police Act 1936, s 85(1)(j) (repealed; see now Summary Offences Act 1953–1986], s 13, (SA)) provides that any person

shall be an idle and disorderly person who (inter alia 'habitually' consorts with thieves, prostitutes, etc.] '"Habitually" requires a continuance and permanence of some tendency, something that has developed into a propensity, that is present from day to day. A habit results from a condition of mind that has become stereotyped. In terms of conduct its presence is demonstrated by the frequency of acts that by repetition have acquired the characteristics of being customary or usual: behaviour that is to be regarded as almost inevitable when the appropriate conditions are present. The tendency will ordinarily be required to be demonstrated by numerous instances of reiteration.' *Dias v O'Sullivan* [1949] ALR 586 at 589, per Mayo J

HABITUAL DRUNKARD

Australia 'It is, of course, true that an habitual drunkard is a person who drinks to excess; the fact that he is a drunkard is a clear indication that he does so. But to say of a man that he is a heavy drinker is to describe his drinking habits; it does not necessarily describe the condition produced by those habits and this is the vital matter for consideration when considering whether a man is an habitual drunkard. It is, of course, as unnecessary as it is fruitless to attempt to define drunkenness or to say what constitutes an habitual drunkard. . . . It suffices in this case to say that the vital question for consideration when the allegation is made that a man is an habitual drunkard is the condition which his addiction to drink produces and not necessarily or solely the extent to which he partakes of liquor.' *Dalgleish v Dalgleish* (1955) 93 CLR 595 at 601, per cur.

Australia '"Habitual drunkard", in my opinion, has a shade of meaning different from that imported by the words "habitual drunkenness". It seems to me that one may well be guilty of habitual drunkenness before he reaches the stage of becoming an habitual drunkard. I think the combination of the two words "habitual drunkard" imports something like his becoming "a sot", which is one of the meanings given to the word in Webster's Dictionary. There are no doubt some highly respectable and otherwise sober people who either by design or misjudgment of their capacity get drunk on every Anzac Day but on no other occasion. That has thus become "habitual". To suggest, however, that the exercise of that habit on two or three successive Anzac Days gave ground for divorce seems to me to be absurd.'

Lehman v Lehman [1969] SASR 357 at 359, per Travers J

New Zealand 'The meaning of the term "habitual drunkard" was discussed by Mr Justice Windeyer in New South Wales in the case *Tate v Tate* [(1893) 14 NSWLR (Div) 1 at 4]. That learned Judge there says, "Drinking habits so confirmed as to lead to the belief that any day of the week the love of indulgence in stimulants will probably render a man liable to becoming incapable of controlling his conduct with a due regard to the feelings and rights of others—such habits, to my mind place him in the category of the habitual drunkard". That expression of opinion has been approved of by two learned Judges in this Court and I agree with them.' *Mackie v Mackie* (1903) 22 NZLR 567 at 567, 568, per Williams J

New Zealand 'I think that when the drinking to excess, with at times resultant serious annoyance to his family, was not infrequent throughout the marriage, a matter of nine years, and was fairly regular, that drinking to excess was habitual. Such a frequency and regularity over a long period appears to me to be sufficient to show that settled disposition or tendency to act in that way which constitutes a habit.' *Smoluch v Smoluch* [1963] NZLR 727 at 728, per Hutchison J

HACKNEY CARRIAGE

Every carriage with two or more wheels which shall be used for the purpose of standing or plying for hire in any public street or road at any place within the distance of five miles from the General Post Office in the City of London, whatever may be the form or construction of such carriage, or the number of persons which the same shall be calculated to convey, or the number of horses by which the same shall be drawn, shall be deemed and taken to be a hackney carriage within the meaning of this Act. (London Hackney Carriage Act 1831, s 4)

The words 'hackney carriage' shall include every carriage (except a stage carriage) which shall stand on hire or ply for a passenger for hire at any place within the limits of the city of London and the liberties thereof, and metropolitan police district. (London Hackney Carriages Act 1843, s 2)

Every wheeled carriage, whatever may be its form or construction, used in standing or plying for hire in any street within the prescribed distance [i.e. within the borough or district], and

every carriage standing upon any street within the prescribed distance, having thereon any numbered plate required . . . to be fixed upon a hackney carriage, or having thereon any plate resembling or intended to resemble any such plate as aforesaid, shall be deemed to be a hackney carriage within the meaning of this Act. . . . Provided always, that no stage coach . . . shall be deemed to be a hackney carriage within the meaning of this Act. (Town Police Clauses Act 1847, s 38)

'Hackney carriage' shall mean any carriage for the conveyance of passengers which plies for hire within the limits of this Act, and is not a stage carriage. (Metropolitan Public Carriage Act 1869, s 4)

It is hereby declared that for the purposes of any act relating to hackney carriages . . . in London, the expressions 'hackney carriage' . . . include any such vehicle, whether drawn or propelled by animal or mechanical power. (London Cab and Stage Carriage Act 1907, s 6)

'Hackney carriage' means a mechanically propelled vehicle standing or plying for hire and includes any mechanically propelled vehicle bailed or (in Scotland) hired under a hire agreement by a person whose trade it is to sell such vehicles or bail or hire them under hire agreements. (Vehicles (Excise) Act 1971, s 38(1), as substituted by the Consumer Credit Act 1974, s 192(3)(a), Sch 4, para 32)

'A hackney carriage is a carriage exposed for hire to the public, whether standing in the public street or exposed for public use in a private gateway. The test is, whether the carriage is held out for the general accommodation of the public.' *Bateson v Oddy* (1874) 43 LJMC 131 at 133, per Lush J

HAIRDRESSING

'Hairdressing' means the following: shaving, cutting, shampooing, tinting, dyeing, bleaching, waving, curling, straightening, setting, or dressing of the hair, upon the scalp or face, with or without the aid of any apparatus or appliance, preparation or substance; the hand or vibro massage of the scalp or face. (Hairdressers (Registration) Act 1964, s 15)

HALF-COMMISSION

'There is no proof of any custom on the Stock Exchange which governs the position of a half-commission man. There are, according to Dr

Richardson, the official assignee of the Stock Exchange, certain practices which prevail on the Stock Exchange with regard to it; but a practice does not make a contract, and the practice is not so general that parties to such a contract must be taken to have contracted with reference to such practice. I think that, whatever might be the position of a half-commission man without a seat in a stockbroker's office, who can hardly be said to be employed at all, the position of a half-commission man who has a seat in an office and who helps to carry out the business in the office, and who is paid in respect of such work by commission and not by salary, is one which gives rise to the relationship of employment, and that prima facie such a person is not entitled to remuneration after the termination of the agreement.' *Bickley v Browning, Todd & Co* (1913) 30 TLR 134 at 134, 135, per Pickford J

HALF COUSIN *See* COUSIN

HALF HOLIDAY *See* HOLIDAY

HALF-YEAR

Australia 'Half a year means half the days of a year, viz 182 days; the odd hours in legal computation are rejected. . . . There is every reason for accepting this meaning in the context of this will; the amount of "£3 per week to commence from the date of my death and to be paid half-yearly". That means, in my opinion, the first payment . . . is to be made, twenty-six weeks "from the date of my death", i.e. on the 25th September 1940; next payment . . . on 26th March 1941, and so on. There is no confusion by paying for odd days or special calculations for leap year. Each half year is simply calculated as a period of 182 days or 26 weeks.' *Re Brewis, Brewis v Brewis* [1946] VLR 199 at 203, 204, per O'Bryan J

HALL *See* LIBRARY

HALLMARK

[A stamp authorised to be impressed on gold or silver articles. The law as to hallmarking was revised by the Hallmarking Act 1973. Hallmarks must be stamped by assay offices (*qv*).

Approved hallmarks for articles composed of a single precious metal made in the United Kingdom are, for the respective assay offices: London, a leopard's head; Edinburgh, a castle; Birmingham, an anchor; Sheffield, a rose. For articles other than those made in the United Kingdom, the approved marks are: London, the sign of the constellation Leo; Edinburgh, St Andrew's Cross; Birmingham, an equilateral triangle; Sheffield, the sign of the constellation Libra. In addition, articles of gold made in the United Kingdom must be marked with a crown, and those of silver with a lion passant (Edinburgh, a lion rampant), and those of platinum with an orb surmounted by a cross. All articles must also be marked with a standard of fineness.]

HALT

'The appellant was charged with failing to conform with a certain sign at a certain road junction. A traffic sign of an approved type stood a little way from the junction, and facing in the correct direction were the words, "Halt at major road ahead". The defendant, as he came near the junction, reduced his speed to walking pace, took observations in both directions, saw a police officer who signalled to him to stop, and stopped in the middle of the road. . . . The justices found that a temporary stop was required. I think they were correct. The Road Traffic Act 1930, s 49 [repealed; see now Road Traffic Act 1988, s 36], makes it an offence to fail to conform to the indication given by a sign regulating the movement of traffic. I do not think there is any doubt that a car should be brought to a momentary standstill before a major road is entered.' *Tolhurst v Webster* [1936] 3 All ER 1020 at 1021, 1022, per Lord Hewart CJ

'Could anything be plainer than "halt"? How could a motorist halt if he proceeded stumblingly or falteringly across?' Ibid at 1022, per Swift J

HAND *See* UNDER HAND AND SEAL

HAND-HOLD

[The Factories Act 1937, s 26(2) (repealed; see now the Factories Act 1961, s 29(2)), provided that where any person was to work at a place from which he would be liable to fall more than a certain distance, unless the place was one which afforded secure foot-hold and, where necessary, secure 'hand-hold', means were to be provided for ensuring his safety.] 'We agree with counsel for the defendants' submission that "hand-hold" in the subsection means something which the man can hold on to or grab from time to time as and when he wishes so to do.' *Wigley v British Vinegars Ltd* [1961] 3 All ER 418 at 424, CA, per cur.

HAND-RAIL

[Regulation 27(1) of the Building (Safety, Health and Welfare) Regulations 1948 (revoked; see now the Construction (Working Places) Regulations 1966, SI 1966 No 94, as amended by SI 1984 No 1593), made it necessary for stairs to be provided with 'hand-rails'.] 'A hand-rail must in my judgment be construed as something different from a guard-rail. A hand-rail—which is not required by reg 27(1) to be of any particular strength—connotes to my mind a rail that can be gripped by the hand. Such a rail need not necessarily act as a physical barrier; it need only be such a rail as will enable any person, by gripping it, to steady himself against falling.' *Carn v Weir's Glass (Hanley) Ltd* [1960] 2 All ER 300 at 303, CA, per Willmer LJ

HANDICRAFTSMAN   *See* ARTIFICER

HANDLE

A person handles stolen goods if (otherwise than in the course of the stealing) knowing or believing them to be stolen goods he dishonestly receives the goods, or dishonestly undertakes or assists in their retention, removal, disposal or realisation by or for the benefit of another person, or if he arranges to do so. (Theft Act 1968, s 22(1))

'Before the Theft Act 1968 came into force on 1 January 1969, there was no offence of handling stolen goods. The governing provision was s 33 of the Larceny Act 1916, which made it an offence for a person to receive stolen property knowing that it had been stolen. Receiving meant receiving property into his possession or control. Section 22 of the Theft Act 1968 [supra] created the offence of handling. This provision is wider than the old one. It embraces two kinds of handling: the first is essentially the old offence of receiving and the second is what I shall call, for brevity, assisting. . . . Inevitably every case in which the question arose prior to 1969 was a case of receiving, and many of these cases therefore touched on, or turned on, the question of

whether it could be said [i.e. inferred] that the goods passed into the possession or control of the defendant. There is, in the view of this court, no reason in logic or justice why, since 1969, it should be permissible to draw the inference where the defendant has received recently stolen goods into his possession, but impermissible to draw it when he is merely assisting somebody else to deal with such goods. The distinction between the two types of handling lies in the relationship between the defendant and the goods. In each his state of mind is the same, and it is in relation to his state of mind that the jury may think it right to draw the inference.' *R v Ball* [1983] 2 All ER 1089 at 1093, CA, per cur.

HARBOUR   *See also* PORT

The word 'harbour' shall include harbours properly so called, whether natural or artificial, estuaries, navigable rivers, piers, jetties, and other works in or at which ships can obtain shelter, or ship and unship goods or passengers. (Merchant Shipping Act 1894, s 742)

'Harbour' means any harbour, whether natural or artificial, and any port, haven, estuary, tidal or other river, canal or inland navigation navigated by sea-going ships and, subject to the provisions of this Act, any dock. (Petroleum (Consolidation) Act 1928, s 23)

'Harbour' means any harbour, whether natural or artificial, and any port, haven, estuary, tidal or other river or inland waterway navigated by sea-going ships, and any dock, including any pier, jetty or other place at which ships can ship or unship goods or passengers. (Transport Act 1962, s 92; General Rate Act 1967, s 32)

'Whether or not s 37 of the Harbours and Passing Tolls Act 1861 [repealed], took the harbour of Ramsgate out of the district of the corporation [for rating purposes], . . . the word "harbour" in that section, in the absence of any special definition, [was] used in its ordinary sense as a place to shelter ships from the winds and the sea, and where ships come for commercial purposes to load and unload goods.' *R v Hannam* (1886) 34 WR 355 at 356, CA, per Lord Esher MR

Canada 'The words "harbour" and "bay" are often loosely applied and the same body of water is sometimes called a "harbour" and sometimes a "bay". But cartographers generally apply the word "harbour" to a body of water wherein there is shelter. . . . Before a body of water can properly be considered a "harbour", it must have the essential element of shelter or safety. Apart altogether from its use to designate a body of water, the word carries the meaning of a place of safety. Generally speaking, the word "bay" connotes a larger body of water with an inward curve something like a saucer and which affords relatively no protection from the sea. A harbour because it must have the essential element of safety (often afforded by its projecting headlands) is to some extent an enclosure.' *Re Dominion Coal Co Ltd and County of Cape Breton* (1963) 40 DLR (2d) 593 at 646, NSSC, per Patterson J

HARBOUR AUTHORITY

'Harbour authority' means any person or body of persons, corporate or unincorporate, being or claiming to be proprietor or proprietors of or intrusted with the duty or invested with the power of improving, managing, maintaining, or regulating any harbour properly so called, whether natural or artificial, and any port, haven, and estuary, or intrusted with the duty of conserving, maintaining, or improving the navigation of any tidal water, and any such harbour, port, haven, estuary, tidal water, and any wharf, dock, pier, jetty, and work, and other area, whether land or water, over which the harbour authority as above defined have control or exercise powers, are in the other portions of this Act included in the expression 'harbour'. (Explosives Act 1875, s 108)

'Harbour authority' means a person or body of persons empowered by an enactment to make charges in respect of vessels entering a harbour in the United Kingdom or using facilities therein. (Prevention of Oil Pollution Act 1971, s 8(2))

HARBOUR BOARD

'Harbour board' means any persons who are otherwise than for private profit intrusted with the duty or invested with the power of constructing, improving, managing, regulating, and maintaining a harbour, whether natural or artificial, or any dock. (Railway and Canal Traffic Act 1888, s 55)

HARBOUR IN UNITED KINGDOM

'Harbour in the United Kingdom' means a port, estuary, haven, dock, or other place which fulfils the following conditions, that is to say—
(a) that it contains waters to which s 2 of this Act applies, and

(b) that a person or body of persons is empowered by an enactment to make charges in respect of vessels entering that place or using facilities therein.
(Prevention of Oil Pollution Act 1971, s 8(2))

[Section 2 applies to (a) the whole of the sea within the seaward limits of the territorial waters of the United Kingdom and (b) all other waters (including inland waters) which are within those limits and are navigable by seagoing ships]

HARBOUR (Verb)

[Section 22 of the Criminal Justice Act 1961 makes it an offence to 'harbour' a person who has escaped from prison.] 'I am of the opinion that the word "harbour" in this context means to shelter a person, in the sense of giving refuge to that person.' *Darch v Weight* [1984] 2 All ER 245 at 247, per Robert Goff LJ

HARDSHIP   *See also* EXCEPTIONAL

'The word "hardship" is not a word of art. It follows that it must be construed by the courts in a common sense way, and the meaning which is put on the word "hardship" should be such as would meet with the approval of ordinary sensible people. In my judgment, the ordinary sensible man would take the view that there are two aspects of "hardship"—that which the sufferer from the hardship thinks he is suffering and that which a reasonable bystander with knowledge of all the facts would think he was suffering. That can be illustrated by a homely example. The rich gourmet who because of financial stringency has to drink *vin ordinaire* with his grouse may well think that he is suffering a hardship; but sensible people would say he was not.' *Rukat v Rukat* [1975] 1 All ER 343 at 351, CA, per Lawton LJ

Australia   'There is no definition of "hardship" in the Act [s 70 (see now s 70(1)) of the Landlord and Tenant (Amendment) Act 1948–1986, as amended (NSW)]. In its context I would be of the opinion that "hardship" would comprehend any matter of appreciable detriment whether financial, personal, or otherwise. Each case must depend upon its own particular facts.' *O'Brien (FG) Ltd v Elliott* [1965] NSWR 1473 at 1475, per Asprey J

Australia   [Section 44(4) of the Family Law Act 1975–1986 (Cth) provides that the court shall not grant leave under sub-s (3) (to commence certain ancillary proceedings more than twelve months after a decree nisi for dissolution of marriage) unless the court is satisfied that 'hardship' would be caused to a party of a marriage or a child of a marriage if leave were not granted.] 'The meaning of "hardship" in s 44(4) is akin to such concepts as hardness, severity, privation, that which is hard to bear or a substantial detriment.' *In the Marriage of Whitford* (1979) 24 ALR 424 at 430, per cur.

New Zealand 'The claim that an accommodation allowance is not paid or payable by reason of hardship depends upon the view that Parliament intended the word "hardship" to be understood with the significance of financial strain or stringency. But this would be to give to that word a particular and so a restricted flavour. The Shorter Oxford Dictionary gives it a general and wider meaning: "the quality of being hard to bear", or alternatively "hardness of need or circumstance"'. *Director-General of Education v Morrison* (1985) 2 NZLR 431 at 433, per Woodhouse P

New Zealand 'In all such cases the justification for any grant is that in modern social conditions it is considered hard that a student undertaking and qualified for a tertiary course should have to do so without assistance from public funds. In a broad sense therefore the assistance is given by reason of hardship. In ordinary usage hardship does not necessarily connote extreme privation or the like. The expression is wide enough to cover the basic ground on which in general tertiary students are assisted' Ibid, at 436, per Cooke J

Greater hardship

[Schedule 1 to the Rent and Mortgage Interest Restrictions (Amendment) Act 1933 (repealed; see now the Rent Act 1977, Sch 15, Part III, para 1), provided (inter alia) as follows: 'A court shall for the purposes of s 3 of this Act, have power to make or give an order or judgment for the recovery of possession of any dwelling-house to which the principal Acts apply or for the ejectment of a tenant therefrom without proof of suitable alternative accommodation (where the court considers it reasonable so to do) if . . . (h) the dwelling-house is reasonably required by the landlord . . . for occupation as a residence for (i) himself; or (ii) any son or daughter of his over eighteen years of age; or (iii) his father or mother: Provided that an order or judgment shall not be made or given on any ground specified in para (h) of the foregoing provisions of this Schedule if the court is satisfied that

having regard to all the circumstances of the case, including the question whether other accommodation is available for the landlord or the tenant, greater hardship would be caused by granting the order or judgment than by refusing to grant it.'] 'I incline to the view that the burden is upon the tenant to prove that greater hardship would be caused by granting the order or judgment than by refusing to grant it. It seems to me that this is the natural construction of the proviso, and, further, if the landlord has satisfied the court that the dwelling-house is reasonably required by him for the occupation of himself or, for instance, as in this case his daughter, it is obvious that some hardship would be caused to the landlord by refusing the order. I think once the landlord has brought himself within the provisions of para (h) it is for the tenant then to satisfy the court that greater hardship would be caused by granting the order than by refusing it. . . . I think that the fact, if it be a fact in any particular case, that an order for possession will confront the tenant with the alternative of either selling his furniture or storing it, is one of the circumstances which a judge is entitled to take into account in arriving at a conclusion on the question of "greater hardship". How much weight should be given to it is not a matter which one can usefully discuss. It must, I think, depend upon the circumstances in each case.' *Sims v Wilson* [1946] 2 All ER 261 at 263, 264, CA, per Morton LJ

Undue hardship

[The Arbitration Act 1950, s 27 provides that where the terms of an agreement to refer future disputes to arbitration provide for claims to be barred unless the proper steps are taken within a time fixed by the agreement, and a dispute arises, the High Court, if it is of opinion that in the circumstances of the case 'undue hardship' would otherwise be caused, may extend the time for such period as it thinks proper.] 'It does appear that in the past the courts have been inclined to emphasise the word "undue", and to say that if a man does not read the contract and is a day or two late, it is a "hardship"; but it is not an "undue hardship", because it is his own fault. I cannot accept this narrow interpretation of the statute. These time-limit clauses used to operate most unjustly. Claimants used to find their claims barred when, by some oversight, they were only a day or two late. In order to avoid that injustice, the legislature intervened so as to enable the courts to extend the time whenever "in the circumstances of the case undue hardship would otherwise be caused". "Undue" there simply means excessive. It means greater hardship than the circumstances warrant. Even though a claimant has been at fault himself, it is an undue hardship on him if the consequences are out of proportion to his fault.' *Liberian Shipping Corpn v King (A) & Sons Ltd* [1967] 1 All ER 934 at 938, CA, per Lord Denning MR

New Zealand [Section 18(6) of the Arbitration Amendment Act 1938 authorises the court to grant an extension of time within which to take some step in an arbitration if 'undue hardship' would be caused by the refusal of such extension.] 'While judges have refrained from attempting to define what undue hardship is, no doubt because there are infinite varieties of circumstances which might constitute undue hardship, it seems clear that the following are relevant matters in considering whether there is undue hardship or not: (a) The mere fact that the claim is barred cannot be held to be an undue hardship; (b) The court will not hold circumstances to constitute an undue hardship where the delay has been due to inadvertence or to an applicant not making himself aware of the terms of his contract or to his negligently letting the time go by; (c) The court will hold there is undue hardship where there has been a misunderstanding or confusion which has been caused or contributed to by the other side; (d) The court will hold there is undue hardship where the failure to give notice in time was due to circumstances over which the applicant had no control or other very special circumstances explaining the delay; (e) The court would hold there to be undue hardship if the refusal of an extension would involve an applicant in actual financial difficulties or perhaps bankruptcy.' *Lower Hutt City v New Zealand Municipalities Co-operative Insurance Co Ltd* [1965] NZLR 24 at 28, per Tompkins J

HARM   *See* ACTUAL BODILY HARM; GRIEVOUS BODILY HARM

HARSH AND OPPRESSIVE

Australia 'Each of the two words in the phrase "harsh and oppressive" must be given its meaning. The test of harshness and oppressiveness is subjective and must relate to the respondent. What is envisaged is not some such concept in the abstract or as applying generally to others, or even to the reasonable man or woman. The phrase connotes some substantial detriment to the party before the

court. It is not satisfied by argument based on generalities or on social philosophy or that the petitioner is at fault or by suggested injustice, e.g. loss of status or such as would be said to result from unsuccessful opposition by the respondent.' *McDonald v McDonald* [1965] ALR 166 at 175, per Herron CJ

Australia 'Should the court be of the opinion that it is proper that financial provision be made for the respondent and the petitioner be in a position to make adequate provision, financial considerations might well be irrelevant to the question of the consequence of harshness and oppressiveness. But should the petitioner, by reason of his own financial situation, be completely unable to make provision for the respondent, when the Court was of the opinion that it was proper that some provision should be made, then it could fairly be said that it would be harsh and oppressive to the respondent to make a decree.' *Ferguson v Ferguson* [1965] ALR 310 at 318, per Selby J

HARSH OR UNJUST

Canada [Divorce decree could be refused where consequences would be unduly harsh or unjust.] 'The test of undue harshness or injustice is subjective, and connotes a real and substantial detriment to the respondent beyond such normal consequences of the granting of a decree. Murray's New English Dictionary, in defining the northern word "harsh" refers to an action "Repugnant or roughly offensive to the feelings; severe, rigorous, cruel, rude, rough, unfeeling". "Unjust" in the Shorter Oxford Dictionary is "not in accordance with justice or fairness". As qualified by the word "unduly", these two words mean something to excess and beyond the due degree of harshness and injustice. The Act therefore impliedly recognises that some decrees will inevitably have a certain degree of harshness or injustice without being unduly harsh or unjust.' *Johnstone v Johnstone* (1969) 7 DLR (3d) 14 at 19, Ont SC, per Lacourciere J

HAULING

Australia 'To decide the critical question, "hauling" must be defined. There is no difficulty about pushing. The Tribunal referred to the definition in the Random House Dictionary of the English Language in which the following meanings of "hauling" appear, namely, "to pull or draw with force, move by drawing, drag", "to cart or transport, carry", "to do carting or transport, or move freight commercially". The Shorter Oxford English Dictionary with respect to the verb "to haul" supplies meanings including, "to pull or drag with force" and "to transport by cart or other conveyance". The New Oxford Dictionary defines "hauling" as "the action of pulling, dragging or traction". "Haulier" is defined as, "a man employed in hauling something e.g. coal in a mine". Although it is true that "hauling" is sometimes applied to the movement of goods by truck such use of the word is, I think, a somewhat strained one. Normally in the concept of hauling there is the notion of pulling. Thus one hauls logs from the forest. And one finds the word "hauling" used as the converse of "pushing".' *Blackwood Hodge (Australia) Pty Ltd v Collector of Customs (New South Wales)* (1980) 47 FLR 131 at 138, per Smithers J

HAVE

Canada 'The gist of the offence under this section [Intoxicating Liquor Act 1927 (NB), c 28, s 56(2) (repealed; see now Liquor Control Act RJNB 1973, cL-10, s 133] is possession of illegal liquor. There is no doubt that the verb "have" is broad enough to include temporary possession. Why should its grammatical meaning be narrowed in this provision? In all the judgments under Liquor Acts to which we have been referred the word "have" is treated as synonymous with "possess".' *R v Theriault* (1951) 28 MPR 412 at 417, NBCA, per Harrison J

HAVE OR KEEP

Australia 'The expression found in s 84 (see now s 84(1)) [of the Police Act 1892–1986 (WA)] is "have or keep". These words are not synonymous. "Have" probably involves having some interest in the premises themselves, perhaps even so small an interest as a revocable licence to occupy. But "keep" need not have any such connotation: it is commonly used to denote no more than one who has effective and lawful physical control, as in the expressions gatekeeper or housekeeper, and in fact the primary meaning of "keeper" given in the Oxford English Dictionary is one who has the charge or care or oversight of something.' *Higgon v O'Dea* [1962] WAR 140 at 144, per Hale J

HAVEN

'Hale describes a haven to be "a place of a large receipt and safe riding of ships, so situate and secured by the land circumjacent that the vessels thereby ride and anchor safely, and are protected by the adjacent land from dangerous and violent winds" [De Port Mar c 2, p 46]. But he afterwards uses the word to denote a portion of the port itself, as in page 54, where he says, "In the consideration of a port there are these two things involved, viz, first, the consideration of the interest of the soil, both of the shore or town, which is the *caput portûs*, and of the soil of the haven itself wherein the ships do ride and apply".' *Gann v Free Fishers of Whitstable* (1865) 11 HL Cas 192 at 219, 220, per Lord Chelmsford

HAWKER

'Hawker' means any person who travels with a horse or other beast bearing or drawing burden, and goes from place to place or to other men's houses carrying to sell or exposing for sale any goods, wares or merchandise, or exposing samples or patterns of any goods, wares, or merchandise to be afterwards delivered, and includes any person who travels by any means of locomotion to any place in which he does not usually reside or carry on business, and there sells or exposes for sale any goods, wares, or merchandise in or at any house, shop, room, booth, stall, or other place whatever hired or used by him for that purpose. (Hawkers Act 1888, s 2)

[Excise licences are no longer required by hawkers, but the above definition is included as of general interest although the Hawkers Act was repealed by the Local Government Act 1966, s 35, Schs 3, 6.]

[A bye-law provided that every person who should 'hawk or expose about the town for sale' certain articles should pay a toll.] 'I think in the bye-law the word "hawk" has a meaning which is more than the words in the definition clauses of the Hawkers Act [1888 (repealed; see supra)]. It means carrying about for sale—offering for sale as you carry them about; it means taking some step which is similar to the idea conveyed by the words "expose for sale". . . . No one would understand that a man was a hawker who took a thing about the town and did not either expose it for sale or cry it, or take some steps which indicated that he had got the thing for sale and was ready to sell to any person who would buy. Therefore, in substance, this man was doing that which was like a tradesman going to his customers asking of them whether they want a supply on that particular day. I think in substance the justices were quite right in saying this man is not within the bye-law.' *Philpott v Allright* (1906) 94 LT 540 at 541, DC, per Lawrence J (Darling J dissenting)

'I do not agree . . . that "hawk" means exactly the same thing as "expose about the town for sale". I think "expose about the town for sale" means one thing and "hawk" another. I think if a man goes about with things not exposed, carries them about and offers to sell them to persons, that he is a hawker. . . . Some of the people who were called hawkers of old time long ago did not expose things; they concealed that they had got them.' *Ibid* at 542, per Darling J

Canada 'A "hawker" is technically one who cries his goods from a wagon or other vehicle. The word "pedlar" may have originally designated one who went on foot with a pack; but in this country the words "hawker" and "pedlar" are generally considered equivalent in law.' *R (Best) v Veniot* (1939) 14 MPR 27 at 31, NSSC, per Graham J

New Zealand 'I think I should be going beyond any decided case if I held that the term "hawker" included tradesmen who by invitation call for, receive, and at the same time supply daily orders for articles of food.' *Duncan v Briarley* (1890) 8 NZLR 79 at 82, per Richmond J

HAY

Canada 'Hay is not an appropriate word to designate grass before it is cut. It is defined to be "grass cut and dried for fodder; grass prepared for preservation".' *R v Good* (1889) 17 OR 725 at 727, Ont Common Pleas, per Rose J

HAZARDOUS *See* RASH

HEALTH *See* GOOD HEALTH

HEARING

'I think that the word "hearing" in that section [15 & 16 Vict c 86, s 39 (repealed)] is used, not in its technical, but in its general sense; and that "upon the hearing" means whenever and wherever a cause is heard.' *Hope v Threlfall* (1854) 2 Eq Rep 307 at 307, CA, per Turner LJ

Canada 'Because the National Energy Board Act [RSC 1970, c N–6] has bestowed upon the Board the attributes of a court and because the statute and the regulations contemplate the panoply of a full adversary hearing it follows that the word "hearing" in s 20 of the Act must have attributed to it the same meaning as it has in a court of law. . . . In that sense, a "hearing" before the Board is analogous to and imports a "trial" before a court of law. . . . That being so the applicant for a licence and the opponents thereto must be treated on an equal footing with no discriminatory advantage being bestowed on one side or the other. Accordingly, if one side is permitted to give oral evidence the facility must be afforded to the opponents with the right by both sides to cross-examine the witnesses giving the oral testimony adverse to the respective positions.' *Re A-G of Manitoba & National Energy Board* (1974) 48 DLR (3d) 73 at 91, 92, Fed Ct, per Cattanach J

New Zealand [Section 43 of the Summary Proceedings Act 1957 provides a court with jurisdiction to amend an information at any time during the 'hearing'. In the Supreme Court it was held that an amendment made after the conclusion of all evidence and where no addresses were to be made by counsel was without jurisdiction as the hearing had already concluded.] 'In brief, we are of the opinion that the hearing of an information continues for the purposes of s 43 in a case in which a District Court judge does not reserve his decision until the point of time when he finds the charge proved or dismisses it.' *Ministry of Transport v Nicol* [1980] 1 NZLR 436 at 441, per McMullin J

New hearing

Canada [Section 55(1) of the Surface Rights Acquisition and Compensation Act 1968 (Sask) c 73 provides that an appeal under s 52 shall take the form of a 'new hearing'.] 'A new hearing may be compared to what under the Criminal Code is styled as a trial de novo. It involves the taking of evidence on the issues involved, which may be the same, similar or with considerable variation from that before the Board. An appellant is not subjected to an additional onus of calling "cogent" evidence to warrant a change in a determination by the Board. The duty and obligation of the appellate judge is to arrive at his decisions on the issues before him based upon the evidence given in this new hearing before him.' *Re Canadian Reserve Oil & Gas Ltd & Lamb* (1974) 49 DLR (3d) 759 at 763, Sask CA, per Maguire JA

Public hearing

Canada 'It was contended that the word "public" as an adjective modifying the word "hearing" means that the proceedings of the Board shall be conducted "in public" as contrasted with the proceedings being held in camera. I do not agree with that contention. The word "public" in the context, in my opinion, means that every member of the public, subject to the qualification that such person has a demonstrable interest in the subject-matter before the Board over and above the public generally, shall have the right to participate in the hearing.' *Re A-G of Manitoba & National Energy Board* (1974) 48 DLR (3d) 73 at 86, Fed Ct, per Cattanach J

Upon the merits

Australia 'A hearing on the merits is one in which the issues of fact or law, or both, between the parties are fought out to a final conclusion binding upon the parties—a decision "upon the merits". It does not seem to matter that the determination of one or some only of the issues may suffice to decide the whole controversy, or that the issues may be decided on facts which are the subject of admission and not of dispute or even of evidence. Without purporting to make an exhaustive enumeration, or to state all the qualifications which may be necessary, a hearing may be said not to have been on the merits if it resulted in a decision which was not final but analogous rather to a nonsuit, or if, for some such reason as withdrawal, want of jurisdiction, non-compliance with some preliminary requirement, defect in the information, or other technical or procedural informality or irregularity, it did not result, or could not have resulted, in a decision on the merits, final in its nature and capable of supporting (in criminal cases) a plea of *autrefois acquit* or *autrefois convict*.' *Bridie v Messina* [1965] NSWR 332 at 337, 338, per Sugerman J

Australia 'In my judgment, taking into account the context in which the phrase "hearing on the merits" is to be found in s 75A(8) [Supreme Court Act 1970 (NSW)] and the apparent purpose of the restriction imposed, that phrase should be construed as meaning the hearing of any interlocutory matter in which both parties appeared and in which the issue between them in that interlocutory matter (whether of fact and/or law) was investigated by the relevant tribunal. There is no need for the issues between the parties in the proceedings as a whole to be investigated or determined for the hearing to be one "on the merits". The issue to be investigated or determined is that which arises between the parties in the particular interlocutory proceedings in question . . .' *Martin v Abbott Australasia Pty Ltd* [1981] 2 NSWLR 430 at 435–436, per Hunt J

HEARING AID

'Hearing aid' means an instrument intended for use by a person suffering from impaired hearing to assist that person to hear better but does not include any instrument or device designed for use by connecting conductors of electricity to equipment or apparatus provided for the purpose of affording means of telephonic communication. (Hearing Aid Council Act 1968, s 14)

HEARSAY EVIDENCE *See* EVIDENCE

HEAT

[Paragraph 2 of a bill of lading contained the words: 'The master, owners or agents of the vessel . . . shall not be responsible for loss, damage, or injury arising from . . . explosion, heat, fire at sea or on shore, at any time or in any place.'] 'I have . . . to consider the effect of the words in paragraph 2, on which the defendants rely. What are those words? They rely first on the word "heat". I think . . . that that word, having regard to its collocation—between the words "explosion" and "fire at sea or on shore"—does not refer to the heating of the cargo from its own spontaneous combustion or generation of heat, through the action of moisture coming against it, or its own moisture causing it to develop heat, but that the word "heat" refers to some extraneous source, such as heat coming from the engine-room.' *The Pearlmoor* [1904] P 286 at 298, per Gorell Barnes J

HEAVY GOODS VEHICLE *See* GOODS VEHICLE

HEAVY LOCOMOTIVE *See* LOCOMOTIVE

HEAVY MOTOR CAR *See* MOTOR CAR

HEIGHT

'Height' in relation to a storey of a building means the level of the surface of the highest point of the floor of that storey measured at the centre of that face of the building where the measurement is greatest from the level of the footway immediately in front of that face or if there is no such footway from the level of the ground before excavation. (London Building Acts (Amendment) Act 1939, s 33)

'Height' means the height of the building measured from the mean level of the ground adjoining the outside of the external walls of the building to the level of half the vertical height of the roof of the building, or to the top of the walls or of the parapet, if any, whichever is the higher (Building Regulations 1985, SI 1985/1065, reg 2(1))

HEIR

'She [the testatrix] gives her real and personal estate to trustees in trust for her nephew for life, and after his death in trust for sale, and after payment of legacies, as to the residue, to pay "one third to the heirs or next of kin of Thomas Lodge, deceased; one third to the heirs or next of kin of John Lodge, deceased; and one third to the heirs or next of kin of Milburn Lodge, deceased". . . . As regards personal estate the word "heirs" is used for statutory next of kin, and as the testatrix meant both descriptions to apply to the same class, it follows that the gift is in favour of the statutory next of kin of the three persons named.' *Re Thompson's Trusts* (1878) 9 Ch D 607 at 609, per Jessel MR

[A testator by his will bequeathed certain articles to his wife, with the proviso that on her death they should be returned to his brothers and sister or their 'heirs and successors'.] 'It seems to me most probable that today, in the case of a gift to a class of person or their heirs, both realty and personalty would be distributed in accordance with the present law of intestate succession, making no distinction between realty and personalty. That, I think, is most probable, but I must not put it higher, because that is not the position here. I have the words "and successors", and, in my view, the words "and successors" are words of a much wider and more general application than the word "heirs". There is about them no flavour or savour of realty. The word "heirs", of course, historically and in a legal vocabulary has a very strong flavour of realty, though no doubt lay people often use it and have used it in connection with personalty; but the word "successors" has no such flavour. It is no more akin to realty than to personalty; and the phrase is "heirs and successors". In my judgment, that does not mean the same as "heirs and successors", which might have suggested a different construction. I think that the words "heirs and successors" should be construed as referring to the persons entitled to the real and personal estate under the law of intestate succession applicable at the date when the testator died.' *Re Kilver (decd), Midland Bank Executor and Trustee Co Ltd v Kilvert* [1957] 2 All ER 196 at 199, per Roxburgh J (also reported in [1957] Ch 388 at 393, 394).

Australia 'So long as a system of law prevails by which, in case of intestacy, realty descends to the heir-at-law, and personalty to the next-of-kin, then, in the case of dispositions which admit of effect being given to apparent intention, the word "heir", since it is a term of art, should prima facie, when used in relation to a disposition of realty, be regarded as intended to refer to the common law heir-at-law. This is so whether it be used alone or reinforced by expressions pointing in the same direction.' *Ex p Price* [1945] NSWSR 53 at 57, per Jordan CJ

Australia 'The word "heir" or "heirs" "right heir" or "right heirs" and other equivalent expressions used as words of purchase in a devise or settlement of land prima facie signify the common law heir.' *Re McIlrath* [1959] VR 720 at 729, (FC)

Canada 'HD left him surviving, as his next-of-kin, his widow . . . and a son age twenty, represented by the Official Guardian. It will be noted that the gift over refers to "his lawful heirs", i.e. the lawful heirs of HD deceased. This expression means the persons who would have taken in case of an intestacy unless a contrary intention appears, which it does not.' *Re Wallis* [1944] 3 DLR 223 at 224, Ont SC, per Urquhart J

Heirs of the body

'The question, in this case, appears to me to be this: The whole will must be examined to ascertain whether the testator has used the words "heirs of the body" in their ordinary legal acceptation; if he has, the devisee takes an estate tail, and all subsequent words controlling that estate will be rejected. But if he has used the words "heirs of the body" as synonymous with "children", then the Court will give effect to his intention. . . . The cases of *Lowe v Davies* [(1729) 2 Ld Raym 1561], *Lisle v Gray* [(1678) T Raym 278] and *North v Martin* [(1833) 6 Sim 266] establish that where the testator uses words interpreting the words "heirs of the body" to mean "children", such interpretation shall have its effect given to it. The only question here is, has the testator so interpreted the words "heirs of the body", and I think that he has. . . . I do not say the case is free from difficulty, but upon the best consideration I have been able to give to it, I think that the testator has expressed his meaning to be, that the words "heirs of the body" are synonymous with children, and accordingly such is my decision. The parents took estates for life only.' *Gummoe v Howes* (1857) 23 Beav 184 at 189, 190, 192, per Romilly MR

'I proceed . . . to consider whether the terms of the devise vested in Mary Harris an estate tail. If the devise had ended with the words "unto and to the use of the heirs of the body and bodies of such child, if more than one, to be equally divided between them", it would have been, I think, beyond controversy that Mary Harris took an estate tail. . . . It is a rule of law that where an estate is devised to the "heirs" or "heirs of the body" of a person to whom a prior estate of freehold has been given, the heirs take by descent, and not by purchase, and that an estate in fee simple or in fee tail is created in the ancestor. A testator can no more make such a devise and direct that it shall not have this operation than he can, in terms, create an estate in fee simple or an estate tail, and then direct that these estates shall not have the incidents which the law annexes to them. . . . I can find nothing in the will which inevitably leads to the conclusion that the testator used the word "heirs" in a sense other than its ordinary legal one. . . . The difficulty said to be occasioned by the use of the words "to be equally divided between them" is a difficulty only if you assume that they are intended to apply in case the testator has only one child, and that child has more than one son—a gratuitous assumption, as it seems to me, for the words are properly applicable in the case of more than one child of the testator having an heir of the body, and this sufficiently explains their presence in the will without supposing that by "heirs of the body" the testator meant something else.' *Van Grutten v Foxwell, Foxwell v Van Grutten* [1897] AC 658 at 662–664, per Lord Herschell

Canada '"Heirs of the body" in its technical legal sense comprehends all the posterity of the donee in succession.' *Re Woodward Estate, Smith v MacLaren* [1945] 1 WWR 722 at 728, BCSC, per Coady J

HEIRLOOMS

[Heirlooms] accompany the inheritance, whether they pass by special custom, such as the best bed or the like, or whether they savour of the inheritance. In the latter class are included title deeds and the chest or box in which they are usually kept, the patent creating a dignity, the garter and collar of a knight, an ancient horn where the tenure is by cornage, and the ancient jewels of the Crown. (17 Halsbury's Laws (4th edn) para 1084)

Heirlooms were articles which, either from their connection with real estate or by special custom, formerly passed, on the death of the ancestor, to the heir. They were connected in this manner with real estate when they were an incident of the tenure of land, or were necessary for maintaining the dignity of the owner of land or the possessor of a title. An ancient horn, where the tenure was by cornage, the garter and collar of a knight, the ancient jewels of the Crown, and a patent creating a dignity, were all heirlooms and may still properly be so styled. However, since descent to the heir has been abolished, and heirlooms devolve, in the first instance, with the real estate, on the ancestor's personal representatives, the vesting in the heir can only be secured by special provision, such as a limitation under which the heir takes by purchase. The title of the heir will then be completed by assent. Chattels may, possibly, also be heirlooms on the ground that they are an essential feature in the ordinary enjoyment of the land, for example, wild deer in a park, assuming that they can be the subject of property at all. If they are so far tame as to be under control, they are personal property.

By special custom, such articles as the best bed and utensils, and other household implements, might be heirlooms, but the custom had to be strictly proved.

Chattels which are not heirlooms at common law may be settled in a manner corresponding to the trusts of a settlement of land so as to be inseparable from the land. These so-called heirlooms are in fact the only heirlooms which usually occur in modern times. (39 Halsbury's Laws (4th edn) paras 390, 391)

Heirlooms are such goods and personal chattels, as, contrary to the nature of chattels, shall go by special custom to the heir along with the inheritance, and not to the executor of the last proprietor. The termination, *loom*, is of Saxon original; in which language it signifies a limb or member; so that an heirloom is nothing else, but a limb or member of the inheritance. They are generally such things as cannot be taken away without damaging or dismembering the freehold; otherwise the general rule is, that no chattel interest whatsoever shall go to the heir, notwithstanding it be expressly limited to a man and his heirs, but shall vest in the executor. But deer in a real authorised park, fishes in a pond, doves in a dove-house, &c, though in themselves personal chattels, yet they are so annexed to and so necessary to the well-being of the inheritance, that they shall accompany the land wherever it vests, by either descent or purchase. For this reason also I apprehend it is, that the ancient jewels of the crown are held to be heirlooms for they are necessary to maintain the state, and support the dignity, of the sovereign for the time being. Charters likewise, and deeds, court-rolls, and other evidences of the land, together with the chests in which they are contained, shall pass together with the land to the heir, in the nature of heirlooms, and shall not go to the executor. By special custom also, in some places, carriages, utensils, and other household implements may be heirlooms; but such custom must be strictly proved. On the other hand, by almost general custom, whatever is strongly affixed to the freehold or inheritance, and cannot be severed from thence without violence or damage, *'quod ab aedibus non facile revellitur'*, is become a member of the inheritance, and shall thereupon pass to the heir; as marble chimney-pieces, pumps, old fixed or dormant tables, benches, and the like. A very similar notion to which prevails in the duchy of Brabant; where they rank certain things movable among those of the immovable kind, calling them, by a very peculiar appellation, *praedia volantia*, or volatile estates: such as beds, tables, and other heavy implements of furniture. (2 Bl Com 427, 428)

'The portion of the will upon which this question turns may be divided into two parts, one which I will denominate the gift of the principal subject, that is of the Quendon Hall estate, and the other the gift of the accessory, that is to say, of certain articles of personalty, which it is directed shall go along with and accompany the principal subject. . . . The accessory is given in the following words: "With my mansion house, furniture, plate, books, linen, and Archbishop Cranmer's portrait by Holbein, the Indian cabinet in drawing-room, and striking watch, and diamond earrings and pins, *as heirlooms with my estate*". From the words which I have read, an intention must be inferred that these articles shall be enjoyed collectively, and not in a divided or separate manner. They are to go "as heirlooms with my estate". Now according to the popular and familiar sense of the term "heirlooms", it indicates things directed to descend by way of inheritance. I collect, therefore, from these words of gift of the heirlooms, the intention that they are to be enjoyed together, collectively, and therefore, of necessity, in a form of individual enjoyment, and that such enjoyment is to be had together "with the estate".' *Byng v Byng* (1862) 10 HL Cas 171 at 175, 176, per Lord Westbury

'The very word "heirlooms" seems to involve in it the principle of descent. It was said at the bar the word "looms" was only a corruption or abbreviation of "limbs", I find that Johnson and Webster both give a different, and, as I believe, a more correct explanation of it. They say it is an old Anglo-Saxon word, signifying goods or chattels. According to either derivation, the word "heirlooms" must mean something which, though not by its own nature heritable, is to have a heritable character impressed upon it.' Ibid at 183, per Lord Cranworth

'An "heirloom" is a limb or member of the inheritance and in very old times, before the law of perpetuities stood on its present basis, there were customs in some parts of the country, by which, irrespective of a devise, certain chattels were "heirlooms", and passed from ancestor to heir in a perpetual course of succession, and were always annexed to the mansion, such as state beds, etc. In this case sums of money in various forms were found in unexpected receptacles, and as heirlooms are intended to be enjoyed in specie manually, and to be kept in the house, it is clear that they cannot pass, although a double sovereign and a half-guinea were found among them, which, per se, might be regarded as curiosities fit for a museum. An heirloom must have a certain degree of durability, although, no doubt, that is a relative term, and it may be said that no chattel is durable in perpetuity, and where an article can only be enjoyed by its consumption, it is not intended as an heirloom—such as live stock, cows, and carriages, or any articles that are perishable in a short time.' *Hare v Pryce* (1864) 11 LT 101 at 102, per Kindersley V-C

HENCEFORTH

'The question we have to decide is whether this order of the justices is bad, because, after ordering the removal of the checkweigher, it continues: "And that from henceforth he shall cease to perform the duties of checkweigher on behalf of the persons employed in the said mine as aforesaid". Now, it is admitted that the justices may remove a checkweigher by making a summary order for his removal if sufficient ground is shown in accordance with s 13 of the Coal Mines Regulation Act 1887. . . . Now, the order made by the justices may possibly in the future not be a bar to the man being re-appointed, but I cannot say that the order is bad because it contains the words which I have quoted above.' *R v Llewellyn, Ex p Squire* (1906) 96 LT 32 at 32, per Lord Alverstone CJ

'The word "henceforth" means from the date of the order, and does not mean "henceforth and for ever".' Ibid at 32, per Darling J

HERALD *See* ARMS

HERBAL REMEDY

'Herbal remedy' means a medicinal product consisting of a substance produced by subjecting a plant or plants to drying, crushing or any other process, or of a mixture whose sole ingredients are two or more substances so produced, or of a mixture whose sole ingredients are one or more substances so produced and water or some other inert substance. (Medicines Act 1968, s 132(1))

HERD

'Herd' includes a flock. (Medicines Act 1968, s 132(1))

HEREAFTER

'The words "hereafter to be begotten" [in a settlement providing for remainder "to the heirs male of his body hereafter to be begotten"] do not confine it to the issue born after but will likewise take in that born before.' *Hebblethwaite v Cartwright* (1734) Cas temp Talb 31 at 32, per Talbot LC

HEREDITAMENT

'Tenements' and 'hereditaments' mean, respectively, whatever can be the subject of tenure, and whatever is capable of devolving upon death, whether as real property or as personal property, to personal representatives; but they are used in a general sense to include both the corporeal things, such as houses and land, and the rights which arise out . of them. Where these rights extend to the exclusive possession of the thing which is the subject of property, they are called corporeal hereditaments, a term which is used to denote both the thing itself and the right of property in the thing; where they fall short of this, as for example in the case of profits à prendre, they are called incorporeal hereditaments. (27 Halsbury's Laws (4th edn) para 131)

Strictly the term 'corporeal' applies to the land itself, while rights in the land are incorporeal; but this is not in accordance with legal usage, and a right in the land, if accompanied by possession, is regarded as corporeal, whereas partial rights which do not entitle the owner of them to possession are regarded as incorporeal. Rights in land whether corporeal or incorporeal are described by the words 'tenements' and 'hereditaments', 'tenements' meaning primarily that they are the subjects of tenure, though the word is not thus restricted, and 'hereditaments' meaning that they were, while rules of inheritance were in force, capable of passing to the heir. 'Tenements' and 'hereditaments' are not the same in scope, and 'land' is not always restricted to land in the physical sense; it may extend to rights in the land. 'Lands, tenements, and hereditaments' comprises both real estate and chattels real; thus, although it does not include personal chattels, it formerly comprised copyholds, and it comprises chattels real as well as freeholds. . . .

Any property which might, on an intestacy occurring before 1926, have devolved upon the heir of the intestate is a hereditament. 'Hereditament' includes land as a physical object, money which is liable to be invested in land and is treated in equity as land, heirlooms, and certain rights in land and other rights. Hereditaments are either corporeal or incorporeal. (39 Halsbury's Laws (4th edn) para 375, 380)

'Hereditaments' means real property which on an intestacy might before the commencement of this Act have devolved on an heir. (Settled Land Act 1925, s 117)

Subject to the next following subsection, in this section 'hereditament', in relation to a project of material development, means the aggregate of the land which at the relevant date forms the subject of a single entry in the valuation list for the time being in force for a rating area.

Where any land is on the boundary between two or more rating areas and accordingly—
(a) different parts of that land form the subject of different entries in the valuation list for the time being in force for those areas respectively, but
(b) if the whole of the land had been in one of those areas it would have formed the subject of a single entry in the valuation list for that area,

the Commission may direct that the whole of that land shall be treated for the purposes of the last preceding subsection as if it formed the subject of a single entry in the valuation list for a rating area. (Land Commission Act 1967, s 65(5), (6))

'By the word "lands" an advowson will not pass, but by hereditaments it may.' *Savil v Savil* (1737) Fortes Rep 351 at 351, per cur.

'The settled sense of that word [hereditaments] is to denote such things as may be the subject-matter of inheritance, but not the inheritance itself, and cannot therefore, by its own intrinsic force enlarge an estate, prima facie a life estate into a fee.' *Moor v Denn d Mellor* (1800) 2 Bos & P 247 at 251, per cur.

'There is no doubt they had a right to include advowson under the word hereditaments.' *Holmes v Seton* (1825) 3 Bing 176 at 176, per cur.

'"Hereditament" is defined in the text-books of authority to signify "all such things, whether corporeal or incorporeal, which a man may have to him and his heirs, by way of inheritance and which, if they be not otherwise bequeathed come to him which is next of blood, and not to the executors or administrators, as chattels do".' *Lloyd v Jones* (1848) 6 CB 81 at 90, per cur.

'If freeholds of inheritance are bought, they are to be settled to the same uses to which the hereditaments, by the sale or exchange of which the purchase-money should have arisen, previously stood settled; the word "hereditaments" alone being used as signifying the subject-matter of the sale, but which might be anything that was part of the settled estates, and "hereditaments" being a word which, after the statute [Wills Act 1837], as I conceive, as well as before, means heritable property.' *Prescott v Barker* (1874) 9 Ch App 174 at 190, per Lord Selborne LC

'In Sheppard's Touchstone at page 91 I find this

statement: "The word 'hereditament' is of as large extent as any word, for whatsoever may be inherited, be it corporeal or incorporeal, real, personal or mixed is a hereditament".' *Basset v St Levan* (1894) 71 LT 718 at 720, 722, per Stirling J

'The word used in the will is "hereditaments". That would seem naturally to mean "things capable of being inherited"; and money subject to a trust for reinvestment in land, held in the hands of trustees, as this money was at the date of the testator's death, satisfies that description. I am assisted in coming to this conclusion by Lindley LJ's judgment in the Court of Appeal in *Re Duke of Cleveland's Settled Estates* [[1893] 3 Ch 244 at 250]. "Money which a testator has not got into his own hands, and which he has no right to have in his own hands, and which is held upon trust for investment in land, is, in our opinion, to be treated as real estate, although, if he has power to dispose of such money, he can dispose of it either as land or money, as he may think right." . . . I am of opinion that without any enlargement the word "hereditaments", in its natural meaning, is sufficiently large to describe money held in trust for investment in land in a case like the present, in which the testator possesses no power to dispose of it, either as money or land, as he pleases.' *Re Gosselin, Gosselin v Gosselin* [1906] 1 Ch 120 at 123, 124, per Farwell J

Australia [The respondent gas company had a statutory right to lay gas pipes under public streets. The appellant Commissioner for Main Roads resumed certain streets under which pipes were laid in order to construct an expressway. The issue was whether the streets were 'land' within the meaning of the Public Works Act 1912–1986 (NSW), s 101 for the taking of which the gas company was required to be compensated.] 'On general principle the exercise by the respondent of its statutory right to occupy part of a street vested in the council by placing its mains and pipes there did not, it seems to me, give it a corporeal hereditament. The hereditament of the whole of the street is in my opinion in the council. It could direct the gas company to alter the mains and pipes and their accessories—which I take it would include moving them and relaying them elsewhere in the street. The word "hereditament" and the word "estate" both appear to me inapt for the respondent's mere right of occupation.' *Mains Roads Comr v*

North Shore Gas Co Ltd (1967) 120 CLR 118 at 133, per Windeyer J

Corporeal hereditament

Land itself, and also such physical objects as are annexed to and form part of it, or are treated as forming part of it, are corporeal hereditaments; and strictly are the only corporeal hereditaments. However, those estates in land, whether legal or equitable, which before 1926 were capable of passing by descent, and which entitled the owner to present possession of the land or to receipt of rents and profits, were classed as corporeal hereditaments, and this applies to the legal estates and equitable interests which now represent the former legal and equitable estates. Whatever the interest may be, if it entitles the owner to present possession or receipt of rents and profits, and would before 1926 have been inheritable, it is treated as taking on corporeal nature and ranks as a corporeal hereditament. (39 Halsbury's Laws (4th edn) para 381)

Hereditaments . . . are of two kinds, corporeal, and incorporeal. Corporeal consist of such as affect the senses; such as may be seen and handled by the body: incorporeal are not the object of sensation, can neither be seen nor handled, are creatures of the mind, and exist only in contemplation. Corporeal hereditaments consist wholly of substantial and permanent objects; all which may be comprehended under the general denomination of land only. (2 Bl Com 17)

Incorporeal hereditament

Incorporeal hereditaments include (1) rights in land which are not accompanied by exclusive possession; these are seigniories, franchises, profits à prendre, advowsons, rentcharges, rights of common, and, possibly, easements; (2) certain heritable rights not necessarily connected with land, such as offices. Reversions, remainders, and executory interests and conditions have usually been classed as incorporeal hereditaments, but the classification is not satisfactory.

Incorporeal hereditaments may be either appendant, as seigniories; appurtenant, as easements; or in gross, as rentcharges. Rights of common and profits à prendre may be either appendant or appurtenant or in gross. Advowsons may be either appendant or in gross. (39 Halsbury's Laws (4th edn) para 382)

Real and personal hereditaments

Hereditaments were . . . formerly divided into real and personal. Real hereditaments included land and estates of inheritance in land, and also all heritable rights which were connected with or incident to land. Heritable rights which had no connection with land were personal hereditaments. Of this nature were personal annuities granted to a man and his heirs. Personal hereditaments, notwithstanding that they were limited to heirs and passed to heirs on an intestacy, were personal estate and passed under a residuary bequest of such estate.

In the case of persons dying after 31st December 1925, the rules of inheritance have been abolished alike for real and personal hereditaments, and according to the proper meaning of 'hereditaments' there can in such cases be no hereditaments of either kind; but the term 'hereditaments' can still be used to denote property which, under the law before 1926, would have fallen in the class of real hereditaments. (39 Halsbury's Laws (4th edn) para 383)

HIGH SEAS   *See also* SEA

At common law, 'high seas' includes the whole of the sea below low-water mark where great ships can go, except for such parts of the sea as are within the body of a county, for the realm of England only extends to the low-water mark, and all beyond is the high seas. In international law 'high seas' means all parts of the sea not included in the territorial sea and internal waters of any state. (49 Halsbury's Laws (4th edn) para 284)

'The high seas' means the seas outside the seaward limits of the territorial waters adjacent to the United Kingdom or to any other country or territory outside the United Kingdom. (Marine &c Broadcasting (Offences) Act 1967, s 9)

'The expression "high seas" [in the Merchant Shipping Act 1894, s 686] has the same meaning as when used with reference to the jurisdiction of the Court of Admiralty, that is, all oceans, seas, bays, channels, rivers, creeks, and waters below low-water mark, and "where great ships can go", except any such of such oceans, etc, as lie within the body of some country.' *R v Liverpool JJ, ex p Molyneux* [1972] 2 All ER 471

HIGH WATER MARK

Canada 'In the instant case the expression used is not merely "high water mark" but "high water mark at ordinary spring tides". The latter expression no more than the former can suggest a freshet mark, for the meaning of the words "spring tides" is clear and unequivocal. Spring tides are simply the tides that happen at, or soon after, the new and full moon, as opposed to neap tides, which happen in the second and last quarters of the moon. One can only assume that here it was not the normal high water mark, viz that medium tide line between the spring and neap tides, which was intended but the high water mark during spring tides.' *Re McNichol* (1976) 20 NBQR (2d) 240 at 251, per Dickson J

HIGHWAY   *See also* ROAD; ROUTE

A highway is a way over which there exists a public right of passage, that is to say a right for all of Her Majesty's subjects at all seasons of the year freely and at their will to pass and repass without let or hindrance. A highway may be dedicated subject to certain restrictions or obstructions; and it may be limited to a recognised class of traffic, that is it need not be a way for vehicles, as, if they are open to the public generally, footpaths, bridleways and driftways are highways. It is, however, an essential characteristic of a highway that every member of the public should have a right to use it for the appropriate class of traffic; there can be no dedication to a limited section of the public, such as the inhabitants of a parish.

No right can be granted, otherwise than by statute, to the public at large to wander at will over an undefined open space, nor can the public acquire such a right by prescription. If there is no regular way, but people merely go where they like, there is no highway. Land is not a highway merely because a limited class of persons have a right of recreation over it. The use of an esplanade for strolling up and down or for amusement is not inconsistent with it being a highway.

There is no rule of law which prevents a cul-de-sac, whether in the town or in the country, from being a highway. However, dedication of a cul-de-sac as a highway is unlikely to be inferred merely from user by the public; this is a rule of common sense based on the fact that members of the public do not claim to use a way as of right unless there is some point in doing so. If there is some kind of attraction at the far end which might cause the public to wish to use the way, that may be sufficient to justify the conclusion that a public highway has been created.

A road which has been a highway does not cease to be a highway merely because one end of it is lawfully stopped up. On the other hand, where both ends are lawfully stopped up so that members of the public cannot have access to the intervening length of it without committing a trespass, that intervening length ceases to be a highway.

There is no general public right of way over the foreshore, but a highway may exist along or across a particular part of it.

A highway may exist over artificial structures, such as embankments, sea walls and piers.

A right of way may exist by custom for parishioners to go to and from their parish church. Such a way is known as a churchway. It is distinguished from a highway insofar as no-one but a parishioner can be legally entitled to use a churchway, whereas every member of the public has the right to use a highway. A way leading to a church as its point of destination may be a highway, and so may a way across a churchyard. Such ways will be highways where dedication by the landowner is inferred from the facts.

In the Highways Act 1980, except where the context otherwise requires, 'highway' means the whole or a part of a highway other than a ferry or waterway; and where a highway passes over a bridge or through a tunnel, that bridge or tunnel is taken for the purposes of that Act to be a part of the highway.

At common law highways are of three kinds according to the degree of the public rights of passage over them. A 'cartway' or 'carriageway' is a highway over which the public has a right of way (1) on foot, (2) riding on or accompanied by a beast of burden, or (3) with vehicles and cattle. A 'bridleway' is a highway over which the rights of passage are cut down by the exclusion of the right of passage with vehicles and sometimes, although not invariably, the exclusion of the right of driftway, that is driving cattle, while a 'footpath' is one over which the only public right of passage is on foot.

Thus a bridleway includes a right of footway, and a carriageway includes both the lesser rights. A carriageway is presumed to include the right of driftway, and a bridleway may include that right; but the right of driftway may in either case be excluded. A bridleway now includes the right to ride a bicycle.

A way may, however, be dedicated to the public for a limited purpose, such as the use of a towpath for towing.

The fact that some vehicles are too wide to use a particular way does not prevent it from being a highway for such vehicles as the way will allow to pass. (21 Halsbury's Laws (4th edn) paras 1–8)

(1) In this Act, except where the context otherwise requires, 'highway' means the whole or a part of a highway other than a ferry or waterway.

(2) Where a highway passes over a bridge or through a tunnel, that bridge or tunnel is to be taken for the purposes of this Act to be a part of the highway.

(3) In this Act 'highway maintainable at the public expense' and any other expression defined by reference to a highway is to be construed in accordance with the foregoing provisions of this section.
(Highways Act 1980, s 328)

'If a way lead to a market, and were a way for all travellers, and did communicate with a great road, etc, it is a highway; but if it lead only to a church, to a private house or village, or to fields, there 'tis a private way. But 'tis a matter of fact, and much depends upon common reputation.' *Austin's Case* (1672) 1 Vent 189 at 189, per Hale CB

'The word "highway" is the genus of all public ways, as well cart, horse, and foot ways, and yet an indictment lies for any one of these ways, if they be common to all the Queen's subjects having occasion to pass there; that is, if it be a foot-way only common to them all, or a horse-way and a prime-way; and these are not *altæ regiæ viæ*, for that is the great highway common to cart, horse, and foot, that please to use it.' *R v Saintiff* (1704) 6 Mod Rep 255 at 255, per Holt CJ

'In Com Dig Chimin (A1), it is said "A navigable river is in the nature of a highway, and if the water alters its course, the way alters, per Thorp, 22 Ass 93", and in that book, it is thus stated '*et nota*. Thorp saith, If a water be a high street, which water by its own force changes its course upon another soil, yet it shall have there the same high street as it had before in its ancient course, so that the lord of the soil cannot disturb the new course".' *R v Montague* (1825) 4 B & C 598 at 604, per Holroyd J

'The common definition of a highway that is given in all the text-books of authority is, that it is a way leading from one market-town or inhabited place to another inhabited place, which is common to all the Queen's subjects. . . . To constitute a highway, there must be some notion of a passage which begins somewhere and ends somewhere, and along which the public have a right to drive or to walk from its beginning to its end.' *Bailey v Jamieson* (1876) 1 CPD 329 at 332, per Lord Coleridge CJ

'It is argued that a cul-de-sac may be a highway. That is so in a street in a town into which houses open and which is repaired, sewered, and lighted by the public authority at the expense of the public. Lord Cranworth instances Connaught Place, which opens into the Edgware Road; *Young v Cuthbertson* [(1854) 1 Macq 455 at 456], and see *Rugby Charity v Merryweather* [(1790) 11 East 375 n]. But I am not aware that this law has ever been applied to a long tract of land in the country on which public money has never been expended.' *Bourke v Davis* (1889) 44 Ch D 110 at 122, 123, per Kay J

'It is a necessary element in the legal definition of a highway that it must lead from one definite place to some other definite place. . . . There must be a definite terminus, and a more or less definite direction.' *Eyre v New Forest Highway Board* (1892) 56 JP 517 at 518, per Wills J

'In their Lordships' opinion it is impossible to say that "route" and "highway" . . . are synonymous terms. . . . A "highway" is the physical track along which an omnibus runs, whilst a "route" appears to their Lordships to be an abstract conception of a line of travel between one terminus and another, and to be something distinct from the highway traversed.' *Kelani Valley Motor Transit Co Ltd v Colombo-Ratnapura Omnibus Co Ltd* [1946] AC 338 at 345, 346, per cur.

'The law of highways forms one of the most ancient parts of the common law. At common law highways are of three kinds according to the degree of restriction of the public rights of passage over them. A full highway or "cartway" is one over which the public have rights of way (1) on foot, (2) riding on or accompanied by a beast of burden, and (3) with vehicles and cattle. A "bridleway" is a highway over which the rights of passage are cut down by the exclusion of the right of passage with vehicles and sometimes, though not invariably, the exclusion of the right of driftway, i.e. driving cattle, while a footpath is one over which the only public right of passage is on foot. At common law too a public right of way of any of the three kinds has the characteristic that once it has come into existence it can be neither extinguished nor diminished by disuse, however long the period that has elapsed since it was last used by any member of the public, a rule of law that is the origin of the brocard "Once a highway, always a highway".' *Suffolk County Council v Mason* [1979] 2 All ER 370 at 371, per Lord Diplock

Canada 'A "highway" is a way over which all members of the public are entitled to pass and repass; and, conversely, every piece of land which is subject to such public right of passage, is a highway or part of a highway.' *Rideout v Howlett* (1913) 13 DLR 293 at 295, 296, NBKB, per Barry J

Canada 'In my opinion, unless its meaning is affected by context or association or definition, "highway" means, in its common use, a public road or way open equally to everyone for travel, and includes the public streets of an urban district equally with connecting roads between urban districts.' *Consumers' Gas Co v Toronto* [1941] OR 175 at 192, Ont CA, per Robertson CJO; affd [1941] SCR 584

Canada 'In view of the many things that are included in the meaning of "public highway" it seems to me that there must be a great deal of overlapping of meanings and that the words should be construed according to their normal usage. The normal use of the word "highway" includes "road", particularly when the reference is to places where "there is a public right of travel".' *R ex rel Johnson v Johansen* (1962) 38 WWR 381 at 383, Alta SC, per Manning J

Canada [The court found that a set of traffic lights did not operate properly and that they went from green to amber to red in a time span shorter than programmed, thereby causing the plaintiff to have a motor vehicle collision in the intersection. One issue before the court was whether or not the lights formed part of the 'highway'.] 'Section 148 of the Urban Municipality Act, RSC 1978, c U-10, imposes a statutory duty on a municipality to keep every "highway" in a reasonable state of repair having regard to the character of the highway and the locality in which it is situated. . . . . I am of the opinion that a stop light or traffic lights which control the traffic flow are an integral part of the highway system and are included in the term "highway". The statutory duty to repair applies to traffic lights as well as

to the surface of roadway or highway.' *Dusablon v Saskatoon City* (1983) 23 Sask R 295 at 298, Sask QB, per Vancise J

Canada [Accused was convicted, but acquitted on appeal, of driving while disqualified; licence was required only in respect of driving on 'highway'.] 'I concluded that the term "highway" in its ordinary and popular sense . . . does not embrace the concept of a parking lot and particularly, a parking lot adjacent to an apartment building, and presumably one which was established primarily for the provision of parking to its inhabitants.' *R v Mansour* [1979] 2 SCR 916 at 921, SCC, per Estey J

HIGHWAY ROBBERY   *See* ROBBERY

HIJACKING

A person on board an aircraft in flight who unlawfully, by the use of force or by threats of any kind, seizes the aircraft or exercises control of it commits the offence of highjacking, whatever his nationality, whatever the State in which the aircraft is registered and whether the aircraft is in the United Kingdom or elsewhere . . . (Aviation Security Act 1982, s 1(1))

[Some modifications of this principle, e.g. in the case of aircraft use in military, customs or police service, are made by sub-s (2) of the section]

HINDER   *See* PREVENTION

HIRE   *See also* PLY FOR HIRE

'In my judgment, hire means engaging the services of a person or the use of a chattel for payment, and it is immaterial, as I see it, whether or not there is in the hiring charge a profit element.' *Corner v Clayton* [1976] 3 All ER 212 at 216, per Boreham J

Canada 'We think that the word "hire" in the Act [Conditional Sales Act, RSO, 1960, c 61] applies only to those situations in which a person acquires goods by a contract under which either the title is obtained subject to being divested on the happening of a certain event or the title remains in him until the happening of a certain event; it does not include the simple leasing of goods.' *CAC Leasing Co v Calce* [1969] 2 OR 707 at 708, per Gale CJO

Private hire

'Private hire-car' means a motor vehicle, other than a licensed cab or public service vehicle, which is used for the purpose of carrying passengers for hire or reward. (London Cab Act 1968, s 4(5))

'Private hire is distinct, in my opinion, from plying for hire, that is to say, using the car as a taxicab, standing in the street or driving about seeking passengers. It is private hire in the way that any private hire car is used, namely, by hiring the vehicle for a defined journey at a defined time.' *Lyons v Denscombe* [1949] 1 All ER 977 at 979, per Lord Goddard CJ

HIRE OR REWARD

'The point . . . is as to the proper construction of the question in the proposal form: "Will passengers be carried for hire or reward;" . . . It appears to me that a distinction falls to be drawn between the word "hire" and the word "reward". The first word necessarily imports, I think, an obligation to pay. The inclusion of the second word is not, in my opinion, merely for the purpose of giving an alternative word to "hire" meaning the same thing, but for the purpose of bringing in a subject-matter which does not include hire and including (I do not say it is confined to that) cases where there is no obligation to pay.' *Bonham v Zurich General Accident & Liability Insurance Co Ltd* [1945] KB 292 at 300, CA, per Uthwatt J

'I shall consider first what is meant by "carried for hire or reward". In my opinion, there is no need to say that in this composite expression the word "hire" and the word "reward" are synonymous. That would be a surprising statement, because it would mean that the words "or reward" add nothing and might as well have been omitted. It is not the practice to insert unnecessary words in an Act of Parliament. The probable explanation of the composite phrase is that the words "for hire" were used because they were the most familiar words to describe remuneration for carriage in some vehicles and the words "or reward" were added because "reward" is a wider word and apt to cover some forms of remuneration or some arrangements for which the words "for hire" might not be appropriate.' *Albert v Motor Insurers' Bureau* [1971] 2 All ER 1345 at 1362, HL, per Lord Pearson

[In the above case, *Coward v Motor Insurers' Bureau* [1962] 1 All ER 531 was disapproved]

Australia 'The expression "hire or reward" has been considered in a good number of reported cases. The precise meaning will often depend upon the context in which the words appear and, most important, the purpose of the legislation in question. . . . I do not think that "hire" necessarily connotes a legally enforceable contract. Certainly "reward" does not. Usually there will be a payment in money, but this is not essential.' *Chegwidden v White* (1985) 38 SASR 440 at 443–444, 447, per Cox J

HIRE PURCHASE

'Hire-purchase agreement' means an agreement, other than a conditional sale agreement, under which—
(a) goods are bailed or (in Scotland) hired in return for periodical payments by the person to whom they are bailed or hired; and
(b) the property in the goods will pass to that person if the terms of the agreement are complied with and one or more of the following occurs:
  (i) the exercise of an option to purchase by that person;
  (ii) the doing of any specified act by any party to the agreement;
  (iii) the happening of any other event;
and 'hire-purchase' shall be construed accordingly. (Health and Safety at Work etc Act 1974, s 53(1); see also Consumer Credit Act 1974, s 189(1))

HIRER

'Hirer' means the individual to whom goods are bailed or (in Scotland) hired under a consumer hire agreement, or the person to whom his rights and duties under the agreement have passed by assignment or operation of law, and in relation to a prospective consumer hire agreement includes the prospective hirer. (Consumer Credit Act 1974, s 189(1))

HISTORIC BUILDING

'Historic building' means any building which in the [Historic Buildings and Monuments]

Commission's opinion is of historic or architectural interest. (Natural Heritage Act 1983, s 35)

HOLD

'What is the meaning of the word "held" [in s 40 of the Companies Act 1867 (repealed; see now Companies Act 1985, s 519(2))]. I think that the word "held" there has no specific technical meaning. I think it is sufficient that the shares have been registered in the contributory's name at the period mentioned, and that if they have been registered within the meaning of the two Acts of Parliament [the Companies Act 1862, and the Companies Act 1867 (both repealed)], which I am entitled to read together, it must be said that the shares are "held" by him for that period.' *Re Wala Wynaad Indian Gold Mining Co* (1882) 21 Ch D 849 at 852, per Chitty J

Australia   [By a codicil a testatrix bequeathed shares 'held' by her in a certain company.] 'The word "hold" is not a word of art. The word must be construed in its ordinary English meaning. In my opinion it is a normal use of English to say that one holds shares when once possesses or owns them and that this is true whether the ownership is by means of a legal or an equitable title.' *Re Bennet (decd)* [1957] VR 113 at 116, per Lowe J

HOLDER

'Holder' means the payee or indorsee of a bill or note who is in possession of it, or the bearer thereof. (Bills of Exchange Act 1882, s 2)

In this Part [Part III: securities] of this Act, the expression 'holder'—
(a) in relation to a security transferable by means of a bearer certificate or to a coupon, includes the person holding the certificate or coupon; and
(b) in relation to a security which is registered in the name of a deceased person or of any person who, by reason of bankruptcy, unsoundness of mind or any other disability is incapable of transferring the security, means the personal representative, trustee in bankruptcy or other person entitled to transfer the security.
(Exchange Control Act 1947, s 20(4))

'Section 77 [of the Bills of Exchange Act 1882], sub-s 3, expressly provides that where a cheque is crossed generally the holder may cross it specially. It was argued that this authority does not extend to mere agents for collection, and that "holder" must be read as meaning only holder for value. I see no reason, however, for limiting the operation of the section in such a way. Holder does not necessarily mean a holder for value. The expression includes every person who is in lawful possession of the instrument, and therefore includes an agent for collection.' *Akrokerri (Atlantic) Mines Ltd v Economic Bank* [1904] 2 KB 465 at 472, per Bigham J

'Now it seems to me to be quite plain that "holder" in article 27 [of the articles of association of a company] does mean "registered holder", and that the word cannot in any reasonable sense or upon any stateable ground, be held to apply to or include a person who may have the radical right to shares, but whose name does not appear upon the company's register as holding them.' *Paul's Trustee v Thomas Justice & Sons Ltd* 1912 SC 1303 at 1307, per Lord Dundas

'Mr Dey was a bookmaker. Mr Mayo made bets with him, and was fortunate enough to win £852 which he received by crossed cheques from Mr Dey. Mr Mayo indorsed the cheques for £852 in blank and paid them into the account standing in the name of his wife. The bank . . . credited the account with them at once, and presented them for payment to Mr Dey's bank, who paid them. Fortune changed, and Mr Mayo lost bets amounting to £320 odd. . . . It seemed right to Mr Mayo not to pay. . . . Mr Dey sued Mr Mayo for the £320 . . . and for the £852 . . . alleging that he, Dey, had paid the amount of cheques given for an illegal consideration to third parties—namely, Mrs Mayo and her bank—to whom Mr Mayo had indorsed them, and that he, Dey, was therefore entitled to recover the sum from Mayo as money paid for and on account of Mayo. . . . If the account in the wife's name is the account of the husband, she receives the cheque indorsed in blank as his agent, and becomes the "holder" of it. So does the bank receiving it for collection. Though neither of them is holder in due course, each of them, in my view, is a "holder", and can, under s 38 of the Bills of Exchange Act 1882, sue in his own name, as indorsee in blank, and therefore bearer and holder. I agree with the view of Bigham J in *Akrokerri (Atlantic) Mines Ltd v Economic Bank* [supra] that holder includes every person who is in lawful possession of the instrument, and therefore includes an agent for collection.' *Dey v Mayo* [1920] 2 KB 346 at 358, 362, CA, per Scrutton LJ

Commercial paper

United States 'Holder' means a person who is in possession of a document of title or an instrument of a certificated investment security drawn, issued, or indorsed to him or his order or to bearer or in blank. (Uniform Commercial Code 1978, s 1–201(20))

In due course

'An examination of ss 20, 21, 29, 30 and 38 [of the Bills of Exchange Act 1882] relating expressly to bills, and ss 83, 84, 88 and 89, relating to promissory notes, will make it quite clear that "a holder in due course" is a person to whom after its completion by and as between the immediate parties, the bill or note has been negotiated.' *Lewis v Clay* (1897) 67 LJQB 224 at 227, per Lord Russell of Killowen CJ

'I do not think that the expression "holder in due course" includes the original payee of a cheque. It is true that under the definition clause in the Act [Bills of Exchange Act 1882] (s 2) the word "holder" includes the payee of a bill unless the context otherwise requires; but it appears from s 29 sub-s 1, that a "holder in due course" is a person to whom the bill has been "negotiated", and from s 31 that a bill is negotiated by being transferred from one person to another and (if payable to order) by indorsement and delivery. In view of these definitions it is difficult to see how the original payee of a cheque can be a "holder in due course" within the meaning of the Act.' *Jones (RE) Ltd v Waring & Gillow Ltd* [1926] AC 670 at 680, per Viscount Cave LC

United States A holder in due course is a holder who takes the instrument
(a) for value; and
(b) in good faith; and
(c) without notice that it is overdue or has been dishonoured or of any defence against or claim to it on the part of any person.
(Uniform Commercial Code 1978, s 3–302(1))

HOLDING   *See* AGRICULTURAL HOLDING; COTTAGE HOLDING

HOLE   *See* PIT

HOLIDAY   *See also* WORKING HOLIDAY

The term 'holidays' used in the larger sense covers the common law holidays, namely, in England, Good Friday, and Christmas Day, and the statutory holidays, which include those established by the Banking and Financial Dealings Act 1971 and by statutes and rules relating to legal procedure. (45 Halsbury's Laws (4th edn) para 1119)

Bank holidays now are (in England and Wales): Easter Monday; 1 May; the *last* Monday in May; the *last* Monday in August; 26 December, if not a Sunday; and 27 December in any year in which the 25 or 26 December is on a Sunday (Act of 1971, supra). From 1974, New Year's Day has been appointed a bank holiday by proclamation in the *London Gazette* ibid, s 1(3)).
(In Scotland): New Year's Day and the following day (if either falls on a Sunday, then 3 January); Good Friday; the *first* Monday in May; the *first* Monday in August; and Christmas Day (if on a Sunday, 26 December) ibid.]

In relation to any person employed about the business of a shop the following expressions have the meanings hereby respectively assigned to them, that is to say,
'whole holiday' means a day on which that person is not employed about the business of that shop;
'statutory half-holiday' means a day on which under s 17 of this Act he is not employed about the business of that shop after half-past one o'clock in the afternoon;
'half-holiday' means a day on which he is either not employed before, or not employed after, half-past one o'clock in the afternoon of that day about the business of that shop. (Shops Act 1950, s 22).

'Holiday', in relation to any part of the United Kingdom, means any day that is a bank holiday in that part of the United Kingdom under the Banking and Financial Dealings Act 1971, Christmas Day, Good Friday, and the day appointed for the purposes of customs and excise for the celebration of Her Majesty's birthday. (Customs and Excise Management Act 1979, s 1(1))

[By a charterparty, the loading of a steamship was to be carried on at a certain rate per running day, Sundays and 'holidays' excepted.] 'On the question of holidays I agree that whether a particular day was a holiday or not is a question of fact. It is unnecessary to show that a holiday was officially decreed or universally recognised. Holidays are not the same in England and in Scotland; different days may be kept as holidays in different places, and holidays are really a local, and only exceptionally a national institution.' *Hain SS Co Ltd v Sociedad Anonima Comercial de Exportacion y Importacion etc* (1932) 48 TLR 363 at 364, per MacKinnon J

[By a charterparty, the loading of another steamship was also to be carried on at a certain rate per running day, 'Sundays and holidays excepted'. The question for the court on a special case was whether Saturday afternoons should be taken into account when computing the lay days, or whether they should be regarded as 'holidays'. 'I think . . . in ascertaining what is the meaning of the language used by the parties here, that quite clearly the period on Saturdays from 1 pm onwards is not included in the Sundays and holidays and must not be taken to be impliedly included merely because in the Argentine a holiday is sanctioned by . . . a local law which says that it is illegal to work. It is, I think, purely a question of what is the meaning of this clause and the language used by the parties, and I think clearly the proper meaning of this is to exclude from the consecutive periods of twenty-four hours only Sundays and full general holidays and not to exclude the period from 1 pm on Saturdays.' *Hain SS Co Ltd v Sociedad Anonima Comercial de Exportacion y Importacion (Louis Dreyfus & Cia) Ltda of Buenos Aires* (1934) 151 LT 305 at 306, 307, per MacKinnon J

HOLOGRAPH

Canada 'Holograph' is described in Wharton's Law Lexicon as derived from two Greek words 'all' and 'to write', and it is a deed or writing written entirely by the grantor himself. In Scotland such a deed is held probative without witnesses, and a holograph will is good. In Manitoba in *Re Nesbitt Estate* [1933] 3 WWR 171, the late Taylor J wrote a very informative judgment on the matter of holograph wills. In that case the supposed holograph will was typewritten by the testator, and Taylor J held, under the Manitoba Statute respecting the interpretation of statutes which is similar to the Saskatchewan statute in that

respect, that so long as the whole of the document has been the personal work of the testator himself, whether it be written by pen and ink or printed or typewritten or painted or engraved or lithographed, so long as it has been the product of his own hand and is signed with his signature, that is a good holograph will. There is a difference between the provisions of the two statutes which would make it possible for a typewritten document to be accepted in Manitoba providing the typewriting was done by the testator, but under our statute the will must be wholly in the handwriting of the testator.' *Re Rigden Estate* [1941] 1 WWR 566 at 567–569, Sask Surr Ct, per McPhee SCJ

HOLY ORDERS

'The part of the will that raises the present questions is in these words: "and my further will . . . is that every such scholar [proceeding from Glasgow College to Balliol College, Oxford] . . . shall be bound . . . to enter into holy orders as soon as he or they shall be respectively capable by the Canons of the Church of England". . . . I think there is no doubt that what he meant by holy orders was something that was consistent with the state of Scotland and the state of England at that time, and that by the expression, "holy orders", he meant holy orders according to the understanding of the Episcopal form of church government.' *Glasgow College v A-G* (1848) 1 HL Cas 800 at 819, 823, per Lord Cottenham LC

HOME

'Home', in relation to any person, means the house, flat or other place where he is living, whether permanently or temporarily. (Extra-Parochial Ministry Measure 1967, s 3)

'The testatrix was minded to establish, as appears from the letter incorporated in the will, a home of rest for lady teachers. . . . I do not find any assistance in the use of the word "lady", but I do find a good deal in the use of the word "home". I need not go into a description of what is meant by a "home"—but it is something very different from a hotel or lodgings for which you pay. It is a place where you find not only the reasonable comforts of life according to your position in life, but where you find the comforts of what is known as a home.' *Re Estlin, Prichard v Thomas* (1903) 72 LJ Ch 687 at 688, 689, per Kekewich J

'The word "home" itself is not easy of exact definition, but the question posed, and to be answered by ordinary common-sense standards, is whether the particular premises are in the personal occupation of the tenant as his or her home, or, if the tenant has more than one home, as one of his or her homes. Occupation merely as a convenience for . . . occasional visits . . . would not, I venture to think, according to the common sense of the matter, be occupation as a home.' *Beck v Scholz* [1953] 1 All ER 814 at 816, CA, per Evershed MR (also reported in [1953] 1 QB 570 at 575, 576)

[A testator left money to his daughter on condition that she would always 'provide a home' for another daughter.] 'I confess to feeling a grave doubt whether the conception of one person, A, providing a home for another, B, is susceptible of any such clear and definite interpretation as to enable anyone to say what it means or what obligations it imposes. Obviously, the provision of a home would involve giving shelter from the elements, but how about board and lodging, clothing etc, and, if these things, food, clothing, and so forth, have to be provided, on what scale or by what standard is the obligation to be discharged? . . . What is meant by the expression "provide a home", without any reference . . . to costs and expenses? It is, I think, an expression which has a certain general significance applicable in various contexts, and having in each case a very different meaning. Of a negligent mother, for example, it may be said: "She does not really provide a home for the children", in the sense that she allows them to run loose. To "provide a home" is not like providing a shelter and allowing a person to reside there. "Home" is a word, in my judgment, of an extremely wide and varied significance. . . . The expression "provide a home" is not only extremely vague, but is one to which it is impossible to attach any intelligible signification. It is not a question of a difficult expression, but a question, I think, of an unintelligible one. I agree that a man may be said to be providing a home for someone when he feeds him, gives him board and lodging, entertains him, and gives him pocket money. In such a case a home is provided to the fullest extent. But what if the pocket money is stopped, what if the food is reduced, what if the person for whom the home is to be provided is compelled to wear shabby clothes while the person who is required to provide the home is handsomely dressed? All those questions seem to me to introduce an element of uncertainty into the conception of "providing a home", which is, in my view, an expression to which no real attention can be paid in so far as it is alleged to create legal obligations.' *Re Brace, Gunton v Clements* [1954] 2 All ER 354 at 356, 358, per Vaisey J

'"Home" is a somewhat nebulous concept, incapable of precise definition. Nor would it be possible to obtain any measure of agreement between reasonable men as to the essential constituents of a real home. For example, uxorious persons might consider that a real home cannot exist without a wife and children; hardened bachelors might take an entirely opposite view. Some people might hold that there can be no real home without television; others that there can be none with it. It would be easy to multiply instances. In my view, if the evidence establishes, as it does here, a substantial degree of regular personal occupation by the tenant of an essentially residential nature, it would be difficult, if not impossible for a court to hold that he was not in occupation of the premises as a home within the meaning of the word as used by this court in *Skinner v Geary* [[1931] 2 KB 546], and in the later authorities.' *Herbert v Byrne* [1964] 1 All ER 882 at 887, CA, per Salmon LJ

'Home' is defined thus in the Shorter Oxford English Dictionary: "A dwelling-house, house, abode: the fixed residence of a family or household; one's own house; the dwelling in which one habitually lives or which one regards as one's proper abode." It is a definition which, in my judgment, contains the essential elements of a "home" as it is to be understood for present purposes [application for an adoption order]. I have no doubt that an individual may have two homes; but each, in my judgment, to be properly so called, must comprise some element of regular occupation (whether past, present or intended for the future, even if intermittent), with some degree of permanency, based on some right of occupation whenever it is required, where, in the words of Kekewich J in *Re Estlin, Prichard v Thomas* [supra], "you find the comforts of what is known as a home", the fixed residence of a family or household.' *Re Y (minors)* [1985] 3 All ER 33 at 37, per Sheldon J

Australia 'A home is a place where the residents ordinarily eat morning and night, and where they usually sleep. With adults it may have the characteristic of permanency. A home is, or used to be, regarded as a place of refuge and rest. With modern conveniences, and under the present conditions of life, these aspects may perhaps be regarded as undergoing change. References to "sharing a home" can be taken to import an intention by the parties to live together under conditions of mutual indulgence and forbearance, of propriety, decorum and friendliness, and, if necessary, of resignation and toleration, as might be reasonably expected in a home.' *Todd v Nicol* [1957] SASR 72 at 86, per Mayo J

New Zealand ' "Home" [for the purpose of s 241(1) of the Income Tax Act 1976] is where the heart is; it is the location of the axis around which for the present, the normal course of one's life revolves. Put another way, it is the place where the centre of gravity of one's domestic life is to be found . . . For the married person who is not separated "home" will generally be where his or her spouse and children are to be found; and some such equivalent centre no doubt can be found for the single or separated person on the basis of the place where the normal course of his or her life occurs. This definition of the concept of "home" would appear to be consistent with and explain those cases in which a person has been found to be resident in a country although he has not actually lived there at any time during the relevant year'. *Geothermal Energy NZ Ltd v Inland Revenue Comr* [1979] 2 NZLR 324 at 341, per Beattie J

HOME OCCUPATION

New Zealand 'An "home occupation" could be conducted in a place other than a home, but it is an occupation which, from the point of view of the person engaged in it can conveniently be carried on at that person's home and which, from the land use planning point of view, is appropriate in that person's home. Why the person finds it convenient to work at home is of no relevance to land use planning: that he does so, is relevant. We expect that in most cases the person who works at home will be self-employed. But not in every case. Taking the definition as a whole we see no reason why those who work at their homes cannot include people remunerated on a contract, salary or wages basis. Outwork is commonly done at home; some kinds of

clerical work can be done at home. Nor do we think the definition excludes an employee who lives and works where he does because the house goes with the job. Again, land use planning is not concerned with why a person lives at a particular place; it is concerned with the consequences should he also work at that place'. *Mt Wellington Borough v Pensioner Funerals* (1983) 9 NZTPA 53 at 62, per Chilwell J

HOME-GOING SHIP   *See* SHIP

HOMELESS

(1) A person is homeless if he has no accommodation in England, Wales or Scotland.
(2) A person shall be treated as having no accommodation if there is no accommodation which he, together with any other person who normally resides with him as a member of his family or in circumstances in which it is reasonable for that person to reside with him–
   (a) is entitled to occupy by virtue of an interest in it or by virtue of an order of a court, or
   (b) has an express or implied licence to occupy, or in Scotland has a right or permission or an implied right or permission to occupy, or
   (c) occupies as a residence by virtue of any enactment or rule of law giving him the right to remain in occupation or restricting the right of another person to recover possession.
(3) A person is also homeless if he has accommodation but–
   (a) he cannot secure entry to it, or
   (b) it is probable that occupation of it will lead to violence from some other person residing in it or to threats of violence from some other person residing in it and likely to carry out the threats, or
   (c) it consists of a movable structure, vehicle or vessel designed or adapted for human habitation and there is no place where he is entitled or permitted both to place it and to reside in it.
(4) A person is threatened with homelessness if it is likely that he will become homeless within 28 days.
(Housing Act 1985, s 58(1))

HOMESTEAD

Australia '"Homestead" means, according to the Standard Dictionary .of the English Language, the place of a home, the house and adjacent land occupied as a home, rarely either house or land separately, a farm occupied by the owner and his family as a permanent abode. Notoriously in Australia, where large areas of land are occupied for grazing, the dwelling-house is called the "homestead", and the paddock nearest to it, usually used for the horses worked on the property, is called the "homestead" paddock, as contrasted with the rest of the property.' *Re Ellen Anderson, Longstaff v Anderson* [1908] VLR 593 at 603, per Madden CJ

Canada 'As I understand it, occupation of the land as a family home is necessary for the establishment as a fact of a homestead. It is not necessary that a permanent dwelling house be erected for that occupation; a box car or tent may be sufficient. There should of course be ownership of the land and a definite *animus manendi*. When the homestead has once been in fact established, residence thereon, as I understand it, becomes of diminishing importance, especially if the absence of residence thereon be only that of either one of the heads of the family. It is homestead notwithstanding that only a small portion, whether urban or farm land, be used in the actual—as distinguished from the legal—occupation.' *Re Real Estate Loan Co of Canada Ltd & Badner* [1941] 3 WWR 730 at 733, per Donovan J

HOMEWORKER

'Homeworker' means a person who contracts with a person, for the purposes of that person's business, for the execution of work to be done in a place not under the control or management of the person with whom he contracts, and who does not normally make use of the services of more than two persons in the carrying out of contracts for the execution of work with statutory minimum remuneration. (Wages Councils Act 1979, s 28)

HOMICIDE

The term homicide is used to describe the killing of a human being by a human being. Such a killing may be lawful or it may be unlawful and criminal. Unlawful homicide includes murder, manslaughter, causing death by dangerous driving, killing in pursuance of a suicide pact, and infanticide. (11 Halsbury's Laws (4th edn) para 1151)

Culpable homicide

'Culpable homicide is the name which is given in Scotland to a crime where death is caused by improper conduct, and where the guilt is less than murder.' *HM Advocate v Kidd* 1960 SLT 82 at 86, per Lord Strachan

HONEST *See also* DISHONEST

'The Legislature has passed the Judicial Trustees Act 1896, excusing trustees for breach of trust, but that Act does not apply here. According to the Act (s 3 [repealed; see now Trustee Act 1925, s 61]) a trustee, if he is to be excused, must act "honestly and reasonably". The word "honest" is used in many senses. In one sense a trustee is honest if he has not done anything dishonest. . . . But in another sense he is not honest. It seems to me that a man who accepts such a trusteeship, and does nothing, swallows wholesale what is said by his co-trustee, never asks for explanation, and accepts flimsy explanations, is dishonest.' *Re Second East Dulwich 745th Starr-Bowkett Building Society* (1899) 68 LJ Ch 196 at 197, 198, per Kekewich J

HONESTLY

Australia 'This background to the language of the section [Companies Act 1961–1986 (Vic) s 124] appears to justify the conclusions, first, that the section is not concerned with the conduct of a director in relation to creditors or other persons dealing with or concerned with the company or anybody else but the company itself; secondly, that it is concerned with the performance of his fiduciary duty to the company; and, thirdly, that to 'act honestly' refers to acting bona fide in the interests of the company in the performance of the functions attaching to the office of director. A breach of the obligation to act bona fide in the interests of the company involves a consciousness that what is being done is not in the interests of the company, and deliberate conduct in disregard of that knowledge.' *Marchesi v Barnes* [1970] VR 434 at 438, per Gowans J

HONORARIUM

Canada 'A common thread running through [the dictionary] definitions is the notion that, while the money paid as an "honorarium" is a compensation for services rendered, it is nevertheless not a payment for which the recipient, if not paid, could sue in a court of law. It is thus in the nature of an ex gratia or gratuitous payment, unlike a salary or wage or other contracted remuneration. Certainly "honoraria" paid to English barristers or to Fellows of the Royal College of Surgeons in England may be very substantial in amount. There is nothing in the use of the word in relation to those professions in England denoting a mere "token" amount.' *Re Vladicka and Board of School Trustees of Calgary School District No 19* (1974) 45 DLR (3d) 442 at 449, Alta SC, per McDonald J

HONOUR

'The declaration is on a guarantee, which states that, in consideration that the plaintiff would receive the promissory note of two persons therein mentioned, and thereby give time for the payment of a debt due from one of those persons, the defendant promised to pay the plaintiff the amount of the debt, if the note were not "duly honoured and paid". . . . Upon this contract of guarantee, therefore, it seems to me that the word "honoured" means no more than the words "duly paid", and that, inasmuch as this note has not been paid the defendant is chargeable.' *Walton v Mascall* (1844) 13 M & W 452 at 457, 458, per Parke B

United States To 'honor' is to pay or to accept and pay, or where a credit so engages to purchase or discount a draft complying with the terms of the credit. (Uniform Commercial Code 1978, s 1–201(21))

HONOUR POLICY *See* POLICY

HORSE *See also* LIVESTOCK

The word 'horse' shall include every mare and gelding. (London Hackney Carriages Act 1843, s 2)

'Horse' includes any mare, gelding, pony, foal, colt, filly, or stallion. (Protection of Animals Act 1911, s 15)

'Horse' includes pony, ass and mule, and 'horseback' is to be construed accordingly. (National Parks and Access to the Countryside Act 1949, s 27; Highways Act 1980, s 329(1))

'Horse' includes stallion, gelding, colt, mare, filly, pony, mule and hinny. (Docking and Nicking of Horses Act 1949, s 3)

'Horse' includes any mare, gelding, pony, foal, colt, filly or stallion and also any ass, mule or jennet. (Riding Establishments Act 1964, s 6)

'Horse' includes ass and mule. (Slaughterhouses Act 1974, ss 34, 35; Animal Health Act 1981, s 89(1))

'Horse' includes pony, mule, donkey or other equine animal. (Farriers (Registration) Act 1975, s 18)

'Foals and fillies are within the statutes 2 & 3 Edw 6 [c 53 (repealed), which related to horse-stealing], and are included in the words "horse, gelding, or mare", and therefore . . . the evidence of stealing a mare filly would support this indictment for stealing a mare.' *R v Welland* (1822) Russ & Ry 494 at 494, per cur.

'The word "horse" is a generic term, and includes a gelding, and wherever there is a well-known generic term or name for property, it may be described by that name in an indictment for stealing it. The same objection was made in a case where the indictment described the animal as a sheep, and the proof was the loss of a lamb. It was decided by all the judges, that the word "sheep" was a generic term, and included lambs.' *R v Aldridge* (1849) 4 Cox CC 143 at 143, per Erle J

HORSE RACE

'Recognised horse race' means a horse race run on an approved horse racecourse on a day when horse races and no other races take place on the racecourse. (Betting, Gaming and Lotteries Act 1963, s 55)

HORSEFLESH

In this section 'horseflesh' means the flesh of horses, asses and mules, and includes any such flesh—
(a) whether cooked or uncooked, and
(b) whether alone or accompanied by, as mixed with, any other substance,
and 'flesh' includes any part of any such animal. (Food Act 1984, s 29(4))

HORTICULTURE   *See also*
AGRICULTURE

Canada [Labour Relations Act, RSO 1960,
c 202, s 2(c) (see now RSO 1980, c 228)
excluded persons employed in horticulture.] 'I
have little difficulty in determining that
"horticulture" means gardening and that in the
statute it covers every kind of garden and
garden work known in Ontario. It includes,
among much else, work in ornamental
gardens, botanical gardens and arboreta, tree
nursery work, the development and care of
civilised parks and urban and suburban
roadsides, the care of individual shrubs and
trees, topiary work, garden designs,
landscaping and garden care. But it only
includes those functions in connection with
gardens of some kind.' *R v Ontario Labour
Relations Board, ex p Cedarvale Tree Services
Ltd* (1970) 15 DLR (3d) 413 at 416, 417, Ont
SC, per Wright J

Horticultural produce

'Horticultural produce' means vegetables
fruit, flowers and plants. (Horticultural
Produce (Sales on Commission) Act 1926, s 3)

'Horticultural produce' means vegetation
intended for purposes of decoration or fruit,
vegetables, flowers or plants. (City of London
(Various Powers) Act 1959, s 6; London
County Council (General Powers) Act 1959,
s 11)

In this Part [Part I] of this Act 'horticultural
produce' means—
(a) fruit
(b) vegetables of a kind grown for human
    consumption including fungi, but not
    including maincrop potatoes or peas
    grown for seed, for harvesting dry or for
    vining,
(c) flowers, pot plants and decorative foliage,
(d) herbs,
(e) seeds other than pea seeds, and bulbs and
    other material, being seeds, bulbs or
    material for sowing or planting for the
    production of fruit, of such vegetables,
    flowers, plants or foliage as aforesaid, or of
    herbs, or for reproduction of the seeds,
    bulbs or other material planted, or
(f) trees and shrubs, other than trees grown
    for the purpose of afforestation;
but does not include hops. (Horticulture Act
1960, s 8)

'Horticultural produce' means—
(a) fresh fruit, dried fruit, frozen fruit and
    fruit preserved in airtight containers;

(b) fresh vegetables, dried vegetables, frozen
    vegetables and vegetables preserved in
    airtight containers;
(c) fresh herbs and dried herbs;
(d) fresh edible fungi, dried edible fungi and
    edible fungi preserved in airtight
    containers;
(e) nuts;
(f) cut flowers;
(g) dried flowers;
(h) decorative foliage;
(i) Christmas trees;
(j) pot plants, bedding plants and herbaceous
    plants;
(k) shrubs and flowering trees;
(l) fruit trees, fruit bushes and fruit plants;
    and
(m) seeds, bulbs, corms, tubers and seed
    potatoes.
(Agriculture and Horticulture Act 1964, s 10)

'Fresh horticultural produce' means—
(a) fruit, vegetables, herbs, nuts and edible
    fungi, whether freshly-gathered or stored
    or taken from store, but not including
    maincrop potatoes or hops or any dried,
    frozen, bottled, canned or preserved
    produce;
(b) cut flowers and decorative foliage;
(c) pot plants, bedding plants and herbaceous
    plants;
(d) shrubs and flowering trees;
(e) fruit trees, fruit bushes and fruit plants;
    and
(f) bulbs, corms and tubers.
(Agriculture and Horticulture Act 1964, s 24)

Horticultural production business

In this Part [Part I] of this Act 'horticultural
production business' means a business which
consists, or so much of a larger business as
consists, of the growing in the United Kingdom
of horticultural produce for sale or the growing
of produce as aforesaid and its storage
preparation for market or transport.
(Horticulture Act 1960, s 8(2))

HOSPITAL

'Hospital' includes any premises for the
reception of the sick. (Public Health Act 1936,
s 343)

'Hospital' includes a clinic, dispensary or other
institution for the reception of the sick whether
as in-patients or as out-patients. (Cancer Act
1939, s 5)

'Hospital' includes a clinic, nursing home or similar institution. (Medicines Act 1968, s 132(1))

'Hospital' means an institution which provides medical or surgical treatment for in-patients or out-patients. (Road Traffic Act 1972, s 12(1))

[See also s 158(1) of the Act of 1972, which gives a different definition applicable to Part VI (third-party liabilities) of the Act.]

'Hospital' means—
(a) any institution for the reception and treatment of persons suffering from illness,
(b) any maternity home, and
(c) any institution for the reception and treatment of persons during convalescence or persons requiring medical rehabilitation,
and includes clinics, dispensaries and outpatient departments maintained in connection with any such home or institution, and 'hospital accommodation' shall be construed accordingly. (National Health Service Act 1977, s 128(1))

'Hospital' means—
(a) any health service hospital within the meaning of the National Health Service Act 1977; and
(b) any accommodation provided by a local authority and used as a hospital by or on behalf of the Secretary of State under that Act.
(Mental Health Act 1983, s 147)

Australia 'The term "hospital" is not a term of art, and may have different meanings in different countries. In Australia it is commonly used to denote an institution for the medical or surgical treatment of persons suffering from bodily ailment or injury. Used without the adjective "private" prefixed, it commonly means a charitable institution of that kind, whether supported wholly, or in part, or not at all, by voluntary contributions. Other charitable institutions which are in some countries included in the term "hospital" are in Australia ordinarily called by other names.' *Re Padbury, Home of Peace for the Dying & Incurable v Solicitor-General* (1908) 7 CLR 680 at 686, per Griffith CJ

Australia 'I do not think that in ordinary Australian parlance . . . a convalescent home or an infirmary attached to a home for the aged or a rest home would have been regarded as a hospital. I think ordinary speech distinguishes

between these conceptions.' *Executor Trustee Co v Warbey* [1971] SASR 255 at 261, per Bray CJ

Australia [A person injured in the course of employment spent some time in an institution where she received constant attention but no curative treatment. The question was whether the institution was a 'hospital' within the Workmen's Compensation Ordinance Act 1951–1986, s 6(1).] 'I am inclined to think that in everyday speech, in Australia at present, the word "hospital" primarily suggests a place to which a person resorts with the intention of being treated for a curable malady or injury. . . . But it is one thing to say what the word primarily suggests, and quite another to decide that a sense lying outside the scope of such primary sense cannot be included for the purpose of the construction of a statute. . . . If it be said that the appellant is not in a hospital because she receives there no more than she could receive in her own home, at the hands of relations or friends endowed by unlimited patience, time and devotion, the answer may be that it does not follow that the institution which provides this is not a hospital. It does not seem to me a misuse of language to say that the appellant is a sick person who is obliged to live in a hospital because she cannot get the care she needs at home.' *Tanner v Marquis Jackson* (1974) 3 ACTR 32 at 38, per Blackburn J

In will

'This, in my judgment, is a question which turns upon the ordinary meaning of the English word "hospital" as the testator must be assumed to have understood it. Little guidance can be derived from the etymological history of the word, but it seems to me, prima facie, to indicate a place in which patients are received for continuous treatment and to exclude places to which patients merely resort for the purpose of occasional medical or surgery aid such as is normally obtained at the out-patients' department of hospitals. In the ordinary sense of the word I am of opinion, that "hospital" signifies a building where in-patients are received and the fact that in ordinary parlance a hospital is regarded as being something different from a dispensary is indicated in the affidavit of the secretary. In reference to the casualty clinics of the applicants, he tells me that they have been set up to treat minor industrial injuries and ailments hitherto catered for by hospitals only. That, in my judgment, is a significant statement and implies, none the less cogently because unconsciously, that the deponent regarded the casualty clinics as such in contradistinction to hospitals.' *Re Ford* [1945] 1 All ER 288 at 289, per Vaisey J

'The testator here made his will in 1931: and at that date, which was long before the National Health Service Act 1946 [repealed; see now National Health Service Act 1977], I am clearly of opinion that the word "hospital" was capable of a narrower meaning than that which the judge gave it. It was capable of meaning a voluntary hospital, without being extended so as to cover a "nursing home" which was a private hospital, or a "sanatorium" for the private treatment of boys in a school. No one at that date would describe such a place as a "hospital". Collections used to be made on "Hospital Sunday" and everyone knew that they would go to the voluntary hospitals, not to the private nursing homes. When an appeal was made for money to erect a "new hospital", it meant a voluntary hospital and not an institution run for profit. In short, when people spoke in 1931 of giving money to a "hospital" or "hospitals" they meant, as of course, voluntary hospitals which were helped by collections and gifts of money from people of good will, and by the free and willing services of doctors and surgeons, and of the nurses who devoted themselves to the work for little reward. Seeing that the word "hospital" is capable of a wide and also a narrower meaning, the question is what meaning did it bear in this will? What was the testator's intention? I am clearly of opinion that when he used the word "hospital" in this will (using it, as he did, in the context of giving money to or for a hospital) the testator meant a voluntary hospital which was not carried on for the private profit of any individual, but for the relief of the sick. Such a "hospital" is clearly a charitable institution.' *Re Smith's Will Trusts, Barclays Bank Ltd v Mercantile Bank Ltd* [1962] 2 All ER 563 at 565, CA, per Lord Denning MR

Special hospital

The duty imposed on the Secretary of State . . . to provide services for the purposes of the health service includes a duty to provide and maintain establishments (in this Act referred to as 'special hospitals') for persons subject to detention under the Mental Health Act 1983 who in his opinion require treatment under conditions of special security on account of their dangerous, violent or criminal propensities. (National Health Service Act 1977, s 4 as amended by the Mental Health Act 1983, s 148, Sch 4, para 47)

HOSPITALITY

'Now the purpose of this legacy therefore is, that the income is to be expended yearly by the mayor in acts of hospitality or charity. The question is, whether that is a good charitable gift. . . . In order to arrive at the determination that this is a charitable gift, I must regard the words "hospitality" or "charity" as meaning charity, or such hospitality as may be considered to be charitable. I am afraid that to do that would be to invert the order of the words. The testator puts "hospitality" before "charity", and the two words are manifestly contra-distinguished; so that I must hold the word "hospitality" as meaning in this bequest hospitality not necessarily for charity.' *Re Hewitt's Estate, Gateshead Corpn v Hudspeth* (1883) 53 LJ Ch 132 at 133, per Kay J

HOSPITIUM

The strict liability in respect of a guest's goods imposed on a hotel proprietor in his capacity as an innkeeper only attaches where the goods of the guest are within the hospitium of the inn. The goods need not be in the special keeping of the hotel proprietor to render him liable, for he is bound to answer for himself and for his family with respect to the chambers and stables, if they are within the hospitium of the inn. The hospitium consists of the inn buildings themselves and precincts so intimately related to those buildings as to be treated for this purpose as forming part of them. (24 Halsbury's Laws (4th edn) para 1228)

HOSTEL

'Hostel' means a building in which is provided for persons generally or for a class or classes of persons–
(a) residential accommodation otherwise than in separate and self-contained sets of premises, and
(b) either board or facilities for the preparation of food adequate to the needs of those persons, or both.
(Housing Associations Act 1985, s 106(1))

[See also Housing Act 1985, s 622]

'No doubt there are a number of hostels of superior quality; and one day, perhaps, I may even encounter the expression "luxury hostel". But without any such laudatory adjective the word "hostel" has to my mind a strong flavour of a building which provides somewhat modest accommodation for those who have some temporary need for it and are willing to accept accommodation of that standard in order to meet the need.' *Re Niyazi's Will Trusts* [1978] 3 All ER 785 at 788, 789, per Megarry V-C

HOSTILE *See* ADVERSE

HOSTILITIES

Hostilities in the f c and s warranty connotes existing hostilities, that is, operations of war, offensive or defensive; it implies enemy nations at war with one another. 'Warlike operations' is said to have been added in order to cover similar acts done when no actual outbreak of war had occurred. It is a wider term, and would probably cover almost any act or movement of combatant forces in the course of their combatant duties while exercised in the area of war, and all those operations of a belligerent power or its agents which form part of or directly lead up to attack or defence. (25 Halsbury's Laws (4th edn) para 158)

'The word "hostilities" [in the f c s clause of a policy of marine insurance] . . . means hostile acts by persons acting as the agents of sovereign powers, or of such organised and considerable forces as are entitled to the dignified name of rebels as contrasted with mobs or rioters, and does not cover the act of a mere private individual acting entirely on his own initiative, however hostile his action may be.' *Atlantic Mutual Insurance Co v King* [1919] 1 KB 307 at 310, per Bailhache J

Australia '[Hostilities] is a word which is used in a number of judgments, and is used at times to indicate that upon the cessation of hostilities the disability which attaches to an alien enemy preventing him from suing in our courts, or perhaps the character of alien enemy itself ceases. . . . To my mind it may well be said that acts of hostility are proceeding when the armed forces of one country occupy another country and control it, and do so after that other country has surrendered its own armed forces and agreed no longer to fight a war.'

Schering AG v Pharmedica Pty Ltd (1952) 52 SR (NSW) 16 at 19, 20, per Roper CJ in Eq

New Zealand [The Patents, Designs, and Trademarks Act 1921–22 (NZ), s 20(6) (repealed; see now the Patents Act 1953, s 32 (NZ)) provides: 'Where, by reason of hostilities between His · Majesty and any foreign State, the patentee as such has suffered loss or damage . . . an application under this section may be made . . .' (reproducing s 18(6) of the Patents and Designs Act 1907 (Eng) repealed; cf Patents Act 1949, s 24 (Eng)).] 'In my view, the plaintiff cannot ask the Court to make allowance in its favour for any reduction of the useful life of the patent which was due to the mere anticipation of hostilities. The loss or damage which the Court may take into account under s 20(6) is the loss or damage suffered "by reason of hostilities". In my opinion, those words mean actual hostilities, not the threat or fear of hostilities. . . . After actual hostilities have occurred, the Court has, no doubt, power to afford relief by reason of the continuance of the effect of hostilities beyond their cessation. . . . In the view which I take of the present application, all that I need decide on the question of the effect of hostilities is that the peace-time benefit of the patent to the applicant continues right up to 3 September 1939. It follows that the war life of the patent ran from that date until the end of the normal term of the patent on 13 April 1942, a period of two years and two hundred and twenty-two days. The question for the Court is as to how much of that life still remains useless by reason of the war. The onus of proving the extent of the effect of the war rests upon the plaintiff. . . . The extent of the plaintiff's loss should be ascertained by reference to the number of articles sold during the war when compared with the average sold before the war.' *Radiation Ltd v Comr of Patents* [1944] NZLR 496 at 499, 500, per Smith J, also reported [1944] GLR 257 at 258

New Zealand [A lease of shop premises was expressed to be for a term commencing on 15 July 1943, and terminating on (a) the expiration of three calendar months after the date upon which the Dominion of New Zealand should have ceased 'active hostilities' with all nations or countries then engaged in the war being waged by the British Commonwealth of Nations with enemy countries, or (b) the expiration of five years from 15 July 1943, whichever date should be the earlier. An action was brought for possession after a month's notice of determination expiring on 15 November 1945.] 'The word "active" must have been intended to modify the meaning which the provision would have borne if the word "hostilities" alone had been used. . . . "Active hostilities" mean in this context "actual belligerent operations by force of arms against an organised government representing, at least, a considerable section of the people of an enemy country". It does not extend to operations against relatively small bodies of armed forces of that country that continue to resist without having any form of civil government, and contrary to the wishes and orders of their own civil government. The nature of the operations has, in such circumstances, changed from hostilities against the enemy country to hostilities against rebels defying their government's authority.' *Mrs Levin Ltd v Wellington Co-operative Book Society* [1947] NZLR 83 at 87, per Fair J; also reported [1946] GLR 365

HOTCHPOT

A clause called 'a hotchpot clause', is often inserted [in a settlement] in order to preclude appointees of a share of the fund from participating in the unappointed fund without treating the appointed shares as received in or towards satisfaction of the shares to which they would be entitled if the whole fund were to go in default of appointment.

The clause applies to appointments of life or reversionary interests. A life interest must be brought into hotchpot on the basis of an actuarial calculation of its value on the date when it fell into possession, irrespective of subsequent events.

The ordinary hotchpot clause in settlements does not apply to advancements. (42 Halsbury's Laws (4th edn) para 929)

This word is in English a pudding; for in this pudding is not commonly put one thing alone but one thing with other things together (*Coke on Littleton*, Sect 267)

Australia 'In my view in legal parlance the word "hotchpot" presupposes that the testator or settlor has advanced or empowered the advancement of one of a class out of property of or derived from the testator or settlor. Of course, in a particular will the word "hotchpot" may be seen from its context to be used in a different sense from a mere accounting for an advance made by the testator. Thus in *Middleton v Windross* [[1873] LR 16 Eq 212] the testator directed that an estate which a daughter had received from her grandfather should be brought into hotchpot and then the will went on to direct that the daughter should actually convey that estate so that it could be enjoyed by all the children as if it had been the testator's absolute property. But such a case as that does not affect the fact that "hotchpot" prima facie presupposes an advance derived from the testator.' *Re Blume (Decd), Fegan v Blume* [1959] Qd R 95 at 118, 119, per Philp J

HOT PURSUIT

'I should not have any right to doubt—and I have not any doubt—that Lord Parker was correct in saying, as he did in *The Roumanian*, [[1916] 1 AC 124 PC], that if property is liable to seizure at sea, and the enemy succeeds in getting ashore and escaping with his property, the belligerent who is trying to capture it has a right to pursue him and to take the property from him. . . . It was contended that I ought to treat this as a case of that kind, which is called sometimes a case of hot pursuit.' *The Anichab* [1919] P 329 at 337, per Lord Sterndale P

HOTEL   *See also* INNKEEPER

A hotel within the meaning of the Hotel Proprietors Act 1956 is, and any other establishment is not, deemed to be an inn. 'Hotel' means an establishment held out by the proprietor as offering food, drink and, if so required, sleeping accommodation, without special contract, to any traveller presenting himself who appears able and willing to pay a reasonable sum for the services and facilities provided and who is in a fit state to be received.

In deciding whether a house is a hotel within the statutory definition, and thus is an inn, the name by which it is designated is not conclusive. A house which is called a hotel or an inn may not be a hotel within the statutory definition even though it is a house of public entertainment, for every alehouse is not such a hotel. If a hotel is used for the common selling of ale, it is an alehouse as well as an inn, and if an alehouse lodges and feeds travellers it is also a hotel. On the other hand, a house which describes itself as a tavern and coffee house may in fact be a hotel within the statutory definition, although 'tavern' is usually understood to mean a house in which wines and other liquors are sold and in which a table is furnished, and 'coffee house' usually means a house where refreshment such as tea or coffee is supplied, and neither a mere tavern nor a mere coffee house is an inn. Nor is a mere restaurant an inn. A place under the same roof as a hotel, with a separate entrance and being in fact a shop in which spirits are sold across a counter is not an inn, even though the hotel is itself an inn. (24 Halsbury's Laws (4th edn) paras 1205, 1207)

'Residential hotel' means premises used for the reception of guests and travellers desirous of dwelling or sleeping therein. (Shops Act 1950, s 74)

(1) An hotel within the meaning of this Act shall, and any other establishment shall not, be deemed to be an inn; and the duties, liabilities and rights which immediately before the commencement of this Act by law attached to an innkeeper as such shall, subject to the provisions of this Act, attach to the proprietor of such an hotel and shall not attach to any other person.
(2) The proprietor of an hotel shall, as an innkeeper, be under the like liability, if any, to make good to any guest of his any damage to property brought to the hotel as he would be under to make good the loss thereof.
(3) In this Act, the expression 'hotel' means an establishment held out by the proprietor as offering food, drink and, if so required, sleeping accommodation, without special contract, to any traveller presenting himself who appears able and willing to pay a reasonable sum for the services and facilities provided and who is in a fit state to be received.

(Hotel Proprietors Act 1956, s 1).

New Zealand 'Upon consideration I think that in normal New Zealand parlance the word "hotel" is not necessarily restricted to premises that supply accommodation. In ordinary usage I think it is quite commonly applied also to a tavern where only liquor and not accommodation is supplied. In this connection one notes, for example, that s 2 of the Hotel Association of New Zealand Act 1969, defines "hotel industry" as including the business of licensed hotel keeping, tourist-house keeping or tavern-keeping. For these reasons I am of opinion that the word "hotel" as used in the context of the three policies [of insurance] is wide enough to include not only premises providing accommodation but also premises

that provide merely for the sale of liquor.' *Daken v Hartford Fire Insurance Co Ltd* [1972] NZLR 971 at 979, per Wild CJ; affd sub nom *Hartford Fire Insurance Co Ltd v Daken* [1972] NZLR 1120

HOTEL KEEPER

'It is impossible to adopt a different construction from that put by the Courts on the words "keepers of hotels". By deliberately using the same words ['keepers of inns, taverns, hotels or coffee-houses'] in the present Act [Bankruptcy Act 1869, s 1 (repealed)], after the Courts had put a certain construction on them, I think the Legislature must be taken to have adopted that construction. It is therefore settled that a keeper of a lodging house, who also supplies board is an hotel keeper within the Bankruptcy Act.' *Re Jones, Ex p Thorne* (1876) 3 Ch D 457 at 458, 459, CA, per James LJ

HOUR   *See also* WORKING HOURS

'Hour' may mean any one of the twenty-four parts of a day or any period of sixty minutes. (45 Halsbury's Laws (4th edn) para 1114)

Where it is stipulated that money is to be paid at a given hour, the whole period between that hour and the next hour is intended; the hour is considered as the twenty-fourth aliquot part of the day. (45 Halsbury's Laws (4th edn) para 1143)

HOURS OF DARKNESS

'Hours of darkness' means the time between half an hour after sunset and half an hour before sunrise. (Highways Act 1980, s 329(1))

HOUSE   *See also* DWELLING HOUSE

'House' includes any curtilage or garden appurtenant to or usually occupied with the house. (Welsh Church Act 1914, s 38(1))

'House' means a dwelling-house, whether a private dwelling-house or not. (Public Health Act 1936, s 343)

'House' means a dwelling-house, whether a private dwelling house or not, and includes any part of a building if that part is occupied as a separate dwelling house. (Water Act 1945, Sch 3, s 1)

'House' includes any part of a building which is occupied or intended to be occupied as a dwelling. (Accommodation Agencies Act 1953, s 1)

'House' includes a public institution. (Births and Deaths Registration Act 1953, s 41)

For purposes of this Part [Part I] of this Act, 'house' includes any building designed or adapted for living in and reasonably so called, notwithstanding that the building is not structurally detached, or was or is not solely designed or adapted for living in, or is divided horizontally into flats or maisonettes; and—
(a) where a building is divided horizontally, the flats or other units into which it is so divided are not separate 'houses', though the building as a whole may be; and
(b) where a building is divided vertically the building as a whole is not a 'house' though any of the units into which it is divided may be.
(Leasehold Reform Act 1967, s 2(1))

'House' includes—
(a) any yard, garden, outhouses and appurtenances belonging thereto or usually enjoyed therewith; and
(b) any part of a building which is occupied or intended to be occupied as a separate dwelling.
(Rent Act 1977, s 15(6))

[See also the Housing Act 1985, ss 56, 207, 457 and the Housing Associations Act 1985, s 106(1).]

[A building comprised a basement, a ground floor, and two upper floors. The ground floor had been let as a betting shop. The question was whether the building was a 'house' within the Leasehold Reform Act 1967 (supra)] 'I believe this is the first Act in which Parliament had endeavoured to give a definition of a "house". There have been many statutes which have used the word "house" without defining it. And the courts have given it a wide interpretation. The first case was the most extreme: *Richards v Swansea Improvement and Tramways Co* [(1878) 9 Ch D 425]. It was under the Lands Clauses Consolidation Act 1845. It was held that a mass of buildings was a "house", although part of it was residence, part cottages, and part manufactory. It was all held to be a "house". That is going a long way. It would not apply, I should think, to the present Act, because of the words "reasonably so called". In the Rent Acts too there was no definition of a "house", [but see supra]; but under them a hotel was held to be a "house", see *Epsom Grand Stand Association Ltd v Clarke* [(1919) 35 TLR 525]; and also a building

which was part dwelling and part business premises, see *Ellen v Goldstein* [(1920) 89 LJ Ch 586]. Quite recently in *Luganda v Service Hotels Ltd* [(1969) 2 All ER 692] this court held that a building (four houses knocked into one) with 88 rooms which were let off in furnished rooms, was a "house". I doubt whether the whole would be a "house" within the Leasehold Reform Act 1967, because of the limitation "reasonably so called", although each one of the four might be. In the Housing Acts there was no definition of a "house", but we considered it in *Ashbridge Investments Ltd v Minister of Housing and Local Government* [[1965] 3 All ER 371]. I ventured to suggest that "a 'house' in the Act [i.e. the Housing Act 1957] means a building which is constructed or adapted for use as, or for the purposes of, a dwelling". It would appear that in the Leasehold Reform Act 1967, Parliament adopted these words, but added the limitation "reasonably so called". It is quite plain that this building was a "house" within all these earlier statutes. The point is: what is the limitation conveyed by the words "reasonably so called"? I would not pretend on this occasion to attempt to define the limitation, but it may be useful to give an illustration. I do not think that a tower block of flats would reasonably be called a "house". But I think that a four-storied building like the present one is reasonably called a "house". Take it in stages. First, if the tenant occupied the building entirely by himself, using the ground floor for his shop premises, that would plainly be a "house" reasonably so called. Secondly, if the tenant, instead of using the ground floor himself for business purposes, sublets it, that does not alter the character of the building. It is still a "house" reasonably so called. And that is this case. But counsel for the respondents says: "It depends on the nature of the business. If one has a business which is a bookmaker's office, financially very profitable, that gives a colour to the whole building. It is not a house but a bookmaker's office". I am afraid that I do not agree. It seems to me that, even though the subletting is financially profitable for the tenant, the character of the building remains the same. It is a "house" within the meaning of the Act.' *Luke v Bennett* [1970] 1 All ER 457 at 459, 460, CA, per Lord Denning MR

Australia 'The primary meaning of the word "house" I take to be a dwelling-house for a family. . . . In my opinion the question whether a building occupied as several residential flats can or cannot be properly described as one dwelling-house depends on the nature of its construction. Two semi-detached houses side by side even though under one roof cannot in my opinion be regarded as one dwelling-house within the meaning of such a [restrictive] covenant.' *Ex p High Standard Constructions Ltd* (1929) 29 SRNSW 274 at 278, per Harvey CJ in Eq

Australia 'What, then, is meant by the "house"? There is a long line of authority, commencing many centuries ago, according to which the presence in a conveyance or lease of the word "house" refers not merely to the building of the house itself but also the surrounding garden occupied in conjunction with it. The conveyancing expression, traditionally used to cover both a house and its garden or surrounds, is "messuage", which has been held to mean—". . . not only the house itself but the outbuildings, courtyard, garden and adjacent land used and occupied with it".' See *Royal Sydney Golf Club v Federal Commissioner of Taxation* (1955) 91 CLR 610, 625. . . . In the case of a standard residential house, the nearest equivalent in current usage in Australia would no doubt be the 'yard' of the house. It may be added that the word 'curtilage' refers to land near a house and 'belonging' to it. 'The concept of curtilage has long existed almost entirely in connection with land closely associated with dwelling houses and messuages, from which context the word has been derived as a matter of philology': *Re St George's Oakdale* [1976] Fam 210, 219. The word 'premises' in popular language is applied to buildings, although in legal language it means the thing previously expressed: see *Beacon Life and Fire Assurance Co v Gibb* (1962) 1 Moo NS 73, 97; 15 ER 630, 639. Sir Owen Dixon, who cited this statement in *Turner v York Motors Proprietary Limited* (1951) 85 CLR 55, 75 subjoined a reference to the dictionary meaning of the word 'premises' as 'a house or building with its grounds or other appurtenances'. All these words therefore embody much the same concept as comprehending both the house itself and the surrounding garden or yard belonging to or occupied along with the house. In 27 Halsbury's Laws of England (4th ed), para 130, it is said that "by a lease of a 'house' outbuildings occupied with and necessary for the convenient occupation of the house will pass, and also a courtyard, garden and orchard." A similar view was taken by the Full Court of South Australia in *Draper v South Australian Rly Commrs* [1903] SALR 150, 156,

where Way CJ observed that "a house includes as much land as is necessary for the convenient and comfortable enjoyment of the premises".' *Thomas v Bergin* [1986] 2 Qd R 478 at 480, per McPherson J

Compulsory purchase proceedings

[The Lands Clauses Consolidation Act 1845, s 92, provided that no party should be required to sell part of a house if the party was willing and able to sell the whole. The section is, however, excluded from various later enactments, e.g. new provisions are substituted for this section in s 8 of the Compulsory Purchase Act 1965.]

'It is clear . . . that the garden and orchard would pass under the term "house". In this case the shrubbery and series of gardens are all connected by doors, and, upon the evidence, it is beyond dispute that the land in question is a garden in the strict sense of the term. It has been attached to the dwelling-house for forty-nine years and taken out of the adjoining lawn by running up a hedge; fig-trees and vines were planted on the walls, and apple-trees and currant-bushes were growing in it, a gravel path from the house running through and connecting the whole series of gardens. . . . Upon the older authorities, as to the meaning of the term "house", and the application of those older authorities as to the construction of s 92 [of the Lands Clauses Consolidation Act 1845 (see supra)], it must be held that this garden formed part of the house.' *Hewson v South Western Rly Co* (1860) 2 LT 369 at 369, 370, per Wood V-C

'The principle is this: That, according to the true construction of the Act [Lands Clauses Consolidation Act 1845 (see supra)], the word "house" includes everything which will ordinarily pass under the word "house" in a conveyance. Consequently, if the company require any part of that which is included under the word "house", they are bound to take the whole. The Courts have, I think very justly, determined that the word "house", as used in the statute, is to be construed liberally, and that it includes all that which properly passes under the word "house".' *King v Wycombe Rly Co* (1860) 28 Beav 104 at 106, per Romilly MR

'The Legislature has enacted [in s 92 of the Lands Clauses Consolidation Act 1845 (see supra)] that "no person shall be required to sell or convey a part only of any house, or other building or manufactory, if such party be willing and able to sell and convey the whole thereof". The construction of the word "house" in the Act of Parliament has been clearly settled by authority to comprise all that would pass by a grant of a house; and this, according to the old authorities, would include not only the curtilage, but also a garden attached to the house; a fortiori, therefore, any building forming part of or appertaining to the messuage would also be included.' *St Thomas's Hospital (Governors) v Charing Cross Rly Co* (1861) 1 John & H 400 at 404, per Page Wood V-C

'I am . . . of opinion that these buildings can be designated by no other term than "houses", unfinished it is true, but if a company give notice to a man who is building his house, that they intend to take it for the purpose of their undertaking, they cannot, if he stops, say it is a mere heap of bricks, and that they are not obliged to take it; the advantage they have is, that it is of less value than if the building had been completed.' *Alexander v Crystal Palace Rly Co* (1862) 30 Beav 556 at 559–562, per Romilly MR

'The question is whether the land in question is to be considered as part of the house within the meaning of the Act [Lands Clauses Consolidation Act 1845 (see supra)]. . . . The strip of land . . . is . . . about two hundred and fifty yards from the house. It is part of a larger field of about six acres, through the middle of which the railway is intended to pass. . . . The question is, whether the strip of land . . . ought to be considered as part of the plaintiff's house. Now, I take the law on that point to be that by the description of a "house", what is necessary for the convenient occupation of the house will pass. . . . I entertain a very decided opinion that this land is not to be considered as part of the house within the meaning of the 92nd section of the Act.' *Steele v Midland Rly Co* (1866) 1 Ch App 275 at 289, 291, per Turner LJ

'The word "house" [within the Lands Clauses Consolidation Act 1845, s 92 (see supra)] does not mean . . . necessarily a mere dwelling house, or a house only used, or exclusively or principally used, for a residence; the word "house" includes a shop, or may consist of a shop. The word "house", beyond all question, as it seems to me, would include a very large inn, or anything of that kind which was built for one purpose. It has been held to include St Thomas' Hospital. . . . A house is not the less a house because it is a public-house or an inn; . . . it is not the less a house because it

comprises or is used for the purpose of a shop, or because it comprises or is used for the purpose of a workshop or storehouse.' *Richards v Swansea Improvement & Tramways Co* (1878) 9 Ch D 425 at 431, 432, per James LJ

'To my mind the clause in the Act [Lands Clauses Consolidation Act 1845, s 92 (see supra)] is distinct, and the law is perfectly distinct. The Legislature, having to frame in words an expression which would cover the subject included in the clause, adopted this word "house", but not affecting to give any description of what a "house" means, because none was necessary. The word "house" had already acquired a legal signification. The passage which has been cited from Lord Coke is not new law in itself, although it is a very plain and distinct definition. The meaning of "house" is domus, residence, possession— what a man has when he talks about "having a house". The meaning of the word "house" in the Act of Parliament, therefore, is the meaning which Lord Coke ascribes to it in Coke upon Littleton, and it includes all that which may be called the domus.' *Barnes v Southsea Rly Co* (1884) 27 Ch D 536 at 542, per Bacon V-C

'The question must be what would pass by a conveyance of, as in this case, "my house" or "the house Buena Vista". If this land here would pass by such a description either in a devise standing alone or by a conveyance, then this garden would pass—this garden, stables, and so on; and if that will not pass, then the company are not compelled [by the Lands Clauses Consolidation Act 1845, s 92 (see supra)] to take the residence, when it takes the garden and stables, as part of the garden and stables. . . . I think the garden and other property would not pass as part of the house. . . . A conveyance of the house or "my house Buena Vista" . . . passes the residence, and does not pass the garden and stables on the other side of the road.' *Kerford v Seacombe Hoylake & Deeside Rly Co* (1888) 57 LJ Ch 270 at 275, per Kekewich J

'It has been laid down ever since that Act [Lands Clauses Consolidation Act 1845 (see supra)] was passed, that by the word "house" is meant, not a mere building, whether for residential or for other purposes, but whatever would pass under the conveyance of a "house".' *Allhusen v Ealing & South Harrow Rly Co* (1898) 78 LT 396 at 397, CA, per Lindley MR

'Had the construction of s 92 [of the Lands

Clauses Consolidation Act 1845 (see supra)] been open, I should rather have demurred to construe "house" as meaning everything that passes on a conveyance. But the point was settled long ago. This paddock would pass by a gift in a will of "my house near Sunbury", or "my house in which I live", or by any phrase of a similar kind which failed in more precise description. The test is this: Is this piece of ground such as might be reasonably attached and is de facto attached, to the "house" in question? Provided it be so attached it does not then matter in the least whether it be used as a garden or an orchard, or for any other use whatever. It is part of the house within the meaning of s 92.' *Low v Staines Reservoirs Joint Committee* (1900) 64 JP 212 at 213, CA, per Rigby LJ

For purposes of Housing Acts

'If those buildings had originally been built, like many buildings are nowadays, with dwelling rooms above, and with a garage below . . . nobody would suggest, I think, that they were not houses. The fact that the whole of the ground floor was occupied by a garage would not make the building any the less a house.' *Re Butler, Camberwell (Wingfield Mews) (No 2) Clearance Order* 1936 [1939] 1 KB 570 at 576, 578–580, CA, per Greene MR

'In s 188 of the Act [Housing Act 1936 (repealed; see now the Housing Act 1985, ss 56, 207, 322, 457)] there is a definition of the word "house". "House" includes any yard, garden, outhouses and appurtenances belonging thereto or usually enjoyed therewith. Then, by sub-s (3), it is provided: "For the purposes of any provisions of this Act relating to the provision of housing accommodation"—that refers to Part V of the Act: the part we are dealing with is Part II—"the expression 'house' includes, unless the context otherwise requires, any part of a building which is occupied or intended to be occupied as a separate dwelling". I think that is not a bad illustration of what I was saying, namely, whether you call it a dwelling or whether you call it a house, for some purposes a particular place may be two houses or two dwellings, but for another purpose it may be one house or one dwelling.' *Benabo v Wood Green Corpn* [1945] 2 All ER 162 at 164, 165, per Humphreys J

'The word "house" has no very precise meaning. There are many types of houses. A tenement house is one type of house, a lodging

house is another; so is a house at one of the public schools, a suburban villa, and Blenheim Palace. The fact that some of these types of houses may be more likely than others to pass the requirements of the Housing Acts with flying colours does not make them any more or less houses. Once it is decided as a fact that a building is a house and there is evidence to support the decision, the question of law arises whether or not it is a type of house to which the relevant section of the Housing Act applies. . . . In my view it is wrong to hold, if words have any meaning, that each tenement in a tenement block is a house. It may be as counsel for the owner suggests that the occupier of a tenement sometimes refers to it loosely as his house, just as it is said figuratively that an Englishman's home is his castle. This however is beside the point for it seems to me as impossible to hold that a single tenement is a house, as it would be to hold that a suburban villa is a castle.' *Okereke v Borough of Brent (Town Clerk)* [1966] 1 All ER 150 at 157, 158, CA, per Davies LJ

In restrictive covenant

'The words [in the restrictive clause in the sale of an interest in a public-house] are peculiar. They extend to a person exercising, carrying on, or being concerned in any house for the sale of wines, etc. Should the meaning of the word "house" in this connection be limited to public or licensed house, or extended to any premises upon which the trade is being carried on? . . . I think that the word "house" is much more applicable to premises where a licensed trade in liquor is being carried on than it is to premises of other traders in liquor, as, for instance, a wine merchant's business. I think, therefore, that having regard to the subject-matter of the sale, I ought to read the word "house" as "licensed house", and hold that the clause is not too wide.' *Cattermoul v Jared* (1909) 53 Sol Jo 244 at 244, per Neville J

Private house

'By "private house" is meant a dwelling-house, where a family reside.' *Barnes v Shore* (1846) 1 Rob Eccl 382 at 397, per Sir Herbert Jenner Fust

Rating and revenue duties

'We all think that the term "house" prima facie means a dwelling-house. The Act of Charles II confined the charge to the inhabitants of the parish. That Act being repealed [by 51 Geo 3, c cl] a new arrangement was substituted by which the charge was imposed upon all occupiers of houses within the parish. It seems to me that this Act was intended to apply only to dwelling houses occupied by individuals as such, and that such buildings as warehouses and counting-houses were not included in it. Neither can we construe it to extend to other buildings which strictly speaking, are not houses, though popularly called so.' *Surman v Darley* (1845) 14 M & W 181 at 185, per Pollock CB

'We have no doubt that the coach-house and stable must be considered as part of the house [for the purpose of deciding under a local paving and lighting Act whether the house was more than 30 yards from the next house].' *R v Warwickshire JJ* (1851) 17 LTOS 183 at 183, per Lord Campbell CJ

'The tax is laid by the Act of 1 Vict c 2 [a local Act], upon all houses within the parish, and there is nothing whatever to put any particular meaning on the word "house", either to restrict it or extend it beyond what is the natural and proper meaning of the word "house". . . . I think that which is occupied by a man for the sake of his business, if it be not part of the house, is not subject to the rate which is imposed on the house only; that which he occupies for the use of his business does not become in any sense part of the house. But it has been laid down as early as the time of Lord Coke—and I think it is good sense that it should be so—that where a house is not confined to stone walls, but if there be a garden or orchard subordinate to the occupation of the house as a residence, and occupied and enjoyed with the house, solely for the sake of an ancillary to the residence, then the garden should be considered as part of the house and enhancing its rateable value.' *Hole v Milton Comrs, Watson v Milton Comrs* (1867) 31 JP 804 at 807, per Blackburn J

'It is very difficult to give an accurate definition of a "house" [under the Customs and Inland Revenue Act 1878, s 13 (repealed)]. One knows practically what it is, and I should be inclined to think as good as any the definition given of it in the books on criminal law, where the question of burglary is discussed, as "a permanent building in which the tenant, or the owner and his family, dwells or lies".' *Chapman v Royal Bank of Scotland* (1881) 7 QBD 136 at 140, per Huddlestone B

'Now what is the building if it is not a house? It may be called a chapel, but that does not prevent the whole building being a "house", and I don't agree that the term "house" [in the Metropolis Management Acts] must be confined to the popular sense of the word. . . . It is no doubt difficult to define exactly what a house is. I suppose a wall, for instance, is not a house. There have been numerous cases under the Registration Acts which throw light on what is and what is not a house within these Acts. But . . . a building, in my judgment, may well be a "house" for the purposes of the Metropolitan Management Acts, though it may not be a "house" under the Registration Acts. When I look at the object of the statutes I feel no hesitation in holding that this building is liable to be assessed. There are caretaker's rooms, lecture and school rooms, and there is nothing to prevent the tenant from receiving money for the use of these rooms.' *Caiger v St Mary, Islington Vestry* (1881) 50 LJMC 59 at 63, DC, per Grove J

'We can see no authority . . . for this court holding in the present case that, under statutes which are . . . passed for fiscal purposes, but are passed in order to make provision for the spiritual wants of the dwellers in a parish by a rate levied on the occupiers of all houses within the parish which are capable of being used as dwelling-houses, a building may not properly be treated as a dwelling-house, although the larger part of the building is used for the time being for the purposes of trade or business, if, in fact, the whole of the building is capable of being used as a dwelling-house and persons, whether caretakers or others, do, in fact, dwell in part of it.' *Lewin v Newnes Ltd, Lewin v Warne & Co* (1904) 90 LT 160 at 162, 163, per Kennedy J

HOUSE OF LORDS   *See* PARLIAMENT

HOUSE OF RESIDENCE
See ECCLESIASTICAL RESIDENCE

HOUSE REFUSE   *See* REFUSE

HOUSE TO HOUSE   *See* COLLECTION

HOUSEBREAKING
See also IMPLEMENT; INSTRUMENT

[Under s 26 of the repealed Larceny Act 1916, every person who: (1) broke and entered any dwelling-house, or any building within the curtilage thereof and occupied therewith, or any school-house, shop, warehouse, counting-house, office, store, garage, pavilion, factory, or workshop, or any building belonging to Her Majesty, or to any Government Department, or to any municipal or other public authority, and committed any arrestable offence therein; or (2) broke out of the same, having committed any arrestable offence therein, was guilty of felony.

The Act of 1916 was repealed by the Theft Act 1968, under which there is no longer a specific offence of housebreaking. See, however, ss 1–10 of the Act, which define theft, robbery, burglary, etc.

The only reference to housebreaking in the Act of 1968 is in the cross-heading to ibid, s 25, 'possession of housebreaking implements, etc.']

HOUSEHOLD

'A man may be related to a household in two ways. He may be a member of the household, or he may be the head of the household. The underwriters, while insuring the assured against his liability to passengers, except in their own favour his liability to a passenger who is a "member of the assured's household". The question is, accordingly, whether, on the true construction of the policy, the exception covers not only the narrower class of members of a household of which the plaintiff is the head, but the wider class of members of a household of which the plaintiff is a member. Branson J, takes the view that the more natural meaning of the phrase covers the wider class, namely, members of the household of which the plaintiff is a member. . . . I find myself bound to hold that the phrase of exception covers only the narrower class, the member of a household of which the plaintiff [the assured] is head.' *English v Western* [1940] 2 KB 156 at 165, 166, CA, per Clauson LJ

[A house maintained as a place of temporary refuge for ill-treated women was held not to be a single 'household' within the Housing Act 1969, s 58(1) (repealed see now Housing Act 1985, s 345).] 'I do not think that every community consisting of temporary migrants housed under a single roof reasonably organised constitutes or can constitute a single household. I do not think this is necessarily true of a hostel, a monastery, or a school, but certainly not of a temporary haven in a storm.'

Simmons v Pizzey [1977] 2 All ER 432 at 442, HL, per Lord Hailsham of St Marylebone

Australia [By s 6(1)(c) of the Matrimonial Causes Act 1959 (Cth), (repealed, but see now s 5(1) of the Family Law Act 1975 (Cth), as amended) a child of either the husband or the wife if, at the relevant time, the child was ordinarily a 'member of the household' of the husband and wife, shall be deemed to be a child of the marriage.] 'Whether a child was ordinarily a member of the household is a question of fact, and whether the child was ordinarily a member of the household immediately before the parties ceased to live together is also a question of fact. . . . The mere fact that a child was not living in the household when it came to an end would in some circumstances not be sufficient to exclude the child from the definition. . . . If there was an intention that the child should . . . return to the household of the husband and wife, a temporary absence . . . would not affect his (or her) membership of the household.' *May v May and Thomas* [1962] VR 123 at 124, per Barry J; also reported in [1962] ALR 317 at 318

Canada 'The "household", in the broad sense of a family, is a collective group living in a house, acknowledging the authority of a head, the members of which, with few exceptions, are bound by marriage, blood affinity or other bond, between whom there is an intimacy and by whom there is felt a concern with and an interest in the life of all that gives it a unity. It may, for example, include such persons as domestic servants, and distant relatives permanently residing within it. To some degree they are all admitted and submit to the collective body, its unity and its conditions, particularly that of the general discipline of the family head. They do not share fully in the more restricted family intimacy or interest or concern, but they participate to a substantial degree in the general life of the household and form part of it.' *Wowanesa Mutual Insurance Co v Bell* [1957] SCR 581 at 584, per Rand J

Canada [Insurance benefits were payable to specified persons residing in household.] 'In the several dictionary definitions of the word "household" it is variously defined as "a family living together", "inmates of a house", "occupants of a house", "those who dwell as a family under one roof". It is also defined in several dictionaries as "a domestic establishment" and in Webster's New World Dictionary as "the home and its affairs".

In *Vaughan v American Alliance Ins Co of New York* (1933) 27 P (2d) 212, the Supreme Court of Kansas referred with approval to an American dictionary definition of "household" as "the place where one holds house, his home".

The word "domestic," used in the expression "domestic establishment", is defined as "having to do with the home".

It therefore appears that while "household" has a broad meaning such as "the inmates of a house" it also has in some of the dictionary definitions a narrower meaning such as a "domestic establishment", "the home and its affairs", "a place where one holds house, his home".' *Muir v Royal Insurance Co* (1981), 125 DLR (3d) 172 at 175, Ont Co Ct, per Phelan, Co Ct J

HOUSEHOLD ARTICLE

In this section . . . 'household article' means an article of furniture, bedding or clothing or any similar article. (Public Health Act 1961, s 37)

HOUSEHOLD EFFECTS *See* EFFECTS

HOUSEHOLD FURNITURE *See*
FURNITURE

HOUSEHOLD GOODS *See* GOODS

HOUSEHOLD STUFF

'Another point was, whether plate should pass by the name of household-stuff; and it being plate that was in common use about the house, the counsel would not stand upon it but that it should; but if it had been plate laid up, it seemeth that it should not.' *Phillips v Phillips* (1676) Freem Ch 11 at 12, per the Lord Chancellor

HOUSEHOLD ORNAMENT

[A testator by his will made a specific bequest of all his furniture, pictures, drawings, and all other articles of personal, domestic, or household use or ornament.] 'A drawing in its nature is an article of household use or ornament, and, prima facie, the elaborate enumeration of the furniture and effects might seem to cover all the drawings. Some of the drawings were framed and hung on the walls of the house, but the great bulk of them were stored in a chest. On the whole I come to the conclusion that the testator intended to pass under the specific bequest those of the drawings which were used as household ornaments, and not those stored in the chest which passed under the residuary bequest.' *Re Du Maurier, Millar v Coles* (1916) 32 TLR 579 at 579, per Neville J

HOUSEHOLDER

'This case depends entirely upon the meaning of the word "householders", as used in the statute 26 Geo 3, c 38 [repealed]. . . . It is sufficient for the purpose of this cause, if five of those who voted for the defendant, and whose right to vote is disputed, shall be found to be householders within the true meaning of this statute. And we think that five such are found. . . . Each of them, with his partners, is the tenant or holder of a dwelling-house; each, either by a servant or partner, sleeps in such house; and each is in the daily habit, for the purposes of business, of resorting to such dwelling-house, or to some of the buildings connected with it.' *R v Hall* (1822) 1 B & C 123 at 136–138, per Abbott CJ

HOUSING ASSOCIATION

In this Act 'housing association' means a society, body of trustees or company–
(a) which is established for the purpose of, or amongst whose objects or powers are included those of, providing, constructing, improving or managing, or facilitating or encouraging the construction or improve-ment of, housing accommodation, and
(b) which does not trade for profit or whose constitution or rules prohibit the issue of capital with interest or dividend exceeding such rate as may be prescribed by the Treasury, whether with or without differentiation as between share and loan capital.
(Housing Associations Act 1985, s 1(1))

HOVERCRAFT

'Hovercraft' means a vehicle which is designed to be supported when in motion wholly or partly by air expelled from the vehicle to form a cushion of which the boundaries include the ground, water or other surface beneath the vehicle. (Hovercraft Act 1968, s 4; Social Security Act 1975, Sch 20)

HOVERPORT

'Hoverport' means any area, whether on land or elsewhere, which is designed, equipped, set apart or commonly used for affording facilities for the arrival and departure of hovercraft. (Hovercraft Act 1968, s 4)

HOVERTRAIN

'Hovertrain' means a hovercraft which is at all times guided by tracks, rails or guides fixed to the ground. (Insurance Companies Act 1982, s 96(1))

HULL AND MACHINERY

'What is the ordinary meaning of an insurance upon the "hull and machinery" of a steamship? Does it cover the coal on board, or the provisions and stores? I think it clear that it does not.' *Roddick v Indemnity Mutual Marine Insurance Co* [1895] 2 QB 380 at 386, CA, per A L Smith LJ

HUMAN HABITATION

Fit for *See* FIT

HUNT

'The word "hunting" does not, in its fair acceptation, extend to shooting feathered game. If one were to give leave to another to hunt over his premises, it would not give him the liberty of shooting there; and many would give another liberty of hunting over their premises, who would be extremely annoyed if he went shooting there.' *Moore v Plymouth (Earl)* (1817) 7 Taunt 614 at 627, per Gibbs CJ

Canada 'I think that if a person searches for game with a loaded gun at night in an area where it is not unreasonable to expect the presence of game, with the intention of capturing or killing that game, he is guilty of the offence of unlawfully hunting game. . . . In

one sense it may be true that the word "hunt" means to "do something more than look for", but, in my opinion, to look for game in certain circumstances is to hunt the game, for example, if the person looking for the game has a weapon, is looking for the game in a place where its presence can reasonably be expected, and intends to kill or take it if he finds it. In my opinion, the word "hunt" for the purposes of this case means to "hunt with intent to kill or take".' *R v Fredericks* (1962) 47 MPR 324 at 328, 329, NSSC, per Ilsley CJ

HURT *See* INJURY

HUSBAND

'I have no hesitation in saying that, in the absence of a controlling context, a gift to an unmarried woman for life, with remainder to her husband in fee, vests an indefeasible estate of inheritance in the person who first answers the description of her husband.' *Radford v Willis* (1871) LR 7 Ch App 7 at 10, per James LJ

'The question is . . . whether the defendant is entitled to a life interest in the residuary estate of the testator as the surviving husband of the testator's daughter. It is necessary to look at the very words of the bequest—they are "in trust for any husband with whom she might intermarry, if he should survive her". The defendant was a husband with whom the testator's daughter intermarried, and he survived her, so that he fulfils all the words of the bequest [although he had divorced her and married again in her lifetime].' *Bullmore v Wynter* (1883) 22 Ch D 619 at 620, per Fry J [A settlement gave a woman power to appoint for the benefit of any 'husband' who might survive her. The appointor married the plaintiff and exercised the power in favour of her husband if he should survive her. The appointor divorced the plaintiff and died without having remarried, and the plaintiff brought an action against the trustees of the settlement, claiming that he was entitled to be paid the appointed fund.] 'The person described as "husband who may survive", or "who shall survive", or "such surviving husband", is a person to be ascertained by the fact of his possessing a certain characteristic—namely, that of being a husband, and in no other way . . . the plaintiff fails.' *Bosworthick v Clegg* (1929) 45 TLR 438 at 439, per Maugham J

HUSBANDRY *See also* FARMING

Rules of good husbandry

(1) For the purposes of this Act, the occupier of an agricultural unit shall be deemed to fulfil his responsibilities to farm it in accordance with the rules of good husbandry in so far as the extent to which and the manner in which the unit is being farmed (as respects both the kind of operations carried out and the way in which they are carried out) is such that, having regard to the character and situation of the unit, the standard of management thereof by the owner and other relevant circumstances, the occupier is maintaining a reasonable standard of efficient production, as respects both the kind of produce and the quality and quantity thereof, while keeping the unit in a condition to enable such a standard to be maintained in the future.

(2) In determining whether the manner in which a unit is being farmed is such as aforesaid, regard shall be had, but without prejudice to the generality of the provisions of the last foregoing subsection, to the extent to which—

  (a) permanent pasture is being properly mown or grazed and maintained in a good state of cultivation and fertility and in good condition;

  (b) the manner in which arable land is being cropped is such as to maintain that land clean and in good state of cultivation and fertility and in good condition;

  (c) the unit is properly stocked where the system of farming practised requires the keeping of livestock, and an efficient standard of management of livestock is maintained where livestock are kept and of breeding where the breeding of livestock is carried out;

  (d) the necessary steps are being taken to secure and maintain crops and livestock free from disease and from infestation by insects and other pests;

  (e) the necessary steps are being taken for the protection and preservation of crops harvested or lifted, or in course of being harvested or lifted;

  (f) the necessary work of maintenance and repair is being carried out.

(3) The responsibilities under the rules of good husbandry of an occupier of an agricultural unit which is not owned by him shall not include an obligation to carry out any work of maintenance or repair which the owner of the unit or any part thereof is under an obligation to carry out in order to fulfil his responsibilities to manage in accordance with the rules of good estate management.
(Agriculture Act 1947, s 11)

[Section 39 of the Finance (No 2) Act 1915 (repealed), excepted 'husbandry' from the trades and businesses to which excess profits duty applied.] 'Husbandry presupposes a connection with land and production of crops or food in some shape. The objects of the society we are dealing with are composite, and no doubt the conversion of milk into butter is one of its primary objects. It has certainly been so in practice, and it is unquestionably a farming operation; but, taking it by itself apart from its association with other branches of farming industry, I cannot conceive how it could be regarded as husbandry. As well might the owner of a machine for threshing corn, or of a steam plough, or of a mill for grinding corn, or of a machine for spraying potatoes, be held to be engaged in the trade or business of husbandry.' *Re Cavan Co-operative Society Ltd* [1917] 2 IR 954 at 608, 609, per Kenny J

'In common parlance lands devoted to grazing sheep are occupied "for purposes of husbandry", and . . . a sheep farmer is a husbandman in the ordinary acceptation of the term.' *Keir v Gillespie* 1920 SC 67 at 69, per the Lord President

'I think that, at the present day, the primal and natural meaning of the term "husbandry" as applied to land includes all those uses of it which are commonly described as "farming".' Ibid at 70, 71, per Lord Skerrington

'"Good husbandry" is roughly the maintenance of a reasonable standard of efficient production having regard . . . to the character of the agricultural unit and the manner in which it is being farmed.' *Lory v London Borough of Brent* [1971] 1 All ER 1042 at 1046, per Ungoed-Thomas J

HYPNOTISM

'Hypnotism' includes hypnotism, mesmerism and any similar act or process which produces or is intended to produce in any person any form of induced sleep or trance in which the susceptibility of the mind of that person to suggestion or direction is increased or intended to be increased but does not include hypnotism, mesmerism or any such similar act or process whch is self-induced. (Hypnotism Act 1952, s 6)

HYPOTHECATION

Subject to certain conditions, the master [of a ship] is entitled, as agent of necessity on behalf of the cargo owner, to hypothecate the cargo for the purpose of raising funds to enable him either to complete the voyage in the same bottom, or to forward the goods to their destination. 'Hypothecation of the cargo' means a pledge of the cargo without immediate change of possession; it gives a right to the person making advances on the faith of it to have the possession of the goods if the advances are not paid at the stipulated time; but it leaves to the owner of the goods hypothecated the power of making such repayment, and thereby freeing them from the obligation. (43 Halsbury's Laws (4th edn) para 635)

New Zealand 'If a person or corporation mortgages or hypothecates debentures, the possession of the debentures is not thereby given to the mortgagee or to the person to whom they are hypothecated. If the possession of the debentures were parted with, then the transaction would not be a hypothecation or mortgage, but a pawn or pledge. The distinction between a hypothecation and a pledge is that possession is given in the one but not in the other. . . . The definition of a mortgage and the definition of an hypothecation are clearly set forth in *Coote's Law of Mortgages* [7th Edn at p 7] where he says, "An hypothecation differs from a mortgage in that there is no actual or executory conveyance or assurance of the property appropriated for payment of the debt or loan, and from a pledge in that there is no actual or constructive delivery of the property".' *Karon Corpn v Australian Mutual Provident Society* (1911) 33 NZLR 438 at 439, 440, per Stout CJ

I

IOU

'In England the purpose of an IOU is to "state the accounts" as between parties, while in Scotland it has been repeatedly observed that its purpose is to give an acknowledgment of debt and an implied undertaking to repay it.' *Winestone v Wolifson* 1954 SLT 153 at 154, per the Lord President (Cooper)

ICE-BOUND

[The rules of a marine insurance association provided that an 'ice-bound' ship should not be considered as lost unless and until there should have been a specified period of open water after the disaster.] 'Ice-bound is a well-known phrase. It is a phrase applicable to the navigation of a ship. It means that ice has so got round the ship that the ship cannot navigate by reason thereof. It does not mean that the ship cannot move. It means that, though the ship may be able to move, she cannot get out of the ice. In other words, it applies if the ice is so close round the ship that she cannot get out of it. A ship is relieved from that position when the water is open—that is, when she can get out of the ice. That being so, the ship will cease to

be "ice-bound" within the meaning of this rule the moment there is open water in which she can navigate, though the ice may still produce difficulties, as, for instance, if the ice breaks up in a storm.' *Re Sunderland SS Co & North of England Iron SS Insurance Assocn* (1894) 11 TLR 106 at 107, CA, per Lord Esher MR

[Clause 16 of a charterparty provided that a steamer should not be ordered to any 'ice-bound' port.] 'The shipowners . . . sued the charterers alleging: (1) that they had ordered her [the ship] to an ice-bound port contrary to clause 16 of the charterparty, and that in consequence she was damaged. . . . The judge below has found, and I agree with him, that Abo was not an ice-bound port. It would be if no artificial measures were taken, but in fact by the use of icebreakers a channel for entrance is kept open from the Aland Islands to Abo. The captain admitted it was kept open the whole year and the defendants' witnesses proved that steamers were running six voyages a week between Stockholm and Abo the whole winter. Such a port kept artificially open the whole winter cannot be said to be ice-bound.' *Limerick SS Co Ltd v Stott & Co Ltd* [1921] 2 KB 613 at 620, CA, per Scrutton LJ

IDIOT   *See also* MENTAL DISORDER

'An idiot is known by his perpetual infirmity of nature, *a nativitate*, for he never had any sense or understanding to contract with any man; but he who was of good memory and understanding, and able to make a contract, and afterwards becomes· by infirmity or casualty of unsound memory, is not so well known to the world as an idiot natural.' *Beverly's Case* (1603) 4 Co Rep 123b at 124b, per cur.

'The Act [Criminal Law Amendment Act 1885 (repealed)] includes the "idiot" or person who from birth has no mind, and the "imbecile" or person who, having once had a mind of some kind, owing to decay or other mental or physical causes, ceases to have a mind.' *R v F——* (1910) 74 JP 384 at 384, per Grantham J

Australia 'Although, in current parlance, an "idiot" is generally regarded as being a person so deficient in mind as to be totally and permanently incapable of rational conduct in contrast to an "imbecile", who has such a want of reason as prevents him from attaining any considerable amount of knowledge or intelligence, the researches of counsel, and my own research, would suggest that, although the defintion of an "idiot" in law was a strict one and a narrow one it was not so strict as to exclude persons who, although severely, or profoundly retarded, were not totally incapable of any rational conduct whatsoever.' *RH v CAH* [1984] 1 NSWLR 694 at 703–705, per Powell J

Australia [Sections 188 and 189 of the Criminal Code of Western Australia make it a crime to indecently deal with or have or attempt to have unlawful carnal knowledge of an 'idiot' or 'imbecile'. It was contended that an imbecile was a person of weak intellect.] 'The words "idiot" and "imbecile" . . . have been the subject of judicial consideration in *F* (1910) 74 JP 384, *Colgan* (1959) SR (NSW) 96 and [an] unreported decision of Heenan DCJ . . . on a submission of no case to answer. In our view the policy behind the relevant sections in Ch XXII of the Code is to protect a person who is either too young or, by reason of mental infirmity, incapable of giving a reasoned judgment as to whether she should consent to an act of a sexual nature being performed in conjunction with her. In the absence of any statutory assistance from the Code of a precise nature as to the meaning of imbecile, it is useful to consider the course

adopted in *Colgan* by the Court of Criminal Appeal in New South Wales. Reference in the joint judgment of their Honours at 98.99 was made to the Mental Deficiency Act 1927 (Imp) which contains the following definitions: "Idiots, that is to say persons in whose case there exists mental defectiveness of such a degree that they are unable to guard themselves against common physical dangers. Imbeciles, that is to say persons in whose case there exists mental defectiveness which, though not amounting to idiocy, is yet so pronounced that they are incapable of managing themselves or their affairs, or in the case of children of being taught to do so." As their Honours state, these definitions are practical, and in our view should be adopted as a satisfactory guide to jurors in this State in cases such as the present.' *R v Jeffrey Archibald Lindsay* (1984) 15 A Crim R 179 at 181 (Full Court)

IDLE AND DISORDERLY

Every petty chapman or pedlar wandering abroad, and trading without being duly licensed, or otherwise authorised by law; every common prostitute wandering in the public streets or public highways, or in any place of public resort, and behaving in a riotous or indecent manner; and every person wandering abroad, or placing himself or herself in any public place, street, highway, court, or passage, to beg or gather alms, or causing or procuring or encouraging any child or children so to do; shall be deemed an idle and disorderly person within the true intent and meaning of this Act. . . . (Vagrancy Act 1824, s 3)

'It seems to me that the proper conclusion to be drawn [from the Vagrancy Act 1824, s 3, supra] is that the statute was directed against a particular habit and mode of life, and that if persons making it their habit and mode of life to wander abroad or place themselves in public places to beg, do wander abroad and beg and gather alms, they fall within the words of the statute.' *Pointon v Hill* (1884) 12 QBD 306 at 308, per Cave J

'An idle and disorderly person is a person who has been convicted of any of the offences mentioned in s 3 of the Vagrancy Act 1824 [supra], one of which is begging.' *R v Johnson* [1909] 1 KB 439 at 443, CCA, per cur.

'I think that the Vagrancy Act 1824, which

enacts that a person infringing its provisions is to be deemed to be an idle and disorderly person, is aimed not at persons collecting for an object of a charitable nature in which possibly they themselves have an interest, but that it is directed at persons of a different type. . . . In my opinion it would be a misuse of language to say that the respondent, simply because he stood in the street and asked for contributions to a fund from which he and others were to profit, they being temporarily out of work, had become an idle and disorderly person. The words of the statute are obviously aimed at persons . . . who are wandering abroad, who are placing themselves at the corners of streets and begging or soliciting alms, such persons as are described in the judgment of Cave J in *Pointon v Hill* [supra] . . . as having given up work and adopted begging as a habit or mode of life. Those persons are clearly, I think, within the statute.' *Mathers v Penfold* [1915] 1 KB 514 at 519–521, DC, per Darling J

IF AND WHEN

[A testator, by a codicil to his will, directed that certain money should be paid to his five grandchildren 'if and when' they should respectively attain the age of twenty-one years.] 'As regards the legacies to the five grandchildren, there is a direction that they are to be paid "if and when" the grandchildren respectively attain the age of twenty-one years. It is conceded by counsel for the residuary legatee that, in the absence of the word "if", a direction as to payment of a legacy when the legatees attain twenty-one would not prevent the legacies from vesting immediately, because the direction in that case would relate only to the time of payment and would not affect the orginal gift of the legacy. . . . I think that the hypothesis of attaining twenty-one, introduced by the word "if" in the direction as to payment, is not merely personal to the legatee, but affects the original gift of the legacy. It is impossible, in my judgment, to hold that a legacy which would not, owing to an express condition attached to it, though in a direction to pay, be payable to the legatee, except contingently on his attaining twenty-one, might yet be paid to the personal representative of the legatee even though the legatee died under twenty-one.' *Re Kirkley, Halligey v Kirkley* (1918) 87 LJ Ch 247 at 247, 248, per Sargant J

IGNORANCE

Of law

'It is said "*Ignorantia juris haud excusat*"; but in that maxim the word "*jus*" is used in the sense of denoting general law, the ordinary law of the country. But when the word "*jus*" is used in the sense of denoting a private right, that maxim has no application.' *Cooper v Phibbs* (1867) LR 2 HL 149 at 170, per Lord Westbury

'With regard to the objection , that the mistake (if any) was one of law, and that the rule "*Ignorantia juris neminem excusat*" applies, I would observe upon the peculiarity of this case, that the ignorance imputable to the party was of a matter of law arising upon the doubtful construction of a grant. This is very different from the ignorance of a well-known rule of law. And there are many cases to be found in which equity, upon a mere mistake of the law, without the admixture of other circumstances, has given relief to a party who has dealt with his property under the influence of such mistake.' *Beauchamp (Earl) v Winn* (1873) LR 6 HL 223 at 234, per Lord Chelmsford

ILLEGAL CONTRACT   See CONTRACT

ILLEGAL PRACTICE   See CORRUPT PRACTICE

ILLEGAL PURPOSE

[Under the Friendly Societies Act 1896 (repealed; see now Friendly Societies Act 1974) the Chief Registrar may cancel the registry of any society if that society exists for an 'illegal purpose'.] 'If a society, the rules of which are on the face of them perfectly legal, has as its real object the doing of something unlawful under the cloak of lawful rules, I think that may well be said to be a society existing for an illegal purpose.' *Re Middle Age Pension Friendly Society* [1915] 1 KB 432 at 437, DC, per Lush J

ILLEGITIMATE   See also LEGITIMATE

'The testatrix was living with the plaintiff, and if I find, when she talks of illegitimate children, persons in existence to answer the description as objects of her bounty, I cannot do less than give the property to them. The law will not contemplate the notion that there can be future illegitimate children, and therefore I must consider that the testatrix meant to give her property to the children which she has had by the plaintiff. . . .' *Bentley v Blizard* (1858) 4 Jur NS 652 at 652, per Stuart V-C

[The Family Law Reform Act 1969, s 14 provides that an illegitimate child or his issue may succeed on the intestacy of his parents to any interest to which he would have been entitled if born legitimate; and similarly that the parents of an illegitimate child, on such child's intestacy, may succeed to any interest in his estate as if he had been born legitimate.]

New Zealand [The concept of illegitimacy was abolished in New Zealand by the Status of Children Act 1969 (NZ). Under s 3 of this Act, for all purposes of the law of New Zealand, the relationship between every person and his father and mother is to be determined irrespective of whether the father and mother are or have been married to each other, and all other relationships are to be determined accordingly.]

ILLICIT

Canada 'I am satisfied that the word "illicit" in that section [Criminal Code, RSC 1970, c C-34, s 195(1)(a) (procuring female to have illicit intercourse with another person)] is used in the sense of not being sanctioned or permitted by law and not necessarily in the sense of constituting a criminal offence.' *R v Turner* (1972) 8 CCC (2d) 76 at 79, BCCA, per McFarlane JA

ILLNESS

'Illness' includes mental disorder within the meaning of the Mental Health Act 1983 and any injury or disability requiring medical or dental treatment or nursing. (National Health Service Act 1977, s 128(1) as amended by the Mental Health Act 1983, s 148, Sch 4)

Australia 'The meaning of the word "illness" is not susceptible of proof by medical evidence, and a failure to appreciate this has complicated the matter. The word "illness" is not synonymous with "disease". In its primary meaning it refers to a bad moral quality, and includes a bad or unhealthy condition of the body.' *Burgess v Brownlow* [1964] NSWR 1275 at 1278, 1279, per Manning J

New Zealand [The Shipping and Seamen's Act Amendment Act 1894, s 5 (repealed; see now the Shipping and Seamen Act 1952, s 67) dealt with the discharge of any seamen by reason of 'illness' or accident.] 'In its widest sense "illness" covers all cases of sickness and suffering, even from accidents. It cannot be said it is used in its widest sense here, for if it were there was no need of using the word "accident". "Illness" must therefore have a limited meaning. A contrast is made between "illness and accident" in the statute, and were I to hold that "illness" was used in its widest sense, then the use of the word "accident" was unmeaning.' *Minister of Marine v Briscoe MacNeil & Co* (1899) 18 NZLR 722 at 724, 725, per Stout CJ; also reported, 2 GLR 161 at 162.

ILL-TREATMENT   *See* CRUELTY

ILL-USAGE

'As to "ill-usage" [of members of the crew of a ship], that is a very undefined term, depending much upon the opinion of the person who uses it, and taking its character out of the provocation given, and the relation in which the parties stand to each other. What in one instance may be the just exercise of authority, or may be moderate correction, or even justifiable defence, may, in another, be intemperate passion, or wanton cruelty. . . . Although it is necessary that the master should be supported in enforcing due sub-ordination and discipline in his ship, yet the law will not countenance his giving way to intemperate passion; for that is not only unjustifiable, but certainly is not the most effectual mode of maintaining proper authority.' *The Lima* (1837) 3 Hag Adm 346 at 353, per Nicholl J

IMBECILE   *See also* IDIOT

Australia [Section 215 of The Criminal Code provides that any person who 'knowing a woman or girl to be an imbecile has or attempts to have unlawful carnal knowledge of her is guilty of a misdemeanour'.] 'There is no definition of "imbecile" in the Code or in any related legislation . . . the term "imbecile" in s 215(2) does not necessarily involve the existence of an incapacity to consent to the act of carnal knowledge. . . an imbecile may be described as a person "of weak character, intellect or will resulting from a mental deficiency". The difference between "idiot" and "imbecile" is a matter of degree. This is apparent from the dictionary definitions of the term to which His Honour referred during the course of his summing-up and I add, merely for the sake of completeness, the meaning given to it in The Macquarie Dictionary (p 884): "a person of defective mentality above the grade of idiocy".' *R v Abbott* [1984] 1 Qd R 342 at 342, 346, per Campbell CJ

IMITATION   *See also* FIREARM;
FRAUDULENT IMITATION

Canada 'To come within s 302(d) [of the Criminal Code, RSC 1970, c C–34] the person charged must be armed with an offensive weapon or an imitation thereof. In this case all that was shown is that the appellant in this adventure simulated the conduct of a man armed with a weapon. He acted a part or played out a pantomime to give the impression that he had a weapon. While this conduct might have justified a conviction under paras (a) or (c) of s 302 of the Code, a question I refrain from deciding, it does not meet the requirements of s 302(d). To arm oneself with a weapon means to equip oneself, to acquire, to become possessed of some instrument which is either a weapon or an imitation of a weapon. I am not of the opinion that in these circumstances a man can be armed with his own finger and I am satisfied that the word "imitation" as used in s 302(d) of the Criminal Code refers to an imitation of the weapon and cannot be stretched to include a simulation of conduct or actions. No arming has been demonstrated here and the Crown being confined to the particulars of the information has in my opinion failed to prove its case.' *R v Sloan* (1974) 19 CCC (2d) 190 at 192, BCCA, per McIntyre JA

IMMATURE

Salmon

'Immature' in relation to salmon means that the salmon is of a length of less than twelve inches, measured from the tip of the snout to the fork or cleft of the tail, and in relation to any other fish, means that the fish is of a length less than such length (if any) as may be prescribed by the byelaws applicable to the water in which the fish is taken. (Salmon and Freshwater Fisheries Act 1975, s 41(1))

Whale

For the purposes of this section [protection for certain classes of whales] a whale of any description shall be deemed to be immature if it is of less than such length as may be prescribed for whales of that description: Provided that the length prescribed for the purposes of this section in relation to blue whales shall not be less than sixty feet, and the length so prescribed in relation to fin whales shall not be less than fifty feet (Whaling Industry (Regulations) Act 1934, s 3(2))

[Whaling Industry (Ship) Regulations have been made under this section prescribing minimum maturity lengths for blue whales, fin whales, sei whales, humpback and sperm whales. For a complete classified list of whales see the Schedule to the Act of 1934.]

IMMEDIATE

[Regulation 6 of the Building (Safety Health and Welfare) Regulations 1948 (revoked; see now the Construction (Working Places) Regulations 1966, SI 1966/94), provided that no scaffold should be erected, etc, except under the 'immediate' supervision of a competent person.] 'I accept counsel for the defendants' submission that, though there must be supervision, the proper extent of that supervision must be a question of degree related to the structure being built, the difficulties and dangers involved. There must be some person—not the workman himself—who is "immediately" responsible. The word "immediate" is, I think, directed to this relationship rather than intended to indicate that every act must be closely supervised. In some cases the supervision may have to be constant and relate to every act that is done—where, for instance, great danger and difficulty are involved. In other cases, where there is no risk and the men are competent, the supervision may be less intensive.' *Moloney v A Cameron Ltd* [1961] 2 All ER 934 at 936, CA, per Holroyd Pearce LJ

[Regulation 79(5) of the Building (Safety, Health and Welfare) Regulations 1948 (revoked; see supra), provided that certain operations should be carried out only under the 'immediate' supervision of a competent foreman or chargehand, etc]. 'What is meant by "immediate"? It has been submitted that "immediate" must mean constant, unremitting supervision of work of this kind. That is not my view of the proper construction of this regulation. The word "immediate", in my judgment, carried no limitation of supervision, other than it must be a direct supervision. There must not be any intermediary between the person supervising and the person being supervised. That, I think, is the meaning of the word "immediate". It means "direct".' *Owen v Evans and Owen (Builders) Ltd* [1962] 3 All ER 128 at 131, CA, per Ormerod LJ

'The word "immediate" does not mean "constant"; it means "immediate" in the sense of being opposed to delegated; or, put in another way, "immediate" in the sense of "direct". In other words, the supervision must be by the competent foreman or chargehand himself, and not by anyone else, and it cannot be delegated.' Ibid at 133, per Upjohn LJ

Canada 'I think that the words "immediate" and "forthwith", which are so familiar to lawyers and in legal affairs, mean not necessarily as some have said "within a reasonable time", but as others have said "without delay". I think that, when the statute puts an immediate duty or requires something to be done *forthwith* by a public officer, he has to establish, if he is not performing that duty, that he is ready to perform it without delay and as promptly as may be.' *R v Dick, ex p Bennett* (1970) 18 DLR (3d) 157 at 159, 160, Ont SC, per Wright J

Immediate binding trust for sale

[The Settled Land Act 1925, s 20(1)(viii) provides that a person entitled to the income of land under a trust or direction for payment thereof to him during his own or any other life, etc, shall, unless the land is subject to an 'immediate binding trust for sale', have the powers of a tenant for life under the Act.] 'The expression "unless the land is subject to an immediate binding trust for sale" must I think mean unless the land that is the total subject-matter of the settlement is subject to a trust for sale which operates in relation to the whole subject-matter of the settlement and is immediately exercisable, although possibly with the limitation, that it is treated as immediately exercisable "whether or not exercisable at the request or with the consent of any person and with or without a power at discretion to postpone the sale".' *Re Leigh's Settled Estates* [1926] Ch 852 at 859, per Tomlin J

IMMEDIATE APPROACHES *See*
APPROACH

IMMEDIATELY (Place)

[The question on a case stated was whether the appellant had erected a stall 'immediately' in front of his house, contrary to the provisions in a section of a local market Act.] '"Immediately", in this section means without any considerable space intervening.' *R v Durham Market Co* (1857) 29 LTOS 247 at 247, per cur.

IMMEDIATELY (Time) *See also* AT ONCE; FORTHWITH; ON DEMAND

There appears to be no material difference between the terms 'immediately' and 'forthwith'. A provision to the effect that a thing must be done 'forthwith' or 'immediately' means that it must be done as soon as possible in the circumstances, the nature of the act to be done being taken into account. (45 Halsbury's Laws (4th edn) para 1148)

'The only material word remaining, is the word immediately. . . . It was said that that word excludes all intermediate time and actions; but it will appear that it has not necessarily so strict a signification: Stevens in his Thesaurus expounds the word, immediate, by *cito et celeriter*; so Cooper's Dictionary renders in English immediately, forthwith, by and by; and Minshew gives it as various meanings, and refers it to the word presently; nor is its signification more confined in legal proceedings, as appears even from 2 Lev 77, in the case of *Pibus* and *Mitford* [*Pybus v Mitford* (1672) 2 Lev 75], which was cited to the contrary, which says thus, though the word immediately, in strictness, excludes all mesne time, yet to make good the deeds and intents of parties it shall be construed such convenient time as is reasonably requisite for doing the thing.' *R v Francis* (1735) Lee temp Hard 113 at 114, per Lord Hardwicke CJ

[Stat (1840) 3 & 4 Vict c 24, s 2 (repealed), enacted that costs should not be recovered in certain actions, where the damages recovered were less than 40s, unless the judge before whom the verdict should be obtained should 'immediately afterwards' certify that the action was brought to try a right, or that the grievance in respect of which the action was brought was wilful and malicious. The judge having adjourned on the finding of a verdict to his lodgings, counsel went to him there, and the judge granted a certificate within a quarter of an hour after the delivery of the verdict.] 'In strict construction, the words "immediately afterwards" exclude the lapse of any interval of time, but their meaning, with reference to a case like the present, must be, that the certificate shall be granted as speedily as conveniently can be. Then I agree that that was done here.' *Thompson v Gibson* (1841) 8 M & W 281 at 289, per Rolfe B

'The word "immediate" occurring in a statute is not to be construed in its strictest sense "on the instant", but . . . it means with reasonable promptness, having regard to all the circumstances of the particular case.' *R v Aston* (1850) 19 LJMC 236 at 239, per cur.

'When a statute requires an act to be done immediately, I do not see how we can construe it to mean that the act may be done some weeks afterwards.' *Leech v Lamb* (1855) 11 Exch 437 at 439, 440, per Pollock CB

'The great question is, whether the condition in this contract, that the goods shall be taken from the vessel immediately she was ready to discharge, has been satisfied or not. . . . The first point is, what is the effect of the word "immediately" here? Under ordinary circumstances, when a man is called upon by a contract to do an act, and no time is specified, he is allowed a reasonable time for doing it; and what is a reasonable time may depend on all the circumstances of the case. But here the word used being "immediately", it implies that there is a more stringent requisition than what is ordinarily implied in the word "reasonable". Still, it must receive a reasonable interpretation, so far that it cannot be considered as imposing an obligation to do what is impossible.' *Alexiadi v Robinson* (1861) 2 F & F 679 at 683, 684, per Cockburn CJ

'It is impossible to lay down any hard and fast rule as to what is the meaning of the word "immediately" in all cases. The words "forthwith" and "immediately" have the same meaning. They are stronger than the expression "within a reasonable time", and imply prompt, vigorous action, without any delay.' *R v Berkshire JJ* (1878) 4 QBD 469 at 471, per Cockburn CJ

[A condition of sale provided that the vendor should 'immediately' after the sale (which took place on 30 December) furnish to the purchaser or his solicitor an abstract of title to the premises.] 'I accede to the purchaser's argument that "immediately" means "forthwith", "instanter", and that the purchaser's solicitor might with reason say that

he expected the abstract at latest on the 1st of January.' *Re Todd & M'Fadden's Contract* [1908] 1 IR 213 at 220, per Kenny J

New Zealand 'Whether something is or is not done immediately is a question of fact. As was said in *Ex p Lamb, Re Southam* [(1881) 19 Ch D 169], dealing with the word "forthwith", it must be construed with reference to the object of the rule and the circumstances of the case.' *Wightman v Land Board of Canterbury & Quirk* (1912) 31 NZLR 799 at 806, per Denniston J; also reported 14 GLR 518 at 521.

IMMEDIATELY BEFORE

[The question was the effect on the poor law settlement of a poor person by an alteration of the area of a local authority.] 'Section 26 [of a local Act] expressly names the class of persons whose settlement is to be dealt with under the conditions, arising from the extension of the boundaries, namely, those who were resident in the added areas immediately before the "appointed day". But [the poor person] was not resident in the added area immediately before the appointed day. He had in fact left that area on 23rd February 1935 and the extension did not take place until April 1935. "Immediately before" cannot cover 23rd of February. That provision, therefore, is of no help whatever to the county of Monmouth. Indeed, that section makes it perfectly plain that this poor person was excluded from the class therein being dealt with.' *Newport Borough Council v Leicester County Council* [1937] 1 All ER 439 at 441, per Lord Hewart LCJ

IMMEMORIAL USAGE   *See* TIME
IMMEMORIAL

IMMIGRANT

Australia 'I do not question that the word 'immigration' in the Constitution [s 51(xxvi)] connotes the entry into Australia of persons coming for the purpose of settling here. I realise that in other contexts the verb "to immigrate" has been used to mean simply moving from one place of settled residence to another within the same country. But in the Constitution immigration means immigration to Australia from places abroad. A person who comes from another country to settle here, if permitted by our law to do so, is thus an immigrant in the ordinary sense of the word. It has been said that to qualify for that description he must intend to make his permanent home in this country. There are weighty statements to that effect. But, notwithstanding them, I am not satisfied that to be an immigrant, within the ordinary sense of that word, a newcomer must have relinquished all hope or expectation of ever returning to live or die in his native land.' *Re De Braic* [1971] ALR 605 at 608, per Windeyer J

Australia 'Clearly a person who has sought and obtained a temporary entry permit cannot during its duration become a member of the Australian community. He remains of necessity an immigrant in fact under the terms of the entry permit, bound to remove himself and liable to be removed.' *R v Forbes, Ex p Kwok Kwan Lee* (1971) 124 CLR 168 at 173, per Barwick CJ

IMMORAL

Canada [Imported book was seized as being 'immoral or indecent'.] 'The appellant observes that the words "immoral" and "indecent" appeared in the first version of customs legislation passed by Parliament in 1867 almost immediately after Confederation. In that Victorian age, he submits, there was a uniformly clear and precise view of ethics and morals and that these words, therefore, had a similarly clear and precise meaning which was universally understood. However, with the complexity of the contemporary views of ethics and morals, these words have lost so much of their former clarity and precision that they are almost impossible to define and virtually incomprehensible to the ordinary citizen. I am in no position to comment on what may or may not have been the simplicity of the Victorian understanding of the words "immoral" and "indecent". But they are capable of definition. Referring again to standard dictionaries, "immoral" is defined by such words as "morally evil", "dissolute", "wicked", "lewd", "unchaste", and "indecent" is defined with such words as "in extremely bad taste", "suggesting or tending to obscenity", "disgusting", "obscene". And, in turn, all of these definitions can be applied only in the light of our contemporary moral or ethical standards, complex as they may be.' *Re Luscher and Deputy Minister, Revenue Canada Customs and Excise* (1983) 149 DLR 13d) 243 at 246, BC Co Ct, per Anderson Co Ct J

IMMORAL PURPOSES

[The Sexual Offences Act 1956, s 32 makes it an offence for a man persistently to solicit or importune in a public place for 'immoral purposes'.] 'In my judgment the words "immoral purposes" in their ordinary meaning connote in a wide and general sense all purposes involving conduct which has the property of being wrong rather than right in the judgment of the majority of contemporary fellow citizens. In that sense . . . the words are, at least arguably, apt to cover the conduct [soliciting] alleged against the respondent in the present case. However I am convinced at least of this. That Parliament cannot be supposed to have used those words in their general sense, as comprising all wrong conduct, in a statute relating solely to sexual offences; soliciting persons to commit non-sexual crime is dealt with by the law relating to accessories before the fact or specifically by statute, e.g. in respect of mutiny, breach of security or Post Office offences. It seems to me to follow that the "immoral purposes" here in question must be immoral in respect of sexual conduct.' *Crook v Edmondson* [1966] 1 All ER 833 at 835, per Winn LJ

IMMOVABLE   *See also* MOVABLE
PROPERTY

Canada [Article 375 of the Quebec Civil Code provides that property is 'immovable' either by its nature, or by its destination, or by reason of the object to which it is attached, or lastly by determination of law, and by art 376, that lands and buildings are 'immovable' by their nature.] 'The word "immovable" in s 521 of the Cities and Towns Act [RSQ 1925] must, in their Lordships' view of the construction of that Act, bear the meaning given to it by the Quebec Civil Code. . . . What then is an "immovable" under the Civil Code? A gas main laid in the earth is an "immovable" in the sense that it is physically a construction fixed in the earth, though the individual pipes of which it is made up were movable before they came to form part of the construction. . . . Gas mains . . . must be regarded as immovable by their nature in the territory in which they are physically situate.' *Montreal Light, Heat & Power Consolidated v Outremont (City)* [1932] AC 423 at 435–437, per cur.

Canada 'The existence of a building which is immovable by its nature under art 376 [of the Quebec Civil Code (see supra)] involves two things, namely, that you have a structure and that such structure is incorporated with or adherent to, the soil.' *Bell Telephone Co of Canada v St Laurent (Ville)* [1936] AC 73 at 83, 84, PC, per cur.

IMMUNITY

Diplomatic immunity

[See now the State Immunity Act 1978, which restricts the immunity which sovereign States can claim from the jurisdiction of civil courts and tribunals in the United Kingdom. The Act enacts provisions which are consistent with the European Convention on State Immunity (Cmnd 5081).

Section 20 of the Act provides that with the necessary modifications the Diplomatic Privileges Act 1964 shall apply to a Sovereign or other head of a State as it applies to the head of a diplomatic mission.]

IMPEDE

[The Mining Industry Act 1926, s 13(2) (repealed; see now the Mines (Working Facilities and Support) Act 1966, s 1), enabled the Railway and Canal Commission to grant legal rights, and to modify existing rights, in cases where the working of coal was 'impeded' by restrictions, etc] 'The sub-section speaks of the working of any coal or of the working of any coal in the most efficient and economical manner being impeded by restrictions, terms or conditions contained in a mining lease. The word "manner" which is to be the subject of the impediment points very much in favour of the impediment of a restrictive method in the process of working or carrying away the coal; something in the nature of a physical and not a financial impediment.' *Consett Iron Co Ltd v Clavering Trustees* [1935] 2 KB 42 at 69, 70, CA, per Slesser LJ

IMPEDIMENT

[The Ordination Service contains the words: 'But yet if there be any of you who knoweth any impediment oʀ notable crime in any of them for which he ought not to be received into this Holy Ministry, let him come forth in the name of God and shew what the crime or impediment is'. The appellant had accordingly come forth and objected to one of the deacons presenting himself for ordination at a service in St Paul's Cathedral on the ground that he had

taken part in certain services, and being overruled he persisted and was convicted and fined at petty sessions for an offence under s 2 of the Ecclesiastical Courts Jurisdiction Act 1860.] 'The word "impediment" related originally to a number of matters, some of which can no longer be regarded as such—as, for instance, bastardy, and certain physical defects as the loss of a limb or eye—but included impediments which would still be considered as a bar to ordination such as the fact that the candidate was an unbaptised person or was not of the requisite age for the orders to which he proposed to be ordained. Without attempting in this judgment to give an exhaustive enumeration of what may be regarded as "notable crimes" or "impediments", there is not a trace to be found in any of the authorities that a mere allegation that a candidate has been a party to, or taken part in, the service in a church in which breaches of prescribed ritual have taken place comes within those words.' *Kensit v St. Paul's (Dean & Chapter)* [1905] 2 KB 249 at 256, 257, per cur. . . .

IMPERCEPTIBLE

'The defendant has pleaded, that the land in question, by the slow, gradual, and imperceptible projection, alluvion, subsidence, and accretion of ooze, soil, sand, and other matter, being slowly, gradually, and by imperceptible increase, in long time cast up, deposited, and settled by and from the flux and reflux of the tide and water of the sea in upon and against the outside and extremity of the demesne lands of the manor, hath been formed, and hath settled grown and accrued upon against and unto the said demesne lands. . . . Considering the word "imperceptible" in this issue, as connected with the words "slow and gradual", we think it must be understood as expressive only of the manner of the accretion, as the other words undoubtedly are, and as meaning imperceptible in its progress, not imperceptible after a long lapse of time.' *R v Yarborough (Lord)* (1824) 3 B & C 91 at 105, 107, per cur.

IMPERIAL STANDARD   *See*
MEASUREMENT

See, generally, 50 Halsbury's Laws (4th edn) paras 59–62.

IMPLEMENT   *See also* COIN; INSTRUMENT

Of housebreaking

[The Prevention of Offences Act 1851, s 1 (repealed; cf now Theft Act 1968, s 25), made it an offence to be found by night with an 'implement of housebreaking'. The accused had been found in possession of ordinary house door keys and a pair of pincers.] 'Every instrument that may be used for house-breaking, and is intended to be so used, is, I think, an implement of housebreaking within the Act of Parliament.' *R v Oldham* (1852) 3 Car & Kir 249 at 251, CCR, per Erle J

New Zealand 'In the direction in the summing-up the learned trial judge refers to implements capable of being used for burglary and includes in such category implements advantageous to the burglar for the purpose of his criminal activities after he has effected an entry into premises. Whatever the position may be when a charge is laid under s 244 of the Crimes Act, we do not think such considerations are pertinent in considering what may be instruments of housebreaking. "Housebreaking" is not in itself a definitive offence, and it must be regarded as having the meaning attributed to it when the section was originally enacted in 1866, the breaking in or out of buildings (including the breaking of interior doors), and cannot include acts in the interior of the premises which are connected only with the commission of another offence.' *R v Hodges* [1965] NZLR 676 at 677, CA, per cur.

Of trade

[The County Courts Act 1888, s 147 (repealed; see now County Courts Act 1984, s 89(1)(a)) provided that, in levying distress on a person's goods and chattels, the 'implements of his trade' to the value of £5 (now £150) should be exempt.] 'We have to decide . . . whether the county court judge was right in taking the view that the cab which was at the time in the possession of, and was being used by, the person who was owing rent for this stable comes within the words of the exception in s 147 . . . as being an implement of his trade. . . . It is contended that it was not an implement of the cabman's trade because he . . . was not necessarily bound to use this particular cab, but could go elsewhere and continue to carry out his business or trade as a cab-driver by hiring a cab from a cab-

proprietor. I do not think that that is a good argument. The case of *Fenton v Logan* [(1833) 9 Bing 676] in my opinion supports the view we are taking. I think this cab which the man had hired by the week and was using was properly regarded by the county court judge as being an implement of his trade.' *Lavell v Richings* [1906] 1 KB 480 at 481, 482, DC, per Lord Alverstone CJ

[*Fenton v Logan*, referred to above, decided that an implement of trade is only privileged from distress if it is in use.]

'What we have to decide is whether a typewriter taken on his rounds by a commercial traveller as a sample of the goods which he is employed to sell comes within the words "the tools and implements of his trade" [within the County Courts Act 1888, s 147 (repealed; see supra)]. In my opinion it does not. I have much doubt whether the trade of a commercial traveller is one which involves the use of any tools or implements at all. . . . Here the typewriter no doubt assists the traveller in earning his living, but it is not essential. He could earn his living as a traveller in typewriters without having a sample with him.' *Addison v Shepherd* [1908] 2 KB 118 at 120, DC, per Lord Alverstone CJ

IMPLICATION

Necessary implication

'Sometimes the rule is stated that the Crown, in order to be bound [by a statute which does not expressly so provide], must be included by necessary implication. But what is "necessary implication" in the construction of a statute? I may cite the words of Lord Eldon in *Wilkinson v Adam* [(1813) 1 Ves & B 422 at 465, 466, where after stating that in construing a will, a particular intention must appear by necessary implication upon the will itself, he continues: "With regard to that expression 'necessary implication', I will repeat what I have before stated from a Note of Lord Hardwicke's judgment in *Coriton v Hellier* [(1745) 2 Cox Eq Cas 340], that in construing a will, conjecture must not be taken for implication, but necessary implication means not natural necessity, but so strong a probability of intention, that an intention contrary to that which is imputed to the testator cannot be supposed".' *Cork County Council & Burke v Public Works Comrs* [1945] IR 561 at 573, per Murnaghan J

IMPLIED COVENANT *See* COVENANT

IMPLIED TERM

See, generally, 9 Halsbury's Laws (4th edn) paras 351–362.

'The expression "implied term" is used in different senses. Sometimes it denotes some term which does not depend on the actual intention of the parties but on a rule of law, such as the terms, warranties or conditions which, if not expressly excluded, the law imports, as for instance under the Sale of Goods Act [1979] and the Marine Insurance Act [1906]. The law also in some circumstances holds that a contract is dissolved if there is a vital change of conditions. . . . There have been several general statements by high authorities on the power of the Court to imply particular terms in contracts. . . . The general presumption is that the parties have expressed every material term which they intended should govern their agreement, whether oral or in writing. But it is well recognised that there may be cases where obviously some term must be implied if the intention of the parties is not to be defeated. . . . The implications must arise inevitably to give effect to the intention of the parties.' *Luxor (Eastbourne) Ltd v Cooper* [1941] AC 108 at 137, per Lord Wright

'Strictly speaking, I think that an implied term is something which, in the circumstances of a particular case, the law may read into the contract if the parties are silent and it would be reasonable to do so; it is something over and above the ordinary incidents of the particular type of contract. . . . But the phrase "implied term" can be used to denote a term inherent in the nature of the contract which the law will imply in every case unless the parties agree to vary or exclude it.' *Sterling Engineering Co Ltd v Patchett* [1955] 1 All ER 369 at 376, HL, per Lord Reid LJ; see also [1955] AC 534.

IMPLIED TRUST *See* TRUST

IMPLIEDLY

New Zealand [The Workers' Compensation Act 1956, s 5 extends the course of a worker's employment to the time when he is travelling to and from work by a means of transport, other than public passenger transport, which use for the purpose the employer has expressly or 'impliedly' authorised.] 'I turn now to the meaning of the words "expressly or impliedly authorised" as they are used in the section under review. The intention of the legislature is clearly to extend the cover of the section where the facts of a particular case justify an inference that the employer had authorised the use of the means of transport used by the worker. To insist in all circumstances that the employer must, as it were, spell out his approval of the form of transport would deny a meaning and effect to the word "impliedly". While I entirely agree with the proposition that mere knowledge that a worker is using a particular form of transport is not implied authorisation, I believe that if the employer has by his own conduct and with knowledge of the facts obliged his worker to use his own vehicle, then this is implied authorisation within the meaning of the section.' *Hayden v Air New Zealand Ltd* [1972] NZLR 149 at 153, per Blair J

IMPORT

Australia 'The Customs Tariff . . . imposes the duties [import duties] on "all goods dutiable . . . imported into Australia", etc . . . Importation does not necessarily include landing the goods. They may be transhipped direct from the ship in which they arrive into the ship or aircraft into which they are to be transhipped, and still be "imported goods". Section 68(1) [of the Customs Act 1901–1986 (Cth)] says: "All imported goods shall be entered either (a) for home consumption; or (b) for warehousing; or (c) for transhipment". Consequently "imported goods" as there used is an expression not confined to goods landed or even to goods to be consumed in Australia. On the other hand it does not include all goods in fact arriving by ship in an Australian port. A vessel, say, with a cargo destined for New Zealand may call in at Melbourne or Sydney and may continue her voyage without it being said that the goods it carries are "imported goods" within the meaning of s 68. . . . In my opinion, having regard to the various sections of the Act—and needless to say the question must be solved by reference to that Act and not to other Acts—the expression "imported goods", in s 68, means goods which in fact are brought from abroad into Australian territory, and in respect of which the carriage is ended or its continuity in some way in fact broken.' *Wilson v Chambers*

& *Co Proprietary Ltd* (1926) 38 CLR at 138, 139, per Isaacs J

Australia 'The word "import" [in s 233B of the Customs Act 1901–1986/9 (Cth)] is not defined. It is my opinion, upon a survey of the Act as a whole, that importing by a ship constitutes either landing goods or bringing them into port. Our attention was drawn . . . to a number of provisions of the Act conferring powers in relation to ships within the three mile limit, but, in my opinion, these conditions do not warrant the conclusion that goods are imported by being brought within that limit.' *R v Bull* (1974) 48 ALJR 232 at 250, per Gibbs J

Canada [The Customs Tariff Act 1894, s 4 (Can), provided that duty should be paid on raw sugar when such goods were 'imported into Canada' or taken out of warehouse for consumption therein. Section 150 of the Customs Act 1886 (see now Customs Tariff Act, RSC 1970, c C–41, directed that the precise time of the importation of goods should be deemed to be the time when they came within the limits of the port at which they ought to be reported.] 'The words "when such goods are imported into Canada" express the time at which the duties are to be paid. If therefore the goods are imported into Canada when the vessel enters a port of call on her way to her ultimate destination, the duties would be payable at that date, which is highly improbable, and contrary to the express provisions of s 31. . . . The words "imported into Canada" must, in order to give any rational sense to the clause, mean imported at the port of discharge. . . . The object of the definition in s 150 is not to define the port of importation, or the meaning of ''imported'', but the time when the goods are to be deemed to be first imported. The words in question apply equally to importation coastwise or by inland navigation in any decked vessel. If made by land or by inland navigation in any undecked vessel, then the time is when such goods are brought within the limits of Canada.' *Canada Sugar Refining Co v R* [1898] AC 735 at 740–742, PC, per cur.

Canada 'To import into Canada means to bring in goods from anywhere outside Canada to anywhere inside Canada. I see no reason in principle or precedent to restrict the relevant location within Canada to the actual point of border crossing. The word "import" should not be stultified by narrow interpretation. Importing is a process which, although it

necessarily includes the act of crossing the border, extends to the point of intended final destination. In my view the test is whether there is a direct link between the place of origin outside Canada and the destination inside Canada.' *Bell v R* [1983] 2 SCR 471 at 477, SCC, per Dickson J

United States The terms 'import' and 'importation' include reimporting a consumer product manufactured or processed, in whole or in part, in the United States. (Consumer Product Safety Act 1972, s 3(a)(13))

IMPORTER

'Importer' in relation to any goods at any time between their importation and the time when they are delivered out of charge, includes any owner or other person for the time being possessed of or beneficially interested in the goods and, in 'relation' to goods imported by means of a pipe-line, includes the owner of the pipe-line. (Customs and Excise Management Act 1929, s 1(1))

'Importer', in relation to an imported article, includes any person who, whether as owner, consignor, consignee, agent or broker, is in possession of the article or in any way entitled to the custody or control of it. (Food Act 1984, s 132(1))

'The importer of goods is the consignor, who sets the adventure afloat, who directs the port to which, and the person to whom it is to be delivered, and who can stop the goods *in transitu.*' *The Matchless* (1822) 1 Hag Adm 97 at 102, per Lord Stowell

New Zealand [The Customs Act 1966, s 2 defines 'importer' as any person by or for whom any goods are imported, including the consignee of any goods and any person who is or becomes the owner or entitled to the possession of or beneficially interested in any goods on or at any time after their importation and before they have ceased to be subject to the control of the Customs. The defendant was a freight forwarding company which contracted to transport goods which had been entered 'for removal for warehousing elsewhere' from Auckland to Wellington. Whilst in transit some of the goods were stolen, and the Collector sued the defendant to recover customs duty on the goods so stolen. The defendant's liability depended on whether or not it was an 'importer' of the goods within the above definition.] 'It is not disputed that the defendant contracted to arrange the removal of the goods pursuant to s 110 [of the Customs Act] and that the defendant duly accepted delivery of the goods for forwarding by rail. In those circumstances the defendant was in my opinion "entitled to the possession of" the goods and accordingly was an importer within the definition contained in the interpretation section.' *Collector of Customs v Daily Freightways Ltd* [1973] 2 NZLR 434 at 437, per White J

IMPOSE   *See also* IMPRISONMENT

[By a covenant in a lease the lessor covenanted with the lessees to pay all rates, taxes and impositions 'imposed' by the corporation of the city of London.] 'The words here are "all rates, taxes, and impositions whatsoever . . . imposed by the corporation of the city of London or otherwise howsoever". The question appears to me to be whether this water-rate can be said to be a rate of imposition "imposed", within the meaning of those words. I do not think that it can. I do not think that a charge to which a person can only be made liable with his own consent can be said to be imposed upon him within the meaning of this covenant. . . . Furthermore, I think that the words "imposed otherwise howsoever" must be construed according to the rule of construction applicable when general words follow specific words, and that therefore they can only include rates or impositions . . . imposed compulsorily upon the person charged.' *Badcock v Hunt* (1888) 22 QBD 145 at 148, CA, per Lord Esher MR

'In my judgment it [the water-rate] is not imposed at all within the meaning of the covenant; it becomes payable by the voluntary action of the person who chooses to take the water and thereby incurs the legal liability to pay for it; it is not, like the rates and charges previously mentioned in the covenant, an imposition by some superior authority which a man becomes liable to pay whether he will or no.' Ibid at 149, per Fry LJ

IMPOSITION

[A lessee covenanted to pay and discharge all taxes, rates, etc, and all 'impositions' whatsoever charged or imposed upon the premises. Notice was given to the lessor by the sanitary authority of the district to abate a nuisance caused by a privy, by removing the privy and constructing a water-closet. The lessor did the work and subsequently sued the lessee to recover his expenses.] 'What . . . is an "imposition" within the meaning of this covenant? I should say, apart from authority, that in this covenant it means a sum of money payable by the landlord or tenant in respect of an imposition. A duty imposed appears to me to be an imposition, and I should say that the word "imposition" is, if anything, rather larger than the word "duty". Therefore I do not think that we ought to treat it as bearing a narrower meaning. I agree that it ought not to be treated as covering a matter which would be beyond anything that the parties to the lease could reasonably be supposed to have contemplated, but I cannot say that the expense incurred by the landlord in this case was something which clearly was not intended to be covered by the covenant.' *Foulger v Arding* [1902] 1 KB 700 at 710, 711, CA, per Romer LJ

'The question I have to determine is whether the tenant can prove against her landlord's estate for a sum of £118 expended by her on the reconstruction of drains in compliance with a notice from the sanitary authority. . . . I am of opinion that the tenant is not entitled to recover. She covenanted to pay the rent "free and clear . . . from all deductions . . ." and to "pay and discharge all . . . impositions. . . ." In my view the duty of complying with the notice . . . and the payment of the costs of the necessary works constituted an "imposition".' *Re Warriner, Brayshaw v Ninnis* [1903] 2 Ch 367 at 369–371, per Swinfen Eady J

IMPOSSIBLE   *See also* FRUSTRATION; IMPRACTICABLE

'In the language of everyday life a thing is impossible when, according to the ordinary course of human events, no expectation can be entertained that it will happen.' *Shepherd v Kottgen* (1877) 2 CPD 585 at 591, CA, per Cotton LJ

IMPOTENCE

'The charge made [of impotence *quoad hanc*], though physical and not moral, is nevertheless a grave and wounding imputation that the respondent is lacking, at least *quoad hanc*, in the power of reproducing his species, a power which is commonly and rightly considered to be the most characteristic quality of manhood. The allegation made in the present case is not that the respondent completely lacks the capacity of reproduction. As in many other cases, it is urged that he is incapable of consummating this particular marriage with this particular woman.' *C (otherwise H) v C* [1921] P 399 at 400, per Lord Birkenhead LC

Canada 'Impotence in my understanding of the word is physical disability for sexual connection. I have not been referred to nor have I been able to find any judicial definition of the word. The cases seem to have arisen entirely upon the existence of some defect or malformation making carnal intercourse impossible and either proved as a physical fact or inferred from a refusal on the part of the alleged impotent to consummate.' *Hale v Hale* [1927] 2 DLR 1137 at 1138, per Walsh J; affd [1927] 3 DLR 481

IMPOUND

'By the 11 Geo 2, c 19 [Distress for Rent Act 1737], s 10, persons making distresses for rent "may impound or otherwise secure the distress, of whatever nature it may be, on such place, or on such part of the premises chargeable with the rent, as shall be most fit and convenient, and may appraise, sell, and dispose of the same upon the premises". The words "or otherwise secure" appear to me to enlarge "impound", and to give a wider meaning to it than if the latter well known term, implying an inclosed place, had alone been used.' *Thomas v Harries* (1840) 1 Man & G 695 at 703, per Tindal CJ

'In order to "impound or otherwise secure" the goods there must be some distinct act manifesting it. Words alone are not enough. To prove the point, it is as well to remember the offence of pound-breach. As soon as the distress is impounded, whether on or off the premises, it is in the custody of the law: and anyone who breaks the pound (as by forcing the lock) or takes the goods out of the pound, is guilty of pound-breach. He is indictable for a misdemeanour for which he can be sent to prison, and is also liable to an action which carries penal consequences, namely, for treble damages [under Stat 2 Will & M c 5 (1689), s 3]. On principle, a man is not to be held guilty of this offence unless he has a guilty mind. He must know that the goods have been impounded or otherwise secured, on or off the premises. How can a stranger be expected to know this unless there is some open and manifest act so as to show it? I am prepared to hold, therefore, that, as against strangers,

goods are not validly impounded unless they are locked up in a room or otherwise secured in such a way that it is manifest that they are not to be taken away. "Walking possession" may be sufficient as against the tenant who agrees to it, but not as against a stranger who knows nothing of it.' *Abingdon RDC v O'Gormon* [1968] 3 All ER 79 at 83, CA, per Lord Denning MR

New Zealand [The Impounding Act 1884, s 11 (NZ) (repealed; see now the Impounding Act 1955, s 45), provided that any person by whom cattle were sent to the pound should specify in writing to the poundkeeper certain particulars—e.g. brands and ear-marks, name of owner, etc]. 'A lawful impounding consists not merely of a delivery of the impounded cattle to the poundkeeper, but of a delivery accompanied by the written particulars required by the statute. The two acts are to be consecutive so as to form the one act of a lawful impounding, and if the first act is not immediately followed by the second, the act of a lawful impounding does not become complete, and the delivery of the cattle to the poundkeeper becomes consequently an illegal impounding within the meaning of s 10 of the Act.' *Mehaffy v Jury* (1906) 25 NZLR 867 at 868, per Edwards J; also reported 8 GLR 553 at 554

IMPRACTICABLE

'In matters of business, a thing is said to be impossible when it is not practicable; and a thing is impracticable when it can only be done at an excessive or unreasonable cost. A man may be said to have lost a shilling, when he has dropped it into deep water; though it might be possible, by some very expensive contrivance to recover it.' *Moss v Smith* (1850) 9 CB 94 at 103, per Maule J

'The trustees have to form an "opinion" that the sharing of a particular institution in the testator's residue is either impracticable or inequitable. What does "impracticable" mean? It means that something cannot be done. . . . What does "inequitable" mean? . . . In this court the word "equitable" is a word of the highest importance. The word "inequitable", which is the contrary of it, is that against which this court by its ancient constitution, and, I hope, by its application of legal principles, is bound to strive. The trustees here have to form an opinion that something is "impracticable", i.e. it cannot be done, or is "inequitable", in the sense of being unfair or unjust.' *Re Hayes' Will Trusts, Dobie v National Hospital Board of Governors* [1953] 2 All ER 1242 at 1245, per Vaisey J

'The first point of law which arises involves the construction of s 135(1) [of the Companies Act 1948, (repealed; see now the Companies Act 1985, s 371(1))], the examination being directed to consider the scope of the phrase: "If for any reason it is impracticable to call a meeting of a company in any manner in which meetings of that company may be called, or to conduct the meeting of the company in manner prescribed by the articles or this Act. . . ." It is to be observed that the subsection opens with the words "If for any reason", and, therefore, it follows that the subsection is intended to have, and, indeed, has by reason of its language, a necessarily wide scope. The next words being "it is impracticable to call a meeting of a company", the question arises, what is the scope of the word "impracticable"? It is conceded . . . that the word "impracticable" is more limited than the word "impossible", and it appears to me that the question necessarily raised by the introduction of the word "impracticable" is merely this: Examine the circumstances of the particular case and answer the question whether, as a practical matter, the desired meeting of the company can be conducted, there being no doubt, of course, that it can be convened and held. On the face of s 135(1), there is no express limitation which would operate to give those words "is impracticable" any less meaning than that which I have stated, and I can find no good reason in the arguments which have been addressed to me on behalf of the respondents for qualifying in any way the force of the word "impracticable" or the interpretation which I have placed on it.' *Re El Sombrero Ltd* [1958] 3 All ER 1 at 4, per Wynn-Parry J; also reported [1958] Ch 900 at 903, 904.

[Regulation 97 of the Building (Safety, Health and Welfare) Regulations 1948 (revoked; see now the Construction (Working Places) Regulations 1966, SI 1966/94), dealt with circumstances where the special nature, etc, of any work rendered it 'impracticable' to comply with safety regulations.] '"Impracticable" in reg 97 is a strong word. It must mean "not possible" or "not feasible". At any rate, it means something very much more than "not reasonably practicable".' *Moorcroft v Thomas Powles & Sons Ltd* [1962] 3 All ER 741 at 746, per Lord Parker CJ

'In my view, "impracticability" is a conception different from that of "impossibility": the latter is absolute, the former introduces at all events some degree of reason and involves at all events some regard for practice. There are, therefore, three theoretical categories into which a set of circumstances requiring precautions may fall, namely, "impossibility", "impracticability" and "not being reasonably practicable". Indeed, if one adds the standard of "reasonableness" required at common law, there are four categories.' *Jayne v National Coal Board* [1963] 2 All ER 220 at 223, per Veale J

IMPRISONMENT *See also* FALSE IMPRISONMENT; LIFE IMPRISONMENT

'Impose imprisonment' means pass a sentence of imprisonment or commit to prison in default of payment of any sum of money or for failing to do or abstain from doing anything required to be done or left undone. (Criminal Justice Act 1948, s 80)

'Impose imprisonment' means pass a sentence of imprisonment or fix a term of imprisonment for failure to pay any sum of money, or for want of sufficient distress to satisfy any sum of money, or for failure to do or abstain from doing anything required to be done or left undone. (Magistrates' Courts Act 1980, s 150(1))

'Imprisonment' includes detention of any description. (Fugitive Offenders Act 1967, s 19).

IMPROPER

[A printed report, dealing with the affairs of a certain 'Society of Guardians for the Protection of Trade against Swindlers and Sharpers', contained a notice to the effect that the plaintiff was an 'improper' person to be ballotted for as a member of the Society.] 'There may be numerous reasons why a person may not be fit to become a member of such a society, even though he be not a swindler or sharper. He may not be a fit person to be a member of the society, if he be old or infirm, or has not a knowledge of such persons as are sharpers and swindlers, and on that account not likely to promote the object of the society. If I am asked whether a certain person be fit for a particular situation, and answer that he is not: I do not mean that he is dishonest, but that he is disqualified for the situation. So here, the being an improper person to be a member of the society, means what it naturally imports, and no more.' *Goldstein v Foss* (1828) 2 Y & J 146 at 155, per cur.

IMPROPER NAVIGATION
See NAVIGATION

IMPROPRIATION   *See* APPROPRIATION

IMPROPRIATOR   *See* LAY
IMPROPRIATOR; VICAR

IMPROVEMENT   *See also*
CONSTRUCTION

Of common

The improvement of a common comprises for the purposes of this Act all or any of the following things; that is to say,
(1) The draining, manuring, or levelling the common; and
(2) The planting trees on parts of such common, or in any other way improving or adding to the beauty of the common; and
(3) The making or causing to be made bye-laws and regulations for the prevention of or protection from nuisances or for keeping order on the common; and
(4) The general management of such common;
(5) The appointment from time to time of conservators of the common for the purposes aforesaid.
(Commons Act 1876, s 5)

Of highway

'Improvement', in relation to a road, includes the widening of the road, the cutting off of corners of the road, and the provision for the road of a cattle-grid and of any works required in connection with a cattle-grid, and 'improve' shall be construed accordingly. (Agriculture (Improvement of Roads) Act 1955, s 5)

'Improvement' means the doing of any act under powers conferred by Part V of this Act, and includes the erection, maintenance, alteration and removal of traffic signs, and the freeing of a highway or road-ferry from tolls. (Highways Act 1980, s 329(1))
[The acts referred to which may be done under Part V of the Act of 1980 include the making of dual carriageways, roundabouts and cycle tracks; the widening or levelling of highways; cutting off of corners; planting trees; lighting, drainage, etc.]

Of land

By 'the improvement of land' shall herein be meant all or any of the following matters:
1. The drainage of land, and the straitening, widening, deepening, or otherwise improving the drains, streams, and watercourses of any land:
2. The irrigation and warping of land:
3. The embanking and weiring of land from the sea or tidal waters, or from lakes, rivers, or streams, in a permanent manner:
4. The inclosing of lands, and the straitening of fences and redivision of fields:
5. The reclamation of land, incuding all operations necessary thereto:
6. The making of permanent farm roads, and permanent tramways and railways and navigable canals, for all purposes connected with the improvement of the estate:
7. The clearing of land:
8. The erection of labourers cottages, farmhouses, and other buildings required for farm purposes, and the improvement of and addition to labourers cottages, farmhouses, and other buildings for farm purposes already erected, so as such improvements or additions be of a permanent nature:
9. Planting for shelter:
10. The constructing or erecting of any engine-houses, water-wheels, saw and other mills, kilns, shafts, wells, ponds, tanks, reservoirs, dams, leads, pipes, conduits, watercourses, bridges, weirs, sluices, floodgates, or hatches, which will increase the value of any lands for agricultural purposes:
11. The construction or improvement of jetties or landing places on the sea coast, or on the banks of navigable rivers or lakes, for the transport of cattle, sheep, and other agricultural stock and produce, and of lime, manure, and other articles and things for agricultural purposes; provided that the Commissioners shall be satisfied that such works will add to the permanent value of the lands to be charged to an extent equal to the expense thereof:
12. The execution of all such works as in the judgment of the Commissioners may be necessary for carrying into effect any matter herein-before mentioned, or for deriving the full benefit thereof. (Improvement of Land Act 1864, s 9)

Australia [A lease in printed form devised by the Commonwealth for use in the case of leases of broad acres of the Australian Capital Territory contains four subclauses which express the respective right and obligation of lessor and lessee concerning compensation for 'improvements' on the event of the demised land or a part of it being withdrawn by the Commonwealth during the term.] 'In my opinion, timber treatment, pasture improvement and the provision of shade and shelter plantings are all "improvements" within the meaning of that word in the clause—and throughout the lease. . . . Griffith CJ in *Morrison v Federal Comr of Land Tax* [(1914) 17 CLR 498] said:—"What operations of man are improvements? . . . Any operation of man upon land which has the effect of enhancing its value comes within the definition of 'improvement'." It appears to me that the word "improvements" has been given a meaning which would include what is done in improvement of the quality of the soil and thereby the usefulness of the land.' *Commonwealth of Australia v Oldfield* (1976) 10 ALR 243 at 248, per Jacobs J

Of premises

[A lessee was entitled by the terms of his lease to remove all such 'improvements' as should be capable of removal without injury to the land itself. He pulled down a brick building which he had erected on the land demised and removed the materials, leaving only the foundations.] 'In the argument before their Lordships, as in the argument before the Supreme Court, it was sought to confine the term "improvements" to erections not affixed to the soil. But that is not the natural or proper meaning of the expression, which seems to be more applicable to something attached to and forming an integral part of the thing improved than to something which is merely added to it or placed upon it without annexation or union.' *London & South African Exploration Co Ltd v De Beers Consolidated Mines Ltd* [1895] AC 451 at 455, PC, per cur.

[The Landlord and Tenant Act 1927, s 19(2) provides that in all leases containing a covenant against the making of 'improvements' without licence or consent, such covenant shall be deemed to be subject to a proviso that such licence or consent is not to be unreasonably withheld.] 'I must be satisfied that the matter required to be done is in fact an improvement. From what point of view am I to consider this? From the point of view of the tenant or of the landlord or of both? I think the answer to the question will be found in the subsection itself. The subsection provides in effect that the landlord may say to the tenant, who asks for leave to make an improvement: "I shall not give my consent to the alteration you are making unless and until you give an undertaking to reinstate at the end of the term". That shows that the question whether it is an improvement or not may be considered from the point of view of the tenant alone. . . . If it is plain that, so far as the tenant is concerned, what is suggested will constitute an improvement, then, although it is not or may not be so from the landlords' point of view, the landlords will be amply protected by the undertaking of the tenant to reinstate at the end of the term.' *Balls Brothers Ltd v Sinclair* [1931] 2 Ch 325 at 331, 332, per Luxmoore J

'I find great difficulty in framing a definition of what is an "improvement" as distinct from a "repair". . . . It seems to me that the test, so far as one can give any test in these matters, is this: If the work which is done is the provision of something new for the benefit of the occupier, that is, properly speaking, an improvement; but if it is only the replacement of something already there, which has become dilapidated or worn out, then, albeit that it is a replacement by its modern equivalent, it comes within the category of repairs and not improvements.' *Morcom v Campbell-Johnson* [1955] 3 All ER 264 at 266, CA, per Denning LJ; see also [1956] 1 QB 106

Works of improvement

For the purposes of this section 'works of improvement' includes the provision of additional or improved fixtures or fittings but not works by way of decoration or repair. (Housing Act 1985, s 310(5))

IN

'In', in a context referring to works, apparatus or other property in a street, controlled land or other place, includes a reference to works, apparatus or other property under, over, across, along or upon it, and, in a context referring to a sewer, drain or tunnel in a street, includes a reference to one thereunder. (Public Utilities Street Works Act 1950, s 39)

'In' in a context referring to things in a road includes a reference to things under, over, across, along or upon the road. (Road Traffic Regulation Act 1984, s 60(4))

'Bye-law 21 [of the bye-laws of a county council] relates directly to the reconstructing of pipes or drains. Every person who shall construct or reconstruct any pipe or drain, or other means of communicating with sewers, or any trap or apparatus connected therewith, so far as he shall effect any such works in any building erected before the confirmation of these bye-laws, shall do the same as if it were a new building. I cannot think that that means that the pipes or drains there referred to, which, in the majority of cases so far as this work is concerned, must be outside the actual walls, are to be limited to works which are inside the building, and that the word "in" there means "inside". In my opinion, the word "in" does mean "in reference to" or "in connection with", and does not mean "inside".' *Kingsland v Haben* (1904) 90 LT 449 at 450, per Lord Alverstone CJ

'The circumstances of this case show that the appellant was not found *in* the building but that he was found *outside* the building trying to get into it. Therefore, of whatever other offence he may have been guilty, he was not guilty of the offence with which he was charged, namely, being found in a building with intent to commit a felony.' *R v Parkin* [1949] 2 All ER 651 at 652, CCA, per Lynskey J; [1950] 1 KB 155 at 156

IN ACCORDANCE WITH

[The Bills of Sale Act (1878) Amendment Act 1882, s 9 enacts that a bill of sale made by way of security for the payment of money is to be void unless made 'in accordance with' the form in the schedule.] 'We have to determine what legal meaning ought to be attached to the words "in accordance with the form". . . . A bill of sale is surely in accordance with the prescribed form if it is substantially in accordance with it, if it does not depart from the prescribed form in any material respect. But a divergence only becomes substantial or material when it is calculated to give the bill of sale a legal consequence or effect, either greater or smaller, than that which would attach to it if drawn in the form which has been sanctioned, or if it departs from the form in a manner calculated to mislead those whom it is the object of the statute to protect. . . . Whatever form the bill of sale takes, the form adopted by it in order to be valid must produce, not merely the like effect, but the same effect—that is to say, the legal effect, the whole legal effect, and nothing but the legal effect which it would produce if cast in the exact mould of the schedule.' *Re Barber, ex p*

Stanford (1886) 17 QBD 259 at 269–271, CA, per cur.

IN ALL RESPECTS

'One has to see what the conditions [on a car park ticket] mean. I will read them again: "The proprietors do not take any responsibility for the safe custody of any cars or articles therein (i.e., in a private parking ground], nor for any damage to the cars or articles however caused, nor for any injuries to any persons, all cars being left in all respects entirely at their owner's risk." . . . The words that have been used . . . are the words "in all respects" which appear to me to be the suitable words to show in a sentence, expressed as this one is, that whatever may happen, whatever may be done with regard to that car, the owner takes the risk of it happening or of it being done. It appears to me that the language is wide enough to produce that result and does on its true construction produce that result. The position, therefore, is that if the owners of the park put their servant there, even if they put him there with instructions to see that he does not hand over the car to anybody but the true owner, and if the servant in the performance of that duty performs it negligently, and, acting under a misapprehension which a little more care might have prevented, hands over the car to the wrong person, that, as it appears to me, is one of the risks which, on the true construction of this document, the car owner takes.' *Ashby v Tolhurst* [1937] 2 KB 242 at 250, 253, CA, per Greene MR

IN ARREAR *See also* ARREARS

[The defendant company's articles of association (art 65) provided that the original preference shares should not confer voting rights upon the holders unless (inter alia) the dividend thereon was 'in arrear' for more than three years after the appropriate date for payment.] 'The plaintiffs say that "in arrear" means if no dividend is paid. . . . On the other hand the defendants say that where, as here, the preferred shares are non-cumulative, there can be no arrears in respect of any year in which there were no profits earned available for dividends. . . . The words . . . "in arrear" connote in the strict sense a reference to a sum which has become due and payable and has not been paid. They may, however, be used in a secondary sense to indicate some deficiency which is capable, either certainly or contingently, of being made good. . . . That secondary meaning may be applicable to the words "in arrear" used in art 65. The secondary sense does not, however, assist the plaintiffs. Is there, then, a third sense wide enough to cover the non-payment of something . . . which never in fact becomes payable, and never can in the future in any contingency become payable or be made good? . . . The words "in arrear" in art 65 cannot, in the context in which they occur, be so construed.' *Coulson v Austin Motor Co Ltd* (1927) 43 TLR 493 at 494, 495, per Tomlin J

IN BALLAST

'This is a short point. . . . It is whether a steamer . . . can be said to be "in ballast" when she is carrying more coal than is necessary to take her from one port to the other. . . . "In ballast" must have a different meaning according to the different circumstances to which it is sought to apply it. . . . Vessels are either in ballast or laden. . . . When a vessel has got nothing on board except these matters which are necessary for her purposes as a travelling vessel, can she be said to be otherwise than in ballast? . . . You cannot say a vessel shall only have so much ballast. There is no regulation prescribing, according to tonnage, how much ballast she shall have. . . . In this case the extra coal the *Tongariro* was carrying, which was to be used entirely by herself and in her own furnaces, was nothing more or less than ballast. In my opinion, the vessel was in ballast.' *The Tongariro* [1912] P 297 at 300–302, per Bargrave Deane J

IN BEING

'In being' means living or en ventre sa mere. (Perpetuities and Accumulations Act 1964, s 15)

IN CASE OF DEATH

New Zealand 'If death—an event which must inevitably happen—is nevertheless referred to in terms of contingency, such as "in case of death", "in the event of death", or the like, without being coupled to some contingency expressed, the testator is presumed to have had

in his mind some unexpressed circumstance which, in combination with death, would create an event which may or may not happen. Therefore in cases of an immediate gift death spoken of in words of contingency, but without any contingent circumstance being expressed in addition, is held to refer to the contingency of death in the lifetime of the testator as the circumstance he had in his mind which will best fit the requirements of the case.' *JE v JP* [1918] 38 NZLR 161 at 164, 165, per Hosking J; also reported [1918] GLR 696 at 697

IN CHARGE OF

A person shall be deemed not to have been in charge of a motor vehicle if he proves that at the material time the circumstances were such that there was no likelihood of his driving it so long as he remained unfit to drive through drink or drugs. (Road Traffic Act 1988, s 4(3))

[Section 5 of the Act of 1972 imposes penalties for driving, or being in charge, when under the influence of drink or drugs]

[Under the Road Traffic Act 1930, s 15 (repealed; see now the Road Traffic Act 1988, s 4) it was an offence for a person to be 'in charge of' a motor vehicle while under the influence of drink.] 'On a fair consideration of section 15 we know quite well what is meant by referring to a person who is driving or attempting to drive a car, and when the section goes on to refer also to a person "in charge" of a car the reference must be to the person in de facto control, even though he may not be at the time actually driving or attempting to drive.' *Crichton v Burrell* 1915 SLT 365 at 366, per the Lord Justice-General (Cooper)

'In my view the words "in charge of" in s 15 of the Act mean being responsible for the control or driving of the car. They do not mean necessarily that the person concerned is driving or is attempting to drive.' Ibid at 367, per Lord Keith

'It may be that, if a man goes to a public house and leaves his car outside or in the car park and, getting drunk, asks a friend to go and look after the car for him or take the car home, he has put it in charge of somebody else, but if he has not put the vehicle in charge of somebody else he is in charge of it [within the Road Traffic Act 1930, s 15(1) (repealed; see supra)] until he does so.' *Haines v Roberts* [1953] 1 All ER 344 at 345, per Lord Goddard CJ

IN CONNECTION WITH

[The first appellants, promoters of football pools, were convicted under the Betting and Lotteries Act 1934, s 26(1)(a) (repealed; see now the Lotteries and Amusements Act 1976, s 14(1)) of having unlawfully conducted in connection with a business of newsagent and tobacconist a competition in which prizes were offered for forecasting football results. The second appellants, the proprietors of the business, were convicted of aiding and abetting.] 'Section 26(1) simply provides: "It shall be unlawful to conduct . . . in connection with any trade or business . . . (a) any competition in which prizes are offered for forecasts of the result . . . of a future event." . . . Here it is said that the appellant company were conducting their competition in connection with the trade or business of the second appellants. The second appellants are carrying on a business, but the Act does not say "in connection with any person who carries on a trade or business". The Act says: "in connection with any trade or business," and there must be some nexus, as it seems to me, between the carrying on of the competition and the trade or business in respect of which it is said to have been carried on. I do not think the words of the subsection are apt to create an offence in the present case.' *ITP (London) Ltd v Winstanley* [1947] 1 All ER 177 at 178, per Lord Goddard CJ

Australia [The appellant granted a lease of a motor service station and garage and received from the lessees the sum of £1,500 as consideration, inter alia, for a covenant by him against competition. The issue was whether that sum was received by the appellant 'for or in connection with' the goodwill acquired by the lessees within the meaning of s 84 of the Income Tax Assessment Act 1936–1986 (see now s 85A(a)).] 'The words "for or in connection with" imply that a consideration may satisfy the definition as being "in connection with" one of the subjects mentioned, although not "for" it. Now, while it is true that a payment cannot be described as a consideration "for" anything but that which is given in exchange for it, to speak of a consideration being "in connection with" an item of property parted with is to use language quite appropriate to the case of a payment received as consideration "for" something other than the property in question, so long as the receipt of the payment has a substantial relation, in a practical business sense, to that

property. A consideration may be "in connection with" more things than that "for" which it is received.' *Berry v Federal Comr of Taxation* (1953) 89 CLR 653 at 658, per Kitto J

New Zealand The Government Railway Act 1908 (NZ), s 10 empowers the Minister of Railways to fix scales of charges to be paid for goods carried on a railway or stored in, etc, any shed, store, etc, 'in connection with' a railway.] 'In the view of their Lordships these words cannot apply to something done on a space or in a building merely contiguous to or abutting upon a railway, even though it be the property of a railway; if the thing done forms no part of or has no connection with the proper business of a railway, as a carrier of passengers and goods by rail, or in other words that the expression "in connection with a railway" means connected with, subserving and being ancillary to, the business of a railway as such carriers. . . . These words . . . must be directed to something different from propinquity or contiguity, and in their Lordships' view, having regard to all the provisions of the statute, mean in s 10 in connection with the business and operations of a railway as a carrier of goods by rail.' *Hatrick (A) & Co v R* [1923] AC 213 at 225–227, PC, per cur.

IN CONSEQUENCE OF

'It has been a well settled rule for over seventy years, in regard to the construction of marine insurance policies, that where, in an added clause in a policy, there are words like "in consequence thereof", you must, in dealing with causation look at the proximate and not the remote cause.' *Hall Brothers SS Co Ltd v Young* [1939] 1 KB 748 at 761, 762, CA, per MacKinnon LJ

[The Agricultural Holdings Act 1923, s 12(1) (repealed; see now s 34 of the Agricultural Holdings Acts 1948 as amended by the Agricultural Holdings (Notices to Quit) Act 1977) provided for the payment of compensation by a landlord in certain cases where a tenant left a holding 'in consequence of' a notice to quit.] 'The question whether or not a tenant who holds over for any period, be it short or be it long, after the expiration of a notice to quit, and subsequently quits the holding, can be said to have quitted the holding "in consequence of" the notice, is really a question of fact on which the finding of an arbitrator under the Act is conclusive, provided that there is evidence to support it. In spite of the fact that a tenant holds over, it may well be that the notice is what causes him to quit the holding. To explain our meaning, we will give two examples. At the expiration of the notice, the tenant may be in bed seriously ill, and incapable of moving. In the absence of permission to remain, he becomes in law a trespasser. Nevertheless, if when he recovers sufficiently to enable him to be moved, he at once quits the holding, the inevitable conclusion would be that he did so "in consequence of" the notice. His temporary failure to comply with the notice could not break the causal link between the notice and his departure which is all that is postulated by the words "in consequence of". The other example is the case of a tenant who disputes the validity of the notice and requires a decision of the court upon it. Either he or the landlord may (subject to the arbitration provisions if they apply) obtain that decision by an originating summons or by an action for a declaration. If in such a case the court decided against the tenant, and the tenant thereupon quitted the holding, the inevitable inference would, we think, be that he had done so "in consequence of" the notice since the notice and nothing but the notice would have been the effective cause of his departure. On the other hand, there may well be cases in which the arbitrator would be at liberty to find on the facts that the necessary causal link between the notice and the quitting of the holding did not exist.' *Preston v Norfolk County Council* [1947] KB 775 at 784, 785, CA, per Lord Greene MR

IN CONTEMPLATION OF   *See*
CONTEMPLATION

IN COURSE OF DELIVERY

[The Sale of Food and Drugs Act Amendment Act 1879, s 3 (repealed; see now Food Act 1984, s 11(1)(*b*)) empowered an inspector to procure samples of milk 'in course of delivery'.] 'The statute empowers the inspector to procure . . . a sample of milk "in course of delivery", its object being to make certain that any adulteration which may have taken place took place not in the shop or premises of the purchaser, but while the milk was still in the custody of the dairyman. In the present case the sheriff's findings in fact shew

that the inspector allowed the appellant's servant to pour the milk into clean cans belonging to the purchaser, and that he immediately and in the presence of the dairyman's servant took the samples in question from them. I think it would be a strained and mischievous interpretation of the statute to hold that the samples were not taken while the milk was in course of delivery.' *Semple v Dunbar* (1904) 6 F 65 at 67, per Lord Moncrieff

'The statute [Sale of Food and Drugs Act Amendment Act 1879, s 3 (repealed see supra)] does not mean that the question whether the milk is "in course of delivery" must be decided as a question of law, but it is a question of fact for the justices in each case. They have to determine whether there was in point of fact, a cessation of delivery,—whether it had come to an end, or whether it was still in course of being perfected when the sample was taken.' *Cox v Evans* [1917] 1 KB 275 at 282, DC, per Ridley J

IN COURSE OF EMPLOYMENT   *See*
COURSE OF EMPLOYMENT

IN DEFAULT OF

'In my opinion, the words "in default of such issue" are, and as a matter of conveyancing always have been, considered and used as apt words for the introduction of a remainder and not as words of contingency.' *White v Summers* [1908] 2 Ch 256 at 271, per Parker J

IN FAVOUR OF

'The words "in favour of", when used in relation to a bill of exchange, do not ordinarily mean that it is payable only to the person in whose favour it is said to be drawn; the words are equally applied when the bill is made payable to his order. The words "in favour of", therefore, are properly paraphrased by "payable to, or to the order of".' *Meyer & Co Ltd v Decroix, Verley et Cie* [1891] AC 520 at 528, 529, per Lord Herschell

'The current phrase whereby the court says that it exercises its discretion "in favour of" one side conveys the impression that the court is saying that that party's conduct is excusable, or, at any rate, not so heinous as that of the other, whereas the court is often saying no such thing. It is only saying what the statute authorises it to say, namely, that it is exercising its discretion to grant a divorce.' *Sydenham v Sydenham* [1949] 2 All ER 196 at 198, CA, per Denning LJ

IN FULL

'In this case the plaintiff was insured with the defendant under a time policy on freight by his steamship *Ivy* valued at £950. To the policy were attached the Institute Time Clauses— Freight—1910, by No 5 of which "In the event of total loss, whether absolute or constructive, of the steamer the amount underwritten by this policy shall be paid in full, whether the steamer be fully or only partly loaded, or in ballast, chartered or unchartered," and the parties desire to have the construction of that clause decided. It is agreed that the ship while on a voyage from the Baltic to Manchester stranded in the Mersey and became a constructive total loss, that she was subsequently towed up to Manchester and discharged her cargo, whereupon the sum of £630 12s was paid to the plaintiff by the cargo owners for freight. Notwithstanding the receipt and retention of that sum by the plaintiff he contends that he is entitled to be paid on the policy "in full". . . . It is argued that the effect of the words "in full" is the same as if they were "without benefit of salvage", but it is to my mind clearly contrary to the intention of the parties to treat this clause as a wagering policy. . . . In my opinion that clause was introduced for the purpose of meeting the hardship that has long been felt to exist that a shipowner, who has given notice of abandonment and has consequently lost his right to the freight subsequently earned, is precluded from suing on the policy on freight. In *United Kingdom Mutual Steamship Assurance Assocn v Boulton* [(1898) 3 Com Cas 330], where the rules of a freight club contained a very similar clause, Bigham J construed it as intended to secure that where freight was lost to the shipowner not by perils of the sea but by operation of the notice of abandonment in transferring to the underwriters on hull the freight which was eventually earned, the assured should nevertheless recover it from the underwriters on freight as though it had been lost entirely by perils of the sea.' *Coker v Bolton* [1912] 3 KB 315 at 318–320, per Hamilton J

IN GOOD FAITH   *See* GOOD FAITH

IN HAND

[The articles of a company provided that dividends should not be paid except out of profits, and that a dividend should be declared as often as the profits 'in hand' were sufficient to pay 5 per cent on the capital, subject to the resolutions of a general meeting.] 'If we were to lay down as a rule that there must be actually cash in hand, or at the bankers of the company, to the full amount of the dividend declared, we should be laying down a rule which, in my judgment, would be inconsistent with what I understand and believe to be the custom of all companies of this description, and also inconsistent with mercantile usage, and we should be laying down a rule which would open the door to and encourage a very great amount of litigation, because there are very few dividends indeed which would not be open to more or less question if such a rule as that were laid down. I think that in the absence of any fraudulent intent as against the shareholders, or as against the creditors or the public, the court ought not to be astute in searching out minute errors in calculation, in an account honestly made out and openly declared; especially as in the present case, where the account was submitted to, and the dividend consequent upon it was ratified, by the general meeting.' *Re Mercantile Trading Co Stringer's Case* (1869) 4 Ch App 475 at 492, 493, per Selwyn LJ

'We do not understand "available balance in hand" merely to mean money in the coffers of the defendant society, but money which without undue loss or undue delay they could realise.' *Brett v Monarch Investment Building Society* [1894] 1 QB 367 at 371, 372, CA, per Lopes LJ

IN LOCO PARENTIS

'As regards a child, a person not the father of the child may put himself in the position of one in loco parentis to the child, and so incur the obligation to make a provision for the child. Now what is the meaning of the expression "a person in loco parentis"? I cannot do better than refer to the definition of it given by Lord Eldon in *Ex p Pye* [(1811) 18 Ves 140], referred to and approved of by Lord Cottenham in *Powys v Mansfield* [(1837) 3 My & Cr 359]. Lord Eldon says it is a person "meaning to put himself in loco parentis; in the situation of the person described as the lawful father of the child". Upon that Lord

Cottenham observes, "but this definition must, I conceive, be considered as applicable to those parental offices and duties to which the subject in question has reference, namely, to the office and duty of the parent to make provision for the child. The offices and duties of a parent are infinitely various, some having no connection whatever with making a provision for a child; and it would be most illogical, from the mere exercise of any such offices or duties by one not the father, to infer an intention of such person to assume also the duty of providing for the child". So that a person in loco parentis means a person taking upon himself the duty of a father of a child to make a provision for that child.' *Bennet v Bennet* (1879) 10 Ch D 474 at 477, per Jessel MR

Canada 'A person in loco parentis to a child is one who has acted so as to evidence his intention of placing himself towards the child in the situation which is ordinarily occupied by the father for the provision of the child's pecuniary wants. In Vol 22 of the Cyclopædia of Law and Procedure, at p 1066 the following definition of the phrase in loco parentis is given "When used to designate a person it means one who puts himself in the situation of a lawful father to a child with reference to the office and duty of making provision for the child".' *Shtitz v Canadian National Rly Co* [1927] 1 WWR 193 at 201, CA, per Turgeon JA

Canada [The Divorce Act, RSC 1970, c D–8, s 2 provides that 'child' of a husband and wife includes any person to whom the husband and wife stand in loco parentis and any person of whom either the husband or the wife is a parent and to whom the other of them stands in loco parentis. 'In the case before me the petitioner, husband, acted as father to this boy right up to the date of trial and while he expressed a suspicion of the boy's paternity it is quite clear from the evidence, particularly of the respondent wife, that she gave him to believe the boy was issue of the marriage. To come within the meaning of "child" as used in the Divorce Act the person must either be the actual issue of the parties or in the position where he is treated in loco parentis in the view I take of the definition. . . . To be in loco parentis it seems to me the husband must "intend" to place himself in the position towards the child ordinarily occupied by the father, which intention must be based on the knowledge that someone else is the father.' *Aksugyuk v Aksugyuk* [1975] 2 WWR 91 at 94, NWTSC, per Morrow J

IN MOTION

[The Factories Act 1937, s 16 (repealed; see now the Factories Act 1961, s 16) provided that all fencing and safeguards provided under the Act should be constantly maintained and kept in position while the protected parts of the machinery were 'in motion'.] 'Using the phrase in its ordinary sense, I do not think that one would naturally say of a man moving parts of a machine round [by hand] to a required position [in order to effect repairs] that he had set the machine or its parts in motion. The phrase "in motion" appears to me to be more apt to describe a continuing state of motion lasting, or intended to last, for an appreciable time.' *Richard Thomas & Baldwins Ltd v Cummings* [1955] 1 All ER 285 at 290, HL, per Lord Reid; see also [1955] AC 32s

'I . . . think it is impossible to prescribe an exhaustive definition of the terms "in motion" or "in use" as they are used in s 16 of the Factories Act 1937 [repealed; see *supra*]. One can say that "in motion" means something more than merely in movement; that a machine may be put "in motion" manually as well as by power; and that a machine may be "in use" notwithstanding some temporary halt in the running of it. Beyond this, general guidance is difficult to give, and any attempt at it might be misconceived. In particular, I do not think that it would be right to say that a machine is "in motion" when it is being run for the industrial purpose it was installed to achieve, but not "in motion" when being run for some preparatory purpose.' *Knight v Leamington Spa Courier Ltd* [1961] 2 All ER 666 at 671, CA, per Donovan J; also reported [1961] 2 QB 253 at 265

'There is, I think, a broad distinction between a thing which is "being moved" slowly and a thing which is "in motion" at a fast pace.' *Stanbrook v Waterlow & Sons Ltd* [1964] 2 All ER 506 at 508, CA, per Lord Denning MR

'In *Richard Thomas & Baldwins Ltd v Cummings* [supra] the House of Lords were unanimous in concluding that some special meaning must be given to the phrase "in motion"; but they were not unanimous as to the exact definition or description of that special meaning. Nevertheless, in my view the prevalent opinion can be found in the speeches of Lord Porter, Lord Reid and Lord Keith of Avonholm. . . . I think that . . . one can deduce from *Richard Thomas & Baldwins Ltd v Cummings* these propositions. First: in ascertaining whether machinery in fact moving is "in motion" for the purposes of the section, regard should be had to the character of the movement more than to its purpose. If machinery is revolving rapidly in a place where a workman may come in contact with it, the guard should be kept in place on the machinery whatever may be the purpose for which the movement is being made, whether it be production, examination, demonstration, adjustment, repairing, testing, or whatever the purpose may be. Secondly: the obvious and typical case of machinery in motion is, of course, machinery running in the usual way in its ordinary course of operation. Thirdly: there must, however, be other cases of machinery which is "in motion", because the object of the statute is to protect the workman, and machinery may be running dangerously even though not in the ordinary course of operation or perhaps even though not running in the usual way. Fourthly: in deciding whether in a particular case the movement is or is not of such a character that the machinery is "in motion", the factors to be taken into account include the speed of the movement, its duration, the method of starting the machinery, and probably to some extent or in some cases also the purpose for which the movement has been instituted. Then, fifthly: when the factors are rightly taken into account, it must be a question of fact and of degree whether or not the machinery is "in motion" within the meaning of the section.' *Mitchell v Westin (WS) Ltd* [1965] 1 All ER 657 at 664, CA, per Pearson LJ

IN ORDER

[A clause in a statute contained the phrase 'with intent, or in order that.'] 'The Attorney-General says that he supposes that the words "in order" were added to avoid some evasion or quibble. I believe that they were added to leave no doubt as to the meaning: the expression "in order" is explained in Todd's Johnson to signify "means to an end", and Jeremy Taylor, Tillotson, and Swift, are quoted as authorities; the passage from Swift, "One man pursues power in order to wealth" that is, power is the "means", wealth is "the end".' *A-G v Sillem* (1864) 2 H & C 431 at 525, per Pollock CB

[Rule 3(2) of the Land Registration (Official Searches) Rules 1969 (revoked; see now SI 1981/1135) provided that an application for an official search should, if 'in order', be entered in the day list.] 'The 1969 rules relating to

official searches ought to be construed, if possible, in such a way as to give them practical efficacy. So great is the number of applications lodged with the Land Registry that if every application had to be in perfect order before it was accepted, a large proportion of the applications would fail to get priority under the 1969 rules owing to formal defects, and the whole official search procedure would be in jeopardy. In my judgment therefore the words "in order" can fairly, and should be, construed as "substantially in order" rather than "in perfect order".' *Smith v Morrison Smith v Chief Land Registrar* [1974] 1 All ER 957 at 973, per Plowman J

IN PUBLIC   *See* PUBLIC; PUBLIC PLACE

IN PURSUANCE OF

Canada 'The phrase "in pursuance of" is much more restrictive than the phrase "by reason of". The one imports a notion of obligation—of duty to do a thing; the other suggests merely the power or authority to do it. The one is mandatory; the other is permissive.' *Dobush v Greater Winnipeg Water District* [1945] 2 WWR 371 at 374, per Dysart J

IN REGULAR TURN

[Article 3 of a charterparty provided that cargo was to be loaded 'in regular turn' as customary.] 'Under art 3 the cargo is to be loaded "in regular turn as customary at the rate of one thousand tons a day." . . . I do not appreciate the special efficacy supposed to belong to the actual words "in regular turn." . . . The . . . words would be satisfied, when she [the ship] was lying in the bay next in turn to go to the berth, as soon as the ship, then loading in the berth, should complete her loading and haul off. It follows that she might be "in regular turn" and yet, at that moment and for some time to come, be unable to load.' *United States Shipping Board v Strick (Frank C) & Co Ltd* [1926] AC 545 at 569, 576, HL, per Lord Sumner

IN RELATION TO

[The Trade Marks Act 1938, provides that the registration of a person as proprietor of a trade mark in respect of goods shall give him the exclusive right to the use of the trade mark in relation to those goods; and that right shall be deemed to be infringed by any person who uses a mark identical with it, or so nearly resembling it as to be likely to deceive or cause confusion, in the course of trade, 'in relation to' any goods in respect of which it is registered.] 'The old phrase "in connection with goods" seems, prima facie, to be intended to deal with the case where for physical reasons the mark cannot be impressed on the goods but is used in such connection as . . . to manifest that the mark is used as an indication of the origin of the particular physical object in connection with which the mark is used. The phrase "in relation to" would seem to be used in order to cover the case of the use of a mark in an advertisement where there is no impression of the mark on an object . . . but the mark is used to indicate the origin not of a specific physical object offered for sale but of the goods advertised; that is, of the products, whether at the moment in physical existence or not, which have or will have their origin in the owner of the mark. In view of the use of this phrase "in relation to" in the section . . . on which this case turns, the change in the language used to define a trade mark is, in my view, not unimportant.' *Bismag Ltd v Amblins (Chemists) Ltd* [1940] 1 Ch 667 at 692, 693, CA, per Clauson LJ

IN RESPECT OF

'During the argument I asked the plaintiff's counsel what meaning could be given to the words "or in respect of", which are in the statute [Gaming Act 1892, s 1] in addition to the word "under". . . . The only suggestion made in answer to my question was that the words "or in respect of" were tautological and meant the same thing as "under". I cannot think so. It is a short Act of Parliament, and the language used is very clear and intelligible. I think that the words were put in purposely; and, if they are to be given any meaning at all, they must be intended to strike at transactions such as this [the placing of bets through an agent]. I do not think it makes any difference whether the plaintiff knew, or did not know, that the payments he made were in payment of bets; because, if those payments were made "in respect of" betting contracts, he is brought within the very words of the Act [and so could not recover the sums paid from the defendant, who had made the original bets].' *Tatam v Reeve* [1893] 1 QB 44 at 48, per Wills J

'The Gaming Act 1892, enacts that "any promise", express or implied, to pay any person any sum of money paid by him under or in respect of any contract or agreement rendered null and void by the Act of 8 & 9 Vict c 109 . . . shall be null and void, and no action shall be brought or maintained to recover any such sum of money.' The ground of the decision in *Tatam v Reeve* [supra] was that effect must be given to the words "in respect of" as well as to the word "under" in the Gaming Act 1892, and that the action in that case was upon an implied promise to repay sums which had been paid "in respect of" gaming or wagering contracts. So likewise in the present case the action is upon an implied promise . . . to pay to the bankrupt a sum of money paid by him "in respect of" contracts or agreements made by way of gaming or wagering.' *Saffery v Mayer* [1901] 1 QB 11 at 18, 19, CA, per Stirling LJ

Australia 'The words "in respect of" are difficult of definition, but they have the widest possible meaning of any expression intended to convey some connection or relation between the two subject-matters to which the words refer.' *Trustees Executors & Agency Co Ltd v Reilly* [1941] VLR 110 at 111, per Mann CJ

IN THE COURSE OF EMPLOYMENT *See* COURSE OF EMPLOYMENT

IN THE FIRST PLACE

'Unless a contrary intent appear upon the will, it must be presumed that a testator considers that he has property sufficient to answer all his legacies; and that he has an equal intention that all should be equally paid. This presumption of equality is not to be repelled by ambiguous expressions, but must prevail, unless there be clear intent to the contrary. . . . The expressions, "In the first place, I direct that my executors shall pay to A, then to B, then to C", are not evidence of such intent, for they mark only the order in which it occurs to the testator to give the directions to his executors. The expressions, "I direct that my executors shall, in the first place, pay to A, in the next place, to B, then to C", are not evidence of such intent, because they do not necessarily import more than the order of payment; that A shall be paid by my executors in the first place, or out of the first monies which they have applicable to the payment of legacies; B in the next place, or next in order; and then, or next in order, C;

and these expressions are therefore consistent with the presumed intention that all shall be equally paid in their order.' *Beeston v Booth* (1819) 4 Madd 161 at 168, 169, per Leach V-C

'In my opinion, by using the words " in the first place" and "in the next place" the testator is merely giving a list or catalogue of the payments which the trustees are to make out of the proceeds of the sale and conversion of his estate; and . . . therefore, the words which the testator has used do not indicate that the nephews are to have any priority of interest over the nieces, and the legacies given to the nephews and . . . to the nieces must accordingly rank pari passu.' *Re Harris, Harris v Harris* [1912] 2 Ch 241 at 248–250, per Warrington J

IN THE LIGHT OF

[A wife applied for the alteration of the terms of a maintenance agreement under s 1(3) of the Maintenance Agreements Act 1957 (repealed; see now the Matrimonial Causes Act 1973, s 35(2)), by reason of a change in the circumstances 'in the light of' which the original financial arrangements were made.] 'The expression "circumstances in the light of which" means, in our judgment, circumstances which influenced the parties, and were within their contemplation.' *K v K* [1961] 2 All ER 266 at 269, CA, per cur.

IN THE PRESENCE OF

The testator's signature must be made or acknowledged by him in the presence of two or more witnesses present at the same time. In the testator's presence, each witness must attest and sign the will or, in the case of a will of a testator who dies on or after 1st January 1983, either attest and sign the will or acknowledge his signature. The testator's complete signature must be made or acknowledged when both the attesting witnesses are actually present at the same time, and both witnesses must attest and subscribe after the testator's signature has been so made or acknowledged. Although it is not essential for the attesting witnesses to sign in the presence of each other, it is usual for them to do so. Each witness should be able to say with truth that he has seen the testator sign the document but it is not necessary that the witness should know that it is the testator's will. However, there is no sufficient acknowledgment unless the witnesses either saw or had the opportunity of seeing the signature, even though the testator expressly states that the paper to be attested is his will or that his signature is inside the will. (50 Halsbury's Laws (4th edn) para 261)

'The statute [Statute of Frauds 1677 (see now the Wills Act 1837, s 9 as substituted by the Administration of Justice Act 1982, s 17] required attesting in his presence, to prevent obtruding another will in place of the true one. It is enough if the testator might see, it is not necessary that he should actually see them signing; for at that rate if a man should but turn his back, or look off, it would vitiate the will. Here the signing was in the view of the testator; he might have seen it, and that is enough. So if the testator being sick should be in bed and the curtain drawn.' *Shires v Glascock* (1685) 2 Salk 688 at 688, per cur.

[The Wills Act 1837 s 9, (as substituted; see supra) enacts that no will shall be valid unless (inter alia) the signature of the testator is made 'in the presence of' two or more witnesses present at the same time.] 'It appears that the testatrix prepared the . . . will herself and then took it to a shop, a photograph of which was produced with a variety of groceries and other things shewn therein, and in particular two counters one on the left and the other on the right hand side of the shop. The two witnesses, or people exceedingly like them, are shewn standing behind the respective counters. The testatrix appears to have proceeded straight to the left-hand counter, where Miss Jeffery was, and asked her to witness her will. She stood with her back towards the other counter, and behind her was a commercial traveller doing business with Mr Read, the other witness in the case. It appears, as far as I understand the evidence, that the testatrix signed her name at the left-hand counter, over which Miss Jeffery was leaning, and then Miss Jeffery signed her name as it appears on the document. Up to this time Mr Read had been engrossed with the commercial traveller, and had not the slightest idea of what was going on at the other counter. It is urged that, even if he were conscious that the testatrix was there, he did not see anything of the transaction at the other counter; he says so himself. In fact, he did not know, and had no opportunity of knowing, what was going on there. The witness, Miss Jeffery, having completed her signature, marched round the shop and asked Mr Read to come from his counter and go round to where the testatrix still was, Miss Jeffery taking up the position which Mr Read vacated. Mr Read accordingly went round, and the testatrix said to him, "This is my will". Mr Read then signed his name to the document. . . . I fail to see how the testatrix's signature can be said to have been affixed to the document in the presence of Mr Read, when, although he was in the shop, he had no idea and saw nothing of what was going on at the time, and, moreover, had no opportunity of seeing, there being, as I have said, another person in the shop between him and the testatrix. . . . The Wills Act is very precise, and must be applied with strictness.' *Brown v Skirrow* [1902] P 3 at 6, 7, per Gorell Barnes J

IN THE PUBLIC INTEREST *See*
PUBLIC INTEREST

INABILITY

To act

Canada '"Inability to act" [of a judge] may or may not involve absence. It is usually accompanied by physical absence; and absence may be due to physical inability to be present.' *Brunet v R* (1918) 57 SCR 83 at 91, per Anglin J

INACCESSIBLE

[A clause in a bill of lading provided that if a port to which goods were to be carried should be 'inaccessible on account of ice', the master might discharge the goods at some other port.] 'This vessel went from Middlesbrough to Japan to deliver most of her cargo, and then sailed for Vladivostock. When she arrived within forty miles of Vladivostock she found she could not get into the port by reason of ice. . . . The vessel tried for three days in vain to get through the ice and then went back to Nagasaki, and, by order telegraphed from England, there discharged her cargo. The next day after her turning back the ice cleared off, the access was safe, and other vessels entered. This vessel went back to Nagasaki, and it is claimed that she was entitled to do so. Is this conduct justifiable within the terms of the fourth clause of the bill of lading? Was the port of Vladivostock "inaccessible" on account of ice? At that moment, and for two or three days, undoubtedly it was; but the meaning of this bill of lading, in my opinion, is that the port must be inaccessible in a commercial sense so that a ship cannot enter without inordinate delay. There is no ground for saying that a delay of three days on a journey so long could

be regarded as inordinate delay.' *SS Knutsford Ltd v Tillmanns & Co* [1908] AC 406 at 407, 408, per Lord Loreburn LC

INACCURATE

South Africa 'The ordinary meaning of inaccurate information is information which is in fact "incorrect", whereas "false" information would ordinarily mean information that is known by the informant to be incorrect.' *R v Kruger* 1943 TPD 36, per Broome J

INADVERTANCE

[The Corrupt and Illegal Practices Prevention Act 1883, s 23(b) and the Municipal Elections (Corrupt and Illegal Practices) Act 1884, s 20 (repealed; see now Representation of the People Act 1983, s 167(2)(b)) empowered the court to except an act or omission of a candidate or election agent at an election from being an illegal practice, if such act or omission arose from 'inadvertence'.] 'The legislature has used the word "inadvertence" to give wide powers to the court. Inadvertence means negligence or carelessness, where the circumstances show an absence of bad faith. In cases of that sort, we will deem that the offence was done inadvertently.' *Re County Council Elections, ex p Lenanton, ex p Pierce* (1889) 53 JP 263 at 263, DC, per Huddleston B

'Inadvertence is a word which is capable of several interpretations and which has been interpreted in various ways not always I think consistent with one another. It may mean mere thoughtlessness, it may mean what is equivalent to a mere mistake, but in this case it was also an ignorance of the law. . . . Persons might be fairly described as acting inadvertently because they did not know the law . . . inadvertence does not cover a case where in the immediate duty which he is performing he ought to have a full knowledge of the law.' *West Bromwich Case* (1911) 6 O'M & H 256 at 287, per Ridley J

'The first question is whether or not ignorance of the law may fall within the word "inadvertence". This is a legal question of ever-recurring practical importance. . . . In several dictionaries—e.g., the Imperial Dictionary, Dr Worcester's Dictionary, and Webster's Dictionary—the word "inadvertent" seems to be treated as substantially equivalent to the words "careless" or "negligent". In Dr Johnson's Dictionary, I see "inadvertence" is defined as "carelessness, negligence, inattention". . . . In my own view it is clear that ignorance of the law may fall within the word "inadvertence".' *Nichol v Fearby, Nichol v Robinson* [1923] 1 KB 480 at 496–498, per McCardie J

'As regards inadvertence, of course, it is a matter of degree. It is not every act of inadvertence which amounts to negligence. Equally, in certain circumstances inadvertence may well amount to negligence. It must depend on all the facts of the case.' *Hicks v British Transport Commission* [1958] 2 All ER 39 at 50, CA, per Sellers LJ

INALIENABLE

[By an ante-nuptial settlement property was settled upon a wife to the intent that the same might be and remain a separate and 'inalienable' provision for her during coverture.] 'Pursuing the trusts of this very remarkable instrument, we find inalienability referred to in a certain way, but in company with such other words and such expressions as to render the argument not wholly unreasonable, that, notwithstanding the word "inalienable", this lady was to have the absolute power over the property, so as in effect to enable her to defeat the settlement by giving the whole over to her husband. I think, however, that there is not enough in the settlement to defeat the plain meaning of the word "inalienable", and in my judgment the true interpretation of the settlement is that during the coverture—during the time as yet existing during which both the husband and the wife are living—the whole income (and I am now only speaking of income and in no way referring to what may become of the capital after the death of either the husband or the wife) of the property was to be for her separate use without power of anticipation, and therefore in that sense inalienable.' *Spring v Pride* (1864) 4 De G J & Sm 395 at 402, 403, per Bruce LJ

INAPPRECIABLE

'We are not prepared to say that the learned judge at nisi prius was correct in his interpretation of the word "inappreciable" when connected with the word "quantity", nor sure that he was not; for the word "inappreciable" or "unappreciable" is one of a new coinage, not to be found in Johnson's Dictionary or Richardson's. The word "appreciate" first appears in our dictionaries in the last edition of Johnson, by Todd, 1827, with the explanation "to estimate", "to value", and assuming that to be the true meaning, which we suppose it is, the compound adjective signifies that the quantities were not capable of being estimated or valued.' *Embrey v Owen* (1851) 6 Exch 353 at 367, per cur.

INATTENTION

'I am of opinion that the words "mismanagement" and "inattention" are not synonymous. The one is active, the other passive; the one denotes commission, the other omission.' *Brooks v Blanshard* (1833) 1 Cr & M 779 at 793, per Vaughan B

INCAPABLE

A person may be treated as being, as the result of an injury or disease or as the joint result of two or more injuries or diseases, totally incapable of work and likely to remain so incapable for a considerable period notwithstanding that the disability resulting from the injury or disease or, as the case may be, from the injuries or diseases taken together is not such as to prevent him from being capable of work, if it is likely to prevent his earnings (including any remuneration or profit derived from a gainful occupation) exceeding in a year such amount as is for the time being prescribed in pursuance of section 58(3) of the Social Security Act [1975]. (Industrial Injuries and Diseases (Old Cases) Act 1975, s 14(4)(b) as amended by s 11(5) of the Social Security (Miscellaneous Provisions) Act 1977)

[The Trustee Act 1850, s 32 (repealed; see now Trustee Act 1925, s 36(1)), enabled the court to appoint a new trustee in the place of a trustee who had become 'incapable' of acting in the trusts.] 'One instance of incapacity is where the trustee is residing abroad. That is a case usually provided for by settlements and wills, but not, in terms, by the 32nd section. If a trustee is in such a condition that he cannot act properly in his trust, and is, in fact, incapable of acting, it is undoubtedly expedient for the court to appoint a new trustee in his place.' *Re Lemann's Trusts* (1883) 22 Ch D 633 at 635, per Chitty J

New Zealand [The Crimes Act 1908, s 431(4) (NZ) (repealed; see now the Crimes Act 1961, s 374(3)) provided, inter alia, procedure in cases where a juror, in the course of a trial, became 'incapable' of continuing to perform his duty.] 'In my opinion, the phrase "incapable of continuing to perform their duty" should be given a reasonable construction, and it is not limited to cases of sudden illness on the part of the juror himself, though that would be the normal and likely situation. We require of a juror his mind, not his body. I am of opinion, supported as I am by the doctor's evidence, that in this case [a juror's wife having died during the course of a trial] it is right that I should hold, and I do hold, that this juryman has been rendered incapable of continuing to perform his duty.' *R v Kelman* [1957] NZLR 904 at 905, 906, per North J

INCAPACITY

Australia 'Consideration of the relevant provisions of the Act [Repatriation Act 1920 (Cth)] leads, in our view, to the conclusion that, in a general sense, the word "incapacity", used in the Act generally and s 101 and Sch 3 table C in particular, refers to a physical or mental disability or impairment rather than inability to work or earn. The consistent references to a person "suffering" an incapacity, the references to an incapacity "from which" a person "has died", the consistent link, as alternatives, between "incapacity" and "death", the terms of the partial definition of incapacity in s 23 as including "incapacity that arose from disease" and the policy underlying the Schedules of paying an increased pension over that payable in respect of "total incapacity" in the event that the incapacitated person is unable to earn other than a negligible percentage of a living wage all point to that conclusion.' *Repatriation Commission v Moss* (1982) 59 FLR 226 at 240, per Deane and Fitzgerald JJ

For work

[The Workmen's Compensation Act 1906, Sch 1, para 1(b) (repealed) dealt with the scale of compensation for injury resulting in 'incapacity' to work.] 'In the ordinary and popular meaning which we are to attach to the language of this statute I think there is incapacity for work when a man has a physical defect which makes his labour unsaleable in any market reasonably accessible to him, and there is a partial incapacity for work when such a defect makes his labour saleable for less than it would otherwise fetch.' *Ball v Hunt*

(William) & Sons Ltd [1912] AC 496 at 499, 500 per Earl Loreburn LC

'"Incapacity for work" as the phrase is used in the schedule seems to me to be a compendious expression meaning inability to earn wages or full wages as the case may be at the work in which the injured workman was employed at the time of the accident.' Ibid at 500, per Lord Macnaghten

Australia [The Workers' Compensation Act 1926–1986 (NSW), s 11(2) deals with the subject of partial 'incapacity' for pre-injury employment.] 'We have come to the conclusion that the words in s 11(2), "partially incapacitated for pre-injury employment", refer to physical incapacity, even though in the Act the words "incapacity for work" have the economic sense which has been established over the years. It seems to us that in s 11(2) the Legislature was looking at the position of a worker who could do some of the work, but not all of the work, which was involved in his pre-injury job. Upon the view which has been adopted, if he is not able to do any of the work then the subsection cannot apply but if he is able to do some of the work then it is the duty of the employer to provide him with some work. We can see no reason for introducing into the concept of incapacity for pre-injury employment some intention of the Legislature that if employers did not like to employ men who were thus partially incapacitated then such a person would have to be regarded as totally incapacitated for pre-injury employment and no obligation would be placed on the employer under s 11(2).' *Sinanoglou v Australian Iron & Steel Pty Ltd* (1967) 68 SR (NSW) 279 at 289, per McLelland and Jacobs JJA

Of infant

An infant is under a general incapacity to exercise the rights of citizenship or perform civil duties, or to hold public or private offices or perform the duties incidental to them.

With certain exceptions, an infant may not hold an office or post of public and pecuniary trust. Accordingly he may not act as the clerk of a court where it is part of the duties to receive money, nor as a bailiff or receiver. If a peer, he may not sit or vote in the House of Lords, nor is an infant eligible for the House of Commons. A person is not qualified to be elected and to be a member of a local authority unless on the relevant day he has attained the age of twenty-one years. For the purposes of the Representation of the People Acts a person is of voting age if he is of the age of eighteen years or over; and, if otherwise qualified, a person who is of voting age on the date of the poll at a parliamentary or local government election is entitled to vote as an elector, whether or not he is of voting age on the qualifying date.

An infant is not qualified to serve on a jury. (24 Halsbury's Laws (4th edn) paras 492, 493).

To consummate marriage

'First the onus of proving that a marriage has not been consummated and that the non-consummation was due to the incurable incapacity of the respondent lies on the petitioner. When one talks of "incapacity" and "incurable incapacity", there does not really appear to be much difference between them; for if incapacity is not incurable, then it is not incapacity. Secondly, if it is established that the marriage has not been consummated and that the petitioner is capable, the fact of non-consummation after a reasonable period gives rise to an inference, especially perhaps in undefended cases, that the non-consummation was due to the incapacity of the respondent; and naturally the longer the period that that state of affairs is continued, the stronger the inference may be.' *S v S (otherwise W)* [1962] 2 All ER 816 at 818, 819, CA, per Davies LJ; also reported in [1963] P 162 at 171

INCENDIARISM

'I am of opinion that the word "incendiarism", as used in the condition in question [a condition in a fire policy], cannot be read in the limited sense which has been contended [i.e. as acts of incendiarism committed in the houses described in the policy], but that it includes any act of incendiarism, wherever committed, which directly caused the loss or damage sued for.' *Walker v London & Provincial Insurance Co* (1888) 22 LR Ir 572 at 575, per Palles CB

INCEST

Man

(1) It is an offence for a man to have sexual intercourse with a woman whom he knows to be his grand-daughter, daughter, sister or mother.
(2) In the foregoing subsection 'sister' includes half-sister, and for the purposes of that subsection any expression importing a

relationship between two people shall be taken to apply notwithstanding that the relationship is not traced through lawful wedlock.
(Sexual Offences Act 1956, s 10)

Woman

(1) It is an offence for a woman of the age of sixteen or over to permit a man whom she knows to be her grandfather, father, brother or son to have sexual intercourse with her by her consent.
(2) In the foregoing subsection 'brother' includes half-brother, and for the purposes of that subsection any expression importing a relationship between two people shall be taken to apply notwithstanding that the relationship is not traced through lawful wedlock.
(Sexual Offences Act 1956, s 11)

INCHMAREE CLAUSE

It is now customary to include in policies [of marine insurance] a clause expressly making the policy cover loss of or damage to the subject matter insured directly caused by accidents in loading, discharging or shifting cargo or fuel; explosions on shipboard or elsewhere; breakdown of or accident to nuclear installations or reactors on shipboard or elsewhere; bursting of boilers, breakage of shafts or any latent defect in the machinery or hull; negligence of master, officers, crew or pilots; negligence of repairers provided those repairers are not the assured; contact with aircraft; contact with any land conveyance, dock or harbour equipment or installation, earthquake, volcanic eruption or lightning; provided that such loss or damage has not resulted from want of due diligence by the assured, owners or managers. Masters, officers, crew or pilots are not to be considered as part owners within the meaning of the clause should they hold shares in the vessel. (25 Halsbury's Laws (4th edn) para 168)

[So called because of an accident, in 1884, to a donkey-pump in the steamer *Inchmaree*, which was held by the House of Lords not to be covered by the words 'perils of the sea' or any other of the general words of the form of marine insurance policy then in use. See *Thames and Mersey Marine Insurance Co Ltd v Hamilton, Fraser and Co* (1887) 12 App Cas 484, HL]

'The clause I have to construe is commonly

known as the "Inchmaree Clause". The machinery of the *Inchmaree* was damaged by an explosion. . . . The House of Lords in *Thames & Mersey Marine Insurance Co v Hamilton, Fraser & Co* [(1887 12 App Cas 484] held that such a damage was not recoverable either as a peril of the sea or under the general words in a Lloyd's policy. The Inchmaree Clause was introduced to give the protection denied by this decision. It covers the negligence of servants, it covers explosion and bursting of boilers, it mentions breakage of shafts, which is rather a damage in itself than a peril causing damage, and it then covers loss or damage through latent defects.' *Hutchins Brothers v Royal Exchange Assurance Corpn* [1911] 2 KB 398 at 403, 404, CA, per Scrutton J

'I am . . . of opinion that clause 7 [in a policy of marine insurance], known as the "Inchmaree" clause, is not to be read as inserted into or expanding the description of risks contained in the policy, but is to be regarded simply as a supplemental and independent clause, adding to the risks covered loss or damage to hull or machinery arising out of the negligence of those managing the ship, or from, among other things, breakage of shafts or latent defects. Clause 7 does not in this view enlarge the genus, but simply provides that if this kind of accident happens it is to be covered independently as an addition to the perils described in the policy.' *Stott (Baltic) Steamers Ltd v Marten* [1916] 1 AC 304 at 308, per Viscount Haldane.

INCIDENTAL TO   *See also* IN

'Strangely enough, there is no authority, so I am told, as to the meaning of the words "and incidental to" and what they add to the words "costs of" in an order for costs. In my judgment the words "and incidental to" as used in the order . . . "costs of and incidental to the negotiations" mean "costs of and consequent on the negotiations", and costs incurred before negotiations commenced cannot be said to be costs incidental to the negotiations.' *Re Fahy's Will Trusts, McKnight v Fahy* [1962] 1 All ER 73 at 75, per Plowman J

INCITE   *See* ENCOURAGE

INCITEMENT   *See also* ENCOURAGE

'It is contended, that the offence charged in the second count, of which the defendant has been

convicted, is no misdemeanor, because it amounts only to a bare wish or desire of the mind to do an illegal act. If that were so, I agree that it would not be indictable. But this is a charge of an act done; namely, an actual solicitation of a servant to rob his master, and not merely a wish or desire that he should do so. A solicitation or inciting of another, by whatever means it is attempted, is an act done; and that such an act done with a criminal intent is punishable by indictment has been clearly established.' *R v Higgins* (1801) 2 East 5 at 22, 23, per Le Blanc J

INCLOSED   *See also* ENCLOSED LAND

'Inclosed land' includes any land in the exclusive occupation of one or more persons for agricultural purposes, though not separated by a fence or otherwise from adjoining land of another person, or from a highway. (Highways Act 1980, s 45(12))

[The Highway Act 1835, s 51 (repealed; see now Highways Act 1980, s 45) enabled a surveyor of highways to take materials from any waste land or common ground, river, or brook, but under s 53 (see now s 45(5)(b) of the Act of 1980) he could not remove materials from any 'inclosed' land or ground without giving written notice to the owner of the premises from which such materials were intended to be taken.] 'The question is whether the powers of a surveyor under s 51 of the Highway Act 1835, extend to rivers or brooks in inclosed lands. In my opinion they do not. I should have been of that opinion apart from the stat 4 & 5 Vict c 51 [Highway Act 1841 (repealed)], because I think the scheme of the Highway Act 1835, was to distinguish between waste or common ground and inclosed ground, or ground held in private occupation, and whereas it gave the surveyor the right of his own motion to take or get stones from the common or waste ground, including the beds of rivers or brooks on common or waste ground, it gave him the like rights on inclosed ground only after giving the owner a month's notice and obtaining the licence of the justices. I think the provisions of s 53 were intended to apply to rivers and brooks in inclosed lands as much as to any other part of such lands. In law the bed of a river is as much a part of the close as the middle of the close.' *Allinson v Cumberland County Council* (1907) 71 JP 398 at 399, DC, per Lawrence J

[The respondent was charged with being found in an 'inclosed' yard for an unlawful purpose, contrary to s 4 of the Vagrancy Act 1824.] 'I am content to take the second part of the New Oxford English Dictionary's definition of a "yard" as the starting-point of my explanation of what is meant by an "inclosed yard" for the purposes of the Act: an "area surrounded by walls or buildings within the precincts of a house, castle, inn, etc." To "walls or buildings" I would add "fences". Such a yard is not often found to be wholly surrounded by walls, buildings and fences so that access can be obtained only through the back door of one of the surrounding buildings. There is almost always a way into the yard, sometimes through an archway. In my view, a yard does not cease to be inclosed within the meaning of this Act because there is access from outside through spaces left between the surrounding buildings, nor is it necessary that there should be means provided of closing those spaces, such as a gate. If gates are provided, it is unnecessary that they should be kept closed. I should add that it is a question of degree whether the space in question is sufficiently surrounded by walls, buildings and fences to justify the description of an "inclosed yard", or whether the buildings or walls cover so small a part of the perimeter that the yard would more reasonably be regarded as an open yard.' *Goodhew v Morton* [1962] 2 All ER 771 at 772, 773, per MacKenna J

Australia [The Dog Act 1928 (Vic), s 19 (repealed; see now Dog Act 1970–1986, s 24(1)), provided that the owner or occupier of any field, paddock, yard, or other place 'enclosed' by a fence in which any sheep, cattle or poultry were confined might destroy any dog found at large therein.] 'It was argued that this section has no application to the case where the killing takes place in a building, and that the language of the section indicates a genus of the places where the dog must be found if the section is to apply and that that genus is confined to open spaces, open to the sky, as a field, paddock or yard is. I think this contention is correct. It is quite impossible, on the proper construction of the section, to read the words, "other place enclosed by a fence", as including buildings.' *Henry v Fisher* [1954] ALR 973 at 974, per Herring CJ

Australia [The defendant was charged with being found in an 'inclosed' area without lawful excuse.] 'I think that the word "inclosed" . . . requires that there must be a barrier of some kind along such of the boundaries of the space in question as are accessible to the public. It need not be a barrier of a kind difficult to surmount or penetrate, but it must be something more than a mere marking out of the boundaries.' *Webb v Epstein* [1956] ALR 154 at 161, per cur.

Australia [The Inclosed Lands Act 1854 (repealed) [see now Inclosed Lands Protection Act 1901 (NSW), s 3] defined 'inclosed lands' as lands either private or public which might be enclosed with any fence, wall or other erection by which the boundaries thereof might be known or recognised. The question was whether it was a breach of the later Inclosed Lands Protection Act 1901 to enter the Sydney Showground arena for the purpose of making a demonstration.] 'The boundaries of land, be they lands of a person, village, shire or other area within the control of some person or body, are in common speech the perimeter of that area. There are still in older countries customs whereby the boundaries are beaten annually in what has become a ceremonial. The boundaries of land of a person exist whether or not there is a fence or other erection or some natural feature such as a river by which the boundaries may be recognised. It seems to me that the effect of the definition is to describe those lands only which are enclosed or surrounded by a fence, or other structure or natural feature which is erected upon or is found to be upon the perimeter of such lands.' *Press v Tuckwell* [1968] 2 NSWR 212 at 215, per Holmes JA

INCLUDE   *See also* MEAN

'The interpretation clauses [of the Towns Improvement Clauses Act 1847 (repealed; see now the Highways Act 1980, s 329(1), where the words are now "includes any part of a street")] . . . provide that "the word 'street' shall extend to and include any road." The intention of the clauses is that in construing the Acts the word, in addition to its ordinary meaning, shall bear the meanings mentioned in the section; the words "shall include" mean "shall have the following meanings in addition to its popular meaning".' *Portsmouth Corpn v Smith* (1883) 13 QBD 184 at 195, CA, per Brett MR

'The word "include" is very generally used in interpretation clauses in order to enlarge the meaning of words or phrases occurring in the body of the statute; and when it is so used these words or phrases must be construed as comprehending, not only such things as they signify according to their natural import, but also those things which the interpretation clause declares that they shall include. But the word "include" is susceptible of another construction, which may become imperative, if the context of the Act is sufficient to shew that it was not merely employed for the purpose of adding to the natural significance of the words or expressions defined. It may be equivalent to "mean and include", and in that case it may afford an exhaustive explanation of the meaning which, for the purposes of the Act, must invariably be attached to these words or expressions.' *Dilworth v Stamps Comrs, Dilworth v Land & Income Tax Comrs* [1899] AC 99 at 105, 106, PC per cur.

'"Included" is a word to which parliamentary draftsmen seem considerably addicted: one reason for this may be that in law it can have, according to its context, not only one or other of simple but in essence quite differing effects (for instance, in relation to the words that follow it may be found to have been used simply to enlarge, to limit, to define exhaustively or for the avoidance of doubts to repeat the preceding word or phrase, but it may also be used to secure on one and the same occasion more than one of those effects, thus putting the draftsman but not necessarily the court, in a happy position.' *Customs & Excise Comrs v Savoy Hotel Ltd* [1966] 2 All ER 299 at 301, per Sachs J

'An interpretation clause in a statute may serve two different purposes. If it states at greater length what an expression used in other provisions in the statute "means", it is no more than a drafting device to promote economy of language. It is a direction to the reader: "Wherever you see this shorter expression in the statute you must treat it as being shorthand for the longer one." Alternatively an interpretation clause may be used by the draftsman not to define the meaning of an expression appearing in the statute but to extend it beyond the ordinary meaning which it would otherwise bear. An indication that this *may* be its purpose is given if it purports to state what the expression "includes" instead of what it "means", but the substitution of the one verb for the other is not conclusive of its being a direction to the reader: "Wherever you see this shorter expression in the statute you may treat it as bearing either its ordinary meaning or this other meaning which it would not ordinarily bear." Where the words used in the shorter expression are in themselves too imprecise to give a clear indication of what is included in it,

an explanation of their meaning which is introduced by the verb "includes" may be intended to do no more than state at greater length and with more precision what the shorter expression means.' *Inland Revenue Comrs v Joiner* [1975] 3 All ER 1050 at 1060, 1061, HL, per Lord Diplock

Canada 'The latter word ['includes' in a statutory definition] in contrast to "means" is inserted in an interpretation section to permit enlargement of the meaning of terms occurring in the body of the statute. It signifies that which is "included" is in addition to something else that is not specifically stated to be so included and may not need to be so "included".' *Wagenstein v Graham*, (1954) 4 DLR 540 at 542, per O'Halloran JA (dissenting)

Canada 'The word "includes" in contrast to "means", signifies that which is included is an addition to something else that is not stated to be included or may not be so included.' *R v Hall* (1954) 14 WWR 241 at 244, per O'Halloran JA

INCOME

In relation to land, income includes rents and profits, and possession includes receipt of income. (Conveyancing Act 1881, s 2)

'Income' includes rents and profits. (Administration of Estates Act 1925, s 55(1))

'Income is an ordinary word in the English language and, unless the context otherwise requires, it should be given its ordinary natural meaning in a statute. I see nothing in the 1952 Act [Income Tax Act 1952 (repealed; see now the Income and Corporation Taxes Act 1988, s 739(1)] to require it to be given anything other than its ordinary natural meaning. . . . So the question to be decided can be simply stated. Did dividends received by Attleborough [a company] constitute income of that company? If they did . . . it matters not how the company applied that income. . . . In *Inland Revenue Comrs v Frere* [[1964] 3 All ER 796] Lord Radcliffe said: "Income that is assessed to tax is neither measured by expenditure nor is it the residual income that lies after expenditure of an income nature. It is not the savings of income. In principle it is gross income as reduced for the purposes of assessment by such deductions only as are actually specified in the tax code or are granted by way of reliefs, usually in the form of fixed sums or proportions."' *Lord Chetwode v Inland Revenue Comrs* [1977] 1 All ER 638 at 645, HL, per Viscount Dilhorne

Australia 'The word "income" is not a term of art, and what forms of receipts are comprehended within it, and what principles are to be applied to ascertain how much of those receipts ought to be treated as income, must be determined in accordance with the ordinary concepts and usages of mankind, except in so far as the statute states or indicates an intention that receipts which are not income in ordinary parlance are to be treated as income, or that special rules are to be applied for arriving at the taxable amount of such receipts.' *Scott v Commissioner of Taxation* (NSW) (1935) 35 SR (NSW) 215 at 219, per Jordan CJ

New Zealand 'I think that compensation for the loss of a profit-making scheme, the profits of which would have been assessable income, is naturally to be regarded as itself assessable income. The one replaces the other.' *Duff v Inland Revenue Comr* [1982] 2 NZLR 710 at 715, 716, CA, per Cooke J

Arising from estate

'Certain sums have been paid over to the testator's estate. There are three sums paid from the Williams syndicate, five sums from the Graham syndicate, and three sums from the Rose-Thompson-Young syndicate. What I have to consider is whether these sums, in so far as they were paid and ascertained after the death of the testator, could be treated as income for the purpose of the trust to pay income to the widow, or whether I should treat them as capital of the estate, in which case the tenant for life receives only the income from them. The first question is on the construction of the will, and on that I have come to the conclusion that, when the testator declared "all income arising from any part of my estate shall at all times be used and applied as income and no part thereof shall be added to capital," he was including income which came to the hands of his executors in the nature of income, and Mr Hodge's argument, that these profits do not come within that clause because they do not "arise from any part of my estate", I cannot agree with, because I find they did arise from a part of his estate, from his business; the profits arose from the fact that he was interested in the syndicates, and I think that that is income

arising from a part of his estate.' *Re Lynch-White, Smith v Lynch-White* [1937] 3 All ER 551 at 553, per Crossman J

Earned income

Subject to subsections (5) and (6) below, in the Income Tax Acts "earned income" means, in relation to any individual—
(a) any income arising in respect of—
  (i) any remuneration from any office or employment held by the individual, or
  (ii) any pension, superannuation or other allowance, deferred pay or compensation for loss of office, given in respect of the past services of the individual or of the husband or parent of the individual in any office or employment, or given to the individual in respect of past services of any deceased person, whether the individual or husband or parent of the individual shall have contributed to such pension, superannuation allowance or deferred pay or not; and
(b) any income from any property which is attached to or forms part of the emoluments of any office or employment held by the individual; and
(c) any income which is charged under Schedule A, B or D and is immediately derived by the individual from the carrying on or exercise by him of his trade, profession or vocation, either as an individual or, in the case of a partnership, as a partner personally acting in the partnership.
In cases where the income of a wife is deemed to be income of the husband, any reference in this subsection to the individual includes either the husband or the wife. (Income and Corporation Taxes Act 1988, s 833(4))

Gross income

New Zealand 'The "income" of a business is, in its ordinary and proper meaning, the gain resulting from the business; the income of an estate is the annual return from the estate. The term "gross income" is the antithesis of "net income". It means, in ordinary language in reference to a business, the gross result of the terminal trading as distinguished from the net result, the net result being what remains of the gross result after all salaries, working-expenses, interest on capital, rent, rates, and outgoings necessary for the management of the business have been deducted. . . .' *Yates v Yates* (1913) 33 NZLR 281 at 284–286, per

Cooper J; also reported 15 GLR 623 at 625

In Income Tax Acts

[A New Brunswick Act imposed a tax upon the amount of 'income' received during the fiscal year.] 'Their Lordships have come to the conclusion, upon consideration of the Act in question, that there is nothing in the enactment imposing the tax, nor in the context which should induce them to construe the word "income", when applied to the income of a commercial business for a year, otherwise than in its natural and commonly accepted sense, as the balance of gain over loss, and consequently . . . where no such gain has been made in the fiscal year, there is no income or fund which is capable of being assessed.' *Lawless v Sullivan* (1881) 6 App Cas 373 at 383, 384, per cur.

'A man may sell his property for a sum which is to be paid in instalments, and when that is the case the payments to him are not income. . . . What I have to do is to see what the sum payable in this case really is. . . . In this case there is no difficulty in seeing what was intended. The property was sold for a certain sum, and in addition the vendor took an annual sum which was dependent upon the volume of business done; that is to say, he took something which rose or fell with the chances of the business. When a man does that he takes an income; it is in the nature of income, and on that ground I decide this case.' *Jones v Inland Revenue Comrs* [1920] 1 KB 711 at 714, 715, per Rowlatt J

'In income tax legislation that word [income] must be construed in its income tax meaning, that is, as income assessed and charged under one or other of the five [now six] schedules, unless it is expressly qualified as "total income", or "total income from all sources", or "aggregate income".' *F P H Finance Trust Ltd v Inland Revenue Comrs* [1943] 1 KB 345 at 348, CA, per Scott LJ

'Income is an ordinary word in the English language and, unless the context otherwise requires, it should be given its ordinary natural meaning in a statute. I see nothing in the 1952 Act [Income Tax Act 1952 (repealed; see now the Income and Corporation Taxes Act 1988, s 739(1))] to require it to be given anything other than its ordinary natural meaning. . . . So the question to be decided

can be simply stated. Did dividends received by Attleborough [a company] constitute income of that company? If they did . . . it matters not how the company applied that income. . . . In *Inland Revenue Comrs v Frere* [[1964] 3 All ER 796] Lord Radcliffe said: "Income that is assessed to tax is neither measured by expenditure nor is it the residual income that lies after expenditure of an income nature. It is not the savings of income. In principle it is gross income as reduced for the purposes of assessment by such deductions only as are actually specified in the tax code or are granted by way of reliefs, usually in the form of fixed sums or proportions".' *Lord Chetwode v Inland Revenue Comrs* [1977] 1 All ER 638 at 645, HL, per Viscount Dilhorne

Australia 'Income is as large a word as can be used to denote a person's receipts (*Re Huggins, ex parte Huggins* [(1882) 51 LJ Ch 935 at 938]); it signifies that which comes in. An "Act to impose a tax upon incomes" is not less general in scope; it must be liberally construed, and include everything which by reasonable understanding might fairly be regarded as income.' *Resch v Federal Comr of Taxation* (1942) 66 CLR 198 at 213, per Starke J

Australia 'The Court was referred on the one hand to *Lawless v Sullivan* [supra], where it was said that the natural meaning of the word "income" was the gain, if any, resulting from the balance of profits and losses of the business in a year; and, on the other hand, to *R v Commissioners of the Port of Southampton* [[1870] LR 4 HL 449], where it was said that "income is that which comes in, not that which comes in less an outgoing". These cases taken together show that the word "income" is ambiguous. It may mean either net income or gross income, according to the context—and there will then sometimes be room for argument as to how net income (or gross income) is to be ascertained. Two men referring to the same state of facts might use the word in quite different senses. One man might say that he had a large income in a given year, but that all his income and more went in meeting expenses and losses. Another man might describe the same facts by saying that he had no income at all in that year, because he made a loss on the year's transactions. In each case the context shows in what sense the word "income" is used.' *Bartlam v Union Trustee Co of Australia Ltd* [1946] ALR 162 at 164, per Latham CJ

Canada 'My brother Ferguson has come to the conclusion that the amount of premiums received yearly at Kingston in the agency office there of the defendants was assessable at that place as "gross" income. . . . "Income" is not perhaps the most appropriate word to use with reference to corporations, but being used for convenience or for comprehensiveness, it must receive the meaning which "income" has in connection with individuals or partnerships. Whatever difficulty one might have in arriving at a conclusion as to this word in its statutory signification, has been obviated by the judgment of the Privy Council in *Lawless v Sullivan*, [supra]. . . . The judgment . . . is definitely and conclusively upon the point, that "income" as commercially used, means the balance of gain over loss in the fiscal year or other period of computation. . . . I see nothing to detract from the ordinary commercial meaning attributable to the word "income", as defined by the highest appellate tribunal of this country.' *Kingston City Corpn v Canada Life Assurance Co* (1890) 19 OR 453 at 456–458, per Boyd C

Canada 'The broad question for decision is whether certain moneys received by the respondents under use and occupancy policies insuring them against loss of profit resulting from the cessation of business consequential upon fire are liable, under the British Columbia Taxation Act 1924, to be brought into account by them for assessment to income tax. . . . This insurance receipt . . . was the product of a revenue payment prudently made by the respondents to secure that the gains which might have been expected to accrue to them had there been no fire should not be lost, but should be replaced by a sum equivalent to their estimated amount. . . . The question is whether within the meaning of the Act the insurance receipt in respect of "loss of net profits" was also "income". . . . In view of the nature and origin of the receipt, . . . their Lordships have reached the conclusion that within the meaning even of the interpretation clause this receipt was "income from a business", and that in ordinary parlance it was income or gain derived from the business of the respondents which had necessarily to be brought into receipt as such in the profit and loss account of the business referred to in s 48, sub-s 3 of the statute. . . . But, however the receipt be described, it is because it is truly "income" of the respondents that it must be brought into charge in their revenue account for the purpose of arriving in respect of the

year of charge at the respondents' net income.' *R v British Columbia Fir & Cedar Lumber Co Ltd* [1932] AC 441 at 442, 443, 447, 450, 451, PC, per cur.

New Zealand 'The "income" of a business is, in its ordinary and popular meaning, the gain resulting from the business; the income of an estate is the annual return from the estate. . . . The term "income" means, as applied to a commercial business, the profits made in that business. It means in its natural and commonly accepted sense the balance of gain over loss. . . . It seems to me to be altogether straining the ordinary signification of the term "income" to say that it means the volume of business. That is the "turnover", not the "income".' *Yates v Yates* (1913) 33 NZLR 281 at 285, 286, per Cooper J; also reported, 15 CLR 623 at 625

New Zealand 'I think that compensation for the loss of a profit-making scheme, the profits of which would have been assessable income, is naturally to be regarded as itself assessable income. The one replaces the other.' *Duff v Inland Revenue Comr* [1982] 2 NZLR 710 at 715, CA, per Cooke J

In rules of building society

[Rule 40 of a building society's rules decided how to meet a deficiency of 'income' by which the society might be prevented from meeting its anticipated expenditure and liabilities.] 'There is no contrast in this clause between "income" and "capital". "Income" here means all that comes in. . . . I . . . hold that "income" includes, for instance, repayments by advanced members, monies borrowed from outsiders, . . . and in fact everything that comes in.' *Re West Riding of Yorkshire Permanent Benefit Building Society* (1890) 43 Ch D 407 at 415, per Chitty J

Income derived

Australia 'The concept of "income derived" is one which will often take its content from the context in which it has to be applied, and may have a very different content and significance when applied to the financial operations of a huge multi-national corporation, or a large trading company or business, or a large professional partnership respectively than it would in the case of a one man professional practitioner. I have come to the conclusion that in the case of a one man professional practitioner, the essential feature of "income derived" is receipt.' *Taxation Comr v Firstenberg* [1977] VR 1 at 14, per McInerney J

Net income *See* GROSS INCOME, supra

Of trustee company

Australia 'It has often been said that "income" is a word of wide import which, in some cases, comprises everything that comes in. That it has not always that meaning is clear from the opinion delivered in *Lawless v Sullivan* [supra]. I think the popular sense of the word, in speaking not only of the income of a business but also of that of an individual, is net income.' *Re De Little, Union Trustee Co of Australia Ltd v De Little* [1945] VLR 198 at 207, per Martin J

Total income

In the Income Tax Acts 'total income', in relation to any person, means the total income of that person from all sources estimated in accordance with the provisions of the Income Tax Acts. (Income and Corporation Taxes Act 1988, s 835(1))

INCOME TAX

'Income tax, if I may be pardoned for saying so, is a tax on income. It is not meant to be a tax on anything else. It is one tax, not a collection of taxes essentially distinct. There is no difference in kind between the duties of income tax assessed under Sched D and those assessed under . . . any of the other schedules of charge. One man has fixed property; another lives by his wits; each contributes to the tax if his income is above the prescribed limit. The standard of assessment varies according to the nature of the source from which taxable income is derived. That is all.' *London County Council v A-G* [1901] AC 26 at 35, per Lord Macnaghten

INCOMMODIOUS

'The plaintiff must rely upon the word "incommodious", and in my opinion his coffee-shop was rendered incommodious by the bad smells arising from . . . horses; when we speak as lawyers we do not always use words in their ordinary and popular significance, and we shall not be doing violence to language by holding that "incommodious" sufficiently describes annoyance by bad smells.' *Benjamin v Storr* (1874) 43 LJCP 162 at 166, 167, per Brett J

INCOMPETENT

[In an action by a painter against his employer for wrongful dismissal, it was contended on behalf of the defendant that competency was an implied condition of the contract of service, and that the plaintiff was 'incompetent'.] 'It seems very unreasonable that an employer should be compelled to go on employing a man who, having represented himself as competent, turns out to be incompetent. An engineer is retained by a railway company to drive an express train for a year, and is found incompetent to drive or regulate the locomotive—are the railway company still bound under pain of an action to entrust the lives of thousands to his dangerous and demonstrated incapacity? A clerk is retained for a year to keep a merchant's books, and it turns out that he is ignorant, not only of book-keeping, but not sufficiently skilled in arithmetic—is the merchant bound to continue him in his employment? Misconduct in a servant is, according to every day's experience, a justification of a discharge. The failure to afford the requisite skill which had been expressly or impliedly promised is a breach of legal duty, and therefore misconduct.' *Harmer v Cornelius* (1858) 22 JP 724 at 724, per Willes J

INCORPOREAL HEREDITAMENT *See* HEREDITAMENT

INCORRIGIBLE ROGUE *See* VAGRANT

INCREASE

Of nominal share capital

'My Lords, I cannot express my view of the case better than it is expressed in the judgment of Ridley J in which he says that the "nominal share capital" means the capital in shares and the figure value attached to it, and that if the company extends the capital and gives it a greater nominal value, that is an increase which requires an additional statement of the amount of such increase to be delivereed by the company.' *Midland Rly Co v A-G* [1902] AC 171 at 174, HL, per Lord Shand

Offspring

[By an indenture of mortgage the defendant assigned as security for a loan certain flocks of sheep, together with their issue, 'increase' and produce.] 'Their Lordships, looking at the deed, and seeing that "increase" is always spoken of as the increase, not of a flock, but as the increase of those sheep which were originally the subject of the mortgage, are clearly of opinion, that it must be taken to mean the natural increase, or the offspring of those original sheep.' *Webster v Power* (1868) LR 2 PC 69 at 80, per Sir James W Colvile

INCREMENT

'The word "increment" is a word of wide meaning. It does not import of itself the limitation that it is referable only to a payment that is annual. In order that it should in a particular case bear such a limited meaning a proper context must be provided.' *Turburville v West Ham Corpn* [1950] 2 KB 208 at 226, CA, per Wynn-Parry J

INCUMBENT

The incumbent of the parish is the clergyman holding the church and its benefice and having, under the bishop, the sole and exclusive cure of souls in the parish. The incumbent is the proper custodian of the keys of the church and of the register books, and has a general control over the church, including the vestry, and over the ringing of the bells. (14 Halsbury's Laws (4th edn) para 541)

The word 'incumbent' means the rector, vicar, or perpetual curate, as the case may be, of a church or ecclesiastical benefice the advowson of which is to be dealt with under this Act, and includes the officiating clergyman for the time being, if the incumbent reside abroad or be incapable of acting. (Sale of Advowsons Act 1856, s 1)

'Incumbent' includes any minister with cure of souls. (New Parishes Measure 1943, s 29)

'Incumbent' includes any minister with a separate cure of souls but shall not include a curate in charge of a conventional district. (Incumbents and Churchwardens (Trusts) Measure 1964 (No 2), s 1)

'Incumbent', in relation to a benefice, means a rector or vicar with cure of souls but does not include the dean or provost of a cathedral church. (Ecclesiastical Offices (Age Limit) Measure 1975, s 6)

INCUMBRANCE

Incumbrance includes a mortgage in fee, or for a less estate, and a trust for securing money, and a lien, and a charge of a portion, annuity, or other capital or annual sum; and incumbrancer has a meaning corresponding with that of incumbrance, and includes every person entitled to the benefit of an incumbrance, or to require payment or discharge thereof. (Conveyancing Act 1881, s 2)

'Incumbrance' includes a legal or equitable mortgage and a trust for securing money, and a lien, and a charge of a portion, annuity, or other capital or annual sum; and 'incumbrancer' has a meaning corresponding with that of incumbrance, and includes every person entitled to the benefit of an incumbrance, or to require payment or discharge thereof. (Law of Property Act 1925, s 205)

'The word "incumbrance" has no strictly technical meaning; but what is usually understood is, that where a person has a right at his pleasure to charge £3,000 upon an estate, that is an incumbrance. In such a state of things nobody could say he had an estate free from incumbrances while his estate was liable at any time to be charged with such a sum of money.' *Evans v Evans* (1853) 22 LJ Ch 785 at 790, CA, per Lord Cranworth LC

[The Settled Land Act 1882, s 21(ii) (repealed; see now Settled Land Act 1925, s 73(1)(ii)), enabled capital trust money to be invested or applied in discharge, purchase, or redemption of 'incumbrances affecting the inheritance' of settled land.] 'I think the words "incumbrances affecting the inheritance of the settled land", must be taken to have been used in their ordinary sense such as mortgages, portions, etc, and not as meaning incumbrances with incidents such as these are [charges for land drainage, etc, under the Improvement of Land Act 1864] which require the tenant for life, if he lives sufficiently long himself to pay off the whole of this charge; and although in one sense this is an incumbrance affecting the inheritance so far as the Commissioners advance their money on a charge upon the inheritance, it is in very numerous cases a charge which to all intents and purposes rather affects the tenant for life than the tenant in remainder.' *Re Knatchbull's Settled Estate* (1884) 27 Ch D 349 at 353, per Pearson J

INCUMBRANCER   *See* MORTGAGE

INCUR

Canada [Paragraphs 35(d) and (e) of the Interpretation Act, RSC 1970, c 1–3 state that where an enactment is repealed the repeal does not 'affect . . . any penalty, forfeiture or punishment incurred under the enactment so repealed' or 'affect any investigation, legal proceeding or remedy in respect of any such right, privilege, obligation, liability, penalty, forfeiture or punishment' and the investigation, legal proceeding or remedy may be instituted, continued or enforced and the penalty, forfeiture or punishment may be imposed as if the enactment had not been so repealed.] 'The Shorter Oxford English Dictionary, 3rd ed, defines the word "incur" as meaning "to render oneself liable to . . .; to bring upon oneself". The definition of "incur" found in Webster's Third International Dictionary includes the following: "become liable or subject to; bring upon oneself". I rely upon these definitions and treat the word "incur" in s 35 of the Interpretation Act as being synonymous with "liable to" or "subject to".' *R v Allan* (1979) 45 CCC (2d) 524 at 529, 530, Ont CA, per Lacourciere JA

New Zealand [Expenditure 'incurred' is deductible from assessable income in terms of s 121 of the Land and Income Tax Act 1954.] 'A deduction may be allowed under that section in respect of "expenditure incurred" although there has been no actual disbursement if, in the relevant income year, the taxpayer is definitely committed to that expenditure.' *King v Inland Revenue Comr* [1974] 2 NZLR 190, per Wild CJ

INCURABLE

'I am concerned to find . . . whether it is true that this respondent . . . is "incurably of

unsound mind". . . . The lady has, in fact, for the last five years had done for her all that medical and nursing skill and care and attention and treatment can do for her. . . . I am satisfied . . . beyond any doubt whatever that this lady is of unsound mind. . . . Having regard to the long history of her illness, . . . in particular having regard to the length of the last onset, which now extends over eleven years, and above all to her age, I am satisfied that there is no prospect of cure.' *Swettenham v Swettenham* [1938] P 218 at 221–223, per Merriman P

'In my judgment, the test to be applied to the word 'incurably' is to be applied with common sense and with regard to the popular understanding of the term. In a sense, no doubt, anyone who has suffered a severe disease, mental or physical, cannot be cured in that he cannot expect to enjoy a mind or body as robust or healthy as before. Nevertheless, we regard such a person as cured when he has left hospital and resumed a normal life. The mere fact that he may have to take prophylactic measures to preserve his cure does not in ordinary language class him as an invalid. . . . I would conclude, therefore, that in deciding whether a person is "incurably of unsound mind" [within s 1(1) of the Matrimonial Causes Act 1950 (repealed)] the test to be applied is whether by reason of his mental condition he is capable of managing himself and his affairs and, if not, whether he can hope to be restored to a state in which he will be able to do so. I would add to the above test the rider that the capacity to be required is that of a reasonable person.' *Whysall v Whysall* [1959] 3 All ER 389 at 397, per Phillimore J

INDEBTED   *See* OWING

INDECENT

[A bye-law provided that no person should in any public place use any profane, obscene, or 'indecent' language to the annoyance of passengers. The language used in this instance was: 'You are too b——y keen; you can report what the b——y hell you like.'] 'The first point taken is that the language used was not indecent, but I do not think that upon the facts it is not possible to say that the magistrates were wrong in law in holding that it was, for I do not think that the word "indecent" is to be taken as ejusdem generis with "profane" and "obscene". Again I do not think that all language that is not decent is within the bye-law, because in that case, the word "obscene" would be surplusage. But when one considers that the person who used it was a publican in his own house, no words seem to me less appropriate to say that it was the use of indecent language in a public place to the annoyance of passengers.' *Russon v Dutton (No 1)* (1911) 104 LT 601 at 602, DC, per Hamilton J

'I do not think that the two words "indecent" and "obscene" are synonymous. The one may shade into the other, but there is a difference of meaning. It is easier to illustrate than define, and I illustrate thus. For a male bather to enter the water nude in the presence of ladies would be indecent, but it would not necessarily be obscene. But if he directed the attention of a lady to a certain member of his body his conduct would certainly be obscene. The matter might perhaps be roughly expressed thus in the ascending scale: Positive—Immodest; Comparative—Indecent; Super-lative—Obscene. These, however, are not rigid categories. The same conduct which in certain circumstances may merit only the milder description, may in other circumstances deserve a harder one. "Indecent" is a milder term than "obscene", and as it satisfies the purposes of this case if the prints in question are indecent, I shall apply that test.' *M'Gowan v Langmuir* 1931 SC (J) 10 at 13, per Lord Sands

'The words "indecent or obscene" convey one idea, namely, offending against the recognised standards of propriety, indecent being at the lower end of the scale and obscene at the upper end of the scale. . . . As it seems to this court, an indecent article is not necessarily obscene, whereas an obscene article almost certainly must be indecent.' *R v Stanley* [1965] 1 All ER 1035 at 1038, 1039, CCA, per cur.; also reported [1965] 2 QB 327

'The sole question here is whether the behaviour of the appellants acting jointly could be said to be indecent behaviour within the meaning of that statute [Ecclesiastical Courts Jurisdiction Act 1860, s 2]. Were it not for the great industry of counsel for the appellants in this case, I for my part should have thought that this was completely unarguable. He refers to the fact that "indecent" has a number of meanings, both dictionary meanings and meanings that can be ascertained from the cases; but the true meaning in any particular statute must naturally depend on the context.

It is quite clear here that indecency is not referring to anything in the nature of tending to corrupt or deprave; it is quite clearly used without any sexual connotation whatsoever, but it is used in the context of riotous, violent or indecent behaviour, to put it quite generally, within the genus of creating a disturbance in a sacred place.' *Abrahams v Carey* [1967] 3 All ER 179 at 182, per Lord Parker CJ

'Indecent exhibitions in public have been widely interpreted. Indecency is not confined to sexual indecency; indeed it is difficult to find any limit short of saying that it includes anything which an ordinary decent man or woman would find to be shocking, disgusting and revolting.' *Knuller (Publishing Printing & Promotions) Ltd v Director of Public Prosecutions* [1972] 2 All ER 898 at 905, HL, per Lord Reid

Australia 'This is an application by an inspector of police for an order under s 3 of the Disorderly Houses Act 1943 (NSW), that certain premises be declared a disorderly house. The evidence simply is that these premises are occupied by a woman who therein carries on the profession of prostitution. Formerly her clients were sought by her in the street but for some time past she has conducted her affairs solely by telephone. She is the only person, so far as the evidence goes, using the premises for this or, indeed, any other purpose. The only ground upon which the premises can be declared a disorderly house is that contained in s 3(1)(a) of the ' Act, namely:—"that drunkenness or disorderly or indecent conduct or any entertainment of a demoralising character takes place on the premises, or has taken place and is likely to take place again on the premises". There is no suggestion of drunkenness and there is no suggestion that the proceedings are other than orderly. It would appear that appointments are made and that men enter and leave the premises in succession at regular, if somewhat short, intervals. There is no element of disorderliness visible to me in this, nor indeed do I think the word "disorderliness" was relied upon in support of the application. The fundamental question is whether indecent conduct takes place on the premises. There is no doubt that sexual intercourse between unmarried persons does occur on the premises. There is no doubt that it occurs for monetary consideration and that it occurs fairly frequently. It may well be that it would be proper to hold that immoral conduct occurs on the premises but the fact that something is immoral does not necessarily mean that it is indecent. In a situation of the sort with which I am here dealing, is the fact that money changes hands a criterion of decency or indecency? Is the number and frequency of visits to the place a criterion of decency or indecency? The act itself, as Mr Bannon has said, done in private is not ordinarily regarded as indecent even if the parties to it are not husband and wife.' *Ex p Fergusson; Re Premises No 13, Charlotte Lane, East Sydney* [1967] 1 NSWR 185 at 185, per Brereton J

New Zealand [The Police Offences Act 1908, s 42 (repealed; see now the Police Offences Act 1927, s 48) made it an offence to use 'indecent' language. In this case the words used were 'bloody calf'.] 'The word "indecent" has no definite legal meaning, and it must be taken, therefore, in its modern and popular acceptation. . . . In the Standard Dictionary "indecent" is defined to be anything that is unbecoming or offensive to common propriety. This definition is wide enough, certainly, to cover the language in question.' *Purves v Inglis* (1915) 34 NZLR 1051 at 1053, per Sim J; also reported 17 GLR 782

New Zealand 'I think that the whole question of indecency falls to be considered to a large extent by reference to the context in which photographs appear. If they appear as part of a nature magazine then the whole setting of the photographs is different from the setting which the same photographs have when concentrated together on the front page of a brochure advertising books on sex and arranged in such a way as to throw emphasis on the private parts of the male figure forming the centrepiece of the brochure. What can be acceptable according to the common standards of the community in one context, can be unacceptable and injurious· to the public in another. Having regard to the way these photographs have been arranged, to their context of lists of publications dealing with sex which they are used to draw attention to, and to the fact that they were mailed without solicitation through the post, I regard the front page of this pamphlet taken as a whole and with particular reference to the centre figure as an indecent document.' *Powell v Police* [1971] NZLR 110 at 111, per Richmond J

New Zealand 'The word "indecent" occurs in a number of sections of the Crimes Act.

Moreover it occurs more than once in s 124 in different subsections. In some of the sections and subsections in which it is to be found, it is obvious that it can only bear its common or general connotation. We do not say, of course, that a construction must always be constant throughout all the sections of an Act, or indeed throughout all the subsections of a particular section; but we would need to be satisfied of good reason before we would place a special meaning in a particular instance on a word so often used in an Act. We see no reason at all why when it appears in s 124(1)(b), the word "indecent" should be given any other meaning than that which it is accorded in general use. . . . Indecency must always be judged in the light of time, place and circumstances.' *R v Dunn* [1973] NZLR 481 at 483, 484, CA, per cur.

New Zealand 'The test which the Tribunal should, in my view, apply in classifying books is whether their publication is injurious to the public good. It is important for the Tribunal in classifying books to deal with them in advance of their release to the public so that the Tribunal must necessarily make its decision on some firm basis rather than on the basis of what might be regarded as commonly accepted standards of decency. It is much more reliable a guide for the Tribunal to determine whether or not a book describes or depicts matter which in its view is injurious to the public good than to endeavour to reach a conclusion as to whether the material is an affront to commonly accepted standards of decency which might prevail.' *Waverley Publishing Company Ltd v Comptroller of Customs* [1980] 1 NZLR 631 at 638, per Davison CJ

INDECENT ASSAULT

'Before you can find that a man has been guilty of an indecent assault, you have to find that he was guilty of an assault, for an indecent assault is an assault accompanied by indecency.' *Director of Public Prosecutions v Rogers* [1943] 2 All ER 644 at 645, per Lord Goddard CJ

[*See*, generally, as to indecent assault, ss 14, 15 of the Sexual Offences Act 1956; also *Beal v Kelley* [1951] 2 All ER 763; *Fairclough v Whipp* [1951] 2 All ER 834; *Director of Public Prosecutions v Rogers* [1953] 2 All ER 644]

'The proper course, where there is an act which no one in their right mind could call an assault but which takes place in an indecent situation, is to prosecute under the Indecency with

Children Act 1960, not under the 1956 Act [Sexual Offences Act 1956]. Juries should . . . be directed, in cases of indecent assault against children under 16, that if there is a touching which is in itself indecent it is indecent assault however willing the child may be, but that if the touching is not in itself indecent there will be no assault and thus no indecent assault unless the touching itself is hostile or threatening or one which the subject has demonstrated a reluctance or unwillingness to accept.' *R v Sutton* [1977] 2 All ER 476 at 480, per cur.

INDEFEASIBLE   *See also* ABSOLUTE AND INDEFEASIBLE

[By the Prescription Act 1832, s 3 the right to light which has been enjoyed for twenty years without interruption shall be deemed absolute and 'indefeasible'.] 'After an enjoyment of an access of light for twenty years without interruption, the right is declared by the statute to be absolute and indefeasible, and it would seem therefore that it cannot be lost or defeated by a subsequent temporary intermission of enjoyment, not amounting to abandonment. Moreover this absolute and indefeasible right, which is the creation of the statute, is not subjected to any condition or qualification; nor is it made liable to be affected or prejudiced by any attempt to extend the access or use of light beyond that which, having been enjoyed uninterruptedly during the required period, is declared to be not liable to be defeated.' *Tapling v Jones* (1865) 11 HL Cas 290 at 304, 305, per Lord Westbury LC

'In that case [*Tapling v Jones* (supra)], Lord Westbury, Lord Cranworth, and Lord Chelmsford all assume that a period of twenty years' enjoyment of the access and use of light to a building creates an absolute and indefeasible right immediately on the expiration of the period of twenty years. No doubt s 3 [of the Prescription Act 1832 (supra)] says so in terms, but s 4 must be read in connection with s 3; and if the two sections are read together, it will be seen that the period is not a period in gross, but a period next before some suit or action wherein the claim or matter . . . shall be brought into question. Unless and until the claim or matter is thus brought into question, no absolute or indefeasible right can arise under the Act. There is what has been described as an inchoate right.' *Colls v home & Colonial Stores*

Ltd [1904] AC 179 at 189, 190, HL, per Lord Macnaghten

INDEMNITY   *See also* GUARANTEE

A contract of indemnity is a contract by which one party agrees to make good a loss suffered by the other. In the widest sense of the term, therefore, it will include most contracts of insurance, and also a contract of guarantee. But it may be limited to describing a contract to save the promissee from loss caused by the claims of third parties, when it will not include a contract of marine insurance against loss or damage to the subject matter of the insurance, and may even be differentiated from those contracts of insurance which have for their object the protection of the assured against liability to third parties. The term 'indemnity' is, however, in law normally used to denote a contract by which the promisor undertakes an original and independent obligation to indemnify, as distinct from a collateral contract in the nature of a guarantee by which the promisor undertakes to answer for the default of another person who is to be primarily liable to the promisee'. (20 Halsbury's Laws (4th edn) para 305)

Most contracts of insurance belong to the general category of contracts of indemnity in the sense that the insurer's liability is limited to the actual loss which is in fact proved. The happening of the event does not of itself entitle the assured to payment of the sum stipulated in the policy; the event must in fact result in a pecuniary loss to the assured, who then becomes entitled to be indemnified subject to the limitations of his contract. He cannot recover more than the sum insured, for that sum is all that he has stipulated for by his premiums and it fixes the maximum liability of the insurers. Even within that limit, however, he cannot recover more than what he establishes to be the actual amount of his loss. The contract being one of indemnity, and of indemnity only, he can recover the actual amount of his loss and no more, whatever may have been his estimate of what his loss would be likely to be and whatever the premiums he may have paid, calculated on the basis of that estimate. However, if he wants to guard against unpredictable fluctuations in values (particularly of goods for which there may be a very variable market) and the consequent danger of paying far too much in premiums for what the goods turn out to be worth at the date of loss, he may persuade his insurers to enter into an agreement at the time of making the insurance, and from time to time afterwards, fixing the value. If recorded in or annexed to the policy, such an agreement makes it a valued or agreed value policy and, in the absence of fraud or circumstances invalidating the agreement, the insurers will be precluded from disturbing the agreed value if and when a loss occurs. In all contracts of insurance, whether marine or non-marine, which are contracts of indemnity the insurer is entitled to be subrogated to the rights of the assured, and to a contribution from other insurers where he has paid the whole of the loss or more than his proportionate share of it. (25 Halsbury's Laws (4th edn) para 3)

'Looking at this guarantie, it is undoubtedly very difficult to say that any sufficient consideration appears, construing it according to its terms, either upon the face of it or according to the existing state of facts. The terms of the guarantie are, "We, the undersigned, hereby indemnify the bank to the extent of £1,000 advanced or to be advanced Mr R Pinney by the Blandford Branch", the terms advanced or to be advanced, in a certain state of facts, might fairly admit of the construction that they applied to future as well as to past advances, but the facts to which they apply here, are, that at the time they were made use of, there was owing to the bank the sum of £1,400, and there is nothing on the face of the guarantie to shew, and certainly nothing when the state of accounts between the parties is considered, that they respectively intended to give and take a security for future advances up to the extent of £1,000. There is £1,000 already advanced, and the terms of the guarantie bind the defendants to the extent of £1,000. What is the consideration for that? The only consideration contended for is, that the word "indemnify" shews that the bank was to run some hazard in future of losing their money by forbearing to sue, and that was a sufficient consideration to make the guarantie attach. The word "indemnify" might mean what is suggested, but, in its ordinary use, in this place it means that the party guaranteeing is to secure and pay to the person guaranteed the sum of £1,000.' *Bell v Welch* (1850) 19 LJCP 184 at 189, per Wilde CJ

INDENTURE

An indenture is a deed to which two or more persons are parties, and which evidences some act or agreement between them other than the mere consent to join in expressing the same active intention on the part of all. An indenture derives its name from the fact that the parchment on which such a deed was written was indented or cut with a waving or indented line at the top (12 Halsbury's Laws (4th edn) para 1303)

INDEPENDENT

'It has been for many years well settled that no one standing in a fiduciary relation to another can retain a gift made to him by that other, if the latter impeaches the gift within a reasonable time, unless the donee can prove that the donor had independent advice, or that the fiduciary relation had ceased for so long that the donor was under no control or influence whatever. . . . The donee does not discharge this burden by showing that his own solicitor acted for both parties. . . . The solicitor, therefore, must be independent of the donee in fact, and not merely in name, and this he cannot be if he is solicitor for both.' *Powell v Powell* [1900] 1 Ch 243 at 246, 247, per Farwell J

'I agree with counsel for the respondent that independence ordinarily denotes financial independence, but I do not think that is the only sense in which the word can be used. I think that the word may be used to refer to a person who is permitted—and, perhaps, indeed required—by the man who employs or retains him to bring an independent mind to bear on a particular problem; for example, a solicitor. The term "independent contractor" conveys what I mean.' *Potato Marketing Board v Merricks* [1958] 2 All ER 538 at 548, per Devlin J; also reported [1958] 2 QB 316 at 335

INDEPENDENT CONTRACTOR

'The question whether a man be a servant or an independent contractor is often a mixed question of fact and law. If, however, the relationship rests upon a written document only, the question is primarily one of law. The contract is to be construed in the light of the relevant circumstances. . . . The distinction between "servant" and "independent contractor" does not seem to rest merely on the magnitude of the task undertaken. . . . I conceive that a general manager, at a high salary, of a partnership, or the managing director of a limited company at an even higher salary, are usually servants and not independent contractors. . . . It seems, however, reasonably clear that the final test, if there be a final test, and certainly the test to be generally applied, lies in the nature and degree of detailed control over the person alleged to be a servant. . . . The point is put well in Pollock on Torts (12th edn) pp 79, 80: "The relation of master and servant exists only between persons of whom the one has the order and control of the work done by the other. A master is one who not only prescribes to the workman the end of his work, but directs or at any moment may direct the means also, or, as it has been put 'retains the power of controlling the work'. . . . A servant is a person subject to the command of his master as to the manner in which he shall do his work. . . . An independent contractor is one who undertakes to produce a given result, but so that in the actual execution of the work he is not under the order or control of the person for whom he does it, and may use his own discretion in things not specified beforehand".' *Performing Right Society Ltd v Mitchell & Booker Palais de Danse Ltd* [1924] 1 KB 762 at 765–768, per McCardie J

See, generally, 16 Halsbury's Laws (4th edn) paras 756–761)

New Zealand 'The tests for deciding the issue [whether a man is a worker or an independent contractor] appear to be changing by placing less emphasis on the element of control and more on viewing all facets of the contract on a broad basis.' *Perry v Satterthwaite* [1967] NZLR 718 at 722, per Blair J

INDEPENDENT SCHOOL   *See* SCHOOL

INDICTABLE OFFENCE

'An "indictable offence" without any qualifying context can mean nothing else but an offence in respect of which an indictment would lie. . . . It is none the less "indictable" because, if the prosecution chose, it could proceed in respect of it summarily.' *Hastings and Folkestone Glassworks Ltd v Kalson* [1949] 1 KB 214 at 220, CA, per Asquith LJ

'The word "indictable" has appeared in innumerable Acts. Very often—probably more often than not—the Act has contained a definition section which makes clear what an indictable offence means in that Act, but it is of course of very little value to look at such

statutes unless closely related to the present one for assistance, and I think the proper approach to this problem is to go straight to the word "indictable" and ask oneself what it means in ordinary common use. I think the answer to that is that you speak of an offence as being "an indictable offence" when it is an offence for which an indictment lies. In other words, it includes offences like murder, which must be tried on indictment, and also hybrid offences. That is my view of the ordinary straightforward meaning of the word and, if that is so, the present offences were indictable offences because they were capable of being tried on indictment, even though not so tried.' *R v Guildhall Justices, ex p Marshall* [1976] 1 All ER 767 at 768, 769, per Lord Widgery CJ

INDICTMENT

An indictment is a written accusation preferred before the Crown Court, signed by the proper officer of that court and charging one or more persons with the commission of one or of a number of offences. (11 Halsbury's Laws (4th edn) para 193)

'It is clear, both upon reason and the authorities, that in old times the word "indictment" included all charges of a criminal nature made upon oath by an inquest which had power to make the inquiry; although the term is now more generally understood to signify such a charge when reduced into writing.' *R v Ingham* (1864) 5 B & S 257 at 274, per Blackburn J

INDIFFERENT

New Zealand [A clause in an insurance policy provided that any difference between the insurance company and the insured as to the amount of any alleged loss should be referred to the arbitration of some 'indifferent' person.] 'An arbitrator ought to be a person who stands indifferent between the parties, and condition 12 of the policy expressly provides that the persons to be nominated by the parties shall be "indifferent" persons. . . . In my opinion the term "indifferent" does not necessarily exclude only those who have an interest in the matters in dispute. It excludes also persons who may be reasonably presumed, owing to their prior relationship with one of the parties to the dispute in connection with the subject-matter of the dispute, to have a bias in favour of such party.' *Re Coleman & Royal Insurance Co* (1905) 24 NZLR 817 at 823, per Cooper J; also reported 7 GLR 414 at 417, 418

New Zealand 'Quite independently of the express requirement that the person to be appointed by the parties shall be "indifferent", it is a general rule of law that inasmuch as an arbitrator is in a quasi-judicial position he must be a person from whom there can be expected complete impartiality and indifference both as between the parties to the arbitration and in regard to the matters which are to be the subject of the arbitration. A pecuniary interest in the result of the arbitration would, of course, be a disqualifying circumstance. But the term "indifferent" connotes more than that. It operates to exclude any person who may be reasonably presumed on account of his prior relationship with the party appointing him to have some bias in favour of that party. Further, it is essential in an arbitrator that he should be free to approach the matter subject to the arbitration with an open mind, free from previously-formed or pronounced views.' *A-G v Wellington Harbour Board* [1959] NZLR 150 at 154, per cur.

INDIGENT

Canada 'The dictionaries distinguish between an "indigent" person and a "pauper". The difference is one of degree. A pauper has no means and is altogether dependent upon charity; an "indigent" person may possess some means.' *National Sanitarium Assocn v Mattawa Corpn* (1925) 56 OLR 474 at 475, per cur.

INDIRECT TAX *See* TAX

INDIRECTLY *See* DIRECTLY

INDISPUTABLE

'The defendants issued a prospectus, by which they represented that all policies effected by them should be indisputable, except in cases of fraud. That was holding out to all the world that they would require no proof of the truth of the matters stated in the proposal, but would only dispute the claim on the ground of fraud.' *Wood v Dwarris* (1856) 11 Exch 493 at 503, per Alderson B

INDIVIDUAL

[The Patents, Designs and Trade Marks Act 1888, s 10 (repealed; see now Trade Marks Act 1938, s 9), provided that a trade mark must contain (inter alia) (a) a name of an 'individual' or firm, or (e) a word or words having no reference to the character or quality of the goods and not being a geographical name.] 'The real difficulty in this case . . . is to determine whether the word "Trilby" is the "name of an individual" within clause (a) of s 10 of the Act of 1888. Clause (a) does not say that the name to be registered need be the name of a living person, nor the name of the applicant for registration. . . . The reference to a firm, however, points rather to real persons than to imaginary persons. In metaphorical language, an imaginary person may perhaps be called an "individual", but such a use of the word is unusual, and to my mind rather fanciful. It is hardly to be supposed that the legislature meant "individual" to be taken in a fanciful or metaphorical sense, or meant it to denote an imaginary person who has not, and never had, any real existence. I do not think that such words as Hamlet, Sam Weller, Jupiter, Venus, etc, can be called names of "individuals" within the meaning of clause (a) of s 10. Such names fall within (e) rather than (a). "Trilby" is clearly a "word" within (e), unless it is the name of an "individual" within (a), and I am not prepared to hold it to be within (a).' *Re Holt & Co's Trade Mark* [1896] 1 Ch 711 at 719, 720, CA, per Lindley LJ

[Section 9 of the Railway and Canal Traffic Act 1888 (repealed), gave the Railway and Canal Commissioners jurisdiction to hear complaints where an enactment in a special Act imposed on a railway company an obligation in favour of the public or any 'individual'.] 'It seems to me that the word "individual" must be construed as extending, not merely to what is commonly called an individual person, but to a company or corporation. Supposing the right to be given by a special Act of Parliament to a limited company, it seems to me impossible to suppose that they would not be within the word "individual". "Individual" seems to me to be any legal person who is not the general public.' *Great Northern Rly Co v Great Central Rly Co* (1899) 10 Ry & Can Tr Cas 266 at 275, per Wright J

INDORSEMENT

Indorsement means the writing on a bill, cheque or note the name of the transferor and its delivery to the transferee.

Indorser means a person who effects an indorsement.

Indorsee means the person to whom a bill of exchange, cheque or promissory note is transferred by indorsement. (4 Halsbury's Laws (4th edn) para 308)

[See also s 2 of the Bills of Exchange Act 1882]

Australia [A policy of insurance provided that the insurance thereby made was and should be subject to the conditions and to the memoranda, if any, 'indorsed' thereon. Typed slips containing terms of the policy were attached to the front of the policy.] 'In my opinion the fact that the slips attached to the policy are attached to the front of it, not the back of it, does not prevent there being "memoranda . . . indorsed thereon" within the meaning of the policy. In relation to modern business documents, the word "indorsed" does not invariably suggest the back of a document rather than the usually far more prominent position upon the face of the document.' *L'Union Fire Accident & General Insurance Co Ltd v Klinker Knitting Mills Proprietary Ltd* (1938) 59 CLR 709 at 728, per Evatt J

INDUCEMENT

[The owner of a freehold estate, worth, beyond a mortgage to which it was subject, about £1,300, was persuaded to make a post-nuptial settlement of it on his wife and children. As an 'inducement' to do this a relative of the wife agreed to advance to him £150 to meet the interest on the mortgage.] 'I think that if a man is induced to do a thing upon the faith of £150 being paid to him, that amounts to a bargain between the parties, whether the word describing the transaction be "inducement" or "bargain".' *Bayspoole v Collins* (1871) 6 Ch App 228 at 234, per Lord Hatherley LC

Australia '"Inducement" [in s 410 of the Crimes Act 1900 (NSW)] is used in its ordinary sense of persuasion aimed at producing some willing action, as opposed to compulsion by force or fear of force to produce some unwilling action. It is not necessary that the prisoner should have been pressed to confess guilt and it has been held that it is sufficient to exclude the statement if he were pressed to say anything whatever: *R v Thompson* [1893] 2 QB 12.' *R v Bodsworth* [1968] 2 NSWR 132 at 138, per cur.

INDUSTRIAL ACCIDENT *See* ACCIDENT

INDUSTRIAL ASSURANCE *See* INSURANCE

INDUSTRIAL BUILDING OR STRUCTURE

(1) Subject to the provisions of this section, in this Chapter [reliefs for capital expenditure on industrial buildings and structures] 'industrial building or structure' means a building or structure in use—

(a) for the purposes of a trade carried on in a mill, factory or other similar premises, or

(b) for the purposes of a transport, dock, inland navigation, water, electricity or hydraulic power undertaking, or

(c) subject to subsection (7) below, for the purposes of a tunnel undertaking, or

(d) subject to subsection (8) below, for the purposes of a bridge undertaking, or

(e) for the purposes of a trade which consists in the manufacture of goods or materials or the subjection of goods or materials to any process, or

(f) for the purposes of a trade which consists in the storage—
   (i) of goods or materials which are to be used in the manufacture of other goods or materials, or
   (ii) of goods or materials which are to be subjected, in the course of a trade, to any process, or
   (iii) of goods or materials which, having been manufactured or produced or subjected, in the course of a trade, to any process, have not yet been delivered to any purchaser, or
   (iv) of goods or materials on their arrival by sea or air into any part of the United Kingdom, or

(g) for the purposes of a trade which consists in the working of any mine, oil well or other source of mineral deposits, or of a foreign plantation, or

(h) for the purposes of a trade consisting in all or any of the following activities, that is to say, ploughing or cultivating land (other than land in the occupation of the person carrying on the trade) or doing any other agricultural operation on such land, or threshing the crops of another person, or

(i) for the purposes of trade which consists in the catching or taking of fish or shellfish, and, in particular, the said expression includes any building or structure provided by the person carrying on such a trade or undertaking for the welfare of workers employed in that trade or undertaking and in use for that purpose.

(2) The provisions of subsection (1) of this section shall apply in relation to a part of a trade or undertaking as they apply in relation to a trade or undertaking:

Provided that where part only of a trade or undertaking complies with the conditions set out in the said provisions, a building or structure shall not, by virtue of this subsection, be an industrial building or structure unless it is in use for the purposes of that part of that trade or undertaking.

(3) Notwithstanding anything in subsection (1) or subsection (2) of this section, but subject to the provisions of subsection (4) of this section, "industrial building or structure" does not include any building or structure in use as, or as part of, a dwelling-house, retail shop, showroom, hotel or office or for any purpose ancillary to the purposes of a dwelling-house, retail shop, showroom, hotel or office:

Provided that this subsection shall not apply to, or to part of, a building or structure which was constructed for occupation by, or for the welfare of, persons employed at, or in connection with the working of, a mine, oil well or other source of mineral deposits, or for occupation by, or for the welfare of, persons employed on, or in connection with the growing and harvesting of the crops on, a foreign plantation, if the building or structure is likely to have little or no value to the person carrying on the trade when the mine, oil well or other source or the plantation is no longer worked, or will cease to belong to such person on the coming to an end of a foreign concession under which the mine, oil well or other source, or the plantation, is worked.

(4) Where part of the whole of a building or structure is, and part thereof is not, an industrial building or structure, and the capital expenditure which has been incurred on the construction of the second mentioned part is not more than one-tenth of the total capital expenditure which has been incurred on the construction of the whole building or structure, the whole building or structure and every part thereof shall be treated as an industrial building or structure. . . .

(7) Subsection (1) (c) above shall not affect any allowance or charge which would have been made under this Part of this Act [Part I: Main reliefs for capital expenditure] if this Act had been enacted without that paragraph and if

section 25 of the Finance Act 1952 (which is the corresponding provision repealed by this Act) had not been passed, and where by virtue of the said paragraph (c) a balancing charge is made on a person in respect of any expenditure, the amount on which it is made shall not exceed the amount of the allowances made to him in respect of that expenditure by virtue of the said paragraph (c) (and the said section 25).

(8) Subsection (1)(d) above shall have effect only in relation to expenditure which is to be treated for the purposes of this Chapter [Chapter I of Part I] as incurred after the end of the year 1956–57. (Capital Allowances Act 1968, s 7)

(1) In this Part [Part IV: control in special cases] of this Act 'industrial building' means a building used or designed for use—
(a) for the carrying on of any process for or incidental to any of the following purposes, that is to say—
   (i)   the making of any article or of part of any article; or
   (ii) the altering, repairing, ornamenting, finishing, cleaning, washing, freezing, packing or canning, or adapting for sale, or breaking up or demolition, of any article; or
   (iii) without prejudice to the preceding sub-paragraphs, the getting, dressing or preparation for sale of minerals or the extraction or preparation for sale of oil or brine;
(b) for the carrying on of scientific research, being a process or research carried on in the course of a trade or business.

(2) For the purposes of subsection (1) of this section, premises which—
(a) are used or designed for use for providing services or facilities ancillary to the use of other premises for the carrying on of any such process or research as is mentioned in the subsection; and
(b) are or are to be comprised in the same building or the same curtilage as those other premises,
shall themselves be treated as used or designed for use for the carrying on of such a process or, as the case may be, of such research.

(3) In this section—
   'article' means an article of any description, including a ship or vessel;
   'building' includes a part of a building;
   'scientific research' means any activity in the fields of natural or applied science for the extension of knowledge.

(Town and Country Planning Act 1971, s 66)

INDUSTRIAL DISPUTE

Australia 'The basic question raised by this case . . . is whether an "industrial dispute" within the meaning of the Federal Constitution is legally possible between the States of Victoria and Tasmania on the one hand and the teachers they employ on the other. . . . The theory [of the employers] was that society is industrially organised for the production and distribution of wealth in the sense of tangible, ponderable, corpuscular wealth, and therefore an industrial dispute cannot possibly occur except where there is furnished to the public—the consumers—by the combined efforts of employers and employed, wealth of that nature. Consequently, say the employers, "education" not being "wealth" in that sense, there never can be an "industrial dispute" between employers and employed engaged in the avocation of education, regardless of the wealth derived by the employers from the joint co-operation. . . . The contention is radically unsound. . . . It . . . neglects the fundamental character of "industrial disputes" as a distinct and insistent phenomenon of modern society. Such disputes are not simply a claim to share the material wealth jointly produced and capable of registration in statistics. At heart they are a struggle, constantly becoming more intense on the part of the employed group engaged in co-operation with the employing group in rendering services to the community essential for a higher general human welfare, to share in that welfare in a greater degree.' *Federated State School Teachers' Assocn of Australia v Victoria* (1929) 41 CLR 569 at 576-578, per Isaacs J

Australia 'To create an industrial dispute the relationship of employer and employee must be directly involved in the demand. Demands which in themselves do not do so will not be industrial in the relevant sense, however much of the relationship of employer and employee may be indirectly affected by the result of acceptance or refusal of the demand. . . . What is sought to be done in this case is to make a demand which directly concerns only the management of the transport system. The subject-matter of the demand is the management of the transport system. This, in my opinion, is not an industrial demand.' *R v Commonwealth Conciliation & Arbitration Commission, ex p Melbourne & Metropolitan Tramways Board* [1966] ALR 722 at 725, 726, per Barwick J

INDUSTRIAL OR INTELLECTUAL PROPERTY

'Industrial or intellectual property' includes, without prejudice to its generality, patents, designs, trade-marks, know-how and copyrights. (Aircraft and Shipbuilding Industries Act 1977, s 56(1))

INDUSTRIAL PLANT

'Industrial plant' includes any still, melting pot or other plant used for any industrial or trade purposes, and also any incinerator used for or in connection with any such purposes. (Clean Air Act 1956, s 34(1))

INDUSTRIAL SCHOLARSHIP   *See* SCHOLARSHIP

INDUSTRIAL UNDERTAKING

For the purpose of this Convention [Nightwork (Women) Convention (Revised) 1934] 'industrial undertaking' includes particularly:
(a) Mines, quarries, and other works for the extraction of minerals from the earth;
(b) Industries in which articles are manufactured, altered, cleaned, repaired, ornamented, finished, adapted for sale, broken up or demolished, or in which materials are transformed, including shipbuilding, and the generation, transformation, and transmission of electricity or motive power of any kind;
(c) Construction, reconstruction, maintenance, repair, alteration, or demolition of any building, railway, tramway harbour, dock, pier, canal, inland waterway, road, tunnel, bridge, viaduct, sewer, drain, well, telegraphic or telephonic installation, electrical undertaking, gas work, water work, or other work of construction, as well as the preparation for or laying the foundations of any work or structure. (Hours of Employment (Conventions) Act 1936, Schedule, Part I, Article 1)

INDUSTRIAL USE

'Industrial use', in relation to any goods, means the use of those goods in the manufacture of, or for incorporation in, goods of a different description in the course of the carrying on of a business. (Weights and Measures Act 1985, s 94(1))

INDUSTRY

Australia 'An industry contemplated by the Act [Commonwealth Conciliation and Arbitration Act 1904] is apparently one in which both employers and employees are engaged, and not merely industry in the abstract sense, or in other words, the labour of the employee given in return for the remuneration received from his employer. As suggested, not only by the words defining "industry" itself, but also by Schedule B, and by such a phrase in the definition of "industrial dispute" as "employment in industries carried on by or under the control of the Commonwealth", etc, an "industry" as intended by Parliament seems to be a business, etc., in which the employer on his own behalf is engaged as well as the employees in his employment. Turning to the specific definition of "industry", it rather appears to mean a business (as merchant), a trade (as cutler), a manufacturer (as a flour miller), undertaking (as a gas company), a calling (as an engineer) or service (as a carrier) or an employment (a general term like "calling"—embracing some of the others, and intended to extend to vocations which might not be comprised in any of the rest), all of these expressions so far indicating the occupation in which the principal, as I may call him, is engaged whether on land or water. If the occupation so described is one in which persons are employed for pay, hire, advantage, or reward, that is, as employees, then, with the exceptions stated, it is an industry within the meaning of the Act.' *Jumbunna Coal Mine v Victorian Coal Miners' Assocn* (1908) 6 CLR 309 at 370, per Isaacs J; approved in *Federated Engine-Drivers & Fireman's Assocn of Australia v Broken Hill Proprietary Co Ltd* (1911) 12 CLR 398

INEQUITABLE   *See* IMPRACTICABLE

INEVITABLE ACCIDENT   *See also* ACT OF GOD

Inevitable accident no longer exists as a separate defence. A person is not liable in negligence unless the plaintiff proves that he failed to take reasonable care. In trespass, too, it now seems that the plaintiff fails unless he proves that the defendant either intentionally or negligently committed the wrongful act. Where the tort is one of strict liability, it will be no defence for the defendant to prove inevitable accident.

Where an injury results from natural causes which could not have been foreseen and could not have been avoided by any amount of foresight and care which could reasonably have been expected, it may be said to result from an act of God. Thus, in one sense, it is merely a type of inevitable accident, but its particular quality is that it affords a defence to common law torts involving strict liability whereas other categories of inevitable accident do not. (45 Halsbury's Laws (4th edn) paras 1250, 1251)

'In my apprehension, an inevitable accident in point of law is this, viz that which the party charged with the offence could not possibly prevent by the exercise of ordinary care, caution and maritime skill.' *The Virgil* (1843) 2 Wm Rob 201 at 205, per cur.

'The definition I have given . . . and to which I must adhere, is this: where a collision takes place when every prudent measure, consistent with ordinary seamanship, has been adopted and carried into effect by the vessel proceeded against. Inevitable accident is not this: where a man proceeds carelessly on his voyage, and afterwards circumstances arise, and it is too late for him to do what is fit and proper to be done.' *The Juliet Erskine* (1849) 6 Notes of Cases 633 at 634, per Dr Lushington

'What is an inevitable accident? Inevitable accident, in the absolute and strict sense of the term, very seldom takes place. "Inevitable" must be considered as a relative term, and must be construed not absolutely, but reasonably, with regard to the circumstances of each particular case. In the strict sense of the term, there are very few cases of collision that can be said to be inevitable, for it is almost always possible, the bare possibility considered, to avoid such an occurrence. It was possible in this case, by going at a slower pace, or lying to during the fog. But the import of the words "inevitable accident", in my view, is this: where a man is pursuing his lawful avocation in a lawful manner, and something occurs which no ordinary skill or caution could prevent, and, as the consequence of that occurrence, an accident takes place.' *The Europa* (1850) 14 Jur 627 at 628, per Dr Lushington

'To constitute an inevitable accident it is necessary that the occurrence shall have taken place in such a manner as not to have been capable of being prevented by ordinary skill and ordinary diligence.' *The Thomas Powell v The Cuba* (1866) 14 LT 603 at 603, per Dr Lushington

'Inevitable accident is that which a party

charged with an offence could not possibly prevent by the exercise of ordinary care, caution, and maritime skill. It is not enough to show that the accident could not be prevented by the party at the very moment it occurred, but the question is, what previous measures have been adopted to render the occurrence of it less probable.' *The Uhla* (1868) 19 LT 89 at 90, per Dr Lushington

'Inevitable accident is where the collision could not possibly have been prevented by proper care and seamanship under the particular circumstances of the case.' *The Calcutta (Owners) v The Emma (Owners), The Calcutta* (1869) 21 LT 768 at 768, PC, per cur.

[A lease of a warehouse provided that the rent should abate if the warehouse should at any time during the term be destroyed or damaged by fire, etc, or other 'inevitable accident'.] 'It is to be observed that the words "inevitable accident" are coupled with the word "other", which seems to shew to some extent that they are to be construed by the rule of ejusdem generis, that is, the inevitable accident pointed at is one of a kind similar to "flood, fire, storm, or tempest", referred to in the earlier words. . . . It is to be an "inevitable accident", but here the accident, according to the defendant's own case, might have been avoided if the building had been properly constructed, and consequently it was not an "inevitable accident".' *Saner v Bilton* (1878) 7 Ch D 815 at 823, per Fry J

'It appears to me that inevitable accident as applied to two vessels both in motion, and to one vessel in motion and another at rest, differs in the sense that it is obvious that the facility with which a stationary body may be avoided is very much greater than the facility with which a moving body may be avoided, especially when the law of that motion is more or less unknown; and therefore, though I think that the principle of law applicable to the two cases is the same, I think the fact makes an important difference in the application of the common principle to the two different cases. . . . If she [the *Albano*] acted in the best manner in which she could act, it follows that whatever rule we adopt in the definition of inevitable accident, inevitable accident has occurred in this case.' *The Schwan, The Albano* [1892] P 419 at 433, 434, CA, per Fry LJ

'"Inevitable accident" was defined by Dr Lushington in the Admiralty case of *The Virgil* [supra], in terms which have since received general acceptance—"that which the party

charged with the offence could not possibly prevent by the exercise of ordinary care, caution, and maritime skill". Omitting the word "maritime" the definition is as applicable to courts of common law as to the Court of Admiralty.' *McBride v Stitt* [1944] NI 7 at 10, per Andews CJ

INFAMOUS CONDUCT

[The Medical Act 1858, s 29 (repealed; see now the Medical Act 1983, s 36 where the expression is now 'serious professional misconduct'), empowered the General Medical Council to direct the registrar to erase from the register the name of any medical practitioner guilty of 'infamous conduct' in any professional respect.] 'The Master of the Rolls [Lord Esher] has adopted a definition which, with his assistance and that of my brother Davey, I prepared. I will read it again: "If it is shewn that a medical man, in the pursuit of his profession, has done something with regard to it which would be reasonably regarded as disgraceful or dishonourable by his professional brethren of good repute and competency", then it is open to the General Medical Council to say that he has been guilty of "infamous conduct in a professional respect". That is at any rate evidence of "infamous conduct" within the meaning of s 29.' *Allinson v General Council of Medical Education & Registration* [1894] 1 QB 750 at 763, CA, per Lopes LJ

'It is a great pity that the word "infamous" is used to describe the conduct of a medical practitioner who advertises. As in the case of the Bar so in the medical profession advertising is serious misconduct in a professional respect and that is all that is meant by the phrase "infamous conduct"; it means no more than serious misconduct judged according to the rules written or unwritten governing the profession.' *R v General Medical Council* [1930] 1 KB 562 at 569, CA, per Scrutton LJ

Australia 'In the case of *Re Kennely* [(1912) 12 SR (NSW) 319] Ferguson J expressed his opinion in no uncertain manner that the word "infamous" in that Act [Dental Act 1900] was used to describe conduct which was notoriously evil, wicked, or vile, and not in any "mild Pickwickian sense". His judgment, however, was a dissenting judgment and the Chief Justice was equally emphatic that the expression "infamous conduct in a professional respect" included conduct which would not necessarily be regarded by the public as infamous, and which would not be classed as vile or disgraceful if tried by non-professional standards but included conduct in the pursuit of a profession which would reasonably be regarded as disgraceful or dishonourable by his professional brethren of good repute and competency. This opinion of the learned Chief Justice was no more than an application to the New South Wales Dental Act of the decision in *Allinson v General Council of Medical Education and Registration* [supra] on the meaning of the same words in the English Medical Act s 29 [see supra].' *Hartnett v Medical Board of Victoria* [1941] VLR 289 at 292, per O'Bryan J

Australia 'I think I should emphasise . . . that it must be a rare case indeed, if such a case can exist at all, in which mere negligence which might found a claim against a medical practitioner for damages for negligence would amount to infamous conduct in a professional respect. This, of course, is far from saying that gross negligence might not amount to infamous conduct especially if such negligence was aggravated by lack of concern for the welfare of the patient.' *Epstein v Medical Board of Victoria* [1945] VLR 309 at 310, per Lowe J

Australia 'It is perhaps a pity that the use has been continued of the word "infamous" which in ordinary speech today has been strengthened. But it is best represented by the words "shameful" or "disgraceful"; and it is as conduct of a medical practitioner in relation to his profession that it must be considered shameful or disgraceful.' *Hoile v Medical Board of South Australia* [1960] ALR 430 at 432, per cur.

Australia 'Consideration of the cases and of the provisions of the legislation in force in this State suggest that the only generalisation as to the meaning in that legislation of "infamous conduct in any professional respect", which can be attempted as capable of application to the varying situations which may arise, is that it refers to conduct which being sufficiently related to the pursuit of the profession, is such as would reasonably incur the strong reprobation of professional brethren of good repute and competence. Like the word "infamous" such suggested alternatives as "disgraceful" or "dishonourable" or "shameful" must be understood by reference to this context of professional disapprobation; and due regard must be had to the varying classes of conduct to which these epithets, used in this special professional sense, may come to

be applied. Some forms of misconduct by medical practitioners may in themselves bear the badge of iniquity, in general as well as in professional estimation, and thus be "infamous" in the ordinary, as well as in the special professional, sense. Other forms of misconduct may be "infamous" in a professional sense and yet not be so regarded in the ordinary and general use of that expression. Then there are those whose infamy is a matter of degree and which, if they are reasonably to be regarded as infamous in a professional respect, must be accompanied by some element of moral turpitude. Deviations from accepted procedures in the actual practice of the art may sometimes become, and with reason, the subject of professional reprobation, although unattended by any taint of moral obliquity. But in this branch also of the subject, decision must be dependent upon the circumstances of the particular case and upon questions of degree. In short, whether moral turpitude is a necessary ingredient of "infamous conduct in any professional respect" is a matter on which no general rule can be laid down, the answer being dependent upon the nature of the conduct which is in question in each instance.' *Ex p Meehan, re Medical Practitioners Act* [1965] NSWR 30 at 35, 36, per Sugerman J

Australia 'These words, as has been pointed out [*Epstein v Medical Board of Victoria* [1945] VLR 309 at 310], require something more than "mere negligence which might found a claim against a medical practitioner for damages". Gross negligence, it was suggested in the same case, might amount to infamous conduct, especially if such negligence was aggravated by lack of concern for the welfare of the patient. So too might departures from elementary and generally accepted standards of which a medical practitioner could scarcely be heard to say that he was ignorant, as in the illustrations given in *Epstein v Medical Board of Victoria,* of operating by a long abandoned technique or in an unclean manner. As not far removed from this, the expression "infamous conduct in any professional respect" was applied in *Ex p Meehan, Re Medical Practitioners Act* [[1965] NSWR 30], to what was there described as departure from an approved surgical practice thereby exposing patients to unnecessary hazard, the infringement being of basic professional tenets as to which there was no suggestion of doubt or difference of opinion and to which the medical practitioner had said that he himself subscribed, and such infringement occurring at intervals over a substantial period of time in a premeditated course of conduct adopted by the doctor. Each case must be judged upon its own circumstances.' *Re Medical Practitioners Act 1938–1964* [1967] 2 NSWR 357 at 370, per Sugerman J

New Zealand The Medical Practitioners Act 1914, s 22(1) (repealed; see now the Medical Practitioners Act 1950, s 44 as substituted by s 7(1) of the Medical Practitioners Amendment Act 1957) was in part as follows: 'If any registered medical practitioner is, in the opinion of the Council, guilty of any grave impropriety or infamous conduct in any professional respect, . . . the Council may . . . apply to the Supreme Court for an order for the removal of the name of that person from the register'.] 'The conclusion that the language of the subsection is both clear and definite is inescapable. The phrases "grave impropriety" and "infamous conduct" are generic terms and are not, in their ordinary grammatical sense, limited to acts or conduct which do not offend against the criminal law. Such a limited interpretation might be attached to them if they were of doubtful meaning, in which case that meaning might properly be adopted which could, with propriety, be assumed to express the intention of Parliament. But here the words are not susceptible of more than one meaning. In any event, to give the words other than their ordinary grammatical meaning would defeat and not give effect to what appears to be the clearly expressed intention of the Legislature. There can be no question but that Parliament was concerned in the public interest to ensure that no unworthy person should enjoy or continue to enjoy the benefits of registration. This was the view expressed by the Full Court in *Re McKinnon* [[1918] NZLR 566, 570], where, in delivering the judgment of the Court, Sir Robert Stout CJ said: "We are of opinion that the whole object of the Legislature is to prevent undesirable persons of bad character obtaining the position of registered medical practitioners". That case covered an application for registration, but the definition of the object of the Legislature is general in character. This being the purpose of the Legislature, it prescribed the various circumstances in which and the method by which the name of any offending person could be removed from the register. It is the duty of the Court to give effect to this clearly demonstrated intention.' *Re Isdale, Isdale v Medical Council* [1945] NZLR 136 at 145, CA, per cur; also reported [1944] GLR 435 at 437

INFANT

[By s 1 of the Family Law Reform Act 1969 the age of majority was reduced from twenty-one years to eighteen years and all statutory references to minority and infancy are to be construed accordingly. Section 9 of the Act of 1969 further provides that the time at which a person attains a particular age expressed in years shall be the commencement of the relevant anniversary of the date of his birth. The old common law rule that a person was deemed to attain a particular age at the first moment of the day immediately preceding the relevant anniversary of his birth has thus been abolished.

In legislation after 1970 the term 'infant' is seldom used. Section 12 of the Act of 1969 provides that a person who is not of full age (eighteen) may be described as a 'minor' instead of as an infant.]

Australia [A testator devised his residuary estate to trustees upon trusts for conversion and investment and to pay to his wife the income for the support of herself and his 'infant children'.] 'The provision in the will admits of two constructions: it may mean that the trust is for the benefit of such of the children of the testator as happened to be infants at the time of his death, or it may mean that the trust is for the benefit of those of his children who are for the time being under the age of twenty-one years; if it has the latter meaning it is clear that the period during which the trust continues is limited to the respective minorities of the infants. If the testator intended the word "infant" to be a word of designation merely, and to have no effect upon the duration of the trust, he could more properly and equally easily have attained that result by naming the children whom he intended to be the objects of his bounty. He, however, has not done so, but has merely said "my infant children", and I have no doubt that he intended by that to indicate his children who for the time being should happen to be infants. . . . The trust for the support and maintenance of the testator's infant children is limited to the respective minorities of such children.' *Re Hart, Hart v Griffiths* (1907) 7 SRNSW 839, at 840, 841, per Simpson CJ in Eq

Australia 'The word "infants" is generally used to refer only to very young children but . . . over several centuries, the legal connotation of the word has extended to all persons who have yet to attain their majority, that is, all persons who are not legally adult. The word is used in this sense in Coke's First Institute 1628, pp 170–71, in Blackstone's Commentaries on the Laws of England 1765, Book I, Chapter XVII, p 463 and in *Morgan v Thorne* (1841) 7 M & W 400 at 408.' *Thurgood v Director Australian Legal Aid Office* (1984) 56 ALR 565 at 571, 572, per Wilcox J

INFANTICIDE

(1) Where a woman by any wilful act or omission causes the death of her child being a child under the age of twelve months, but at the time of the act or omission the balance of her mind was disturbed by reason of her not having fully recovered from the effect of giving birth to the child or by reason of the effect of lactation consequent upon the birth of the child, then, notwithstanding that the circumstances were such that but for this Act the offence would have amounted to murder, she shall be guilty of felony, to wit of infanticide and may for such offence be dealt with and punished as if she had been guilty of the offence of manslaughter of the child.

(2) Where upon the trial of a woman for the murder of her child, being a child under the age of twelve months, the jury are of opinion that she by any wilful act or omission caused its death, but that at the time of the act or omission the balance of her mind was disturbed by reason of her not having fully recovered from the effect of giving birth to the child or by reason of the effect of lactation consequent upon the birth of the child, then the jury may, notwithstanding that the circumstances were such that but for the provisions of this Act they might have returned a verdict of murder, return in lieu thereof a verdict of infanticide. (Infanticide Act 1938, s 1)

[All distinctions between felonies and misdemeanours were abolished by s 1(1) of the Criminal Law Act 1967. The word 'felony' in this section should accordingly be read as 'offence' (see s 12(5)(a) of the Act of 1967).]

INFECTION

Of goods

Under the doctrine of infection, goods, not in themselves liable to condemnation, which belong to the same owner as other cargo in the same vessel, which latter cargo is liable to condemnation, are liable to seizure and condemnation as lawful prize. (37 Halsbury's Laws (4th edn) para 1326)

'That the so-called doctrine of infection does not really rest, in spite of many passages which suggest it, on the personal culpability or complicity of the owner of the goods is shewn by the fact that, if it were so, excusable ignorance would be an answer, and for this there is no authority. The term is as old as the Treaty of Utrecht, but the doctrine is perhaps unfortunately named. From the figure which describes the goods as contaminated when seized, the mind passes to the analogy of a physical taint, which runs through the entire cargo in consequence of its being in one bottom, and begins on shipment or at least on sailing. Hence, "once infected always infected", is assumed to be the rule, and a buyer would get a tainted parcel, even though he became owner before seizure, and was recognised as such. This is inconsistent with the view that the rule is a penal rule, as it certainly has been said to be, but it is argued that the penal effect is only accidental and that the real foundation is the belligerent's right of capture, which may arise as soon as the ship gets out to sea. "Infection" has then attached to all the goods afloat in one common ownership, and to purge it by a subsequent transaction and transfer of ownership on land would be to defeat an accrued belligerent right. This reasoning is answered as soon as it is appreciated that "infection"—that is, the liability of a particular owner to a derivative condemnation of his goods—is not a quality of the goods themselves, but is an incident of the owner's position, when the seizure is made and the captor's right arises.' *The Kronprinsessan Margareta, The Parana* [1921] 1 AC 486 at 496, PC, per cur.

INFERIOR COURT   *See also* COURT

'We are concerned to determine whether [a] local valuation court is an "inferior court". This is the expression used in RSC Ord 52, r 1, but that order does not create a jurisdiction where none existed before. It uses the expression "inferior court" to describe the tribunal which the Queen's Bench Divisional Court is concerned to protect from interference by committal for contempt. Those tribunals are aptly described as inferior courts for the expression contemplates a superior court, namely a court of record. So one looks for a comparable tribunal but at an inferior level, that is, with limited jurisdiction. What then are the attributes of such a tribunal? In my opinion the first is that it should have been created by the state. At one time courts were created or recognised by the monarch. Now they are created by Parliament. Thus, while an arbitration tribunal may contain many of the attributes of a court, it will lack this first essential one. Secondly, it must conduct its procedure in accordance with the rules of natural justice. Thirdly, that procedure will involve a public hearing with the power at least to receive evidence orally, to permit the oral examination and cross-examination of witnesses and to hear argument on the issues before it. Fourthly, it arrives at a decision which is final and binding as long as it stands. Fifthly, there will be two parties at least before it, one of whom may be the Crown, who are interested in the decision. Sixthly, the decision will be concerned with legal rights.' *A-G v British Broadcasting Corpn* [1979] 3 All ER 45 at 55, CA, per Eveleigh LJ

[It was held that local valuation courts are courts of record.]

INFESTATION

'Infestation' means the presence of rats, mice, insects or mites in numbers or under conditions which involve an immediate or potential risk of substantial loss of or damage to food, and 'infested' shall be construed accordingly. (Prevention of Damage by Pests Act 1949, s 28)

INFIRMITY

'As regards "infirmity" [under the rules of a Friendly Society], that means some permanent disease, accident, or anything of that kind, rendering the member an object deserving of the assistance of the society.' *Re Buck, Bruty v Mackey* [1896] 2 Ch 727 at 734, per Kekewich J

INFLAMMABLE

Australia 'The word "inflammable" is an ordinary English word, and . . . it is sufficient for me to say that in ordinary parlance it means that which is very easily set alight, and dry paper and dry cardboard are things which, of course, fall within that category.' *Ex p N Ormsby & Sons Pty Ltd, Re Strathfield Municipal Council* [1963] NSWR 1167 at 1170, per McClemens J

INFLICT

'If a man by a grasp of the hand infects another with small-pox, it is impossible to trace out in detail the connection between the act and the disease, and it would, I think, be an unnatural use of language to say that a man by such an act "inflicted" small-pox on another. It would be wrong in interpreting an Act of Parliament to lay much stress on etymology, but I may just observe that "inflict" is derived from "*infligo*", for which, in Faeciolati's Lexicon three Italian and three Latin equivalents are given, all meaning "to strike", viz "*dare, ferire*, and *percuotere*" in Italian, and "*infero impingo*, and *percutio*" in Latin.' *R v Clarence* (1888) 22 QBD 23 at 42, CCR, per Stephen J

INFLUENCE   *See* UNDUE INFLUENCE

INFORM

Canada [After sentencing an accused to six months' imprisonment and two years' probation, the court was requested by Crown counsel to explain the significance and consequence of being on probation, but declined to do so.] 'There is a significant difference between "inform" in s 663(4)(c) [of the Criminal Code (RSC 1970, c C-34)] and "address" in s 469. In the latter, the Code makes it perfectly clear that the justice shall verbally communicate in open court the statutory warning at the conclusion of the Crown's case on a preliminary enquiry. In the former, there is no clear expression that the information be given *viva voce* in open court by the trial judge. . . . In *Leguilloux* [*R v Leguilloux* (1979) 51 CCC (2d) 99 BCCA)], all justices agreed that "inform" was not always confined to a direct verbal communication by the trial judge at the time. . . . If "inform" in s 663(4)(c) is defined to include a less direct communication, then it cannot be mandatory that the trial judge personally communicate the significance and consequences of being on probation to the offender. . . . What is clear from the Criminal Code is that "address" and "inform" have different meanings. . . . It would appear that the Newfoundland Court of Appeal gives the word "inform" broader meaning than "address".' *R v Oliver* (1981) 29 Nfld & PEIR 443 at 448, 449, Nfld Prov Ct, per Luther PCJ

INFORMAL WILL   *See* WILL

INFORMATION   *See also* ACTION

In criminal proceedings

'The term "information" is of well-defined meaning; and, whether it be in writing or *ore tenus*, is understood to be the initiary step in proceedings of a criminal nature, which are to be disposed of summarily.' *Re Dillon* (1859) 11 ICLR 232 at 238, per Hayes J

Australia 'The term "information" is most frequently understood in New South Wales to be the initiatory step before a magistrate in proceedings of a criminal nature which may be disposed of summarily or later on indictment after committal. But the term has an older meaning. In *R v Slator* (1881) 8 QBD 267 at p 274, Bowen J referred to this other meaning of "information". ". . . The distinction between an indictment and an information is one founded in the history of the law and liberties of this country. There are two great ways of proceeding against and bringing to trial a person accused of a crime; one is by proceeding against him before a grand jury, and time out of mind that proceeding has been known as an 'indictment'; the other mode is by proceeding without a grand jury upon an information, which is initiated either by the law officers of the Crown or by a private prosecutor with the leave of the Court." In the same case Hawkins J said (at p 272): "A well-defined distinction exists and has long existed between an indictment and an information. An indictment is 'an accusation found by an inquest of twelve or more upon their oath' . . . whilst an information is a proceeding by the Attorney-General of his own motion without the intervention of a grand jury." The distinction between an information in the usual sense of an initiatory step before a magistrate and an indictment is clearly made in the Justices Act 1902. An information may be laid before a justice in any case where a person has committed or is suspected to have committed any treason or other indictable offence in various specified places: Justices Act, s 21. One of those places is "on land beyond the seas, when for such offences an *indictment* may legally be preferred in New South Wales." An information may also be laid before a justice in any case where a person has committed or is suspected of having committed an offence or act in New South Wales which is liable to be summarily punished: Justices Act, s 52.

The Justices Act, s 41, dealing with the procedure on the hearing of an information concerning an indictable offence, also draws a distinction between an information against a person and the presentation of an indictment against him. In New South Wales the term "information" in its older meaning and the term "indictment", however, are frequently used interchangeably.' *Fraser v The Queen (No 2), Meredith v The Queen (No 2)* (1985) 1 NSWLR 680 at 689–690, per McHugh JA

[See also Costs in Criminal Cases Act 1967 (NSW), s 2]

Official information

New Zealand 'The most outstanding feature of the definition [in the Official Information Act, s 2(1)] is that the word "information" is used which dramatically broadens the scope of the whole Act. The stuff of what is held by Departments, Ministers, or organisations is not confined to the written word but embraces any knowledge, however gained or held, by the named bodies in their official capacities. The omission, undoubtedly deliberate, not to define the word "information" serves to emphasise the intention of the legislature to place few limits on relevant knowledge.' *Comr of Police v Ombudsman* [1985] 1 NZLR 578 at 586, HC, per Jeffries J

INFRINGEMENT   *See also* COPYRIGHT

Of copyright

In this Part [Part III: Remedies for infringements of copyright] of this Act "infringing copy"—
(a) in relation to a literary, dramatic, musical or artistic work, or to such a published edition as is mentioned in section fifteen of this Act, means a reproduction otherwise than in the form of a cinematograph film,
(b) in relation to a sound recording, means a record embodying that recording,
(c) in relation to a cinematograph film, means a copy of the film, and
(d) in relation to a television broadcast or a sound broadcast or a cable programme means a copy of a cinematograph film of it or a record embodying a sound recording of it,
being (in any such case) an article the making of which constituted an infringement of the copyright in the work, edition, recording, film, broadcast or programme, or, in the case of an

imported article, would have constituted an infringement of that copyright if the article had been made in the place into which it was imported. (Copyright Act 1956, s 18(3), as amended by the Cable and Broadcasting Act 1984, s 57(1), Sch 5, para 6(11))

Of patent

Subject to the provisions of this section, a person infringes a patent for an invention if, but only if, while the patent is in force, he does any of the following things in the United Kingdom in relation to the invention without the consent of the proprietor of the patent, that is to say—
(a) Where the invention is a product, he makes, disposes of, offers to dispose of, uses or imports the product or keeps it whether for disposal or otherwise;
(b) where the invention is a process, he uses the process or he offers it for use in the United Kingdom when he knows, or it is obvious to a reasonable person in the circumstances, that its use there without the consent of the proprietor would be an infringement of the patent;
(c) where the invention is a process, he disposes of, offers to dispose of, uses or imports any product obtained directly by means of that process or keeps any such product by disposal or otherwise.
(Patents Act 1977, s 60(1))

[The remainder of the section also makes it an infringement to supply a person other than a licensee with the means for putting an invention into effect; but declares that certain acts do not amount to infringement, as e.g. where such an act is done privately and for purposes which are not commercial, or is done for experimental purposes, etc]

INGREDIENT

'Ingredient', in relation to the manufacture or preparation of a substance, includes anything which is the sole active ingredient of that substance as manufactured or prepared. (Medicines Act 1968, s 132(1))

INGRESS

'I must have recourse to the very words which are used in the grant. After the grant of the allotment the following are the words: "Together with full and free liberty of ingress, egress, and regress . . . to and from the road which adjoins to and abounds the said land on the north and west sides thereof". . . . Now, what is the meaning of "ingress to and from the road", that is to say, the private road? I read it to mean the right of going from the close on to the road, or the right of going from the road on to the close. That appears to me to be the meaning of the word "ingress" to the road and from the road. The next words are these: "egress from the road". What is the meaning of "egress from the road"? It is plainly going out from the road—going forth from the road. . . . Then it is said, and said no doubt truly, that the word "regress" is tautological, for you have already sufficient words to enable you to go from the close to the road, and from the road on to the close, and therefore that word does not seem to require special attention.' *Somerset v Great Western Rly Co* (1882) 46 LT 883 at 884, per Fry J

INHABIT—INHABITANT *See also* PARISHIONER

'Inhabited' in relation to any room means that the room is one in which some person passes the night or which is used as a living room or with respect to which there is a presumption until the contrary is shown that some person passes the night therein or that it is used as a living room. (London Building Acts (Amendment) Act 1939, s 4)

'It is difficult to assign a meaning to the word "inhabitants". Under the Statute of Bridges [1530–1, s 3 (repealed)], it means persons holding lands in the county. In the grant of a way over a field to church it would extend to all persons in the parish. It must be taken according to the subject-matter, and be explained, as circumstances allow, sometimes by usage, sometimes by the context or object of a charter. It cannot be said to have any fixed meaning. It ought, therefore, to have been shewn, on this application, who, beyond tenants, were meant by the words "tenants and inhabitants". It might be lodgers, inmates, servants or, perhaps, other descriptions of persons. Those who rely upon the term ought to have shewn what was the character of those whom they seek to introduce under it.' *R v Mashiter* (1837) 6 Ad & El 153 at 165, per Littledale J

[Under s 9 of Stat (1835) 5 & 6 Will 4 c 76 (repealed), a person was not entitled to be on the burgess-list, unless he occupied a house within the borough and was also an 'inhabitant' householder within the borough, or within seven miles thereof.] 'The defendant is occupier of an entire house, and is therefore within s 9 if he also inhabits the house. I agree . . . that he must inhabit a house within the borough, or within seven miles; and looking at the facts, I am of opinion that Mr Boycott does so inhabit this house in Worcester-street, Kidderminster. He has no other fixed residence; he takes his meals there, has his furniture, wines, and library there; his son, his friends, and servants sleep there, and he only does not sleep there himself because of the state of his wife's health. It is impossible to say that a man must always sleep in the house he inhabits.' *R v Boycott* (1866) 14 LT 599 at 600, per Lush J

'A person may inhabit a place without sleeping there, or he may sleep there without inhabiting it. The fact that a person sleeps in a place is generally a very important ingredient in deciding whether he inhabits it, but it is not conclusive.' *R v Exeter (Mayor), Dipstale's Case* (1868) LR 4 QB 114 at 115, 116, per Blackburn J

'The word "inhabit" simply means to dwell in.' *Atkinson v Collard* (1885) 16 QBD 254 at 266, per cur.

'The word "inhabit" does not have an exact meaning. It connotes more than merely occupying a building. Whether an occupant of a building is inhabiting that building depends upon the use he makes of the building. He inhabits a building if he uses it for the purposes for which a dwelling is usually used, namely as a source of sustenance, a place which provides shelter and a place in which to sleep. There may be cases which a person can be said to inhabit a building notwithstanding that he does not use it for all those purposes. I can see no justification for adding a requirement that a person must intend to permanently reside in a building, or must reside or intend to reside in it for a particular period of time before it can be said that he is inhabiting that building. If during a period as short as, say, twenty-four hours a person prepares and eats a meal and sleeps the night in a house, I think that it would unreasonably restrict the meaning of the word to suggest that the house was not inhabited during that period.' *Vass v GRE Insurance Ltd* (1982) Tas R 77 at 78-79, per Green CJ

Canada 'It would appear that, speaking generally, to be an "inhabitant" one might be a permanent resident or a temporary resident having a permanent dwelling within the area.

There appears to be no reason for holding that a person cannot be an inhabitant of two places at the same time, or that a person ceases to be an inhabitant due to temporary absence from the area.' *Ingleby v Innisfil Township* [1958] OWN 349 at 352, per Gibson JA

New Zealand 'The word "inhabit" does not have an exact meaning. It connotes more than merely occupying a' building. Whether an occupant of a building is inhabiting that building depends upon the use he makes of the building. He inhabits a building if he uses it for the purposes for which a dwelling is usually used, namely as a source of sustenance, a place which provides shelter and a place in which to sleep. There may be cases in which a person can be said to inhabit a building notwithstanding that he does not use it for all those purposes. I can see no justification for adding a requirement that a person must intend to permanently reside in a building, or must reside or intend to reside in it for a particular period of time before it can be said that he is inhabiting that building. If during a period as short as, say, 24 hours a person prepares and eats a meal and sleeps the night in a house. I think that it would unreasonably restrict the meaning of the word to suggest that the house was not inhabited during that period.' *Vass v GRE Insurance Ltd* [1982] 2 ANZ Insurance Cases 60, 473, per Green CJ

INHERENT VICE

As regards the inherent vice or nature of the subject matter, unless the policy [of marine insurance] otherwise provides, the underwriter is not liable for loss or damage that is not the consequence of some casualty which can properly be considered a peril of the seas. He is, therefore, not liable for loss or damage arising solely from decay or corruption of the subject matter insured, as when fruit becomes rotten or flour heats, not from external causes, but from internal decomposition; nor is he liable for spontaneous combustion generated by some chemical change in the thing insured, arising from its being put on board in a wet or otherwise damaged condition, or for some damage caused by inadequate packing of the goods. (25 Halsbury's Laws (4th edn) para 177)

'The plaintiff, being the owner of two horses, and having occasion to send them from London to Aberdeen, shipped them on board a steamship belonging to the company of which the defendant is the representative, plying regularly as a general ship between the two ports. The horses were shipped without any bill of lading. In the course of the voyage a storm of more than ordinary violence arose; and partly from the rolling of the vessel in the heavy seas, partly from struggling caused by excessive fright, one of the animals, a mare, received injuries from which she died. . . . If the fright which led to the struggling of the mare was in excess of what is usual in horses on ship-board in a storm, then the rule applies that the carrier is not liable where the thing carried perishes or sustains damage, without any fault of his, by reason of some quality inherent in its nature, and which it was not possible for him to guard against. If, on the other hand, the fright was the natural effect of the storm and of the agitation of the ship, then it was the immediate consequence of the storm, and the injuries occasioned by the fright are sufficiently closely connected with the storm, in other words with the act of God, to afford protection to the carrier.' *Nugent v Smith* (1876) 1 CPD 423 at 425, 426, 438, 439, CA, per Cockburn CJ

INHIBITION

The censures to which a person found guilty of an offence under this Measure renders himself liable are the following, namely . . . (b) inhibition, that is to say, disqualification for a specified time from exercising any of the functions of his Order. (Ecclesiastical Jurisdiction Measure 1963 (No 1), s 49)

INITIAL

'Initial' includes any recognised abbreviation of a name. (Business Names Act 1985, s 8(1))

INJUNCTION

An injunction is a judicial remedy by which a person is ordered to refrain from doing or to do a particular act or thing. In the former case it is called a restrictive injunction, and in the latter a mandatory injunction. It is a remedy of an equitable nature, and since equity acts in personam, an injunction affecting land does not run with the land. (24 Halsbury's Laws (4th edn) para 901)

Mandatory

Formerly the Court of Chancery would not direct the performance of a positive act, but by restraining a defendant from allowing things to remain as they were, as, for example, from allowing buildings to remain on land, indirectly accomplished the same result. An order so framed was called a mandatory order; but now all mandatory injunctions should be in the direct mandatory form, as, for example, by directing buildings to be pulled down and removed. (25 Halsbury's Laws (4th edn) para 902)

'The jurisdiction of this court, so far as it partakes of the nature of a preventive remedy, that is, prohibition of further damage or an intended damage, is a jurisdiction that may be exercised without difficulty, and rests upon the clearest principles. But there has been superadded to that the power of the Court to grant what has been denominated a mandatory injunction, that is, an order compelling a defendant to restore things to the condition in which they were at the time when the plaintiff's complaint was made.' *Isenberg v East India House Estate Co Ltd* (1863) 3 De G J & Sm, 263 at 272, per Lord Westbury LC

Mareva injunction

[The plaintiffs claimed damages against the defendants for repudiation of a charterparty, and for unpaid hire. There was a danger that the defendants, in order to defeat the plaintiff's claim, might transfer assets out of the jurisdiction. The plaintiffs were granted an injunction to prevent this from happening.] 'If it appears that the debt is due and owing, and there is a danger that the debtor may dispose of his assets so as to defeat it before judgment, the court has jurisdiction in a proper case to grant an interlocutory judgment so as to prevent him disposing of those assets. It seems to me that this is a proper case for the exercise of this jurisdiction. There is money in a bank in London which stands in the name of these charterers. The charterers have control of it. They may at any time dispose of it or remove it out of this country. If they do so, the shipowners may never get their charter hire. The ship is now on the high seas. It has passed Cape Town on its way to India. It will complete the voyage and the cargo will be discharged. And the shipowners may not get their charter hire at all. In face of this danger, I think this court ought to grant an injunction to restrain the charterers from disposing of these moneys now in the bank in London until the trial or judgment in this action. If the charterers have any grievance about it when they hear of it, they can apply to discharge it. But meanwhile the shipowners should be protected. It is only just and right that this court should grant an injunction.' *Mareva Companiana Naviera SA v International Bulk Carriers SA, The Mareva* [1975] 2 Lloyd's Rep 509, CA; *see also* [1980] 1 All ER 213 at 215, CA, per Lord Denning MR

'I would not limit the Mareva principle. It seems to me, as Lord Hailsham of St Marylebone indicated in the *Siskina* case [*Siskina (Owners) v Distos Compania Naviera SA, The Siskina* [1977] 3 All ER 803, HL], that the law is developing in this field. Even when a defendant may be present in this country and is served here, it is quite possible that a Mareva injunction can be granted. Counsel for the Chartered Bank told us that it has already been done from time to time in the Commercial Court. Eveleigh LJ made this suggestion: suppose a person was able to be served here because he was on a short visit for a weekend, or had dropped in for an hour or two, and was served, would that make all the difference as to whether a Mareva injunction could be granted or not? That cannot be. The law should be that there is jurisdiction to grant a Mareva injunction, even though the defendant may be served here. If he makes a fleeting visit, or if there is a danger that he may abscond or that the assets or moneys may disappear and be taken out of the reach of the creditors, a Mareva injunction can be granted.' *Chartered Bank v Daklonche* [1980] 1 All ER 205 at 210, CA, per Lord Denning MR

Perpetual

A perpetual injunction is based on a final determination of the rights of the parties, and is intended permanently to prevent infringement of those rights and obviate the necessity of bringing action after action in respect of every such infringement. (25 Halsbury's Laws (4th edn) para 903)

INJURE *See also* CONSPIRACY; INJURY

'An intent to "injure" in strictness means more than an intent to harm. It connotes an intent to do wrongful harm.' *Mogul SS Co Ltd v McGregor Gow & Co* (1889) 23 QBD 598 at 612, CA, per Bowen LJ; affd [1892] AC 25

INJURIOUS AFFECTION

[Section 6 of the Railways Clauses Consolidation Act 1845 provides for the assessment and payment of compensation to the owners and occupiers of land 'injuriously

affected' by the construction of a railway pursuant to a special Act.] 'The damage contemplated in s 6 must, I think, be *damnum cum injuria*. It must be a damage occasioned by the land having been injuriously affected. Both principle and authority seems to me to shew that no case comes within the purview of the statute, unless where some damage has been occasioned to the land itself, in respect of which, but for the statute, the complaining party might have maintained an action. The injury must be actual injury to the land itself, as by loosening the foundation of buildings on it, obstructing its light, or its drains, making it inaccessible by lowering or raising the ground immediately in front of it, or by some such physical deterioration.' *Ricket v Metropolitan Rly Co (Directors etc)* (1867) LR 2 HL 175 at 198, per Lord Cranworth

'I approach the consideration of the statute [Lands Clauses Consolidation Act 1845, s 68] . . . with the belief that the true construction is in the plaintiff's favour. Now I agree that the word "injuriously" does not mean "wrongfully" affected. What is done is rightful under the powers of the Act. It means hurtfully or "damnously" affected. As when we say of a man that he fell and injured his leg. We do not mean that his leg was wrong, but that it was hurt. We mean he fell, and his leg was injuriously, that is to say hurtfully affected. At the same time I am clearly of the opinion that to entitle the parties interested to compensation, the injury or hurt must be such as could not lawfully be inflicted except by the powers of the Act.' *McCarthy v Metropolitan Board of Works* 8 LRCP 191 at 208, 209, per Bramwell B affd (1874) LR 7 HL 243

Canada [Amount payable by expropriating authority to respondent farmer for land expropriated was settled and included sum in compensation for disturbance or business damages.] 'It is common ground between the parties, and I accept as valid, the proposition that the board may only award interest on such elements of compensation as are provided for under s 35(1) of the Act. That section reads in part: "35(1) . . . the owner of lands expropriated is entitled to be paid interest on the portion of the market value of his interest in the land and on the portion of any allowance for injurious affection to which he is entitled, outstanding from time to time, at the rate of 6 per cent a year calculated from the date the owner ceases to reside on or make productive use of the lands." By s 1(1)(e) the Act defines injurious affection as follows: "(e) 'injurious affection' means, (i) where a statutory authority acquires part of the land of an owner, (A) the reduction in market value thereby caused to the remaining land of the owner by the acquisition or by the construction of the works thereon or by the use of the works thereon or any combination of them, and (B) such personal and business damages, resulting from the construction or use, or both, of the works as the statutory authority would be liable for if the construction or use were not under the authority of a statute." . . . The statutory definition limits the claim for injurious affection by way of business damages, to such damages as directly result from the construction or use of the works (in this case a public highway) for which the statutory authority would have been liable at common law, presumably in nuisance. Damages for injurious affection do not result from the mere taking or expropriation of the land, but there must be a causal connection between the construction or use of the public works and the loss sustained.' *Re Van den Elzen & Ministry of Transportation and Communications* (1985) 52 OR (2d) 261 at 263, 264, per Griffiths J

INJURY *See also* DAMAGE; DEATH; IRREPARABLE INJURY; LATENT; WAR INJURY

'The word injury is a general and large word, and comprehends in itself all manner of wrongs, be it in debt, in not paying of it, or in detinue, in the detaining of rent, . . . *injuria* and *damnum* are the two grounds for the having all actions, and without these, no action lieth: if there be *damnum absque injuria*, or *injuria absque damno*, no action lieth, but where there is injury, *injuria* and *damnum*, and so both of them do run together, there an action well lyeth: also this word injury, in itself comprehends all demands; the words of the submission [submission of all debts, trespasses and 'injuries'] comprehends all wrong, which one man by any way may do unto another, being an injury, and includes in it all matters of equity, and also of law.' *Cable v Rogers* (1625) 3 Bulst 311 at 312, per Dodderidge J

'I shall try to distinguish between "damage" and "injury", following the stricter diction, derived from the civil law, which more especially prevails in Scottish jurisprudence. So used, "injury" is limited to actionable wrong, while "damage", in contrast with injury, means loss or harm occurring in fact,

whether actionable as an injury or not. "An intent to injure, in strictness", said Bowen LJ in the *Mogul* case [*Mogul SS Co v McGregor, Gow & Co* (1889) 23 QBD 598], "means more than intent to harm. It connotes an intent to do wrongful harm".' *Crofter Hand Woven Harris Tweed Co Ltd v Veitch* [1942] AC 435 at 442, per Lord Simon LC

Australia 'It does not strain the English language to use the word "injury" for both physical and psychological harm. The object of the legislation [Child Protection Act 1974 (Tas)] leads to the conclusion that such use was intended. It would be unreasonable to conclude that parliament did not intend to give a young child suffering from a psychosis the same protection as that given to a child suffering from physical injury when both were caused by cruel treatment. Accordingly, I reach the conclusion that the word "injury" in s 10 includes both physical and psychological injury.' *Re P (an infant)* (1986) 10 Fam LR 999 at 1002–1003, per Underwood J

Canada 'The distinction between "injury" and "damage" is fundamental. One can only justify a quotation pointing up the distinction on the basis that the draftsman of the policy here seems not to have appreciated it (Jowitt, Dictionary of English Law, p 973): "*Injuria; Injury*, the infringement of some right. Hence 'injury' is opposed to 'damage,' because a right may be infringed without causing pecuniary loss (*injuria sine damno*): thus, the pollution of a clear stream is to a riparian proprietor below both injury and damage . . ." *Hildon Hotel (1963) Ltd v Dominion Insurance Corpn* (1968) 1 DLR (3d) 214 at 217, BCSC per Rae J

Bodily injury

'Bodily injury' includes injury to health. (Factories Act 1961, s 176)

Australia [The Government Railways Act 1912–1986 (NSW), s 116, provides that 'a gratuity . . . shall be payable to any officer who is incapacitated from the further discharge of his duties by reason of bodily injuries received in the course of his duty, and who retires from the service'.] 'The words "bodily injuries" in s 116 of the Act cannot be confined to external bodily or traumatic injuries, but extend to any injuries to the material body of man and its properties, or, in short, to any physical injuries. The evidence is clear that the appellant was incapacitated from the further discharge of his duties and that he had retired from the service. And there is ample evidence that the appellant suffered from some organic disease, some physical degeneration of the brain involving destruction of nerve cells. Fear just as well as sudden terror or nervous shock may, it is now recognised, affect the physical state of the body as well as mental, nervous, or other functions.' *Deeble v Nott* (1941) 65 CLR 104 at 109, 110, per Starke J

'There have been many decisions upon clauses in insurance policies and provisions in workmen's compensation Acts which have contained expressions such as "bodily injury", "personal injury" and "injury". They show the three expressions have been used indiscriminately to mean the same thing and to cover all cases where a person suffers a physiological injury or change as a result of the happening of the event insured against. They have been held to include many diseases, including bodily disability resulting from the nervous consequences of an accident.' Ibid at 113, per Williams J

Hurt or injury

The Merchant Shipping Act 1854, s 28 (repealed; cf, now Merchant Shipping Act 1970, ss 25, 26), provided that if a seaman received any 'hurt or injury' in the service of the ship to which he belonged, the expense of providing the necessary surgical and medical advice with attendance and medicines should be defrayed by the shipowner without deduction from the seaman's wages. A seaman was attacked by illness caused by the bad provisions supplied to him.] 'The illness here is an illness brought upon the respondent while in the service of the ship [within the above section]. . . . The word "injury" may include illness, and therefore we must interpret it as distinguished from "hurt"; and such clearly ought to be the interpretation where a man receives a gross injury of this kind while in the service of the ship. With regard to the latter phrase, I am of opinion that the words "in the service of the ship" are intended to distinguish such a case as this from a hurt or injury which a man may receive while on shore.' *Board of Trade Secretary v Sundholm* (1879) 41 LT 469 at 470, per Cockburn CJ

Physical injury

For the removal of doubt it is hereby declared that the expression 'physical injury', in the principal Act [Pensions (Navy, Army, Air Force and Mercantile Marine) Act 1939] and in this Act, and in the Personal Injuries (Emergency Provisions) Act 1939, includes tuberculosis and any other organic disease, and the aggravation thereof. (Pensions (Mercantile Marine) Act 1942, s 5)

To person

In this Act the expression 'personal injury' includes any disease and any impairment of a person's physical or mental condition, and the expression 'injured' shall be construed accordingly. (Law Reform (Personal Injuries) Act 1948, s 3)

'Personal injury' includes any disease and any impairment of a person's physical or mental condition. (Defective Premises Act 1972, s 6(1); cf also s 14 of the Unfair Contract Terms Act 1977)

[See also s 1(5) of the Fatal Accidents Act 1976.]

'Personal injuries' includes any disease and any impairment of a person's physical or mental condition, and 'injury' and cognate expressions shall be construed accordingly. (Limitation Act 1980, s 38(1))

'A physiological injury or changes occurring in the course of a man's employment by reason of the work in which he is engaged at or about that moment is an injury by accident arising out of his employment, and this is so even though the injury or change be occasioned partly, or even mainly, by the progress or development of an existing disease if the work he is doing at or about the moment of the occurrence of the physiological injury or change contributes in any material degree to its occurrence. Moreover, this is none the less true though there may be no evidence of any strain or similar cause other than that arising out of the man's ordinary work.' *Oates v Fitzwilliam's (Earl) Collieries Co* [1939] 2 All ER 498 at 502, CA, per cur.

'In ordinary parlance the term "injuries" is used to describe both the initial blows and some of the more immediate consequences. Bruises would, normally, be comprehended in the term "injuries" in its ordinary use. Tumours might be; mental changes might not. The ordinary meaning is, for the purposes of the Act of 1948 [Law Reform (Personal Injuries) Act 1948], supplemented by a statutory definition in s 3 of that Act which provides that the expression "personal injury" is to include "any disease and any impairment of a person's physical or mental condition".' *Flowers v George Wimpey & Co Ltd* [1955] 3 All ER 165 at 170, per Devlin J; see also [1956] 1 QB 73

'The justices have taken much too narrow a view of the words "causes injury", because the accused obviously did intend to cause injury; frightening a person or intimidating a person is causing injury.' *Woodward v Koessler* [1958] 3 All ER 557 at 558, per Lord Goddard CJ

'In the context of the statute [National Insurance (Industrial Injuries) Act 1965 (repealed; see now the Social Security Act 1975, Part II, Chapter IV)] "accident" is used as descriptive of the first event in three chains of causation: (1) Accident—personal injury—incapability of work. (2) Accident—personal injury—loss of capacity—disablement. (3) Accident—personal injury—death. . . . "Personal injury" is only an intermediate link in each of the three chains of causation of which the final result is incapability of work, death or disablement. It is used in this statute as a generic term embracing all adverse physical or mental consequences of an "accident".' *Jones v Secretary of State for Social Services* [1972] 1 All ER 145 at 185, HL, per Lord Diplock

Australia 'Section 7(1)(b)(c) [of the Workers Compensation Act 1926–1986 (NSW)] provides that where a worker has received injury without his own default or wilful act on any of the daily or periodic journeys between his place of abode and place of employment, the worker . . . shall receive compensation from the employer in accordance with the Act. . . . It is plain, I think, that the definition of injury in s 6 is wholly inapplicable to the word injury as used in s 7(1)(b), the definition dealing, as it does, with personal injuries arising out of or in the course of employment . . . whilst s 7(1)(b) is concerned only with injury received on any daily or periodic journey, before employment has begun or after it has ended. In these circumstances, I can see nothing to justify us in not giving to the word "injury" in this context the non-colloquial sense, wide enough to include disease generally, which it has been held to have in this scheme of legislation by the English authorities when there is nothing to indicate that it is intended to have a narrower significance. . . . Upon the authorities the word "injury", when used in its present connection without any definition or context to control it, extends to injury by the contracting

of a disease or the accentuation of an existing disease.' *Peart v Hume Steel Ltd* (1947) 47 SR (NSW) 384 at 386, 387, per Jordan CJ

Australia 'In order that a worker may become entitled to receive compensation, it is necessary, inter alia, (1) that he should receive a personal injury, and (2) that the injury should incapacitate him, totally or partially, for work, for a minimum period. Personal injury means, in my opinion, injury to his person, that is, to some part of his body.' *Storey v McCawley* (1948) 48 SR (NSW) 474 at 475, per Jordan CJ

Australia [The Limitation of Actions Act 1958 (Vic), s 23(A) provides for an extension of the limitation period in certain cases where a person is unaware of any material fact relating to the cause of action. By s 23(A)(3) it is provided that material facts in relation to a cause of action include the nature and extent of personal 'injuries'.] 'In the first place, "injury" in paragraphs (f) and (g) of sub-s (3) means the physical injury and not the signs and symptoms thereof. Pain and stiffness do not constitute the injury. They are merely evidentiary of it. . . . In the second place, "injury" within paragraphs (f) and (g) does not comprehend effects on the working capacity of the injured person. Such effects are consequences of the injury but, although they may constitute evidence of the nature or extent of the injury, they are in themselves neither "the nature of the personal injury" nor the extent of the personal injury".' *Hevey v Leonard* [1976] VR 624 at 632, per cur.

New Zealand [Section 7(1)(a) of the Deaths by Accidents Compensation Act 1952 (NZ), provides for the awarding of damages proportioned to 'injuries' resulting from the death to the person or persons for whose benefit action is brought.] 'For a period of over one hundred years "injury" has been construed as limited to existing or prospective pecuniary loss suffered or likely to be suffered by the family of the deceased.' *McCarthy v Palmer* [1957] NZLR 442 at 447, per McGregor J; affd, ibid, at 620

To property

[Section 14 of the Land Drainage Act 1847 (repealed; cf now the similar provision (as to cleaning of ditches) in the Land Drainage Act 1976, s 40), enacted that where, by reason of the neglect of an occupier of land, 'injury' was caused 'to any other land' by reason of failure to clean and scour a stream, the occupier of such other land might cleanse and scour the channel himself and recover his expenses from the occupier whose neglect had caused the injury.] 'I have come to the conclusion, though not without some doubt, that the expression "injury to any other land" in s 14 does not covet the damage to a mill owner which was complained of in the present case. It is not necessary now to define the cases to which the provisions were intended to apply. It is sufficient, I think, to say that, the object of the Act being to facilitate the drainage of land, the injury which is contemplated by the section is the injury to or the interference with the drainage of other land rather than the interference with land which has been covered with buildings such as a mill.' *Finch v Bannister* [1908] 1 KB 485 at 489, per Channell J; affd, [1908] 2 KB 441, CA

[See also s 17(5) of the Act of 1976, as to injury caused by the carrying out of drainage works.]

'It is not necessary for present purposes to attach any limitation to the word "injury" in s 34(3) of the Land Drainage Act 1930 [repealed; see now s 17(5) of the Land Drainage Act 1976]. It is sufficient to say that, in my view, it includes damage to property suffered by a riparian owner.' *Marriage v East Norfolk Rivers Catchment Board* [1949] 2 All ER 1021 at 1026, per Tucker LJ; *see also* [1950] 1 KB 284 at 292

INJUSTICE

[By the Law of Property Act 1925, s 171 (repealed) where the court was satisfied that any person might suffer an 'injustice' if the property were allowed to devolve as undisposed of on the death intestate of a mental patient, or under any testamentary disposition executed by him, the court might direct a settlement to be made of his property.] 'In my judgment . . . "an injustice" must be construed in a wider sense. It must connote unfairness, and import a sense of grievance, at "the hand of stern injustice and confused wrong" (Shakespeare, King John, Act V, sc 2). It must be used of such a case as where by a change of the law property would go awry; so that those who use the term "injustice" colloquially might think it not appropriate for the purpose of conveying the meaning that the new legislation had worked regrettably, and against the interests of those who would otherwise have enjoyed advantages.' *Re Freeman* [1927] 1 Ch 479 at 486, 487, CA, per Lord Hanworth MR

[The Mental Health Act 1983, s 96, which deals with the powers of justices as to a patient's property and affairs, no longer uses the term 'injustice']

INLAND PACKET

'Inland packet' means anything which is posted within the United Kingdom for delivery at a place in the United Kingdom to the person to whom it is addressed. (Post Office Act 1969, s 30(7), as substituted by SI 1973/960)

INLAND WATERS   *See also* SHIP

'Inland water' means any canal, river, navigation, lake, or water which is not tidal water. (Explosives Act 1875, s 108)

'Inland waters' includes rivers, harbours and creeks. (Public Health Act 1936, s 343)

'Inland waters' includes any part of the sea adjacent to the coast of the United Kingdom, certified by the Secretary of State to be waters falling by international law to be treated as within the territorial sovereignty of Her Majesty apart from the operation of that law in relation to territorial waters. (Supreme Court Act 1981, s 22(2); County Courts Act 1984, s 30(3))

'Inland water' means any of the following, that is to say—
(a) so much of any river, stream or other watercourse, whether natural or artificial and whether tidal or not, as is within any of the river authority areas;
(b) any lake or pond, whether natural or artificial, and any reservoir or dock, in so far as any such lake, pond, reservoir or dock does not fall within the preceding paragraph and is within any of the river authority areas; and
(c) so much of any channel creek, bay, estuary or arm of the sea as does not fall within the preceding paragraphs and is within any of the river authority areas,
and any reference in this Act to an inland water includes a reference to part of an inland water. (Water Resources Act 1963, s 135)

[See the similar definition in s 32(5) of the Land Drainage Act 1976. The principal difference is that in the latter the expression 'Great Britain' is substituted for the words 'any of the river authority areas', wherever they occur.]

In this section . . . 'inland waters' means waters within Great Britain which do not form part of the sea or of any creek, bay or estuary or of any river as far as the tide flows. (Diseases of Fish Act 1983, s 7(8))

INLAND WATERWAY *See* WATERWAY

INMATE

[The Copyright Act 1956, s 12(7) affords protection from infringement of copyright in cases (inter alia) where sound recordings are caused to be heard in public at any premises where persons reside or sleep, as part of the amenities provided exclusively or mainly for such residents or 'inmates'.] 'One asks oneself at once why is there this distinction drawn between residing and sleeping and between residents and inmates? The plaintiffs suggest, and I am inclined to agree, that what Parliament had in mind was that some of the premises to which this subsection was meant to apply were not places which could be said to contain "residents". Take, for example, a prison or an asylum. One would not ordinarily speak of the people in a prison or an asylum as residing in or residents in those establishments. So I think that probably the words "inmates" and "sleeping" were used in contra-distinction to "residents" and "residing" to cover that sort of institution.' *Phonographic Performance Ltd v Pontin's Ltd* [1967] 3 All ER 736 at 738, 739, per Cross J

INN-INNKEEPER *See also* HOTEL

'Innkeeper' is not defined by statute, although the term is used in relation to the proprietor of a hotel to describe the capacity in which duties attach to such persons. At common law an innkeeper was a person who received travellers and provided lodging and necessaries for them and their attendants, and who employed people for this purpose and for the protection of travellers lodging in his inn and of their goods. Where the proprietor of a hotel is a company, and the hotel is carried on by means of a manager, the innkeeper is the company and not the manager, even though the licence for the sale of intoxicating liquor is in the name of the manager. All the duties, liabilities and rights which formerly attached to

an innkeeper as such now attach to the proprietor of a hotel and to no other person. (24 Halsbury's Laws (4th edn) para 1206)

[By s 1 of the Hotel Proprietors Act 1956 an hotel within the meaning of the Act is to be deemed an inn, and any other establishment shall not be so deemed. Further, the duties, liabilities and rights which prior to the Act attached to an innkeeper as such by the common law (as modified by the Innkeepers' Liability Act 1863, now repealed) now attach to the proprietor of such an hotel, ie 'innkeeper' and 'hotel proprietor' are now synonymous.

Under the Act of 1956 'hotel' (and so 'inn') means 'an establishment held out by the proprietor as offering food, drink and, if so required, sleeping accommodation, without special contract, to any traveller presenting himself who appears able and willing to pay a reasonable sum for the services and facilities provided and who is in a fit state to be received']

'The plaintiff's house . . . is no inn; for the verdict finds he lets lodgings only, which shews him not compellable to entertain anybody, and that none can come there without a previous contract; that he is not bound to sell at reasonable rates, or to protect his guests; but contrary it is in all the said points in the case of an innkeeper.' *Parker v Flint* (1699) 12 Mod Rep 254 at 254, per cur.

'An inn is a house, the owner of which holds out that he will receive all travellers and sojourners who are willing to pay a price adequate to the sort of accommodation provided, and who come in a situation in which they are fit to be received. . . . A lodging-house keeper, on the other hand, makes a contract with every man that comes; whereas an innkeeper is bound, without making any special contract, to provide lodging and entertainment for all, at a reasonable price.' *Thompson v Lacy* (1820) 3 B & Ald 283 at 287, per Best J

'The defendant was only the manager of the hotel company, who were the real innkeepers. The circumstances that the licence was taken out in her name does not, in my opinion, alter her position; and there is nothing in the Licensing Acts which prevents it from being shewn that the real "innkeeper" is not the person licensed, but someone else.' *Dixon v Birch* (1873) LR 8 Exch 135 at 136, per Martin B

'The indictment charges the defendant that, being an innkeeper, and under the obligation to receive the prosecutor in his inn, he refused to do so without having any reasonable cause or excuse for such refusal. . . . The defendant was the proprietor of an hotel, and if the prosecutor had been refused accommodation in the hotel the case might have been different. But he was not. The place in question, known as the Carlton, was under the same roof as the hotel, but was entirely separate from it, with a separate entrance, and appears to have been a mere shop in which spirits are retailed across a counter. . . . Such a place is not an inn within the meaning of the common-law rule. An inn is a place "instituted for passengers and way-faring men": *Calye's* case [(1584) 8 Co Rep 32a]. A tavern is not within the definition. In such a place as this no one has a right to insist on being served any more than in any other shop.' *R v Rymer* (1877) 2 QBD 136 at 139, 140, CCR, per Kelly CB

'An hotel-keeper by opening his house as an hotel offers it to the use of the public as such, and thereupon the common law of England imposes on him certain duties, and gives him certain rights. He has no right to refuse to take into his house any one of the public who offers himself as a guest, if he has room for him in his house; and, in return for this obligation which it imposes on him, the common law gives him a lien for his charges upon the goods of the guest which are in the house. If the innkeeper has no room in his house, then he is not bound to take in any person who offers himself as a guest.' *Medawar v Grand Hotel Co* [1891] 2 QB 11 at 19, 20, CA, per Lord Esher MR

INNOCENCE

Presumption of *See* PRESUMPTION

INNOCENT

[A contract for the supply of whisky stipulated that it should be coloured with burnt sugar or other 'innocent' material.] 'The word "innocent" is no doubt a word of many meanings, but in this particular context it is used in connection with a commodity which is referred to, burnt sugar; and the meaning obviously is this: The whisky, it is suggested, was to be coloured either with burnt sugar, which was itself a material which could produce no ill effect upon the spirit, or else with some other innocent material, that is to say, some other material *ejusdem generis*, which would be equally free from any charge of injuring the material into which it was introduced. In other words, the term "innocent" would correctly represent a material which would not be injurious to the commodity by rendering it unfit for the purpose for which it was intended.' *Macfarlane & Co v Taylor & Co* (1868) 18 LT 214 at 217, per Lord Cairns LC

INNOCENT MISREPRESENTATION
See MISREPRESENTATION

INNUENDO   *See also* LIBEL

Words may have not only a literal meaning but also an inferential meaning which goes beyond the literal meaning but is inherent in them and may depend upon the context in which they were published. The literal meaning and any inferential meaning are known as the natural and ordinary meaning. The words may also have a secondary or extended meaning which depends upon knowledge of special or extrinsic facts. The secondary or extended meaning is known as the innuendo, or true or legal innuendo. . . . Confusion has been caused because 'innuendo' has been used to describe both the inferential defamatory meaning of words and their secondary defamatory meaning. However, it is now clear that the secondary defamatory meaning is the true or legal innuendo and that the inferential defamatory meaning is the natural and ordinary meaning, or part of it, the distinction being that the true or legal innuendo depends on knowledge of special facts or circumstances either extrinsic to the words themselves or relating to a special meaning of the words, whereas the inferential meaning must be deduced or inferred from the words themselves and the context in which they were published. (28 Halsbury's Laws (4th edn) paras 44, 46)

'An innuendo is an averment, that such a one, means such a particular person; or, that such a thing, means such a particular thing: and, when coupled with the introductory matter, it is an averment of the whole connected proposition, by which the cognisance of the charge will be submitted to the jury, and the crime appear to the court.' *R v Horne* (1777) 2 Cowp 672 at 683, per de Grey CJ

'"Innuendo" means a secondary meaning, a meaning because of something which is known to particular people.' *Thomson v Chain Libraries Ltd* [1954] 2 All ER 616 at 618, per Lord Goddard CJ

'The word "innuendo" is used in at least two meanings in the law of defamation. First, it is applied to facts and matters tending to show that the alleged libel or slander . . . refers to the plaintiff. Second, it is applied to a secondary or extended or expanded meaning of the alleged libel, as based on and proved by the existence of extrinsic facts and matters. Of these usages, only the second is, in my view, strictly accurate. . . . The second usage is . . . an allegation that, by reason of extrinsic facts, the alleged libel was understood to be such though not defamatory in its natural and ordinary meaning, or though defamatory in its natural and ordinary meaning, was understood in a further or extended defamatory sense. The difference between the two usages may be illustrated by a simple example. Suppose it were written that "the curate of Extown is a regular Casanova". It would, of course, be necessary for the plaintiff to aver and prove that he was at all material times the Curate of Extown. That is the first usage. But, unless it could be said that the pejorative sense of the name "Casanova" has become part of the English language, the plaintiff would go on to allege that by the said words the defendant meant and was understood to mean that the plaintiff was a fornicator, and adulterer, etc. And in such a case particulars would have to be given under RSC Ord 19, r 6(2) [now RSC 1965 Ord 82, r 3], which would, no doubt, consist of a short description of the life and habits of the notorious character referred to. That is the true meaning of an innuendo. Perhaps an even better example of an innuendo was one given by . . . counsel for the defendants. Suppose it to be written that "the advertising of Mr X is in extremely bad taste and indeed grossly vulgar". Those words would probably be defamatory in their natural and ordinary meaning. But, in addition, it would be open to the plaintiff to allege an innuendo, viz, that to those who knew he was a member of the Bar and were familiar with the etiquette of the profession the libel amounted to an allegation of professional misconduct. In the present case counsel for the plaintiff suggests that there is a third kind of innuendo, derived, I suppose, from the ordinary use of that word in common parlance as connoting the sting of, or obvious inference or implication to be drawn from, the libel in its natural and ordinary meaning. That, in my judgment, is not what is properly meant in the law of libel by the expression "innuendo", though unquestionably . . . it is often so used in the decided cases. If the words are defamatory on their face in their natural and ordinary meaning, no innuendo is required. If they are not, then the plaintiff must allege and prove a secondary meaning by an innuendo based on evidence.' *Grubb v Bristol United Press Ltd* [1962] 2 All ER 380 at 395, 396, CA, per Davies LJ also reported in [1963] 1 QB 309 at 336

'No one doubts that it is for the jury to decide the meaning of words, not as a question of pure construction but as a question of fact, as Lord Tenterden CJ put it in *Harvey v French* [(1932) 1 Cr & M 11], "a court must read these words in the sense in which ordinary persons or in which we ourselves out of court . . . would understand them". Whether the words are capable of defamatory meaning is for the judge, and where the words, whether on the face of them they are or are not innocent in themselves, bear a defamatory or more defamatory meaning because of extraneous facts known to those to whom the libel has been published, it is the duty of the judge to rule whether there is evidence of such extraneous facts fit to be left to the jury. It is in conjunction with secondary meanings that much of the difficulty surrounding the law of libel exists. These secondary meanings are covered by the word "innuendo" which signifies pointing out what and who is meant by the words complained of. . . . Libels are of infinite variety and the literal meaning of the words even of such simple phrases as "X is a thief" does not carry one very far for they may have been spoken in play or other circumstances showing that they could not be taken by reasonable persons as imputing an accusation of theft. Conversely to say that a man is a good advertiser only becomes capable of a defamatory meaning if coupled with proof, for example, that he was a professional man whose reputation would suffer if such were believed of him. The first subdivision of the innuendo has lately been called the false innuendo as it is no more than an elaboration or embroidering of the words used without proof of extraneous facts. The true innuendo is that which depends on extraneous facts which the plaintiff has to prove in order to give the words the secondary meaning of which he complains.' *Lewis v Daily Telegraph Ltd* [1963] 2 All ER 151 at 165, HL, per Lord Hodson; also reported in [1964] AC 234 at 271

[See also the speech of Lord Devlin, ibid at 169–171]

'Words may be defamatory in their ordinary and natural meaning. They may also, or in the alternative, bear a defamatory innuendo. A "true" or "legal" innuendo is a meaning which is different from the ordinary and natural meaning of the words, and defamatory because of special facts and circumstances known to those to whom the words are published.' *Slim v Daily Telegraph* [1968] 1 All ER 497 at 511, CA, per Salmon LJ

New Zealand 'An innuendo may be of two kinds. The first kind, commonly called a "false" innuendo, is no more than an explicit pleading of one or more defamatory meanings which the plaintiff alleges that the actual words published by the defendant are capable of bearing in their ordinary and natural sense. The second kind of innuendo, commonly called a "true" innuendo, is a defamatory meaning alleged to have been conveyed by the published words when read in the light of extraneous circumstances.' *Yelash v In Print Publishing Co Ltd* [1972] NZLR 83 at 85, per Richmond J

INPUT TAX

Subject to subsection (4) below, 'input tax', in relation to a taxable person, means the following tax, that is to say—
(a) tax on the supply to him of any goods or services; and
(b) tax paid or payable by him on the importation of any goods, being (in either case) goods or services used or to be used for the purpose of any business carried on or to be carried on by him; and 'output tax' means tax on supplies which he makes. Value Added Tax 1983, s 14(3))

[Subsection (4) of the section deals with the case where the goods or services are supplied or imported partly for the purpose of a business and partly for other purposes.]

INQUEST *See* INQUISITION

INQUIRY *See also* DUE INQUIRY

In this Act the word 'inquiry' shall mean any inquiry held under the authority of any Royal Commission or by any committee of either House of Parliament, or pursuant to any statutory authority, whether the evidence at such inquiry is or is not given on oath, but shall not include any inquiry by any court of justice. (Witnesses (Public Inquiries) Protection Act 1892, s 1)

[The sixth condition in a lease provided (inter alia) that no requisition or 'inquiry' should be made respecting title.] 'The condition is: "It shall form no objection to the title that such indenture is an underlease, and no requisition or inquiry shall be made respecting the title". . . . The word "inquiry" there is not used for the purpose of precluding all inquiry *aliunde*, but is used as a convertible expression with the word "requisition", and does not extend beyond the word "requisition". . . . It seems to me, therefore, that the sixth condition does not preclude all inquiry, because it does not amount to anything like what has been held in several of the cases to amount to an agreement precluding all inquiry from every quarter.' *Waddell v Wolfe* (1874) LR 9 QB 515 at 521, 522, per Quain J

INQUISITION

'The coroner's inquisition is not like a judgment in rem. Nothing is done which is conclusive upon any person affected by it. . . . An inquiry before a coroner is merely in the nature of a preliminary investigation. It is not of any binding force. . . . I am of opinion that the result of an investigation conducted by the coroner, however valuable for certain purposes, cannot in law be treated as *prima facie* evidence against any person of the facts found by the jury.' *Bird v Keep* [1918] 2 KB 692 at 698, 699, CA, per Swinfen Eady MR

INSANITY *See* DELUSION, MENTAL DISORDER

INSCRIBE

'Inscribing' includes the producing of marks on or in a surface by whatsoever means. (London County Council (General Powers) Act 1954, s 20)

INSECTICIDE

Australia 'In my opinion, the term insecticide, as commonly used in English, means, or at any rate includes, any preparation in the nature of a drug or chemical adapted solely or mainly to the destruction of insect life, and the effect of which is produced either by immediate contact with the insect or by some influence fatal to insect life inherent in or emanating from the preparation.' *Markell v Wollaston* (1906) 4 CLR 141 at 147, 148, per Griffith CJ

INSET

'Inset' means, in relation to a shaft or outlet of a mine, a heading chamber or other space driven or excavated from the shaft or outlet, being a heading, chamber or space to which access can only be had from the shaft or outlet and not being a heading, chamber or space the sole or main purpose of the driving or excavation of which is the getting of minerals or products of minerals. (Mines and Quarries Act 1954, s 182)

INSIDER

Bankruptcy

United States 'Insider' includes—
(A) if the debtor is an individual—
  (i) relative of the debtor or of a general partner of the debtor;
  (ii) partnership in which the debtor is a general partner;
  (iii) general partner of the debtor; or
  (iv) corporation of which the debtor is a director, officer, or person in control;
(B) if the debtor is a corporation—
  (i) director of the debtor;
  (ii) officer of the debtor;
  (iii) person in control of the debtor;
  (iv) partnership in which the debtor is a general partner;
  (v) general partner of the debtor; or
  (vi) relative of a general partner, director, officer, or person in control of the debtor;
(C) if the debtor is a partnership—
  (i) general partner of the debtor;
  (ii) relative of a general partner in, general partner of, or person in control of the debtor;
  (iii) partnership in which the debtor is a general partner;
  (iv) general partner of the debtor; or
  (v) person in control of the debtor;
(D) if the debtor is a municipality, elected official of the debtor or relative of an elected official of the debtor;

(E) affiliate, or insider of an affiliate as if such affiliate were the debtor; and
(F) managing agent of the debtor. . . .
(Bankruptcy Act 1978, s 101(25))

INSOLVENCY PROCEEDINGS

United States 'Insolvency proceedings' includes any assignment for the benefit of creditors or other proceedings intended to liquidate or rehabilitate the estate of the person involved. (Uniform Commercial Code 1978, s 1–201(22))

INSOLVENT   *See also* BANKRUPTCY

A person is deemed to be insolvent within the meaning of this Act if he has either ceased to pay his debts in the ordinary course of business, or he cannot pay his debts as they become due, whether he has committed an act of bankruptcy or not. (Sale of Goods Act 1979, s 61(4))

'I admit that a man is not insolvent, because he postpones the payment of a demand for a week or ten days, during which the creditor consents to wait, or renews a bill; and yet these are indications of a want of present power to fulfil his engagements. These, however, are cases to be decided by a jury upon the whole matter. My understanding of insolvency is a man's not being in a condition to pay 20s [now 100 pence] in the pound, in satisfaction of all demands.' *Teale v Younge* (1825) M'Cle & Yo 497 at 506, per Garrow B

'The ordinary import of the word insolvency is an incapability of paying the party's just debts.' *Parker v Gossage* (1835) 2 Cr M & R 617 at 620, per Parke B

[By a marriage settlement real property was vested in trustees upon trust for the wife for life, and after her death to pay the rents to the husband, until he should be bankrupt or 'insolvent', with a gift over to the children.] 'The settlement here creates a series of vested estates, the interest of the children taking effect in remainder upon the bankruptcy or insolvency of their father. On his becoming bankrupt in the lifetime of his wife, his interest in remainder, unless it went over, would have passed to his assignees, and the intention of the gift over was to preserve the property to the children in the event in which it would otherwise pass to the assignees. Neither can there be any question that what took place was an insolvency within the meaning of the settlement. The word insolvent has no technical meaning in such cases, but simply means incapable of paying debts that are due. . . . It is impossible to say that there was not an insolvency in this case, although no doubt a mere request for time, or a compromise of disputed claims, would not amount to an insolvency.' *Re Muggeridge's Trusts* (1860) John 625 at 627, per Page Wood V-C

'I cannot help thinking it quite clear that the term "insolvent" means public insolvency; not necessarily the taking the benefit of, or being made liable to, the Insolvent Act, but being incapable to pay his debts in ordinary course; or, in other words, having "stopped payment". . . . It may at least mean "not paying" as well as "being incapable of paying".' *R v Saddlers' Co* (1863) 10 HL Cas 404 at 463, per Lord Wensleydale

'There are decisions as to the meaning of the word "insolvent". They all state that "insolvency" means commercial insolvency, that is to say, inability to pay debts as they become due.' *London & Counties Assets Co Ltd v Brighton Grand Concert Hall & Picture Palace Ltd* [1915] 2 KB 493 at 501, 503, per Buckley LJ

Australia '"Insolvent" is a word that has no technical meaning in the law of England; it simply means "unable to pay debts". In this State [South Australia], iń consequence of the laws for the relief of insolvent debtors using the term insolvent where in England the term "bankrupt" is used, the word has, in my opinion acquired, in addition to its primary meaning, as above, the technical meaning of subject to legal process under those laws. . . . So well established has this meaning become in popular usage in this State that if anyone were told that a certain individual—I am not speaking of companies, which are not subject to the Insolvent Acts—had "become insolvent", he would, I believe, understand by that expression not that he was merely unable to pay his debts, but that he had become subject to the process of the Court of Insolvency.' *Re Salom, Salom v Salom* [1924] SASR 93 at 95, 97, per Murray CJ

Canada 'The question . . . is, was the debtor "in insolvent circumstances" or "unable to pay his debts in full" when he executed the mortgage in question? The authorities shew that these two phrases denote the same financial condition. . . . Various tests of insolvency have been from time to time formulated and applied, but the one which has been received with most favour in this province is that given by Vice-Chancellor Spragge in *Davidson v Douglas* [(1868) 15 Gr 347 at 351]. He there says that in considering the question of the solvency or insolvency of a debtor the proper course is "to seé and examine whether all his property, real and personal, be sufficient if presently realised for the payment of his debts, and in this view we must estimate his land, as well as his chattel property, not at what his neighbours or others may consider to be its value, but at what it would bring in the market at a forced sale; or at a sale when the seller cannot await his opportunities, but must sell". . . . The Spragge test seems to me the proper one as applied at least to a non-trader.' *Trotter v Pedlar* [1921] 1 WWR 233 at 235, 236, per Mathers CJKB

United States A person is 'insolvent' who either has ceased to pay his debts in the ordinary course of business or cannot pay his debts as they become due or is insolvent within the meaning of the federal bankruptcy law. (Uniform Commercial Code 1978, s 1–201(23))

Bankruptcy

United States '[I]nsolvent means—
(A) with reference to an entity other than a partnership, financial condition such that the sum of such entity's debts is greater than all of such entity's property, at a fair valuation, exclusive of—
  (i) property transferred, concealed, or removed with intent to hinder, delay, or defraud such entity's creditors; and
  (ii) property that may be exempted from property of the estate under s 522 of this title; and
(B) with reference to a partnership, financial condition such that the sum of such partnership's debts is greater than the aggregate of, at a fair valuation—
  (i) all of such partnership's property, exclusive of property of the kind specified in subparagraph (A)(i) of this paragraph; and
  (ii) the sum of the excess of the value of each general partner's separate property, exclusive of property of the kind specified in subparagraph (A)(ii) of this paragraph, over such partner's separate debts . . .
(Bankruptcy Act 1978, s 101(26))

INSPECTION   *See* EXAMINATION;
MEDICAL INSPECTION

INSPECTION OF DOCUMENTS   *See*
DISCOVERY

INSTALL—INSTALLATION

'First, installation—"installation . . . of machinery or plant". Now, "installation" is a metaphorical word. It is not a word of any great precision. It was well put in the Court of Appeal in Manitoba in *City of Winnipeg v Brian Investments Ltd* [infra] by Coyne J when he said: "'Installed' is not a word of art nor a word of precision. Indefiniteness gives it, as it gives any word, a chameleon-like character so that associate words show through and give their colour and meaning to it." It conveys putting in place something already made so that it can be used. There may be an element of assembly required; but basically a thing installed is ready to work when it is put in its place and, if necessary, connected up.' *Engineering Industry Training Board v Foster Wheeler John Brown Boilers Ltd* [1970] 2 All ER 616 at 620, CA, per Lord Wilberforce

Canada 'The word "install" which in mediaeval times meant to perform a formal ceremony of induction to a position or office, has been taken in modern times for use in the mechanical and structural trades. There it means more than to bring in or merely to place an article somewhere for service. . . . In those trades, the word is used in respect of a system of ventilation, lighting, plumbing, heating water or electrical service, or a fire place, etc, to be put into a building, or of an engine, steering gear or carburettor into a motor car or other similar use. On the contrary, it would seem that "install" cannot properly be used where a chair or desk or rug is brought into a room and left there; nor does it apply to a portable electric heater or radio or to a stove, whether electric or other, which a tenant brings in and is entitled to take away again with him, or to any other thing that remains personal property in the general acceptance of that term. "Install" would seem to connote the doing of something of some complexity, difficulty and importance, probably requiring some skill, involving the integration of an article or articles into the building or machine in which the installing takes place, and causing

a change of some importance in the building or machine.' *Winnipeg v Brian Investments Ltd* (1952) 60 Man R 416 at 439, per Coyne JA; on appeal [1953] 1 DLR 270

Mobile offshore installation

In this Part [Part III: credits and grants for construction of ships and offshore installations] of this Act . . . 'mobile offshore installation' means any installation which is intended for underwater exploitation of mineral resources or exploration with a view to such exploitation and can move by water from place to place without major dismantling or modification, whether or not it has its own motive power. (Industry Act 1972, s 12(1))

INSTANTLY

[A coroner's inquisition found that the deceased person, a fireman, had received a shock from the bursting of a boiler, 'of which said mortal shock', etc, he 'instantly' died.] 'It is contended that instantly is equivalent to then, which word was employed immediately before in connection with the shock described; and that word is admitted to be sufficient. We think it not equivalent. "Then", "*adtunc*", means the very time at which the other event happened; it therefore involves the same day; and such is the known sense of the term in pleading. But of instantly the more natural and usual sense is, instantly after; we do not know what the pleader may mean by that allegation; possibly five minutes, or an hour, some time on the succeeding day, or even a longer time. By the course of precedents such words as instanter and incontinenter do not dispense with a direct allegation of time: we repeatedly find them associated with it.' *Re v Brownlow* (1839) 11 Ad & El 119 at 127, 128, per cur.

INSTEAD

'What effect ought I to give to the codicil? The conclusion I come to is that the testator has not thereby entirely revoked the gift by the will, but has only modified it to the extent shewn by that codicil. It is noticeable that by the codicil the payment of £1,000 provided for by the will is clearly revoked. But when the testator comes to deal with the residuary personal estate he only says that, instead of the bequest in the manner expressed in the will to his daughters absolutely, he directs his executors to stand possessed of the residuary personal estate upon trusts which are for the benefit of the daughters, their children and appointees. That is certainly not clearly a total revocation. . . . I quite feel the force of the word "instead" used in the codicil; but the other words used, "in the manner expressed in my said will to my daughters absolutely", seem to me to point, not to a total substitution of the new gift for the old, but to a modification of the old gift.' *Re Wilcock, Kay v Dewhirst* [1898] 1 Ch 95 at 99, per Romer J

INSTITUTE

Canada 'In my opinion the word "instituted" in "instituted vexatious legal proceedings" in s 1(1) [of Vexatious Proceedings Act, RSO 1970, c 481; see now RSO 1980, c 523] only applies to the commencement of an action or proceeding by writ or originating notice of motion or similar originating proceedings. It would not apply in any event to proceedings which were a response to, or a participation in, proceedings instituted by another party.' *Foy v Foy (No 2)* (1979) 102 DLR (3d) 342 at 352, 353, Ont CA, per Howland CJ

INSTITUTION

This Act applies to every institution established, whether before or after the passing of this Act, for effecting all or any of the following purposes, that is to say: (i) To give technical instruction . . . ; (ii) To provide the training, mental or physical, necessary for the above purpose; (iii) In connection with the purposes before mentioned, to provide workshops, tools, scientific apparatus and plant of all kinds, libraries, reading rooms, halls for lectures, exhibitions, and meetings, gymnasiums, and swimming baths, and also general facilities for mental and physical training, recreation and amusement, and also all necessary and proper accommodation for persons frequenting the institutions. (Technical and Industrial Institutions Act 1892, s 2)

'Institution' includes any trust or undertaking. (Charities Act 1960, s 46)

'It is a little difficult to define the meaning of the term "institution" in the modern acceptation of the word. It means, I suppose, an undertaking formed to promote some defined purpose having in view generally the instruction or education of the public. It is the

body (so to speak) called into existence to translate the purpose as conceived in the minds of the founders into a living and active principle. . . . A public library may, I think, be properly called an "institution" in that sense.' *Manchester Corpn v McAdam* [1986] AC 500 at 511, 512, per Lord Macnaghten

Canada [The Income War Tax Act (Canada) 1927, s 4(e) exempted from taxation the income of (inter alia) any charitable 'institution'.] 'It is by no means easy to give a definition of the word "institution" that will cover every use of it. Its meaning must always depend upon the context in which it is found. It seems plain, for instance, from the context in which it is found in the subsection in question that the word is intended to connote something more than a mere trust. . . . In view of the language that has in fact been used, it seems to their Lordships that the charitable institutions exempted are those which are institutions in the sense in which boards of trade and chambers of commerce are institutions, such, for example, as a charity organisation society, or a society for the prevention of cruelty to children.' *Minister of National Revenue v Trusts & Guarantee Co Ltd* [1940] AC 138 at 149, 150, PC, per cur.

Public institution

'Public institution' means a prison, lock-up or hospital, and such other public or charitable institution as may be prescribed. (Births and Deaths Registration Act 1953, s 41)

'The question . . . is whether this school, which is established and chiefly maintained by Freemasons for the benefit entirely of those who belong to their own body, is a "public institution" within the meaning of s 1 of the Factories and Workshop Act 1907 [repealed; see now Factories Act 1961, s 175(2)(e)] . . . and . . . whether the laundry of this school is carried on incidentally to the purposes of a "public institution". This school is an "institution". . . . I think that this is the kind of institution which they [the legislature] contemplated when they provided safeguards for persons employed in laundries. . . . Is there anything "public" about this institution? I think that there is. To be a Freemason does not appear to me to be an entirely private matter. . . . The appellants solicit contributions from a very large body of people, that is, all Freemasons; . . . and when that is habitually done I cannot come to any other conclusion than that . . . the word "public" is as good a word to indicate the kind of institution at which they were aiming as any word which I can think of. In my opinion therefore, this is a public institution, and this laundry which is carried on incidentally to its purposes comes within the provisions of the Factory Acts.' *Royal Masonic Institution for Boys Trustees v Parkes* [1912] 3 KB 212 at 215–217, DC, per Darling J

INSTRUMENT (Document)   *See also* STATUTORY INSTRUMENT

The word 'instrument' as applied to a writing may . . . include documents which affect the pecuniary position of parties although they do not create rights or liabilities recognised in law; but usually it applies to a document under which some right or liability, whether legal or equitable, exists. (12 Halsbury's Laws (4th edn) para 47)

The expression 'instrument' includes every written document. (Stamp Act 1891, s 122(1))

'Instrument' (without prejudice to the generality of that expression) includes in particular Orders in Council, Letters Patent, judgments, decrees, orders, rules, regulations, bye-laws, awards, contracts, certificates and other documents. (Atomic Energy Authority Act 1954, s 8)

Subject to subsection (2) below in this Part of this Act [Part I: Forgery and Related Offences] 'instrument' means—
(a) any document, whether of a formal or informal character;
(b) any stamp issued or sold by the Post Office;
(c) any Inland Revenue stamp; and
(d) any disc, tape, sound track or other device on or in which information is recorded or stored by mechanical, electronic or other means.
(Forgery and Counterfeiting Act 1981, s 8(1))

[Subsection (2) provides that a currency note is not an instrument. 'Currency note' itself is defined in s 27(1).]

Canada 'The Crown's case is that the cheques and unemployment insurance card are "instruments or other writings" within the meaning of s 312(b) [of the Criminal Code; see now RSC 1970, c C–34, s 327] adapted and intended to be used to commit forgery. . . . The words "other writing" give colour to the word "instrument" and plainly indicate to me

that "instrument" is used in the sense of "written document" and has that meaning.' *R v Evans* (1962) 132 Can CC 271 at 272, per Tysoe JA

Commercial paper

United States 'Instrument' means a negotiable instrument. (Uniform Commercial Code 1978, s 3–102(1)(e))

Secured transactions

United States 'Instrument' means a negotiable instrument . . ., or a certificated security . . ., or any other writing which evidences a right to the payment of money and is not itself a security agreement or lease and is of a type which is in ordinary course of business transferred by delivery with any necessary indorsement or assignment. . . . (Uniform Commercial Code 1978, s 9–105(1)(i))

Under hand

An instrument under hand only is a document in writing which either creates or affects legal or equitable rights or liabilities, and which is authenticated by the signature of the author, but is not sealed by him. Such documents are used in a great variety of transactions, including contracts, assignments, acknowledgments of title, and notices. The expression is not limited to documents of a formal character, and it extends to any duly signed document which is intended by the author to be the means of producing a result recognised in law. (12 Halsbury's Laws (4th edn) para 1436)

INSTRUMENT (Tool)

Of housebreaking   *See also* IMPLEMENT

Canada 'An instrument "of" or "for" housebreaking is an instrument capable of being used for breaking into buildings or structures housing stores of merchandise, articles of commerce, or documents, or capable of housing a great many other things besides people, who may or may not dwell therein.' *R v Singleton* [1956] OWN 455 at 456, per Aylesworth JA

New Zealand [Section 282 of the Crimes Act 1908 (NZ) (repealed; see now s 244 of the Crimes Act 1961) created the offence of having in possession, without lawful excuse, any 'instrument of housebreaking'.] 'The word "instrument" is used in this section in a wide and not a narrow sense, and . . . it comprehends all those things (to use as colourless a term as possible) which are or can be applied to advantage by those resorting to housebreaking. It will consequently include such articles as may be of use to a housebreaker either in more efficiently effecting an entrance, or in effecting his escape, or concealing his identity. All such things may constitute the equipment of a housebreaker, and the word "instrument" should so be interpreted as to include all these.' *R v Allingham, R v Bandy* [1954] NZLR 1223 at 1226, CA, per cur.

New Zealand 'No doubt these must be material objects capable of physical use; objects whose use is effected through a mental rather than a physical process (such as plans of a shop) can hardly be included. . . . But all physical objects capable of physical use as part of a burglar's equipment will in our opinion be included. A torch is within this definition, for it may be physically used to facilitate the process both of breaking and of entering. For the same reasons we are of the opinion that the pair of gloves found in this case was also an article or articles capable of being used for burglary.' *R v Martin* [1965] NZLR 228 at 232, CA, per Turner J

INSUBORDINATION

'On behalf of the owners it has been alleged that when the crew were informed of the intention to take the ship to Holland, they declined to perform their duty in pumping, and also in other matters requiring their exertions as sailors. Assuming the fact to be as stated, such conduct would be insubordination; it would not be desertion. The distinction and difference between the two offences must be borne in mind. The utmost that could be said of it is, that it may be a fact explanatory of their subsequent conduct; and assuredly, whether the sailors were right or wrong as to other matters, it was misconduct on their part.' *The Westmorland* (1841) 1 Wm Rob 216 at 222, 223, per Dr Lushington

'The short point for my decision . . . becomes whether he [the plaintiff] was sentenced for "highly insubordinate conduct". . . . The plaintiff's counsel contends . . . that wilfully disobeying a lawful command of a superior officer does not and cannot amount to highly insubordinate conduct. . . . Counsel for the plaintiff suggests that highly insubordinate conduct is the equivalent of gross insubordination, and I agree, but the adjective seems to me to relate merely to the quality of the insubordination, and not to render highly insubordinate conduct a different offence from insubordinate conduct or a different offence from wilful disobedience, if insubordinate conduct is not a different offence from wilful disobedience.' *Jenkins v Shelley* [1939] 2 KB 137 at 143, 145, 146, per Hallet J

'Everybody knows what insubordination means. It means a refusal to subordinate oneself to authority, and it does not follow that a mere failure to obey an order amounts to insubordination. One would not say either in military or civilian circles that that was so. A schoolboy might be told he was not to go to a certain place to buy sweets at a shop, and if he disobeyed the order it does not at all follow that he would be insubordinate or that it would be proper to call him insubordinate. So, too, if a soldier was told that he was not to go to a place described as out of bounds, he might disobey the order and be guilty of disobedience, but it could hardly be said he was insubordinate merely because he did it. If, however, he met an officer who said: "Turn back, you are going where you ought not to," and the soldier said: "I intend to go on and I will go on," then he is showing he will not subordinate himself to military authority and he becomes insubordinate.' *R v Grant* [1957] 2 All ER 694 at 696, per cur.

INSULT

[The Public Order Act 1936, s 5 (as amended) made it an offence for a person, in any public place or at any public meeting, to use threatening, abusive or 'insulting' words or behaviour.] 'We were referred to a number of dictionary meanings of "insult" such as treating with insolence or contempt or indignity or derision or offensive disrespect. Many things otherwise unobjectionable may be said or done in an insulting way. There can be no definition. But an ordinary sensible man knows an insult when he sees or hears it. . . . "Affront" is much too vague a word to be helpful; there can often be disrespect without insult, and I do not think that contempt for a person's rights as distinct from contempt for the person himself would generally be held to be insulting. Moreover there are many grounds other than insult for feeling resentment or protesting. I do not agree that there can be conduct which is not insulting in the ordinary sense of the word but which is "insulting for the purpose of this section". If the view of the Divisional Court was that in this section the word "insulting" has some special or unusually wide meaning, then I do not agree. Parliament has given no indication that the word is to be given any unusual meaning. Insulting means insulting and nothing else.' *Brutus v Cozens* [1972] 2 All ER 1297 at 1300, HL, per Lord Reid

[Although s 7 of the Act of 1965 was repealed by the Race Relations Act 1976, s 5 of the Public Order Act 1936 continues to have effect as substituted.]

Australia 'The Police Offences Act 1935 in s 12(d) provides that "No person shall, in any public place, or within the hearing of any person passing therein . . . (iv) Use any threatening, abusive, or insulting words or behaviour with intent or calculated to provoke a breach of the peace, . . ." "Insulting" is a very large term, and in a statement of this kind is generally understood to be a word not cramped within narrow limits. In the Oxford Dictionary under the word "insult", we find it means in a transitive sense "to assail with offensively dishonouring or contemptuous speech or action; to treat with scornful abuse or offensive disrespect; to offer indignity to; to affront, outrage". We find in the same dictionary: "Hence 'insulted', treated with contemptuous abuse, outraged". There is, therefore, in this case no warrant for saying that the words complained of and found to have been used were not legally capable of being regarded as insulting words.' *Thurley v Hayes* (1920) 27 CLR 548 at 550, per Knox CJ, Gavan Duffy and Rich JJ

INSURABLE INTEREST

A person may be said to be interested in an event when, if the event happens, he will gain an advantage, and if it is frustrated he will suffer a loss, and it may be stated as a general principle that to constitute an insurable interest it must be an interest such that the peril would by its proximate effect cause damage to the assured, that is to say, cause him to lose a benefit or incur a liability. (25 Halsbury's Laws (4th edn) para 190)
  (1) Subject to the provisions of this Act, every person has an insurable interest who is interested in a marine adventure.
  (2) In particular a person is interested in a marine adventure where he stands in any

legal or equitable relation to the adventure or to any insurable property at risk therein, in consequence of which he may benefit by the safety or due arrival of insurable property, or may be prejudiced by its loss, or damage thereto, or by the detention thereof, or may incur liability in respect thereof. (Marine Insurance Act 1906, s 5)

'A man is interested in a thing to whom advantage may arise or prejudice happen from the circumstances which may attend it. . . . And whom it importeth, that its condition as to safety or other quality should continue: interest does not necessarily imply a right to the whole, or a part of the thing, nor necessarily and exclusively that which may be the subject of privation, but the having some relation to, or concern in the subject of the insurance, which relation or concern by the happening of the perils insured against may be so affected as to produce a damage, detriment, or prejudice to the person insuring: and where a man is so circumstanced with respect to matters exposed to certain risks or dangers, as to have a moral certainty of advantage or benefit, but for those risks or dangers, he may be said to be interested in the safety of the thing. To be interested in the preservation of a thing, is to be so circumstanced with respect to it as to have benefit from its existence, prejudice from its destruction. The property of a thing and the interest devisable from it may be very different: of the first the price is generally the measure, but by interest in a thing every benefit and advantage arising out of or depending on such thing may be considered as being comprehended.' *Lucena v Craufurd* (1806) 2 Bos & PNR 269 at 302, per Lawrence J

'In my opinion, the result of the authorities is that, although an interest to be insurable is not necessarily a right, legal or equitable, in or charge upon or arising out of the ownership of the thing exposed to the risks insured against, and any interest may be insured which is dependent on the safety of the thing exposed to such risks, still it must in all cases at the time of the loss be an interest legal or equitable, and not merely an expectation, however probable.' *Moran, Galloway & Co v Uzielli* [1905] 2 KB 555 at 562, per Walton J

'An insurable interest [in a life policy] means that the person effecting the policy must by the happening of the death of the person insured be likely to sustain some pecuniary loss or liability.' *Morris v Britannic Assurance Co Ltd* [1931] 2 KB 125 at 129, per Mackinnon J

INSURANCE *See also* ALL RISKS;
CONTRIBUTION; FIRE; POLICY; LIFE
POLICY; POLICY OF INSURANCE

Every insurance, whatever its nature, postulates that a sum of money will be paid by the insurers on the happening of a specified event. There must be uncertainty as to the happening of the event, either as to whether it will happen or not, or, if it is bound to happen, like the death of a human being, uncertainty as to the time at which it will happen. There must also be an insurable interest in the assured which is normally, that the event must be one which is prima facie adverse to his interest. (25 Halsbury's Laws (4th edn) para 2)

For the purposes of this Act 'insurance business' includes—
(a) the effecting and carrying out, by a person not carrying on a banking business, of contracts for fidelity bonds, performance bonds, administration bonds, bail bonds or customs bonds or similar contracts of guarantee, being contracts effected by way of business (and not merely incidentally to some other business carried on by the person effecting them) in return for the payment of one or more premiums;
(b) the effecting and carrying out of tontines;
(c) the effecting and carrying out, by a body (not being a body carrying on a banking business) that carries on business which is insurance business apart from this paragraph, of—
　(i) capital redemption contracts;
　(ii) contracts to manage the investments of pension funds (other than funds solely for the benefit of its own officers or employees and their dependants or, in the case of a company, partly for the benefit of those persons and partly for the benefit of officers or employees and their dependants of its subsidiary or holding company or a subsidiary of its holding company);
(d) the effecting and carrying out of contracts to pay annuities on human life.
(Insurance Companies Act 1982, s 95)

'Insurance is a contract upon speculation. The special facts, upon which the contingent chance is to be computed, lie most commonly in the knowledge of the *insured* only: the underwriter trusts to his representation, and proceeds upon confidence that he does not keep back any circumstance in his knowledge, to mislead the underwriter into a belief that the circumstance does not exist, and to induce him to estimate the risque, as if it did not exist. The keeping back such circumstances is a *fraud*, and therefore the policy is *void* . . . . Good faith forbids either party by concealing what he privately knows, to draw the other into a bargain, from his ignorance of that fact, and his believing the contrary. . . . Either party may be innocently silent. . . . The underwriter . . . needs not to be told general topics of speculation.' *Carter v Boehm* (1766) 3 Burr 1905 at 1909, 1910, per cur.

'Insurance is a contract by which the one party in consideration of a price paid to him adequate to the risk becomes security to the other that he shall not suffer loss, damage, or prejudice by the happening of the perils specified in certain things which may be exposed to them.' *Lucena v Craufurd* (1806) 2 Bos & PNR 269 at 301, per Lawrence J

Australia 'In *Seaton v Heath* [[1899] 1 QB 782, 792] . . . Romer LJ . . . says: "The difference between these two classes of contract does not depend upon any essential difference between the word 'insurance' and the word 'guarantee'. There is no magic in the use of those words. The words, to a great extent, have the same meaning and effect; and many contracts, like the one in the case now before us, may with equal propriety be called contracts of insurance or contracts of guarantee." The distinction in substance, in cases in which the loss insured against is simply the event of the non-payment of a debt, seems to be, as I read the judgment of Romer LJ between contracts in which the person desiring to be insured has means of knowledge as to the risk and the insurer has not the same means, and those cases in which the insurer has the same means.' *Re Australian & Overseas Insurance Ltd* [1966] 1 NSWR 558 at 564, per McLelland CJ in Eq.

Consumer credit insurance

United States 'Consumer credit insurance' means insurance, other than insurance on property, by which the satisfaction of debt in whole or in part is a benefit provided, but does not include
(a) insurance provided in relation to a credit transaction in which a payment is scheduled more than 10 years after the extension of credit;
(b) insurance issued as an isolated transaction on the part of the insurer not related to an agreement or plan for insuring debtors of the creditor; or

(c) insurance indemnifying the creditor against loss due to the debtor's default.
(Uniform Consumer Credit Code 1969, s 4.103(1))

Contingency insurance

In one sense all insurances are related to a contingency; in life or endowment insurance the contingency is death or the survival of the assured to a particular date; in personal accident or sickness insurance the contingency is injury by accident or disablement by disease; in property insurance the contingency is the peril to the property which is insured against; in liability insurance the contingency is incurring the specified liability to a third party. However, apart from the contingencies covered by these particular types of insurance there remains a wide field representing (1) what a person would or might have earned or acquired but for the happening of a particular event, and (2) the danger, in the sense of the possibility of a loss being incurred if a particular event happens. Therefore, pecuniary loss insurance may be defined in general terms as an insurance, not falling within any of the classes of insurance previously mentioned, which provides for the making of a payment in the event of a specified event occurring, the payment representing either the loss, or the possibility of loss, which that event entails. (25 Halsbury's Laws (4th edn) para 791)

Double insurance

Double insurance exists in the strict sense where two or more policies are effected by or on behalf of the same assured in respect of the same interest and the total of the sums assured exceeds what is required to secure to the assured a full indemnity. Generally, the existence of double insurance is important only insofar as it may affect the amount recoverable under a particular policy in the case of indemnity insurance; it does not necessarily invalidate any of the policies concerned. (25 Halsbury's Laws (4th edn) para 534)

Where two or more policies are effected by or on behalf of the assured on the same adventure and interest or any part thereof, and the sums insured exceed the indemnity allowed by this Act, the assured is said to be over-insured by double insurance. (Marine Insurance Act 1906, s 32(1))

Industrial assurance

A somewhat specialised form of life insurance has developed where premiums are payable, usually in very small sums, at short intervals. Such insurances, where the premiums are received by means of collectors and are payable at intervals of less than two months, are called industrial assurance, and are subject to certain special statutory provisions. The industrial assurance legislation applies to industrial assurance companies and registered friendly societies which carry on industrial assurance business, and such societies are known as collecting societies. Registered friendly societies are also subject generally to certain provisions of friendly society legislation affecting their power to effect life insurances. (25 Halsbury's Laws (4th edn) para 550)

For the purposes of this Act, 'industrial assurance business' means the business of effecting assurances upon human life premiums in respect of which are received by means of collectors:
Provided that such business shall not include—
(a) assurances the premiums in respect of which are payable at intervals of two months or more;
(b) assurances effected whether before or after the passing of this Act by a society or company established before the date of the passing of this Act which at that date had no assurances outstanding the premiums on which were payable at intervals of less than one month so long as the society or company continues not to effect any such assurances;
(c) assurances effected before the passing of this Act, premiums in respect of which are payable at intervals of one month or upwards, and which have up to the commencement of this Act been treated as part of the business transacted by a branch other than the industrial branch of the society or company;
(d) assurances for twenty-five pounds or upwards effected after the passing of this Act, premiums in respect of which are payable at intervals of one month or upwards, and which are treated as part of the business transacted by a branch other than the industrial branch of the society or company, in cases where the Commissioner hereinafter mentioned [the Industrial Assurance Commissioner] certifies that the terms and conditions of such assurances are on the whole not less

favourable to the assured than those imposed by this Act.
(Industrial Assurances Act 1923, s 1(2))

Life assurance

'The contract commonly called life-assurance, when properly considered, is a mere contract to pay a certain sum of money on the death of a person, in consideration of the due payment of a certain annuity for his life,—the amount of the annuity being calculated, in the first instance, according to the probable duration of the life: and, when once fixed, it is constant and invariable. The stipulated amount of annuity is to be uniformly paid on one side, and the sum to be paid in the event of death is always (except when bonuses have been given by prosperous offices) the same, on the other. This species of insurance in no way resembles a contract of indemnity.' *Dalby v India & London Life Assurance Co* (1854) 15 CB 365 at 387, per cur.

Australia 'A policy of life assurance in its characteristics is "a contract . . . for money. It is a purchase of a reversionary sum in consideration of a present payment of money, or, as is generally the case, on payment of an annuity during the life of the person insuring" (per Jessel MR in *Fryer v Morland* [[1876] 3 Ch D 675 at 685].) . . . In form the contract may be, and I think usually is, for the entire life subject to defeasance, or lapse, upon non-payment of any of the periodic premiums, provided the surrender value (if any) does not sustain rights of the accused. . . . But there may be policies, which in substance are life policies, but which take other forms. . . . The view has been expressed that the form may even be an annual insurance with annual rights of renewal; in effect a series of contracts.' *Re Kerr* [1943] SASR 8 at 18, 19, per Mayo J

Australia 'Marine, fire, burglary, personal accident, motor vehicle, and other miscellaneous insurances indemnify the insured against loss from events which may or may not occur. Life insurance, on the other hand, is related to a contingency, death, which must occur. It is not a risk, it is a certainty; the only uncertainty is when it will occur. This does not mean that the aim of the life policyholder is always provision against the inevitable rather than precaution against the possible. He may wish to insure the life of a creditor for a term, or he may be concerned with the risk of death depriving dependants of support, or of the loss of income in old age; so that it has been said that a whole life policy is an insurance against dying too soon, an endowment policy an insurance against living too long. But they have a common difference from other forms of insurance; and endowment policies in various forms are today as properly called life insurances as are whole of life policies.' *National Mutual Life Assocn of Australia Ltd v Federal Taxation Comr* [1959] ALR 467 at 474, per Windeyer J

Marine insurance

A contract of marine insurance is a contract whereby the insurer undertakes to indemnify the assured, in manner and to the extent thereby agreed, against marine losses, that is to say, the losses incident to marine adventure. (Marine Insurance Act 1906, s 1)

'This document . . . is a contract for sea insurance in a particular form—that is to say, it purports to be a reinsurance of the original underwriters in respect of part of the interest which they acquire by undertaking the liability. It is a contract of insurance on excesses, and the risks insured against are marine risks. It is therefore a contract for sea insurance.' *Home Marine Insurance Co Ltd v Smith* [1898] 2 QB 351 at 357, CA, per Rigby LJ

'The word "insured" in a policy of marine insurance prima facie covers all insurances against sea risks, including war risks; and there is in the policy in question in this case no context sufficient to cut down the natural meaning of the word. It is true that the insurer of a ship against ordinary marine risks is not directly interested in the amount of the insurance of the freight against war risks. But it is said that an over-insurance of freights by honour policies against war risks may tempt the owner to throw away his ship with a view to claiming under the war risks policies and alternatively under the ordinary marine policies, and so may involve the marine underwriters in litigation and loss; and certainly the course of events in the present case supports that view. Upon the whole I think that the word "insured" must be construed in its natural and ordinary sense, and as including all kinds of marine insurance.' *Samuel (P) & Co v Dumas* [1924] AC 423 at 441, 442, per Lord Cave

Reinsurance

'A gentleman wants to insure his country house, say, for £30,000. He goes to one of the insurance companies and says he wishes to effect that insurance. The insurance company takes it without a word of objection if the risk be a proper one, and if they are satisfied as to the condition of the property. But their own limit is probably £10,000 . . . and the way in which they protect themselves is this: they arrange with another company to do what they call "reinsure"—that is, to contract with them to take so much of that risk as exceeds their own limit. In the case of £30,000 probably they would arrange for two reinsurances. The ordinary limit being £10,000, they would arrange with one company to take one £10,000 and with another company to take another £10,000; so that, if the mansion should happen to be burnt down, they would have to pay to the owner of course the whole £30,000, but they would be recouped £10,000 by one reinsurance office and £10,000 by another. That is the ABC of insurance business.' *Re Norwich Equitable Fire Assurance Society, Royal Insurance Co's Claim* (1887) 57 LT 241 at 243, per Kay J

'A main object of reinsurance is to relieve the reinsured from a portion of the risk previously undertaken by him.' *Re Eddystone Marine Insurance Co ex p Western Insurance Co* [1892] 2 Ch 423 at 427, per Stirling J

'Is the clause that the insured value shall be taken as the repaired value to be read into the reinsurance policy? I will first examine this policy as though it contained no express reference of any kind to this clause—that is to say, as though the clause had never appeared in print in the margin and had never been struck through in ink, as already described. What then would have been the meaning of the policy? Now I think the meaning quite plain, it is a "reinsurance", that expression connotes the idea of something already insured.' *Marten v Steamship Owners' Underwriting Assocn* (1902) 71 LJKB 718 at 721, per Bigham J

'What is the contract which a reinsurer enters into when he underwrites a policy . . . such as exists here? It consists of a promise to indemnify the reassured against any liability that he may come under to the shipowner in respect of the risk reinsured, and "to pay as may be paid thereon". What is the effect of such a promise? What is the position as between reassured and reinsurer? It is, in my opinion, this. The reinsurer, when called upon to perform his promise, is entitled to require the reassured first to shew that a loss of the kind reinsured has in fact happened; and, secondly,

that the reassured has taken all proper and businesslike steps to have the amount of it fairly and carefully ascertained. That is all. He must then pay. . . . So long as liability exists, the mere fact of some honest mistake having occurred in fixing the exact amount of it will afford no excuse for not paying. He has promised "to pay as may be paid thereon".' *Western Assurance Co of Toronto v Poole* [1903] 1 KB 376 at 386, per Bigham J

'The clause "to pay as may be paid thereon" [in a reinsurance policy] means as legally paid, though no doubt the settlement of the amount of the liability cannot be questioned.' *Fireman's Fund Insurance Co v Western Australian Insurance Co Ltd* (1927) 138 LT 108 at 113, per Bateson J

INSURANCE BUSINESS

For the purposes of this Act 'insurance business' includes—
(a) the effecting and carrying out, by a person not carrying on a banking business, of contracts for fidelity bonds, performance bonds, administration bonds, bail bonds or customs bonds or similar contracts of guarantee, being contracts effected by way of business (and not merely incidentally to some other business carried on by the person effecting them) in return for the payment of one or more premiums;
(b) the effecting and carrying out of tontines;
(c) the effecting and carrying out, by a body (not being a body carrying on a banking business) that carries on business which is insurance business apart from this paragraph, of—
(i) capital redemption contracts;
(ii) contracts to manage the investments of pension funds (other than funds solely for the benefit of its own officers or employees and their dependants or, in the case of a company, partly for the benefit of those persons and partly for the benefit of officers or employees and their dependants of its subsidiary or holding company or a subsidiary of its holding company);
(d) the effecting and carrying out of contracts to pay annuities on human life.
(Insurance Companies Act 1982, s 95)

INSURANCE COMPANY

'Insurance company' means a person or body of persons (whether incorporated or not)

carrying on insurance business. (Insurance Companies Act 1982, s 96(1))

United States The term 'insurance company' means a company which is organised as an insurance company, whose primary and predominant business activity is the writing of insurance or the reinsuring of risks underwritten by insurance companies, and which is subject to the supervision by the insurance commissioner, or a similar official or agency, of a State or territory or the District of Columbia; or any receiver or similar official or any liquidating agent for such company, in his capacity as such. (Securities Act of 1933, s 2(13))

INSURED

Canada [A fire insurance policy defined 'insured' as including the named insured, his spouse and relatives of both living in the household. A son of the named insured caused a fire which damaged the insured property. The insurer relied on an exemption clause which stated that the policy did not cover loss caused by the wilful act of the insured.] 'It is my opinion that the word "insured" in the exception clause means, where as here more than one person is insured, the person who is making the claim under the policy. In the present case, the son was separately insured for his own personal effects, but had no interest in the house or the contents owned by the appellants for which loss was proved. The appellants are not affected, in respect of their interests, by the wrongful act of their son.' *Rankin v North Waterloo Farmers Mutual Insce Co* 25 OR (2d) 102 at 107, Ont CA, per Weatherston JA

INTEGRAL PART

'An integral part' is, I apprehend, something which is necessary to the completeness of the whole.' *Dixon (Inspector of Taxes) v Fitch's Garage Ltd* [1975] 3 All ER 455 at 458, per Brightman J

INTELLECTUAL PROPERTY *See* INDUSTRIAL OR INTELLECTUAL PROPERTY

INTENT *See also* INTENTION; MOTIVE

'The word "intent" denotes a state of mind. A man's intention is a question of fact. Actual intent may unquestionably be proved by direct evidence or may be inferred from surrounding circumstances. Intent may also be imputed on the basis that a man must be presumed to intend the natural consequences of his own act.' *Lloyds Bank Ltd v Marcan* [1973] 2 All ER 359 at 367, per Pennycuick V-C

'I am firmly of opinion that foresight of consequences, as an element bearing on the issue of intention in murder, or indeed any other crime of specific intent, belongs not to the substantive law but to the law of evidence. Here . . . I am happy to find myself aligned with Lord Hailsham in *Hyam v DPP* [[1974] 2 All ER 41, 43] where he said: "Knowledge or foresight is at the best material which entitles or compels a jury to draw the necessary inference as to intention." A rule of evidence which judges for more than a century found of the utmost utility in directing juries was expressed in the maxim, "A man is presumed to intend the natural and probable consequences of his acts". In *DPP v Smith* [[1960] 3 All ER 161] your Lordships' House, by treating this rule of evidence as creating an irrebuttable presumption and thus elevating it, in effect, to the status of a rule of substantive law, predictably provoked the intervention of Parliament by s 8 of the Criminal Justice Act 1967 to put the issue of intention back where it belonged, viz in the hands of the jury, "drawing such inferences from the evidence as appear proper in the circumstances". I do not by any means take the conjunction of the verbs "intended or foresaw" and "intended or foresee" in that section as an indication that Parliament treated them as synonymous; on the contrary, two verbs were needed to connote two different states of mind. I think we should now no longer speak of presumptions in this context but rather of inferences. In the old presumption that a man intends the natural and probable consequences of his acts the important word is "natural". This word conveys the idea that in the ordinary course of events a certain act will lead to a certain consequence unless something unexpected supervenes to prevent it. One might almost say that, if a consequence is natural, it is really otiose to speak of it as also being probable. . . . In the rare cases in which it is necessary to direct a jury by reference to foresight of consequences, I do not believe it is necessary for the judge to do more than invite the jury to consider two questions. First, was death or really serious injury in a murder case (or whatever relevant consequence must be proved to have been intended in any other case) a natural consequence of the defendant's voluntary act? Second, did the defendant foresee that consequence as being a natural consequence of his act? The jury should then be told that if they answer Yes to both questions it is a proper inference for them to draw that he intended that consequence.' *R v Moloney* [1985] 1 All ER 1025 at 1038, 1039, HL, per Lord Bridge of Harwich

Australia [Proviso (c) to s 23(2) (see now s 23(2)(b)) of the Crimes Act 1900–1986 (NSW) enacts that on a trial for murder the crime shall not be reduced to manslaughter by reason of provocation unless the jury find that the act causing death was done suddenly, in the heat of passion caused by the provocation, and without 'intent' to take life.] 'Their lordships consider . . . that in its context the word "intent" must denote a purpose of the accused which is distinct from a purpose which is the product of a state of passion caused by a provocative act.' *Parker v R* [1964] 2 All ER 641 at 651, PC, per cur; also reported [1964] AC 1369

INTENT TO DEFRAUD   *See* FRAUD

INTENTION   *See also* CONSPIRACY;
   MOTIVE

'In some branches of the law, "intention" may be understood to cover results which may reasonably flow from what is deliberately done, on the principle that a man is to be treated as intending the reasonable consequence of his acts.' *Crofter Hand Woven Harris Tweed Co Ltd v Veitch* [1942] AC 435 at 444, per Lord Simon LC

'An "intention" to my mind connotes a state of affairs which the party "intending"—I will call him X—does more than merely contemplate: it connotes a state of affairs which, on the contrary, he decides, so far as in him lies, to bring about, and which, in point of possibility, he has a reasonable prospect of being able to bring about, by his own act of volition. X cannot, with any due regard to the English language, be said to "intend" a result which is wholly beyond the control of his will. He cannot "intend" that it shall be a fine day tomorrow: at most he can hope or desire or pray that it will. Nor, short of this, can X be said to "intend" a particular result if its occurrence, though it may be not wholly

uninfluenced by X's will, is dependent on so many other influences, accidents, and cross-currents of circumstance that, not merely is it quite likely not to be achieved at all, but, if it is achieved, X's volition will have been no more than a minor agency collaborating with, or not thwarted by, the factors which predominantly determine its occurrence.' *Cunliffe v Goodman* [1950] 2 KB 237 at 253, CA, per Asquith LJ

'It is not now in doubt that the import of the word "intend" in s 30(1)(f) of the Act [Landlord and Tenant Act 1954] is that at the appropriate date or dates . . . there must be a firm and settled intention not likely to be changed, or in other words that the proposal for doing the work has moved "out of the zone of contemplation . . . into the valley of decision". The language that I have just used is part of the felicitous language used by Asquith LJ, in *Cunliffe v Goodman* [supra], a case concerning the Landlord and Tenant Act 1927, s 18(1), in which in point of actual fact the word "intends" or "intention" did not appear at all. Recent decisions, however, under the present Act of 1954 have, I think, now laid it down for us to follow that the language which Asquith LJ used is appropriate to a question under s 30(1)(f). Indeed in more than one very recent case . . . this court made it clear that the test for "intention" within the meaning of s 30(1)(f) is to be found in this langauge taken from Asquith LJ's judgment in *Cunliffe v Goodman*.' *Fleet Electrics Ltd v Jacey Investments Ltd* [1956] 3 All ER 99 at 102, CA, per Lord Evershed MR

'Asquith LJ in *Cunliffe v Goodman* [supra], examined the precise signification of this word in connection with the provisions of s 18(1) of the Landlord and Tenant Act 1927. I do not at the moment cite from this classic judgment; it is enough to note that, in the lord justice's view, "intend" imports a fixed and settled, as distinct from a provisional, purpose. The word "intend" does not, in fact, appear in s 18(1) of the Act of 1927, but the definition of it given by Asquith LJ has been adopted as applicable to its use in s 30 of the Act [Landlord and Tenant Act] of 1954: see *Fisher v Taylors Furnishing Stored Ltd* [[1956] 2 All ER 78], *Roehorn v Barry Corpn* [[1956] 2 All ER 742], and *Fleet Electrics Ltd v Jacey Investments Ltd* [supra]. It is, accordingly, quite clear, as I think, that if a lessor is to succeed in establishing the ground of opposition on which the landlord company relies in the present case [viz, that the landlord company, on the termination of the current tenancy, 'intended' to reconstruct the premises], he must satisfy the court, when the tenant's application is before it, that his intention is of the quality which Asquith LJ described; and, indeed, that such intention is reasonably capable of being carried into effect.' *Betty's Cafés Ltd v Phillips Furnishing Stores Ltd* [1957] 1 All ER 1 at 12, CA, per Romer LJ; also reported in [1957] Ch 67 at 90

'The words in the Wills Act 1837, s 27, are "contrary intention", and, though the word "intention" has been construed and re-construed, and shaved round and round by judicial decisions in quite a different context, to my mind a person cannot be said to have an intention in relation to something which is not even in his mind.' *Re Thirlwell's Will Trusts, Evans v Thirlwell* [1957] 3 All ER 465 at 467, per Roxburgh J

'If a landlord desires to rely on s 30(1)(g) of the Landlord and Tenant Act 1954, he has to shew that on the termination of the current tenancy he "intends" to occupy the holding for business purposes; and it has been well established now, on the authorities, first that such an intention must exist at the hearing of the tenant's application, and, secondly, that the intention must be a real intention, fixed and settled.' *Espresso Coffee Machine Co Ltd v Guardian Assurance Co Ltd* [1959] 1 All ER 458 at 463, CA per Romer LJ

[By s 253(1) of the Road Traffic Act 1960 a motor vehicle means a mechanically propelled vehicle 'intended' or adapted for use on roads.] 'For my part, I think that the expression "intended" . . . does not mean "intended by the user of the vehicle either at the moment of the alleged offence or for the future". I do not think that it means the intention of the manufacturer or the wholesaler or the retailer; and it may be, as Salmon J said in [*Daley v Hargreaves* [1961] 1 All ER 552], that it is not referring to the intention as such of any particular purpose. Salmon J suggested that the word "intended" might be paraphrased as "suitable or apt". It may be merely a difference of wording but I prefer to make the test whether a reasonable person looking at the vehicle would say that one of its users would be a road user. In deciding that question, the reasonable man would not, as I conceive, have to envisage what some man losing his senses would do with a vehicle; nor an isolated user or a user in an emergency. The real question is: is some general use on the roads contemplated as one of the users?' *Burns v Currell* [1963] 2 All ER 297 at 300, per Lord Parker CJ; also reported in [1963] 2 QB 433 at 440

Australia 'Their Lordships . . . venture to question whether, as a matter of strict terminology, a man can be said to entertain conflicting "intentions". A man may well have incompatible desires. He may have an in-tention which conflicts with a desire, i.e., he may will one thing, and wish another, as when he renounces some cherished article of diet in the interest of health. But "intention" necessarily connotes an element of volition: desire does not.' *Lang v Lang* [1954] 3 All ER 571 at 580, PC, per Lord Porter; see also [1955] AC 402

Australia 'The mental element which must be proved when a case of murder goes to the jury under s 302(1) [Criminal Code Act 1899 (Qld)] is intention to cause death or to do grievous bodily harm. The ordinary and natural meaning of the word "intends" is "to mean, to have in mind". Relevant definitions in The Shorter Oxford English Dictionary show that what is involved in the directing of the mind, having a purpose or design. The notion of desire is not involved as the learned judge rightly held. A person may do something, fully intending to do it, although he does not in the least desire to do it.' *R v Willmot* [1985] 2 Qd R 413 at 418, per Campbell J

South Africa 'The main object always is to ascertain what the parties intended; but we can only adopt what we think was their intention so far as the words of the contract permit us to do so.' *Van der Merwe v Jumpers Deep Ltd* 1902 TS 207, per Innes CJ

INTERCOURSE *See* SEXUAL INTERCOURSE

INTEREST

Canada [The Estate Tax Act 1958 (Can), c 29, s 3(1)(j) (now RSC 1970, c E–9, amended 1970–71–72, c 43) provides that property passing on death includes any annuity or other 'interest' purchased or provided by the deceased.] 'I have only been referred to one sense that the English word "interest" has that is in anyway appropriate. That sense appears in the Concise Oxford Dictionary, 5th edition, at p 635, as follows: (1) Legal concern, title, right (in property). . . . Used in this sense, section

3(1)(j) refers to an "interest" *in something*, which interest has been purchased or provided by the deceased. A common use of the word "interest" in such a context is to refer to a life interest in property, a reversionary interest in property, or a leasehold interest in property. I have no doubt that the word can also be used to refer to the "interest" of an absolute owner of property but it would be a rare use. A much more common use of the word would be to refer to such interest as a beneficiary may have in trust property. The word "interest" is not, however, according to my understanding of the ordinary use of English language, appropriate to refer to an obligation to pay money upon the happening of an event some time in the future or to the actual payment when made. Such an obligation is not an "interest" in property. It is an obligation to find and transfer (pay) unascertained property (money) at some as yet undetermined time in the future. There is no interest in any property created by entering into the contract. The contract merely creates a conditional obligation to pay money. Finally, there is no sense of the word "interest" that extends to a payment of money as such. . . . My conclusion is, therefore, that the inclusion of the two amounts paid under the accident policies cannot be justified under section 3(1)(j).' *Minister of National Revenue v Shaw Estate* [1971] CTC 15 at 22, 23 (Ex Ct), per Jackett J

Dissenting shareholder

United States 'Interest' means interest from the effective date of the corporate action until the date of payment, at the average rate currently paid by the corporation on its principal bank loans or, if none, at a rate that is fair and equitable under all the circumstances. (Revised Model Business Corporation Act 1984, s 13.01(4))

General interest

'The law of England lays down the rule that, on the trial of issues of fact before a jury, hearsay evidence is to be excluded, as the jury might often be misled by it; but makes exceptions where a relaxation of the rule tends to the due investigation of truth and the attainment of justice. One of these exceptions is where the question relates to matters of public or general interest. The term "interest" here does not mean that which is "interesting" from gratifying curiosity or a love of information or amusement, but that in which a class of the community have a pecuniary interest, or some

interest by which their legal rights or liabilities are affected.' *R v Bedfordshire (Inhabitants)* (1855) 4 E & B 535 at 541, 542, per Lord Campbell CJ

In business

'When a person sells a business and agrees not to carry on, or be in any way interested in, any similar business, the word "interested" is used to prevent him, not only from carrying it on, but also from having any proprietary or pecuniary interest in it.' *Smith v Hancock* [1894] 2 Ch 377 at 386, CA, per Lindley LJ

[By an agreement under seal made between the plaintiffs and the defendant, it was agreed that the defendant should serve as manager of one of the plaintiffs' branches for three years, and that, after the determination by notice or otherwise of his engagement he would not for three years directly or indirectly become 'interested in any similar trade or business' within twenty miles of Regent Street.] 'The covenant departs materially from the common form. It does not provide that the covenantor shall not be "engaged or concerned or interested" in a similar business, but merely that he shall not be "interested" therein. Nor does it contain the usual provision against accepting employment as a servant in a similar business. . . . The covenant, fairly construed, prohibits the defendant from being interested, directly or indirectly, in a similar business in the sense that he must not have a proprietary or pecuniary interest in the success or failure thereof. If his remuneration in any way depended on the profits or gross returns, he would be "interested" in the business, but the mere fact that he is employed as a servant at a fixed salary gives him no such interest and constitutes no breach of his covenant.' *Gophir Diamond Co v Wood* [1902] 1 Ch 950 at 952, 953, per Swinfen Eady J

'When it is put that you are interested if you lend money to a person, if you supply him with capital, if you do this, that, and the other which enables a business to be carried on, in a certain wide sense it cannot be denied that you are "interested", and "being interested" might include the fact that you are on affectionate terms with the person carrying on the business. But . . . the mere fact of being a creditor of the firm is not being "concerned or interested in" it.' *Cory (William) & Son Ltd v Harrison* [1906] AC 274 at 276, per Lord Halsbury LC

In contract

[The Municipal Corporations Act 1882, s 12 (repealed; cf now the Local Government Act 1972, s 94) enacted (inter alia) that a person should be disqualified from being a councillor if he had any 'interest in a contract' with the council.] 'An "interest" within the meaning of the section must . . . be something more than a sentimental interest, such as arises from the natural love and affection of a man for his son; it must be a pecuniary or, at least, a material interest; but I do not see on what principle it must necessarily be a pecuniary advantage.' *England v Inglis* [1920] 2 KB 636 at 639, DC, per Salter J

In defence of privilege

Australia 'The ground on which the defendants seek to establish that the admittedly defamatory publication complained of was made on an occasion of qualified privilege is that it was made by persons who were promoting a legitimate interest of their own in making it and that they made it to persons who had a legitimate interest to receive it. To succeed in this contention, it was necessary that they should show by evidence that both the givers and the receivers of the defamatory information had a special and reciprocal interest in its subject matter, of such a kind that it was desirable as a matter of public policy, in the general interests of the whole community of New South Wales, that it should be made with impunity, notwithstanding that it was defamatory of a third party. The word "interest" as used in the cases, is not used in any technical sense. It is used in the broadest popular sense, as when we say that a man is "interested" in knowing a fact—not interested in it as a matter of gossip or curiosity, but as a matter of substance apart from its mere quality as news (*Howe v Lees* (1910) 11 CLR 361 at 398). The interest relied on as a foundation of privilege must be definite. It may be direct or indirect, but it must not be vague or unsubstantial. So long as the interest is of so tangible a nature that for the common convenience and welfare of society it is expedient to protect it, it will come within the rule.' *Andreyevich v Kosovich and Publicity Press Pty Ltd* (1947) 47 SR (NSW) 357 at 363, 364, per Jordan CJ

In insurance policy

[The 'held covered' clause in a policy of marine insurance was in these words: 'In the event of deviation being made from the voyage hereby insured or of any incorrect definition of the interest insured it is agreed to hold the assured covered at a premium (if any) to be arranged.'] 'The appellants say that the words "interest insured" refer only to the insurable interest which the assured had in goods the subject-matter of the policy. But that is not a matter which is required to be specified in or dealt with by the policy, and the assured need not even have any insurable interest in the subject-matter at the time when the insurance is effected (see s 6, sub-s 1 of the Marine Insurance Act 1906). In my opinion the words "interest insured" in the "held covered" clause have reference, not to "insurable interest", but to "subject-matter insured".' *Hewitt Brothers v Wilson* [1915] 2 KB 739 at 746, CA, per Swinfen Eady LJ

In land

'Interest', in relation to land, includes any estate in land and any right over land, whether the right is exercisable by virtue of the ownershp of an interest in land or by virtue of a licence or agreement, and in particular includes sporting rights. (National Parks and Access to the Countryside Act 1949, s 114)

'I confess I am quite unable to see the impropriety of describing the interest of a person beneficially entitled to money invested on mortgage held by his trustee as an interest in land. The interest of the cestui que trust is not confined to the money, but extends to the security for it, ie to the land held by his trustee. Such land is vested in the trustee, but upon trust for whom? The only possible answer is, upon trust for those persons who are beneficially entitled to the money. If there is only one such person, and he is sui juris, the trustee can be required to transfer the security to him, ie to assign the debt and convey the land to him. . . . Interest in the £1,100 in question might in my opinion be properly regarded either as an interest in land or as an incumbrance upon or affecting it.' *Miller v Collins* [1896] 1 Ch 573 at 586, 589, CA, per Lindley LJ

Australia 'By definition "interest" in relation to land means (a) a legal or equitable estate in the land, or (b) a right, power or privilege over or in connexion with the land. "Land" includes an interest in land.' *Maddalozzo v Commonwealth* (1978) 34 FLR 332 at 334, per Gallop J

Canada 'A common use of the word "interest" . . . is to refer to a life interest in property, a reversionary interest in property, or a leasehold interest in property. I have no doubt that the word can also be used to refer to the "interest" of an absolute owner of property but it would be a rare use. A much more common use of the word would be to refer to such interest as a beneficiary may have in trust property. The word "interest" is not, however, according to my understanding of the ordinary use of English language, appropriate to refer to an obligation to pay money upon the happening of an event some time in the future or to the actual payment when made.' *Minister of National Revenue v Shaw Estate* [1971] CTC 15 at 22, 23 (Ex Ct), per Jackett J

Canada [The plaintiff lessee made a lease with the original owner, and when the property was sold to the defendants, the plaintiff registered a notice of lease and later a *lis pendens*. The issue was whether a leasehold interest was an 'interest in land' under s 41(1) of the Judicature Act (Ont), (see now Courts of Justice Act 1984 (Ont), c 11, s 116(1)) thereby enabling a party to register a *lis pendens* on title.] 'Counsel have been unable to cite any case where this issue has been specifically dealt with. In *Procopio v D'Abbondanza* [[1970] 1 OR 127 (CA)], one issue was the vacating of a certificate of *lis pendens*. There, as in the case at bar, the subject-matter of the litigation was a lease and assignment thereof for which the plaintiff claimed a certificate of *lis pendens*. The Court of Appeal found that there was a "triable issue *as to an interest in the lands* in question" (italics are mine), so that a certificate of *lis pendens* should not be vacated on that ground. In other words, the court in determining whether there was sufficient evidence to raise a triable issue (one test for vacating a certificate of *lis pendens*) assumed that a lease was an interest in land for the purpose of s 41 of the Judicature Act. I quote from the judgment of MacKay JA, at 128: "It is clear from the evidence before the learned trial judge on the motion and before us that there is a triable issue as between the parties as to an interest in the lands in question and we are therefore all of the opinion that the *lis pendens* should not have been vacated and in respect to the order as to *lis pendens*, the appeal is allowed and the *lis pendens* restored." I have therefore concluded that the plaintiff lessee in this case does have an interest in land and the certificate of *lis pendens* issued will not be set aside on this ground.' *Peppe's Pizza Factory Ltd v Stacey* (1980) 14 CPC 235 at 237, 238, 241, Ont SC, per DuPont J

In proceedings

[Application was made to admit two statements (the maker of which had since died) under the Evidence Act 1938, s 1 (repealed; as to hearsay evidence, see now the Civil Evidence Act 1968, Pt I). Section 1(3) of the Act of 1938 provides that nothing in the section shall render admissible as evidence any statement made by a person 'interested' at a time when proceedings were pending or anticipated involving a dispute as to any fact which the statement might tend to establish.] 'The word "interest" is not a word which has any well-defined meaning, and anybody who was asked what it meant would at once want to know the context in which it was used before he could venture an opinion. It may mean a direct financial interest on the one hand, or on the other hand it may mean nothing more than the ordinary human interest which everybody has in the outcome of proceedings in which he is likely to be a witness. Just as in ordinary speech one would require to know the context, so in construing the word in an Act of Parliament it is essential . . . to look at the scope and purpose of the Act; and I think that if one does that one will be led to the conclusion that sub-s (3) is to be given a narrow rather than a broad meaning. . . . I would suggest this negative approach: that no witness ought to be held to be "a person interested" on a ground which would not be taken into consideration as affecting the weight of his evidence if he was actually called in court.' *Bearmans Ltd v Metropolitan Police District Receiver* [1961] 1 All ER 384 at 391, 393, CA, per Devlin J

INTEREST (Return on capital)

Interest is the return or compensation for the use or retention by one person of a sum of money belonging to or owed to another. Interest accrues from day to day even if payable only at intervals, and is, therefore, apportionable in respect of time between persons entitled in succession to the principal. (32 Halsbury's Laws (4th edn) para 106)

'Interest is not an apt word to express the return to which a shareholder is entitled in respect of shares paid up in due course and not by way of advance. Interest is compensation for delay in payment and is not accurately applied to the share of profits of trading, although it may be used as an inaccurate mode of expressing the measure of the share of those profits.' *Bond v Barrow Hæmatite Steel Co* [1902] 1 Ch 353 at 363, per Farwell J

'I think that interest payable on an advance from a bank means interest on an advance made to the person paying. The guarantor does not pay on an advance made to him, but pays under his guarantee. It is true that he pays a sum which pays all interest due by the person to whom the advance is made, but his debt is his debt under the guarantee, not a debt in respect of the advance made to him.' *Holder v Inland Revenue Comrs* [1932] AC 624 at 627, 628, per Viscount Dunedin

'The question which the House has to decide has not, it seems, come previously before the courts. It is whether a sum of money awarded, under the powers conferred by s 3, sub-s 1, of the Law Reform (Miscellaneous Provisions) Act 1934, as interest, and included in the total sum for which judgment is given, is "interest of money" within the meaning of Sched D to the Income Tax Act 1918 [repealed; see now the Income and Corporation Taxes Act 1988, s 18]. . . . I see no reason why, when the judge orders payment of interest from a past date on the amount of the main sum awarded (or on a part of it), this supplemental payment, the size of which grows from day to day by taking a fraction of so much per cent. per annum of the amount on which interest is ordered, and by the payment of which further growth is stopped, should not be treated as interest attracting income tax. It is not capital. It is rather the accumulated fruit of a tree which the tree produces regularly until payment.' *Riches v Westminster Bank Ltd* [1947] AC 390 at 396, 398, HL, per Viscount Simon

'The essence of interest is that it is a payment which becomes due because the creditor has not had his money at the due date. It may be regarded either as representing the profit he might have made if he had had use of the money, or, conversely, the loss he suffered because he had not that use. The general idea is that he is entitled to compensation for the deprivation.' Ibid at 400, per Lord Wright

Australia 'It has frequently been held in relation to various taxing Acts that the word "interest" is not necessarily to be taken as a technical term, and that it is frequently used in such Acts in a popular sense.' *Craig v Federal Comr of Taxation* (1945) 70 CLR 441 at 446, per Latham CJ

'The word "interest" is not a technical term: the law does not give the word the same specific application in all contexts in which it is used. . . . In its ordinary or popular sense, the word "interest" as applied to property may include a contingent interest.' Ibid at 454, per McTiernan J

'The word "interest" which has a popular rather than a technical meaning . . . is a word of wide import and includes contingent as well as vested interests.' Ibid at 457, per Williams J

Canada 'Interest is, in general terms, the return or compensation for the use or retention by one person of a sum of money belonging to, in a colloquial sense, or owed to, another.' *Re Farm Security Act 1944* [1947] SCR 394 at 411, per Rand J

INTEREST OR NO INTEREST

'Take it that the law is settled, that if a man has no interest, and insures, the insurance is void, although it be expressed in the policy interested or not interested and the reason the law goes upon, is that these insurances are made for the encouragement of trade, and not that persons unconcerned in trade, nor interested in the ship, should profit by it.' *Goddart v Garrett* (1692) 2 Vern 269 at 269, per cur.

INTERESTED PARTY

Canada 'A point was raised as to the possible difference between the words "interested person" and "interested party"; the latter, it being contended, indicated a more restricted classification than the former, but it is noted, and was admitted on the hearing, that the words "person" and "party" seemed to be used interchangeably in some of the authorities cited and not too much argument was directed to that contention, with which I am not impressed. . . . A restricted application of the word "party" might be justified when used in certain contexts or with respect to certain subject-matter, e.g. in reference to court actions or to contracts, but there is no such limiting factor present here.' *Re Consumers' Gas Co & Public Utilities Board* [1971] 8 DLR (3d) 749 at 761, 762, Alta CA, per Allen JA

Canada 'The question [for purposes of subdivision approval] is whether other property owners in the neighbourhood are "interested parties". At law, the word "interest" is typically used to connote legal concern, title or right in property, rather than in the larger sense of concern or curiosity. The objectors in the case at bar claim no legal interest, title or right in the property, although as neighbours, they are generally concerned in the outcome of this application. In my opinion, they are not "parties interested".' *Re Crittenden and City of Vancouver* (1984) 14 DLR (4th) 599 at 601, BCSC, per McLachlin J

INTERFERENCE

In this Act, the expression 'interference', in relation to wireless telegraphy, means the prejudicing by any emission or reflection of electromagnetic energy of the fulfilment of the purposes of the telegraphy. (Wireless Telegraphy Act 1949, s 19)

In this Act 'wrongful interference', or 'wrongful interference with goods', means—
(a) conversion of goods (also called trover),
(b) trespass to goods,
(c) negligence so far as it results in damage to goods or to an interest in goods,
(d) subject to section 2, any other tort so far as it results in damage to goods or an interest in goods.
(Torts (Interference with Goods) Act 1977 s 1)

[Section 2 of the Act abolishes detinue.]

'Every man's business is liable to be "interfered with" by the action of another, and yet no action lies for such interference. Competition represents "interference", and yet it is in the interest of the community that it should exist. A new invention utterly ousting an old trade would certainly "interfere with" it. If, too, this loose language is to be held to represent a legal definition of liability, very grave consequences would follow. Of course the conduct of the boiler-makers [in threatening to strike] in the case before your Lordships amounted to an interference with the plaintiffs' business, and yet, as has been pointed out, it is not said that an action lies against them. Every organiser of a strike, in order to obtain higher wages, "interferes with" the employer carrying on his business; also every member of an employers' federation who persuades his co-employer to lock out his workmen must "interfere with" those workmen. Yet I do not think it will be argued that an action can be maintained in either case on account of such interference. But whatever meaning may be attached to the words

"interfere with", I see no ground for saying that any different rule should be applied to cases of interference with a man when carrying on his trade or business, or when he is engaged in any other pursuit. In the *Mogul Steamship Co* case [[1892] AC 25], there was an extreme case of interference with the plaintiffs' business by methods which directly injured the plaintiffs in their trade for the express purpose of benefiting the defendants. The admitted interference was carried on by several defendants in a combination which in one sense amounted to a conspiracy, yet it was held by ·this House that no action could be maintained, for the acts done were not unlawful and the combination was not a criminal conspiracy.' *Allen v Flood* [1898] AC 1 at 179, 180, per Lord James Hereford

'Interference, to my mind, connotes intermeddling with something which is not one's business, rather than acting negligently in the performance of some duty properly undertaken.' *Burden (RB) Ltd v Swansea Corpn* [1957] 3 All ER 243 at 253, HL, per Lord Tucker

Australia 'Section 33 of the Act [Customs Act 1901–1986 (Cth) [see now s 33(1)]] provides that no goods subject to the control of the Customs shall be moved, altered, or interfered with without authority. . . . I think the expression "interfered with" in the context in which it is found should be construed as connoting some physical dealing with the goods, something in the nature of a movement of the goods or an alteration of their character.' *Wilson v Chambers & Co Proprietary Ltd* (1926) 38 CLR 131 at 136, 137; per Knox CJ

Australia [The proceedings were for a declaration that a barrister had been guilty of professional misconduct which amounted to 'interference' with the proper administration of justice.] 'To my mind it [interference with proper administration of justice] denotes the doing of something which, if successful, would bring about consequences in the working of the system of justice in this State by improper means. It is wrongful behaviour whether or not it is successful. Obvious examples are actual or attempted bribery of someone who has a material part to play in the decision of litigation. Such persons include any of the lawyers concerned in the case, jurors, witnesses and even, in cases with a number of parties, some of the parties themselves. Less obvious examples are where persons material to the decision of litigation are subjected to influences upon their judgment or, if witnesses, their evidence, quite external to the particular litigation, as for instance prejudicial media comment. Other examples away from the courtroom are where persons who may have information or potential evidence relevant to projected proceedings whether they be by way of litigation or in these days some form of Royal Commission, are subjected to pressures of various kinds not to make their information or evidence available to relevant authorities. On the other hand, interruptions and delays to litigation are not of themselves necessarily interference with the proper administration of justice. . . . Similarly, objections to evidence however misguided they may be are not regarded as interfering with the proper administration of justice, although it is conceivable that a barrister could so conduct himself as for example by objecting to every question asked throughout a long trial that the court would have to take steps to prevent the barrister continuing to behave in that way. . . . Similarly, conflict in court between opposing barristers or between the court and one or more barristers is not per se an interference with the proper administration of justice. The courtroom is a place where conflicts of many kinds are intended to take place and, at the end of the process, to be decided. In the progress of the case towards decision it is part of rather than interference with the proper administration of justice that opposing views are expressed. It is inevitable that expressions of view sometimes become very forceful and, when met with opposition cause heat between the people putting the differing views forward. Heat leads to sharp words and sometimes rude exchanges. These things are regrettable and usually regretted by the participants. In the overwhelming number of cases it never occurs to anyone that these incidents constitute interference with the proper administration of justice. They are part of it. When matters become extreme the power to punish for contempt is available. The comparative rarity of the use of this power in contrast to the innumerable incidents of heated behaviour in courtrooms shows how fully accepted it is that conflict in court is part of the ordinary routine of the proper administration of justice. Whether behaviour in court goes so far beyond a tolerable degree of heat and conflict as to justify the description of interference with the proper administration of justice will be a question of fact in each case.' *Prothonotary of Supreme Court of New South Wales v Costello* [1984] 3 NSWLR 201 at 208–209, per Priestley JA

Patents

United States An interference is a proceeding instituted for the purpose of determining the question of priority of invention between two or more parties claiming substantially the same patentable invention and may be instituted as soon as it is determined that common patentable subject matter is claimed in a plurality of applications or in an application and a patent. (Title 37 Code of Federal Regulations, s 1.201(a))

INTERIM

'What does the word "interim" mean? Counsel for the applicant has said that it is only a classical way of saying "temporary". That may be true. I suppose it is another way of saying "for the time being".' *Algar v Middlesex County Council* [1945] 2 All ER 243 at 246, per Cassels J

'In my view, the word "interim" means nothing more than "for the time", "in the meantime", that is all it means. I asked the question in the course of the argument: Is the dividend which is declared to be an interim dividend any less a dividend? It cannot be recalled afterwards. A very much better illustration was at once afforded by counsel for the applicant, who said: Can an injunction which is granted by the court be said to be not an injunction because it is only an interim injunction? The answer surely must be that it is an injunction, and just as much an injunction as a permanent injunction, with this qualification, that it is to last only for a certain time, but otherwise it is just as effective as is, in truth and in fact and in law, an injunction. I think the word "interim", as part of the description of an appointment, does not qualify the position of the appointee in any way whatever except as regards the limit of time for which he is appointed.' Ibid at 250, per Humphreys J

INTERLINEATION

[The Wills Act 1837, s 21 provides that no obliteration, 'interlineation', or other alteration made in a will shall be valid except in certain cases, unless such alteration is executed in the manner required for the execution of the will.] 'I am not prepared to say that . . . the word "interlineation" in the Act is to be confined to something written between the lines. Undoubtedly, that is its etymological meaning, or one of its meanings. But I think it has acquired a secondary signification, namely, the introduction of something into the will, and I think it would be equally an interlineation within the meaning of the Act if something were put into one of the lines written on the line.' *Bagshawe v Canning* (1888) 52 JP 583 at 583, per Hannen P

INTERLOCUTORY   *See also* ORDER

'Those applications only are considered interlocutory which do not decide the rights of parties, but are made for the purpose of keeping things in statu quo till the rights can be decided, or for the purpose of obtaining some direction of the Court as to how the cause is to be conducted, as to what is to be done in the progress of the cause for the purpose of enabling the Court ultimately to decide upon the rights of the parties.' *Gilbert v Endean* (1875) 9 Ch D 259 at 268, 269, CA, per Cotton LJ

'The whole matter depends on the construction of sub-s 8 of s 25 of the Judicature Act of 1873 [repealed; see now Supreme Court Act 1981, s 18(1)(h)] . . . I think the proper meaning of "interlocutory order" in this subsection is an order other than the final judgment or decree in an action.' *Smith v Cowell* (1880) 29 WR 227 at 228, CA, per Brett LJ

INTERLOCUTORY INJUNCTION   *See* INJUNCTION

INTERMIXTURE   *See* CONFUSION

INTERNAL LAW

'Internal law' in relation to any territory or state means the law which would apply in a case where no question of the law in force in any other territory or state arose. (Wills Act 1963, s 6)

[A similar definition is to be found in the Adoption Act 1968, s 11 and the Adoption Act 1976, s 71(1).]

INTERNATIONAL VOYAGE   *See* VOYAGE

INTERPLEADER

Where a person, for example a sheriff who has levied under a writ of execution, is in possession of property or its proceeds of sale and he is, or expects to be, sued in respect thereof by two or more persons making adverse claims thereto, he may apply to the court for an order requiring the claimants to litigate their differences and to abide by the court's final order in respect thereof. He is thereafter safeguarded by being able to act in respect of the property or its proceeds of sale consistently with, or as may be directed by, the court's final order. In these circumstances he is said to apply to the court for relief by way of interpleader. (25 Halsbury's Laws (4th edn) para 1001)

'The foundation of the right to file a bill of interpleader is, that there is a conflict between two or more persons claiming the same debt or obligation. That is stated in all the cases and in all the treatises of authority on the subject, and is a matter which admits of no doubt. Where such a state of things exists, and when that double claim has not been occasioned by the conduct of the person who is liable to discharge the debt or obligation, he may obtain the assistance of this court, and upon bringing into court the amount of the debt in dispute, the court will relieve him, and put the conflicting claimants to litigate their rights between one another. I guard myself thus in saying, that when the liability is not occasioned by the act of the person liable, for otherwise there is no case of interpleader.' *Desborough v Harris* (1855) 5 De GM & G 439 at 455, per Lord Cranworth LC

'The principle of interpleader is, that when two persons are concerned in a dispute, and a third person has that which is to be the fruit of the dispute, and has no part in it, but is willing to give it up according to the result of the dispute, if that third person is sued, he is not obliged to be at the expense or risk of defending the action, but on giving up what is sometimes called "the thing *in medio*", he is relieved, and the court directs that the persons, between whom the dispute really exists, should fight it out at their expense.' *Evans v Wright* (1865) 5 New Rep 331 at 333, per Willes J

INTERPRETATION *See also*
CONSTRUCTION; INCLUDE

South Africa 'That interpretation should be adopted . . . which is most calculated to attain the object and most in accordance with the mind of the law-giver; and not a hide-bound interpretation, nor one which circumvents the aim of the law so as to allow that which the law does not wish to be done though it has not expressly prohibited it.' *Dadoo Ltd v Krugersdorp Municipality* 1920 AD 547, per Innes CJ

South Africa 'It is an ordinary rule of construction that when *words* of *general* application are used they must be applied generally, unless there is something . . . in the subject matter of the enactment or the context, to show that they are intended in a more limited sense.' *Misa v Rex* 1924 NPD 309 per Dove-Wilson JP

[In England, see generally the Interpretation Act 1978.]

INTERROGATORIES

Interrogatories are a mode of discovery of facts under which, with the leave of the court, written questions may be served by one party on another party relating to any matter in question between them in the cause or matter, which that other party is by order of the court to answer on affidavit within the time specified in the order.

The function of interrogatories is to enable a party to obtain from the opposite party admissions of evidence of material facts to be adduced at the trial or to appraise the strength or weakness of the case before the trial and thereby to assist in the fair disposal of the proceedings at or before the trial or in saving costs. The utility and propriety of orders for interrogatories in suitable cases is unquestionable but the practice in recent years has tended to discourage general resort to interrogatories, particularly in simple cases and in cases where other means of information are available or where the necessity for · interrogatories has not been clearly made out.

Interrogatories should be distinguished from the discovery of documents, from particulars of pleadings which are designed to ascertain or narrow the issues in the action, and from the voluntary admission of facts, though these are matters which the court will take into account in deciding whether or not to give leave for interrogatories to be served. (13 Halsbury's Laws (4th edn) para 100)

'The plaintiff wishes to maintain his questions, and to insist upon answers to them, in order that he may find out something of which he knows nothing now, which might enable him to make a case of which he has no knowledge at present. If that is the effect of the interrogatories, it seems to me that they come within the description of "fishing" interrogatories, and on that ground cannot be allowed.' *Hennessy v Wright (No 2)* (1888) 24 QBD 445 at 448n, CA, per Lord Esher MR

INTERRUPTION

'It seems to me . . . that we are driven to a pure question of construction of the meaning of this covenant for quiet enjoyment which is in a very usual form; and it must be remembered that these covenants for quiet enjoyment must be construed with reference to the transaction, which is one of lease, and so as to give effect to what may be reasonably supposed to be intended by the lessor and the lessee. . . . I think that an interruption under such a covenant is not caused by the lessor or by those claiming under him, unless it is either a direct act of interruption, or unless it is some act of which it either was foreseen or ought by reasonable care to have been foreseen that the consequence in the particular case would be an interruption.' *Harrison, Ainslie & Co v Muncaster* [1891] 2 QB 680 at 688, 689, CA, per Bowen LJ

[The Prescription Act 1832, s 3 confers an absolute and indefeasible right to light after enjoyment for twenty years without 'interruption'. Section 4 enacts that 'no act or matter shall be deemed to be an 'interruption' unless it has been submitted to or acquiesced in for one year after notice.] 'The term "interruption", . . . in s 3 bears the same meaning as in s 4, and refers to an adverse obstruction, and not a mere discontinuance of user.' *Smith v Baxter* [1900] 2 Ch 138 at 143, per Stirling J

'Section 1(1) [of the Rights of Way Act 1932 (repealed; see now the Highways Act 1980, s 31(1))] says: "Where a way . . . upon or over any land has been actually enjoyed by the public as of right and without interruption for a full period of twenty years, such way shall be deemed to have been dedicated as a highway". . . . "Without interruption", means that the enjoyment of the right must not have been interrupted. If for the statutory period members of the public have used the way as of right, and their exercise of that right has in fact not been interrupted, then the statutory consequences follow. The word "interruption" must be given its proper import in its grammatical context. A mere absence of continuity in the de facto user proved will not prevent the statute from running. If that were not so, the necessary proof in public right-of-way cases would often break down . . . simply because witnesses were not available to fill all the gaps in such proof. No interruption comes within the statute unless it is shown to have been an interference with the enjoyment of the right of passage.' *Jones v Bates* [1938] 2 All ER 237 at 245, 246, CA, per Scott LJ

'It seems to me that the reference to interruption in the subsection [now the Highways Act 1980, s 31(1) (supra)] is to the fact of an interruption and that the question of intention is primarily relevant if, and only if, the owner, against whom the right of way is asserted, seeks to prove no intention to dedicate. None the less, intention may be involved in the question whether a particular act is or is not interruption. Thus, padlocking a gate is prima facie an act of interruption; but I doubt whether it could be held to be so if the interruptor fixed on the gate a notice that the key would be found hanging on the gatepost.' *Lewis v Thomas* [1950] 1 KB 438 at 447, CA, per Cohen LJ

Australia 'Interruption in this context [Workers' Compensation Act 1926–1986, s 7 (see now s 7(1)(b)(i))], which includes also the word "deviation", is a temporary "break" in the continuity of the journey—a temporary suspension of motion towards its goal—which requires no departure from its route. Deviation in this context, which includes also the word "interruption", is such a departure, not necessarily accompanied by interruption. It is a "break" in the journey which consists of divergence from its route or some portion of it; the motion towards the destination continues, but the route is departed from. There may be both interruption and deviation, that is, an interruption may occur during the course of a deviation.' *Joseph Reid Pty Ltd v Watters* [1970] 1 NSWR 148 at 156, CA, per Sugerman JA

INTERSECTION

Canada 'The accident [in which a car struck a pedestrian] occurred at the junction of College

Avenue and Toronto Street in Regina. . . . The learned trial judge instructed the jury that the junction of these two streets was not an "intersection" within the meaning of . . . s 68 [of the Vehicles Act 1935 (see now s 137 of RSS 1965, c 377 amended by 1968 (Sask) c 83)]. . . . In making this statement the learned trial judge referred to the dictionary definition of the word "intersection" and held that because Toronto Street does not run across and beyond College Avenue but comes to an end when it runs into it, the space formed at the junction is not an intersection. I am of opinion, with all respect, that the learned trial judge placed his interpretation upon too narrow a ground. . . . My opinion that the Legislature intended these junctions to be considered as intersections is fortified by the consideration that otherwise great inconvenience would result to drivers of vehicles.' *Baker v Johnson (No 2)* [1940] 3 WWR 251 at 252, 253, per cur.

INTERSTATE COMMERCE

United States The term 'interstate commerce' means trade or commerce in securities or any transportation or communication relating thereto among the several States or between the District of Columbia or any Territory of the United States and any State or other Territory, or between any foreign country and any State, Territory, or the District of Columbia, or within the District of Columbia. (Securities Act of 1933, s 2(7))

United States The term 'interstate commerce' means trade, commerce, transportation, or communication among the several States, or between any foreign country and any State, or between any State and any place or ship outside thereof. The term also includes interstate use of (A) any facility of a national securities exchange or of a telephone or other interstate means of communication, or (B) any other interstate instrumentality. (Securities Exchange Act of 1934, s 3(a)(17))

INTERVENING CAUSE

[By the terms of a policy of insurance the insurance company undertook to pay a sum in the case of an injury which directly caused the death of the insured. A proviso in the policy provided that the policy only insured against death where accident was the direct or proximate cause thereof, but not where the direct or proximate cause was disease or other 'intervening cause'.] 'I will read the first words used by Channell J in giving judgment [in the court below]: "Now the first question one has to consider is what is meant by the term 'intervening cause', when used in connection with the well-known doctrine about the *causa proxima*, in order that you may say in law that the effect is caused by another thing, and not directly caused by the accident. I think that the expression 'new cause intervening' is practically the same as that used here, 'other intervening cause', and that it means some new and independent thing started, which together with the existing cause in some way or other— the one cause, possibly, in greater degree than the other cause, but the two acting together— ultimately causes a certain result; you must have something that may be called a new intervening cause, in order to prevent the existing cause which is operating to produce a well-known result from being said to be the real effective cause of what has happened". In my opinion the view expressed by Channell J is quite right. . . . The counsel for the company contended that, instead of saying that the new thing or new cause intended by the words "disease or other intervening cause" in the proviso must be something new and independent of the accident, we ought to read the words as meaning a new intervening cause, whether dependent on or independent of the accident. I do not agree. When the disease or other cause is dependent on the accident, I think it is right to say that the term "direct or proximate cause" covers in such a case not only the immediate result of the accident, but also all those things which may be fairly considered as results usually attendant upon the particular accident in question.' *Re Etherington & Lancashire & Yorkshire Accident Insurance Co* [1909] 1 KB 591 at 597, 598, CA, per Vaughan Williams LJ

'The gist, as it seems to me, of the view put forward by the defendants is that the word "intervening", as used in this document, means "supervening", or following. The argument on the other side is that it does not mean that, but is used in the sense in which Channell J read it, as equivalent to something independent of and unconnected with the accident as it happened at the time. . . . To put it in the way in which the matter presents itself to me, I should say that the words mean something which cannot . . . be described as a "*sequela*" of the accident.' Ibid at 603, per Kennedy LJ

INTESTACY

'Intestate' includes a person who leaves a will but dies intestate as to some beneficial interest in his real or personal estate. (Administration of Estates Act 1925, s 55(1))

'Intestacy can only arise when a person dies without legally bequeathing his property, that is, without a will. If a man by will declares he dies intestate, and that his property shall go as in the case of intestacy, such paper does not constitute an intestacy but a bequest of the property to *personæ designate*—designated by the statute, as it might be by any other description.' *Brenchley v Lynn* (1852) 2 Rob Eccl 441 at 468, per Dr Lushington

INTIMIDATION   *See also* THREAT

[The Conspiracy and Protection of Property Act 1875, s 7 imposes a penalty for 'intimidation' or annoyance by violence or otherwise.] 'I am . . . of opinion that the word intimidation may mean any kind of threat, provided it made the person against whom it was used reasonably afraid, and if so, then it is contrary to the statute.' *Judge v Bennett* (1887) 52 JP 247 at 248, per Stephen J

'The justices appear to have followed my ruling in *R v McKeevit* [Liverpool Assizes, 16 December 1890, unreported], which was that to constitute intimidation within the meaning of this section [s 7 of the Conspiracy and Protection of Property Act 1875 (see supra)] personal violence must be threatened.' *R v McKeevit* (1890), cited by Cave J (*arguendo*) in *Gibson v Lawson* [1891] 2 QB 545 at 550

'If a man says to another, "I am going to hit you when I get you alone", it is undoubtedly a threat; and an injunction can be obtained to restrain him from carrying out his threat. But the threat itself does not give rise to a claim for damages. It is only when he delivers the blow that it is actionable; and then as an assault, not as intimidation. Very recently it has become clear that the tort of intimidation exists not only in threats or violence, but also in threats to commit a tort or a breach of contract. The essential ingredients are the same throughout; there must be a coercive threat to use unlawful means, so as to compel a person into doing something that he is unwilling to do, or not doing something that he wishes to do; and the party so threatened must comply with the demand rather than risk the threat being carried into execution. In such case, the party damnified by the compliance can sue for damages for intimidation.' *Stratford (J T) & Son Ltd v Lindley* [1964] 2 All ER 209 at 216, CA, per Lord Denning MR; *revd on other grounds* [1964] 3 All ER 102; [1965] AC 269, HL

'The essence of intimidation is damage caused by a coercive threat to do some unlawful act.' Ibid at 227, per Salmon LJ

New Zealand 'Essential to the definition of this tort [intimidation] is the intention on the part of one person to compel another to take a particular course of action. "Threat" in this connection means "an intimation by one to another that unless the latter does or does not do something the former will do something which the latter will not like".' *Huljich v Hall* [1973] 2 NZLR 279 at 285, per McCarthy J

New Zealand 'I agree with McCarthy J that a threat to commit a tort does not generally give rise to an action in damages unless that tort is committed—and then the damages arise, not from the threat, but from the tort itself. One exception to this rule may be found in a threat to commit an assault—this may itself be an assault, and then it is a tort; if it does not itself amount to a tort it gives rise to no claim. Another is to be found where the threat itself amounts to the tort of intimidation—but the threat must be of the "or else" kind—the tort lies in coercing the person threatened, by means of the threat, to act in a desired manner, with the result that loss ensues.' Ibid at 288, per Turner P

INTO

'The question comes to be what is pilotage "into" Harwich harbour. Does it mean that the ship is to be brought to any point in Harwich harbour at which she is compelled to stop, and then the pilotage ceases to be compulsory? Or does it mean compulsory so long as she is still proceeding to the destination in the port to which she has to go? . . . It seems to me that what is pilotage into a harbour, where it is left general, must be determined by the place in that harbour to which the vessel is intended and destined to go.' *The Ole Bull* [1905] P 52 at 64, 65, per Gorell Barnes J

Canada 'It would seem that the prepositions "into" and "through" are complementary, the "into" dealing spatially with the Province in the aspect of entry, and the preposition

"through" connoting exit or departure, as well as traversing the whole from end to end and such an interpretation appears to be supported by all the several dictionaries and authorities on words and word origins that I have consulted.' *R v Beaney* (1969) 4 DLR (3d) 369 at 380, 381, Ont Co Ct, per Matheson Co Ct J

INTOXICATED

Canada 'The word "intoxicated" is not defined under the Act [Intoxicated Persons Act Detention 1980]. I accept the submission on behalf of the Government of Manitoba that in the context in which it is used in this particular enactment, it means intoxicated by liquor—as opposed to intoxication by poisons or drugs.' *Reference Re Intoxicated Persons Detention Act* (1980) 116 DLR (3d) 91 at 96, Man CA, per Hubard JA

INTOXICATING LIQUOR

'Intoxicating liquor' means spirits, wine, beer, cider, and any other fermented, distilled or spirituous liquor, but does not include—
(a) any liquor, which, whether made on the premises of a brewer for sale or elsewhere, is found on analysis of a sample thereof at any time to be of an original gravity not exceeding 1016° and of a strength not exceeding 1.2 per cent;
(b) perfumes;
(c) flavouring essences recognised by the Commissioners [of Customs and Excise] as not being intended for consumption as or with dutiable alcoholic liquor;
(d) spirits, wine or made-wine so medicated as to be, in the opinion of the Commissioners, intended for use as a medicine and not as a beverage.
(Licensing Act 1964, s 201(1) as substituted by the Finance Act 1967, s 5(1)(c), Sch 7, para 22 and amended by the Finance Act 1981, s 11(1), Sch 8, Part III, para 25)

INTOXICATION   *See also* DRUNK

'A drunken woman in the streets excited by spirituous liquors, forgets the modesty of her sex, is guilty of every sort of extravagance, talks irrationally, is hooted and pursued and pulled about by boys, so that every person who sees her says,—"she is a mad woman" or, "she must be either drunk or mad". There is hardly an act of which an insane person can be guilty which may not arise from intoxication. Intoxication is in truth temporary insanity: the brain is incapable of discharging its proper functions; there is temporary mania—but that species of derangement, when the exciting cause is removed, ceases; sobriety brings with it a return to reason.' *Wheeler & Batsford v Alderson* (1831) 3 Hag Ecc 574 at 602, per Sir John Nicholl

'The condition attached to the public-house certificate in question was that "the licensee shall not be in a state of intoxication on the premises" these being the words of the second form in Schedule 6 [repealed] to the Licensing (Scotland) Act 1903. . . . I stress the words "state of intoxication" because they occur immediately afterwards in the form of certificate in relation to the prohibition against selling or supplying excisable liquor to persons who are in a "state of intoxication", and the phrase also falls to be read in contradistinction to such terms as "drunk" or "drunken" or "under the influence of drink", which are used elsewhere in this and related statutes in describing various stages of the condition of inebriation. My view is that the words "state of intoxication", prima facie suggest a condition graver and more extreme than that which is suggested by such words as "drunk" or "under the influence of drink", and it is desirable that that distinction should be kept clearly in view for the purposes of prosecutions based upon an alleged breach of a condition in the certificate.' *Keith v Bell* 1944 SLT 31 at 32, 33, per the Lord Justice-Clerk (Lord Cooper)

'I wish to take, and make, public note of the fact that, as argued for the respondent to us, there was a distinct attempt to involve the words "state of intoxication on the premises" as meaning exactly the same as—no more and no less than—the words "drunk" or "drunken", or even as "under the influence of excisable liquor". Where in varying sections of several Acts of Parliament variant words are found employed, it is a sound general principle to presume that they express different things or at least different degrees. I am of opinion for my part—and wish to express it, that where the words "state of intoxication" are used, as they are, in only three parts of this long Act, they are intended to be used of a different condition from that indicated by the mere words "under the influence of drink" or the mere word "drunk". That is so much so that, in my opinion, s 70, to which we were referred, very clearly established two classes of offence in open public places and streets. One involves

the words "state of intoxication", in which case a person may be arrested, if he is incapable, or not under the charge of a suitable person, and no more is required. No rowdyism, no disorder. The other cases in the later part of said section are cases in which every person who is "drunk while in charge in any street or public place", or other named premises involving duty, can be charged, and in that case, in my opinion, the word "drunk" is used as in specific contrast with the words "state of intoxication", used a little way above. . . . In my opinion it would be wrong to give any different significance to that expression "state of intoxication" in these two or three different significances and uses within the self-same Act of Parliament. Therefore I think it is clear that some particular static state, of a higher degree than that which in an ordinary person and day-to-day circumstances is often described as "drunk", may be necessary for such a conviction. Stated very generally, a publican, to incur this disqualification, must himself be in that befuddled state in which if he found a customer he must refuse him any more excisable liquor.' Ibid at 33, 34, per Lord Mackay

Australia 'It appears that a man is to be regarded as "under the influence" if he has taken such a quantity of intoxicating liquor as disturbs the balance of his mind, or the quiet, calm, intelligent exercise of his faculties.' *Cassidy v State Government Insurance Office* [1965] WAR 81 at 81, per Negus J

Australia 'When dealing as in this case with a liquid which is clearly a beverage it is not, in my opinion, correct to say that it is of an intoxicating nature only if it is such that an ordinary man could consume it in such quantities as to become intoxicated without other adverse effects. I think that if its alcoholic content is within the range found in beverages commonly used for, inter alia, their alcoholic stimulation, then it must be classed as "of an intoxicating nature", for the simple reason that it may be used to contribute to or if used may contribute to intoxication.' *McKnight v Onusco* [1966] VR 591 at 594, per Lush J

Canada 'The meaning to be attached to the word "intoxicated" in the policy [of accident insurance] is important. Is an insured person to be deemed intoxicated within the meaning of the policy when a certain number of parts of alcohol per thousand are found in his blood, although discoverable clinical symptoms of intoxication are absent, or, on the other hand, are such symptoms necessary to a finding of intoxication? . . . Is there not still the possibility that some persons are not affected at all to any appreciable degree by the consumption of a large quantity of whisky? It may well be that until more is known with certainty, it is unsafe to build too much upon a blood-test uncorroborated by other symptoms. In the meantime it may be prudent to confine the application of the word "intoxicated" to cases where recognisable symptoms of it are observable.' *Earnshaw v Dominion of Canada General Insurance Co* [1943] OR 385 at 398 (CA), per Robertson CJO

Canada 'Intoxication is the stupefied condition of a person who has imbibed alcoholic liquor in sufficient quantity to make him lose totally or partially the use of his mental or nervous faculties. To be intoxicated in the legal sense, it is not necessary to be dead drunk any more than to be ill it is necessary to be dying. It suffices that an individual be affected by alcohol to the point of no longer having his normal control, his judgment, or, in a word, that he no longer has the use of all his intellectual or physical faculties.' *Desbiens v R* (1951) 103 Can CC 36 at 41, per Bienvenue J

New Zealand 'What is the meaning of the words in s 146 of the Licensing Act 1881 [repealed; see now s 243 of the Sale of Liquor Act 1962] under which this conviction has been obtained? The words of the section are, "If any innkeeper permits drunkenness . . . or sells any liquor to any person already in a state of intoxication . . . he shall be liable", etc. What is meant by "already in a state of intoxication"? In my opinion the words mean that state in which, through intoxicating liquors, a person has lost the normal control of his bodily and mental faculties. In my opinion, in a state of intoxication both are more or less affected. It is, no doubt, a difficult matter to draw the line so as to determine when a man ceases to be sober, and becomes intoxicated. It ever is difficult to distinguish between states which come on gradually. To do so is akin to the difficulty of solving the old problem of the Sorites—when, as between two heaps of grain, one large and one small, does the large one cease to be large, and the small become large, if a grain from time to time is taken from the one and added to the other. The decision in such a case as this must rest on the evidence of impartial men of common-sense who are

themselves sober. I do not think the words "drunk and incapable" are an exact equivalent of "in a state of intoxication". It seems to me that these words signify some degree less than absolute incapacity from drunkenness. It is, in fact, assumed that this "person already in a state of intoxication" is capable of asking for more drink, and, apparently, capable of paying for it; for it cannot be assumed that a man who is thoroughly drunk could either ask for a drink or pay for it. The state pointed out by the statute is therefore, in my opinion, a degree less than absolute drunkenness; and that is, I think, apparent from the use of the words in the section, and the fact that the word "drunkenness", though used in another part of the section, is differentiated from "in a state of intoxication".' *Brown v Bowden* (1900) 19 NZLR 98 at 102, 103, per Stout CJ; also reported 2 GLR 374

New Zealand 'It has been held, and is obvious, that the state of intoxication mentioned in s 146 of the Licensing Act 1881 [repealed; see supra] does not mean a state of complete intoxication involving an almost entire suspension of the faculties of the body or of the mind. A person is, I think, intoxicated within the meaning of the section when either his mental or his bodily faculties are so far disturbed by the influence of liquor that an average man who is neither a publican nor a prohibitionist would say that it was improper for him to be supplied with more liquor.' *Laffey v Magorian* (1903) 22 NZLR 577 at 578, 579, per Williams J

New Zealand 'A man is in a state of intoxication . . . when as a result of his consumption of intoxicating liquor, his physical or mental faculties, or his judgment, are appreciably and materially impaired in the conduct of the ordinary affairs or acts of daily life.' *R v Ormsby* [1945] NZLR 109 at 109, per Fair J; also reported [1945] GLR 23

New Zealand 'Liquor is of an intoxicating nature if it is such as to affect to an extent appreciable in his conduct, the control of a person's physical or mental faculties, such person being fairly representative of a considerable section of the community, and not so exceptional in conduct or physique as to make him an anomalous test.' *Graham v Adams* [1945] NZLR 147 at 150, per Fair J; also reported [1945] GLR 14

New Zealand 'In my opinion, capacity to

drive with care and safety negatives intoxication, and, whilst so holding, the magistrate was not justified in convicting the appellant. A man is intoxicated when he is so much under the influence of alcohol as to have lost control of his faculties to such an extent as to render him incapable of executing safely the occupation in which he was engaged at the material time.' *Wood v Ellis* [1949] NZLR 312 at 314, per Gresson J (citing *Smith's Forensic Medicine* (3rd Edn) 483)

New Zealand [Under a policy of personal accident insurance no compensation was payable to the insured in respect of any event happening to him whilst 'intoxicated'.] 'I hold . . . that the insured was "intoxicated" in terms of exception 2(c) to the policy if he was [as was cited (see supra) by Gresson J in *Wood v Ellis*] "so much under the influence of alcohol as to have lost control of his faculties to such an extent as to render him incapable of executing safely the occupation in which he was engaged at the material time".' *Farmer's Mutual Insurance Association v Parsons* [1970] NZLR 795 at 803, per Wilson J

INTRODUCTION

Canada [Real estate agent was entitled to commission if purchaser was introduced to property during currency of agreement.] "Introduction" is not a term of art or a technical word. It is a word in common usage and should be given its ordinary and accepted meaning. . . . The word "introduction" carries the connotation of "initial" or "first" presentation.' *Terry Martel Real Estate Ltd v Lovette Investments Ltd* (1981) 123 DLR (3d) 387 at 390, Ont CA, per Houlden JA

INVALID CARRIAGE

'Invalid carriage' means a vehicle, whether mechanically propelled or not, constructed or adapted for use for the carriage of one person, being a person suffering from some physical defect or disability. (Chronically Sick and Disabled Persons Act 1970, s 20(2))

In this Act 'invalid carriage' means a mechanically propelled vehicle of which the weight unladen does not exceed 254 kilograms and which is specially designed and constructed,

and not merely adapted, for the use of a person suffering from some physical defect or disability and is used solely by such a person. (Road Traffic Regulation Act 1984, s 136(5))

INVENTED WORD

[Section 64(1)(d) of the Patents, Designs and Trade Marks Act 1888 (repealed; see now Trade Marks Act 1938, s 9(1)(c)), enacted that a trade mark must contain or consist of at least one of a number of essentials, one of which was an 'invented word'.] 'In one sense *Apollinaris* has been invented no doubt—that is to say, there has been appropriated to the water issuing from this spring the name of a saint well known in the neighbourhood, . . . and whose name had been already given to a hill and a church. It was not invented in that way, but it was invented no doubt as applied to water. I am far from saying . . . that you may not take some word used for an entirely different purpose, some foreign word it may be, or a combination of foreign words, or even a combination of English words, which would be applicable to some entirely different purpose, and still say it is invented for the purpose in hand. . . . But here there is nothing approaching to invention, but merely an application to the spring of that which was already applied to other things in the immediate neighbourhood.' *Re Apollinaris Co's Trade Marks* [1891] 2 Ch 186 at 202, 203, CA, per Kekewich J

'There is no statutory definition or description of an "invented word" [within the Patents, Designs and Trade Marks Act 1888 (repealed; see supra)]; and I cannot myself see any legitimate ground for limiting its ordinary meaning. Any word which is in fact new, and not what may be called a colourable imitation of an existing word, is, in my opinion, an "invented word" within the meaning of the statute under consideration.' *Re Farbenfabriken Application* [1894] 1 Ch 645 at 652, CA, per Lindley LJ

[In this case the word 'Eboline' was the subject of the action. Eboli is the name of a town in Italy.] 'The applicants' manager says that he invented the word "Eboline", and no doubt he is speaking honestly according to his belief. But it appears that "Eboli" is the name of an Italian town of 11,000 inhabitants, mentioned in the Gazetteer. The mere addition of the common English termination "ne" is not sufficient to make the word an invented word—a word already in existence cannot properly be said to be an invented word because the person claiming to have invented it was not aware of its existence. If it were otherwise, the fewer words a man knows the more readily could he invent. . . . What the Act [Patents, Designs and Trade Marks Act 1888 (repealed; see supra)] requires is that the word should be an invented word in fact, and not merely in the belief of the person claiming to register it as a trade mark.' *Re Salt (Sir Titus) Sons & Co's Application* [1894] 3 Ch 166 at 168, per Chitty J

'A word that does not exist in any language, and as far as all the evidence goes, and as far as one's own common sense goes, had no previous existence before it was used for the purposes of the Trade Marks Acts by the person who then had it registered, is an invented word.' *Re Densham's Trade Mark* [1895] 2 Ch 176 at 189, 190, CA, per Lopes LJ

'The present Act [Patents, Designs and Trade Marks Act 1888 (repealed; see supra)] provides, among other things, by s 10, that a trade mark must consist of or contain at least one of certain particulars, one of which is "an invented word or invented words". This word "Solio" is claimed to be an invented word; and it has been adjudged not to be an invented word, and apparently . . . because it is a word which has reference to the character or quality of the goods. My lords, I think it is an invented word within the meaning of this statute. I know of no such word as "Solio" in any sense which would make it intelligible here, although it is an Italian word meaning a throne, and although it is a Latin word in the ablative case with the same meaning. . . . I am satisfied in this case to say that the word "Solio" is an invented word.' *Eastman Photographic Materials Co v Comptroller-General of Patents, Designs, & Trade Marks* [1898] AC 571 at 576, 578, per Lord Halsbury LC

'I do not think we shall deprive the trade of any advantage . . . by holding that this word "Absorbine" is not an invented word. . . . In my opinion "Absorbine" is a mere variation of the word "absorb", and is used in precisely the same sense, and with the intention of indicating that this preparation . . . effects its cure by absorbing. . . . I am of opinion that there is no invention whatsoever in this word "Absorbine". I may mention that, so far as the "Solio" case [*Eastman Photographic Materials*

Co v Comptroller-General (supra)] is concerned, that case is obviously different from the present. "Solio" may have been derived from "Sol", but there is no word in the English language of which one could say that "Solio" was a mere variation.' *Christy v Tipper* [1905] 1 Ch 1 at 2, 3, CA, per Vaughan Williams LJ

'I come . . . to consider whether this word [the word "cyclostyle"] could be registered under s 9 of the Act of 1905 [Trade Marks Act 1905 (repealed; see now Trade Marks Act 1938, s 9(1)(c))]. The first question is whether it is an "invented word" within the meaning of sub-s (3) of that section. I think that it is not. It has been decided that words which have become part of the stock of human knowledge as describing a particular thing are not invented words within the meaning of that enactment.' *Re Gestetner's Trade Mark* [1908] 1 Ch 513 at 519, per Lord Alverstone CJ

'Dealing with the words in para 3 [of s 9 of the Trade Marks Act 1905 (repealed; see supra)] "An invented word or invented words", I confess that I should regret very much to come to the conclusion that a word wholly unknown to an ordinary Englishman was not an invented word merely because on investigation in some gazetteer or atlas or anything of that kind it was found that there existed in a foreign country a place or a person whose name was identical with or substantially identical with the word proposed to be registered. No one except Parker J has ever attempted to define the meaning of those words used in that paragraph. In the case . . . which is usually mentioned as the *Diabolo* case [*Philippart v William Whiteley Ltd, Re Philippart's Trade Mark 'Diabolo'* [1908] 2 Ch 274], Parker J, who knew more about trade mark law than most people, said this: "To be an invented word, within the meaning of the Act, a word must not only be newly coined in the sense of not being already current in the English language, but must be such as not to convey any meaning, or at any rate any obvious meaning, to ordinary Englishmen". It will be observed that his language is quite general, He said that the word must be newly coined in the sense of not being already current in the English language, and I cannot help thinking that a word which happens to be the name of some foreign place or resident, and which is not in use in this country as an ordinary English word, comes within that definition.' *Re Boots Pure Drug Co Ltd's Registered Trade Mark No 530, 535* [1938] Ch 54 at 71, CA, per Romer LJ

INVENTION

A patent may be granted only for an invention in respect of which the following conditions are satisfied, that is to say—
(a) the invention is new;
(b) it involves an invented step;
(c) it is capable of industrial application;
(d) the grant of a patent for it is not excluded by subsections (2) and (3) below;
and references in this Act to a patentable invention shall be construed accordingly. (Patents Act 1977, s 1(1))

[Subsection excepts certain things from the definition, eg scientific theories, computer programs, etc. Subsection (3) provides that no patent shall be granted if it would encourage offensive or immoral, etc behaviour, or for any variety of animal or plant or biological process.]

'It is extremely desirable that when a beneficial idea has been started by one man, he should have the benefit of his invention, and that it should not be curtailed and destroyed by another man simply improving upon that idea; but if the idea be nothing in the world more than the discovery of a road to attain a particular end, it does not at all interfere with another man discovering another road to attain to that end, any more than it would be reasonable to say, that if one man has a road to go to Brighton by Croydon, another man shall not have a road to go to Brighton by Dorking. They are roads, and means of attaining the end, and unless you can prove that one is a colourable imitation of the other, or unless you can prove that one bodily incorporate the other, with merely an addition, it is impossible to say they shall not be coexistent subjects of contemporaneous patents. Now, that is the conclusion that I come to in this case. I am sorry to find these inventions in collision, but I am bound to say that merit is due to the one, and the merit is due to the other. I am bound also to say, that the invention of the one appears to me to have been arrived at originally by a process of thought in which the one did not derive assistance from the knowledge of the other.' *Curtis v Platt* (1864) 11 LT 245 at 249, CA, per Westbury LC

'It appears to their Lordships that it is not proved that any invention in the true sense of the word was made. . . . It is not enough for a man to say that an idea floated through his brain; he must at least have reduced it to a definite and practical shape before he can be said to have invented a process.' *Permutit v*

Borrowman (1926) 135 LT 742 at 743, PC, per Lord Cave LC

'The only definition of "invention" contained in the Patents Act 1949 is by reference to the phrase "any manner of new manufacture" in the Statute of Monopolies 1623. This statute has never been construed as confining the grant of patents to processes which would have been within the contemplation of Parliament in the early seventeenth century as constituting a new manner of manufacture. The concept of "invention" as an activity which entitles the person who undertakes it to a patent monopoly of a process or its product has been continually changing by applying the social policy which underlay the Statute of Monopolies 1623 in the seventeenth century to the changing conditions resulting from advances in technology and the sciences.' *American Cyanamid Co v Upjohn Co* [1970] 3 All ER 785 at 802, HL, per Lord Diplock

First and true inventor

'The Act of Parliament on which all these patents are founded, says that in order to come within the exception of the statute of monopolies [(1623) 21 Jac 1, c 3] the person to whom the patent is granted, must be the first and true inventor and he must describe something in his specification which is not already known and used. What is the meaning of a first and true inventor? . . . As I understand, shortly after the passing of the statute, the question arose whether a man could be called a first and true inventor, who in the popular sense, had never invented anything, but who having learned abroad (that is, out of the realm in a foreign country, because it has been decided that Scotland is within the realm for this purpose) that somebody else had invented something, quietly copied this invention and brought it over to this country and then took out a patent. As I said before, in a popular sense, he had invented nothing. But it was decided, and now, therefore, is the legal sense and meaning of the statute, that he was the first and true inventor, if the invention being in other respects novel and useful, was not previously known in this country, known being used in that particular sense as being part of what has been called the common or public knowledge of the country. That was the first point. Then there was a second point. Suppose there were two people actual inventors in this country, who simultaneously invented the same thing, could either be said to be the first and true inventor?

It was decided that the man who first took out the patent was the first and true inventor. Then came another point. If the man who took out the patent was not in popular language the first and true inventor, because somebody had invented it before but had not taken out a patent for it, would he still in law be the first and true inventor? And it was decided that he would, provided the invention of the first inventor had been kept secret or without being actually kept secret had not been made known in such a way as to become a part of the common knowledge or of the public stock of information. Therefore, in that case also, we have a person who was legally the first and true inventor, although in common language he was not, because one person or more had invented it before him, but had not sufficiently disclosed it.' *Plimpton v Malcolmson* (1876) 45 LJ Ch 505 at 506, 507, per Jessel MR

INVENTORY

Secured transactions

United States Goods are 'inventory' if they are held by a person who holds them for sale or lease or to be furnished under contracts of service or if he has so furnished them, or if they are raw materials, work in process or materials used or consumed in a business. Inventory of a person is not to be classified as his equipment (Uniform Commercial Code 1978, s 9–109)

INVESTMENT   *See also* INCOME

'The term "investment" implies investment for a given term, but that cannot be applied to a balance in the bankers' hands, using it in a technical or popular sense.' *Archibald v Hartley* (1852) 21 LJ Ch 399 at 400, per Kindersley V-C

'It may be . . . that the word "investments" is of rather vague meaning, but the testator here has, I think, clearly shown that he regarded it as including debentures and perference and ordinary shares. . . . It is true that he was peculiarly ill-informed of the exact nature of his holdings in the various companies and that in endeavouring to particularise his investments he has made many mistakes, but the word he has used and the context in which he has used it are, in my opinion, sufficiently comprehensive to cover the debenture stock.' *Re Connolly, Walton v Connolly* (1914) 110 LT 688 at 691, per Eve J

'Without attempting to give an exhaustive definition of the words "invest" and "investment" I think that the verb "to invest" when used in an investment clause may safely be said to include as one of its meanings "to apply money in the purchase of some property from which interest or profit is expected and which property is purchased in order to be held for the sake of the income which it will yield".' *Re Wragg, Wragg v Palmer* [1919] 2 Ch 58 at 64, 65, per P O Lawrence J

'The word "investment", though it primarily means the act of investing, is in common use as meaning that which is thereby acquired; and the primary meaning of the transitive verb "to invest" is to lay out money in the acquisition of some species of property.' *Inland Revenue Comrs v Rolls-Royce Ltd* [1944] 2 All ER 340 at 341, 342, per Macnaghten J

'I think it is clearly stated by Lawrence J as he then was, in the case of *Re Wragg* [*Re Wragg, Wragg v Palmer* (supra)], that . . . there is a distinction between purchasing freehold property for the sake of the income one is going to get from it and purchasing freehold property for the sake of occupying it or permitting somebody else to occupy it. In the former case, the purchase is . . . accurately described as an "investment". In the latter case, it is not necessarily an investment, for it is a purchase for some other purpose than the receipt of income. It may be a purchase which would not be, from the financial point of view, attractive or indeed at all beneficial, because part of the price may be attributable to the special benefit represented by the acquisition of a suitable place in which to live.' *Re Power, Public Trustee v Hastings* [1947] Ch 572 at 575, per Jenkins J

'What did this testator mean when he excepted "investments" and "securities for money"? I think he meant stock exchange investments—stocks and shares—and things which were not stocks or shares but were securities, such as debentures. I do not think he intended to include policy moneys in that phrase.' *Re Lilly's Will Trusts, Public Trustee v Johnstone* [1948] 2 All ER 906 at 907, per Harman J

'The meaning of "investment" is its meaning, not in the vernacular of the man in the street, but in the vernacular of the business man. It is a form of income-yielding property which the business man, looking at the total assets of the company, would single out as an investment.' It certainly does not include all the property of the company and I am unable to accede to the proposition . . . that every item of the company's property is an investment, and that while the company uses those items itself the profit it derives from them is a profit of trade, but, if it hands one of them over to others to use in return for a periodic payment, it begins to receive an income from an investment. The business man would not limit income from investments to income from the kinds of securities which are quoted on the stock exchange, and he would, I think, regard as income from investment a profitable rent from a sub-lease of office premises or the like surplus to the company's requirements.' *Tootal Broadhurst Lee Co Ltd v Inland Revenue Comrs* [1949] 1 All ER 261 at 265, 266, HL, per Lord Normand

New Zealand [A fine was paid to an insurance company to reinstate a lapsed policy. The question was whether this could be said to be an 'investment'.] 'What, then, is an "investment"? It is defined by Webster in his dictionary as meaning "The laying-out of money in the purchase of some species of property, usually of a permanent character". Skeat, in his Etymological Dictionary, says "invest" means "to lay out money", and in Wharton's Law Lexicon the same meaning is given. In Latham's "Johnson's English Dictionary" the meaning given of "invest" is "Putting out capital (ie establishing a vested interest in it) for the purpose of obtaining interest for it". The root idea is the "putting-out of money". In this transaction no money is put out. The cash account is not depleted by one penny by the entry of the premium paid. As understood by the compilers of dictionaries, and as ordinarily understood amongst business men, there is no "investment". No money passes.' *Taxes Comr v Australian Mutual Provident Society* (1902) 22 NZLR 445 at 450, CA, per Stout CJ; also reported 5 GLR 106 at 107

New Zealand 'There is no statutory definition of the word "investment". The word must therefore be read in its popular meaning. That popular meaning embraces, I think, every mode of application of money which is intended to return interest, income, or profit. Money employed as capital in a business is, in popular language, money invested in a business; money used for the purchase of negotiable instruments is an investment; so also money lent upon a bond or other personal security; so money deposited with a bank or other financial institution at interest.' Ibid at 456, 457, per Edwards J; ibid at 111

New Zealand [The terms of a will referred to 'my investments of every description'.] 'I do not think in popular parlance the word "investment" covers money lodged in a post-office savings-bank. Such money is withdrawable at will just as money in a current account with a bank is. The only difference is until recent times the Post Office Savings Bank has paid a low rate of interest—that is, a rate of interest lower in comparison with the rate obtainable elsewhere on what are sometimes termed gilt-edged investments. An investment is, I think, the antithesis of ready money, and ready money is usually used in a sense including money on current account or money withdrawable on demand. Money lodged with a post-office savings-bank and withdrawable at will in a broad sense still retains the characteristics of unconverted money.' *Re Ferry, Ferry v Allen* [1945] NZLR 448 at 451–454, per Kennedy J

INVESTMENT COMPANY *See* COMPANY

INVESTMENT TRUST

'Investment trust' means a company which is not a close company and which is approved for these purposes by the Commissioners of Inland Revenue for a particular accounting period. The commissioners may not approve any company unless it is shown to their satisfaction:

(1) that it is resident in the United Kingdom;
(2) that its income is derived wholly or mainly from shares or securities;
(3) that no holding in a company, other than an investment trust or a company which would qualify as an investment trust but for head (4), represents more than 15 per cent by value of the investing company's investments;
(4) that the shares of the company making up its ordinary share capital, or, if there are such shares of more than one class, those of each class, are listed in the Official List of The Stock Exchange;
(5) that the distribution as dividend of surpluses arising from realisation of investments is prohibited by the company's memorandum or articles of association; and
(6) that the company does not retain in respect of any accounting period more than 15 per

cent of the income it derives from shares and securities.

(23 Halsbury's Laws (4th edn) para 1185)

INVITATION

To public

Australia 'An invitation can be conveyed or communicated to the public in many ways: in writing, by a notice in the press or posted in a public place conveying an invitation to any reader: orally, by an address to a public meeting or an announcement in a public place: by handing leaflets to passers-by in a public street: by circulars sent through the post: by going indiscriminately from house to house repeating the invitation. The essence of an invitation to the public [within the Registration of Business Names Act 1928–1961 (SA), s 4(a) [see now Business Names Act 1963–1986, s 26(1)] is not in the manner of its communication or in the number of the persons to whom it is communicated. The criteria are rather, are the recipients of the invitation persons chosen at random, members that is of the general public, the public at large, all and sundry: or are they a select group to whom and to whom alone the invitation is addressed, so that if an outsider sought to respond to it he would be told that he was not one of those invited to come in.' *Lee v Evans* (1964) 112 CLR 277 at 292, per Windeyer J

INVITEE

[The distinction between the duty owed to invitees and that owed to licensees was abolished, in England, by the Occupiers' Liability Act 1957, which imposed a 'common duty of care' to all visitors. The common law rules continue, however, to determine who is an occupier and to whom the duty of care is owed, and 'visitors' in the Act of 1957 include only those categories who would at common law be treated as invitees or licensees. As to the duty of an occupier to persons other than his visitors (eg trespassers) see the Occupiers' Liability Act 1984.]

'The question of what is an invitee and what is a licensee has been considered many times and I suppose the best definition is that an invitee is a person "invited to the premises by the owner or occupier for the purposes of business or of manifest interest"; that is to say, he is a person who receives permission from the occupier as a matter of business and not as a matter of grace. The words quoted are taken from the speech of Lord Buckmaster in *Fairman v Perpetual Investment Building Society* [[1923] AC 74 at p 80].' *Stowell v Railway Executive* [1949] 2 KB 519 at 523, per Lynskey J

'The general principles on which persons coming on the premises of an occupier with his consent are classified as invitees and licensees, respectively, are easy to formulate, but not always easy to apply. They are somewhat over-simplified in the formula in *Salmond's Law of Tort* [10th Edn, p 476] justly commended by MacKinnon LJ [in *Ellis v Fulham Borough Council* [1938] 1 KB 212]: "The invitor says 'I ask you to enter upon my business'. The licensor says: 'I permit you to enter on your own business'." Succinct and vivid as is this formula, it might suggest that the visitor is an invitee only if the business on which he comes is exclusively that of the occupier. This is, of course, not what is meant. It is more exact to say that an invitee is a person who comes on the occupier's premises with his consent on business in which the occupier and he have a common interest; eg a shopper has an interest to buy and a shopkeeper an interest to sell.' *Pearson v Lambeth Borough Council* [1950] 2 KB 353 at 366, CA, per Asquith LJ

'The Law Reform Committee has recently recommended that the distinction between invitee and licensee should be abolished [see supra], but this result has already been virtually attained by the decisions of the courts. The classic distinction was that the invitor was liable for unusual dangers of which he knew or ought to know, whereas the licensor was only liable for concealed dangers of which he actually knew. This distinction has now been reduced to vanishing point. . . . The duty of the occupier is nowadays simply to take reasonable care to see that the premises are reasonably safe for people lawfully coming on to them: and it makes no difference whether they are invitees or licensees.' *Slater v Clay Cross Co Ltd* [1956] 2 All ER 625 at 627, CA, per Denning LJ

'The law as to the duties owed by the owner of heritable property to those called "invitee" or "licensee" respectively seems to have developed in relation to the following circumstances. The landowner considered was one who had devoted his land to his own purposes. If then he asked someone to visit his land for a purpose which was his business or material interest, it was just that he should take reasonable care to guard his "invitee" against dangers existing on the land of which he knew or ought to have known. If, however, he merely permitted a person to visit his land for a purpose in which he had no material interest, it was considered just that his "licensee", being there for a purpose, should take the lands as he found them. The landowner was under no duty to him save one, dictated as much by moral considerations as enforced by the law, to warn the "licensee, of concealed dangers of which he" the landowner, had actual knowledge.' *Plank v Magistrates of Stirling* 1956 SLT 83 at 89, per Lord Patrick

INVOLUNTARY

Australia 'Such phrases as "reflex action" and "automatic reaction" can, if used imprecisely and unscientifically, be, like "black out", mere excuses. They seem to me to have no real application to the case of a fully conscious man who has put himself in a situation in which he has his finger on the trigger of a loaded rifle levelled at another man. If he then presses the trigger in immediate response to a sudden threat or apprehension of danger, as is said to have occurred in this case, his doing so is, it seems to me, a consequence probable and foreseeable of a conscious apprehension of danger, and in that sense a voluntary act. The latent time is no doubt barely appreciable, and what was done might not have been done had the actor had time to think. But is an act to be called involuntary merely because the mind worked quickly and impulsively? I have misgivings in using any language descriptive of pyschological processes and phenomena, especially as I doubt whether all those skilled in this field employ their descriptive terms uniformly. Guided however by what has been said in other cases and by writers on criminal law whose works I have read . . . I have come to the conclusion that if the applicant, being conscious of the situation in which he had put himself, pressed the trigger as a result, however spontaneous, of the man whom he was threatening making some sudden movement, it could not be said that his action was involuntary so as to make the homicide guiltless. The act which caused the death was, it seems to me, using the language of s 18 of the statute [Crimes Act 1900–1986 (NSW)], an act of the accused.' *Ryan v R* (1967) 121 CLR 205 at 245, 246, per Windeyer J

IRON

'The document which we have to construe is a time policy of marine insurance upon the hull and boilers of the steamship *Celtic Monarch*, and it contains warranties which were intended to exclude certain sources of danger to the ship, amongst others this: "Warranted no iron or ore or phosphate cargoes". We have now to construe the words "no iron" in this warranty. The first question we have to ask ourselves is, What is the meaning of "iron" in the English language as used by ordinary men, amongst others by merchants? It is perfectly well known to every Englishman familiar with the common objects of life that steel is a form of iron; it is plain, therefore, that when the expression "no iron" is used the meaning must be that steel is excluded. . . . In the present case there is no evidence which tends to cut down the ordinary meaning of the word "iron". Then we are bound to take into consideration the object and scope of the clause in question, and it seems to me to be plain that . . . steel goods must fall within the object of this clause quite as much as iron goods.' *Hart v Standard Marine Insurance Co* (1889) 58 LJQB 284 at 287, CA, per Fry LJ

IRREDEEMABLE

'I agree that, prima facie, the true legal meaning of the word "redeemable" when applied to stock is stock liable to redemption, that is to say, liable to be redeemed at the option of the mortgagor or person who has the right to redeem. . . . If that be the prima facie meaning of the word "redeemable", the prima facie meaning of the word "irredeemable" when applied to stock is stock that the mortgagor has no power to redeem. . . . I think in whatever sense the word "redeemable" is used in the resolution the word "irredeemable" must be held to be used in the contrary sense. The word "redeemable" is used in this resolution in reference to stock which in any event must be paid off. It is not used to describe stock which the company has the option of paying off. It describes stock which the company is bound to pay off, and applying to the word "irredeemable" the contrary meaning, it describes stock which the company is not bound to pay off.' *Re Stocks (Joseph) & Co Ltd, Willey v Stocks (Joseph) & Co Ltd* (1909), reported in [1912] 2 Ch 134n at 140n, per Eve J

IRREGULAR EXECUTION   *See*
EXECUTION

IRREGULARITY

[Section 166 of the Public Health (Scotland) Act 1897 provided that a board of management of a hospital should not be liable in damages for any 'irregularity' committed by its officers.] 'Prima facie "irregularity" seems to indicate something less than negligence. . . . I take the view that in that context the word "irregularity" was intended to mean an irregularity in the procedure and method by which the powers given to a local authority and its officers were to be carried into execution.' *Davies v Board of Management for Glasgow Victoria Hospitals* 1950 SLT 392 at 394, per Lord Strachan

'So far as the first part of the section [s 166 of the Public Health (Scotland) Act 1897 (supra)] is concerned, it was contended that "irregularity" must be given an extended meaning and that it covered acts of negligence. I do not think that this is so. This part appears to perform a very modest function. What seems to be contemplated is the case where a servant does something which the Act empowers him to do but is guilty of some technical fault in carrying it out, eg fails to go through all the prescribed formalities.' *M'Ginty v Board of Management for Glasgow Victoria Hospitals* 1951 SLT 92 at 98, per the Lord Justice-Clerk (Thomson)

IRREPARABLE INJURY

[An information filed by the Attorney-General prayed that the defendant might be restrained from cutting down trees or undergrowth in the royal forest of Waltham.] 'We are all agreed that this is not a case in which the court can interfere by injunction before trial. The principle upon which our refusal proceeds is, that an injunction is not granted in the case of an ordinary trespass; though in instances where, looking at all the circumstances, it appears that the act complained of or threatened falls under the description of irreparable injury, it will. The defendant's act of cutting the vert will amount to waste, if the lands on which it grew are within the forest; but . . . it has not been shown that the cutting . . . would be irreparable injury to the forest, viz such an injury as could not be compensated in damages.' *A-G v Hallett* (1847) 16 M & W 569 at 581, per Parke B

'I take the meaning of irreparable injury to be that which, if not prevented by injunction, cannot be afterwards compensated by any decree which the Court can pronounce in the result of the cause.' Ibid at 581, per Alderson B

'Although there might be no equity on the part of these plaintiffs, it appeared to me that, if they were right in contending that the proceedings were legally invalid, it would be a case of irreparable injury (using the word "irreparable" in the sense in which the Court uses it, that is, not that there would be no physical possibility of repairing it, but that it would be a very grievous injury indeed), to allow the defendants to proceed.' *Pinchin v London & Blackwall Rly Co* (1854) 5 De GM & G 851 at 860, per Lord Cranworth LC

[The plaintiffs contended that a conference of shipowners had combined and conspired to exclude from the China markets the ships of the plaintiffs. They asked for an interim injunction to prevent the defendants from pursuing this course.] 'This does not appear to me to be a case in which . . . the plaintiffs can sustain irreparable injury by our declining to grant the relief prayed. It may be that they will suffer some damage; it may be that they will for a time have a difficulty in carrying on their China trade, or may have to carry it on at a loss. But injury of that sort differs altogether from the injury which is called "irreparable", to prevent which injunctions have heretofore been granted in the Court of Chancery, and are now allowed to issue from this court. For instance, if a fine old ornamental tree in a nobleman's park be cut down, the injury is practically irreparable, and cannot be compensated in damages. It is in cases of that nature that an interim injunction issues. The injury here, if it be made out, obviously is not one of that character.' *Mogul SS Co v M'Gregor, Gow & Co* (1885) 15 QBD 476 at 486, per cur; affd [1892] AC 25

Canada '"Irreparable injury" in injunction applications means an injury that cannot be adequately remedied by damages.' *Hooper v North Vancouver* [1921] 3 WWR 878 at 830, per Murphy J; revd on other grounds [1922] 1 WWR 1249

Canada 'Have the plaintiffs established that they will suffer "irreparable injury" in the event of the injunction prayed for not being granted? The "irreparable injury" must be material and one which cannot be adequately remedied by damages. . . . In 17 Halsbury's Laws 218 [see now 24 Halsbury's Laws (4th edn) para 926], the following appears under the heading, "Irreparable injury": "The plaintiff must also as a rule be able to show that an injunction until the hearing is necessary to protect him against irreparable injury; mere inconvenience is not enough. By the term 'irreparable injury' is meant, substantially, injury which could never be adequately remedied or atoned for by damages". . . . In the affidavit of A G Spooner [the plaintiff], it is stated "that if the order of the board is carried into effect the plaintiff will suffer irreparable injury by the cutting down of its production and the consequent loss of revenue and in my opinion will not be able to continue in business". It is to be noticed that, while the words "irreparable injury" are used, they mean nothing more in the setting in which they are used than that there will be a loss in production and revenue which the company's financial position is unable to support. . . . It seems to me that the plaintiffs must fail on the ground of having failed to establish "irreparable injury" in the sense in which these words are judicially used.' *Spooner Oils Ltd & Spooner v Turner Valley Gas Conservation Board & A-G for Alberta (No 2)* [1932] 2 WWR 641 at 646, 648, 649, per McGillivray JA

IS

New Zealand 'I am of opinion that the word "is" is used [in an Act] . . . without any temporal significance at all. This can be the case with the use of the word "is", and in a different context this proposition formed the basis of the advice of the Privy Council per Lord Porter in *Pye & Others v Minister of Lands for New South Wales* [[1954] 1 WLR 1410 at 1425; [1954] 3 All ER 514 at 525]. There the words under consideration were "provided that where any such resumption *is* made . . .''; and it was argued that this expression should be read as equivalent to "where any such resumption *has been* made". Lord Porter said: "In their Lordships' opinion, no such meaning need be, or should be, ascribed to it. The words, in their view, are descriptive of the purpose of resumption, *and have no temporal connotation*." So again in *Hargreaves v Hopper* [(1875) 1 CPD 195] the Court of Common Pleas, in construing the words "is of full age" had no hesitation in reading "is" as "was"

feeling it unnecessary to read any notion of contemporaneousness into the word "is". This same question is not unusual when the word "is" is encountered in statutes.' *Public Trustee v McKay* [1969] NZLR 995 at 1005, per Turner J

ISSUANCE

Canada [Claim for dependants' relief was required to be by action commenced within specified period from date of 'issuance' of probate.] 'I hold that the word "issuance" in s 11 of the Testator's Family Maintenance Act [now Wills Variation Act, RSBC 1979, c 435, s 10(a)] means the date upon which the grant of letters probate was entered in the Court Registry. On that date nothing further was required to perfect the grant. On that date the grant of letters probate was given out officially and publicly.' *Re Hirsch* (1977) 76 DLR (3d) 558 at 561, BCSC, per Hinds LJSC

Canada [The Alberta Labour Act, RSA 1970, c 196, s 71(4) provides for an application to review a Board's decision no later than 30 days after the 'issuance' of the Board's decision.] 'Where issuance is used to define the commencement of the period within which a party affected by an order may move to have it questioned or reviewed, and the word has more than one meaning, I am of the opinion that the meaning adopted should be one that gives effect to the intention of the legislature. In my view to hold that issuance is effected merely by placing the decision in the mail or in the hands of a delivery service, without reference to the date on which it is received by or on behalf of a party, does not carry out the intention of the legislature. Such a definition could result in a party being deprived of the right granted under s 71(4) if for any reason the decision was not received by or on behalf of that party within 30 days of the date it was placed in the mail or with the delivery service. It also could substantially reduce the 30-day period the Legislature intended a party would have to consider its position before it had to move under s 71(4). I am therefore of the opinion that the word "issuance" as found in s 71(4) involves the idea of passing from the Board to a party, such as when it is communicated to them at the conclusion of a hearing if an oral decision is delivered or when received by or on behalf of a party if it is placed with an agency of the Board for the purpose of delivering, whether that agency be the mails, a delivery service or a telegraph company.'

United Assocn of Journeymen & Apprentices of Plumbing & Pipe Fitting Industry of United States & Canada v Board of Industrial Relations [1975] 2 WWR 470 at 475, Alta CA, per Prowse JA

ISSUE (Offspring) *See also* CHILD

In settlement

[By marriage articles J M covenanted to convey lands to trustees in trust for J M for life, and afterwards to the use of his intended wife for life, and after their deaths to the 'issue' of the match.] 'I must take the articles as they are, and the plain meaning of the words. I am of opinion it was the intention of the articles the issue, whether male or female, should have the whole of this estate amongst them. . . . What does issue of the marriage mean? Issue female, as well as male; and therefore if it had gone no farther than to the issue of the marriage, and a bill had been brought for carrying the articles into execution, the settlement must have been to all the issue, to the first and every other son, and for default of such issue to the daughters, with proper remainders following one after another.' *Hart v Middlehurst* (1746) 3 Atk 371 at 374, per Lord Hardwicke LC

'The word "issue" is ambiguous; it may mean either "children"; or "issue *in infinitum*". In the present case I think it impossible upon the words "to the issue of the said John and Anne", not to say that the word "issue" was used as synonymous to a child and was not meant to express issue indefinitely. The issue were to take in such shares as John Campbell should appoint, which could not apply to issue indefinitely, nor did the power of appointment extend to any limitation of estate; and the next clause, which disposes of the property in default of appointment, uses the word "children" as describing the same persons before described by the word "issue", and the subsequent words "for default of such issue", must therefore, I think, receive the same construction.' *Campbell v Sandys* (1803) 1 Sch & Lef 281 at 292, 293, per Lord Redesdale LC

'It is clearly settled, that the word "issue" unconfined by any indication of intention, includes all descendants. Intention is required for the purpose of limiting the sense of that word, restraining it to children only.' *Leigh v Norbury* (1807) 13 Ves 340 at 344, per Grant MR

[By marriage articles H T covenanted that he would, within six months of his intended marriage, by conveyance settle property so

that on his death it should vest in the 'issue' of H T and his intended wife, and that such 'issue' should also be entitled to a sum of £1,000, failing any appointment by H T or his intended wife, in equal shares if there were more than one of such 'issue' born in H T's lifetime or in a reasonable time after his death.] 'I think upon the construction of these articles, it would be difficult to say that the word "issue" does not mean children; that is the natural import of the expression in such a settlement, and particularly where it is referred to issue "living in the lifetime of the husband, or born in a reasonable time after his death".' *Thompson v Simpson* (1841) 1 Dr & War 459 at 480, per Sugden LC

'I am of opinion that the rule which I adopted in the case of *Ross v Ross* [(1855) 20 Beav 645] is that which is applicable to the present case, and where I, acting upon the principle that though the word "issue" is *nomen generalissimum* and includes all the remotest descendants, nevertheless, held, that where issue are pointed out as persons to take with reference to the share of the parent, a gift which, so far as regards the parent, fails, they take on the principle which may be called a quasi representative principle, that is, that the children of each parent whose share fails takes that parent's share, but not admitting the grandchildren to take in competition with the children, to participate in the share of that deceased parent. The scope and object of the settlement . . . all appear to me to point to this construction, viz. that though the word "issue" undoubtedly includes all the remotest descendants, yet that when each share is divisible, the division of that share must take place, in this manner:— amongst a class in the same generation, and that each share of a parent which fails is divisible amongst his children, if he has any, or if not amongst his grandchildren, excluding in the former case the grandchildren, if there should be any, and in the latter case, great grandchildren, if there should be any in existence at the time of the division.' *Robinson v Sykes* (1856) 23 Beav 40 at 51, 52, per Romilly MR

[A settlement provided that certain trust estates should be transferred or assigned to certain children or such of them as should be living at the time of the decease of the spouses and the 'issue' of such of them as might be then dead leaving issue.] 'I am, as to the construction to be put upon the word "issue" in this case, concluded by authority. The principle which governs the decision in *Sibley v*

Perry [(1802) 7 Ves 522] and of that in *Harrington v Lawrence* [(1814), cited in 11 Sim 138] before Sir W Grant, applies equally here; and, looking at the language of the instrument before me, I find no words sufficiently strong to justify me in deciding that the grandchildren are included in the word "issue", and consequently entitled to a share in the property. The primary meaning of this word . . . indeed, embraces descendants however remote; but such meaning is upon the authority of Lord Eldon, controlled by the word "parent", namely, father or mother, as distinguished from ancestors in general. Upon the face of the deed I feel I am bound to decide that no other issue than children are entitled to take; and though I should be glad to adopt a more enlarged construction, I am not at liberty, upon the ground of mere hardship, to disturb a settled doctrine of the Court, namely, that the word "issue", used in conjunction with that of "parent", implies children only, and does not include a more remote descendant.' *Anderson v St Vincent (Viscount)* (1856) 2 Jur NS 607 at 608, per Stuart V-C

[Property was settled by a marriage settlement in trust for A H during so long as he should live and should not marry a second time, and in case he married a second time and there should be any 'issue' of the intended marriage then on certain other trusts.] 'Now one point that arises here is, whether the word "issue" which occurs here, means anything but children. The word is "issue", but looking to the subsequent part of the settlement, I think it is plain that this is a trust limited for the benefit of the children only. The word issue may be used generally in a will, and it is frequently so, and it may be used, in one sense or another in a settlement, but here, although it is "leave any issue", the subsequent part shews that the only issue in the contemplation of the author of the settlement were issue of the first generation, or the children. It is therefore in my opinion a trust for the children only, and not for the grandchildren or more remote issue.' *Frewen v Hamilton* (1877) 47 LJ Ch 391 at 393, per Malins V-C

'I see no difference between the case of a will and that of a deed. I shall follow *Harrington v Lawrence* [(1814), cited in 11 Sim 138], and hold that the word "issue" as used in the case before me must be limited to meaning children, and that the grandchildren take nothing under the substitutional gift.' *Barraclough v Shillito* (1884) 53 LJ Ch 841 at 841, per Chitty J

'The proper objects of the marriage settlement are the children of the intended marriage; grandchildren and great-grandchildren are never thought of on such occasions as objects of intending provision; portions are provided for the children, and they are enabled thereby, when their own turn comes to be married, to make provision for their children. But issue more remote than children are rarely, if ever, directly within the scope of a marriage treaty; and therefore it is that when dealing with such an instrument the very occasion suggests that if "issue" be the word used, it is meant in the sense to which it so easily lends itself, of children.' *Re Bromhead's Trusts, Public Trustee v Bromhead* [1922] 1 IR 75 at 79, per Powell J

'In my judgment, the phrase "issue of our marriage" ought to mean to the court, as it undoubtedly would mean to any layman, the children of the husband and his wife. Though the grandchildren are, in one sense, issue of the marriage between the husband and his wife, since there could have been no grandchildren if there had been no children, the grandchildren are not really issue of the marriage of the husband and his wife, but are issue of the son or daughter and his wife or her husband, who have been able to have issue by reason of the circumstance, among other things, that the grandfather had issue.' *Re Noad, Noad v Noad* [1951] 1 All ER 467 at 469, per Roxburgh J; [1951] Ch 553 at 557

In will

'The word "issue", in a will, prima facie means the same thing as heirs of the body, and is to be construed as a word of limitation; but this prima facie construction will give way, if there be on the face of the will sufficient to show that the word was intended to have a less extended meaning, and to be applied only to children, or to descendants of a particular class or at a particular time.' *Slater v Dangerfield* (1846) 15 M & W 263 at 272, per cur.

'The word "issue" may be restricted so as to mean children; and, conversely, the word "children" may, from the context, be enlarged so as to be construed "issue" generally. . . . In this particular case, the trust is declared "for all and every the respective issues of his said daughters, whether sons or daughters", etc etc. On the meaning of these words, standing by themselves, I can have no doubt; the testator speaks of the issue of his daughters "whether sons or daughters". The subsequent words "such issue" is a relative expression, and the general rule is to go back to the last antecedent, and we there find the "issue" limited to "sons or daughters". I think that the testator must be understood to have put his own construction on the word "issue", and to mean the "sons or daughters" of his daughters.' *Farrant v Nichols* (1846) 9 Beav 327 at 330, per Lord Langdale MR

'I am of opinion, that the word "issue" means "children". There are many cases where the word issue is so restricted. I admit the proposition, that the primary meaning of the word "issue" includes every possible class of issue to the remotest generation, and that the burden of proof lies on those who ask to restrict its ordinary meaning; but I think the plaintiffs have discharged that obligation on the present occasion. . . . I find . . . on five separate occasions, the testator uses the word "issue" as equivalent to children. It is a canon of construction, that where the testator has affixed a particular meaning to a word in one part of his will, it shall be construed as having the same meaning in all other parts of his will, if it do not violate the sense.' *Rhodes v Rhodes* (1859) 27 Beav 413 at 416, 417, per Romilly MR

'Every part of the will must be considered in order to gather the intention of the testator. The inconvenience of construing the word "issue" to mean descendants generally is so great that the court lays hold of any circumstance to cut it down. It is clear that when the testator speaks of "issue of her issue" he meant by the word "issue" children only, or issue of the first generation. He has, therefore, said in effect, "be it understood by the word 'issue' I mean children only, issue of the first generation only".' *Livesay v Walpole* (1875) 23 WR 825 at 826, per Malins V-C

'The child was en ventre sa mère at the time of the death of its grandmother, and was plainly then living, so as to bring it within the words of the will "in the case she has issue living".' *Re Burrows, Cleghorn v Burrows* [1895] 2 Ch 497 at 498, per Chitty J

'It is now firmly established that in devises of real estate "issue" is prima facie a word of limitation and equivalent to "heirs of the body".' *Re Simcoe, Vowler-Simcoe v Vowler* [1913] 1 Ch 552 at 557, per Swinfen Eady J

'The first question here, and the first part of the second question, are concerned with the familiar difficulty whether, in a gift to certain persons and their issue, the term "issue" is to have its normal prima facie meaning of descendants of all generations, or is to be limited, on the context of the particular document, to children. . . . One must, however, undoubtedly start with this, namely, that as a matter of legal construction the word "issue" has the prima facie meaning I have mentioned. . . . Starting, then, with this prima facie, though no doubt flexible, meaning of the word "issue", it is to be noted here that all through the settlement of the residue on the testator's daughter there is a very careful and marked distinction between the use of the word "issue" and the use of the word "children", and that the former word is used throughout in its strict meaning of descendants generally. . . . On the whole, having regard to the very careful distinction between children and issue that has been drawn and preserved in the previous part of the will, and to the studied character of the language of the two gifts immediately in question, I think that more violence would be done to the language of the will, taken as a whole, by abruptly changing the use of the word "issue" from its full meaning to its more limited meaning than by reading the words of substitution as applying generally rather than as being limited to a single generation. And, accordingly, I am of opinion that in these two gifts the word "issue" includes grandchildren as well as children.' *Re Burnham, Carrick v Carrick* [1918] 2 Ch 196 at 201, 202, 204, per Sargant J

'The will seems to be a carefully drawn document and in several places . . . the testator used, as it seems, the word "children" as a word of different meaning from the word "issue". He refers in the power of appointment to "the children of the respective daughter or the issue of any such child". Later he refers to the power of appointment "provided for such of my daughters and their children and issue". Later he refers to "child or issue of such son", and so on. It seems to me that this is a testator who said "issue" when he meant "issue"—ie when he meant issue to have its primary meaning, with all descendants of every degree; and he used the word "children" when he meant "children".' *Re Hipwell, Hipwell v Hewitt* [1945] 2 All ER 476 at 480, CA, per Morton LJ

'In the law of Scotland the term "issue" or "lawful issue" has no technical meaning. The words are merely words of popular signification and their meaning is to be gathered from the terms of the clause in which they are used.' *Murray's Trustees v Mackie* 1959 SLT 129 at 130, per Lord Guest

Australia 'The terms of the testator's codicil . . . were these: "I hereby declare that the issue of any child of mine shall be entitled by way of substitution as tenants in common in equal shares per stirpes if more than one to the share to which the parent of such issue would have been entitled under the preceding trust had such parent survived such deceased child of mine." . . . The word "issue" in the passage I have read must in this codicil be interpreted as "children"; that is to say, the great-grandchildren of the testator do not take under it. This interpretation, it seems to me, necessarily arises by reason of the use made of the word "parent", in relation to the issue, and I do not think there is anything to lessen the force of that word to be found in the presence of the words "per stirpes" in the passage read.' *Re Dougharty, National Trustees Executors & Agency Co of Australasia Ltd v Brentnall* [1935] VLR 333 at 338, 340, 341, per Mann J

Australia '"Issue" is a word with a clear prima facie legal meaning. It means descendants or progeny. No doubt "issue" is a flexible word and its prima facie application may be restricted by any sufficient indications appearing in the documents: cf *Re Birks* [[1900] 1 Ch 417 at 418, 420]. But "the essence of the word 'issue', which primarily means all descendants, is totality rather than succession" (*Re Cust, Glasgow v Campbell* [[1919] VLR 221 at 254, 255] per Cussen J distinguishing "issue" from "heirs of the body"). . . . The word "issue" therefore ought not to receive a secondary or restricted meaning unless, upon a consideration of the whole document, it satisfactorily appears that it was intended.' *Matthews v Williams* (1941) 65 CLR 639 at 650, 651, per cur.

Australia 'It must be conceded that, whatever may be the sense in which the word "issue" is used in popular parlance, in a will or settlement, at any rate if apparently drawn up by a lawyer, it means descendants of all degrees unless there is sufficient indication to the contrary.' *Re Matthews* [1941] SASR 9 at 17, per Richards J

Australia 'The word "issue" . . . is more flexible than the expression "heirs of the body", and its prima facie meaning as a word of limitation is more easily displaced by the context in which it is found.' *Plunkett v Plunkett* (1947) 46 NSWSR 483 at 486, per Roper J

Australia 'The only question in controversy is the meaning given to the phrase [in a will] "the lawful female issue". The full phrase is not to be found in any decided case or legal dictionary, but there is no doubt that the word "issue" must be taken to mean "lineal descendants of every degree", unless there is something in the context or in other provisions of the will to indicate that, in the circumstances, it was intended to mean "children".' *Re Irish (decd)* [1962] SASR 73 at 75, per Chamberlain J

Lawful issue

[The Law Reform (Miscellaneous Provisions) (Scotland) Act 1940, s 5(1) (repealed) enacted that 'the surviving husband of any woman domiciled in Scotland who . . . dies wholly or partially intestate leaving no lawful issue shall have the like rights to or in her estate as a widow has in her deceased husband's estate under the Intestate Husband's Estate (Scotland) Acts 1911 and 1919.'] 'The condition for the application of s 5 of the Act of 1940 is that the woman in question shall have died "leaving no lawful issue". These words are very familiar words in our law and in our statutes dealing with rights of succession, and it seems to me to involve an insupportable strain upon any legitimate principle of statutory construction to read them as if they said not "leaving no lawful issue" but "leaving no issue, whether lawful or not".' *Osman v Campbell* 1946 SC 204 at 208, per the Lord Justice-Clerk (Cooper)

Canada 'The narrow question for determination is whether or not an "adopted son" of a now-deceased cestui que trust is the "lawful issue" of that beneficiary. . . . The combined term, "lawful issue", does not coincide in meaning with natural born children. It may include a child who is not the natural offspring of a man, and may exclude another child who is his natural offspring. Thus in law, every child born of a couple during their marriage is "lawful issue" of the couple, even though the husband is not in fact the child's natural father. This rule of law is based, not upon truth or fact, but upon public policy, which seeks to uphold the purity of the marriage relationship and to protect children born in wedlock. On the other hand a child, which is born of an unmarried woman, and of which a specific man is admittedly the natural father, is not the lawful issue of the man; and even the subsequent marriage of the child's father and mother does not of itself legitimize the child so as to make it the "lawful issue" of its natural father. If then the law, in declaring that all children born in wedlock are lawful issue of a husband, can disregard the actual paternity, why may not the law also declare that a child adopted into a man's family is also his lawful issue? This is precisely what the Child Welfare Act does. That public Act expressly declares that a child so adopted shall be deemed and held, for every purpose, to be the child of its adopting parents as fully as if born to them. That declaration of law makes the child lawful issue of its adopting parents. The declaration is clear and explicit and must control the present case. . . . I hold that the adopted child of the settlor's grandson is, within the meaning of the trust agreement, "lawful issue" of that grandson.' *Re Clark Trust* [1946] 3 WWR 490 at 491–493, per Dysart J

ISSUE (Proceedings)

'An issue is that which, if decided in favour of the plaintiff, will in itself give a right to relief, or would, but for some other consideration, in itself give a right to relief; and if decided in favour of the defendant will in itself be a defence.' *Howell v Dering* [1915] 1 KB 54 at 62, CA, per Buckley LJ

'Arbitration, like litigation, is concerned only with the legal rights and duties of the parties thereto. It is concerned with facts only in so far as they give rise to legal consequences. The final resolution of a dispute between parties as to their respective legal rights or duties may involve the determination of a number of different "issues", that is to say, a number of decisions as to the legal consequences of particular facts, each of which decisions constitutes a necessary step in determining what are the legal rights and duties of the parties resulting from the totality of the facts. To determine an "issue" in this sense, which is that in which I shall use the word "issue" throughout this judgment, it is necessary for the person adjudicating on the issue first to find out what are the facts, and there may be a dispute between the parties as to this. But while an issue may thus involve a dispute about facts, a mere dispute about facts divorced from their legal consequences is not an "issue".'

Fidelitas Shipping Co Ltd v V/O Exportchleb [1965] 2 All ER 4 at 9, 10, CA, per Diplock LJ

Australia 'The defendant in this case obtained judgment with costs, and the order of the court was that the plaintiff should be allowed the costs of the issues upon which he succeeded. . . . The real trouble is what is meant by "issues"—a point which has not received any judicial interpretation since the coming into force of the Judicature Act so far as I am aware. At the time when the Common Law Procedure Statute was in force, and under the old common law pleading, the matter was clear and definite. The plaintiff could have put in his declaration one or more counts, and defendant could plead to those counts. If, for instance, the plaintiff sued for goods sold and delivered and for money lent, defendant might plead the general issue, and, in addition, might plead special defences. He might, for example, plead denying the delivery, and allege that the goods were not up to sample. To the count for money lent he might plead that the money was not lent, or that it was paid. Each of these would be a distinct issue, and the jury would try these issues and determine them each by itself, subject of course, to the direction of the judge. . . . The main question is whether that question still exists. I think it does. I think that, under our present system, when an order is made as to costs of certain issues, the order means the costs of substantial defences, and does not mean the costs of each material fact disputed by either side.' *Ferne v Wilson* (1901) 26 VLR 829 at 830, 831, per Hood J

ISSUE (Verb)

Certificate

Australia 'Plainly enough a certificate is not "issued" to the person until it is delivered to him, which means that it must pass from the possession of the authorities either into his manual custody or under his control or into his legal possession so as to be at his command.' *Koon Wing Lau v Calwell* (1949) 80 CLR 533 at 574, per Dixon J

Commercial paper

United States 'Issue' means the first delivery of an instrument to a holder or a remitter. (Uniform Commercial Code 1978, s 3–102(1)(a))

Debentures

'The first matter that I have to consider is sub-s (k) of s 3 of the memorandum of association. That says that one of the objects for which the company is founded is to borrow money by the issue of debentures, debenture stocks, bonds, mortgages, obligations, and other securities upon all or any part of the company's undertaking, revenues, and property, including uncalled capital, with or without any security. . . . I do not know that there is anything in the meaning of the word "issue" which is inconsistent with an issue of an obligation or security which is oral. The word "issue", as a mere English word, does apply to words as well as to writings; and although when one looks at the catalogue here of "debentures, debenture stocks, bonds, mortgages, obligations, and other securities", those words do all of them suggest to one's mind written securities, yet, with regard at all events to mortgages, it is plain you might have a mortgage without any writing, and you might have a security in the nature of a pledge without any writing whatever.' *Re Tilbury Portland Cement Co Ltd* (1893) 62 LJ Ch 814 at 815, per Williams J

Negotiable instrument

'I think that there cannot be an issue in point of law of a negotiable instrument unless and until it comes into the hands of some person entitled to treat it as a security available in law.' *Brown v Inland Revenue Comrs, Gordon v Inland Revenue Comrs* (1900) 84 LT 71 at 79, CA, per Collins LJ

Notes

[Section 11 (repealed in part) of the Bank Charter Act 1844, prohibits the 'issue' of notes by bankers. (As to the issuing powers of the Bank of England, see now Currency and Bank Notes Act 1954.)] 'Section 11 prohibits the issue of notes by bankers. . . . The legislature provides that there shall be kept in the issue department of the bank [the Bank of England] a specified amount of securities, coin, and bullion, not to exceed, except in certain cases, the sum of fourteen million pounds. Bank of England notes are to be delivered out of the issue department into the banking department to such an amount as, when taken with the notes then in circulation, to make up fourteen million pounds. If any banker, who in 1844 was issuing his own notes, ceases to issue them, the bank may issue an equivalent number in addition to the fourteen millions. These provisions taken together shew clearly what is meant by the "issue" of notes. The word means the delivery of the notes to persons who are willing to receive them in exchange for value in gold, in bills, or otherwise; the person who delivers them being prepared to take them up when they are presented for payment.' *A-G v Birbeck* (1884) 12 QBD 605 at 609–611, per cur.

Prospectus

[The Companies (Consolidation) Act 1908, s 81 (repealed; see now Companies Act 1985, s 56), provided for certain particulars to be contained in every prospectus 'issued' by or on behalf of a company, etc.] 'The question is whether in the circumstances of this case a "prospectus" was "issued" to the respondent. . . . This involves two inquiries, first, the meaning of the word "issued". . . . It is difficult to think of a prospectus being issued without some measure of publicity, however modest, and I think it is also impossible to do so, unless the steps taken are taken with the intention of inducing a subscription by the person invited to subscribe for the securities. I do not think that the term is satisfied by a single private communication between friends, even if they are business friends, or even though preparations have been made for other documents to be used in other communications, if none such take place. In the present case all that constituted the "issue" was that one of the directors, in the course of a general endeavour to find money, was furnished with some copies of these typewritten documents and gave one of them to a friend who, as requested, passed it on to a friend of his own. I cannot believe that any one in business would call this the issue of a prospectus.' *Nash v Lynde* [1929] AC 158 at 165, 168, per Lord Sumner

Shares

'I find, turning to a dictionary, that the popular meaning of issue is "sending out, as of notes from a bank". The legal meaning of the word "issue" we have in the decision in *Re Imperial Rubber Co, Bush's Case* [(1874) 9 Ch App 554], which shews that the time of issue is the period when the company part with the control or power over the shares, the period when, in fact, the property vests in the allottee.' *Grenfell v Inland Revenue Comrs* (1876) 1 Ex D 242 at 250, per Huddleston B

'The defendant subscribed the memorandum of association for one share of £500, and, according to *Fothergill's* case [*Re Pen 'Allt Silver Lead Mining Co, Fothergill's Case* (1873) 8 Ch App 270], he became upon the registration of the company the actual and legal owner of that share, and became a member of the company. It is impossible to contend that this share was not "issued" to him at that moment.' *Dalton Time Lock Co v Dalton* (1892) 66 LT 704 at 706, CA, per Lopes LJ

'The Paris Company agreed to issue 250,000 shares of the increased capital. What does that mean? It means they agreed to offer to the public those shares, agreed to place them on the market in the usual way, agreed to invite the public to take them in the usual way—that is, by prospectuses, circulars, advertisements, and such like.' *Re London-Paris Financial Mining Corpn Ltd* (1897) 13 TLR 569 at 571, CA, per Lord Ludlow LJ

Australia 'Speaking generally the word "issue" used in relation to shares means, where an allotment has taken place, that the shareholder is put in control of the shares allotted. A step amounts to issuing shares if it involves the investing of the shareholder with complete control over the shares.' *Central Piggery Co Ltd v McNicoll* (1949) 78 CLR 594 at 598, per Dixon J

Canada 'What we have here . . . is a contract, and the substance of it is to purchase from the company the shares in question. . . . The covenant is to take them when issued and allotted. As applied to a fixed quantity of anything, or a fixed number of shares, the word "allot" can mean nothing more than to give, to assign, to set apart, to appropriate. The word has all these meanings. Nor does the word "issue" in the present case mean the doing of any particular act, and I think "issue" and "allot", taken together, mean no more than some signification by the company of its assent that the appellant now was or had become the owner of the number of shares which he agreed to take.' *Nelson Coke & Gas Co v Pellatt* (1902) 1 OWR 595 at 596, 597, CA, per Maclennan JA

ISSUE ESTOPPEL   *See* ESTOPPEL

ISSUED CAPITAL   *See* CAPITAL

ITEM

Bank deposits and collections

United States 'Item' means any instrument for the payment of money even though it is not negotiable but does not include money. . . . (Uniform Commercial Code 1978, s 4–104(1)(g))

J

JETSAM   *See also* WRECK

'Jetsam' are goods thrown into the sea to lighten a ship which nevertheless sinks. (1 Halsbury's Laws (4th edn) para 350n)

'Jetsam is when the ship is in danger of being sunk, and to lighten the ship the goods are cast into the sea, and afterwards notwithstanding the ship perish.' *Constable's Case* (1601) 5 Co Rep 106a at 106b, per cur.

JETTISON

'Jettisons' clearly includes the general average sacrifice consisting of the throwing overboard of cargo in time of peril for the common safety, but there is little authority on whether the meaning of the term is wider than this, and includes any throwing overboard not amounting to such a sacrifice. (25 Halsbury's Laws (4th edn) para 163)

'Jettison, in its largest sense . . . signifies any throwing overboard; but, in its ordinary sense it means a throwing overboard for the preservation of the ship and cargo, and most of the jurists treat of it in this sense, under the head of general average.' *Butler v Wildman* (1820) 3 B & Ald 398 at 402, per Abbott CJ

JEW

'The word "Jew" in English law has almost always been confined to persons practising the

Jewish religion; the disabilities of Jews have not attached to persons of Jewish race who have become baptised. Thus, they are generally described in Acts of Parliament and in legal documents as persons practising the Jewish religion, and Jewish religious endowments and trusts are now recognised and executed by the courts and regarded as charitable purposes: *Re Michel's Trust* [(1860) 28 Beav 39]. The Ballot Act of 1872 [repealed] speaks of voters of Jewish persuasion. In *Re Cohen* [(1919) 36 TLR 16], Peterson J appears to have treated a bequest for the benefit of deserving Jewish girls on their marriage as being for the benefit of Jewish religion, and thus gave to the word "Jewish" its religious denotation.' *Keren Kayemeth Le Jisroel Ltd v Inland Revenue Comrs* [1931] 2 KB 465 at 494, per Slesser LJ; on appeal, [1932] AC 650

'There are many associations consisting of members whose identity can be ascertained with absolute or reasonable certainty, such as the House of Commons, a club, an inn of court, a college, or, as we may gather from the testator's will, a synagogue. But there are other associations of which membership may be predicated only in a general sort of way, such as a political party, or, in most cases, a religious body. . . . I think it is possible for a man to be, and properly to call himself, a member of, say, the socialist party, at election time, although he has never been a member of that party in the sense that its chiefs would recognise him as such, or that he has subscribed to the party funds, or has supported it in some other way. I am sure that, for some purposes, a man may well be a member of the Church of England and for other purposes not a member. If a Jew were to be asked whether he was a member of the Jewish faith or a member of the Jewish community, he might well be puzzled as to how to give a truthful answer, and would be almost certain, if he were wise, to counter the question by asking in what sense it was being put to him. . . . It seems to me that "the Jewish faith", whatever be the sense in which the words are used, is an expression of complete uncertainty, and in the expression "a member of the Jewish faith" I find a double or perhaps a multiple uncertainty.' *Re Moss's Trust, Moss v Allen*, [1945] 1 All ER 207 at 209, per Vaisey J

JEWELLERY

'The definition of "jewellery" in the Shorter Oxford Dictionary—and for present purposes

the definition in the larger dictionary is the same—is as follows: "Jewellers' work, gems or ornaments made or sold by jewellers; jewels collectively or as a form of adornment." From that definition it seems to me clear that in the ordinary use of English language the word "jewellery" would cover jewels collectively and gems sold by jewellers just as it covers jewels made up into articles of adornment such as a brooch.' *Re Whitby, Public Trustee v Whitby* [1944] Ch 210 at 213, CA, per Lord Greene MR

JOB

'Job', in relation to an employee, means the nature of the work which he is employed to do in accordance with his contract and the capacity and place in which he is so employed. (Employment Protection (Consolidation) Act 1978, s 153(1))

JOB CONTROL

Australia 'A term of an award . . . provided that "The claimant organisation" (the present respondent) "shall not during the term of the award, order, encourage, or aid any strike or job control by any of its members". . . . The term is a comparatively recent expression, and is of American origin. . . . The word "job" hardly permits of final definition, because what is selected as the thing to be controlled, and called the "job", is naturally not susceptible of prior delimitation. It must vary with circumstances and with the progress of industrial operations. It may be a house, or a shop, or a ship, or a waterworks. "Job control", so far as we understand that phrase to have acquired any definite meaning, connotes the control by employees, whether already engaged or not, or by some organisation representing them, of some single enterprise or portion of an enterprise of an employer, which is selected as an isolated unit of industrial operations; the effective method of enforcing the control being, not a general strike in the industry or of the union, or even in the general service of the employer, but a strike of the employees engaged on that unit or a refusal to engage on it at all.' *Commonwealth SS Owners' Assocn v Federated Seamen's Union of Australasia* (1923) 33 CLR 297 at 304, 305, per Isaacs and Rich JJ

JOBBER

'. . . I will put a case of a trade such as that of a jobber who sells to anyone who comes to him at a fraction above the market price, and buys of anyone at a fraction below the market price.' *Mollet v Robinson* (1872) 7 LRCP 84 at 104, 105, per Blackburn J

JOIN

'A professional man may well "join" an "undertaking" on the terms that he is to be free to exercise his professional skill without being under the obligation to conform to any directions as to how he is to do his work.' *Faraday v Auctioneers' & Estate Agents' Institute of United Kingdom* [1936] 1 All ER 496 at 498, 503, CA, per cur.

'To "join" means to associate or combine, so that if five or more persons do associate or combine with the common object of intimidating or injuring someone . . . they not only form an unlawful assembly, but simultaneously and knowingly join it as members. Whether or not they continue to be members may be gathered from their subsequent acts.' Ibid at 403, per Davidson J

Australia [The Crimes Act 1900–1986 (NSW), s 545c(1) imposes a penalty on anyone who knowingly 'joins' an unlawful assembly or continues in it. Subsection (3) provides that any assembly of five or more persons whose common object is by means of intimidation or injury to compel any person to do what he is not legally bound to do or to abstain from doing what he is legally entitled to do, shall be deemed to be an unlawful assembly.] '"Join", according to one of its dictionary meanings, signifies "become a member of". It is obvious that it is in this sense that it is used here. A person is guilty of the offence of knowingly "joining" if he becomes one of an assembly of at least five persons who, to his knowledge, have the common object described in sub-s (3). If he so "joins" he is deemed to be a member of it and is liable to summary conviction.' *R v O'Sullivan* (1948) 48 SR (NSW) 400 at 401, per Jordan CJ

JOINT AND SEVERAL

'In this case we ought to look at the whole instrument: and if we do so, there is no doubt what the meaning of it is. Here, a power is given to fifteen persons jointly and severally to execute such policies as they or any of them shall jointly or severally think proper. The true construction of this is, as it seems to me, that the power is given to all or any of them to sign such policies, as all or any of them should think proper.' *Guthrie v Armstrong* (1822) 5 B & Ald 628 at 629, per Abbott CJ

JOINT AUTHOR   *See* AUTHOR

JOINT FUNDS

Australia 'In my opinion "joint funds of the club" includes such moneys as may be lent to it from time to time and does not presuppose an excess of assets over liabilities.' *Taylor v Hayes* [1969] 2 NSWR 523 at 523, per Brereton J

JOINT TORTFEASORS

'The substantial question in the present case is: What is meant by "joint tortfeasors"? and one way of answering it is: "Is the cause of action against them the same?" Certain classes of persons seem clearly to be "joint tortfeasors": the agent who commits a tort within the scope of his employment for his principal, and the principal; the servant who commits a tort in the course of his employment, and his master; two persons who agree in common action, in the course of, and to further which one of them commits a tort. These seem clearly joint tortfeasors; there is one tort committed by one of them on behalf of, or in concert with another.' *The Koursk* [1924] P 140 at 155, CA, per Scrutton LJ; also reported [1924] All ER Rep 168

JOINT VENTURE

Australia 'The term "joint venture" is not a technical one with a settled common law meaning. As a matter of ordinary language, it connotes an association of persons for the purposes of a particular trading, commercial, mining or other financial undertaking or endeavour with a view to mutual profit, with each participant usually (but not necessarily) contributing money, property or skill. Such a joint venture (or, under Scots' law, "adventure") will often be a partnership. The term is, however, apposite to refer to a joint undertaking or activity carried out through a medium other than a partnership: such as a company, a trust, an agency or joint ownership.' *United Dominions Corporation Ltd v Brian Pty Ltd* (1985) 60 ALR 741 at 746–747, per Mason Brennan and Deane JJ

JOINT WORK

Copyright

United States A 'joint work' is a work prepared by two or more authors with the intention that their contributions be merged into inseparable or interdependent parts of a unitary whole. (Copyright Act of 1976, s 101)

JOINTLY

'In the Shorter Oxford English Dictionary the word "joint" is defined in relation to "a thing, action, etc" as: "Held, done, made, etc. by two or more persons, parties, or things, in conjunction; common to two or more". The word "jointly" is defined as: "In a joint manner; so as to be joined . . . unitedly, conjunctly". No authority was cited to me showing that in English law the word "jointly" has a technical meaning, though of course the words "as joint tenants" do have a technical meaning. In my judgment, "jointly" in its ordinary sense means "common to two or more", and therefore is wide enough to include an equitable tenancy in common of English real property. If the word "jointly" was confined to joint tenants and excluded tenants in common, an extraordinary position would arise where one joint tenant severed an equitable joint tenancy and thus they became tenants in common in equity. Up to the moment of severance, it would not be settled property and the individuals would be chargeable, while after severance it would be settled property and the trustees would be chargeable. Such an extraordinary result should be avoided if a permissible construction is available which leads to a different result.' *Kidson (Inspector of Taxes) v Macdonald* [1974] 1 All ER 849 at 858, per Foster J

JOINTURE

A jointure is prima facie an estate for life given to a wife to take effect immediately upon the death of her husband. The power to jointure is not a 'usual power' within the meaning of an agreement to make a settlement with all the usual powers. (36 Halsbury's Laws (4th edn) para 847)

'What is a jointure? I think, according to the common acceptation of the word both popularly and by legal writers, it means a provision made for the wife after the death of the husband. I will refer to some of the text-writers in order to shew that. First of all, I will go back to Lord Coke. He says at p 36b this: "By the Statute of 27 Hen VIII, if a joynture be made to the wife, according to the purview of that Statute, it is a barre of her dower, so as the woman shall not have both joynture and dower, and to the making of a perfect joynture within the Statute six things are to be observed. First, her joynture by the first limitation is to take effect for her life possession or profit presently after the decease of her husband. Secondly, that it be for the terme of her owne life, or greater estate." The other points I need not mention. In Blackstone's Commentaries, Vol ii, p 137, there is this statement: "A jointure, which strictly speaking signifies a joint estate, limited to both husband and wife, but in common acceptation extends also to a sole estate, limited to the wife only, is thus defined by Sir Edward Coke,—'a competent livelyhood of freehold for the wife, of lands and tenements; to take effect, in profit or possession, presently after the death of the husband; for the life of the wife at least'." The same definition is to be found in Bacon's Abridgment, Vol ii, p 744. In another book which is very accurate, namely, Burton's Compendium 8th Ed, at p 125, I find this: "Before the Statute of Uses, the use or equitable estate was subject neither to curtesy nor to dower. Hence settlements upon marriage became necessary; of which the most simple form was to make the husband and wife joint tenants, that the whole might go to the survivor. This seems to be the origin of the word 'jointure', as applicable to the provision made for a woman upon marriage in the event of her husband's death; though it has been more usual, as being more secure, to make this provision by way of remainder, expectant upon a life estate in the husband." Lastly, in Sugden on Powers, 8th Ed, at p 484, Lord St Leonards, in speaking of jointuring powers, says this: "Jointure, like leases, will supersede all the estates in the settlement, which would prevent the jointress from taking her jointure upon the death of her husband, which is the period at which it should arise." I take it, therefore, prima facie, that a jointure is a provision for the wife after the death of her husband. It is, no doubt, true that the word is not necessarily confined to a provision only to commence at the death of the husband.' *Re De Hoghton, De Hoghton v De Hoghton* [1896] 2 Ch 385 at 392, 393, CA, per Stirling J

JOURNEYMAN

'The question is, whether saying that such a one is a man's journeyman, is as much as to say, that he is such a man's servant; that is, whether the jury by finding him to be the plaintiff's journeyman do not *ex vi termini* find him to be his servant? A journeyman is a servant by the day; and it makes no difference whether the work is done by the day or by the piece.' *Hart v Aldridge* (1774) 1 Cowp 54 at 55, 56, per Lord Mansfield CJ

JUDGE   *See also* COURT

Canada 'It is sufficient to notice that throughout the Supreme Court Act wherever it was intended that the Court, or any judge of the Court, may exercise some jurisdiction the wording is invariably "the Court . . . or any judge thereof". In s 58 [see now s 58 of RSC 1970, c S–19] on the contrary, the language is: "the Court or judge". Taking into account the context in which this language is found, the "judge" there referred to is the judge before whom the application for habeas corpus was brought, and while such application is still before him,—and no other. After he has disposed by judgment of the habeas corpus petition, he becomes *functus officio*. The Court alone then has jurisdiction to grant bail, provided the application for habeas corpus is brought before it by way of appeal. *Re Brown* [1946] SCR 537 at 538, per Rinfret CJ

JUDGMENT

The terms 'judgment' and 'order' in the widest sense may be said to include any decision given by a court on a question or questions at issue between the parties to a proceeding properly before the court. (26 Halsbury's Laws (4th edn) para 501)

The expression 'judgment' means any judgment or order given or made by a court in any civil proceedings, whether before or after the passing of this Act, whereby any sum of money is made payable, and includes an award in proceedings on an arbitration if the award has, in pursuance of the law in force in the place where it was made, become enforceable in the same manner as a judgment given by a court in that place. (Administration of Justice Act 1920, s 12)

'Judgment' means a judgment or order given or made by a court in any civil proceedings, or a judgment or order given or made by a court in any criminal proceedings for the payment of a sum of money in respect of compensation or damages to an injured party. (Foreign Judgments (Reciprocal Enforcement) Act 1933, s 11)

'Judgment' includes a decree. (Supreme Court Act 1981, s 151(1))

'The maxim *expressio unius, exclusio alterius* is not a canon of construction that is applicable to judgments. To construe a judgment as if its function were to lay down a code of law is a common error into which the English reliance on precedent makes it easy to fall. A cautious judge expresses a proposition of law in terms that are wide enough to cover the issue in the case under consideration; the fact that they are not also wide enough to cover an issue that may arise in some subsequent case does not make his judgment an authority against any wider proposition.' *D v National Society for Prevention of Cruelty to Children* [1977] 1 All ER 589 at 596, 597, HL, per Lord Diplock

Canada [The plaintiff appealed against an order of an Ontario County Court Judge in a mechanics' lien action to the Divisional Court. The appeal was dismissed and the plaintiff appealed to the Court of Appeal. Some respondents made a preliminary objection that under the Mechanics Lien Act, s 43(1) (see now Construction Lien Act 1983 (Ont), c 6, s 73(1) only a judgment or report may be appealed to the Divisional Court.] 'In our view the word "judgment" in s 43(1) of the Mechanics' Lien Act applies to any decision by the appropriate judge or master by which the rights of a party to the mechanics' lien proceedings are finally disposed of, and that the matter is not to be tested by the name which is given to that disposition nor by the terminology within it. Much was sought to be made in this case of the fact that the disposition by His Honour Judge Sullivan was referred to internally as an "order", was referred to as an "order" in the appeal to the Divisional Court, and has been referred to in the same way in the notice of appeal to this Court. As I have said we do not think that this is conclusive of the matter, but that the substance of the disposition sought to be appealed is what governs.' *Durall Construction Ltd v McDougall (WA) Ltd* (1979) 25 OR (2d) 371 at 373, 374, Ont CA, per Arnup JA

Canada [Application was brought to set aside a judgment pursuant to Queen's Bench

Rule 390(1) (Alta) which provided that 'an order may be set aside . . . on notice, by the judge who granted it'. It was argued that the rule applied only to orders and not to judgments.] 'Williston & Rolls, The Law of Civil Procedure, vol 2 pp 1020–21, refer to authorities that distinguish between judgments and orders. One of the references is to *Loring v Ilsley* [1 Cal 27] and the following quotation from that case is included: "What then is the distinction between an order and a final judgment? . . . The former is a decision made during the progress of the cause, either prior or subsequent to final judgment settling some point of practice or some question collateral to the main issue presented by the pleadings and necessary to be disposed of before such issue can be decided upon by the court, or necessary to be determined in carrying the execution into effect." The authors say that where the controversy between the parties is determined it is a judgment and every other decision is an order.' *Canadian Imperial Bank of Commerce v Bury* (1980) 14 CPC 189 at 192, Alta Ct, of QB, per Stevenson J

Declaratory

Judgments and orders are usually determinations of rights in the actual circumstances of which the court has cognisance, and give some particular relief capable of being enforced. It is, however, sometimes convenient to obtain a judicial decision upon a state of facts which has not yet arisen, or a declaration of the rights of a party without any reference to their enforcement. Such merely declaratory judgments may now be given, and the court is authorised to make binding declarations of right whether any consequential relief is or could be claimed or not. (1 Halsbury's Laws (4th edn) para 185)

Final

In general a judgment or order which determines the principal matter in question is termed 'final'. A final judgment has been defined as 'a judgment obtained in an action by which a previously existing liability of the defendant to the plaintiff is ascertained or established' and as 'a judgment obtained in an action by which the question whether there was a pre-existing right of the plaintiff against the defendant is finally determined in favour either of the plaintiff or of the defendant'. A final order is none the less final by reason that it is subject to appeal, and a judgment may be final even though it directs inquiries, or deals with

costs only, or is made on an interlocutory application, or reserves liberty to apply. (26 Halsbury's Laws (4th end) para 505)

'No order, judgment, or other proceeding can be final which does not at once affect the status of the parties, for whichever side the decision may be given; so that if it is given for the plaintiff it is conclusive against the defendant, and if it is given for the defendant it is conclusive against the plaintiff; whereas if the application for leave to enter final judgment had failed, the matter in dispute would not have been determined.' *Standard Discount Co v La Grange* (1877) 3 CPD 67 at 71, per Brett LJ

'To constitute an order a final judgment nothing more is necessary than that there should be a proper *litis contestatio*, and a final adjudication between the parties to it on the merits. That this order [for the payment of costs] was a judgment is plain, and it is equally plain that it was final. Nothing further remains but the question, whether the fact of there being in the same judgment a direction for an enquiry as to damages, in respect of which the judgment was not final until the amount of the damages was ascertained . . . makes any difference as to the finality of the remainder of the judgment. It appears to me that this can make no difference when the right of the plaintiff to this amount [the amount of the taxed costs] . . . is wholly independent of the inquiry.' *Re Faithfull, ex p Moore* (1885) 14 QBD 627 at 632, CA, per Lord Selborne LC

'In my opinion, "a final judgment" means a judgment obtained in an action by which the question whether there was a pre-existing right of the plaintiff against the defendant is finally determined in favour either of the plaintiff or of the defendant.' *Re Riddell, ex p Strathmore (Earl)* (1888) 20 QBD 512 at 516, CA, per Lord Esher MR

'Nothing can be a final judgment by which there is not a final and conclusive adjudication between the parties of the matters in controversy in the action.' Ibid at 517, per Fry LJ

'I believe the definition I am about to give of the term "final judgment" as used in this subsection [Bankruptcy Act 1883, s 4(1) (repealed)] is a substantially good definition, though I do not say it is exhaustive. I think a "final judgment" is a final adjudication of the matters in contest in the action, between the parties to the action.' Ibid at 518, per Lopes LJ

'It is urged that the judgment of the Scotch Court of Session is not a final judgment; but when the word "final" is used, as I think it is in some authorities with reference to judgments that does not mean, I apprehend, a judgment which is not open to appeal, but merely "final" as opposed to "interlocutory". A judgment is, in my opinion, not the less an estoppel between the parties to the action because it may be reversed on appeal to the House of Lords.' *Huntly (Marchioness) v Gaskell* [1905] 2 Ch 656 at 667, CA, per Cozens-Hardy LJ

Australia [The Northern Territory Supreme Court Act (1961–73), s 46(1) provides that the High Court has jurisdiction to hear and determine appeals from every 'judgment' (whether final or interlocutory) of the Supreme Court. This section is substantially the same as s 35 of the Judiciary Act.] 'The form of s 35 of the Judiciary Act is dictated by circumstances that s 73 of the Constitution gives the High Court jurisdiction to hear and determine appeals from all judgments, decrees, orders and sentences of . . . the Supreme Court, but with such exceptions and subject to such regulations as the Parliament prescribes. Section 35 does so prescribe. But it is important to observe that the judgments etc. to which it refers are the judgments to which s 73 refers. The words "judgments, etc" there refer to the formal orders which the Supreme Court may make, whether in the form of a judgment strictly so called or a decree, order or sentence. That is the accepted meaning of the word "judgment" in such a context as the present. The constitutional reference to such judgments is unqualified: it is not concerned with their subject matter or the reason which prompted the making of them.' *Moller v Roy* (1975) 49 ALJR 311 at 312, 313, per Barwick CJ

Canada 'A judgment is final when it does, if allowed to stand, finally dispose of the rights of the parties.' *Seibel & Day v Cummins* (1922) 16 SLR 405 at 412, per cur.

In personam

A judgment in personam determines the rights of the parties among themselves to or in the subject matter in dispute, whether it be corporeal property of any kind whatever, or a liquidated or unliquidated demand, but does not affect the status of either persons or things, or make any disposition of property, or declare or determine any interest in it except as between the parties litigant. Judgments in personam include all judgments which are not judgments in rem, but, as many judgments in rem deal with the status of persons and not of things, the description 'judgments inter partes' is preferable to 'judgments in personam'. (26 Halsbury's Laws (4th edn) para 503)

In rem

A judgment in rem may be defined as the judgment of a court of competent jurisdiction determining the status or the disposition of a thing, as distinct from the particular interest in it of a party to the litigation. (26 Halsbury's Laws (4th edn) para 503)

Legislative judgment

Australia 'The notion of a legislative judgment, as I apprehend it, is the enactment by a legislature of a statute in a form which so exercises judicial power that the powers of the judicial tribunal, to which the enactment is directed, to arrive at a judgment by the essential procedures of true judicial process in a case coming before it are wholly absorbed by the legislative Act, thus leaving the tribunal nothing to do but to put its judicial stamp on the case in the terms of a judgment already formulated by the provisions of the statute. In such a situation there would, in truth, be no judicial functions for the tribunal to perform.' *Clyne v East* [1967] 2 NSWR 483 at 496, per Asprey JA

JUDGMENT CREDITOR

The expression 'judgment creditor' means the person by whom the judgment was obtained, and includes the successors and assigns of that person. (Administration of Justice Act 1920, s 12)

'Judgment creditor' means the person in whose favour the judgment was given and includes any person in whom the rights under the judgment have become vested by succession or assignment or otherwise. (Foreign Judgments (Reciprocal Enforcement) Act 1933, s 11)

JUDGMENT DEBT

In this Part [Part II: enforcement of debt] of this Act, 'judgment debt' means a sum payable under—
(a) a judgment or order enforceable by a court in England and Wales (not being a magistrates' court); or

(b) an order of a magistrates' court for the payment of money recoverable summarily as a civil debt; or

(c) an order of any court which is enforceable as if it were for the payment of money so recoverable.

but does not include any sum payable under a maintenance order or an administration order. (Administration of Justice Act 1970, s 13(3); Attachment of Earnings Act 1971, s 2)

JUDGMENT DEBTOR

The expression 'judgment debtor' means the person against whom the judgment was given, and includes any person against whom the judgment is enforceable in the place where it was given. (Administration of Justice Act 1920, s 12)

'Judgment debtor' means the person against whom the judgment was given, and includes any person against whom the judgment is enforceable under the law of the original court. (Foreign Judgments (Reciprocal Enforcement) Act 1933, s 11)

JUDGMENT SUMMONS

'Judgment summons' means a summons issued on the application of a person entitled to enforce a judgment or order under s 5 of the Debtors Act 1869, requiring a person, or where two or more persons are liable under the judgment or order, requiring any one or more of them, to appear and be examined on oath as to his or their means. (County Courts Act 1984, s 147(1))

JUDICIAL

'The word "judicial" has two meanings. It may refer to the discharge of duties exercisable by a judge or by justices in court, or to administrative duties which need not be performed in court, but in respect of which it is necessary to bring to bear a judicial mind—that is, a mind to determine what is fair and just in respect of the matters under consideration.' *Royal Aquarium & Summer & Winter Garden Society Ltd v Parkinson* [1892] 1 QB 431 at 452, CA, per Lopes LJ

Australia 'The assessment of compensation, as it is the determination of a question affecting the rights of subjects, is a judicial function. . . . In *Frome United Breweries Co*

Ltd v Bath Justices [[1926] AC 898 at 914] Lord Atkinson cited with approval the following definition by May CJ in the Irish case of *The Queen v Corporation of Dublin* [(1878) 2 LR Ir 371 at 377]: "The term 'judicial' does not necessarily mean acts of a judge or legal tribunal sitting for the determination of matters of law, but for the purpose of this question a judicial act seems to be an act done by competent authority, upon consideration of facts and circumstances, and imposing liability or affecting the rights of others".' *Australian Apple & Pear Marketing Board v Tonking* (1942) 66 CLR 77 at 83, per Williams J

JUDICIAL LIEN

Bankruptcy

United States '[J]udicial lien' means lien obtained by judgment, levy, sequestration, or other legal or equitable process or proceeding . . . (Bankruptcy Act 1978, s 101(27))

JUDICIAL NOTICE

'Judges are entitled and bound to take judicial notice of that which is the common knowledge of the great majority of mankind and of the greater majority of men of business.' *R v Aspinall* (1876) 3 QBD 48 at 61, 62, per Brett JA

JUDICIAL POWER

Australia 'I am not satisfied that the words of Griffith CJ [in *Huddart Parker & Co Pty Ltd v Moorehead* (1909) 8 CLR 330] are properly interpreted when it is said that they mean that a power to make binding and authoritative decisions as to facts is necessarily judicial power. I direct attention to the concluding words—"is called upon to take action". In my opinion these words are directed to action to be taken by a tribunal which has power to give a binding and authoritative decision. The mere giving of the decision is not the action to which the learned Chief Justice referred. If a body which has power to give a binding and authoritative decision is able to take action so as to enforce that decision, then, but only then, according to the definition quoted, all the attributes of judicial power are plainly present. I refer to what I say more in detail hereafter, that the Privy Council, in the *Shell Case* [[1931]

AC 275] in which approval was given to the definition quoted, expressly held that a tribunal was not necessarily a court because it gave decisions (even final decisions) between contending parties which affected their rights.'
Rola Co (Aus) Pty Ltd v Commonwealth (1944) 69 CLR 185 at 198, per Latham CJ

JUDICIAL PROCEEDING

The expression 'judicial proceeding' includes a proceeding before any court, tribunal or person having by law power to hear, receive, and examine evidence on oath. (Perjury Act 1911, s 1(2))

JURISDICTION   *See also* ADMIRALTY JURISDICTION

By 'jurisdiction' is meant the authority which a court has to decide matters that are litigated before it or to take cognisance of matters presented in a formal way for its decision. The limits of this authority are imposed by the statute, charter, or commission under which the court is constituted, and may be extended or restricted by similar means. If no restriction or limit is imposed the jurisdiction is said to be unlimited. A limitation may be either as to the kind and nature of the actions and matters of which the particular court has cognisance, or as to the area over which the jurisdiction extends, or it may partake of both these characteristics. If the jurisdiction of an inferior court or tribunal (including an arbitrator) depends on the existence of a particular state of facts, the court or tribunal must inquire into the existence of the facts in order to decide whether it has jurisdiction; but, except where the court or tribunal has been given power to determine conclusively whether the facts exist, the Queen's Bench Divisional Court will inquire into the correctness of its decision by means of proceedings for mandamus, prohibition or certiorari. Where a court takes it upon itself to exercise a jurisdiction which it does not possess, its decision amounts to nothing. Jurisdiction must be acquired before judgment is given. The jurisdiction of an inferior court is not lost by mere non-user. (10 Halsbury's Laws (4th edn) para 715)

'Courts (even inferior courts) have "jurisdiction" to be wrong in law; that is why we hear appeals on questions of law and not merely applications for certiorari. A court may lack "jurisdiction" to hear and determine a particular action or application because (i) of the composition of the court (for example, the bias of the judge), or (ii) the subject-matter of the proceedings (for example, title to foreign land), or (iii) the parties to the proceedings (for example, diplomatic immunity); or, although having jurisdiction to hear and determine the proceedings, it may lack jurisdiction to make the kind of order made. . . . A mere error of law, however, made by a county court judge or an application of a kind, which he is entitled to entertain between parties between whom he is entitled to adjudicate, resulting in an order of a kind which he is entitled to make, does not affect his "jurisdiction" to make the order.'
Oscroft v Benabo [1967] 2 All ER 548 at 557, CA, per Diplock LJ

'"Jurisdiction" is an expression which is used in a variety of senses and takes its colour from its context. In the present appeal . . . we are concerned only with statutory jurisdiction in the sense of an authority conferred by statute on a person to determine, after inquiry into a case of a kind described in the statute conferring that authority and submitted to him for decision, whether or not there exists a situation, of a kind described in the statute, the existence of which is a condition precedent to a right or liability of an individual who is party to the inquiry, to which effect will or may be given by the executive branch of government.'
Anisminic Ltd v Foreign Compensation Commission [1967] 2 All ER 986 at 994, CA, per Diplock LJ

JURY

Juries are bodies of persons convened by process of law to represent the public, and to discharge upon oath or affirmation defined public duties. . . .
    The jury's duty may be defined as making to the Crown declarations of fact on the reception of evidence. Presentments are now abolished or obsolete except for the 'verdict' of a coroner's jury in cases of murder, manslaughter or infanticide where a person is named and committed for trial, which is strictly a presentment. Inquisitions in lunacy have been abolished, as have assessments of compensation under the Land Clauses Consolidation Act 1845 and all special juries. Therefore the jury's principal duty now is to return verdicts upon issues joined in courts of civil and criminal jurisdiction or findings of fact at coroners' courts. . . . (26 Halsbury's Laws (4th edn) paras 601, 602)

[The verdict of a jury in the Crown Court or the High Court need not be unanimous if (a) in a case where there are not less than eleven jurors, ten of them agree on the verdict; and (b) in a case where there are ten jurors, nine of them agree on the verdict. In the county court, it is sufficient if seven out of eight agree. Such a verdict is known as a majority verdict. A court may not accept a majority verdict of guilty unless the foreman of the jury has stated in open court the number of jurors who respectively agreed to and dissented from the verdict, nor unless it appears to the court that the jury have had such period of time for deliberation as the court thinks reasonable having regard to the nature and complexity of the case. See s 17 of the Juries Act 1974.]

JUST

'The expression "just" . . . must mean that which is right and fitting with regard to the public interests.' *Re An Application under Solicitors Act 1843* (1899) 80 LT 720 at 720, 722, per Wills J

Australia 'Clause 3 [of a building contract] provides: "The architect, during the progress of the works, shall be the sole judge of all matters arising out of the contract . . .; and against his decision, providing it be just and impartial, there shall be no appeal." . . . I cannot accept the plaintiff's interpretation of the word "just" in this clause as meaning simply honesty in the architect. What is required is that the decision shall be just, which I take to mean that his decision shall be right and fair, having reasonable and adequate grounds to support it, well founded and conformable to a standard of what is proper and right.' *Loxton v Ryan* [1921] St R Qd 79 at 84, 88, per Lukin J

JUST AND EQUITABLE

'Under the Law Reform (Married Women and Tortfeasors) Act 1935, by s 6, sub-s 2, it is provided that: "In any proceedings for contribution under this section the amount of the contribution recoverable from any person shall be such as may be found by the court to be just and equitable having regard to the extent of that person's responsibility for the damage; and the court shall have power to exempt any person from liability to make contribution, or to direct that the contribution shall be recovered from any person shall amount to a complete indemnity." I am told that nobody, up to the present, has decided what is the proper interpretation to put upon the words "just and equitable", appearing in that subsection. We are not accustomed to finding the word "just" in a statute. . . . I must, therefore, do what I can to construe those words, "just and equitable", having regard to the context in which I find them, and I cannot believe that they are intended to be used here strictly as terms of art. When I see those words are coupled with "having regard to the extent of what person's responsibility", I think the meaning of the subsection is that exercising a judicial discretion in the matter I am intended to do that which I think is right between the parties, having regard to what I think, on the true facts of the case, is the fair division of responsibility between them.' *Daniel v Rickett, Cockerell & Co Ltd & Raymond* [1938] 2 KB 322 at 325, 326, per Hilbery J

Australia [The Companies Act 1931 (Qd), (repealed; see now Companies (Queensland) Code, s 364(1)(j)), provided that a company might be wound up by the Court if the Court was of opinion that it was 'just and equitable' that the company should be wound up.] 'The words "just and equitable" are words of the widest significance and do not limit the jurisdiction of the Court to any case. It is a question of fact and each case must depend on its own circumstances.' *Re Kurilpa Protestant Hall Pty Ltd* [1946] St R Qd 171 at 183, per Macrossan CJ

JUST AND REASONABLE

Australia [The Common Carriers Act 1902–1986, s 9 (NSW) prohibits a common carrier from restricting his liability except by conditions found 'just and reasonable' and embodied in a written contract signed by the affected party.] 'There is no fixed criterion of what is just and reasonable; the extent and the nature of the condition must be considered and all the surrounding circumstances. It is not intrinsically unjust nor unreasonable that claims for loss or damage to goods carried by the Commissioner [of Railways] should not be allowed unless lodged in writing within a fixed period of time.' *Comr of Railways v Quinn* [1946] ALR 249 at 254, per Starke J

JUST CLAIM

Australia 'In my opinion, the expression "just claim" [in s 13D(2)(a) of the Trading with the Enemy Act 1939–1986 (Cth)] should be understood, in the absence of a controlling context, as referring only to demands which are justified on legal grounds—rights to payments or to property "not by the caprice of the judge, but according to sufficient legal reasons or on settled legal principles". *Beddow v Beddow* (1878) 9 Ch D 89 at 93.' *A-G of the Commonwealth of Australia v Schmidt (No 1)* [1963] ALR 276 at 277, per Kitto J

JUST OR CONVENIENT

'We should be sorry to limit by construction the beneficial jurisdiction of the Court to grant an injunction or make an order for a receiver where it is "just or convenient" to do so; but we conceive those well-known words do not confer an arbitrary or unregulated discretion on the Court, and do not authorise the Court to invent new modes of enforcing judgments in substitution for the ordinary modes.' *Harris v Beauchamp Brothers* [1894] 1 QB 801 at 809, CA, per cur.

JUST TERMS

Australia 'Our Constitution, when it refers to "just terms", is placing a qualification on the legislative power it bestows to acquire property compulsorily. But it is, I think, difficult to say that it makes it necessary for the legislature to give more than the full content of "compensation", as compensation is understood in English law, and we know from the House of Lords that a right to interest on the amount payable for the thing is not always or necessarily included.' *Commonwealth v Huon Transport Pty Ltd* (1945) 70 CLR 293 at 326, per Dixon J

JUSTIFICATION

The defence of justification is that the words complained of were true in substance and in fact. (28 Halsbury's Laws (4th edn) para 81)